NEW FEATURES:

- ALL CHAPTERS HAVE BEEN REVISED AND UPDATED TO REFLECT THE LATEST RESEARCH ON GLOBAL BUSINESSES. MOST CONTAIN 20-30 NEW REFERENCES, AS WELL AS REAL-WORLD EXAMPLES AND RESEARCH RESULTS, IN EACH OF THE CHAPTERS.

- THE FIRST FOUR CHAPTERS ON THE ENVIRONMENT HAVE BEEN GREATLY REVISED AND INCLUDE MENTION OF THE RECENT U.S. TRAGEDY WHERE APPROPRIATE TO THE TOPIC OR CONTEXT UNDER DISCUSSION.

BusinessWeek ALL-NEW CHAPTER OPENING VIGNETTES COME FROM *BUSINESS WEEK* MAGAZINE. THESE RECENT, RELEVANT SHORT NEWS STORIES SHOW HOW CHAPTER TOPICS RELATE TO THE REAL WORLD OF BUSINESS AND GET STUDENTS IMMEDIATELY INTERESTED IN THE CHAPTER MATERIAL, WHICH LEADS TO ACTIVE AND ATTENTIVE READING.

International Management

Culture, Strategy, and Behavior

International Management

Culture, Strategy, and Behavior

Fifth Edition

Richard M. Hodgetts
Florida International University

Fred Luthans
University of Nebraska

McGraw-Hill
Irwin

Boston   Burr Ridge, IL   Dubuque, IA   Madison, WI   New York   San Francisco   St. Louis
Bangkok   Bogotá   Caracas   Kuala Lumpur   Lisbon   London   Madrid   Mexico City
Milan   Montreal   New Delhi   Santiago   Seoul   Singapore   Sydney   Taipei   Toronto

McGraw-Hill Higher Education
*A Division of The **McGraw-Hill** Companies*

INTERNATIONAL MANAGEMENT: CULTURE, STRATEGY, AND BEHAVIOR
Published by McGraw-Hill/Irwin, a business unit of The McGraw-Hill Companies, Inc., 1221 Avenue of the
Americas, New York, NY, 10020. Copyright © 2003, 2000, 1997, 1994, 1991 by The McGraw-Hill Companies,
Inc. All rights reserved. No part of this publication may be reproduced or distributed in any form or by any
means, or stored in a database or retrieval system, without the prior written consent of The McGraw-Hill
Companies, Inc., including, but not limited to, in any network or other electronic storage or transmission, or
broadcast for distance learning.

Some ancillaries, including electronic and print components, may not be available to customers outside
the United States.

This book is printed on acid-free paper.

domestic 1 2 3 4 5 6 7 8 9 0 VNH/VNH 0 9 8 7 6 5 4 3 2
international 1 2 3 4 5 6 7 8 9 0 VNH/VNH 0 9 8 7 6 5 4 3 2

ISBN 0-07-248854-9

Publisher: *John E. Biernat*
Sponsoring editor: *Marianne C. P. Rutter*
Editorial assistant: *Tammy Higham*
Marketing manager: *Lisa Nicks*
Project manager: *Anna M. Chan*
Production supervisor: *Debra Sylvester*
Senior designer: *Pam Verros*
Cover image: © *Digital Vision*
Media producer: *Craig Atkins*
Lead supplement producer: *Cathy L. Tepper*
Senior digital content specialist: *Brian Nacik*
Photo research coordinator: *Jeremy Cheshareck*
Photo researcher: *Catherine Nance*
Typeface: *10/12 Times Roman*
Compositor: *ElectraGraphics, Inc.*
Printer: *Von Hoffmann Press, Inc.*

Library of Congress Cataloging-in-Publication Data

Hodgetts, Richard M.
    International management : culture, strategy, and behavior / Richard M. Hodgetts, Fred
Luthans.—5th ed.
      p. cm.
    Includes bibliographical references and index.
    ISBN 0-07-248854-9 (alk. paper)—ISBN 0-07-119559-9 (international)
     1. International business enterprises—Management. 2. International business
enterprises—Management—Case studies. I. Luthans, Fred. II. Title.
HD62.4 .H63 2003
658'.049—dc21

                                                      2002016544

INTERNATIONAL EDITION ISBN 0-07-119559-9
Copyright © 2003. Exclusive rights by The McGraw-Hill Companies, Inc. for manufacture and export.
This book cannot be re-exported from the country to which it is sold by McGraw-Hill. The International
Edition is not available in North America.

www.mhhe.com

Dedicated to

Henry H. Albers
Scholar, Mentor, and Friend

Richard M. Hodgetts
by Fred Luthans

On November 17, 2001, Richard M. Hodgetts passed away after a battle with cancer. His immediate family lost a devoted husband (over 30 years of marriage to his wife Sally), father (two grown children Steven and Jennifer), brother (to John and William) and uncle. In addition, many, many of us lost a great friend and colleague, and the field of management lost a very significant contributor.

Richard was a prolific author. In addition to this text—he completed his portion of this new edition a few weeks before his untimely death—he authored or co-authored over 25 different college texts in numerous editions and languages. In addition, he published well over a hundred articles in practitioner and research journals such as *AMJ*. He was also the editor of *Journal of Leadership Studies* and served on a number of editorial boards.

Richard was an active Academy of Management member his whole career, serving among many other activities as program chair and chair of the management history division, recent editor of the New Time special issue of *AME,* and was elected Fellow in 1983, Board of Governors 1993–1996, and received the Distinguished Educator Award in 1999. At the time of his death, he was on the Executive Organizing Committee and Chair of the All-Academy Symposia for the 2002 meeting.

Besides his tremendous contribution to the management body of knowledge, he was known as a truly outstanding classroom teacher. He won every Distinguished Teaching Award offered at both his first job for 10 years at the University of Nebraska and his home school for the past 25 years at Florida International University. For example, this year he was voted Faculty Member of the year by the Executive MBA students. He literally developed thousands of students at all levels—undergraduate, MBA, executive development, and doctoral—and millions across the world were influenced by his texts and innovative distance education materials and courses.

Although the above is just a sampling of Richard's distinguished career as a scholar and educator, those who knew him will never forget his humor, his dedication to the Academy, his genuine interest in you and your work, his compassion, and since his illness struck, his true courage. He brought a zest and fun to life and, to the end, did it his way. His family (which was always number one in his life), friends, students, colleagues, Academy members, and the field of management will miss him very much. However, we are all better off for having known him and he will always be with us. If you would like to honor Richard's legacy, please send your contributions to:

FIU Foundation/Richard Hodgetts Scholarship
Attn: Annabelle Rojas, Office of the Dean
College of Business Administration
Florida International University
Miami, FL 33199

Preface

What can be said about the new, globalized, borderless economy facing international managers today and in the future that has not already been said before? Perhaps only this—uncertainty. When we first conceived the need for an international management text well over 10 years ago, we were operating from a premise of unlimited world economic growth and opportunity. Then came the implosion of Eastern Europe, the economic crisis in Southeast Asia, the bursting of the dot-com bubble, and then 9/11 that left the world never the same. The result of these defining events has been a roller-coaster ride for international managers around the world. Going into this fifth edition, the premise has changed from unlimited growth to uncertainty and caution, but importantly, the premise of opportunity in global business remains unchanged. The uncertain economy and increasing geopolitical complexity simply levels the playing field for managers around the world. How managers respond, how they manage and turn the increasing threats into opportunities, becomes vital to success in today's environment.

Now, more than ever, all students must recognize that they will have the qualifier "international" in front of whatever their chosen career field. The whole world is now connected electronically and psychologically; it is hard to imagine any business or nonbusiness organization that is not directly affected by globalization. The challenge in the uncertain global economy is to learn and effectively practice international management. Nothing can be taken for granted, and international managers no longer have the luxury of burying their inadequacies and mistakes in a robust world economy. Those with the knowledge and skills to apply the contents of this text on international management will be taking a big step toward gaining a competitive advantage in today's uncertain, unprecedented environment.

We continue to take a *balanced approach* to this fifth edition of *International Management: Culture, Strategy, and Behavior.* We emphasize this balanced approach in the subtitle. Whereas other texts stress one of these, we feel that balance and the resulting synergy is needed for a true international management text and course. Thus, we have the following chapter distribution: Environment (4 chapters), Culture (4 chapters), Strategy (4 chapters), and organizational behavior/human resource management (5 chapters). Obviously, since international management is such a dramatically changing field, all the chapters have been completely updated and improved. For example, for most chapters there are at least 20–30 new references (and thus real-world examples and research results) in each of the chapters.

An exciting dimension of this edition is the addition of all new chapter opening articles from *Business Week.* These are very recent, relevant, short news stories to get the readers' interest and attention before going into the chapter topic. A transition paragraph for the chapter follows these opening stories and at the end of each chapter, there is a pedagogical feature titled *The World of Business Week—Revisited.* This has a few discussion questions based on the opening news article that require drawing from the chapter material in order to answer. As a teaching tool, suggested answers to these discussion questions are placed in the Instructor's Manual and also some multiple choice and true–false questions directly from the story can be used by instructors who want to include this material in their tests.

Another end-of-chapter feature is an *Internet Exercise.* The purpose of these exercises is to use the Internet to find information from websites on prominent MNCs needed to answer relevant questions about the chapter topic. An end-of-book feature is *International Manager Skill Building.* These in-class exercises represent the various parts of the text (culture, strategy, and behavior) and give hands-on experience and actual skill building. Finally, the use of cases is featured. The two short end-of-chapter cases remain (and are updated). There are also intermediate length (3–4 pages) integrative cases positioned at the end of each part. About half of these cases are new to this edition. These cases were retained or newly selected for high-interest discussion and strategic analysis. Unlike the shorter end-of-chapter cases on a specific country (In the International Spotlight) and cases covering specific topics in the preceding chapter (You Be the International Management Consultant), which can be read and discussed in class, these longer, end-of-part cases normally would be read outside of class and then discussed in depth. Along with the new or updated boxed application examples within each chapter and other pedagogical features at the end of each chapter (e.g., Key Terms, Review and Discussion Questions, The World of *Business Week*—Revisited, and Internet Exercise), the longer end-of-part cases, and the end-of-book skill-building exercises provide the complete package for relating text material to the real world of international management.

To help instructors teach international management, this text is accompanied by a revised and expanded Instructor's Resource Manual and Test Bank. This edition includes power-point presentation slides for each chapter and a set of videos complementing many of the key concepts and examples from the text.

International Management is generally recognized to be the first "mainline" text of its kind (strategy case books and specialized books in organizational behavior, human resources, and, of course, international business, finance, marketing, and economics preceded it, but there were no international management texts before this one) and is the market leader. We have had sustainability because of the effort and care put into the revisions. We hope you agree this Fifth Edition continues the tradition and remains the best "world-class" text for the study of international management.

We would like to acknowledge those who have helped to make this book a reality. Special thanks go to our growing number of colleagues throughout the world who have given us many ideas and inspired us to think internationally. Closer to home, we would like to give special recognition to two international management scholars who have had a direct influence on both of us. First is Henry H. Albers, former Chair of the Management Department at the University of Nebraska and former Dean at the University of Petroleum and Minerals, Saudi Arabia, to whom we have dedicated this book. He had a significant influence on our early careers and stimulated us to research and write in the field of management but, most importantly, to think globally. More recently, we would like to acknowledge the influence of Sang M. Lee, currently Chair of the Management Department at Nebraska and President of the Pan Pacific Business Association. He is a true "Global-Academic," and we appreciate his stimulation, advice, and support. Also, we would like to thank Cathy Watson for her work on various stages of the manuscript.

In addition, we would like to acknowledge the help that we received from the many reviewers from around the globe, whose feedback guided us in preparing the fifth edition of the text.

Our thanks, too, to the reviewers of previous editions of the text: Yohannan T. Abraham, Southwest Missouri State University; Kibok Baik, James Madison University; R. B. Barton, Murray State University; Mauritz Blonder, Hofstra University; Gunther S. Boroschek, University of Massachusetts-Boston; Charles M. Byles, Virginia Commonwealth University; Helen Deresky, SUNY Plattsburgh; Val Finnigan, Leeds Metropolitan University; David M. Flynn, Hofstra University; Robert T. Green, University of Texas at Austin; Jean M. Hanebury, Salisbury State University; Richard C. Hoffman, Salisbury State University; Johan Hough, University of South Africa; Mohd Nazari Ismail, University of Malaya; Robert Kuhne, Hofstra University; Robert C. Maddox, University of Tennessee; Douglas M. McCabe, Georgetown University; Jeanne M. McNett, Assumption College; Ray Montagno, Ball State University; Rebecca J. Morris, University of Nebraska-Omaha; Ernst W. Neuland, University of Pretoria; Yongsun Paik, Loyola Marymount University; Richard B. Peterson, University of Washington; Suzanne J. Peterson, University of Nebraska-Lincoln; Joseph A. Petrick, Wright State University; Richard David Ramsey, Southeastern Louisiana University; Mansour Sharif-Zadeh, California State Polytechnic University, Pomona; Jane H. Standford, Texas A&M-Kingsville University; Dale V. Steinmann, San Francisco State University; Randall Stross, San Jose State University; George

Sutija, Florida International University; David Turnipseed, Georgia Southern College; Katheryn H. Ward, Chicago State University; Aimee Wheaton, Regis College; Marion M. White, James Madison University; Corinne Young, University of Tampa; and Anatoly Zhuplev, Loyola Marymount University.

Thanks to the team at McGraw-Hill who worked on this book: John Biernat, Publisher; Marianne Rutter, Sponsoring Editor; Tammy Higham, Editorial Assistant; Lisa Nicks, Marketing Manager; Anna Chan, Project Manager; Debra Sylvester, Production Supervisor; Cathy Tepper, Supplement Producer; Craig Atkins, Media Producer; Jeremy Cheshareck, Photo Research Coordinator; and Pam Verros, Designer.

Last, but by no means least, we greatly appreciate the love and support provided by our families—Sally, Steven, Emily, Jennifer and Steven; and Kay, Kristin, Todd, Brett, Angie, Kyle, Dina, Paige, Kourtney, Taylor, Emma, and Ashley.

Richard M. Hodgetts
Fred Luthans

About the Authors

For RICHARD M. HODGETTS see IN
REMEMBRANCE, p. vii.

FRED LUTHANS is the George Holmes Distinguished Professor of Management at the University of Nebraska-Lincoln. He is also a senior research scientist with Gallup, Inc. He received his BA, MBA, and PhD from the University of Iowa, where he received the Distinguished Alumni Award in 2002. While serving as an officer in the U.S. Army from 1965–1967, he taught leadership at the U.S. Military Academy at West Point. He has been a visiting scholar at a number of colleges and universities and has lectured in most European and Pacific Rim countries. He has taught international management as a visiting faculty member at the Universities of Bangkok, Hawaii, Henley in England, Norwegian Management School, Monash in Australia, Macau, Chemnitz in the former East Germany, and Tirana in Albania. A past president of the Academy of Management, in 1997 he received the Academy's Distinguished Educator Award. In 2000 he became an inaugural member of the Academy's Hall of Fame for being one of the "Top Five" all-time published authors in the prestigious Academy journals. Currently, he is co-editor-in-chief of the *Journal of World Business,* editor of *Organizational Dynamics,* co-editor of *Journal of Leadership and Organization Studies,* and the author of numerous books. His book *Organizational Behavior* (Irwin/McGraw-Hill) is now in its ninth edition. He is one of very few management scholars who is a Fellow of the Academy of Management, the Decision Sciences Institute, and the Pan Pacific Business Association, and he has been a member of the Executive Committee for the Pan Pacific Conference since its beginning 18 years ago. This committee helps to organize the annual meeting held in Pacific Rim countries. He has been involved with some of the first empirical studies on motivation and behavioral management techniques and the analysis of managerial activities in Russia; these articles have been published in the *Academy of Management Journal, Journal of International Business Studies, Journal of World Business,* and *European Management Journal.* Since the very beginning of the transition to a market economy after the fall of communism in Eastern Europe, he continues to be actively involved in management education programs sponsored by the U.S. Agency for International Development in Albania and Macedonia, and U.S. Information Agency programs involving the Central Asian countries of Kazakhstan, Kyrgyzstan, and Tajikistan. Professor Luthans's most recent international research involves the relationship between psychological variables and attitudes and performance of managers and entrepreneurs across cultures. He is applying his positive approach to organization behavior (POB) and leadership (PAL) to effective global management.

Brief Contents

Organizational Behavior
and Human Resource Management   Part Four

Experiential Exercises
for International Management   Skill Building

Contents

Part Two   The Role of Culture

International Strategic Management   **Part Three**

Part Four

Organizational Behavior and Human Resource Management

Skill Building   Experiential Exercises for International Management

Part One

Environmental Foundation

Objectives of the Chapter

The global economy has arrived. In the United States, a dramatically increasing number of not only large corporations, but medium and small firms, are going international, and a growing percentage of overall revenue is coming from overseas markets. The same is true throughout Europe, Asia, and the rest of the world. As a result, international management, the process of applying management concepts and techniques in a multinational environment, is rapidly gaining importance.

Although there has been considerable historical evolution, the overriding focus of this opening chapter is to examine the worldwide developments of the last few years. The end of the cold war and the onset of the Information Age has created a new world and true global competition. These developments both create and influence the opportunities, challenges, and problems that managers in the international arena will face during the years ahead. Since the environment facing international management is so all encompassing, this chapter is mostly concerned with the economic dimensions and the next chapter is focused more on the political, legal and technological dimensions. The specific objectives of this chapter are:

1. **REVIEW** current trends in international investment and trade.

2. **EXAMINE** the present economic status in the major regions of the global community.

3. **ANALYZE** some of the major developments and issues in the various regions of the world.

BusinessWeek

The World of *Business Week*

The New Economy

Old Virtues

The worldwide proliferation of mobile phones and Web accounts by itself will not bring about a more vibrant global economy. What's also needed are dramatic changes in core institutions that will translate technology into faster productivity growth. That means financial markets better able to fund innovation, more flexibility in corporations and labor markets, a faster pace of deregulation, and increased competition (table).

The Road to the New Economy

Here's what countries must do to get a high-productivity, low-inflation economy

BOOST INVESTMENT SPENDING on information technology as a share of GDP

RESTRUCTURE CORPORATIONS to cut costs, improve flexibility, and make better use of technology

OPEN FINANCIAL MARKETS to direct capital to the best uses

DEVELOP VENTURE CAPITAL and IPO markets to aid innovative companies

ENCOURAGE AN ENTREPENEURIAL CULTURE and make it easier to start new businesses

INCREASE THE PACE OF DEREGULATION especially in telecom and labor markets

ADJUST MONETARY POLICY to the realities of the New Economy by waiting for inflation to appear before raising interest rates

---

The process of shifting to a fast-growth track is still in its early stages in most of the world. Europe is at least two or three years behind the United States with Asia lagging even farther behind. While there are pockets of entrepreneurial vigor in places such as Finland, it has turned out to be an enormous challenge to reshape cultures to allow more risk-taking in Europe and Asia, where caution is a virtue.

Moreover, investment in risky innovation—a linchpin of the New Economy—depends on open global markets, since national markets do not provide a big enough payoff for taking big risks. But as shown by the demonstrations against the World Trade Organization in Seattle, there are groups in every country who feel threatened by free trade. A widespread backlash against globalization could remove a key underpinning of the New Economy.

Open Access

The global economy is not a zero-sum game: Faster growth in the rest of the world would have a big payoff for the United States as well. Commodity prices might rise at first, but so would exports, bringing down the swelling trade deficits and creating manufacturing jobs at home. U.S. companies would start to see overseas profits accelerate.

And then there's the innovation factor. For corporations, the most important justification for spending big bucks on information technology is that it supports restructuring and cost-cutting. But from a global

perspective, a critical benefit of the Information Revolution is that for the first time it makes data available worldwide. Historically it has taken years, if not decades, for even the most important technological and business innovations to spread across national borders.

But that's changing. Now, an engineer in China, say, can log on to the Internet and have immediate access to the treasure trove of data on U.S. Web sites. More important, engineers in developing countries can communicate much more quickly with counterparts in other countries and learn what works and what doesn't. The gains from faster transmission of innovation can add up to 1% to global growth rates, according to research by economists Jonathan Eaton and Samuel S. Kortum of Boston University. That's an enormous potential boost.

But new technology has to be nourished within a larger framework of institutional changes. For one thing, openness of domestic markets to foreign trade is vital for turning innovations into real improvements in output. Without competition from overseas, companies make changes slowly and reluctantly.

American Advantage

One area where the U.S. excels is the ability to fund innovative companies at an early stage. Other countries in Europe and Asia are trying to catch up. In China, for example, the southern city of Shenzhen has put together its own $120 million venture-capital fund in an effort to stimulate local high-tech development—just one of several Chinese cities that has done so. The problem is that the new venture funds in Europe and Asia often have corporate or government affiliations, which tend to make them less effective.

And even if the funding is available, it's a slow process to adopt a culture that favors risk-taking and makes it easier for new businesses to start up. "This won't take six months," says Bernard P. Vergnes, chairman of Microsoft Europe. "We'll have to start in the schools to change the bankers and the politicians of the future and make them less averse to risk."

It may become easier in the future to entice politicians to jump aboard the New Economy bandwagon, as the political advantages become clearer. In India, for example, the Bharatiya Janata Party government decided to use the vision of an IT-literate India as an election promise. In Sweden, Björn Rosengren, the minister for industry, employment, and communications, is promising broadband in every home.

There is a growing willingness to back away from central control over national economies, even in the most hidebound of regulated industries. The wave of telecom mergers in Europe shows that the old idea of national monopolies is dead. And in Japan, where high telecom charges were holding back e-commerce, Nippon Telegraph & Telephone introduced a flat-rate high-usage Internet access service—aimed primarily at small offices and heavy individual users—for $75 a month in parts of Tokyo and Osaka, the two largest cities. Now it's contemplating cutting the price, possibly by 50%, by the time it launches the service in major centers around Japan.

What could stop the New Economy from going global? Simultaneous rapid expansion in Europe, the United States, and Asia could push up the prices on world commodity markets. But unless there is a cartel that holds supply down—as in the case of oil—such increases are likely to be temporary and not result in lasting inflation. Take steel, for example. With the world's mills operating at close to full capacity, "we are forecasting a shortage of steel," says Peter Marcus, managing partner of World Steel Dynamics, an Englewood Cliffs (N.J.)-based consulting firm.

But as buyers and suppliers of industrial products and tools increasingly move onto the Web, it will hold down prices. "Improvement in e-commerce will make the pricing structure more competitive," notes Marcus.

Similarly, soaring demand for the core products of the Information Revolution—memory chips, microprocessors, and liquid-crystal displays—is likely to push up prices in the short run. Companies such as Gateway Inc. have already complained of shortages. But recent experience shows that new capacity can be quickly created in these industries.

The biggest constraint on the spread of the New Economy globally will not be commodity inflation or product shortages. Rather, the main problem will be finding enough highly skilled and computer-literate workers to staff rapidly growing information industries. Europe and Japan will have to find a lot of highly skilled workers—quickly—as they try to beef up their New Economy industries. "The one big inhibitor is the shortage of skilled labor," says Andrew Milroy of International Data Corp. in London. IDC estimates that the demand for skilled workers will exceed supply by 20% in Western Europe in 2002.

It will be necessary to draw on the enormous supply of college-educated workers in countries such as India and China. Asia accounts for two-thirds of the global increase in college and other post-high-school enrollments in the 1990s. Indian universities turn out 122,000 engineers every year, compared with 63,000 in the U.S. And engineers comprise some 40% of China's enormous crop of annual graduates.

The growth of the U.S. high-tech industry has been fueled by a steady flow of highly educated immigrants and foreign students. Between 1985 and 1996, foreign students accounted for two-thirds of the growth in science and engineering doctorates at U.S. universities. Most of them planned to stay and work in the country.

Like many other aspects of the New Economy, opening up the doors to foreign workers won't come easily in many countries. But the genie is out of the bottle—no country will be able to resist it. In the end, the benefits will be well worth the pain.

By Michael J. Mandel in New York, with bureau reports

Source: **Reprinted from January 31, 2000, pp. 73–77 issue of *Business Week* by special permission, copyright © 2000 by McGraw-Hill Companies, Inc.**

The news story that opens this chapter provides a thumbnail sketch of the "new economy." Will the American model with its emphasis on high technology, international investment, the development of a skilled labor force, innovative decision making, and free-market capitalism prove to be the right one for economic success? Even with the bursting of the dot-com bubble and the resulting uncertain economy of recent years, one thing is certain: the old ways of doing things have to change. Japan and Germany, for example, two of the nations that were the most competitive in the world market a decade ago have now slipped badly. Japan's economy has been in recession for about 10 years and Germany's economy has not fared much better. In turning things around, as noted in the article, both of these countries are going to have to increase their skilled labor force, and, because they cannot do this by relying exclusively on their home market, they are going to have to tap the international labor market. The United States has been able to meet this challenge by complementing its high-tech college graduate pool with a steady flow of highly educated immigrants and international students. Additionally, the American model did not produce immediate results; the U.S. had to stay the course—a major challenge for countries that are looking for a quick fix. This chapter examines internationalization and worldwide developments on a region-by-region basis. Most economies are up and down in recent times, but are generally under-performing. However, all would like to emulate the vigorous and sustained economic growth that America had in the late nineties. As you read this chapter, note the role that globalization will be playing in this quest and some of the things that all nations, including the U.S., are going to have to do differently in improving their economic performance in the years ahead.

■ Introduction

International management is the process of applying management concepts and techniques in a multinational environment. Today more firms than ever are earning some of their revenue from international operations. Many of these companies are multinational corporations (MNCs, for short). An **MNC** is a firm that has operations in more than one country, international sales, and a nationality mix of managers and owners. One example is BP Amoco PLC, the giant British petroleum firm that recently committed $2 billion in a joint venture with PetroChina, which owns most of China's gas reserves and the infrastructure to transport and deliver the product.[1] Another is Dell Computer which now has three manufacturing plants in Ireland, passing Intel as the country's largest foreign employer.[2] A third is the Solectron Corporation of Milpitas, California, known worldwide for its high quality manufacturing processes, which bought a Japanese-based auto electronics plant from the Sony Corporation.[3] A fourth is IBM whose Global Services division has helped the company provide quality service to clients in more countries than any industry rival.[4] A fifth is General Electric which has operations in every major market worldwide including China where its businesses run the gamut from medical-imaging equipment to plastics to insurance.[5] And in the automobile industry, every major manufacturer has multinational operations. In the last five years in Latin America alone, Ford built a car plant in Brazil, Volkswagen retooled its Mexico facilities to launch the New Beetle, and DaimlerChrysler built a new plant to produce engines in Brazil.[6] General Motors has not only been actively investing in Latin America, but is making pickup trucks and sport utility vehicles in China and Buicks in Shanghai and recently agreed to spend $99 million

International management
Process of applying management concepts and techniques in a multinational environment.

MNC
A firm having operations in more than one country, international sales, and a nationality mix of managers and owners.

on a joint venture with Russian auto maker Avtovaz to sell cars in emerging markets world-wide. In recent years GM has also paid $125 million to buy the remaining 50 percent of Saab, laid out $2.4 billion for a 20 percent stake in Fiat, $1.3 billion for 20 percent of Fuji Heavy Industries, and $653 million to double its 10 percent position in Suzuki Motor.[7]

These companies are not alone. In recent years such well-known American MNCs as Avon Products, Chevron, Citicorp, Coca-Cola, Colgate Palmolive, DuPont, Exxon, Eastman Kodak, Gillette, Hewlett-Packard, McDonald's, Mobil, Motorola, Ralston Purina, Texaco, the 3M Company, and Xerox have all earned more annual revenue in the international arena than they have stateside. As a result, increasingly firms are finding that they must develop international management expertise. Managers from today's MNCs must learn to work effectively with those from many different countries. Moreover, as this decade unfolds, more and more small and medium-sized businesses will find that they are being affected by the trend toward internationalization. Many of these companies will be doing business abroad and those who do not will find themselves doing business with MNCs operating locally. In either event, these growing businesses will need to be concerned with international management if only to improve their ability to interact and work well with MNCs that they are supplying and/or are supplying them on a local basis.

■ Increasing Internationalization

International business is not a new phenomenon; however, the volume of international trade has increased dramatically over the last decade. Today, every nation and an increasing number of companies buy and sell goods in the international marketplace. A number of developments in regions around the world have helped to fuel this activity.

Regional Developments Impacting Internationalization

Although the status and issues facing major regions of the global economy are given detailed attention in the last part of this chapter, several important developments have had a direct impact on internationalization and should be noted. Obviously, the horrific consequences of terrorism and its threat around the world have made a permanent mark on how and where international business is conducted. However, some of the more routine, but still important developments have been:

North American Free Trade Agreement (NAFTA)
A free trade agreement between the United States, Canada, and Mexico which has in essence removed all barriers to trade.

1. The United States, Canada, and Mexico make up the **North American Free Trade Agreement (NAFTA),** which in essence has removed all barriers to trade between these countries and created a huge North American market. Although not occurring as fast as once assumed, this market eventually will be expanded to include Latin American countries as well. Chile will probably join NAFTA in the near future, and others, such as Argentina and Brazil, are likely to follow. The result may be a giant "American Market" that would parallel similar developments in Europe and Asia. In the early 1990s an "Alliance of the Americas" was proposed. During the first six months of his presidency, President Bush has echoed this basic idea. He wants to win negotiating authority with the Congress to build a free trade area from Alaska to Argentina. His goal, as well as that of other leaders in the western hemisphere, is to create the world's largest free trade zone, encompassing over 800 million people, by January 2005.[8]

2. The European Union (EU) is now well on its way to creating a unified market that many have described as the United States of Europe. This group consists of 15 nations including Austria, Belgium, Denmark, Finland, France, Germany, Great Britain, Greece, Holland, Ireland, Italy, Luxembourg, Portugal, Spain, and Sweden. Not only have most trade barriers between the members been removed, but the group has adopted a unified currency called the "euro." As a result of this agreement, it will now be possible for customers to compare prices between countries because everything can be done in a uniform currency. In other words, business done in the EU will be in euros.[9] Even though long standing cultural

differences remain, the EU is better integrated as a single market than either NAFTA or the allied Asian countries. Additionally, other nations such as Turkey have applied for membership. In the near future, the former communist bloc countries of Central and Eastern Europe undoubtedly also will become part of the EU. For example, Poland, Hungary, and the Czech Republic are already making progress toward membership, and others such as Albania, Romania, Slovakia, Lithuania, Latvia, Estonia, and Bulgaria have the goal to become members. Once East and West join together, the result will be a giant economic market that no major MNC can afford to ignore.

3. Although Japan has experienced economic problems for about 10 years, it continues to be the primary economic force in the Pacific Rim. Japan recently has invested relatively more in its own backyard of Asia than in any other part of the world. Japanese MNCs want to take advantage of the underdeveloped and huge Asian markets. At the same time, China is proving to be a major economic force (some experts forecast that China eventually will be the biggest economy in the world). Although all of the economies in Asia are now feeling the impact of the economic uncertainty similar to the rest of the world, the Four Tigers (Hong Kong, Taiwan, South Korea, and Singapore) have been doing relatively well and the Southeast Asia countries of Malaysia, Thailand, Indonesia, and even Vietnam should bounce back to become major export-driven economies. As in other parts of the world, an economic bloc called ASEAN (Association of Southeast Asian Nations) made up of Indonesia, Malaysia, the Philippines, Singapore, Brunei, Thailand, and in recent years Cambodia, Myanmar, and Vietnam, promotes exports to other countries.

4. Central and Eastern Europe, Russia, and the other republics of the former Soviet Union currently are still trying to make the transition to market economies. Although the Czech Republic, Slovenia, Poland, and Hungary have a start, but remaining problems, the others (the Balkan countries, Russia, and the other republics of the former Soviet Union) still have a long way to go. However, all are a target for MNCs looking for expansion opportunities. For example, after the fall of the Berlin Wall in 1989, Coca-Cola quickly began to sever its relations with most of the state-run bottling companies in the former communist bloc countries. The soft drink giant began investing heavily to import its own manufacturing, distribution, and marketing techniques. To date, Coca-Cola has pumped billions into Central and Eastern Europe—and this investment is beginning to pay off. Its business in Central and Eastern Europe has been expanding at twice the rate of its other foreign operations.

5. Economic activity in Latin America continues to be up and down. Despite the continuing political and economic setbacks these countries periodically experience, economic growth and exports continue in Brazil, Chile, Venezuela, and Mexico. Additionally, while outside MNCs continually target this geographic area, there also is a great deal of cross-border investments between Latin American countries. Regional trade agreements are helping in this cross-border process, including NAFTA which ties the Mexican economy more closely to the U.S. than Latin America. Within South America there is Mercosur, a common market created by Argentina, Brazil, Paraguay, and Uruguay, and the Andean Common Market, a subregional free trade compact that is designed to promote economic and social integration and cooperation between Bolivia, Colombia, Ecuador, Peru, and Venezuela.[10]

6. There also is recent economic progress among less developed nations. A good example is India, which for years has had a love–hate relationship with multinational businesses. The Indian government has been known for its slow-moving bureaucracy and this has been a major stumbling block in attracting foreign capital. In recent years, however, there has been a dramatic turnaround

in government policy, and a growing number of multinationals recently have been attracted to India. Much of this spurt has resulted from the current Indian government's willingness to reduce the bureaucratic red tape that accompanies the necessary approvals to move forward with investments.

These are specific, geographic examples of emerging internationalism. Equally important to this new climate of globalization, however, are the recent developments in both international investment and trade.

International Investment and Trade

Approximately 80 percent of all international investments come from developed countries. For example, foreign direct investment (FDI), the term used to indicate the amount invested in another country, in the United States currently stands at almost $1 trillion, while U.S. FDI is $1.1 trillion. The largest investors in the United States in recent years have been Great Britain, Japan, the Netherlands, Germany, and Canada. Conversely, the major stake for U.S. investors has been the EU, followed by Canada, and then Japan. Tables 1–1 and 1–2 provide additional information on FDI in the United States and by U.S. investors.

As nations become more affluent, they begin looking for countries with economic growth potential where they can invest funds. Over the last two decades, for example, Japanese MNCs have invested not only in their Asian neighbors, but in both the United

Table 1–1
Foreign Direct Investment in the United States 1998–1999
(in millions of dollars)

	1998	1999
All Countries	793,748	986,668
Canada	74,143	79,716
Europe	528,601	685,845
(select countries)		
United Kingdom	143,165	183,145
Germany	94,404	111,138
France	58,051	77,622
South and Central America	9,819	10,606
(select countries)		
Mexico	2,432	3,612
Brazil	635	651
Other Western Hemisphere	18,034	33,984
(select countries)		
Bermuda	3,740	13,054
Netherlands Antilles	2,844	2,695
Bahamas	2,077	2,163
Africa	882	1,545
Middle East	6,346	7,087
(select countries)		
Israel	2,084	2,680
Kuwait	n.a.	3,391
Saudi Arabia	n.a.	949
Asia and Pacific	155,943	167,884
(select countries)		
Japan	134,590	148,947
Australia	12,883	10,818
Taiwan	3,144	2,983
South Korea	974	1,520
Singapore	1,561	1,049
Hong Kong	1,578	1,210

Source: Bureau of Economic Analysis: U.S. Department of Commerce, 2001.

States and the EU. European MNCs, meanwhile, have made large financial commitments in Japan, and more recently in China, because they see Asia as having continued growth potential. American multinationals have followed a similar approach in regard both to Europe (Table 1–3 shows some of the most recent acquisitions there) and Asia. For example, GE Capital has gone to Asia to acquire a majority stake in a charge-card issuer, boost to 100 percent its ownership of an auto financing business, purchase a 49 percent stake in a consumer finance company, and enter Japan's insurance market with a $575 million investment in a joint venture with Toho Mutual Life Insurance.[11] Other U.S. MNCs such as Merrill Lynch acquired 33 branches of the Japanese Yamaichi Securities firm, Coca-Cola bought a 50 percent interest in a Thai bottler, and Microsoft recently purchased 60 percent of Titus Communications, Japan's second-largest cable operator.[12] In addition, U.S. auto firms hold substantial ownership positions in the Japanese car industry. For example, General Motors owns 49 percent of Isuzu and 10 percent of Suzuki and Ford holds a 33.4 percent equity position in Mazda.[13]

In addition to these types of investments, international trade had increased substantially over the last two decades. For example, in 1983 the United States exported slightly over $200 billion of goods and services and imported $269 billion of goods and services. At the end of the century U.S. exports were in the range of $700 billion annually and imports were over $1 trillion. In other words, during this period, the United States more than tripled its trade with the rest of the world.

Table 1–2
Foreign Direct Investment by the United States 1998–1999
(in millions of dollars)

	1998	1999
All Countries	1,104,012	1,132,622
Canada	101,871	111,707
Europe	528,113	581,791
(select countries)		
United Kingdom	192,663	213,070
Germany	46,405	49,617
France	42,064	39,984
South and Central America	74,254	74,839
(select countries)		
Mexico	28,396	34,265
Brazil	38,195	35,003
Other Western Hemisphere	68,459	77,569
(select countries)		
Bermuda	40,403	45,959
Netherlands Antilles	4,372	4,377
Bahamas	1,065	1,065
Africa	14,241	15,062
Middle East	10,632	11,137
(select countries)		
Saudi Arabia	4,276	4,231
Israel	2,922	3,199
United Arab Emirates	687	543
Asia and Pacific	155,364	185,912
(select countries)		
Japan	35,633	47,786
Australia	31,150	33,662
Singapore	18,427	24,781
Hong Kong	18,421	20,848
Taiwan	6,262	6,860
South Korea	7,395	8,749

Source: Bureau of Economic Analysis: U.S. Department of Commerce, 2001.

Table 1–3
Recent European Acquisitions of U.S. Firms

Investor	Acquirer's Nation	Company Acquired	Purchase Price (in billions of dollars)
BP Amoco	United Kingdom	ARCO	$28.22
Cap Gemini	France	Ernst & Young consulting business	11.77
France Telecom	France	NTL	5.50
British Telecom, worldwide assets	United Kingdom	AT&T worldwide assets, operations	5.04
France Telecom	France	Global One	4.35
National Grid Group	United Kingdom	New England Electric System	4.22
BASF	Germany	American Cyanamid agricultural products	3.90
Royal Ahold	Netherlands	US Foodservice	3.62
Dexla	Belgium	Financial Security Assurance Holdings	2.55
Bayer	Germany	Lyondell Chemical polyols business	2.45

EU trade has also increased sharply. This is particularly true for exports and imports between EU members both of which are now in excess of $2 trillion annually.[14] Japan, despite its ongoing economic problems, has also seen continual increases in its annual exports and imports. In the early 1980s exports and imports were around $440 billion and $335 billion respectively; by the end of the century imports and exports were in the neighborhood of $450 and $325 billion respectively with a large amount of this positive trade balance accounted for by its sales to the United States.

When international trade statistics for all countries are examined, what is particularly interesting about these data is that the *percentage* of world trade that is accounted for by the three major trading blocs—the United States, the EU, and Japan—has remained fairly consistent. Over the last two decades this group's share of world exports and imports has remained in the range of 55–59 percent. Simply stated, this triad accounts for most of the world's international trade, and the United States is the major economic power among the three. As seen in Table 1–4, the U.S. sells over $450 billion of goods and services to its top 10 trading partners and, in turn, buys over $730 billion of goods and services from them. And in the future, the amount of international trade by all countries will continue to rise, making an understanding of international management even more important than it has been in the past.

Finally, it is important to note that foreign investment and trade do not rely exclusively on MNCs exporting or setting up operations locally. In some cases, it is far easier to buy a domestic firm. Beer companies, for example, are finding that customers like local products, so rather than trying to sell them an imported beer, the MNC will invest in or buy a local brewery. Moreover, the name of the local company may remain the same, so that many local residents are unaware that the firm has changed hands. To illustrate this point, answer the following questions about well-known products sold in the United States, then check your answers at the end of the chapter:

1. Where is the parent company of Braun household appliances (electric shavers, coffee makers, etc.) located?

   a. Switzerland   *b.* Germany   *c.* the United States   *d.* Japan

2. The BIC pen company is

   a. Japanese   *b.* British   *c.* U.S.-based   *d.* French

Table 1–4
The Top 10 Trading Partners of the United States: 1999

Rank	Importing Country	U.S. Exports (in millions of dollars)	Rank	Exporting Country	U.S. Imports (in millions of dollars)
1	Canada	166,600.0	1	Canada	198,711.1
2	Mexico	86,908.9	2	Japan	130,863.9
3	Japan	57,465.7	3	Mexico	109,720.5
4	United Kingdom	38,407.1	4	China	81,788.2
5	Germany	26,800.2	5	Germany	55,228.4
6	South Korea	22,958.4	6	United Kingdom	39,237.2
7	Netherlands	19,436.6	7	Taiwan	35,204.4
8	Taiwan	19,131.4	8	South Korea	31,178.6
9	France	18,877.4	9	France	25,708.6
10	Singapore	16,247.3	10	Italy	22,356.5

Source: Office of Trade and Economic Analysis, U.S. Department of Commerce, 2001.

3. The company that owns Häagen-Dazs ice cream is in
   a. Germany   *b.* the U.S.   *c.* Sweden   *d.* Japan

4. RCA television sets are produced by a company based in
   a. France   *b.* the United States   *c.* Malaysia   *d.* Taiwan

5. The firm that owns Green Giant vegetables is
   a. U.S.-based   *b.* Canadian   *c.* British   *d.* Italian

6. The owners of Godiva chocolate are
   a. U.S.-based   *b.* Swiss   *c.* Dutch   *d.* Swedish

7. The company that produces Vaseline is
   a. French   *b.* Anglo-Dutch   *c.* German   *d.* U.S.-based

8. Wrangler jeans are made by a company that is
   a. Japanese   *b.* Taiwanese   *c.* British   *d.* U.S.-based

9. The company that owns Holiday Inn is headquartered in
   a. Saudi Arabia   *b.* France   *c.* the United States   *d.* Britain

10. Tropicana orange juice is owned by a company that is headquartered in
    a. Mexico   *b.* Canada   *c.* the United States   *d.* Japan

This quiz helps to illustrate how transnational today's MNCs have become. This trend is not restricted to firms in North America, Europe, or Asia. An emerging global community is becoming increasingly interdependent economically. Although there may be a true, totally integrated global market in the near future, at present regionalization, as represented by North America, Europe, Asia, and the less developed countries, is most descriptive of the world economy.

■ The Economic Status and Issues of the Major Regions

International investment and trade are more likely to occur between nations in close geographic proximity; for example, in North America, Mexico and Canada are two of the United States' largest trading partners. However, there also is a growing trend toward expanding these horizons and doing business with nations thousands of miles away. For example, Japan is a major trading partner of the United States, and China does more business with the United States than with most other nations. The following sections examine trends that are occurring in each major region of the world and the impact of these developments on international management.

North America

As noted earlier, North America constitutes one of the three largest trading blocs in the world. The combined purchasing power of the United States, Canada, and Mexico is close to $11 trillion. In 1989, the United States and Canada officially had a free trade agreement, and in 1994, Mexico officially joined, thereby creating the North American Free Trade Agreement (NAFTA). A number of economic developments have occurred because of this agreement, and all are designed to remove trade barriers and promote commerce between these three countries. Some of the more important include: (1) the elimination of tariffs as well as import and export quotas; (2) the opening of government procurement markets to companies in the other two nations; (3) an increase in the opportunity to make investments in each others' country; (4) an increase in the ease of travel between countries; and (5) the removal of restrictions on agricultural products, auto parts, and energy goods.

The NAFTA provisions will take place over time. For example, in the case of Mexico, quotas on Mexican products in the textile and apparel sectors were phased out over time with customs duties on all textile and apparel products completely eliminated by the year 2004. Similarly in 2001 outside investors were allowed to own no more than 51 percent of auto and truck companies but in 2004 these limitations are totally eliminated. Steps such as these are helping to create a unified trading bloc. Even though there will be more integration both globally and regionally, effective international management still requires knowledge of individual countries.

United States   U.S. MNCs have holdings throughout the world. In Europe, General Motors and Ford command dominant market positions, and they are finally beginning to make inroads in Asia as well. U.S. MNCs also do extremely well in the European computer market and are a major force in this industry throughout the Pacific Rim. Telecommunications is another high-tech area where the United States has a large international market share. U.S. firms compete with each other in the international arena as well. For example, AT&T now finds itself getting international competition from the U.S. "Baby Bells" (the regional firms that used to be part of AT&T). These firms are becoming more interested in expanding their market coverage and meeting the growing worldwide demand for higher-quality telephone services.

U.S. consumer-goods companies also are finding overseas markets to be very attractive. For example, Coca-Cola has a soft drink plant and distribution operation in Moscow and has a huge presence throughout Eastern Europe. Toys "R" Us has expanded in Germany and Japan, and it is gaining market share in both locales. U.S. airline companies, such as Delta, United, and American, also are expanding into Europe.

At the same time, foreign MNCs are finding the United States to be a lucrative market for expansion. BMW has set up operations in South Carolina, and Mercedes produces a lower-priced car ($20,000 range) in Alabama designed to help it gain U.S. market share. Other examples of outside investment in the United States include SmithKline Beecham PLC of Britain, which paid almost $3 billion to acquire the over-the-counter drug business of Sterling Winthrop, Inc., an Eastman Kodak unit. Hoechst AG of Germany paid over $7 billion for Marion Merrell Dow, Inc., a Dow Chemical subsidiary. France Telecom and Deutsche Telecom combined to pay over $4 billion for a 20 percent stake in the Sprint Corporation.

Even though Japanese firms are going to Asia more than in the past, they now are turning to the United States to find suppliers who can help increase the quality of their products while keeping down costs. For example, Toyota, Isuzu, and Suzuki all are buying antilock brake systems from General Motors. IBM is selling computers to Mitsubishi Electric, and Sun Microsystems Inc. is selling workstations to Japanese firms. Understanding these developments in the United States contributes to the field of international management.

Canada   Canada is the United States' largest trading partner, a position it has held for many years. The United States also has considerable foreign direct investment in Canada, more than in any other country except the United Kingdom. This helps to explain why most of the largest foreign-owned companies in Canada are totally, or heavily, U.S.-owned.

The legal and business environment in Canada is similar to that in the United States, and this similarity helps to promote trade between the two countries. Geography, language, and culture also help, as does NAFTA, which will assist Canadian firms in becoming more competitive worldwide. They will have to be able to go head-to-head with their U.S. and Mexican competitors as trade barriers are removed. This should result in greater efficiency and market prowess on the part of the Canadian firms, which must compete successfully or go out of business.

In recent years, Canadian firms have begun investing heavily in the United States. For example, Canadian Pacific has purchased the Delaware & Hudson Railway, and Bombardier, Inc., has bought the Learjet Corporation of Wichita, Kansas. Meanwhile, Bronfman, Inc., best known for its Canadian whiskeys, sold its large stake in Du Pont for $1.4 billion (less than market value) to buy 80 percent of MCA (now called Universal) and purchased Polygram, the largest music company in the world.[15] Canadian firms also do business in many other countries, including Mexico, Great Britain, Germany, and Japan, where they find ready markets for Canada's vast natural resources, including lumber, natural gas, crude petroleum, and agriproducts.

At the same time, Canada is becoming a target for increased international investment, especially by firms from the United States. American, Delta, and Northwest airlines all have expanded their Canadian routes. DaimlerChrysler, Ford, and General Motors all have plants in Canada, and so do other major U.S. MNCs, including IBM, Kodak, and Xerox. Again, a major reason for this outside investment is to tap Canada's vast natural resources, which offer a potential bonanza to enterprising firms. Another reason is the growing population and increasing purchasing power of the country. Still another is the chance to take advantage of the opportunities provided under the NAFTA provisions.

Mexico   By the early 1990s, Mexico had recovered from its economic problems of the previous decade and become the strongest economy in Latin America. In 1994, Mexico became part of NAFTA, and it appeared to be on the verge of becoming the major economic power in Latin America. The country's economic optimism proved to be short-lived, however. By late 1994, the value of the peso collapsed, and the economy took a nosedive. By early 1995, the United States, the International Monetary Fund, and the Bank for International Settlements were teaming up to create a $50 billion assistance package. At the same time, the government of Mexico was instituting a number of important economic changes, which included cutting the federal budget (thus holding down the country's spiraling deficit), instituting wage and price controls to limit growing inflation, and privatizing more state-held businesses to raise money and stimulate economic growth. These moves helped to bring the Mexican economy back on its course, and the loans were paid back before they were due.

In 2000 the 71-year hold of the Institutional Revolutionary Party on the presidency of the country came to an end and many investors believe that under the new administration of Vicente Fox the government will be more pro-business than ever. Economic growth in 2001 was in the range of 3 percent[16] and the country is now producing almost 2 million light vehicles annually.[17] In addition, Mexico now has a highly competitive textile industry that has replaced China as the major exporter of garments to the U.S.[18] However, like the U.S. and other countries of the world, Mexico's economy faces an uncertain future.

In the mean time, Mexico has built a very strong **maquiladora industry.** Long before NAFTA, this was an arrangement by the Mexican government that permitted foreign manufacturers to send materials to their Mexican-based plants, process or assemble the products, and then ship them back out of Mexico with only the value added being taxed. Ford Motor, for example, took advantage of this opportunity and annually exports engines from its Chihuahua plant to the United States. General Motors assembles car

Maquiladora industry
Derived from the Spanish word for the fee that a miller collected for processing grain that now represents the arrangement created by the Mexican government that permits the flow of materials and products in and out of Mexico with only the value added being taxed.

radios in its Matamoros plant for shipment north. Hundreds of other large firms have followed suit, taking advantage of the low-cost, but quality conscious, Mexican workforce.

U.S. labor unions argue that this arrangement has cost many jobs in the United States, but the U.S. Department of Labor reports that *maquiladora* operations actually support jobs by helping U.S. firms maintain their international competitiveness. For example, Packard Electric has noted that without *maquiladora* operations, it would have closed its Warren, Ohio, plant and moved everything to Southeast Asia.

Because of NAFTA, Mexican businesses are finding themselves able to take advantage of the U.S. market by replacing goods that were previously purchased from Asia. Mexican firms are now able to produce products at highly competitive prices thanks to lower cost labor and proximity to the American market. Location has helped hold down transportation costs and allows for fast delivery. As a result, Hewlett-Packard has increased imports of copier products from Mexican manufacturers; and IBM is pushing its Asian suppliers to set up joint ventures in Mexico, so that its own costs and inventories can be reduced.[19] Overseas auto producers are also turning their attention to this market location opportunity. Volkswagen, Nissan, and DaimlerChrysler have production facilities in Mexico. As a result, when coupled with the American auto firms that have operations there, almost 1 million cars and trucks for the U.S. market are now being made in Mexico.[20]

Mexican firms are also expanding their worldwide operations. A retail group controlled by billionaire Carlos Slim Helu recently bought CompUSA, the largest chain of personal computer stores in the United States.[21] Grupo Industrial Bimbo SA, a large food company that provides all of the buns for McDonald's units in Mexico, Peru, Colombia, and Venezuela, has built a factory in the Czech Republic to manufacture candy for the local market.[22] Mexican firms, taking advantage of a new arrangement which the government has negotiated with the EU, can now export goods into the European community without having to pay a tariff. So Volkswagen of Mexico, as long as the Mexican content of the cars is in the prescribed 45–60 percent range, can export cars to the EU and save the 7 percent duty it used to pay.[23]

Today Mexican companies employ approximately 70,000 workers in more than two dozen countries and generate almost $8 billion in revenues.[24] In addition, the country's trade with both the EU and Asia is on the rise which is important to Mexico because it wants to reduce its overreliance on the U.S. market.

South America

Over the years, countries in South America have had difficult economic problems. They have accumulated heavy foreign debt obligations and experienced severe inflation. Although most have tried to implement economic reforms, reducing their debt, the last few years have again seen a downturn in the economy.[25]

Brazil is a case in point. From 1992 to 1995, the country's GDP rose by 5 percent annually, and inflation, which was running as high as 50 percent in some months, had dropped to 5 percent by mid-1998. Most important, Brazil attracted outside investors. Examples include Compaq Computer, which opened a factory capable of producing 400,000 personal computers annually. Anheuser-Busch spent $105 million on a brewery to market Budweiser to Brazilians, and General Electric constructed $9 billion worth of coal-fired power electricity plants in the southern part of the country. At the same time, many other well-known companies have set up operations in Brazil, including Arby's, J.C. Penney, Kentucky Fried Chicken, McDonald's, and Wal-Mart.[26] All of this international business activity should spell success. However, by the turn of the century, Brazil was experiencing difficulties in the volatile world economy and its future is uncertain.

Chile has been an economic success story in South America. Annual average growth of GDP in 1997 was 8.1 percent, which was higher than that for any other country in South America except Argentina.[27] In addition, Chile's export volume increased dramatically and the amount of foreign direct investment was on the rise. However, in the last couple of years the economy has weakened, GDP has declined, and its future is uncertain.

Despite the ups and downs, a major development in South America is the growth of intercountry trade, spurred on by the progress toward free market policies. For example, beginning in 1995, 90 percent of trade among Mercosur members was duty free. Also, members of the Andean Pact formed a customs union by adopting common external tariffs and eliminating most duties between the members. Currently, negotiations are under way for merging Mercosur and the Andean Pact into a South American Free Trade Association. Because of such developments, intercountry trade is increasing sharply.

At the same time, South American countries are increasingly looking to do business with the United States.[28] In fact, a survey of businesspeople from Argentina, Brazil, Chile, Colombia, and Venezuela found that the U.S. market, on average, was more important for them than any other. Some of these countries, however, also are looking outside of the Americas for growth opportunities. Mercosur has begun talks with the EU to create free trade between the two blocs, and Chile has joined the Asia-Pacific Economic Cooperation group.[29] These developments help to illustrate the economic dynamism of South America and, especially in light of Asia's recent economic problems, explain why so many multinationals are interested in doing business within this part of the world.

Europe

Although often in the past overshadowed because of Asia's spectacular growth, major economic developments have occurred in Europe over the past decade. One interesting development has been the privatization of traditionally nationalized industries (see the accompanying box, "Privatization in Great Britain"). Another has been the full emergence of the EU as an operational economic union, and yet another the close economic linkages established between the EU and newly emerging Central and Eastern European countries. Including the former communist bloc, today Greater Europe is a trading area of about 550 million, mostly middle-class consumers in at least 25 countries.

The EU   The ultimate objective of the EU is to eliminate all trade barriers among member countries (like between the states in the United States). This economic community eventually will have common custom duties as well as unified industrial and commercial policies regarding countries outside the union. Another goal that has finally largely become a reality is a single currency and a regional central bank.

Such developments will allow companies based in EU nations that are able to manufacture high-quality, low-cost goods to ship them anywhere within the EU without paying duties or being subjected to quotas. This helps to explain why many North American and Pacific Rim firms have established operations in Europe; however, all these outside firms are finding their success tempered by the necessity to address local cultural differences.

As a result of differing local tastes, EU-based firms follow the international strategy adage, "plan globally, act locally." Although this strategy also applies to other parts of the world and will be covered in subsequent chapters, it must be given special consideration if unity in Europe is to become a reality. For example, EU appliance makers will add a self-cleaning option to those ovens for the French market, but leave this option out of units for the German market, where food generally is cooked at lower temperatures. Another interesting strategy is to draw heavily on a network of factories in the EU that can produce both components and finished goods. For example, the Philips television factory in Brugge, Belgium, uses tubes that are supplied from a factory in Germany, transistors that come from France, plastics that are produced in Italy, and electronic components that come from another factory in Belgium.

The most common way that foreign MNCs have gained a foothold in the EU is by using two strategy approaches: acquisitions and alliances. Also, co-operative research and development (R&D) programs are becoming increasingly common as firms team up to share expenses. Siemens and Philips have used this approach to develop computer chips, and IBM has a number of agreements with European firms for developing advanced computer technology. EU-based firms also are able to obtain financial assistance through the

International Management in Action

Privatization in Great Britain   www.cgtd.com/global/europe/gbritain.htm

Many people think that privatization is a strategy confined to former communist governments that now are transforming to free enterprise. In fact, a number of Western countries have been selling off their state-owned properties, and they are finding that this economic strategy can be extremely profitable. Great Britain is an excellent example.

By the late 1970s, the British government had nationalized a sizable number of industries, including steel, coal, electricity generation, trucking, and railways. The government also owned most of the telecommunications industry, as well as aircraft, shipbuilding, car manufacture, silicon-chip production, and North Sea oil holdings. The borrowings and losses of these operations were running 3 billion pounds annually. A number of reasons can be cited for these results, including high cost, low productivity, poor labor relations, inefficient use of resources, and unsatisfactory customer service. It was at this time the government embarked on a new strategy: Sell these industries and businesses to private buyers, and let them operate the companies based on market economy principles.

By the early 1990s, many of the national firms had been privatized, and the results were astounding. In virtually all cases, the operations were profitable, and productivity, labor relations, and customer service had improved. For example, at British Airways and British Gas, productivity per employee was up 20 percent. At Associated British Ports, there were virtually no labor disputes, in sharp contrast to the major disruptions of earlier years. At British Telecom, the call failure rate (a quality service measure) had declined from 4 percent to one-half of 1 percent, and the long waiting list for telephone installation, so common before privatization, had all but disappeared. Moreover, while under government ownership, the company reported that three-quarters of its public telephones were operational (a statistic vigorously denied as overinflated by most members of the general public). In contrast, today, with many more public telephones in existence, 96 percent of them work.

The transition of Great Britain from government-owned enterprises to privatization has greatly improved the nation's economic performance. No wonder so many other countries, both in the EU and outside, are currently following a similar strategy. As one ex-government minister who was part of Britain's privatization effort put it, "The worldwide collapse of state socialism has created a new inevitability—the rise of free economic institutions."

Of course, this is not to say that all privatization efforts have dramatically increased productivity, and not everyone agrees that all state-owned businesses should be sold. For example, research shows that only 16 percent of the British population believe the railway system should be privatized, while 64 percent oppose such action. Nevertheless, the question facing nations—"is no longer whether to introduce or expand the practice of capitalism but only how to do it." For many privatization will be an important part of how to accomplish the transition to a market economy; and this is a goal that the elected Labor government supports.

European Research Cooperation Agency (Eureka)
An EU agency that funds projects in a number of fields with the objective of making Europe more productive and competitive in the world market.

European Research Cooperation Agency (Eureka), which funds projects in the fields of energy, medical technology, biotechnology, communications, information technology, transportation, new materials, robotics, production automation, lasers, and the environment. The objective of Eureka is to make Europe more productive and competitive in the world market. In the years ahead, the EU will continue to be a major focal point for international investment; U.S. firms in particular have been buying businesses in the EU, joining in strategic alliances with EU firms, and exporting into the European market.

The challenge for the future of the EU is to absorb their Eastern neighbors, the former communist bloc countries. This could result in a giant, single European market. In fact, a unified Europe could become the largest economic market in terms of purchasing power in the world. Such a development is not lost on Asian and U.S. firms, which are working to gain a stronger foothold in Eastern European countries as well as the existing EU. In recent years, foreign governments have been very active in helping to stimulate and develop the market economies of Central and Eastern Europe to enhance their economic growth as well as world peace.

Central and Eastern Europe   In December 1989, the Berlin Wall came down, and 2 years later, on December 8, 1991, the Soviet Union ceased to exist. Each of the individual republics that made up the U.S.S.R. in turn declared its independence. The Russian Republic has the most population, territory, and influence, but others, such as Ukraine, also are industrialized and potentially can be important in the global economy. Of the ideas promoted by former Soviet president Mikhail Gorbachev, *glasnost* (openness) has been

Table 1–5
The Three Eras of the Soviet Union

Traditional Russian Society (Pre-1917)	Red Executive Managers (1917–1987)	Market-Oriented (1987–present)
Centralization of authority and responsibility	Centralized leadership	Sharing of power with numerous stakeholders in state enterprises
Collective action	Communist domination	Responsibility for private enterprise success
Dual ethical standards (honesty in personal relationships, deception in business relationships)	Party service	Effective delegation of responsibility to employees
Feelings ranging from helplessness (only a religious savior will deliver people from their plight) to bravado (belief in one's ability to outsmart others)	Rise of collective enterprises	Use of informal influence to obtain favors
	Dual ethical standards (honesty in personal conduct with employees, dishonesty in business dealings)	Bipolar extremes of cynicism in problem solving
	Use of informal influence to obtain favors	Use of overpromising to both clients and business partners
	Feelings of helplessness due to producing inferior products and bravado in operating some of the world's largest organizations	A high degree of achievement motivation regarding quality service and products but social contempt for success

Source: Adapted from Sheila Puffer, "Understanding the Bear: A Portrait of Russian Business Leaders," *Academy of Management Executive,* February 1994, pp. 41–61. Used with permission.

achieved, but *perestroika* (economic and political restructuring) is still having major problems. A brief overview of the historical developments in Russia is shown in Table 1–5. Of most importance to the study of international management are the Russian economic reforms, the dismantling of Russian price controls (allowing supply and demand to determine prices), and privatization (converting the old communist-style public enterprises to private ownership).

Clearly, Russia still has tremendous problems.[30] In fact, by the turn of the century, once-mighty Russia's economy was not nearly as strong as those of its once-dominated neighbors, the Czech Republic, Hungary, and Poland. Even with rapid economic progress, closing the gap with their Western European neighbors will take many more years.

One of the ways that Russia is attempting to get its economy going is by removing many administered prices and subsidies and letting free market forces take over. The problem with this strategy is that it results in very high inflation (demand is much greater than supply). Hyperinflation is very hard on the people, and for political expediency, this slows down price reforms.

On the positive side, many efforts are under way to help stimulate the Russian economy. Russia has been given membership in the International Monetary Fund (IMF), which has pledged development loans to help the country make the transition to a free market economy, and also put together a loan package to help keep the economy from collapsing.[31] In addition, the Group of Seven (the United States, Germany, France, England, Canada, Japan, and Italy) has pledged billions for humanitarian and other types of assistance. So, while the Russian economy likely will have a number of years of painfully slow economic recovery and many current problems, most economic experts predict that if the Russians can hold things together politically and maintain social order, things should get better in the long run.

Besides freeing up prices, the other major development that is needed for Russia to transform into a market economy is privatization. Russian enterprises no longer are fully subsidized, and they no longer can automatically sell all their output to the state. Enterprises are increasingly becoming more self-sustaining and are operating in more of a market-based environment. Privatization has taken a number of different forms, including turning a large number of state-run businesses over to the workers and managers, letting them set up a board of directors and run the operation. In addition, an increasing number of public enterprises issued stock, and both employees and outside investors purchased ownership. Shareholders not only get equity but also a vote in how the company is run.

Although these economic reforms are being implemented slowly, there are significant problems in Russia associated with growing crime of all kinds as well as political uncertainty. Many foreign investors feel that the risk is still too high.[32] Russia is such a large market, however, and has so much potential for the future, many MNCs feel they must get involved. For example, DaimlerChrysler of Germany has a contract for a $140 million plant to build buses. The Carroll Group of Britain is constructing a $250 million hotel-trade center. Alcatel, the giant French telecommunications company, has a $2.8 billion contract to supply advanced digital telephone equipment switches. McDonald's opened a restaurant in Moscow about 10 years ago and now operates more than 50 restaurants throughout the country. Overall, however, Russia still has a long way to go in becoming like its Western neighbors. The *Economist* Intelligence Unit (EIU) has reported that Russia was one of the least successful countries in Central and Eastern Europe in making the transition to a market economy, and it also was ranked as one of the most politically risky countries in the world.[33]

Former communist countries that have become most visible in the international arena include the Czech Republic, Hungary, and Poland. All three initially were battered by inflation, unemployment, and slow economic growth during their transition efforts. All three made significant progress, and they have been successful in attracting Western capital. Although recently they have been experiencing economic problems as will be discussed in the next chapter, they have been able to attract outside investors, including: (1) Volkswagen taking a $6.6 billion stake in the Skoda Auto Works; (2) Japan's Fravalex purchasing the glass manufacturer Sklo-Union Teplice for $1 billion; (3) Linde of Germany investing $106 million in Technoplyn, a natural gas company; (4) US West and Bell Atlantic entering into an $80 million telecommunications joint venture with the Czech government to produce telephone switches; (5) Swedish furniture maker Ikea investing $60 million in a furniture production plant in Trnava; and (6) Siemens of Germany investing $35 million for an interest in Electromagnetica, a medical equipment company, and $15 million in Tesla Karin, a telecommunications firm. There also has been a movement toward teaching Western-style business courses, as well as MBA programs in all the Central European countries.

In Hungary, state-owned hotels have been privatized, and Western firms, attracted by the low cost of highly skilled, professional labor, have been entering into joint ventures with local companies. MNCs also have been making direct investments, as in the case of General Electric's purchase of Tungsram, the giant Hungarian electric company. Another example is Britain's Telfos Holdings, which paid $19 million for 51 percent of Ganz, a Hungarian locomotive and rolling stock manufacturer. Still others include Suzuki's investment of $110 million in a partnership arrangement to produce cars with local manufacturer Autokonzern, Ford Motor's construction of a new $80 million car component plant, and Italy's Ilwa $25 million purchase of the Salgotarjau Iron Works.

Poland had a head start on the other former communist bloc countries. General political elections were held in June 1989, and the first noncommunist government was established, well before the fall of the Berlin Wall. In 1990, the Communist Polish United Workers Party dissolved, and Lech Walesa was elected President. Earlier than its neighbors, Poland instituted radical economic reforms (characterized as the so-called "shock therapy"). Although the relatively swift transition to a market economy has been very difficult for the Polish people, with very high inflation initially, continuing unemployment, and the decline of public services, Poland's economy has done relatively well. However, political instability and risk, large external debts, a still-deteriorating infrastructure, and only modest education levels have led to continuing economic problems.

Although Russia, the Czech Republic, Hungary, and Poland are the largest and receive the most media coverage, the other former communist countries also are struggling to right their economic ships. A small but particularly interesting example is Albania. Ruled ruthlessly by the Stalinist-style dictator Enver Hoxha for over four decades following World War II, Albania was the last, but most devastated, Eastern European country to abandon communism and institute radical economic reforms. At the beginning of the 1990s, Albania started from zero. Industrial output initially fell over 60 percent, and inflation reached 40 percent monthly. Today, Albania still struggles but is slowly making progress.[34]

The key for Albania and the other Eastern European countries is to maintain the social order, establish the rule of law, rebuild the collapsed infrastructure, and get factories and other value-added, job-producing firms up and running. Foreign investment must be forthcoming for these countries to join the global economy. A key challenge for Albania and the other "have-not" Eastern European countries will be to make themselves less risky and more attractive for international business.

Asia

Despite the severe economic downturn starting in 1997, Asia in general has bounced back and promises to continue being one of the major players in the world economy.[35] Because there are far too many nations to allow for comprehensive coverage here, the following provides insights into the economic status and international management challenges of selected Asian countries.

Japan During the 1970s and 1980s, Japan's economic success had been without precedent. The country had a huge positive trade balance, the yen was strong, and in manufacturing and consumer goods the Japanese became recognized as a world leader.

Analysts ascribe Japan's phenomenal success to a number of factors. Some areas that have received a lot of attention are the Japanese cultural values supporting a strong work ethic and group/team effort, consensus decision making, the motivational effects of guaranteed lifetime employment, and the overall commitment that Japanese workers have to their organizations. However, as seen in "International Management in Action: Separating Myths from Reality," at least some of these assumptions about the Japanese workforce have turned out to be more myth than reality and some of the former strengths have become weaknesses in the new economy. For example, consensus decision making turns out to be too time-consuming in the speed-based new economy.

Some of the early success of the Japanese economy can be attributed to the **Ministry of International Trade and Industry (MITI).** This is a governmental agency that identifies and ranks national commercial pursuits and guides the distribution of national resources to meet these goals. In recent years, MITI has given primary attention to the so-called ABCD industries: automation, biotechnology, computers, and data processing.

Another major reason for Japanese success was the use of **keiretsus.** This Japanese term stands for the large, vertically integrated corporations whose holdings provide much of the assistance needed in providing goods and services to end users. Being able to draw from the resources of the other parts of the keiretsu, a Japanese MNC often can get things done more quickly and profitably than its international competitors.

Over the years, Japanese multinationals have invested billions of dollars abroad. In both the United States and the EU, Japanese auto firms have built new assembly plants. Japanese MNCs have made controversial acquisitions as well, including such well-known U.S. landmarks as Rockefeller Center, the Pebble Beach golf course, and Columbia Pictures. Beginning in the 1990s, however, there was a marked slowdown in overseas investment, and Japan's international holdings declined. This decline was mostly attributable to the slowing of the Japanese economy; however, poor management decisions also played an important role. For example, in the case of Rockefeller Center, Mitsubishi found that it was unable to generate sufficient revenue to pay the huge interest on its mortgage. As a result, it sought protection under American bankruptcy laws, causing a furor among the investors who held the mortgage and demanded the company dip into its corporate coffers and make the payments.[36]

Now for over 10 years, the Japanese economy has endured a serious recession.[37] The government has had great difficulty correcting the situation. During the 1980s many major

Ministry of International Trade and Industry (MITI)
A Japanese government agency that identifies and ranks national commercial pursuits and guides the distribution of national resources to meet these goals.

Keiretsus
An organizational arrangement in Japan in which a large group of vertically integrated companies bound together by cross-ownership, interlocking directorates, and social ties provide goods and services to end users.

International Management in Action

Separating Myths from Reality   http://fuji.stanford.edu/jguide

One objective of multicultural research is to learn more about the customs, cultures, and work habits of people in other countries. After all, a business can hardly expect to capture an overseas market without knowledge of the types of goods and services the people there want to buy. Equally important is the need to know the management styles that will be effective in running a foreign operation. Sometimes this information can be quite surprising. For example, recent analysis of Japanese management styles and techniques reveals that much of what Americans "know" about the Japanese may not always be true. Here are some examples that provide food for thought about Japanese management:

1. Many people believe that the Japanese are hardworking by nature. However, recent research shows that there is little difference in productivity among workers in Japanese plants throughout the world. Moreover, many of the differences that do exist are a result of factors such as subcontracting, vendors, and labor regulation. In addition, research among workers at Japanese municipal offices and the national railways shows that many of these workers are not industrious at all.

2. Most Japanese do not have lifelong employment. In fact, about the one-third that did in the past no longer have this security in recent years of the economic downturn. In addition, because of compulsory retirement, many workers must leave their jobs between the ages of 55 and 60. If they do not have a good retirement program

or have not saved enough for their later years, they may have to get another job at a greatly reduced salary.

3. Many Japanese managers are not participative managers; they tend to be autocratic. One study found that almost half of all Japanese executives indicated that they autocratically set annual goals for their division; in contrast, only 32 percent of U.S. managers follow this practice.

4. Young Japanese college graduates entering the workforce express a desire to stay with their firm for a lifetime and say they are willing to work hard to get ahead. After only a few years on the job, however, these attitudes change, and only about one-third feel this way. In short, company loyalty among many Japanese may not be as high as commonly believed.

5. Most Japanese do not work long hours because they enjoy work. The most common reason is that their family needs the money for living expenses. A second common reason is that the boss works long hours, and the staff are afraid to leave the office until the manager does. As a result, many employees end up staying at the office until late in the evening.

These examples show the importance of studying international management and learning via systematic analysis and firsthand information how managers in other countries really do behave toward their employees and their work. Such analysis is critical in separating international management myths from reality.

Japanese banks made large loans to local businesses. Some of these loans were backed up with real estate, while others were based on projected revenues. In the early 1990s when the Japanese real estate market collapsed, these loans were no longer fully collateralized and the borrowers, in most cases, could not afford to pay the debt. At the same time, the economy began slowing up and many businesses found that with reduced profits they could not meet their loan obligations to the banks. By the turn of the century the situation was so bad that most of the major banks had billions of dollars in uncollectible loans on their books and lacked the financial resources to make additional loans that could help turn around the economy.[38] At the same time the government began insisting that the banks write off their bad loans and straighten out their portfolios. Coupled with these problems, international competition increased and small and medium-sized Japanese firms found themselves scurrying to stay afloat and corporate[39] bankruptcies have reached record levels.[40] Yet, despite these setbacks, Japan remains a formidable international competitor (the second largest economy behind the U.S.) and is well poised in all three major economic regions: the Pacific Rim, North America, and Europe.

Japan also has been the target of foreign investment. Automakers such as BMW and Mercedes annually dominate foreign auto sales in the Japanese market. Meanwhile, Ford and General Motors, among others, are working on building market share in the Japanese auto market. IBM, Coca-Cola, Dow, McDonald's, and Toys "R" Us also do well in Japan, collectively accounting for annual sales of over $150 billion. Moreover, the future likely will see even greater progress. Other MNCs, particularly those from the EU and newly industrialized Pacific Rim countries, are targeting the Japanese market as well. Given that Japan relies heavily on exporting to sustain its economic growth, the years ahead should prove to be interesting as international managers from around the world continue to compete against the down but not out Japan, Inc.

China During the 1980s, China's average annual real economic growth was about 10 percent. From 1990 to 1995 GDP maintained this spectacular rate of growth and by the turn of the century, despite a severe economic downturn in the late nineties by its Asian neighbors, the awakened giant China reported an annual GDP growth of 8 percent.[41] This continuing growth in tough times shows that its economy is healthy and growing stronger. At the same time, however, some international economists believe that China may overstate its growth rate[42] and that it is really closer to 6 percent. Others contend that even if the country has been growing at a healthy rate, China will be unable to maintain it and, in fact, the Asian Development Bank recently forecasted the country's growth rate for the early years of the new century at 6 to 6.5 percent.[43] The ruling communist government has set 8 percent as a target which is needed to handle the continual influx of workers from the countryside.

Despite being caught up in the economic problems facing all of Asia, China continues to attract foreign investment.[44] Among others, Motorola has put $120 million into facilities producing semiconductors and mobile phones; General Motors has a $100 million investment in a truck assembly plant, and Procter & Gamble has invested $10 million in a joint-venture factory to produce laundry and personal care products. Additionally, the country's exports remain high with the U.S., Japan, and the EU importing billions of dollars of goods from China every year.[45]

At the same time, however, China remains a major political risk for investors.[46] The one country, two systems (communism and capitalism) is a delicate balance to maintain and foreign businesses are often caught in the middle. Most MNCs find it very difficult to do business in and with China and have yet to make a profit. Many of them have also found that product pirating is still common, and while the government has promised to prosecute companies that engage in this illegal and unethical practice, much remains to be done about it. Perhaps even more disconcerting for MNCs is that contractual agreements often prove to be worthless.[47] For example, McDonald's received a long-run lease on property in Beijing and built a large restaurant there; since then the government has told the company that it must move because the entire area is to be razed and turned into a huge office and retail complex. This is not an isolated incident. Outside chemical producers have found themselves facing $10,000-per-product "registration fees," and U.S. law firms operating in Shanghai were forced to close until the government granted them new licenses. German and Japanese banks have found that collecting loans from the government can be extremely difficult as well. In addition, some securities firms have learned that Chinese clients sometimes refuse to pay for trades that turn out to be losers, and there is no government protection for such actions. Simply put, China remains a complicated and high-risk venture. Even so, MNCs know that China with its 1.3 billion people will be a major world market and that they must have a presence there.

The Four Tigers In addition to Japan and China, there are four other widely recognized economic powerhouses in Asia. Note that the traditionally used term "newly industrialized countries" (NICs) is not used, because they are not really new anymore. South Korea, Hong Kong, Singapore, and Taiwan have arrived as major economic powers and probably now should be referred to more accurately as the "Four Tigers." The GDP of all four had grown rapidly up until the problems starting in the Southeast Asian countries of Thailand, Indonesia, and Malaysia in 1997 began to affect them also.

In South Korea, the major conglomerates, called **chaebols,** include such internationally known firms as Samsung, Daewoo, Hyundai, and the LG Group. Many key managers in these huge firms have attended universities in the West, where in addition to their academic

Chaebols
The very large, family-held Korean conglomerates that have considerable political and economic power.

programs, they learned the culture, customs, and language. Now they are able to use this information to help formulate competitive international strategies for their firms. This will be very helpful for South Korea, which among the Four Tigers was hardest hit by the 1997 Southeast Asian economic crisis. Its GDP declined in the late 1990s and the value of its currency dropped almost 50 percent against the dollar.[48] This led the government to announce plans for investigating the ethical and even illegal practices of the chaebols, privatizing a wide range of industries, and withdrawing some of the restrictions on overall foreign ownership.[49] Since then things have started improving. GDP increased by more than 7 percent at the turn of the century and new company formations reached an all-time high.[50] Additionally, auto exports rose sharply with Hyundai and Daewoo, in particular, dramatically increasing their U.S. market share.[51]

Bordering southeast China and now part of the PRC (People's Republic of China), Hong Kong has been the headquarters for some of the most successful multinational operations in Asia. Hong Kong has had some economic problems like its neighbors but has bounced back. Although it can rely heavily on southeast China for manufacturing, there is still uncertainty about the future and the role that the Chinese government intends to play in local governance.[52] Although the transition has gone smoothly so far, there is the risk that the business climate could radically change. However, the former British colony should continue to play a strong international role in the Pacific Rim.

Singapore is a major success story. It has been hurt least by the economic downturn because of its solid foundation. A major problem Singapore now faces is how to continue expanding this economic foundation in the face of increasing international competition. To date, however, Singapore has emerged as an urban planner's ideal model and the leader and financial center of Southeast Asia. As shown in Table 1–6, Singapore continues to be near the top of the list of the world's most competitive nations.

The fourth Tiger, Taiwan, has progressed from a labor-intensive economy to one that is dominated by more technologically sophisticated industries, including banking, electricity generation, petroleum refining, and computers. Although its economy has also been hit by the downturn in Asia, like the other Tigers it has bounced back and remains a major

Table 1–6
The World's Most Competitive Nations 2000 Rank

Country	
United States	1
Singapore	2
Finland	3
Netherlands	4
Switzerland	5
Luxembourg	6
Ireland	7
Germany	8
Sweden	9
Iceland	10
Canada	11
Denmark	12
Australia	13
Hong Kong	14
United Kingdom	15

Source: World Competitiveness Scoreboard, 2000.

economic power in the Pacific Rim. China considers Taiwan to be a breakaway province and this continues to be a real threat not only to geopolitics but also contributes to risk in doing business there. However, Taiwan's government continues to work out its relationship with the mainland to at least maintain the status quo.

Each of the Four Tigers has been the target of foreign MNCs. For example, IBM and Hewlett-Packard, determined to build their local shares of the computer market, have invested in laboratories and factories within these countries. Motorola has followed the same strategy in enlarging its telecommunications market. Other major MNCs in "Tiger Country" range from the Japanese (Matsushita, Nissan, and Sharp) to the Europeans (Volkswagen, Philips, and Nestlé). As a result, the amount of trade and investment occurring between the Four Tigers and the rest of the world continues to expand.

Southeast Asian Countries Besides Singapore, other countries of Southeast Asia also should be recognized. Although not yet having the economic prowess of the Four Tigers and suffering economic problems starting in 1997, Thailand, Malaysia, Indonesia (sometimes called the "Baby Tigers"), and now Vietnam[53] have economically developed along the lines of the Four Tigers. All have a relatively large population base, inexpensive labor, and, unlike the Four Tigers, they do have considerable natural resources. These countries were also known to have social stability, but in the aftermath of the economic crisis there has been considerable turmoil in this part of the world, especially the fourth largest populated country in the world, Indonesia. Nevertheless, as Japan and the Four Tigers have begun to level off and mature, these export-driven Southeast Asian countries remain attractive to outside investors. MNCs from Japan, the Four Tigers, North America, and the EU all want to have a presence in these countries.

Less Developed Countries

In contrast to the fully developed countries of North America, Europe, and Asia are the less developed countries (LDCs) around the world. An LDC typically is characterized by two or more of the following: low GDP, slow (or negative) GDP growth per capita, high unemployment, high international debt, a large population, and a workforce that is either unskilled or semiskilled. In some cases, such as in the Middle East, there also is considerable government intervention in economic affairs. In recent years, some of these LDCs have shown improvement, but they still have a long way to go to fully compete in the world marketplace. Although complete coverage of all LDCs is beyond the scope of this chapter, the following focuses on representative LDCs and regions.

India With a population of about 1 billion and growing, India has traditionally had more than its share of political and economic problems. Per-capita GDP remains low, but there is still a large middle- and upper-class market for goods and services. Although India's economic growth does not compare with that of countries such as China, there has been a steady growth in recent years. The government continues its attempt to attract investors and further stimulate economic growth.

For a number of reasons, India is attractive to multinationals, and especially to U.S. and British firms. Many Indian people speak English and are very well educated and are known for advanced information technology expertise. Also, the Indian government is providing funds for economic development. For example, India is expanding its telecommunication systems and increasing the number of phone lines fivefold, a market that AT&T is vigorously pursuing. Many frustrations remain in doing business in India (see "In the International Spotlight" at the end of this chapter), but there is little question that the country will receive increased attention in the years ahead.

Middle East and Central Asia Israel, the Arab countries, Iran, Turkey, and the Central Asian countries of the former Soviet Union are considered by the World Bank to be LDCs. Because of their oil, however, some people would consider these countries to be economically rich. Recently, this region has been in the world news because of the aftermath of the September 11, 2001 terrorism attack on the U.S. However, these countries continue to try to balance the geopolitical, religious forces with economic viability. For example, Israel has been hard hit by inflation, and although the GDP per capita is well over $18,000, there are balance-of-payment problems. Economic problems continue to plague all the countries in the region. Despite the tragedies and economic problems, the Middle East countries continue to be active in the international business arena, and students of international management should have a working knowledge of these countries' customs, culture, and management practices.

The Arab and Central Asian countries rely almost exclusively on oil production. The price of oil greatly fluctuates and the Organization of Petroleum Exporting Countries (OPEC) has trouble holding together its cartel. In recent years the price has been relatively high and world demand is likely to keep it there.

Most industrial nations rely, at least to some degree, on imported oil and Arab countries have invested billions of dollars in U.S. property and businesses. Many people around the world, including those in the West, work for Arab employers. For example, the bankrupt United Press International was purchased by the Middle East Broadcasting Centre, a London-based MNC owned by the Saudis.

Africa   Even though they have considerable natural resources, on the whole African nations remain very poor and undeveloped, and international trade is not a major source of income. Although African countries do business with developed countries, it is on a limited scale. One major problem of doing business in the African continent is the overwhelming diversity of about 750 million people divided into 3,000 tribes that speak 1,000 languages and dialects. Also, there is political instability in many countries with the associated risks, especially as far as direct foreign investment is concerned.

In recent years, Africa, especially sub-Saharan Africa, has had a number of severe problems. In addition to tragic tribal wars, there has been the spread of terrible diseases such as AIDS and Ebola. Other big problems include poverty, starvation, illiteracy, corruption, social breakdown, vanishing resources, overcrowded cities, drought, and homeless refugees. There is still hope in the future for Africa despite this bleak situation, however, because African countries remain virtually untapped. Not only are there considerable natural resources, but the diversity can also be used to advantage. For example, many African people are familiar with the European cultures and languages of the former colonial powers (e.g., English, French, Dutch, and Portuguese), which can serve them well in international business. Also, the spirit of these emerging countries has not been broken. There are continuing efforts to stimulate economic growth.[54] Examples of what can be done include Togo, which has sold off many of its state-owned operations and leased a steel-rolling mill to a U.S. investor, and Guinea, which has sold off some of its state-owned enterprises and cut its civil service force by 30 percent. A special case is South Africa, where apartheid, the former white government's policies of racial segregation and oppression, has been dismantled and the healing process is progressing. Long-jailed former black president Nelson Mandela is recognized as a world leader. These significant developments have led to an increasing number of the world's MNCs returning to South Africa; however, there continue to be both social and economic problems which, despite Mandela's and his successors' best efforts, signal uncertain times for the years ahead.

The World of *Business Week*—Revisited

Having read this chapter, you should now be more cognizant of worldwide economic developments. After a great first few years, when the dot-com bubble burst at the end of 2000, the new economy is now best characterized by considerable uncertainty and ups and downs around the world. North America is still doing relatively well, and the creation of a free trade market that economically solidified all of the Americas could be beneficial in helping jump-start and sustain the economies of the Caribbean and South America. The EU economies are also uncertain, especially those in central and eastern European countries that have emerged from behind the iron curtain of communism. In Asia, Japan has been bogged down for over a decade and China's economy offers mixed signals. However, the Four Tigers and Southeast Asian Baby Tigers have generally bounced back from the late nineties' economic crisis and now are uncertain like the rest of the world. Less developed countries have not fared particularly well during the past decade, although India shows perennial signs of slow improvement. In light of these developments which you read about in the chapter, answer these three questions: (1) How useful could the American economic model be for EU countries such as the UK, Germany, and France? (2) What would be the biggest challenge for China in adopting this model? and (3) Could Russia benefit from following more the example of China or the Western European countries and the U.S.?

Summary of Key Points

1. International trade and investment have been increasing dramatically over the years. Major multinational corporations (MNCs) have holdings throughout the world, from North America to Europe to the Pacific Rim to Africa. Some of these holdings are a result of direct investment; others are partnership arrangements with local firms. Small firms also are finding that they must seek out international markets to survive in the future. The internationalization of nearly all business has arrived.

2. International economic activity is most pronounced in the triad of North America, Europe, and the Pacific Rim. In North America, the United States, Canada, and Mexico have the North American Free Trade Agreement (NAFTA) that is turning the region into one giant market. In South America, there is an increasing amount of intercountry trade, sparked by Mercosur and the Andean Pact nations. Additionally, others such as Chile have been projected to may be part of NAFTA. In Europe, the 15 countries of the European Union (EU) form a major economic power, and the former communist countries to the east are seeking membership in the EU. The Central European countries of the Czech Republic, Poland, and Hungary already are becoming trading partners, and if Russia and the other Eastern European countries make progress in their transformation efforts, then Greater Europe will be an even more formidable market in the future. Although having economic problems and uncertainty like the rest of the world, Asia is another major regional power, as shown not only by Japan but also the economies of China and the Four Tigers (Singapore, South Korea, Hong Kong, and Taiwan). Other areas of the world, including India, the Middle East and Central Asia, and Africa, continue to have complex problems, but still hold economic promise for the future.

Key Terms

international management, 5

European Research Corporation Agency (Eureka), *16*

MNC, 5

North American Free Trade Agreement (NAFTA), 6

Ministry of International Trade and Industry (MITI), *19*

keiretsus, 19

maquiladora industry, *13*

chaebols, 21

Review and Discussion Questions

1. How does NAFTA have an impact on the economies of North America? What importance does this economic pact have for international managers in Europe and Asia?

2. How has the formation of the EU created new opportunities for member countries? Of what importance are these opportunities to international managers in other geographic regions such as North America or Asia?

3. Why are Russia and Eastern Europe of interest to international managers? Identify and describe some reasons for such interest.

4. Many MNCs have secured a foothold in Asia, and many more are looking to develop business relations there. Why does this region of the world hold such interest for international management? Identify and describe some reasons for such interest.

5. Why would MNCs be interested in South America, India, the Middle East and Central Asia, Africa, the LDCs of the world? Would MNCs be better off focusing their efforts on more industrialized regions? Explain.

Answers to the In-Chapter Quiz

1. **c.** Gillette, a U.S.-based MNC, owns the Braun company.
2. **d.** Bic SA is a French company.
3. **b.** The British MNC Grand Metropolitan PLC recently sold Häagen-Dazs to The Pillsbury Company of the U.S.
4. **a.** Thomson SA of France produces RCA televisions.
5. **a.** Britain's Grand Metropolitan PLC also sold the Green Giant product line to The Pillsbury Company of the U.S.
6. **a.** Godiva chocolate is owned by Campbell Soup, an American firm.
7. **b.** Vaseline is manufactured by the Anglo-Dutch MNC Unilever PLC.
8. **d.** Wrangler jeans are made by the VF Corporation based in the United States.
9. **d.** Holiday Inn is owned by Britain's Bass PLC, recently renamed Six Continents.
10. **c.** Tropicana orange juice was purchased by U.S.-based PepsiCo.

Internet Exercise: Franchise Opportunities at McDonald's

One of the best-known franchise operations in the world is McDonald's; and in recent years the company has been working to expand its international presence. Why? Because the U.S. market is becoming saturated and the major growth opportunities lie in the international arena. Visit the McDonald's web site **www.mcdonalds.com** and find out what is going on in the company. Begin by perusing their latest annual report and see how well they are doing both domestically and internationally. Then turn to the franchise information that is provided and find out how much it would cost to set up a franchise in the following countries: Belgium, Brazil, South Korea, Mexico, Slovenia, and Turkey. Which seems like the most attractive international investment? In addition to this group, in what other countries is the firm seeking franchisees? Would any of these seem particularly attractive to you as investor? Which ones? Why?

Then, based on this assignment and the chapter material, answer these last two questions: (1) Will the fact the euro has become the standard currency in the EU help or hinder a new McDonald's franchisee in Europe? (2) If there are exciting worldwide opportunities, why does McDonald's not exploit these itself instead of looking for franchisees? (3) What is the logic in McDonald's expansion strategy?

India

India is located in southern Asia, with the Bay of Bengal on the east and the Arabian Sea on the west. One-sixth of the world's population (approximately 1 billion people) lives within the country's 1.27 million square miles. Over 80 percent of the population are Hindus, and the official language is Hindi, although many people also speak English. Because the literacy rate is less than 40 percent, radio and television are the most influential media. The country operates as a democratic republic, and for the most part, one party has dominated the government since independence in 1947. At that time, India was born of the partition of the former British Indian empire into the new countries of India and Pakistan. This division has been a source of many problems through the years. For example, much to the dismay of the world community, both countries had nuclear tests in a cold war atmosphere. Also, many millions of Indians still live at the lowest level of subsistence, and the per-capita income is very low.

In the past, doing business in India has been quite difficult. For example, it took PepsiCo 3 years just to set up a soft drink concentrate factory, and Gillette, the U.S. razor blade company, had to wait 8 years for its application to enter the market to be accepted. Additionally, many MNCs have complained that there are too many barriers to effective operations. In the mid-1970s, the country changed its rules and required that foreign partners hold no more than 40 percent ownership in any business. As a result, some MNCs left India.

In recent years, the government has been relaxing its bureaucratic rules, particularly those relating to foreign investments. From 1981 to 1991, total foreign direct investment in India increased by $250 million, and between 1991 and 1993, it jumped by an additional $2.5 billion. In 2000 foreign direct investment was over $3 billion and the pace continues. Most of this new investment has come from the United States and nonresident Indians. One reason for this change in the nation's policies toward business is that the government realizes many MNCs are

making a critical choice: India or China? Any monies not invested in India may be lost to China forever. Additionally, it can be seen that foreign investments are having a very positive effect on the Indian economy. After the first big year of new investments (1991), India's annual GDP jumped to over 4 percent. In 2000 annual GDP increased by more than 5 percent.

The relaxation of rules definitely has encouraged more foreign investment. Coca-Cola was able to get permission for a 100-percent-owned unit in India in 8 weeks, and Motorola received clearance in 2 days to add a new product line—and did all of this via fax. Other companies that have reported rapid progress include DaimlerChrysler, Procter & Gamble, and Whirlpool. At the same time, however, not everything is roses. Many MNCs are still reporting problems.

Nevertheless, the Indian government's new approach is helping a great deal. In addition, there are other attractions that entice MNCs to India. These include: (1) a large number of highly educated people, especially in critically short supply areas such as in medicine, engineering and computer science; (2) widespread use of English, long accepted as the international language of business; and (3) low wages and salaries, which often are 10 to 30 percent of those in the world's economic superpowers.
www.ib-net.com

Questions

1. What is the climate for doing business in India? Is it supportive of foreign investment?

2. How important is a highly educated human resource pool for MNCs wanting to invest in India? Is it more important for some businesses than for others?

3. Given the low per-capita income of the country, why would you still argue for India to be an excellent place to do business in the coming years?

Here Comes the Competition

The Wadson Company is a management research firm headquartered in New Jersey. The company was recently hired by a large conglomerate with a wide range of products, ranging from toys to electronics and financial services. This conglomerate wants Wadson to help identify an acquisition target. The conglomerate is willing to spend up to $2.5 billion to buy a major company anywhere in the world.

One of the things the research firm did was to identify the amount of foreign direct investment in the United States by overseas companies. The research group also compiled a list of major acquisitions by non-U.S. companies. It gathered these data to show the conglomerate the types of industries and companies that are currently attractive to the international buyers. "If we know what outside firms are buying," the head of the research firm noted, "this can help us identify similar overseas businesses that may also have strong growth potential. In this way, we will not confine our list of recommendations to U.S. firms only." In terms of direct foreign investment by industry, the researchers found that the greatest investment was being made in manufacturing (almost $100 billion). Then, in descending order, came wholesale trade, petroleum, real estate, and insurance.

On the basis of this information, the conglomerate has decided to purchase a European firm. "The best acquisitions in the United States have already been picked," the president told the board of directors. "However, I'm convinced that there are highly profitable enterprises in Europe that are ripe for the taking. I'd particularly like to focus my attention on France and Germany." The board gave the president its full support, and the research firm will begin focusing on potential European targets within the next 30 days.

Questions

1. Is Europe likely to be a good area for direct investment during the years ahead?

2. Why is so much foreign money being invested in U.S. manufacturing? Based on your conclusions, what advice would be in order for the conglomerate?

3. If the conglomerate currently does not do business in Europe, what types of problems is it likely to face?

The Political, Legal, and Technological Environment

Objectives of the Chapter

The environment that international managers face is changing rapidly. The past is proving to be a poor indicator of what will happen in the future. Changes are not only more common now but also more significant than ever before, and these dramatic forces of change are creating new challenges. Although there are many dimensions in this new environment, most relevant to international management would be the economic environment that was covered in the last chapter and the cultural environment covered in the chapters of Part 2. Also important are the political, legal and regulatory, and technological dimensions of the environment. The objective of this chapter is to examine how the political, legal and regulatory, and technological environments have changed in recent years. Some major trends in each that will help dictate the world in which international managers will compete also are presented. The specific objectives of this chapter are:

1. **EXAMINE** some of the major changes that are currently taking place in the political environment of China, Europe, Russia, and Central and Eastern Europe.

2. **PRESENT** an overview of the legal and regulatory environment in which MNCs operate worldwide.

3. **REVIEW** key technological developments as well as their impact on MNCs now and in the future.

BusinessWeek

The World of *Business Week*

China: Coping with Its New Power

As has happened so often in the dozen years since the Tiananmen Square crackdown, every time Washington and Beijing seem to be building positive momentum, diplomatic disaster strikes. The emergency landing of a U.S. EP-3E spy plane on Hainan Island, following a midair collision with a fighter some 70 miles off China's coast, quickly snowballed into another crisis. A Gallup poll shows more than 80% of Americans view China as dangerous. Temperatures are likely to get much hotter. Among the potential flash points: the Bush Administration's imminent decision on whether to sell destroyers equipped with advanced Aegis radar to Taiwan, its plans to sponsor a U.N. resolution condemning Beijing's human rights record, and what promises to be another hot congressional debate over China's trade status.

China's transformation since 1989 has been breathtaking. State-owned industries, which then accounted for about two-thirds of economic output, are now responsible for just 28%. The once-minuscule private sector, which the government only endorsed three years ago, now accounts for one-third of output and is the main driver of job growth. A decade ago, Shanghai was a drab, isolated city stuck in a time warp. Walk the streets near the Nanjing Road shopping thoroughfare today, and you will see Buick sedans, Esprit boutiques, and Starbucks coffee shops.

You'll also hear plenty of frank criticism of the government: Prosperity has loosened the strict controls on information and expression that characterized the much poorer Maoist regime.

Even though WTO entry has just become a done deal, it already has become a catalyst for change. After two decades of steady but halting reforms, Beijing is now racing to dismantle the last vestiges of a command economy. "There is a revolution under way," says Brookings Institution China economist Nicholas Lardy. Beijing's leaders "really have come to appreciate the benefits of plugging China into the global economy." China is breaking up state monopolies in telecom and distribution. Protections aimed at nurturing national champions in cars, electronics, and machinery are crumbling, and multinationals are gaining unprecedented market access. "The government wants to keep control of only the biggest state enterprises" and privatize the rest, says Beijing University political scientist Wang Yong.

All of these changes will accelerate under the commitments China has made to the WTO—which in many cases it is implementing ahead of schedule. Except in a few sectors, most nontariff barriers to imports will disappear. Duties, which already have dropped from an average of 44%, in 1992, to around 15% now, will plunge below 10% in five years. North America, Europe, and Australia will be able to export millions of extra tons of wheat, corn, cotton, and soybeans.

The market openings Beijing has agreed to were unimaginable a decade ago. China's imports of U.S. high-tech gear, which have swelled from $970 million in 1992 to $4.6 billion last year, could really explode: Computers, telecom equipment, and semiconductors will come in duty-free. With WTO in force, multinationals in China no longer will be forced to give technology to state-controlled partners. Foreign auto makers will be able to sell their cars anywhere, while foreign banks also will be able to open 100%-owned branches and lend directly to consumers. No longer will foreigners have to rely on middlemen to distribute and retain their products.

Of course, WTO membership won't be a magic wand that will make all trade frictions disappear. The next few years may well be marked by anti-dumping suits, counterfeiting charges, and cries of protectionism. That's partly because the deal with the U.S. gives trading partners wide latitude to curb growth in certain Chinese imports if they rise too rapidly and to file antidumping charges.

China is fast becoming integral to the global economy. Its share of world trade has nearly quadrupled, to 3.6%, since 1978. It now supplies 7.3% of the goods America imports, and nearly 14% of what Japan imports. The shares are likely to grow. The Development Research Center of China's State Council estimates that in a decade, annual world trade would be 3.2% higher than it would if China didn't enter the WTO. Some Western economists think that even this projection is a big understatement, since it does not take into account the leap in productivity that greater competition and inflows of foreign equipment and technology will provoke. World Bank economist Will Martin calculates China's share of world trade will double by 2005.

The biggest impact of WTO entry will be felt in industries like garments, toys, and consumer electronics. China's enormous pool of $2-a-day labor, as well as its well-developed industrial parks, give it a huge edge. In 2005, the U.S. and Europe will be required to drop all remaining import quotas on garments and shoes. That could enable China to boost its share of global apparel exports, from 20% to 47%, according to the World Bank. That will send shockwaves through Mexico, India, Indonesia, and other nations whose exports rely on cheap labor. The most profound changes, however, will be in China itself. Brookings' Lardy notes that China is still "shallowly integrated" into the global economy. Half of its exports come from companies in which foreign corporations own stakes—even though they account for just one-eighth of manufacturing output. When foreign-invested companies are excluded, China drops from being the world's 9th-largest exporter to the 15th. China's growth rate, meanwhile, has fallen from 10% five years ago to a projected 7% this year. Even that number is puffed up by heavy public spending and overproduction.

Dramatic Downsizing

Chinese leaders know that greater trade and more foreign capital are essential if they are to achieve their goal of doubling the size of the $1.1 trillion economy in a decade. Trade also is vital in order to create jobs for up to 9 million people entering the workforce each year, especially since downsizing at bloated state industries and the civil service is throwing millions of others out of work. The Chinese are confident they will get that capital: Central Bank Governor Dai Xianglong told *BusinessWeek* he expects China to lure $45 billion in foreign direct investment annually for the next five years, trailing only the U.S. as a recipient of investment.

And that means much deeper economic engagement by America's biggest corporations. After years of travails, many are finding that the China market finally is living up to its hype. In the past three years, Kodak has invested more than $1.2 billion into factories acquired from ailing Chinese film manufacturers. It has opened more than 6,000 franchised Kodak shops around the country. Now, China is Kodak's second-largest market for consumer film and paper, and it should overtake the U.S. in a decade. "China is the potential opportunity of a lifetime," says Kodak Asia President Henri Petit. After 12 years of steadily investing in plant and equipment, Motorola Inc. now has one-third of China's huge 53 million-unit annual market for cell phones. It will plow an additional $1.9 billion into new plants for semiconductors, mobile handsets, and networking equipment.

Multinationals also are finding state companies, now worried about getting buried by imports when duties fall, to be eager partners. General Motors' deepening involvement in the once-cosseted auto industry is evidence of China's new thinking. Just a couple of years ago, Beijing strictly controlled which and how many foreign auto makers could operate in China, which models they could produce, and with whom they teamed up. The authorities until recently confined GM's new $1.5 billion joint venture in Shanghai to making $40,000 Buicks.

Now, Beijing is letting GM and other foreign carmakers into the sectors they really covet: vehicles that meet the modest budgets of Chinese consumers. Soon, GM is to buy a 34% stake in Liuzhou Wuling Motor Co., located in impoverished Guangxi province. In contrast to the money-losing state-owned behemoths foreign carmakers usually are stuck with, Wuling is doing well. It commands a quarter of China's 400,000-unit minivan market.

But with local competition intensifying and with car duties set to plunge, Wuling needs help. "We've been making cars for 10 years, but our production volume isn't big enough for us to compete in the global market," explains Wuling General

Manager Shen Yang. With the aid of dozens of GM experts, Wuling already has started to redesign its factory along the lines of GM's in Shanghai, down to the bulletin board that tracks materials, defects, and output.

What the leadership really wants to achieve by opening up, though, is to enable China's own companies to learn to stand on their own and compete globally. That's starting to happen in consumer electronics, where domestic competition has long been fierce. Now Chinese air conditioners, televisions, and microwave ovens hold their own against imports from Japan and Korea. And brands like Haier, TCL, Galantz, and Konka are starting to be exported around Asia and even to the West. Yukio Shohtoku, managing director of overseas electronics for Matsushita Electronics, says these producers have "very strong advantages" that will enable them soon to take over the low-end market in Japan.

Ambitious Goal

While the outside world may be watching China nervously as a rising economic rival, many Chinese state enterprises simply won't be able to shape up before foreign competition arrives in force. Their weakness will open enormous opportunities for the private sector, even in such sensitive industries as finance. Chengdu-based New Hope Group, a $500 million conglomerate whose interests range from animal feed to real estate, now runs a publicly listed bank that is opening branches across China. President Liu Yonghao credits the deal on WTO for paving the way for his success: In five years, institutions such as Citibank and HSBC will be able to open wholly owned branches in any city, presenting a huge challenge for China's shaky and backward state banks. So authorities are tearing down hurdles for entrepreneurs like Liu. "The WTO is a great opportunity for private companies," he says.

All true, providing political spats get settled quickly. What U.S. business leaders don't want is a repeat of 1996, when Beijing discriminated against Boeing and other companies, after the Clinton administration granted a visa to Taiwan's then-President Lee Tenghui. Even then, the damage got repaired, so much so that after the next serious rupture, the accidental bombing of the Chinese embassy in Belgrade, the two sides were able to sign a WTO agreement six months later. "That shows how we've matured in our relationship," suggests Tim Stratford, chairman of the American Chamber of Commerce in Beijing.

There's no doubt that Beijing will assert itself on the global stage. Leaders from Zhu Rongji down repeatedly stress to visiting Americans that they see freer trade as vital to China's own emergence. A China that competes peacefully in free markets is something no other nation can really oppose. The concern for U.S. policymakers is that China's economic rise fuels its growing military might. That formula guarantees more confrontations. For the West, dealing with this new power is the great foreign policy challenge of the new century.

By Mark Clifford and Dexter Roberts in Beijing and Pete Engardio in New York, with Alysha Webb in Liuzhou, and bureau reports.

This news article provides interesting insights into how the political, legal, and technological environments in China present challenges for the United States government as well as for multinational corporations. To date, many of the political problems that were identified have been resolved or faded from interest. However, the main issue remains. How can China resolve the dilemma it faces? On the one hand, the country wants to modernize and to double the size of its economy within the next decade and to do this it needs foreign investment and technology as well as a strong export program. On the other hand, one of the prices that China will have to pay to attain its economic goals is the opening of its own markets to international goods and services. As free trade becomes a reality, the government's centralized control and power will weaken and many local businesses and industries will be driven out by international competition. MNCs doing business in China see a great opportunity here, but they also realize that the government creates a risky climate for business and they must proceed with caution. Many of the ideas that are discussed in this chapter are critical to the effective international management operations that will be needed in gaining and holding market share in the emerging Chinese economy.

■ Political Environment

The domestic and international political environment has a major impact on MNCs. As government policies change, MNCs must adjust their strategies and practices to accommodate the new perspectives and actual requirements. Moreover, in a growing number of geographic regions and countries, governments appear to be less stable; therefore, these areas carry more risk than they have in the past. The assessment of political risk will be given specific attention in Chapter 10, but the following examines political developments in selected areas and countries that are particularly relevant to today's international management.

China

As discussed in the opening news article, China is such an emerging economic power that it cannot be ignored by international business. The Chinese political environment, however, is very complex and risky because of the government's desire to balance national, immediate needs with the challenge of a free market economy and globalization. For example, at the present time the Chinese government is trying to sustain its economic growth. If growth is slower than 7 percent, the economy will likely not be able to generate enough jobs to take in the 9 million Chinese that enter the workforce each year, as well as the millions being laid off by restructured state enterprises. In the past, economic growth was not a problem. In 1992, for example, the country's GDP increased by 14 percent. However, since then this rate has been continually declining.[1]

In order to ensure that the economy does not fall into the economic malaise that has been sweeping the rest of Asia, the Chinese government has stepped up efforts to encourage foreign investment. Yet, by 2000–2001 there were indications that the country's economic strength was showing signs of fatigue. For example, foreign investment is slowing up because cash-starved Asian companies can no longer afford to build in China; and Chinese exporters are seeing overseas business customers shift to less expensive factories in Thailand and Malaysia. At the same time, local unemployment is starting to rise and bad loans are piling up in the state-owned banks.

In response, the government has begun giving the green light to projects that had been bogged down in bureaucratic red tape and announced a series of steps to open up the economy.[2] Some of these include: (1) speeding up a program to convert state enterprises, which still account for a significant amount of industrial output, into corporations owned by shareholders; (2) dramatically expanding the size of capital markets by authorizing hundreds of new stock listings annually in Shanghai and Shenzhen; (3) allowing government bodies to sell off all but 1,000 of the country's 305,000 state enterprises and letting those that could not be sold go bankrupt; (4) accelerating worker retraining, building low-cost housing, and creating other social services to relieve burdens on state enterprises and care for millions of workers who would lose their jobs; and (5) reducing tariffs to 15 percent.[3]

Despite these developments, MNCs face a host of major obstacles when doing business with and in China. For example, government regulations severely hamper multinational activity and favor domestic companies.[4] Additionally, it is difficult to find qualified people and when a multinational does and then invests money in training these individuals, it is common to find them leaving for jobs with other companies.[5] Yet the biggest problem may well be that the government does not know what it wants from multinational investors and this is what accounts for the mixed signals and changes in direction that it continually sends. Those who have studied China's economic transition over the past decade have noted that this transition is unusual in that it is planned by the state that maintains an active involvement of governmental institutions in business affairs. This approach is so different from anything that MNCs have previously encountered that the experiences of these firms in other emerging economies is often insufficient to provide them the guidelines and insights that they need to do business in China. In fact, the researchers found, the peculiarities of China's system not only generate uncertainties for MNCs, but the nature of the transition challenges the capabilities of current international business theory.[6]

Typical of the problems faced by multinationals in China is provided by the Qualcomm Corporation. The firm had wanted to sell China narrow band CDMA (code division multiple access) technology. However, Qualcomm was unsuccessful in convincing the government that it could build enough products locally and this doomed its plans for CDMA production in China, a technology that is in use in the United States and a few other countries. Instead, China's current mobile phone network, which has over 30 million subscribers, will use the GSM technology that is popular in Europe.[7] This was a big blow to Qualcomm, but the company is not alone. Most MNCs have found that doing business in China is both challenging and frustrating. Here is a recent report of auto firms trying to do business in China:

> The auto companies are especially instructive, because they are some of the highest-profile foreign investors in China. Like most multinationals lured by China's fabled masses, auto companies have wrung their hands in frustration over the strict central control of business deals, the unpredictable unwritten rules and the lack of a functioning legal system. Peugeot, which had an early venture, gave up. DaimlerChrysler has threatened to leave. Profits are non-existent, except for the biggest players; about 100 companies, including scores of inefficient domestic makers, compete.[8]

Yet the auto firms remain because of the huge market there. In 1990 approximately 58,000 cars were made and sold in China. A decade later this total was about 10 times greater. The government allows only a small number of imports, so local production is important and companies like General Motors, Ford, DaimlerChrysler, Mercedes, Toyota, and other major manufacturers are determined to stay the course. For the time being, however, largely due to the political environment, China remains an elusive, uncertain prize for most MNCs.

Europe

Far away from Chinese politics, the political situation in Europe also continues to change. One reason is that leaders in major countries, as well as the EU itself, are finding it difficult to firmly establish a foothold of power. As a result, international managers must remain alert as to how political changes may impact their business. For example, in France, the 12-year reign of the Socialists under François Mitterand ended in mid-1995. Mitterand was replaced by Jacques Chirac, a more conservative Gaullist, and this heralded a host of political changes impacting on doing business in France.

The same kind of changes are occurring in the other major European countries. In Germany, Helmut Kohl was re-elected in late 1994 but soon was having troubles. Three months into his new term, he was forced to consider forming a coalition with the opposition Social Democrats, who already controlled the upper house of Parliament. More recently, Gerald Schröder, subsequent to his 1998 election as Chancellor succeeding Kohl, faced a similar situation involving the Green Party. In Great Britain, political change has been even more pronounced. The Labor Party swept into power in 1997 with a strong majority. Since then, under the leadership of Tony Blair, Britain's economy continued to improve and the government moved more into the middle of the political continuum as seen by one of its recent programs designed to reduce the welfare roles by offering work incentives to the unemployed.[9] This strategy is a strong reversal of earlier Labor party philosophy and shows that the winds of political change can alter very quickly. For example, by 2001 the Blair government's popularity was waning even though the economy continued to be one of the strongest in Europe.[10]

That the nations of Western Europe, with the exception of Norway and Switzerland, now are part of the EU only adds to the complexity of the political environment. MNCs cannot avoid political risks even when doing business with individual countries because of what the EU may dictate. It is important to realize that there are vast cultural differences, as will be pointed out in Chapter 5, but also that the fate of the EU members is interdependent. Now, what happens to one can often influence the others. A good example is provided by France and Germany. Today, Franco-German relations are the cornerstone of a united Europe. The two are tied closely together in a number of ways. For example, each is the other's major trading partner; each has a vested interest in the other doing well. MNCs doing business in either country find that they must focus on developments in both nations, as well as in the EU at large. Simply put, Europe is no longer a series of fragmented countries; it is a giant, interwoven region in which international management must be aware of what is happening politically both in the immediate area of operations as well as throughout the continent.[11]

Russia

Along with China, Russia presents one of the most extreme examples of how the political environment impacts on international management. Boris Yeltsin governed Russia throughout the 1990s, and when he resigned in 2000 and turned the reigns over to Vladimir Putin, the economy was in shambles. Neglect, corruption, and confusing changes in economic policy had taken their toll.[12] The country's infrastructure was literally falling apart. Electricity was regularly cut off throughout the country, gas pipelines sprung leaks on a daily basis, industrial accidents were common place, toxic waste seeped from industrial plants into drinking water supplies, and almost half of the country's freight and passenger railroad cars needed to be replaced. Worse yet, the little funds that were available to begin rebuilding the infrastructure were in the hands of inefficient managers.[13] By one estimate, it will take at least $100 billion to minimally rebuild Russia's infrastructure, a sum that is four times the country's current annual budget.

What makes the international business situation even worse is that infrastructure reform such as in the legal, financial, and trade sectors is a political quagmire. For example, President Putin approved an ambitious plan of reform to spur growth by improving conditions for investment and by deregulating the giant Soviet-era enterprises such as the United Energy Systems, the giant electric company, and the Railways Ministry. However, many people are concerned that this will result in higher prices, and they have appealed to top Kremlin officials who have stalled these types of reforms. At the same time, machinery and equipment is breaking down all over the country because there are no funds to pay for repairs, many trains no longer operate, and most roads are pitted with potholes. Highly educated individuals such as scientists and engineers, such as those who work in the atomic energy sector, are so poorly paid that many of them are looking for other jobs.

Despite such a bleak picture, the economic outlook for Russia is still cautiously optimistic. Real GDP growth in 1999 was 3 percent and it rose to 6 percent in 2000. Moreover, monthly inflation that stood at almost 40 percent in August 1998 had fallen to around 1 percent by mid-2000.[14] In addition, Putin's administration has gotten a tax reform bill enacted that both simplifies the tax code and slashes tax rates. Under the new law individuals pay a flat tax of 13 percent on income and business payroll taxes have been cut. This is good news for the country's middle class that has weathered the economic crisis of 1998 and is looking for a stable economy. Many of these people are entrepreneurs who own their own shops, restaurants, hotels, bakeries, and computer software firms or are managers of large Russian enterprises or multinational firms. In this country of 145 million, there are around 30 million people in the middle, and according to the Russian business magazine *Expert,* this group accounts for 30 percent of the country's $220 billion gross domestic product.[15] So there is a large, productive group of people in Russia that can also be a market for outside MNC goods and services.

The challenge for the Russian government is to keep the economy on an even keel while attracting more foreign investment. One of the big problems is corruption. The

European Bank for Reconstruction and Development report that almost a third of firms doing business in Russia indicate that they are required to give bribes in order to do business and that these monies add more than 4 percent to the overall cost of doing business there.[16] As more MNCs invest in Russia, these unethical practices will face increasing scrutiny.[17] To date, many multinationals feel that the risk is too great. Still most view Russia as they do China; it is too large and potentially lucrative a market to ignore. This is why General Motors recently struck a deal to manufacture cars in Russia. GM is going to team up with Avtovaz, the country's largest domestic carmaker, to produce sport utility vehicles under the Chevrolet brand name. GM will invest about $100 million to build a new assembly line.[18] The giant automaker joins others including BMW, Fiat, Ford, and Renault that currently have Russian operations. There is a big demand for cars. Only 12 percent of Russians now own an auto, compared to Poland where 25 percent of the population have cars. However, most Russians cannot afford to pay much for an auto. Analysts estimate that no more than 30,000 people can buy a car that costs $10,000 or more. On the other hand, if the economy continues to improve, these auto firms, like other foreign investors, will find that their decision to invest now was a wise one. A lot of what happens, however, will be determined by the political environment.[19]

Central and Eastern Europe

Besides Russia, the political situation in the rest of the post-communist countries in Central and Eastern Europe is also in a state of flux. Many problems remain as these nations work to make the transition from a centrally planned to a market economy. A good example is Poland.

In late 1997 Polish voters replaced a government of former communists and brought in a coalition of trade unionists, nationalists, and free marketers. Since then, the government's plan to streamline the economy and get the country moving has been fraught with problems. By the end of 2000, the unemployment rate stood at 15 percent and there were high unemployment pockets in the agriculture and industrial sectors. The Russian crisis and an economic slowdown in the EU had dampened Polish exports, and inflation was running at a 10 percent annual rate. Nevertheless, the country's economy has proven resilient in the past and, as the EU economies begin to improve, things will hopefully get better.

Hungary, one of the strongest economies in Central Europe, had annual GDP increases of over 5 percent in both 2000 and 2001. Unemployment was below 7 percent and consumer price inflation, which was as high as 30 percent in 1995, is now in the range of 10 percent. The government is trying to maintain a positive investment image, which will be important given that foreign investors have put more money per capita into Hungary than anywhere else in post-communist Europe and they want to see results. The future success of Hungary will depend heavily on the ability of the government to maintain this economic momentum.[20]

The Czech Republic in its transition privatized very quickly, gambling that private owners could reorganize and manage firms more effectively than the state. The government also allowed Czech citizens to bid for shares in newly privatized firms—and for a time the country was pointed to as one of the success stories in Central Europe. However, in the late 1990s the country went into a recession, its trade deficit ballooned, and there was negative economic growth of almost 3 percent. Since then things have started to turn around. By late 2000 the economy was growing at an annual rate of almost 4 percent and the finance ministry predicted that this rate would continue for at least the next couple of years. In addition, while the country's trade gap was widening because of high demand for investment goods and a weakening demand for its exports in western Europe, economic activity in the private sector remained high.[21]

The governments of the Balkan countries (e.g., Buglaria, Romania, and Albania) and, with the possible exception of the Baltic states (Estonia, Latvia, and Lithuania), the republics of the former Soviet Union still face severe problems. The governments of these former communist countries all went at the necessary economic reforms (freeing up prices, privatization, elimination of subsidies, and building the needed financial and legal systems and supporting infrastructure) at a much slower pace than Poland, Hungary, or the Czech Republic. Now, they are paying the price with generally depressed economies and lack of foreign investment. Only time will tell what will happen, but the outlook of most experts on the region is generally pessimistic.

■ Legal and Regulatory Environment

One reason that today's international environment is so confusing and challenging for MNCs is because there are so many different laws and regulations. There are four foundations on which laws are based around the world. Briefly summarized, these are:

Islamic law
Law that is derived from interpretation of the *Qur'an* and the teachings of the Prophet Mohammed and is found in most Islamic countries.

1. **Islamic law.** This is law derived from interpretation of the *Qur'an* and the teachings of the Prophet Mohammed. It is found in most Islamic countries in the Middle East and Central Asia.

Socialist law
Law that comes from the Marxist socialist system and continues to influence regulations in countries formerly associated with the Soviet Union as well as China.

2. **Socialist law.** This law comes from the Marxist socialist system and continues to influence regulations in former communist countries, especially those from the former Soviet Union, as well as present-day China, Vietnam, North Korea, and Cuba.

Common law
Law that derives from English law and is the foundation of legislation in the United States, Canada, and England, among other nations.

3. **Common law.** This comes from English law, and it is the foundation of the legal system in the United States, Canada, England, Australia, New Zealand, and others.

Civil or code law
Law that is derived from Roman law and is found in the non-Islamic and nonsocialist countries.

4. **Civil or code law.** This law is derived from Roman law and is found in the non-Islamic and nonsocialist countries such as France, some countries in Latin America, and even Louisiana in the United States.

With these broad statements serving as points of departure, the following sections discuss basic principles and examples of the international legal environment facing MNCs today.

Basic Principles of International Law

Principle of sovereignty
An international principle of law which holds that governments have the right to rule themselves as they see fit.

When compared with domestic law, international law is less coherent, because its sources embody not only the laws of individual countries concerned with any dispute but also treaties (universal, multilateral, or bilateral) and conventions (such as the Geneva Convention on Human Rights or the Vienna Convention of Diplomatic Security). In addition, international law contains unwritten understandings that arise from repeated interactions among nations. Conforming to all the different rules and regulations can create a major problem for MNCs. Fortunately, much of what they need to know can be subsumed under several broad and related principles that govern the conduct of international law.

Nationality principle
A jurisdictional principle of international law which holds that every country has jurisdiction over its citizens no matter where they are located.

Sovereignty and Sovereign Immunity   The **principle of sovereignty** holds that governments have the right to rule themselves as they see fit. In turn, this implies that one country's court system cannot be used to rectify injustices or impose penalties on another unless that country agrees. So, while U.S. laws require equality in the workplace for all employees, U.S. citizens who take a job in Japan cannot sue their Japanese employer under the provisions of U.S. law for failure to provide equal opportunity for them.

Territoriality principle
A jurisdictional principle of international law which holds that every nation has the right of jurisdiction within its legal territory.

International Jurisdiction   International law provides for three types of jurisdictional principles. The first is the **nationality principle,** which holds that every country has jurisdiction (authority or power) over its citizens no matter where they are located. Therefore, a U.S. manager who violates the American Foreign Corrupt Practices Act while traveling abroad can be found guilty in the United States. The second is the **territoriality principle,** which holds that every nation has the right of jurisdiction within its legal territory. Therefore, a German firm that sells a defective product in England can be sued under English law even though the company is headquartered outside of England. The third is the **protective principle,** which holds that every country has jurisdiction over behavior that adversely affects its national security, even if that conduct occurred outside the country. Therefore, a French firm that sells secret U.S. government blueprints for a satellite system can be subjected to U.S. laws.

Protective principle
A jurisdictional principle of international law which holds that every country has jurisdiction over behavior that adversely affects its national security, even if the conduct occurred outside that country.

Doctrine of Comity   The **doctrine of comity** holds that there must be mutual respect for the laws, institutions, and government of other countries in the matter of jurisdiction over their own citizens. Although this doctrine is not part of international law, it is part of international custom and tradition.

Act of State Doctrine   Under the **act of state doctrine,** all acts of other governments are considered to be valid by U.S. courts, even if such acts are inappropriate in the United States. As a result, for example, foreign governments have the right to set limits on the repatriation of MNC profits and to forbid companies from sending more than this amount out of the host country.

Treatment and Rights of Aliens   Countries have the legal right to refuse admission of foreign citizens and to impose special restrictions on their conduct, right of travel, where they can stay, and what business they may conduct. Nations also can deport aliens. For example, the United States has the right to limit the travel of foreign scientists coming into the U.S. to attend a scientific convention and can insist they remain within 5 miles of the hotel.

Forum for Hearing and Settling Disputes   This is a principle of U.S. justice as it applies to international law. At their discretion, U.S. courts can dismiss cases brought before them by foreigners; however, they are bound to examine issues such as where the plaintiffs are located, where the evidence must be gathered, and where property to be used in restitution is located. One of the best examples of this principle is the Union Carbide pesticide plant disaster in Bhopal, India. Over 2,000 people were killed and thousands left permanently injured when a toxic gas enveloped 40 square kilometers around the plant. The New York Court of Appeals sent the case back to India for resolution.

Examples of Legal and Regulatory Issues

The principles described above help to form the international legal and regulatory framework within which MNCs must operate. The following examines some examples of specific laws and situations that can have a direct impact on international business.

Foreign Corrupt Practices Act   During the special prosecutor's investigation of the Watergate scandal in the early 1970s, a number of questionable payments made by U.S. corporations to public officials abroad were uncovered. These bribes became the focal point of investigations by the U.S. Internal Revenue Service, Securities and Exchange Commission (SEC), and Justice Department. This concern over bribes in the international arena eventually culminated in the 1977 passage of the **Foreign Corrupt Practices Act (FCPA),** which makes it illegal to influence foreign officials through personal payment or political contributions. The objectives of the FCPA were to stop U.S. MNCs from initiating or perpetuating corruption in foreign governments and to upgrade the image of both the United States and its businesses abroad.

Critics of the FCPA feared the loss of sales to foreign competitors, especially in those countries where bribery is an accepted way of doing business. Nevertheless, the U.S. government pushed ahead and attempted to enforce the act. Some of the countries that were named in early bribery cases under the law included Algeria, Kuwait, Saudi Arabia, and Turkey. The U.S. State Department tried to convince the SEC and Justice Department not to reveal countries or foreign officials who were involved in its investigations for fear of creating internal political problems for U.S. allies. Although this political sensitivity was justified, for the most part, several interesting developments occurred: (1) MNCs found that they could live within the guidelines set down by the FCPA; and (2) many foreign governments actually applauded these investigations under the FCPA, because it helped them to crack down on corruption in their own country.

One analysis reported that since passage of the FCPA, U.S. exports to "bribe prone" countries actually increased.[22] Investigations reveal that once bribes were removed as a key competitive tool, more MNCs were willing to do business in that country. This proved to be true even in the Middle East, where many U.S. MNCs always assumed that bribes were

Doctrine of comity
A jurisdictional principle of international law which holds that there must be mutual respect for the laws, institutions, and government of other countries in the matter of jurisdiction over their own citizens.

Act of state doctrine
A jurisdictional principle of international law which holds that all acts of other governments are considered to be valid by U.S. courts, even if such acts are illegal or inappropriate under U.S. law.

Foreign Corrupt Practices Act (FCPA)
Made into U.S. law in 1977 because of concerns over bribes in the international business arena, this act makes it illegal to influence foreign officials through personal payment or political contributions.

required to ensure contracts. There is evidence showing that this is no longer true in most cases, and where it is those companies that engage in bribery face a strengthened FCPA that now allows the courts to both fine and imprison guilty parties.[23]

Bureaucratization   Very restrictive foreign bureaucracies are one of the biggest problems facing MNCs. This is particularly true when bureaucratic government controls are inefficient and not corrected. A good example is Japan, whose political parties feel more beholden to their local interests than to those in the rest of the country. As a result, it is extremely difficult to reorganize the Japanese bureaucracy and streamline the ways things are done, because so many politicians are more interested in the well-being of their own districts than in the long-run well-being of the nation as a whole. In turn, parochial actions create problems for MNCs trying to do business there. The election of Junichiro Koizumi as the new prime minister of Japan may help reduce some of this bureaucracy.[24] Certainly the long-running recessionary economy of the country is leading to the beginning of change in the nation's antiquated banking system and is likely to make the markets there more open to competition.[25]

Japanese businesses are also becoming more aware of the fact that they are dependent on the world market for many goods and services and when bureaucratic red tape drives up the costs of these purchases, local consumers pay the price. These businesses are also beginning to realize that government bureaucracy can create a false sense of security and leave them unprepared to face the harsh competitive realities of the international marketplace.

A good example was provided during the mid-1990s when the value of the yen rose sharply and resulted in a decline in international sales by local businesses. Foreign purchasers were unwilling to buy Japanese products that cost 30–40 percent more than they did just a few years earlier. At the same time, foreign firms exporting goods into the Japanese market found that they could easily compete because their prices were lower than those of Japanese producers whose costs were pegged to the high-value yen. As a result, Chrysler cut the price of its Jeep Cherokee by 10 percent and sales rose; and American computer manufacturers such as Compaq and IBM, largely on the basis of price, were able to double their share of the Japanese market. Since this time the yen has declined in market value and local businesses have been able to recapture some lost market share. However, local firms still face greater international competition than ever before.

Additionally, Japan now faces new problems. One of these is that the cost of doing business in Japan is often higher than in other Asian countries. As a result, there has been a recent trend by MNCs toward buying from these less expensive sources. In an effort to deal with this new challenge, the Japanese will have to continue to cut bureaucratic red tape and open their markets to foreign competition. The accompanying "International Management in Action: The United States Goes to the Mat" shows the pressure that has been put on Japan to open its markets. Only in this way in the long run will they drive down their own costs of doing business and remain competitive against world-class organizations.

Privatization   Another example of the changing international regulatory environment is the current move toward privatization by an increasing number of countries. The German government, for example, has sped up deregulation of its telecommunications market. This has opened a host of opportunities for MNCs looking to create joint ventures with local German firms. Additionally, as noted in Chapter 1, the British government continues selling off state-run operations; and in France the government is putting some of its businesses on the sale block. Meanwhile, in China the government has ordered the military to close or sell off between 10,000 and 20,000 companies that earn an estimated $9.5 billion annually. Known collectively as PLA Inc., the Chinese Army's business interests stretch from Hong Kong to the United States and include five-star hotels, paging services to golf courses, and Baskin-Robbins ice cream franchises. When the government cut the military budget during the early 1990s, it allowed the Army to make up this shortfall by earning commercial revenue. However, now the government has decided that the Army must get out of this end of the business and let the free market take over.[26]

International Management in Action

The U.S. Goes to the Mat

For a number of years, the United States has demanded that Japan open its markets and provide the same access that Japanese MNCs are accorded. One of the strategies used by the U.S. government has been to negotiate purchasing targets. For example, in the case of automobiles, the Japanese government several years ago agreed to buy a specific amount of U.S.-made auto parts. This strategy now seems to be a thing of the past, however. Japanese negotiators believe it was a mistake and say they will hold fast in future negotiations.

For their part, the current U.S. administration is pushing hard to level the playing field for trading with Japan. In the past, the United States threatened to impose a major import tax on luxury Japanese cars coming into America. Some observers noted, however, that the U.S. government immediately tempered its hard line with a willingness to set an early date for talks with the Japanese about the trade impasse. The administration countered that this concession was quite minor and used simply to meet a condition set forth by the World Trade Organization (WTO). According to WTO rules, in the absence of a mutual agreement on a date to meet, the parties are required to get together before new sanctions are instituted. This does not mean that there will be a settlement, however, only that the two parties will discuss their differences.

One major roadblock to an early resolution of U.S. demands is that EU countries want to be included in these negotiations. They argue that any arrangement between the United States and Japan will result in their being denied market access. After all, if the Japanese agree to buy $6 billion of U.S.-made auto parts, this is market share that cannot be captured by EU MNCs. The EU wants Japan to open its markets to all countries and let each compete on the level playing field.

How far will Japan go in giving concessions? How determined is the United States to wrestle additional agreements from the Japanese? These questions are yet unanswered. One thing is certain, however: Japan is a major world market, and its citizens have enormous purchasing power. Therefore, all nations will continue efforts to break down trade walls and get into the lucrative Japanese market. For example, General Motors sells its Saturn line in Japan through a network of stand-alone dealerships. The cost of distributing and retailing vehicles in Japan is extremely high, but GM feels that the strong market there is worth this risk. Additionally, GM has been selling Saturns in Taiwan and believes this experience has helped reduce the risk in the Japanese market.

The steps being taken by the U.S. government and some of the major MNCs, such as GM, are important in opening up the Japanese market. Much needs to be done, however, and the U.S. government believes that success in this area will require it to "go to the mat" with Japan. The outcome promises to be not only interesting, but vital to the success of world trade.

■ Technological Environment

The technological environment is changing at lightning speed. For example, while semiconductor firms are now working to develop new memory chips for personal computers,[27] other high-tech firms are trying to create technologies that will replace the PC with even better computing architecture.[28] At the same time, computers, telephones, televisions, and wireless forms of communication are being merged to create multimedia products and to allow users anywhere in the world to communicate with each other. Today the number of people who use cellular phones is greater than ever and in countries like Finland, Norway, and Sweden over half the population are cellular subscribers.[29] In addition, a growing number of people have access to the Internet, allowing them to obtain information from literally millions of sources, and the number of websites is rising sharply. In the United States recent reports are that two-thirds of those 12 years of age or older went online during the past year[30] and more than half of them went online every day.[31] In addition to Internet access, other specific ways in which technology will affect international management in the next decade include:

1. Rapid advances in biotechnology that are built on the precise manipulation of organisms, which will revolutionize the fields of agriculture, medicine, and industry.

2. The emergence of nanotechnology, in which nanomachines will possess the ability to remake the whole physical universe.

3. Satellites that will play a role in learning. For example, communication firms will place tiny satellites into low orbit, thus making it possible for millions of people, even in remote or sparsely populated regions like Siberia, the Chinese desert, and the African interior, to send and receive voice, data, and digitized images through handheld telephones.

4. Automatic translation telephones, which will allow people to communicate naturally in their own language with anyone in the world who has access to a telephone.

5. Artificial intelligence and embedded learning technology, which will allow thinking that formerly was felt to be only the domain of humans to occur in machines.

6. Silicon chips containing up to 100 million transistors, allowing computing power that now rests only in the hands of supercomputer users to be available on every desktop.

7. Supercomputers that are capable of 1 trillion calculations per second, which will allow advances such as simulations of the human body for testing new drugs and computers that respond easily to spoken commands.[32]

Although all these technological wonders will affect international management, more specific technologies will have an even more direct impact. The following discussion highlights some specific dimensions of the technological environment currently facing international management.

E-Business

As the Internet becomes increasingly common, it is having a dramatic effect on international commerce. For example, millions of Americans have purchased books from Amazon.com and the company has now expanded its operations into Europe. So have a host of other electronic retailers (e-tailers) who are discovering that their home-grown retailing expertise can be easily transferred and adapted for the international market.[33] Dell Computer has been offering B2C (electronic business to consumer) goods and services in Europe for a number of years, and the auto makers are now beginning to move in this direction. General Motors, for example, has plans to sell custom cars online and cut the time from order to delivery from eight weeks, the current period, to as few as four days.[34] Other firms are looking to use e-business to improve their current operations. For example, the Deutsche Bank is overhauling its retail network with the goal of winning affluent customers across the Continent.[35] Yet the most popular form of e-business is for business-to-business or B2B dealings such as placing orders and interacting with suppliers worldwide. Recent estimates of B2B global transactions by 2004 put the figure in excess of $7 trillion.[36] Business to consumer (B2C) transactions will not be as large, but this is an area where many MNCs are trying to improve their operations. In 2000 B2C transactions in the United States were around $25 billion and are forecasted to be approximately $135 billion by 2004. In Europe B2C transactions in 2000 were over $2.75 billion and are forecasted by some analysts to increase to over $165 billion in the next five years.

The area of e-business that will most affect global customers is e-retailing and financial services. For example, customers can now use their keyboard to pay by credit card, although security remains a problem. However, the day is fast approaching when electronic cash (e-cash) will be common. When this happens, there will be a convergence of money, business transactions, and personal computers. Here is a brief description of how e-cash might work:

> To see how e-cash might evolve on the Internet, start with the rudimentary transaction scheme run by Mr. Stein's First Virtual Holdings. Both buyer and seller must have accounts at the "bank." In the case of the buyer, this amounts to an authority for First Virtual to make charges against his credit card. When the buyer, having investigated the seller's wares on the Internet and found something that he likes, makes a purchase, he gives his account number to the

seller, who ships the product. Each day or each week the merchant sends his list of who-bought-what to First Virtual, which sends e-mail messages to buyers asking them to confirm the transactions. Once a buyer confirms, his (conventional) credit card is charged and the money is transferred to the seller's account. If the buyer withholds confirmation, First Virtual withholds settlement.[37]

This scenario already occurs in a number of not-as-sophisticated forms. A good example is prepaid smart cards, which are being used mostly for telephone calls and public transportation. An individual can purchase one of these cards and use it in lieu of cash. This idea is blending into the Internet, allowing individuals to buy and sell merchandise and transfer funds electronically. The result will be global digital cash, which will take advantage of existing worldwide markets that allow buying and selling on a 24-hour basis.

This technological development also will have a major impact on financial institutions. After all, who will need the local corner ATM when they can tap into their funds through the Internet? Similarly, companies will not have to wait for their money from buyers, thus eliminating (or at least substantially reducing) bad debts while increasing their working capital. Therefore, if General Electric shipped $12 million of merchandise to Wal-Mart in Hong Kong with payment due on delivery, the typical 7- to 10-day waiting period between payment and collection of international transactions would, for all intents and purposes, be eliminated.[38]

Of course, e-cash will create many problems, and it will take some time for these to be resolved. For example, if a Mexican firm pays for its merchandise in pesos, there must be some system for converting these pesos into U.S. dollars. At present, such transactions are handled through regulated foreign exchange markets. In the near future, these transactions likely will be denominated in a single, conventional currency and exchanged at conventional market rates. It is equally likely, however, that the entire system of transactions eventually will become seamless and require no processing through foreign exchange markets. One expert explained it this way:

> Ideally, the ultimate e-cash will be a currency without a country (or a currency of all countries), infinitely exchangeable without the expense and inconvenience of conversion between local denominations. It may constitute itself as a wholly new currency with its own denomination—the "cyber dollar," perhaps. Or, it may continue to fix itself by reference to a traditional currency, in which case the American dollar would seem to be the likeliest possibility. Either way, it is hard to imagine that the existence of an international, easy-to-use, cheap-to-process, hard-to-tax electronic money will not then force freer convertibility on traditional currencies.[39]

Telecommunications

The most obvious dimension of the technological environment facing international management today is telecommunications. To begin with, it no longer is necessary to hardwire a city to provide residents with telephone service. This can be done wirelessly, thus allowing people to use cellular phones, beepers, and other telecommunications services. As a result, a form of technologic leapfrogging is occurring, in which regions of the world are moving from a situation where phones were unavailable to one where cellular is available everywhere, including rural areas, because the infrastructure needed to support this development can be installed both quickly and relatively inexpensively. In addition, technology is merging the telephone and the computer. As a result, in Europe and Asia a growing number of people are now accessing the web through their cell phone. While this development has not attracted a large market in the U.S., over 125 million Asians and 50 million Europeans now use this service.[40] Over the next decade, the merging of the Internet and wireless technology will radically change the ways people communicate.[41] Wireless technology is also proving to be a boon for less developed countries such as in South America and Eastern Europe where customers once waited years to get a telephone installed.

One reason for this rapid increase in telecommunications services is many countries believe that without an efficient communications system, their economic growth may stall. Additionally, governments are accepting the belief that the only way to attract foreign investment and know-how in telecommunications is to give up control to private industry. As a result, while most telecommunications operations in the Asia-Pacific region were state-run a decade ago, a growing number are now in private hands. Singapore Telecommunications, Pakistan Telecom, Thailand's Telecom Asia, Korea Telecom, and Globe Telecom in the Philippines all have been privatized, and MNCs have helped in this process by providing investment funds. Today, NYNEX holds a stake in Telecom Asia; Bell Atlantic and Ameritech each own 25 percent of Telecom New Zealand; and Bell South has an ownership position in Australia's Optus. At the same time, Australia's Telestra is moving into Vietnam; Japan's NTT is investing in Thailand, and Korea Telecom is in the Philippines and Indonesia.

Many governments are reluctant to allow so much private and foreign ownership of such a vital industry; however, they also are aware that foreign investors will go elsewhere if the deal is not satisfactory. The Hong Kong office of Salomon Brothers, a U.S. investment bank, estimates that to meet the expanding demand for telecommunication service in Asia, companies will need to considerably increase the investment, most of which will have to come from overseas. MNCs are unwilling to put up this much money unless they are assured of operating control and a sufficiently high return on their investment.

A good example occurred in China, where the government announced that foreign investors who were interested in building and operating power plants would have their annual rate of return (ROI) capped at 12 percent. Investors immediately began looking for more lucrative opportunities in other power-hungry Asian nations, and now China has increased the ROI cap to continue attracting deals. China presently is facing a similar backlash from telecommunications firms as well, which are only allowed to provide advice and to supply and manufacture telecommunication equipment for the Chinese market and are banned from the potentially more lucrative business of owning and/or operating these services.

Unlike China, however, other developing countries are eager to attract telecommunication firms and offer liberal terms. Cable & Wireless of Great Britain has opened an office in Hanoi. In Hong Kong, while the local telephone monopoly will not lose its grip on international services until 2006, its monopoly on local services has ended, and private groups are competing to provide service.

The Employment Fallout from Technology

In international management, technology also impacts the number of employees who are needed to carry out operations effectively. As MNCs use advanced technology to help them communicate, produce, and deliver their goods and services internationally, they face a new challenge: how technology will affect the nature and number of their employees. Some informed observers note that technology already has eliminated much, and in the future will eliminate even more of the work now being done by middle management and white-collar staff. In the past century, machines replaced millions of manual laborers, but those who worked with their minds were able to thrive and survive. During the past two decades in particular, blue-collar, smoke-stack industries such as steel and autos have been downsized by technology, and the result has been a permanent restructuring of the number of employees needed to run factories efficiently. In the 1990s, the same thing happened in the white-collar service industries (insurance, banks, and even government). Most recently, the same has occurred with the dot-com bubble bursting with the fallout being hundreds of thousands of jobs being lost, probably forever.

Some experts predict that in the future technology has the potential to largely displace employees in all industries, from those doing low-skilled jobs to those holding positions traditionally reserved for human thinking. For example, voice recognition is helping to replace telephone operators; the demand for postal workers has been reduced severely by address-reading devices; and cash-dispensing machines can do 10 times more transactions in a day than bank tellers, so the number of tellers can be reduced, or even eliminated entirely, in the future. Also, expert (sometimes called "smart") systems can eliminate human thinking completely. For example, American Express has an expert system that performs the credit analysis formerly done by college-graduate financial analysts. In the medical field, expert systems can diagnose some illnesses as well as doctors, and robots capable of performing certain operations are starting to be used.

Emerging information technology also makes work more portable. This is especially true for work that can be easily contracted with overseas locations. For example, low-paid workers in India and Asian countries now are being given subcontracted work such as labor-intensive software development and writing code jobs. A restructuring of the nature of work and of employment is resulting from such information technology; Figure 2–1 provides some winners and losers in the workforce in recent years.

The new technological environment has both positives and negatives for MNCs and societies as a whole. On the positive side, the cost of doing business worldwide should decline thanks to the opportunities that technology offers in substituting lower-cost machines for higher-priced labor. Over time, productivity should go up, and prices should go down. On the negative side, many employees will find either their jobs eliminated or their wages and salaries reduced because they have been replaced by machines and their skills are no longer in high demand. This job loss from technology can be especially devastating in developing countries. However, it doesn't have to be this way. A case in point is

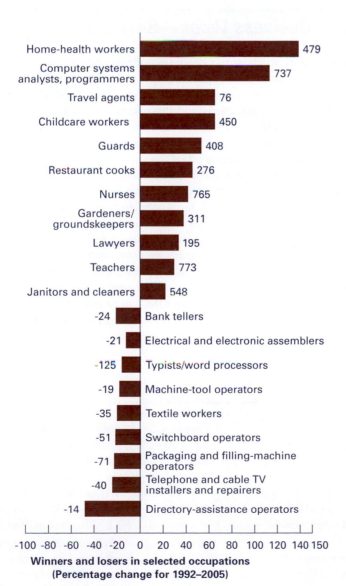

Figure 2–1

Winners and Losers in Selected Occupations (Percentage Change Forecasts for 1992–2005)

Winners and losers in selected occupations
(Percentage change for 1992–2005)

Source: U.S. Bureau of Labor Statistics.

South Africa's showcase for automotive productivity, the Delta Motor Corporation's Opel Corsa plant in Port Elizabeth. To provide as many jobs as possible, this world-class operation automated only 23 percent compared to more than 85 percent of European and North American auto assembly.[42] Also, some industries can add jobs. For example, in the computer and information technology industry, even with its ups and downs, the negative has been offset by the positive. For example, over the last decade, employment in the U.S. computer-software industry has increased. In less developed countries such as India, a high-tech boom in recent years has created jobs and opportunities for a growing number of people.[43] Additionally, even though developed countries such as Japan and the United States are most affected by technological displacement of workers, both nations still lead the world in creating new jobs and shifting their traditional industrial structure toward a high-tech, knowledge-based economy.

The precise impact that the advanced technological environment will have on international management over the next decade is difficult to forecast. One thing is certain, however; there is no turning back the technological clock. MNCs and nations alike must evaluate the impact of these changes carefully and realize that their economic performance is closely tied to keeping up, or ahead, of rapidly advancing technology.

World of *Business Week*—Revisited

As the *Business Week* article at the beginning of this chapter illustrated, many of the political and regulatory barriers in China are now changing. At the same time, as China plays an increasingly greater role in the global economy, it will also have to conform to international regulatory standards and the rule of widely accepted laws in a wide number of areas from importing and exporting to patent and copyright protection to the end of the use of child and prison labor to manufacture products. The country will also find that technology will greatly affect the way its people live and e-business and telecommunications will change the communication and general living patterns of its society. At the same time, multinationals doing business in China will face a wide variety of challenges as the political, legal, and technological environments change dramatically. The international management skills of these businesses will be severely tested. In light of the information you have learned from reading this chapter, you should have a good understanding of these environments and some of the ways that they will affect companies doing business here. Based on this knowledge, answer the following questions: (1) If the Chinese economy only grows at a 6–7 percent annual rate, how might this present a problem for MNCs in China? (2) How might the Foreign Corrupt Practices Act make it more difficult for American MNCs to do business in China than for other multinationals? (3) How will an increase in e-business and telecommunications present opportunities for banks and e-tailers in China?

Summary of Key Points

1. Today's political environment presents a myriad of challenges for MNCs. China is going through a transition as the old guard passes from the scene. The political situation in Europe also continues to change. Russia is facing economic problems and social upheaval, and the rest of Central and Eastern Europe has had varying degrees of success with their newfound freedom and continue to struggle with their past.

2. The current legal and regulatory environment is both complex and confusing. There are many different laws and regulations to which MNCs doing business internationally must conform, and each nation is unique. Also, MNCs must abide by the laws of their own country. For example, U.S. MNCs must obey the rules set down by the Foreign Corrupt Practices Act. MNCs doing business in Japan and the EU face a wide range of bureaucratic rules and regulations that often are both time-wasting and inefficient.

3. The technological environment is changing quickly and is having a major impact on international business. This will continue in the future. For example, money transfers and exchange are changing dramatically.

Also, areas such as telecommunications offer developing countries new opportunities to leapfrog into the twenty-first century. New markets are being created for high-tech MNCs that are eager to provide telecommunications service. Technological developments also impact on both the nature and the structure of employment, shifting the industrial structure toward a more high-tech, knowledge-based economy. MNCs who understand and take advantage of this high-tech environment should prosper, but they also must keep up, or ahead, to survive the highly competitive years ahead.

Key Terms

Islamic law, *38*

socialist law, *38*

common law, *38*

civil or code law, *38*

principle of sovereignty, *38*

nationality principle, *38*

territoriality principle, *38*

protective principle, *38*

doctrine of comity, *39*

act of state doctrine, *39*

Foreign Corrupt Practices Act (FCPA), *39*

Review and Discussion Questions

1. In what way does the political environment around the world create challenges for MNCs? Would these challenges be less for those operating in the EU than for those in Russia or China? Why or why not?

2. How do the following legal principles impact on MNC operations: the principle of sovereignty, the nationality principle, the territoriality principle, the protective principle, and principle of comity?

3. How could the national and local government bureaucracy in Japan impede the operations of a U.S. MNC doing business there? What are some Japanese laws or regulations that would reduce the MNC's effectiveness?

4. Why are developing countries interested in privatizing their telecommunications industries? What opportunities does this privatization have for telecommunication MNCs?

Internet Exercise: Hitachi Goes Worldwide

Hitachi products are well-known in the United States, as well as in Europe and Asia. However, in an effort to continue maintaining its international momentum, the Japanese MNC is continuing to push forward into new markets, while also developing new products. Visit the MNC at its web site **www.hitachi.com** and examine some of the latest developments that are taking place. Begin by reviewing the firm's current activities in Asia, specifically Hong Kong and Singapore. Then look at how it is doing business in North America. Finally, read about its European operations. All of these are available at this web site. Then answer these three questions: (1) What kinds of products does the firm offer? What are its primary areas of emphasis? (2) In what types of environments does it operate? Is Hitachi primarily interested in developed markets or is it also pushing into newly emerging markets? (3) Based on what it has been doing over the last 2–3 years, what do you think Hitachi's future strategy will be in competing in the environment of international business during the first decade of the new millenium?

Vietnam

Located in Southeast Asia, the Socialist Republic of Vietnam is bordered to the north by the People's Republic of China, to the west by Laos and Cambodia, and to the east and south by the South China Sea. The country is a mere 127,000 square miles but has a population of almost 80 million. The language is Vietnamese and the principal religion Buddhism, although there are a number of small minorities, including Confucian, Christian (mainly Catholic), Caodist, Daoist, and Hoa Hao. In recent years, the country's economy has been up and down, but average per-capita income still is in the hundreds of dollars as the peasants still remain very poor.

One of the reasons that Vietnam has lagged behind its fast-developing neighbors in Southeast Asia, such as Thailand and Malaysia, is its isolation from the industrial west, and the United States in particular, because of the Vietnam war. From the mid-1970s, the country had close relations with the U.S.S.R., but the collapse of communism there forced the still-communist Vietnamese government to work on establishing stronger economic ties with other countries. The nation recently has worked out many of its problems with China, and today, the Chinese have become a useful economic ally. Vietnam would most like to establish a vigorous trade relationship with the United States, however. Efforts toward this end began over a decade ago, but because of lack of information concerning the many U.S. soldiers still unaccounted for after the war, it was not until 1993 that the United States permitted U.S. companies to take part in ventures in Vietnam that were financed by international aid agencies. Then, in 1994, the U.S. trade embargo was lifted, and a growing number of American firms began doing business in Vietnam.

Caterpillar began supplying equipment for a $2 billion highway project. Mobil teamed with three Japanese partners to begin drilling offshore. Exxon, Amoco, Conoco, Unocal, and Arco negotiated production-sharing contracts with Petro Vietnam. General Electric opened a trade office and developed plans to use electric products throughout the country. AT&T began working to provide long-distance service both in and out of the country. Coca-Cola began bottling operations. Within the first 12 months, 70 U.S. companies obtained licenses to do business in Vietnam. Besides the U.S., the largest investors have been Singapore, Taiwan, Japan, South Korea, and Hong Kong which collectively have put over $22 billion into the country.

In July 2000 the U.S. and Vietnam signed a bilateral trade agreement which opens up trade and foreign investment in Vietnam and gives Vietnamese exporters access to the U.S. market. The agreement is also likely to increase U.S. investment in the country over the next decade. Similar to China, many U.S. firms find doing business in Vietnam frustrating because of the numerous and changing bureaucratic rules imposed by the communist government officials, but if relations between the two countries continue on their present course, more and more opportunities should open up for American multinationals.

www.vietnam.com

Questions

1. In what way does the political environment in Vietnam pose both an opportunity and a threat for American MNCs seeking to do business there?

2. Why are U.S. multinationals so interested in going into Vietnam? How much potential does the country offer? Conversely, how much benefit can Vietnam derive from a business relationship with U.S. MNCs?

3. Would there be any opportunities in Vietnam for high-tech American firms? Why or why not?

A Chinese Venture

The Darby Company is a medium-size communications technology company headquartered on the west coast of the United States. Among other things, Darby holds a patent on a mobile telephone that can operate effectively within a 5-mile radius. The phone does not contain state-of-the-art technology, but it can be produced extremely cheaply. As a result, the Chinese government has expressed interest in manufacturing and selling this phone throughout their country.

Preliminary discussions with the Chinese government reveal that some major terms of the agreement that it would like include: (1) Darby will enter into a joint venture with a local Chinese firm to manufacture the phones to Darby's specifications; (2) these phones would be sold throughout China at a 100 percent markup, and Darby will receive 10 percent of the profits; (3) Darby will invest $35 million in building the manufacturing facility, and these costs will be recovered over a 5-year period; and (4) the government in Beijing will guarantee that at least 100,000 phones are sold every year, or it will purchase the difference.

The Darby management is not sure whether this is a good deal. In particular, Darby executives have heard all sorts of horror stories regarding agreements that the Chinese government has made and then broken. The company also is concerned that once its technology is understood, the Chinese will walk away from the agreement and start making these phones on their own. Because the technology is not state-of-the-art, the real benefit is in the low production costs, and the technological knowledge is more difficult to protect.

For its part, the Chinese government has promised to sign a written contract with Darby, and it has agreed that any disputes regarding enforcement of this contract can be brought, by either side, to the World Court at the Hague for resolution. Should this course of action be taken, each side would be responsible for its own legal fees, but the Chinese have promised to accept the decision of the court as binding.

Darby has 30 days to decide whether to sign the contract with the Chinese. After this time, the Chinese intend to pursue negotiations with a large telecommunications firm in Europe and try cutting a deal with them. Darby is more attractive to the Chinese, however, because of the low cost of producing its telephone. In any event, the Chinese are determined to begin mass producing cellular phones in their country. "Our future is tied to high-tech communication," the Chinese Minister of Finance recently told Darby's president. "That is why we are so anxious to do business with your company; you have quality phones at low cost." Darby management is flattered by these kind words but still not sure if this is the type of business deal in which it wants to get involved.

Questions

1. How important is the political environment in China for the Darby Company? Explain.

2. If a disagreement arises between the two joint-venture partners and the government of China reneges on its promises, how well protected is Darby's position? Explain.

3. Are the economic and technological environments in China favorable for Darby? Why or why not?

Chapter 3

Global Competitiveness

As MNCs continue to expand their operations and begin to do business in every part of the globe, the competitive pressures will mount. In competitive battles, MNCs will try to gain an advantage (i.e., gain a competitive advantage) over rivals in attracting and maintaining targeted customers and obtaining a larger share of the global market. In the type of environment outlined in Chapters 1 and 2, all MNCs must become increasingly competitive. They must be able to compete with anybody, anywhere, anytime (the "Three Any's"). Being third or fourth in an industry or the world market in this competitive environment is not sufficient in the long run. Organizations must strive to be the best: a world-class organization (WCO).

The overriding objective of this chapter is to examine how MNCs are trying to become WCOs. First, attention is given to the issues of quality and why MNCs must strive to develop the highest-quality goods and services anywhere. Next, the discussion shifts beyond quality to learning organizations and their major characteristics. Finally, the characteristics of WCOs and some specific, real-world examples of how some MNCs are becoming WCOs are considered. These MNCs are able to compete with anybody, anywhere, anytime. The specific objectives of this chapter are:

1. **DESCRIBE** the importance of quality in helping multinational organizations in Three Any's competitiveness.

2. **DEFINE** learning organizations and their key characteristics.

3. **DESCRIBE** the major pillars of world-class organizations (WCOs) and how these pillars are critical in Three Any's competitiveness.

BusinessWeek

The World of *Business Week*

Machete Time

Toyota vs. Nissan: It's one of the oldest rivalries in the auto business—and one of the most lopsided. For years, Toyota Motor Corp. has steadily grabbed share in Japan and the U.S. from its main competitor, ramped up record profits while Nissan Motor Co. lost billions, and helped shove Nissan to the edge of bankruptcy. Even now, with Nissan in the middle of an impressive turnaround under the aegis of its European partner Renault, Toyota still walks away with top honors in sales and profits.

Yet, Nissan can lay claim to one surprising accomplishment: cost-cutting. Nissan is on track to slice 10% off its car parts, thanks to a brutal decision to drop its most inefficient suppliers and consolidate orders with the most cost-conscious ones. That adds up to at least $2.25 billion in savings—savings that go straight to the bottom line. Mighty Toyota, in contrast, expects to shave $1.5 billion off its procurement costs, much less than Nissan, whose sales amount to less than half its rival's.

Quick Results

Company executives in Toyota City hate losing at anything, so this achievement of Nissan's has set off loud alarm bells. To keep its competitive edge, Toyota is jettisoning the traditional approach to cost-savings that won it fame: *kaizen,* the slow and steady approach to chipping away at expenses. *Kaizen* will still be applied to factory operations. But in parts purchasing, Toyota is no longer content to tinker: It wants 30% cuts in the cost of almost every type of auto part sourced from outside. "Toyota wants nothing less than to be the world's lowest-cost producer of the highest-quality automobiles," says analyst Noriyuki Matsushima of the Tokyo office of Nikko Salomon Smith Barney.

The sweeping undertaking is the cornerstone of a plan dubbed CCC21, or Construction of Cost Competitiveness for the 21st century. The goal of the drive is to chop costs by $8 billion by the end of fiscal 2005. That's a huge change: Before, it would normally take Toyota a decade to squeeze out that much in savings. According to Toyota Senior Managing Director Akio Watanabe, the point man in the drive, the company has no choice. "It may come as a shock," he says, "but if we're content with the little-by-little approach of *kaizen,* then we can't win."

That may sound overdramatic, given Toyota's awesome strengths. Yet the company has made some disturbing discoveries. At about the same time Nissan announced its widely publicized plan to slash jobs, close factories, and wring huge savings from its supplier network, Toyota learned from internal studies that is was paying prices well above those charged for similar parts used in General Motors Corp. and Volkswagen vehicles. "We thought we had the world's cheapest parts, but we were wrong," says Tadaaki Jagawa, Toyota's

executive vice-president for corporate planning and purchasing.

How did Toyota get caught flat-footed? It stuck with the old ways—asking local Japanese suppliers it has used for decades to bid against each other for parts contracts every time Toyota rolled out a new model. Toyota also spurned the growing industry practice of installing standardized parts in a range of car models: No sharing of door locks in Camrys and Corollas, if you please.

But in the past five years, the worldwide auto-parts business has undergone massive change. Foreign auto-parts makers such as Delphi Automotive Systems Corp. and Robert Bosch Corp. now enjoy gigantic economies of scale by providing similar parts to a host of U.S. and European carmakers. Nissan, for example, has teamed up with Renault to buy standardized parts at big savings from fewer suppliers. "We are going more and more for global contracts," says Nissan CEO Carlos Ghosn.

Toyota so far has turned down offers from GM and Volkswagen to team up on parts purchases. But that means it's new cost-cutting drive has to work, or it risks a steady erosion in margins. A key part of the exercise: Figuring out the lowest prices paid by carmakers for 173 commodity-type components, from rear-view mirrors to the bearings inside shock absorbers. Once Toyota learns these benchmark prices, it asks suppliers to match them as closely as possible without sacrificing quality.

No Handouts

So far, Toyota's procurement team has used the pricing data uncovered on about 85 of these parts to devise new ways to save money. For example, Toyota wants to cut the number of bearings it buys to as little as $\frac{1}{20}$ of current levels by asking suppliers to design simpler parts.

The broader message is clear: If Toyota is ditching its old habits, longtime suppliers had better follow. "We won't give handouts anymore," says Jagawa. That kind of talk is aimed squarely at the 213 companies that make up the Kyohokai, an organization of Toyota suppliers that was founded during World War II. "We thought our products were already low-cost," says Yoshihei Iida, president of Tokai Rika, which supplies 90% of Toyota's turn signals and other switches. "Now we have to work even harder at it to maintain our business." Toyota may be turning up the heat in another way: Reports are surfacing that the giant wants its three biggest brake suppliers to set aside their rivalry and combine their manufacturing operations.

The effect of these changes is already being felt. Tokai Rika is now developing standardized parts for joint use in different models: All five variations of the Toyota Vitz subcompact, for example, now share the same dashboard knobs for adjusting temperature. Tokai Rika has also simplified its turn-signal levers, which are being installed on cars of entirely different classes.

No part is too mundane to escape scrutiny. One of the first successes under ccc21 involves the plastic grips installed above a car's doors on the inside—passengers grab them to brace themselves on sharp turns. Toyota found out that Volkswagen was procuring much cheaper, but still high-quality, grips. So by knocking heads at major suppliers such as Kojima Press Kogyo, Watanabe says his team has come up with a way to use simpler designs and cheaper materials to produce grips for upper-end car models for $4 a piece, half the earlier price. The number of grips used will also be cut from 30 or so to just 3 main types.

Of course, there are limits to how far you can standardize basic parts before customers start to notice. But for the senior managers at Toyota, the war on costs is just beginning. If Nissan can do it, they say, Toyota can—and will. Suppliers, prepare to be squeezed.

By Chester Dawson in Tokyo

Source: **Reprinted from April 9, 2001, pp. 42–43 issue of** *Business Week* **by special permission, copyright © 2001 by the McGraw-Hill Companies, Inc.**

The opening news story focuses on a competitive strategy that is being used by most multinationals. If they can purchase something from an outside supplier at a lower price or with better quality than they can make it themselves, they will outsource it. As a result, MNCs, especially in manufacturing, are now focusing on their core business while relying on outsiders to provide the rest of what they need. In the case of auto manufacturers like Toyota, for example, it is common to find them purchasing most of the interior of the car from suppliers including seats, door locks, steering wheels, air conditioners, radios, and CDs. Outsourcers also provide most of the exterior of the car including the lights, windshields, windows, tires, fenders, and bumpers. Much of what is under the hood or below the car is also provided by outsourcers including such things as the shock absorbers, the battery, and the electrical system. In addition, by using some of the same parts in all of their models, these companies are able to achieve still further cost savings. As a result, the window price of a Toyota Camry today is slightly less than the price for this same car a half dozen years ago. How was the company able to hold the line on costs over a six-year period? One part of the answer is the use of global sourcing. Another is that MNCs in every field are driving down costs by learning how to do things ever better, thus greatly increasing their efficiency. In order to compete in the international arena, multinationals like Toyota have learned how to be globally competitive.

■ The Total Quality Issue

Total quality remains a major issue for MNCs today. One major reason is because in the international marketplace customers do not care who provides the goods and services they want; they simply want their expectations to be met or exceeded. This is why auto consumers across the world now pay little attention to where the company is headquartered. International consumers are more concerned that the autos perform well, have few (if any) mechanical defects, last a long time, and are competitively priced, than whether the firm is Japanese, Korean, U.S. or German based. The same is true for many other products, from cameras and televisions to computers and shoes. To meet or exceed customer expectations, at minimum the MNC must give attention to quality as well as cost. Accordingly, a technology paradox is inherent in this total quality emphasis, and, of course, innovation takes on new importance.

The Technology Paradox Facing MNCs

A **paradox** is a statement that appears to be contradictory but is not. For example, when Motorola began developing a worldwide strategy for its cellular telephones and pagers, it faced the "quality versus cost" dilemma. If the firm increased the quality of its products to unprecedented levels, would their price not become prohibitive? For years, engineers contended that it would, and they explained this idea in terms of a "bath tub" diagram, an example of which is provided in Figure 3–1. As the number of failures is reduced, the cost of achieving these quality levels goes up dramatically. As a result, the company at first attempted to balance quality and cost by producing products that offered "sufficient" quality and fairly low price.

Faced with increasing competition with Japan, however, Motorola began to challenge this thinking by asking: How much will it cost to increase quality to ever-higher levels? In particular, the MNC decided to reduce the number of errors to as low a level as possible and compute the cost of producing these quality products. In doing so, Motorola engineers began measuring quality in terms of defective parts per million. This answer can be expressed in terms of sigma, and the higher the sigma, the lower the number of defects per million parts. Here are four examples:

Paradox
A statement that appears to be contradictory but is not, such as "increases in product quality often result in a decline of the cost of producing the goods."

Sigma	Errors per million
3	66,810.0
4	6,210.0
5	233.0
6	3.4

Now Motorola began to examine the costs associated with these various levels of sigma. As the error rate fell, so did the cost of producing the product. For example, the cost of rework and the amount of scrap decreases, and of course there is an indirect but very

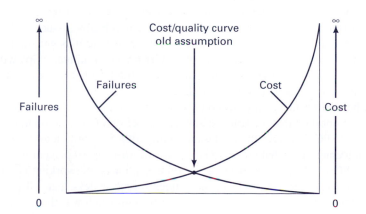

Figure 3–1

The Quality/Cost Curve as Initially Perceived

Figure 3–2

Quality/Cost Curve as Determined Through Research

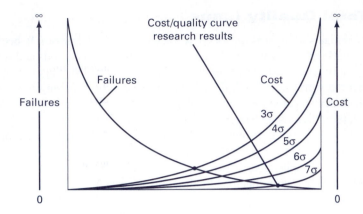

significant impact on customer satisfaction and demand/loyalty. Figure 3–2 shows this graphically. Clearly, what this amazingly showed was that quality and cost are inversely related! In other words, MNCs that produce quality products can do so at a lower cost per unit than for products with higher error rates. The reason that so many MNCs did not see this relationship earlier is that they were blindsided by the old quality/cost paradox. Now the idea is becoming widespread. In recent years both General Electric and Ford Motor have announced that they are implementing "six sigma" programs throughout their operations. These quality efforts have saved the firms billions of dollars. A growing number of multinationals are implementing similar quality-focused strategies.

Technology also presents MNCs with a paradox, but this one is far more significant. For many years, multinational firms believed that new technology could be exploited best by getting to the market first and charging premium prices. Now, however, they are learning that the best way to exploit their advantage is often to lower their prices as quickly as possible. In turn, this strategy helps them grow their international market share while also increasing overall revenues and profits. An excellent example is provided by Intel which has begun an aggressive pricing strategy designed to increase market share and to drive less efficient competitors from the market. In November 2000, the price of its 1.3 gigahertz chip was $332 and the 1.5 gigahertz version sold for $637. By April 2001, the prices of these chips had been reduced to $193 and $256 respectively. At that time the company introduced its new 1.7 gigahertz chip at $352 for volume purchases by PC makers, and planned on making still more price cuts on the other chips it was selling.[1] While competitors such as Advanced Micro Devices Inc. announced that they would meet or beat these prices, Intel's strategy clearly illustrates what is known as the technology paradox.

Technology paradox
The situation where high-tech businesses can thrive at the very moment that their prices are falling the fastest.

The **technology paradox** holds that high-tech businesses can thrive at the very moment that their prices are falling the fastest. Simply put, in order to be successful high-tech companies have to cut their prices sharply at the same time that they are offering products that contain ever greater amounts of advanced technology. Of course, this strategy can result in razor-thin margins and those firms that dominate the market may find their returns on investment sharply reduced because of the radical price cuts. In order to prevent this from happening, however, successful high-tech MNCs such as Intel are also using technological breakthroughs in a variety of products and thus generating more revenue from their technology. So while sharply lower-priced computer chips will undoubtedly stimulate demand for personal computers (PCs), Intel cannot rely exclusively on this market because competitors may soon emulate their breakthrough technology and, in any event, will be willing to severely discount their own chips in order to maintain market share. So it is important that the firm expand its sales efforts into other markets and not be overly reliant on PCs. As a result, in addition to investing $7.5 billion to develop the latest chip-making technologies that will cut manufacturing costs by 30 percent, Intel is expanding into non-PC products such as chips for mobile phones, networking equipment, and consumer electronics. Revenues from these lines represent less than 10 percent of the firm's annual total, but in 2000 they stood at $6.5 billion which was three times what they were in 1996 and collectively accounted for over 19 percent of the company's sales that year.[2] Intel believes that in the future these non-PC products will generate a much greater percentage of overall revenues.

Keeping up in terms of technology is the major challenge that face many MNCs. Motorola again is a good example. The company stumbled badly by failing to anticipate the industry's switch from analog to digital cell phones; and since then its share of the worldwide mobile phone market has declined. At the turn of the century, Motorola held only 17 percent of the world market and its share in Europe which stood at 30 percent in 1995 had dropped to under 15 percent.[3]

How can MNCs continue to increase their technology and keep their prices low? One way is by outsourcing more and more of their manufacturing, while focusing their own efforts on developing new technologies that will change the type or performance of the products they are selling. For example, Motorola now outsources a large percentage of its cellular phone, pager, and switch production to Singapore-based Flextronics International Ltd.,[4] which has worldwide operations so it can manufacture these products and quickly ship them to the requisite Motorola location. As seen in the news story that opened this chapter, Toyota and Nissan both use outsourcing to cut costs.[5] So, too, do Ericsson,[6] NEC, Mitsubishi, NCR Japan[7] and most other multinational manufacturing and electronic firms. In 1996 approximately $40 billion of electronic goods were outsourced by manufacturers; in 2003 this total will be $160 billion.[8] In the process, a new form of world-class organization (WCO) has emerged: the high technology outsourcer. These outsourcers produce world-class quality goods at prices that others cannot match. MNCs from Europe to Asia rely heavily on these world-class outsourcers and many industrial giants are willing to give them long-term contracts to handle a variety of tasks from designing new products to taking care of after-sales service. Notes one industry expert:

> As yesterday's industrial giants slim down, leading contract manufacturers are bulking up, flouting some key tenets of New Economy wisdom. While many gurus rave about virtual corporations, Flextronics and its rivals have been quietly picking up the abandoned brick-and-mortar pieces and reassembling them into new versions of vertically integrated empires. The new age production experts are happily shelling out billions to acquire competitors along with factories once owned by Siemens, IBM, and Nortel. To broaden their services, they are also acquiring design and engineering firms—specialists in creating anything from customized semiconductors to prototypes of futuristic wireless-Web phones. Some outside contractors are buying parts suppliers and stakes in distributors.[9]

Successful MNCs understand the impact of the technology paradox and the need to keep driving down their costs as they improve the quality of their output. They also understand that they need to combine value-added features so that they can add to their initial package and keep their product from becoming a generic offering sold strictly on price. A good example is Dell Computer which tailor-makes its computers to meet the expectations of international customers. This strategy, commonly referred to as **mass customization,** helps maintain product uniqueness and prevents it from being viewed as a generic offering. A major part of the success equation also is the MNC's ability to develop and maintain its innovative capacity.

Mass customization
Tailor-making mass-production products to meet the expectations of the customer.

The Innovative Challenge Facing MNCs

Strategy guru Michael Porter has emphasized that the key to succesful multinational efforts in global competitive battles is the ability to continually innovate.[10] For example, 3M has a goal of generating 30 percent of annual revenues from products that it has brought to market in the last four years. One of 3M's most innovative products in recent years has been SelfCheck, a computerized system that allows users to check out library books without assistance.[11] Other new developments include electrochemical devices that convert fuel into electricity without using combustion; radiant color film that produces such brilliant color that objects appear to be lit from inside; and radiant mirror film that reflects more than 98 percent of visible light that hits the surface from any angle, making it ideal for use in day lighting through light pipes that transmit natural light to building interiors and general lighting applications.[12] Another good example of innovation is provided by Nintendo that continues to dominate the handheld video game market. Its ability to offer units that easily fit into a book bag and which offer a high color quality screen allow the game maker to easily outdistance its many competitors.[13] And innovation need not be restricted to products. Ryanair, the Irish airline, has proven to be a major competitor in Europe by offering no-frills service at low price. By paring costs to the bone, the airline is able to attract a rapidly growing number of passengers, and in an industry where competitors need to fill 75 percent of the seats in order to break even, Ryanair can make money while flying almost half empty thanks to its innovative cost cutting and marketing.[14]

The Importance of Vision   The approaches of other successful MNCs in developing quality products often are quite similar. One such approach to stimulate innovation involves having a vision. The MNC will develop an idea of how the market will look in the future, then create products or services based on this vision. For example, Canon of Japan envisioned a world in which photocopiers were small, cheap, and ubiquitous, then used this vision to drive its developmental and production strategies. Harley-Davidson has its senior-level executives spend time in the field with bikers, visiting rallies, and discussing with customers what they like about their bikes and what changes they would like to see.

The Need to Benchmark   Another approach commonly used by MNCs in their relentless effort to develop innovative products is the effective use of **benchmarking.** This is the process of identifying what leading-edge competitors are doing, then using this information to produce improved products or services. Among the best MNCs, benchmarking often entails competing against oneself and producing products that outmode those the MNC sells currently.

New Versions of Products   Still another innovative approach is **product proliferation,** which involves the creation of a wide array of products that the competition cannot copy quickly enough. Additionally, as the firm begins offering different versions of a product, the customer often becomes confused and is not sure which is the best buy. As a result, the company offering the large number of products often succeeds, because it gains market share at the expense of its competitors, which offer far fewer products. Moreover, this process of creating new versions of current products is ongoing; for example, Canon started planning its second-generation personal copier before the first had even come off the assembly line.

Importantly, product development need not come just from in-house research and development (R&D). Today the trend is to acquire more and more help from other firms. As noted earlier, suppliers like Flextronics provide assistance to manufacturers by not only producing products for them but by actually designing and engineering some of them. Similarly, outsourcers continually work to improve the products they make for their customers. Companies that manufacture auto seats for car companies, for example, now build stronger, more durable units so that the seats better withstand wear and tear as well as impact during a crash.

Quality Pays Off for MNCs

Besides recognizing the technology paradox and creating a climate of innovation, quality goods and services simply pay off. International Management in Action: Quality Wins Out provides some examples of high quality goods and services. The following sections examine some specific examples of the importance of quality.

Auto Manufacturing   Auto firms that produce quality products appeal to customers worldwide, and quality products can lead to increased market share and profits. In the United States, the big automakers (General Motors, Ford, and DaimlerChrysler) have all increased their quality in the last decade. This has been very helpful because overall auto industry quality has continued to increase[15] and Japanese manufacturers, in particular, are still leading the way. According to J.D. Power & Associates, well-known for their independent research on

Benchmarking
The process of identifying what leading-edge competitors are doing and then using this information to produce improved products or services.

Product proliferation
The creation of a wide array of products that the competition cannot copy quickly enough.

International Management in Action:

Quality Wins Out

Quality is proving to be a major factor in winning the global competitiveness battle. In the auto industry, for example, some companies that have long had a difficult time competing are now moving to the fore. Korean auto makers, in particular, have sharply increased the quality of their cars and their share of the U.S. market is beginning to reflect these changes. Hyundai, Daewoo, and Kia are having excellent success here in the small car market. In fact, Hyundai has now overtaken Mazda to become the fifth-largest Asian brand in the American market.

For many years Korean carmakers had a quality image problem. However, as the quality of their cars has improved, these firms have been able to offer extremely generous terms to buyers and this helped generate sales. For example, Hyundai has been able to capture the attention of car buyers with its 10-year or 100,000-mile warranty on engines and transmissions, five-year bumper-to-bumper warranty, and free roadside service. And Daewoo offers its buyers free maintenance for the first three years. In the small car market, where buyers shop on price and cannot afford expensive repairs, these are very attractive features. But they are only possible because of the recent improvements in quality that these companies have been able to achieve. Now, armed with these quality improvements, the Korean automakers are preparing to move up the line into the mid-price range with new, sleek and sporty models that will directly attack Japanese offerings.

At the same time, a number of other multinational automakers that produce high quality cars are beginning to offer less expensive models for the mid-range market. For example, Mercedes recently rolled out a $26,000 two-door hatchback with cloth seats. Jaguar has a model that sells for under $30,000; and BMW intends to roll out its small 1-Series sedan for less than $25,000. These firms realize that there is a limited market for their cars at the $50,000-and-up price, but there are many potential buyers in the $25,000–$35,000 range. These companies also know that they can manufacture high quality cars and the sheer volume of this mid-price market will more than offset the lower profit per unit that they are earning. Jaguar, for example, introduced its S-Type for $44,000 and within a year it was selling 90,000 units. The company is now forecasting sales of 200,000 by 2005. The revenue and profits from this line are substantially greater than what it earns in the high-end market. Simply put, when high quality and affordable price come together, customers tend to respond.

At the same time, this does not mean that there is no market for high quality and high-priced goods. Rolls Royce and Bentley have been successful for generations with their small production of high quality, high-priced cars. And DaimlerChrysler is getting ready to offer a super-luxurious Maybach in the $200,000 to $300,000 range. Once again, customers will buy quality products.

Take the case of Starbucks, the Seattle-based coffee company. Who would have thought a decade ago that people would be willing to pay $4 for a high quality cup of coffee? Yet today, across the United States, thousands of people pay this price and more every day at a Starbucks. And in recent years the firm has expanded internationally and now has units in more than 20 countries including China, Japan, the United Kingdom, Switzerland, and the United Arab Emirates. Annual sales are over $700 million and the company has yet to tap the full potential of these markets. A good example is China where coffee has never been popular. This, however, is beginning to change. In the past four years coffee consumption has doubled and although this amounts to only one cup per person per year, Starbucks believes that there are many Chinese who will appreciate high quality coffee and pay for it. The same is true in Continental Europe, where the firm is only now starting to set up units. Italy and France are viewed as high potential areas, although they have their own coffee cultures and may well resist Starbucks' offerings. On the other hand, the company believes that its product is unique and will appeal to a large segment of the European coffee-drinking market. Executives are convinced that its quality will carry the day.

auto quality, the gap between Japanese and American car manufacturers has again begun to widen. Honda's Accura brand, Toyota's Lexus car line, and Nissan's Infiniti brand are now judged as the best cars by consumers.[16] German automakers such as BMW and Mercedes also fare very well. So while U.S. car quality has been improving over the years, the competition has been doing even better. In particular, the Power group found that two-thirds of quality defects are traceable to engineering, not assembly plant mistakes. As a result, U.S. auto makers will have to do a better job of designing not only attractive cars, but also quality cars as well. In Europe, Ford has been losing market share because customers feel their cars are simply not appealing,[17] and both it and GM are now struggling to remake their dowdy images,[18] although they certainly are not alone; a growing number of multinationals including Toyota have had trouble making money there.[19]

It will be difficult for American manufacturers to meet the ever-rising quality expectations of customers around the globe, but if they fail to do so they will continue to lose market share. In Europe, for example, customers tend to be very loyal and gaining lost market share is extremely difficult. One strategy in dealing with the quality challenge is to start from scratch and do it right. A good example is the way General Motors designed the Saturn from the ground up. Another approach has been to revamp old car lines or simply get rid of them. GM completely redesigned the Chevrolet Lumina and Chevrolet Cavalier, both of which have far fewer defects than their previous versions; and it has now dropped its Oldsmobile line.

Aircraft Manufacturing   Another example that quality pays is Boeing, the giant commercial aircraft manufacturer. The firm has been long known for its quality aircraft and this has paid off in big international sales. The MNC has sold planes to a wide number of airline carriers and has done particularly well in Asia where its customers include Cathay Pacific Airlines, Japan Air Lines, Korean Airlines, All Nippon Airways, and Thai International Airways. Other worldwide customers include Air Europa, Saudia, the Saudi Arabian state-run carrier, United Parcel Service, Lauda Air, and Eurobelgian.[20]

However, Boeing does not have the aircraft market to itself. In recent years Airbus Industrie of Europe has been producing high quality aircraft and has landed large orders not only from European carriers such as Iberia Airlines and Belgium's Sabena Airlines, but also from American companies such as US Airway Group and Northwest Airlines, and more recently from China. As a result, Airbus now holds slightly more than half of the world's aircraft market.[21]

Emerging Chinese High Tech   Many MNCs have entered the Chinese market in hopes of selling high-tech equipment. To their chagrin, they are finding that local Chinese firms are producing quality that is often superior and more cost effective than that offered by them. As a result, local Chinese firms are beginning to win back market share. An example is the PC market. By the mid-1990s western PC makers had captured more than 50 percent of this market, but by the turn of the century Chinese firms held the lion's share and were continuing to gain ground. Moreover, noted the *Economist*:

> The same is true in medical technology, where Chinese firms are now beating foreigners in sales of CAT scanners and radiation therapy machines. In power generation, the state company no longer buys foreign equipment below 600 MW now that Chinese firms can make it themselves. Even Chinese car makers are improving. Sales of the Alto are growing more rapidly than those of any other car in China; it is designed by Suzuki, but made efficiently by an all-Chinese company, Norinco.[22]

How are the Chinese managing to compete effectively with international WCOs? One way is by learning how to drive down costs. A second, and complementary, way is by hiring young engineers who are willing to work around the clock in exchange for a promise of stock options. A third is by partnering with high-tech WCOs and using the joint venture to share costs and information useful for penetrating the local market.

At present, Chinese high-tech firms are focusing exclusively on the domestic market. However, as they continue to increase their market share they are likely to begin moving into the international arena and competing with such well-known giants as Motorola, Ericsson, and Sony.[23]

Asian Services   Still another good example of how quality pays off is Asia's service industry, which has become internationally competitive. When most people think of Asia, they picture countries that produce competitively manufactured products; however, these countries also are becoming very competitive in the services area. For example, the national airlines of Malaysia, Singapore, and Thailand regularly top the quality-service rankings in polls of international businesspeople; and Singapore's Changi International Airport has been ranked number one in the world in recent years. Asian hotel groups such as the Shangri-La and Mandarin Oriental chains also receive high ratings for quality service. Now an increasing number of Asian governments and businesses hope to build on such successes and create a service sector that is just as competitive as their manufacturing sector.

Because of such activity throughout Asia, the total trade in services of the 10 largest Asian economies increased almost 300 percent in the last 10 years. Much of this was accounted for by small firms, and many Asian governments have been slow to open up their service industries to foreign competition. This is slowly beginning to change, however, because governments realize that if they are going to have other industries such as manufacturing compete worldwide, they must withstand international competition for their service industry as well. As a result, Thailand has granted a number of banking licenses to foreign firms, the Philippine government has concluded that it cannot revamp its domestic telecommunication system without outside help and allowed a number of foreign firms into this marketplace, and India has opened cellular and basic telephone service to foreign investors.

These developments all point to the fact that if countries close themselves to outside competition, they will be unable to compete worldwide. This is because they become isolated and fail to develop state-of-the-art goods and services. By opening their markets to the outside world, Asian nations are able to attract MNCs that place a premium on knowledge, technology, and financial and human capital. Additionally, while these MNCs are anxious to sell things such as environmental services, computer software, and health care, these outputs also help Asian nations to develop low-tech services industries, such as retailing.

■ Beyond Quality in Order to Compete

What are MNCs doing to develop and sustain a competitive edge? They are employing a number of strategies that best can be summarized in terms of three stages or paradigm shifts through which organizations must progress to compete in today's environment. Although there is a fine line of distinction and some obvious overlap between total quality, learning, and world-class organizations. However, there are some longitudinal differences, as Figure 3–3 illustrates, as firms move from total quality, adaptive organizations to anticipative, learning organizations to being simply the best, world-class organizations (WCOs). So far attention has been given to total quality organizations, and the rest of the chapter is devoted to the emerging learning and world-class organizations in the global economy.

MNCs as Learning Organizations

Increasingly common are MNCs that achieve quality and excellence but then slip back either because they were too slow in keeping up with needed changes or did not anticipate changes. These MNCs typically are referred to as **adaptive organizations,** which are

Adaptive organizations
Organizations that are characterized by reaction to required changes but failure to anticipate them and stay on or ahead of the cutting edge.

Figure 3–3

New Paradigm Organizations

Source: Fred Luthans, Richard Hodgetts, and Sang M. Lee, "New Paradigm Organizations: From Total Quality to Learning to World-Class," *Organizational Dynamics,* Winter 1994, p. 10. Used with permission of the publisher, © 1994, American Management Association, New York. All rights reserved.

characterized by reaction to required changes but a failure to anticipate and stay on or ahead of the cutting edge. Those MNCs such as General Electric or Sony that do succeed in keeping ahead are learning organizations.

A **learning organization** is able to transform itself by anticipating change and discovering new ways of creating products and services; it has learned how to learn. Kodak is a good example. This MNC has changed direction and is now engaging in large-scale implementation with new technologies that move across the boundaries of traditional silver-based film and into the area of electronic photography, now possible by high-resolution imaging. Importantly, Kodak is focusing on digital technology, which it anticipates will be the wave of the future.

Another example of an MNC that is a learning organization is Gruppo GFT, the world's largest manufacturer of designer clothing. Unlike its competitors, who tend to view the world market in terms of standardized apparel with universal appeal, GFT focuses on designing products in response to a host of local differences in key markets. This MNC learned the needs of those markets and anticipated appropriately—redefining the way it did business in the process. In other words, GFT learned how to learn; and they anticipated the needed changes.

Three common characteristics of learning organizations are openness, creativity, and self-efficacy.[24] The following discussion examines each of these, and Table 3–1 provides additional comparisons between MNCs that are traditional adaptive and generative learning organizations.[25]

Openness   Learning organizations not only are prepared to accept new trends, they encourage and anticipate changes. Rather than fight change, they learn how to accommodate, create, and profit from it.[26] Although the chapters in Part II on the cultural context will point out the need to understand and apply concepts such as openness differently across cultures, MNCs that are learning organizations will in general try to suspend their need to control all aspects of operations as well as the people who run the place and interact with customers. Their managers empower associates, flatten the structure, and allow flexibility on everything; they examine their core values and try to identify how these must change for the MNC to grow and prosper.

Whirlpool is an example of a firm that reinvented itself. Several years ago, this MNC analyzed its markets and structure, and it concluded that the U.S. market no longer would be the largest, nor would it provide enough business for them to grow and prosper. They found that growth would come from untapped markets in Central and Eastern Europe, Mexico, and Asia. So Whirlpool reoriented itself to a new vision and set about translating this vision into action. All senior managers were required to have global experience so that they would better understand the international markets where the company was doing business. In addition, the firm created a joint venture with N.V. Philips to capture the European market and started joint ventures in India and Mexico. Moreover, to build shared cross-cultural values, the company held a worldwide leadership conference in Europe so that its managers could get to know each other and better understand their varied cultural backgrounds. In addition, to achieve what it called a "one company" culture, Whirlpool established cross-national–functional teams to establish and implement specific plans of action.[27]

Creativity   Of all the requisite skills and abilities for learning, creativity is the most widely and readily acknowledged, and two of the most important aspects of creativity are critical to effective learning: personal flexibility and a willingness to take risks. MNCs that are learning organizations nurture and promote both of these dimensions.

In the case of flexibility, MNCs such as Emerson and RCA missed the boat in their analysis of changes in the radio market. They believed that sales would follow a natural growth curve, eventually reach maturity and decline. In contrast, learning organizations such as Sony were highly flexible and saw a variety of different alternative possibilities for the radio. Sony believed that it could alter the product life cycle through creative innovation; the result was the Sony Walkman, which changed how, where, and when people listened to radios. MNCs lacking the flexibility to anticipate and make such changes end up losing out. Examples are provided in the accompanying "International Management in Action: Bit Players Bite the Dust."

Learning organizations
Organizations that are able to transform themselves by anticipating change and discovering new ways of creating products and services; they have learned how to learn.

Table 3–1
Characteristics of Traditional Adaptive and Generative Learning Organizations

Characteristics	Adaptive	Generative
Strategic		
Core competence	Better sameness	Meaningful difference
Source of strength	Stability	Change
Output	Market share	Market creation
Organizational perspective	Compartmentalization (SBU)	Systemic
Developmental dynamic	Change	Transformation
Structural		
Structure	Bureaucratic	Network
Control systems	Formal rules	Values, self-control
Power bases	Hierarchic position	Knowledge
Integrating mechanisms	Hierarchy	Teams
Networks	Disconnected	Strong
Communications flow	Hierarchic	Lateral
Human resource practices		
Performance appraisal system	Rewards stability	Flexibility
Reward basis	Short-term financial	Long-term financial and human resource development
Focus of rewards	Distribution of scarcity	Determination of synergy
Status symbols	Rank and title	Making a difference
Mobility patterns	Within division or function	Across divisions or functions
Mentoring	Not rewarded	Integral part of performance appraisal process
Culture	Market	Clan
Managers' behaviors		
Perspective	Controlling	Openness
Problem-solving orientation	Narrow	Systemic thinking
Response style	Conforming	Creative
Personal control	Blame and acceptance	Efficacious
Commitment	Ethnocentric	Empathetic

Source: Michael E. McGill, John W. Slocum, Jr., and David Lei, "Management Practices in Learning Organizations," *Organizational Dynamics,* Summer 1992, p. 14. Used with permission of the publisher, © 1992. American Management Association, New York. All rights reserved.

In the case of risk-taking, many MNCs are losing out because they remain overly conservative. Japanese automakers conducted market research in the United States and found no support from U.S. customers for minivans. As a result, they decided not to enter this market. Chrysler also conducted market research and received the same results, but this MNC was convinced there was a market for these vehicles and decided to take the risk. This decision proved to be one of the most profitable in Chrysler's history, helping the firm to attain record annual profits.

Self-Efficacy Drawn from well-known psychologist Albert Bandura's social cognitive theory, **self-efficacy** is a person's belief or confidence in his or her abilities to marshall the motivation, resources, and courses of action needed to successfully accomplish a specific task. [28] In the workplace, here is a description of how this self-efficacy applies to employees:

> Before they select their choices and initiate their effort, employees tend to weigh, evaluate, and integrate information about their perceived capabilities. Expectations of personal efficacy determine whether an employee's coping behavior will be initiated, how much task-related effort will be expended, and how long that effort will be sustained despite disconfirming evidence. [29]

Stajkovic and Luthans in a meta-analysis of 114 empirical studies found a strong positive correlation (.38) between this self-efficacy and work-related performance. [30]

Self-efficacy
A person's belief or confidence in his or her abilities to marshall the motivation, resources, and courses of action needed to successfully accomplish a specific task.

International Management in Action

Bit Players Bite the Dust   http://www.toyota.com

Keeping up with the competition can be difficult, especially for small MNCs that lack the resources and flexibility to change quickly. Small Japanese exporters that in recent years have found their competitiveness being slowly eroded provide a good example.

For many of these small MNCs the downhill slide began when the Japanese yen started rising against the U.S. dollar. As exports to the United States and other countries that were tied to the dollar became more expensive for buyers, Japanese MNCs, large and small, quickly realized they needed to control costs. Many of Japan's small manufacturing firms are suppliers to large MNCs such as Toyota, Nissan, and Sony, and they soon found these giant MNCs beginning to demand that products be produced at a lower price.

In the last decade, thousands of small Japanese enterprises have been driven out of business. One primary reason is that these small companies borrowed large sums of money during the early 1990s to upgrade their equipment and remain state-of-the-art for their big domestic customers. This strategy appeared to be very effective, because it meant these firms would be able to design, develop, and manufacture all sorts of output, from specialized machine parts to high-tech components. However, this strategy was premised on the companies continuing to garner orders from their giant customers. As the yen's value increased sharply and the large Japanese MNCs saw that the only way to protect their overseas markets was by remaining price competitive, these giant customers began demanding that their suppliers cut prices or lose their business—and this is exactly what happened to many of them. As an example, one small firm that made lenses and other camera parts found that when it could no longer drive down prices, the orders stopped coming. At its peak, this company made 5,000 lenses a month, but this eventually dropped to under 2,000 and the firm had trouble surviving. In the case of run-of-the-mill parts, many Japanese MNCs found they could easily replace their domestic producers by outsourcing to cheaper, offshore resources. As a result, Ricoh, the big Japanese office-equipment MNC, now imports 10 percent of its parts from China and other low-cost world locations, in contrast to the 2 percent the MNC used to purchase just a few years ago.

Those small Japanese manufacturers that have survived and prospered have market niches where more sophisticated parts and components are needed and face very limited competition. In these markets, the small firms are not bit players. They are mainstream competitors, and this makes all the difference for their present survival. However, they also must anticipate future changes and learn how to learn. In other words, they must become learning organizations.

Importantly, learning organizations can and do promote and develop such self-efficacy to take advantage of the positive impact on human performance and thus competitive advantage through people. There are a number of specific ways that self-efficacy can be developed (e.g., making sure employees experience success, verbal persuasion, or training through vicarious learning/modeling), but learning organizations also use a more general approach of creating a climate or culture that teaches and promotes associated self-awareness and active problem solving.

Self-awareness is fostered by a clear organizational vision that gives direction regarding critical choices and provides feedback about results. In particular, associates are taught to actively seek information about the impact of their behavior on others, and on issues that are important to others, as a means of maximizing their own efficacy. In other words, "information seeking" is turning out to be an important characteristic of effective employees in learning organizations. At Whirlpool, for example, the assessment of managerial talent is multiple and conducted on a worldwide basis. They conduct what are termed "360 (degree) evaluations," which include self-assessments as well as assessments from peers, subordinates, direct supervisors, and managers a level above one's own supervisor. These 360 assessments are not performance reviews per se. Instead, they focus on people's potential and capability, and they help individuals to understand themselves better. Most often, only the target individual, not his or her boss, receives the feedback.[31]

Proactive problem solving is used to teach managers in learning organizations how to anticipate and become more efficacious with issues before these issues become serious. Managers also learn how to prevent these problems from recurring. For example, IBM used to rely on customer feedback to help identify service problems. The MNC eventually discovered, however, that most customers who are dissatisfied with service do not fill out questionnaire surveys—they simply stop doing business with the firm. Now, IBM handles customer problems proactively by contacting customers who have stopped doing business with them and finding out what went wrong and how they can win back this customer. This proactivity is characteristic of a learning organization.

World-Class Organizations

Today, the very best MNCs are going beyond even the learning organization and have become what can be called "world-class organizations." **World-class organizations (WCOs)** are enterprises that are able to compete with anybody, anywhere, anytime. In most cases, WCOs have operations throughout the globe. IBM and Sony, discussed so far as total quality and learning organizations, are also WCOs, but so are MNCs such as General Electric, Toyota, and ABB. In a few cases, WCOs may focus heavily on only one geographic locale and have only limited worldwide operations. In either case, however, WCOs are able to compete effectively against all comers, foreign or domestic.

> **World-class organizations (WCOs)**
> Enterprises that are able to compete with anybody, anywhere, anytime.

To become a WCO, an organization must excel in a number of dimensions that in both an additive and synergistic way create a new level of competitive excellence that goes beyond the total quality and learning organizations. As shown in Figure 3–4, some major pillars forming the basis of WCOs include: (1) a customer-based focus; (2) continuous improvement; (3) fluid, flexible or "virtual organizations"; (4) creative human resources; (5) egalitarian climate; and (6) technological support. The details of each of these characteristics of the world-class organization will be discussed in the remainder of the chapter.

Customer-Based Focus   WCOs are customer-driven. They have identified their internal and external customers and have determined how to serve them effectively. In doing so, WCOs tend to have flat structures, so that everyone can be closer to the customer. Additionally, WCOs go beyond just satisfying their customers; they work very hard to delight their customers and have a bond with them. In the process, they also create new demands for their goods and services. A good example again is Sony's Walkman. The buyers were impressed not only with the innovativeness of the product but also with the CD version, and how much value they were receiving.

Another example is Wal-Mart, which has dominated the U.S. retail market and now has made in-roads in Mexico, Europe, and China, among other international markets. Focusing heavily on the customer, this firm has helped to break the old retailing model in which manufacturers would "push" their goods to retail stores and the latter in turn would push them onto customers. Wal-Mart, relying heavily on its ability to identify customer needs and negotiate competitive prices from suppliers, has created a "pull" system, in which customers buy things they need and thus pull the goods from the store. This strategy is not unique to Wal-Mart. Successful retailers in other parts of the world such as Metro International of Germany, Ito-Yokado of Japan, and Carrefour of France also employ customers-driven, market-pull strategies.

Figure 3–4   **Some Major Pillars of World-Class Organizations**

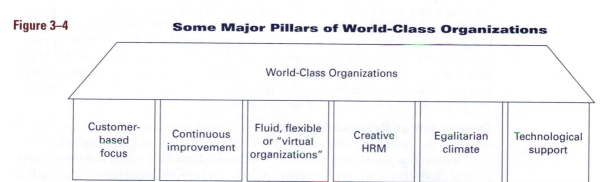

Source: Fred Luthans, Richard M. Hodgetts, and Sang M. Lee, "New Paradigm Organizations: From Total Quality to Learning to World-Class," *Organizational Dynamics,* Winter 1994, p. 15. Used with permission of the publisher, © 1994, American Management Association, New York. All rights reserved.

Continuous Improvement   A second distinctive characteristic of WCOs is their commitment to continuous improvement (CI). In contrast to their competitors, WCOs can improve faster, more efficiently, and more effectively. A good example is Ford Motor, which found that it took weeks to process vendor receipts because so many people had to approve the payment. By carefully studying this process, Ford was able to reduce sharply the number of individuals who needed to sign off on payments and cut the processing time by 90 percent.

Microsoft, although recently undergoing scrutiny for being a monopoly in the computer services and software industry, feels it must continually improve in order to compete with the likes of Netscape, IBM, Novell, Oracle, and UNIX. To counter the antitrust argument, chairman and CEO Bill Gates points out that Windows continuously, dramatically improves.

Use of Flexible or Virtual Organizations   Another characteristic of WCOs is their use of flexible or virtual organizations. A **virtual organization** is one that is able to conduct business as if it were a very large enterprise with major facilities while in fact it is much smaller, made up of core business competencies with the rest outsourced or partnered. How is this possible? One major way when taken into the international arena is global sourcing, a topic introduced earlier in the chapter.

Global sourcing is the use of worldwide suppliers, regardless of where they are located geographically, who are best able to provide the needed output.[32] For example, Japanese automakers today rely increasingly on U.S. suppliers for their cars. Similarly, U.S. laptop computer firms rely on Japanese sources to provide screen technology. Where possible, however, MNCs prefer home-based suppliers because of the benefit this provides them in maintaining their worldwide competitive advantage. Michael Porter explains it this way:

> Perhaps the most important benefit of home-based suppliers . . . is the *process of innovation and upgrading.* Competitive advantage emerges from close working relationships between world-class suppliers and the industry. Suppliers help firms perceive new methods and opportunities to apply new technology. Firms gain quick access to information to new ideas and insights and to supplier innovations. They have the opportunity to influence suppliers' technical efforts as well as to serve as test sites for development work. The exchange of R&D and joint problem solving lead to faster and more efficient solutions. Suppliers also tend to be a conduit for transmitting information and innovations from firm to firm. Through this process the pace of innovation within the entire national industry is accelerated. All these benefits are enhanced if suppliers are located in proximity to firms, shortening the communication lines.[33]

This also helps to explain why suppliers often locate near their major customers. When Ford Motor decides to set up new facilities in Europe, its U.S.-based suppliers will locate nearby so that they can continue to work closely with the giant automaker. This strategy helps Ford to become, essentially, a virtual organization because it does not have to produce these supplies in-house but derives the same benefits as if it did. Other firms have taken this concept further. For example in Argentina, Metalurgica Romet SA makes and assembles doors at Volkswagen's new plant. In fact, VW workers at the factory are responsible for building only the chassis, powertrain, and a few other parts. The rest of the car is produced and assembled by suppliers working in the factory. These suppliers buy the equipment they need to do their jobs and are responsible for their own inventory and carrying costs. As a result, VW is now able to manufacture a car in half the time it took at its old plant in Argentina, and the firm has reduced total costs in the factory by 50 percent.[34] In the coming years, an increasing number of MNCs will rely on global sourcing to provide materials and products that once were produced in-house. As a result, these companies can act like larger enterprises when in fact they are smaller and depend on partnering and global sourcing to take care of many of their needs.

Creative Human Resource Management   Human resources generally are given lip service to be the most important asset for any organization. Yet, as Pfeffer recently pointed out, "Rather than putting their people first, numerous firms have sought solutions to competitive challenges in places and means that have not been very productive—treating their businesses as portfolios of assets to be bought and sold in an effort to find the right competitive niche, downsizing and outsourcing in a futile attempt to shrink or transact their

---

Virtual organization
An organization that is able to conduct business as if it were a very large enterprise when, in fact, it is much smaller, made up of core business competencies and the rest outsourced or partnered.

Global sourcing
The use of worldwide suppliers, regardless of where they are located geographically, who are best able to provide the needed output.

way to profit, and doing myriad other things that weaken or destroy their organizational culture in efforts to minimize labor costs—even as they repeatedly proclaim, 'people are our most important asset.' "[35] Yet, there is growing research evidence that human resources and how they are managed do make the difference. In Pfeffer's recent book *The Human Equation,* he summarizes these substantial findings: The returns from managing people in ways that build high commitment, involvement, and learning and organizational competence are typically on the order of 30 to 50 percent.[36]

World-class organizations such as Southwest Airlines, Virgin Airlines, ABB, and Gallup, Inc. do recognize the importance of their people. The relative value of human resources is becoming increasingly important as knowledge-based organizations are replacing traditional asset-based MNCs. WCOs know they must compete based on what their human resources are capable of doing rather than on mere physical assets, such as buildings, machinery, and equipment. WCOs have state-of-the-art, creative approaches to managing their human resources, and they effectively stimulate and have a supportive climate for employee creativity. More specifically, their human resource management (HRM) programs are designed to help their people share ownership of problems and solutions, achieve a strong commitment and involvement by top management, communicate consistent goals and objectives to all levels and functions in the organization, and help develop an effective use of recognition and reward programs.

There are many examples of creative HRM practices. One is the use of empowered teams with the authority to make all decisions in their own work area. For example, at the world-class Ritz-Carlton Hotels, employees can spend up to $1,000 on customer service-related matters. Another example is the creation of suggestion systems that generate new, useful ideas for better serving clients. Wainwright Industries, a small but world-class U.S. manufacturer, has a suggestion system so effective that it annually generates 55 suggestions per employee, which is sharply higher than the 12 generated by typical Japanese MNCs and the 0.3 by the typical U.S. firm.[37]

Another important aspect of WCO HRM strategy is effective recognition and monetary reward systems. In particular, WCOs ensure that rewards are positive, given openly, and highly publicized. At the Ritz-Carlton chain any employee can send a "First Class" card—a 3" × 5" card designed with the company logo, to express his or her appreciation to anyone else in the organization for a job well done. The company also uses "Lightning Strikes"—monetary rewards granted by a member of the Executive Committee to any employee for outstanding service. In addition, individuals who submit the best ideas for improvement are listed on a bulletin board and given a dinner for two, and those who generate the greatest number of useful ideas are honored at quarterly receptions.

Egalitarian Climate   WCOs create an egalitarian climate in which all stakeholders— employees, customers, owners, suppliers, and the community—are treated with dignity and respect. This is done in a number of ways. At Wal-Mart, everyone is referred to as an "associate," there are no subordinates or employees. Another common approach is the way in which customers are treated. At the Ritz-Carlton chain, when a guest asks for directions to a particular locale in the hotel, the associate will stop whatever he or she is doing and become a personal escort to that location.

Another sign of an egalitarian approach is the way in which WCOs treat their suppliers. In the past, companies would negotiate with vendors and pit one against the other to get the lowest possible price. Under an egalitarian approach, this strategy is abandoned in favor of a team approach, in which the supplier is regarded as an integral part of the in-house team. For example, at IBM, suppliers participate in new product design, learn the company's needs, and work with the firm to provide materials and parts at the highest quality levels and most competitive prices. In the process, suppliers learn their customer's culture and how the organization operates. Suppliers then are in a better position to integrate their own approach with that of their partner company. Japanese WCOs such as Sony and Mitsubishi take this idea a step further, getting suppliers involved in helping cost the product and continually working together to drive down expenses. Figure 3–5 provides an example.

Figure 3–5

Cost Reduction Approaches: The United States versus Japan

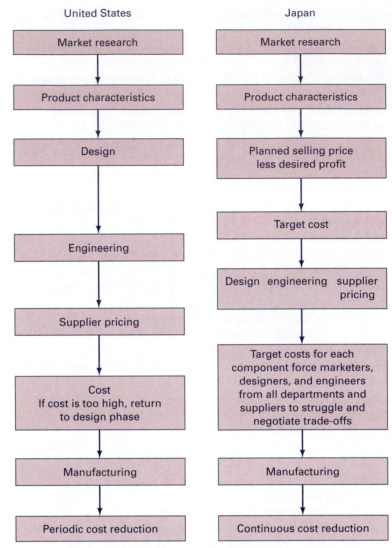

Source: Adapted from Ford S. Worthy, "Japan's Smart Secret Weapon," *Fortune,* August 12, 1991, p. 73.

Technological Support Most of the creative, innovative, and effective approaches of WCOs are supported by advanced, cutting-edge technological support. Examples of such technology include computer-aided design and computer-aided manufacturing (CAD/CAM), telecommunications networks, expert or "smart" systems, distributed information systems, multimedia systems, intranets, and executive or management information systems. One good example is found in the retailing industry, where competition is fierce and profit margins are typically low.

Information technology (IT) is critical to e-tailing discussed in the last chapter, but also to the operations of retailing WCOs. Thanks to IT, retailers can tell instantly what they are selling in each of their hundreds of stores, how much money they are making on each sale, and increasingly, who their customers are. Additionally, an effective IT system can help a company to minimize its inventory but still reduce the likelihood of stockouts. Wal-Mart uses such a just-in-time (JIT) inventory system to reduce costs and increase revenue-producing sales space in their stores, thus allowing the firm to keep its international prices low.[38]

Computers also have helped world-class retailers to exercise closer control over their international units and thus transform themselves into truly global firms. Again, the best example is Wal-Mart, which has been the leader in blending IT with operations. More recently, other big retailers have followed suit. Tesco, the giant British supermarket chain, has used IT to cut the amount of stock in its supply chain to a mere 2 weeks' supply. Tesco is using automated picking and sorting systems to break down deliveries into smaller units and believes that within 5 years, it will be operating with only 1 week's supply. Like Wal-Mart, Tesco also is using computer modeling derived from electronic point-of-sale data to predict future demand.

Thanks to inexpensive yet powerful PC-based computer systems, WCO retailers now can identify small suppliers that offer special niche products. For example, a small, local cheese producer now can supply a single Tesco supermarket in York, England. Five years ago, it would not have been economically feasible to identify such a small supplier and negotiate a contract; Tesco would have opted for a larger supplier who could provide a wider range of products to a greater number of stores. Because of effective technological support, WCOs are able to increase their market coverage while simultaneously reducing price and improving customer service.

In the years ahead, all MNCs will begin to recognize and attempt to adopt the types of WCO characteristics discussed in this chapter. If MNCs do not become world class, they may not survive in the long run. If they take on the characteristics of WCOs, however, they increasingly should be able to compete with anybody, anywhere, anytime.

The World of *Business Week*—Revisited

The *Business Week* article that opened this chapter provided an excellent example of a world-class organization (WCO) that can compete with anybody, anywhere, anytime. Having read this chapter, you should now be aware of some of the innovative techniques used by WCOs to gain competitive advantage. In addition, you should now understand the relationship between quality and cost and know the importance of the technology paradox in creating and sustaining a competitive advantage. WCOs in all fields from auto manufacturing to chemical processing to retailing are using this knowledge to create worldwide market niches. Reflecting on what you have read in this chapter and using Toyota as your reference, answer the following questions: What will happen to the quality and price of a Toyota automobile over the next five years? How is the company using innovation to maintain its competitive position? What are three things that the firm does that clearly show it to be a WCO?

Summary of Key Points

1. Quality is having a major impact on international operations. One reason is because it transcends national boundaries and allows firms to compete in a borderless world. Another is because, paradoxically, as technology increases, costs tend to be driven down, and only the most effective MNCs succeed. This emphasis on quality is leading MNCs to become increasingly more competitive in terms of both products and services.

2. One way in which successful MNCs are going beyond total quality to sustain, and even increase, their world competitiveness is through learning. Total quality has become just the cost of entry into today's highly competitive world economy. Now, MNCs not only must adapt, they must anticipate and even create change. They must transform themselves into learning organizations. Three of the major characteristics of learning organizations are openness, creativity, and self-efficacy.

3. World-class organizations (WCOs) are able to compete with anybody, anywhere, anytime. There are several major pillars that form the basis for WCOs: customer-based focus, continuous improvement, flexible or virtual organizations, creative human resource management practices, an egalitarian climate, and technological support. Today, more and more firms are adopting the characteristics of WCOs, because they realize this is the only way of ensuring that they can compete, and in the long run even survive, in today's Three Any's environment.

Key Terms

adaptive organizations, *59*

benchmarking, *56*

global sourcing, *64*

learning organizations, *60*

mass customization, *55*

paradox, *53*

product proliferation, *56*

self-efficacy, *61*

technology paradox, *54*

virtual organizations, *64*

world-class organizations
  (WCOs), *63*

Review and Discussion Questions

1. What is the relationship between quality and cost? Why is this relationship important to MNCs that want to develop products for the international market?

2. Why would an understanding of the technology paradox be valuable to high-tech MNCs? What practical value would it offer these firms regarding how to price and market their products?

3. How do learning organizations differ from traditional adaptive organizations? Why would MNCs be inter-ested in developing the characteristics of learning organizations? What value would it have for stake-holders? In your answer, be sure to identify and incorporate the three characteristics of learning organizations.

4. As MNCs try to become world-class organizations, what are some of the steps that they should take? In your answer, be sure to identify and incorporate the six pillars.

Internet Exercise: Going Worldwide with Wal-Mart

When it comes to competing with anybody, anywhere, anytime, there are few companies that can surpass Wal-Mart, the world's largest discount retailer. In recent years the company has continued to expand its coverage of the U.S. market. At the same time it has begun moving into the international arena and has plans to become the world's leading discount retailer. How will it accomplish this feat? Visit the company at **www.wal-mart.com** and read about their expansion plans. Then answer these three questions:

(1) What has Wal-Mart been doing over the last couple of years to increase its international presence? In particular, concentrate your attention on Argentina, Brazil, Canada, Mexico, China, and the United Kingdom. How well is the company doing in these countries? (2) Is its sales in these international locations increasing faster or slower than in the U.S. market? (3) Will the fact that Wal-Mart has been able to meet the criteria of a world-class organization be of value to it in these expansion activities? Why or why not?

France

The French Republic is situated in Western Europe. It is bounded on the north by the English Channel; to the east by Belgium, Luxembourg, Germany, Switzerland, and Italy; to the south by the Mediterranean Sea and Spain; and to the west by the Atlantic Ocean. The island of Corsica is part of metropolitan France, while four overseas departments, two overseas *collectivites territoriales,* and four overseas territories also form an integral part of the Republic. The principal language is French, which has numerous regional dialects; small minorities speak Breton and Basque. There are approximately 60 million residents in France.

France is one of the most economically powerful countries in Europe, and it is one of the G-7 nations. According to United Nations estimates, the country currently has a GDP of over $1.2 trillion and a per-capita GDP of about $20,000. During recent years, the GDP has continued to grow at an annual rate of 3.0 to 3.5 percent.

Mining, manufacturing, construction, and power provide around 30 percent of French GDP, and industrial production continues to grow. Manufacturing in particular accounts for a sizable portion of economic activity, and the country is a net exporter. In 1999, France had a trade surplus of over $11 billion, and the nation typically has a favorable balance of trade with the United States. Its major trading partner is Germany, however, which buys 18 percent of all France's exports and accounts for about 19 percent of French imports. Most of the rest of the country's import and export activity occurs between other EU nations.

Because of France's recent steady economic growth, the country has been the target of much MNC activity. The purchasing power of an average French family is far higher than that in many other EU nations, including Spain, Portugal, Greece, and Finland. Additionally, MNCs from around the world doing business in Germany have found that the French economy is so interrelated that France becomes a second market. France also is a target for new expansion, as in the case of the big German auto firm DaimlerChrysler, which has recently built a new factory in France because of its faith in the workers' productivity and work ethic. On the negative side, the near future may see difficult economic times for the country. In particular, the unemployment rate in France is higher than that in other economic powers, and in 2000 it stood at around 2.5 million. Additionally, the country has been running deficits in recent years.

To get the French economy moving, President Jacques Chirac promised to give tax breaks, speed up privatization, and institute pension reform. Recently there have been demonstrations against these reforms and many French businesspeople still complain that the government has too much control and prevents them from making needed changes to ensure the efficiency of their operations. For example, when Perrier, the world-famous French bottling MNC, wanted to cut 600 jobs to boost efficiency, the government turned down its request. When Michelin, the tire maker, tried to increase productivity by running its plants 24 hours a day, the government delayed a long time before giving the MNC permission to run one of its five plants continuously. The other four must still close on weekends, conforming to the current rules requiring French businesses to operate only five days a week. These bureaucratic rules have a negative effect on productivity and could weaken France's competitive position in the world economy. **www.france.com**

Questions

1. Why would MNCs be interested in doing business in France?

2. How would French customers be likely to measure quality in products such as cars? Computers? Televisions? What would they be looking for?

3. Why would MNCs need to have a total quality commitment if they hoped to succeed in the French market?

4. Would successful MNCs in France need to be learning organizations? Why or why not?

5. If a WCO were successful in France, might it also do well throughout the EU? Why or why not?

It's a Price and Quality Issue

A German high-tech firm has just achieved a major break-through in cellular technology that likely will drive down the cost of such phones. The company estimates that it can manufacture a phone for less than $4 that will retail for approximately $15, and these units will have higher quality and more features than any others on the market. The company intends to have a prototype completed within 60 days and is planning a worldwide launch within 4 months.

The initial market will be Germany and then the European Union; however, the company also intends to begin selling these phones in the United States and Japan within 6 months. At present, the firm is focusing on three key areas. First are the distribution channels that will be needed to successfully market the product in Europe, North America, and Japan. Second is continuing research and development (R&D) efforts to increase the quality of the product even further. Third are the manufacturing processes that will be used to build the units, because the company wants to continue driving down the cost. To senior-level management, these three areas constitute the major opportunities and threats for the firm. The head of R&D put it this way:

> When we first release this product, there will be a wave of initial demand that will sustain us through the first 90 days. However, we will not be able to rest on this initial success. We must continue improving our technology. Ideally, we would like to come out with a new version of the phone within 6 months, and we have to continue this improvement for the indefinite future. At the same time, we must work to drive down our costs, so that it becomes less and less expensive for people to purchase our product.

If we don't do this, the competition will be able to reverse engineer our product and soon have a similar offering on the market that will be just as good as ours, but at a lower price. To achieve these goals, we must be flexible and pre-pared to change and rethink everything we are doing. We are in a fast-moving industry, and if we cannot keep up, we are going to fall behind and not even survive. This new product should thrust us into the lead, but the real chal-lenge will be sustainability and, hopefully, growth.

The head of manufacturing agreed with this statement but also believes that the firm can meet the challenge. "We have been carefully designing the production processes that will be needed to produce this product," he recently told the board of directors, "and if we continue to impro-vise and modify our manufacturing approaches, we will be able to drive down costs by 40 percent within 12 months while maintaining a sigma level of close to six." The board members agree that if this can be done, the company likely will do very well indeed. As one board member put it, "it's all a matter of controlling price and quality."

Questions

1. How would the technology paradox help to shape the strategy of this German firm?

2. Why would the company need to become a learning organization if it hopes to dominate the cellular phone market?

3. If the firm wanted to become a WCO, what are some steps it would need to take? Identify and describe four of the most important.

Chapter 4

Ethics and Social Responsibility

Objectives of the Chapter

The current concern that all businesses and the general public have for ethical behavior and social responsibility is not restricted to the domestic situation. In this era of a global economy, MNCs must be concerned with how they carry out their business and their social role in host countries. This chapter examines business ethics and social responsibility in the international arena, and it looks at some of the critical social issues that will be confronting MNCs in the years ahead. The discussion includes ethical decision making in various countries, regulation of foreign investment, and current responses to social responsibility by today's multinationals. The specific objectives of this chapter are:

1. **EXAMINE** some of the major ethical issues and problems confronting MNCs in selected countries.

2. **EXPLAIN** some of the ways that host countries are attempting to regulate foreign investments and why reciprocity is such an important trade issue.

3. **DISCUSS** some of the action being taken by selected industrialized countries to be more socially responsive to world problems.

BusinessWeek

The World of *Business Week*

Invasion of the Cartel Cops

The European Commission antitrust SWAT teams arrived without warning at dawn. In a coordinated raid in Italy and the Netherlands, they sealed off exits at offices of some of Europe's leading brewers, including Heineken, Carlsberg, Peroni, and Interbrew, flashed subpoenas, and demanded entry. After two days of rummaging through desks and computers, they carted off thousands of documents. Why? An investigation into charges of price-fixing and market division. "We're looking for evidence of cozy meetings where the CEOs carve up markets and agree not to hurt each other," says EC competition official Michael Tscherny.

The brewery inquiry is the latest sally in Europe's rapidly widening war against cartels. While the 15 countries in the European Union have had a long history of tolerating price-fixing, that attitude is quickly changing. Since early last year, the EU's competition police have cracked down on cartels in the shipping, automobile, steel-pipe, and cement industries, among others.

The shift has been prompted in large part by the move to a single currency and a unified market. Major industries from airlines to telephones have been deregulated and national monopolies privatized. As countries open to free trade, they're stepping up the fight against powerful cartels that have artificially raised prices and limited consumer choice. If a company wants to complain about being shut out of a foreign market, it has recourse in Brussels. "We now have a single market and need a new competition policy," says the EC's antitrust commissioner, Mario Monti, a Yale University-trained economist.

That's welcome news for American antitrust cops, who have long been frustrated by Europe's lax attitude toward price-fixing. Even though the key players in the worldwide vitamin cartel were Germany's BASF, Switzerland's F. Hoffmann-La Roche, and France's Rhône Poulenc, the job of breaking it up fell primarily on the U.S., which fined the companies $242 million.

Europe's trustbusters are fighting tradition. Since the trade guilds of the Middle Ages, cozy cooperation has been the norm. "Industries, particularly in small countries where everyone knew everyone else, banded together," says Stephen Kinsella, a partner at Brussels law firm Herbert Smith. Even governments have supported price-fixing to protect small shops. Germany doesn't let retailers shave more than 3% off manufacturers' suggested prices—and it forbids any discounting of books. In the Netherlands, cartels were legal until 1996.

Indeed, there's little evidence of vigorous competition in the beer industry. In their home markets, Europe's big brewers enjoy huge and growing market shares. Interbrew, owner of the brands Stella Artois and Abbaye de Leffe, makes almost 60% of the beer consumed in Belgium. Heineken's market share in the Netherlands is about the same. Big brewers own large numbers of bars and often strike exclusive deals with them that last up to 10 years, shutting out new entrants. "Most cafés won't even talk to me," complains Jean-Pierre Van Roy, CEO of Cantillon Brewery, a small Brussels producer.

Coincidence?

The breweries deny they ever fixed prices, conspired to divide markets, or unlawfully hurt consumers. Heineken spokesman Michael Berssenbrugge says "there is fierce competition in beer in the Netherlands" and notes that there were no price hikes in that country from 1992 to 1998. The companies also say the practice of signing exclusive distribution deals with bars has declined and note that in June, a new EC law takes effect that prevents brewers dominant in their home markets from owning restaurants or cafés. "We are forced to carry all types of beers in our pubs," says Interbrew spokesman Jan Coucke.

Monti is also targeting the telecommunications industry. Mobile phones in Europe work across the entire region, yet charges are high. After receiving numerous complaints, Monti last year opened an investigation into whether mobile-phone companies have been colluding to keep roaming charges high.

Additionally, Monti wants to help consumers take advantage of Europe's new single market, where they can cross borders and buy products in the

Bucking a History of Collusion

Europe has traditionally been far more tolerant of price-fixing than the U.S.
But as the EU tries to encourage free trade, that attitude is rapidly changing.

BEER
EU regulators raided Heineken, Carlsberg, Peroni, Interbrew, and other major breweries, seeking evidence of price-fixing.

SHIPPING
Fifteen shippers, including Britain's P&O Nedlloyd, Denmark's Maersk Line, and the U.S.'s Sea-Land Service, were fined a record $314 million.

MOBILE PHONES
EU Competition Commissioner Monti opened an investigation into whether mobile-phone companies have been colluding to keep roaming charges high.

STEEL PIPE
Eight steel producers were fined $95 million for conspiring to fix prices of seamless-steel tubes.

BANKS
Monti announced that he is investigating whether European banks have conspired to fix charges for currency transactions.

Data: *Business Week*

cheapest markets. Carmakers long have keep domestic prices 30% higher or more than they are abroad. When Volkswagen tried in 1998 to prevent German dealers from importing cheaper cars from Italy, the EC fined it more than $100 million. Now Monti has opened new investigations into the carmaker's exclusive distribution arrangements. Soon, he could order the entire system disbanded.

Unlike American trustbusters, Monti cannot bring criminal charges and threaten cartel offenders with jail, which makes it harder to crack tough cases. But he can fine companies up to 10% of their worldwide sales if they are found guilty of participating in a cartel. And the penalties are getting bigger. Monti fined a group of shipping companies controlling freight across the Atlantic $314 million—a new record.

The EC has also set up a whistleblower program that gives a nearamnesty to the first company that rats on fellow conspirators. And it's working. "People are pointing so many fingers that it has become open slaughter," says Peter Alexiadus, an antitrust specialist at Squires, Sanders & Dempsey in Brussels. That's making Europe's remaining cartels squirm. But they've had things too easy for too long.

By William Echikson in Brussels

Source: Reprinted from May 8, 2000, pp. 130, 132 issue of *Business Week* by special permission, copyright © 2000 by the McGraw-Hill Companies, Inc.

The news article that opens this chapter helps emphasize the importance of ethical and socially responsible behavior by multinationals. The article also underscores the fact that what is illegal in one country may be totally acceptable in another. About 100 years ago, when the U.S. government started breaking up the big business trusts, those who objected said that the government was interfering with business and it had no right to regulate commerce this way. However, the Supreme Court sided with the government and today U.S. firms all know that they must not do anything to restrain trade. If the government thinks they are guilty of such action, as Microsoft recently learned, the Justice Department will take action. Simply put, the creation of cartels for the purpose of dominating an industry is outlawed; and the use of price-fixing can result in both fines and imprisonment for those involved.

From the article, however, it is clear that the use of cartels and price-fixing have long been common in Europe. Only now with the emergence of the European Union (EU) and the creation of rules and regulations for governing the business behaviors of member nations have these activities become illegal. Of course, getting EU businesses to stop these practices can be difficult. In fact, many of them may have created their strategies based on the continued use of price-fixing and other questionable ethics.

This development is good news for U.S. MNCs that have long had to compete under these types of restrictions in their home market. Certainly the EU crackdown will make it easier for noncartel members to compete. At the same time, however, it is important to remember that the news article relates only to the EU. Asian companies doing business in their geographic areas of the world have their own ways of doing things and their cultural and regulatory systems are quite different from those in the U.S. and EU. So, for example, if a publishing house in Canton, Ohio, were to print a best-selling novel that belonged to another publisher, it would be sued for copyright infringement. However, if a publishing house in Canton (Guangzhou), China, were to print this same book, the publisher with the copyright might find it a waste of time to bring legal action against the Chinese publisher. In fact, both authors of this text have had books they wrote translated into Chinese and published there with no permission from the U.S. publisher with the copyright and no payment of royalties to either the publisher or the authors. Simply put, the legal and ethical rules that govern business practices in one country may have absolutely no impact on the practices of businesses in another. As this chapter will illustrate, worldwide differences in ethics and the views of social responsibility can leave MNCs in a difficult position when trying to determine how they should behave internationally. What is unethical conduct in one nation may be totally acceptable in another. For instance, in some countries the payment of a bribe to secure a contract may be common place, but this activity can get a U.S. firm into legal trouble back home because of American laws that affect the way U.S. companies can do things worldwide. As a result, it is extremely important for MNCs to understand the role and impact of ethics and social responsibility on their business operations not only at home, but also as they do business across the globe.

■ Ethics Around the World

The ethical behavior of business has become a major issue. Not only in the United States but all countries around the world have received considerable media attention and aroused the public's concern about ethics in international business.

Ethics is the study of morality and standards of conduct. In recent years a growing number of MNCs have formulated codes of ethics to guide their behavior and ensure that their operations conform to these standards worldwide. Part of the corporate credo of Johnson & Johnson, the giant MNC, reads as follows:

Ethics
The study of morality and standards of conduct

> We are responsible to our employees, the men and women who work with us throughout the world. Everyone must be considered as an individual. We must respect their dignity and recognize their merit. They must have a sense of security in their jobs. Compensation must be fair and adequate, and working conditions clean, orderly and safe. We must be mindful of ways to help our employees fulfill their family responsibilities. Employees must feel free to make suggestions and complaints. There must be equal opportunity for employment, development and advancement for those qualified. We must provide competent management, and their actions must be just and ethical.
>
>   We are responsible to the communities in which we will live and work and to the world community as well. We must be good citizens—support good works and charities and bear our fair share of taxes. We must encourage civic improvements and better health and education. We must maintain in good order the property we are privileged to use, protecting the environment and natural resources.[1]

Ethics is important in the study of international management, because ethical behavior in one country sometimes is viewed as unethical behavior in other countries. Considerable attention has been given in the management literature to ethical problems in the United States; not so well-known are the ethical issues in other parts of the world.[2] The following sections examine some of the ethical problems that occur in international business in selected countries.

Ethical Problems and Concerns in Japan

In terms of both internal and external business relations, Japan, like the United States, has had more than its share of ethical problems in recent years. Some of the most devastating and widely publicized have occurred in both the political and business arenas.

Political and Business Scandals   In recent years not only has Japan struggled economically, but has also been rocked by a number of political scandals. In one recent case, a Japanese cabinet member was forced to resign after admitting that he had received $1.8 million for advisory work from the Mitsubishi Trust and Banking Corporation and had also accepted $800,000 from a condominium developer.[3] A few days later the chief cabinet secretary, the second highest ranking job after the prime minister, acknowledged that he had accepted a political donation of $68,000 from two people, an amount far in excess of the $12,000 limit.[4] In another case, the finance director for the Japanese Public Highway Corporation was accused of accepting lavish entertainment from a stock brokerage firm. Tokyo prosecutors charged the official with being influenced by this largesse and, in turn, selecting the brokerage as the chief underwriter of $800 million worth of bonds issued by the Highway Corporation.[5] As a result of the investigation, more than 30 executives of Japanese financial institutions were arrested. Additionally, four officials of the Finance Ministry and one from the Bank of Japan were taken into custody on charges of having accepted bribes in the form of entertainment. However, very little happened as a result of these actions except that the chief prosecutor in Tokyo was transferred to a remote coastal city and the investigation came to a halt.[6]

Another scandal that has rocked Japan in recent years has been the failure of its banking system to take corrective action and help out the country's drawn-out recession. This problem seems to have been caused by both the government and business. The government failed to institute strong procedures designed to prevent the banks from taking large, dangerous risks and the banks failed to adjust their loan policies, write off bad loans, and accept the responsibility for their errors. As a result, the total amount of uncollectible loans by major Japanese banks was greater than their total equity. Simply put, many of them were technically bankrupt![7]

Another Japanese scandal is the alleged relationship between politicians and organized crime. Critics contend that the major Japanese shipping ports are controlled by gangsters. In support of their claims, they point to the fact that it costs $3,619 to ship a 20-foot container from Yokohama Port to Tokyo (24 miles) while to ship that same container from Yokohama to Los Angeles (5,400 miles) is only $2,761.[8] Why does the government not investigate? One high-ranking crime lord, interviewed by *Forbes* magazine, has said that politicians in both major political parties are given kickbacks by the mob which the politicians then use to fund their political campaigns. Here is a reported example:

> When the $14 billion Kansai airport was built near Osaka, mob members were informed of where access roads would go. They then intimidated residents along the proposed routes into selling their property. Parcels were resold to the government for a premium, much of which was plowed back into politicians' pockets. In an assertion strongly disputed by the Kansai Airport Authority, the gangster says mob-controlled companies also substituted industrial waste for the uncontaminated landfill that was supposed to have been used. Again, huge kickbacks went from the gangs to the ruling [political party], he says—common public-works practice.[9]

Japanese business firms have also come under scrutiny for unethical and illegal practices. Mitsubishi Motors, for example, has admitted that it systematically concealed customer complaints in Japan for more than 20 years and some top managers knew about the cover-up.[10] The company failed to inform car owners about possible auto defects and did not file this information with the government. One of the ways Mitsubishi did this was by maintaining two sets of records of customer complaints: those to be reported to the authorities and those to be hidden.[11] The police launched an investigation into allegations that the firm was criminally negligent in covering up these defects[12] and the company began a massive recall of over 600,000 vehicles in Japan and another 200,000 in overseas markets.

In another instance, Nissan Motors was charged with encouraging employees to mislead government inspectors. In a manual distributed to employees, the company told the workers to "put away secret materials" when government officials held surprise inspections and to switch their computer screens to the one designed for inspection.[13] In its defense, the firm responded by saying that these instructions were meant to apply only to materials that had not been completed and approved by a supervisor.

Hostile Work Environment Issues   Japanese firms have also been facing charges of sexual harassment in the workplace, an issue on which more and more Japanese women are fighting back. Several years ago, a Japanese woman won a judgment of $12,500 from her company. This was the first lawsuit ever filed in Japan charging sexual harassment, and it set off a wave of concern. Within 48 hours of the verdict, the government had issued 10,000 copies of a booklet on sexual harassment, and all were quickly snapped up.

Despite a heightened sensitivity in recent years, sexual harassment remains a major social issue in Japan. A good example is provided by a Japanese saleswoman for a large bank, who was visiting clients with a male deputy branch manager. This manager made improper advances toward her, but when she reported the incident the only thing the company did was to give her a new work partner. Soon afterwards the branch manager approached the woman and told her that her previous partner had been having work problems and he would like the two of them to again become job partners. The woman refused, quit her job, and filed a sexual harassment lawsuit against the firm.

One of the major reasons why sexual harassment remains a problem in Japan is that traditionally many male managers regard female employees as mere assistants and, following a stereotype, feel that women employees will soon marry and leave the firm. So women are often not given the opportunity for promotion and are not considered for management positions. Additionally, sexual harassment is a new concept to many Japanese managers. One labor economist recently tried to put the issue into perspective by noting that most Japanese managers do not consider it a moral issue or think about why it happens or of improving the work environment. In fact, while many Japanese know that there are sexual harassment lawsuits filed in the United States, they fail to grasp why it is such an important issue for Americans. One analyst recently conveyed this idea by noting that in Japan, "There is no specific law against sexual harassment, so those suing must use general civil law. Suits can take years in the courts, and awards are typically only a few thousand dollars. And victory can be difficult."[14]

Equal Opportunity Issues   There are a number of equal opportunity issues that Japanese firms face. One of the most prominent is the refusal to hire women or promote them into management positions. Many women who are in the last year of their college program, for example, find that company interviewers are interested in hiring them only for secretarial or other dead-end jobs. They quickly learn that there is a two-track recruiting process in many Japanese firms: one for men and one for women. Labor market experts say that the business rationale for excluding women from professional jobs is the belief that they will quit to get married after only a few years. One college graduate, who applied to almost 50 firms and got just three job offers, summed up her experience by saying, "What I've learned is that if a company has a choice between a man and a woman, they will choose the man, even if he is of lesser ability."[15]

This type of thinking has also created problems for Japanese firms doing business overseas. For example, a few years ago the U.S. Equal Employment Opportunity Commission filed a lawsuit against Mitsubishi charging the firm with sexual harassment of more than 300 women. The company eventually settled the case agreeing, among other things, to donate $100,000 to women's causes as well as to make substantial cash payments to some of the women who had brought lawsuits of their own.[16] In yet another lawsuit, Honda of America Manufacturing, Inc., agreed to give 370 African-Americans and women a total of $6 million in back pay to resolve a federal discrimination complaint.

Social Responsibility Implication from Lobbying   Another area of ethical concern has been the Japanese lobbying effort in the United States.[17] Japan, more than other countries, spends millions of dollars every year for lobbying in Washington. For this money, Japanese firms have been able to hire very savvy, effective lobbyists. Is this ethical for Japanese firms to hire bank-rolled, well-connected, talented lobbyists to argue their case in Washington? Is it ethical for former U.S. cabinet officers and elected officials to become lobbyists for Japan? Certainly, these activities are legal. Many Americans feel that the interests of the United States and Japan are not the same when it comes to business dealings, however, and that Americans are being shortchanged in the process. To the extent that these feelings persist, Japanese lobbying will continue to be an area of ethical concern during the years ahead.

Ethical Problems and Concerns in Europe

Ethical behavior in European countries is an important area of interest in international management, because in some respects, these countries differ sharply from Japan and the United States. Although ethical issues are a concern throughout the world and all European countries, France and Germany seem to get most of the attention in the literature.

One study surveyed 124 U.S., 72 French, and 70 German managers.[18] Each was asked to respond to a series of five vignettes that examined ethical situations related to coercion and control, conflict of interest, the physical environment, paternalism, and personal integrity. In most cases, the U.S. managers' responses were quite different from those of their European counterparts. The following is an example of one of the vignettes:

> Rollfast Bicycle Company has been barred from entering the market in a large Asian country by collusive efforts of the local bicycle manufacturers. Rollfast could expect to net 5 million dollars per year from sales if it could penetrate the market. Last week a businessman from the country contacted the management of Rollfast and stated that he could smooth the way for the company to sell in his country for a price of $500,000.[19]

The executives from the three countries were asked how they would respond to the request for payment. The Americans were opposed to paying the money; 39 percent of them said that a bribe was unethical or illegal under the Foreign Corrupt Practices Act. Only 12 percent of the French managers felt that way, and none of the Germans agreed. However, 55 percent of the French and 29 percent of the Germans said that paying the money was not unethical but merely the price to be paid for doing business.

In each of the other four vignettes, the managers were given situations that presented them with a variety of ethical dilemmas such as conflicts of interest or questionable behaviors. Summing up the responses of managers to all five scenarios, the researchers concluded:

> If one were to generalize, the U.S. managers were noticeably more concerned with ethical and legal questions. Their French and German counterparts appeared to worry more about maintaining a successful business posture. To be sure, there was some overlapping of responses; however, the differences remained.[20]

This cross-national research on ethical behavior shows that MNCs must be aware that the ethical practices of their home country may be quite different from those of countries where they do business. A number of reasons account for these differences, including culture, personal values, incentives, and the obvious legal restrictions.

The Status of Women Managers in Europe

Because most European countries have experienced only limited population growth in recent years, integration of women into the workforce has become a critical goal. Similar to the United States and Japan, however, European women have encountered equal opportunity problems and a "glass ceiling" in the managerial ranks. The following discussion examines the current status of women managers in three of the largest European nations: France, Germany, and Great Britain.

France   The proportion of French women in the labor force from 1900 until 1970 remained at about 35 percent. Since then, however, more than 2.5 million women have entered the workforce, compared with less than 300,000 men. This trend would seem to indicate that women now should be gaining a greater foothold in the managerial ranks—and to a degree, this is true. Over the last 40 years, the number of women managers has increased almost twice as fast as the number of managerial positions has increased. The greatest gains have been in product promotion and sales, import-export, sales administration, real estate, urban planning and architecture, socioeconomic studies, and chemistry.

Although French women are making strides in the management ranks, they still are underrepresented in corporate management. Women still are far behind men in terms of corporate management and the traditional functions of manufacturing and sales. A number of reasons are given for this underrepresentation. One is that promotion into top management depends on more than diplomas, abilities, and ambitions. As in the United States and Japan, French women face many obstacles when trying to break the glass ceiling. As one analysis of women managers in France notes:

> Being a manager includes having to work long hours, travel, make difficult decisions, motivate people, and achieve high objectives—most often with limited resources and strong business competitors. For women managers, it also often means fighting within their own company to establish a reputation as a leader—since women are rarely spontaneously seen as leaders, avoiding or responding appropriately to sexist criticisms, motivating employees to accept and execute their decisions, and sometimes hiding their family problems. Women frequently have more difficulty than men getting access to information necessary to make wise career decisions. Although it is important for women to understand the organization's career criteria, few companies in France provide such information through either equal opportunity managers or assertiveness courses.[21]

From a legal standpoint, French law guarantees equal treatment and equal professional opportunities. Enforcement of these guarantees is fairly weak, however, and organizations that could be valuable to women generally are uninvolved. For example, unions have generally resisted taking on women's issues, and there are no organizations in France comparable to the National Organization of Women in the United States that could promote equal opportunity issues. Even French associations of women managers are limited in their efforts and, for the most part, focus primarily on social networking. So, while some French companies have promoted women into higher-level positions and have affirmative action programs in place, these firms unfortunately still are the exception rather than the rule. As one analyst recently put it, "Companies' needs for the best possible managers will favor highly qualified women; but to succeed, these women will most likely have to accept even more difficult working conditions."[22]

Germany   Before unification, about half of working-age women in West Germany and almost all of those in East Germany were in the workforce. In both West and East, however, women held few top management positions. Studies of large West German firms found that less than 10 percent of top managers and only a slightly higher percent of managers at the next level were women, and only a handful were members of managing boards of public companies. In East Germany, one-third of all management positions were held by women, but these primarily were low-level jobs. With the unification of Germany, the status of women in management does not look any more promising. One reason is that professional qualifications appear to relate inversely to hierarchical position. Antal and Krebsbach-Gnath explained this seeming paradox as follows:

> The higher the position, the less significance the organization attaches to . . . "objective" criteria. The factors that receive more weight in promotion decisions for senior management positions are both less objective and more often based on traditional male career patterns. In effect, therefore, they discriminate against women. Among the factors listed in one study for promotion into upper-level management were professional competence, effectiveness, professional experience, length of experience, time with the company, commitment to the job, and professional and regional mobility. To the extent that "objective" factors and qualifications, such as education and training that women can consciously acquire, play a lesser role in decision making, other sociopsychological and systemic factors assume increasing importance and create less easily surmountable barriers to career development for women.[23]

Unlike some other countries, Germany has introduced laws that mandate equal opportunity and the creation of equal opportunity positions throughout the public sector.

Today, all German states must ensure that their legislation provides for equal treatment of men and women in the workplace. On the other hand, use of quotas is unacceptable, and this makes the legislation difficult to enforce. Additionally, those individuals who are designated as equal opportunity officers typically have difficulty carrying out their tasks, because they often lack the needed authority to enforce their decisions.

In the private sector, there has been some progress toward increasing the number of women in upper-level management positions through the introduction of voluntary equal opportunity programs. Some German firms also have nominated individuals or groups and assigned them the responsibility of ensuring equal opportunity for all personnel. Another, and more recent, development is the inclusion of company-level, work-family agreements between employers and workers' representatives regarding parental leave and return plans. These plans allow employees to take a longer parental leave than is granted by law, and to attract these employees back, these plans guarantee an equivalent job on returning from the extended leave.

Some analysts believe that Germany's growing need for competent managers likely will increase the number of women in management and the opportunity for them to achieve higher-level positions. On the other side, critics argue this is wishful thinking and that what is needed is stronger legislation. Still others contend that until there is a fundamental change in the way that male managers view the role and status of women, nothing significant will happen. These arguments all point to one conclusion: Opportunities for women managers in Germany remain limited and do not seem likely to improve significantly in the near future.

Great Britain   By the turn of the century, approximately 13 million women were in the British workforce, which was about 45 percent of the country's total workforce. The number of women in management and related occupations has been steadily increasing over the last two decades. Once again, however, as in other countries, British women are not well represented at the highest levels of organizations.

Most women managers in Britain are employed in retail distribution, hotel and catering, banking, finance, medical and other health services, and food, drink, and tobacco. Almost all of these managers are at the lowest levels, and they have a long way to go if they hope to reach the top. Legislation designed to prevent discrimination in the workplace is proving to be of limited value; however, a number of steps are being taken to help British women attain equal opportunity in employment.

In recent years, British women have been setting up their own associations, such as the Women's Engineering Society, to develop sources for networking and to increase their political lobbying power. There also is a national association, known as The 300 Group, that campaigns for women seeking election to Parliament. In addition, women have become very active in joining management and professional associations, such as the Hotel, Catering and Institutional Management Association; the Institute of Personnel Management; and the Institute of Health Service Management. Women now constitute 50 percent or more of the membership in these professional associations.

At the same time, a growing number of British companies are proactively trying to recruit and promote women into the management ranks. They are introducing career development programs specifically for women and are prepared to take whatever steps are necessary to ensure that outstanding women remain with the company. For example, the National Westminster Bank allows women managers to leave for up to 5 years to raise their children and then return to a management position at their previous level. Firms also are designing strategies to ensure that equal opportunities are, in fact, being implemented. Chief executives and directors of leading companies recently have formed a group known as Opportunity 2000. One of the group's goals is to provide a wide range of assistance to women who are interested in business careers; in particular, the focus is on helping firms to demonstrate a commitment to these goals, change their old ways of doing business, communicate their desires to potential women managers, and make the necessary financial and time commitments that are needed to ensure success.

At the same time discrimination lawsuits are becoming more common place in the UK. In 1994 approximately 4,500 sex and race discrimination lawsuits were filed with Employment Tribunals in England and Wales. In 2000 this number was in excess of 8,000, an increase of over 75 percent.[24] In one lawsuit, a woman working as an investment banker at Deutsche Bank's London office and earning over $400,000 annually resigned and sued the company for sex discrimination. She won her case before a tribunal and received an out-of-court settlement of over $1.4 million. Most settlements involve much smaller sums and, unlike the United States, in the UK there are limits for compensation from legal actions. Nevertheless, with the large increase in the number of lawsuits many British companies are realizing that they need to take action to ensure that they are not sued. Among large firms one of the most popular approaches is that taken by the British branch of UBS A.G. of Switzerland. The company has created a new position, global head of diversity, and it is this person's job to ensure that all employees are treated fairly. Meanwhile, the legal system in the UK continues to change, making it easier to sue for bias, raising the amounts that can be awarded, shifting the burden of proof from claimants to defendants, and allowing third parties such as the British Equal Opportunity Commission to sue on behalf of individuals. Given the changing legal and social environment, a growing number of firms are starting to adopt a much more proactive stance regarding discrimination.

Ethical Problems and Concerns in China

Along with the tremendous opportunities offered in China, MNCs doing business there face a variety of ethical problems. After the violent, June 1989 crackdown on the student protestors in Beijing's Tiananmen Square, many MNCs questioned whether any business should be conducted in China until more freedom and human rights were restored.

Despite continuing ethical issues such as piracy of intellectual property and human rights violations such as the use of prisoner and child labor, most MNCs still feel there are too many opportunities in China to be ignored. One of these is low-cost labor. Workers in China are not well paid, and to meet the demand for output, they often are forced to work 12 hours a day, 7 days a week. In some cases, children are used for this work and are paid very little, usually only one-half of the already very low adult's wages. The government also has been using prison labor to produce goods for the export market. In addition, with China now totally open to the outside world, there has been a rush to get rich under the market reforms and this has been accompanied by a dramatic increase in crime and illegal business activities.

These developments have led to friction between the U.S. Congress and China. A closer look at the existing piracy, counterfeit, and industrial spying problems and the current status of women in the workplace illustrate some of the major ethical challenges facing MNCs in China.

Piracy, Counterfeiting, and Industrial Spying Problems
In recent years the U.S. government has been taking a hard line on Chinese piracy of intellectual property (e.g., patents, copyrights, and trademarks) and demanding that China crack down on those who are copying illegally. The music business is a good example. The International Federation of Phonographic Industries estimates that music piracy in China cost the industry $620 million in a recent year.[25] Figure 4–1 provides an opaque index which, among other things, measures the effect of unclear legal systems and regulations. China's system is the most opaque, which means that it lacks transparency and does the least to enforce rules against piracy and other unethical practices than in any other country in the world. Commenting on this, one analyst recently noted:

> China's legal system is riddled with loopholes. In much of the world, counterfeiting refers to the unauthorized production and sale of exact copies of genuine goods, down to the trademarks, and there is a growing trend to enact comprehensive anticounterfeiting criminal laws. But in China there isn't even a clear definition of counterfeiting. An old trademark law utilizes vague terms like "large" and "relatively large" to determine whether cases rise to a criminal level. In 1993, China issued more specific regulations (*i.e.,* suggesting the prosecution of

thrice-captured offenders), but a criminal-code amendment in 1997 leaves enforcement officials scratching their heads as to whether the . . . regs still apply. In most countries possession and intent to sell are enough for a counterfeiter to face criminal liability. But in China evidence of prior sales is required—a high hurdle considering that few counterfeiters keep records. The bottom line is that few offenders ever go to prison. And those who knowingly assist counterfeiters by providing transportation, storage, and raw materials are largely ignored.[26]

Besides music, in film, software, and most popular consumer products of all kinds pirating is rampant. For example, within a week of the U.S. release of the film *Dr. Seuss: How the Grinch Stole Christmas,* videodisc copies were selling on China streets for about $1.20 each,[27] and Hollywood hits such as *Gladiator* and *Shanghai Noon* could be purchased on DVD for $2 soon after they were first shown in American theatres.[28] In an effort to deal with this problem, the U.S. government has been putting pressure on the Chinese government to close down factories that produce pirated films, and there has been some progress to date.

In addition to taking direct action against pirating, the Chinese government has been offering rewards to those who provide information leading to the closing of an illegal operation.[29] However, the problem is not easily resolved.[30] For example, Macau near Hong Kong is a nucleus of Asia's fake CD-ROM manufacturing, but law enforcement personnel give it wide latitude because of the personal danger they face in trying to enforce piracy laws there.[31] The accompanying sidebar, "Get Tough . . . or Else," gives some more specific examples of the huge pirating problem in China.

Figure 4–1

The Opaque Index (Lack of Transparency, Unclear Legal Systems)

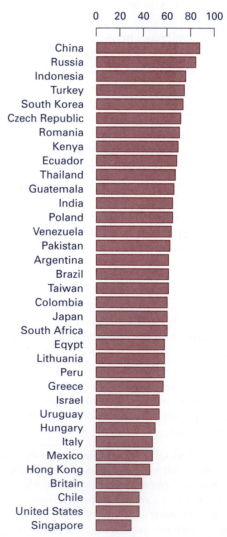

Source: Reported in the *Economist,* March 3, 2001, p. 100.

In addition to piracy and counterfeiting problems, Chinese-backed industry spying on outside MNCs has increased dramatically. A survey of 1,300 major U.S. MNCs now see China as its major foreign economic-espionage threat. Some examples include:

- Amgen discovered that a Chinese spy had infiltrated its organization and was trying to steal a vial of cell cultures for Epogen, now a $1.2 billion-a-year anemia drug.

- A Chinese spy in Hong Kong was recently caught using sophisticated telecommunications software to secretly listen in on sensitive phone conversations between American executives.

- A Chinese engineer at a Boulder, Colorado, software company allegedly stole proprietary source code and peddled it to a Chinese company. As a result, the U.S. company went out of business.[32]

A related problem is joint ventures in which Chinese partners break the agreement and walk off with patents and/or capital or simply start an operation that is in direct competition with the venture. Kimberly-Clark is a good example.

> Its plant in Handan, which is 97% owned by [Kimberly-Clark] produces around $10 million annually of feminine-care pads. Located in the northeastern province of Hebei, it is one of 12 company factories in China. The operation seemed to be running smoothly until last spring, when plant officials noticed a nearby factory was making a similar product. Worse, the Americans discovered that the head of the rival operation was Li Hongzhi, who was picked by Kimberly-Clark's Chinese partner, Xingha Factory Co., to be the manager of the joint venture. Li was "stealing" and "diverting materials" such as spare parts and pulp from the venture to the new factory, alleged . . . Kimberly-Clark's vice-president for corporate communications.[33]

Kimberly-Clark went to the American Embassy to complain and eventually the situation was satisfactorily resolved. The same was not true for Chicago-based Borg-Warner Automotive, Inc. Soon after this company signed a joint venture agreement, the firm realized that its Chinese partner had no intention of making the deal work. In fact, the partner intended to set up a rival operation. So Borg-Warner filed a request with the requisite Chinese agency to end the joint venture, pointing out that its partner had not fulfilled its obligation to provide utilities such as water and electricity and so the company was unable to accept the factory site that had been given to it. The Chinese regulatory agency rejected Borg-Warner's request, and in the interim the Chinese partner filed a lawsuit against the firm for rejecting the plant site. In the judgment that ensued, a Chinese court awarded all of the joint venture assets of $2.2 million, 60 percent of which came from Borg-Warner, to the Chinese partner. By the time the American MNC found out about the judgment, it was too late to appeal the decision at the local level.

The examples discussed are only representative of the many that are coming out of China and the rest of the world. And they all reinforce the same point: Doing international business can be very risky and even joint ventures with in-country partners do not ensure that the MNC will be protected from the adverse effects of unethical and illegal actions.[34]

The Status of Women Managers in China   As in other countries, women managers in China confront a "glass ceiling" when trying to reach top management ranks. There are a number of reasons for this, including cultural stereotypes, restricted opportunities, and of course, discrimination.

Cultural stereotypes are deep-rooted and very prevalent in China, and they go a long way toward hindering women's preparation for managerial roles as well as their more direct opportunities for promotion. Women have been socialized to be shy and unassertive. As a result, they often are viewed as being unprepared to assume leadership positions. A common stereotype is that Chinese women are disorganized, narrow-minded, and hard to work with compared to men. Such widespread thinking greatly inhibits the advancement of women in management.

Coupled with this are restricted opportunities. For example, Chinese women are not well represented in the Communist party, which is one of the fastest ways to gain upward mobility. Additionally, Chinese women are less likely to be chosen for education

International Management in Action

Get Tough . . . or Else   www.chinatoday.com

A growing number of multinationals are very concerned about doing business in China. For example, within hours of the time their goods are on the street, many find that counterfeiters are already working on developing their own version of the product—and in many cases, these clones look just like the original. Today, there are fake cans of Coca-Cola, fake McDonald's hamburger restaurants, fake versions of the Jeeps that Chrysler manufactures with a joint-venture partner in Beijing, and fake Gillette razor blades.

Personal-care product companies such as Henkl of Germany and Procter & Gamble of the U.S. estimate that about a quarter of the goods bearing their names in China are fake. Nike says that its potential annual losses in China resulting from counterfeit operations are about the size of its legitimate business in the United States. And pharmaceutical firms find that their drugs are often copied and distributed under their own name. Pfizer began selling Viagra in China in July 2000. By the end of the year, three local producers had introduced ripped-off versions of the pill and within the next 90 days another 30 companies had done so.

Even more disconcerting is that when counterfeiters are caught, the Chinese government often does very little about it. The Gillette Razor Blade Company is a good example of this. The Huaxing Razor Blade Factory was producing Gillette look-alike blades and packaging them in the same blue package as that used by Gillette. After Chinese authorities raided the factory, they fined the company $3,500 and told management that it was illegal to produce counterfeit blades and they were to stop. Five months later, when it became evident that the company was still manufacturing the blades, there was a second raid, followed by a fine of $3,300. At that time, the manager was asked why he not only kept producing

the blades but also used the same packaging as before. He remarked that he did not want to throw away packaging that had already been printed. "We didn't want to waste it," he said.

Will such a "slap on the wrist" type of enforcement stop the counterfeiting? This is unlikely, because the fines are small compared with the revenues being generated. The Chinese government also does not seem to be very interested in taking sterner measures. In fact, in some cases when MNCs have complained that counterfeiters have gone back to their old ways, inspectors have refused to take any additional action, arguing that "we already addressed that issue and we are now moving on to other matters." Such an attitude worries MNCs, because they feel there is no protection for their intellectual properties. A lawyer who has represented several U.S. companies in trademark disputes in China put it this way:

> In most countries, if you have 10 pirates, you can go after one, expect seven to stop, and then figure out how to get the remaining two. But in China, when you go after one the other nine see exactly what you're doing. Not only do they keep pirating, but you invite 10 more to join in.

Unless the government of China takes more stringent steps to do something about pirating and counterfeiting, MNCs likely will take action of their own. One of the most commonly mentioned steps is to demand that Chinese exports to the United States be limited and that levies be assessed on these goods to offset the loss of revenues being sustained by the U.S. MNCs. In the final analysis, it appears that China will have to get tough on pirates and counterfeiters . . . or else.

and training programs, again restricting their opportunity to enter the upper-managerial ranks. In particular, women typically are required to have higher test scores on university entrance exams to ensure their admission. They also face segregation on the job and, as a result, often end up with the less meaningful tasks. For example, men typically operate the high-tech equipment and processes, while women do the routine work.

Discrimination in the workplace is both blatant and subtle. For example, women often are given additional workplace favors, such as extra rest periods, but in turn, these serve as the basis for bypassing them for promotions, which go instead to men who work longer hours. Additionally, women are required to retire at the age of 60, while men can work until 65. This inhibits their career advancement and helps to prevent them from reaching senior management positions. Drawing together many of these perceptions and stereotypes, Korabik has summed up the series of interviews that she conducted with women managers in the People's Republic of China by noting:

> Stereotypes in China are particularly insidious because no research exists to show them to be inaccurate. Many Chinese therefore believe them to represent the "true" nature of women and men. Government campaigns to eradicate such stereotypes have been largely ineffective, and

their consequences are often not redressed because they are not viewed as discriminatory. Thus, despite many laws intended to insure equality in the workplace, Chinese women managers are still at a disadvantage compared to men.[35]

■ Regulating Foreign Investment

The regulation of foreign investment is another area of international business that has at least indirect implications for ethics and social responsibility. Many countries have a growing concern regarding the ethics of an MNC's gaining an economic foothold and then taking the resources and profits back home. This concern focuses on reciprocity between the home country of MNCs and the host country. The United States again provides a good example. The latest available data (presented in Chapter 1) reveal that foreigners have invested triple-digit billions in the United States, and U.S. investments abroad also are in triple-digit billions. Moreover, foreign investors have put more money into this country than U.S. investors have put overseas.[36]

The rapid increase of foreign investment in the United States has raised ethical concerns among many Americans, who believe that such foreign investment needs to be regulated more closely. In addition, some are concerned that countries like Japan seem much more interested in selling to the United States than in buying from U.S. firms. These concerns have ethical and social responsibility implications, and they have led to regulation of acquisitions and reciprocal trade agreements in the United States. Other countries are following the U.S. lead by also looking more closely at these two areas and how they affect their own country.

Regulation of Acquisitions

In the United States, under preliminary regulations published by the Treasury Department, most foreign investors now must obtain formal approval before acquiring a U.S. company. The primary exceptions are industries such as toys and games, food products, hotels and restaurants, and legal services. Acquisition requests are reviewed by the interagency Committee on Foreign Investment, which is made up of eight agencies and headed by the Treasury Department. The stated objective of the regulation is to prevent foreign firms from gaining control of U.S. businesses that are important to U.S. security.

Other countries are following the U.S. lead and implementing similar regulatory practices. For example, many less developed nations now refuse to allow MNCs to establish new operations or purchase ongoing businesses unless they first obtain governmental clearance. This ensures that the government remains in control of the economy and is not overly reliant on foreign companies. In practice, however, many of these countries need MNC operations and are willing to accede to most requests for setting up, acquiring, or expanding local operations.

The countries in the European Union also are beginning to limit the business dealings of foreign multinationals. In particular, in the EU new regulations are making it more difficult for MNCs not located in Europe to do business there. The EU, except for England, is particularly sensitive to the rise of Japanese industrialism and the likelihood that Japanese auto manufacturers will dominate the world market. The EU also is trying to support local companies by mandating that certain parts and equipment, such as computer chips, that are to be sold in Europe also be built there by firms from the EU.

These regulatory developments show that countries around the globe are concerned about the increasingly large amount of foreign investment being made in their economies. This is particularly true in the case of those nations that are viewed as **nonreciprocal trade partners,** or those which sell goods to others but do not buy from them.

Nonreciprocal trade partners
Nations that sell (export) goods to other countries but do not buy (import) from them.

The Implications of Reciprocity

Is there an ethical and social responsibility to engage in reciprocal trade? This question is at the forefront of current trade talks between many countries, but especially between the United States and Japan. How much of an obligation does Japan have to import U.S. goods and services in light of its tremendous volume of exports to the United States? Every year, the Japanese have massive trade surpluses with the United States. The 1990s provided an excellent example. Despite some success in reducing barriers in areas such as tobacco and telecommunications and the weakening of the dollar against the yen for most of the decade, the annual trade deficit remained in the $50 to $60 billion range.

In recent years, the executive branch has undertaken a review of U.S.–Japanese trade relations. One primary source of information for the analysis was a voluminous report prepared by a special task force consisting of members from both government and business. The group recommended a 1-year trial period during which trade negotiations would be conducted with Japan. If no substantive results were achieved, the group suggested using Super 301, which is a provision of the Omnibus Trade and Competitiveness Act of 1988 that allows for sanctions against "unfair traders."

In the past few years, the United States has targeted Japan, China, and Brazil, among others, for retaliatory action. Whether or not this approach will work, the important thing to remember is that the United States feels it is unethical and irresponsible for countries such as Japan, China, and Brazil to behave in trade relations as they do.[37] Most European countries disagree with the United States and believe there are more effective ways of negotiating trade problems than the use of sanctions. However, as long as the U.S. administration believes that the United States is not being treated ethically in the international trade arena, retaliation will continue to be a means to obtain reciprocity in international trade.

■ Response to Social Obligations

So far, the discussion has focused on differences in ethical standards between countries and why nations such as the United States are concerned about trade reciprocity. However, many countries are responsive to their international social obligations. For example, the United States is pushing for higher ethical codes, and others, such as Italy and China, which have a tradition of questionable ethics, are putting forth considerable effort to clean things up.

Foreign Corrupt Practices Act Revisited

As noted in the previous chapter, the Foreign Corrupt Practices Act (FCPA) makes it illegal for U.S. companies and their managers to attempt to influence foreign officials through personal payments or political contributions. Prior to passage of the FCPA, some American multinationals had engaged in this practice, but realizing that their stockholders were unlikely to approve of these tactics the firms typically disguised the payments in the form of entertainment expenses, consulting fees, etc. The FCPA not only prohibits these activities but the U.S. Internal Revenue Service continually audits the books of MNCs. Those firms that take deductions for such illegal activities are subject to high financial penalties, and individuals who are involved can even end up going to prison.

Strict enforcement of the FCPA has been applauded by many people. At the same time some critics wonder if such a strong social responsibility stance has not hurt the competitive ability of American MNCs. On the positive side, many U.S. multinationals have now increased the amount of business in countries where they used to pay bribes. Additionally, many institutional investors in the United States have made it clear that they will not buy stock in companies that engage in unethical practices; and if they hold stock in these firms, they will sell their holdings. Given that these institutions have hundreds of billions of dollars invested, senior-level management must be responsive to their needs.

Looking at the effect of the FCPA on U.S. multinationals, it appears that the law has had far more of a positive effect than a negative one. In fact, some observers wonder if companies did not overstate the importance of such covert activities. And given the growth of American MNCs in recent years, it seems fair to conclude that bribes are not a basic part of business in many countries as seen by the fact that when they stopped this activity, these multinationals were still able to sell in that particular market.

On the other hand, this does not mean that bribery and corruption is a thing of the past. Figure 4–2 gives the latest corruption index of countries around the world. Notice that the U.S. ranks 16th by this independent analysis. However, a report issued by the U.S. Commerce Department contends that since 1994, foreign companies have used bribes to edge out U.S. MNCs on a large number of international business deals. The report describes a case of bribery involving the contract for a power-generating plant in Central Europe as follows:

> A European company was awarded the multimillion-dollar contract even though the Central European government's own review board had recommended the contract be awarded to a U.S. firm. The report says there was clear evidence that a power-company official had been given a cash bribe by the European company that won the contract. The company used the same practice to win other contracts in Eastern and Central Europe, according to the report.[38]

These experiences reveal that bribery continues to be a problem for U.S. MNCs. At the same time, to comply with the provisions of the FCPA, U.S. firms must be careful not to follow suit and resort to bribery themselves. In particular, changes in the law make FCPA violators subject to Federal Sentencing Guidelines. As a result, when two Lockheed Corporation executives were found guilty of paying a $1 million bribe to a member of the Egyptian parliament in order to secure the sale of aircraft to the Egyptian military, one of the executives was sentenced to probation and fined $20,000 and the other, who initially fled prosecution, was fined $125,000 and sentenced to 18 months in prison.[39]

Another development that promises to give teeth to "anti-bribing" is the recent formal agreement by a host of industrialized nations that have agreed to outlaw the practice of bribing foreign government officials. The treaty, signed in Paris by 29 nations that belong to the Organization for Economic Cooperation and Development, marked a victory for the United States, which outlawed foreign bribery two decades previously, but had not

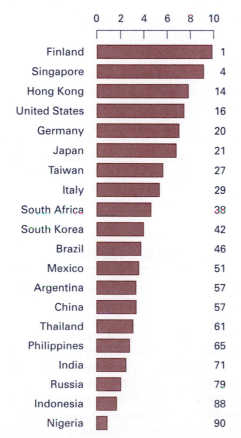

Figure 4–2

Corruption Index: Ranking of Least Corrupt to Most

Country	Index
Finland	1
Singapore	4
Hong Kong	14
United States	16
Germany	20
Japan	21
Taiwan	27
Italy	29
South Africa	38
South Korea	42
Brazil	46
Mexico	51
Argentina	57
China	57
Thailand	61
Philippines	65
India	71
Russia	79
Indonesia	88
Nigeria	90

Source: Adapted from Transparency International and *The Economist,* June 30th, 2001, p. 98.

been able to persuade other countries to follow its lead. As a result, American firms had long complained that they lost billions of dollars in contracts each year to rivals that bribed their way to success.[40]

This treaty does not outlaw most payments to political party leaders. In fact, the treaty provisions are much narrower than U.S. negotiators wanted, and there will be undoubtedly ongoing pressure from the American government to expand the scope and coverage of the agreement. For the moment, however, it is a step in the direction of a more ethical level playing field in global business. Additionally, in summing up the impact and value of the treaty, one observer noted that:

> For their part, business executives say the treaty . . . reflects growing support for anti-bribery initiatives among corporations in Europe and Japan that have openly opposed the idea. Some of Europe's leading industrial corporations, including a few that have been embroiled in recent allegations of bribery, have spoken out in favor of tougher measures and on the increasingly corrosive effect of corruption.[41]

International Assistance

Besides fighting unethical practices, another way to meet social responsibilities is to provide assistance to underdeveloped countries. For many years, governments did this by providing foreign aid in the form of food, machinery, and equipment to help feed the people of less-developed countries and to stimulate their economies. In addition, many less-developed countries tried to improve their own conditions by borrowing large sums of money for economic development. The problem was that these monies were often not wisely spent, and the country ended up with billions of dollars of debt and no realistic hope of ever repaying the funds. In recent years the United States, Japan, and other developed countries have begun forgiving these debts so that a struggling country can move on from here.

MNCs are not in a position to give foreign aid to countries. However, a growing number of them are taking direct steps to help the local economies of countries where they do business. This philanthropic role is not only a pragmatic approach to protecting their investments and improving their corporate image, but is also a way of helping meet their social responsibilities. Japanese firms doing business and having factories in the United States, for example, have financially contributed in a wide variety of ways including scholarships for minority students, funds to help expand local libraries, and contributions to the United Way. By integrating themselves into the local community and becoming good local citizens, these firms have also showed themselves to be good corporate citizens. The same is true for U.S. multinationals that have done similar things from China to Brazil and from Austria to Australia. European and other worldwide MNCs can boast similar records. Quite clearly, multinational corporate assistance directed at host countries is a two-way street. Each side stands to benefit economically through MNCs meeting their social responsibilities, and the coming years should see even more efforts in this direction.

World of *Business Week*—Revisited

The *Business Week* article that opened this chapter discussed some of the actions being taken by the European Commission's antitrust group. For years the United States has outlawed cartels because they are detrimental to fair competition, but in Europe price-fixing cartels have existed for generations. Now the EU is cracking down and moving ever closer to the American position of encouraging free trade. Activities that used to go unnoticed or unpunished are now becoming focal points for both scrutiny and legal action. Of course, it won't be easy to eliminate all of these activities. However, as the EU continues to function more and more like one giant common market, price-fixing and other forms of collusion will have to end. The old message of "this is how we've always done business" will have to give way to new standards of ethical conduct. Based on this article and what you have read in the chapter, answer the following questions: (1) Why would American MNCs applaud these antitrust actions? (2) Are these actions necessary, or would price-fixing eventually fade away because of increased competition in the EU marketplace? (3) In Europe, who stands to benefit most from this new development? Who stands to benefit least?

Summary of Key Points

1. Ethics is the study of morality and standards of conduct. It is important in the study of international management because ethical behavior often varies from one country to another. For example, in recent years in Japan, political and business scandals and apparent cases of avoiding minority hiring have drawn attention to the need for another look at ethical and socially responsible behavior. Japan's lobbying efforts in Washington also have been questioned from an ethical standpoint.

2. Research in France and Germany reveals that European and U.S. MNCs seem to have different standards of ethics that result in different types of decisions and business practices. For example, U.S. MNCs do not believe in bribing businesspeople or politicians to gain favors, while some studies find that more respondents in samples of both German and French managers were not as concerned with bribes as being unethical and instead felt payoffs were merely a cost of doing business. In the area of equal opportunity for women, the Europeans have goals for fully integrating women into the workforce and even EU legislation to ensure equal pay and equal treatment in employment. However, similar to U.S. women, European women are still being deprived of equal opportunities and are underrepresented in the managerial ranks of European firms, although some progress is being made.

3. Ethics also is a problem in countries such as China. Since the violent crackdown at Tiananmen Square and continued ethical and human rights violations, many MNCs have questioned whether they should do business with the Chinese. Those that found the low labor cost attractive too often overlooked the fact that the Chinese factory employees work long hours for very low pay and that some of these workers are underaged or prisoners. These types of exploitive practices have ethical implications. So, too, does the status of women managers. As in many other countries, women managers in China face a "glass ceiling" blocking their advancement into top management. Three of the main reasons are cultural stereotypes, restricted opportunities, and discrimination.

4. A more indirect area of ethics and social responsibility deals with the regulation of foreign investment. In the United States, for example, the interagency Committee on Foreign Investment, which involves eight agencies headed by the Treasury Department, was set up to curb the indiscriminant buying of U.S. firms by foreign investors. The committee regulates the acquisition of U.S. companies by foreign multinationals. A similar, indirect area of ethics and social responsibility is reciprocal trade and the desire of countries such as the United States to get trading partners such as Japan to open their markets to U.S. goods.

5. During the years ahead, multinationals likely will become more concerned about being socially responsive, and legislation such as the U.S. Foreign Corrupt Practices Act is forcing the issue. Other countries also are passing laws to regulate the ethical practices of their MNCs. MNCs are being more proactive (often because they realize it makes good business sense) in providing international assistance in the form of philanthropy and direct community involvement as well.

Key Terms

ethics, *75*

nonreciprocal trade partners, *85*

Review and Discussion Questions

1. What lessons can U.S. multinationals learn from the political and bribery scandals in Japan that can be of value to them in doing business in this country? Discuss two.

2. In recent years, some prominent spokespeople have argued that those who work for the U.S. government in trade negotiations should be prohibited for a period of 5 years from accepting jobs as lobbyists for foreign firms. Is this a good idea? Why?

3. How do ethical practices differ among the United States and European countries such as France and Germany? What implications does your answer have for U.S. multinationals operating in Europe?

4. Why are many MNCs reluctant to produce or sell their goods in China? What role can the Chinese government play in helping to resolve this problem?

5. In what way is trade reciprocity an ethics or social responsibility issue? How important is this issue likely to become during the current decade?

6. Why are MNCs getting involved in philanthropy and local communities? Are they displaying a sense of social responsibility, or is this merely a matter of good business? Defend your answer.

Internet Exercise: Mitsubishi's Philanthropy

In this chapter some of the social responsibility problems that Mitsubishi has had in recent years were discussed. However, on the other side of the coin, the huge Japanese MNC has been trying very hard to improve its image and to address its social responsibility shortcomings. Visit the company's web site at **www.mitsubishi.com** and learn some of the latest social-type of activities in which the firm has been engaged. In particular, look closely at the "philanthropy" and "environment" sections of the web site. Then answer these questions: (1) What are some of the most recent things that Mitsubishi is doing in terms of philanthropy? Do you think these actions represent sincere concern for the community or do you think that Mitsubishi is simply trying to create a positive image for itself to offset past bad coverage by the press? (2) What steps is the MNC taking in its environmental efforts and of what value are these actions? (3) Based on your responses to these questions, what conclusions can you draw regarding the current social responsibility stance of Mitsubishi?

Saudi Arabia

Saudi Arabia is a large Middle Eastern country covering 865,000 square miles. Part of its east coast rests on the Persian Gulf, and much of the west coast rests along the Red Sea. One of the countries on its borders is Iraq. After Iraq's military takeover of Kuwait in August 1990, Iraq next threatened to invade Saudi Arabia. This, of course, did not happen, but only time will tell what will happen next in this explosive part of the world.

There are approximately 22 million people in Saudi Arabia, and the per-capita income is around $10,000. This apparent prosperity is misleading, because most Saudis are poor farmers and herders who tend their camels, goats, and sheep. In recent years, however, more and more have moved to the cities and have jobs connected to the oil industry. Nearly all are Arab Muslims. The country has the two holiest cities of Islam: Mecca and Medina. The country depends almost exclusively on the sale of oil (it is the largest exporter of oil in the world) and has no public debt. The government is a monarchy, and the king makes all important decisions but is advised by ministers and other government officials. Royal and ministerial decrees account for most of the promulgated legislation. There are no political parties.

Earlier this week, Robert Auger, the executive vice president of Skyblue, a commercial aircraft manufacturing firm based in Kansas City, had a visit with a Saudi minister. The Saudi official explained to Auger that the government planned to purchase 10 aircraft over the next 2 years. A number of competitive firms were bidding for the job. The minister went on to explain that despite the competitiveness of the situation, several members of the royal family were impressed with Auger's company. The firm's reputation for high-quality performance aircraft and state-of-the-art technology gave it the inside track. A number of people are involved in the decision, however, and in the minister's words, "anything can happen when a committee decision is being made."

The Saudi official went on to explain that some people who would be involved in the decision had recently suffered large losses in some stock market speculations on the London Stock Exchange. "One relative of the King, who will be a key person in the decision regarding the purchase of the aircraft, I have heard, lost over $200,000 last week alone. Some of the competitive firms have decided to put together a pool of money to help ease his burden. Three of them have given me $100,000 each. If you were to do the same, I know that it would put you on a par with them, and I believe it would be in your best interests when the decision is made." Auger was stunned by the suggestion and told the minister that he would check with his people and get back with the minister as soon as possible.

As soon as he got back to his temporary office, Auger sent a coded message to headquarters asking management what he should do. He expects to have an answer within the next 48 hours. In the interim, he has had a call from the minister's office, but Auger's secretary told the caller that Auger had been called away from the office and would not be returning for at least 2 days. The individual said he would place the call again at the beginning of this coming week. In the interim, Auger has talked to a Saudi friend whom he had known back in the United States who was currently an insider in the Saudi government. Over dinner, Auger hinted at what he had been told by the minister. The friend seemed somewhat puzzled about what Auger was saying and indicated that he had heard nothing about any stock market losses by the royal family or pool of money being put together for certain members of the decision-making committee. He asked Auger, "Are you sure you got the story straight, or as you Americans say, is someone pulling your leg?"

Questions

1. What are some current issues facing Saudi Arabia? What is the climate for doing business in Saudi Arabia today?

2. Is it legal for Auger's firm to make a payment of $100,000 to help ensure this contract?

3. Do you think other firms are making these payments, or is Auger's firm being singled out? What conclusion can you draw from your answer?

4. What would you recommend that Skyblue do?

It Sounds a Little Fishy

For the past 2 years, the Chicago-based Brattle Company has been thinking about going international. Two months ago, Brattle entered into negotiations with a large company based in Paris to buy one of its branches in Lyon, France. This would give Brattle a foreign subsidiary. Final arrangements on the deal should be completed within a month, although a few developments have occurred that concern the CEO of Brattle, Angela Scherer.

The most serious concern resulted from a conversation that Scherer had with one of the Lyon firm's largest customers. This customer had been introduced to Scherer during a dinner that the Paris headquarters gave in her honor last month. After the dinner, Scherer struck up a conversation with the customer to assure him that when Brattle took over the Lyon operation, they would provide the same high-quality service as their predecessor. The customer seemed interested in Scherer's comments and then said, "Will I also continue to receive $10,000 monthly for directing my business to you?" Scherer was floored; she did not know what to say. Finally she stammered, "That's something I think you and I will have to talk about further." With that, the two shook hands and the customer left. Scherer has not been back in touch with the customer since the dinner and is unsure of what to do next.

The other matter that has Scherer somewhat upset is a phone call from the head of the Lyon operation last week. This manager explained that his firm was very active in local affairs and donated approximately $5,000 a month to charitable organizations and philanthropic activities. Scherer is impressed with the firm's social involvement but wonders whether Brattle will be expected to assume these obligations. She then told her chief financial officer, "We're buying this subsidiary as an investment and we are willing to continue employing all the local people and paying their benefits. However, I wonder if we're going to have any profits from this operation after we get done with all the side payments for nonoperating matters. We have to cut back a lot of extraneous expenses. For example, I think we have to cut back much of the contribution to the local community, at least for the first couple of years. Also, I can't find any evidence of payment of this said $10,000 a month to that large customer. I wonder if we're being sold a bill of goods, or have they been paying him under the table? In any event, I think we need to look into this situation more closely before we make a final decision on whether to buy this operation."

Questions

1. If Scherer finds out that the French company has been paying its largest customer $10,000 a month, should Brattle back out of the deal? If Brattle goes ahead with the deal, should it continue to make these payments?

2. If Scherer finds out that the customer has been making up the story and no such payments were actually made, what should she do? What if this best customer says he will take his business elsewhere?

3. If Brattle buys the French subsidiary, should Scherer continue to give $5,000 monthly to the local community? Defend your answer.

Integrative Case 1

China

William Fung is a practical man. As group managing director at Hong Kong's Li & Fung Ltd., a giant Hong Kong trading company, his job is to find ways to produce and ship goods to global markets the fastest and cheapest way possible. So he already has a plan for China's now being a member of the World Trade Organization, the global body that enforces free-trade rules. One of the trade barriers that Li expects to fall is U.S. and European import quotas on clothes made in China for children up to 2 years old. Most of the apparel Li & Fung trades in that category is now produced in Egypt, Thailand, Sri Lanka, Honduras, and Guatemala. Fung plans to shut operations in all those countries and move baby-clothes production to southern China. Sure, the labor will cost a bit more in China, "but the productivity!" he says. Moreover, transportation to the key U.S. market is faster: "Shipment time from China to California is 14 days, vs. 30 days from Sri Lanka."

The same kind of cold calculation is under way inside corporations across the world. In their race to slash costs as the global economy slows and profits plunge, companies are looking anew for lowest-cost manufacturing centers. And after they do the math, the winner, very often, is China. Even as the new war against terrorism is realigning the political world, China's arrival as a manufacturing superpower is reshaping world trade. Its advantages are formidable: abundant cheap labor, millions of talented engineers, good infrastructure. And thanks to the terms Beijing formally accepted on Sept. 17 in order to enter the WTO, that enormous market will eventually be thrown wide open to foreign competition. So multinationals in industries from semiconductors to Internet routers to passenger cars are increasingly beating a path to China's door.

There's a dark side to this story, though. For every gleaming factory on the China coast that's producing world-class goods, there's a rusting hulk of a state-owned enterprise that's barely holding on. While many Chinese are now joining the middle class, millions are slipping into a new underclass of displaced peasants, unemployed factory workers, and low-level laborers whose wages barely sustain them. Beijing has managed to keep the lid on these mounting social problems by pumping out billions of dollars' worth of exports, which in turn have sustained government social spending and eased the pain of transition to a market economy.

"Unstoppable Force"

That balancing act is now going to get very hard. In the aftermath of the U.S. military actions in Afghanistan, still more uncertainty has been introduced to already shaky markets. "This war will have a major impact on the world economy," says Michelle Wang, a sales rep at an office-supplies shop in Beijing. "And because China is now a member of the WTO, China is becoming a part of the world. So it's clear we will be affected, too."

The short-term effect could be nasty indeed. Last year, China's exports grew 30%; this year, they will be flat. Slowing growth means China has fewer jobs for its growing legions of unemployed. China's executives and policymakers are aware of these risks. So are the multinationals involved in the mainland. But they are willing to make a big bet—that Beijing, which has managed over 20 years to transform its economy, can maintain enough stability to make their investments pay off. The new Chinese industrial machine "is an unstoppable force," says Michael E. Marks, CEO of contract-manufacturing giant Flextronics Corp. in San Jose, Calif.

And it will affect every region of the world. Flextronics is rapidly expanding its two sprawling manufacturing complexes in China, where it now makes cell phones and computer products. Within seven years, Mexico and the Caribbean will lose thousands of garment-industry jobs to China as the U.S. and Europe lift their last restraints on Chinese-made textile products. In Taiwan and Malaysia, two of the high-tech export hot spots of the 1990s, new investment in semiconductor, disk drive, and computer plants is drying up as companies such as Intel, Motorola, and Dell Computer move production to China. Matsushita, Sony, and Samsung are preparing a wholesale transfer of production facilities to the mainland. At a time when most emerging markets are desperate for outside capital, direct foreign investment in China was up 20.4%, year-on-year, for the first eight months of 2000, to $27.4 billion. That's more than the rest of non-Japan Asia combined.

Beijing is holding a big bash to celebrate its entry into the WTO when it hosts the Asia-Pacific Economic Cooperation meeting in Shanghai from Oct. 15–21. A number of world leaders, including President George W. Bush, are scheduled to attend. Of course, the military action in Central Asia has taken some of the bloom off that occasion.

But even if the summit is low key, China's leaders are justified in raising a glass to their achievements. When China first launched its quest to join what is now the WTO back in 1986, it asked for special favors, citing its poverty and backwardness. Beijing demanded the right to control key industries tightly, limit foreign ownership of factories,

As China Grows...

Data: World Bank, Borgan Stanley Dean Witter & Co.

...Its Share of World Trade Rises

Data: World Bank

...But So Does Unemployment

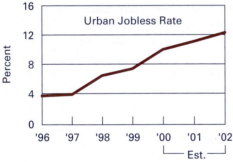

Data: Goldman, Sachs & Co. estimates

and protect access to telecom and financial services. U.S. and European negotiators wouldn't budge. A wise move: As time passed, President Jiang Zemin and Premier Zhu Rongji increasingly saw the market discipline required by WTO rules as an opportunity to force reform on industries and bureaucracies.

Jiang and Zhu hope the restructuring has prepared China's entry into the WTO. At that point, new trading rules start to kick in. Over the next five years, China will eliminate all the quotas and other nontariff mechanisms that have kept out foreign goods. Duties, which have already dropped from an average of 44% in 1992 to 15% today, will fall to 9%. Foreign banks will have the right to open 100%-foreign-owned branches anywhere in China and take deposits from Chinese in local currency. "We will provide finance services to individuals for the first time and contribute to the creation of a consumer class," says Lionel Johnson, director of international government relations for Citigroup.

Foreign telecom operators will be able to freely own parts of Chinese networks. Multinationals will have the right to set up their own distribution networks rather than work through Chinese corporate middlemen, as they must now. Foreign carmakers will make and sell whichever models they wish and set up nationwide dealerships and service networks. In telecom gear, computers, and semiconductors—sectors that Beijing tried to protect for decades—imports will be duty-free by 2005.

Part of the incentive for foreign investors is that after WTO rules kick in, they can operate in China with a greater measure of legal protection. Nobody expects China to develop institutions to enforce WTO rules overnight. Still, the arbitrary power that Communist Party cadres long wielded over foreign investors can be challenged. "The key thing is that the rules will now be on paper," says Andy Xie, chief economist at Morgan Stanley & Co. in Hong Kong. "That will be the biggest shock."

Assuming Beijing lives up to its promises, the opportunities are tremendous. One study of the WTO deal, by U.S. Agriculture Dept. economist Zhi Wang, estimates that China will import some $264 billion worth of capital-intensive manufacturing goods such as vehicles, machinery, and electronics over the next 10 years. Half of those goods will be exported from Western Europe, the U.S., and Japan. Exports from Hong Kong, Taiwan, Singapore, and South Korea will surge as well. Western farmers will win big. China's pledge to sharply limit import barriers on wheat, corn, rice, and other agricultural commodities could boost its food imports by $73 billion over 10 years.

In information technology, China has already passed the U.S. as the world's biggest user of mobile phones. By 2005, the number of cell-phone users in China is expected to more than double, to at least 260 million. In personal computers, China should pass Japan this year, with 10 million PCs sold. Jun Ma, a Deutsche Bank economist based in Hong Kong, predicts that a decade from now, the China effect will raise world economic growth by a quarter percentage point.

In China, Beijing is betting that the new boost from trade—and from more dynamic domestic industries—will prolong the upward march in living standards. Although hundreds of millions of Chinese still live in poverty, economists say that about 100 million have now joined the middle class, which in China means earning at least $2,500 a year.

You can see this affluence when you cross the border from Hong Kong. Mainland Chinese are now buying homes in leafy suburbs that are sprouting on the edges of coastal metropolises such as Guangzhou. To move to and from those cities, Chinese are traveling on new highways and will soon be riding on high-speed trains designed to reduce the country's fabled congestion. Chinese play golf at private clubs and educate their children at private schools. In glitzy Hong Kong-style shopping malls, consumers are buying up the latest in home appliances and IT gadgetry.

Low-Cost Producer

What makes China such a formidable manufacturing center? It has an abundant pool of young, high school-educated workers earning about $1.50 a day, with millions more entering the workforce each year. China's many universities and institutes are turning out well-trained yet relatively low-paid engineers. The cost of industrial land is among the cheapest in the world—about $25 per square meter in Shanghai, half the price of that in Kuala Lumpur and Bangkok and 60 times cheaper than in Yokohama, Japan. Phone service, ports, electrical power, and other infrastructure in China's key coastal cities are among the best in the developing world. China's bureaucracy has become so streamlined that officials sometimes grant the necessary approvals for new factories in days.

In electronics, as recently as the mid-1990s, Chinese factories did little more than screw together radios, telephone handsets, and electronic toys from components shuttled in from Hong Kong, Taiwan, and Japan. Now, foreign manufacturers are relocating semiconductor, high-end circuit-board, and other sophisticated electronics plants to China. Intel Corp. operates a big memory-chip plant in Shanghai, and on Sept. 21 the company announced that it will spend $300 million to double its size, mostly to serve the mobile-phone industry. "China is already the No. 1 wireless market in the world," says Jason Chen, vice-president and general manager of Intel's China operation. "We have to be there to work with that industry."

China's success comes at the expense of workers and companies throughout the developing world that offer cheap labor but not much else. Even in India, which has some of the planet's lowest wages, low-tech industries can't compete with the Chinese in productivity. Shops in Bombay and Calcutta are flooded with Chinese goods. The Indian government is so worried about China that it has refused to allow Chinese software companies to locate in the high-tech center of Bangalore and scotched plans by software powerhouse Infosys Technologies to train 200 Chinese employees in India.

Hardest hit is Southeast Asia. A decade ago, the Association of Southeast Asian Nations took half of the foreign direct investment in non-Japan Asia, compared with just

The Global Impact
China's entry into the WTO will affect trade everywhere

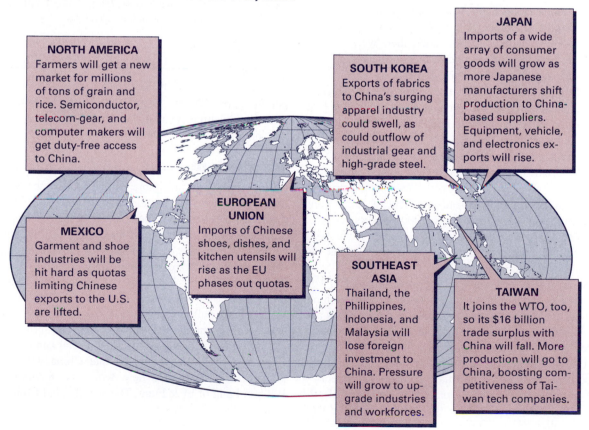

NORTH AMERICA
Farmers will get a new market for millions of tons of grain and rice. Semiconductor, telecom-gear, and computer makers will get duty-free access to China.

MEXICO
Garment and shoe industries will be hit hard as quotas limiting Chinese exports to the U.S. are lifted.

EUROPEAN UNION
Imports of Chinese shoes, dishes, and kitchen utensils will rise as the EU phases out quotas.

SOUTH KOREA
Exports of fabrics to China's surging apparel industry could swell, as could outflow of industrial gear and high-grade steel.

JAPAN
Imports of a wide array of consumer goods will grow as more Japanese manufacturers shift production to China-based suppliers. Equipment, vehicle, and electronics exports will rise.

SOUTHEAST ASIA
Thailand, the Phillippines, Indonesia, and Malaysia will lose foreign investment to China. Pressure will grow to upgrade industries and workforces.

TAIWAN
It joins the WTO, too, so its $16 billion trade surplus with China will fall. More production will go to China, boosting competitiveness of Taiwan tech companies.

20% for China. Now, those numbers are reversed. "Our products out of ASEAN will become less competitive because of the surge of made-in-China goods," says Yukio Shohtoku, managing director in charge of global business for Japanese electronics giant Matsushita Electric Industrial Co.

Taiwan is both a victim and a long-term benefactor of China's rise. True, the mainland is sucking factory jobs out of its island rival by the thousands. But Taiwan has become a member of the WTO at the same time as China, which means Taiwan's own restrictions on trade with the mainland will fall, too. "There are 50,000 Taiwanese-owned factories in mainland China screaming for banking services," says Jeffrey Koo Sr., chairman of Taipei-based Chinatrust Commercial Bank, which hopes to open its first office in China soon.

Struggling Farmers

China's WTO debut is not uniformly good news for the 1.3 billion Chinese. The threat of social instability is real. In the poverty-stricken countryside, the situation is only going to deteriorate after WTO entry triggers imports of cheap foreign grain. "Everybody is saying that the WTO is both a challenge and an opportunity for China," says Xia Ying, a research fellow at the China Academy of Agricultural Science in Beijing. "But for agriculture, the challenge is very real, and the opportunities are largely invisible."

Already, more than 100 million peasants have flocked to the cities in search of work, and that number is likely to increase, adding to China's angry underclass. Frank Lu, director of the Hong Kong-based Information Center for Human Rights & Democracy, says that in 1999, the most recent year for which he has statistics, there were 100,000 demonstrations by workers and farmers protesting against low wages, unpaid pensions, and corruption.

As Beijing struggles with the social pressures aggravated by greater import competition, a big question is how faithfully policymakers will honor their WTO commitments. Old ways won't die quickly. Many foreign companies operating in China have long complained that locals enjoy unfair advantages thanks to their *guanxi*, or connections. "They pay less tax, they get cheaper electricity," gripes Sam Lo, the 39-year-old president of Hong Kong toymaker Tai Sun, which employs 2,000 workers in China. After WTO, Lo predicts that it will be easier for Hong Kong companies to compete. "But still," he says, "I think our costs will be much higher."

One reason is that the Chinese government will still own a stake in many companies. Take TCL International Holdings, a Guangdong-based producer of televisions and other consumer electronics that had $1.1 billion in sales last year. In late August, TCL said that first-half profits were off 31%. So even as he talks bravely about taking on the competition overseas, Chairman Tomson Li expects a boost from the state, since a Guangdong municipality still owns a big stake in TCL. "We will continuously be supported by the Chinese government," says Li. While WTO entry should eliminate many barriers, "some things are visible, others are not," he says.

Skepticism

Such resistance is inevitable, which is why many critics doubt whether Beijing has the wherewithal to push through the necessary changes. "There is a great deal of skepticism regarding China's willingness and ability to carry through on its commitments," says Fred Hu, chief economist at Goldman, Sachs & Co. in Hong Kong.

But there are also reasons to believe that China will honor its WTO membership more than it will abuse it. The Chinese have built up a solid track record of more than two decades of economic reform. And the long-term stability of the country depends on the growth that can come only when foreigners are convinced that China will play by global rules. "A whole new world is opening," says William Fung of Li & Fung. The world—and China—had better be ready.

The Long March

1972 U.S. President Richard Nixon visits Mao Zedong, setting the stage for normal diplomatic contacts.

1978 Two years after Mao's death, Deng Xiaoping rises to power and ushers in economic reforms.

1979 China emerges as a new low-wage manufacturing base for Hong Kong and other countries.

1982 Communes are dismantled in the countryside

1985 Beijing slashes average tariffs from 56% to 43%, beginning a gradual reduction of import barriers.

Mid-1980s First foreign joint ventures begin production for the Chinese market.

1989 Bloody suppression of pro-democracy protests in Tiananmen Square freezes relations with the world. Foreign investment plunges, and market reforms are put on hold.

1992 Deng Xiaoping reignites economic reform, sparking new boom in exports and investment. State enterprises are given wider latitude to deal with foreigners.

1993 Shanghai Mayor Zhu Rongji, a favorite of foreign companies, becomes economic czar and starts urging faster reforms. He is now premier.

1997 Beijing leadership's 15th Party Congress opens the way for a sell-off of state enterprises and gives more rights to private entrepreneurs.

1999 China and U.S. initial agreement spelling out terms for China's entry into the World Trade Organization. Beijing to dramatically lower barriers to foreign goods and services. U.S. agrees to halt annual reviews of China's trade status.

2001 On Sept. 17, last barriers fall to China's entry into WTO, and becomes official Dec. 11, 2001.

Data: *BusinessWeek*

By Bruce Einhorn in Hong Kong, with Chester Dawson and Irene M. Kunii in Tokyo, Dexter Roberts in Beijing, Alysha Webb in Shanghai, and Pete Engardio in New York.

1. Do you agree that China is or will be the lowest-cost manufacturing center in the global economy? What are the strengths? What are the problems of doing business in China?

2. What impact does and will China's entry into the WTO have on the economies of other countries? Give some specific examples.

3. Explain the statement that "Taiwan is both a victim and a long-term benefactor of China's rise."

4. Explain the statement that "China's WTO debut is not uniformly good news for the 1.3 billion Chinese."

5. What if any changes have occurred in China since this case was written at the end of 2001?

Source: Reprinted from October 29, 2001, pp. 48–50, 52 of *Business Week* by special permission, copyright © 2001 by the McGraw-Hill Companies, Inc.

Will the EU Go for Microsoft's Jugular?

It was a lesson Bill Gates couldn't miss. Last summer, General Electric Co.'s John F. Welch flew to Brussels and lobbied for approval of a deal Washington had already O.K.'d, GE's $42 billion merger with Honeywell International Inc. Yet by the time Welch emerged from his meeting with Europe's powerful Commissioner for Competition, Mario Monti, the merger was dead.

Now it's Gates's turn to deal with Monti. Just as Microsoft appears to be nearing the conclusion of its battle with Washington, the debate over its conduct is heating up in Europe, where the software giant pulls in one-third of its sales. By mid-November, Microsoft attorneys must respond to charges in Brussels that it is using its desktop dominance to steamroll a host of rivals in everything from server software to online music.

So how serious a threat does the software giant face? Chances are Monti will steer clear of any attempt to break up Microsoft or order it to release its precious source code, the digital foundation of its empire. But he could well force Microsoft to rip its Windows Media Player, the heart of its multimedia push, out of its operating system, or hit the company with a big fine.

The American and European cases are similar. Both focus on Microsoft's attempts to leverage its strength in desktop. But while the American case focused on the browser wars that raged in the mid-'90s, Monti is looking closely at servers. These powerful computers are at the core of Microsoft's .NET strategy, the giant's bid to extend its dominance from PCs to the entire networked world.

Monti issued preliminary findings in a confidential document in August, and announced that he would "make every effort" to prevent "monopolization through illegal practices." Two days of closed-door hearings are scheduled for December—which means by February, Monti could well be in a position to rule on the case and impose whatever sanctions he deems needed. Here's a look at what could happen:

Microsoft Breakup

It's a remote possibility, but EU officials insist they have the power to break up the company. But such a hardball tactic could spark a titanic struggle with Washington, since U.S. regulators shelved their breakup proposal two months ago. Moreover, it would be seen as draconian, since Microsoft has yet to even defend itself against EU charges filed only weeks ago.

Open the Source Code

For now, a move to force Microsoft to release its source code also looks like a long shot. Opening the source code would enable competitors to clone Microsoft's Windows arsenal—a disaster for Redmond. But to Microsoft's relief, the words "source code" did not appear in Monti's statement of objections. What's more, many of Microsoft's rivals lobbying on both sides of the Atlantic aren't calling for a source-code remedy. Why? The code is so complex and convoluted that few appear eager to wrestle with it. "It's 30 million lines of spaghetti," says one rival lobbyist.

Unbundle Windows

Prospects appear greater that the EU may push Microsoft to take features out of Windows that compete with rival stand-alone products. The most likely: Windows Media Player, which competes with RealPlayer from RealNetworks Inc. Microsoft crushed Netscape Communications Corp., in part, by bundling the Internet Explorer browser with Windows.

Insist on Access

The commission also seems keen on pushing Microsoft to give rivals technical data they need to compete effectively with Redmond. That means timely disclosure of so-called application program interfaces, the hooks developers use to make programs work with Windows. Competitors have accused Microsoft of withholding APIs from rivals, so that developers from Microsoft or its partners can get products to market faster, or make them work better with Windows. Monti is likely to force Microsoft to disclose those APIs earlier.

Levy a Big Fine

The commission has the authority to impose a fine of up to 10% of annual sales. That could amount to $2.5 billion— Microsoft's entire projected profit for the current year. Still, money means far less to it than market dominance. Moreover, few in Brussels believe the EU, which has never imposed a fine of more than $100 million, would ask for anywhere near the maximum. That said, few believe Microsoft will walk away with a slap on the wrist, either.

By Stephen Baker with Renée Cordes in Brussels, Jim Kerstetter in San Mateo, and Jay Greene in Seattle

1. Why do Bill Gates and Microsoft, a U.S. multinational, have to deal with the EU and worry about their concerns about Microsoft being a monopoly?

2. What can the EU do to Microsoft? Evaluate the possibilities of each alternative.

3. Do you think the EU's stranglehold on U.S. multinationals is fair? What if anything can be done about it?

Source: Reprinted from November 5, 2001, p. 48 of *Business Week* by special permission, copyright © 2001 by the McGraw-Hill Companies. Inc.

Colgate's Distasteful Toothpaste

Colgate is a well-known consumer products company based in New York. Its present products are in the areas of household and personal care, which include laundry detergents such as Ajax and Fab, health-care products manufactured for home health care, and specialty products such as Hill pet food. The household products segment represents approximately 75 percent of company revenues, while the specialty segment accounts for less than 7 percent. Colgate's value has been set in excess of $5.6 billion. Through both recessionary and recovery periods in the United States, Colgate has always been advocated by investment analysts as a good long-term stock.

Colgate's lagging domestic market share has been present for several years. In the 1970s, when diversification seemed to be the tool to hedge against risk and sustain profits, Colgate bought companies in various industries, including Kosher hot dogs, tennis and golf equipment, and jewelry. However, such extreme diversification diverted the company's attention away from its key money-making products: soap, laundry detergents, toothpaste, and other household products. The product diversification strategy ended in 1984 when Reuben Mark became CEO. At the young age of 45, he ordered the sale of parts of the organization that deviated too far from Colgate's core competency of personal and household products. He followed consultant Tom Peters's prescription for excellence of "stick to the knitting."

Colgate's International Presence

Colgate traditionally has had a strong presence overseas. The company has operations in Australia, Latin America, Canada, France, and Germany. International sales presently represent one-half of Colgate's total revenue. In the past, Colgate always made a detailed analysis of each international market for demand. For instance, its entry into South America required an analysis of the type of product that would be most successful based on the dental hygiene needs of South American consumers. Because of this commitment to local cultural differences, the company has the number-one brand of toothpaste worldwide, Total.

To create a strong share of the Asian market without having to build its own production plant, Colgate bought a 50 percent partnership in the Hawley and Hazel group in August 1985 for $50 million. One stipulation of this agreement was that Colgate had no management prerogatives; Hawley and Hazel maintained the right to make the major decisions in the organization. This partnership turned out to be very lucrative for Colgate, with double-digit millions in annual sales.

Enter the Distasteful Toothpaste

Hawley and Hazel is a chemical products company based in Hong Kong. The company was formed in the early part of the twentieth century, and its only product of note, believe it or not, was called "Darkie" toothpaste. Over the years, this had been one of the popular brands in Asia and had a dominant presence in markets such as Taiwan, Hong Kong, Singapore, Malaysia, and Thailand.

"Darkie" toothpaste goes back to the 1920s. The founder of this product, on a visit to the United States, loved Al Jolson, then a very popular black-faced entertainer (i.e., a white person with black makeup on his face). The founder decided to re-create the spirit of this character in the form of a trademark logo for his toothpaste because of the character's big smile and white teeth. When the founder returned to Asia, he copyrighted the name "Darkie" to go along with the logo. Since the 1920s, there has been strong brand loyalty among Asians for this product. One housewife in Taipei whose family used the product for years remarked, "The toothpaste featuring a Black man with a toothy smile is an excellent advertisement."

The Backlash against Colgate

"Darkie" toothpaste had been sold in Asia for about 65 years. After Colgate became partners with Hawley and Hazel and its distasteful product, however, there was a wave of dissatisfaction with the logo and name from U.S. minorities and civil rights groups. There really has been no definite source on how this issue was passed to U.S. action groups and the media; however, a book entitled *Soap Opera: The Inside Story of Procter and Gamble* places responsibility in the hands of Procter and Gamble in an effort to tarnish Colgate's image and lower its market share.

The Americans' irate response to "Darkie" was a surprise to the Hawley and Hazel group. They reasoned that the product had always been successful in their Asian markets, and there had been no complaints. In fact, the success of "Darkie" had led the firm to market a new product in Japan called "Mouth Jazz," which had a similar logo. A spokesperson for Hawley and Hazel remarked, "There had been no problem before, you can tell by the market share that it is quite well received in Asia."

ICCR, the Interfaith Center on Corporate Responsibility, started the fight against Colgate about 10 years ago when it received a package of "Darkie" toothpaste from a consumer in Thailand. ICCR is composed of institutional investors that influence corporations through stock ownership. At the time the movement against Colgate's racially offensive product started, three members of ICCR already owned a small amount of stock in the company, and they filed a shareholder petition against Colgate requesting a change in the logo and name.

In a letter to Colgate, the ICCR Executive Director summarized the position against the distasteful toothpaste as follows:

> "Darkie" toothpaste is a 60-year-old product sold widely in Hong Kong, Malaysia, Taiwan and other places in the Far East. Its packaging includes a top-hatted and gleaming-toothed smiling likeness of Al Jolson under the words "Darkie" toothpaste. As you know the term "Darkie" is deeply offensive. We would hope that in this new association with the Hawley and Hazel Chemical Company, that immediate action will be taken to stop this product's name so that a U.S. company will not be associated with promoting racial stereotypes in the Third World.

In response to this letter, R.G.S. Anderson, Colgate's director of corporate development, replied, "No plans exist or are being contemplated that would extend marketing and sales efforts for the product in Colgate subsidiaries elsewhere or beyond this Far East area." Anderson then went on to explain that Darkie's founder was imitating Al Jolson and that in the Chinese view, imitation was the "highest form of flattery." The ICCR then informed Colgate that if the logo was not changed, the organization would create a media frenzy and help various civil rights action groups in a possible boycott.

Because Colgate still refused to remove the logo, ICCR did form a coalition with civil rights groups such as the NAACP and National Urban League to start protest campaigns. The protest took all forms, including lobbying at both the state and local levels. At one point, after heavy lobbying by the ICCR, the House of Representatives in Pennsylvania passed a resolution urging Colgate to change the name and logo. Also, similar resolutions had been proposed in the U.S. Congress.

The pressures at home placed Colgate in a difficult position, especially as it had no management rights in its agreement with Hawley and Hazel. In the Asian market, neither Colgate nor Hawley and Hazel had any knowledge of consumer dissatisfaction because of racial offensiveness, despite the fact that the local Chinese name for "Darkie" (pronounced *hak ye nga goh*) can be translated as "The Black Man" toothpaste. The logo seemed to enhance brand loyalty. One Asian customer stated, "I buy it because of the Black man's white teeth."

The demographics of the Asian market may help to explain the product's apparent acceptance. There are a relatively small number of Africans, Indians, Pakistanis, and Bangladeshis in the region; therefore, the number of people who might be offended by the logo is low. Also, some people of color did not seem disturbed by the name. For example, when asked about the implications of "Darkie"

toothpaste, the secretary of the Indian Chamber of Commerce noted, "It doesn't offend me, and I'm sort of dark-skinned."

Initially, Colgate had no intentions of forcing Hawley and Hazel to change the product. R.G.S. Anderson issued another formal statement to the ICCR as follows: "Our position . . . would be different if the product were sold in the United States or in any Western English-speaking country; which, as I have stated several times, will not happen." Hawley and Hazel concurred with the stance. The alliance was very fearful of a loss of market share and did not believe that the complaints were issues relevant to Pacific Rim countries. A spokesperson for the alliance referred to the protest campaign as "a U.S. issue." The trade-off for revamping a successful product was deemed to be too risky and costly.

Colgate's Change of Heart

The issue did not go away. As U.S. leaders in Congress began to learn about this very offensive logo and name, the pressure on Colgate mounted. Interestingly, however, the value of Colgate's stock increased throughout this period of controversy. Wall Street seemed oblivious to the charges against Colgate, and this was another reason why Colgate took no action. Colgate management believed that an issue about overseas products should not have a negative effect on the company's domestic image. However, pressures continued from groups such as the Congressional Black Caucus, a strong political force. Colgate finally began to waver, but because of its agreement with Hawley and Hazel, it felt helpless. As one Colgate executive remarked, "One hates to let exogenous things drive your business, but you sometimes have to be aware of them."

Colgate CEO Reuben Mark eventually became very distressed over the situation. He was adamantly against racism of any kind and had taken actions to exhibit his beliefs. For instance, he and his wife had received recognition for their involvement in a special program for disadvantaged teenagers. He commented publicly about the situation as follows: "It's just offensive. The morally right thing dictates that we must change. What we have to do is find a way to change that is least damaging to the economic interests of our partners." He also publicly stated that Colgate had been trying to change the package since 1985, when it bought into the partnership.

Colgate's Plan of Action to Repair the Damage

The protest campaign initiated by ICCR and carried further by others definitely caused Colgate's image to be tarnished badly in the eyes of not only African-Americans but of all Americans. To get action, some members of the Congressional Black Caucus (including Rep. John Conyers, D-Mich.) even bypassed Colgate and tried to negotiate directly with Hawley and Hazel. To try to repair the damage, Colgate, in cooperation with Hawley and Hazel, finally developed, although two years after ICCR's initial inquiry, a plan to change the product. In a letter to ICCR, CEO Mark stated, "I and Colgate share your concern that the caricature of a minstrel in black-face on the package and the name 'Darkie' itself could be considered racially offensive." Colgate and Hawley and Hazel then proposed some specific changes for the name and logo. Names considered included Darlie, Darbie, Hawley, and Dakkie. The logo options included a dark, nondescript silhouette and a well-dressed Black man. The alliances decided to test market the options among their Asian consumers; however, they refused to change the Chinese name ("Black Man Toothpaste"), which is more used by their customers.

They decided that changes would be implemented over the course of a year to maintain brand loyalty and avoid advertising confusion with their customers. There was the risk that loyal customers would not know if the modified name/logo was still the same toothpaste that had proven itself through the years. Altogether, the process would take approximately 3 years, test marketing included. Colgate also decided to pay for the entire change process, abandoning their initial suggestion that the change be paid for by Hawley and Hazel.

Colgate and Hawley and Hazel then made a worldwide apology to all insulted groups. Although Hawley and Hazel was slow to agree with the plan, a spokesperson for the group emphasized that racial stereotyping was against its policy. It also helped that Hawley and Hazel would pay no money to make the needed changes. They felt that the product was too strong to change quickly; thus, three years was not too long to implement the new logo and name fully into all Asian markets. Further, they insisted that as part of the marketing campaign, the product advertising use the following statement in Chinese, "Only the English name is being changed. Black Man Toothpaste is still Black Man Toothpaste."

Response Worldwide

Colgate and Hawley and Hazel still suffer from the effects of their racially offensive product. In 1992, while dealing with its own civil rights issues, the Chinese government placed a ban on Darlie toothpaste because of the product's violation of China's trademark laws. Although the English name change was implemented across all markets, the retained Chinese name and logo still were deemed derogatory by the Chinese, and the government banned the product. Also, Eric Molobi, an African National Congress representative, was outraged at the toothpaste's logo on a recent visit to the Pacific Rim. When asked if Darlie toothpaste would be marketed in his country, the South African representative replied, "If this company found itself in South Africa it would not be used. There would be a permanent boycott."

Today, the name of Colgate cannot be found anywhere on the packaging of what is now called Darlie toothpaste. In a strategic move, Colgate has distanced itself completely away from the controversial product. In the Thailand and Indonesia health-products markets, Colgate even competes against Darlie toothpaste with its own brand.

1. Identify the major strategic and ethical issues faced by Colgate in its partnership with Hawley and Hazel.

2. What do you think Colgate should have done to handle the situation?

3. Is it possible for Colgate and Hawley and Hazel to change the toothpaste's advertising without sacrificing consumer brand loyalty? Is that a possible reason for Colgate's not responding quickly to domestic complaints?

4. In the end, was a "no management rights" clause good for Colgate? What could have happened during the negotiations process to get around this problem?

Source: This case was written specially for this book by Professor Alisa L. Mosley, Jackson State University.

Dark Days for a Black Market

Ever since the September 11 terrorist attacks on the U.S., life at Pakistan's Karkhanai Bazaar near the border with Afghanistan hasn't been the same. Normally the market is thronged with people shopping for Japanese TVs, Chinese bicycles, and Korean household goods smuggled across the border to avoid onerous Pakistani customs duties of up to 100%. But these days, in the wake of stepped-up border controls, smugglers are leery of sneaking across. As a result, Sharif Ullah, a 19-year-old Afghan porter, has too little work and too much time to fret about the situation back home in Kabul. "People are afraid of the U.S. attacks," he says, leaning against his empty handcart. "Uncertainty is everywhere."

The uncertainty is a threat to the livelihood of tens of thousands of people like Ullah. That's because the free flow of contraband and drugs plays a critical role in the fragile, ragtag economies of Pakistan and Afghanistan. If the illicit trade is disrupted, it could ultimately determine the fate of the governments on both sides of the border.

Militancy

Trouble is, any long-term interruption in smuggling will just "compound the problems" of Pakistani President Pervez Musharraf, says Barnett R. Rubin, a New York University professor and leading authority on the region. A worsening economy could stoke Islamic militancy among the underclass and worsen an already chaotic law-and-order situation along the border. That's the last thing Musharraf needs as he contends with a populace deeply divided between pro- and anti-U.S. sentiment. Already the slowdown is spreading through Pakistan, where everything from car parts and Sony PlayStations to heroin is sold in black-market bazaars, or *baras*. The stealth economy is said to be worth at least $30 billion, or half Pakistan's official gross domestic product.

In Afghanistan, the underground economy plays an even larger role. In a country that for years has produced nothing more than food and opium, smuggling is an economic driver. Electronics from Dubai, cosmetics from Iran, tires from Turkmenistan, food processors from Japan—all move through Afghanistan and into Pakistan. The slowdown in smuggling will put thousands of traders out of work.

Smuggling has been a feature of this trading crossroads for millennia. And it got a boost in the 1950s when landlocked Afghanistan negotiated a deal with Islamabad that allowed goods to pass from the port of Karachi through Pakistan and over the Afghan border duty-free. The pact

has a fancy name: the Afghan Trade Transit Agreement (ATTA). But it merely provided a cover for smugglers. Nearly all of the goods bound for Afghanistan find their way back into Pakistan.

The scheme is called the "U-Turn." It works like this: A buyer in Afghanistan issues a letter of credit to import, say, a load of air conditioners through Karachi port (map). The appliances are then transported across the Afghan border 620 miles away. The trucks unload on the Afghan side and drive back across to Pakistan empty to wait while the air conditioners reenter Pakistan illegally, carried by camels, donkeys, or on the backs of tribesmen living along the rugged, 1,550-mile border. The goods, which sell for far less than legally imported items in Pakistan, are distributed via a trucking industry largely controlled by Afghan refugees. According to the World Bank, the illegal trade amounted to $2.5 billion in 1997; about $75 million went to the Taliban.

Pakistan's government has made half-hearted attempts to crack down on the contraband. A few years ago, acting under pressure from local manufacturers, it banned the import of TVs and other electronics under the ATTA system. Smugglers simply chartered planes to fly the goods directly from Dubai into Kandahar in Afghanistan. From there they were smuggled into Pakistan.

Money-Spinner

Nor has Islamabad responded effectively to pleas from locally based multinationals. Lever Brothers Pakistan Ltd., for example, says it could sell 20% more Lux soap, Sunsilk shampoo, and Lipton tea if the black market were curtailed. Company Chairwoman Musharaf Hai says 20,000 tons of tea were smuggled in over the past 12 months. "If we cannot constrain or eliminate this problem, maybe we should source somewhere else," she says.

Drugs are another major money-spinner. The gangs moving heroin through Afghanistan, Pakistan, and Iran are as sophisticated as the cocaine traffickers of Colombia. Smugglers drive in convoys of Land Cruisers equipped with satellite phones and rocket launchers. And they enjoy the protection of some of the most powerful people in Pakistan; millions of dollars in kickbacks flow right to the top of the political establishment, says a former Pakistani intelligence agent. A 2000 report by the United Nations Office for Drug Control & Crime Prevention said Afghanistan accounted for more than 70% of global opium production. "Afghanistan is to Europe what Colombia is to the U.S.," says a U.S. official.

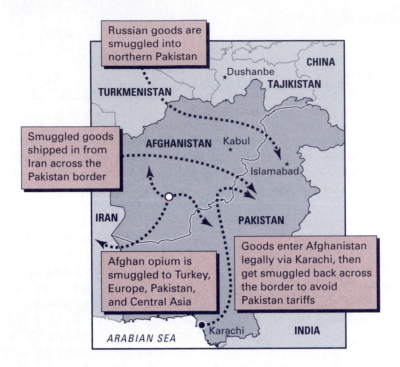

And despite the Taliban's high-profile ban on poppy cultivation in 2000, law enforcement agents say the religious sect has benefited from the drug trade. UNODCCP representative Bernard Frahi says the Taliban raised at least $18 million in 1999 through 10% Islamic levies, called *usha,* imposed on poppy farmers. How much more the Taliban took in from labs and traffickers is anyone's guess. Some even speculate that the Taliban imposed the ban on poppy farming because it feared a glut would drive down prices. Indeed, earlier this year the wholesale price of heroin soared tenfold, to $600 a kilogram (2.2 pounds), says a U.S. official.

Now, however, the drug revenues are at risk. Not because the border is more tightly controlled—heroin is smuggled more easily than consumer durables—but because prices have fallen to $100 a kilo. In a drug den near Peshawar, Tajali, a green-eyed 16-year-old Afghan trader, says many traffickers are now dumping their stocks. Of course, by the time the poppies bloom next April, the

Taliban are history. However, some other group will appear to take its cut from the flow of drugs and contraband—and the underground economies of Pakistan and Afghanistan will thrive once again.

By Frederik Balfour in Peshawar

1.   Do you have any sympathy for the Black Market smugglers? Why or why not?

2.   How can long-term interruption in smuggling "compound the problems" of Pakistani President Pervez Musharraf?

3.   How does the so-called "U-Turn" work? Knowing this exists, what impact would it have in your recommendation to do business in this part of the world?

Source: Reprinted from October 15, 2001, pp. 60–61 of *Business Week* by special permission, copyright © 2001 by the McGraw-Hill Companies, Inc.

Part Two

The Role of Culture

Chapter 5

The Meanings and Dimensions of Culture

Objectives of the Chapter

A major challenge of doing business internationally is to adapt effectively to different cultures. Such adaptation requires an understanding of cultural diversity, perceptions, stereotypes, and values. In recent years, a great deal of research has been conducted on cultural dimensions and attitudes, and the findings have proved useful in providing integrative profiles of international cultures. However, a word of caution must be given when discussing these country profiles. It must be remembered that stereotypes and overgeneralizations should be avoided; there are always individual differences and even subcultures within every country.

This chapter examines the meaning of culture as it applies to international management, reviews some of the value differences and similarities of various national groups, studies important dimensions of culture and their impact on behavior, and finally, examines attitudinal dimensions and country clusters. The specific objectives of this chapter are:

1. **DEFINE** the term "culture," and discuss some of the comparative ways of differentiating cultures.

2. **DESCRIBE** the concept of cultural values, and relate some of the international differences, similarities, and changes occurring in terms of both work and managerial values.

3. **IDENTIFY** the major dimensions of culture relevant to work settings, and discuss their effect on behavior in an international environment.

4. **DISCUSS** the value of country cluster analysis and relational orientations in developing effective international management practices.

BusinessWeek

The World of *Business Week*

The Mark of Zara

It's early Thursday evening, and almost all 250,000 residents of La Coruña, Spain, seem to be out on Calle Real, either downing glasses of the pungent local white wine in bars or eyeing fashion boutiques. One shop attracts a crowd—Zara. Twice a week, the store receives a delivery of clothes, and today is Z-day. "I come every week to see what's new," says Pilar Alonso Risteos, a 23-year-old tax collector standing in line to purchase a snazzy frilled dress.

Can Z-day cross the ocean? In the two decades since its founding in this rainy northwestern port city, Zara's parent, Inditex, has used a powerful combination of sophisticated fashion, budget pricing, fast logistics, and unconventional marketing—that is, almost none—to build a chain of 937 stores in 31 countries. The company rings up some $2 billion a year in sales, almost exclusively in Europe.

Now, Zara, with its legions of European fans— mostly twenty-something women—is hoping to make a similar splash in the U.S. It plans to build up its current four U.S. stores to 40 within three years. And some analysts predict that that number could grow tenfold. Inditex CEO José María Castellano is also thinking big, comparing Zara to some of the biggest fish in the retail sea. "Even though Gap is more casual, both of us share the goal of becoming global retailers," he says.

Tight Control

Zara, which competes side by side with Gap in many European malls, has a long way to go before catching up with its much larger rival. It offers "disposable fashion," with prices ranging from $33 for a red tank top to a black blazer for $145. But European retailers have often found the U.S. market notoriously tough, says retail consultant Howard Davidowitz. "Galleries Lafayette? A disaster. Benetton? Closed three-quarters of its U.S. stores," he notes. "The U.S. is not an easy game."

Believers insist that Zara will be a contender. One reason is its accelerated fashion schedule. Employing an army of 200-plus designers, Zara produces 12,000 different items a year. The fabric is cut in Zara's factory, then subcontracted out to local workshops for stitching. The company offsets the higher costs of European labor by avoiding markdowns, keeping inventory to a minimum, and spending little on marketing. "If anything, Zara is nimbler and faster to the market than Gap," says retail analyst Keith Willis of Goldman, Sachs & Co. in London. "That will be important as fashion trends globalize."

Tight control over design and production allows Zara to take a trend from catwalk to store shelf in as little as two weeks. Rival Gap Inc. takes about a year, albeit on a much larger scale, and the company is trying hard to get that process down to six months. "Gap is quite aware of Zara and knows that it must focus on reducing its time to market," says Marcia

Aaron, a retail analyst at Deutsche Bank. Gap officials declined to comment.

The chain's most potent advantage may be its salespeople, who act as grass-roots market researchers. Each carries a Casio wireless organizer that is used to punch in trends, customer comments, and orders to headquarters. If an item does not sell, it can be off shelves in weeks. If it is successful, Zara designers know immediately and can churn out new versions in myriad colors. This year, Zara sold a pink men's dress shirt. Customers suggested they would prefer purple. Zara's in-house manufacturing sped into action. "We were able to get the new shirt into the stores within two weeks," says José Toledo, director of Zara Homme.

Zara has already tapped its sales-staff research to adapt to the U.S. As a result of the trend toward casual attire, new products such as T-shirts and khakis, which compete with Gap's basic look, joined Zara's European look.

Still, Zara isn't tinkering much with its basic model. It plans to continue its no-advertising policy, for instance. Zara depends mainly on its stores' elegant front windows to sell its merchandise. In New York, Zara has four outlets, including one on Fifth Avenue and one in SoHo. At the store on 34th Street, the company tore out the entire interior, added marble-like floors and high-tech lights to create a stunning 10,000-square-foot emporium. The crowd, mostly in their 20s, also includes more mature businesswomen.

"You feel like you're in a classy European boutique," says Dyann Klein, owner of a theater-props company, as she eyes a $33 pair of black stretch pants. "This would cost $350 at Prada," she says.

Zara's management does worry about how to maintain lean logistics as the company grows. Zara supplies its American stores by air from Spain. CEO Castellano says he plans to add stores primarily in major U.S. cities. "If we had a bigger American network, we would have to open a factory in Mexico," he says.

So far, Zara is a niche player in the U.S. "Not a heavyweight—more like a wannabe," says Kurt Barnard of Barnard's Retail Consulting Group. But shoppers are finding Zara's mix of fast fashion appealing. Barbara Marreo, a shopper in a New York Zara, came in wearing a Gap T-shirt. "I like Gap for casual clothes, but this is much sexier," she says. And that may be how Zara makes its mark.

By William Echikson
in La Coruña, Spain

Source: **Reprinted from May 29, 2000, pp. 98, 100 issue of** *Business Week* **by special permission, copyright © 2000 by McGraw-Hill Companies, Inc.**

This opening news article provides an excellent example of how multinationals have to take culture into account if they are to be successful in their worldwide efforts. Clothing is a culturally influenced product. Suits that sell well in Italy often have little market in the rest of Europe. Styling is not universally accepted on the Continent. The same is true worldwide; what sells well in the United States often has a limited market elsewhere. As a result, clothing companies have to address the regional and local tastes of their customers. As the article explains, the firm's most important asset is its salespeople who serve as grass-roots market researchers. They find out what the customers want and they pass this information on to management for appropriate action. As a result, Zara now does business in more than 30 countries. None of this would be possible, however, if the company did not understand the importance of culture and its impact on buyer behavior. But because it does, the firm is able to gross more than $2 billion annually without spending a dime on advertising!

■ Nature of Culture

Culture
The acquired knowledge that people use to interpret experience and generate social behavior. This knowledge forms values, creates attitudes, and influences behavior.

The word "culture" comes from the Latin *cultura*, which is related to cult or worship. In its broadest sense, the term refers to the result of human interaction.[1] For the purposes of the study of international management, then **culture** is acquired knowledge that people use to interpret experience and generate social behavior.[2] This knowledge forms values, creates attitudes, and influences behavior. Most scholars of culture would agree on the following characteristics of culture:

1. *Learned.* Culture is not inherited or biologically based; it is acquired by learning and experience.
2. *Shared.* People as members of a group, organization, or society share culture; it is not specific to single individuals.
3. *Transgenerational.* Culture is cumulative, passed down from one generation to the next.
4. *Symbolic.* Culture is based on the human capacity to symbolize or use one thing to represent another.
5. *Patterned.* Culture has structure and is integrated; a change in one part will bring changes in another.
6. *Adaptive.* Culture is based on the human capacity to change or adapt, as opposed to the more genetically driven adaptive process of animals.[3]

Because different cultures exist in the world, an understanding of the impact of culture on behavior is critical to the study of international management.[4] If international managers do not know something about the cultures of the countries they deal with, the results can be quite disastrous. For example, a partner in one of New York's leading private banking firms tells the following story:

> I traveled nine thousand miles to meet a client and arrived with my foot in my mouth. Determined to do things right, I'd memorized the names of the key men I was to see in Singapore. No easy job, inasmuch as the names all came in threes. So, of course, I couldn't resist showing off that I'd done my homework. I began by addressing top man Lo Win Hao with plenty of well-placed Mr. Hao's—sprinkled the rest of my remarks with a Mr. Chee this and a Mr. Woon that. Great show. Until a note was passed to me from one man I'd met before, in New York. Bad news. "Too friendly too soon, Mr. Long," it said. Where diffidence is next to godliness, there I was, calling a room of VIPs, in effect, Mr. Ed and Mr. Charlie. I'd remembered everybody's name—but forgot that in Chinese the surname comes *first* and the given name *last*.[5]

Cultural Diversity

There are many ways of examining cultural differences and their impact on international management. Culture can affect technology transfer, managerial attitudes, managerial ideology, and even business–government relations. Perhaps most important, culture affects how people think and behave. Table 5–1, for example, compares the most important cultural values of the United States, Japan, and Arab countries. A close look at this table shows a great deal of difference among these three cultures. Culture affects a host of business-related activities, even including the common handshake. Here are some contrasting examples:

Culture	Type of Handshake
United States	Firm
Asian	Gentle (shaking hands is unfamiliar and uncomfortable for some; the exception is the Korean, who usually has a firm handshake)
British	Soft
French	Light and quick (not offered to superiors); repeated on arrival and departure
German	Brusk and firm; repeated on arrival and departure
Latin American	Moderate grasp; repeated frequently
Middle Eastern	Gentle; repeated frequently[6]

Table 5–1
Priorities of Cultural Values: United States, Japan, and Arab Countries

United States	Japan	Arab Countries
1. Freedom	1. Belonging	1. Family security
2. Independence	2. Group harmony	2. Family harmony
3. Self-reliance	3. Collectiveness	3. Parental guidance
4. Equality	4. Age/seniority	4. Age
5. Individualism	5. Group consensus	5. Authority
6. Competition	6. Cooperation	6. Compromise
7. Efficiency	7. Quality	7. Devotion
8. Time	8. Patience	8. Patience
9. Directness	9. Indirectness	9. Indirectness
10. Openness	10. Go-between	10. Hospitality

Note: "1" represents the most important cultural value, "10" the least.

Source: Adapted from information found in F. Elashmawi and Philip R. Harris, *Multicultural Management* (Houston: Gulf Publishing, 1993), p. 63.

International Management in Action

Business Customs in Japan

When doing business in Japan, foreign businesspeople should follow certain customs if they wish to be as effective as possible. Experts have put together the following guidelines:

1. Always try to arrange for a formal introduction to any person or company with which you want to do business. These introductions should come from someone whose position is at least as high as that of the person whom you want to meet or from someone who has done a favor for this person. Let the host pick the subjects to discuss. One topic to be avoided is World War II.

2. If in doubt, bring a translator along with you. For example, the head of Osaka's $7 billion international airport project tells the story of a U.S. construction company president who became indignant when he discovered that the Japanese project head could not speak English. By the same token, you should not bring along your lawyer, because this implies a lack of trust.

3. Try for a thorough personalization of all business relationships. The Japanese trust those with whom they socialize and come to know more than they do those who simply are looking to do business. Accept afterhours invitations.

However, a rollicking night out on the town will not necessarily lead to signing the contract to your advantage the next morning.

4. Do not deliver bad news in front of others, and if possible, have your second-in-command handle this chore. Never cause Japanese managers to lose face by putting them in a position of having to admit failure or say they do not know something that they should know professionally.

5. How business is done often is as important as the results. Concern for tradition, for example, is sometimes more important than concern for profit. Do not appeal solely to logic, because in Japan, emotional considerations often are more important than facts.

6. The Japanese often express themselves in a vague and ambiguous manner, in contrast to the specific language typically used in the United States. A Japanese who is too specific runs the risk of being viewed as rudely displaying superior knowledge. The Japanese avoid independent or individual action, and they prefer to make decisions based on group discussions and past precedent. The Japanese do not say no in public, which is why foreign businesspeople often take away the wrong impression.

In overall terms, the cultural impact on international management is reflected by these basic beliefs and behaviors. Here are some specific examples where the culture of a society can directly affect management approaches:

- *Centralized vs. decentralized decision making.* In some societies, all important organizational decisions are made by top managers. In others, these decisions are diffused throughout the enterprise, and middle- and lower-level managers actively participate in, and make, key decisions.

- *Safety vs. risk.* In some societies, organizational decision makers are risk-aversive and have great difficulty with conditions of uncertainty. In others, risk-taking is encouraged, and decision making under uncertainty is common.

- *Individual vs. group rewards.* In some countries, personnel who do outstanding work are given individual rewards in the form of bonuses and commissions. In others, cultural norms require group rewards, and individual rewards are frowned on.

- *Informal vs. formal procedures.* In some societies, much is accomplished through informal means. In others, formal procedures are set forth and followed rigidly.

- *High vs. low organizational loyalty.* In some societies, people identify very strongly with their organization or employer. In others, people identify with their occupational group, such as engineer or mechanic.

- *Cooperation vs. competition.* Some societies encourage cooperation between their people. Others encourage competition between their people.

- *Short-term vs. long-term horizons.* Some cultures focus most heavily on short-term horizons, such as short-range goals of profit and efficiency. Others are more interested in long-range goals, such as market share and technologic development.

- *Stability vs. innovation.* The culture of some countries encourages stability and resistance to change. The culture of others puts high value on innovation and change.

These cultural differences influence the way that international management should be conducted. The accompanying box, "Business Customs in Japan," provides some examples in a country where many international managers are unfamiliar with day-to-day business protocol.

Another way of depicting cultural diversity is through concentric circles. Figure 5–1 provides an example. The outer layer consists of the explicit artifacts and products of the culture. This level is observable and consists of such things as language, food, buildings, and art. The middle layer contains the norms and values of the society. These can be both formal and informal, and they are designed to help people understand how they should behave. The inner layer contains the basic, implicit assumptions that govern behavior. By understanding these assumptions, members of a culture are able to organize themselves in a way that helps them increase the effectiveness of their problem-solving processes and interact well with each other. In explaining the nature of this inner layer, Trompenaars and Hampden-Turner have noted that:

> The best way to test if something is a basic assumption is when the [situation] provokes confusion or irritation. You might, for example, observe that some Japanese bow deeper than others .
> . . . if you ask why they do it the answer might be that they don't know but that the other person

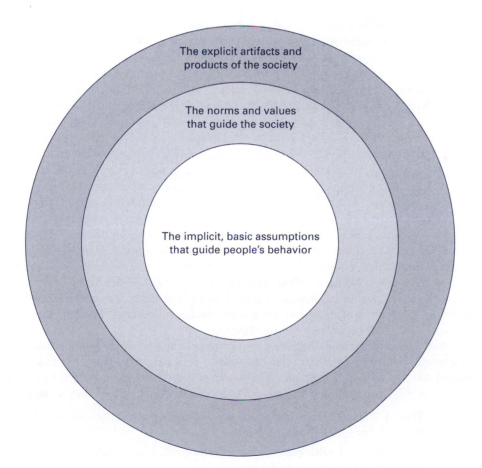

Figure 5–1

A Model of Culture

The explicit artifacts and products of the society

The norms and values that guide the society

The implicit, basic assumptions that guide people's behavior does it too (norm) or that they want to show respect for authority (value). A typical Dutch question that might follow is: "Why do you respect authority?" The most likely Japanese reaction would be either puzzlement or a smile (which might be hiding their irritation). When you question basic assumptions you are asking questions that have never been asked before. It might lead others to deeper insights, but it also might provoke annoyance. Try in the USA or the Netherlands to raise the question of why people are equal and you will see what we mean.[7]

A supplemental way of understanding cultural differences is to compare culture as a normal distribution, as in Figure 5–2, and then to examine it in terms of stereotyping, as in Figure 5–3. French and American culture, for example, have quite different norms and values. So the normal distribution curves for the two cultures have only limited overlap. However, when one looks at the tail ends of the two curves, it is possible to identify stereotypical views held by members of one culture about the other. The stereotypes are often exaggerated and used by members of one culture in describing the other, thus helping reinforce the differences between the two while reducing the likelihood of achieving cooperation and communication. This is one reason why an understanding of national culture is so important in the study of international management.

Values in Culture

Values
Basic convictions that people have regarding what is right and wrong, good and bad, important or unimportant.

A major dimension in the study of culture is values. **Values** are basic convictions that people have regarding what is right and wrong, good and bad, important or unimportant. These values are learned from the culture in which the individual is reared, and they help to direct the person's behavior. Differences in cultural values often result in varying management practices. Table 5–2 provides an example. Note that U.S. values can result in one set of business responses, and alternative values can bring about different responses.

Value Differences and Similarities across Cultures

Personal values have been the focus of numerous intercultural studies. In general, the findings show both differences and similarities between the work values and managerial values of different cultural groups. For example, one study found differences in work values between Western-oriented and tribal-oriented black employees in South Africa.[8] The Western-oriented group accepted most of the tenets of the Protestant work ethic, but the tribal-oriented group did not. The results were explained in terms of the differences of the cultural backgrounds of the two groups.

Differences in work values also have been found to reflect culture and industrialization. Researchers gave a personal-values questionnaire (PVQ) to over 2,000 managers in five countries: Australia ($n = 281$), India ($n = 485$), Japan ($n = 301$), South Korea ($n = 161$), and the United States ($n = 833$).[9] The PVQ consisted of 66 concepts related to business goals, personal goals, ideas associated with people and groups of people, and ideas about general topics. Ideologic and philosophic concepts were included to represent major value systems of all groups. The results showed some significant differences between the managers in each group. U.S. managers placed high value on the tactful acquisition of influence and regard for others. Japanese managers placed high value on deference to superiors, on company commitment, and on the cautious use of aggressiveness and control. Korean managers placed high value on personal forcefulness and aggressiveness and low value on recognition of others. Indian managers put high value on the nonaggressive pursuit of objectives. Australian managers placed major importance on values reflecting a low-keyed approach to management and a high concern for others.[10] In short, value systems across national boundaries often are different.

At the same time, value similarities exist between cultures. In fact, research shows that managers from different countries often have similar personal values that relate to success. England and Lee examined the managerial values of a diverse sample of U.S. ($n = 878$), Japanese ($n = 312$), Australian ($n = 301$), and Indian managers ($n = 500$). They found that:

1. There is a reasonably strong relationship between the level of success achieved by managers and their personal values.

2. It is evident that value patterns predict managerial success and could be used in selection and placement decisions.

Figure 5–2

**Comparing
Cultures as
Overlapping
Normal
Distributions**

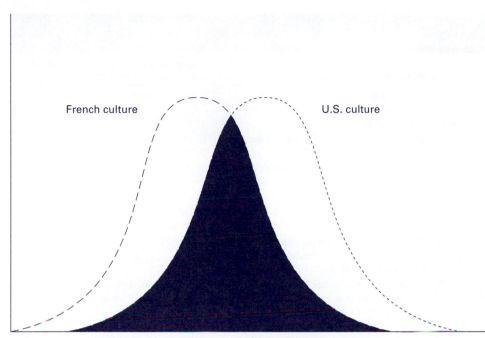

French culture   U.S. culture

Source: Adapted from Fons Trompenaars and Charles Hampden-Turner, *Riding the Waves of Culture: Understanding Diversity in Global Business,* 2nd ed. (New York: McGraw-Hill, 1998), p. 25.

Figure 5–3

**Stereotyping from
the Cultural
Extremes**

How the Americans see the French:

- arrogant
- flamboyant
- hierarchical
- emotional

How the French see the Americans:

- naive
- aggressive
- unprincipled
- workaholic

French culture   U.S. culture

Source: Adapted from Fons Trompenaars and Charles Hampden-Turner, *Riding the Waves of Culture: Understanding Diversity in Global Business,* 2nd ed. (New York: McGraw-Hill, 1998), p. 23.

3. Although there are country differences in the relationships between values and success, findings across the four countries are quite similar.

4. The general pattern indicates that more successful managers appear to favor pragmatic, dynamic, achievement-oriented values, while less successful managers prefer more static and passive values. More successful managers favor an achievement orientation and prefer an active role in interaction with other

---

Table 5–2
U.S. Values and Possible Alternatives

U.S. Cultural Values	Alternative Values	Examples of Management Function Affected
Individuals can influence the future (when there is a will there is a way).	Life follows a preordained course, and human action is determined by the will of God.	Planning and scheduling.
Individuals should be realistic in their aspirations.	Ideals are to be pursued regardless of what is "reasonable."	Goal-setting and career development.
We must work hard to accomplish our objectives (Puritan ethic).	Hard work is not the only prerequisite for success. Wisdom, luck, and time also are required.	Motivation and reward system.
A primary obligation of an employee is to the organization.	Individual employees have a primary obligation to their family and friends.	Loyalty, commitment, and motivation.
Employees can be removed if they do not perform well.	The removal of an employee from a position involves a great loss of prestige and will rarely be done.	Promotion.
Company information should be available to anyone who needs it within the organization.	Withholding information to gain or maintain power is acceptable.	Organization, communication, and managerial style.
Competition stimulates high performance.	Competition leads to unbalances and disharmony.	Career development and marketing.
What works is important.	Symbols and the process are more important than the end point.	Communication, planning, and quality control.

Source: Adapted from information found in Philip R. Harris and Robert T. Moran, *Managing Cultural Differences* (Houston: Gulf Publishing, 1991), pp. 79–80.

---

individuals who are instrumental to achieving the managers' organizational goals. Less successful managers have values associated with a static and protected environment in which they take relatively passive roles.[11]

"International Management in Action: Common Personal Values" discusses these findings in more depth.

Values in Transition   Do values change over time? George England found that personal value systems are relatively stable and do not change rapidly.[12] However, changes are taking place in managerial values as a result of both culture and technology. A good example is the Japanese. Reichel and Flynn examined the effects of the U.S. environment on the cultural values of Japanese managers working for Japanese firms in the United States. In particular, they focused attention on such key organizational values as lifetime employment, formal authority, group orientation, seniority, and paternalism. Here is what they found:

1. Lifetime employment is widely accepted in Japanese culture, but the stateside Japanese managers did not believe that unconditional tenure in one organization was of major importance. They did believe, however, that job security was important.

2. Formal authority, obedience, and conformance to hierarchic position are very important in Japan, but the stateside managers did not perceive obedience and conformity to be very important and rejected the idea that one should not question a superior. However, they did support the concept of formal authority.

3. Group orientation, cooperation, conformity, and compromise are important organizational values in Japan. The stateside managers supported these values but also believed it was important to be an individual, thus maintaining a balance between a group and a personal orientation.

International Management in Action

Common Personal Values

One of the most interesting findings about successful managers around the world is that while they come from different cultures, many have similar personal values. Of course, there are large differences in values within each national group. For example, some managers are very pragmatic and judge ideas in terms of whether they will work; others are highly ethical-moral and view ideas in terms of right or wrong; still others have a "feeling" orientation and judge ideas in terms of whether they are pleasant. Some managers have a very small set of values; others have a large set. Some have values that are related heavily to organization life; others include a wide range of personal values; others have highly group-oriented values. There are many different value patterns; however, overall value profiles have been found within successful managers in each group. Here are some of the most significant:

U.S. managers

- Highly pragmatic
- High achievement and competence orientation
- Emphasis on profit maximization, organizational efficiency, and high productivity

Japanese managers

- Highly pragmatic
- Strong emphasis on size and growth
- High value on competence and achievement

Korean managers

- Highly pragmatic
- Highly individualistic
- Strong achievement and competence orientation

Australian managers

- High moral orientation
- High humanistic orientation
- Low value on achievement, success, competition, and risk

Indian managers

- High moral orientation
- Highly individualistic
- Strong focus on organization compliance and competence

The findings listed here show important similarities and differences. Most of the profiles are similar in nature; however, note that successful Indian and Australian managers have values that are distinctly different. In short, although values of successful managers within countries often are similar, there are intercountry differences. This is why the successful managerial value systems of one country often are not ideal in another country.

---

4. In Japan, organizational personnel often are rewarded based on seniority, not merit. Support for this value was directly influenced by the length of time the Japanese managers had been in the United States. The longer they had been there, the lower their support for this value.

5. Paternalism, often measured by a manager's involvement in both personal and off-the-job problems of subordinates, is very important in Japan. Stateside Japanese managers disagreed, and this resistance was positively associated with the number of years they had been in the United States.[13]

Other researchers have found supporting evidence that Japanese values are changing—and not just among managers outside the country. One study examined value systems among three groups of managers in Japan: (1) a group of Japanese managers who had graduated from the Japanese Institute for International Studies and Training at least 10 years previously; (2) a group of Japanese management trainees who currently were enrolled in the institute; and (3) a group of U.S. M.B.A. students who were taking M.B.A. courses at the institute.[14] The results showed that the Japanese managers were greatly concerned with job security, whereas the U.S. M.B.A. students valued achievement. The Japanese managers put great importance on group success; the U.S. M.B.A. students highly valued personal success. Although there were some exceptions, the two groups had contrasting values. The profiles of the Japanese students, meanwhile, fell between these two extremes. Two-thirds of responses were in this middle range. The researchers therefore concluded that "the data seem to indicate a significant difference in values between Japanese respondents who have already attained responsible managerial positions in their organization and the Japanese management trainees, who have held lower positions and been employed less long with their present company or government agency."[15]

Recently there is increasing evidence that individualism in Japan is on the rise. The country's long economic slump has convinced many Japanese that they cannot rely on the large corporations or the government to ensure their future. They have to do it for themselves. As a result, today a growing number of Japanese are starting to embrace what is being called the "era of personal responsibility." Instead of denouncing individualism as a threat to society, they are proposing it as a necessary solution to many of the country's economic ills. A vice-chairman of the nation's largest business lobby summed up this thinking at the opening of a recent conference on economic change when he said, "By establishing personal responsibility, we must return dynamism to the economy and revitalize society."[16] This thinking is supported by Lee and Peterson's research which reveals that a culture with a strong entrepreneurial orientation is important to global competitiveness, especially in the small business sector of an economy. So this current trend may well be helpful to the Japanese economy in helping it meet foreign competition at home.[17]

■ Cultural Dimensions

Some researchers have attempted to provide a composite picture of culture by examining its subparts, or dimensions. In particular, Dutch researcher Geert Hofstede found there are four dimensions of culture that help to explain how and why people from various cultures behave as they do.[18] His initial data were gathered from two questionnaire surveys with over 116,000 respondents from over 70 different countries around the world—making it the largest organizationally based study ever conducted. The individuals in these studies all worked in the local subsidiaries of IBM. As a result, Hofstede's research has been criticized because of its focus on just one company; however, he has recently countered this criticism. Hofstede is well aware of

> the amazement of some people about how employees of a very specific corporation like IBM can serve as a sample for discovering something about the culture of their countries at large. "We know IBMers," they say, "they are very special people, always in a white shirt and tie, and not at all representative of our country." The people who say this are quite right. IBMers do not form representative samples from national populations. . . . However, samples for cross-national comparison need not be representative, as long as they are functionally equivalent. IBM employees are a narrow sample, but very well matched. Employees of multinational companies in general and of IBM in particular form attractive sources of information for comparing national traits, because they are so similar in respects other than nationality: their employers . . . , their kind of work, and—for matched occupations—their level of education. The only thing that can account for systematic and consistent differences between national groups *within* such a homogenous multinational population is nationality itself. The national environment in which people were brought up *before* they joined this employer. Comparing IBM subsidiaries therefore shows national culture differences with unusual clarity.[19]

Hofstede's massive study continues to be a focal point for additional research. The four now-well-known dimensions that Hofstede examined were: (1) power distance, (2) uncertainty avoidance, (3) individualism, and (4) masculinity.

Power Distance

Power distance
The extent to which less powerful members of institutions and organizations accept that power is distributed unequally.

Power distance is "the extent to which less powerful members of institutions and organizations accept that power is distributed unequally."[20] Countries in which people blindly obey the orders of their superiors have high power distance. In many societies, lower-level employees tend to follow orders as a matter of procedure. In societies with high power distance, however, strict obedience is found even at the upper levels; examples include Mexico, South Korea, and India. For example, a senior Indian executive with a Ph.D. from a prestigious U.S. university related the following story:

What is most important for me and my department is not what I do or achieve for the company, but whether the [owner's] favor is bestowed on me. . . . This I have achieved by saying "yes" to everything [the owner] says or does. . . . To contradict him is to look for another job. . . . I left my freedom of thought in Boston.[21]

The effect of this dimension can be measured in a number of ways. For example, organizations in low power-distance countries generally will be decentralized and have flatter organization structures. These organizations also will have a smaller proportion of supervisory personnel, and the lower strata of the work force often will consist of highly qualified people. By contrast, organizations in high power-distance countries will tend to be centralized and have tall organization structures. Organizations in high power-distance countries will have a large proportion of supervisory personnel, and the people at the lower levels of the structure often will have low job qualifications. This latter structure encourages and promotes inequality between people at different levels.[22]

Uncertainty Avoidance

Uncertainty avoidance is "the extent to which people feel threatened by ambiguous situations, and have created beliefs and institutions that try to avoid these."[23] Countries populated with people who do not like uncertainty tend to have a high need for security and a strong belief in experts and their knowledge: examples include Germany, Japan, and Spain. Cultures with low uncertainty avoidance have people who are more willing to accept that risks are associated with the unknown, that life must go on in spite of this. Examples here include Denmark and Great Britain.

> **Uncertainty avoidance**
> The extent to which people feel threatened by ambiguous situations and have created beliefs and institutions that try to avoid these.

The effect of this dimension can be measured in a number of ways. Countries with high uncertainty-avoidance cultures have a great deal of structuring of organizational activities, more written rules, less risk-taking by managers, lower labor turnover, and less ambitious employees.

Low uncertainty-avoidance societies have organization settings with less structuring of activities, fewer written rules, more risk-taking by managers, higher labor turnover, and more ambitious employees. The organization encourages personnel to use their own initiative and assume responsibility for their actions.

Individualism

Individualism is the tendency of people to look after themselves and their immediate family only.[24] Hofstede measured this cultural difference on a bipolar continuum, with individualism on one end and collectivism on the other. **Collectivism** is the tendency of people to belong to groups or collectives and to look after each other in exchange for loyalty.[25]

> **Individualism**
> The tendency of people to look after themselves and their immediate family only.
>
> **Collectivism**
> The tendency of people to belong to groups or collectives and to look after each other in exchange for loyalty.

Similar to those of the other cultural dimensions, the effects of individualism and collectivism can be measured in a number of different ways.[26] Hofstede has found that wealthy countries have higher individualism scores and poorer countries higher collectivism scores (see Table 5–3 for the country abbreviations used in Figure 5–4 and subsequent figures). Note that in Figure 5–4, the United States, Canada, Australia, Denmark, and Sweden, among others, have high individualism and high GNP. Conversely, Indonesia, Pakistan, and a number of South American countries have low individualism (high collectivism) and low GNP. Countries with high individualism also tend to have greater support for the Protestant work ethic, greater individual initiative, and promotions based on market value. Countries with low individualism tend to have less support for the Protestant work ethic, less individual initiative, and promotions based on seniority.

Masculinity

Masculinity is defined by Hofstede as "a situation in which the dominant values in society are success, money, and things."[27] Hofstede measured this dimension on a continuum ranging from masculinity to femininity. Contrary to some stereotypes and connotations,

> **Masculinity**
> A culture in which the dominant values in society are success, money, and things.

Table 5–3
Countries and Regions Used in Hofstede's Research

ARA	Arab countries (Egypt, Lebanon, Libya, Kuwait, Iraq, Saudi Arabia, U.A.E.)	JPN	Japan
		KOR	South Korea
ARG	Argentina	MAL	Malaysia
AUL	Australia	MEX	Mexico
AUT	Austria	NET	Netherlands
BEL	Belgium	NOR	Norway
BRA	Brazil	NZL	New Zealand
CAN	Canada	PAK	Pakistan
CHL	Chile	PAN	Panama
COL	Colombia	PER	Peru
COS	Costa Rica	PHI	Philippines
DEN	Denmark	POR	Portugal
EAF	East Africa (Kenya, Ethiopia, Zambia)	SAF	South Africa
EQA	Equador	SAL	Salvador
FIN	Finland	SIN	Singapore
FRA	France	SPA	Spain
GBR	Great Britain	SWE	Sweden
GER	Germany	SWI	Switzerland
GRE	Greece	TAI	Taiwan
GUA	Guatemala	THA	Thailand
HOK	Hong Kong	TUR	Turkey
IDO	Indonesia	URU	Uruguay
IND	India	USA	United States
IRA	Iran	VEN	Venezuela
IRE	Ireland	WAF	West Africa (Nigeria, Ghana, Sierra Leone)
ISR	Israel		
ITA	Italy		
JAM	Jamaica	YUG	Yugoslavia

Source: Adapted from Geert Hofstede, *Cultures and Organizations: Software of the Mind* (London: McGraw-Hill U.K., Ltd., 1991), p. 55. Used with permission.

Femininity
A culture in which the dominant values in society are caring for others and quality of life.

femininity is the term used by Hofstede to describe "a situation in which the dominant values in society are caring for others and the quality of life."[28] Countries with a high masculinity index, such as the Germanic countries, place great importance on earnings, recognition, advancement, and challenge. Individuals are encouraged to be independent decision makers, and achievement is defined in terms of recognition and wealth. The workplace is often characterized by high job stress, and many managers believe that their employees dislike work and must be kept under some degree of control.

Countries with a low masculinity index (Hofstede's femininity dimension), such as Norway, tend to place great importance on cooperation, a friendly atmosphere, and employment security. Individuals are encouraged to be group decision makers, and achievement is defined in terms of layman contacts and the living environment. The workplace tends to be characterized by low stress, and managers give their employees more credit for being responsible and allow them more freedom.

Cultures with a high masculinity index such as the Japanese tend to favor large-scale enterprises, and economic growth is seen as more important than conservation of the environment. The school system is geared toward encouraging high performance. Young men expect to have careers, and those who do not often view themselves as failures. Fewer women hold higher-level jobs, and these individuals often find it necessary to be assertive. There is high job stress in the workplace, and industrial conflict is common.

Figure 5–4   **Individualism Index vs. Per Capita GNP**

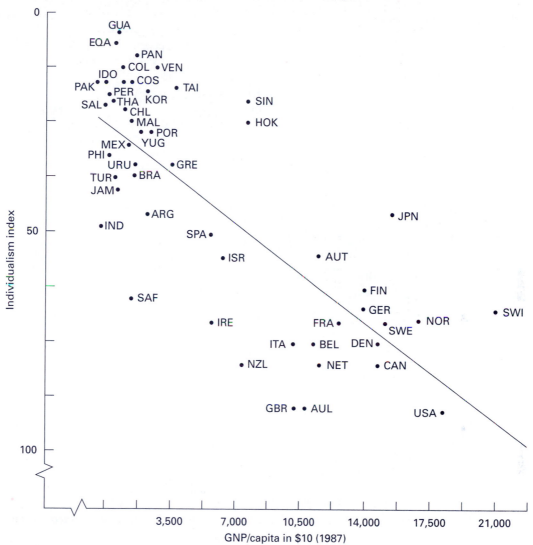

Source: Geert Hofstede, *Cultures and Organizations: Software of the Mind* (London: McGraw-Hill U.K., Ltd., 1991), p. 75. Used with permission.

Cultures with a low masculinity index (high femininity) tend to favor small-scale enterprises, and they place great importance on conservation of the environment. The school system is designed to teach social adaptation. Some young men and women want careers; others do not. Many women hold higher-level jobs, and they do not find it necessary to be assertive. Less job stress is found in the workplace, and there is not much industrial conflict.

Integrating the Dimensions

A description of the four dimensions of culture is useful in helping to explain the differences between various countries, and Hofstede's research has extended beyond this focus and showed how countries can be described in terms of pairs of dimensions. Figure 5–5, which incorporates power distance and individualism, provides an example.

In Figure 5–5, the United States is located in the lower left-hand quadrant. Americans have very high individualism and relatively low power distance. They prefer to do things for themselves and are not upset when others have more power than they do. In fact, Americans are taught to believe that everyone is equal, so they are not overly impressed by individuals with important titles or jobs. Australians, Canadians, British, Dutch, and New

Figure 5–5   **A Power Distance and Individualism-Collectivism Plot**

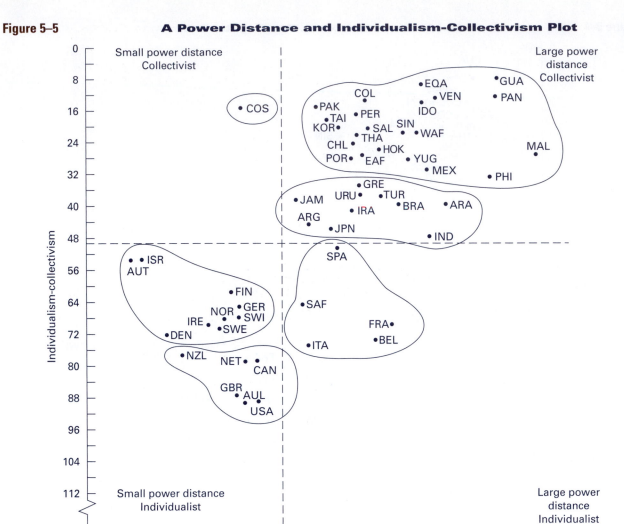

Source: Geert Hofstede, *Cultures and Organizations: Software of the Mind* (London: McGraw-Hill U.K., Ltd., 1991), p. 54. Used with permission.

Zealanders have the same basic values. Conversely, many of the underdeveloped or newly industrialized countries, such as Colombia, Hong Kong, Portugal, and Singapore, are characterized by large power distance and low individualism. These nations tend to be collectivist in their approach.

Figure 5–6 plots the uncertainty avoidance index for the 53 countries against the power-distance index. Once again, there are clusters of countries. Many of the Anglo nations tend to be in the upper left-hand quadrant, which is characterized by small power distance and weak uncertainty avoidance (they do not try to avoid uncertainty). These countries tend to be moderately unconcerned with power distance, and they are able to accept conditions of uncertainty. In contrast, many Latin countries (both in Europe and the Western hemisphere), Mediterranean countries, and Asian nations (*e.g.,* Japan and Korea) are characterized by high power distance and strong uncertainty avoidance. Most other Asian countries are characterized by large power distance and weak uncertainty avoidance.

Figure 5–7 plots the position of 53 countries in terms of uncertainty avoidance and masculinity-femininity. The most masculine country is Japan, followed by the Germanic countries (Austria, Switzerland, Germany) and Latin countries (Venezuela, Mexico, Italy).

Figure 5–6

A Power Distance and Uncertainty Avoidance Plot

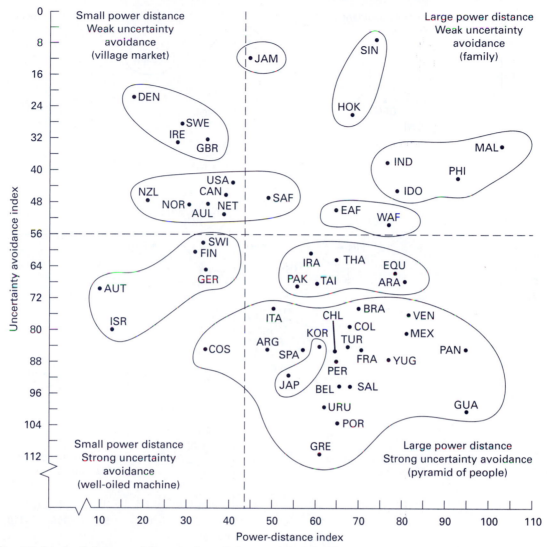

Source: Geert Hofstede, *Cultures and Organizations: Software of the Mind* (London: McGraw-Hill U.K., Ltd., 1991), p. 141. Used with permission.

Many countries in the Anglo cluster, including Ireland, Australia, Great Britain, and the United States, have moderate degrees of masculinity. So do some of the former colonies of Anglo nations, including India, South Africa, and the Philippines. The Northern European cluster (Denmark, Sweden, Norway, the Netherlands) has low masculinity, indicating that these countries place high value on factors such as quality of life, preservation of the environment, and the importance of relationships with people over money.

The integration of these cultural factors into two-dimensional plots helps to illustrate the complexity of understanding culture's effect on behavior. A number of dimensions are at work, and sometimes, they do not all move in the anticipated direction. For example, at first glance, a nation with high power distance would appear to be low in individualism, and vice versa, and Hofstede found exactly that (see Figure 5–5). However, low uncertainty avoidance does not always go hand-in-hand with high masculinity, even though those who are willing to live with uncertainty will want rewards such as money and power and accord low value to the quality of work life and caring for others (see Figure 5–7). Simply put, empirical evidence on the impact of cultural dimensions may differ from commonly held beliefs or stereotypes. Research-based data are needed to determine the

Figure 5–7 **A Masculinity-Femininity and Uncertainty Avoidance Plot**

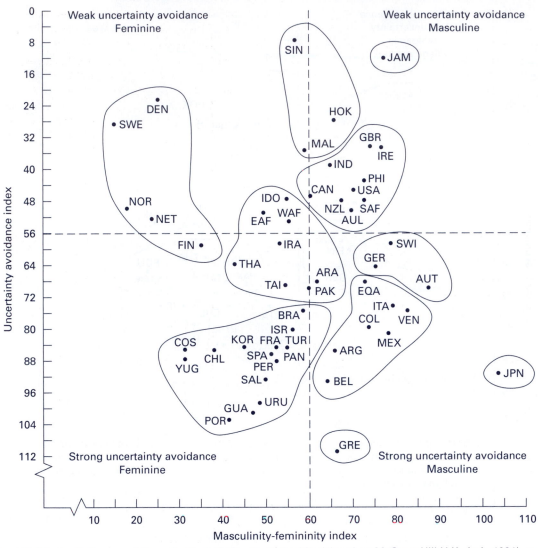

Source: Geert Hofstede, *Cultures and Organizations: Software of the Mind* (London: McGraw-Hill U.K., Ltd., 1991), p. 123. Used with permission.

full impact of differing cultures. However, some interesting attempts have been made to classify countries in uniform clusters on variables such as attitudes and deal with cultures on a more structured basis. These efforts are described in the next section.

■ Attitudinal Dimensions of Culture

For well over two decades, researchers have attempted to cluster countries into similar cultural groupings for the purpose of studying similarities and differences. Such research also helps us to learn the reasons for cultural differences and how they can be transcended. Much of the initial research in this area examined similarities among countries based on employee work values and attitudes.

Work Value and Attitude Similarities

Drawing on his extensive data, Hofstede was able to use the four cultural dimensions discussed in the last section to compile a series of country clusters, as shown in Figures 5–5, 5–6, and 5–7. His work was only preliminary, but it served as a point of departure for other multicultural research, which revealed many similarities in both work values and attitudes among certain countries. For example, early research by Ronen and Kraut reported that "countries could be clustered into more or less homogeneous groups based on intercorrelations of standard scores obtained for each country from scales measuring leadership, role descriptions, and motivation."[29] These researchers then attempted to cluster the countries by use of the mathematic technique of nonparametric multivariate analysis, known as **smallest space analysis (SSA).** Simply put, this approach maps the relationships of various culture dimensions among the countries by showing the distance between each. By looking at the resulting two-dimensional map, one can see those countries that are similar to each other and those that are not.

Drawing on the work of many earlier researchers as well as that of 4,000 technical employees in 15 countries, Ronen and Kraut were able to construct SSA maps of various countries, including the United States, France, India, Sweden, and Japan. These maps showed five country clusters: (1) Anglo-American (United States, United Kingdom, Australia); (2) Nordic (Norway, Finland, Denmark); (3) South American (Venezuela, Mexico, Chile); (4) Latin European (France and Belgium); and (5) Germanic (Germany, Austria, and Switzerland). Commenting on the overall value of their research, Ronen and Kraut concluded:

> An important aspect of this study is the potential for practical application by multinational organizations. For example, knowledge of relative similarities among countries can guide the smooth placement of international assignees and the establishment of compatible regional units, and predict the ease of implementing various policies and practices across national boundaries.[30]

Since Ronen and Kraut, additional multicultural studies have been conducted, and the number of countries and clusters has increased. These country clusters are particularly important in providing an overall picture of international cultures.[31]

Country Clusters

To date, perhaps the most integrative analysis of all available findings has been provided by Ronen and Shenkar.[32] After conducting a thorough review of the literature, they found that eight major cluster studies had been conducted over the previous 15 years. These studies examined variables in four categories: (1) the importance of work goals; (2) need deficiency, fulfillment, and job satisfaction; (3) managerial and organizational variables; and (4) work role and interpersonal orientation. Each of the eight country cluster studies had produced different results. Some had focused only on one part of the world, such as the Far East or the Middle East, others had been more international in focus but arrived at different cluster groupings. Based on careful analysis of these research efforts, Ronen and Shenkar identified eight country clusters and four countries that are independent and do not fit into any of the clusters (see Figure 5–8).

Each country in Figure 5–8 that has been placed in a cluster is culturally similar to the others in that cluster. In addition, the closer a country is to the center of the overall circle, the greater its per-capita gross national product (GNP). Those countries with similar GNPs will not necessarily have intercluster similarity, but to the extent that GNP influences values and culture, these countries will have converging cultural values.

Not everyone agrees with the synthesis presented in Figure 5–8. Some researchers place India and Israel in the Anglo culture because of the strong Anglo ties of these countries. Others combine the Nordic and Germanic clusters into one. Still others believe that some of the Latin European countries, such as Italy, Portugal, and Spain, are culturally much closer to those of the South American culture and cluster them there. Nevertheless, Figure 5–8 does provide a useful model and point of departure for examining international culture. The concept of country clusters is useful to those studying multinational management as well. Ronen and Shenkar note:

> As multinational companies increase their direct investment overseas, especially in less developed and consequently less studied areas, they will require more information concerning their local employees in order to implement effective types of interactions between the organization

Smallest space analysis (SSA)
A nonparametric multivariate analysis. This mathematic tool maps the relationship among the countries by showing the distance between each. By looking at this two-dimensional map, it is possible to see those countries that are similar to each other and those that are not.

Figure 5–8

**A Synthesis of
Country Clusters**

Source: Simcha Ronen and Oded Shenkar, "Clustering Countries on Attitudinal Dimensions: A Review and Synthesis," *Academy of Management Journal,* September, 1985, p. 449. Used with permission.

and the host country. The knowledge acquired thus far can help one to understand better the work values and attitudes of employees throughout the world. American theories work very well for Western nations. Are they equally applicable in non-Western countries? Clearly, more cluster research is called for, including research in countries from all parts of the globe.[33]

Empirical evidence shows that international managers share a common international culture, so there may well be much more convergence than previously has been believed. There also may be much more recent adaptation to the local culture by national firms than many outside observers realize. In short, although recognizing cultural diversity still is vital, convergence and flexibility in the international arena are gaining momentum.

■ Trompenaars' Cultural Dimensions

Both the Hofstede cultural dimensions and the Ronen and Shenkar country clusters are widely recognized and accepted in the study of international management. A more recent description of how cultures differ, by another Dutch researcher, Fons Trompenaars, is receiving increasing attention as well. Trompenaars' research was conducted over a 10-year period and published in 1994.[34] He administered research questionnaires to over 15,000 managers from 28 countries and received usable responses from at least 500 in each nation; the 23 countries in his research are presented in Table 5–4. Building heavily on value orientations and the relational orientations of well-known sociologist Talcott

Table 5–4
Trompenaars' Country Abbreviations

Abbreviation	Country
ARG	Argentina
AUS	Austria
BEL	Belgium
BRZ	Brazil
CHI	China
CIS	Former Soviet Union
CZH	Former Czechoslovakia
FRA	France
GER	Germany (excluding former East Germany)
HK	Hong Kong
IDO	Indonesia
ITA	Italy
JPN	Japan
MEX	Mexico
NL	Netherlands
SIN	Singapore
SPA	Spain
SWE	Sweden
SWI	Switzerland
THA	Thailand
UK	United Kingdom
USA	United States
VEN	Venezuela

Parsons,[35] Trompenaars derived five relationship orientations that address the ways in which people deal with each other; these can be considered to be cultural dimensions that are analogous to Hofstede's dimensions. Trompenaars also looked at attitudes toward both time and the environment, and the result of his research is a wealth of information helping to explain how cultures differ and offering practical ways in which MNCs can do business in various countries. The following discussion examines each of the five relationship orientations as well as attitudes toward time and the environment.[36]

Universalism vs. Particularism

Universalism is the belief that ideas and practices can be applied everywhere without modification. **Particularism** is the belief that circumstances dictate how ideas and practices should be applied. In cultures with high universalism, the focus is more on formal rules than on relationships, business contracts are adhered to very closely, and people believe that "a deal is a deal." In cultures with high particularism, the focus is more on relationships and trust than on formal rules. In a particularist culture, legal contracts often are modified, and as people get to know each other better, they often change the way in which deals are executed. In his early research, Trompenaars found that in countries such as the United States, Australia, Germany, Sweden, and the United Kingdom, there was high universalism, while countries such as Venezuela, the former Soviet Union, Indonesia, and China were high on particularism. Figure 5–9 shows the continuum.

In follow-up research Trompenaars and Hampden-Turner uncovered additional insights regarding national orientations on this universalism-particularism continuum. They did this by presenting the respondents with a dilemma and asking them to make a decision. Here is one of these dilemmas along with the national scores of the respondents:[37]

Universalism
The belief that ideas and practices can be applied everywhere in the world without modification.

Particularism
The belief that circumstances dictate how ideas and practices should be applied and something cannot be done the same everywhere.

Figure 5–9

**Trompenaars'
Relationship
Orientations
on Cultural
Dimensions**

Universalism vs. Particularism

Individualism vs. Communitarianism

Neutral vs. Emotional

Specific vs. Diffuse

Achievement vs. Ascription

Source: Adapted from information found in Fons Trompenaars, *Riding the Waves of Culture* (New York: Irwin, 1994) and Charles M. Hampden-Turner and Fons Trompenaars, "A World Turned Upside Down: Doing Business in Asia," in Pat Joynt and Malcolm Warner (eds.), *Managing across Cultures: Issues and Perspectives* (London: International Thomson Business Press, 1996), pp. 275–305.

You are riding in a car driven by a close friend. He hits a pedestrian. You know he was going at least 35 miles per hour in an area of the city where the maximum allowed speed is 20 miles per hour. There are no witnesses. His lawyer says that if you testify under oath that he was driving 20 miles per hour it may save him from serious consequences. What right has your friend to expect you to protect him?

(*a*) My friend has a definite right as a friend to expect me to testify to the lower figure.

(*b*) He has some right as a friend to expect me to testify to the lower figure.

(*c*) He has no right as a friend to expect me to testify to the lower figure.

With a high score indicating strong universalism (choice *c*) and a low score indicating strong particularism (choice *a*), here is how the different nations scored:

Universalism (no right)

Canada	96
United States	95
Germany	90
United Kingdom	90
Netherlands	88
France	68
Japan	67
Singapore	67
Thailand	63
Hong Kong	56

Particularism (some or definite right)

China	48
South Korea	26

As noted earlier, respondents from universalism cultures (*e.g.,* North America and Western Europe) felt that the rules applied regardless of the situation, while respondents from particularism cultures were much more willing to bend the rules and help their friend.

Based on these types of findings, Trompenaars recommends that when individuals from particularist cultures do business in a universalist culture, they should be prepared for rational, professional arguments and a "let's get down to business" attitude. Conversely, when individuals from universalist cultures do business in a particularist environment, they should be prepared for personal meandering or irrelevancies that seem to go nowhere and should not regard personal, get-to know-you attitudes as mere small talk.

Individualism vs. Communitarianism

Individualism and communitarianism are key dimensions in Hofstede's earlier research. Although Trompenaars derived these two relationships differently than Hofstede, they still have the same basic meaning, although in his more recent work Trompenaars has used the word "communitarianism" rather than "collectivism." For him, individualism refers to people regarding themselves as individuals, while **communitarianism** refers to people regarding themselves as part of a group. As shown in Figure 5–9, the United States, former Czechoslovakia, Argentina, the former Soviet Union (CIS), and Mexico have high individualism. These findings of Trompenaars are particularly interesting, because they differ somewhat from those of Hofstede, as reported in Figure 5–5. Although the definitions are not exactly the same, the fact that there are differences (e.g., Mexico and Argentina are collectivistic in Hofstede's findings but individualistic in Trompenaars' research) points out that cultural values may be changing (i.e., Hofstede's findings may be dated). For example, with Mexico now part of NAFTA and the global economy, this country may have moved from dominant collectivistic or communitarianistic cultural values to more individualist values. Trompenaars also found that the former communist countries of Czechoslovakia and the Soviet Union now appear to be quite individualistic, which of course is contrary to assumptions and conventional wisdom about the former communist bloc. In other words, Trompenaars points out the complex, dynamic nature of culture and the danger of overgeneralization.

In his most recent research, and again using the technique of presenting respondents with a dilemma and asking them to make a decision, Trompenaars posed the following situation. If you were to be promoted, which of the two following issues would you emphasize most: (a) the new group of people with whom you will be working; or (b) the greater responsibility of the work you are undertaking and the higher income you will be earning. The following reports the latest scores associated with the individualism of option b— greater responsibility and more money.[38]

Communitarianism
Refers to people regarding themselves as part of a group.

Individualism (emphasis on larger responsibilities and more income)

Canada	77
Thailand	71
United Kingdom	69
United States	67
Netherlands	64
France	61
Japan	61
China	54
Singapore	50
Hong Kong	47

Communitarianism (emphasis on the new group of people)

Malaysia	38
Korea	32

These findings are somewhat different from those presented in Figure 5–9 and show that cultural changes may be occurring more rapidly than many people realize. For example, the latest findings show Thailand very high on individualism (possibly indicating an increasing entrepreneurial spirit/cultural value) whereas the Thais were found to be low on individualism a few years before as shown in Figure 5–9. At the same time, it is important to remember that there are major differences between people in high individualism societies and those in high communitarianism societies. The former stress personal and individual matters; the latter value group-related issues. Negotiations in cultures with high individualism typically are made on the spot by a representative, people ideally achieve things alone, and they assume a great deal of personal responsibility. In cultures with high communitarianism, decisions typically are referred to committees, people ideally achieve things in groups, and they jointly assume responsibility.

Trompenaars recommends that when people from cultures with high individualism deal with those from communitarianism cultures, they should have patience for the time taken to consent and to consult, and they should aim to build lasting relationships. When people from cultures with high communitarianism deal with those from individualist cultures, they should be prepared to make quick decisions and commit their organization to these decisions. Also, communitarianistics dealing with individualists should realize that the reason they are dealing with only one negotiator (as opposed to a group) is that this person is respected by his or her organization and has its authority and esteem.

Neutral vs. Emotional

Neutral culture
A culture in which emotions are held in check.

Emotional culture
A culture in which emotions are expressed openly and naturally.

A **neutral culture** is one in which emotions are held in check. As seen in Figure 5–9, both Japan and the United Kingdom are high neutral cultures. People in these countries try not to show their feelings; they act stoically and maintain their composure. An **emotional culture** is one in which emotions are openly and naturally expressed. People in emotional cultures often smile a great deal, talk loudly when they are excited, and greet each other with a great deal of enthusiasm. Mexico, the Netherlands, and Switzerland are examples of high emotional cultures.

Trompenaars recommends that when individuals from emotional cultures do business in neutral cultures, they should put as much as they can on paper and submit it to the other side. They should realize that lack of emotion does not mean disinterest or boredom, but rather that people from neutral cultures do not like to show their hand. Conversely, when those from neutral cultures do business in emotional cultures, they should not be put off stride when the other side creates scenes or grows animated and boisterous, and they should try to respond warmly to the emotional affections of the other group.

Specific vs. Diffuse

A **specific culture** is one in which individuals have a large public space they readily let others enter and share and a small private space they guard closely and share with only close friends and associates. A **diffuse culture** is one in which both public and private space are similar in size and individuals guard their public space carefully, because entry into public space affords entry into private space as well. As shown in Figure 5–9, Austria, the United Kingdom, the United States, and Switzerland all are specific cultures, while Venezuela, China, and Spain are diffuse cultures. In specific cultures, people often are invited into a person's open, public space; individuals in these cultures often are open and extroverted; and there is a strong separation of work and private life. In diffuse cultures, people are not quickly invited into a person's open, public space, because once they are in, there is easy entry into the private space as well. Individuals in these cultures often appear to be indirect and introverted, and work and private life often are closely linked.

An example of these specific and diffuse cultural dimensions is provided by the United States and Germany. A U.S. professor, such as Robert Smith, Ph.D., generally would be called Dr. Smith by students when at his U.S. university. When shopping, however, he might be referred to by the store clerk as Bob, and he might even ask the clerk's advice regarding some of his intended purchases. When golfing, Bob might just be one of the guys, even to a golf partner who happens to be a graduate student in his department. The reason for these changes in status is that, with the specific U.S. cultural values, people have large public spaces and often conduct themselves differently depending on their public role. At the same time, however, Bob has private space that is off-limits to the students who must call him Doctor in class. In high diffuse cultures, on the other hand, a person's public and private life often are similar. Therefore, in Germany, Herr Professor Doktor Schmidt would be referred to this way at the university, local market, and bowling alley—and even his wife might address him formally in public. A great deal of formality is maintained, often giving the impression that Germans are stuffy or aloof.

Trompenaars recommends that when those from specific cultures do business in diffuse cultures, they should respect a person's title, age, and background connections, and they should not get impatient when people are being indirect or circuitous. Conversely, when individuals from diffuse cultures do business in specific cultures, they should try to get to the point and be efficient, learn to structure meetings with the judicious use of agendas, and not use their titles or acknowledge achievements or skills that are irrelevant to the issues being discussed.

Achievement vs. Ascription

An **achievement culture** is one in which people are accorded status based on how well they perform their functions. An **ascription culture** is one in which status is attributed based on who or what a person is. Achievement cultures give high status to high achievers, such as the company's number one salesperson or the medical researcher who has found a cure for a rare form of bone cancer. Ascription cultures accord status based on age, gender, or social connections. For example, in an ascription culture, a person who has been with the company for 40 years may be listened to carefully because of the respect that others have for the individual's age and longevity with the firm, and an individual who has friends in high places may be afforded status because of whom she knows. As shown in Figure 5–9, Austria, the United States, Switzerland, and the United Kingdom are achievement cultures, while Venezuela, Indonesia, and China are ascription cultures.

Trompenaars recommends that when individuals from achievement cultures do business in ascription cultures, they should make sure that their group has older, senior, and formal position-holders who can impress the other side, and they should respect the status and influence of their counterparts in the other group. Conversely, he recommends that when individuals from ascription cultures do business in achievement cultures, they should make

Specific culture
A culture in which individuals have a large public space they readily share with others and a small private space they guard closely and share with only close friends and associates.

Diffuse culture
A culture in which both public and private space are similar in size and individuals guard their public space carefully, because entry into public space affords entry into private space as well.

Achievement culture
A culture in which people are accorded status based on how well they perform their functions.

Ascription culture
A culture in which status is attributed based on who or what a person is.

sure that their group has sufficient data, technical advisers, and knowledgeable people to convince the other that they are proficient, and they should respect the knowledge and information of their counterparts on the other team.

Time

Aside from the five relationship orientations, another major cultural difference is the way in which people deal with the concept of time. Trompenaars has identified two different approaches: sequential and synchronous. In cultures where sequential approaches are prevalent, people tend to do only one activity at a time, keep appointments strictly, and show a strong preference for following plans as they are laid out and not deviating from them. In cultures where synchronous approaches are common, people tend to do more than one activity at a time, appointments are approximate and may be changed at a moment's notice, and schedules generally are subordinate to relationships. People in synchronous-time cultures often will stop what they are doing to meet and greet individuals coming into their office.

A good contrast is provided by the United States, Mexico, and France. In the United States, people tend to be guided by sequential-time orientation and thus set a schedule and stick to it. Mexicans operate under more of a synchronous-time orientation and thus tend to be much more flexible, often building slack into their schedules to allow for interruptions. The French are similar to the Mexicans and, when making plans, often determine the objectives they want to accomplish but leave open the timing and other factors that are beyond their control; this way, they can adjust and modify their approach as they go along. As Trompenaars noted, "For the French and Mexicans, what was important was that they get to the end, not the particular path or sequence by which that end was reached."[39]

Another interesting time-related contrast is the degree to which cultures are past- or present-oriented as opposed to future-oriented. In countries such as the United States, Italy, and Germany, the future is more important than the past or the present. In countries such as Venezuela, Indonesia, and Spain, the present is most important. In France and Belgium, all three time periods are of approximately equal importance. Because different emphases are given to different time periods, adjusting to these cultural differences can create challenges.

Trompenaars recommends that when doing business with future-oriented cultures, effective international managers should emphasize the opportunities and limitless scope that any agreement can have, agree to specific deadlines for getting things done, and be aware of the core competence or continuity that the other party intends to carry with it into the future. When doing business with past- or present-oriented cultures, he recommends that managers emphasize the history and tradition of the culture, find out whether internal relationships will sanction the types of changes that need to be made, and agree to future meetings in principle but fix no deadlines for completions.

The Environment

Trompenaars also examined the ways in which people deal with their environment. Specific attention should be given to whether they believe in controlling outcomes (inner-directed) or letting things take their own course (outer-directed). One of the things he asked managers to do was choose between the following statements:

1. What happens to me is my own doing.
2. Sometimes I feel that I do not have enough control over the directions my life is taking.

Managers who believe in controlling their own environment would opt for the first choice; those who believe that they are controlled by their environment and cannot do much about it would opt for the second. Here is an example by country of the sample respondents who believe that what happens to them is their own doing:[40]

United States	89%
Switzerland	84%
Australia	81%

Belgium	76%
Indonesia	73%
Hong Kong	69%
Greece	63%
Singapore	58%
Japan	56%
China	35%

In the United States, managers feel strongly that they are masters of their own fate. This helps to account for their dominant attitude (sometimes bordering on aggressiveness) toward the environment and discomfort when things seem to get out of control. Many Asian cultures do not share these views. They believe that things move in waves or natural shifts and one must "go with the flow," so a flexible attitude, characterized by a willingness to compromise and maintain harmony with nature, is important.

Trompenaars recommends that when dealing with those from cultures that believe in dominating the environment, it is important to play hard ball, test the resilience of the opponent, win some objectives, and always lose from time to time. When dealing with those from cultures that believe in letting things take their natural course, it is important to be persistent and polite, maintain good relationships with the other party, and try to win together and lose apart.

Cultural Patterns or Clusters

Like Hofstede's and the earlier work of Ronen and Shenkar, Trompenaars' research lends itself to cultural patterns or clusters. Table 5–5 relates his findings to the five relational orientations, categorized into the same types of clusters that Ronen and Shenkar used (see Figure 5–5). There is a great deal of similarity between the Trompenaars and the Ronen and Shenkar clusters. Both the United States and United Kingdom profiles are the same, except for the neutral (U.K.) and emotional (U.S.) dimension. So are those in most of the Asian countries, including Japan, which was left out of the Ronen and Shenkar clusters and labeled an independent. Brazil, which also was left out of the Ronen and Shenkar clusters, continues to be sufficiently different from other members of the Latin American group in the Trompenaars-derived Table 5–5. In other words, Brazil still appears to be independent. Additionally, while France and Belgium, in the Latin European Trompenaars group, have identical profiles, Spain is significantly different from both of them as well as from Italy. This shows that earlier cluster groups, such as that of Ronen and Shenkar, may need to be revised in light of more recent data.

Overall, Table 5–5 shows that a case can be made for cultural similarities between clusters of countries. With only small differences, Trompenaars' research helps to support, and more importantly, to extend, the work of Hofstede as well as Ronen and Shenkar. Such research provides a useful point of departure for recognizing cultural differences, and it provides guidelines for doing business effectively around the world.

The World of *Business Week*—Revisited

The article that opened this chapter illustrated how important it is for the chic clothes retailer Zara to understand the culture of the countries where it does business. For example, because of the trend in the U.S. toward casualwear, the company sells attire such as T-shirts and khakis. The company caters also heavily to customers in their 20s and this includes young business women, so there is more to their line than casualwear. Based on your reading of the article and Hofstede's and Trompenaars' work on cultural dimensions, answer the following questions: (1) In what way could an understanding of American values be useful to the company? (2) How might individualism play a role in the types of clothes that Americans buy? (3) If a particular style of clothing sold well in the U.K., would it also be popular in the U.S.?

Table 5–5
Cultural Groups Based on Trompenaars' Research

Anglo cluster

Relationship	United States	United Kingdom
Individualism	X	X
Communitarianism		
Specific relationship	X	X
Diffuse relationship		
Universalism	X	X
Particularism		
Neutral relationship		X
Emotional relationship	X	
Achievement	X	X
Ascription		

Asian cluster

Relationship	Japan	China	Indonesia	Hong Kong	Singapore
Individualism					
Communitarianism	X	X	X	X	X
Specific relationship					
Diffuse relationship	X	X	X	X	X
Universalism					
Particularism	X	X	X	X	X
Neutral relationship	X		X	X	X
Emotional relationship		X			
Achievement					
Ascription	X	X	X	X	X

Latin American cluster

Relationship	Argentina	Mexico	Venezuela	Brazil
Individualism	X	X		X
Communitarianism			X	
Specific relationship				X
Diffuse relationship	X	X	X	
Universalism				X
Particularism	X	X	X	
Neutral relationship	X	X	X	
Emotional relationship				X
Achievement	X	X		
Ascription			X	X

Latin European cluster

Relationship	France	Belgium	Spain	Italy
Individualism			X	
Communitarianism	X	X		X
Specific relationship	X	X		
Diffuse relationship			X	X
Universalism	X	X		X
Particularism			X	
Neutral relationship			X	
Emotional relationship	X	X		X
Achievement			X	
Ascription	X	X		X

Table 5–5 *(continued)*
Cultural Groups Based on Trompenaars' Research

	Germanic cluster			
Relationship	**Austria**	**Germany**	**Switzerland**	**Czechoslovakia**
Individualism	X			
Communitarianism		X	X	X
Specific relationship	X		X	X
Diffuse relationship		X		
Universalism	X	X	X	X
Particularism				
Neutral relationship	X			X
Emotional relationship		X	X	
Achievement	X	X		X
Ascription			X	

Source: Adapted from information in Fons Trompenaars, *Riding the Waves of Culture* (New York: Irwin, 1994).

Summary of Key Points

1. Culture is acquired knowledge that people use to interpret experience and generate social behavior. Culture also has the characteristics of being learned, shared, transgenerational, symbolic, patterned, and adaptive. There are many dimensions of cultural diversity, including centralized vs. decentralized decision making, safety vs. risk, individual vs. group rewards, informal vs. formal procedures, high vs. low organizational loyalty, cooperation vs. competition, short-term vs. long-term horizons, and stability vs. innovation.

2. Values are basic convictions that people have regarding what is right and wrong, good and bad, important and unimportant. Research shows that there are both differences and similarities between the work values and managerial values of different cultural groups. Work values often reflect culture and industrialization, and managerial values are highly related to success. Research shows that values tend to change over time and often reflect age and experience.

3. Hofstede has identified and researched four major dimensions of culture: power distance, uncertainty avoidance, individualism, and masculinity. Each will affect a country's political and social system. The integration of these factors into two-dimensional figures can illustrate the complexity of culture's effect on behavior.

4. In recent years, researchers have attempted to cluster countries into similar cultural groupings to study similarities and differences. Through use of smallest space analysis, they have constructed two-dimensional maps that illustrate the similarities in work values and attitudes between countries. These syntheses, one of which is provided in Figure 5–8, help us to understand intercultural similarities.

5. Recent research by Trompenaars has examined five relationship orientations: universalism-particularism, individualism-communitarianism, affective-neutral, specific-diffuse and achievement-ascription. Trompenaars also looked at attitudes toward time and the environment. The result is a wealth of information helping to explain how cultures differ as well as practical ways in which MNCs can do business effectively in these environments. In particular, his findings update those of Hofstede while at the same time help to support the previous work by both Hofstede and Ronen and Shenkar on clustering countries.

Key Terms

achievement culture, *129*

ascription culture, *129*

collectivism, *117*

communitarianism, *127*

culture, *108*

diffuse culture, *129*

emotional culture, *128*

femininity, *118*

individualism, *117*

masculinity, *117*

neutral culture, *128*

particularism, *125*

power distance, *116*

smallest space analysis (SSA), *123*

specific culture, *129*

uncertainty avoidance, *117*

universalism, *125*

values, *112*

Review and Discussion Questions

1. What is meant by the term "culture"? In what way can measuring attitudes about the following help to differentiate between cultures: centralized or decentralized decision making, safety or risk, individual or group rewards, high or low organizational loyalty, cooperation or competition? Use these attitudes to compare the United States, Germany, and Japan. Based on your comparisons, what conclusions can you draw regarding the impact of culture on behavior?

2. What is meant by the term "value"? Are cultural values the same worldwide, or are there marked differences? Are these values changing over time, or are they fairly constant? How does your answer relate to the role of values in a culture?

3. What are the four dimensions of culture studied by Geert Hofstede? Identify and describe each. What is the cultural profile of the United States? Of Asian countries? Of Latin American countries? Of Latin European countries? Based on your comparisons of these four profiles, what conclusions can you draw regarding cultural challenges facing individuals in one group when they interact with individuals in one of the other groups?

4. Of what value is Figure 5–8 on country clusters to the study of international management? Offer at least three advantages or benefits of the figure.

5. As people engage in more international travel and become more familiar with other countries, will cultural differences decline as a roadblock to international understanding, or will they continue to be a major barrier? Defend your answer.

6. What are the characteristics of each of the following pairs of cultural characteristics derived from Trompenaars' research: universalism vs. particularism, neutral vs. emotional, specific vs. diffuse, achievement vs. ascription? Compare and contrast each pair.

7. In what way is time a cultural factor? In what way is the need to control the environment a cultural factor? Give an example for each.

Internet Exercise: BMW Goes National and International

BMW is an internationally known auto firm. However, in recent years the company has been finding that its success in Europe does not necessarily translate into the American market, the largest, richest target for overseas sales. Visit the BMW site at **www.bmw.com** and look at what the big automaker is doing in both Europe and the United States. Compare and contrast both the similarities and the differences in these markets. Then answer these three questions: (1) How do you think cultural differences affect the way the firm operates in Europe vis-à-vis the United States? (2) In what way is culture a factor in auto sales? (3) Is it possible for a car company to transcend national culture and produce a global automobile that is accepted by people in every culture? Why or why not?

Taiwan

Taiwan is an island located 100 miles off the southeast coast of the China mainland. Taiwan is only 13,900 square miles, and with a population of approximately 23 million, it has one of the highest population densities in the world. In 1949, the communists under Mao Zedong defeated the Nationalists under Chiang Kai-shek and the latter government moved to Taiwan where it established dominance. The People's Republic of China still considers Taiwan to be a breakaway province.

The government of Taiwan was totally controlled by the Nationalists until 1996 when the first democratic election was held. In 2000 the Democratic Progressive party candidate, Chen Shui-bian, was elected president for a four-year term, although the Nationalist party continued to hold over 50 percent of the seats in the country's parliament, the Legislative Yuan.

The country's gross domestic product is approximately $375 billion and per capita GDP is around $16,500. In the late 1990s many Asian economies slowed down sharply, caught in a vicious economic crisis. Japan, South Korea, Indonesia, Thailand, and Malaysia all saw their GDP growth decline, and some of them, especially Japan, are still running budget deficits as high as 10 percent of GDP. Taiwan, on the other hand, had steady GDP growth in the range of 6 percent throughout this period. In particular, the country's economy has been managed carefully through a combination of tight exchange controls, low foreign debt, conservative fiscal policies, and relatively austere and transparent banking.

Taiwan is one of the 15 largest trading powers in the world, and one of the strongest sectors of its economy is information technology. The value of computer-related products produced in Taiwan is over $30 billion annually. Taiwanese manufacturers build two-thirds of the motherboards and keyboards sold worldwide, in addition to 60 percent of the monitors, and almost 40 percent of the notebook PCs. A number of major high-tech firms have set up operations on the island, including Sun Microsystems, Microsoft, and Intel. All three realized that costs here are lower than in most other places and the quality of the workforce would allow them to produce state-of-the-art products. Other firms, including locally based manufacturers, also followed this strategy. As a result, by the mid-1990s Taiwan had leapfrogged South Korea in the production of PCs. Some of this success was a result of Taiwanese firms entering into a series of private-label contracts with U.S. importers.

By the late 1990s Taiwan-based chipmakers were investing billions of dollars annually in semiconductor fabrication plants. By 2001 annual investment in research, development, and new capacity was in excess of $15 billion. The world is so dependent on Taiwan for computer-related equipment that when a devastating earthquake hit the island in September 1999, the global informational technology (IT) market shuddered and the price of PC chips immediately rose sharply. Although the IT companies emerged relatively unscathed, the incident served to underscore the importance of Taiwan's semiconductor, electronic components, and PC industry. During the first decade of the millennium Taiwan's importance in these areas is likely to grow.

www.asiapages.com

Questions

1. What are some current issues facing Taiwan? What is the climate for doing business in Taiwan today?

2. In terms of cultural dimensions, is Taiwan much different from the United States? (Use Figure 5–8 in your answer.) Why or why not?

3. In what way might culture be a stumbling block for firms seeking to set up businesses in Taiwan?

4. How are the three high-tech firms in this case managing to sidestep or overcome cultural barriers?

A Jumping-Off Place

A successful, medium-sized U.S. manufacturing firm in Ohio has decided to open a plant near Madrid, Spain. The company was attracted to this location for three reasons. First, the firm's current licensing agreement with a German firm is scheduled to come to an end within 6 months, and the U.S. manufacturer feels that it can do a better job of building and selling heavy machinery in the EU than the German firm. Second, the U.S. manufacturer has invested almost $300 million in R&D over the last three years. The result is a host of new patents and other technological breakthroughs that now make this company a worldwide leader in the production of specialized heavy equipment. Third, labor costs in Spain are lower than in most other EU countries, and the company feels that this will prove extremely helpful in its efforts to capture market share in Greater Europe.

Because this is the manufacturer's first direct venture into the EU, it has decided to take on a Spanish partner. The latter will provide much of the on-site support, such as local contracts, personnel hiring, legal assistance, and governmental negotiations. In turn, the U.S. manufacturer will provide the capital for renovating the manufacturing plant, the R&D technology, and the technical training.

If the venture works out as planned, the partners will expand operations into Italy and use this location as a jumping-off point for tapping the Central and Eastern European markets. Additionally, because the cultures of Spain and Italy are similar, the U.S. manufacturer feels that staying within the Latin European cultural cluster can be synergistic. Plans for later in the decade call for establishing operations in northern France, which will serve as a jumping-off point for both Northern Europe and other major EU countries, such as Germany, the Netherlands, and Belgium. However, the company first wants to establish a foothold in Spain and get this operation working successfully; then it will look into expansion plans.

Questions

1. In what way will the culture of Spain be different from that of the United States? In answering this question, refer to Figures 5–5, 5–6, 5–7, and 5–8.

2. If the company expands operations into Italy, will its experience in Spain be valuable, or will the culture be so different that the manufacturer will have to begin anew in determining how to address cultural challenges and opportunities? Explain.

3. If the firm expands into France, will its previous experiences in Spain and Italy be valuable in helping the company address cultural challenges? Be complete in your answer.

Chapter 6

Managing across Cultures

Objectives of the Chapter

Traditionally, both scholars and practitioners have assumed the universality of management. There was a tendency to take those management concepts and techniques that worked at home into other countries and cultures. It is now clear, both from practice and cross-cultural research, that this universality assumption of management, at least across cultures, does not hold up. Although there is a tendency in a borderless economy and with global integration strategies of MNCs to promote a universalist approach, there is enough evidence from cross-cultural researchers such as Nancy Adler and others to conclude that the universalist assumption that may have held for U.S. organizations and employees is not generally true in other cultures.[1]

The overriding purpose of this chapter is to examine how MNCs can and should manage across cultures. This chapter puts into practice the previous Chapter 5 on the meaning and dimensions of culture and serves as a foundation and point of departure for subsequent Chapters 9 and 10 on strategic management. The first part addresses the traditional tendency to attempt to replicate successful home country operations overseas without addressing cultural differences. Next, attention is given to cross-cultural challenges, focusing on how differences can impact on multinational management strategies. Finally, the cultures in specific countries and geographic regions are examined. The specific objectives of this chapter are:

1. **EXAMINE** the impact of globalization and national responsiveness on international strategic management.

2. **DISCUSS** cross-cultural differences and similarities.

3. **REVIEW** cultural differences in select countries and regions, and note some of the important strategic guidelines for doing business in each.

BusinessWeek

World of *Business Week*

India 3.0

These days when Vivek Paul heads to work, he often wears a blue denim shirt with the letters "FF" stitched to the pocket. The letters stand for Fast Forward. And they neatly sum up Paul's ambitions for Wipro Technologies, the Bangalore-based company of which he is president. Wipro over the past half-century has transformed itself from a vegetable and edible-oils trader into India's largest listed software services company. Today, Wipro routinely wins multimillion-dollar contracts from the likes of General Electric, Home Depot, and Nokia.

Now, Paul is thinking bigger. Much bigger. His goal: to change Wipro from a provider of unglamorous, back-office code-writing into a $4 billion multinational that offers end-to-end software solutions. The idea is to take on IBM Global Consulting, Accenture, and Electronic Data Service, the leviathans of the industry. "We want to be a tech powerhouse," says Paul, a former GE executive who has been Wipro vice-chairman and president since July of 1999. By 2004, Paul wants Wipro to rank among the top 10 IT service companies on the planet. Even he concedes that "it's a completely audacious goal."

That it is. But Paul is not some lonely maverick. Like Wipro, other leading Indian companies such as Infosys Technologies, Tata Consultancy Services (TCS), and Satayam Computer are no longer content to dominate the anonymous but low-risk business of writing code on contract. All are pushing upstream into more lucrative full-service consulting. Not only that, restless young Indians are leaving secure jobs at Indian companies to create original software for Western markets.

Scaling the value chain is a matter of survival. While the likes of Wipro and Infosys continue to report triple-digit profit increases, they are facing increasing competition from such low-cost Asian nations as China, the Philippines, and Vietnam. While a Bangalore programmer earns just $800 a month, salaries are rising 15% a year.

Squeeze

At the same time, such Western consulting firms as PricewaterhouseCoopers (PWC) and Accenture, formerly Andersen Consulting, are entering the low-margin coding business. In the past two years, both companies have opened Asian software centers, in Calcutta and Manila, respectively. The Indians, says Ravi Trivedy, head of IT strategy for PWC in India, "are getting squeezed on all sides." So before the vise tightens, Bangalore's best are attempting to break out beyond their core services business.

Yet much of the new work is project-based. What Indian companies now want are wider-ranging long-term contracts that encompass a client's entire IT needs. This means consulting on IT strategy as well as designing and implementing it. For the likes of Wipro and Infosys, the ultimate money-spinner is what the industry calls "business process consulting." That involves advising clients how to adjust their management and work flow to mesh effectively with their technical systems.

The Western giants already provide a plethora of such services to a roster of blue-chip clients. To catch up, the Indians must bring in outside marketing, management, and top-drawer consulting expertise. Doing so means Bangalore's executives will have to transform their insular companies into true multinationals. That perhaps is the biggest challenge—learning to run a far-flung enterprise that includes everyone from Indian engineers to American marketers to Vietnamese code-jockeys. PWC's Trivedy reckons "all that stuff is out of their reach."

Perhaps, but U.S. and European firms are according the Indians growing respect. If the leading IT companies of Bangalore and Bombay can transform themselves into all-round IT-solutions providers, they might challenge IBM, PWC, and Sapient. Moreover, with corporate layoffs again the fashion in the U.S., a more powerful Indian software industry could become a growing threat to American white-collar workers—or even a new source of employment for those workers.

Big Steps

Already, companies such as Wipro and Infosys are plotting strategy. For his part, Wipro's Paul divides the process into three steps. Step one is building what he calls industry "verticals"—groups that combine the talents of engineers and business process consultants. Wipro now has 1,200 staff specializing in finance and insurance. But so far it has hired only 60 or so business process consultants, most of them in

India. Step two is recruiting such people. Paul figures Wipro needs to add 30,000 employees over the next three years.

Step three: the acquisitions required to grow into a globally competitive enterprise. Both Infosys and Wipro have cast an acquisitive eye on U.S. e-commerce consulting firms, but neither has moved because, despite falling stock markets, many of these companies remain expensive. Paul knows he can't wait forever. "With acquisitions we can move faster," he says. "To do it organically will take time."

While Indian companies continue to chase big multinationals, they also are targeting midsize businesses. One is EveryD.com, a new online community for Japanese housewives that provides everything from shopping to banking. EveryD paid Infosys $9 million to set it all up—from devising the business plan to designing the portal to writing the software it runs on.

Moving Abroad

To get close to customers, Indian executives are shifting overseas. One is Rajesh Hukku, the 42-year-old chairman of Bombay-based i-Flex Solutions, a financial-services software maker. In 1997, Hukku moved to Parsippany, N.J. He regularly goes on sales calls, seals deals, and pushes his product at industry forums. To bring a more global complexion to the company, Hukku has been hiring managers from London to Buenos Aires, and has posted about a quarter of his 1,450 employees to four continents.

A year ago, when Pradeep Singh formed Talisma Corp., a customer-relations-management software maker, he based it in Seattle, where he could get U.S. salespeople to push his made-in-India product. The global approach seems to be working. Talisma has 19 offices in 7 countries serving such clients as GE, Citibank, and EMI Records. The latter purchased Talisma software that lets the London-based company communicate with artists' fans and boost its customer database. "We like its sophistication and simplicity," says Fergal Gara, EMI's director of new media. "We think it's going to give us a good payback."

To succeed in their breakout bid, the Indians will have to overcome their conservatism. Entering the product business means being willing to lose money in the short term. "That's anathema to Indian investors," says the managing director for a major Western securities house in Bombay. Moreover, companies that aspire to enter the high-end consulting business will need to part with cash to acquire U.S. or European companies—another challenge for cautious Indian managers. "They study an acquisition to death," the analyst says.

But Indians realize they must change. Aware of the pain that mighty companies like Daimler have encountered on taking over U.S. companies, Wipro's Paul says he's been reluctant to take the plunge. But he knows he must. "We're not going to be a $4 billion company doing the work we're doing today," he says. So he's preparing to start making deals. "Luck favors the brave," he says. As India's software companies try to climb the world's IT ladder, they'll need all the bravery they can muster.

By Bruce Einhorn and Manjeet Kripalani in Bangalore,
with Pete Engardio in New York.

Source: Reprinted from February 26, 2001, pp. 44–46 of *Business Week* by special permission, copyright © 2001 by the McGraw-Hill Companies, Inc.

The news story that opens this chapter highlights the importance of being able to manage across cultures. Wipro Technologies is doing well in India. If the company is going to meet its goal of becoming a $4-billion multinational that offers end-to-end software solutions, however, it will need an international presence. In particular, Wipro is going to have to locate near its major customers which means, among other things, setting up operations in the U.S. and the EU. The firm is also going to have to hire more engineers and business process consultants worldwide, as well as make some acquisitions of e-business consulting firms outside of India. In short, Wipro is going to have to expand rapidly over the next three years. At present the company's strategy is too conservative and limited. The firm needs to develop a much greater international focus. If it cannot do this, Wipro will be unable to challenge the likes of IBM Global and EDS. In doing so, the company will have to be able to effectively manage across cultures, a challenge that it and most other MNCs will have to meet in the coming years.

■ The Strategy for Managing across Cultures

As MNCs become more transnational, their strategies must address the cultural similarities and differences in their varied markets.[2] A good example is provided by Renault, the French auto giant. For years Renault manufactured a narrow product line which it sold primarily in France. Because of this limited geographic market and the fact that its cars continued to have quality-related problems, the company's performance was at best mediocre. Several years ago, however, Renault made a number of strategic decisions that dramatically changed the way it did business. Among other things, it bought controlling stakes in Nissan Motor of Japan, Samsung of South Korea, and Dacia, the Romanian automaker. The company also built a $1 billion factory in Brazil to produce its successful Megane sedan and acquired an idle factory near Moscow to manufacture Renaults for the eastern European market.

Today, Renault is a multinational automaker with operations on four continents. The challenge the company now faces is to make all of these operations profitable. This will not be easy. Nissan's annual losses have been running in triple-digit millions in recent years and Samsung has to be brought back from bankruptcy. Meanwhile Dacia is operating in one of Europe's most dismal economies. Fortunately, Renault is grossing over $40 billion annually from its own businesses, so it has the necessary funds to implement turnaround strategies for these acquisitions. Now it needs to straighten out its international operations and get everything working in harmony.[3] One of the recent steps it has taken to do this is the decision to meld its own sales organizations with those of Nissan in Europe, thus creating one well-integrated, efficient sales force on the Continent. Another step has been to start producing Nissan models in the Brazilian plant so that it can expand its South American offerings by more efficiently using current facilities. One of the company's long-run goals is by 2010 to have 10 common platforms, or underbodies, that will allow it to build Renaults and Nissans everywhere, while maintaining the look, feel, and identity of their separate brands.[4] At the same time the firm is working to improve its effectiveness in dealing with governments, unions, and employees, as well as to understand the cultural differences in customer preferences in Europe, Asia, and the Americas.

This Renault example helps to illustrate one of the major problems facing MNCs as they attempt to manage across cultures: a natural tendency to do things abroad the way they are done at home. This commonly is referred to in strategic international management as the "globalization vs. national responsiveness conflict." As used here, **globalization** is the production and distribution of products and services of a homogeneous type and quality on a worldwide basis. To a growing extent, the customers of MNCs have homogenized tastes, and this has helped to spread international consumerism. For example, throughout North America, the EU, and Japan, there has been a growing acceptance of standardized, yet increasingly personally customized goods such as automobiles and computers. This goal of efficient economic performance through a globalization and mass customization strategy, however, has left MNCs open to the charge that they are overlooking the need to address national responsiveness through Internet and intranet technology.

National responsiveness is the need to understand the different consumer tastes in segmented regional markets and respond to different national standards and regulations imposed by autonomous governments and agencies. For example, in designing and building cars, international manufacturers now carefully tailor their offerings in the American market. Toyota's "full size" T100 pickup proved much too small to attract U.S. buyers. So

Globalization
The production and distribution of products and services of a homogeneous type and quality on a worldwide basis.

National responsiveness
The need to understand the different consumer tastes in segmented regional markets and respond to different national standards and regulations imposed by autonomous governments and agencies.

the firm went back to the drawing board and created a full-size Tundra pickup that is powered by a V-8 engine and has a cabin designed to "accommodate a passenger wearing a 10-gallon cowboy hat." Honda has developed its new Model X SUV with more Americanized features including enough interior room so that travelers can eat and sleep in the vehicle. Mitsubishi has abandoned its idea of making a global vehicle and has brought out its new Montero Sport sport-utility vehicle in the U.S. market with the features it learned that Americans want: more horsepower, more interior room, more comfort. Meanwhile, Nissan is doing what many foreign carmakers would have thought to be unthinkable just a few years ago. Today, U.S. engineers and product designers are now completely responsible for the development of most Nissan vehicles sold in North America. Among other things, they are asking children between the ages of eight and 15, in focus-group sessions, for ideas on storage, cup holders, and other refinements that would make a full-size minivan more attractive to them.[5]

National responsiveness also relates to the need to adapt tools and techniques for managing the local workforce. Sometimes what works well in one country does not work in another, as seen by the following example:

> An American computer company introduced pay-for-performance in both the USA and the Middle East. It worked well in the USA and increased sales briefly in the Middle East before a serious slump occurred. Inquiries showed that indeed the winners among salesmen in the Middle East had done better, but the vast majority had done worse. The wish for their fellows to succeed had been seriously eroded by the contest. Overall morale and sales were down. Ill-will was contagious. When the bosses discovered that certain sales people were earning more than they did, high individual performances also ceased. But the principal reason for eventually abandoning the system was the discovery that customers were being loaded up with products they could not sell. As A tried to beat B to the bonus, the care of customers began to slip, with serious, if delayed, results.[6]

Globalization vs. National Responsiveness Matrix

The issue of globalization vs. national responsiveness can be analyzed conceptually via a two-dimensional matrix. Figure 6–1 provides an example.

The vertical axis in the figure measures the need for economic integration, frequently referred to as globalization. Movement up the axis results in a greater degree of economic integration. Globalization generates economies of scale (takes advantage of large size) and also capital on further lower unit costs (through experience curve benefits) as a firm moves into worldwide markets selling its products or services. These economies are captured through centralizing specific activities in the value-added chain. They also occur by reaping the benefits of increased coordination and control of geographically dispersed activities.

The horizontal axis measures the need for multinationals to respond to national responsiveness or differentiation. This suggests that MNCs must address local tastes and government regulations. The result may be a geographic dispersion of activities or a decentralization of coordination and control for individual MNCs.

Figure 6–1 depicts four basic situations in relation to the degrees of globalization vs. national responsiveness. Quadrants 1 and 4 are the simplest cases. In quadrant 1, the need for integration is high and for awareness of differentiation low. In terms of economies of scale, this situation leads to globalization strategies based on price competition. In this quadrant 1-type of environment, mergers and acquisitions often occur. The opposite situation is represented by quadrant 4, where the need for differentiation is high but the concern for integration low. Besides the term "national responsiveness," this quadrant is also referred to as "multi-domestic" strategies. In this case, niche companies adapt products to satisfy the high demands of differentiation and ignore economies of scale because integration is not very important.

Quadrants 2 and 3 reflect more complex environmental situations. Quadrant 2 incorporates those cases in which both the need for integration and awareness of differentiation

National responsiveness (differentiation)

Source: Adapted from information in Christopher A. Bartlett and Sumantra Ghoshal, *Managing across Borders: The Transnational Solution,* 2nd ed. (Boston: Harvard Business School Press, 1998).

are low. Both the potential to obtain economies of scale and the benefits of being sensitive to differentiation are of little value. Typical strategies in quadrant 2 are characterized by increased international standardization of products and services. This mixed approach is often referred to as just international strategies. This situation can lead to lower needs for centralized quality control and centralized strategic decision making, while simultaneously eliminating requirements to adapt activities to individual countries.

In quadrant 3, the needs for integration and differentiation are high. There is a strong need for integration in production along with higher requirements for regional differentiation in marketing. MNCs trying to simultaneously achieve these objectives often refer to them as their transnational strategies. Quadrant 3 is the most challenging quadrant and one where successful MNCs seek to operate. The problem for many MNCs, however, is the cultural challenges associated with "localizing" a global focus.

Meeting the Challenge

Research reveals that far from addressing regional differentiation issues, many MNCs are committed to a **globalization imperative,** which is a belief that one worldwide approach to doing business is the key to both efficiency and effectiveness. One study, involving extensive examination of 115 medium and large MNCs and 103 affiliated subsidiaries in the United States, Canada, France, Germany, Japan, and the United Kingdom, found an overwhelming preponderance to use the same strategies abroad as at home.[7]

Despite these tendencies to use home strategies, effective MNCs are continuing their efforts to address local needs. A number of factors are helping to facilitate this need to develop unique strategies for different cultures, including:

1. The diversity of worldwide industry standards such as those in broadcasting, where television sets must be manufactured on a country-by-country basis.

Globalization imperative
A belief that one worldwide approach to doing business is the key to both efficiency and effectiveness.

2. A continual demand by local customers for differentiated products, as in the case of consumer goods that must meet local tastes.

3. The importance of being an insider, as in the case of customers who prefer to "buy local."

4. The difficulty of managing global organizations, as in the case of some local subsidiaries that want more decentralization and others that want less.

5. The need to allow subsidiaries to use their own abilities and talents and not be restrained by headquarters, as in the case of local units that know how to customize products for their market and generate high returns on investment with limited production output.

By responding to the cultural needs of local operations and customers, MNCs find that regional strategies can be used effectively in capturing and maintaining worldwide market niches. One of the best examples is Warner-Lambert, which has manufacturing facilities in Belgium, France, Germany, Italy, Ireland, Spain, and the United Kingdom. Each plant is specialized and produces a small number of products for the entire European market; in this way, each can focus on tailoring products for the unique demands of the various markets.

The globalization vs. national responsiveness challenge is even more acute when marketing cosmetics and other products that vary greatly in consumer use. For example, marketers sell toothpaste as a cosmetic product in Spain and Greece but as a cavity-fighter in the Netherlands and United States. Soap manufacturers market their product as a cosmetic item in Spain but as a functional commodity in Germany. Moreover, the way in which the marketing message is delivered also is important. For example:

- Germans want advertising that is factual and rational; they fear being manipulated by "the hidden persuader." The typical German spot features the standard family of two parents, two children, and grandmother.

- The French avoid reasoning or logic. Their advertising is predominantly emotional, dramatic, and symbolic. Spots are viewed as cultural events—art for the sake of money—and are reviewed as if they were literature or films.

- The British value laughter above all else. The typical broad, self-deprecating British commercial amuses by mocking both the advertiser and consumer.[8]

Meanwhile, in China McDonald's has worked hard to befriend young children and make them feel special. One way is by recording their names and birthdates in a special list called "The Book of Little Honorary Guests," and then sending them cards and urging them to drop by their local McDonald's.

> The burger joints are all run by locals. And far from accepting the same McDonald's that Americans do, Asian consumers gradually twist McDonald's to their own purposes. Rather than being fast, efficient take-out joints, many McDonald's restaurants are more akin to Seattle coffee houses—places to hang out for the young. In several places, McDonald's has gone so native that many of its customers do not realize it is American. In China, one of its appeals is the fact that its menu is so limited; there is no danger of losing face because the table next door orders a more expensive dish. As [one observer] concludes, people come for the experience, not the product; and they make sure that it is their experience—not one foisted upon them by an American juggernaut.[9]

In some cases, however, both the product and the marketing message are similar worldwide. This is particularly true for high-end products, where the lifestyles and expectations of the market niche are similar regardless of the country. Heineken beer, Hennessey brandy, Porsche cars, and the *Financial Times* all appeal to consumer niches that are fairly homogeneous, regardless of geographic locale. The same is true at the lower end of the market for goods that are impulse purchases, novel products, or fast foods, such as Coca-Cola's soft drinks, Levi's jeans, pop music, and ice-cream bars. In most cases, however, it is necessary to modify products as well as the market approach for the regional or local market. One analysis noted that the more marketers understand about the way in which a

---

International Management in Action

Ten Key Factors for MNC Success

Why are some international firms successful while others are not? Some of the main reasons are that successful multinational firms take a worldwide view of operations, support their overseas activities, pay close attention to political winds, and use local nationals whenever possible. These are the overall findings of a report that looked into the development of customized executive education programs. Specifically, there are 10 factors or guidelines that successful global firms seem to employ. Successful global competitors:

1. See themselves as multinational enterprises and are led by a management team that is comfortable in the world arena.

2. Develop integrated and innovative strategies that make it difficult and costly for other firms to compete.

3. Aggressively and effectively implement their worldwide strategy and back it with large investments.

4. Understand that technologic innovation no longer is confined to the United States and develop systems for tapping technologic innovation abroad.

5. Operate as if the world is one large market rather than a series of individual, small markets.

6. Have organization structures that are designed to handle their unique problems and challenges and thus provide them the greatest efficiency.

7. Develop a system that keeps them informed about political changes around the world and the implications of these changes on the firm.

8. Have management teams that are international in composition and thus better able to respond to the various demands of their respective markets.

9. Allow their outside directors to play an active role in the operation of the enterprise.

10. Are well managed and tend to follow such important guidelines as sticking close to the customer, having lean organization structures, and encouraging autonomy and entrepreneurial activity among the personnel.

---

particular culture tends to view emotion, enjoyment, friendship, humor, rules, status, and other culturally based behaviors, the more control they have over creating marketing messages that will be interpreted in the desired way.

Figure 6–2 provides an example of the role that culture should play in advertising by recapping the five relationship orientations identified through Trompenaars' research (see Chapter 5). Figure 6–2 shows how value can be added to the marketing approach by carefully tailoring the advertising message to the particular culture. For example, advertising in the United States should target individual achievement, be expressive and direct, and appeal to U.S. values of success through personal hard work. On the other hand, the focus in China and other Asian countries should be much more indirect and subtle, emphasizing group references, shared responsibility, and interpersonal trust.

The need to adjust global strategies for regional markets presents three major challenges for most MNCs. First, the MNC must stay abreast of local market conditions and sidestep the temptation to assume that all markets are basically the same. Second, the MNC must know the strengths and weaknesses of its subsidiaries so that it can provide these units with the assistance needed in addressing local demands. Third, the multinational must give the subsidiary more autonomy so that it can respond to changes in local demands. "International Management in Action: Ten Key Factors for MNC Success" provides additional insights into the ways that successful MNCs address these challenges.

■ Cross-Cultural Differences and Similarities

As shown in Chapter 5, culture can be similar or quite different across countries. The challenge for MNCs is to recognize and effectively manage these similarities and differences. For instance, the way in which MNCs manage their home businesses often should be different from the way they manage their overseas operations.[10] After recognizing the danger

Figure 6–2

**Trompenaars'
Cultural
Dimensions
and Advertising:
Adjusting the
Message for
Local Meaning**

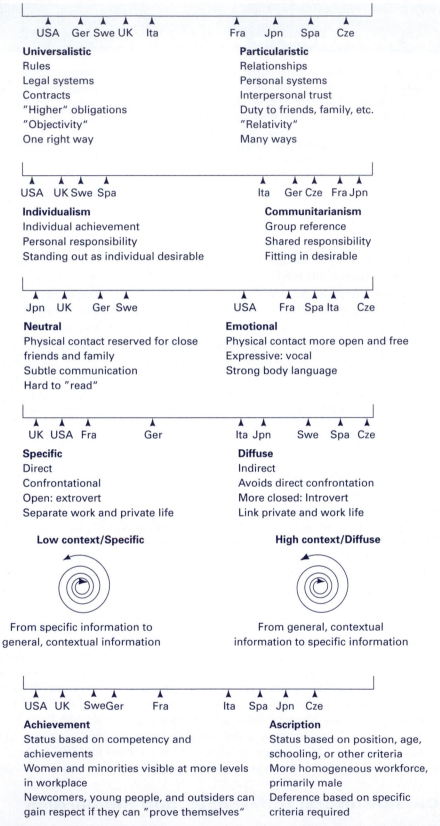

USA Ger Swe UK Ita   Fra   Jpn   Spa   Cze

Universalistic

Rules

Legal systems

Contracts

"Higher" obligations

"Objectivity"

One right way

Particularistic

Relationships

Personal systems

Interpersonal trust

Duty to friends, family, etc.

"Relativity"

Many ways

USA   UK Swe Spa   Ita   Ger Cze Fra Jpn

Individualism

Individual achievement

Personal responsibility

Standing out as individual desirable

Communitarianism

Group reference

Shared responsibility

Fitting in desirable

Jpn   UK   Ger Swe   USA   Fra Spa Ita   Cze

Neutral

Physical contact reserved for close
friends and family

Subtle communication

Hard to "read"

Emotional

Physical contact more open and free

Expressive: vocal

Strong body language

UK USA Fra   Ger   Ita Jpn   Swe   Spa Cze

Specific

Direct

Confrontational

Open: extrovert

Separate work and private life

Diffuse

Indirect

Avoids direct confrontation

More closed: Introvert

Link private and work life

Low context/Specific

From specific information to
general, contextual information

High context/Diffuse

From general, contextual
information to specific information

USA UK   SweGer   Fra   Ita   Spa Jpn Cze

Achievement

Status based on competency and
achievements

Women and minorities visible at more levels
in workplace

Newcomers, young people, and outsiders can
gain respect if they can "prove themselves"

Ascription

Status based on position, age,
schooling, or other criteria

More homogeneous workforce,
primarily male

Deference based on specific
criteria required

Source: Lisa Hoecklin, *Managing Cultural Differences* (Workingham, England: Addison-Wesley,
1995), p. 107, which is drawn from information found in Fons Trompenaars, *Riding the Waves
of Culture* (New York: Irwin, 1994).

for MNCs to drift toward parochialism and simplification because of cultural differences, the discussion shifts to some examples of both cultural similarities and differences and how to effectively manage across cultures by a contingency approach.

Parochialism and Simplification

Parochialism is the tendency to view the world through one's own eyes and perspectives. This can be a difficult problem for many international managers, who often come from advanced economies and believe that their state-of-the-art knowledge is more than adequate to handle the challenges of doing business in lesser-developed countries. In addition, many of these managers have had a parochial point of view fostered by their background.[11] A good example is provided by Randall and Coakley, who studied the impact of culture on successful partnerships in the former Soviet Union. Initially after the breakup of the Soviet Union, the republics called themselves the Commonwealth of Independent States or CIS. This term will be used to refer to the former Soviet Union. They found that while outside MNC managers typically entered into partnerships with CIS enterprises with a view toward making them efficient and profitable, the CIS managers often brought a different set of priorities to the table. As a result, some of the practices that were implemented by the CIS managers did not generate profit—but they were culturally acceptable in the CIS. These included:

> **Parochialism**
> The tendency to view the world through one's own eyes and perspectives.

1. Some managers laid off as much as 30–40 percent of their workforces in order to reduce overemployment. While this was a good start, many more needed to be let go, but the managers kept them on because they felt a social obligation to help provide employment and services for the workers and their families.

2. Many high-tech CIS managers and their scientists wanted to produce and sell products in the international arena, but they downplayed the need for making a systematic analysis of the competition and evaluating the needs of customers. They believed that if they could simply build a technologically superior product they would be able to succeed in the world marketplace.

3. Most CIS managers believed that the first responsibility of the partnership was to provide jobs to people. So even when it came to maximizing core competencies and remaining competitive in this area, the company was viewed as a vehicle for providing health care, education, social goods and services, and basic full-time employment to the personnel. In fact, CIS managers were adamant regarding the fact that profits were not as important in achieving a successful partnership arrangement.[12]

Commenting on their research, Randall and Coakley noted that the way CIS managers do business is sharply different from that of their American counterparts. In particular, there is an inconsistency between CIS cultural norms, their past training, and their work experiences, and the emerging economic structure and way in which they must do business if they hope to succeed in the international arena. This led the researchers to conclude:

> As behavioral change continues to lag behind structural change, it becomes imperative to understand that this inconsistency between what economic demands and cultural norms require manifests problems and complexities far beyond mere structural change. In short, the implications of the different perspectives on technology, labor, and production . . . for potential partnerships between U.S. and CIS companies need to be fully grasped by all parties entering into any form of relationship.[13]

Simplification is the process of exhibiting the same orientation toward different cultural groups. For example, the way in which a U.S. manager interacts with a British manager is the same way in which he or she behaves when doing business with an Asian executive. Moreover, this orientation reflects one's basic culture. Table 6–1 provides an example, showing several widely agreed-on, basic cultural orientations and the range of variations for each. Asterisks indicate the dominant U.S. orientation. Quite obviously, U.S. cultural values are

> **Simplification**
> The process of exhibiting the same orientation toward different culture groups.

Table 6–1
Six Basic Cultural Variations

Orientations	Range of Variations
What is the nature of people?	Good (changeable/unchangeable)
	A mixture of good and evil*
	Evil (changeable/unchangeable)
What is the person's relationship to nature?	Dominant*
	In harmony with nature
	Subjugation
What is the person's relationship to other people?	Lineal (hierarchic)
	Collateral (collectivist)
	Individualist*
What is the modality of human activity?	Doing*
	Being and becoming
	Being
What is the temporal focus of human activity?	Future*
	Present
	Past
What is the conception of space?	Private*
	Mixed
	Public

Note: *Indicates the dominant U.S. orientation.
Source: Adapted from the work of Florence Rockwood Kluckhohn and Fred L. Stodtbeck.

not the same as those of managers from other cultures; as a result, a U.S. manager's attempt to simplify things can result in erroneous behavior. Here is an example of a member of the purchasing department of a large European oil company who was negotiating an order with a Korean supplier.

> At the first meeting, the Korean partner offered a silver pen to the European manager. The latter, however, politely refused the present for fear of being bribed (even though he knew about the Korean custom of giving presents). Much to our manager's surprise, the second meeting began with the offer of a stereo system. Again the manager refused, his fear of being bribed probably heightened. When he gazed at a piece of Korean china on the third meeting, he finally realized what was going on. His refusal had not been taken to mean: "let's get on with business right away," but rather: "If you want to get into business with me, you had better come up with something bigger."[14]

Understanding the culture in which they do business can make international managers more effective.[15] Unfortunately, when placed in a culture with which they are unfamiliar, most international managers are not culturally knowledgeable, so they often misinterpret what is happening. This is particularly true when the environment is markedly different from the one in which they live. Consider, for example, the difference between the cultures in Japan and the United States. Japan has what could be called a high-context culture, which possesses characteristics such as:

1. Relationships between people are relatively long-lasting, and individuals feel deep personal involvement with each other.
2. Communication often is implicit, and individuals are taught from an early age to interpret these messages accurately.
3. People in authority are personally responsible for the actions of their subordinates, and this places a premium on loyalty to both superiors and subordinates.

4. Agreements tend to be spoken rather than written.

5. Insiders and outsiders are easily distinguishable, and outsiders typically do not gain entrance to the inner group.

These Japanese cultural characteristics are markedly different from those of low-context cultures such as the United States, which possess the following characteristics:

1. Relationships between individuals are relatively short in duration, and in general, deep personal involvement with others is not valued greatly.

2. Messages are explicit, and individuals are taught from a very early age to say exactly what they mean.

3. Authority is diffused throughout the bureaucratic system, and personal responsibility is hard to pin down.

4. Agreements tend to be in writing rather than spoken.

5. Insiders and outsiders are not readily distinguished, and the latter are encouraged to join the inner circle.[16]

These differences help to explain why Japanese managers in the United States often have trouble managing local operations, and vice versa.[17] At the same time, it is important to realize that while there are cultural differences, there also are similarities. Therefore, in managing across cultures, not everything is totally different. Some approaches that work at home also work well in other cultural settings.

Similarities across Cultures

When internationalization began to take off in the 1970s, many companies quickly admitted that it would not be possible to do business in the same way in every corner of the globe. There was a secret hope, however, that many of the procedures and strategies that worked so well at home could be adopted overseas without modification. This has proved to be a false hope. At the same time, some similarities across cultures have been uncovered by researchers. For example, the co-author of this text (Luthans) and his associates studied through direct observation a sample of managers ($n = 66$) in the largest textile factory in Russia to determine their activities.[18] Similar to U.S. managers studied earlier, Russian managers carried out traditional management, communication, human resources, and networking activities. The study also found that again similar to U.S. managers, the relative attention given to the networking activity increased the Russian managers' opportunities for promotion, and communication activity was a significant predictor of effective performance in both Russia and the United States.[19]

Besides the similarities of managerial activities, another study at the same Russian factory tested whether organizational behavior modification (O.B. Mod.) interventions that led to performance improvements in U.S. organizations would hold true in Russia.[20] As with the applications of O.B. Mod. in the United States, Russian supervisors were trained to administer contingently social rewards (attention and recognition) and positive feedback when they observed workers engaging in behaviors that contributed to the production of quality fabric. In addition, Russian supervisors were taught to give corrective feedback for behaviors that reduced product quality. The researchers found that this O.B. Mod. approach, which had worked so well in the United States, also produced positive results in the Russian factory, and they concluded that "the class of interventions associated with organizational behavior modification are likely to be useful in meeting the challenges faced by Russian workers and managers is given initial support by the results of this study."[21]

In another cross-cultural study, this time using a large Korean sample (1,192 employees in 27 large Korean firms), Luthans and colleagues analyzed whether demographic and situational factors identified in the U.S.-based literature had the same antecedent influence on the commitment of Korean employees.[22] As in the U.S. studies, Korean employees' position in the hierarchy, tenure in their current position, and age all related to organizational commitment. Other similarities with U.S. firms included: (1) as organizational size increased, commitment declined; (2) as structure became more employee-focused, commitment increased; and (3) the more positive the perceptions of organizational climate, the greater the employee commitment. The following conclusion was drawn:

> This study provides beginning evidence that popular constructs in the U.S. management and organizational behavior literature should not be automatically dismissed as culture bound. Whereas some organizational behavior concepts and techniques do indeed seem to be culture specific . . . a growing body of literature is demonstrating the ability to cross-culturally validate other concepts and techniques, such as behavior management. . . . This study contributed to this cross-cultural evidence for the antecedents to organizational commitment. The antecedents for Korean employees' organizational commitment was found to be similar to their American counterparts.[23]

Many Differences across Cultures

Despite similarities between cultures in some studies, far more differences than similarities have been found. In particular, MNCs are discovering that they must carefully investigate and understand the culture where they intend to do business and modify their approaches appropriately.

Sometimes these cultures are quite different from the United States—as well as from each other! One human resource management (HRM) example has been offered by Trompenaars, who examined the ways in which personnel in international subsidiaries were appraised by their managers. The head office had established the criteria to be used in these evaluations, but left the prioritization of the criteria to the national operating company. As a result, the outcome of the evaluations could be quite different from country to country because what was regarded as the most important criterion in one subsidiary might be ranked much lower on the evaluation list of another subsidiary. In the case of Shell Oil, for example, Trompenaars found that the firm was using a HAIRL system of appraisal. The five criteria in this acronym stood for: (a) Helicopter—the capacity to take a broad view from above; (b) Analysis—the ability to evaluate situations logically and completely; (c) Imagination—the ability to be creative and think outside the box; (d) Reality—the ability to use information realistically; and (e) Leadership—the ability to effectively galvanize and inspire personnel. When Shell's operating companies were asked to prioritize from top to bottom these five criteria, the results were as follows:

Netherlands	France	Germany	Britain
Reality	Imagination	Leadership	Helicopter
Analysis	Analysis	Analysis	Imagination
Helicopter	Leadership	Reality	Reality
Leadership	Helicopter	Imagination	Analysis
Imagination	Reality	Helicopter	Leadership

Quite obviously, personnel in different operating companies were being evaluated differently. In fact, none of the operating companies in the above four countries had the same criterion at the top of their list. Moreover, the criterion that was at the top of the list for operating companies in the Netherlands—reality—was at the bottom of the list for those in France; and the one at the top of the list in French operating companies—imagination— was at the bottom of that of the Dutch firms. Similarly, the German operating companies put leadership at the top of their list and helicopter at the bottom, while the British companies did just the opposite! In fact, the whole list for the Germans are in the exact reverse order from the British.[24]

Other HRM differences can be found in areas such as wages, compensation, pay equity, and maternity leave. Here are some representative examples.

1. The concept of an hourly wage plays a minor role in Mexico. Labor law requires that employees receive full pay 365 days a year.

2. In Austria and Brazil, employees with 1 year of service are automatically given 30 days of paid vacation.

3. Some jurisdictions in Canada have legislated pay equity—known in the United States as comparable worth—between male- and female-intensive jobs.

4. In Japan, compensation levels are determined using the objective factors of age, length of service, and educational background rather than skill, ability, and performance. Performance does not count until after an employee reaches age 45.

5. In the United Kingdom, employees are allowed up to 40 weeks of maternity leave, and employers must provide a government-mandated amount of pay for 18 of those weeks.

6. In 87% of large Swedish companies, the head of human resources is on the board of directors.[25]

These HRM practices certainly are quite different from those in the United States, and U.S. MNCs need to modify their approaches when they go into these countries if they hope to be successful. Compensation plans in particular provide an interesting area of contrast across different cultures.

Drawing on the work of Hofstede (see Chapter 5), it is possible to link cultural clusters and compensation strategies. Table 6–2 shows a host of different cultural groupings, including some in Asia, the EU, and Anglo countries. Each cluster requires a different approach to formulating an effective compensation strategy, and after analyzing each such cluster, we suggest that:

1. In Pacific Rim countries, incentive plans should be group-based. In high masculinity cultures (Japan, Hong Kong, Malaysia, the Philippines, Singapore), high salaries should be paid to senior-level managers.

2. In EU nations such as France, Spain, Italy, and Belgium, compensation strategies should be similar. In the latter two nations, however, significantly higher salaries should be paid to local senior-level managers because of the high masculinity index. In Portugal and Greece, both of which have a low individualism index,

Table 6–2
Cultural Clusters in the Pacific Rim, EU, and United States

	Power Distance	Individualism	Masculinity	Uncertainty Avoidance
Pacific Rim				
Hong Kong, Malaysia, Philippines, Singapore	+	–	+	–
Japan	+	–	+	+
South Korea, Taiwan	+	–	–	+
EU and United States				
France, Spain	+	+	–	+
Italy, Belgium	+	+	+	+
Portugal	+	–	–	+
Greece	+	–	+	+
Denmark, Netherlands	–	+	+	–
Germany	–	+	+	+
Great Britain, Ireland, United States	–	+	+	–

Note: + indicates high or strong; – indicates low or weak.

Source: Based on research by Hofstede and put together in Richard M. Hodgetts and Fred Luthans, "U.S. Multinationals' Compensation Strategies for Local Management: Cross-Cultural Implications," *Compensation & Benefits Review,* March–April 1993, p. 47. Used with permission of the publisher, © 1993. American Management Association, New York. All rights reserved.

profit-sharing plans would be more effective than individual incentive plans, while in Denmark, the Netherlands, and Germany, personal-incentive plans would be highly useful because of the high individualism in these cultures.

3. In Great Britain, Ireland, and the United States, managers value their individualism and are motivated by the opportunity for earnings, recognition, advancement, and challenge. Compensation plans should reflect these needs.[26]

Additionally, some MNCs have found that compensation plans that are very attractive to their local workforce have no value for members of their international workforce.[27] For example, when the Gillette Company decided to offer stock to its 33,000 employees worldwide, the firm discovered that its plan was not global in terms of worker interest.[28] Other companies have had similar experiences. Some of the reasons are provided in Table 6–3; others include low employee disposable income and a feeling that stocks are risky investments. Simply put, workers in other cultures often do not have the same view of compensation plans as U.S. workers do. This is why many MNCs now are developing their own contingency-based compensation strategies that are geared toward meeting the needs of the local workers.

Figure 6–3 shows how specific HRM areas can be analyzed contingently on a country-by-country basis. Take, for example, the information on Japan. When contrasted with U.S. approaches, a significant number of differences are found. Recruitment and selection in Japanese firms often are designed to help identify those individuals who will do the best job over the long run. In the United States, people often are hired based on what they can do for the firm in the short run, because many of them eventually will quit or be downsized. Similarly, the Japanese use a great deal of cross-training, while the Americans tend to favor specialized training. The Japanese use group performance appraisal and reward people as a group; at least traditionally, Americans use manager–subordinate performance appraisal and reward people as individuals. In Japan, unions are regarded as partners; in the United States, both management and unions view each other in a much more adversarial way. Only in the area of job design,

---

Table 6–3
Problems with U.S. Employee Stock Plans in Select Countries

Country	Reasons for Lack of Success
Belgium	Problematic. Some stock plans conflict with a government-imposed wage freeze.
Brazil	Impossible. Foreign-exchange controls prohibit out-of-country stock investment; phantom stock plans are a headache.
Britain	Easy. But sometimes labor unions can get in the way.
Eastern Europe	Forget it. Even if you get government permission, chances are you talked to the wrong bureaucrat.
Germany	Can I get that in deutsche marks? U.S. plans suffer when the dollar is weak.
Israel	Difficult. Exchange controls forced National Semiconductor to a third-party system, but the plan has only scant participation.
Luxembourg	Tax haven. Great place to set up a trust to administer stock plans.
Mexico	May regret it. Labor laws can force a one-time stock grant into an annual event.
Netherlands	No thanks. Employees may like the stock options, but they will not appreciate a hefty tax bill up front.
Philippines	Time-consuming. Requires government approval and lots of worker education.

Source: Adapted from information found in Tara Parker-Pope, "Culture Clash," *Wall Street Journal,* April 12, 1995, p. R7.

where the Japanese use a great deal of participative management and autonomous work teams, are the Americans beginning to employ a similar approach. The same types of differences can be seen in the matrix of Figure 6–3 among Japan, Germany, Mexico, and China.

These differences should not be interpreted to mean that one set of HRM practices are superior to another. In fact, recent research from Japan and Europe shows these firms often have a higher incidence of personnel-related problems than U.S. companies. For example, one study found that Japanese MNCs ($n = 34$) and European MNCs ($n = 23$) had more problems than U.S. MNCs ($n = 24$) in areas such as: (1) home-country personnel who possessed sufficient international management skills; (2) home-country personnel who wanted to work abroad; (3) difficulty in attracting high-caliber local nationals; and (4) high turnover of local employees. Additionally, when compared with Japanese MNCs, U.S. multinationals had less friction and better communication between their home-country expatriates and local employees, and there were fewer complaints by local employees regarding their ability to advance in the company.[29]

Figure 6–3   **A Partially Completed Contingency Matrix for International Human Resource Management**

	Japan	Germany	Mexico	China
Recruitment and selection	• Prepare for long process • Ensure that your firm is "here to stay" • Develop trusting relationship with recruit	• Obtain skilled labor from government subsidized apprenticeship program	• Use expatriates sparingly • Recruit Mexican nationals at U.S. colleges	• Recent public policy shifts encourage use of sophisticated selection procedures
Training	• Make substantial investment in training • Use general training and cross-training • Training is everyone's responsibility	• Reorganize and utilize apprenticeship programs • Be aware of government regulations on training	• Use bilingual trainers	• Careful observations of existing training programs • Utilize team training
Compensation	• Use recognition and praise as motivator • Avoid pay for performance	• Note high labor costs for manufacturing	• Consider all aspects of labor cost	• Use technical training as reward • Recognize egalitarian values • Use "more work more pay" with caution
Labor relations	• Treat unions as partners • Allow time for negotiations	• Be prepared for high wages and short work week • Expect high productivity from unionized workers	• Understand changing Mexican labor law • Prepare for increasing unionization of labor	• Tap large pool of labor cities • Lax labor laws may become more stringent
Job design	• Include participation • Incorporate group goal setting • Use autonomous work teams • Use uniform, formal approaches • Encourage co-worker input • Empower teams to make decision	• Utilize works councils to enhance worker participation	• Approach participation cautiously	• Determine employee's motives before implementing participation

Source: Fred Luthans, Paul A. Marsnik, and Kyle W. Luthans, "A Contingency Matrix Approach to IHRM," *Human Resource Management Journal,* © 1997. Reprinted with permission of John Wiley & Sons, Inc.

Figure 6–3 clearly indicates the importance of MNCs using a contingency approach to HRM across cultures. Not only are there different HRM practices in different cultures, there also are different practices within the same cultures. For instance, one study involving 249 U.S. affiliates of foreign-based MNCs found that in general, affiliate HRM practices closely follow local practices when dealing with the rank-and-file but even more closely approximate parent-company practices when dealing with upper-level management.[30] In other words, this study found that a hybrid approach to HRM was being used by these MNCs.

Aside from the different approaches used in different countries, it is becoming clear that common assumptions and conventional wisdom about HRM practices in certain countries no longer are valid. For example, for many years, it has been assumed that Japanese employees do not leave their jobs for work with other firms. They are loyal to their first employer, and it would be virtually impossible for MNCs operating in Japan to recruit talent from Japanese firms. Recent evidence, however, reveals that job-hopping among Japanese employees is increasingly common. One report concluded:

> While American workers, both the laid-off and the survivors, grapple with cutbacks, one in three Japanese workers willingly walks away from his job within the first 10 years of his career, according to the Japanese Institute of Labor, a private research organization. And many more are thinking about it. More than half of salaried Japanese workers say they would switch jobs or start their own business if a favorable opportunity arose, according to a survey by the Recruit Research Corporation.[31]

These findings clearly illustrate one important point: managing across cultures requires careful understanding of the local environment, because common assumptions and stereotypes may not be valid. Cultural differences must be addressed, and this is why cross-cultural research will continue to be critical in helping firms learn how to manage across cultures.[32]

■ Cultural Differences in Selected Countries and Regions

Chapter 5 introduced the concept of country clusters, which is the idea that certain regions of the world have similar cultures. For example, the way that Americans do business in the United States is very similar to the way that British do business in England. Even in this Anglo culture, however, there are pronounced differences, and in other clusters, such as in Asia, these differences become even more pronounced. The accompanying box, "Managing in Hong Kong," depicts such differences. Chapter 1 examined some important worldwide developments, and the following sections focus on cultural highlights and differences in selected countries and regions that provide the necessary understanding and perspective for effective management across cultures.

Doing Business in China

The People's Republic of China (PRC or China, for short) has had a long tradition of isolation. In 1979, Deng Xiaoping opened his country to the world. Although his bloody 1989 put-down of protestors in Tiananmen Square was a definite setback for progress, China is rapidly trying to close the gap between itself and economically advanced nations and to establish itself as a power in the world economy. As noted in Chapter 1, China is actively trading in world markets, is a member of the WTO, and is a major trading partner of the United States. Despite this global presence, many U.S. and European multinationals still find that doing business in the PRC can be a long, grueling process.[33] Very few outside firms have yet to make a profit in China. One primary reason is that Western-based MNCs do not appreciate the important role and impact of Chinese culture.

Experienced travelers report that the primary criterion for doing business in China is technical competence. For example, in the case of MNCs selling machinery, the Chinese want to know exactly how the machine works, what its capabilities are, and how repairs

International Management in Action

Managing in Hong Kong   **www.asiapages.com.sg/vgt/welcome.htm**

Managing across cultures has long been recognized as a potential problem for multinationals. To help expatriates who are posted overseas deal with a new culture, many MNCs offer special training and coaching. Often, however, little is done to change expatriates' basic cultural values or specific managerial behaviors. Simply put, this traditional approach could be called the *practical school of management thought,* which holds that effective managerial behavior is universal and a good manager in the United States also will be effective in Hong Kong or any other location around the world. In recent years, it generally has been recognized that such an approach no longer is sufficient, and there is growing support for what is called the *cross-cultural school of management thought,* which holds that effective managerial behavior is a function of the specific culture. As Black and Porter point out in a recent article, successful managerial action in Los Angeles may not be effective in Hong Kong.

Black and Porter investigated the validity of these two schools of thought by surveying U.S. managers working in Hong Kong, U.S. managers working in the United States, and Hong Kong managers working in Hong Kong. Their findings revealed some interesting differences. The U.S. managers in Hong Kong exhibited managerial behaviors similar to those of their counterparts back in the United States; however, Hong Kong managers had managerial behaviors different from either group of U.S. managers. Commenting on these results, the researchers noted:

> This study . . . points to some important practical implications. It suggests that American firms and the practical school of thought may be mistaken in the assumption that a good manager in Los Angeles will necessarily do fine in Hong Kong or some other foreign country. It may be that because firms do not include in their selection criteria individual characteristics such as cognitive flexibility, cultural flexibility, degree of ethnocentricity, etc., they end up sending a number of individuals on international assignments who have a tendency to keep the same set of managerial behaviors they used in the U.S. and not adjust or adapt to the local norms and practices. Including the measurement of these characteristics in the selection process, as well as providing cross-cultural training before departure, may be a means of obtaining more effective adaptation of managerial behaviors and more effective performance in overseas assignments.

Certainly the study shows that simplistic assumptions about culture are erroneous and that what works in one country will not necessarily produce the desired results in another. If MNCs are going to manage effectively throughout the world, they are going to have to give more attention to training their people about intercultural differences.

and maintenance must be handled. Sellers must be prepared to answer these questions in precise detail. This is why successful multinationals send only seasoned engineers and technical people to the PRC. They know that the questions to be answered will require both knowledge and experience, and young, fresh-out-of-school engineers will not be able to answer them.

A major cultural difference between the PRC and many Western countries is the issue of time. The Chinese tend to be punctual, so it is important that those who do business with them arrive on time. During meetings, such as those held when negotiating a contract, the Chinese may ask many questions and nod their assent at the answers. This nodding usually means that they understand or are being polite; it seldom means that they like what they are hearing and want to enter into a contract. For this reason, when dealing with the Chinese, one must keep in mind that patience is critically important. The Chinese will make a decision in their own good time, and it is common for outside businesspeople to make several trips to China before a deal is finally concluded. Moreover, not only are there numerous meetings, sometimes these are unilaterally canceled at the last minute and rescheduled. This often tries the patience of outsiders and is inconvenient in terms of rearranging travel plans and other problems.

Another important dimension of Chinese culture is **guanxi,** which means "good connections."[34] In turn, these connections can result in such things as lower costs for doing business.[35] Yet *guanxi* goes beyond just lower costs. Yi and Ellis surveyed Hong Kong ($n = 68$) and PRC Chinese ($n = 30$) managers and found that both groups agreed that *guanxi* networking offered a number of potential benefits including increased business, higher

Guanxi
In China, it means good connections.

sales revenue, more sources of information, greater prospecting opportunities, and the facilitation of future transactions.[36] In practice, *guanxi* resembles nepotism where individuals in authority make decisions on the basis of family ties or social connections rather than objective indices. Tung has reported that:

> In a survey of 2,000 Chinese from Shanghai and its surrounding rural community, 92% of the respondents confirmed that *guanxi* played a significant role in their daily lives. Furthermore, the younger generation tended to place greater emphasis on *guanxi*. In fact, *guanxi* has become more widespread in the recent past. . . . Most business practitioners who have experience in doing business with East Asians will readily agree that in order to succeed in these countries "who you know is more important than what you know." In other words, having connections with the appropriate individuals and authorities is often more crucial than having the right product and/or price.[37]

Additionally, outsiders doing business in China must be aware that Chinese people will typically argue that they have the *guanxi* to get a job done, when in reality they may or may not have the necessary connections.

In China, it is important to be a good listener. This may mean having to listen to the same stories about the great progress that has been made by the PRC over the past decade. The Chinese are very proud of their economic accomplishments and want to share these feelings with outsiders.

When dealing with the Chinese, one must realize they are a collective society in which people pride themselves on being members of a group. This is in sharp contrast to the situation in the United States and other Western countries, where individualism is highly prized. For this reason, one must never single out a Chinese and praise him or her for a particular quality, such as intelligence or kindness, because this may well embarrass the individual in the presence of his or her peers. It is equally important to avoid using self-centered conversation, such as excessive use of the word "I," because it appears that the speaker is trying to single him- or herself out for special consideration.

The Chinese also are much less animated than Westerners. They avoid open displays of affection, do not slap each other on the back, and are more reticent, retiring, and reserved than North or South Americans. They do not appreciate loud, boisterous behavior, and when speaking to each other, they maintain a greater physical distance than is typical in the West.

Cultural highlights that affect doing business in China can be summarized and put into some specific guidelines as follows:

1. The Chinese place values and principles above money and expediency.[38]

2. Business meetings typically start with pleasantries such as tea and general conversation about the guest's trip to the country, local accommodations, and family. In most cases, the host already has been briefed on the background of the visitor.

3. When a meeting is ready to begin, the Chinese host will give the appropriate indication. Similarly, when the meeting is over, the host will indicate that it is time for the guest to leave.

4. Once the Chinese decide who and what is best, they tend to stick with these decisions. Therefore, they may be slow in formulating a plan of action, but once they get started, they make fairly good progress.

5. In negotiations, reciprocity is important. If the Chinese give concessions, they expect some in return. Additionally, it is common to find them slowing down negotiations to take advantage of Westerners desiring to conclude arrangements as quickly as possible. The objective of this tactic is to extract further concessions. Another common ploy used by the Chinese is to pressure the other party during final arrangements by suggesting that this counterpart has broken the spirit of friendship in which the business relationship originally was established. Again, through this ploy, the Chinese are trying to gain additional concessions.

6. Because negotiating can involve a loss of face, it is common to find Chinese carrying out the whole process through intermediaries. This allows them to convey their ideas without fear of embarrassment.[39]

7. During negotiations, it is important not to show excessive emotion of any kind. Anger or frustration, for example, are viewed as antisocial and unseemly.

8. Negotiations should be viewed with a long-term perspective. Those who will do best are the ones who realize they are investing in a long-term relationship.[40]

Doing Business in Russia

As pointed out in Chapter 1, the Russian economy has experienced severe problems[41] and the risks of doing business there can not be understated.[42] At the same time, however, by following certain guidelines, MNCs can begin to tap the potential opportunities. Here are some suggestions for being successful in Russia:

1. Build personal relationships with partners. Business laws and contracts do not mean as much in Russia as they do in the West. When there are contract disputes, there is little protection for the aggrieved party because of the time and effort needed to legally enforce the agreement. Detailed contracts can be hammered out later on; in the beginning, all that counts is friendship.

2. Use local consultants. Because the rules of business have changed so much in recent years, it pays to have a local Russian consultant working with the company. Russian expatriates often are not up-to-date on what is going on and, quite often, are not trusted by local businesspeople who have stayed in the country. So the consultant should be someone who has been in Russia all the time and understands the local business climate.

3. Consider business ethics. Ethical behavior in the United States is not always the same as in Russia. For example, it is tradition in Russia to give gifts to those with whom one wants to transact business, an approach that is often regarded as bribery in the United States.

4. Be patient. In order to get something done in Russia, it often takes months of waiting. Those who are in a hurry to make a quick deal are often sorely disappointed.

5. Stress exclusivity. Russians like exclusive arrangements and often negotiate with just one firm at a time. This is in contrast to Western businesspeople who often "shop" their deals and may negotiate with a half dozen firms at the same time before settling on one.

6. Remember that personal relations are important. Russians like to do business face-to-face. So when they receive letters or faxes, they often put them on their desk but do not respond to them. They are waiting for the businessperson to contact them and set up a personal meeting.

7. Keep financial information personal. When Westerners enter into business dealings with partners, it is common for them to share financial information with these individuals and to expect the same from the latter. However, Russians wait until they know their partner well enough to feel comfortable before sharing financial data. Once trust is established, then this information is provided.

8. Research the company. In dealing effectively with Russian partners, it is helpful to get information about this company, its management hierarchy, and how it typically does business. This information helps ensure the chances for good relations because it gives the Western partner a basis for establishing a meaningful relationship.

9. Stress mutual gain. The Western idea of "win-win" in negotiations also works well in Russia. Potential partners want to know what they stand to gain from entering into the venture.

10. Clarify terminology. For-profit business deals are new in Russia, so the language of business is just getting transplanted there. As a result, it is important to double-check and make sure that the other party clearly understands the proposal, knows what is expected and when, and is agreeable to the deal.[43]

11. Be careful about compromising or settling things too quickly because this is often seen as a sign of weakness. During the Soviet Union days, everything was complex and so they are suspicious of anything that is conceded easily. If agreements are not reached after a while, a preferred tactic on their part is to display patience and then wait it out. However, they will abandon this approach if the other side shows great patience because they will realize that their negotiating tactic is useless.

12. Written contracts are not as binding in their minds as they are among westerners. Like Asians, Russians view contracts as binding only if they continue to be mutually beneficial. One of the best ways of dealing with this is to be able to continually show them the benefits associated with sticking to the deal.[44]

These dozen steps can be critical to the success of a business venture in Russia. They require careful consideration of cultural factors and it often takes a lot longer than initially anticipated. However, the benefits may be worth the wait. And when everything is completed, there is a final cultural tradition that should be observed: Fix and reinforce the final agreements with a nice dinner together and an invitation to the Russians to visit your country and see your facilities.[45]

Doing Business in India

In recent years, a growing number of MNCs have been attracted to India.[46] The government continues to play an important role in this process,[47] although recently many of the bureaucratic restrictions have been lifted as India works to attract foreign investment and raise its economic growth rate.[48] In addition, although most Indian businesspeople speak English, many of their values and beliefs are markedly different from those in the West. Thus, understanding Indian culture is critical to successfully doing business in India.

Shaking hands with male business associates is almost always an acceptable practice. U.S. businesspeople in India are considered equals, however, and the universal method of greeting an equal is to press one's palms together in front of the chest and say *namaste,* which means "greetings to you." Therefore, if a handshake appears to be improper, it always is safe to use *namaste.*

Western food typically is available in all good hotels. Most Indians do not drink alcoholic beverages, however, and many are vegetarians or eat chicken but not beef. Therefore, when foreign businesspeople entertain in India, the menu often is quite different from that back home. Moreover, when a local businessperson invites an expatriate for dinner at home, it is not necessary to bring a gift, although it is acceptable to do so. The host's wife and children usually will provide help from the kitchen to ensure that the guest is well treated, but they will not be at the table. If they are, it is common to wait until everyone has been seated and the host begins to eat or asks everyone to begin. During the meal, the host will ask the guest to have more food. This is done to ensure that the person does not go away hungry; however, once one has eaten enough, it is acceptable to politely refuse more food.

For Western businesspeople in India, shirt, trousers, tie, and suit are proper attire. In the southern part of India, where the climate is very hot, a light suit is preferable. In the north during the winter, a light sweater and jacket are a good choice. Indian businesspeople, on the other hand, often will wear local dress. In many cases, this includes a *dhoti,* which is a single piece of white cloth (about 5 yards long and 3 feet wide) which is passed around the waist up to half its length, then the other half is drawn between the legs and tucked at the waist. Long shirts are worn on the upper part of the body. In some locales, such as Punjab, Sikhs will wear turbans, and well-to-do Hindus sometimes will wear long coats like the Rajahs. This coat, known as a *sherwani,* is the dress recognized by the government for official and ceremonial wear. Foreign businesspeople are not expected to dress like locals, and in fact, many Indian businesspeople will dress like Europeans. Therefore, it is unnecessary to adopt local dress codes.

When doing business in India, one will find a number of other customs useful to know. Some of the most useful include:

1. It is important to be on time for meetings.
2. Personal questions should not be asked unless the other individual is a friend or close associate.
3. Titles are important, so people who are doctors or professors should be addressed accordingly.
4. Public displays of affection are considered to be inappropriate, so one should refrain from backslapping or touching others.
5. Beckoning is done with the palm turned down, while pointing often is done with the chin.
6. When eating or accepting things, use the right hand, because the left is considered to be unclean.
7. The *namaste* gesture can be used to greet people; it also is used to convey other messages, including a signal that one has had enough food.
8. Bargaining for goods and services is common; this contrasts with Western traditions, where bargaining might be considered rude or abrasive.[49]

Finally, it is important to remember that Indians are very tolerant of outsiders and understand that many are unfamiliar with local customs and procedures. Therefore, there is no need to make a phony attempt to conform to Indian cultural traditions. Making an effort to be polite and courteous is sufficient.[50]

Doing Business in France

Many in the United States believe that it is more difficult to get along with the French than with other Europeans. This feeling probably reflects the French culture, which is markedly different from that in the United States. In France, one's social class is very important, and these classes include the aristocracy, the upper bourgeoisie, the upper-middle bourgeoisie, the middle, the lower-middle, and the lower. Social interactions are affected by class stereotypes, and during their lifetime, most French people do not encounter much change in social status. Unlike an American, who through hard work and success can move from the lowest economic strata to the highest, a successful French person might, at best, climb one or two rungs of the social ladder. Additionally, the French are very status conscious, and they like to provide signs of this status, such as a knowledge of literature and the arts; a well-designed, tastefully decorated house; and a high level of education.

The French also tend to be friendly, humorous, and sardonic (sarcastic), in contrast to Americans, for example, who seldom are sardonic. The French may admire or be fascinated with people who disagree with them; in contrast, Americans are more attracted to those who agree with them. As a result, the French are accustomed to conflict and during negotiations accept that some positions are irreconcilable and must be accepted as such. Americans, on the other hand, believe that conflicts can be resolved and that if both parties make an extra effort and have a spirit of compromise, there will be no irreconcilable differences. Moreover, the French often determine a person's trustworthiness based on their firsthand evaluation of the individual's character. This is in marked contrast to Americans, who tend to evaluate a person's trustworthiness based on past achievements and other people's evaluations of this person.

In the workplace, many French people are not motivated by competition or the desire to emulate fellow workers. They often are accused of not having as intense a work ethic as, for example, Americans or Asians. Many French workers frown on overtime, and statistics show that on average, they have the longest vacations in the world (4 to 5 weeks annually). On the other hand, few would argue that they work extremely hard in their regularly scheduled time and have a reputation for high productivity. Part of this reputation results from the French tradition of craftsmanship. Part of it also is accounted for by a large percentage of the workforce being employed in small, independent businesses, where there is widespread respect for a job well done.

Most French organizations tend to be highly centralized and have rigid structures. As a result, it usually takes longer to carry out decisions. Because this arrangement is quite different from the more decentralized, flattened organizations in the United States, both middle- and lower-level U.S. expatriate managers who work in French subsidiaries often find bureaucratic red tape a source of considerable frustration. There also are marked differences at the upper levels of management. In French companies, top managers have far more authority than their U.S. counterparts, and they are less accountable for their actions. While top-level U.S. executives must continually defend their decision to the CEO or board of directors, French executives are challenged only if the company has poor performance. As a result, those who have studied French management find them to take a more autocratic approach.[51]

In countries such as the United States, a great deal of motivation is derived from professional accomplishment. Americans realize there is limited job and social security in their country, so it is up to them to work hard and ensure their future. The French do not have the same view. While they admire Americans' industriousness and devotion to work, they believe that quality of life is what really matters. As a result, they attach a great deal of importance to leisure time, and many are unwilling to sacrifice the enjoyment of life for a dedication to work.

The values and beliefs discussed here help to explain why French culture is so different from that in other countries. Some of the sharp contrasts with the United States, for example, provide insights regarding the difficulties of doing business in France. Additional cultural characteristics, such as the following, also help to explain the difficulties that outsiders may encounter in France:

1. When shaking hands with a French person, use a quick shake with some pressure in the grip. A firm, pumping handshake, which is so common in the United States, is considered to be uncultured.

2. It is extremely important to be on time for meetings and social occasions. Being "fashionably late" is frowned on.

3. During a meal, it is acceptable to engage in pleasant conversation, but personal questions and the subject of money are never brought up.

4. Great importance is placed on neatness and taste. Therefore, visiting businesspeople should try very hard to be cultured and sophisticated.[52]

5. The French tend to be suspicious of early friendliness in the discussion and dislike first names, taking off jackets, or disclosure of personal or family details.

6. In negotiations they try to find out what all of the other side's aims and demands are at the beginning, but reveal their own hand only late in the negotiations.

7. They do not like being rushed into making a decision and they rarely make important decisions inside the meeting. In fact, the person who is ultimately responsible for making the decision is often not present.

8. They tend to be very precise and logical in their approach to things, and will often not make concessions in negotiations unless their logic has been defeated. If a deadlock results, unlike Americans who will try to break the impasse by suggesting a series of compromises by both sides, they tend to remain firm and simply restate their position.[53]

Doing Business in Arab Countries

The intense media attention given to continuing conflicts in the Middle East have pointed out that Arab cultures are distinctly different from Anglo cultures. Americans often find it extremely hard to do business in Arab countries, and a number of Arab cultural characteristics can be cited for this difficulty.

One is the Arabian view of time. In the United States, it is common to use the cliche "time is money." In Arab countries, a favorite expression is *Bukra insha Allah,* which means "tomorrow if God wills," an expression that explains the Arabs' fatalistic approach to time. Arabs believe that Allah controls time, in contrast to Westerners, who believe that they control their own time. As a result, if Arabs commit themselves to a date in the future and fail to show up, there is no guilt or concern on their part, because they have no control over time in the first place.

A word of caution on overgeneralizing is needed here and in all of the examples used throughout this chapter's discussion of cultural characteristics. There are many Arabs that are very particular about promises and appointments. There are also many Arabs that are very proactive and not fatalistic. The point is that there are always exceptions and stereotyping in cross cultural dealings is unwarranted.

Another Arab cultural belief that generally holds is that destiny depends more on the will of a supreme being than on the behavior of individuals. A higher power dictates the outcome of important events, so individual action is of little consequence. This thinking affects not only Arabs' aspirations but also their motivation. Also of importance is that the status of Arabs largely is determined by family position and social contact and connections, not necessarily by their own accomplishments. This view helps to explain why some Middle Easterners take great satisfaction in appearing to be helpless. In fact, helplessness can be used as a source of power, for in this area of the world, the strong are resented and the weak compensated. Here is an example:

> In one Arab country, several public administrators of equal rank would take turns meeting in each other's offices for their weekly conferences, and the host would serve as chairman. After several months, one of these men had a mild heart attack. Upon his recovery, it was decided to hold the meetings only in his office, in order not to inconvenience him. From then on, the man who had the heart attack became the permanent chairman of the conference. This individual appeared more helpless than the others, and his helplessness enabled him to increase his power.[54]

This approach is quite different from that in the United States, where the strong tend to be compensated and rewarded. If a person were ill, such as in this example, the individual would be relieved of this responsibility until he or she had regained full health. In the interim, the rest of the group would go on without the sick person, and he or she may have lost power.

Another important cultural contrast between Arabs and Americans is that of emotion and logic. Arabs often act based on emotion; in contrast, those in an Anglo culture are taught to act on logic. Many Arabs live in unstable environments where things change constantly, so they do not develop trusting relationships with others. Americans, on the other hand, live in a much more predictable environment and develop trusting relationships with others.

Arabs also make wide use of elaborate and ritualized forms of greetings and leave-takings. A businessperson may wait past the assigned meeting time before being admitted to an Arab's office. Once there, the individual may find a host of others present; this situation is unlike the typical one-on-one meetings that are so common in the United States. Moreover, during the meeting, there may be continuous interruptions, visitors may arrive and begin talking to the host, and messengers may come in and go out on a regular basis. The businessperson is expected to take all this activity as perfectly normal and remain composed and ready to continue discussions as soon as the host is prepared to do so.

Business meetings typically conclude with an offer of coffee or tea. This is a sign that the meeting is over and that future meetings, if there are to be any, should now be arranged.

Unlike the case in many other countries, titles are not in general use on the Arabian Peninsula, except in the case of royal families, ministers, and high-level military officers. Additionally, initial meetings typically are used to get to know the other party. Business-related discussions may not occur until the third or fourth meeting. Also, in contrast to the common perception among many Western businesspeople who have never been to an Arab country, it is not necessary to bring the other party a gift. If this is done, however, it should be a modest gift. A good example is a novelty or souvenir item from the visitor's home country.

Arabs attach a great deal of importance to status and rank. When meeting with them, one should pay deference to the senior person first. It also is important never to criticize or berate anyone publicly. This causes the individual to lose face, and the same is true for the person who makes these comments. Mutual respect is required at all times.

Other useful guidelines for doing business in Arab cultures include:

1. It is important never to display feelings of superiority, because this makes the other party feel inferior. No matter how well someone does something, the individual should let the action speak for itself and not brag or put on a show of self-importance.

2. One should not take credit for joint efforts. A great deal of what is accomplished is a result of group work, and to indicate that one accomplished something alone is a mistake.

3. Much of what gets done is a result of going through administrative channels in the country. It often is difficult to sidestep a lot of this red tape, and efforts to do so can be regarded as disrespect for legal and governmental institutions.

4. Connections are extremely important in conducting business. Well-connected businesspeople can get things done much faster than their counterparts who do not know the ins and outs of the system.

5. Patience is critical to the success of business transactions. This time consideration should be built into all negotiations, thus preventing one from giving away too much in an effort to reach a quick settlement.

6. Important decisions usually are made in person, not by correspondence or telephone. This is why an MNC's personal presence often is a prerequisite for success in the Arab world. Additionally, while there may be many people who provide input on the final decision, the ultimate power rests with the person at the top, and this individual will rely heavily on personal impressions, trust, and rapport.[55]

The World of *Business Week*—Revisited

As the *Business Week* article at the beginning of the chapter indicated, doing business in different cultures presents multinationals with a variety of challenges. In the case of Wipro, the main customers are in the U.K. and the U.S., two nations with similar cultures. However, Wipro will still face a host of problems related to managing across cultures. For one thing, the company is going to have to establish on-site operations, something it has not done before. In addition, the firm estimates that it will have to hire 30,000 new employees over the next three years, and many of these people will be located in the overseas markets. At the same time, the company will be facing stiff competition from IBM Global and EDS for upper-end business and from Pricewater-houseCoopers and Accenture for lower-end business in international markets where workforces are being downsized and clients are demanding more from their IT out-sourcers. In particular, the international competitive environment is heating up and Wipro must succeed here if it hopes to reach its annual revenue goal of $4 billion. Now that you have read this chapter, you should have a good understanding of the difficulties of managing across cultures. Using this knowledge as a platform, answer the following questions: (1) How can Wipro Technologies' past success prove to be a major problem in its multinational expansion efforts? (2) In what way does the globalization and national responsiveness conflict help explain some of the company's challenges? (3) What are some of the cultural differences between doing business in India and in the U.S. that Wipro is going to have to address if it is to be successful?

Summary of Key Points

1. One major problem facing MNCs is that they attempt to manage across cultures just the way they do in their home country. Globalization is given greater attention than national responsiveness or sovereignty; however, in recent years, under strategic international management, this globalization imperative has begun to be de-emphasized and the need for local focus has gained in importance. A number of factors help to account for this new strategy: (1) the need to address diverse worldwide standards; (2) the importance of differentiating products for local markets; (3) the need to become an insider rather than relying solely on export policies; and (4) the need to give subsidiaries more authority to respond to local conditions.

2. One major challenge when dealing with cross-cultural problems is that of overcoming parochialism and simplification. Parochialism is the tendency to view the world through one's own eyes and perspectives. Simplification is the process of exhibiting the same orientation toward different cultural groups. Another problem is that of doing things the same way in foreign markets as they are done in domestic markets. Research shows that in some cases, this approach can be effective; however, effective cross-cultural management more commonly requires approaches different than those used at home. One area where this is particularly evident is human resource management. Recruitment, selection, training, and compensation often are carried out in different ways in different countries, and what works in the United States may have limited value in other countries and geographic regions.

3. Doing business in various parts of the world requires the recognition and understanding of cultural differences. Some of these differences revolve around the importance the society assigns to time, status, control of decision making, personal accomplishment, and work itself. These types of cultural differences help to explain why effective managers in China or Russia often are quite different from those in France, and why a successful style in the United States will not be ideal in Arab countries.

Key Terms

globalization, *141*

globalization imperative, *143*

guanxi, 155

national responsiveness, *141*

parochialism, *147*

simplification, *147*

Review and Discussion Questions

1. Define "globalization" as used in strategic international management. In what way might globalization be a problem for a successful national organization that is intent on going international? In your answer, provide an example of the problem.

2. Some international management experts contend that globalization and national responsiveness are diametrically opposed forces, and that to accommodate one, a multinational must relax its efforts in the other. In what way is this an accurate statement? In what way is it incomplete or inaccurate?

3. In what way are parochialism and simplification barriers to effective cross-cultural management? In each case, give an example.

4. Many MNCs would like to do business overseas in the same way that they do business domestically. Do research findings show that any approaches that work well in the United States also work well in other cultures? If so, identify and describe two.

5. In most cases, local managerial approaches must be modified when doing business overseas. What are three specific examples that support this statement? Be complete in your answer.

6. What are some categories of cultural differences that help make one country or region of the world different from another? In each case, describe the value or norm and explain how it would result in different behavior in two or more countries. If you like, use the countries discussed in this chapter as your point of reference.

Internet Exercise: Sony's Approach

Sony is a multinational corporation that sells a wide variety of goods in the international marketplace. These range from electronics to on-line games to music—and the Japanese MNC is even in the entertainment business (Sony Pictures Entertainment), producing offerings for both the big screen as well as for television. Visit the MNC's web site at **www.sony.com** and read about some of the latest developments in which the company is engaged. Pay close attention to its new offerings in the areas of electronics, television shows, movies, music, and on-line games. Then answer these three questions: (1) What type of cultural challenges does Sony face when it attempts to market its products worldwide? Is demand universal for all of these offerings or is there a "national responsiveness/ globalization" challenge, as discussed in the chapter, that must be addressed? (2) Investigate the Sony credit card that the company is now offering on-line. Is this a product that will have worldwide appeal, or is it more likely to be restricted to more economically advanced countries? (3) In managing its far-flung enterprise, what are two cultural challenges that the company is likely to face and what will it need to do to respond to these?

Mexico

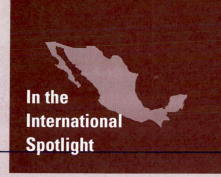

Located directly south of the United States, Mexico covers an area of 756,000 square miles. It is the third-largest country in Latin America and the thirteenth-largest in the world. The most recent estimates place the population at around 100 million and this number is increasing at a rate of about 1.84 percent annually. As a result, today Mexico is one of the "youngest" countries in the world. Approximately 55 percent of the population is under the age of 20, while a mere 4 percent is 65 years of age or older.

Today, even though the economy is uncertain like the rest of the world and has political risk, Mexico has made itself attractive for foreign investment. Multinationals in a wide variety of industries from computers to electronics and from pharmaceuticals to manufacturing have invested billions of dollars in the country. Telefonica, the giant Spanish telecommunications firm, is putting together a wireless network across Latin America and Mexico is one of the countries that it has targeted for investment. Meanwhile, manufacturers not only from the U.S. but also from Asia to Europe have helped sustain Mexico's booming maquiladora assembly industry. By the turn of the century over 1.2 million people were employed in this industry including 600,000 in the two border states of Baja California and Chihuahua.

Thomson SA, the French consumer electronics firm, has three plants in the border states that make export TVs and digital decoder boxes. And like a growing number of MNCs located in Mexico, the firm is now moving away from importing parts and materials from outside and producing everything within the country. One reason for this move is that under the terms of the North American Free Trade Agreement only parts and materials originating in one of the three NAFTA trading partners is now allowed to enter the processing zones duty free. Anything originating outside these three countries is subject to tariffs of as much as 25 percent. So the French MNC Thomson is building a picture-tube factory in Baja, California so that it will no longer have to import dutiable tubes from Italy. In many cases imported items from the European Union, however, are allowed to enter duty free because in 1999 Mexico signed a free-trade agreement with the EU. As a result, a host of firms including Philips Electronics and Siemens poured large amounts of investment into the country. At the same time Mexico also has begun negotiating another free trade pact with the four Nordic countries, raising the likelihood that firms like Nokia, Ericsson, and Saab-Scania will also invest heavily in the country.

While many European MNCs are now investing in Mexico, the United States still remains the largest investor. Over 60 percent of all outside investment is by U.S. firms. Asian companies, in particular Japanese MNCs, also have large holdings in the country, although these firms have been scaling back in recent years because of the import duties and the fact that Mexican labor costs are beginning to rise, thus making it more cost-effective to produce some types of goods in Asia and export them to North America. The largest investments in Mexico are in the industrial sector (around 60 percent of the total) and services (around 30 percent).

One of the major benefits of locating in Mexico is the highly skilled labor force that can be hired at fairly low wages when compared with those paid elsewhere, especially in the United States. Additionally, manufacturing firms that have located there report high productivity growth rates and quality performance. A study by the Massachusetts Institute of Technology on auto assembly plants in Canada, the United States, and Mexico reported that Mexican plants performed well. Another by J. D. Power and Associates noted that Ford Motor's Hermisillo plant was the best in all of North America. Computer and electronic firms are also finding Mexico to be an excellent choice for new expansion plants.

www.mexicool.com

Questions

1. Why would multinationals be interested in setting up operations in Mexico? Give two reasons.

2. In what way would national responsiveness be a strategic issue that these MNCs would have to face?

3. Would cultural differences be a major stumbling block for U.S. MNCs doing business in Mexico? For European firms? For Japanese firms? Explain your answer.

4. Why might MNCs be interested in studying the organizational culture in Mexican firms before deciding whether to locate there? Explain your logic.

Beijing, Here We Come!

A large toy company located in Canada is considering a business arrangement with the government of China (PRC). Although company representatives have not yet visited the PRC, the president of the firm recently met with their representatives in Ottawa and discussed the business proposition. The Canadian CEO learned that the PRC government would be quite happy to study the proposal, and the company's plan would be given a final decision within 90 days of receipt. The toy company now is putting together a detailed proposal and scheduling an on-site visit.

The Canadian firm would like to have the mainland Chinese manufacture a wide variety of toys for sale in Asia as well as in Europe and North America. Production of these toys requires a large amount of labor time, and because the PRC is reputed to have one of the largest and least expensive workforces in the world, the company believes that it can maximize profit by having the work done there. For the past 5 years, the company has had its toys produced in Taiwan. Costs there have been escalating recently, however, and because 45 percent of the production expense goes for labor, the company is convinced that it will soon be priced out of the market if it does not find another source.

The company president and three officers plan on going to Beijing next month to talk with government officials. They would like to sign a 5-year agreement with a price that will not increase by more than 2 percent annually. Production operations then will be turned over to the mainland Chinese, who will have a free hand in manufacturing the goods.

The contract with the Taiwanese firm runs out in 90 days. The company already has contacted this firm, and the latter understands that its Canadian partner plans to terminate the arrangement. One major problem is that if it cannot find another supplier soon, it will have to go back to the Taiwanese firm for at least 2 more years. The contract stipulates that the agreement can be extended for another 24 months if the Canadian firm makes such a request; however, this must be done within 30 days of expiration of the contract. This is not an alternative that appeals to the Canadians, but they feel they will have to take it if they cannot reach an agreement with the mainland Chinese.

Questions

1. What is the likelihood that the Canadians will be able to reach an agreement with the mainland Chinese and not have to go back to their Taiwanese supplier? Explain.

2. Are the Canadians making a strategically wise decision in letting the Chinese from the PRC handle all the manufacturing, or should they insist on getting more actively involved in the production process? Defend your answer.

3. What specific cultural suggestions would you make to the Canadians regarding how to do business with the mainland Chinese?

Chapter 7

Organizational Cultures and Diversity

Objectives of the Chapter

The previous two chapters focused on national cultures. The overriding objective of this chapter is to examine the interaction issues of national culture (diversity) versus organizational cultures and to discuss ways in which MNCs can manage the often inherent conflicts between national and organizational cultures. Many times, the cultural values and resulting behaviors that are common in a particular country are not the same as those needed for a successful MNC; therefore MNCs must learn to deal with this diversity/challenge. Although the field of international management has long recognized the impact of national cultures, only recently has attention been given to the importance of managing organizational cultures and diversity. This chapter first examines common organizational cultures that exist in MNCs, then presents and analyzes ways in which multiculturalism and diversity are being addressed by the best, world-class multinationals. The specific objectives of this chapter are:

1. **DEFINE** exactly what is meant by "organizational culture," and discuss the interaction between national and MNC culture.

2. **IDENTIFY** the four most common categories of organizational culture that have been found through research, and discuss the characteristics of each.

3. **PROVIDE** an overview of the nature and degree of multiculturalism and diversity in today's MNCs.

4. **DISCUSS** common guidelines and principles that are used in building multicultural effectiveness at the team and the organizational levels.

BusinessWeek

The World of *Business Week*

This Euro Brew's for You

It's a hot, muggy summer day in the Belgian city of Leuven. Inside the wood-paneled De Lantaarn café on Vaartstraat, residents are cooling off with the favorite local drink—beer. One customer gulps a cold Stella Artois lager. Another sips a creamy wheat beer called Hoegaarden, while his companion downs a rich amber brew called Abaye de Leffe. Yet another enjoys a bright red cherry-flavored concoction called Belle-Vue.

Such labels convey the richness of Belgium's centuries-old beer heritage, providing enough variety to satisfy even the most demanding beer drinker. Every one is produced by a single company: Leuven's Interbrew. "They supply me with all the brands I need," says café manager Marina Walters.

As the owner of more than 200 brands, Interbrew is ubiquitous in Europe and its products are gaining popularity in Asia and America, even though few customers have ever heard the parent's name. In the past five years, Interbrew has made 17 acquisitions in 11 countries, most recently British alemaker Bass PLC. Along the way, it has remade itself from a small, family-owned company into the world's second-largest brewer. Only Anheuser-Busch Cos. is bigger.

Now, Interbrew CEO Hugo Powell, who holds both Canadian and British citizenship, has set his sights on the U.S., where imported beer consumption is on the rise. Although the sales of domestic microbrews have slowed in recent years, imports have more than taken up the slack—in what analysts call the super-premium market. High-margin import labels, in fact, are growing at about a 10% clip, compared with 3% for beer in general. "Super-premium beers are pulling consumers from wine and spirits," explains Michael Branca, who follows beer companies for Lehman Brothers Inc. Says Powell: "We are hitting the market's sweet spot."

To crack the U.S. market, Interbrew is adapting its tried-and-true European strategy: buy up local brewers, keep those brands, and use their distributor to sell high-margin specialty labels such as Stella and Leffe. The push began quietly in 1995 when Interbrew purchased Canadian brewer Labatt, where Powell was an executive. He and others set about revamping Labatt's Rolling Rock label with new ads that made much of the brewery's homespun origins in rural Latrobe, PA., and began distributing it more aggressively than its former owner. The strategy worked. Last year, sales rose 4%, compared with a 5% drop for other domestic specialty beers.

If Powell has his way, Rolling Rock will be just the beginning. Powell brings a decade of North American marketing experience to Interbrew. And he has hired a team of North American-trained executives to carry out the push. He plans to attack not only fellow importers such as Heineken but also to try to take share from marginal domestic players such as Pabst, Stroh, and Lone Star. In the next few years, he plans to boost distribution of Interbrew's Labatt and Stella

labels, perhaps in a deal that would share distributor networks with Anheuser-Busch or another big U.S. brewer. "We have a giant opportunity," Powell says.

But building a name in the land of light suds won't be easy. Anheuser-Busch, Miller, and Coors control 80% of the market. And instead of having one flagship brand, Interbrew will sell multiple labels, making its strategy more complex. Even importers tend to stick to one big brand. And although imported beers are popular in the U.S., experts wonder how many more minilabels the market will be able to support. Many of Interbrew's brands, moreover, contain more alcohol and tend to be heavier than domestic brews. "You can't drink a 12-pack of Bass or Leffe," says Mitch Meyers, a beer marketing consultant at Zipatoni Co. in St. Louis.

Still, U.S. beermakers are watching Interbrew's invasion with a mixture of anxiety and respect. "They are very competent marketers," says C. James Koch, founder of Boston Beer Co., maker of Samuel Adams, a beer brand that will likely go head to head with Interbrew's quirky lineup. Koch predicts that expansion by the European brewer will help wrest market share from light-beer makers. "Good marketing educates drinkers to choices," he says.

Smart marketing has been an Interbrew strong point since the company was created 13 years ago from the merger of two regional Belgian brewers, Jupiter and Stella Artois. Its first big scores were in France, where Abbaye de Leffe became and remains the No. 1 import, and in Britain, where Stella soared thanks to its snobbish slogan "Reassuringly Expensive." "Stella is a textbook example of premium marketing," says Alex Batchelor, a managing director at consultancy Interbrand.

Elitism, though, can be a tougher sell in the U.S. Still, Interbrew has stealthily moved in the U.S. beer market with early success. Now Powell's goal is to turn Miller time into Interbrew time.

By William Echikson in Leuven, Belgium

Source: **Reprinted from July 24, 2000, pp. 120, 122 issue of** *Business Week* **by special permission, copyright © 2000 by McGraw-Hill Companies, Inc.**

This opening news article focuses on the challenges that a multinational company faces as it expands its worldwide operations. Interbrew's basic strategy is to buy local brewers and then use their brand, operations, and distribution network to market high-margin, specialty beer. This strategy has worked well for the company in Europe. However, in recent years the firm has acquired companies in the U.K., Canada, and the U.S., as well as in Asia, and these new acquisitions are going to present challenges. In particular, the way things are done in Belgian organizations is going to be different from the way they must be done in the U.S. or Asia. The marketing strategy may be the same but the way that business operations are handled will not be the same. Moreover, to continue its growth and to replace Anheuser-Busch as the world's largest brewer, Interbrew is going to have to continue its acquisition strategy. As a result, managing effectively in a host of different country and, equally important, organizational cultures is going to be one of the keys to its success. This will not be easy because the competition that the firm will face in markets such as the United States, where Anheuser-Busch, Miller, and Coors are dominant, is going to challenge the firm's ability to operate in a diverse environment. If Interbrew cannot do this, it will not achieve its major objective of being the world's leading brewer.

■ The Nature of Organizational Culture

The chapters in Part One provided the background on the external environment, and the chapters so far in this part have been concerned with the external culture. Regardless of this environment or cultural context impacting on the MNC, when individuals join an MNC, they not only bring their national culture, which greatly affects their learned beliefs, attitudes, values, and behaviors, with them, but at the same time, they enter into an organizational culture. Employees of MNCs are expected to "fit in." For example, at PepsiCo, personnel are expected to be cheerful, positive, enthusiastic, and have committed optimism; at Ford, they are expected to show self-confidence, assertiveness, and machismo.[1] Regardless of the external environment or their national culture, managers and employees must understand and follow their organization's culture to be successful. After first defining organizational culture, the interaction between national and organizational culture is analyzed. An understanding of this interaction has become recognized as vital to effective international management.

Definition and Characteristics

Organizational culture
A pattern of basic assumptions that are developed by a group as it learns to cope with problems of external adaptation and internal integration and that are taught to new members as the correct way to perceive, think, and feel in relation to these problems.

Organizational culture has been defined in several different ways. Widely recognized organizational cultural theorist Edgar Schein defines it as a pattern of shared basic assumptions that the group learned as it solved its problems of external adaptation and internal integration, that has worked well enough to be considered valid and, therefore, to be taught to new members as the correct way to perceive, think, and feel in relation to those problems.[2]

Regardless of how the term is defined, a number of important characteristics are associated with an organization's culture. These have been summarized as:

1. Observed behavioral regularities, as typified by common language, terminology, and rituals;

2. Norms, as reflected by things such as the amount of work to be done and the degree of cooperation between management and employees;

3. Dominant values that the organization advocates and expects participants to share, such as high product and service quality, low absenteeism, and high efficiency;

4. A philosophy that is set forth in the MNC's beliefs regarding how employees and customers should be treated;

5. Rules that dictate the do's and don'ts of employee behavior relating to areas such as productivity, customer relations, and intergroup cooperation; and

6. Organizational climate, or the overall atmosphere of the enterprise as reflected by the way that participants interact with each other, conduct themselves with customers, and feel about the way they are treated by higher-level management.[3]

These characteristics are not intended to be all-inclusive, but they do help to illustrate the nature of organizational culture.[4] The major problem is that sometimes, an MNC's organizational culture in one country's facility differs sharply from those in other countries. For example, managers who do well in England may be ineffective in Germany, despite the fact that they work for the same MNC. In addition, the cultures of the English and German subsidiaries may differ sharply from those of the home U.S. location. Effectively dealing with this multiculturalism within the various locations of an MNC is a major challenge for international management.

A good example is provided by the German MNC Hoechst AG, the very large chemical company that employs more people on the other side of the Atlantic than in Germany. As its chairman has noted, "We are not merely a German company with foreign interests. One could almost say we are a nonnational company." And because of the high labor costs in Germany, the firm has been expanding its operations to lower-cost regions. It has also been selling some of its German operations, while purchasing businesses in other countries. In the process, Hoechst has also made its top management less German. For example, a Brazilian and an American are members of the firm's nine-member board. The company is also trying to change its culture through new performance-based pay programs. However, getting people to buy into the new culture has proven a challenge. For example:

> After Hoechst integrated its German, French, and American drug operations, German workers feared the American side would have the upper hand. A group of scientists in Frankfurt tried to block a conference to decide which of the company's 55 research projects to eliminate. "For the German employees, it was difficult to hear that what they were doing was not good enough," says research chief Frank Douglas. . . . "There were only a lot of suspicions." As it turned out, only three American projects were given high priority while German projects fared well. Now, Mr. Douglas says, "the German scientists welcome the scrutiny." But the German scientists remain wary of the emphasis on marketing, fearing that it will stifle innovative research. "Everything has to be backed up by 5,000 market studies," one researcher says. But he conceded that Hoechst thought too little about sales in the past.[5]

In some cases companies have deliberately maintained two different business cultures because they do not want the culture of one influencing the other. A good example is J.C. Penney, the giant department store chain. A couple of years ago, the well-known retailer bought control of Renner, a Brazilian retail chain with 20 stores. Rather than impose its own culture on the chain, however, Penney's management took a back seat. Recognizing Renner's reputation for value and service among its middle-class customers, Penney let the Brazilian managers continue to run the stores while it provided assistance in the form of backroom operations, merchandise presentation, logistics, branding, and expansion funds. In a country where fashion is constantly evolving, Renner is able to keep up with the market by changing fashion lines seven to eight times a year. The company also provides rapid checkout service and credit cards to individuals who earn as little as $150 a month, and interest-free installment plans that allow people to pay as little as $5 a month toward their purchase. Thanks to Penney's infusion of capital, in the first two years Renner's opened 30 more stores and sales jumped from $150 million to over $300 million. The culture is totally different from that of Penney's in the U.S., but it is very successful in Brazil.[6]

Interaction Between National and Organizational Cultures

There is a widely held belief that organizational culture tends to moderate or erase the impact of national culture. The logic of such conventional wisdom is that if a U.S. MNC set up operations in say France, it would not be long before the French employees began to "think like Americans." In fact, evidence is accumulating that just the opposite may be true. Hofstede's research found that the national cultural values of employees have a significant impact on their organizational performance, and that the cultural values employees bring to the workplace with them are not easily changed by the organization. So, for example, while some French employees would have a higher power distance than Swedes and some a lower power distance, chances are "that if a company hired locals in Paris, they would, on the whole, be less likely to challenge hierarchical power than would the same number of locals hired in Stockholm."[7]

Andre Laurent's research supports Hofstede's conclusions.[8] He found that cultural differences actually are more pronounced among foreign employees working within the same multinational organization than among personnel working for firms in their native lands. Nancy Adler summarized these research findings as follows:

> When they work for a multinational corporation, it appears that Germans become more German, Americans become more American, Swedes become more Swedish, and so on. Surprised by these results, Laurent replicated the research in two other multinational corporations, each with subsidiaries in the same nine Western European countries and the United States. Similar to the first company, corporate culture did not reduce or eliminate national differences in the second and third corporations. Far from reducing national differences, organization culture maintains and enhances them.[9]

There often are substantial differences between the organizational cultures of different subsidiaries, and of course, this can cause coordination problems. For example, when the Upjohn Company of Kalamazoo, Michigan merged with Pharmacia AB of Sweden, which also has operations in Italy, the Americans failed to realize some of the cultural differences between themselves and their new European partners. As was reported in the *Wall Street Journal,* "Swedes take off the entire month of July for vacation, virtually en masse, and Italians take off August. Everyone in *Europe* knows, that is, but apparently hardly anyone in Kalamazoo, Mich., does."[10] As a result, a linkup that was supposed to give a quick boost to the two companies, solving problems such as aging product lines and pressure from giant competitors, never got off the ground. Things had to be rescheduled and both partners ended up having to meet and talk about their cultural differences, so that each side better understood the "dos and don'ts" of doing business with the other.

When the two firms first got together, they never expected these types of problems. Upjohn, with household names such as Rogaine and Motrin, had no likely breakthroughs in its product pipeline, so it was happy to merge with Pharmacia. The latter had developed a solid roster of allergy medicines, human-growth hormone, and other drugs, but its distribution in the United States was weak and its product line was aging. So a merger seemed ideal for both firms. The big question was how to bring the two companies together. Given that Pharmacia had recently acquired an Italian firm, there was a proposal by the European group that there be three major centers—Kalamazoo, Stockholm, and Milan—as well as a new headquarters in London. However, this arrangement had a number of built-in problems. For one, the executives in Italy and Sweden were accustomed to reporting to local bosses. Second, the people in London did not know a great deal about how to coordinate operations in Sweden and Italy. American cultural values added even more problems in that at Upjohn workers were tested for drug and alcohol abuse, but in Italy waiters pour wine freely every afternoon in the company dining room and Pharmacia's boardrooms were stocked with humidors for executives who liked to light a cigar during long meetings. Quite obviously, there were cultural differences that had to be resolved by the companies. In the end, Pharmacia & Upjohn said, it would meld the different cultures and attitudes and get on with its growth plans. However, one thing is certain: The different cultures of the merged firms created a major challenge.

In examining and addressing the differences between organizational cultures, Hofstede has provided the early database of a set of proprietary cultural-analysis techniques and programs known as DOCSA (Diagnosing Organizational Culture for Strategic Application). This approach has identified the dimensions of organizational culture summarized in Table 7–1. It was found that when cultural comparisons were made between different subsidiaries of an MNC, different cultures often existed in each one. Such cultural differences within an MNC could reduce the ability of units to work well together; an example is provided in Figure 7–1, which shows the cultural dimensions of a California-based MNC and its European subsidiary as perceived by the Europeans. A close comparison of these perceptions reveals some startling differences.

The Europeans viewed the culture in the U.S. facilities as only slightly activities-oriented (see Table 7–1 for a description of these dimensions), but they saw their own European operations much more heavily activities-oriented. The U.S. operation was viewed as moderately people-oriented, but their own relationships were viewed as very job-oriented. The Americans were seen as having a slight identification with their own organization, while the Europeans had a much stronger identification. The Americans were perceived as being very open in their communications; the Europeans saw themselves as moderately closed. The Americans were viewed as preferring very loose control, while the Europeans felt they preferred somewhat tight control. The Americans were seen as somewhat conventional in their conduct, while the Europeans saw themselves as somewhat pragmatic. If these perceptions are accurate, then it obviously would be necessary for both groups to discuss their cultural differences and carefully coordinate their activities to work well together.

Table 7–1
Dimensions of Corporate Culture

Motivation	
Activities	**Outputs**
To be consistent and precise. To strive for accuracy and attention to detail. To refine and perfect. Get it right.	To be pioneers. To pursue clear aims and objectives. To innovate and progress. Go for it.
Relationship	
Job	**Person**
To put the demands of the job before the needs of the individual.	To put the needs of the individual before the needs of the job.
Identity	
Corporate	**Professional**
To identify with and uphold the expectations of the employing organizations.	To pursue the aims and ideals of each professional practice.
Communication	
Open	**Closed**
To stimulate and encourage a full and free exchange of information and opinion.	To monitor and control the exchange and accessibility of information and opinion.
Control	
Tight	**Loose**
To comply with clear and definite systems and procedures.	To work flexibly and adaptively according to the needs of the situation.
Conduct	
Conventional	**Pragmatic**
To put the expertise and standards of the employing organization first. To do what we know is right.	To put the demands and expectations of customers first. To do what they ask.

Source: Reported in Lisa Hoecklin, *Managing Cultural Differences: Strategies for Competitive Advantage* (Workingham, England: Addison-Wesley, 1995), p. 146.

Figure 7–1

Europeans' Perception of the Cultural Dimensions of U.S. Operations (A) and European Operations (B) of the Same MNC

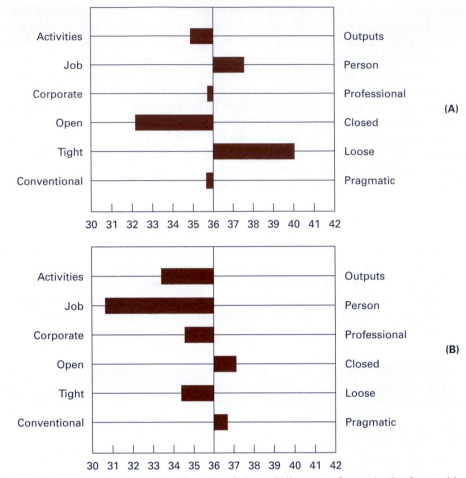

Source: Reported in Lisa Hoecklin, *Managing Cultural Differences: Strategies for Competitive Advantage* (Workingham, England: Addison-Wesley, 1995), pp. 147–148.

This analysis is relevant to multinational alliances. It shows that even though an alliance may exist, the partners will bring different organizational cultures with them. Lessem and Neubauer, who have portrayed Europe as offering four distinct ways of dealing with multiculturalism (based on the United Kingdom, French, German, and Italian characteristics), provide an example, and Table 7–2 briefly describes each of these sets of cultural characteristics. A close examination of the differences highlights how difficult it can be to do business with two or more of these groups, because each perceives things differently from the others. Another example is the way in which negotiations occur between groups; here are some contrasts between French and Spanish negotiators[11]:

French	Spanish
Look for a meeting of minds.	Look for a meeting of people.
Intellectual competence is very important.	Social competence is very important.
Persuasion through carefully prepared and skilled rhetoric is employed.	Persuasion through emotional appeal is employed.
Strong emphasis is given to a logical presentation of one's position coupled with well-reasoned, detailed solutions.	Socialization always precedes negotiations, which are characterized by an exchange of grand ideas and general principles.
A contract is viewed as a well-reasoned transaction.	A contract is viewed as a long-lasting relationship.
Trust emerges slowly and is based on the evaluation of perceived status and intellect.	Trust is developed on the basis of frequent and warm interpersonal contact and transaction.

Table 7–2
European Management Characteristics

| | Characteristic | | | |
Dimension	Western (United Kingdom)	Northern (France)	Eastern (Germany)	Southern (Italy)
Corporate	Commercial	Administrative	Industrial	Familial
Management attributes				
Behavior	Experiential	Professional	Developmental	Convivial
Attitude	Sensation	Thought	Intuition	Feeling
Institutional models				
Function	Salesmanship	Control	Production	Personnel
Structure	Transaction	Hierarchy	System	Network
Societal ideas				
Economics	Free market	Dirigiste	Social market	Communal
Philosophy	Pragmatic	Rational	Holistic	Humanistic
Cultural images				
Art	Theatre	Architecture	Music	Dance
Culture	(Anglo-Saxon)	(Gallic)	(Germanic)	(Latin)

Source: Reported in Lisa Hoecklin, *Managing Cultural Differences: Strategies for Competitive Advantage* (Workingham, England: Addison-Wesley, 1995), p. 149.

Such comparisons also help to explain why it can be difficult for an MNC to break into foreign markets where there is only local competition. The accompanying box "McDonald's Tackles Eating Habits in Brazil," provides an illustration. When dealing with these challenges, MNCs must work hard to understand the varying nature of the organizational cultures in their worldwide network and to both moderate and adapt their operations in a way that accommodates these individual units. A large part of this process calls for carefully understanding the nature of the various organizational cultures, and the next section examines the different types in detail.

■ Organizational Cultures in MNCs

Organizational cultures of MNCs are shaped by a number of factors, including the cultural preferences of the leaders and employees. In the international arena, some MNCs have subsidiaries that, except for the company logo and reporting procedures, would not be easily recognizable as belonging to the same multinational.[12]

Given that many recent international expansions are a result of mergers or acquisition, the integration of these organizational cultures is a critical concern in international management. Numeroff and Abrahams have suggested that there are four steps that are critical in this process: (1) The two groups have to establish the purpose, goal, and focus of their merger; (2) Then they have to develop mechanisms to identify the most important organizational structures and management roles; (3) They have to determine who has authority over the resources needed for getting things done; and (4) They have to identify the expectations of all involved parties and facilitate communication between both departments and individuals in the structure.

> Companies all over the world are finding out firsthand that there is more to an international merger or acquisition than just sharing resources and capturing greater market share. Differences in workplace cultures sometimes temporarily overshadow the overall goal of long-term success of the newly formed entity. With the proper management framework and execution, successful integration of cultures is not only possible, but the most preferable paradigm in which to operate. It is the role of the sponsors and managers to keep sight of the necessity to create, maintain, and support the notion of a united front. It is only when this assimilation has occurred that an international merger or acquisition can truly be labeled a success.[13]

International Management in Action

McDonald's Tackles Eating Habits in Brazil   www.mcdonalds.com

People in Brazil like to buy American goods. This is one reason why McDonald's, with perhaps the strongest organizational culture representing American values, is rapidly expanding its investment in this country. Over the last three years the firm has spent almost $500 million to nearly double the number of restaurants in Brazil. At the same time, sales growth has been slow and when the inflation rate is factored into the investment equation, McDonald's is not taking home a great deal of profit. Nor have things been helped along by the fact that the firm has had to discount its prices in order to increase demand. This Brazilian experience by McDonald's is an example where organizational culture, no matter how strong, is affected by national culture.

A challenge is how to get more Brazilians to eat at their local McDonald's. Over the last 36 months the company's Brazilian revenues have more than doubled to about $800 million. However, much of this demand has come from upper- and middle-class customers. As the company begins to further penetrate the market, it will have to begin making inroads among those consumers for whom a milkshake and a hamburger seem exotic. An accompanying challenge is that of changing the culture and getting people to eat breakfast at a local unit. In Brazil people have breakfast at home, thus making it next to impossible to market offerings such as Egg McMuffins. And even getting people to come to the unit for lunch can be difficult. Most workers are accustomed to going home for lunch—and then taking a nap.

The company is currently facing a big gamble that the economy will remain sufficiently strong and it can change the eating habits of millions of people and get

them to come to Mickey D's on a regular basis. Unfortunately, some of this may be wishful thinking. As one observer recently noted:

> Especially in the lower-income areas, McDonald's finds that old habits die hard. Just a couple of blocks from a McDonald's in a working-class Rio neighborhood, delivery man Manoel Ribeiro stands at the counter of a typical Brazilian greasy spoon feasting on a baked ham-and-cheese wrap and a boiled egg—a meal that costs half the $2.80 or so that he would pay for a Big Mac. "I work too hard for my money to experiment on American food," he says, between bites. His attitude isn't uncommon in a country where per-capita income runs about $3,500 a year.[15]

The challenge for McDonald's is going to be to keep its prices low and to convince a growing number of people that a Big Mac and a milkshake can be a meal for everybody—not just for North Americans. The firm also hopes that by lowering its prices, it will be able to break down some of these cultural barriers. Recent research, however, shows that even with these lower prices, annual sales have been flat in dollar terms. Moreover, while the company continues to open more and more new stores, current unit owners believe that this strategy is simply drawing business away from them. As one of them explained it, "There is a definite limit as to how much fast food in this market is ready to consume now."[16] Obviously Mickey D, regardless of its strong organizational culture, has work cut out for it to penetrate the Brazilian market (culture).

In addition, there are three aspects of organizational functioning that seem to be especially important in determining MNC organizational culture: (1) the general relationship between the employees and their organization; (2) the hierarchical system of authority that defines the roles of managers and subordinates; and (3) the general views that employees hold about the MNC's purpose, destiny, goals, and their places in them.[14] When examining these dimensions of organizational culture, Trompenaars has suggested the use of two continua. One distinguishes between equity and hierarchy; the other examines orientation to the person and the task. Along these continua, which are shown in Figure 7–2, he identifies and describes four different types of organizational cultures: family, Eiffel Tower, guided missile, and incubator.

In practice, of course, organizational cultures do not fit neatly into any of these four, but the groupings can be useful in helping to examine the bases of how individuals relate to each other, think, learn, change, are motivated, and resolve conflict. The following discussion examines each of these cultural types.

Family culture
A culture that is characterized by a strong emphasis on hierarchy and orientation to the person.

Family Culture

Family culture is characterized by a strong emphasis on the hierarchy and orientation to the person. The result is a family-type environment that is power-oriented and headed by a leader who is regarded as a caring parent and one who knows what is best for the personnel.

Figure 7–2

**Organizational
Cultures**

Source: Adapted from Fons Trompenaars, *Riding the Waves of Culture: Understanding Diversity in Global Business* (Burr Ridge, IL: Irwin, 1994), p. 154.

Trompenaars has found that this organizational culture is common in countries such as Turkey, Pakistan, Venezuela, China, Hong Kong, and Singapore.

In this culture, personnel not only respect the individuals who are in charge but look to them for both guidance and approval as well. In turn, management assumes a paternal relationship regarding their personnel, looks after them, and tries to ensure that they are treated well and have continued employment. These cultures also are characterized by traditions, customs, and associations that bind together the personnel and make it difficult for outsiders to become members.

When it works well, the family culture can catalyze and multiply the energies of the personnel and appeal to their deepest feelings and aspirations. When it works poorly, members of the organization end up supporting a leader who is ineffective and drains their energies and loyalties.

This type of culture is foreign to most in the United States, who believe in valuing people based on their abilities and achievements, not on their age or position in the hierarchy. As a result, many managers in U.S.-based MNCs fail to understand why senior-level managers in overseas subsidiaries might appoint a relative to a high-level, sensitive position even though that individual might not appear to be the best qualified for the job. They fail to realize that family ties are so strong that the appointed relative would never do anything to embarrass or let down the family member who made the appointment. Here is an example:

> A Dutch delegation was shocked and surprised when the Brazilian owner of a large manufacturing company introduced his relatively junior accountant as the key coordinator of a $15 million joint venture. The Dutch were puzzled as to why a recently qualified accountant had been given such weighty responsibilities, including the receipt of their own money. The Brazilians pointed out that the young man was the best possible choice among 1,200 employees since he was the nephew of the owner. Who could be more trustworthy than that? Instead of complaining, the Dutch should consider themselves lucky that he was available.[17]

Other characteristics of family culture include the emphasis given to intuitive rather than rational knowledge. More concern is given to the development of people rather than their deployment or use. Personal knowledge of others is more important than empirical knowledge about them. Conversations are more important than research questionnaires, and subjective data are superior to objective data. In addition, people in family cultures tend to be motivated more by praise and appreciation than by money. They tend to socialize risk by spreading it among the members, and they resist motivation programs that threaten family bonds. These cultural values suggest that human-resource approaches such as pay-for-performance plans may be ineffective in this type of culture.

Eiffel Tower Culture

Eiffel Tower culture is characterized by a strong emphasis on the hierarchy and orientation to the task. Under this organizational culture, jobs are well defined, employees know what they are supposed to do, and everything is coordinated from the top. As a result, this culture is steep, narrow at the top, and broad at the base, thus the term "Eiffel Tower," which is constructed in this manner.

Unlike family culture, where the leader is revered and considered to be the source of all power, the person holding the top position in the Eiffel Tower culture could be replaced at any time, and this would have no effect on the work that organization members are doing or on the organization's reasons for existence. In this culture, relationships are specific, and status remains with the job. Therefore, if the boss of an Eiffel Tower subsidiary were playing golf with a subordinate, the subordinate would not feel any pressure to let the boss win. In addition, these managers seldom create off-the-job relationships with their people, because they believe this could affect their rational judgment. In fact, this culture operates very much like a formal hierarchy—impersonal and efficient.

> Each role at each level of the hierarchy is described, rated for its difficulty, complexity, and responsibility, and has a salary attached to it. There then follows a search for a person to fill it. In considering applicants for the role, the personnel department will treat everyone equally and neutrally, match the person's skills and aptitudes with the job requirements, and award the job to the best fit between role and person. The same procedure is followed in evaluations and promotions.[18]

Eiffel Tower cultures most commonly are found in Northwest European countries. Examples include Denmark, Germany, and the Netherlands. The way that people in this culture learn and change differs sharply from that in the family culture. Learning involves the accumulation of skills necessary to fit a role, and organizations will use qualifications in deciding how to schedule, deploy, and reshuffle personnel to meet their needs. The organization also will employ such rational procedures as assessment centers, appraisal systems, training and development programs, and job rotation in managing its human resources. All these procedures help to ensure that a formal hierarchic or bureaucracy-like approach works well. When changes need to be made, however, the Eiffel Tower culture often is ill-equipped to handle things. Manuals must be rewritten, procedures changed, job descriptions altered, promotions reconsidered, and qualifications reassessed.

This same, methodic approach is used in motivating and rewarding people and in resolving conflict. Carefully designed rules and policies are relied on, and things are done "by the book." Conflicts are viewed as irrational and offenses against efficiency; criticisms and complaints are handled through channels. The organizational participants carry out these tasks by viewing them as obligations to their jobs, not as responsibilities to specific individuals. Because the Eiffel Tower culture does not rely on values that are similar to those in most U.S. MNCs, U.S. expatriate managers often have difficulty initiating change in these cultures. As Trompenaars notes:

> An American manager responsible for initiating change in a German company described to me the difficulties he had in making progress, although the German managers had discussed the new strategy in depth and made significant contributions to its formulation. Through informal channels, he had eventually discovered that his mistake was not having formalized the changes to structure or job descriptions. In the absence of a new organization chart, this Eiffel Tower company was unable to change.[19]

Guided Missile Culture

Guided missile culture is characterized by a strong emphasis on equality in the workplace and orientation to the task. This organizational culture is oriented to work, which typically is undertaken by teams or project groups. Unlike the Eiffel Tower culture, where job assignments are fixed and limited, personnel in the guided missile culture do whatever it takes to get the job done. This culture derived its name from high-tech organizations such as the National Aeronautics and Space Administration (NASA), which pioneered the use of project groups working on space probes that resembled guided missiles. In these large project teams, more than a hundred different types of engineers often were responsible for building, say, a lunar landing module. The team member whose contribution would be crucial at any given time in the project typically could not be known in advance. Therefore, all types of engineers had to work in close harmony and cooperate with everyone on the team.

To be successful, the best form of synthesis must be used in the course of working on the project. For example, in a guided missile project, formal hierarchical considerations are given low priority, and individual expertise is of greatest importance. Additionally, everyone in the team is equal (or at least potentially equal), because their relative contributions to the project are not yet known. All teams treat each other with respect, because they may need the other for assistance. This egalitarian and task-driven organizational culture fits well with the national cultures of the United States and United Kingdom, which helps to explain why high-tech MNCs commonly locate their operations in these countries.

Guided missile organizational cultures generally are made up of professionals who are formed into cross-disciplinary teams. Moreover, the objectives of project teams are time bound; once objectives are accomplished, the team members move to other groups. An interesting situation sometimes develops in MNCs where an operation with a guided missile culture is combined (superimposed) with another unit having a more traditional, Eiffel Tower culture into what is called a "matrix structure." Of course, given the nature of both organizations, there can be a culture clash, because the bureaucratic design of the Eiffel Tower arrangement contrasts sharply with the flexible, changing design of the guided missile group.

The way in which members of a guided missile organizational culture learn and change differs sharply from that of either family or Eiffel Tower cultures. The missile structure could be called "cybernetic," meaning that the focus is on a particular objective and there is direct feedback to measure progress. Additionally, changes typically are corrective and conservative, because the overall goal remains constant. Learning involves finding out how to get along with people; playing the role of an active, contributing team member; being practical rather than theoretic; and focusing on problem solving. Moreover, in these missile cultures, performance appraisal often is carried out by peers and subordinates rather than just the boss. When bosses, peers, and subordinates all have an input into the evaluation, this is called "360-degree feedback," which is becoming increasingly popular in these organizations.

Unlike the family and Eiffel Tower cultures, change in the guided missile culture comes quickly. Goals are accomplished, and teams are reconfigured and assigned new objectives. People move from group to group, and loyalties to one's profession and project often are greater than those to the organization per se.

Trompenaars found that the motivation of those in guided missile cultures tends to be more intrinsic than just concern for money and benefits. Team members become enthusiastic about, and identify with, the struggle toward attaining their goal. For example, a project team that is designing and building a new computer for the Asian market may be highly motivated to create a machine that is at the leading edge of technology, user friendly, and will sweep the market. Everything else is secondary to this overriding objective. Thus, both intragroup and intergroup conflicts are minimized and petty problems between team members set aside; everyone is so committed to the project's main goal that they do not have time for petty disagreements. As Trompenaars notes:

> This culture tends to be individualistic since it allows for a wide variety of differently specialized persons to work with each other on a temporary basis. The scenery of faces keeps changing. Only the pursuit of chosen lines of personal development is constant. The team is a vehicle for the shared enthusiasm of its members, but is itself disposable and will be discarded when the project ends. Members are garrulous, idiosyncratic, and intelligent, but their mutuality is a means, not an end. It is a way of enjoying the journey. They do not need to know each other intimately, and may avoid doing so. Management by objectives is the language spoken, and people are paid for performance.[20]

Table 7–3
Summary Characteristics of the Four Corporate Cultures

Characteristic	Corporate Culture			
	Family	**Eiffel Tower**	**Guided Missile**	**Incubator**
Relationships between employees	Diffuse relationships to organic whole to which one is bonded	Specific role in mechanical system of required interaction	Specific tasks in cybernetic system targeted on shared objectives	Diffuse, spontaneous relationships growing out of shared creative process
Attitude toward authority	Status is ascribed to parent figures who are close and powerful	Status is ascribed to superior roles that are distant yet powerful	Status is achieved by project group members who contribute to targeted goal	Status is achieved by individuals exemplifying creativity and growth
Ways of thinking and learning	Intuitive, holistic, lateral and error-correcting	Logical, analytical, vertical, and rationally efficient	Problem centered, professional, practical, cross-disciplinary	Process oriented, creative, ad hoc, inspirational
Attitudes toward people	Family members	Human resources	Specialists and experts	Co-creators
Ways of changing	"Father" changes course	Change rules and procedures	Shift aim as target moves	Improvise and attune
Ways of motivating and rewarding	Intrinsic satisfaction in being loved and respected	Promotion to greater position, larger role	Pay or credit for performance and problems solved	Participation in the process of creating new realities
	Management by subjectives	Management by job description	Management by objectives	Management by enthusiasm
Criticism and conflict resolution	Turn other cheek, save other's face, do not lose power game	Criticism is accusation of irrationalism unless there are procedures to arbitrate conflicts	Constructive task-related only, then admit error and correct fast	Improve creative idea, not negate it

Source: Adapted from Fons Trompenaars and Charles Hampden-Turner, *Riding the Waves of Culture: Understanding Diversity in Global Business,* 2nd ed. (Burr Ridge, IL: Irwin, 1998), p. 183.

Incubator Culture

Incubator culture
A culture that is characterized by a strong emphasis on equality and orientation to the person.

Incubator culture is the fourth major type of organizational culture that Trompenaars identified, and it is characterized by a strong emphasis on equality and personal orientation. This culture is based heavily on the existential idea that organizations per se are secondary to the fulfillment of the individuals within them. This culture is based on the premise that the role of organizations is to serve as incubators for the self-expression and self-fulfillment of their members; as a result, this culture often has little formal structure. Participants in an incubator culture are there primarily to perform roles such as confirming, criticizing, developing, finding resources for, and/or helping to complete the development of an innovative product or service. These cultures often are found among start-up firms in Silicon Valley, California, or Silicon Glen, Scotland. These incubator-type organizations typically are entrepreneurial and often founded and made up by a creative team who left larger, Eiffel-Tower-type employers. They want to be part of an organization where their creative talents will not be stifled.

Incubator cultures often create environments where participants thrive in an intense, emotional commitment to the nature of the work. For example, the group may be in the process of gene splitting that could lead to radical medical breakthroughs and extend life. Often, personnel in such cultures are overworked, and the enterprise typically is underfunded. As breakthroughs occur and the company gains stability, however, it starts moving down the road toward commercialization and profit. In turn, this engenders the need to hire more people and develop formalized procedures for ensuring the smooth flow of operations.

Figure 7–3

National Patterns of Corporate Culture

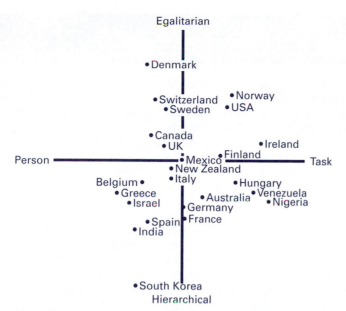

Source: Adapted from Fons Trompenaars and Charles Hampden-Turner, *Riding the Waves of Culture: Understanding Diversity in Global Business,* 2nd ed. (New York: McGraw-Hill, 1998), p. 184.

In this process of growth and maturity, the unique characteristics of the incubator culture begin to wane and disappear, and the culture is replaced by one of the other types (family, Eiffel Tower, or guided missile).

As noted, change in the incubator culture often is fast and spontaneous. All participants are working toward the same objective. Because there may not yet be a customer who is using the final output, however, the problem itself often is open to redefinition, and the solution typically is generic in that it is aimed at a universe of applications. Meanwhile, motivation of the personnel remains highly intrinsic and intense, and it is common to find them working 70 hours a week-and loving it. The participants are more concerned with the unfolding creative process than they are in gathering power or ensuring personal monetary gain. In sharp contrast to the family culture, leadership in this incubator culture is achieved, not gained by position.

Organizational Cultures and Country Preferences

The four organizational cultures described by Trompenaars are "pure" types and seldom exist in practice. Rather the types are mixed and, as shown in Table 7–3, overlaid with one of the four major types of culture dominating the corporate scene.

Recently, Trompenaars and his associates have created a questionnaire designed to identify national patterns of corporate culture as shown in Figure 7–3. Commenting on the instrument and the results of the analysis, he has explained that:

> Sixteen questions were devised which deal with general concepts of egalitarianism versus hierarchy, degrees of formality, different forms of conflict resolution, learning, and so on. Respondents are asked to choose between four possible descriptions of their company, which are geared respectively to the power-priority of the family, the role-dominance of the Eiffel Tower, the task-orientation of the guided missile and the person-orientation of the incubator. This work is fairly new; the database currently totals 13,000 and we have significant samples for 42 countries. These show very marked distinctions. . . . [They show] the highest scores for guided missile companies in the USA and the UK, and the highest for family companies in France and Spain. Sweden scores highest for incubators and Germany for Eiffel Towers.[21]

This analysis would suggest that MNCs who have operations in a number of different countries should adjust their local organizational cultures to fit that country's culture. At the same time, however, these subsidiaries must be able to coordinate their local operations

In recent years, a growing number of multinationals have begun to expand their operations, realizing that if they do not increase their worldwide presence now, they likely will be left behind in the near future. In turn, this has created a number of different challenges for these MNCs, including making a fit between their home organizational culture and those at local levels in the different countries where the MNC operates. Matsushita provides an excellent example in how they have handled this challenge with their macro/micro approach. This huge, Japanese MNC has developed a number of guidelines that it uses in setting up and operating its more than 150 industrial units. At the same time, the company complements these macro guidelines with on-site micro techniques that help to create the most appropriate organizational culture in the subsidiary.

At the macro level, Matsushita employs six overall guidelines that are followed in all locales. They include: (1) be a good corporate citizen in every country, among other things, by respecting cultures, customs, and languages; (2) give overseas operations the best manufacturing technology the company has available; (3) keep the expatriate head count down, and groom local management to take over; (4) let operating plants set their own rules, fine-tuning manufacturing processes to match the skills of the workers; (5) create local research and development to tailor products to markets; and (6) encourage competition between overseas outposts and with plants back home.

Working within these macro guidelines, Matsushita then allows each local unit to create its own culture. The Malaysian operations are a good example. Since 1987, Matsushita has set up 13 new subsidiaries in Malaysia, and employment there has more than quadrupled,

to approximately 25,000 people. Only 230 of these employees, however, are Japanese. From these Malaysian operations, Matsushita currently produces 1.3 million televisions and 1.8 million air conditioners annually, and 90 percent of these units are shipped overseas. To produce this output, local plants reflect Malaysia's cultural mosaic of Muslim Malays, ethnic Chinese, and Indians. To accommodate this diversity, Matsushita cafeterias offer Malaysian, Chinese, and Indian food, and to accommodate Muslim religious customs, Matsushita provides special prayer rooms at each plant and allows two prayer sessions per shift.

How well does this Malaysian workforce perform for the Japanese MNC? In the past, the Malaysian plants' slogan was "Let's catch up with Japan." Today, however, these plants frequently outperform their Japanese counterparts in both quality and efficiency. The comparison with Japan no longer is used. Additionally, Matsushita has found that the Malaysian culture is very flexible, and the locals are able to work well with almost any employer. Commenting on Malaysia's multiculturalism, Matsushita's managing director notes, "They are used to accommodating other cultures, and so they think of us Japanese as just another culture. That makes it much easier for us to manage them than some other nationalities."

Today, Matsushita faces a number of important challenges, including remaining profitable in a slow-growth, high-cost Japanese economy. Fortunately, this MNC is doing extremely well overseas, which is buying it time to get its house in order back home. A great amount of this success results from the MNC's ability to nurture and manage overseas organizational cultures (such as in Malaysia) that are both diverse and highly productive.

with other organizational groups in the MNC so that all units operate in harmony and unity of purpose. A good example is provided by the accompanying "International Management in Action: Matsushita Goes Global."

■ Managing Multiculturalism and Diversity

As the "International Management in Action" box on Matsushita indicates, success in the international arena often is greatly determined by an MNC's ability to manage both multiculturalism and diversity.[22] Both domestically and internationally, organizations find themselves leading workforces that have a variety of cultures (and subcultures) and consist of a largely diverse population of women, men, young and old people, blacks, whites, Latins, Asians, Arabs, Indians, and many others.

Phases of Multicultural Development

The effect of multiculturalism and diversity will vary depending on the stage of the firm in its international evolution. Table 7–4 depicts the characteristics of the major phases in this evolution. For example, Adler has noted that international cultural diversity has minimal impact on domestic organizations, although domestic multiculturalism has a highly signif-

Table 7–4
The Evolution of International Corporations

Characteristics/ Activities	Phase I (Domestic Corporations)	Phase II (International Corporations)	Phase III (Multinational Corporations)	Phase IV (Global Corporations)
Primary orientation	Product/service	Market	Price	Strategy
Competitive strategy	Domestic	Multidomestic	Multinational	Global
Importance of world business	Marginal	Important	Extremely important	Dominant
Product/service	New, unique	More standardized	Completely standardized (commodity)	Mass-customized
	Product engineering emphasized	Process engineering emphasized	Engineering not emphasized	Product and process engineering
Technology	Proprietary	Shared	Widely shared	Instantly and extensively shared
R&D/sales	High	Decreasing	Very low	Very high
Profit margin	High	Decreasing	Very low	High, yet immediately decreasing
Competitors	None	Few	Many	Significant (few or many)
Market	Small, domestic	Large, multidomestic	Larger, multinational	Largest, global
Production location	Domestic	Domestic and primary markets	Multinational, least cost	Imports and exports
Exports	None	Growing, high potential	Large, saturated	Imports and exports
Structure	Functional divisions	Functional with international division	Multinational lines of business	Global alliances, hierarchy
	Centralized	Decentralized	Centralized	Coordinated, decentralized
Primary orientation	Product/service	Market	Price	Strategy
Strategy	Domestic	Multidomestic	Multinational	Global
Perspective	Ethnocentric	Polycentric/ regiocentric	Multinational	Global/multicentric
Cultural sensitivity	Marginally important	Very important	Somewhat important	Critically important
With whom	No one	Clients	Employees	Employees and clients
Level	No one	Workers and clients	Managers	Executives
Strategic assumption	"One way"/ one best way"	"Many good ways," equifinality	"One least-cost way"	"Many good ways," simultaneously

Source: Nancy J. Adler, *International Dimensions of Organizational Behavior,* 2nd ed. (Boston: PWS-Kent Publishing, 1991), pp. 7–8.

icant impact. As firms begin exporting to foreign clients, however, and become what she calls "international organizations" (Phase II in Table 7–4), they must adapt their approach and products to those of the local market. For these international firms, the impact of multiculturalism is highly significant. As companies become what she calls "multinational firms" (Phase III), they often find that price tends to dominate all other considerations, and the direct impact of culture may lessen slightly. For those who continue this international evolution, however, and become full-blown "global companies" (Phase IV), the impact of culture again becomes extremely important. Notes Adler:

> Global firms need an understanding of cultural dynamics to plan their strategy, to locate production facilities and suppliers worldwide, to design and market culturally appropriate products and services, as well as to manage cross-cultural interaction throughout the organization—from senior executive committees to the shop floor. As more firms today move from domestic, international, and multinational organizations to operating as truly global organizations and alliances, the importance of cultural diversity increases markedly. What once was "nice to understand" becomes imperative for survival, let alone success.[23]

Figure 7–4

Location of International Cross-Cultural Interaction

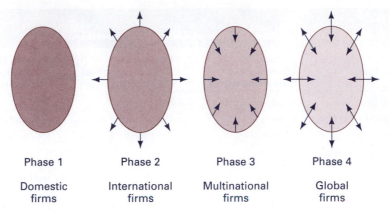

Phase 1	Phase 2	Phase 3	Phase 4
Domestic firms	International firms	Multinational firms	Global firms

Source: Nancy J. Adler, *International Dimensions of Organizational Behavior,* 2nd ed. (Boston: PWS-Kent Publishing, 1991), p. 123.

As shown in Figure 7–4, international culture diversity traditionally affects neither the domestic firm's organizational culture nor its relationship with its customers or clients. These firms work domestically, and only domestic multiculturalism has a direct impact on their dynamics as well as their relationship to the external environment.

Conversely, among international firms, which focus on exporting and producing abroad, cultural diversity has a strong impact on their external relationships with potential buyers and foreign employees. In particular, these firms rely heavily on expatriate managers to help manage operations; as a result, the diversity focus is from the inside out. This is the reverse of what happens in multinational firms, where there is less emphasis on managing cultural differences outside the firm and more on managing cultural diversity within the company. This is because multinational firms hire personnel from all over the world. Adler notes that these multinational firms need to develop cross-cultural management skills up the levels of the hierarchy. As shown in Figure 7–4, this results in a diversity focus that is primarily internal.

Global firms need both an internal and an external diversity focus (again see Figure 7–4). To be effective, everyone in the global organization needs to develop cross-cultural skills that allow them to work effectively with internal personnel as well as external customers, clients, and suppliers.

Types of Multiculturalism

For the international management arena, there are several ways of examining multiculturalism and diversity. One is to focus on the domestic multicultural and diverse workforce that operates in the MNC's home country. In addition to domestic multiculturalism, there is the diverse workforce in other geographic locales, and increasingly common are the mix of domestic and overseas personnel found in today's MNCs. The following discussion examines both domestic and group multiculturalism and the potential problems and strengths.

Domestic Multiculturalism   It is not necessary for today's organizations to do business in another country to encounter people with diverse cultural backgrounds. Culturally distinct populations can be found within organizations almost everywhere in the world. In Singapore, for example, there are four distinct cultural and linguistic groups: Chinese, Eurasian, Indian, and Malay. In Switzerland, there are four distinct ethnic communities: French, German, Italian, and Romansch. In Belgium, there are two linguistic groups: French and Flemish. In the United States, millions of first-generation immigrants have brought both their language and their culture. In Los Angeles, for example, there are more Samoans than on the island of Samoa, more Israelis than in any other city outside Israel, and more first- and second-generation Mexicans than in any other city except Mexico City. In Miami, over one-half the population is Latin, and most residents speak Spanish fluently. More Puerto Ricans live in New York City than in Puerto Rico.

It is even possible to examine domestic multiculturalism within the same ethnic groups. For example, Lee, after conducting research in Singapore among small Chinese

Table 7–5
Perspectives of Older and Younger Generations in Small Chinese Family Businesses in Singapore

Older Generation	Younger Generation
Claim that they have more experiences.	Claim that they have more education.
Perceive that their role is to intervene for the workers and help them.	Perceive that their role is to hire competent workers and expect them to perform.
Believe that it is the boss's responsibility to solve problems.	Believe that it is the individual's responsibility to solve problems.
Stress that a boss has the obligation to take care of the workers.	Stress that workers have responsibility to perform the job well.
Emphasize that individuals should conform to the majority.	Emphasize that individuals should maximize his/her talents and potentials.
Believe that work cannot be divided clearly and like to be involved in everything.	Believe that a boss should mind his own work and leave the workers to do their jobs.
Perceive that work is more important than designation and organizational structure.	Perceive that designation and organizational structure are important in order to get the work done.
Believe that managers should help the workers to solve their problems.	Believe that managers should set objectives and achieve them.
Complain that the younger generation likes to use complicated management methods.	Complain that the old generation does things on an ad hoc basis.
Perceive that the younger generation likes to change and expects immediate results.	Perceive that the old generation is static and resistant to change.
Worry that the young generation is not experienced in running the business.	Frustrated that the old generation still holds on strongly to their power.
Emphasize that they have to take care of the old workers in the process of the company's growth.	Emphasize that they have to gain acceptance from their customers in order to enhance its image as a modern company.
Emphasize that ethics are important in business.	Emphasize that strategy is important in business.
Anticipate that the young generation is going to have many difficulties if they adopt Western concepts of management.	Frustrated that the old generation does not let them test out their concepts of management.
Believe that one's ability is limited and one should be contented with what one has.	Believe that there are a lot of opportunities for achievement and growth.

Source: Adapted from Jean Lee, "Culture and Management—A Study of Small Chinese Family Business in Singapore," *Journal of Small Business Management,* July 1996, p. 65.

family businesses, found that the viewpoints of the old generation differ sharply from those of the younger generation. Table 7–5 provides specific contrasts between the old and young generations of Chinese.

In short, there is considerable multicultural diversity domestically in organizations throughout the world, and this trend will continue. For example, the U.S. civilian labor force of the next decade will change dramatically in ethnic composition. In particular, there will be a significantly lower percentage of white males in the workforce and a growing percentage of women, African-Americans, Hispanics, and Asians.

Group Multiculturalism   There are a number of ways that diverse groups can be categorized. Four of the most common include:

1. **Homogeneous groups,** which are characterized by members who share similar backgrounds and generally perceive, interpret, and evaluate events in similar ways. An example would be a group of male German bankers who are forecasting the economic outlook for a foreign investment.

2. **Token groups,** in which all members but one have the same background. An example would be a group of Japanese retailers and a British attorney who are looking into the benefits and shortcomings of setting up operations in Bermuda.

Homogeneous group
A group that is characterized by members who share similar backgrounds and generally perceive, interpret, and evaluate events in similar ways.

Token group
A group in which all members but one have the same background, such as a group of Japanese retailers and a British attorney.

Bicultural group

A group in which two or more members represent each of two distinct cultures, such as four Mexicans and four Taiwanese who have formed a team to investigate the possibility of investing in a venture.

Multicultural group

A group in which there are individuals from three or more different ethnic backgrounds, such as three U.S., three German, three Uruguayan, and three Chinese managers who are looking into mining operations in South Africa.

3. **Bicultural groups,** which have two or more members of a group represent each of two distinct cultures. An example would be a group of four Mexicans and four Canadians who have formed a team to investigate the possibility of investing in Russia.

4. **Multicultural groups,** in which there are individuals from three or more different ethnic backgrounds. An example is a group of three American, three German, three Uruguayan, and three Chinese managers who are looking into mining operations in Chile.

As the diversity of a group increases, the likelihood of all members perceiving things in the same way decreases sharply. Attitudes, perceptions, and communication in general may be a problem. On the other hand, there also are significant advantages associated with the effective use of multicultural, diverse groups. The following sections examine the potential problems and the advantages.

Potential Problems Associated with Diversity

Overall, diversity may cause a lack of cohesion that results in the unit's inability to take concerted action, be productive, and create a work environment that is conducive to both efficiency and effectiveness. These potential problems are rooted in people's attitudes.

An example of an attitudinal problem in a diverse group may be the mistrust of others. For example, many U.S. managers who work for Japanese operations in the United States complain that Japanese managers often huddle together and discuss matters in their native language. The U.S. managers wonder aloud why the Japanese do not speak English. What are they talking about that they do not want anyone else to hear? In fact, the Japanese often find it easier to communicate among themselves in their native language, and because no Americans are present, the Japanese managers ask why they should speak English. If there is no reason for anyone else to be privy to our conversation, why should we not opt for our own language? Nevertheless, such practices do tend to promote an attitude of mistrust.

Another potential problem may be perceptual. Unfortunately, when culturally diverse groups come together, they often bring preconceived stereotypes with them. In initial meetings, for example, engineers from economically advanced countries often are perceived as more knowledgeable than those from less advanced countries. In turn, this can result in status-related problems, because some of the group initially are regarded as more competent than others and likely are accorded status on this basis. As the diverse group works together, erroneous perceptions often are corrected, but this takes time. In one diverse group consisting of engineers from a major Japanese firm and a world-class U.S. firm, a Japanese engineer was assigned a technical task because of his stereotyped technical educational background. The group soon realized that this particular Japanese engineer was not capable of doing this job, however, because for the last 4 years, he had been responsible for coordinating routine quality and no longer was on the technologic cutting edge. His engineering degree from the University of Tokyo had resulted in the other members perceiving him as technically competent and able to carry out the task; this perception proved to be incorrect.

A related problem is inaccurate biases. For example, it is well-known that Japanese companies depend on groups to make decisions. Entrepreneurial behavior, individualism, and originality are typically downplayed.[24] However, in a growing number of Japanese firms this stereotype is proving to be incorrect.[25] Here is an example.

Mr. Uchida, a 28-year-old executive in a small software company, dyes his hair brown, keeps a sleeping bag by his desk for late nights in the office and occasionally takes the day off to go windsurfing. "Sometimes I listen to soft music to soothe my feelings, and sometimes I listen to hard music to build my energy," said Mr. Uchida, who manages the technology-development division of the Rimnet Corporation, an Internet access provider. "It's important that we always keep in touch with our sensibilities when we want to generate ideas." The creative whiz kid, a business personality often prized by corporate America, has come to Japan Inc. Unlikely as it might seem in a country renowned for its deference to authority and its devotion to group solidarity, freethinkers like Mr. Uchida are popping up all over the workplace. Nonconformity is suddenly in.[26]

Still another potential problem with diverse groups is inaccurate communication, which could occur for a number of reasons. One is misunderstandings caused by words used by a speaker that are not clear to other members. For example, in a diverse group in which one of the authors was working, a British manager told her U.S. colleagues, "I will fax you this report in a fortnight." When the author asked the Americans when they would be getting the report, most of them believed it would be arriving in 4 days. They did not know that the common British word "fortnight" (14 nights) means 2 weeks.

Another contribution to miscommunication may be the way in which situations are interpreted. Many Japanese nod their heads when others talk, but this does not mean that they agree with what is being said. They merely are being polite and attentive. In many societies, it is impolite to say no, and if the listener believes that the other person wants a positive answer, the listener will say yes even though this is incorrect. As a result, many U.S. managers find out that promises made by individuals from other cultures cannot be taken at face value—and in many instances, the other individual assumes that the American realizes this!

Diversity also may lead to communication problems because of the different uses of time. For example, many Japanese will not agree to a course of action on-the-spot. They will not act until they have discussed the matter with their own people, because they do not feel empowered to act alone. Many Latin managers refuse to be held to a strict timetable, because they do not have the same time-urgency that U.S. managers do. Here is another example, as described by a European manager:

> In attempting to plan a new project, a three-person team composed of managers from Britain, France, and Switzerland failed to reach agreement. To the others, the British representative appeared unable to accept any systematic approach; he wanted to discuss all potential problems before making a decision. The French and Swiss representatives agreed to examine everything before making a decision, but then disagreed on the sequence and scheduling of operations. The Swiss, being more pessimistic in their planning, allocated more time for each suboperation than did the French. As a result, although everybody agreed on its validity, we never started the project. If the project had been discussed by three Frenchmen, three Swiss, or three Britons, a decision, good or bad, would have been made. The project would not have been stalled for lack of agreement.[27]

Advantages of Diversity

While there are some potential problems to overcome when using culturally diverse groups in today's MNCs, there also are a host of benefits to be gained.[28] In particular, there is growing evidence that culturally diverse groups can enhance creativity, lead to better decisions, and result in more effective and productive performance.[29]

One main benefit of diversity is the generation of more and better ideas. Because group members come from a host of different cultures, they often are able to create a greater number of unique (and thus creative) solutions and recommendations. For example, a U.S. MNC recently was preparing to launch a new software package aimed at the mass consumer market. The company hoped to capitalize on the upcoming Christmas season with a strong advertising campaign in each of its international markets. A meeting of the sales managers from these markets in Spain, the Middle East, and Japan helped the company to revise and better target its marketing effort. The Spanish manager suggested that the company focus its campaign around the coming of the Magi (January 6) and not Christmas (December 25), because in Latin cultures, gifts typically are exchanged on the date that the Magi brought their gifts. The Middle East manager pointed out that most of his customers were not Christians, so a Christmas campaign would not have much meaning in this area. Instead, he suggested the company focus its sales campaign around the value of the software and how it could be useful to customers and not worry about getting the product shipped by early December. The Japanese manager concurred with his Middle

East colleague, but additionally suggested that some of the colors being proposed for the sales brochure be changed to better fit with Japanese culture. Thanks to these ideas, the sales campaign proved to be one of the most effective in the company's history.

A second major benefit is that culturally diverse groups can prevent **groupthink,** which is social conformity and pressures on individual members of a group to conform and reach consensus. When this occurs, group participants believe that their ideas and actions are correct and that those who disagree with them are either uninformed or deliberately trying to sabotage their efforts. Multicultural diverse groups often are able to avoid this problem, because the members do not think similarly or feel pressure to conform. As a result, they typically question each other, offer opinions and suggestions that are contrary to those held by others, and must be persuaded to change their minds. Therefore, unanimity is achieved only through a careful process of deliberation. Unlike homogeneous groups, where everyone can be "of one mind," diverse groups may be slower in reaching a general consensus; however, the decision may be more effective.

Groupthink
Social conformity and pressures on individual members of a group to conform and reach consensus.

Building Multicultural Team Effectiveness

Multiculturally diverse teams have a great deal of potential to be either very effective or very ineffective.[30] As shown in Figure 7–5, Kovach reports that if cross-cultural groups are led properly, they can indeed be highly effective; unfortunately, she also found that if they are not managed properly, they can be highly ineffective. In other words, diverse groups are more powerful than single-culture groups. They can hurt the organization, but if managed effectively, they can be the best.[31] The following sections provide the conditions and guidelines for managing diverse groups in today's organizations effectively.

Understanding the Conditions for Effectiveness   Multicultural teams are most effective when they face tasks requiring innovativeness. They are far less effective when they are assigned to routine tasks. As Adler explains:

> Cultural diversity provides the biggest asset for teams with difficult, discretionary tasks requiring innovation. Diversity becomes less helpful when employees are working on simple tasks involving repetitive or routine procedures. Therefore, diversity generally becomes more valuable during the planning and development of projects (the "work" stage) and less helpful during their implementation (the "action" stage). The more senior the team members, the more likely they are to be working on projects that can benefit from diversity. Diversity is therefore extremely valuable to senior executive teams, both within and across countries.[32]

In achieving the greatest amount of effectiveness from diverse teams, activities must be determined by the stage of team development (e.g., entry, working, and action). For example, in the entry stage, the focus should be on building trust and developing team cohesion. This can be a difficult task for diverse teams, whose members are accustomed to

Figure 7–5

Group Effectiveness and Culture

Source: Based on Dr. Carol Kovach's research, conducted at the Graduate School of Management, University of California at Los Angeles (UCLA), and reported in Nancy J. Adler, *International Dimensions of Organizational Behavior,* 2nd ed. (Boston: PWS-Kent Publishing, 1991), p. 135.

working in different ways. For example, Americans, Germans, and Swiss typically spend little time getting to know each other; they find out the nature of the task and set about pursuing it on their own without first building trust and cohesion. This contrasts sharply with individuals from Latin America, Southern Europe, and the Middle East, where a great deal of initial time is spent getting to know each other. This contrast between task-oriented and relationship-oriented members of a diverse team may cause difficulty in creating cohesion. To counteract this problem, it is common in the entry stage of development to find experienced multicultural managers focusing attention on the team members' equivalent professional qualifications and status. Once this professional similarity and respect are established, the group can begin forming itself into a cohesive team.

In the work stage of development, attention may be directed more toward describing and analyzing the problem or task that has been assigned. This stage often is fairly easy for managers of multicultural teams, because they can draw on the diversity of the members in generating ideas. As noted earlier, diverse groups tend to be most effective when dealing with situations that require innovative approaches.

In the action stage, the focus shifts to decision making and implementation. This can be a difficult phase, because it often requires consensus building among the members. In achieving this objective, experienced managers work to help the diverse group recognize and facilitate the creation of ideas with which everyone can agree. In doing so, it is common to find strong emphasis on problem-solving techniques such as the nominal group technique (NGT), where the group members individually make contributions before group interaction and consensus is reached.

Using the Proper Guidelines   Besides some overall conditions, a number of specific guidelines for effectively managing culturally diverse groups have been identified. Here are some of the most useful:

1. Team members must be selected for their task-related abilities and not solely based on ethnicity. If the task is routine, homogeneous membership often is preferable; if the task is innovative, multicultural membership typically is best.

2. Team members must recognize and be prepared to deal with their differences. The goal is to facilitate a better understanding of cross-cultural differences and generate a higher level of performance and rapport. In doing so, members need to become aware of their own stereotypes, as well as those of the others, and use this information to better understand the real differences that exist between them. This can then serve as a basis for determining how each individual member can contribute to the overall effectiveness of the team.

3. Because members of diverse teams tend to have more difficulty agreeing on their purpose and task than members of homogeneous groups, the team leader must help the group to identify and define its overall goal. This goal is most useful when it requires members to cooperate and develop mutual respect in carrying out their tasks.

4. Members must have equal power so that everyone can participate in the process; cultural dominance always is counterproductive. As a result, managers of culturally diverse teams distribute power according to each person's ability to contribute to the task, not according to ethnicity.

5. It is important that all members have mutual respect for each other. This often is accomplished by managers choosing members of equal ability, making prior accomplishments and task-related skills known to the group, and minimizing early judgments based on ethnic stereotypes.

6. Because teams often have difficulty determining what is a good or a bad idea or decision, managers must give teams positive feedback on their process and output. This feedback helps the members to see themselves as a team, and it teaches them to value and celebrate their diversity, recognize contributions made by the individual members, and trust the collective judgment of the group.

These guidelines can be useful in helping leaders to manage culturally diverse teams effectively. World-class organizations use such an approach, and one good example is NUMMI (New United Motor Manufacturing), a joint venture between General Motors and Toyota that transformed an out-of-date GM plant in Fremont, California, into a world-class organization. This joint-venture partnership, formed over 10 years ago, continues to be a success story of how a culturally diverse workforce can produce state-of-the-art automobiles. The successful approach to culturally diverse work teams at NUMMI was built around four principles:

1. Both management and labor recognized that their futures were interdependent, thus committing them to a mutual vision.
2. Employees felt secure and trusted assurances that they would be treated fairly, thus enabling them to become contributors.
3. The production system formed interdependent relationships throughout the plant, thus helping to create a healthy work environment.
4. The production system was managed to transform the stress and conflict of everyday life into trust and mutual respect.[33]

In achieving success at NUMMI, Toyota sent trainers from Japan to work with its U.S. counterparts and teach the production system that would be used throughout the plant. During this period, both groups searched for points of agreement, establishing valuable relationships in the process. In addition, the Japanese taught the Americans some useful techniques for increasing productivity, including how to focus on streamlining operations, reduce waste, and learn how to blame mistakes on the situation or themselves (not on team members).

In overcoming multicultural differences at NUMMI, several changes were introduced, including: (1) reserved dining rooms were eliminated, and all managers now eat in a communal cafeteria; (2) all reserved parking spaces were eliminated; and (3) GM's 80 job classifications were collapsed into only 3 to equalize work and rewards and ensure fairness. Commenting on the overall success of the joint venture, it was noted that

> Toyota managers resisted temptations to forge ahead with a pure version of the system. Both the Japanese and Americans learned as they went. By adopting a "go slow" attitude, the Japanese and Americans remained open to points of resistance as they arose and navigated around them. By tolerating ambiguity and by searching for consensus, Toyota managers established the beginnings of mutual respect and trust with the American workers and managers.[34]

NUMMI is only one example of the many successful multicultural workforces producing world-class goods and services. In each case, however, effective multinationals rely on the types of guidelines that have been highlighted in this discussion.

The World of *Business Week*—Revisited

The *Business Week* article at the beginning of this chapter offered an excellent example of how an MNC can face challenges from both national and organizational culture. Now that you have read this chapter, you should have a better understanding of how national culture can potentially inhibit or enhance the effects of organizational culture. While Interbrew is a Belgian firm, its culture is similar to that of France, a country that was examined in many examples in this chapter. Both of these nations are in the Latin European cultural cluster (see Figure 5–8). So when the article pointed out that Interbrew did very well when it expanded operations into France, this is readily understandable. The organizational cultures in the two countries are likely to be quite similar. On the other hand, now Interbrew is moving into other major markets including the U.K., the U.S., and Asia where the organizational cultures will be quite different. The article also notes that the firm makes acquisitions so that it can produce beer locally and also have a distribution network for marketing its high-margin imported offerings. From the chapter material, it is evident that Interbrew cannot use the same operational approach in the U.S. that it employs in Belgium because the organizational cultures will be quite different. The same is true in its other worldwide operations. Given these facts and drawing on the information in this chapter, answer these three questions: (1) Using Figure 7–2 as your guide, how would the organizational culture of a Belgian firm differ from that of an American firm? (2) Using Figure 7–3 as a reference point, how would the national pattern of a Belgian firm differ from that of an American firm? (3) What would be two of the major organization culture challenges faced by Interbrew in managing its U.S. operations?

Summary of Key Points

1. Organizational culture is a pattern of basic assumptions that are developed by a group as it learns to cope with its problems of external adaptation and internal integration and that are taught to new members as the correct way to perceive, think, and feel in relation to these problems. Some important characteristics of organizational culture include observed behavioral regularities, norms, dominant values, philosophy, rules, and organizational climate.

2. Organizational cultures are shaped by a number of factors. These include the general relationship between employees and their organization, the hierarchic system of authority that defines the roles of managers and subordinates, and the general views that employees hold about the organization's purpose, destiny, goals, and their place in them. When examining these differences, Trompenaars has suggested the use of two continua: equity/hierarchy, and person/task orientation, resulting in four basic types of organizational cultures: family, Eiffel Tower, guided missile, and incubator.

3. The family culture is characterized by a strong emphasis on hierarchic authority and orientation to the person. The Eiffel Tower culture is characterized by a strong emphasis on hierarchy and orientation to the task. The guided missile culture is characterized by a strong emphasis on equality in the workplace and orientation to the task. The incubator culture is characterized by a strong emphasis on equality and orientation to the person.

4. Success in the international arena often is heavily determined by a company's ability to manage multiculturalism and diversity. There are four phases through which firms progress in their international evolution: (1) domestic corporation; (2) international corporation; (3) multinational corporation; and (4) global corporation.

5. There are a number of ways to examine multiculturalism and diversity. One is by looking at the domestic multicultural and diverse workforce that operates in the MNC's home country. Another is by examining the variety of diverse groups that exist in MNCs, including homogeneous groups, token groups, bicultural groups, and multicultural groups. Several potential problems as well as advantages are associated with multicultural, diverse teams.

6. A number of guidelines have proved to be particularly effective in managing culturally diverse groups. These include careful selection of the members, identification of the group's goals, establishment of equal power and mutual respect among the participants, and delivering positive feedback on performance. A good example of how these guidelines have been used is the NUMMI joint venture created by General Motors and Toyota.

Key Terms

bicultural group, *186*

Eiffel Tower culture, *178*

family culture, *176*

groupthink, *188*

guided missile culture, *178*

homogeneous group, *185*

incubator culture, *180*

multicultural group, *186*

organizational culture, *170*

token group, *185*

Review and Discussion Questions

1. Some researchers have found that when Germans work for a U.S. MNC, they become even more German, and when Americans work for a German MNC, they become even more American. Why would this knowledge be important to these MNCs?

2. When comparing the negotiating styles and strategies of French versus Spanish negotiators, a number of sharp contrasts are evident. What are three of these, and what could MNCs do to improve their position when negotiating with either group?

3. In which of the four types of organizational cultures—family, Eiffel Tower, guided missile, incubator—would most people in the United States feel comfortable? In which would most Japanese feel comfortable? Based on your answers, what conclusions could you draw regarding the importance of understanding organizational culture for international management?

4. Most MNCs need not enter foreign markets to face the challenge of dealing with multiculturalism. Do you agree or disagree with this statement? Explain your answer.

5. What are some potential problems that must be overcome when using multicultural, diverse teams in today's organizations? What are some recognized advantages? Identify and discuss two of each.

6. A number of guidelines can be valuable in helping MNCs to make diverse teams more effective. What are five of these? Additionally, what underlying principles guided NUMMI in its effective use of multicultural teams? Were the principles used by NUMMI similar to the general guidelines identified in this chapter, or were they significantly different? Explain your answer.

Internet Exercise: Hewlett-Packard's International Focus

Mention the name Hewlett-Packard, or HP for short, and people are likely to think of printers—an area where the MNC has managed to excel worldwide in recent years. However, HP has many other offerings besides printers and has rapidly expanded its product line into the international arena over the last decade. Visit its Web site at **www.hp.com** and review some of the latest developments. In particular, pay close attention to its product line and international expansion. Then choose three different countries where the firm is doing business: one from the Americas, one from Europe, and one from Southeast Asia or India. (Since the sites are all presented in the local language, you might want to make India your choice, since this one is in English.) Compare and contrast the product offerings and ways in which HP goes about marketing itself over the Web in these locations. What do you see as some of the major differences? Second, using Figure 7–2 and Table 7–3 as your guide, in what way are national cultures likely to present significant challenges to HP's efforts to create a smooth-running international enterprise? What would you see as two of the critical issues with which the management will have to deal? Third, what are two steps that you think HP will have to take in order to build multicultural team effectiveness? What are two guidelines that can help them do this?

Japan

Japan is located in eastern Asia, and it comprises a curved chain of more than 3,000 islands. Four of these—Hokkaido, Honshu, Shikoku, and Kyushi—account for 89 percent of the country's land area. The population of Japan is approximately 128 million, with over 8 million people living in the nation's capital, Tokyo. According to the World Bank, the country's gross domestic product at the turn of the century was approximately $23,500 per capita. At the same time, the country has been in the throes of an economic recession that has been going on for over 10 years. However, most economists believe that things will turn around and Japan will once again have an expanding economy.

This optimistic outlook is shared by two multinationals, one from the United States and the other from Germany. These two MNCs recently joined forces with a large Japanese MNC to create a new retailing chain throughout Japan. The joint venture will limit its merchandise selection to clothing and toys, which are two product areas where Japanese prices are relatively higher than those paid by consumers in other countries. The U.S. and German partners will design the clothing and toys, but they will be produced in Japan by local labor and sold there. The U.S. and German partners will contribute most of the capital needed for the venture and they also will help design the production and distribution system as well as the retail store layout. The Japanese partner will be responsible for choosing the type of merchandise to be produced, manage and/or coordinate (for subcontractors) the production facilities, and handle the marketing.

To provide a managerial presence in Japan, the two foreign partners will share a new headquarters building with their local partner. Located approximately 60 miles outside of Tokyo, this building will house the senior-level management from all three MNCs as well as key finance, production, and marketing personnel. The plan is to have strategy and major decisions made at this headquarters, then disseminated to the production facilities and retail stores. The joint venture hopes to have six stores operating within 24 months, and 20 more within five years.

www.japanlink.com

Questions

1. What type of organizational culture is each of the three partners likely to have? (Use Figure 7–3 as a guide in answering this question.)

2. Which of the organizational cultures will be most different from that of the other two? Explain.

3. What types of problems might the culturally diverse top-management team at headquarters create for the joint venture? Give some specific examples. How could these problems be overcome?

4. In terms of organizational culture, what is your estimate of success for this joint venture?

A Good Faith Effort Is Needed

Excelsior Manufacturing is a medium-sized firm located in the northeast part of the United States. Excelsior has long been known as a high-quality, world-class producer of precision tools. Recently, however, this MNC has been slowly losing market share in Europe, because many EU companies are turning to other European firms to save on taxes and transportation costs. Realizing that it needed a European partner if it hoped to recapture this lost ground, Excelsior began looking to buy a firm that could provide it a strong foothold in this market. After a brief search, the MNC made contact with Quality Instrumentation, a Madrid-based firm that was founded five years ago and has been growing at 25 percent annually. Excelsior currently is discussing a buyout with Quality Instrumentation, and the Spanish firm appears to be interested in the arrangement as it will provide them with increased technology, a quality reputation, and more funding for European expansion.

Next week, owners of the two companies are scheduled to meet in Madrid to discuss purchase price and potential plans for integrating their overall operations. The biggest sticking point appears to be a concern for meshing the organizational cultures and the work values and habits of the two enterprises. Each is afraid that the other's way of doing business might impede overall progress and lead to wasted productivity and lost profit. To deal with this issue, the president of Excelsior has asked his management team to draft a plan that could serve as a guide in determining how both groups could coordinate their efforts.

On a personal level, the head of Excelsior believes that it will be important for the Spanish management team to understand that if the Spaniards sell the business, they must be prepared to let U.S. managers have final decision-making power on major issues, such as research and development efforts, expansion plans, and customer segmentation. At the same time, the Americans are concerned that their potential European partners will feel they are being told what to do and resist these efforts. "We're going to have to make them understand that we must work as a unified team," the president explained to his planning committee, "and create a culture that will support this idea. We may not know a lot about working with Spaniards and they may not understand a great deal about how Americans do things, but I believe that we can resolve these differences if we put forth a good faith effort."

Questions

1. What do you think some of the main organizational culture differences between the two companies would be?

2. Why might the cultural diversity in the Spanish firm not be as great as that in the U.S. firm, and what potential problems could this create?

3. What would you recommend be done to effectively merge the two organizational cultures and ensure they cooperate harmoniously? Offer some specific recommendations.

Chapter 8

Intercultural Communication

Objectives of the Chapter

Communication takes on special importance in international management because of the difficulties in conveying meanings between parties from different cultures. The problems of misinterpretation and error are compounded in the international context. Chapter 8 examines how the communication process in general works, and it looks at the downward and upward communication flows that commonly are used in international communication. Then, the chapter examines the major barriers to effective international communication and reviews ways of dealing with these communication problems. The specific objectives of this chapter are:

1. **DEFINE** the term "communication," and examine some examples of external and internal communication.

2. **REVIEW** examples of verbal communication styles and explain the importance of message interpretation.

3. **ANALYZE** the common downward and upward communication flows used in international communication.

4. **EXAMINE** the language, perception, culture, and nonverbal barriers to effective international communications.

5. **PRESENT** the steps that can be taken to overcome international communication problems.

BusinessWeek

The World of *Business Week*

GM Tries to Show Who's Boss

For a company run by conservative finance guys, General Motors Corp. is making some big wagers these days. Case in point: GM agreed to spend $99 million on a joint venture with beleaguered Russian auto maker Avtovaz. The Detroit giant will put its reputation on the line by selling an Avtovaz-designed sport utility vehicle as the Chevrolet Niva, for $7,500 or so, in emerging markets worldwide.

Betting on such overseas ventures with other auto makers has become standard procedure for GM. The grand design is to exploit emerging markets and develop small vehicles for Europe and North America. So, since buying the remaining 50% of Saab for $125 million early last year, GM spent $2.4 billion for a 20% stake in Fiat, $1.3 billion for a fifth of Subaru parent Fuji Heavy Industries, and $653 million to double its 10% position in Suzuki Motor. To put this spending in perspective, the $4.6 billion acquisition spree is twice GM's earnings target for this year.

Pricey as it is, this global hunt is key to CEO G. Richard Wagoner Jr.'s vow to build market share and find new technology fast. GM in the U.S., for example, has proven inept at making successful small cars for entry-level buyers, an area where Suzuki and Fiat excel. Tapping such expertise and building a global presence is worth the effort to Wagoner. "Sure, there's risk," he concedes. But "I would challenge [anyone] to find a better overseas footprint than we have."

A skeptic would point out that last year, GM's international operations lost almost $900 million, mostly from the travails of Isuzu and Adam Opel, the German operation. Revenue from outside North America is essentially flat at around $35 billion. And overseas cooperation with Detroit has resulted in some notable duds like the Cadillac Catera and the Saturn L-series—both jointly developed with Opel.

Wagoner's response has been a major review of GM's overseas management. Before, foreign alliances tended to be loosely monitored. To rectify this sloppiness, over the past year GM has installed a much tighter network of senior managers who work in the headquarters and product development centers of its partners and report directly to the top-ranking GM executive in each region of the world. Those executives send ideas to Lawrence D. Burns, GM's vice-president of research & development in Detroit. Wagoner now meets regularly with top executives at partner companies. In a sign he is getting serious, he has finally forced a tough recovery plan on Isuzu.

The new approach is paying off in some areas. GM has had success with the Opel-designed Celta in Brazil and the Suzuki-designed, Polish-built Opel Agila compact wagon in Europe. In the U.S., GM is jointly designing an entry-level Chevrolet with Suzuki.

Too Distant

But the approach may not solve a kind of psychological complex GM has: It often declines to buy outright control of a partner, as Renault has essentially done

with Nissan Motor. And when GM does acquire control, the process can be so ponderous that benefits are lost. Says Prudential Securities Inc. auto analyst Michael Bruynestyne: "When you can't control a company, that means making compromises."

Many of these issues are apparent in GM's forays in Europe. Witness Saab. GM bought half of the struggling Swedish carmaker in 1990. A decade later, Saab still has a measly two-car lineup, and it has lost $1 billion since GM bought it. In all, say sources close to the deal, GM spent nearly $1 billion to get all of Saab. Yet GM often let the operation sputter along without giving Saab the new products it needed to transcend its status as a niche player. Undaunted, GM plans to double Saab sales, to 250,000 a year, by 2005.

Saab is just the start of GM's troubles in Europe. Opel badly misread the shift to diesel-powered cars. A lack of sharp styling hurt, too. To fix Opel, GM cut 15% of its capacity and is sacking salaried workers. Concedes Michael Burns, head of GM Europe: "Our goal is to be profitable by [yearend], but a lot has to go our way to make that happen."

Opel's crying need for more diesel engines offers GM a chance to test its new strategy of close coordination. GM ally Isuzu Motors Ltd. has a Polish plant that can crank out 200,000 small diesel engines a year, and it will share the output with Opel. GM will start putting Fiat diesels in its cars, including the Opel lineup. There could be a Fiat payoff for GM North America, too, if it follows through on plans to sell Fiat's Alfa Romeo cars in the U.S. The Italian marque could be the third leg of a premium-car strategy in America that would include Cadillac and Saab, says Ronald L. Zarrella, president of GM 's North American operations.

This is just what Wagoner envisioned. But there are signs that the old GM way of doing things may slow the execution of the alliance. Opel insiders bemoan all the levels of decision-making, with GM Europe executives and now Fiat managers all in the mix. GM executives say the synergies emerging from the Fiat deal will put these concerns to rest.

GM has similar troubles in Asia, where weak oversight has built up the problems. GM owns 49% of Isuzu, which accounted for nearly all of GM's recent loss in Asia. Rudolph A. Schlais Jr., president of Asia-Pacific operations, told Wall Street analysts that Isuzu lacked good cost controls. Hence GM's decision to install a new president at Isuzu.

A Few Hits

Apart from the Isuzu hassle, GM has found East Asia and Japan nearly impossible to crack. GM decided to yank Saturn from its Japanese dealerships after a three-year attempt to build the brand there. GM has less than 4% of the 11 million-vehicle market in Asia. So GM is again turning to its partners. With Suzuki, it developed the YGM1 subcompact, a car built expressly for Asia that seats five. In China, GM is looking at some of Suzuki's subcompacts and minicars to sell besides its Opel-based Buick Sail compact, says Philip Murtaugh, head of GM China. GM has invested $2 billion in China, selling the Buick Century sedan, minivans, and Chevrolet Blazer SUVs, but has just 3% of the market.

If General Motors gets the green light to build other cars in China, its partners would be the source for some of the vehicles. It might be a while, though, before any agreement is struck. "We would like them to move faster," says Koichi Arasawa, Fuji's senior vice-president of product planning. "GM's structure can be very bureaucratic." The Fuji partnership has yet to announce a jointly designed vehicle that they can market.

Sometimes cooperation produces clear hits. The Brazil-built, Opel-derived Celta minicar should push GM's profits in South America, says Frederick A. "Fritz" Henderson, group vice-president of operations in Latin America, Africa, and the Middle East. In the U.S., pickup trucks jointly designed with Isuzu could liven up GM's line. But no matter how clear the vision at the top, there's always the problem of the GM bureaucracy. Wagoner has the right idea. He needs the right organization.

By David Welch in Detroit, with bureau reports.

Source: **Reprinted from March 12, 2001, pp. 54–55 of** *Business Week* **by special permission, copyright © 2001 by the McGraw-Hill Companies, Inc.**

This opening news story provides an excellent example of some of the challenges presented by intercultural communication. General Motors is the world's largest auto firm. In order to maintain this position, however, the company will have to more effectively tap the expertise of its global operations. This will not be an easy chore, but it is one that is crucial to the company's future. In recent years GM's worldwide market share has been slipping and the firm is losing money in its international operations. In order to turn things around, GM is now trying to better communicate with and coordinate worldwide operations in order to get all units to work in harmony. This is going to require the auto giant to do two things: (a) develop a clear picture of what it wants done and (b) clearly communicate this message to everyone. If the company cannot do this, its worldwide market share will continue to decline and losses from international operations will continue to increase.

■ The Overall Communication Process

Communication
The process of transferring meanings from sender to receiver.

Communication is the process of transferring meanings from sender to receiver. On the surface, this appears to be a fairly straightforward process. On analysis, however, there are a great many problems in the international arena that can result in the failure to transfer meanings correctly. One of these is the inability to effectively establish rapport with the other side. For example, many expatriates who have not been adequately trained will bring up conversation topics that more experienced international managers know should be avoided. Table 8–1 provides a brief list of some of the "dos" and the "don'ts." When an inappropriate topic arises, communication breakdown likely will result, because the other party interprets the message differently from what was intended.[1]

In gaining some insights into the overall communication process, it is helpful to examine Figure 8–1. As shown, the sender of a message will determine what he or she wants to say and then encode the message to convey his or her meanings. The communiqué then is transmitted using some medium, such as telephone, e-mail, or face-to-face verbal interaction. Finally, the message is decoded and interpreted by the receiver. If the message is unclear or the receiver feels that a response is required, the process then is reversed: The receiver now becomes the sender, and the sender becomes the receiver. This reverse flow of information is achieved through feedback, which creates a two-way process. In practice, this back-and-forth flow of meanings is used to clarify, elaborate, and monitor actions by one or more parties to the communication. Unfortunately, this process often is interrupted by what is called "noise," which is the deliberate or nondeliberate distortion of the communication process. (This so-called noise problem is discussed later.)

External and Internal Communications

Organizational communication involves both the external and internal flow of information. In international management, this flow becomes particularly important, because parties to messages often are located in different geographic areas and/or have been born and raised in different cultures. This international context can create communication problems that are quite different from those faced by companies operating within one country.

Examples of External Communication   One major form of external communication during the years ahead will be government attempts to secure agreements with other nations regarding international trade. For example, the United States has been engaged in prolonged discussions with China regarding reciprocal trade agreements. The United States feels that China is not opening up for imports, is lagging behind in doing business with foreign firms, and is exporting goods to virtually every corner of the globe.

This perception of the problem greatly influences the way that the U.S. government communicates with China during trade negotiations and helps explain some of the concerns that America had regarding China's entry into the World Trade Organization. There

Table 8–1 **Topics of Conversation in Select Countries**		
Country	**Appropriate Topic**	**Inappropriate Topic**
Austria	Cars, skiing, music	Money, religion, divorce/separation
France	Music, books, sports, theater	Prices of items, person's work, income, age
Germany	Travel abroad, hobbies, soccer, international politics	World War II, questions about personal life
Great Britain	History, architecture, gardening	Politics, money, prices
Japan	History, culture, art	World War II, government policies that help to exclude foreign competition
Mexico	Family, social concerns	Politics, debt or inflation problems, border violations

Source: Lillian H. Chaney and Jeanette S. Martin, *Intercultural Business Communication* © 1995, p. 102. Reprinted by permission of Prentice-Hall, Inc., Englewood Cliffs, New Jersey.

Figure 8–1

The Communication Process

are other interpretations of international trade strategy, however, and the Chinese have their own version. They believe that Americans are overrating the danger to their own economy and are failing to see that many of the steps being taken by U.S. business will make the United States a dominant economic power in China for the indefinite future.

Other external communication is more one-way in that it does not directly involve all the parties affected by the message. A good example is the EU's rules designed to ensure that member firms are not forced out of their home markets. The EU's Competition Directorate has been empowered to approve mergers between large European firms. This action will help to ensure that U.S. and Japanese companies do not dominate the European market.

Examples of Internal Communication   Although the communication process is the same worldwide, its internal use often is influenced by cultural differences. How U.S. managers communicate may be quite different from how European or Asian managers do, and these differences are important to recognize. For example, a Harvard research team made a comparative study of the management of Russian and U.S. factories, and they found that Russian managers make greater use than U.S. managers of direct, face-to-face communications. U.S. managers rely more heavily on informal, written communication and the telephone.[2] On the other hand, a more recent observational study found both Russian and U.S. managers spend approximately one-third of their time carrying out communication activities.[3]

In another study, Pascale investigated communication techniques used by U.S. and Japanese managers operating both at home and in each other's country. He found that in some ways, the two national groups used similar communication techniques. For example, U.S. managers in the United States made an average of 37 phone calls daily, and U.S. managers in Japan averaged 34 calls a day. Japanese managers in Japan made 35 calls a day, and the Japanese managers in the United States averaged 30 calls daily. Therefore, use of the telephone to convey information really did not vary between the two groups; however, Pascale did find some important differences. For example, Japanese managers in Japan made much greater use of face-to-face contacts than U.S. or Japanese managers in the United States. Pascale's study also found greater use of upward and lateral communication in Japanese-based Japanese firms, but managers in U.S.-based Japanese firms used communication patterns similar to those used in U.S. firms.[4] Were there any perceived differences in the quality of decision making among the various groups of managers? Pascale found none. Each group gave itself a high score on decision quality; however, the Japanese-based Japanese firms perceived the quality of decision implementation as higher than that of the other three groups.[5]

Verbal Communication Styles

Context

Information that surrounds a communication and helps to convey the message.

Another way of examining the ways in which individuals convey information is by looking at their communication styles. In particular, as has been noted by Hall, context plays a key role in explaining many communication differences.[6] **Context** is the information that surrounds a communication and helps convey the message. In high-context societies, such as Japan and many Arab countries, messages are often highly coded and implicit. As a result, the sender's job is to interpret what the message means by correctly filtering through what is being said and the way in which the message is being conveyed. This approach is in sharp contrast to low-context societies such as the United States and Canada where the message is explicit and the speaker says precisely what he or she means. Figure 8–2 provides an international comparison of high context/implicit and low context/explicit societies. In addition, Table 8–2 presents some of the major characteristics of communication styles.

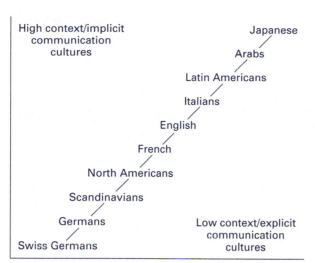

Source: Adapted from Martin Rosch, "Communications: Focal Point of Culture," *Management International Review,* vol. 27, no. 4, 1987, p. 60. Used with permission.

Figure 8–2

Explicit/Implicit Communication: An International Comparison

Table 8–2
Major Characteristics of Verbal Styles

Verbal Style	Major Variation	Cultures in Which Characteristic	It Is Found
Indirect vs. direct	Indirect	Implicit messages	Collective, high context
	Direct	Explicit messages	Individualistic, low context
Succinct vs. elaborate	Elaborate	High quantity of talk	Moderate uncertainty avoidance, high context
	Exacting	Moderate amount of talk	Low uncertainty avoidance, low context
	Succinct	Low amount of talk	High uncertainty avoidance, high context
Contextual vs. personal	Contextual	The focus is on the speaker and role relationships	High power distance, collective, high context
	Personal	The focus is on the speaker personal relationships	Low power distance, individualistic, low context
Affective vs. instrumental	Affective	Language is process oriented and receiver focused	Collective, high context
	Instrumental	Language is goal oriented and sender focused	Individualistic, low context

Indirect and Direct Styles   In high-context cultures, messages are implicit and indirect. One reason is because those who are communicating—family, friends, coworkers, clients—tend to have both close personal relationships and large information networks. As a result, each knows a lot about others in their communication network; they do not have to rely on language alone to communicate. Voice intonation, timing, and facial expressions can all play roles in conveying information.

In low-context cultures, people often meet only to accomplish objectives. Since they do not know each other very well, they tend to be direct and focused in their communications.

A good example comparing these two kinds of culture—high context and low context—is the types of questions that are typically asked when someone is contacted and told to attend a meeting. In a high-context culture it is common for the person to ask, "Who will be at this meeting?" The individual wants to be prepared to interact correctly. This is in contrast to low-context cultures where the individual is likely to ask, "What is the meeting going to be about?" In the high-context society, the person focuses on the environment in which the meeting will take place; in the low context, the individual is most interested in the objectives that are to be accomplished at the meeting.

Elaborate and Succinct Styles   There are three degrees of communication quantity—elaborate, exacting, and succinct. In high-context societies the elaborate style is often very common. There is a great deal of talking, description includes much detail, and people often repeat themselves. This elaborate style is widely used in Arabic countries.

The exacting style is more common in nations such as England, Germany, and Sweden, to name three. This style focuses on precision and the use of the right amount of words to convey the message. If a person uses too many words, this is considered exaggeration; if the individual relies on too few, the result is an ambiguous message.

The succinct style is most common in Asia where people tend to say few words and allow understatements, pauses, and silence to convey meaning. In particular, in unfamiliar situations communicators are succinct in order to avoid risking a loss of face.

Researchers have found that the elaborating style is more popular in high-context cultures that have a moderate degree of uncertainty avoidance. The exacting style is more common in low-context, low uncertainty avoidance cultures. The succinct style is more common in high-context cultures with considerable uncertainty avoidance.

Contextual and Personal Styles   A contextual style is one that focuses on the speaker and relationship of the parties. For example, in Asian cultures people use words that reflect the role and hierarchical relationship of those in the conversation. As a result, in an organizational setting speakers will choose words that indicate their status relative to those of the others. Commenting on this idea, Yoshimura and Anderson have noted that white collar, middle management employees in Japan, commonly known as salarymen, quickly learn how to communicate with others in the organization by understanding the context and reference group of the other party.

> A salaryman can hardly say a word to another person without implicitly defining the reference groups to which he thinks both of them belong. . . . [This is because] failing to use proper language is socially embarrassing, and the correct form of Japanese to use with someone else depends not only on the relationship between the two people, but also on the relationship between their reference groups. Juniors defer to seniors in Japan, but even this relationship is complicated when the junior person works for a much more prestigious organization (for example, a government bureau) than the senior. [As a result, it is] likely that both will use the polite form to avoid social embarrassment.[7]

A personal style focuses on the speaker and the reduction of barriers between the parties. In the United States, for example, it is common to use first names and to address others informally and directly on an equal basis.

Researchers have found that the contextual style is often associated with high power distance, collective, high-context cultures. Examples include Japan, India, and Ghana. In contrast, the personal style is more popular in low power distance, individualistic, low-context cultures. Examples include the United States, Australia, and Canada.

Affective and Instrumental Styles   The affective style is characterized by language which requires the listener to carefully note what is being said and to observe how the sender is presenting the message. Quite often the meaning that is being conveyed is nonverbal and requires the receiver to use his or her intuitive skills in deciphering what is being said. The part of the message that is being left out may be just as important as the part that is being included. In contrast, the instrumental style is goal-oriented and focuses on the sender. The individual clearly lets the other party know what he or she wants them to know.

The affective style is common in collective, high-context cultures such as the Middle East, Latin America, and Asia. The instrumental style is more commonly found in individualistic, low-context cultures such as Switzerland, Denmark, and the United States.

Table 8–3 provides a brief description of the four verbal styles that are used in select countries. A close look at the table helps explain why managers in Japan can have great difficulty communicating with their counterparts in the United States and vice versa. The verbal styles are completely opposite.

Interpretation of Communications

The effectiveness of communication in the international context often is determined by how closely the sender and receiver have the same meaning for the same message.[8] If this meaning is different, effective communication will not occur. A good example was the U.S. firm that wanted to increase worker output among its Japanese personnel. This firm put an individual incentive plan into effect, whereby workers would be given extra pay based on their work output. The plan, which had worked well in the United States, was a total flop. The Japanese were accustomed to working in groups and to being rewarded as a group. In another case, a U.S. firm offered a bonus to anyone who would provide suggestions that resulted in increased productivity. The Japanese workers rejected this idea, because they felt that no one working alone is responsible for increased productivity. It is always a group effort. When the company changed the system and began rewarding group productivity, it was successful in gaining support for the program.

A related case is when both parties agree on the content of the message, but one party believes it is necessary to persuade the other to accept the message. Here is an example:

> Motorola University recently prepared carefully for a presentation in China. After considerable thought, the presenters entitled it "Relationships do not retire." The gist of the presentation was that Motorola had come to China in order to stay and help the economy to create wealth. Relationships with Chinese suppliers, subcontractors and employees would constitute a permanent commitment to building Chinese economic infrastructure and earning hard currency through exports. The Chinese audience listened politely to this presentation but was quiet when invited to ask questions. Finally one manager put up his hand and said: "Can you tell us about pay for performance?"[9]

Table 8–3
Verbal Styles Used in 10 Select Countries

Country	Indirect vs. Direct	Elaborate vs. Succinct	Contextual vs. Personal	Affective vs. Instrumental
Australia	Direct	Exacting	Personal	Instrumental
Canada	Direct	Exacting	Personal	Instrumental
Denmark	Direct	Exacting	Personal	Instrumental
Egypt	Indirect	Elaborate	Contextual	Affective
England	Direct	Exacting	Personal	Instrumental
Japan	Indirect	Succinct	Contextual	Affective
Korea	Indirect	Succinct	Contextual	Affective
Saudi Arabia	Indirect	Elaborate	Contextual	Affective
Sweden	Direct	Exacting	Personal	Instrumental
United States	Direct	Exacting	Personal	Instrumental

Source: Reported in Anne Marie Francesco and Barry Allen Gold, *International Organizational Behavior* (Upper Saddle River, NJ: Prentice-Hall, 1998), p. 60.

Quite obviously, the Motorola presenter believed that it was necessary to convince the audience that the company was in China for the long run. Those in attendance, however, had already accepted this idea and wanted to move on to other issues.

Still another example has been provided by Adler, who has pointed out that people doing business in a foreign culture often misinterpret the meaning of messages. As a result, they arrive at erroneous conclusions as seen by the following story of a Canadian doing business in the Middle East. The Canadian was surprised when his meeting with a high-ranking official was not held in a closed office and was constantly interrupted.

> Using the Canadian-based cultural assumptions that (a) important people have large private offices with secretaries to monitor the flow of people into the office, and (b) important business takes precedence over less important business and is therefore not interrupted, the Canadian interprets the . . . open office and constant interruptions to mean that the official is neither as high ranking nor as interested in conducting the business at hand as he had previously thought.[10]

■ Communication Flows

Communication flows in international organizations move both down and up. However, as Figure 8–3 humorously, but in many ways accurately, portrays, there are some unique differences in organizations around the world.

Downward Communication

Downward communication
The transmission of information from superior to subordinate

Downward communication is the transmission of information from manager to subordinate. The primary purpose of the manager-initiated communication flow is to convey orders and information. Managers use this channel to let their people know what is to be done and how well they are doing. The channel facilitates the flow of information to those who need it for operational purposes.

Figure 8–3

Communication Epigrams

There are a number of different "organization charts" that have been constructed to depict international organizations. An epigram is a poem or line of verse that is witty or satirical in nature. The following organization designs are epigrams that show how communication occurs in different countries. In examining them, remember that each contains considerable exaggeration and humor, but also some degree of truth.

In America, everyone thinks he or she has a communication pipeline directly to the top.

America

There are so many people in China that organizations are monolithic structures characterized by copious levels of bureaucracy. All information flows through channels.

China

In Asian countries, as noted earlier, downward communication is less direct than in the United States. Orders tend to be implicit in nature. Conversely, in some European countries, downward communication is not only direct but extends beyond business matters. For example, one early study surveyed 299 U.S. and French managers regarding the nature of downward communication and the managerial authority they perceived themselves as having. This study found that U.S. managers basically used downward communication for work-related matters. A follow-up study investigated matters that U.S. and French managers felt were within the purview of their authority.[11] The major differences involved work-related and nonwork-related activities: U.S. managers felt that it was within their authority to communicate or attempt to influence their people's social behavior only if it occurred on the job or it directly affected their work. For example, U.S. managers felt that it was proper to look into matters such as how much an individual drinks at lunch, whether the person uses profanity in the workplace, and how active the individual is in recruiting others to join the company. The French managers were not as supportive of these activities. The researcher concluded that "the Americans find it as difficult [as] or more difficult than the French to accept the legitimacy of managerial authority in areas unrelated to work."[12]

Harris and Moran have noted that when communicating downward with nonnative speakers, it is extremely important to use language that is easy to understand and allows the other person to ask questions. Here are 10 of the suggestions that not only apply for downward, but for all types of communication:

1. Use the most common words with their most common meanings.
2. Select words that have few alternative meanings.
3. Strictly follow the basic rules of grammar—more so than would be the case with native speakers.

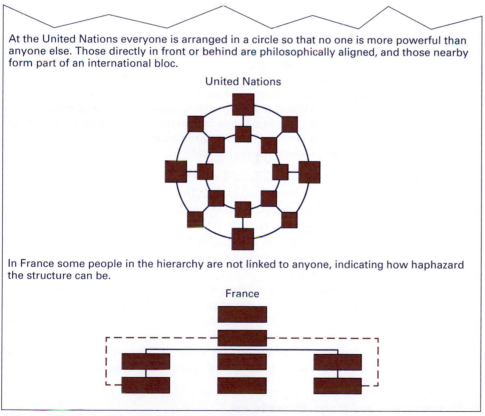

At the United Nations everyone is arranged in a circle so that no one is more powerful than anyone else. Those directly in front or behind are philosophically aligned, and those nearby form part of an international bloc.

United Nations

In France some people in the hierarchy are not linked to anyone, indicating how haphazard the structure can be.

France

Source: Adapted from Simcha Ronen, *Comparative and Multinational Management* (New York: Wiley, 1986), pp. 318–319. The epigrams in turn were derived from a variety of sources, including Robert M. Worchester of the U.K.-based Market and Opinion Research International (MORI), Ole Jacob Raad of Norway's PM Systems, and anonymous managers.

4. Speak with clear breaks between the words so that it is easier for the person to follow.

5. Avoid using words that are esoteric or culturally biased such as "he struck out" or "the whole idea is Mickey Mouse" because these cliches often have no meaning for the listener.

6. Avoid the use of slang.

7. Do not use words or expressions that require the other person to create a mental image such as "we were knee deep in the Big Muddy."

8. Mimic the cultural flavor of the nonnative speaker's language, for example, by using more flowery communication with Spanish-speaking listeners than with Germans.

9. Continually paraphrase and repeat the basic ideas.

10. At the end, test how well the other person understands by asking the individual to paraphrase what has been said.[13]

Upward Communication

Upward communication
The transfer of meaning from subordinate to superior.

Upward communication is the transfer of information from subordinate to superior. The primary purpose of this subordinate-initiated upward communication is to provide feedback, ask questions, or obtain assistance from higher-level management. In recent years, there has been a call for and a concerted effort to promote more upward communication in the United States. In other countries, such as in Japan, Hong Kong, and Singapore, upward communication has long been a fact of life. Managers in these countries have extensively used suggestion systems and quality circles to get employee input and always are available to listen to their people's concerns. For example, here are some observations from the approach the Japanese firm Matsushita uses in dealing with employee suggestions:

> Matsushita views employee recommendations as instrumental to making improvements on the shop floor and in the marketplace. [It believes] that a great many little people, paying attention each day to how to improve their jobs, can accomplish more than a whole headquarters full of production engineers and planners.
>
> Praise and positive reinforcement are an important part of the Matsushita philosophy. . . . Approximately 90 percent of . . . suggestions receive rewards; most only a few dollars per month, but the message is reinforced constantly: "Think about your job; develop yourself and help us improve the company." The best suggestions receive company-wide recognition and can earn substantial monetary rewards. Each year, many special awards are also given, including presidential prizes and various divisional honors.[14]

This company has used the same approach wherever it has established plants worldwide, and the strategy has proved very successful. The company has all its employees begin the day by reciting its basic principles, beliefs, and values, which are summarized in Table 8–4, to reinforce in all employees the reason for the company's existence and to provide a form of spiritual fabric to energize and sustain them. All employees see themselves as important members of a successful team, and they are willing to do whatever is necessary to ensure the success of the group.

Outside these Asian countries, upward communication is not as popular. For example, in South America, many managers believe that employees should follow orders and not ask a lot of questions. German managers also make much less use of this form of communication. In most cases, however, evidence shows that employees prefer to have downward communication at least supplemented by upward channels. Unfortunately, such upward communication does not always occur because of a number of communication barriers.

■ Communication Barriers

A number of common communication barriers are relevant to international management. The more important include language, perception, culture, and nonverbal communication.

Table 8–4
Matsushita's Philosophy

Basic Business Principles

To recognize our responsibilities as industrialists, to foster progress, to promote the general welfare of society, and to devote ourselves to the further development of world culture.

Employees Creed

Progress and development can be realized only through the combined efforts and cooperation of each member of the Company. Each of us, therefore, shall keep this idea constantly in mind as we devote ourselves to the continuous improvement of our Company.

The Seven Spiritual Values

1. National service through industry
2. Fairness
3. Harmony and cooperation
4. Struggle for betterment
5. Courtesy and humility
6. Adjustment and assimilation
7. Gratitude

Language Barriers

Knowledge of the home country's language (the language used at the headquarters of the MNC) is important for personnel placed in a foreign assignment. If managers do not understand the language that is used at headquarters, they likely will make a wide assortment of errors. Additionally, many MNCs now prescribe English as the common language for internal communication, so that managers can more easily convey information to their counterparts in other geographically dispersed locales.[15] Despite such progress, however, language training continues to lag in many areas, although in an increasing number of European countries, more and more young people are becoming multilingual.[16] Table 8–5 shows the percentage of European students who are studying the major languages.

Language education is a good beginning, but it is also important to realize that just the ability to speak the language used at MNC headquarters is often not enough to ensure that the personnel are capable of doing the work. Stout recently noted that many MNCs worldwide place a great deal of attention on the applicant's ability to speak English without considering if the person has other necessary skills such as the ability to interact well with others and the technical knowledge demanded by the job.[17] Additionally, in interviewing people for jobs he has noted that many interviewers fail to take into account the applicant's culture. As a result, interviewers misinterpret behaviors such as quietness or shyness and use them to conclude that the applicant is not sufficiently confident or self-assured. Still another problem is that nonnative speakers may know the language but not be fully fluent. So they end up asking questions or making statements that convey the wrong message. After studying Japanese for only one year, Stout reports that he began interviewing candidates in their local language and made a number of mistakes. In one case, he reports, "a young woman admitted to having an adulterous affair—even though this was not even close to the topic I was inquiring about—because of my unskilled use of the language."[18]

More recently, written communication has been getting increased attention, because poor writing is proving to be a greater barrier than poor talking. For example, Hildebrandt has found that among U.S. subsidiaries studied in Germany, language was a major problem when subsidiaries were sending written communications to the home office. The process often involved elaborate procedures associated with translating and reworking the report. Typical steps included: (1) holding a staff conference to determine what was to be

Table 8–5
Multilingualism in the EU Classroom

	Percentage of pupils in general secondary education learning English, French, or German as a foreign language, 1991–1992		
	English	**French**	**German**
Holland	96	65	53
Germany	93	23	—
Denmark	92	8	58
Spain	92	10	0.3
France	84	—	27
Belgium (Flemish)	68	98	22
Belgium (French)	58	1	6
Italy	61	33	3
Portugal	55	25	0.4
Britain	—	59	20
Ireland	—	69	24

Source: Eurostat, 1995.

included in the written message; (2) writing the initial draft in German; (3) rewriting the draft in German; (4) translating the material into English; (5) consulting with bilingual staff members regarding the translation; and (6) rewriting the English draft a series of additional times until the paper was judged to be acceptable for transmission. The German managers admitted that they felt uncomfortable with writing, because their command of written English was poor. As Hildebrandt noted:

> All German managers commanding oral English stated that their grammatical competence was not sufficiently honed to produce a written English report of top quality. Even when professional translators from outside the company rewrote the German into English, German middle managers were unable to verify whether the report captured the substantive intent or included editorial alterations.[19]

Problems associated with the translation of information from one language to another have been made even clearer by Schermerhorn, who conducted research among 153 Hong Kong Chinese bilinguals who were enrolled in an undergraduate management course at a major Hong Kong university. The students were given two scenarios written in either English or Chinese. One scenario involved a manager who was providing some form of personal support or praise for a subordinate. The research used the following procedures:

> [A] careful translation and back-translation method was followed to create the Chinese language versions of the research instruments. Two bilingual Hong Kong Chinese, both highly fluent in English and having expertise in the field of management, shared roles in the process. Each first translated one scenario and the evaluation questions into Chinese. Next they translated each other's Chinese versions back into English, and discussed and resolved translation differences in group consultation with the author. Finally, a Hong Kong professor read and interpreted the translations correctly as a final check of equivalency.[20]

The participants were asked to answer eight evaluation questions about these scenarios. A significant difference between the two sets of responses was found. Those who were queried in Chinese gave different answers from those who were queried in English. This led Schermerhorn to conclude that language plays a key role in conveying information between cultures, and that in cross-cultural management research, bilingual individuals should not be queried in their second language.

Cultural Barriers

Closely related to the language barriers are cultural barriers. For example, research by Sims and Guice compared 214 letters of inquiry written by native and nonnative speakers of English to test the assumption that cultural factors affect business communication. Among other things, the researchers found that nonnative speakers used exaggerated politeness, provided unnecessary professional and personal information, and made inappropriate requests of the other party. Commenting on the results and implications of their study, the researchers noted that their investigation

> indicates that the deviations from standard U.S. business communication practices were not specific to one or more nationalities. The deviations did not occur among specific nationalities but were spread throughout the sample of nonnative letters used for the study. Therefore, we can speculate that U.S. native speakers of English might have similar difficulties in international settings. In other words, a significant number of native speakers in the U.S. might deviate from the standard business communication practices of other cultures. Therefore, these native speakers need specific training in the business communication practices of the major cultures of the world so they can communicate successfully and acceptably with readers in those cultures.[21]

Research by Scott and Green has extended these findings, showing that even in English-speaking countries, there are different approaches to writing letters. In the United States, for example, it is common practice when constructing a bad-news letter to start out "with a pleasant, relevant, neutral, and transitional buffer statement; give the reasons for the unfavorable news before presenting the bad news; present the refusal in a positive manner; imply the bad news whenever possible; explain how the refusal is in the reader's best interest; and suggest positive alternatives that build goodwill."[22] In Great Britain, however, it is common to start out by referring to the situation, discussing the reasons for the bad news, conveying the bad news (often quite bluntly), and concluding with an apology or statement of regret (something that is frowned on by business-letter experts in the United States) designed to keep the reader's goodwill. Here is an example:

> Lord Hanson has asked me to reply to your letter and questionnaire of February 12 which we received today.
> As you may imagine, we receive numerous requests to complete questionnaires or to participate in a survey, and this poses problems for us. You will appreciate that the time it would take to complete these requests would represent a full-time job, so we decided some while ago to decline such requests unless there was some obvious benefit to Hanson PLC and our stockholders. As I am sure you will understand, our prime responsibility is to look after our stockholders' interests.
> I apologize that this will not have been the response that you were hoping for, but I wish you success with your research study.[23]

U.S. MNC managers would seldom, if ever, send this type of letter; it would be viewed as blunt and tactless. However, the indirect approach that Americans use would be viewed by their British counterparts as overly indirect and obviously insincere.

On the other hand, when compared to Asians, many American writers are far more blunt and direct. For example, Park, Dillon, and Mitchell recently reported that there are pronounced differences between the ways in which Americans and Asians write business letters of complaint. They compared the approach used by American managers, for whom English is a first language, who wrote international business letters of complaint, with that of Korean managers, for whom English is a second language, who wrote the same types of letters. They found that American writers used a direct organizational pattern and tended to state the main idea or problem first before sharing explanatory details that clearly related to the stated problem. In contrast, the standard Korean pattern was indirect and tended to delay the reader's discovery of the main point. This led the researchers to conclude that the U.S.-generated letter could well be regarded as rude by Asian readers, while American readers might regard the letter from the Korean writer as vague, emotional, and accusatory.[24]

Perceptual Barriers

Perception
A person's view of reality.

Perception is a person's view of reality. How people see reality can vary and will influence their judgment and decision making.[25] One example involves Japanese stockbrokers who now perceive that the chances of improving their career are better with U.S. firms, so they have changed jobs. Another involves Hong Kong hoteliers who have begun buying U.S. properties, because they have the perception that if they can offer the same top-quality hotel service as back home, they can dominate their U.S. markets. These are examples of how perceptions can play an important role in international management. Unfortunately, misperceptions also can become a barrier to effective communication. For example, when the Clinton administration decided to allow Taiwan President Lee Tenghui to visit the United States, the Chinese (PRC) government perceived this as a threatening gesture and took actions of its own. Besides conducting dangerous war games very near Taiwan's border as a warning not to become too bold in its quest for recognition as a sovereign nation, the PRC also snubbed U.S. car manufacturers and gave a much-coveted, $1 billion contract to Mercedes-Benz of Germany.[26] The following sections provide examples of perception barriers in the international arena.

Advertising Messages   One way that perception can prove to be a problem in international management communication is when one person uses words that are misinterpreted by the other. Many firms have found to their dismay that a failure to understand home-country perceptions can result in disastrous advertising programs. Here are two examples:

> Ford . . . introduced a low cost truck, the "Fiera," into some Spanish-speaking countries. Unfortunately, the name meant "ugly old woman" in Spanish. Needless to say, this name did not encourage sales. Ford also experienced slow sales when it introduced a top-of-the-line automobile, the "Comet," in Mexico under the name "Caliente." The puzzling low sales were finally understood when Ford discovered that "caliente" is slang for a street walker.[27]
>
> One laundry detergent company certainly wishes now that it had contacted a few locals before it initiated its promotional campaign in the Middle East. All of the company's advertisements pictured soiled clothes on the left, its box of soap in the middle, and clean clothes on the right. But, because in that area of the world people tend to read from the right to the left, many potential customers interpreted the message to indicate the soap actually soiled the clothes.[28]

View of Others   Perception influences communication when it deals with how individuals "see" others. A good example is provided by the perception of foreigners who reside in the United States. Most Americans see themselves as extremely friendly, outgoing, and kind, and they believe that others also see them in this way. At the same time, many are not aware of what negative impressions they give to others. Another example is the way in which people act, or should act, when initially meeting others. "International Management in Action: Doing It Right the First Time" provides some insights regarding how to conduct oneself when doing business in Japan.

Another example of how the perceptions of others affect communication occurs in the way that some international managers perceive their subordinates. For example, a study examined the perceptions that German and U.S. managers had of the qualifications of their peers (those on the same level and status), managers, and subordinates in Europe and Latin America.[29] The findings showed that both the German and U.S. respondents perceived their subordinates to be less qualified than their peers. However, although the Germans perceived their managers to have more managerial ability than their peers, the Americans felt that their South American peers in many instances had equal or better qualifications than their own managers. Quite obviously, this perception will affect how U.S. expatriates communicate with their South American peers as well as how the expatriates communicate with their bosses.

Another study found that Western managers have more favorable attitudes toward women as managers than Asian or Saudi managers do.[30] This perception obviously affects the way these managers interact and communicate with their female counterparts. The same is true in the case of many Japanese managers, who according to one survey still regard women as superfluous to the effective running of their organizations and generally continue to not treat women as equals.[31]

International Management in Action
Doing It Right the First Time

Like other countries of the world, Japan has its own business customs and culture. And when someone fails to adhere to these traditions, the individual runs the risk of being perceived as ineffective or uncaring. The following addresses three areas that are important in being correctly perceived by one's Japanese counterparts.

Business Cards

The exchange of business cards is an integral part of Japanese business etiquette, and Japanese businesspeople exchange these cards when meeting someone for the first time. Additionally, those who are most likely to interface with non-Japanese are supplied with business cards printed in Japanese on one side and a foreign language, usually English, on the reverse side. This is aimed at enhancing recognition and pronunciation of Japanese names, which are often unfamiliar to foreign businesspeople. Conversely, it is advisable for foreign businesspeople to carry and exchange with their Japanese counterparts a similar type of card printed in Japanese and in their native language. These cards can often be obtained through business centers in major hotels.

When receiving a card, it is considered common courtesy to offer one in return. In fact, not returning a card might convey the impression that the manager is not committed to a meaningful business relationship in the future.

Business cards should be presented and received with both hands. When presenting one's card, the presentor's name should be facing the person who is receiving the card so the receiver can easily read it. When receiving a business card, it should be handled with care and if the receiver is sitting at a conference or other type of table, the card should be placed in front of the individual for the duration of the meeting. It is considered rude to put a prospective business partner's card in one's pocket before sitting down to discuss business matters.

Bowing

Although the handshake is increasingly common in Japan, bowing remains the most prevalent formal method of greeting, saying goodbye, expressing gratitude, or apologizing to another person. When meeting foreign businesspeople, however, Japanese will often use the handshake or a combination of both a handshake and a bow, even though there are different forms and styles of bowing, depending on the relationship of the parties involved; foreign businesspeople are not expected to be familiar with these intricacies, and therefore a deep nod of the head or a slight bow will suffice in most cases. Many foreign businesspeople are unsure whether to use a handshake or to bow. In these situations, it is best to wait and see if one's Japanese counterpart offers a hand or prefers to bow and then to follow suit.

Attire

Most Japanese businessmen dress in conservative dark or navy blue suits, although slight variations in style and color have come to be accepted in recent years. As a general rule, what is acceptable business attire in virtually any industrialized country is usually regarded as good business attire in Japan as well. Although there is no need to conform precisely to the style of dress of the Japanese, good judgment should be exercised when selecting attire for a business meeting. If unsure about what constitutes appropriate attire for a particular situation, it is best to err on the conservative side.

The Impact of Culture

Besides language and perception, another major barrier to communication is culture, a topic that was given detailed attention in Chapter 5. Culture can affect communication in a number of ways, and one way is through the impact of cultural values.

Cultural Values   One expert on Middle Eastern countries notes that people there do not relate to and communicate with each other in a loose, general way as do those in the United States. Relationships are more intense and binding in the Middle East, and a wide variety of work-related values influence what people in the Middle East will and will not do.

> In North American society, the generally professed prevalent pattern is one of nonclass-consciousness, as far as work is concerned. Students, for example, make extra pocket money by taking all sorts of part-time jobs—manual and otherwise—regardless of the socioeconomic stratum to which the individual belongs. The attitude is uninhibited. In the Middle East, the overruling obsession is how the money is made and via what kind of job.[32]

These types of values indirectly, and in many cases directly, affect communication between people from different cultures. For example, one would communicate differently with a "rich college student" from the United States than with one from Saudi Arabia. Similarly, when negotiating with managers from other cultures, knowing the way to handle the deal requires an understanding of cultural values.[33]

Another cultural value example is the way that people use time. In the United States, people believe that time is an asset and is not to be wasted, which is an idea that often has limited meaning in other cultures. Various values are reinforced and reflected through the use of proverbs that Americans are taught from an early age. These proverbs help to guide people's behavior. Table 8–6 lists some examples.

Misinterpretation Cultural differences can cause misinterpretations both in how others see expatriate managers and in how the latter see themselves. For example, U.S. managers doing business in Austria often misinterpret the fact that local businesspeople always address them in formal terms. They may view this as meaning that they are not friends or are not liked, but in fact, this formalism is the way that Austrians always conduct business. The informal, first-name approach used in the United States is not the style of the Austrians.

Culture even affects day-to-day activities of corporate communications.[34] For example, when sending messages to international clients, American managers have to keep in mind that there are many things that are uniquely American and overseas managers may not be aware of them. As an example, Daylight Savings Time is known to all Americans, but many Asian managers have no idea what the term means. Similarly, it is common for American managers to address memos to their "international office" without realizing that the managers who work in this office regard the American location as the "international" one! Other suggestions that can be of value to American managers who are engaged in international communications include:

- Be careful not to use generalized statements about benefits, compensation, pay cycles, holidays, or policies in your worldwide communications. Work hours, vacation accrual, general business practices, and human resource issues vary widely from country to country.
- Since most of the world uses the metric system, be sure to include converted weights and measures in all internal and external communications.
- Keep in mind that even in English-speaking countries, words may have different meanings. Not everyone knows what is meant by "counterclockwise," or "quite good."
- Remember that letterhead and paper sizes differ worldwide. The 8½ by 11-inch page is a U.S. standard, but most countries use an A4 (8¼ × 11½-inch) size for their letterhead, with envelopes to match.

Table 8–6
U.S. Proverbs Representing Cultural Values

Proverb	Cultural Value
A penny saved is a penny earned	Thriftiness
Time is money	Time thriftiness
Don't cry over spilt milk	Practicality
Waste not, want not	Frugality
Early to bed, early to rise, makes one healthy, wealthy, and wise	Diligence; work ethic
A stitch in time saves nine	Timeliness of action
If at first you don't succeed, try, try again	Persistence; work ethic
Take care of today, and tomorrow will take care of itself	Preparation for future

Source: Drawn from Nancy J. Adler, *International Dimensions of Organizational Behavior,* 2nd ed. (Boston: PWS-Kent Publishing, 1991), pp. 79–80.

- Dollars are not unique to the United States. There are Australian, Bermudian, Canadian, Hong Kong, Taiwanese, and New Zealand dollars, among others. So in referring to American dollars it is important to use "US$."

Many Americans also have difficulty interpreting the effect of national values on work behavior. For example, why do French and German workers drink alcoholic beverages at lunch time? Why are many European workers unwilling to work the night shift? Why do overseas affiliates contribute to the support of the employees' work council or donate money to the support of kindergarten teachers in local schools? These types of actions are viewed by some people as wasteful, but to those who know the culture of these countries, such actions promote the long-run good of the company. It is the outsider who is misinterpreting why these culturally specific actions are happening, and such misperceptions can become a barrier to effective communication.

Nonverbal Communication

Another major reason for perception problems is accounted for by **nonverbal communication,** which is the transfer of meaning through means such as body language and use of physical space. Table 8–7 summarizes a number of dimensions of nonverbal communication. The general categories that are especially important to communication in international management are kinesics, proxemics, chronemics, and chromatics.

Kinesics   **Kinesics** is the study of communication through body movement and facial expression. Primary areas of concern include eye contact, posture, and gestures. For example, when one communicates verbally with someone in the United States, it is good manners to look the other person in the eye. This area of communicating through the use of eye contact and gaze is known as **oculesics.** In some areas of the world oculesics is an important consideration because of what people should not do such as stare at others or maintain continuous eye contact because it is considered impolite to do these things.

Another area of kinesics is posture which can also cause problems. For example, when Americans are engaged in prolonged negotiations or meetings, it is not uncommon for them to relax and put their feet up on a chair or desk, but this is insulting behavior in the Middle East. Here is just such an example from a classroom situation:

Nonverbal communication
The transfer of meaning through means such as body language and the use of physical space.

Kinesics
The study of communication through body movement and facial expressions.

Oculesics
The area of communication that deals with conveying messages through the use of eye contact and gaze.

Table 8–7
Common Forms of Nonverbal Communication

1. Hand gestures, both intended and self-directed (autistic), such as the nervous rubbing of hands
2. Facial expressions, such as smiles, frowns, and yawns
3. Posture and stance
4. Clothing and hair styles (hair being more like clothes than like skin, both subject to the fashion of the day)
5. Interpersonal distance (proxemics)
6. Eye contact and direction of gaze, particularly in "listening behavior"
7. "Artifacts" and nonverbal symbols, such as lapel pins, walking sticks, and jewelry
8. Paralanguage (though often in language, just as often treated as part of nonverbal behavior-speech rate, pitch, inflections, volume)
9. Taste, including symbolism of food and the communication function of chatting over coffee or tea, and oral gratification such as smoking or gum chewing
10. Cosmetics: temporary-powder; permanent-tattoos
11. Time symbolism: what is too late or too early to telephone or visit a friend, or too long or too short to make a speech or stay for dinner
12. Timing and pauses within verbal behavior

Source: This information is found in J. C. Condon and F. S. Yousef, *An Introduction to Intercultural Communication* (Indianapolis, IN: Bobbs-Merrill, 1975), pp. 123–124.

In the midst of a discussion of a poem in the sophomore class of the English Department, the professor, who was British, took up the argument, started to explain the subtleties of the poem, and was carried away by the situation. He leaned back in his chair, put his feet up on the desk, and went on with the explanation. The class was furious. Before the end of the day, a demonstration by the University's full student body had taken place. Petitions were submitted to the deans of the various facilities. The next day, the situation even made the newspaper headlines. The consequences of the act, that was innocently done, might seem ridiculous, funny, baffling, incomprehensible, or even incredible to a stranger. Yet, to the native, the students' behavior was logical and in context. The students and their supporters were outraged because of the implications of the breach of the native behavioral pattern. In the Middle East, it is extremely insulting to have to sit facing two soles of the shoes of somebody.[35]

Haptics
Communicating through the use of bodily contact.

Gestures are also widely used and take many different forms. For example, Canadians shake hands, Japanese bow, Middle Easterners of the same sex kiss on the cheek. Communicating through the use of bodily contact is known as **haptics,** and it is a widely used form of nonverbal communication.

Proxemics
The study of the way people use physical space to convey messages.

Sometimes gestures present problems for expatriate managers because these behaviors have different meanings depending on the country. For example, in the United States, putting the thumb and index finger together to form an "O" is the sign for "okay." In Japan, this is the sign for money; in southern France, the gesture means "zero" or "worthless"; and in Brazil, it is regarded as a vulgar or obscene sign. In France and Belgium, snapping the fingers of both hands is considered vulgar; in Brazil, this gesture is used to indicate that something has been done for a long time. In Britain, the "V for victory" sign is given with the palm out; if the palm is in, this roughly means "shove it"; in non-British countries, the gesture means two of something and often is used when placing an order at a restaurant.[36] Gibson, Hodgetts, and Blackwell found that many foreign students attending school in the United States have trouble communicating, because they are unable to interpret some of the most common nonverbal gestures.[37] A survey group of 44 Jamaican, Venezuelan, Colombian, Peruvian, Thai, Indian, and Japanese students at two major universities were given pictures of 20 universal cultural gestures, and each was asked to describe the nonverbal gestures illustrated. In 56 percent of the choices the respondents either gave an interpretation that was markedly different from that of Americans or reported that the nonverbal gesture had no meaning in their culture. These findings help to reinforce the need to teach expatriates about local nonverbal communication.

Intimate distance
Distance between people that is used for very confidential communications.

Personal distance
In communicating, the physical distance used for talking with family and close friends.

Social distance
In communicating, the distance used to handle most business transactions.

Proxemics   **Proxemics** is the study of the way that people use physical space to convey messages. For example, in the United States, there are four "distances" people use in communicating on a face-to-face basis (see Figure 8–4.) **Intimate distance** is used for very confidential communications. **Personal distance** is used for talking with family and close friends. **Social distance** is used to handle most business transactions. **Public distance** is used when calling across the room or giving a talk to a group.

Public distance
In communicating, the distance used when calling across the room or giving a talk to a group.

Figure 8–4

Personal Space Categories for Those in the United States

Source: Adapted from Richard M. Hodgetts and Donald F. Kuratko, *Management,* 2nd ed. (San Diego, CA: Harcourt Brace Jovanovich, 1991), p. 384.

One major problem for Americans communicating with those from the Middle East or South America is that the intimate or personal distance zones are violated. Americans often tend to be moving away in interpersonal communication with their Middle Eastern or Latin counterparts, while the latter are trying to physically close the gap. The American cannot understand why the other is standing so close; the latter cannot understand why the American is being so reserved and standing so far away. The result is a breakdown in communication.

Office layout is another good example of proxemics. In the United States, the more important the manager, the larger the office, and often a secretary screens visitors and keeps away those whom the manager does not wish to see. In Japan, most managers do not have large offices, and even if they do, they spend a great deal of time out of it and with the employees. Thus, the Japanese have no trouble communicating directly with their superiors. A Japanese manager's staying in his office would be viewed as a sign of distrust or anger toward the group.

Another way that office proxemics can affect communication is that in many European companies, there is no wall between the space allocated to the senior-level manager and that of the subordinates. Everyone works in the same large room. These working conditions often are disconcerting to Americans, who tend to prefer more privacy.

Chronemics   **Chronemics** refers to the way in which time is used in a culture. When examined in terms of extremes, there are two types of time schedules: monochronic and polychronic. A **monochronic time schedule** is one in which things are done in a linear fashion. A manager will address Issue A first and then move on to Issue B. In these societies, time schedules are very important and time is viewed as something that can be controlled and should be used wisely. In individualistic cultures such as the United States, Great Britain, Canada, and Australia, as well as many of the cultures in Northern Europe, managers adhere to monochronic time schedules.

This is sharp contrast to **polychronic time schedules** which are characterized by people tending to do several things at the same time and placing higher value on personal involvement than on getting things done on time. In these cultures, schedules are subordinated to personal relationships. Regions of the world where polychronic time schedules are common include Latin America and the Middle East.

When doing business in countries that adhere to monochronic time schedules, it is important to be on time for meetings. Additionally, these meetings typically end at the appointed time so that participants can be on time for their next meeting. When doing business in countries that adhere to polychronic time schedules, it is common to find business meetings starting late and finishing late.

Chromatics   **Chromatics** is the use of color to communicate messages. Every society uses chromatics, but colors that mean one thing in the United States may mean something entirely different in Asia. For example, in the United States it is common to wear black when one is in mourning, while in some locations in India people where white when they are in mourning. In Hong Kong red is used to signify happiness or luck and traditional bridal dresses are red; in the United States it is common for the bride to wear white. In many Asian countries shampoos are dark in color because users want the soap to be the same color as their hair and if it were a light color, they believe it would remove color from their hair. In the United States shampoos tend to be light colored because people see this as a sign of cleanliness and hygiene. In Chile a gift of yellow roses conveys the message "I don't like you," while in the United States just the opposite message would be conveyed by this gift.

Knowing the importance of chromatics can be very helpful because, among other things, it can avoid embarrassing situations. A good example is the American manager in Peru who upon finishing a one-week visit to the Lima subsidiary decided to thank the assistant who was assigned to him. He sent her a dozen red roses. The lady understood the faux pas, but the American manager was somewhat embarrassed when his Peruvian counterpart smilingly told him, "It was really nice of you to buy her a present. However, red roses indicate a romantic interest!"

Chronemics
The way in which time is used in a culture.

Monochronic time schedule
A time schedule in which things are done in a linear fashion.

Polychronic time schedule
A time schedule in which people tend to do several things at the same time and place higher value on personal involvement than on getting things done on time.

Chromatics
The use of color to communicate messages.

■ Achieving Communication Effectiveness

A number of steps can be taken to improve communication effectiveness in the international arena. These include providing feedback systems, providing language and cultural training, and increasing flexibility and cooperation.

Improve Feedback Systems

One of the most important ways of improving communication effectiveness in the international context is to open up feedback systems. Such feedback is particularly important between parent companies and their affiliates. There are two basic types of feedback systems: personal (e.g., face-to-face meetings, telephone conversations and personalized e-mail) and impersonal (e.g., reports, budgets, and plans). Both of these systems help affiliates to keep their home office aware of progress and, in turn, help the home office to monitor and control affiliate performance as well as set goals and standards.

At present, there seem to be varying degrees of feedback between the home offices of MNCs and their affiliates. For example, one study evaluated the communication feedback between subsidiaries and home offices of 63 MNCs headquartered in Europe, Japan, and North America.[38] A marked difference was found between the way that U.S. companies communicated with their subsidiaries and the way that European and Japanese firms did. Over one-half of the U.S. subsidiaries responded that they received monthly feedback from their reports, in contrast to less than 10 percent of the European and Japanese subsidiaries. In addition, the Americans were much more inclined to hold regular management meetings on a regional or worldwide basis. Seventy-five percent of the U.S. companies had annual meetings for their affiliate top managers, compared with less than 50 percent for the Europeans and Japanese. These findings may help to explain why many international subsidiaries and affiliates are not operating as efficiently as they should. The units may not have sufficient contact with the home office. They do not seem to be getting continuous assistance and feedback that are critical to effective communication.

Provide Language Training

Besides improving feedback systems, another way to make communication more effective in the international arena is through language training. Many host-country managers cannot communicate well with their counterparts at headquarters. Because English has become the international language of business, those who are not native speakers of English should learn the language well enough so that face-to-face and telephone conversations and e-mail are possible. If the language of the home office is not English, this other language also should be learned. As a U.S. manager working for a Japanese MNC recently told one of the authors, "The official international language of this company is English. However, whenever the home office people show up they tend to cluster together with their countrymen and speak Japanese. That's why I'm trying to learn Japanese. Let's face it. They say all you need to know is English, but if you want to really know what's going on you have to talk *their* language."

Written communication also is extremely important in achieving effectiveness. As noted earlier, when reports, letters, and e-mail messages are translated from one language to another, preventing a loss of meaning is virtually impossible. Moreover, if the communications are not written properly, they may not be given the attention they deserve. The reader will allow poor grammar and syntax to influence his or her interpretation and subsequent actions. Moreover, if readers cannot communicate in the language of those who will be receiving their comments or questions about the report, their messages also must be translated and likely will lose further meaning. Therefore, the process can continue on and on, each party failing to achieve full communication with the other. Hildebrandt has described the problems in this two-way process when an employee in a foreign subsidiary writes a report and then sends it to his or her boss for forwarding to the home office:

The general manager or vice president cannot be asked to be an editor. Yet they often send statements along, knowingly, which are poorly written, grammatically imperfect, or generally unclear. The time pressures do not permit otherwise. Predictably, questions issued from the States to the subsidiary and the complicated bilingual process now goes in reverse, ultimately reaching the original . . . staff member, who receives the English questions retranslated.[39]

Language training would help to alleviate such complicated communication problems.

Provide Cultural Training

It is very difficult to communicate effectively with someone from another culture unless at least one party has some understanding of the other's culture.[40] Otherwise, communication likely will break down. This is particularly important for multinational companies that have operations throughout the world.[41] Although there always are important differences between countries, and even between subcultures of the same country, firms that operate in South America find that the cultures of these countries have certain commonalities. These common factors also apply to Spain and Portugal. Therefore, a basic understanding of Latin cultures can prove to be useful throughout a large region of the world. The same is true of Anglo cultures, where norms and values tend to be somewhat similar from one country to another. When a multinational has operations in South America, Europe, and Asia, however, multicultural training becomes necessary. The box "Communicating in Europe" provides some specific examples of cultural differences.

As Chapter 5 pointed out, it is erroneous to generalize about an "international" culture, because the various nations and regions of the globe are too different. Training must be conducted on a region or country-specific basis. Failure to do so can result in continuous communication breakdown.[42] Chapters 15 and 16 will give considerable attention to cultural training as part of selection for overseas assignments and human resource development.

Increase Flexibility and Cooperation

Effective international communications require increased flexibility and cooperation by all parties.[43] To improve understanding and cooperation, each party must be prepared to give a little.[44] Take the case of International Computers Ltd., a mainframe computer firm that does a great deal of business in Japan. This firm urges its people to strive for successful collaboration in their international partnerships and ventures. To drive home the point of flexibility and cooperation, the company gives all its people who are involved in a joint partnership with an overseas firm a list of "dos" that are designed to make the arrangement work. These guidelines, listed in Table 8–8, are designed to ensure the requisite amount of flexibility and cooperation in intercompany interaction and negotiation. At the heart of this process is effective communication. As put by Kenichi Ohmae:

> We must recognize and accept the inescapable subtleties and difficulties of intercompany relationships. This is the essential starting point. Then we must focus not on contractual or equity-related issues but on the quality of the people at the interface between organizations. Finally, we must understand that success requires frequent, rapport-building meetings by at least three organizational levels: top management, staff, and line management at the working level.[45]

The World of *Business Week*—Revisited

The *Business Week* article that opened this chapter presented a number of intercultural communication challenges. One was the desire by GM to more effectively communicate and coordinate its international operations, something that the firm had not done previously because it felt that bureaucratic controls would be good enough. This latest decision means that the communication channels between GM and its overseas holdings and partners will now become more effective and the senior

Communicating in Europe

In Europe, many countries are within easy commuting distance of their neighbors, so an expatriate who does business in France on Monday may be in Germany on Tuesday, Great Britain on Wednesday, Italy on Thursday, and Spain on Friday. Each country has its own etiquette regarding how to greet others and conduct oneself during social and business meetings. The following sections examine some of the things that expatriate managers need to know to communicate effectively.

France

When one is meeting with businesspeople in France, promptness is expected, although tardiness of 5 to 10 minutes is not considered a major gaffe. The French prefer to shake hands when introduced, and it is correct to address them by title plus last name. When the meeting is over, a handshake again is proper manners.

French executives try to keep their personal and professional lives separate. As a result, most business entertaining is done at restaurants or clubs. When gifts are given to business associates, they should appeal to intellectual or aesthetic pursuits as opposed to being something that one's company produces for sale on the world market. In conversational discussions, topics such as politics and money should be avoided. Also, humor should be used carefully during business meetings.

Germany

German executives like to be greeted by their title, and one should never refer to someone on a first-name basis unless invited to do so. Business appointments should be made well in advance, and punctuality is important. Like the French, the Germans often entertain clients outside their house, so an invitation to a German manager's home is a special privilege and always should be followed with a thank-you note. Additionally, as is the case in France, one should avoid using humor during business meetings.

Great Britain

In Britain, it is common to shake hands on the first meeting, and first names are always used in introductions. Unlike the custom in France and Germany, it is common

practice in Britain to arrive a little late for business and social occasions, and invitations to British homes are more likely than in some other European cultures. A typical gift for the host is flowers or chocolates.

During business meetings, suits and ties are common dress; however, striped ties should be avoided if they appear to be a copy of those worn by alumni of British universities and schools or by members of military or social clubs. Additionally, during social gatherings it is a good idea not to discuss politics, religion, or gossip about the monarchy unless the British person brings the topic up first.

Italy

In traditional companies, executives are referred to by title plus last name. It is common to shake hands when being introduced, and if the individual is a university graduate, the professional title *dottore* should be used.

Business appointments should be made well in advance, although punctuality is not essential. In most cases, business is done at the office, and when someone is invited to a restaurant, this invitation is usually done to socialize and not to continue business discussions. If an expatriate is invited to an Italian home, it is common to bring a gift for the host, such as a bottle of wine or a box of chocolates. During the dinner conversation, there is a wide variety of acceptable topics, including business, family matters, and soccer.

Spain

It is common to use first names when introducing or talking to people in Spain, and close friends typically greet each other with an embrace. Appointments should be made in advance, but punctuality is not essential.

If one is invited to the home of a Spanish executive, flowers or chocolates for the host are acceptable gifts. If the invitation includes dinner, any business discussions should be delayed until after coffee is served. During the social gathering, some topics that should be avoided include religion, family, and work. Additionally, humor rarely is used during formal occasions.

managers who work at headquarters and in the product development centers of its partners will be reporting directly to the top-ranking GM executive in each region of the world. This is a new communication channel and one that basically alters the way things have been done in the past; and, as noted in the article, GM 's bureaucracy drastically slows execution of new ideas. So, on the one hand, closer communication and interaction with its worldwide partners and operations could well provide the firm with market advantage while, on the other hand, the company's inability to act

Table 8–8
International Computer Ltd.'s Guidelines for Successful Collaboration

1. Treat the collaboration as a personal commitment. It's people that make partnerships work.
2. Anticipate that it will take up management time. If you can't spare the time, don't start it.
3. Mutual respect and trust are essential. If you don't trust the people you are negotiating with, forget it.
4. Remember that both partners must get something out of it (money, eventually). Mutual benefit is vital. This will probably mean you've got to give something up. Recognize this from the outset.
5. Make sure you tie up a tight legal contract. Don't put off resolving unpleasant or contentious issues until "later." Once signed, however, the contract should be put away. If you refer to it, something is wrong with the relationship.
6. Recognize that during the course of a collaboration, circumstances and markets change. Recognize your partner's problems and be flexible.
7. Make sure you and your partner have mutual expectations of the collaboration and its time scale. One happy and one unhappy partner is a formula for failure.
8. Get to know your opposite numbers at all levels socially. Friends take longer to fall out.
9. Appreciate that cultures—both geographic and corporate—are different. Don't expect a partner to act or respond identically to you. Find out the true reason for a particular response.
10. Recognize your partner's interests and independence.
11. Even if the arrangement is tactical in your eyes, make sure you have corporate approval. Your tactical activity may be a key piece in an overall strategic jigsaw puzzle. With corporate commitment to the partnership, you can act with the positive authority needed in these relationships.
12. Celebrate achievement together. It's a shared elation, and you'll have earned it!

Source: This information is found in Kenichi Ohmae, "The Global Logic of Strategic Alliances," *Harvard Business Review,* March–April 1989, p. 149.

quickly on information could well result in lost opportunities and a perception of ineptness by its partners and overseas personnel. The key to the success of this new organizational arrangement is going to be the company's ability to deal effectively with intercultural communication. In linking the communication concepts discussed in this chapter with the obstacles facing GM, answer these questions: (1) In dealing with its Asian partners, what are two ways that verbal communication styles might prove to be a communication barrier? (2) How might GM 's decision to more closely monitor its worldwide operations create perception problems for the company? (3) What are two things that GM might do to increase international cooperation?

Summary of Key Points

1. Communication is the transfer of meaning from sender to receiver. This process can involve both the external and internal flow of information as well as verbal communication styles. The key to the effectiveness of communication is how accurately the receiver interprets the intended meaning.

2. Communicating in the international business context involves both downward and upward flows. Downward flows convey information from superior to subordinate; these flows vary considerably from country to country. For example, the downward system of organizational communication is much more prevalent in France than in Japan. Upward communication conveys information from subordinate to superior. In the United States and Japan, the upward system is more common than in South America or some European countries.

3. The international arena contains a number of communication barriers. Some of the most important are language, perception, culture, and nonverbal communication. Language, particularly in written communications, often loses considerable meaning during interpretation. Perception and culture can result in people's seeing and interpreting things differently, and as a result, communication can break down. Nonverbal communication such as body language, facial expressions, and use of physical space, time, and even color often varies from country to country and, if improper, often results in communication problems.

4. A number of steps can be taken to improve communication effectiveness. Some of the most important include improving feedback, providing language and cultural training, and encouraging flexibility and cooperation. These steps can be particularly helpful in overcoming communication barriers in the international context and can lead to more effective international management.

Key Terms

chromatics, *215*

chronemics, *215*

communication, *198*

context, *200*

downward communication, *204*

haptics, *214*

intimate distance, *214*

kinesics, *213*

monochronic time schedule, *215*

nonverbal communication, *213*

oculesics, *213*

perception, *210*

personal distance, *214*

polychronic time schedule, *215*

proxemics, *214*

public distance, *214*

social distance, *214*

upward communication, *206*

Review and Discussion Questions

1. How does explicit communication differ from implicit communication? What is one culture that makes wide use of explicit communication? Implicit communication? Describe how one would go about conveying the following message in each of the two cultures you identified: "You are trying very hard, but you are still making too many mistakes."

2. One of the major reasons that foreign expatriates have difficulty doing business in the United States is that they do not understand American slang. A business executive recently gave the authors the following three examples of statements that had no direct meaning for her because she was unfamiliar with slang: He was laughing like hell. Don't worry; it's a piece of cake. Let's throw these ideas up against the wall and see if any of them stick. Why did the foreign expat have trouble understanding these statements, and what could be said instead?

3. Yamamoto Iron & Steel is considering setting up a minimill outside Atlanta, Georgia. At present, the company is planning to send a group of executives to the area to talk with local and state officials regarding this plant. In what way might misperception be a barrier to effective communication between the representatives for both sides? Identify and discuss two examples.

4. Diaz Brothers is a winery in Barcelona. The company would like to expand operations to the United States and begin distributing its products in the Chicago area. If things work out well, the company then will expand to both coasts. In its business dealings in the Midwest, how might culture prove to be a communication barrier for the company's representatives from Barcelona? Identify and discuss two examples.

5. Why is nonverbal communication a barrier to effective communication? Would this barrier be greater for Yamamoto Steel & Iron (question 3) or the Diaz Brothers (question 4)? Defend your answer.

6. For U.S companies going abroad for the first time, which form of nonverbal communication barrier would be the greatest, kinesics or proxemics? Why? Defend your answer.

Internet Exercise: Working Effectively at Toyota

In 2001 Toyota's Camry was the best-selling car in the United States and the firm's share of the American automobile market was solid. However, the company is not resting on its laurels. Toyota has expanded worldwide and is now doing business in scores of countries. Visit the firm's web site and find out what it has been up to lately. The address is: **www.toyota.com**. Then take a tour of the company's products and services including cars, air services, and sports vehicles. Next, go to the jobs section site and see what types of career opportunities there are at Toyota. Finally, find out what Toyota is doing in your particular locale and those in the immediate area. Then, drawing upon this information and the material you read in the chapter, answer these three questions: (1) What type of communication challenges do you think you would face if you worked for Toyota and were in constant communication with their home office personnel in Japan? (2) What type of communication training do you think the firm would need to provide to you to ensure that you were effective in dealing with senior-level Japanese managers in the hierarchy? (3) Using Table 8–2 as your guide, what conclusions can you draw regarding communicating with the Japanese managers and what guidelines would you offer to a non-Japanese employee who just entered the firm and is looking for advice and guidance regarding how to communicate more effectively?

Gulf States

The Gulf States comprise Bahrain, Kuwait, Oman, Qatar, and the United Arab Emirates (U.A.E.). These countries lie along the eastern coast of the Arabian Peninsula, with Saudi Arabia bordering on the west and Iran on the east across the Arabian Gulf (called the Persian Gulf by Westerners). Each of the Gulf States countries is very small, but their desert land is strategically located in one of the largest oil-producing regions of the world.

Oil has made these nations some of the richest in the world, with very high per-capita income. They generally have free education, free health and social services, and no income tax. Because of the heat, business hours from May to October tend to be from 7 to 1 and from 4 to 7. During the rest of the year, the hours are from 8 to 2 and from 4 to 6. The largely government-owned oil industry dominates the economies but does not provide many jobs. The governments are trying to promote economic activities other than oil production to get their people off welfare.

Herman Kerdling's firm has had a very profitable business supplying the Gulf countries with oil-production machinery. Last month, Kerdling learned that he would be going to Oman for a 1-year assignment servicing the firm's contract. He was delighted, because he knows that all the top managers at headquarters have had similar international assignments. Moreover, Oman is one of the company's most important accounts. Kerdling was determined to be successful in this assignment.

Unfortunately, after several weeks in Oman, things have not worked out quite as he expected. Specifically, Kerdling is finding that doing business with the Arabs is difficult, because their approach is so different from that of Americans. One of the most disconcerting things is the fact that people stand so close when they talk. He often tries to back away and put some room between them, but the other person usually follows and closes the distance again.

Another problem is the way that meetings are conducted. Last week, Kerdling went to talk to an Arab customer about some new equipment that was to be delivered and installed within the next few weeks. He and the customer talked for about 5 minutes when someone in the next office suddenly barged in and interrupted the conversation. The customer talked to this individual for almost 5 minutes and then turned back to Kerdling and picked up the conversation where he had left off. Within a few minutes, however, someone else came in, and another interruption ensued. The meeting, which should have taken approximately 30 minutes, took over 2 hours to complete. As Kerdling left, he turned and saw another person start a conversation with the customer only to be interrupted by a third party. "How does anyone get anything done around here?" he wondered to himself.

A third problem are the letters and e-mails that Kerdling receives from his customers. These messages are translated by company-paid Arabic interpreters, and the interpreted copy is attached to the original. Herman sometimes has trouble with the interpretation, because the interpreters are not very good. Unfortunately, no one on the company's staff is fluent in Arabic, and no better interpreters can be found. There seems to be no way around this problem. Kerdling is convinced that there are many communication breakdowns caused by this lack of language fluency, but he is unsure of how to resolve the matter.
www.arab.net/kuwait/kuwait_contents.html

Questions

1. What are some current issues facing the Gulf States? What is the climate for doing business in the Gulf States today?

2. Why is Kerdling upset that his Arab hosts stand so close when they talk to him? What can he do about this?

3. Should Kerdling feel insulted when his conversation is interrupted by outsiders?

4. Is Kerdling right regarding communication breakdowns caused by a lack of language fluency? Can anything be done about the problem?

Foreign or Domestic?

Connie Hatley is a very successful businesswoman who has holdings in a wide variety of industries. Hatley recently was approached by one of the Big Three automakers and offered a multidealership arrangement. In return for investing $50 million in facilities, the auto manufacturer would be willing to give her five dealerships spread throughout the United States. These locations, for the most part, are in rural areas, but over the next decade, these locales likely will become much more populated. In addition, the company pointed out that a large percentage of new cars are purchased by individuals who prefer to buy in rural locations, because prices at these dealerships tend to be lower. Hatley has been seriously considering the offer, although she now has a competitive alternative.

A South Korean auto manufacturer has approached Hatley and offered her the same basic deal. Hatley indicated that she was wary of doing business with a foreign firm so far away, but the Korean manufacturer presented her with some interesting auto sales data, including: (1) between 1981 and 2001, the South Korean share of the U.S. auto market went from 0 to over 3 percent; (2) South Korean automakers are capturing market share in the United States at a faster rate than any other competitor; (3) new technology is being incorporated into these Korean-built cars at an unprecedented rate, and the quality is among the highest in the industry; (4) although the Big Three (GM, Ford, and DaimlerChrysler) hold a large share of the U.S. auto market, their market among those 45 years of age or younger is declining and being captured by foreign competitors; and (5) the South Korean firm intends to increase its share of the U.S. market by 20 percent annually.

Hatley is very impressed with these data and forecasts. Recently, however, the Korean auto company's sales and market share are declining; she is uneasy about having to deal with someone located halfway around the world. "If I don't receive scheduled deliveries, whom do I call?" she asked one of her vice presidents. "Also, we don't speak their language. If there is a major problem, how are we going to really communicate with each other? I like the proposal, and I'd take it if I were sure that we wouldn't have communication problems. However, $50 million is a lot of money to invest. If a mistake is made, I'm going to lose a fortune. They did experience some problems last year, and their sales were off that year. Of course, if the South Koreans are right in their long-range forecasts and I have no major problems dealing with them, my return on investment is going to be almost 50 percent higher than it will be with the U.S. manufacturer."

Questions

1. What specific types of communication problems might Hatley encounter in dealing with the South Koreans?

2. Can these communication problems be resolved, or are they insurmountable and will simply have to be tolerated?

3. Based on communication problems alone, should Hatley back away from the deal or proceed? Give your recommendation, then defend it.

IKEA: Managing Cultural Diversity

After firmly attaining leadership within Sweden, where it holds more than 20 percent of the overall market, IKEA has succeeded over the last 25 years in doing what no furniture distributor has ever attempted: to become a global player in an industry formerly considered by nature to be local.

Today IKEA delivers low-priced quality furniture to key markets throughout the world. It is the only distributor in its field to have successfully established itself in all parts of Europe, including southern and eastern Europe, and more notably in North America, including the USA. It has stores today in the Middle East, Singapore, and Hong Kong and is preparing to enter the Chinese market some time in the early part of the next century. Recently Ingvar Kamprad, the company's founder, secured his position in Europe with the acquisition of British-based Habitat, IKEA's chief rival in the UK and France.

To provide some idea of its worldwide presence, IKEA receives annually over 120 million visitors in its 125 stores, and distributes 35 million catalogs. Its sales revenues increased steadily over the last 10 years by an average of 12 percent annually, in spite of the flattening out of

its business in Western Europe which still represents nearly 80 percent of its annual volume (see Exhibit 1).

Ingvar Kamprad's stubborn insistence that people would buy more furniture if the price was low enough and the furniture was of decent quality, with no delays in delivery has gradually revolutionized the conservative national furniture markets in Europe and beyond. Kamprad intuitively anticipated the rise of consumerism in the 1950s and 1960s and virtually invented the practices of cash and carry, self-service, and volume buying in Europe.

IKEA was to invent many other concepts and new ways of dealing with logistics sourcing and retailing. Many of these innovations have become industry standards: knock-down furniture that can be stored and shipped in flat boxes; the involvement of customers in the value-adding process of handling the transportation and doing home-assembly themselves; and turning shopping into a family event by creating attractive open store environments that contain IKEA trademarks like the children's areas with brightly colored plastic balls and the buffet style restaurants where you can eat Swedish meatballs.

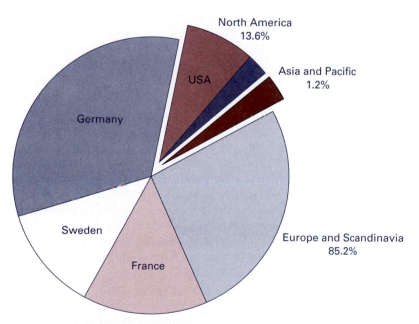

Exhibit 1

IKEA's Sales by Region, 1995–1996

Number of active articles: 11,400
Number of suppliers: 2,353 in 65 countries
Number of distribution centers: 14

IKEA has affected the way furniture is sold and distributed in every country where it is doing business, inspiring imitation and drawing respect, sometimes begrudgingly, from traditional furniture dealers.

One aspect of IKEA's success has been the development of unique product design capabilities, based on an almost religious dedication to the simple yet graceful design of contemporary Swedish furniture. In so doing, it has introduced millions of households around the world to the Swedish style that it, more than others, has come to typify.

IKEA's strength today comes from its mastery of three key aspects of the value chain: unique design capabilities, unique sourcing, and tightly controlled logistics. This means the company is able to produce products that are distinctive enough to provide market recognition, secure sourcing for long runs at profitable levels, and reduce inventory costs through regional warehouses which work very closely with stores. In this way it has been able to buck industry trends and steadily increase its share of slow growth, sometimes shrinking, markets.

IKEA has become a household name as much in Warsaw as in Los Angeles, attracting customers who just want to come to a store, look around, and have some fun. Something universally irresistible about IKEA makes it very difficult for people to come away from one of its stores without making a purchase and instills unprecedented loyalty among its customers and employees.

IKEA's successful development, particular organizational capacities, and the bold and inspired leadership of its entrepreneur-founder have all been largely written up and commented. Its organization, communication, marketing, product range, and store layouts, all tell the same story—the story of the "IKEA Way." A way strongly rooted in the personality of founder Ingvar Kamprad and the Swedish (regional) culture that he grew up in.

The "IKEA Way": Doing Things Differently

What is it that makes IKEA so different? Is it just a matter of "quality goods at affordable prices"? Or is there a deeper explanation? When asked these questions, IKEA managers and personnel become mystical and somewhat vague. "It is really a winning combination of price and merry feeling, a feeling of delight," a Dutch marketing manager answers. This feeling and a conscious awareness that, in addition to the competitive advantage, there is something strong and intangible at IKEA that drives and motivates its success, is shared by Ikeans throughout the organization. Could it be that the "IKEA Way's" combination of vision, charismatic leadership, sound business principles is subtly reinforced by the influence of Swedish culture? Could it be that Swedish, or Scandinavian, culture contains elements that facilitate international expansion?

Can a company's national culture in this case be a competitive advantage? Throughout our investigation of IKEA we have kept these questions in the back of our minds, and we invite you to consider them as we explore the "IKEA Way" more closely.

How It All Started

IKEA's name is derived from the initials of the company's founder, architect, and driving force, Ingvar Kamprad, those of the farm where he was raised, Elmtaryd, and those of his native village Agunnaryd, located in Smaland, a poor farming region in the south-east of Sweden. Coming from a modest background, Kamprad began as a trader in everything from matches to Christmas cards. He got into the furniture business almost accidentally after buying out a furniture plant which had to close down in the early 1950s. He demonstrated from the very beginning a combination of strong salesmanship, practical business acumen, thrift, an identity with ordinary people, and an unconventional perseverance in the face of adversity. Always modest he was nonetheless a true entrepreneur and, more significantly, a nonconformist who was not the least bit restrained by the conventions and traditions of the contemporary Swedish furniture trade.

His habit of staying close to his customers and his reluctance to own manufacturing furniture plants gave him the freedom to focus and innovate on all the facets of distribution. With nearby furniture producers he codesigned furniture to meet very specific requirements for quality products that average customers could afford, and then printed them up in catalogs, which he had discovered as an economical and effective way of marketing to a growing customer base in his early days as a trader.

In 1953 he opened his first showroom at the furniture plant he had bought earlier in Almhult which has become the heart of his furniture empire. The only transportation link to the factory was by road but, at a time when more and more working class Swedes were purchasing their first automobiles, what was originally a problem would become a solution.

Kamprad was obsessed with low prices and the only way to offer them was to keep costs as low as possible—this conviction became a driving force of his business development. He would constantly seek new ways to lower prices. For example, he bought fabrics for his furniture directly from textile mills, placing large orders and then supplying the material himself to his network of small furniture manufacturers. In this way at the same time he was able to cut costs a bit more, and ensure that his customers would have a wider selection of upholstery to choose from in the catalog. Unwittingly he had introduced the notion of vertical integration, which provided IKEA even then with a strong competitive advantage compared to traditional distributors who only displayed and sold furniture.

Such practices enabled him to maintain close contact with his suppliers, and eventually to learn intimately the parameters of furniture production. The relationship between Kamprad and his suppliers was so good that to obtain their commitment he needed only to draw rough sketches of the furniture he wanted and discuss with them how to adapt production to their capabilities. In so doing, he established over the years another cornerstone of his business philosophy: marrying the customers' need for low prices with the suppliers' need for profit through efficiency and long production runs. This was a strong departure from the kind of relationship that distributors traditionally maintained with their suppliers, buying furniture as it was ordered piece by piece at high prices with long waiting periods for delivery.

Balancing customers' requirements and producers' needs, which enabled him to sell furniture at prices 30 to 50 percent below traditional distributors, is now the foundation of the "IKEA Way." This notion is so basic and imperative that a store manager in Germany told me, when walking through the accessories department where some Chinese gadgets were displayed, that this balancing of optimal product design with the supplier with the needs of the customer is the "Yin and Yang" of the IKEA strategy. It was already present in the way Ingvar Kamprad developed his business through the 1950s when his innovative ways provoked stubborn counterattacks from his more established Swedish competitors.

A legendary showdown took place at the Sankt Erik's Fair in Stockholm where, for the first time, IKEA introduced its products. Feeling threatened by Kamprad's unexpected success and many new customers, the Swedish furniture cartel tried to block IKEA's entry at the fair. They failed, but soon thereafter managed a successful boycott of IKEA by Swedish furniture manufacturers, accusing Kamprad of unfair practices. Undaunted by this seemingly insurmountable obstacle, Kamprad looked for and found new suppliers in Poland at the height of the Cold War.

Although Polish manufacturers were willing to sell at prices well below their counterparts in Sweden, the cost of transportation offset this advantage. This new obstacle was at the origin of yet another IKEA invention, as Kamprad discovered that by "knocking down" furniture into disassembled parts it could be packed and shipped in flat cardboard cartons, reducing by more than 80 percent the cost of transportation. To further save on costs, the furniture could be sold directly to customers in these same flat boxes. To help customers participate in the distribution cycle, IKEA offered to rent roof racks and invented the simple assembly tool which has become another of its trademarks.

To reach the largest possible market and benefit fully from volume sales, in 1964 IKEA opened Europe's first large "warehouse scale" store in Stockholm. Unexpectedly large crowds of people attended the grand opening causing yet another problem. Seemingly endless queues formed at the checkout stands as employees scurried to the storage areas to fetch the purchased furniture. Instead of hiring more employees, Kamprad simply opened the storage area to customers and invited them to fetch the furniture themselves. Such practices were unheard of then, but understanding that

this would lead to lower prices, customers willingly complied. In just a few years IKEA had invented the concept of "prosumers," whereby customers actively participate in the distribution cycle.

Suddenly the whole system was in place: Customers were able to purchase attractive quality furniture at low prices; furniture suppliers benefited from long production runs; and IKEA, through volume sales, was able to make a considerable profit from small margins.

IKEA's business strategy did not evolve from "strategic planning," which is still scorned today in the company as "too sophisticated." It evolved from creative responses to difficult problems, turning them into solutions pragmatically and often with considerable risk. Not going by the book, or adopting conventional solutions, and learning by doing appears to be a distinguishing trait of Ingvar Kamprad's and IKEA's intuitive way of doing business.

The IKEA Mission

As IKEA grew, Ingvar Kamprad found ways to explain his unique way of doing business, always using simple language and metaphors He has consistently maintained that IKEA's mission is to offer "a wide range of home furnishing items of good design and function, at prices so low that the majority of people can afford to buy them." This statement is at the heart of the IKEA's philosophy and has shaped all the phases of its business, particularly product range. The concept is protected through numerous guidelines and special legal entities. Changes in the criteria for product range can only be made by joint decisions of INGKA Holding BV and Inter IKEA Systems BV, both of which are outside the sphere of management.

The essential guidelines appear in a 1976 publication, *Testament of a Furniture Dealer*, in which Kamprad emphasizes the company's ambition to cover the furnishing and decorative needs of the total home area with a distinctive style that reflects "our thoughts and is as simple and straightforward as ourselves." The guidelines also express such modern ideals as furniture that is durable and easy to live with, reflects a natural and free life style, and appeals to youthfulness with color and joy. Most of IKEA's products are designed by Swedes in Almhult, who consciously reproduce designs that reflect these values—values which are very consistent with Swedish culture. At the same time there is something in that specific design which has universal appeal throughout the markets of the world.

Business Principles

IKEA has developed unique competencies and an ability to deliver products which are distinctly Swedish, attractively presented in warm value-adding environments, and at prices consistently lower than its competitors.

What has made IKEA so different from other distributors is the balanced focus it has maintained on product range, sourcing, vertical integration, mass marketing, cost leadership, and a distinctive image. As such, the company is not market driven, and tends to react rather slowly to new consumer trends, studying them to see how they can be fitted into its operating systems and what value IKEA can add within its proven framework before adopting them into the company's range. The issue of range is vital for IKEA as, when it introduces new products, it must insure that the volumes it produces are leveraged from within: sourcing—logistics—store layouts.

The Yin/Yang metaphor, mentioned earlier, illustrates the imperative balance of strategic sourcing and marketing mix.

In the area of strategic sourcing, IKEA has established a long-standing competitive advantage. The durable partnerships that it has developed with furniture producers and other suppliers is based on the producers' capacity to provide long runs of parts, and their willingness to comply with IKEA's quality standards, and IKEA's guaranteed purchase of all parts produced. IKEA considers its producers as key stakeholders and provides them with technical assistance to increase their productivity, sometimes under-

The balance and complementariness of:

Strategic Sourcing and the Marketing Mix

writing investments in new technology. Together they actively contribute to both cost reduction and quality enhancement, which in turn optimizes the marketing mix.

Through such partnerships IKEA has virtually integrated production into its value-added chain without the heavy investments of actually owning and running its own furniture plants.

Management Style and Practices

IKEA's management style is described by non-Swedish members as informal, open, and caring. Hierarchy is not emphasized and in a typical store there are only three levels of responsibility between the store manager and coworkers (which is what employees are called, see Exhibit 2 for the worldwide distribution).

A pragmatic approach to problem solving and consensus-based decision making are also strongly imbedded in IKEA management practice.

Coworkers at all levels are encouraged to take initiatives, and making mistakes is considered a necessary part of "learning by doing." Managers are expected not only to share information with coworkers but also their knowledge and skills. IKEA wants its coworkers to feel important: They can express their ideas, and should feel responsible for improving the way things are done.

An entrepreneurial zeal for getting the job done in the most direct way and a distaste for bureaucratic procedures are basic managerial attitudes that have long been promoted within IKEA. Managers are expected to be close to their coworkers, with few if any status barriers, and not to take themselves seriously. This egalitarian approach to management has also made it easy for motivated employees to work their way up the organization with little formal

Exhibit 2

Distribution of IKEA's Coworkers

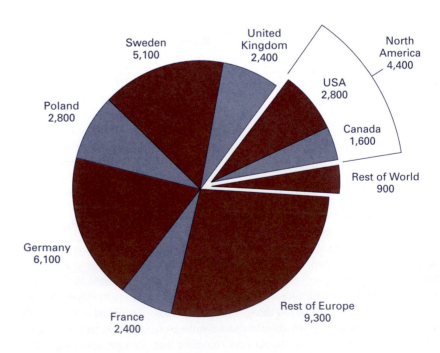

Sweden 5,100
United Kingdom 2,400
North America 4,400
USA 2,800
Poland 2,800
Canada 1,600
Germany 6,100
Rest of World 900
Rest of Europe 9,300
France 2,400

training. It is significant that Swedish managers' titles do not appear on their business cards, and that company cars are the same economy models for all of those who need them for work or business regardless of their position.

Rather than establish extensive training programs and detailed rules and procedures to propagate its unique culture, IKEA prefers a softer approach through discussion and explanation. The IKEA way has been spelled out through wide distribution of Kamprad's *Testament* which has been translated into a dozen languages. Kamprad himself explains that IKEA has "a strong and living culture" based on doing things differently. "It has grown step by step," and together with its business principles is the "cornerstone of our operations . . . which helps us retain the spirit and vitality of the early years . . . and create a feeling of belonging in a large international organization. Our corporate culture binds us together." To ensure that the IKEA Way is understood, the organization relies heavily on managers to act as "missionaries" carrying all that it embodies through their example and willingness to explain to new and senior employees why things are done the way they are. This, as much as anything else, provides the reason for the extensive presence of Swedish managers in IKEA's international units, as their knowledge stems from their direct exposure to Ingvar Kamprad and IKEA's subtle way of doing business and managing people. For those managers who do not have this exposure, week-long "IKEA Way" seminars are organized periodically in Almhult, the IKEA equivalent of Mecca and the heart of its culture.

IKEA's Strategy of International Expansion: Flexibility within Establishment Parameters

Patterns of International Expansion

IKEA's international expansion has taken place progressively over years with a focus on markets in countries with growth potential (see Exhibit 3). Expansion outside of Scandinavia was driven by Ingvar Kamprad's intuitive quest for new opportunities and his previous successful search for suppliers outside of Sweden more than any formal development strategy. Some insights are provided by one of IKEA's Swedish executives, an early companion of Ingvar Kamprad. "When we opened our first store outside Scandinavia, in Switzerland, people asked why there? It was a difficult market. Ingvar said that if we could succeed there, we should succeed anywhere. He had intuitions, he spoke to people on the streets to learn what they were looking for." Such an empirical experiential approach goes against the orthodox rules of international retailing, which preach extensive market studies before entering a new market, catering to local tastes, and gaining expertise through acquisitions and joint ventures.

When IKEA expanded into Germany, competition was strong and German distributors didn't take them seriously. "They called us 'those crazy Swedes,' but we didn't mind; we even used this label in our advertising. It took them five years to really react, but by then we had eight stores and were setting the standards."

Charting its own course, IKEA has developed internationally by finding cheap land for stores, checking sourcing possibilities and proximity to central warehouses, or lowering marketing costs. When, in the late 1970s, the company decided to go into Belgium because it was cost effective to serve that country from its central warehouse in Germany, it ran into problems with building permits and so decided to develop in France instead. The preference has been for leveraging market costs by concentrating several stores in the same area. This explains why IKEA opened four stores in the Philadelphia/Washington DC/New Jersey area, sometimes in locations that were rather isolated. Similarly, the company also preferred to concentrate four stores in the Paris area, even if this could dilute individual store sales and create potential competition between stores.

Typically development has been done on a store-by-store basis. IKEA opens a beachhead in a given country with a group of trusted and experienced Swedish "Missionaries." Together they form a tight-knit group which can

Exhibit 3 **The IKEA Expansion**

	No. of Outlets	No. of Countries	No. of Coworkers	Turnover (NLG)[d]
1954	1	1	15	2,200,000
1964	2	2	250	55,500,000
1974	10	5	1,500	372,900,000
1984	66	17	8,300	2,678,700,000
1994	120(125[a])	25 (26[a])	26,600[b]	8,350,000,000
1996	129(136[a])	27 (28[a])	33,400[b]	9,626,000,000[c]

Note: [a]Including stores opening after September 1, 1996.

[b]20% of coworkers are part time.

[c]Corresponding to net sales of the IKEA Group of companies.

[d]The holding company is in the Netherlands which explains the use of NLG.

solve problems and make decisions quickly. They supervise the building work, lead operational teams who open the store, and run the store until local management has learned how the system works. After a short time, store management is turned over to local managers, while most of the key national positions remain in the hands of Swedes until the operation and market have reached maturity.

Adapting to National Markets

Adapting to new markets in western Europe throughout the 1970s and early 1980s was fairly simple. Catalog offerings were virtually the same. However, concessions had to be made, particularly in bedroom furnishings since bedding could be substantially different from country to country.

"When we entered a new country we did things our way. The idea was to be IKEA everywhere: After all, our furniture is a cultural statement. But as the years went by we learned to be more flexible, particularly when demand in Sweden declined and we became more dependent on our non-Scandinavian markets," recalls one IKEA manager.

Adapting to the U.S. market was a real learning experience for IKEA, since many standards were different. Few product managers from IKEA of Sweden had traveled to North America because the price of air travel was prohibitive in terms of IKEA's cost-conscious policies. They expected their European range to sell just as easily in the United States, but this did not turn out to be the case. As a former U.S. country manager explains: "IKEA ran into problems in the United States so we had to ask ourselves

what we could offer to Americans. Should we become an American company, or merely adapt our merchandising to American customers? We finally decided on a solution: merchandising to the American customer by speaking English with a Swedish accent; capitalizing on our strengths as an outsider."

Development of the range is now closely monitored by IKEA of Sweden (IOS) and the board of directors of INGKA Holding. The issue of range is vital for them as, when they introduce new products, they must insure that the volumes they produce are balanced from within (sourcing—logistics—store layout). It took IKEA of Sweden several years to introduce "futons" in Europe, and American store managers had to work hard to convince the company that a "Home Entertainment" line was feasible in North America.

As a former French country manager described, obtaining concessions from product managers to take into account specific national preferences was a consensual process that required many negotiation skills. "Some room is allowed for national considerations in our catalog range. But, since changes mean that it will be more expensive for the country manager, only limited numbers are allowed. Still, 90 percent of our range is the same all over the world: only 5 to 10 percent is country specific. The product manager has the final word, but he usually listens to the country manager. There is a healthy tension between the two and this enables us to adapt but not to over-adapt and weaken our cost effectiveness."

Although IKEA's stated mission is to provide home furnishing for the "greatest number" and its business is

Exhibit 4

The Organization of the IKEA Group

Supervisory Board, Ingka Holding B.V.
Ingvar Kamprad, *Chairman*
Jan I. Carlsson
Jan Ekman
Per Lindblad
Steffan Persson
Hans-Göran Stennert

Group Management
Anders Moberg, *Group President*
Lars Bråberg
Göran Carstedt
Hans Gydell
Mikael Ohlsson

Stichtingy Ingka Foundation
The Netherlands

Ingka Holding B.V.
The Netherlands

IKEA International A/S

IKEA of Sweden AB and Trading Companies

Retail Companies   **Wholesale Companies**   **Other Companies**

conducted on a volume basis, outside of Scandinavia it is in reality a niche player, appealing to the educated population with mid- to upper-level incomes. This segment is looking for nontraditional lines of furniture, and finds the Swedish style of IKEA suited to its modern taste.

"In spite of our image as the 'common man's store,' the majority of our customers have a university degree," admits a French store manager. This may appear paradoxical considering IKEA's avowed mission statement, but the paradox has proven successful as it keeps IKEA, at the same time, close to its roots and still makes it highly distinctive in foreign marketplaces. It also plays neatly into its strengths of sourcing, volume, long runs, and cost-efficient distribution.

Human Resource Management

Management of international operations has largely followed the IKEA Way and its strong Swedish flavor. The belief of those in IKEA is that their way of managing people has universal appeal. "People like to participate in making decisions. They like to feel respected, and that they can take responsibility," one Swedish expatriate states.

When recruiting, IKEA looks for people who have good communication skills, open minds, positive work attitudes, and good potential without necessarily having diplomas. It attracts people with its pleasant working environment, job security, and the caring attitude it shows towards the individual. IKEA employees, regardless of nationality, are more than likely to have strong preferences for cooperative informal relations, with a high degree of independence, and have tolerant approach to others. "We look for people who know how to listen, and who are able to transmit their knowledge to others. They should not feel they are better than others and be curious about what is going on around them."

Being an IKEA manager overseas isn't solely about running the stores and distribution systems smoothly. He or she must be able to explain to employees and managers why things are done in the way they are and win people's hearts and minds to the "IKEA Way." They are expected to be ambassadors and must educate their non-Swedish coworkers through patience, common understanding, and example. It is not always easy to transmit IKEA's egalitarian management style. While it goes down easily in the Netherlands, it is less acceptable in Germany or France, and for different reasons. In the United States, long-term employees generally feel more comfortable with Scandinavian managers than with Americans—younger American managers don't seem to know how to show "equalness."

The challenge IKEA may be facing is that, with its extended international network, it is becoming more difficult to find enough Swedish IKEA managers who are willing to work overseas for long periods. IKEA has had to hire Swedes from outside the company. Also in the past the company has not systematically searched out and developed at an early stage its international "high potentials," although it does send its most loyal and successful foreign managers to week-long seminars in Sweden and encourage its coworkers to learn something about the culture.

It is still very difficult for non-Scandinavians to work their way up the corporate ladder. To do so they need to have learned all of IKEA's key trades: retailing, logistics, product design, and purchasing. Non-Swedes can work their way up in retailing through the national organizations and sometimes in the logistical organizations which are run regionally, but very few have gone into product management because this function is part of IKEA of Sweden in Almhult, where IKEA's product managers and furniture schools are located. It is a very remote area and only Swedish is spoken. So, speaking the language as well and knowing the culture become prerequisites that very few managers from foreign branches have been able to fulfill.

There are no formal career paths, as a long-term Swedish expatriate executive admits. "To get ahead in IKEA you first have to know the range intimately, then you have to know and use the informal internal network, and then you have to understand the subtleties of the 'IKEA Way,' its cultural roots. It is really difficult for outsiders to know their way around. In reality it is a difficult company to understand. Humbleness is not a sign of weakness. It comes from Ingvar. People are expected to learn from their experience, and this takes time and patience. You can't be in a hurry to move up the ladder."

Dealing with the Europeans

Germany   Germany is the largest national organization in the IKEA group, accounting for ±30 percent of the total group sales through more than 20 stores, including the newly opened stores in former East Germany.

Although IKEA has been established in Germany for more than two decades (its first store was opened in Munich in 1974), Swedish management is still perceived by German IKEA members as peculiar. As described by Thomas Larson, the store manager in Cologne: "Some senior coworkers still have problems addressing me by my first name, or using the German *du* (the informal equivalent for you, like *tu* in French). "*Dutzen*," using the informal you, is often felt as undermining the respect and prestige of the boss. As Heike Oestreich, the personnel manager said: "There are two different *du's*, the IKEA *du* and the *du* which is used between friends."

The Germans are very disciplined and precise. They do exactly what the boss asks them to do and what is agreed or put down in writing. A problem is that the Swedish notion of "taking on responsibilities for yourself," the cornerstone of their work policy, is not perceived in the same way by the Germans, who have a tendency to adhere very closely to precisely defined rules and instructions. When IKEA translated the corporate brochure *The IKEA Way* into German, a need was felt to sharpen and make more explicit the original Swedish text which presented key IKEA concepts in sometimes vague terms in order to give freedom to people to adapt them and take personal responsibility for carrying them out. Once, Anders Moberg, Kamprad's successor, suggested in a letter that certain merchandising displays could be used in a variety of places. In Germany, department managers interpreted this as an order, and systematically set up the displays in every part of their stores.

In general, German employees feel that the Swedes are more result-oriented and treat every problem as a challenge that should be met. However, they believe that Swedish management does not sufficiently assess risks before taking action. According to Heike Oestreich: "The Swedes, to reduce bureaucracy, would like to dump all our office desks in the back yard." The lack of formality is also dismaying to Germans. To implement a decision "some notes on the back of a cigarette packet are often sufficient" for the Swedes. In contrast, Germans are more comfortable adhering to formal procedures: "We need procedures and forms. Germans love administration because it provides us with security."

France   Development in France, which has fewer than half the number of stores in Germany, was always considered problematic because of the numerous administrative regulations on the retail trade, and a hostile attitude towards discounters that prevailed in the late 1970s and early 1980s. By carefully avoiding too much public attention and with only a limited number of store openings IKEA managed to secure a safe place for itself in the market and develop an 8 percent share.

The main challenge for IKEA management in France is the French tendency to judge informality as a sign of weakness, or indecisiveness. French people are accustomed to formal rules and strong hierarchy. In the words of a former Swedish country manager, when IKEA first started in France: "Some French managers felt that the Swedish informality meant they could do whatever they wanted. When we told them that they should inform their subordinates they did not take us seriously." Some aspects of the informality can even be irritating to the French, such as the lack of formal job descriptions and written procedures. Whereas Swedish managers will justify this by saying that they don't like to limit responsibility, and that they get more out of people with an informal approach, the French tend to be suspicious of informality for the same reasons.

In the view of IKEA's French human resource manager: "Working here isn't for everyone. It is particularly difficult for people over 35 because IKEA is different from all other workplaces in France. When you join IKEA, you enter another world—we do not behave like a normal French company. Status is not recognized, which can cause an identity problem: Everyone is put on the same level—no one stands out, and you can get lost in the crowd. It is hard

to explain what IKEA is, everyone will give a different answer. One shouldn't freeze the system, it is flexible, and it should stay that way."

Two of the main reasons given for IKEA's appeal to French candidates are:

1. The esthetics of the stores—they look nice and are pleasant to work in.
2. The intelligent way in which IKEA works—it makes sense.

To make things clearer to employees, a formal communication platform has been developed in France to spell things out in facts and figures by comparing IKEA's benefits with those of competitors. Also, more formal training programs are being developed because in France "learning by doing" is not perceived as a credible way of developing competency. Typically, a boss would not be trusted to develop one's skills in France, and more faith is placed in "off-site programs." In France tolerance has its limits and when IKEA hired "too many" people of non-French origin, the company received complaints from customers, so now it makes a point of keeping non-French workers to a minimum.

Some years ago, relations with unions were hostile. There was a bitter strike and widespread discontent. French labor unions did not trust or understand IKEA's Swedish management style, with its tendency to seek consensus. More recently, IKEA's management has taken a more affirmative attitude, and relations have improved notably. They may continue to improve now that IKEA France is run by a Frenchman, Jean Louis Baillot, whose wife is Swedish and who has worked in Almhult.

Doing Things Differently in the United States

Expanding into the U.S. market was certainly the boldest developmental decision that IKEA had made up to that time. From an historical perspective the venture seemed unlikely to succeed. First, the culturally specific requirements for home furnishing in the United States are considerably different than the European markets, particularly in terms of the size and functions of furniture. Second, the American market had come to be known as the "graveyard" of European retailers with a long list of unfortunate ventures by such successful firms as Casino, Carrefour, and Marks & Spencer. But somehow, IKEA seemed confident that going about it in their own way would prove an exception to the laws of failure that seemed to doom European entrants to the U.S. market.

Initially, development in the United States was quite consistent with IKEA's pattern in Europe: Identify prime markets with volume potential; purchase cheap land on the periphery of big cities; use mass advertising with a unique message emphasizing IKEA's Swedishness; focus on range and price through the catalog, establishing a beachhead from which to launch and develop the organization. Also, its approach was empirical and pragmatic. It did not set out to take the United States by storm, but merely to test its existing formula and learn through experience how success could be achieved. In fact, from the mid-1970s to the early 1980s IKEA opened a series of franchised stores in Canada, developing during this time its logistics capabilities and demonstrating that its European range could sell in America's backyard, before it finally entered the U.S. market in 1985.

Its first stage of development in the United States began on the East Coast with the opening of Plymouth Meeting in Philadelphia's northwest suburbs, followed by a cluster of four other stores. "Development was initially based on the potato field approach. Find some place where there is cheap land, build, and the people will follow." This approach ignored the rule of American retailing based on fine-tuned segmentation and targeting. The choice of locations, driven by cost-consciousness, led IKEA to establish its stores in shopping centers that had no prestige "anchor stores" to draw the high-income customers that IKEA appeals to. This should have been a relative disadvantage, since competitors like Home Depot locate their stores in prime centers with "anchor stores" like Nordstroms and Macy's. But by maintaining the profile of a "different kind of store," very Swedish, with a wide range of products, it apparently has overcome this obstacle. Here, the catalog has served them well, as people can plan their purchases before they come and thus optimize their time investment.

Up until the late 1980s IKEA enjoyed a honeymoon of sorts. The American public was attracted by the novelty of Scandinavian style and IKEA's unique merchandising, which resembles in many ways a European village marketplace. Its advertising was a success. People drove six to eight hours to come to the stores and they initially came in large numbers. Riding on a high dollar, IKEA had appeared to have gotten off to as fast a start as they had in Germany and other European markets. The honeymoon ended suddenly when the dollar went down, revealing multiple weaknesses.

First and foremost, even though Americans were initially attracted by IKEA's advertising and novelty, the company's range of furniture was unsuited to American standards and sold poorly. One often told anecdote illustrates just how far from those standards they really were: Customers would purchase flower vases thinking they were American-size drinking glasses. Americans furnish their master bedrooms with king size beds, whereas IKEA's largest beds were five inches narrower. Also, Americans are harder on sitting room furniture, and IKEA's sofa and armchair offerings proved too lightly designed Additionally, IKEA did not offer furniture suitable for the "home entertainment centers" that blossomed throughout the 1980s and into the 1990s in American households with the proliferation of widescreen televisions, VCRs, and hi-fi equipment. With declining sales revenues and shrinking profits, by 1989 the "graveyard effect" seemed to have caught up with IKEA.

A courageous decision was then made by Anders Moberg and a new management team was brought in to head the organization. Faced with the alternatives of holding on and waiting for better times, withdrawing humbly, or fighting back, the latter course of action was chosen. In 1990, the American retail management group, under the leadership of Göran Carstedt, recently hired from Volvo, convinced the product managers at IKEA of Sweden that the IKEA European range had to be adapted and American-based sourcing stepped up. At the same time, he reassured them that IKEA would not prostitute itself. In the words of Carstedt: "The IKEA strategy in North America will still be blue and yellow, but we will put more stars and stripes and more maple leaves in it."

It was not easy but they succeeded in changing the design of many household products. To make the point, one U.S. manager brought a plastic American-size turkey with him to Almhult and before a surprised group of product managers placed it on one of the best-selling dining tables in the European range. Given the size of the bird there was only room for two table settings instead of the normal six. He had made his point.

However there was a condition attached to adapting the range, and that condition was volume. Lines of furniture specifically designed for the American market would have to be produced in long enough runs to meet IKEA's commitment to suppliers and be priced at the lowest levels possible.

A combination of luck and bold counterattacking led to an unexpected expansion on the West Coast that was to ease pressure on its pricing and provide much needed growth in its retail business. An imitator, "Stor," inspired by IKEA's success, had illicitly acquired intimate knowledge of IKEA's floor plan and merchandising schemes and successfully opened four stores primarily around Los Angeles, far from IKEA's base on the East Coast. Responding as much to the threat to the company's image as to the opportunity to capitalize on Stor's advertising of Swedish style furniture, IKEA decided to counterattack. It opened a store in Los Angeles and eventually, through its price and sourcing advantage, drove Stor to the brink of bankruptcy. It then bought out its imitator at a bargain price and established a solid base in a prime market on the West Coast. If IKEA's low-profile stance stressed its humble origins and culture, it definitely did not mean that the company was a weakling. IKEA showed that it could be tough and decisive in that toughest of tough markets. The current U.S. country manager, Jan Kjellman, in comparing the U.S. market to his previous European experience used the following words: "The biggest difference is competition. Competitors are everywhere, and they are strong. The market is crowded, but still there always seem to be new competitors. Even with a million and a half customers, we are small. It is a total struggle for us, and it is tough to survive." Could IKEA adapt to such competition and still remain faithful to the "IKEA Way"?

Swedish managers are impressed with the professionalism of American salesmanship. "Over here, retailing is a profession. Salespersons are subjected to a lot of pressure for short-term results because large retailers are publicly owned and shareholders measure quarterly results. So they are very time-efficient and masters of the hard sell," relates Kjellman. IKEA has always maintained a soft approach believing that people know what they want, so that sales personnel are there to help them find it. Moreover, the strategy is that most of the selling is done by the catalog so that people arrive with specific purchases in mind. Impulse buying takes place for smaller items like candle holders, or accessories which are sought for as bargains. On this point IKEA has stood firm, and sales personnel from competitors such as Macy's or Bloomingdale's have to unlearn the hard sell approach.

Americans are always looking for convenience, which means more space, more information, anything that reduces effort and saves time. To respond to these demands, IKEA had to redesign its store layouts, providing more directions, and short cuts for people who don't want to just wander through the store. "Customers were screaming 'let us out' before we remodeled our layout," reported one store manager. "They couldn't find their way out of our maze of displays, there were no windows or signs, they felt lost and panicky." While making these adjustments in store layout, which have been criticized by IKEA International headquarters, IKEA has maintained its policy of minimal service. Customers who want home delivery or someone to assemble their furniture must pay the full add-on cost. In fact, IKEA stores carefully outsource these services to local providers and they never promote such services in their advertising. Instead, they encourage their customers to do it the "IKEA Way," which means renting a roof rack and assembling it yourself.

Adapting IKEA's floor plans and furniture to American dimensions paid off, and sales increased by 25 to 30 percent in comparison with the late 1980s. By 1994 IKEA had turned around the situation in the United States. Through its acquisition of Stor and by adapting its range to U.S. requirements, sales have increased steadily by about 10 percent annually, providing IKEA with the volume base necessary to sustain long production run and to keep prices low. Whereas at first only 15 percent of the furniture in American stores was produced locally, the figure is now about 50 percent.

In the view of several IKEA senior U.S. managers, the key to this successful turnaround was the granting of more autonomy to the American country management than their European counterparts had enjoyed. "You can't steer America from Europe," admitted Anders Moberg in 1994. "When we went in we hadn't planned a clear strategy of how to supply the American market at a low cost." Learning how to succeed in the United States through its own painful expense took more than five years. Although its

U.S. operation showed a profit over the subsequent three years it still has not recovered its initial investment. With flat growth in Europe, and heavy investment in longer term expansion into eastern Europe and China putting pressure on IKEA's capital reserves, the focus in the United States is now on developing sales and profit from its existing stores before expanding into new regions. Following its bold actions in the early 1990s, IKEA has entered a more conservative phase of consolidation. Perhaps it has also learned that the price of being different means that you also have to be more careful about where you invest.

Unresolved Issues: Management and Human Resource Development

From an American perspective, Swedish managers don't show emotion in the workplace. "Praise is given for looking calm in all situations. They do not feel comfortable in conflictual situations. Also, they tend not to set themselves apart, and self-promotion is frowned upon. They don't like drum beating or cheerleading in a culture where both are common ways of motivating workers."

"The biggest conflicts here stem from the Americans who need to know who's in charge. People expect their managers to tell them what to do here." However, at IKEA the manager's role is more subtle and they tend to have a long-term approach to management. "It takes longer to do things our way but we want to train people to know how to do things the right way." Since there are few written procedures, the golden rule for managers is to help people understand why things are done in a particular way. This can be viewed as indecision by American employees new to IKEA who are more used to rules and procedures spelled out clearly and managers who take responsibility for quick decision making.

American employees perceive IKEA as being more employee-oriented than average American employers. IKEA attracts and selects people who value security, job enrichment, and benefits which are more generous than typical American employers (like five weeks of paid holiday) more than career advancement. However, with full employment in the United States it is becoming more difficult to find candidates, particularly for management positions, who have the necessary job qualifications and whose values match IKEA's.

Although IKEA has recently initiated an American style performance review procedure, which requires documenting employees' individual performance strengths and weaknesses, Swedish managers feel uncomfortable with the formality of the system and the need to provide negative feedback. Since they hold the more senior positions, their ambivalence has resulted in little real discrimination in pay increases which are directly linked to the reviews. Although turnover at IKEA is lower than the industry average, and coworkers generally appreciate IKEA's caring environment, there is some latent discontent with the way pay increases are distributed, even among long-term employees who feel that their individual achievements are not always rewarded.

In the opinion of one American manager, "A lot of people have left IKEA because they can't move up fast enough here. Some left the store to go to the Service Center (IKEA's national headquarters) then left because it was too hard for them to adjust, there was no clear frame of reference in terms of policies and procedures. We have lost some key American managers because they didn't have a clear idea of their role or future in the organization."

Acknowledging that there are not enough American managers in senior positions, IKEA is trying to attract management trainees through presentations at business schools. However, its low-key image and lack of structured career paths are not easy to sell to "high potentials" more attuned to the packages offered by retailers such as Home Depot which forcefully push rapid promotion and individualize pay incentives. There is a general consensus that IKEA needs to develop young American managers who can play a bigger role in the organization than at present. However, there is no agreement yet on how critical the need is, nor on how to solve the problem.

Two differing views that could be overheard in a fictitious debate between two long-term Ikeans illustrate the unresolved issues facing IKEA USA at the end of 1996.

The View of a Young American Manager   "There is a glass ceiling here. I am at a level at which my growth will stop because I'm not Swedish. IKEA should be made less complicated for Americans, easier for us to adapt to, and develop in. Our management needs to be much more professional in managing human resources. We need to bring new people into the organization, and reward individual accountability for results. This requires a better balance between the IKEA Way and American management. Becoming a successful manager at IKEA requires a lot of time and effort to understand how everything fits together. Yet not everyone can go to Sweden or learn Swedish, and today too many talented Americans choose to go to competitors. Competition is catching up on us in terms of benefits, and with full employment we should be much more competitive than we are on the American job market."

The Swedish View   "Being the underdog, not doing things the traditional way over here is vital to IKEA's success in the United States. We must keep a unique image and work better at getting our message across to employees and customers so that they understand why we are successful. Pride in being a part of IKEA must be built locally and since our system is unique, this takes time. The real danger is assimilation. We are becoming too American. Giving people bonuses and pay incentives doesn't make them more intelligent; people are motivated by learning and improving in an organization that provides them with room to grow. Rewards should be more on a give and take

basis—when the company makes more, it can give more—but we must remain flexible. Although we must seek a balance between adapting and sticking to our proven ways, we must protect our unique concepts and way of doing things. This means that we will always need a strong Swedish presence in the United States. They are our 'on-site missionaries' who can develop loyalty to an understanding of our uniqueness."

Clouds on the Horizon

By the mid-1990s, in spite of its undisputed international success and expansion over the past 25 years, signs appeared that the pattern of growth and steady profit was slowing down. Costs were rising, complaints on quality were more frequent, and unaccustomed delays appeared in product delivery. External factors had changed from the early times in Europe. Economic growth slowed as baby boomers moved into middle age, with new tastes and demands, and fewer new homes were being sold. Competitors had also learned from IKEA's pioneering distribution and were offering better furniture at lower prices, seeking low-cost furniture suppliers in eastern Europe, which put pressure on IKEA's unique sourcing.

IKEA had become a large international organization and, in an effort to adapt to the requirements of its many domestic markets, its product range had grown from 10,000 to 14,000 items, thus weakening returns from long production runs and overburdening logistic supply lines. Increasingly greater attention had to be given to bringing costs down, often through productivity gains which put unprecedented pressure on retail staffs to improve sales to staff ratios. During the years of rapid growth, many recruits were brought in from outside the company, and were therefore not steeped in IKEA culture. Its extended network made it difficult to provide employees and mid-level managers with a clear perception of how their local business impacted on the corporation as a whole. Local initiatives were taken without regard to their impact on the whole system. Was this the price of diversity or was IKEA suffering in many ways from too much decentralization?

In 1993, to cope with this situation, Andreas Mober and IKEA's senior management launched a company-wide operation *Nytt Läge* (New Situation), with the formation of task forces and project teams to suggest ways of improving communication and eliminating snags in distribution. Many suggestions were implemented, including the creation of new regional divisions in Europe for closer coordination of country operations and the hiring of more professionals at headquarters to provide guidelines and more efficient corporate control systems. Although the *Nytt Läge* program met with a lot of enthusiasm and did achieve improvements in some areas it soon became clear to Ingvar Kamprad that a more radical change in the organization was needed.

In early 1996, a major organizational change was introduced to "shorten the value chain" between customers and suppliers. Regional organizations were eliminated to bring stores in more direct contact with IKEA of Sweden. New emphasis was given to the importance of a living corporate culture based on the IKEA values of simplicity and self-discipline, rather than relying on formal policies and procedures. At the same time, IKEA's expansion plans in Europe and the United States were delayed. The fear at corporate headquarters was that IKEA had drifted too far away from the basic principles that were behind its legendary success.

Back to the Roots

In May, Ingvar Kamprad gathered IKEA's 250 worldwide store managers and senior managers at an important meeting in Poland to plan IKEA's need to refocus and redirect its efforts. He actually used the word *rejuvenate*.

> Our product range and purchasing people often have an unequal battle with retailers and their far too many interests. Many of our suppliers got stuck in the middle. Our IKEA idea as one of the world's few production-oriented companies is under threat.
>
> Perhaps we were blinded by the booming years of the 1980s which increased the geographical spread of our operations to new markets, both on the retail and trading sides. Internal communication also became difficult, our administration expanded and our overheads became increasingly heavy. Our costs rose, and our customers and suppliers felt lost many of them got in touch with me directly.
>
> Decision making took longer and longer, and endless discussions took place. It became more difficult to see the company as a whole. Far too much of our product development had too little to do with the tastes and wallets of the majority of people. Our product range expanded in every direction and could not be handled in a reasonable way on our sales floors. Our price advantage compared to competitors began to shrink. Even IKEA's soul, our fine corporate culture, was in danger. Have we forgotten to explain to our new workers about the IKEA Way? Have our desks prevented us from being involved enough in the commercial activity? Have we lost our way?

The managers who attended that meeting felt galvanized by the founder's strong message, and their confidence and belief in the IKEA Way had been doubtlessly reinforced. In an increasingly complex world environment, simplicity indeed appeared to be a true virtue that had guided the company in the past. Several wondered, as they left, how Kamprad's intuitive ability to see through the complexity of a worldwide organization and reignite the dynamics of IKEA's success could be transmitted throughout the organization? Others wondered if they would have as much autonomy as they had previously enjoyed in adapting to very different markets. Some wondered if the company could regain its developmental thrust through the late 1990s?

1. What type of organizational culture is most representative of IKEA: family, Eiffel Tower, guided missile, or incubator? Explain.

2. In what way has international culture proved to be a challenge for IKEA?

3. What are three things that IKEA had to learn in order to do business effectively in the United States?

4. How well has the company been able to deal with the diversity issue? What else does it still need to do?

Integrative Case 2

Euro Disneyland

On January 18, 1993, Euro Disneyland chairperson Robert Fitzpatrick announced he would leave that post on April 12 to begin his own consulting company. Quitting his position exactly one year after the grand opening of Euro Disneyland, Fitzpatrick's resignation removed U.S. management from the helm of the French theme park and resort.

Fitzpatrick's position was taken by a Frenchman, Philippe Bourguignon, who had been Euro Disneyland's senior vice president for real estate. Bourguignon, 45 years old, faced a net loss of FFr 188 million for Euro Disneyland's fiscal year, which ended September 1992. Also, between April and September 1992, only 29 percent of the park's total visitors were French. Expectations were that closer to half of all visitors would be French.

It was hoped that the promotion of Philippe Bourguignon would have a public relations benefit for Euro Disneyland—a project that has been a publicist's nightmare from the beginning. One of the low points was at a news conference prior to the park's opening when protesters pelted Michael Eisner, CEO of the Walt Disney Company, with rotten eggs. Within the first year of operation, Disney had to compromise its "squeaky clean" image and lift the alcohol ban at the park. Wine is now served at all major restaurants.

Euro Disneyland, 49 percent owned by Walt Disney Company, Burbank, California, originally forecasted 11 million visitors in the first year of operation. In January 1993 it appeared attendance would be closer to 10 million. In response, management temporarily slashed prices at the park for local residents to FFr 150 ($27.27) from FFr 225 ($40.91) for adults, and to FFr 100 from FFr 150 for children in order to lure more French during the slow, wet winter months. The company also reduced prices at its restaurants and hotels, which registered occupancy rates of just 37 percent.

Bourguignon also faced other problems, such as the second phase of development at Euro Disneyland, which was expected to start in September 1993. It was unclear how the company planned to finance its FFr 8–10 billion cost. The company had steadily drained its cash reserves (FFr 1.9 billion in May 1993) while piling up debt (FFr 21 billion in May 1993). Euro Disneyland admitted that it and the Walt Disney Company were "exploring potential sources of financing for Euro Disneyland." The company was also talking to banks about restructuring its debts.

Despite the frustrations, Eisner was tirelessly upbeat about the project. "Instant hits are things that go away quickly, and things that grow slowly and are part of the culture are what we look for" he said. "What we created in France is the biggest private investment in a foreign country by an American company ever. And it's gonna pay off."

In the Beginning

Disney's story is the classic American rags-to-riches story which started in a small Kansas City advertising office, where Mickey was a real mouse prowling the unknown Walt Disney floor. Originally, Mickey was named Mortimer, until a dissenting Mrs. Disney stepped in. How close Mickey was to Walt Disney is evidenced by the fact that when filming, Disney himself dubbed the mouse's voice. Only in later films did Mickey get a different voice. Disney made many sacrifices to promote his hero-mascot, including selling his first car, a beloved Moon Cabriolet, and humiliating himself in front of Louis B. Mayer. "Get that mouse off the screen!" was the movie mogul's reported response to the cartoon character. Then, in 1955, Disney had the brainstorm of sending his movie characters out into the "real" world to mix with their fans and he battled skeptics to build the very first Disneyland in Anaheim, California.

When Disney died in 1966, the company went into virtual suspended animation. Their last big hit of that era was 1969's *The Love Bug*, about a Volkswagen named Herbie. Today, Disney executives trace the problem to a tyrannical CEO named E. Cardon Walker who ruled the company from 1976 to 1983, and to his successor, Ronald W. Miller. Walker was quick to ridicule underlings in public and impervious to any point of view but his own. He made decisions according to what he thought Walt would have done. Executives clinched arguments by quoting Walt like the Scriptures or Marx, and the company eventually supplied a little book of the founder's sayings. Making the wholesome family movies Walt would have wanted formed a key article of Walker's creed. For example, a poster advertising the unremarkable *Condorman* featured actress Barbara Carrera in a slit skirt. Walker had the slit painted over. With this as the context, studio producers ground out a thin stream of tired, formulaic movies that fewer and fewer customers would pay to see. In mid-1983, a similar low-horsepower approach to television production led to CBS's cancellation of the hour-long program *Walt Disney*, leaving the company without a regular network show for the first time in 29 years. Like a reclusive hermit, the company lost touch with the contemporary world.

Ron Miller's brief reign was by contrast a model of decentralization and delegation. Many attributed Miller's ascent to his marrying the boss's daughter rather than to any special gift. To shore Miller up, the board installed Raymond L. Watson, former head of the Irvine Co., as part-time chairperson. He quickly became full time.

Miller sensed the studio needed rejuvenation and he managed to produce the hit film, *Splash,* featuring an apparently (but not actually) bare-breasted mermaid, under the newly devised Touchstone label. However, the reluctance of freelance Hollywood talent to accommodate Disney's narrow range and stingy compensation often kept his sound instincts from bearing fruit. "Card [Cardon Walker] would listen but not hear," said a former executive. "Ron [Ron Miller] would listen but not act."

Too many box office bombs contributed to a steady erosion of profit. Profits of $135 million on revenues of $915 million in 1980 dwindled to $93 million on revenues of $1.3 billion in 1983. More alarmingly, revenues from the company's theme parks, about three-quarters of the company's total revenues, were showing signs of leveling off. Disney's stock slid from $84.375 a share to $48.75 between April 1983 and February 1984.

Through these years, Roy Disney, Jr. simmered while he watched the downfall of the national institution that his uncle, Walt, and his father, Roy Disney, Sr., had built. He had long argued that the company's constituent parts all work together to enhance each other. If movie and television production weren't revitalized, not only would that source of revenue disappear but the company and its activities would also grow dim in the public eye. At the same time the stream of new ideas and characters that kept people pouring into the parks and buying toys, books, and records would dry up. Now his dire predictions were coming true. His own personal shareholding had already dropped from $96 million to $54 million. Walker's treatment of Ron Miller as the shining heir apparent and Roy Disney as the idiot nephew helped drive Roy to quit as Disney vice president in 1977, and to set up Shamrock Holdings, a broadcasting and investment company.

In 1984, Roy teamed up with Stanley Gold, a tough-talking lawyer and a brilliant strategist. Gold saw that the falling stock price was bound to flush out a raider and afford Roy Disney a chance to restore the company's fortunes. They asked Frank Wells, vice chairperson of Warner Bros., if he would take a top job in the company in the event they offered it. Wells, a lawyer and a Rhodes scholar, said yes. With that, Roy knew that what he would hear in Disney's boardroom would limit his freedom to trade in its stock, so he quit the board on March 9, 1984. "I knew that would hang a 'For Sale' sign over the company," said Gold.

By resigning, Roy pushed over the first of a train of dominoes that ultimately led to the result he most desired. The company was raided, almost dismantled, greenmailed, raided again, and sued left and right. But it miraculously emerged with a skilled new top management with big plans for a bright future. Roy Disney proposed Michael Eisner as the CEO but the board came close to rejecting Eisner in favor of an older, more buttoned-down candidate. Gold stepped in and made an impassioned speech to the directors. "You see guys like Eisner as a little crazy . . . but every studio in this country has been run by crazies. What do you think Walt Disney was? The guy was off the goddamned wall. This is a creative institution. It needs to be run by crazies again."*

Meanwhile Eisner and Wells staged an all-out lobbying campaign, calling on every board member except two, who were abroad, to explain their views about the company's future. "What was most important," said Eisner, "was that they saw I did not come in a tutu, and that I was a serious person, and I understood a P&L, and 1 knew the investment analysts, and I read *Fortune.*"

In September 1984, Michael Eisner was appointed CEO and Frank Wells became president. Jeffrey Katzenberg, the 33-year-old, maniacal production chief followed Fisher from Paramount Pictures. He took over Disney's movie and television studios. "The key," said Eisner "is to start off with a great idea."

Disneyland in Anaheim, California

For a long time, Walt Disney had been concerned about the lack of family-type entertainment available for his two daughters. The amusement parks he saw around him were mostly filthy traveling carnivals. They were often unsafe and allowed unruly conduct on the premises. Disney envisioned a place where people from all over the world would be able to go for clean and safe fun. His dream came true on July 17, 1955, when the gates first opened at Disneyland in Anaheim, California.

Disneyland strives to generate the perfect fantasy. But magic does not simply happen. The place is a marvel of modern technology. Literally dozens of computers, huge banks of tape machines, film projectors, and electronic controls lie behind the walls, beneath the floors, and above the ceilings of dozens of rides and attractions. The philosophy is that "Disneyland is the world's biggest stage, and the audience is right here on the stage," said Dick

Exhibit 1   How the Theme Parks Grew

1955	Disneyland
1966	Walt Disney's death
1971	Walt Disney World in Orlando
1982	Epcot Center
1983	Tokyo Disneyland
1992	Euro Disneyland

---

* Stephen Koepp, "Do You Believe in Magic?" *Time* (April 25, 1988): pp. 66–73.

Hollinger, chief industrial engineer at Disneyland. "It takes a tremendous amount of work to keep the stage clean and working properly."

Cleanliness is a primary concern. Before the park opens at 8 A.M., the cleaning crew will have mopped and hosed and dried every sidewalk, every street, and every floor and counter. More than 350 of the park's 7,400 employees come on duty at 1 A.M. to begin the daily cleanup routine. The thousands of feet that walk through the park each day and chewing gum do not mix, and gum has always presented major clean up problems. The park's janitors found long ago that fire hoses with 90 pounds of water pressure would not do the job. Now they use steam machines, razor scrapers, and mops towed by Cushman scooters to literally scour the streets and sidewalks daily.

It takes one person working a full eight-hour shift to polish the brass on the Fantasyland merry-go-round. The scrupulously manicured plantings throughout the park are treated with growth retarding hormones to keep the trees and bushes from spreading beyond their assigned spaces and destroying the carefully maintained five-eighths scale modeling that is utilized in the park. The maintenance supervisor of the Matterhorn bobsled ride personally walks every foot of track and inspects every link of tow chain every night, thus trusting his or her own eyes more than the $2 million in safety equipment that is built into the ride.

Eisner himself pays obsessive attention to detail. Walking through Disneyland one Sunday afternoon, he peered at the plastic leaves on the Swiss Family Robinson tree house noting that they periodically wear out and need to be replaced leaf by leaf at a cost of $500,000. As his family strolled through the park, he and his eldest son Breck stooped to pick up the rare piece of litter that the cleanup crew had somehow missed. This old-fashioned dedication has paid off. Since opening day in 1955. Disneyland has been a consistent money-maker.

Disney World in Orlando, Florida

By the time Eisner arrived, Disney World in Orlando was already on its way to becoming what it is today—the most popular vacation destination in the United States. But the company had neglected a rich niche in its business: hotels. Disney's three existing hotels, probably the most profitable in the United States, registered unheard-of occupancy rates of 92 percent to 96 percent versus 66 percent for the industry. Eisner promptly embarked on an ambitious $1 billion hotel expansion plan. Two major hotels, Disney's Grand Floridian Beach Resort and Disney's Caribbean Beach Resort, were opened during 1987–89. Disney's Yacht Club and Beach Resort along with the Dolphin and Swan Hotels, owned and operated by Tishman Realty & Construction, Metropolitan Life Insurance, and Aoki Corporation opened during 1989–90. Adding 3,400 hotel rooms and 250,000 square feet of convention space, this made it the largest convention center east of the Mississippi.

In October 1982, Disney made a new addition to the theme park—the Experimental Prototype Community of Tomorrow or EPCOT Center. E. Cardon Walker, then president of the company, announced that EPCOT would be a "permanent showcase, industrial park, and experimental housing center." This new park consists of two large complexes: Future World, a series of pavilions designed to show the technological advances of the next 25 years, and World Showcase, a collection of foreign "villages."

Tokyo Disneyland

It was Tokyo's nastiest winter day in four years. Arctic winds and eight inches of snow lashed the city. Roads were clogged and trains slowed down. But the bad weather didn't keep 13,200 hardy souls from Tokyo Disneyland. Mikki Mausu, better known outside Japan as Mickey Mouse, had taken the country by storm.

Located on a fringe of reclaimed shoreline in Urayasu City on the outskirts of Tokyo, the park opened to the public on April 15, 1983. In less than one year, over 10 million people had passed through its gates, an attendance figure that has been bettered every single year. On August 13, 1983, 93,000 people helped set a one-day attendance record that easily eclipsed the old records established at the two parent U.S. parks. Four years later, records again toppled as the turnstiles clicked. The total this time: 111,500. By 1988, approximately 50 million people, or nearly half of Japan's population, had visited Tokyo Disneyland since its opening. The steady cash flow pushed revenues for fiscal year 1989 to $768 million, up 17 percent from 1988.

The 204-acre Tokyo Disneyland is owned and operated by Oriental Land under license from the Walt Disney Co. The 45-year contract gives Disney 10 percent of admissions and 5 percent of food and merchandise sales, plus licensing fees. Disney opted to take no equity in the project and put no money down for construction.

Exhibit 2 Investor's Snapshot: The Walt Disney Company (December 1989)

Sales	
(latest four quarters)	$4.6 billion
Change from year earlier	Up 33.6%
Net profit	$703.3 million
Change	Up 34.7%
Return on common stockholders' equity	23.4%
Five year average	20.3%
Stock price average	
(last 12 months)	$60.50–$136.25
Recent share price	$122.75
Price/Earnings Multiple	27
Total return to investors	
(12 months to 11/3/89)	90.6%

Source: Fortune, December 4, 1989

"I never had the slightest doubt about the success of Disneyland in Japan," said Masatomo Takahashi, president of Oriental Land Company. Oriental Land was so confident of the success of Disney in Japan that it financed the park entirely with debt, borrowing ¥180 billion ($1.5 billion at February 1988 exchange rates). Takahashi added, "The debt means nothing to me," and with good reason. According to Fusahao Awata, who co-authored a book on Tokyo Disneyland: "The Japanese yearn for [American culture]."

Soon after Tokyo Disneyland opened in April 1983, five Shinto priests held a solemn dedication ceremony near Cinderella's castle. It is the only overtly Japanese ritual seen so far in this sprawling theme park. What visitors see is pure Americana. All signs are in English, with only small *katakana* (a phonetic Japanese alphabet) translations. Most of the food is American-style, and the attractions are cloned from Disney's U.S. parks. Disney also held firm on two fundamentals that strike the Japanese as strange-no alcohol is allowed and no food may be brought in from outside the park.

However, in Disney's enthusiasm to make Tokyo a brick-by-brick copy of Anaheim's Magic Kingdom, there were a few glitches. On opening day, the Tokyo park discovered that almost 100 public telephones were placed too high for Japanese guests to reach them comfortably. And many hungry customers found countertops above their reach at the park's snack stands.

"Everything we imported that worked in the United States works here," said Ronald D. Pogue, managing director of Walt Disney Attractions Japan Ltd. "American things like McDonald's hamburgers and Kentucky Fried Chicken are popular here with young people. We also wanted visitors from Japan and Southeast Asia to feel they were getting the real thing," said Toshiharu Akiba, a staff member of the Oriental Land publicity department.

Still, local sensibilities dictated a few changes. A Japanese restaurant was added to please older patrons. The Nautilus submarine is missing. More areas are covered to protect against rain and snow. Lines for attractions had to be redesigned so that people walking through the park did not cross in front of patrons waiting to ride an attraction. "It's very discourteous in Japan to have people cross in front of somebody else," explained James B. Cora, managing director of operations for the Tokyo project. The biggest differences between Japan and America have come in slogans and ad copy. Although English is often used, it's "Japanized" English-the sort that would have native speakers shaking their heads while the Japanese nod happily in recognition. "Let's Spring" was the motto for one of their highly successful ad campaigns.

Pogue, visiting frequently from his base in California, supervised seven resident American Disney managers who work side by side with Japanese counterparts from Oriental Land Co. to keep the park in tune with the Disney doctrine. American it may be, but Tokyo Disneyland appeals to such deep-seated Japanese passions as cleanliness, order, outstanding service, and technological wizardry. Japanese executives are impressed by Disney's detailed training manuals, which teach employees how to make visitors feel like VIPs. Most worth emulating, say the Japanese, is Disney's ability to make even the lowliest job seem glamorous. "They have changed the image of dirty work," said Hakuhodo Institute's Sekizawa.

Disney Company did encounter a few unique cultural problems when developing Tokyo Disneyland:

The problem: how to dispose of some 250 tons of trash that would be generated weekly by Tokyo Disneyland visitors?

The standard Disney solution: trash compactors.

The Japanese proposal: pigs to eat the trash and be slaughtered and sold at a profit.

James B. Cora and his team of some 150 operations experts did a little calculating and pointed out that it would take 100,000 pigs to do the job. And then there would be the smell . . .

The Japanese relented.

The Japanese were also uneasy about a rustic-looking Westernland, Tokyo's version of Frontierland. "The Japanese like everything fresh and new when they put it in." said Cora. "They kept painting the wood and we kept saying, 'No, it's got to look old.'" Finally the Disney crew took the Japanese to Anaheim to give them a firsthand look at the Old West.

Tokyo Disneyland opened just as the yen escalated in value against the dollar and the income level of the Japanese registered a phenomenal improvement. During this era of affluence, Tokyo Disneyland triggered an interest in leisure. Its great success spurred the construction of "leisurelands" throughout the country. This created an increase in the Japanese people's orientation towards leisure. But demographics are the real key to Tokyo Disneyland's success. Thirty million Japanese live within 30 miles of the park. There are three times more than the number of people in the same proximity to Anaheim's Disneyland. With the park proven such an unqualified hit, and nearing capacity, Oriental Land and Disney mapped out plans for a version of the Disney-MGM studio tour next door. This time, Disney talked about taking a 50 percent stake in the project.

Building Euro Disneyland

On March 24, 1987, Michael Eisner and Jacques Chirac, the French Prime Minister, signed a contract for the building of a Disney theme park at Marne-la-Vallee. Talks between Disney and the French government had dragged on for more than a year. At the signing, Robert Fitzpatrick, fluent in French, married to the former Sylvie Blondet and the recipient of two awards from the French government, was introduced as the president of Euro Disneyland. He was expected to be a key player in wooing support from the French establishment for the theme park. As one analyst put it, Disney selected him to set up the park because he is "more French than the French."

Disney had been courted extensively by Spain and France. The Prime Ministers of both countries ordered their governments to lend Disney a hand in its quest for a site. France set up a five-person team headed by a Special Advisor to Foreign Trade & Tourism Minister, Edith Cresson, and Spain's negotiators included Ignacio Vasallo, Director-General for the Promotion of Tourism. Disney pummeled both governments with requests for detailed information. "The only thing they haven't asked us for is the color of the tourists' eyes," moaned Vasallo.

The governments tried other enticements, too. Spain offered tax and labor incentives and possibly as much as 20,000 acres of land. The French package, although less generous, included spending of $53 million to improve highway access to the proposed site and perhaps speeding up a $75 million subway project. For a long time, all that smiling Disney officials would say was that Spain had better weather while France had a better population base.

Officials explained that they picked France over Spain because Marne-la-Vallee is advantageously close to one of the world's tourism capitals, while also being situated within a day's drive or train ride of some 30 million people in France, Belgium, England, and Germany. Another advantage mentioned was the availability of good transportation. A train line that serves as part of the Paris Metro subway system ran to Torcy, in the center of Marne-la-Vallee, and the French government promised to extend the line to the actual site of the park. The park would also be served by A-4, a modern highway that runs from Paris to the German border, as well as a freeway that runs to Charles de Gaulle airport.

Once a letter of intent had been signed, sensing that the French government was keen to not let the plan fail, Disney held out for one concession after another. For example, Disney negotiated for VAT (value added tax) on ticket sales to be cut from a normal 18.6 percent to 7 percent. A quarter of the investment in building the park would come from subsidized loans. Additionally, any disputes arising from the contract would be settled not in French courts but by a special international panel of arbitrators. But Disney did have to agree to a clause in the contract which would require it to respect and utilize French culture in its themes.

The park was built on 4,460 acres of farmland in Marne-la-Vallee, a rural corner of France 20 miles east of Paris known mostly for sugar beets and Brie cheese. Opening was planned for early 1992 and planners hoped to attract some 10 million visitors a year. Approximately $2.5 billion was needed to build the park making it the largest single foreign investment ever in France. A French "pivot" company was formed to build the park with starting capital of FFr 3 billion, split 60 percent French and 40 percent foreign, with Disney taking 16.67 percent. Euro Disneyland was expected to bring $600 million in foreign investment into France each year.

As soon as the contract had been signed, individuals and businesses began scurrying to somehow plug into the Mickey Mouse money machine—all were hoping to benefit from the American dream without leaving France. In fact, one Paris daily, *Liberation,* actually sprouted mouse ears over its front-page flag.

The $1.5 to $2 billion first phase investment would involve an amusement complex including hotels and restaurants, golf courses, and an aquatic park in addition to a European version of the Magic Kingdom. The second phase, scheduled to start after the gates opened in 1992, called for the construction of a community around the park, including a sports complex, technology park, conference center, theater, shopping mall, university campus, villas, and condominiums. No price tag had been put on the second phase, although it was expected to rival, if not surpass, the first phase investment. In November 1989, Fitzpatrick announced that the Disney-MGM Studios, Europe would also open at Euro Disneyland in 1996, resembling the enormously successful Disney-MGM Studios theme park at Disney World in Orlando. The new studios would greatly enhance the Walt Disney Company's strategy of increasing its production of live action and animated filmed entertainment in Europe for both the European and world markets.

"The phone's been ringing here ever since the announcement," said Marc Berthod of EpaMarne, the government body that oversees the Marne-la-Vallee region. "We've gotten calls from big companies as well as small—everything from hotel chains to language interpreters all asking for details on Euro Disneyland. And the individual mayors of the villages around here have been swamped with calls from people looking for jobs." he added.

Euro Disneyland was expected to generate up to 28 000 jobs, providing a measure of relief for an area that had suffered a 10 percent plus unemployment rate for the previous year. It was also expected to light a fire under France's construction industry which had been particularly hard hit by France's economic problems over the previous year. Moreover, Euro Disneyland was expected to attract many other investors to the depressed outskirts of Paris. International Business Machines (IBM) and *Banque National de Paris* were among those already building in the area. In addition one of the new buildings going up was a factory that would employ 400 outside workers to wash the 50 tons of laundry expected to be generated per day by Euro Disneyland's 14,000 employees.

The impact of Euro Disneyland was also felt in the real estate market. "Everyone who owns land around here is holding on to it for the time being, at least until they know what's going to happen," said Danny Theveno, a spokesman

Exhibit 3   Chronology of the Euro Disneyland Deal

1984–85	Disney negotiates with Spain and France to create a European theme park Chooses France as the site
1987	Disney signs letter of intent with the French government
1988	Selects lead commercial bank lenders for the senior portion of the project Forms the *Societe en Nom Collectif* {SNC) Begins planning for the equity offering of 51% of Euro Disneyland as required in the letter of intent
1989	European press and stock analysts visit Walt Disney World in Orlando Begin extensive news and television campaign Stock starts trading at 20–25 percent premium from the issue price

Source: From Geraldine E. Willigan, "The value-adding CFO: an interview with Disney's Gary Wilson," *Harvard Business Review,* January–February 1990, pp. 85–93.

for the town of Villiers on the western edge of Marne-la-Vallee. Disney expected 11 million visitors in the first year. The break-even point was estimated to be between seven and eight million. One worry was that Euro Disneyland would cannibalize the flow of European visitors to Walt Disney World in Florida, but European travel agents said that their customers were still eagerly signing up for Florida lured by the cheap dollar and the promise of sunshine.

Protests of Cultural Imperialism

Disney faced French communists and intellectuals who protested the building of Euro Disneyland. Ariane Mnouchkine, a theater director, described it as a "cultural Chernobyl." "I wish with all my heart that the rebels would set fire to Disneyland," thundered a French intellectual in the newspaper *La Figaro.* "Mickey Mouse," sniffed another, "is stifling individualism and transforming children into consumers." The theme park was damned as an example of American "neoprovincialism."

Farmers in the Marne-la-Vallee region posted protest signs along the roadside featuring a mean looking Mickey Mouse and touting sentiments such as "Disney go home," "Stop the massacre," and "Don't gnaw away our national wealth." Farmers were upset partly because under the terms of the contract, the French government would expropriate the necessary land and sell it without profit to Euro Disneyland development company.

While local officials were sympathetic to the farmers' position, they were unwilling to let their predicament interfere with what some called "the deal of the century." "For many years these farmers have had the fortune to cultivate what is considered some of the richest land in France," said Berthod. "Now they'll have to find another occupation."

Also less than enchanted about the prospect of a magic kingdom rising among their midst was the communist dominated labor federation, the *Confédération Générale du Travail* (CGT). Despite the job-creating potential of Euro Disney, the CGT doubted its members would benefit. The union had been fighting hard to stop the passage of a bill which would give managers the right to establish flexible hours for their workers. Flexible hours were believed to be a prerequisite to the profitable operation of Euro Disneyland, especially considering seasonal variations.

However, Disney proved to be relatively immune to the anti-U.S. virus. In early 1985, one of the three state-owned television networks signed a contract to broadcast two hours of dubbed Disney programming every Saturday evening. Soon after, *Disney Channel* became one of the top-rated programs in France.

In 1987, the company launched an aggressive community relations program to calm the fears of politicians, farmers, villagers, and even bankers that the project would bring traffic congestion, noise, pollution, and other problems to their countryside. Such a public relations program was a rarity in France, where businesses make little effort to establish good relations with local residents. Disney invited 400 local children to a birthday party for Mickey Mouse, sent Mickey to area hospitals, and hosted free trips to Disney World in Florida for dozens of local officials and children.

"They're experts at seduction, and they don't hide the fact that they're trying to seduce you," said Vincent Guardiola, an official with *Banque Indosuez,* one of the 17 banks wined and dined at Orlando and subsequently one of the venture's financial participants. "The French aren't used to this kind of public relations—it was unbelievable." Observers said that the goodwill efforts helped dissipate initial objections to the project.

Financial Structuring at Euro Disneyland

Eisner was so keen on Euro Disneyland that Disney kept a 49 percent stake in the project, while the remaining 51 percent of stock was distributed through the London, Paris, and Brussels stock exchanges. Half the stock under the offer was going to the French, 25 percent to the English, and the remainder distributed in the rest of the European community. The initial offer price of FFr 72 was considerably higher than the pathfinder prospectus estimate because the capacity of the park had been slightly extended. Scarcity of stock was likely to push up the price, which was expected to reach FFr 166 by opening day in 1992. This would give a compound return of 21 percent.

Walt Disney maintained management control of the company. The U.S. company put up $160 million of its own capital to fund the project, an investment which soared in value to $2.4 billion after the popular stock offering in Europe. French national and local authorities, by comparison, were providing about $800 million in low-interest loans and poured at least that much again into infrastructure.

Other sources of funding were the park's 12 corporate sponsors, and Disney would pay them back in kind. The "autopolis" ride, where kids ride cars, features coupes emblazoned with the "Hot Wheels" logo. Mattel Inc., sponsor of the ride, is grateful for the boost to one of its biggest toy lines.

The real payoff would begin once the park opened. The Walt Disney Company would receive 10 percent of admission fees and 5 percent of food and merchandise revenue, the same arrangement as in Japan. But in France, it would also receive management fees, incentive fees, and 49 percent of the profits.

A Saloman Brothers analyst estimated that the park would pull in three to four million more visitors than the 11 million the company expected in the first year. Other Wall Street analysts cautioned that stock prices of both Walt Disney Company and Euro Disney already contained all the Euro optimism they could absorb. "Europeans visit Disneyworld in Florida as part of an 'American experience,'" said Patrick P. Roper, marketing director of Alton Towers, a successful British theme park near Manchester. He doubted they would seek the suburbs of Paris as eagerly as America and predicted attendance would trail Disney projections.

The Layout of Euro Disneyland

Euro Disneyland is determinedly American in its theme. There was an alcohol ban in the park despite the attitude among the French that wine with a meal is a God-given right. Designers presented a plan for a Main Street USA based on scenes of America in the 1920s, because research indicated that Europeans loved the Prohibition era. Eisner decreed that images of gangsters and speak-easies were too negative. Though made more ornate and Victorian than Walt Disney's idealized Midwestern small town, Main Street remained Main Street. Steamships leave from Main Street through the Grand Canyon Diorama en route to Frontierland.

The familiar Disney Tomorrowland, with its dated images of the space age, was jettisoned entirely. It was replaced by a gleaming brass and wood complex called Discoverland, which was based on themes of Jules Verne and Leonardo da Vinci. Eisner ordered $8 or $10 million in extras to the "Visionarium" exhibit, a 360-degree movie about French culture which was required by the French in their original contract. French and English are the official languages at the park, and multilingual guides are available to help Dutch, German, Spanish, and Italian visitors.

With the American Wild West being so frequently captured on film, Europeans have their own idea of what life was like back then. Frontier land reinforces those images. A runway mine train takes guests through the canyons and mines of Gold Rush country. There is a paddle wheel steamboat reminiscent of Mark Twain, Indian explorer canoes, and a phantom manor from the Gold Rush days.

In Fantasyland, designers strived to avoid competing with the nearby European reality of actual medieval towns, cathedrals, and chateaux. While Disneyland's castle is based on Germany's Neuschwanstein and Disney World's is based on a Loire Valley chateau, Euro Disney's *Le Château de la Belle au Bois Dormant,* as the French insisted Sleeping Beauty be called, is more cartoon-like with stained glass windows built by English craftsmakers and depicting Disney characters. Fanciful trees grow inside as well as a beanstalk.

The park is criss-crossed with covered walkways. Eisner personally ordered the installation of 35 fireplaces in hotels and restaurants. "People walk around Disney World in Florida with humidity and temperatures in the 90s and they walk into an air-conditioned ride and say, 'This is the greatest,'" said Eisner. "When it's raining and miserable, I hope they will walk into one of these lobbies with the fireplace going and say the same thing."

Children all over Europe were primed to consume. Even one of the intellectuals who contributed to Le Figaro's Disney-bashing broadsheet was forced to admit with resignation that his ten-year-old son "swears by Michael Jackson." At Euro Disneyland, under the name "Captain EO," Disney just so happened to have a Michael Jackson attraction awaiting him.

Food Service and Accommodations at Euro Disneyland

Disney expected to serve 15,000 to 17,000 meals per hour, excluding snacks. Menus and service systems were developed so that they varied both in style and price. There is a 400-seat buffeteria, 6 table service restaurants, 12 counter service units, 10 snack bars, 1 Discovery food court seating

---

Exhibit 4　The Euro Disneyland Resort

5,000 acres in size
30 attractions
12,000 employees
6 hotels (with 5,184 rooms)
10 theme restaurants
414 cabins
181 camping sites

Source: Roger Cohen, "Threat of strikes in Euro Disney debut," *New York Times,* April 10, 1992, p. 20.

850, 9 popcorn wagons, 15 ice-cream carts, 14 specialty food carts, and 2 employee cafeterias. Restaurants were, in fact, to be a showcase for American foods. The only exception to this is Fantasyland which re-creates European fables. Here, food service will reflect the fable's country of origin: Pinocchio's facility having German food; Cinderella's, French; Bella Notte's, Italian; and so on.

Of course recipes were adapted for European tastes. Since many Europeans don't care much for very spicy food, Tex-Mex recipes were toned down. A special coffee blend had to be developed which would have universal appeal. Hot dog carts would reflect the regionalism of American tastes. There would be a ball park hot dog (mild, steamed, a mixture of beef and pork), a New York hot dog (all beef, and spicy), and a Chicago hot dog (Vienna-style, similar to bratwurst).

Euro Disneyland has six theme hotels which would offer nearly 5,200 rooms on opening day, a campground (444 rental trailers and 181 camping sites), and single family homes on the periphery of the 27-hole golf course.

Disney's Strict Appearance Code

Antoine Guervil stood at his post in front of the 1,000 room Cheyenne Hotel at Euro Disneyland, practicing his "Howdy!" When Guervil, a political refugee from Haiti, said the word, it sounded more like "Audi." Native French speakers have trouble with the aspirated "h" sound in words like "hay" and "Hank" and "Howdy." Guervil had been given the job of wearing a cowboy costume and booming a happy, welcoming Howdy to guests as they entered the Cheyenne, styled after a Western movie set.

"Audi," said Guervil, the strain of linguistic effort showing on his face. This was clearly a struggle. Unless things got better, it was not hard to imagine objections from Renault, the French car company that was one of the corporate sponsors of the park. Picture the rage of a French auto executive arriving with his or her family at the Renault-sponsored Euro Disneyland, only to hear the doorman of a Disney hotel advertising a German car.

Such were the problems Disney faced while hiring some 12,000 people to maintain and populate its Euro Disneyland theme park. A handbook of detailed rules on acceptable clothing, hairstyles, and jewelry, among other things, embroiled the company in a legal and cultural dispute. Critics asked how the brash Americans could be so insensitive to French culture, individualism, and privacy. Disney officials insisted that a ruling that barred them from imposing a squeaky-clean employment standard could threaten the image and long-term success of the park.

"For us, the appearance code has a "real effect from a product identification standpoint," said Thor Degelmann, vice president for human resources for Euro Disneyland. "Without it we wouldn't be presenting the Disney product that people would be expecting."

The rules, spelled out in a video presentation and detailed in a guide handbook, went beyond height and weight standards. They required men's hair to be cut above the collar and ears with no beards or mustaches. Any tattoos must be covered. Women must keep their hair in one "natural color" with no frosting or streaking and they may make only limited use of make-up like mascara. False eyelashes, eyeliners, and eye pencil were completely off limits. Fingernails can't pass the end of the fingers. As for jewelry, women can wear only one earring in each ear, with the earring's diameter no more than three-quarters of an inch. Neither men nor women can wear more than one ring on each hand. Further, women were required to wear appropriate undergarments and only transparent panty hose, not black or anything with fancy designs. Though a daily bath was not specified in the rules, the applicant's video depicted a shower scene and informed applicants that they were expected to show up for work "fresh and clean each day." Similar rules are in force at Disney's three other theme parks in the United States and Japan.

In the United States, some labor unions representing Disney employees have occasionally protested the company's strict appearance code, but with little success. French labor unions began protesting when Disneyland opened its "casting center" and invited applicants to "play the role of [their lives]" and to take a "unique opportunity to marry work and magic." The CGT handed out leaflets in front of the center to warn applicants of the appearance code which they believed represented "an attack on individual liberty." A more mainstream union, the *Confédération Française Démocratique du Travail* (CFDT) appealed to the Labor Ministry to halt Disney's violation of "human

Exhibit 5   What Price Mickey?

	Euro Disneyland	Disney World, Orlando
	Peak season hotel rates	
4-person room	$97 to $345	$104–$455
	Campground space	
	$48	$30–$49
	One-day pass	
Children	$26	$26
Adults	$40	$33

Source: Business Week, March 30, 1992.

dignity." French law prohibits employers from restricting individual and collective liberties unless the restrictions can be justified by the nature of the task to be accomplished and are proportional to that end.

Degelmann, however, said that the company was "well aware of the cultural differences" between the United States and France and as a result had "toned down" the wording in the original American version of the guidebook. He pointed out that many companies, particularly airlines, maintained appearance codes just as strict. "We happened to put ours in writing," he added. In any case, he said that he knew of no one who had refused to take the job because of the rules and that no more than 5 percent of the people showing up for interviews had decided not to proceed after watching the video which also detailed transportation and salary.

Fitzpatrick also defended the dress code, although he conceded that Disney might have been a little naive in presenting things so directly. He added, "Only in France is there still a communist party. There is not even one in Russia any more. The ironic thing is that I could fill the park with CGT requests for tickets."

Another big challenge lay in getting the mostly French "cast members," as Disney calls its employees, to break their ancient cultural aversions to smiling and being consistently polite to park guests. The individualistic French had to be molded into the squeaky-clean Disney image. Rival theme parks in the area, loosely modeled on the Disney system, had already encountered trouble keeping smiles on the faces of the staff, who sometimes took on the demeanor of subway ticket clerks.

The delicate matter of hiring French citizens as opposed to other nationals was examined in the more than two-year-long preagreement negotiations between the French government and Disney. The final agreement called for Disney to make a maximum effort to tap into the local labor market. At the same time, it was understood that for Euro Disneyland to work, its staff must mirror the multicountry make-up of its guests. "Casting centers" were set up in Paris, London, Amsterdam, and Frankfurt. "We are concentrating on the local labor market, but we are also looking for workers who are German, English, Italian, Spanish, or other nationalities and who have good communication skills, are outgoing, speak two European languages—French plus one other—and like being around people," said Degelmann.

Stephane Baudet, a 28-year-old trumpet player from Paris refused to audition for a job in a Disney brass band when he learned he would have to cut his ponytail. "Some people will turn themselves into a pumpkin to work at Euro Disneyland." he said. "But not me."

Opening Day at Euro Disneyland

A few days before the grand opening of Euro Disneyland, hundreds of French visitors were invited to a pre-opening party. They gazed perplexed at what was placed before them. It was a heaping plate of spare ribs. The visitors were at the Buffalo Bill Wild West Show, a cavernous theater featuring a panoply of "Le Far West," including 20 imported buffaloes. And Disney deliberately didn't provide silverware. "There was a moment of consternation," recalls Fitzpatrick. "Then they just kind of said, 'The hell with it,' and dug in." There was one problem. The guests couldn't master the art of gnawing ribs and applauding at the same time. So Disney planned to provide more napkins and teach visitors to stamp with their feet.

On April 12, 1992, the opening day of Euro Disneyland, *France-Soir* enthusiastically predicted Disney dementia. "Mickey! It's madness," read its front-page headline, warning of chaos on the roads and suggesting that people may have to be turned away. A French government survey indicated that half a million might turn up with 90,000 cars trying to get in. French radio warned traffic to avoid the area.

By lunchtime on opening day, the Euro Disneyland car park was less than half full, suggesting an attendance of below 25,000, less than half the park's capacity and way below expectations. Many people may have heeded the advice to stay home or, more likely, were deterred by a one-day strike that cut the direct rail link to Euro Disneyland from the center of Paris. Queues for the main rides, such as Pirates of the Caribbean and Big Thunder Mountain railroad, were averaging around 15 minutes less than on an ordinary day at Disney World, Florida.

Disney executives put on a brave face, claiming that attendance was better than at first days for other Disney theme parks in Florida, California, and Japan. However, there was no disguising the fact that after spending thousands of dollars on the pre-opening celebrations, Euro Disney would have appreciated some impressively long traffic jams on the auto route.

Other Operating Problems

When the French government changed hands in 1986, work ground to a halt, as the negotiator appointed by the Conservative government threw out much of the ground work prepared by his Socialist predecessor. The legalistic approach taken by the Americans also bogged down talks, as it meant planning ahead for every conceivable contingency. At the same time, right-wing groups who saw the park as an invasion of "chewing-gum jobs" and U.S. pop-culture also fought hard for a greater "local cultural context."

On opening day, English visitors found the French reluctant to play the game of queuing. "The French seem to think that if God had meant them to queue, He wouldn't have given them elbows," they commented. Different cultures have different definitions of personal space, and Disney guests faced problems of people getting too close or pressing around those who left too much space between themselves and the person in front.

Disney placed its first ads for work bids in English, leaving smaller and medium-sized French firms feeling like foreigners in their own land. Eventually, Disney set up a data bank with information on over 20,000 French and European firms looking for work and the local Chamber of Commerce developed a video text information bank with Disney that small- and medium-sized companies through France and Europe would be able to tap into. "The work will come, but many local companies have got to learn that they don't simply have the right to a chunk of work without competing," said a Chamber official.

Efforts were made to ensure that sooner, rather than later, European nationals take over the day-to-day running of the park. Although there were only 23 U.S. expatriates amongst the employees, they controlled the show and held most of the top jobs. Each senior manager had the task of choosing his or her European successor.

Disney was also forced to bail out 40 subcontractors, who were working for the Gabot-Eremco construction contracting group which had been unable to honor all of its commitments. Some of the subcontractors said they faced bankruptcy if they were not paid for their work on Euro Disneyland. A Disney spokesperson said that the payments would be less than $20.3 million and the company had already paid Gabot-Eremco for work on the park. Gabot-Eremco and 15 other main contractors demanded $157 million in additional fees from Disney for work that they said was added to the project after the initial contracts were

signed. Disney rejected the claim and sought government intervention. Disney said that under no circumstances would they pay Gabot-Eremco and accused its officers of incompetence.

As Bourguignon thought about these and other problems, the previous year's losses and the prospect of losses again in the current year, with their negative impact on the company's stock price, weighed heavily on his mind.

1. Using Hofstede's four cultural dimensions as a point of reference, what are some of the main cultural differences between the United States and France?

2. In what way has Trompenaars' research helped explain cultural differences between the United States and France?

3. In managing its Euro Disneyland operations, what are three mistakes that the company made? Explain.

4. Based on its experience, what are three lessons the company should have learned about how to deal with diversity? Describe each.

This case was prepared by Research Assistant Sonali Krishna under the direction of Professors J. Stewart Black and Hal B. Gregersen as the basis for class discussion. Reprinted by permission of the authors.

Integrative Case 3

Will Tokyo Embrace Another Mouse?

Disney's second park is facing a swarm of challenges

It features a choreographed parade of boats, a Pacific Island volcano, seasalt flavor ice cream—and, of course, the world's most famous rodent. Welcome to Disney & Co.'s big second act in Japan. On Sept. 4, Disney and its Japanese partner, Oriental Land, threw open the gates to DisneySea, a $2.8 billion marine-themed attraction built right next door to Tokyo Disneyland, which opened in 1983.

Disney and Oriental Land are betting that Mickey Mouse in an admiral's uniform will lift Disney's Tokyo fortunes. Attendance at the original park peaked in 1998 (chart), and daily spending per guest, while still the highest of any Disney park, slid 5 percent over the last two years, after a 13-year streak of gains. In May, Oriental Land reported that group net profit fell 52.2 percent, to $395 million, for the year ended in March, despite a 15 percent gain in sales, to $1.7 billion. "Over the past decade, Tokyo Disneyland has managed to shield itself from [Japan's ailing] economy," says Hiroshi Okubo, an analyst in the Tokyo office of UBS Warburg. "But the drop in guest spending suggests those days may be ending."

Disney needs to goose receipts in Tokyo because it wants to show the Mouse franchise is alive and well even as U.S. parks struggle to attract visitors. Disney and Oriental Land expect both Japanese parks to host a combined 25 million visitors a year, up from the current 17.3 million for Tokyo Disneyland alone. Tokyo-based Mitsubishi Research Institute Inc. estimates that Tokyo DisneySea will generate

$15 billion a year in economic activity, if one includes such related businesses as area malls, gas stations, and support services. For its part, Disney, which put up a paltry $20 million for basic pre-construction design work, gets about 10 percent of the gate, 5 percent of food and merchandise sales, and 10 percent of corporate sponsorships.

While advance tickets for the grand opening sold out in hours, some wonder if DisneySea will live up to all the hype. One fear is that it will cannibalize visitors from the original park. Disney's record of adjacent attractions is not reassuring. For example, the company's surf-and-sand-themed California Adventure park is right next door to the original Disneyland in Anaheim, Calif. It has failed to generate the anticipated traffic. Not a problem in Tokyo, asserts Oriental Land. It says Tokyo DisneySea will act as a catalyst, increasing the number of visitors to both parks and how much they spend on mouse-ear caps and gourmet popcorn. "We're confident that guest spending levels have bottomed out and will pick up from here on out," says company spokesman George Yasuoka.

Booze and Backrubs

The key is to make DisneySea sufficiently different from its neighbor. Oriental Land is pitching it to a slightly older, more male clientele than the original park, where about 70 percent of guests are female, mostly 20- to 30-year-olds—some with kids, others with dates or girlfriends. DisneySea offers booze, a hair-raising roller coaster ride in a mock Incan temple, and an on-site spa. Visitors can even get married in the park.

But DisneySea faces other challenges. As the economy sinks back into recession, Japanese may become hesitant to pay the $46 entry fee. And there's the increasing competition. In March, Universal Studios Japan opened in Osaka. The $1.4 billion movie-theme park is a potential threat because it offers residents of western Japan a closer alternative than Tokyo Disney.

Still, thanks in part to field trips that introduce legions of kids to Mickey and his friends, the Disney experience has become ingrained in Japanese life. In his 1993 book, *Disneyland as Holy Land,* University of Tokyo professor Masako Notoji wrote: "The opening of Tokyo Disneyland

Mickey Fatigue
Disney hopes its new Tokyo park will boost attendance

Disneyland Attendance

Data: Oriental Land Co.

was, in retrospect, the greatest cultural event in Japan during the '80s." Or at any rate the most profitable. The $2.8 billion question is whether DisneySea can engender similar enthusiasm—and keep the turnstiles spinning.

By Chester Dawson in Tokyo

1. Do you think starting DisneySea is a good decision? What would indicate this is a good move? A bad move?
2. How does the Japanese culture enter into this decision to open DisneySea?

3. Do you agree with the Tokyo professor's statement that "The opening of Tokyo Disneyland was, in retrospect, the greatest cultural event in Japan during the '80s." How do you explain that Tokyo Disneyland was a success but Euro Disneyland had such problems (see the previous case)?

Source: Reprinted from September 10, 2001, p. 55 of *Business Week* by special permission, copyright © 2001 by the McGraw-Hill Companies, Inc.

Part Three

International
Strategic
Management

Chapter 9

Strategic Planning

Objectives of the Chapter

All major MNCs employ strategic planning, a plan which results from a careful analysis of both the external and internal environments. In this process an MNC will identify the market environment for its goods and services and then evaluate its ability and competitive advantage to capture this market. The success of this strategic planning effort will largely depend on accurate forecasting of the external environment and a realistic appraisal of internal company strengths and weaknesses. In recent years, MNCs have relied on their strategic plans to help refocus their efforts by abandoning old domestic markets and entering new global markets. This strategic global planning process has been critical in their drive to gain market share, increase profitability, and in some cases, even survive.

Chapter 6 addressed overall strategic management across cultures. This chapter focuses on strategic planning in the international context, and the basic steps by which a strategic plan is formulated and implemented are examined. The specific objectives of this chapter are:

1. **DISCUSS** the meaning, needs, benefits, approaches, and predispositions of the strategic planning process for today's MNCs.

2. **IDENTIFY** the basic steps in strategic planning, including environmental scanning, internal resource analysis of the MNC's strengths and weaknesses, and goal formulation.

3. **DESCRIBE** how an MNC implements the strategic plan, such as how it chooses a site for overseas operations.

4. **EXPLAIN** how an MNC implements an ownership and/or entry strategy.

5. **REVIEW** the three major functions of marketing, production, and finance that are used in implementing a strategic plan.

BusinessWeek

The World of *Business Week*

Toyota Unbound

It was a skunk-works project Toyota Motor Corp. executives found hardly worth mentioning. In 1996, in a small office in Toyota city, engineers Shigeki Tomoyama and Akio Toyoda, son of Honorary Chairman Shoichiro Toyoda, constructed a rudimentary computer network that enabled dealers to display photos of used Toyota models in cyberspace. By hooking into the Net, Tomoyama and Toyoda dramatically increased the number of consumer eyeballs checking out those cars: In test markets the average stay of a used car on the lot dropped from 90 days to 10.

Nice job. But that was just the start. Now called Gazoo.com, the Toyota site has become one of Japan's most popular cyber gateways, peddling everything from brake pads to hit compact discs to horoscopes. Toyota's Gazoo.com division boasts more than 50 vendors, 500,000 members, and 2,000 new subscribers every day. It's so popular that almost 13,000 convenience stores want Gazoo.com terminals to go in their locations: Consumers will order stuff at Gazoo kiosks, then pay and pick up their deliveries later at the store. "Gazoo.com is becoming the AOL.com of Japan," says Yasushi Tachikawa, a manager of DigiCube, which sells CDs, DVDs, and videos on the site.

Pace of Change

That may be a bit of a stretch: Gazoo.com has plenty of tough rivals. But there's no denying something momentous is happening at Toyota. The steady-as-you-go maker of some of the world's most popular, blandest cars is turning into one of Japan's most daring New Economy players. Gazoo.com is bold enough—could anyone imagine General Motors Corp. running one of America's hot Web sites? But there's plenty more. The giant will be the second-biggest shareholder in a new telecom company being formed in Japan, KDDI. And the pace of change is picking up. Recently, the company announced the creation of a finance arm to manage Toyota customers' credit cards, arrange loans and mortgages, and peddle higher-paying bond funds to clients. Analysts estimate that in five years, Toyota could be earning up to 20% of its profit from nonauto businesses worldwide.

Because of Toyota's high-tech and financial assets, the market is awarding it a market capitalization of $192 billion. That makes Toyota worth more than General Motors and Ford Motor Co. combined, even though its vehicle sales trail far behind both players. Indeed, Toyota's moves are being taken so seriously that one local report carried the headline: "The day when the word Motor will disappear from Toyota's name."

But wait a minute. Toyota the dot-com? A car company mixing it up in the phone wars? To long-time investors in U.S. auto makers, at least, these strategic thrusts bear an uncomfortable resemblance to the plans of Detroit's Big Three to diversity. General Motors bought Hughes Electronics and Electronic Data Services. Ford ran First Nationwide, the big savings and loan. Chrysler Corp., maker of the lowly K cars, peddled luxury Gulfstream jets. We all know what happened. Ford and Chrysler aren't in those businesses anymore. Even GM, whose investments prospered, has spun off EDS and is reducing its stake in Hughes to concentrate on the car business. And back in Japan, Toyota's earlier forays into housing and riding clubs (yes, riding clubs) were duds. "We have made many mistakes," observes Executive Vice-President Tadaaki Jagawa.

Yet here's Japan's biggest carmaker, with $120 billion in sales, getting ready to spend big money, possibly billions, on dot-coms, cell phones, and financial services. And it will be years before the company sees substantial returns on these investments. Toyota certainly runs the risk of losing its tight focus on the car business that has made it a terrifying force to compete against. "I hope they do end up working more on dot-coms than cars," says one rival auto exec.

But Hiroshi Okuda, Toyota's chairman, sees plenty more opportunity than danger. "In the past, we over-concentrated on making cars," says the 67-year-old executive. He wants to have a big, visible presence in different businesses, even while the auto company rolls out better, more stylish models.

As Okuda sees it, Toyota has a rare opportunity to ride the wave of several major changes. The Internet is starting to affect the way ordinary Japanese live, shop, and work. Deregulation is giving dramatic openings to new players in telecom and financial services, just when individual Japanese investors are searching for higher yields.

Next, technology is transforming the auto business. Soon, consumers will be consulting on-board computers for everything from traffic directions to e-mail. "Until now, Toyota has sold 1.8 million vehicles per year," explains Gazoo's Tomoyama. "But from now on, it will sell 1.8 million computers [in its cars]." Navigation systems already operate in a third of the cars Toyota sells. The day is fast approaching when a car's electronics performance may count more for customers than the engine under the hood. And Toyota does not want Microsoft Corp. or Sony Corp. dictating to Toyota what shape its onboard PCs will take.

Finally, Okuda knows Toyota has one of the best customer bases anywhere: 20 million affluent consumers in Japan alone, with perhaps 30 million abroad. To Okuda and his top execs, there just has to be a way to coax more revenues out of these customers.

Exploding

Take all these factors, and you can see where Okuda is going when he instructs the troops. The Internet is a big new opportunity: Grab a piece of the action. Cell-phone use is exploding in Japan: Get into the game with the telecom venture. Individual investing is accelerating in Japan: Set up a finance operation Japanese can trust.

Most important, Toyota wants to tie all these ventures back to the core car company. Take Gazoo. It has yet to turn a profit, and it's still improving its shopping service, which lags that of Rakuten, a rival site. "I've gone to the Gazoo mall, but the prices aren't low," says Shuichi Okabe, a 46-year-old civil servant.

Nonetheless, Okabe loves Gazoo's chat rooms, which have spawned fan clubs nationwide. More important, Gazoo has hooked consumers like Okabe, who already knows Toyota as the owner of a Toyota Hi-Ace station wagon. Gazoo will be able to alert Okabe to new cars he might be interested in buying—and car insurance policies or car loans from Toyota's new finance arm. And the day will come when Toyota has Gazoo.com installed in all the onboard PCs in its cars.

That's where telecom comes in. To morph into a mobile commercial hub, Toyota will take a 13% stake in a newly forming telecommunications player called KDDI. It's a merger of a tiny but profitable telecom company, IDO Corp., which Toyota controlled, with several other players. The result will be Japan's second-biggest telecom company.

The investments in telecom tie into Toyota's plans to develop wired cars, which will sport built-in cell phones tuned to KDDI signals, and wireless Internet access provided by KDDI. "Toyota's active participation in telecom will set it apart from its competitors," says Stephen Usher, automotive analyst with Jardine Fleming.

Vastly Ambitious

And of course, there's finance. Toyota next year will introduce its own credit card, as opposed to a card it now jointly offers with local partners to almost 3 million Japanese. Toyota wants to issue an independent card so that it can keep track of fast-changing consumer preferences and handle online settlements. "Toyota has concentrated on engines and components," says Takaki Nakanishi, car analyst at Merrill Lynch & Co. "But it basically doesn't know its customers' faces. It needs to." Eventually, Toyota could offer even more financial services over the card, such as loan and insurance products. And Gazoo.com could offer Toyota customers a way to buy life insurance and mutual funds online.

It all makes for a vastly ambitious plan. Inside the company, executives are starting to compare Toyota's aggressive moves to the company's momentous decision in the 1930s to switch from making textile looms to manufacturing cars. Okuda has publicly reckoned that no company can flourish longer than 100 years, and he's defying his managers to prove the conventional wisdom wrong. Indeed, about the only great leap Toyota is not making is the one most of its rivals are pursuing—merging with a foreign auto maker. Toyota isn't looking. "Every 5 or 10 years we're asked if we're interested in buying BMW," Okuda notes. "But I think it's difficult to proceed with a different culture."

There's plenty happening in Toyota's auto business to keep the company busy. Toyota's cars will still drive its operating profits. While Okuda has been racing around pushing managers to think beyond cars, recently named President Fujio Cho has been relentlessly raising the bar in the core auto business. "The base of the car is manufacturing," says Cho. "We cannot forget that."

The strategy is starting to pay off. Two years ago, Toyota's bland sedans weren't moving from its Japanese showrooms, and domestic market share had slipped below 40% for the third year in a row. Mild-mannered engineer Yasuhiko Ichihashi received orders to turn Toyota's fortunes around by producing a killer compact. When Ichihashi showed his design for the Vitz to Okuda, Toyota's chief thought it looked like a squashed bug. Says Ichihashi: "Everyone in the older generation in the company was worried."

Now, dealers are scrambling to get their hands on Vitz, which is selling at the rate of 14,000 a month for about $10,000 each. Dealers are also clamoring for four other distinct models developed from the Vitz platform, ranging from a boxy compact minivan called the bB to a futuristic compact for Tokyo trendsetters called the

Will Vi. All sell in the $12,000 range. The Will Vi, vaguely reminiscent of the Volkswagen Beetle, comes in six metallic shades, including pink. "It doesn't look like a Toyota," says Kimiyo Fujiwara, 33, an office worker checking out the lineup at a showroom in Tokyo's chic Omotesando district. That, of course, is the point.

The experience with the Vitz is paving the way for future strides in manufacturing and cutting costs. After designing an engine with 15% fewer parts than its predecessor, and eliminating nuts and bolts from the car's new transmission and suspension, Ichihashi was able to cut 70 kilograms from the Vitz's weight. "Toyota could not make money [on the Vitz] up to 5 years ago," observes Koji Endo, automotive analyst at Credit Suisse First Boston. "Somehow, they reduced production cost by as much as 25%.

Truck Offensive

Toyota is also dramatically cutting the time it takes to design cars. It broke its own record when it took only 12 months from settling on the bB's final design to launching the minivan into the mass market. Now, Toyota plans to cut its passenger car platforms from 28 to 7 while pumping out the same number of models annually, if not more.

Toyota now has its 40% share in Japan back. In North America, it has used its Tundra pickup to launch a light-truck offensive that could prove a new nightmare for Detroit. This year, Toyota's total share of the auto market is up nearly a point, to 9%, fueled by a 22.5% jump in car and light-truck sales. Light trucks now account for 38.5% of its U.S. sales. But Toyota division general manager Don Esmond wants the North American product mix to be half cars, and half minivans, sport utes, and pickups.

Ultimately, Toyota hopes to respond better to fast-changing consumer preferences by tapping into the zeitgeist through its Web site and other services. The goal is to be the first auto maker to build cars to order and deliver them to the customer within two weeks. And of course, these cars will come with every high-tech gizmo and service offering possible. You want a cell phone with that? How about a mutual fund? The possibilities are endless.

By Emily Thornton in Tokyo, with Larry Armstrong in Los Angeles,
Kathleen Kerwin in Detroit, and bureau reports.

Strategic management is critical to international management. As seen in the opening *Business Week* story, within this decade Toyota is going to expand its operations into a variety of different industries. If the firm is successful, revenues and profits will increase sharply. However, Toyota will need an effective strategic plan in order to coordinate and implement all of these efforts. In particular, the company is branching into areas where, at best, it has limited experience. The firm knows a great deal about selling high quality cars, but will its customers be interested in buying nonauto-related products such as wireless PCs built into the dashboard? Will they sign up for a Toyota credit card? The myriad of ideas that the company is pursuing has great potential, but to bring them to fruition will take a very carefully crafted strategic plan. This chapter is going to examine how multinationals use strategic management in their worldwide operations. The topics covered are the same ones that Toyota is now addressing as it formulates its international strategy. They are also the same ones being used by General Motors, Ford, DaimlerChrysler, and all other major auto manufacturers who are competing in the auto industry. And like Toyota, these competitors are scanning their environment and trying to determine what they need to offer their customers in order to increase their own market share and profitability. As you read this chapter, think of yourself as a manager in a large auto firm. How might you go about developing a strategic plan to capture greater market share and expand the types of products you are selling?

■ International Strategic Planning

Strategic planning
The process of determining an organization's basic mission and long-term objectives, then implementing a plan of action for attaining these goals.

Strategic planning is the process of determining an organization's basic mission and long-term objectives, and then implementing a plan of action for pursuing this mission and attaining these objectives. As companies go international, this strategic process takes on added dimensions. A good example is provided by Citibank which opened offices in China in 1902 and continued to do business there until 1949 when the communists took power. However, in 1984 Citibank quietly returned and over the last two decades the firm has been slowly increasing its presence in China.[1] The Chinese banking environment is closely regulated by the government, and Citibank's activities are currently restricted to making local currency loans to foreign multinationals and their joint venture partners. As a result, the bank does only about 20 percent as much business here as it does in South Korea. However, China's admission into the World Trade Organization (WTO) is changing all of this. Under WTO provisions, elite local corporations such as the personal computer maker Legend, electronic goods manufacturer Konda, consumer appliance maker Haier, and telecom service provider China Telecom will all be able to turn to foreign banks for local currency loans. This will give Citibank a major opportunity to expand operations. Additionally, under WTO rules the bank is allowed to offer consumer financial services such as credit cards and home mortgages. Citibank believes that there is a large pent-up demand for credit cards especially among business people and yuppies who now carry around thick wads of currency to pay their bills and make purchases. Another opportunity Citibank sees is in the area of business-to-business (B2B) commerce. As more Chinese firms conduct commerce over the Internet, there will be an increase in Net-related financial services. Citibank has now hooked up with U.S.-based B2B site Commerce One to run its Net-based payment systems, and the bank believes that it can provide this same service for Chinese exporters.

Despite the huge potential market in China, however, Citibank is aware of the risks. In 1995 the firm was chosen as one of the first foreign banks to be issued a local-currency license. The bank felt certain that this was the opportunity it needed to break into the retail market, but this did not happen. In order to protect its domestic banks from competition, the government imposed a limit on the number of branches that foreign banks could open as well as to whom they could lend money and in what amounts. Quite simply, Citibank's opportunities were very limited. Will China being a member of the WTO change all of this? It might, but there are still a great many risks associated with doing business here. In particular, executives know that if foreign banks are given unrestricted access to China's retail customers, havoc could develop. It is estimated that Chinese customers have over $500 billion in savings. If these customers were to begin taking their money out of local banks and putting it into foreign ones, China's banks would be forced to stop lending to the country's state-owned enterprises (SOEs), most of which are losing money. In turn, these SOEs would go bankrupt and unemployment would skyrocket. The four major state-owned commercial banks currently control 70 percent of all financial assets in China and approximately 30 percent of all their loans are uncollectible. So the Chinese government is unlikely to move quickly to open up the banking market. Nevertheless, Citibank sees China as a major market and is developing strategies to increase its presence there and ride out any financial storms. In order to do this, the bank will need a well-formulated strategic plan.

The Growing Need for Strategic Planning

One of the primary reasons that MNCs such as Toyota or Citibank need strategic planning is to keep track of their increasingly diversified operations in a continuously changing international environment. This need is particularly obvious when one considers the amount of foreign direct investment (FDI) that has occurred in recent years. Recent statistics reveal that FDI has grown three times faster than trade and four times faster than world gross domestic product (GDP).[2] These developments are resulting in a need to coordinate and integrate diverse operations with a unified and agreed-on focus. There are many examples of firms that are doing just this.

One is Ford Motor which has reentered the market in Thailand and, despite a shrinking demand for automobiles there, is beginning to build a strong sales force and to garner market share. The firm's strategic plan here is based on offering the right combination of price and financing to a carefully identified market segment. In particular, Ford is working to keep down the monthly payments so that customers can afford a new vehicle. This is the same approach that Ford used in Mexico, where the currency crises of 1994 resulted in problems for many multinationals. However, this was not true for Ford which rolled out a carefully formulated strategy that allowed it to increase its vehicle market share in Mexico from 14 percent in 1994 to 20 percent three years later.[3]

Another example of the growing need for strategic planning is provided by Bertelsmann AG, the giant German book publisher that has now entered the Chinese market.[4] Bertelsmann has created a giant book club that could dramatically change the way Chinese buy books. In the past two years this club has signed up over 600,000 members, opened a handful of retail stores, and sold almost 5 million volumes. Moreover, Bertelsmann is now adding 2,000 new members every day, a growth rate that is easily sustainable given that approximately 180 million Chinese read books on a regular basis. The company's strategic plan calls for continual expansion well into the new millennium, driven by a wide assortment of books, low costs, and home delivery. In fact, things are going so well for Bertelsmann in China that the company has now sent salespeople to South Korea to lay the groundwork for a book club there and has plans for expanding to Japan, India, and Thailand.[5]

A third example of the growing need for strategic planning is provided by the German MNC Siemens. The firm used to make mobile phones but its costs were so high that it could not compete effectively. Today, thanks to its strategic plan, Siemens is back in the race. The company can now produce a phone in five minutes and the lightweight unit with long battery life sells for half that of competitive models. Notes one observer:

> Siemen's mobile-phone business shows why the Munich company is being taken seriously again. Siemens, which makes everything from gas-turbine generators to streetcars to light bulbs, has always had great engineers. But it only recently found that it takes more than that to beat competitors such as General Electric Co. and Nokia Co. "In the past, we developed our products, then threw them over the fence and hoped somebody would catch them," says Rudi Lamprecht, who gets credit for turning around the mobile-phone business. Siemens has since learned that success also requires marketing, up-to-date design, and ruthless attention to costs.[6]

At the heart of the company's turnaround has been a focus on speed, innovation, and customer-pleasing products. Today joint committees of engineers and marketers oversee new product development. When they spot a product that they believe customers want, they quickly outsource the manufacturing that is not essential to the firm and begin formulating the plan for getting the unit into the marketplace. As a result, Siemens is now a major player in most markets where it competes.

Still another example of the growing need for strategic planning is offered by the highly profitable GE Capital, which has been expanding rapidly in Europe. Since the mid-1980s the company has amassed assets in excess of $50 billion, much of this in the last several years. The firm began years ago by helping customers purchase General Electric products, but it has now expanded widely and provides diverse services from equipment financing for middle-market firms, to consumer finance, to reinsurance. Relying on a well-coordinated strategic plan, the company sets targets for each of its stand-alone businesses. Overall, GE Capital looks for at least a 20 percent annual return on capital and strong growth. The approach flouts some time-honored traditions as seen by the fact that each business handles its customers independently. So one customer can have multiple relationships with GE Capital.[7] And while this type of strategic planning approach may seem questionable to some, the company has been very successful using it. Revenues have been growing sharply and annual earnings in recent years have been in excess of $5 billion.[8]

Benefits of Strategic Planning

Now that the needs for strategic planning have been explored, what are some of the benefits? Many MNCs are convinced that strategic planning is critical to their success, and these efforts are being conducted both at the home office and in the subsidiaries. For example, one study found that 70 percent of the 56 U.S. MNC subsidiaries in Asia and Latin America had comprehensive 5- to 10-year plans.[9] Others found that U.S., European, and Japanese subsidiaries in Brazil were heavily planning-driven[10] and that Australian manufacturing companies use planning systems that are very similar to those of U.S. manufacturing firms.[11]

Do these strategic planning efforts really pay off? To date, the evidence is mixed. Certainly, that the strategic plan helps an MNC to coordinate and monitor its far-flung operations must be viewed as a benefit. Similarly, that the plan helps an MNC to deal with political risk problems (see Chapter 10), competition, and currency instability cannot be downplayed.

Despite some obvious benefits, there is no definitive evidence that strategic planning in the international arena always results in higher profitability. Most studies that report favorable results were conducted at least a decade ago. Moreover, many of these findings are tempered with contingency-based recommendations. For example, one study found that when decisions were made mainly at the home office and close coordination between the subsidiary and home office was required, return on investment was negatively affected.[12] Simply put, the home office ends up interfering with the subsidiary, and profitability suffers.

Another study found that planning intensity (the degree to which a firm carries out strategic planning) is an important variable in determining performance.[13] Drawing on results from 22 German MNCs representing 71 percent of that country's multinational enterprises, the study found that companies with only a few foreign affiliates performed best with medium planning intensity. Those firms with high planning intensity tended to exaggerate the emphasis, and profitability suffered. Companies that earned a high percentage of their total sales in overseas markets, however, did best with a high-intensity planning process and poorly with a low-intensity process. Therefore, although strategic planning usually seems to pay off, as with most other aspects of international management, the specifics of the situation will dictate the success of the process.

Approaches to Formulating and Implementing Strategy

Four common approaches to strategic planning are: (1) focusing on the economic imperative; (2) addressing the political imperative; (3) emphasizing the quality imperative; and (4) implementing an administrative coordination strategy.

Economic Imperative
A worldwide strategy based on cost leadership, differentiation, and segmentation.

Economic Imperative   MNCs that focus on the **economic imperative** employ a worldwide strategy based on cost leadership, differentiation, and segmentation. Many of these companies typically sell products for which a large portion of value is added in the upstream activities of the industry's value chain. By the time the product is ready to be sold, much of its value has already been created through research and development, manufacturing, and distribution. Some of the industries in this group include automobiles, chemicals, heavy electrical systems, motorcycles, and steel. Because the product is basically homogeneous and requires no alteration to fit the needs of the specific country, management uses a worldwide strategy that is consistent on a country-to-country basis.

The strategy also is used when the product is regarded as a generic good and therefore does not have to be sold based on name brand or support service. A good example is the European PC market. Initially, this market was dominated by such well-known companies as IBM, Apple, and Compaq. However, more recently, clone manufacturers have begun to gain market share. This is because the most influential reasons for buying a PC have changed. A few years ago, the main reasons were brand name, service, and support. Today, price has emerged as a major input into the purchasing decision. Customers now are much more computer literate, and they realize that many PCs offer identical quality performance.

Therefore, it does not pay to purchase a high-priced name brand when a lower-priced clone will do the same things. As a result, the economic imperative dominates the strategic plans of computer manufacturers.

Another economic imperative concept that has gained prominence in recent years is global sourcing, which is proving very useful in formulating and implementing strategy.[14] A good example is provided by the way in which manufacturers are reaching into the supply chain and shortening the buying circle. Li & Fung, Hong Kong's largest export trading company, is one of the world's leading innovators in the development of supply chain management and the company has managed to use its expertise to whittle costs to the bone. Instead of buying fabric and yarn from one company and letting that firm work on keeping its costs as low as possible, for example, Li & Fung gets actively involved in managing the entire process. In the case of how it keeps costs down for orders it receives from The Limited, for example, the chairman of the company has explained the firm's economic imperative strategy this way:

> We come in and look at the whole supply chain. We know The Limited is going to order 100,000 garments, but we don't know the style or the colors yet. The buyer will tell us that five weeks before delivery. The trust between us and our supply network means that we can reserve undyed yarn from the yarn supplier. I can lock up capacity at the mills for the weaving and dying with the promise that they'll get an order of a specified size; five weeks before delivery, we will let them know what colors we want. Then I say the same thing to the factories, "I don't know the product specs yet, but I have organized the colors and the fabric and the trim for you, and they'll be delivered to you on this date and you'll have three weeks to produce so many garments."
>
> I've certainly made life harder for myself now. It would be easier to let the factories worry about securing their own fabric and trim. But then the order would take three months, not five weeks. So to shrink the delivery cycle, I go upstream to organize production. And the shorter production time lets the retailer hold off before having to commit to a fashion trend. It's all about flexibility, response time, small production runs, small minimum-order quantities, and the ability to shift direction as the trends move.[15]

Political Imperative   MNCs using the **political imperative** approach to strategic planning are country-responsive; their approach is designed to protect local market niches. "International Management in Action: Point/Counterpoint" demonstrates this political imperative. The products sold by MNCs often have a large portion of their value added in the downstream activities of the value chain. Industries such as insurance and consumer packaged goods are examples—the success of the product or service generally depends heavily on marketing, sales, and service. Typically, these industries use a country-centered or multidomestic strategy.

A good example of a country-centered strategy is provided by Thums Up, a local drink that Coca-Cola bought from an Indian bottler in 1993. This drink was created back in the 1970s, shortly after Coca-Cola pulled up stakes and left the country. In the ensuing two decades the drink, which is similar in taste to Coke, made major in-roads in the Indian market. But when Coca-Cola returned and bought the company it decided to put Thums Up on the back burner and began pushing its own soft drink. However, local buyers were not interested. They continued to buy Thums Up and Coca-Cola finally relented. Today Thums Up is the firm's biggest seller and fastest growing brand in India, and the company spends more money on this soft drink than it does on any of its other product offerings including Coke.[16] As one observer noted, "In India the 'Real Thing' for Coca-Cola is its Thums Up brand."

Quality Imperative   As Chapter 3 discussed, there has been a quality revolution among both domestic companies and MNCs. This **quality imperative** is taking two interdependent paths: (1) a change in attitudes and a raising of expectation for service quality; and (2) the implementation of management practices that are designed to make quality improvement an ongoing process.[17] Commonly called "total quality management," or simply TQM, the approach takes a wide number of forms, including cross-training personnel to do

Political imperative
Strategic formulation and implementation utilizing strategies that are country-responsive and designed to protect local market niches.

Quality imperative
Strategic formulation and implementation utilizing strategies of total quality management to meet or exceed customers' expectations and continuously improve products and/or services.

International Management in Action

Point/Counterpoint

A good example of the political imperative in action is the ongoing Kodak/Fuji dispute. Kodak has accused Fuji of blocking its growth in the Japanese market. Fuji has responded by arguing that Kodak has long held a monopoly-type position in the United States. This debate began when Kodak complained to the U.S. government and asked for help in further opening the door to the Japanese market. Kodak's argument included the following points:

1. Unlike the United States, film manufacturers in Japan do not sell directly to retailers or photo-finishers but to distributors, and Fuji has close ties with the four dominant distributors. Fuji holds an equity position in two of them and gives all four both rebates and cash payments.

2. Fuji controls 430 Japanese wholesale photofin-ishing labs through ownership, loans, rebates, and other forms of operational support. Additionally, the Japanese government has helped to establish the system to impede Kodak.

3. Kodak has invested $750 million in Japan and garnered less than 10 percent of the market.

4. Fuji uses profits from the Japanese market to subsidize the dumping of its products in other countries, thus effectively reducing Kodak's worldwide market share.

5. The Japanese government has not vigorously enforced antimonopoly legislation, and this has helped Fuji to establish distribution dominance.

These charges are answered by Fuji, which contends that Kodak uses many tactics that prevent Fuji from gaining U.S. market share. These include:

1. Kodak gives U.S. retailers rebates and upfront payments that effectively exclude competitors. For example, Kodak offered Genovese Drug Stores of Glen Cove, NY, $40,000 plus rebates if the company would carry no branded film but Kodak, use only Kodak paper and processing chemicals, and give Kodak 80 percent of the chain's shelfspace allotment for film.

2. Kodak holds 70 percent of the U.S. wholesale photofinishing market through ownership and by giving discounts, advertising dollars, and other investments to land exclusive accounts.

3. Fuji has invested $2 billion in the United States and holds less than 11 percent of the market.

4. Kodak's worldwide operating profit margin over the last two decades is 13 percent, close to Fuji's 15.5 percent.

5. The U.S. government has not vigorously enforced consent decrees that were created to limit Kodak's U.S. marketing practices and ensure that it did not gain an unfair advantage over competitors.

Will the U.S. government prevail in its efforts to help Kodak? Will Fuji be able to make further gains in the U.S. market? What role will political intervention play? These questions are yet to be answered. In the meantime, the two firms continue to compete—and cooperate. Together, they currently are developing a so-called "smart film," which is a new system that offers small cameras and film that can record information to improve the quality of processing. Whatever the outcome of their market-share argument, this strategic cooperative effort likely will continue.

the jobs of all members in their work group, process re-engineering designed to help identify and eliminate redundant tasks and wasteful effort, and reward systems designed to reinforce quality performance.

TQM covers the full gamut, from strategy formulation to implementation. Chapter 3 covered the environment of quality, but as an approach to strategy, TQM briefly can be summarized as follows:

1. Quality is operationalized by meeting or exceeding customer expectations. Customers include not only the buyer or external user of the product or service, but also the support personnel both inside and outside the organization who are associated with the good or service.

2. The quality strategy is formulated at the top management level and is diffused throughout the organization. From top executives to hourly employees, everyone operates under a TQM strategy of delivering quality products and/or services to internal and external customers.

3. The techniques range from traditional inspection and statistical quality control to cutting-edge human resource management techniques, such as self-managing teams and empowerment.[18]

Many MNCs make quality a major part of their overall strategy, because they have learned that this is the way to increase market share and profitability. For example, while the U.S. automakers have dramatically increased their overall quality in recent years to close the gap with Japanese auto quality, Japanese firms continue to have fewer safety recalls. Toyota and Honda continue to be ranked very high by American consumers, and Nissan's recent market performance shows that the firm is also a major competitor in this market.[19]

Another example of firms using quality as an integral part of their strategy is provided by Nortel, the Canadian telecom equipment manufacturer. A few years ago Nortel concluded that there would be a growing demand for optical networking technology to send and retrieve data. Investing heavily in research and development and acquiring companies with the technologies needed to complement these efforts, the company was able to create a reliable and affordable system just in time to meet a huge demand.

> Fiber-optic networks per se are nothing new. Major phone companies like AT&T, WorldCom, and Sprint have been installing fiber for years, mostly across long distances—spanning continents and crossing the ocean floors. . . . But in the past few years the rise of the Internet has created an explosion in data traffic and hence in the demand for bandwidth, or carrying capacity, by the world's telecom companies. Instead of just transporting phone conversations from Tupelo to Topeka, telecom networks are also being used to transmit e-mail, Web pages, and video to multiple locations all over the world. This vast quantity of information eats up enormous amounts of network capacity. So telecoms need to start lighting up all their fiber to handle the burgeoning load.[20]

Today Nortel's high quality system helps account for the fact that by 2001 the firm controlled over 40 percent of the global market for optical equipment. Its nearest competitor, Lucent, had a mere 15 percent share.

Still another example of a firm making quality a major part of its overall strategy is provided by Electrolux, the Swedish appliance maker. The company owns a number of familiar names in the appliance industry including Frigidaire, White Westinghouse, Eureka, and Kelvinator, all of which had been sold because this industry is notorious for low profitability. However, Electrolux has been quite profitable by focusing on the production of high quality products for upper income buyers. An example is refrigerators with wood paneling and computer touch screens. The company also sells lawn mowers, tractors, trimmers, blowers, and chain saws and, in a joint effort with Toshiba, recently introduced a new series of home appliances under the "Electrolux by Toshiba" brand. The firm's profit has been rising sharply and its quality emphasis has paid off very well especially in the North American market which currently accounts for over half of the company's operating income.[21]

At the same time a growing number of MNCs are finding that they must continually revise their strategies and make renewed commitment to the quality imperative because they are being bested by emerging market forces. Motorola, for example, found that its failure to anticipate the industry's switch to digital cell technology was a costly one.[22] In 1998 the company dominated the U.S. handset market and its StarTAC was popular worldwide. Three years later the firm's share of the $129 billion global market for handsets had shrunk from 22 percent to 13 percent and was continuing to fall, while Nokia and Ericsson, in particular, with smaller, lighter, and more versatile offerings were now the dominant players.[23] The lesson is clear: the quality imperative is never ending and MNCs such as Motorola must meet this strategic challenge or pay the price.

Administrative Coordination   An **administrative coordination** approach to formulation and implementation is one in which the MNC makes strategic decisions based on the merits of the individual situation rather than using a predetermined economic or political strategy. A good example is provided by Wal-Mart, which has expanded rapidly into Latin America in recent years. While many of the ideas that worked well in the North American

Administrative coordination
Strategic formulation and implementation in which the MNC makes strategic decisions based on the merits of the individual situation rather than using a predetermined economically or politically driven strategy.

market served as the basis for operations in the southern hemisphere, the company soon realized that it was doing business in a market where local tastes were different and competition was strong.

Wal-Mart is counting on its international operations to grow 25–30 percent annually and Latin American operations are critical to this objective. For the moment, however, the company is reporting losses in Latin America, as it strives to adapt to the local markets. The firm is learning, for example, that the timely delivery of merchandise in places such as Sao Paulo, where there are continual traffic snarls and the company uses contract truckers for delivery, is often far from ideal. Another challenge is finding suppliers who can produce products to Wal-Mart's specification for easy-to-handle packaging and quality control. A third challenge is learning to adapt to the culture. For example, in Brazil Wal-Mart brought in stock-handling equipment that did not work with standardized local pallets. It also installed a computerized bookkeeping system that failed to take into account Brazil's wildly complicated tax system. And the problems do not end here.

> Wal-Mart has also been slow to adapt to Brazil's fast-changing credit culture. Not until last February did the company start accepting postdated checks, which have become the most common form of credit since Brazil stabilized its currency in 1995. Pao de Acucar, whose Extra hypermarkets compete with Wal-Mart, has been taking postdated checks since they first became popular and has installed a sophisticated credit-checking system at its registers. Wal-Mart is hurrying to do so, too.
>
> The six South American Sam's Club locations, the members-only warehouse stores that sell merchandise in bulk, got off to a slow start largely because shoppers weren't used to paying a membership and don't have enough room at home to store bulk purchases. In Argentina, the clubs have faced another barrier: Small business customers are reluctant to sign up for fear Wal-Mart could provide information to tax authorities on their purchases.[24]

Many large MNCs work to combine the economic, political, quality, and administrative approaches to strategic planning. For example, IBM relies on the economic imperative when it has strong market power (especially in less developed countries), the political and quality imperatives when the market requires a calculated response (European countries), and an administrative coordination strategy when rapid, flexible decision making is needed to close the sale. Of the four, however, the first three approaches are much more common because of the firm's desire to coordinate its strategy both regionally and globally.

Strategic Predispositions

In addition to the economic, political, quality, and administrative approaches, most MNCs also have a strategic predisposition toward doing things in a particular way. This orientation or predisposition helps to determine the specific steps the MNC will follow. Four distinct predispositions have been identified: ethnocentric, polycentric, regiocentric, and geocentric.

A company with an **ethnocentric predisposition** allows the values and interests of the parent company to guide the strategic decisions. Firms with a **polycentric predisposition** make strategic decisions tailored to suit the cultures of the countries where the MNC operates. A **regiocentric predisposition** leads a firm to try to blend its own interests with those of its subsidiaries on a regional basis. A company with a **geocentric predisposition** tries to integrate a global systems approach to decision making. Table 9–1 provides details of each of these orientations.

If an MNC relies on one of these profiles over an extended time, the approach may become institutionalized and greatly influence strategic planning. By the same token, a predisposition toward any of these profiles can provide problems for a firm if it is out of step with the economic or political environment. For example, a firm with an ethnocentric predisposition may find it difficult to implement a geocentric strategy, because it is unaccustomed to using global integration. Commonly, successful MNCs use a mix of these predispositions based on the demands of the current environment described in the chapters in Part One.

Ethnocentric predisposition
A nationalistic philosophy of management whereby the values and interests of the parent company guide the strategic decisions.

Polycentric predisposition
A philosophy of management whereby strategic decisions are tailored to suit the cultures of the countries where the MNC operates.

Regiocentric predisposition
A philosophy of management whereby the firm tries to blend its own interests with those of its subsidiaries on a regional basis.

Geocentric predisposition
A philosophy of management whereby the company tries to integrate a global systems approach to decision making.

Table 9–1
Orientation of an MNC under Different Profiles

	Orientation of the Firm			
	Ethnocentric	**Polycentric**	**Regiocentric**	**Geocentric**
Mission	Profitability (viability)	Public acceptance (legitimacy)	Both profitability and public acceptance (viability and legitimacy)	Same as regiocentric
Governance	Top-down	Bottom-up (each subsidiary decides on local objectives)	Mutually negotiated between region and its subsidiaries	Mutually negotiated at all levels of the corporation
Strategy	Global integration	National responsiveness	Regional integration and national responsiveness	Global integration and national responsiveness
Structure	Hierarchical product divisions	Hierarchical area divisions, with autonomous national units	Product and regional organization tied through a matrix	A network of organizations (including some stakeholders and competitor organizations)
Culture	Home country	Host country	Regional	Global
Technology	Mass production	Batch production	Flexible manufacturing	Flexible manufacturing
Marketing	Product development determined primarily by the needs of home country customers	Local product development based on local needs	Standardize within region, but not across regions	Global product, with local variations
Finance	Repatriation of profits to home country	Retention of profits in host country	Redistribution within region	Redistribution globally
Personnel practices	People of home country developed for key positions everywhere in the world	People of local nationality developed for key positions in their own country	Regional people developed for key positions anywhere in the region	Best people everywhere in the world developed for key positions everywhere in the world

Source: Adapted from Balaji S. Chakravarthy and Howard V. Perlmutter, "Strategic Planning for a Global Business," *Columbia Journal of World Business,* Summer 1985, pp. 5–6. Copyright 1985, Columbia Journal of World Business. Used with permission.

■ The Basic Steps in Formulating Strategy

The needs, benefits, approaches, and predispositions of strategic planning serve as a point of departure for the basic steps in formulating strategy. In international management, strategic planning can be broken into the following steps: (1) scanning the external environment for opportunities and threats; (2) conducting an internal resource analysis of company strengths and weaknesses; and (3) formulating goals in light of the external scanning and internal analysis. These steps are graphically summarized in Figure 9–1. The following sections discuss each step in detail.

Environmental Scanning

Environmental scanning attempts to provide management with accurate forecasts of trends that relate to external changes in geographic areas where the firm is currently doing business and/or considering setting up operations. These changes relate to the economy, competition, political stability, technology, and demographic consumer data.

Typically, the MNC will begin by conducting a forecast of macroeconomic and industry performance dealing with factors such as markets for specific products, per-capita income of the population, and availability of labor and raw materials. A second common forecast will predict likely trends in monetary exchange rates, exchange controls, balance of payments, and inflation rates. A third is the forecast of the company's potential market

Environmental scanning
The process of providing management with accurate forecasts of trends related to external changes in geographic areas where the firm currently is doing business and/or is considering setting up operations.

Figure 9–1

Basic Elements of Strategic Planning for International Management

share in a particular geographic area as well as that of the competitors. Other considerations include political stability, government pressure, nationalism, and related areas of political risk. These assessments are extremely important in determining the risk profile and profit potential of the region, which always is a major consideration when deciding where to set up international operations.

OpenTV Inc. provides an example of how this environmental scanning process works. The firm analyzed the environment in China and concluded that the market in Shanghai was ideal for its software. As a result, it signed a deal with Shanghai Cable Network to provide this company with "middle ware." When this software is installed in a subscriber's set-top box, it allows the user to interact with the television and do a number of different things from shopping on line to ordering a movie for viewing. Shanghai Cable has over three million customers and one-third of them have broadband cable that lets them access the Internet and interact with television programs in what industry analysts say is one of the world's most advanced cable systems. If OpenTV's scan of the environment is correct, this business arrangement will help the firm become extremely profitable.[25] Another example of the effects of environmental scanning is Microsoft's recent purchase of 60 percent of Japan's second largest cable firm, Titus Communication. After analyzing the environment, Microsoft concluded that there is going to be a shift to high-speed broadband services and it needs to have this technological capability in order to provide its customers with state-of-the-art services.[26] As a result, Microsoft made the decision to take an ownership position in Titus Communication.

Many other firms also have profited from astute environmental scanning. For example, Alcatel Alsthom of France made a series of clever acquisitions and alliances and now is the world's largest telephone equipment company. This has put Alcatel in an ideal position to garner market share in the rapidly growing telecommunications market.

Internal Resource Analysis

When formulating strategy, some firms wait until they have completed their environmental scanning before conducting an internal resource analysis. Others perform these two steps simultaneously. Internal resource analysis helps the firm to evaluate its current managerial, technical, material, and financial strengths and weaknesses. This assessment then is used by the MNC to determine its ability to take advantage of international market opportunities. The primary thrust of this analysis is to match external opportunities (gained through the environmental scan) with internal capabilities (gained through the internal resource analysis).

Key factor for success (KFS)

A factor necessary for a firm to effectively compete in a market niche.

An internal analysis identifies the key factors for success that will dictate how well the firm is likely to do. A **key factor for success (KFS)** is a factor that is necessary for a firm to compete effectively in a market niche. For example, a KFS for an international airline is price. An airline that discounts its prices will gain market share vis-à-vis those that do not. A second KFS for the airline is safety, and a third is quality service in terms of on-time departures and arrivals, convenient schedules, and friendly, helpful personnel. In the automobile industry, quality of products has emerged as the number-one KFS in world markets. Japanese firms have been able to invade the U.S. auto market successfully, because they have been able to prove that the quality of their cars is better than the average domestically built U.S. car. Toyota and Honda have had such a quality edge over the competition in recent years in the eyes of U.S. car buyers. A second KFS is styling. The redesigned VW Beetle has been successful because customers like its looks.

The key question for the management of an MNC is: Do we have the people and resources that can help us to develop and sustain the necessary KFSs, or can we acquire them? If the answer is yes, the recommendation would be to proceed. If the answer is no, management would begin looking at other markets where it has, or can develop, the necessary KFSs.

Goal Setting for Strategy Formulation

In practice goal formulation often precedes the first two steps of environmental scanning and internal resource analysis. As used here, however, the more specific goals for the strategic plan come out of external scanning and internal analysis. MNCs pursue a variety of such goals; Table 9–2 provides a list of the most common ones. These goals typically serve as an umbrella beneath which the subsidiaries and other international groups operate.

Profitability and marketing goals almost always dominate the strategic plans of today's MNCs. Profitability, as shown in Table 9–2, is so important because MNCs generally need higher profitability from their overseas operation than they do from their domestic operations. The reason is quite simple: Setting up overseas operations involves greater

---

Table 9–2
Areas for Formulation of MNC Goals

Profitability

Level of profits
Return on assets, investment, equity, sales
Yearly profit growth
Yearly earnings per share growth

Marketing

Total sales volume
Market share—worldwide, region, country
Growth in sales volume
Growth in market share
Integration of country markets for marketing efficiency and effectiveness

Operations

Ratio of foreign to domestic production volume
Economies of scale via international production integration
Quality and cost control
Introduction of cost-efficient production methods

Finance

Financing of foreign affiliates—retained earnings or local borrowing
Taxation—minimizing tax burden globally
Optimum capital structure
Foreign exchange management—minimizing losses from foreign fluctuations

Human Resources

Recruitment and selection
Development of managers with global orientation
Management development of host-country nationals
Compensation and benefits

risk and effort. In addition, a firm that has done well domestically with a product or serv-ice usually has done so because the competition is minimal or ineffective. Firms with this advantage often find additional lucrative opportunities outside their borders. Moreover, the more successful a firm is domestically, the more difficult it is to increase market share without strong competitive response. International markets, however, offer an ideal alter-native to the desire for increased growth and profitability.

Another reason that profitability and marketing top the list is that these tend to be more externally environmentally responsive, whereas production, finance, and personnel functions tend to be more internally controlled. Thus, for strategic planning, profitability and marketing goals are given higher importance and warrant closer attention. Ford's European operations offer an example. In recent years the auto maker has been losing mar-ket share in the EU. In an effort to turn things around, the MNC scaled back production capacity and announced that it intends to push market share above 10 percent, reversing a trend that has seen its slice of the European auto pie drop from almost 12 percent in the 1980s to just over 8 percent recently.[27] In order to reach this objective, Ford has closed plants, cut its European workforce, and transferred vehicle production to more efficient factories. Now after cutting costs the company is launching a proactive strategy to increase market share.[28] Ford in Europe is working to create a fresh image by offering new models, designing a totally revised advertising campaign, and developing a revised dealership net-work. Given that Ford earns approximately $30 billion of revenue in Europe and makes less than 1 percent profit there, the company needs to grow this market share or face becoming a minor player in the EU auto industry. Whether Ford can go back to 12 percent of this market is questionable, but top management believes a goal of 10 percent is both realistic and necessary.

Once the strategic goals are set, the MNC will develop specific operational goals and controls, usually through a two-way process at the subsidiary or affiliate level (organiza-tion is covered in Chapter 12). Home office management will set certain parameters, and the overseas group will operate within these guidelines. For example, the MNC headquar-ters may require periodic financial reports, restrict on-site decisions to matters involving less than $100,000, and require that all client contracts be cleared through the home office. These guidelines are designed to ensure that the overseas group's activities support the goals in the strategic plan and that all units operate in a coordinated effort.

■ Strategy Implementation

Strategy implementation
The process of providing goods and services in accord with a plan of action.

Once formulated, the strategic plan next must be implemented. **Strategy implementation** provides goods and services in accord with a plan of action. Quite often, this plan will have an overall philosophy or series of guidelines that direct the process. In the case of Japanese electronic-manufacturing firms entering the U.S. market, Chang has found a common approach:

> To reduce the risk of failure, these firms are entering their core businesses and those in which they have stronger competitive advantages over local firms first. The learning from early entry enables firms to launch further entry into areas in which they have the next strongest competi-tive advantages. As learning accumulates, firms may overcome the disadvantages intrinsic to foreignness. Although primary learning takes place within firms through learning by doing, they may also learn from other firms through the transfer or diffusion of experience. This process is not automatic, however, and it may be enhanced by membership in a corporate net-work: in firms associated with either horizontal or vertical business groups were more likely to initiate entries than independent firms. By learning from their own sequential entry experience as well as from other firms in corporated networks, firms build capabilities in foreign entry.[29]

International management must consider three general areas in strategy implementa-tion. First, the MNC must decide where to locate operations. Second, the MNC must carry out entry and ownership strategies. Finally, management must implement functional strate-gies in areas such as marketing, production, and finance.

Location Considerations for Implementation

In choosing a location, today's MNC has two primary considerations: the country, and the specific locale within the chosen country. Quite often, the first choice is easier than the second, because there are many more alternatives from which to choose a specific locale.

The Country   Traditionally, MNCs have invested in highly industrialized countries and research reveals that annual investments have been increasing substantially. In 1993 over $325 billion was spent on mergers and acquisitions worldwide. By 1997 the annual total had jumped to $1.6 trillion[30] and today it is well in excess of $2 billion. Much of this investment, especially by American MNCs, has been in Europe, Canada, and Mexico.

In the case of Japan, multinational banks and investors from around the world have been looking for properties that are being jettisoned by Japanese banks that are trying to unload some of their distressed loans. The Japanese commercial property market collapsed starting in the mid-1990s, creating many opportunities for investors. One was U.S.-based MNC Bankers Trust which bought a large plot of properties of a failed affiliate of Nippon Credit Bank Ltd. Bankers Trust paid $220 million for properties that had a face value of $2.2 billion.[31] Nonbanking MNCs are also actively engaged in mergers and acquisitions in Japan. Intuit Inc. of Menlo Park, California purchased a financial software specialist in Japan for $52 million in stock and spent $30 million for the Nihon Mikon Company, which sells small business accounting software. These purchases point to a new trend in Japan— the acquisition of small firms. However, many larger purchases have also been made, as seen in Table 9–3.

Foreign investors are also pouring into Mexico.[32] One reason is because it is a gateway to the American and Canadian markets. A second reason is because Mexico is a very cost effective place in which to manufacture goods. A third is that the declining value of the peso in the late 1990s hit many Mexican businesses hard and left them vulnerable to mergers and acquisitions—an opportunity that was not lost on many large multinationals.

> Britain's B.A.T. Industries PLC took control of Cigarrera La Moderna, Mexico's tobacco giant, in a $1.5 billion deal. A few days earlier, Philip Morris Cos. increased its stake in the second-largest tobacco company, Cigarros La Tabacalera Mexicana SA, to 50% from about 29% for $400 million. In June, Wal-Mart Stores Inc., announced plans to acquire control of Mexico's largest retailer, Cifra SA, in a deal valued at more than $1 billion. In July, Procter & Gamble Co. acquired a consumer-products concern, Loreto y Pena Pobre, for $170 million. Bell Atlantic Co. has acquired full control of its cellular-phone partner, Grupo Iusacell SA, with total investments of more than $1 billion. The list goes on and on and is expected to keep growing.[33]

MNCs often invest in advanced industrialized countries because they offer the largest markets for goods and services. In addition, the established country or geographic locale may have legal restrictions related to imports, encouraging a local presence. Japanese firms, for example, in complying with their voluntary export quotas of cars to the United States as

Table 9–3 **Representative MNC Acquisitions in Japan**	
Glaxo Wellcome	Has purchased the remaining 50 percent of its Nippon Glaxo affiliate for $537 million.
Ford Motor	Has picked up an additional 9 percent of Mazda, bringing its stake to 33.4 percent, for $430 million.
BASF	The German drugmaker has purchased 51 percent of Hokuriku Seiyaku for $294 million.
Grande Group	The Singapore firm has acquired 70 percent of Nakamichi for $286 million.
GE Capital	Has bought 80 percent of Narubeni Car System, an auto-loan business, for $80 million.
Semi-Tech Group	The Hong Kong high-tech company has put out $167 million for an additional 11 percent of Akai Electric.
Boehringer Ingelheim	The German firm acquired 9 percent of SS Pharmaceutical for $71 million.
Amersham International	The British drug maker acquired 30 percent of Nihon Mediphysics for $76 million.

well as responding to dissatisfaction in Washington regarding the continuing trade imbalance with the United States, have established U.S.-based assembly plants. In Europe, because of EU regulations for outsiders, most U.S. and Japanese MNCs have operations in at least one European country, thus ensuring access to the European community at large. In fact, the huge U.S. MNC ITT now operates in each of the original 12 EU countries.

Another consideration in choosing a country is the amount of government control. Traditionally, MNCs from around the world refused to do business in Eastern European countries with central planning economies. The recent relaxing of the trade rules and move toward free market economies in the republics of the former Soviet Union and the other Eastern European nations, however, have encouraged MNCs to rethink their positions; more and more are making moves into this largely untapped part of the global market. The same is true in India, although the political climate can be volatile and MNCs must carefully weigh the risks of investing here.

Still another consideration in selecting a country is restrictions on foreign investment. Traditionally, countries such as China and India have required that control of the operation be in the hands of local partners. MNCs that are reluctant to accept such conditions will not establish operations there.

In addition to these considerations, MNCs will examine the specific benefits offered by host countries, including low tax rates, rent-free land and buildings, low-interest or no-interest loans, subsidized energy and transportation rates, and a well-developed infrastructure that provides many of the services found back home (good roads, communication systems, schools, health care, entertainment, and housing). These benefits will be weighed against any disincentives or performance requirements that must be met by the MNC, such as job-creation quotas, export minimums for generating foreign currency, limits on local market growth, labor regulations, wage and price controls, restrictions on profit repatriation, and controls on the transfer of technology.

Commenting on the overall effect of these potential gains and losses, Garland and Farmer noted:

> These incentives and disincentives often make operations abroad less amenable to integration on a global basis; essentially they may alter a company's strategy for the region. They affect, for example, a firm's make-or-buy decision, intracorporate transfer policies (e.g., between subsidiaries or between headquarters and the subsidiaries), both horizontal and vertical sourcing arrangements, and so on. In effect, they weaken the MNC's mandate for global efficiency by encouraging the firm to suboptimize.[34]

Local Issues   Once the MNC has decided the country in which to locate the firm must choose the specific locale. A number of factors influence this choice. Common considerations include access to markets, proximity to competitors, availability of transportation and electric power, and desirability of the location for employees coming in from the outside.

One study found that in selecting U.S. sites, both German and Japanese firms place more importance on accessibility and desirability and less importance on financial considerations.[35] However, financial matters remain important: Many countries attempt to lure MNCs to specific locales by offering special financial packages.

Another common consideration is the nature of the workforce. MNCs prefer to locate near sources of available labor that can be readily trained to do the work. A complementary consideration that often is unspoken is the presence and strength of organized labor (Chapter 17 covers this topic in detail). Japanese firms in particular tend to avoid heavily unionized areas.

Still another consideration is the cost of doing business. Manufacturers often set up operations in rural areas, commonly called "green field locations," which are much less expensive and do not have the problems of urban areas. Conversely, banks often choose metropolitan areas, because they feel they must have a presence in the business district.

Some MNCs opt for locales where the cost of running a small enterprise is significantly lower than that of running a large one. In this way, they spread their risk, setting up many small locations throughout the world rather than one or two large ones. Manufacturing firms are a good example. Some production firms feel that the economies of scale associated with a large-scale plant are more than offset by potential problems that can result should economic or political difficulties develop in the country. These firms' strategy is to spread the risk by opting for a series of small plants throughout a wide geographic region.[36] This location strategy can also be beneficial for stockholders. Research has found that MNCs with a presence in developing countries have significantly higher market values than MNCs that operate only in countries that have advanced economies.[37]

Ownership and Entry Considerations for Implementation

There are a number of common forms of ownership in international operations. Figure 9–2 reports some of the latest information regarding global expansion strategies in select world markets. Depending on the region of the world, some approaches are more popular than others. For example, as shown, in Australia and New Zealand alliances and the expansion of facilities are common approaches, while in China joint ventures are widely used

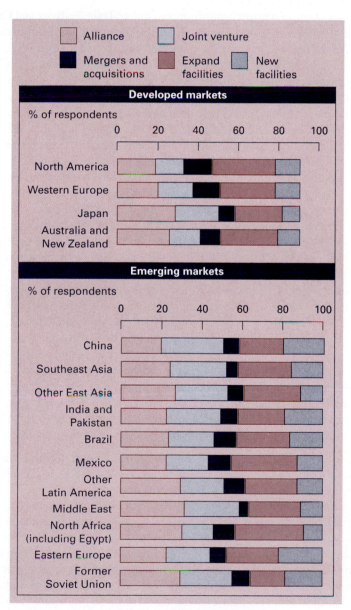

Figure 9–2

Preferred Strategies for Global Expansion

Source: Reported in the *Economist,* April 11, 1998, p. 82.

(although in recent years the Chinese have been reversing its trend toward more open markets and limiting joint ventures in some areas such as between foreign companies and Chinese telecom firms).[38] However, the most widely recognized are wholly owned subsidiaries acquired through acquisitions and alliances/mergers, joint ventures, licensing agreements, franchising, and basic export and import operations. Depending on the situation, any one of these can be a very effective way to implement an MNC's strategy.

Wholly owned subsidiary
An overseas operation that is totally owned and controlled by an MNC.

Wholly Owned Subsidiary   A **wholly owned subsidiary** is an overseas operation that is totally owned and controlled by an MNC. In recent years a growing number of multinationals have acquired (fully own) their subsidiaries through alliances or mergers. One of the largest, in terms of acquisition price, was the British Petroleum (BP) Company's recent purchase of Amoco for $48.2 billion.[39] The merger made BP Amoco one of the biggest oil producers in the United States with operations in Alaska, the Gulf of Mexico, and parts of the 48 contiguous states. Additionally, both BP and Amoco have petrochemical operations which are among the largest in the world. The next few years should see the emergence of a strategic plan that will streamline BP Amoco operations and, if all goes well, make it one of the most profitable oil firms in the world.

Another example of a major acquisition was that of Daimler-Benz and Chrysler, now called DaimlerChrysler. In a deal valued at $39 billion, the German automaker bought Chrysler and, in the process, gained a lucrative North American market, while opening the door in Europe for a Chrysler expansion. The strategic plan of the merged companies calls for each to contribute a series of strengths toward making the firm a highly competitive operation. In particular, Daimler-Benz has luxury cars, heavy-duty trucks, modern V8 engines and diesel technology, and classic designs that are recognized worldwide. Chrysler has minivans, sports utility vehicles, pickup trucks, small cars, and niche vehicles such as the Dodge Viper sports car. Each also has complementary expertise that can be of value to the other. Daimler-Benz has advanced research into fuel cells, intelligent highway guidance systems, and a host of safety features that include skid control and protection of passengers in the case of a crash. Chrysler has new auto technologies, the ability to bring new models to market in under 24 months, and the ability to create new markets by developing innovative designs that exploit gaps in rival car offerings.[40] The challenge for Daimler-Chrysler is to make the merger an effective reality for the two firms. In the last few years Chrysler has suffered severe losses in North America and Daimler's management has come under severe scrutiny by both stockholders and analysts.[41]

The primary reason for the use of fully owned subsidiaries is a desire by the MNC for total control and the belief that managerial efficiency will be better without outside partners. Host countries, however, often feel that the MNC is trying to gain economic control by setting up local operations but refusing to take in local partners. Some countries are concerned that the MNC will drive out local enterprises. In dealing with these concerns, many newly developing countries prohibit fully owned subsidiaries. A second drawback is that home country unions sometimes oppose the creation of foreign subsidiaries, which they see as an attempt to "export jobs," particularly when the MNC exports goods to another country and then decides to set up manufacturing operations there. As a result, today many multinationals opt for a joint venture rather than a fully owned subsidiary.[42]

Joint venture
An agreement in which two or more partners own and control an overseas business.

Joint Venture   As it relates to international operations, a **joint venture** is an agreement in which two or more partners own and control an overseas business. This business typically is located in the home country of one of the partners.

There are two types of joint ventures. The least common is the *nonequity venture,* which is characterized by one group's merely providing a service for another. The group providing the service typically is more active than the other. Examples include a consulting firm that is hired to provide analysis and evaluation and then make its recommendations to the other party, an engineering or construction firm that contracts to design or build a dam or series of apartment complexes in an undeveloped area of a partner's country, or a mining firm that has an agreement to extract a natural resource in the other party's country.

The more common arrangement is the *equity joint venture,* which involves a financial investment by the MNC in a business enterprise with a local partner. Many variations of this arrangement adjust the degree of control that each of the parties will have and the amount of money, technological expertise, and managerial expertise each will contribute.[43]

Most foreign firms are more interested in the amount of control they will have over the venture than in their share of the profits. Many local partners feel the same way, and this can result in problems. Nevertheless, joint ventures have become very popular in recent years because of the benefits they offer to both parties. Some of the most commonly cited advantages include:

1. *Improvement of efficiency.* The creation of a joint venture can help the partners achieve greater economies of scale and scope, something which can be difficult to accomplish by one firm operating alone. Additionally, the partners can spread the risks among themselves and profit from the synergies which arise from the complementarity of their resources.[44]

2. *Access to knowledge.* In joint ventures each partner has access to the knowledge and skills of the others. So one partner may bring financial and technological resources to the venture while another will bring a knowledge of the customer and market channels.

3. *Political factors.* A local partner can be very helpful in dealing with political risk factors such as a hostile government and/or restrictive legislation.

4. *Collusion or restriction in competition.* Joint ventures can help partners overcome the effects of local collusion or limits that are being put on foreign competition. By becoming part of an "insider" group, foreign partners manage to transcend these barriers.[45]

As noted above, joint venture partners often complement each other and can thus reduce the risks associated with their undertaking. A good example is European truck manufacturing and auto component industries. Firms in both groups have found that the high cost of developing and building their products can be offset through joint ventures. In particular, some partners to these ventures have contributed financial assistance while others provide the distribution networks needed to move the product through channels. Another recent example is Alcatel and Fujitsu that have formed a joint venture to develop third-generation cellular equipment.[46]

Although much negotiation may be necessary before a joint-venture agreement is hammered out, the final result must be one that both sides can accept.[47] Many successful examples of such agreements have emerged in recent years. One of the most complex was the General Motors–Toyota agreement, which involved scores of groups and thousands of individuals. Other examples include General Motors' venture with the Polish government to build Opels in that country, L. L. Bean's decision to sell clothing and equipment under a joint-venture agreement with two Japanese companies in Tokyo, Occidental Petroleum's joint venture in a northern China coal mining project, and Sony and America Online's joint venture for linking Sony's PlayStation 2 video game machine to the Internet.[48]

Joint ventures are proving to be particularly popular as a means for doing business in emerging market economies. For example, in the early 1990s, foreigners had signed more than 3,000 joint-venture agreements in Eastern Europe and the former republics of the Soviet Union, and interest remains high today. Careful analysis must be undertaken to ensure that the market for the desired goods and services is sufficiently large and that all parties understand their responsibilities, and that all are in agreement regarding the overall operation of the venture. If these problems can be resolved, the venture stands a good chance of success. The accompanying box, "Joint Venturing in Russia," illustrates some of the problems that need to be overcome for a joint venture to be successful. Some of the other suggestions that have been offered by researchers regarding participation in strategic alliances include:

1. Know your partners well before an alliance is formed.

2. Expect differences in alliance objectives among potential partners headquartered in different countries.

International Management in Action

Joint Venturing in Russia   www.russiatoday.com

Joint venturing is becoming an increasingly popular strategy for setting up international operations. Russia is particularly interested in these arrangements because of the benefits they offer for attracting foreign capital and helping the country tap its natural resource wealth. However, investors are finding that joint venturing in Russia and the other republics of the former Soviet Union can be fraught with problems. For example, Chevron, which has agreed to invest $10 billion over the next 25 years in developing the Tengiz oil field in Kazakhstan, found itself having to renegotiate the contract and drop its share of profits from 28 percent to under 20 percent. This became necessary because the original contract was negotiated with the Soviet Union under then President Mikhail Gorbachev; after the breakup, the new government was unwilling to abide by the previous terms. Renegotiation is not the only problem facing joint-venture investors in Russia. Others include the following:

1. Many Russian partners view a joint venture as an opportunity to travel abroad and gain access to foreign currency; the business itself often is given secondary consideration.

2. Finding a suitable partner, negotiating the deal, and registering the joint venture often take up to a year, mainly because the Russians are unaccustomed to some of the basic steps in putting together business deals.

3. Russian partners typically try to expand joint ventures into unrelated activities, while foreign investors are more prone to minimizing risk and not overextending operations by getting into new areas.

4. Russians do not like to declare profits, because there is a 2-year tax holiday on profits that starts from the moment the first profits are declared. Foreign partners, on the other hand, are not influenced by this fact and often point out that because taxes must be paid in rubles, which have very little value, taxes are not a problem.

5. The government sometimes allows profits to be repatriated in the form of countertrade. However, much of what can be taken out of the country has limited value, because the government keeps control of those resources that are most salable in the world market.

These representative problems indicate why there is a growing reluctance on the part of some MNCs to enter into joint ventures in Russia. As one of them recently put it, "The country may well turn into an economic sink hole." As a result, many MNCs are very reluctant and are proceeding with caution.

---

3. Realize that having the desired resource profiles does not guarantee that they are complementary to your firm's resources.

4. Be sensitive to your alliance partner's needs.

5. After identifying the best partner, work on developing a relationship that is built on trust.[49]

License

An agreement that allows one party to use an industrial property right in exchange for payment to the other party.

Licensing   Another way to gain market entry is to acquire the right to a particular product by getting an exclusive license to make and/or sell the good in a particular geographic locale. A **license** is an agreement that allows one party to use an industrial property right in exchange for payment to the other party. In a typical arrangement, the party giving the license (the licensor) will allow the other (the licensee) to use a patent, trademark, or proprietary information in exchange for a fee. The fee usually is based on sales, such as 1 percent of all revenues earned from an industrial motor sold in Asia. The licensor typically restricts licensee sales to a particular geographic locale and limits the time period covered by the arrangement. Therefore, the firm in this example may have an exclusive right to sell this patented motor in Asia for the next 5 years. This allows the licensor to seek licensees for other major geographic locales, such as Europe, South America, and Australia.

Licensing is used under a number of common conditions. For example, the product typically is in the mature stage of the product life cycle, competition is strong, and profit margins are declining. Under these conditions, the licensor is unlikely to want to spend money to enter foreign markets. However, if the company can find an MNC that is already there and willing to add the product to its own current offerings, both sides can benefit from the arrangement. A second common instance of licensing is when foreign governments require newly entering firms to make a substantial direct investment in the country. By licensing to a firm already there, the licensee avoids entry costs. A third common condition is that the licensor usually is a small firm that lacks financial and managerial resources. Finally, companies that spend a relatively large share of their revenues on research and development (R&D) are likely to be licensors, and those who spend very little on R&D are more likely to be licensees. In fact, some small R&D firms make a handsome profit every year by developing and licensing new products to large firms with diversified product lines.

Some licensors use their industrial property rights to develop and sell goods in certain areas of the world and license others to handle other geographic locales. This provides the licensor with a source of additional revenues, but the license usually is not good for much more than a decade. This is a major disadvantage of licensing. In particular, if the product is very good, the competition will develop improvement patents that allow it to sell similar goods or even new patents that make the current product obsolete. Nevertheless, for the period during which the agreement is in effect, a license can be a very low-cost way of gaining and exploiting foreign markets. Table 9–4 provides some comparisons between licensing and joint ventures and summarizes the major advantages and disadvantages of each.

Franchising A **franchise** is a business arrangement under which one party (the franchisor) allows another (the franchisee) to operate an enterprise using its trademark, logo, product line, and methods of operation in return for a fee. Franchising is widely used in the fast-food and hotel/motel industries. The concept is very adaptable to the international arena, and with some minor adjustments for the local market, it can result in a highly profitable business. In fast foods, McDonald's, Burger King, and Kentucky Fried Chicken have used franchise arrangements to expand their markets from Paris to Tokyo and from Cairo to Caracas. In the hotel business, Holiday Inn, among others, has been very successful in gaining worldwide presence through the effective use of franchisees.

Franchise agreements typically require payment of a fee up front and then a percentage of the revenues. In return, the franchisor provides assistance and, in some instances, may require the purchase of goods or supplies to ensure the same quality of goods or services worldwide. Franchising can be beneficial to both groups: It provides the franchisor with a new stream of income and the franchisee with a time-proven concept and products or services that can be quickly brought to market.

Export/Import Exporting or importing often are the only available choices for small firms wanting to go international.[50] These choices also provide an avenue for larger firms that want to begin their international expansion with a minimum of investment. The paperwork associated with documentation and foreign-currency exchange can be turned over to an export management company to handle, or the firm can handle things itself by creating its own export department. The firm can turn to major banks or other specialists who, for a fee, will provide a variety of services, including letters of credit, currency conversion, and related financial assistance.

A number of potential problems face firms that plan to export. For example, if a foreign distributor does not work out well, some countries have strict rules about dropping that distributor. So an MNC with a contractual agreement with the distributor could be stuck with the distributor. If the firm decides to get more actively involved, it may make direct investments in marketing facilities, such as warehouses, sales offices, and transportation equipment, without making a direct investment in manufacturing facilities overseas.

When importing goods, many MNCs make deals with overseas suppliers who can provide a wide assortment. It is common to find U.S. firms purchasing supplies and components from Korea, Taiwan, and Hong Kong. In Europe, there is so much trade between EU countries that the entire process seldom is regarded as "international" in focus by the MNCs that are involved.

Exporting and importing can provide easy access to overseas markets; however, the strategy usually is transitional in nature. If the firm continues to do international business, it will get more actively involved in terms of investment.

Franchise
A business arrangement under which one party (the franchisor) allows another (the franchisee) to operate an enterprise using its trademark, logo, product line, and methods of operation in return for a fee.

Table 9–4
Partial Comparison of Global Strategic Alliances

Strategy	Organization Design	Advantages	Disadvantages	Critical Success Factors	Strategic Human Resources Management
Licensing—manufacturing industries	Technologies	Early standardization of design Ability to capitalize on innovations Access to new technologies Ability to control pace of industry evolution	New competitors created Possible eventual exit from industry Possible dependence on licensee	Selection of licensee unlikely to become a competitor Enforcement of patents and licensing agreements	Technical knowledge Training of local managers on-site
Licensing—servicing and franchises	Geography	Fast market entry Low capital cost	Quality control Trademark protection	Partners compatible in philosophies/values Tight performance standards	Socialization of franchisees and licensees with core values
Joint ventures—specialization across partners	Function	Learning a partner's skills Economics of scale Quasivertical integration Faster learning	Excessive dependence on partner for skills Deterrent to internal investment	Tight and specific performance criteria Entering a venture as "student" rather than "teacher" to learn skills from partner Recognizing that collaboration is another form of competition to learn new skills	Management development and training Negotiation skills Managerial rotation
Joint venture—shared value-adding	Product or line of business	Strengths of both partners pooled Faster learning along value chain Fast upgrading of technologic skills	High switching costs Inability to limit partner's access to information	Decentralization and autonomy from corporate parents Long "courtship" period Harmonization of management styles	Team-building Acculturation Flexible skills for implicit communication

Source: David Lei and John W. Slocum, Jr., "Global Strategic Alliances: Payoffs and Pitfalls," *Organizational Dynamics,* Winter 1991, p. 48. Used with permission.

The Role of the Functional Areas in Implementation

To implement strategies, MNCs must tap the primary functional areas of marketing, production, and finance. The following sections examine the roles of these functions in international strategy implementation.

Marketing   The implementation of strategy from a marketing perspective must be determined on a country-by-country basis. What works from the standpoint of marketing in one locale may not necessarily succeed in another. In addition, the specific steps of a marketing approach often are dictated by the overall strategic plan, which in turn is based heavily on market analysis.

German auto firms in Japan are a good example of using marketing analysis to meet customer needs. Over the past 15 years, the Germans have spent millions of dollars to build dealer, supplier, and service-support networks in Japan, in addition to adapting their cars to Japanese customers' tastes. Volkswagen Audi Nippon has built a $320-million import facility on a deep-water port. This operation, which includes an inspection center and parts warehouse, can process 100,000 cars a year. Mercedes and BMW both have introduced lower-priced cars to attract a larger market segment, and BMW now offers a flat-fee, 3-year service contract on any new car, including parts. At the same time, German manufacturers work hard to offer first-class service in their dealerships. As a result, German automakers in recent years sell almost three times as many cars in Japan as their U.S. competitors do.

The Japanese also provide an excellent example of how the marketing process works. In many cases, Japanese firms have followed a strategy of first building up their market share at home and driving out imported goods. Then, the firms move into newly developed countries, honing their marketing skills as they go along. Finally, the firms move into fully developed countries, ready to compete with the best available. This pattern of implementing strategy has been used in marketing autos, cameras, consumer electronics, home appliances, petrochemicals, steel, and watches. For some products, however, such as computers, the Japanese have moved from their home market directly into fully developed countries and then on to the newly developing nations. Finally, the Japanese have gone directly to developed countries to market products in some cases, because the market in Japan was too small. Such products include color TVs, videotape recorders, and sewing machines. In general, once a firm agrees on the goods it wants to sell in the international marketplace, then the specific marketing strategy is implemented.

The implementation of marketing strategy in the international arena is built around the well-known "four Ps" of marketing: product, price, promotion, and place. As noted in the example of the Japanese, firms often develop and sell a product in local or peripheral markets before expanding to major overseas targets. If the product is designed specifically to meet an overseas demand, however, the process is more direct. Price largely is a function of market demand.[51] For example, the Japanese have found that the U.S. microcomputer market is price-sensitive; by introducing lower-priced clones, the Japanese have been able to make headway, especially in the portable laptop market. The last two Ps, promotion and place, are dictated by local conditions and often left in the hands of those running the subsidiary or affiliate. Local management may implement customer sales incentives, for example, or make arrangements with dealers and salespeople who are helping to move the product locally.

Production   Although marketing usually dominates strategy implementation, the production function also plays a role. If a company is going to export goods to a foreign market, the production process traditionally has been handled through domestic operations. In recent years, however, MNCs have found that whether they are exporting or producing the goods locally in the host country, consideration of worldwide production is important. For example, goods may be produced in foreign countries for export to other nations. Sometimes, a plant will specialize in a particular product and export it to all the MNC's markets;

other times, a plant will produce goods only for a specific locale, such as Western Europe or South America. Still other facilities will produce one or more components that are shipped to a larger network of assembly plants. This latter option has been widely adopted by pharmaceutical firms and automakers such as Volkswagen and Honda.

If the firm operates production plants in different countries but makes no attempt to integrate its overall operations, the company is known as a **multidomestic.** A recent trend has been away from this scattered approach and toward global coordination of operations.

Multidomestic
A firm that operates production plants in different countries but makes no attempt to integrate overall operations.

Finally, if the product is labor-intensive, as in the case of microcomputers, then the trend is to farm the product out to low-cost sites such as Mexico or Brazil, where the cost of labor is relatively low and the infrastructure (electric power, communications systems, transportation systems) is sufficient to support production. Sometimes, multiple sources of individual components are used; in other cases, one or two sources are sufficient. In any event, careful coordination of the production function is needed when implementing the strategy, and the result is a product that is truly global in nature.

Finance   Use of the finance function to implement strategy normally is developed at the home office and carried out by the overseas affiliate or branch. When a firm went international in the past, the overseas operation commonly relied on the local area for funds, but the rise of global financing has ended this practice. MNCs have learned that transferring funds from one place in the world to another, or borrowing funds in the international money markets, often is less expensive than relying on local sources. Unfortunately, there are problems in these transfers.

Such a problem is representative of those faced by MNCs using the finance function to implement their strategies. One of an MNC's biggest recent headaches when implementing strategies in the financial dimension has been the re-evaluation of currencies. For example, in the late 1990s the U.S. dollar increased in value against the Japanese yen. American overseas subsidiaries that held yen found their profits (in terms of dollars) declining. The same was true for those subsidiaries that held Mexican pesos when that government devalued the currency several years ago. When this happens, a subsidiary's profit will decline. More recently, the declining value of the euro has impacted the profit picture of American and Japanese MNCs doing business in the EU.

When dealing with the inherent risk of volatile monetary exchange rates, some MNCs have bought currency options that (for a price) guarantee convertibility at a specified rate. Others have developed countertrade strategies, whereby they receive products in exchange for currency. For example, PepsiCo received payment in vodka for its products sold in Russia. Countertrade continues to be a popular form of international business, especially in less developed countries and those with nonconvertible currencies.

The World of *Business Week*—Revisited

Looking back to the *Business Week* article that opened this chapter, it is easy to see why Toyota needs effective global strategic planning. In addition to the quality emphasis that has been so instrumental in helping the firm increase its worldwide automobile share, the company is now in the throes of formulating and implementing plans to take it beyond the automotive market. In the process, Toyota is assessing environmental opportunities and threats and examining its internal strengths and weaknesses so that the firm's strategic thrust will exploit its strengths and sidestep any shortcomings. At the same time major competitors, GM and Ford in particular, are conducting similar forms of analysis. One of the markets where these two U.S. carmakers have yet to do well is the EU. So Toyota can expect a major battle in Europe from both EU-based manufacturers and U.S. auto makers. In addition, GM and Ford are determined to hold market share in America, while increasing their share of the Asian market. As a result, Toyota can expect strong competition in this decade in the auto market and effective strategic planning is going to be critical to the firm's success in autos and beyond. Drawing upon the need and benefits of strategic planning, answer these questions: (1) Which imperative is likely to be relatively most important to MNCs in this decade: economic, political, or quality? (2) In scanning the environment, what are two key areas of consideration that MNCs must address? (3) Will joint ventures increase or decrease in popularity during this time period?

Summary of Key Points

1. There is a growing need for strategic planning among MNCs. Some of the primary reasons include: foreign direct investment is increasing, planning is needed to coordinate and integrate increasingly diverse operations via an overall focus, and emerging international challenges require strategic planning.

2. A strategic plan can take on an economic focus, a political focus, a quality focus, an administrative coordination focus, or some variation of the four. In addition, an MNC typically is predisposed toward an ethnocentric, polycentric, regiocentric, or geocentric orientation. Companies may use a combination of these orientations in their strategic planning, but geocentric is the one employed most commonly by global companies.

3. Strategic planning is used by more MNCs every year, although no definitive evidence proves that this process always results in higher profitability. As with other aspects of international management, the particular situation largely will dictate the success of a strategic plan.

4. Strategy formulation consists of several steps. First, the MNC carries out external environmental scanning to identify opportunities and threats. Next, the firm conducts an internal resource analysis of company strengths and weaknesses. Strategic goals then are formulated in light of the results of these external and internal analyses.

5. Strategy implementation is the process of providing goods and services in accord with the predetermined plan of action. This implementation typically involves such considerations as: deciding where to locate operations, carrying out an entry and ownership strategy, and using functional strategies to implement the plan. Functional strategies focus on marketing, production, and finance.

Key Terms

administrative coordination, *257*

economic imperative, *254*

environmental scanning, *259*

ethnocentric predisposition, *258*

franchise, *269*

geocentric predisposition, *258*

joint venture, *266*

key factor for success (KFS), *260*

license, *268*

multidomestic, *272*

political imperative, *255*

polycentric predisposition, *258*

quality imperative, *255*

regiocentric predisposition, *258*

strategic planning, *252*

strategy implementation, *262*

wholly owned subsidiary, *266*

Review and Discussion Questions

1. Of the four imperatives discussed in this chapter—economic, political, quality, and administration—which would be most important to IBM in its efforts to make inroads in the Pacific Rim market? Would this emphasis be the same as that in the United States, or would IBM be giving primary attention to one of the other imperatives? Explain.

2. If a locally based manufacturing firm with sales of $350 million decided to enter the EU market by setting up operations in France, which orientation would be the most effective: ethnocentric, polycentric, regiocentric, or geocentric? Why? Explain your choice.

3. When a large MNC such as Ford Motor sets strategic goals, what areas are targeted for consideration? Incorporate the information from Table 9–2 in your answer. Would this list of strategic goals be very different from that formulated by the manufacturing firm in question 2? Why or why not?

4. One of the most common entry strategies for MNCs is the joint venture. Why are so many companies opting for this strategy? Would a fully owned subsidiary be a better choice?

5. In recent years McDonald's has found that its international franchise operation has been producing more

revenue per unit than its domestic operations. What might account for this? Is it likely that the firm will continue its international expansion? Why?

6. Mercedes changed its U.S. strategy by announcing that it is developing cars for the $30,000 to $45,000 price range (as well as its typical upper-end cars). What might have accounted for this change in strategy? In your answer, include a discussion of the implications from the standpoints of marketing, production, and finance.

Internet Exercise: Dropping In on Dell Computer

One of the largest computer firms in the world is Dell Computer. Dell does not sell its products in retail stores. In order to purchase a Dell computer, it is necessary to go to the firm's web site, indicate the desired machine's configuration, and then arrange for the financing. Go to Dell's web site at **www.dell.com** and examine some of the background on the firm and the computers it is now offering. Then answer these questions: How do you think international strategic planning is reflected in what you see in the web site? What major strategic planning steps would Dell need to carry out in order to remain a world leader in this direct marketing niche? What potential threat, if it occurred, would prove most disastrous for Dell, and what could the company do to deal with the possibility of this negative development?

Poland

Poland is the sixth-largest country in Europe. It is bordered by Germany, the Czech Republic, and Slovakia in the west and south and by the former Soviet Union republics of the Ukraine in the south, Belarus in the east, and Lithuania in the northeast. The northwest section of the country is located on the Baltic Sea. Named after the Polane, a Slavic tribe that lived more than a thousand years ago, Poland has beautiful countryside and rapidly growing cities. Rolling hills and rugged mountains rise in southern Poland. There are approximately 40 million Poles, and GNP is around $270 billion. The country still is highly agricultural, and up to one-third of the population engages in farm work. The people have a rich heritage (at one point, the Poles ruled an empire that stretched across most of central Europe), have many folk traditions (which the former communist government discouraged), and strong loyalty to the Roman Catholic church. The government is now dominated by former communists (socialists), and Lech Walesa, the democratic hero, was defeated in the 1995 presidential election by Aleksander Kwasniewski who was reelected in 2000. Today the government is still working to establish a free-market system. Predictions are that the coming years will remain very difficult as Poland continues to try to undo some of the major problems from the past.

The Poles, despite continuing problems, indeed have made some progress in establishing a viable economy. To take advantage of this economic situation, a medium-sized Canadian manufacturing firm has begun thinking about renovating a plant near Warsaw and building small power tools for the expanding Central and Eastern European market. The company's logic is fairly straightforward. There appears to be no competition in this niche, because there has been little demand for power tools in this area. As the post-communist countries continue to struggle in their transition to a market economy, they will have to increase their productivity if they hope to compete with Western European nations. Small power tools are one of the products they will need to accomplish this goal.

A second reason for the Canadian firm's interest in setting up operations in Poland is that the price of labor is still relatively low. Other nearby countries have lower wage rates, but Warsaw, the company's specific choice, has a cadre of well-trained factory workers that could be recruited to this renovated factory. Product quality in the production of these tools is critical to success, so for this Canadian firm, Poland seems an ideal location.

In addition, Poland likely will continue receiving economic and moral support from Western Europe as well as Canada and the United States. Exporting from Poland to Western Europe or the United States therefore should be easier than from more developed countries. Moreover, the manufacturing firm is convinced that its proximity to Russia will open up that market as well. Transportation costs to Russia will be low vis-à-vis competitors, and the Russians currently are looking for ways to increase their own worker productivity.

Finally, there likely will be little competition for the next couple of years, because small power tools do not carry a very large markup and no other manufacturer is attempting to tap what the Canadian firm views as "an emerging market for the twenty-first century." However, a final decision on this matter is going to have to wait until the company has made a thorough evaluation of the market and the competitive nature of the industry.

www.poland.pl

Questions

1. What are some current issues facing Poland? What is the climate for doing business in Poland today?

2. Is the Canadian manufacturing firm using an economic, political, or quality imperative approach to strategy?

3. How should the firm carry out the environmental scanning process? Would the process be of any practical value?

4. What are two key factors for success that will be important if this project is to succeed?

Go East, Young People, Go East

Amanda Brendhart, Jose Gutierrez, and Rhoda Schreiber founded and are partners in a small electronics firm, Electronic Visions, that has developed and patented some state-of-the-art computer components. Visions has had moderate success selling these components to large U.S.-based computer manufacturers. The biggest problem is that in recent months, the computer market has begun to turn soft, and many of the manufacturers are offering substantial discounts to generate sales. Therefore, although Visions has found an increasing demand for its product, it now is grossing less money than it was several months ago.

To increase both sales and profit, the partners have decided to expand into Asia. Although this region is known for its low-cost computer production, the group believes that countries such as China, Malaysia, and Thailand soon will become more lucrative markets, because the U.S. government will make these countries open their doors to imports more fully. If trade barriers are removed, the partners are convinced that they can export the goods at very competitive prices. In addition, the partners intend to find a partner in each market so that they have someone to help with the marketing and financing of the product. Of course, if the components can be produced more cheaply with local labor, the partnership is willing to forgo exporting and have everything produced locally.

At present, the group is trying to answer three questions. First, what is the best entry strategy to use in reaching the Asian markets? Second, what type of marketing strategy will be most effective? Third, if production must be coordinated between the United States and an overseas country, what is the best way to handle this? The partners believe that over the next 2 months, they will have a very good idea of what is going to happen regarding the opening of Asian markets. In the interim, they intend to work up a preliminary strategic plan that they can use to guide them.

Questions

1. What type of entry and ownership approach would you recommend? Defend your choice.

2. How could the partners use the four Ps of marketing to help implement strategy?

3. If production must be globally coordinated, will Visions have a major problem? Why or why not?

Chapter 10

Managing Political Risk and Negotiations

Objectives of the Chapter

Firms go international to become more competitive and profitable. Unfortunately, many risks accompany this internationalization. One of the biggest involves the political situation of the countries in which the MNC does business, and MNCs must be able to assess political risk and conduct skillful negotiations. An overview of the political environment in selected areas of the world has already been provided, but this chapter specifically examines what political risk is all about and how MNCs try to manage this risk. One major way is through effective evaluation and risk reduction. This process extends from risk identification and quantification to the formulation of appropriate responses, such as integration and protective and defensive techniques. This chapter also examines how negotiations are managed and actually carried out, and it reviews some of the common tactics that are used. The specific objectives of this chapter are:

1. **EXAMINE** how MNCs evaluate political risk.

2. **PRESENT** some common methods used for managing and reducing political risk.

3. **DISCUSS** how the negotiation process works, and how cultural differences can affect this process.

4. **DESCRIBE** some common negotiation tactics.

BusinessWeek

The World of *Business Week*

Korea's Digital Quest

When Kim In Kyung graduated from college and got ready to enter the job market a few years ago, her prospects didn't look bright. One problem was that she hailed from rural Korea, where her parents toiled as farmers—not the sophisticated background a young woman usually needs to land an elite job in Seoul. High-prestige, high-pay positions had always been the exclusive province of the young men who attended Seoul National University or those lucky enough to know a member of one of the dynastic families that controlled the nation's all-powerful industrial conglomerates.

But startling things are going on in Seoul circa 2000. Today, Kim, 24, has a dream job with Samsung Co. that includes world travel and a smart apartment in central Seoul. She's an internationally ranked player of a popular intergalactic-conquest Web game called Star Craft; for her job, she travels, with a Samsung-sponsored team, to Internet-gaming events around Europe, Asia, and the U.S. It's all part of Samsung's strategy to promote its new focus on the Internet. Although Kim has tried to explain her work—which pays her $80,000 to $100,000 a year in salary, competition prizes, and endorsements—to her tech-challenged parents, they still don't understand what she does. "They don't know I'm living in the Internet world," says Kim. "They just know I have a good job."

Kim is the lucky beneficiary of a remarkable turn-around in South Korea's economic fortunes since the

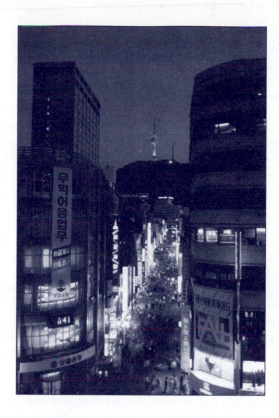

gut-gripping recession of 1998. In the wake of the late-1997 foreign-exchange crisis, tens of thousands of people were thrown out of work, and soup kitchens sprouted in city parks. Families strapped for gas money left their cars in the garage, and Seoul's fabled traffic jams vanished for a time. The economy shrank in 1998 by 6.7%, its worst trauma since the Korean War, and the government had to accept a humiliating bailout from the International Monetary Fund.

Those bad memories have now begun to dissipate. The jobless rate, which peaked in early 1999 at 8.4%, has been cut in half. And the high-tech surge has been astounding. Korea's increasingly vibrant information-technology sector is churning out world-class personal computers, mobile phones, Palm clones, and other devices at an accelerating rate.

Info tech now makes up nearly 8% of South Korea's $400 billion economy. That is expected to hit 11% by the end of the year and 20% by 2010, according to Samsung Economic Research Institute. And it's not just glamorous jobs such as Kim In Kyung's that are being created. For the first time, executives are defecting in large numbers from the huge conglomerates, or *chaebol,* to apply their high-tech expertise to startups in everything from telecoms to liquid-crystal displays. Once obscure companies such as mobile-phone maker Appeal Corp. are teaming up with global leaders such as Motorola Co. and cracking export markets.

Time to celebrate? Not quite yet. Skeptics of the Korean tech revolution urge outsiders to look at other figures. The chief source of concern is the Korean corporate sector, led by debt-burdened *chaebol* such as Daewoo and Hyundai, which are freighted with $630 billion in debt—150% of the country's annual gross domestic product. Some $100 billion of that liability is listed by Seoul banks as nonperforming loans. Meanwhile, the production of high-tech items still employs only 5% of the workforce. Most workers labor on in the smokestack industries of companies such as Daewoo, Hyundai, and Syangyong, plus assorted middling companies in slow-growth areas such as textiles, chemicals, distribution, and basic manufacturing. At heart, Korea is still an industrial economy with loads of unproductive players.

There are thus two Koreas at war with each other, making competing claims on capital and talent. Which will win? That's still not clear. The survival of the *chaebol* and the future employment of the millions of Koreans who work for them is anything but certain. Their failure, and that of the big banks, could drag the whole South Korean economy into a new crisis. Or, an economic downturn in the U.S., the biggest market for many of Korea's high-tech products, could send the information-technology sector into a tailspin. Even optimists such as Woo Cheon Sik, an economist at Korea Development Institute, concede that "Korea is situated at a critical point between making a new digital champion" or falling back from the pack.

No wonder South Korea's progress is being watched with fascination by global investors and policymakers throughout the developing world. It is a test case for whether a state-managed industrial economy can make a quick and seamless transition to a knowledge-based, high-tech model. It's doubtful that Korea can make a clean leap to a U.S.-style New Economy, with innovation spurring high productivity gains. But the South Korean economy could emulate countries such as Ireland and Finland, which have built up computer-literate workforces to transform their industrial base, create new businesses, and attract investment.

South Korea is, arguably, already the most wired nation in Asia—and by some measures, such as online stock trading and broadband access, a world leader. Some 60% of its 46 million people already use mobile phones, and nearly half will be logging onto the Internet by yearend. Over 60% of all trading in Korea is now done online. By 2002, 3 million Korean households will be using high-speed Internet connections such as asymmetric digital subscriber lines (ADSL) and cable-television modems, vs. 2 million in the U.S. and 300,000 in Japan.

More important, South Korea has a well-trained and literate workforce. The illiteracy rate is less than 1%, and 25% of high school graduates go on to four-year colleges. A recent World Bank report lauds South Korea's educational achievement, saying that its success "in improving the education level of its population would appear to be unmatched by any other country." Industry has clearly benefited. Every year, universities and technical schools turn out 5,000 engineers; most of them are working in Korea's information-technology sector.

Cyber Cafes

This deep strength in educated workers is complemented by a consumer-driven craze for all things digital—an obsession that is already showing signs of changing the lives of ordinary Koreans. Teenagers who used to hang out at the mall are now flocking to the country's 20,000 PC parlors, where for as little as $1 an hour they can watch movies, check e-mail, and surf the Net. "This is how many Koreans become versed in the Internet," says Won Jun Young, manager of Yeca Station, a parlor that sells the use of PCs for games, stock trading, and temporary offices.

The passion for tech extends beyond teenagers. Korean housewives make up the lion's share of the current five-month waiting list for ADSL lines. They will all get their chance to hit the Net after the government finishes a $35 billion high-speed telecommunications-infrastructure project that is now under way.

Global investors are looking for local partners to exploit a booming domestic market and use South Korea as an export platform for the rest of Asia, particularly China. Mobile-phone powerhouse Nokia has teamed up with Telson Electronics Co. for production and development of wireless handsets. Ericsson is partnering with LG, while NTT DoCoMo wants to take a 10% equity stake in SK Telecom as part of an alliance to sell telecom products across the region. Thorsten Freitag, vice-president of Cisco Systems in Korea, says South Korea is now Cisco's fastest-growing foreign market for its routers and servers.

Meanwhile, there are scores of success stories starring local businessmen bold enough to strike out on their own. James Kim, President of Locus Corp., gave up a promising academic career back in the early 1990s, borrowed money from his wife and friends, and launched a company specializing in automated corporate voice systems. Now, he's branching out into Internet and wireless-phone services.

Talented executives used to shun companies such as Locus, but Kim has had no trouble recruiting over the past two years. Locus' offices are full of not only recent college graduates sporting California-casual threads but also refugees from the *chaebol.* "You can now get good people from top schools and conglomerates," Kim says.

Easier Access

Thus, Kim is no longer a lonely entrepreneur. Since early 1998, some 7,700 new companies have started, helped by a government willing to extend tax breaks and loans. The Kim administration even exempted some engineers at startups from mandatory military service. It also streamlined the paperwork needed to register a new company.

And though major Seoul banks won't touch such companies, innovative venture-capital networks are starting to crop up. One is the Korean Venture Business Assn. headed by Lee Min Hwa, founder of Medison Co., which pioneered work in three-dimensional ultrasound technology that is used in medical-equipment manufacturing. Founded in 1985, Medison now boasts $185 million in revenues and competes with Toshiba and Siemens.

Will it all be enough to transform the economy permanently? In America, companies and workers had to go through 20 years of wrenching restructuring and a technology revolution had to take place before the New Economy emerged. Korea, by contrast, has done little on the restructuring side. With the exception of well-run companies such as Samsung and LG, Corporate Korea has been slow so far to use information technology to cut costs and improve efficiency. Business-to-business portals to buy parts and supplies online, for instance, are still in their infancy. And an estimated 2 million workers are holding jobs that probably should not exist.

Granted, President Kim Dae Jung's government is out to change this mind-set. It is offering to pay 50% of the cost of setting up databases and online parts exchanges in such industries as shipping, chemicals, and steel. That will be crucial if the smokestack industries are to improve their global competitiveness. But government prodding alone will not suffice. "I'm still quite doubtful that enough Korean chief executives are focused on the issue," says Lim Young Hak, executive director of Samsung Corp.'s Internet and e-commerce business.

The sluggishness of reform at the big *chaebol* is worrisome for the New Economy adventurers. Just about everybody in the business world is focused on whether Korea can work through the last vestiges of the crisis. Chief among the challenges is avoiding a chain reaction of financial-market defaults if the dismemberment of the ailing Hyundai Group fails. Another concern: If Ford Motor Co.'s talks to buy Daewoo Motors fail, it would be a severe blow to confidence.

The unanswered question is whether the flowering of an Internet economy can somehow break through decades of deeply entrenched business practices. Korea's banks still would rather lend to their favorite lumbering *chaebol* than to risky start-ups. And corporations still love to make expensive, debt-fueled forays into new markets instead of crafting targeted business plans that focus on profitable growth.

Certainly, the success of Korea's vibrant sector of small and midsize companies is heartening. Ironically, the transformation would have been much slower to develop if not for the 1998 financial trauma. That opened the way for radical changes that were unthinkable three years ago. "We had a lot of suppressed energy in Korea," says Korea Development Institute's Woo. "The crisis was a way to unleash it." Sometimes, good things do come out of upheaval. The prize of a digital economy awaits Korea. Now, it has to win it.

By Brian Bremner in Tokyo and Moon Ihlwan in Seoul

This opening article helps illustrate how political risk can affect global operations. MNCs doing business in South Korea must compete against the struggling *chaebols* such as Daewoo and Hyundai which are heavily in debt and unlikely to repay all of their loans. If these companies were headquartered in the United States or the EU, their bankers would have stepped in long ago and forced them to repay their loans and sell some of their assets in order to straighten out their finances. However, to date Daewoo and Hyundai are still largely protected by the government and so they remain as competitors to MNCs doing business there. In perspective, there is an "old" Korea that is weighing down the economy, but it is unlikely to be replaced very soon by the "new" Korea with its vibrant information technology sector that promises to make the country a leading Asian economy. The attractiveness of South Korea, especially for those firms that are looking to the country as a jumping-off point for the rest of Asia, will require a solid understanding by MNCs of the political risk both here and throughout the continent. In particular, MNCs will have to be able to evaluate and manage this risk and effectively negotiate with governmental and business personnel as well as with customers. In this chapter some of the most effective ways of managing such political risk and negotiation will be explored.

■ The Nature and Analysis of Political Risk

Political risk
The likelihood that a business's foreign investment will be constrained by a host government's policy.

Applied to international management, **political risk** is the likelihood that a multinational corporation's foreign investment will be constrained by a host government's policies. In the past, this risk was typified by the probability that the company's investment would be expropriated, as in the case of when Castro took over in Cuba, seizing the assets of private investors. However, over the past decade and in the aftermath of the recent terrorist attack on the U.S., political risk has become a much more sophisticated and challenging area facing international management. Few governments today are interested in outright seizing the assets of multinational corporations. On the contrary, almost all countries are interested in attracting and sustaining MNC investment.[1] The problem today facing MNCs is emerging economies, which are attractive markets for MNCs, may begin to badly falter. Then the governments of these struggling economies may make policy decisions that negatively impact on the MNCs. Examples include freezing the movement of assets out of the country, placing limits on remittance of profits or capital, devaluing of the currency, refusing to give import licenses needed for the acquisition of materials and equipment, and refusing to abide by the contractual terms of agreements that have been previously signed with the MNC. These forms of political risk are unfortunately becoming increasingly common for today's MNCs.

In the case of China, for example, the government has been for the past few years very anxious to be admitted to the World Trade Organization (WTO). When this did not happen right away, China began making decisions that were in its own best short-run interests, but which created new political risks for MNCs doing business there. One analysis noted:

> A series of recent moves by Chinese authorities—price controls, currency restrictions, limits on sale of state-owned companies—seem to reflect a slowdown in the nation's effort to shift from a planned to a market economy. Whether such steps are justifiably cautious or simply timid, economists and business executives agree that they are likely to further deter trade and investment in the near future. Today, China's central bank announced new restrictions on foreign exchange transactions, an attempt to control the flow of convertible currency out of the country. Officially described as a crackdown on illegal transactions, the moves will effectively make it more difficult for both domestic and international companies to move money in and out of China.[2]

These actions by the Chinese demonstrate the restrictions on foreign investment in the telecommunications industry, one of the fastest growing industries in China and one that had attracted a great deal of attention from international investors.

Now that China has been admitted into the WTO, political risk still continues to be a major consideration for multinationals doing business there. As was brought out in Chapter 4, industrial piracy continues to be a big problem and the government has yet to take effective action against these unacceptable practices. For example, Procter & Gamble estimates that it loses $150 million in sales annually because of counterfeit brands, and DaimlerChrysler reports that fake brake disks, windshields, oil filters, and shock absorbers for Mercedes cars are being made and sold throughout the country. One reason for the reluctance of the government to take action may well be that state-owned factories are some of the biggest counterfeiters. Yamaha estimates that five of every six JYM 150-A motorcycles and ZY125 scooters bearing its name in China are fake and some state-owned factories turn out copies four months after Yamaha introduces a new model.[3] Another common complaint is the way rules and regulations are interpreted. A Mitsubishi factory manager, commenting on the fact that customs officials continually offer contradictory rulings, recently said "One day one official will say I do not need to pay duty, the next day, a different official will say I have to."[4] Another growing concern is government censorship. All advertisements must be approved by censors who carefully screen ads to ensure that they are culturally and politically correct.[5] Multinationals are also concerned about the pressure that the government puts on businesses to do things a particular way. MNCs in Hong Kong now governed by the PRC have reported quiet meddling by Beijing.[6]

These types of actions by the Chinese increase the political risk of doing business there. On the other side of the coin, however, Chinese MNCs must also assess the political risk inherent in doing business in the United States. The U.S. government has begun to review its trade policy with China. In particular, American trade officials claim that China has taken for granted its relationship with the United States and if markets there are not opened for American goods there will be reciprocal action against Chinese firms that are selling in the United States.[7] Given the enormous trade deficit that the Americans now have with China, this situation could end up creating major political risks for Chinese MNCs doing business in the politically stable, but very risky, United States.

Macro and Micro Analysis of Political Risk

Firms evaluate political risk in a number of ways. One is through **macro political risk analysis,** which reviews major political decisions that are likely to affect all business conducted in the country. For example, China's decision regarding restrictions on foreign exchange transactions is a macro political risk because it affects all MNCs. **Micro political risk analysis** is directed toward government policies and actions that influence selected sectors of the economy or specific foreign businesses. China's government policies regarding investment in the telecommunications industry fall into the micro political risk category. Figure 10–1 reports the riskiness of investing in select countries. This risk rating is based on a series of criteria including the nation's political structure, economic policies, and the state of the country's banking system. The following examines both of these areas—macro and micro political risk—in more depth.

Macro Risk Issues and Examples   In recent years macro risk analysis has become of increasing concern to MNCs because of the growing number of countries that are finding their economies in trouble as in Southeast Asia, or, even worse, unable to make the transition to a market-driven economy. A good example of the latter is Russia, which has been tightening controls on the flow of foreign currencies. This represents a change in direction to the free market principles that the Russians had been following in order to insure that it continued to receive assistance from the International Monetary Fund.

Other examples of developments that fall within the realm of macro political risk are provided by India, a country whose legal system is typified by a labyrinth of laws and bureaucratic red tape. In recent years, the Indian high courts have had a backlog of over 3 million cases. Moreover, approximately one-third of these cases have been winding their way through the legal system for more than 5 years. So while the government touts the fact that Indian law offers strong protection to foreign firms against counterfeiters, an MNC finding that it must rely on the Indian judicial system to enforce its proprietary rights is likely to be sadly disappointed. As a result, many MNCs accept this risk as a price of doing business in India and formulate strategies for managing the problem. A good example is provided by the Timken Company of Canton, Ohio, which makes bearings and alloy steel. When Timken found that the Indian market was rampant with fake Timken products, the MNC's initial reaction was to sue the counterfeiters. However, after realizing how long this would take, the MNC opted for a different strategy. Management switched the packaging of its products from cardboard boxes to heat-sealed plastic with eight-color printing and a hologram which could not be forged. Result: Within months the counterfeit market began drying up.

Timken is not alone, there are many counterfeit operations in India because the slow-moving judicial system encourages noncompliance. In fact, some counterfeiters have found that by filing counter suits they can tie up the case in court for years. For example, Ziff Davis Publishing, an American unit of Japan's Softbank Corporation, brought suit against a former Indian licensee for continuing to publish one of its computer magazines

Macro political risk analysis
Analysis that reviews major political decisions likely to affect all enterprises in the country.

Micro political risk analysis
Analysis directed toward government policies and actions that influence selected sectors of the economy or specific foreign businesses in the country.

Figure 10–1

Country Risk

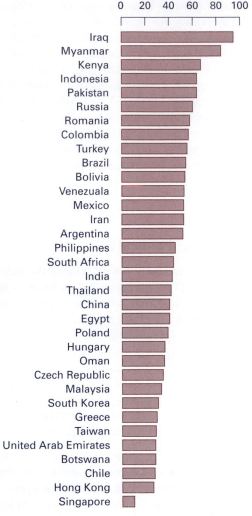

Source: Economist Intelligence Unit. Reported in *Economist,* March 10, 2001, p. 112.

even though the license had expired. The defendant frivolously countersued, arguing that the magazine was generic and not proprietary. A similar brazen example hit Time Warner, owner of cable-television movie channel Home Box Office (HBO). This MNC won a temporary injunction preventing an Indian company from calling its movie channel Cable Box Office or CBO for short. So that firm changed its name to CVO standing for Cable Video Opera. Time Warner is pursuing damages for trademark infringement, but it will probably be years before there is a final settlement of the suit.[8]

Many other newly emerging economies besides the big countries of China, Russia and India also present macro political risks for MNCs. In Vietnam, for example, the communist government there has earned a bad name among foreign investors because of all the pitfalls they have to face. In fact, until very recently the Vietnamese government required all foreign investors to establish joint ventures with local partners. And even with this arrangement, getting things done proved to be extremely slow and difficult because many levels of bureaucracy must be dealt with. One international manager described his MNCs experience this way, "The negotiations would follow a serpentine path, with breakthroughs in one session often being erased in the next."[9] To date, macro political risks in Vietnam remain high and investors find themselves proceeding with caution.[10]

Another example of a macro consideration of political risk is an analysis of what would happen to a company's investment if opposition government leaders were to take control. Many years ago U.S. companies in Iran failed to forecast the fall of the Shah and rise of Khomeini. As a result, they lost their investment. Because of this Iranian experience, the situation in Iraq under militant dictator Saddam Hussein, and the terrorist attack of New York by ethnic Middle Easterners, many multinationals now are very reluctant to invest very heavily in most Middle Eastern countries. Recently, the government of Iran appeared to be interested in attracting foreign investment, but there is still a great deal of concern that this region is too politically explosive. Central, if not Eastern, Europe appears to be a better bet, as seen by the millions of dollars that MNCs have poured into transitionary postcommunist countries such as Hungary and Poland. This geographic region also is regarded as politically risky, however, as shown in the continuing conflict in the Balkans, the breakup of Czechoslovakia, the continuing problems in the former Soviet Republics, and the political instability in the entire region. As a result, many multinationals have been tempering their expansion plans in these transitionary, still emerging economies.

Still another area of consideration in macro political risk is that of government corruption. Common examples include bribery and the use of government rules and regulations that require the inclusion of certain locals in lucrative business deals. In fact, one of the most commonly cited reasons for the severe economic problems in Indonesia in recent years is the corrupt practices of the government. Because the family of former President Suharto was involved in virtually every big business deal that took place under his regime, many loans and major projects were approved by banks and government agencies simply because these family members were part of the process. However, when these loans or projects ran into trouble, more money was poured in to shore up things—and no one dared to challenge these unsound decisions.

What are the most and the least corrupt nations in the world? Table 10–1 provides the results of a recent survey of 85 nations that ranked the countries based on a wide variety of criteria. About half of the nations in the world were omitted from the survey because of the absence of reliable data. The United States ended up in 17th position. One reason for this apparent low ranking, in the view of analysts, is because the American press is very good at ferreting out stories about corruption; so in the United States practices that would go unnoticed in other countries ranked ahead of it, end up widely publicized in the local newspaper or reported on television and thus make the United States appear relatively worse than it may really be.

Micro Risk Issues and Examples   Micro risk issues often take forms such as industry regulation, taxes on specific types of business activity, and various restrictive local laws. The essence of these micro risk issues is that some MNCs are treated differently from others. A good recent example is the situation faced by MNCs importing steel into the U.S. market. In 1992 American steelmakers filed more than 80 complaints against 20 nations on a single day. They charged that foreign steelmakers were dumping their products in the U.S. market at artificially low prices. By 1998, the industry again demanded action against foreign producers who, in the first six months of that year, doubled their imports into the American market. Domestic producers charged that Brazil, Japan, and Russia steelmakers were dumping steel in the United States at unfairly low prices. What was even more troubling was that the American producers were in the process of negotiating with big auto and appliance makers for the steel that is sold under long-term contracts. Since steel prices had dropped sharply because of the alleged "dumping," the American firms were concerned that they would end up getting locked into contracts that offered very little, if any, profit. The American steelmakers were insisting that their government force foreign producers to raise their prices.[11] Recently, after reviewing the facts the U.S. International Trade Commission decided, on a vote of 5 to 1, that the imports from Brazil, Japan, and Russia were not a threat to the U.S. steel industry. So in this case the risk for these international firms was far less than they might have initially anticipated.[12]

A related development is the impact of the WTO and EU regulations on American MNCs. For example, the WTO recently ruled that the United States' 1916 Anti-dumping Act violates global trade regulations and cannot be used by American firms to fend off imports.[13] Meanwhile on the Continent, the European Commission is investigating complaints by

Table 10–1
Corruption Rankings of Select Countries (Least to Most)

Ranking	Country	Ranking	Country
1	Denmark	42	Uruguay
2	Finland	43	South Korea, Zimbabwe
3	Sweden	45	Malawi
4	New Zealand	46	Brazil
5	Iceland	47	Belarus
6	Canada	48	Slovak Republic
7	Singapore	49	Jamaica
8	Netherlands, Norway	50	Morocco
10	Switzerland	51	El Salvador
11	Australia, Britain, Luxembourg	52	China, Zambia
14	Ireland	54	Turkey
15	Germany	55	Ghana, Mexico, Philippines, Senegal
16	Hong Kong	59	Cote d'Ivoire, Guatemala
17	Austria, United States	61	Argentina, Nicaragua, Romania, Thailand, Yugoslavia
19	Israel		
20	Chile	66	Bulgaria, Egypt, India
21	France	69	Bolivia, Ukraine
22	Portugal	71	Latvia, Pakistan
23	Botswana, Spain	73	Uganda
25	Japan	74	Kenya, Vietnam
26	Estonia	76	Russia
27	Costa Rica	77	Ecuador, Venezuela
28	Belgium	79	Colombia
29	Malaysia, Namibia, Taiwan	80	Indonesia
32	South Africa	81	Nigeria, Tanzania
33	Hungary, Mauritius, Tunisia	83	Honduras
36	Greece	84	Paraguay
37	Czech Republic	85	Cameroon
38	Jordan		
39	Italy, Poland		
41	Peru		

Source: Reported in *Miami Herald,* September 23, 1998, p. 8A.

PepsiCo and other competitors that Coca-Cola has improperly attempted to shut down sales of its rivals.[14] The EU also examines all major mergers and acquisitions and has the authority to block such actions as seen by its refusal to allow the G.E. and Honeywell merger, one of the best examples of globalization (the EU was able stop the actions of perhaps the most powerful U.S. firm) as well as political risk (G.E. needed to better assess and manage the risk posed by the politicians and government bureaucrats in Brussels). Other examples include the EU's denying Volvo and Scania to merge and to prevent Alcan Aluminum of Canada, Pechiney of France, and the Alusuisse Lonza Group of Switzerland, the world's three largest aluminum companies, from merging.[15] These regulatory actions are good examples of the types of micro risk issues that MNCs face from industry regulation.

Still another example of micro political risk is provided by countries in South America that face continued indebtedness and have introduced a variety of policies to promote exports and discourage imports. MNCs that feel they cannot abide by these policies will stay out; however, some that are looking for a location from which to produce and export goods will view these same government policies as very attractive. Table 10–2 lists criteria that MNCs could use to evaluate the degree of political risk.

Table 10–2
A Guide to Evaluation of Political Risk

External factors affecting subject country
Prospects for foreign conflict
Relations with border countries
Regional instabilities
Alliances with major and regional powers
Sources of key raw materials
Major foreign markets
Policy toward United States
U.S. policy toward country
Internal groupings (points of power)

Government in power:
  Key agencies and officials
  Legislative entrenched bureaucracies
  Policies—economic, financial, social, labor, etc.
  Pending legislation
  Attitude toward private sector
  Power networks

Political parties (in and out of power):
  Policies
  Leading and emerging personalities
  Internal power struggles
  Sector and area strengths
  Future prospects for retaining or gaining power

Other important groups:
  Unions and labor movements
  Military, special groups within military
  Families
  Business and financial communities
  Intelligentsia
  Students
  Religious groups
  Media
  Regional and local governments
  Social and environmental activists
  Cultural, linguistic, and ethnic groups
  Separatist movements
  Foreign communities
  Potential competitors and customers

Internal factors
Power struggles amongst elites
Ethnic confrontations
Regional struggles
Economic factors affecting stability (consumer inflation, price and
  wage controls, unemployment, supply shortages, taxation, etc.)
Anti-establishment movements
Factors affecting a specific project
(Custom-designed for each project)

Note: Information in the table is an abridged version of Probe's Political Agenda Worksheet, which may serve as a guide for corporate executives initiating their own political evaluations. Probe International is located in Stamford, Conn.
Source: Benjamin Weinger, "What Executives Should Know about Political Risk," *Management Review,* January 1992, p. 20.

Analyzing the Expropriation Risk

Expropriation is the seizure of businesses with little, if any, compensation to the owners. Such seizures of foreign enterprises by developing countries were quite common in the old days. In addition, some takeovers were caused by **indigenization laws,** which required that nationals hold a majority interest in the operation. In the main, expropriation is more likely to occur in non-Western governments that are poor, relatively unstable, and suspicious of foreign multinationals.

Some firms are more vulnerable to expropriation than others. Those at greatest risk often are in extractive, agricultural, or infrastructural industries such as utilities and transportation because of the importance of these industries to the country. In addition, large firms often are more likely targets than small firms, because more is to be gained by expropriating from large firms.

MNCs can take a wide variety of strategies to minimize their chances of expropriation. They can bring in local partners. They can limit the use of high technology so that if the firm is expropriated, the country cannot duplicate the technology. They also can acquire an affiliate that depends on the parent company for key areas of the operation, such as financing, research, and technology transfer, so that no practical value exists in seizing the affiliate.

Expropriation
The seizure of businesses by a host country with little, if any, compensation to the owners.

Indigenization laws
Laws that require that nations hold a majority interest in the operation.

The Role of Operational Profitability in Risk Analysis

Although expropriation is a major consideration, most MNCs are more directly concerned with operational profitability. Will they be able to make the desired return on investment? A number of government regulations can have a negative impact on their profitability. Requiring MNCs to use domestic suppliers instead of bringing in components or raw materials from other company-owned facilities or purchasing them more cheaply in the world market is one such regulation. Another is a restriction on the amount of profit that can be taken out of the country. A third is the wages and salaries that must be paid to the employees. Despite these difficulties, MNCs have become very interested in designing models and frameworks for helping them to better understand and manage their political risk.

■ Managing Political Risk

For well over two decades, businesses have been looking for ways to manage their political risk. Quite often, the process begins with a detailed analysis of the various risks with which the MNC will be confronted, including development of a comprehensive framework that identifies the various risks and then assigns a quantitative risk or rating factor to them.

Developing a Comprehensive Framework

A comprehensive framework for managing political risk should consider all political risks and identify those that are most important. Schmidt has offered a three-dimensional framework that combines political risks, general investments, and special investments.[16] Figure 10–2 illustrates this framework, and the following sections examine each dimension in detail.

Political Risks Political risks can be broken down into three basic categories: transfer risks, operational risks, and ownership-control risks. **Transfer risks** stem from government policies that limit the transfer of capital, payments, production, people, and technology in or out of the country. Examples include tariffs on exports and imports as well as restrictions on exports, dividend remittance, and capital repatriation. **Operational risks** result from government policies and procedures that directly constrain the management and performance of local operations. Examples include price controls, financing restrictions, export commitments, taxes, and local-sourcing requirements. **Ownership control risks** are brought about by government policies or actions that inhibit ownership or control of local operations. Examples include foreign ownership limitations, pressure for local participation, confiscation, expropriation, and abrogation of proprietary rights. For example, the Russian government cancelled an agreement with the Exxon Corporation that would have allowed the firm to tap huge oil deposits in the country's far north. The Russian minister for natural resources cited "legal irregularities" as the reason for the decision. As a result, the $1.5 billion project came to a grinding halt. Commenting on the government's action, one Western investment banker in Russia said that "it raises the question of whether a deal is a

Transfer risks
Government policies that limit the transfer of capital, payments, production, people, and technology in and out of the country.

Operational risks
Government policies and procedures that directly constrain management and performance of local operations.

Ownership-control risks
Government policies or actions that inhibit ownership or control of local operations.

Figure 10–2

A Three-Dimensional Framework for Assessing Political Risk

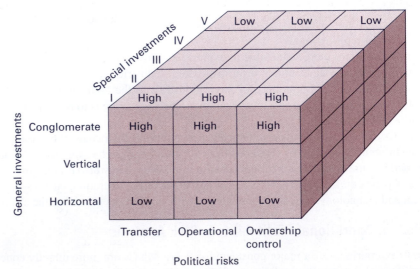

Source: David A. Schmidt, "Analyzing Political Risk," *Business Horizons*, July–August 1986, p. 50. Copyright 1986 by the Foundation for the School of Business at Indiana University. Used with permission.

International Management in Action

Sometimes It's All Politics

One of the biggest problems in doing business internationally is that yesterday's agreement with a government may be cancelled or delayed by today's politicians who disagree with that earlier decision. Enron, the now bankrupt Houston-based U.S. energy consortium, discovered this when its power project in Dabhol, India, became the focal point of political interest. India's economic nationalists began accelerating a campaign to scrap a high-profile, U.S.-backed power project despite warnings of potential damage to the confidence of foreign investors in the country. These politicians wanted to abandon the $28 billion deal as well as all other power projects in the country that had been approved under the government's "fast track" provisions. The contract for the two-stage, 2,000+ megawatt plant was signed before the current politicians came to power in Maharashtra, the state where Dabhol is located.

What effect would this political move have on foreign investment in India? A number of foreign investors indicated that if the Enron project were cancelled, they would review their investment plans for the country. A survey of international energy companies by the East-West Center in Hawaii found that of 13 Asian economies, India's investment climate ranked fifth from the bottom for power-sector investment. This seemed to have little effect on the politicians, who proceeded to cancel the project. Members of the political opposition, who supported the project, called it a mere political ploy designed to appeal to voters in the upcoming elections, and they urged foreign investors to sit tight and ride out the political storm. Many of these investors appeared to be apprehensive about taking such advice, and Enron announced plans for taking the case to international arbitration to reclaim the $300 million they have invested in the project—as well as $300 million in damages.

Eventually things were straightened out, but only for a while. More recently the Maharashtra State Electric Board defaulted on $64 million in unpaid power bills. The Board said that the company was charging too much for power and Enron served notice that it would terminate the power supply contract and pull out.

The political climate in India is not unique. Russia also offers its share of jitters to investors. In particular, many joint ventures that were created during the Gorbachev era now are having problems. A good example is Moscow's Radisson-Slavjanskaya Hotel venture, in which American Business Centers of Irvine, California, owns a 40 percent stake. American Business Centers manages several floors of offices in the hotel, and now that the venture is making money, it appears that the Irvine firm's Russian partners and the Radisson hotel people are trying to oust them. The president of American Business Centers claims that his partners feel they do not need him any longer.

The dilemma faced by American Business Centers is becoming increasingly common in Russia. For example, the Seattle-based firm Radio Page entered into a joint venture with Moscow Public Telephone Network and another Russian company to offer paging services. Together, they built a system of telephone pagers in the Moscow region. Radio Page held a 51 percent stake. When annual revenues hit $5 million and the venture was on the verge of making $1 million, however, the agreement began to unravel. The Russian partners demanded control of the operation and even threatened to pull the critical radio frequencies if they did not get their way.

There is little that foreign joint-venture firms doing business in high-risk countries can do except try to negotiate with their partners. For instance, the political situation in Russia is so unstable that support from one government ministry may be offset by opposition from another, or worse yet, the individuals supporting the foreign firm may be ousted from their jobs tomorrow. Economic considerations tend to be the main reason why firms seek international partners, but sometimes, it seems that everything boils down to politics and the risks associated with dealing in this political environment.

---

deal in Russia because Exxon is meticulous to a fault in following the letter of the law."[17] In any event, the decision provides a good example of ownership control risks. Still another is provided in "International Management in Action: Sometimes It's All Politics."

General Nature of Investment   The general nature of investment examines whether the company is making a conglomerate, vertical, or horizontal investment (see Figure 10–2). In a **conglomerate investment,** the goods or services produced are not similar to those produced at home. These types of investments usually are rated as high risk, because foreign governments see them as providing fewer benefits to the country and greater benefits to the MNC than other investments. **Vertical investments** include the production of raw materials or intermediate goods that are to be processed into final products. These investments run the risk of being taken over by the government because they are export-oriented,

Conglomerate investment
A type of high-risk investment in which goods or services produced are not similar to those produced at home.

Vertical investment
The production of raw materials or intermediate goods that are to be processed into final products.

Horizontal investment
An MNC investment in foreign operations to produce the same goods or services as those produced at home.

and governments like a business that helps it to generate foreign capital. **Horizontal investments** involve the production of goods or services that are the same as those produced at home. These investments typically are made with an eye toward satisfying the host country's market demands. As a result, they are not very likely to be takeover targets.

Special Nature of Investment   The special nature of foreign direct investment relates to the sector of economic activity, technological sophistication, and pattern of ownership. There are three sectors of economic activity: (1) the primary sector, which consists of agriculture, forestry, and mineral exploration and extraction; (2) the industrial sector, consisting of manufacturing operations; and (3) the service sector, which includes transportation, finance, insurance, and related industries. Technological sophistication consists of science-based industry and non-science-based industry; the difference between the two is that science-based industry requires the continuous introduction of new products and/or processes. Patterns of ownership relate to whether the business is wholly or partially owned.

The special nature of foreign direct investments can be categorized as one of five types (see Figure 10–2). Type I is the highest-risk venture; type V is the lowest-risk venture. This risk factor is assigned based on sector, technology, and ownership. Primary sector industries usually have the highest risk factor, service sector industries have the next highest, and industrial sector industries have the lowest. Firms with technology that is not available to the government should the firm be taken over have lower risk than those with technology that is easily acquired. Wholly owned subsidiaries have higher risk than partially owned subsidiaries.

Using a framework similar to that provided in Figure 10–2 helps MNCs to manage their political risks. A way to complement this framework approach is to give specific risk ratings to various criteria.

Quantifying the Variables in Managing Political Risk

Some MNCs attempt to manage political risk through a quantification process that identifies important factors and then compares the results from different geographic locales. This comparison allows them, for example, to identify how risky a venture is in Argentina versus Russia.

Factors that typically are quantified reflect the political and economic environment, domestic economic conditions, and external economic conditions. Each factor is given a minimum and maximum score, and the person(s) responsible for making the evaluation will determine the score for each. When this process is complete, a total risk evaluation number is computed by simply adding the individual scores. Table 10–3 provides an example of a quantitative list of political risk criteria.

Formulating Appropriate Response

Once political risk has been analyzed by either the framework or quantitative approach, or both, the MNC then will attempt to manage the risk further by minimizing or limiting it through carefully formulated responses. Two such common approaches are the use of relative bargaining power and the use of integrative as well as protective and defensive techniques.

Relative Bargaining Power   The theory behind relative bargaining power is quite simple. The MNC works to maintain a stronger bargaining power position than that of the host country. A good example is when the MNC has proprietary technology that will be unavailable to the host country if the operation is expropriated or the firm is forced to abide by government decisions that are unacceptable to it. Over time, of course, this technology may become common, and the firm will lose its bargaining power. To prevent this from happening, however, the firm will work to develop new technology that again establishes the balance of power in its favor. As long as the host country stands to lose more than it will gain by taking action against the company, the firm has successfully minimized its political risk by establishing an effective bargaining position. Figure 10–3 provides an example.

Table 10–3
Criteria for Quantifying Political Risk

Major Area	Criteria	Scores	
		Minimum	Maximum
Political and economic environment	1. Stability of the political system	3	14
	2. Imminent internal conflicts	0	14
	3. Threats to stability emanating from the outside world	0	12
	4. Degree of control of the economic system	5	9
	5. Reliability of the country as a trading partner	4	12
	6. Constitutional guarantees	2	12
	7. Effectiveness of public administration	3	12
	8. Labor relations and social peace	3	15
Domestic economic conditions	9. Size of population	4	8
	10. Per capita income	2	10
	11. Economic growth during previous 5 years	2	7
	12. Prospective growth during next 3 years	3	10
	13. Inflation during previous 2 years	2	10
	14. Accessibility of domestic capital market to foreigners	3	7
	15. Availability of high-quality local labor	2	8
	16. Possibility of giving employment to foreign nationals	2	8
	17. Availability of energy resources	2	14
	18. Legal requirements concerning environmental protection	4	8
	19. Traffic system and communication	2	14
External economic relations	20. Restrictions imposed on imports	2	10
	21. Restrictions imposed on exports	2	10
	22. Restrictions imposed on foreign investments in the country	3	9
	23. Freedom to set up or engage in partnerships	3	9
	24. Legal protection for brands and products	3	9
	25. Restrictions imposed on monetary transfers	2	8
	26. Reevaluations against the DM during previous 5 years	2	7
	27. Development of the balance of payments	2	9
	28. Drain on foreign funds through oil and other energy imports	3	14
	29. International financial standing	3	8
	30. Restrictions imposed on the exchange of local money into foreign currencies	2	8

Source: Adapted from E. Dichtl and H. G. Koglmayr, "Country Risk Ratings," *Management International Review,* vol. 26, no. 4, 1986, p. 6. Used with permission.

As long as the MNC's bargaining power remains at or above the diagonal line, the government will not intervene. At point E in the figure, however, this power declines, and the host country will begin to intervene.[18]

Integrative as well as Protective and Defensive Techniques

Another way that MNCs attempt to protect themselves from expropriation and/or minimize government interference in their operations is to use integration and the implementation of protective and defensive techniques. **Integrative techniques** are designed to help the overseas operation become part of the host country's infrastructure. The objective is to be perceived as "less foreign" and thus unlikely to be the target of government action. Some of the most integrative techniques include: (1) developing good relations with the host government and other local political groups; (2) producing as much of the product locally as possible with the use of in-country suppliers and subcontractors, thus making it a "domestic" product; (3) creating joint ventures and hiring local people to manage and run the operation; (4) doing as much local research and development as possible; and (5) developing effective labor-management relations.

Protective and defensive techniques are designed to discourage the host government from interfering in operations. In contrast to the integrative techniques, these actually encourage nonintegration of the enterprise in the local environment. Examples include: (1)

Integrative techniques
Techniques that help the overseas operation become a part of the host country's infrastructure.

Protective and defensive techniques
Techniques that discourage the host government from interfering in operations.

Figure 10–3

Relative Bargaining Power over Time

Source: Adapted from Thomas A. Pointer, "Political Risk: Managing Government Intervention," in Paul W. Beamish, J. Peter Killing, Donald J. LeCraw, and Harold Crookell, *International Management: Text and Cases* (Homewood, IL: Irwin, 1991), p. 125.

doing as little local manufacturing as possible and conducting all research and development outside the country; (2) limiting the responsibility of local personnel and hiring only those who are vital to the operation; (3) raising capital from local banks and the host government as well as outside sources; and (4) diversifying production of the product among a number of countries.

When should a company use integrative techniques? Under what conditions should it employ protective and defensive techniques? Analysis reveals that this choice will be heavily influenced by characteristics such as the MNC's technology, management skills, and logistics and labor transmission. In all, four basic types of firms can be described using these characteristics.

The first type consists of dynamic, high-technology MNCs that have unique knowledge that the host country would like. Computer companies are a good example. As seen in Figure 10–4, these firms do not rely very much on integrative techniques. They attempt to keep their distance from the host country and rely heavily on protective and defensive strategies.

The second type consists of MNCs with low or stable technology. These MNCs make products that require little innovation or use relatively unsophisticated technology. Steel firms are an example. As seen in Figure 10–4, these firms typically use both high integration and high protective and defensive strategies, although they generally rely more on integration than the defensive approach.

The third type consists of MNCs whose managers need to be highly skilled. For example, food production firms require advanced marketing and management skills to be competitive. These MNCs typically use a balanced approach of integration and protective and defensive techniques, but they are less concerned with either than low or stable technology firms are.

The fourth type consists of MNCs characterized by highly labor-intensive products, high value in relation to weight and/or volume, and the need for a strong global marketing system for selling the product. Sewing machine companies are an example. Firms in this category tend to rely more heavily on protective and defensive measures than any of the other three groups and to employ only moderate concern for integrative techniques (again, see Figure 10–4).

The strategic response that a firm takes in managing its political risk will be influenced by a variety of factors besides the firm's technology, management skills, logistics, and labor transmission. Others include the nature of the industry, local conditions in the host country, and philosophy of the management. Whatever variables are considered, however, firms are going to use a combination of integrative and protective and defensive techniques.

Source: Adapted from Ann Gregory, "Firm Characteristic and Political Risk Reduction in Overseas Ventures," *National Academy of Management Proceedings,* 1982, p. 77. Used with permission.

■ Managing International Negotiations

Closely related to managing political risk, but deserving special attention, is managing negotiations.[19] **Negotiation** is the process of bargaining with one or more parties to arrive at a solution that is acceptable to all. Negotiation often follows assessing political risk and can be used as an approach to conflict management. If the risk is worth it, then the MNC must negotiate with the host country to secure the best possible arrangements. The MNC and the host country will discuss the investment the MNC is prepared to make in return for certain guarantees and/or concessions. The initial range of topics typically includes critical areas such as hiring practices, direct financial investment, taxes, and ownership control. Negotiation also is used in creating joint ventures with local firms and in getting the operation off the ground. After the firm is operating, additional areas of negotiation often include expansion of facilities, use of more local managers, additional imports or exports of materials and finished goods, and recapture of profits.

On a more macro level of international trade are the negotiations conducted between countries. The current balance-of-trade problem between the United States and China is one example. The massive debt problems of less developed countries and the opening of trade doors with Eastern European and newly emerging economies are other current examples.

Negotiation
The process of bargaining with one or more parties for the purpose of arriving at a solution that is acceptable to all.

The Negotiation Process

There are several basic steps that can be used in managing the negotiation process. Regardless of the issues or personalities of the parties involved, this process typically begins with planning.

Planning Planning starts with the negotiators' identifying those objectives they would like to attain. Then, they explore the possible options for reaching these objectives. Research shows that the greater the number of options, the greater the chances for successful negotiations. While this appears to be an obvious statement, research also reveals that many negotiators do not alter their strategy when negotiating across cultures.[20] Next, consideration is given to areas of common ground between the parties. Other major areas include: (1) the setting of limits on single-point objectives, such as deciding to pay no more than $10 million for the factory and $3 million for the land; (2) dividing issues into short- and long-term considerations and deciding how to handle each; and (3) determining the sequence in which to discuss the various issues.

Impersonal Relationship Building   The second phase of the negotiation process involves getting to know the people on the other side. This "feeling out" period is characterized by the desire to identify those who are reasonable and those who are not. In contrast to negotiations in many other countries, those in the United States often give little attention to this phase; they want to get down to business immediately, which often is an ineffective approach. Adler notes:

> Effective negotiators must view luncheon, dinner, reception, ceremony, and tour invitations as times for interpersonal relationship building, and therefore as key to the negotiating process. When American negotiators, often frustrated by the seemingly endless formalities, ceremonies, and "small talk," ask how long they must wait before beginning to "do business," the answer is simple: wait until your opponents bring up business (and they will). Realize that the work of conducting a successful negotiation has already begun, even if business has yet to be mentioned.[21]

Exchanging Task-Related Information   In this part of the negotiation process, each group sets forth its position on the critical issues. These positions often will change later in the negotiations. At this point, the participants are trying to find out what the other party wants to attain and what it is willing to give up.

Persuasion   This step of negotiations is considered by many to be the most important. No side wants to give away more than it has to, but each knows that without giving some concessions, it is unlikely to reach a final agreement. The success of the persuasion step often depends on: (1) how well the parties understand each other's position; (2) the ability of each to identify areas of similarity and differences; (3) the ability to create new options; and (4) the willingness to work toward a solution that allows all parties to walk away feeling they have achieved their objectives.

Agreement   The final phase of negotiations is the granting of concessions and hammering out a final agreement. Sometimes, this phase is carried out piecemeal, and concessions and agreements are made on issues one at a time. This is the way those from the United States like to negotiate. As each issue is resolved, it is removed from the bargaining table and interest focused on the next. Asians and Russians, on the other hand, tend to negotiate a final agreement on everything, and few concessions are given until the end. Simply put, to negotiate effectively in the international arena, it is necessary to understand how cultural differences between the parties affect the process.

Cultural Differences Affecting Negotiations

In negotiating effectively, it is important to have a sound understanding of the other side's culture. This includes consideration of areas such as communication patterns, time orientation, and social behaviors.[22] A number of useful steps can help in this process. One negotiation expert recommends the following:

1. Do not identify the counterpart's home culture too quickly. Common cues (e.g., name, physical appearance, language, accent, location) may be unreliable. The counterpart probably belongs to more than one culture.
2. Beware of the Western bias toward "doing." In Arab, Asian, and Latin groups, ways of being (e.g., comportment, smell), feeling, thinking, and talking can shape relationships more powerfully than doing.
3. Try to counteract the tendency to formulate simple, consistent, stable images.
4. Do not assume that all aspects of the culture are equally significant. In Japan, consulting all relevant parties to a decision is more important than presenting a gift.
5. Recognize that norms for interactions involving outsiders may differ from those for interactions between compatriots.

6. Do not overestimate your familiarity with your counterpart's culture. An American studying Japanese wrote New Year's wishes to Japanese contacts in basic Japanese characters, but omitted one character. As a result, the message became "Dead man, congratulations."[23]

Other useful examples have been offered by Trompenaars and Hampden-Turner, who note that a society's culture often plays a major role in determining the effectiveness of a negotiating approach. This is particularly true when the negotiating groups come from decidedly different cultures such as an ascription society and an achievement society. As noted in Chapter 5, in an ascription society status is attributed based on birth, kinship, gender, age, and personal connections. In an achievement society status is determined by accomplishments. As a result, each side's cultural perceptions can affect the outcome of the negotiation. Here is an example:

> sending whiz-kids to deal with people 10–20 years their senior often insults the ascriptive culture. The reaction may be: "Do these people think that they have reached our own level of experience in half the time? That a 30-year-old American is good enough to negotiate with a 50-year-old Greek or Italian?" Achievement cultures must understand that some ascriptive cultures, the Japanese especially, spend much on training and in-house education to ensure that older people actually are wiser for the years they have spent in the corporation and for the sheer number of subordinates briefing them. It insults an ascriptive culture to do anything which prevents the self-fulfilling nature of its beliefs. Older people are held to be important **so that** they will be nourished and sustained by others' respect. A stranger is expected to facilitate this scheme, not challenge it.[24]

U.S. negotiators have a style that often differs from that of negotiators in many other countries. Americans believe it is important to be factual and objective. In addition, they often make early concessions to show the other party that they are flexible and reasonable. Moreover, U.S. negotiators typically have authority to bind their party to an agreement, so if the right deal is struck, the matter can be resolved quickly. This is why deadlines are so important to Americans. They have come to do business, and they want to get things resolved immediately.

A comparative example would be the Arabs, who in contrast to Americans, with their logical approach, tend to use an emotional appeal in their negotiation style. They analyze things subjectively and treat deadlines as only general guidelines for wrapping up negotiations. They tend to open negotiations with an extreme initial position. However, the Arabs believe strongly in making concessions, do so throughout the bargaining process, and almost always reciprocate an opponent's concessions. They also seek to build a long-term relationship with their bargaining partners. For these reasons, Americans typically find it easier to negotiate with Arabs than with representatives from many other regions of the world.

Another interesting comparative example is provided by the Chinese. In initial negotiation meetings, it is common for Chinese negotiators to seek agreement on the general focus of the meetings. The hammering out of specific details is postponed for later get-togethers. By achieving agreement on the general framework within which the negotiations will be conducted, the Chinese thus seek to limit and focus the discussions. Many Westerners misunderstand what is happening during these initial meetings and believe the dialogue consists mostly of rhetoric and general conversation. They are wrong and quite often are surprised later on when the Chinese negotiators use the agreement on the framework and principles as a basis for getting agreement on goals—and then insist that all discussions on concrete arrangements be in accord with these agreed upon goals. Simply put, what is viewed as general conversation by many Western negotiators is regarded by the Chinese as a formulation of the rules of the game which must be adhered to throughout the negotiations. So in negotiating with the Chinese, it is important to come prepared to ensure that one's own agenda, framework, and principles are accepted by both parties.

Before beginning any negotiations, negotiators should review the negotiating style of the other parties. (Table 10–4 provides some insights regarding negotiation styles of the

Table 10–4
Negotiation Styles from a Cross-Cultural Perspective

Element	United States	Japanese	Arabians	Mexicans
Group composition	Marketing oriented	Function oriented	Committee of specialists	Friendship oriented
Number involved	2–3	4–7	4–6	2–3
Space orientation	Confrontational; competitive	Display harmonious relationship	Status	Close, friendly
Establishing rapport	Short period; direct to task	Longer period; until harmony	Long period; until trusted	Longer period; discuss family
Exchange of information	Documented; step-by-step; multimedia	Extensive; concentrate on receiving side	Less emphasis on technology, more on relationship	Less emphasis on technology, more on relationship
Persuasion tools	Time pressure; loss of saving/making money	Maintain relationship references; intergroup connections	Go-between; hospitality	Emphasis on family and on social concerns; goodwill measured in generations
Use of language	Open, direct, sense of urgency	Indirect, appreciative, cooperative	Flattery, emotional, religious	Respectful, gracious
First offer	Fair ±5 to 10%	±10 to 20%	±20 to 50%	Fair
Second offer	Add to package; sweeten the deal	–5%	–10%	Add an incentive
Final offer package	Total package	Makes no further concessions	–25%	Total
Decision-making process	Top management team	Collective	Team makes recommendation	Senior manager and secretary
Decision maker	Top management team	Middle line with team consensus	Senior manager	Senior manager
Risk taking	Calculated personal responsibility	Low group responsibility	Religion based	Personally responsible

Source: Lillian H. Chaney and Jeanette S. Martin, *Intercultural Business Communication* © 1995, pp. 183–184. Reprinted by permission of Prentice Hall, Inc. Englewood Cliffs, New Jersey.

Americans, Japanese, Arabs, and Mexicans.) This review should help to answer certain questions: What can we expect the other side to say and do? How are they likely to respond to certain offers? When should the most important matters be introduced? How quickly should concessions be made, and what type of reciprocity should be expected? These types of questions help effectively prepare the negotiators. In addition, the team will work on formulating negotiation tactics. The accompanying sidebar, "Negotiating with the Japanese," demonstrates such tactics, and the following discussion gets into some of the specifics.

Negotiation Tactics

A number of specific tactics are used in international negotiation. The following discussion examines some of the most common.

Location   Where should negotiations take place? If the matter is very important, most businesses will choose a neutral site. For example, U.S. firms negotiating with companies from the Far East will meet in Hawaii, South American companies negotiating with European firms will meet halfway, in New York City. A number of benefits derive from using a neutral site. One is that each party has limited access to its home office for receiving a great deal of negotiating information and advice and thus gaining an advantage on the other. A second is that the cost of staying at the site often is quite high, so both sides have an incentive to conclude their negotiations as quickly as possible. (Of course, if one side enjoys the

International Management in Action

Negotiating with the Japanese

Some people believe that the most effective way of getting the Japanese to open up their markets to the United States is to use a form of strong-arm tactics, such as putting the country on a list of those to be targeted for retaliatory action. Others believe that this approach will not be effective, because the interests of the United States and Japan are intertwined and we would be hurting ourselves as much as them. Regardless of which group is right, one thing is certain: U.S. MNCs must learn how to negotiate more effectively with the Japanese. What can they do? Researchers have found that besides patience and a little table pounding, a number of important steps warrant consideration.

First, business firms need to prepare for their negotiations by learning more about Japanese culture and the "right" ways to conduct discussions. Those companies with experience in these matters report that the two best ways of doing this are to read books on Japanese business practices and social customs and to hire experts to train the negotiators. Other steps that are helpful include putting the team through simulated negotiations and hiring Japanese to assist in the negotiations.

Second, U.S. MNCs must learn patience and sincerity. Negotiations are a two-way street that require the mutual cooperation and efforts of both parties. The U.S. negotiators must understand that many times, Japanese negotiators do not have full authority to make on-the-spot decisions. Authority must be given by someone at the home office, and this failure to act quickly should not be interpreted as a lack of sincerity on the part of the Japanese negotiators.

Third, the MNC must have a unique good or service. So many things are offered for sale in Japan that unless the company has something that is truly different, persuading the other party to buy it is difficult.

Fourth, technical expertise often is viewed as a very important contribution, and this often helps to win concessions with the Japanese. The Japanese know that the Americans, for example, still dominate the world when it comes to certain types of technology and that Japan is unable to compete effectively in these areas. When such technical expertise is evident, it is very influential in persuading the Japanese to do business with the company.

These four criteria are critical to effective negotiations with the Japanese. MNCs that use them report more successful experiences than those who do not.

facilities and would like to stay as long as possible, the negotiations could drag on.) A third is that most negotiators do not like to return home with nothing to show for their efforts, so they are motivated to reach some type of agreement.

Time Limits Time limits are an important negotiation tactic when one party is under a time constraint. This is particularly true when this party has agreed to meet at the home site of the other party. For example, U.S. negotiators who go to London to discuss a joint venture with a British firm often will have a scheduled return flight. Once their hosts find out how long these individuals intend to stay, the British can plan their strategy accordingly. The "real" negotiations are unlikely to begin until close to the time that the Americans must leave. The British know that their guests will be anxious to strike some type of deal before returning home, so the Americans are at a disadvantage.

Time limits can be used tactically even if the negotiators meet at a neutral site. For example, most Americans like to be home with their families for Thanksgiving, Christmas, and the New Year holiday. Negotiations held right before these dates put Americans at a disadvantage, because the other party knows when the Americans would like to leave.

Buyer–Seller Relations How should buyers and sellers act? As noted earlier, Americans believe in being objective and trading favors. When the negotiations are over, Americans walk away with what they have received from the other party, and they expect the other party to do the same. This is not the way negotiators in many other countries think, however.

The Japanese, for example, believe that the buyers should get most of what they want. On the other hand, they also believe that the seller should be taken care of through reciprocal favors. The buyer must ensure that the seller has not been "picked clean." For example, when many Japanese firms first started doing business with large U.S. firms, they were unaware of U.S. negotiating tactics. As a result, the Japanese thought the Americans were taking advantage of them, whereas the Americans believed they were driving a good, hard bargain.

The Brazilians are quite different from both the Americans and Japanese. Researchers have found that Brazilians do better when they are more deceptive and self-interested and their opponents more open and honest than they are.[25] Brazilians also tend to make fewer promises and commitments than their opponents, and they are much more prone to say no. However, Brazilians are more likely to make initial concessions. Overall, Brazilians are more like Americans than Japanese in that they try to maximize their advantage, but they are unlike Americans in that they do not feel obligated to be open and forthright in their approach. Whether they are buyer or seller, they want to come out on top.

Bargaining Behaviors

Closely related to the discussion of negotiation tactics are the different types of bargaining behaviors, including both verbal and nonverbal behaviors. Verbal behaviors are an important part of the negotiating process, because they can improve the final outcome. Research shows that the profits of the negotiators increase when they make high initial offers, ask a lot of questions, and do not make many verbal commitments until the end of the negotiating process. In short, verbal behaviors are critical to the success of negotiations.

Use of Extreme Behaviors Some negotiators begin by making extreme offers or requests. The Chinese and Arabs are examples. Some negotiators, however, begin with an initial position that is close to the one they are seeking. The Americans and Swedes are examples here.

Is one approach any more effective than the other? Research shows that extreme positions tend to produce better results. Some of the reasons relate to the fact that an extreme bargaining position: (1) shows the other party that the bargainer will not be exploited; (2) extends the negotiation and gives the bargainer a better opportunity to gain information on the opponent; (3) allows more room for concessions; (4) modifies the opponents' beliefs about the bargainer's preferences; (5) shows the opponent that the bargainer is willing to play the game according to the usual norms; and (6) lets the bargainer gain more than would probably be possible if a less extreme initial position had been taken.

Although the use of extreme position bargaining is considered to be "unAmerican," many U.S. firms have used it successfully against foreign competitors. When Peter Ueberroth managed the Olympic Games in the United States in 1984, he turned a profit of well over $100 million—and that was without the participation of Soviet bloc countries, which would have further increased the market potential of the games. In past Olympiads, sponsoring countries have lost hundreds of millions of dollars. How did Ueberroth do it? One way was by using extreme position bargaining. For example, the Olympic Committee felt that the Japanese should pay $10 million for the right to televise the games in the country, so when the Japanese offered $6 million for the rights, the Olympic Committee countered with $90 million. Eventually, the two sides agreed on $18.5 million. Through the effective use of extreme position bargaining, Ueberroth got the Japanese to pay over three times their original offer, an amount well in excess of the committee's budget.

Promises, Threats, and Other Behaviors Another approach to bargaining is the use of promises, threats, rewards, self-disclosures, and other behaviors that are designed to influence the other party. These behaviors often are greatly influenced by the culture. Graham conducted research using Japanese, U.S., and Brazilian businesspeople and found that they employed a variety of different behaviors during a buyer-seller negotiation simulation.[26] Table 10–5 presents the results.

The table shows that Americans and Japanese make greater use of promises than Brazilians. The Japanese also rely heavily on recommendations and commitment. The Brazilians use a discussion of rewards, commands, and self-disclosure more than Americans and Japanese. The Brazilians also say no a great deal more and make first offers that have higher-level profits than those of the others. Americans tend to operate between these two groups, although they do make less use of commands than either of their opponents and make first offers that have lower profit levels than their opponents.

Table 10–5

Cross-Cultural Differences in Verbal Behavior of Japanese, U.S., and Brazilian Negotiators

Behavior and Definition	Number of Times Tactic Was Used in a Half-Hour Bargaining Session		
	Japanese	United States	Brazilian
Promise. A statement in which the source indicated an intention to provide the target with a reinforcing consequence which source anticipates target will evaluate as pleasant, positive, or rewarding.	7	8	3
Threat. Same as promise, except that the reinforcing consequences are thought to be noxious, unpleasant, or punishing.	4	4	2
Recommendation. A statement in which the source predicts that a pleasant environmental consequence will occur to the target. Its occurrence is not under the source's control.	7	4	5
Warning. Same as recommendation except that the consequences are thought to be unpleasant.	2	1	1
Reward. A statement by the source that is thought to create pleasant consequences for the target.	1	2	2
Punishment. Same as reward, except that the consequences are thought to be unpleasant.	1	3	3
Positive normative appeal. A statement in which the source indicates that the target's past, present, or future behavior was or will be in conformity with social norms.	1	1	0
Negative normative appeal. Same as positive normative appeal, except that the target's behavior is in violation of social norms.	3	1	1
Commitment. A statement by the source to the effect that its future bids will not go below or above a certain level.	15	13	8
Self-disclosure. A statement in which the source reveals information about itself.	34	36	39
Question. A statement in which the source asks the target to reveal information about itself.	20	20	22
Command. A statement in which the source suggests that the target perform a certain behavior.	8	6	14
First offer. The profit level associated with each participant's first offer.	61.5	57.3	75.2
Initial concession. The differences in profit between the first and second offer.	6.5	7.1	9.4
Number of no's. Number of times the word "no" was used by bargainers per half-hour.	5.7	9.0	83.4

Source: Adapted from John L. Graham, "The Influence of Culture on the Process of Business Negotiations in an Exploratory Study," *Journal of International Business Studies,* Spring 1983, pp. 84, 88. Used with permission.

Nonverbal Behaviors Nonverbal behaviors also are very common during negotiations. These behaviors refer to what people do rather than what they say. Nonverbal behaviors sometimes are called the "silent language." Typical examples include silent periods, facial gazing, touching, and conversational overlaps. As seen in Table 10–6, the Japanese tend to use silent periods much more often than either Americans or Brazilians during negotiations. In fact, in this study, the latter did not use them at all. The Brazilians did, however, make frequent use of other nonverbal behaviors. They employed facial gazing almost four times more often than the Japanese, and almost twice as often as the Americans. In addition, although the latter two groups did not touch their opponents, the Brazilians made wide use of this nonverbal tactic. They also relied heavily on conversational overlaps, employing them more than twice as often as the Japanese and almost three times as often as Americans. Quite obviously, the Brazilians rely very heavily on nonverbal behaviors in their negotiating.

Table 10–6
Cross-Cultural Differences in Nonverbal Behavior of Japanese, U.S., and Brazilian Negotiators

Behavior and Definition	Number of Times Tactic Was Used in a Half-Hour Bargaining Session		
	Japanese	United States	Brazilian
Silent period. The number of conversational gaps of 10 seconds or more per 30 minutes.	5.5	3.5	0
Facial gazing. The number of minutes negotiators spend looking at their opponent's face per randomly selected 10-minute period.	1.3 minutes	3.3 minutes	5.2 minutes
Touching. Incidents of bargainers' touching one another per half-hour (not including handshakes).	0	0	4.7
Conversational overlaps. The number of times (per 10 minutes) that both parties to the negotiation would talk at the same time.	12.6	10.3	28.6

Source: Adapted from John L. Graham, "The Influence of Culture on the Process of Business Negotiations in an Exploratory Study," *Journal of International Business Studies,* Spring 1983, p. 84. Used with permission.

The important thing to remember is that in international negotiations, people use a wide variety of tactics, and the other side must be prepared to counter or find a way of dealing with them. The response will depend on the situation. Managers from different cultures will give different answers. Table 10–7 provides some examples of the types of characteristics needed in effective negotiators. To the extent that international managers have these characteristics, their success as negotiators should increase.

The World of *Business Week*—Revisited

There were a far-ranging number of political risks that were discussed in this chapter. However, as MNCs do business in the new millennium, it is becoming evident that some of these risks are more common and more critical than others. For example, there is less risk associated with the expropriation of an MNC's assets. On the other hand, there is increasing risk that an MNC will find itself embedded in an emerging economy that is stagnant and cannot be easily jump-started. There is also the possibility, as seen in the case of South Korea, that a country's economy will be split into two groups: old and new. The old economy consists of businesses and industries that were healthy and profitable a decade ago but are now stagnant or declining while the new economy is made up of companies in emerging, high technology and other cutting-edge areas. Beginning in the mid-1980s the United States faced this same situation and it resulted in a restructuring of the economy. Many old-line businesses ceased to exist and people who had worked with these firms for most of their career found themselves having to find employment elsewhere. Fortunately, new jobs, new companies, and new industries emerged and the economy grew and prospered. One reason was because the government, for the most part, let the marketplace decide what would happen. In South Korea in particular, and Asia in general, the government's view of its responsibility is less market-driven than that in the U.S. So political risk will continue to be a big concern for MNCs doing business there. So too will effective negotiating. Based on your reading of this chapter and the opening news story, answer these questions: (1) What are two of the main concerns that MNCs should evaluate when examining political risk in South Korea? (2) How could an MNC protect itself from government action? (3) What are some useful things to know about negotiating in Asia?

Table 10–7

Culture-Specific Characteristics Needed by International Managers for Effective Negotiations

U.S. managers	Preparation and planning skill Ability to think under pressure Judgment and intelligence Verbal expressiveness Product knowledge Ability to perceive and exploit power Integrity
Japanese managers	Dedication to job Ability to perceive and exploit power Ability to win respect and confidence Integrity Listening skill Broad perspective Verbal expressiveness
Chinese managers (Taiwan)	Persistence and determination Ability to win respect and confidence Preparation and planning skill Product knowledge Interesting Judgment and intelligence
Brazilian managers	Preparation and planning skill Ability to think under pressure Judgment and intelligence Verbal expressiveness Product knowledge Ability to perceive and exploit power Competitiveness

Source: Adapted from Nancy J. Adler, *International Dimensions of Organizational Behavior,* 2nd ed. (Boston: PWS-Kent Publishing, 1991), p. 187, and from material provided by Professor John Graham, School of Business Administration, University of Southern California, 1983.

Summary of Key Points

1. Political risk is the likelihood that the foreign investment of a business will be constrained by a host government's policies. In dealing with this risk, companies conduct both macro and micro political risk analyses. Specific consideration is given to changing host government policies, expropriation, and operational profitability risk.

2. MNCs attempt to manage their political risk in two basic ways. One is by developing a comprehensive framework for identifying and describing these risks. This includes consideration of political, operational, and ownership-control risks. A second is by quantifying the variables that help constitute the risk.

3. Two common risk formulation strategies are the use of relative bargaining power and of integrative as well as protective and defensive techniques. Figure

10–4 illustrates how firms in various industries use a combination of the integrative and the protective and defensive techniques in developing an overall response strategy.

4. Negotiation is the process of bargaining with one or more parties to arrive at a solution that is acceptable to all. This process involves five basic steps: planning, interpersonal relationship building, exchanging task-related information, persuasion, and agreement. The way in which the process is carried out often will vary because of cultural differences.

5. There are a wide variety of tactics used in international negotiating. These include location, time limits, buyer-seller relations, verbal behaviors, and nonverbal behaviors.

Key Terms

conglomerate investment, *289*

expropriation, *287*

horizontal investment, *290*

indigenization laws, *287*

integrative techniques, *291*

macro political risk analysis, *283*

micro political risk analysis, *283*

negotiation, *293*

operational risks, *288*

ownership-control risks, *288*

political risk, *282*

protective and defensive
techniques, *291*

transfer risks, *288*

vertical investment, *289*

Review and Discussion Questions

1. What types of political risk would a company entering Russia face? Identify and describe three. What types of political risk would a company entering France face? Identify and describe three. How are these risks similar? How are they different?

2. Most firms attempt to quantify their political risk, although they do not assign specific weights to the respective criteria. Why is this approach so popular? Would the companies be better off assigning weights to each of the risks being assumed? Defend your answer.

3. If a high-tech firm wanted to set up operations in Iran, what steps might it take to ensure that the subsidiary would not be expropriated? Identify and describe three strategies that would be particularly helpful.

4. If a company new to the international arena was negotiating an agreement with a potential partner in an overseas country, what basic steps should it be prepared to implement? Identify and describe them.

5. Wilsten, Inc., has been approached by a Japanese firm that wants exclusive production and selling rights for one of Wilsten's new, high-tech products. What does Wilsten need to know about Japanese bargaining behaviors to strike the best possible deal with this company? Identify and describe five.

Internet Exercise: Motorola in China

Asia still offers great opportunities for multinational firms. However, given the slowdown that has occurred in this region in recent years, there are also great risks associated with doing business there. The large American-based MNC Motorola has determined that the opportunities are worth the risk and has staked a large claim in China and is determined to be a major player in the emerging Asian market. Visit Motorola's web site at **www.motorola.com** and focus your attention on what this well-known MNC is now doing in Asia. Drawing from specific information obtained from the web site, this chapter, and your reading of the current news answer these questions: What political risks is Motorola facing in Asia, particularly China? How can Motorola manage these risks? How can effective international negotiating skills be of value to the firm in reducing its political risk and increasing its competitive advantage in this area of the world?

Peru

Peru is located on the west coast of South America. It is the third-largest nation on the continent (only Brazil and Argentina have more area), and it covers almost 500,000 square miles (about 14 percent of the size of the United States). The land has enormous contrasts, with a desert (drier than the Sahara), the towering snow-capped Andes Mountains, sparkling grass-covered plateaus, and thick rain forests. Peru has approximately 27 million people, of which about 20 percent live in Lima, the capital. More Indians (one-half of the population) live in Peru than any other country in the Western Hemisphere. The ancestors of Peru's Indians are the famous Incas, who built a great empire. The rest of the population is mixed, and a small percentage is white. The economy depends heavily on agriculture, fishing, mining, and services. GDP is approximately $115 billion and per-capita income in recent years has been around $4,300. In recent years the economy has gained some relative strength and multinationals are now beginning to again consider investing in the country.

One of these potential investors is a large New York bank that is considering a $25 million loan to the owner of a Peruvian fishing fleet. The owner wants to refurbish the fleet and add one more ship.

During the 1970s, the Peruvian government nationalized a number of industries and factories and began running them for the profit of the state. In most cases, these state-run ventures became disasters. In the late 1970s, the fishing fleet owner was given back his ships and allowed to operate his business as before. Since then, he has managed to remain profitable, but the biggest problem is that his ships are getting old and he needs an influx of capital to make repairs and add new technology. As he explained it to the New York banker: "Fishing is no longer just an art. There is a great deal of technology involved. And to keep costs low and be competitive on the world market, you have to have the latest equipment for both locating as well as catching and then loading and unloading the fish."

Having reviewed the fleet owner's operation, the large multinational bank believes that the loan is justified. The financial institution is concerned, however, that the Peruvian government might step in during the next couple of years and again take over the business. If this were to happen, it might take an additional decade for the loan to be repaid. If the government were to allow the fleet owner to operate the fleet the way he has over the last decade, the loan could be repaid within 7 years.

Right now, the bank is deciding the specific terms of the agreement. Once these have been worked out, either a loan officer will fly down to Lima and close the deal or the owner will be asked to come to New York for the signing. Whichever approach is used, the bank realizes that final adjustments in the agreement will have to be made on the spot. Therefore, if the bank sends a representative to Lima, the individual will have to have the authority to commit the bank to specific terms. These final matters should be worked out within the next 10 days.

www.peru-explorer.com

Questions

1. What are some current issues facing Peru? What is the climate for doing business in Peru today?

2. What type of political risks does this fishing company need to evaluate? Identify and describe them.

3. What types of integrative and protective and defensive techniques can the bank use?

4. Would the bank be better off negotiating the loan in New York or in Lima? Why?

Going to Gdansk

When Poland made the necessary reforms to move toward a market economy, Andrzej Jaworski from Chicago, Illinois, began thinking this might be an excellent place to set up an overseas operation. Andrzej and his two brothers own a firm that produces specialized computer chips. The company has a series of patents that provide legal protection and allow it to dominate a small but growing segment of the computer market. Their sales estimates reached $147 million within 3 years, but they believe that this could rise to $200 million if they were to expand internationally. They have thought about setting up a plant in Belgium so that they could take advantage of the European market growth. They would prefer Poland, however, because their parents grew up there before leaving for the United States in 1948. "We feel that we know the Poles because we have grown up in a Polish household here in the Midwest," Andrzej explained to his banker. "We would like to see if the government would allow us to set up a small plant in Gdansk, train the necessary workers, and then export our product into the European Union."

One of the primary reasons that Andrzej believes that the Polish government would be agreeable to the plan is that not only is Poland moving to a market economy, but the country is still struggling with foreign debt, inflation, and outmoded technology. A state-of-the-art plant could help to reduce unemployment and provide an inflow of needed capital. However, the banker is concerned that because of the political risks and uncertainty in Central Europe in general and Poland in particular, the company may either lose its investment through government expropriation or find itself unable to get profits out of the country. Given that the company will have to invest approximately $20 million, the venture could seriously endanger the company's financial status.

Andrzej understands these risks but believes that with the help of an international management consultant, he can identify and minimize the problems. "I'm determined to push ahead," he told the banker, "and if there is a good chance of making this project a success, I'm going to Gdansk."

Questions

1. What are some of the political risks that Andrzej's firm will face if he decides to go ahead with this venture? Identify and describe two or three.

2. Using Figure 10–1, what strategy would you recommend that the firm use? Why?

3. In his negotiations with the Polish government, what suggestions or guidelines would you offer to Andrzej? Identify and describe two or three.

Chapter 11

Organizing International Operations

Objectives of the Chapter

The success of an international firm can be greatly affected by the overall structure and design of operations. There are a wide variety of organizational structures and designs from which to choose. Selecting the most appropriate structure depends on a number of factors, such as the desire of the home office for control over its foreign operations and the demands placed on the overseas unit by both the local market and the personnel who work there.

This chapter first presents and analyzes traditional organizational structures for effective international operations. Then, it explores some of the new, nontraditional organizational arrangements stemming from mergers, joint ventures, and the Japanese concept of *keiretsu*. The specific objectives of this chapter are:

1. **EXAMINE** the major types of organizational structures used in handling international operations.

2. **ANALYZE** the advantages and disadvantages of each type of organizational structure, including the conditions that make one preferable to others.

3. **DESCRIBE** the recent, nontraditional organizational arrangements coming out of mergers, joint ventures, *keiretsus,* and other new designs including electronic networks and product development structures.

4. **DISCUSS** the value of subsidiary boards of directors in overseas operations.

5. **EXPLAIN** how organizational characteristics such as formalization, specialization, and centralization influence how the organization is structured and functions.

BusinessWeek

The World of *Business Week*

Can Kraft Be A Big Cheese Abroad?

When Aussies stroll down the aisles of their local supermarket, what catches their eyes are snacks from Unilever and Nestlé. Kraft Macaroni & Cheese and Oscar Mayer hot dogs, on the other hand, are hard to find and far from first choice. "They would be classified as a slow-moving line," says Terry Walters, the owner of an IGA store in Cairns, Queensland, about the classic American macaroni-and-cheese dinner. As for hot dogs: "We have the meat pie."

Kraft may be ubiquitous in U.S. grocery stores, but overseas it's a far different picture. Kraft isn't one of Walters' top five food suppliers, ranking below even H.J. Heinz Co., despite its ownership of Australia's famed Vegemite spread. Only 27% of its total revenues come from overseas, vs. 44% for Heinz, more than 50% for McDonald's Corp., and more than 80% for Coca-Cola Co.

That will have to change. As Kraft embarks on a giant initial public offering, its challenge is to once again become a growth company. Widely admired for the astute management of its brand lineup, Kraft is nevertheless stuck in a slow-growth industry in the U.S. Smart marketing and methodical cost-cutting helped it boost earnings, but Kraft's sales actually have dipped slightly. The company took a big step toward building revenues with its $19.2 billion purchase of Nabisco Group Holdings Corp., whose cookie and cracker brands are growing faster than Kraft's top brands.

Analysts say that if Kraft is to spark long-term growth, it must do a better job of tapping foreign consumers. Kraft acknowledged as much when it announced that once the IPO is completed, Betsy D. Holden, CEO of Kraft Foods North America, will share the chief executive office with Roger K. Deromedi, a 13-year Kraft veteran who has been president and CEO of Kraft Foods International Inc.

American Icons

The largest food company in North America by far, Kraft has dominated U.S. grocery-store shelves for decades. Its powerhouse brands are American icons: Philadelphia Cream Cheese, Oreo cookies, Tang, Jell-O, Kool-Aid, Life Savers, Planters peanuts, Lunchables prepackaged meals for kids. Its portfolio comprises a remarkable 61 brands with more than $100 million in sales. Supermarket consultants say it would be nearly impossible to run a U.S. grocery store without its products.

Tobacco Taint

Boosting sales will become even more urgent once Kraft has outside shareholders to answer to. Cigarette maker Philip Morris, which has owned Kraft since 1988, is putting 16.1% of the company on the market in an offering that could raise as much as $8.4 billion. That would be the second-largest IPO on record,

behind only AT&T Wireless Group's $10.5 billion stock market debut last year. Philip Morris will remain firmly in control, but its goal is to realize more of Kraft's value by distancing the business from the tobacco taint that has held Philip Morris' stock price down.

The first concern for investors might be whether Kraft's co-CEO structure can work. Deromedi, 47, and Holden, 45, who started at Kraft as an assistant product manager in 1982, will both report to Geoffrey Bible, chairman of Philip Morris. Analysts wonder how long the arrangement will last, citing a long list of prominent companies, from DaimlerChrysler to Citigroup, where co-CEO setups fizzled. "The co-CEO structure calls into question if this is truly an independent company," says Goldman, Sachs & Co. analyst Romitha S. Mally. "At the end of the day, it will be the chairman and the board, which is controlled by Philip Morris, who will be the ultimate decision-makers for Kraft."

In this case, though, the co-CEOs have well-defined management areas. Another plus: Their personalities seem to complement each other. James J. Drury, vice-chairman of Spencer Stuart, an executive-search firm in Chicago, describes Deromedi, who holds a math degree, as "more focused on problem-solving and more likely to make tough decisions in complex situations." Holden, he says, is creative, charismatic, and more people-oriented: "She's more the one to take into consideration how a business situation may impact people."

A top task for the new CEOs will be figuring out how to expand outside North America. Overseas,

Kraft faces a lineup of tough global competitors—Unilever, Nestlé, Groupe Danone—that were quicker to break into fast-growing markets in Asia, Latin America, and Eastern Europe. Unilever and Nestlé, for example, each get 32% of their sales in developing countries. Western Europe, Kraft's strongest international market, is almost as saturated as the U.S. Even in Great Britain, Kraft is only the eighth-largest food company. "A truly global organization would have a quarter to one-third of their business in North America, not three-quarters," says Adrian Richardson, global consumer and retail-sector head at BT Funds Management, a large money manager in Sydney.

Fortress

One problem is that Kraft's strength, convenience products, don't go over well in emerging markets, where scarce shopping dollars are concentrated on necessities. Unilever, for example, sells staples in India such as rice with added protein and salt with iodine. Kraft, on the other hand, has only a tiny presence there. But Kraft plans to jump-start sales in emerging markets by introducing additional snack, beverage, cheese, and other brands in countries where it already has a presence. It also plans to enter countries where it has no operations and to make acquisitions, especially in snacks and beverages, according to its filings with the Securities & Exchange Commission. Richardson believes Kraft could make up to three significant acquisitions in the next few years to beef up its offshore operations: "If they just build, build, build [new plants], they won't meaningfully move the dial," he says. For Kraft, "the U.S. domestic base is an absolute fortress that provides a very good cash cow" with which to go shopping. "They're not too late."

Close to home, Kraft is getting a much-needed shot of adrenaline from the Nabisco purchase. Many older Kraft products are in aging categories with flat or declining volumes, such as cereal and traditional store-bought coffee. But with Nabisco, Kraft picked up faster-growing product lines such as Chips Ahoy! cookies and Ritz crackers that will fuel earnings growth. Overnight, Kraft moved from a 6% to a 20% market share in crackers and cookies, a category that's expanding at more than twice the rate of the food-industry average.

Kraft has long been a leader in product development—in 1989 it launched the novel Lunchables line that's now a $750 million-a-year product. Innovations like that put Kraft on top of the U.S. food industry. Now investors will be counting on Deromedi and Holden to sprinkle some of that magic overseas.

By Julie Forster in Chicago, with Becky Gaylord in Sydney

Source: **Reprinted from June 4, 2001, pp. 63–67, pp. 130, 132 issue of *Business Week* by special permission, copyright © 2001 by the McGraw-Hill Companies, Inc.**

The opening news story on Kraft presents a challenge that is facing many multinationals. Their home markets are maturing and becoming increasingly more competitive. In order to grow, these firms must turn to the international marketplace. Even here, however, competition in the food business is very keen and in order to gain market share and be as efficient as possible, a well-designed structure will be critical. Kraft's acquisition of Nabisco has provided it with more products to sell, but the company must organize its international operations to deal with the varied demands of the international arena. Additionally, the role that Philip Morris will play in monitoring Kraft's activities is unclear. In short, Kraft has many factors to consider in determining how to organize its international operations.

■ Organizational Challenges

During the past decade, an increasing number of large and small MNCs have been rethinking their approach to organizing international operations. Motorola, Coca-Cola, Mazda, and Li & Fung, a well-known Hong Kong firm, are examples.

In recent years Motorola's share of the worldwide cellular market has been declining. In an effort to turn things around, the firm has been revamping its structure, replacing some of the top management team,[1] and committing itself to an increased presence both in Europe and Asia. For example, Motorola is building a $150 million plant in Flensburg, Germany. While the German labor costs are relatively high compared to the United States as well as other European locations, Motorola believes that it must be a major player in the growing European market, so it wants to have a local presence.[2] The same is true for Motorola's decision to expand operations in Asia, most notably in China, Korea, the Philippines, and Taiwan. Motorola is building a $750 million high-tech semiconductor factory in the coastal city of Tianjin, China. This plant will be more advanced than any other company facility, and it is structured to help the firm gain the dominant position it once enjoyed in the region. Motorola estimates that by 2010 China will be the world's second largest semiconductor market and by establishing a strong presence there today, it will be in a good position to become the leading player there in the future.[3]

Another example of worldwide reorganizing is provided by Coca-Cola which recently changed its organizing philosophy and now delegates a great deal of authority for operations to the local level. This move is designed to increase the ability of the worldwide divisions to respond to their local markets. As a result, decisions related to advertising, products, and packaging that used to be made in Atlanta are now being handled by international division managers for their own geographic regions. As an example, in Turkey the regional division recently introduced a new pear-flavored drink, while Coke's German operation launched a berry-flavored Fanta.[4] This "local" approach is designed to help Coke improve its international reputation and the firm is convinced that this new structure will translate into higher sales and profits.

Mazda offers a third example of recent reorganizing efforts by MNCs. When Ford Motor gained operating control of this company, the American MNC put in a new executive team. One of the group's first decisions was to change Mazda's old supplier system and require competitive bidding on all supply contracts. This decision resulted in all firms in the supply network having to reorganize themselves to cut expenses in order to remain competitive. In addition, Mazda and its suppliers all began downsizing and closing inefficient operations.[5] As a result of these organizing efforts, Mazda has become stronger than ever.

A fourth example of how firms are meeting international challenges through reorganization is provided by Li & Fung, Hong Kong's largest export trading company and an innovator in the development of supply chain management. The company has global suppliers worldwide who are responsible for providing the firm with a wide range of consumer goods ranging from toys to fashion accessories to luggage. In recent years Li & Fung has reorganized and now manages its day-to-day operations through a group of product managers who are responsible for their individual areas. This new organizational arrangement emerged in a series of steps. Beginning in the late 1970s the company was a regional sourcing agent. Big international buyers would come to Li & Fung for assistance in getting materials and products because the MNC was familiar with the producers throughout Asia and it knew the complex government regulations and how to successfully work through them. The MNC then moved into a more sophisticated stage in which it began developing the entire process for the buyer from concept to prototype to delivery of the goods. By the late 1980s, however, Hong Kong had become a very expensive place to manufacture products and Li & Fung changed its approach and began organizing around a new concept called "dispersed manufacturing," which draws heavily on dissection of the value chain and coordinating the operations of many suppliers in different geographic locations. For example, when the MNC receives an order from a European retailer to produce a large number of dresses, it has to decide where to buy the yarn in the world market, which companies should get the orders to weave and dye the cloth, where supplemental purchases such as buttons and zippers should be made, and how final shipment must be made to the customer. Commenting on this overall process, the company president noted:

> This is a new type of value added, a truly global product that has never been seen before. The label may say "Made in Thailand," but it's not a Thai product. We dissect the manufacturing process and look for the best solution at each step. We're not asking which country can do the

best job overall. Instead, we're pulling apart the value chain and optimizing each step—and we're doing it globally. Not only do the benefits outweigh the costs of logistics and transportation, but the higher value added also lets us charge more for our services. We deliver a sophisticated product and we deliver it fast. If you talk to the big global consumer products companies, they are all moving in this direction—toward being best on a global scale.[6]

■ Basic Organizational Structures

The above examples of Motorola, Coca-Cola, Mazda, and Li & Fung show how MNCs are dramatically reorganizing their operations to compete more effectively in the international arena. As with other MNCs following this strategic route, a number of basic organization structures need to be considered. In many cases, the designs are similar to those used domestically; however, significant differences may arise depending on the nature and scope of the overseas businesses and the home office's approach to controlling the operation. Ideally, an overseas affiliate or subsidiary will be designed to respond to specific concerns, such as production technology or the need for specialized personnel. The overall goal, however, is to meet the needs of both the local market and the home-office strategy of globalization.

Figure 11–1 illustrates how the pressures for globalization versus local responsiveness play out in a host of industries. As an MNC tries to balance these factors, an if–then contingency approach can be used. *If* the strategy needed to respond quickly to the local market changes, *then* there will be accompanying change in the organizational structure. Despite the need for such a flexible, fast-changing, contingency-based approach, most MNCs still slowly evolve through certain basic structural arrangements in international operations. The following sections examine these structures, beginning with initial, preinternational patterns.[7]

Initial Division Structure

Many firms make their initial entry into international markets by setting up a subsidiary or by exporting locally produced goods or services. A subsidiary is a common organizational arrangement for handling finance-related businesses or other operations that require an on-site presence from the start. In recent years, many service organization have begun exporting their

Figure 11–1

Organizational Consequences of Internationalization

Source: Adapted from Paul W. Beamish, J. Peter Killing, Donald J. LeCraw, and Harold Crookell, *International Management: Text and Cases* (Homewood, IL: Irwin, 1991), p. 99.

expertise. Examples include architectural services, legal services, advertising, public relations, accounting, and management consulting. Research and development firms also fall into this category, exporting products that have been successfully developed and marketed locally.

An export arrangement is a common first choice among manufacturing firms, especially those with technologically advanced products. Because there is little, if any, competition, the firm can charge a premium price and handle sales through an export manager. If the company has a narrow product line, this export manager usually reports directly to the head of marketing, and international operations are coordinated by this department. If the firm has a broad product line and intends to export a number of different products into the international market, the export manager will head a separate department and often report directly to the president. These two arrangements work well as long as the company has little competition and is using international sales only to supplement domestic efforts.

If overseas sales continue to increase, local governments often exert pressure in these growing markets for setting up on-site manufacturing operations. A good example is the General Motors joint venture in China where a large percent of all parts are made locally. Additionally, many firms find themselves facing increased competition. Establishing foreign manufacturing subsidiaries can help the MNC to deal with both local government pressures and the competition. The overseas plants show the government that the firm wants to be a good local citizen. At the same time, these plants help the MNC greatly reduce transportation costs, thus making the product more competitive. This new structural arrangement often takes a form similar to that shown in Figure 11–2. Each foreign subsidiary is responsible for operations within its own geographic area, and the head of the subsidiary reports either to a senior executive who is coordinating international operations or directly to the home-office CEO.

International Division Structure

If international operations continue to grow, subsidiaries commonly are grouped into an **international division structure,** which handles all international operations out of a division that is created for this purpose. This structural arrangement is useful as it takes a great deal of the burden off the chief executive officer for monitoring the operations of a series of overseas subsidiaries as well as domestic operations. The head of the international division coordinates and monitors overseas activities and reports directly to the chief executive on these matters. Figure 11–3 provides an example. PepsiCo reorganized its international soft drink division into six such geographic business units covering 150 countries in which Pepsi does business. These geographic units each have self-sufficient operations and broad local authority.

Companies still in the developmental stages of international business involvement are most likely to adopt the international division structure. Others that use this structural arrangement include those with small international sales, limited geographic diversity, or few executives with international expertise.

International division structure
A structural arrangement that handles all international operations out of a division created for this purpose.

Figure 11–2

Use of Subsidiaries during the Early Stage of Internationalization

Home-office departments — Chief Executive Officer — Production, Marketing, Finance, Human Resources — V.P. International Operations — Overseas subsidiaries — France, Japan, Egypt, Australia, Argentina

Figure 11–3

An International Division Structure

(Partial Organization Chart)

A number of advantages are associated with use of an international division structure. The grouping of international activities under one senior executive ensures that the international focus receives top management attention. The structural arrangement allows the company to develop an overall, unified approach to international operations, and the arrangement helps the firm to develop a cadre of internationally experienced managers.

Use of this structure does have a number of drawbacks, however. The structure separates the domestic and international managers, which can result in two different camps with divergent objectives. Also, as the international operation grows larger, the home office may find it difficult to think and act strategically and to allocate resources on a global basis; thus, the international division is penalized. Finally, most research and development efforts are domestically oriented, so ideas for new products or processes in the international market often are given low priority.

Global Structural Arrangements

MNCs typically turn to global structural arrangements when they begin acquiring and allocating their resources based on international opportunities and threats. This international perspective signifies a major change in management strategy, and it is supported by the requisite changes in organization structure. Global structures come in three common types: product, area, and functional.

Global product division
A structural arrangement in which domestic divisions are given worldwide responsibility for product groups.

Global Product Division   A **global product division** is a structural arrangement in which domestic divisions are given worldwide responsibility for product groups. Figure 11–4 provides an illustration. As shown, the manager who is in charge of product division C has authority for this product line on a global basis. This manager also has internal functional support related to the product line. For example, all marketing, production, and finance activities associated with product division C are under the control of this manager.

The global product divisions operate as profit centers. The products generally are in the growth stage of the product life cycle, so they need to be promoted and marketed carefully. In doing so, global product division managers generally run the operation with considerable autonomy; they have the authority to make many important decisions. However, corporate headquarters usually will maintain control in terms of budgetary constraints, home-office approval for certain decisions, and mainly "bottom-line" (i.e., profit) results.

(Partial Organization Chart)

Figure 11–4

A Global Product Division Structure

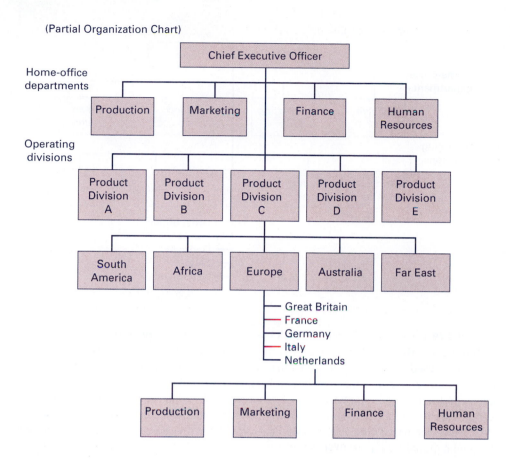

A global product structure provides a number of benefits. If the firm is very diverse (e.g., it produces products using a variety of technologies or has a wide variety of customers), the need to tailor the product to specific demands of the buyer becomes important. A global product arrangement can help to manage this diversity. Another benefit is the ability to cater to local needs. If many geographic areas must have the product modified to suit their particular desires (e.g., foods, toys, or electric shavers), a global product division structure can be extremely important. Still another benefit is that marketing, production, and finance can be coordinated on a product-by-product global basis. Firms also use a product division structure when a product has reached the maturity stage in the home country or similar markets but is in the growth stage in others, such as less developed countries. An example might be color televisions or VCRs. These differing life cycles require close technologic and marketing coordination between the home and foreign market, which is best done by a product division approach. Other advantages of a global product division structure can be summarized as follows:

> It preserves product emphasis and promotes product planning on a global basis; it provides a direct line of communication from the customer to those in the organization who have product knowledge and expertise, thus enabling research and development to work on development of products that serve the needs of the world customer; and it permits line and staff managers within the division to gain an expertise in the technical and marketing aspects of products assigned to them.[8]

Unfortunately, the approach also has some drawbacks. One is the necessity of duplicating facilities and staff personnel within each division. A second is that division managers may pursue currently attractive geographic prospects for their products and neglect other areas with better long-term potential. A third is that many division managers spend too much time trying to tap the local rather than the international market, because it is more convenient and they are more experienced in domestic operations.

Figure 11–5

A Global Area Division Structure

(Partial Organization Chart)

Global Area Division   Instead of a global product division, some MNCs prefer to use a **global area division.** In this structure, illustrated in Figure 11–5, global operations are organized based on a geographic rather than a product orientation. This approach often signals a major change in company strategy, because now international operations are put on the same level as domestic operations. In other words, European or Asian operations are just as important to the company as North American operations. For example, when British Petroleum purchased Standard Oil of Ohio, the firm revised its overall structure and adopted a global area division structure.

Global area division

A structure under which global operations are organized on a geographic rather than a product basis.

Under this arrangement, global division managers are responsible for all business operations in their designated geographic area. The chief executive officer and other members of top management are charged with formulating strategy that ensures that the global divisions all work in harmony.

A global area division structure most often is used by companies that are in mature businesses and have narrow product lines. These product lines often are differentiated based on geographic area. For example, the product has a strong demand in Europe but not in South America, or the type of product that is offered in France differs from that sold in England. In addition, the MNC usually seeks high economies of scale for production, marketing, and resource-purchase integration in that area. Thus, by manufacturing in this region rather than bringing the product in from somewhere else, the firm is able to reduce cost per unit and get the good to market at a very competitive price. Alcatel, the French telecommunications MNC, for example, recently set up its Asian headquarters in Shanghai, underscoring the company's confidence in China's booming telecommunications industry. The firm has invested over $400 million in China and believes that this regional base will be critical in tapping a market where still less than 15 percent of the population have their own telephones.[9]

The geographic structure allows the division manager to cater to the tastes of the local market and make rapid decisions to accommodate environmental changes. A good example is food products. In the United States, soft drinks have less sugar than in South America, so the manufacturing process must be slightly different in these two locales. Similarly, in England, people prefer bland soups, but in France, the preference is for mildly spicy. In Turkey, Italy, Spain, and Portugal, people like dark, bitter coffee; in the United States, people prefer a milder, sweeter blend. In Europe, Canada, and the United States, people prefer less spicy food; in the Middle East and Asia, they like more heavily spiced food. A global area structure allows the geographic unit in a foods company to accommodate such local preferences.

The primary disadvantage of the global area division structure is the difficulty encountered in reconciling a product emphasis with a geographic orientation. For example, if a product is sold worldwide, a number of different divisions are responsible for sales.

(Partial Organization Chart)

Figure 11–6

A Global Functional Structure

This lack of centralized management and control, however, can result in increased costs and duplication of effort on a region-by-region basis. A second drawback is that new research and development efforts often are ignored by division groups, because they are selling goods that have reached the maturity stage. Their focus is not on the latest technologically superior goods that will win in the market in the long run but on those that are proven winners and now are being marketed conveniently worldwide.

Global Functional Division A **global functional division** organizes worldwide operations based primarily on function and secondarily on product. This approach is not widely used other than by extractive companies, such as oil and mining firms. Figure 11–6 provides an example.

A number of important advantages are associated with the global functional division structure. These include: (1) an emphasis on functional expertise; (2) tight centralized control; and (3) a relatively lean managerial staff. Some important disadvantages include: (1) coordination of manufacturing and marketing often is difficult; (2) managing multiple product lines can be very challenging because of the separation of production and marketing into different departments; and (3) only the chief executive officer can be held accountable for the profits. As a result, the global functional process structure typically is favored only by those firms that need tight, centralized coordination and control of integrated production processes and those that are involved in transporting products and raw materials from one geographic area to another.

Mixed Organization Structures Some companies find that neither a global product, area, or functional arrangement is satisfactory. They opt for a **mixed organization structure,** which combines all three into an MNC that supplements its primary structure with a secondary one and, perhaps, a tertiary one. For example, if a company uses a global area approach, committees of functional managers may provide assistance and support to the various geographic divisions. Conversely, if the firm uses a global functional approach, product committees may be responsible for coordinating transactions that cut across functional lines. In other cases, the organization will opt for a matrix structure that results in managers' having two or more bosses. Figure 11–7 illustrates this structure. In this arrangement, the MNC coordinates geographic and product lines through use of a matrix design.

In recent years, mixed organization structures have become increasingly popular. Sony, for example, recently reorganized its varied operations.[10] Under the new arrangement, all of Sony's electronic businesses, including personal computers and cable-television set-top boxes, will be unified in one group. The company has also created a new division that will focus exclusively on the mobile phone business. In addition, the firm has created a management group called the "Global Hub" that will coordinate strategy across a host of Sony units including financial services, games, Internet services, and entertainment. Quite clearly, the company feels that it needs a mixed structure in order to juggle all of its worldwide holdings.

Global functional division
A structure which organizes worldwide operations primarily based on function and secondarily on product.

Mixed organization structure
A structure that is a combination of a global product, area, or functional arrangement.

Figure 11–7

A Multinational Matrix Structure

(Partial Organization Chart)

Many other companies use a mixed structure and one survey has found that more than one-third of the responding firms employ this organizational arrangement. The respondents reported the following:[11]

International operations organized into national subsidiaries with local coordination for production/services, marketing, human resources, etc.	11.8%
International division structure with senior management reporting to the president or CEO of the company.	14.7%
One or more regional headquarters used to coordinate production/ services, marketing, and human resources among national operations.	20.6%
World-production or world-matrix structure used for coordination of international operations.	17.6%
Mixed forms of structure.	35.3%

Many advantages can be gleaned from a mixed organization structure. In particular, it allows the organization to create the specific type of design that best meets its needs. However, there are shortcomings associated with matrix structures. The most important is that as the matrix design's complexity increases, coordinating the personnel and getting everyone to work toward common goals often become difficult. Too many groups are going their own way. Thus, many MNCs have not opted for a matrix structure; they have found that simple, lean structures are the best design for them.

Transnational Network Structures

Transnational network structure

A multinational structural arrangement that combines elements of function, product, and geographic designs, while relying on a network arrangement to link worldwide subsidiaries.

Besides matrix structures, another alternative international organizational design to recently emerge is the **transnational network structure.** This is designed to help MNCs take advantage of global economies of scale while also being responsive to local customer demands. The design combines elements of classic functional, product, and geographic elements, while relying on a network arrangement to link the various worldwide subsidiaries. At the center of the transnational network structure are nodes, which are units charged with coordinating product, functional, and geographic information. Different product line units and geographical area units have different structures depending on what is best for their particular operations. A good example of how the transnational network structure works is provided by N.V. Philips, which has operations in more than 60 countries and produces a diverse product line ranging from light bulbs to defense systems. In all, the company has eight product divisions with a varying number of subsidiaries in each—and the focus of these subsidiaries varies considerably. Some specialize in manufacturing, others in sales; some are closely controlled by headquarters, others are highly autonomous.

Figure 11–8 **The Network Structure of N.V. Philips**

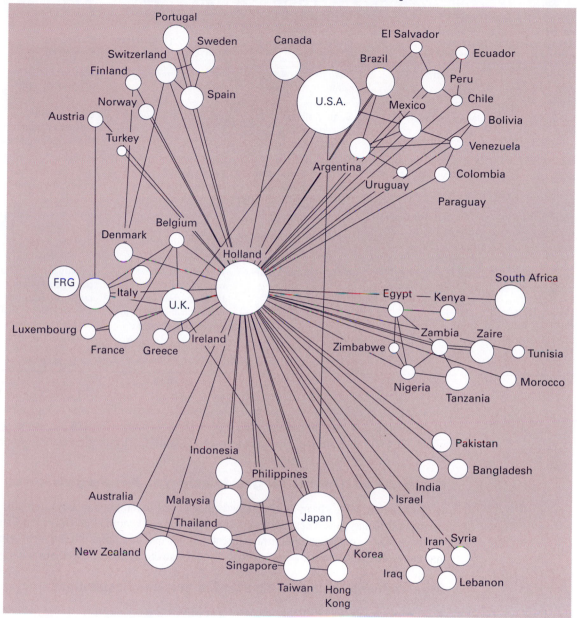

Source: See S. Ghoshal and C. A. Bartlett, "The Multinational Corporation as an Interorganizational Network," *Academy of Management Review,* October 1990, pp. 603–625.

The basic structural framework of the transnational network consists of three components: dispersed subunits, specialized operations, and interdependent relationships. *Dispersed subunits* are subsidiaries that are located anywhere in the world where they can benefit the organization. Some are designed to take advantage of low factor costs, while others are responsible for providing information on new technologies or consumer trends. *Specialized operations* are activities carried out by subunits that focus on particular product lines, research areas, and marketing areas, and are designed to tap specialized expertise or other resources in the company's worldwide subsidiaries. *Interdependent relationships* are used to share information and resources throughout the dispersed and specialized subunits.

The transnational network structure is difficult to draw in the form of an organization chart because it is complex and continually changing. However, Figure 11–8 provides a

Table 11–1
Control Mechanisms Used in Select Multinational Organization Structures

Type of Multinational Structure	Output Control	Bureaucratic Control	Decision-Making Control	Cultural Control
International division structure	Profit control	Have to follow company policies	Typically there is some centralization	Treated like all other divisions
Global area division	Use of profit centers	Some policies and procedures are necessary	Local units are given autonomy	Local subsidiary culture is often the most important
Global product division	Unit output for supply; sales volume for sales	Tight process controls are used to maintain product quality and consistency	Centralized at the product-division headquarters level	Possible for some companies, but not always necessary
Matrix structure	Profit responsibility is shared with product and geographic units	Not very important	Balanced between the global area and product units	Culture must support the shared decision making
Transnational network structure	Used for supplier units and for some independent profit centers	Not very important	Few decisions are centralized at headquarters; most are centralized in the key network nodes	Organization culture transcends national cultures, supports sharing and learning, and is the most important control mechanism

view of N.V. Philips' network structure. These complex networks can be compared to some of the others that have been examined earlier in this chapter by looking at the ways in which the enterprise attempts to exercise control. Table 11–1 provides such a comparison.

■ Nontraditional Organizational Arrangements

In recent years, MNCs have increasingly expanded their operations in ways that differ from those used in the past. These include acquisitions, joint ventures, *keiretsus,* and strategic alliances. These organizational arrangements do not use traditional hierarchical structures and therefore cannot be shown graphically. The following sections describe how they work.

Organizational Arrangements from Mergers and Acquisitions

A recent development affecting the way that MNCs are organized is the increased use of mergers and acquisitions (M&As). In a recent year, as seen in Figure 11–9, the total value of worldwide M&As was over $6 trillion! One reason for this large figure is that a growing number of major MNCs are merging with, or being acquired by, other giant multinationals. In the past decade, for example, British Petroleum acquired Amoco for $48.2 billion, Daimler-Benz bought the Chrysler Corporation for $40.5 billion, while on a smaller scale Renault took over Samsung Motors for $350 million and the assumption of $200 million of Samsung debt.[12] In other cases, MNCs have taken an equity position but have not purchased the entire company. For example, Ford Motor owns 75 percent of Aston Martin Lagonda of Britain, 49 percent of Autolatina of Brazil, and 34 percent of Mazda of Japan; and DaimlerChrysler recently acquired one-third of Mitsubishi.[13]

In each of these examples, the purchasing MNCs have fashioned a structural arrangement that attempts to promote synergy while encouraging local initiative by the acquired firm. The result is an organization design that draws on the more traditional structures that have been examined here but still has a unique structure specifically addressing the needs of the two firms.

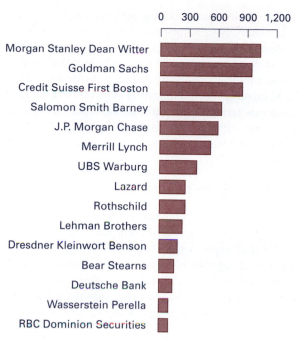

Source: Reported in the *Economist,* January 13, 2001, p. 109.

Figure 11–9

Global Mergers & Acquisitions Handled by Major Investment Houses (in billions of dollars)

Organizational Arrangements from Joint Ventures and Strategic Alliances

Other examples of recent organizational arrangements include joint-venture and strategic alliance agreements in which each party contributes to the undertaking and coordinates its efforts for the overall benefit of the venture.[14] These arrangements can take a variety of forms,[15] although the steps that are followed in creating and operating them often have a fair amount of similarity.[16] One good example of a joint venture is CALICA, which has two partners: Vulcan Materials, the leading firm in the U.S. aggregate materials market, and Grupo ICA of Mexico.[17] Working together, the two companies coordinate their activities in mining, shipping, distributing, and marketing gravel for use in highway and building construction. Another example is provided by Coca-Cola and Procter & Gamble (P&G). Coke has run behind Pepsi in snacks and noncarbonated drinks and recently considered buying Quaker Oats in order to strengthen itself in these areas. However, the $16 billion sales price was too high. So Coke now has entered into a joint venture with P&G.

> Into the 50–50 joint venture, Coke is putting in drink brands like Hi-C and Fruitopia. P&G puts in Pringles chips and healthful noncarbonated drinks like Sunny Delight. P&G also tosses in a new GrowthPlus vitamin fortification technology and 1,300 other patents. The partnership will start off with sales of $4 billion. An early dividend from the joint venture will come soon when Pringles chips are offered to Coke's 16 million outlets.[18]

A third example is the Morgan Stanley Group, which has entered a joint venture with the People's Construction Bank of China to create the China International Capital Corporation. Other partners in this venture include the Singapore government and a Hong Kong holding company. The objective is to help win deals involving project financing, direct investment, and both equity and bond offerings at a time when China needs to finance enormous infrastructure projects.[19]

These joint ventures require carefully formulated structures that allow each partner to contribute what it does best and efficiently coordinate their efforts. In the case of Coke and P&G, this calls for clearly spelling out the responsibilities of all parties and identifying the authority that each will have for meeting specific targets. In the case of China International Capital Corporation, the organizational structure will be used not only to raise capital but to network with the political structure.[20]

One of the main objectives in developing the structure for joint ventures is to help the partners address and effectively meld their different values, management styles, action orientation, and organization preferences. Figure 11–10 illustrates how Western and Asian firms differ in terms of these four areas; the figure also is useful in illustrating the types of considerations that need to be addressed by MNCs from the same area of the world. Consider, for example, Matsushita Electric Industrial and Hitachi Ltd. The two have agreed to join forces to develop new technology in three areas: smart cards, home network systems, and recyclable and energy-efficient consumer electronics.[21] The two firms will need to structure their organizational interface carefully to ensure effective interaction, coordination, and cooperation.

Organizational Arrangements from *Keiretsus*

Still another type of newly emerging organizational arrangement is the **keiretsu,** which is a large, often vertically integrated group of companies that cooperate and work closely with each other. A good example is the Mitsubishi Group, a *keiretsu* which consists of companies that are bound together not by authority relationships but rather by cross-ownership, long-term business dealings, interlocking directorates, and social ties (many of the senior executives are college classmates). There are three flagship firms in the group: Mitsubishi Corporation, which is a trading company; Mitsubishi Bank, which finances

Keiretsu
In Japan, an organizational arrangement in which a large, often vertically integrated group of companies cooperate and work closely with each other to provide goods and services to end users; members may be bound together by cross-ownership, long-term business dealings, interlocking directorates, and social ties.

Figure 11–10

A Comparison of Asian and Western Management Features

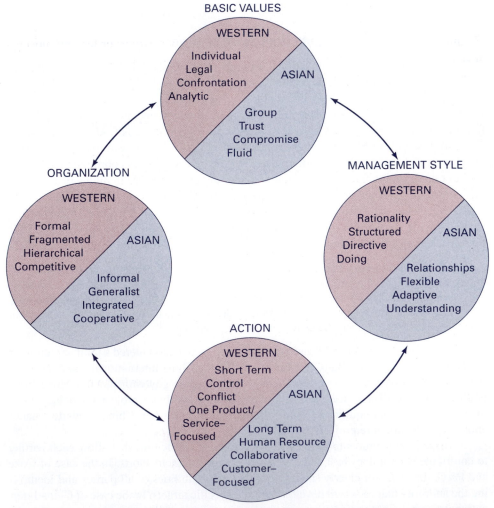

Source: Reprinted from *European Management Journal,* June, Frederic Swierczek and Georges Hirsch, "Joint Ventures in Asia and Multicultural Management," p. 203, © 1994, with kind permission from Elsevier Sciences Ltd., The Boulevard, Langford Lane, Kidlington, OX5 IGB, U.K.

the *keiretsu's* operations; and Mitsubishi Heavy Industries, which is a leading worldwide manufacturer. In addition, hundreds of other Mitsubishi-related companies contribute to the power of the *keiretsu.*

The Japanese are not the only ones using this organizational arrangement, however. Even large U.S. MNCs are creating their own type of *keiretsus.* Ford Motor, for example, now focuses its attention only on automotive and financial services and has divested itself of most other businesses. In the process of reorganizing, Ford has created a giant, *keiretsu-* like arrangement that includes research and development (R&D), parts production, vehicle assembly, financial services, and marketing. For example, in R&D, Ford belongs to eight consortia that conduct research in areas such as improved engineering techniques, materials, and electric-car batteries. In parts production, Ford has equity stakes in Cummins (engines), Excel Industries (windows), and Decoma International (body parts, wheels), and it relies on these firms as major suppliers. In vehicle assembly, Ford has ownership interests in Europe, South America, and Asia and uses these arrangements to both manufacture and sell autos in these parts of the world. In financial services, Ford has seven wholly-owned units that cover a wide gamut, from consumer credit to commercial lending.

Ford is not alone. Today, more and more U.S. firms are cooperating to improve their competitiveness and offset the impact of foreign *keiretsus* that have been rapidly moving across the continuum of business activity, from upstream R&D to downstream marketing. For example, in the area of research, there now are more than 250 R&D consortia in the United States that are sharing both costs and information.[22] In design and production, manufacturers and suppliers are becoming partners; for example, at John Deere, workers now team up with their counterparts at suppliers such as the McLaughlin Body Company to improve quality and cut costs. In the financing area, large companies such as Digital Equipment, IBM, and Novellus Systems are taking equity positions or lending money to their strategic suppliers to ensure high-quality parts and on-time delivery. In the marketing area, manufacturers and suppliers are selling and servicing each other's products. For example, Mazda buys vehicles from Ford for sale in the United States, and vice versa.

In fact, strategic partners and outsourcers are so important to the success of many MNCs that it is common to find them giving their partners direct access to their own computer systems. In this way, for example, an outsourcer can quickly determine the MNC's supply needs and adjust its own production schedule to meet these demands. This same type of close working B2B arrangement is used when providing services. For example, IBM works closely with the giant French MNC Thomson Multimedia SA, managing the firm's data centers, desktops, help desk, disaster recovery, and support services.[23]

Many companies are finding that M&As do not work out or they involve a considerable financial risk because of the high sales price. Joint ventures and strategic alliances are a good alternative. They provide MNCs with the opportunity to access a wide variety of competencies, thus reducing their own costs while ensuring that they have a reliable provider. Eircom, Ireland's dominant telecom provider, for example, has outsourced much of the support work associated with providing phone service, thus allowing the company to focus its primary attention on core telecommunications.[24] In addition, joint ventures and strategic alliances help promote cooperation between the participating organizations; and as the positive effects of these *keiretsu*-like arrangements continue to spread, more and more MNCs will be drawn to them.[25] The organizational arrangement that is used by many of these companies may be difficult to draw on paper, but it is proving to be very effective in practice.

The Emergence of the Electronic Network Form of Organization

Over the last few years there has been a major increase in the number of "electronic freelancers"—individuals who work on a project for a company, usually via the Internet, and when the assignment is done they move on to other employment. In a way, these individuals represent a new type of electronic network organization, "temporary companies" that serve a particular, short-term purpose and then go on to other assignments. There are numerous examples.

Consider the way many manufacturers are today pursuing radical outsourcing strategies, letting external agents perform more of their traditional activities. The U.S. computer-display division of the Finnish company Nokia, for example, chose to enter the U.S. display market with only five employees. Technical support, logistics, sales, and marketing were all subcontracted to specialists around the country. The fashion accessories company Topsy Tail, which has revenues of $80 million but only three employees, never even touches its products through the entire supply chain. It contracts with various injection-molding companies to manufacture its goods; uses design agencies to create its packaging; and distributes and sells its products through a network of independent fulfillment houses, distributors, and sales reps. Nokia's and Topsy Tail's highly decentralized operations bear more resemblance to the network model of organization than to the traditional industrial model.[26]

Many multinationals are beginning to rely increasingly on electronic freelancers (e-lancers, for short) to perform key tasks for them. In the case of General Motors, for example, outsourcers via computers work very closely with the company in providing both design and engineering assistance. The rise of the multinational university is yet another example. A growing number of academic institutions from Europe to North America are now offering both undergraduate and graduate courses, and in some cases full-fledged degree programs, via the Internet. In staffing these courses, the universities rely heavily on e-lancers with PhD degrees who are responsible for delivering the course on-line. In most cases, the university has little face-to-face contact with these e-lancers. Everything is done via computers.

These electronic network organizations are now becoming increasingly prominent. MNCs are realizing that the outsourcing function can be delivered on-line. Examples include design specifications, analytical computations, and consulting reports. So, in a way, this new structure is a version of the matrix design discussed earlier in the chapter. The major difference, however, is that many of the people in the structure are not only temporary, contingent employees but often never see each other and communicate exclusively in an electronic environment.

The New Role of Organizational Synergy

As MNCs increase their globalization, they must meet the challenge of leveraging their knowledge and resources worldwide. The whole becomes greater than the sum of its parts because there is a synergy effect.[27] This synergy effect for knowledge management can take a number of different forms. Some of the most common include the following:

1. Sharing know-how by having personnel in one geographic region pool their insights, knowledge, and information into a particular process or function with those in another region.

2. Sharing tangible resources such as by creating a research lab that serves the needs of all worldwide units.

3. Pooling purchases so that the company is able to achieve greater negotiating power and quantity discounts with its suppliers.

4. Coordinating strategies between units and divisions so that each is more efficient and profitable.

5. Using vertical integration to coordinate the flow of products or services from one unit to another, thus reducing inventory costs, speeding product development, increasing capacity utilization, and improving market access.

6. Creating new businesses by taking discrete activities from various units and combining them into new units or by establishing internal joint ventures or alliances.[28]

Unfortunately, many MNCs have found that the achievement of organizational synergy can be extremely difficult. Some companies, for example, have tried to attain this synergy by coordinating their main product lines and rolling out standardized offerings worldwide—and the outcomes have been very disappointing. In one case, pressured by the chief executive officer who wanted to promote collaboration and standardization across countries in order to leverage the firm's brands internationally, managers launched a succession of high-profile synergy initiatives that resulted in dismal results. Here are the specifics:

> A leading U.K. cookie brand was launched with considerable expense in the United States. It promptly flopped. A past promotion that had worked well in Germany was rolled out in Italy and Spain. It backfired, eroding both margins and market shares. An attempt was made to standardize ingredients across Europe for some confectionery products in order to achieve economies of scale in purchasing and manufacturing. Consumers balked at buying the reformulated products.[29]

Many MNCs have had similar experiences. As a result, there is now an increased movement toward making synergy work correctly. One of the emerging trends is that of conducting detailed analysis before deciding to pursue synergistic programs. This approach helps companies deal with the all-too-common belief that home-office personnel know that synergies can be achieved in the international market but local managers in these geographic regions do not want to make the changes that will be necessary in bringing about these synergies. In truth, many markets do not lend themselves to standardized, worldwide approaches. The culture of the local environment requires a specially designed program that works well here—but not necessarily anywhere else.

A second emerging trend is a focus on determining the types of skills needed in individuals who will be heading synergistic programs. Rather than simply assigning someone based on technical knowledge, MNCs are now looking very closely at the person's ability to create trust, empathize, listen, and achieve meaningful collaboration between all involved parties. The personal characteristics of these managers are now getting more attention than ever.

A third emerging trend is to focus on the downside of introducing synergy programs. In the past it was common for organizations to have an upside bias in which shortcomings were downplayed. Now MNCs are organizing the analysis of the program so that both the positive and negative effects are carefully examined.

A fourth approach that is gaining in popularity is the disaggregation of the various parts of synergy programs. For example, one manager who was charged with leveraging her firm's international brands found that the task had three separate components: (1) make the brand recognizable across borders; (2) reduce duplicated effort; and (3) increase the flow of marketing know-how. Each of these three components, in turn, could be further disaggregated. For example, to make the brand recognizable would involve a number of different efforts including brand positioning, pricing, packaging, ingredients, and advertising. And each of these could be broken down even farther. Packaging, for example, required attention to such things as product material, size, shape, and color of the unit, and size of the label. By carefully examining all of these disaggregated parts, the executive was able to create a synergistic program that was acceptable to the product managers worldwide and resulted in reduced cost and higher profits. As a result of such successes, many MNCs are now organizing their synergy efforts around disaggregation activities.

Organizing for Product Integration

Another recent organizing development is the emergence of designs that are tailored toward helping multinationals integrate product development into their worldwide operations. In the recent past the use of cross-functional coordination has been helpful in achieving this goal. However, MNCs have also found that this arrangement results in people spending less time within their functions and thus becoming less knowledgeable regarding developments that are occurring in their specialized areas. A second shortcoming of the cross-functional approach is that it has often led to product teams becoming autonomous and thus failing to integrate their overall efforts with the organization at large. Most recently Toyota has created a structure that combines a highly formalized system with new structural innovations which ensure that projects are flexibly managed and, at the same time, able to benefit from the learning and experiences of other projects. In accomplishing this, Toyota employs six organizational mechanisms.

One of these is called mutual adjustment. In most companies this is achieved by assigning people to a specific project and having them meet face-to-face and work out a plan of action for designing the new product. At Toyota, however, design engineers are not assigned to specific projects; rather they remain in their functional area and they typically communicate through written messages. This approach ensures that all members remain dedicated to their primary functional area and that they communicate succinctly and directly with each—thus saving time.

A second mechanism employed by Toyota is the use of direct, technically skilled supervisors. In a typical arrangement design engineers are led by individuals who are no longer doing engineering work; they are primarily responsible for seeing that others do this work. However, at Toyota supervisors remain highly skilled in the technical side of the work and are responsible for mentoring, training, and developing their engineers. So if anyone has a design-related problem, the supervisor is technically skilled and can provide this assistance.

A third mechanism is the use of integrative leadership. In typical product design structures, the manager in charge has full authority and relies on the engineering personnel to get the work done according to time, cost, and quality parameters. At Toyota, however, these managers are responsible for coordinating the work of the functional specialists and serving less as a manager than a lead designer on the entire project. In this way, they serve as the glue that binds together the whole process.

In typical design operations, engineers are hired from universities or from other companies where they have gained experience and they remain in their engineering position indefinitely. At Toyota most of the technical training is provided in-house and people are rotated within only one function such as body engineers who work on auto-body subsystems for most, if not all, of their careers. As a result, they are able to get more work done faster because they do not have to communicate and coordinate continually with their counterparts regarding what needs to be done. They are so familiar with their jobs that they know what needs to be done.

Another organizational difference is that in typical design work each new product calls for a new development process and there are complex forms and bureaucratic procedures for ensuring that everything is done correctly. At Toyota standard milestones are created by the project leader and simple forms and procedures are employed so that the work can be done simply and efficiently.

A final difference is that in many organizations design standards are obsolete and rigid. At Toyota these standards are maintained by the people who are doing the work and are continually changed to meet new design demands.

The organizational approach used at Toyota is now being carefully studied by other world-class auto manufacturers, who are coming to realize that the old way of organizing for product design is not sufficiently effective for dealing with the competitive challenges of the new millennium. In particular, a new organizational emphasis has to be placed on better blending the personnel and the work. Commenting on all of this, a group of experts who studied Toyota's approach recently wrote:

> the success of Toyota's system rides squarely on the shoulders of its people. Successful product development requires highly competent, highly skilled people with a lot of hands-on experience, deep technical knowledge, and an eye for the overall system. When we look at all the things that Toyota does well, we find two foundations for its product-development system: chief engineers using their expertise to gain leadership, and functional engineers using their expertise to reduce the amount of communication, supervision, trial and error, and confusion in the process. All the other coordinating mechanisms and practices serve to help highly skilled engineers do their job effectively. By contrast, many other companies seem to aspire to develop systems "designed by geniuses to be run by idiots." Toyota prefers to develop and rely on the skill of its personnel, and it shapes its product-development process around this central idea: people, not systems, design cars.[30]

The Changing Role of Information Technology in Organizing

Another major change that is taking place in the way multinationals organize themselves is related to the role of information technology (IT). After a slow start, Japanese firms, in particular, are now leading the way in redefining how IT will be used in the future. One of the major differences between IT in American multinationals and their Japanese counterparts is that in Japan IT is not seen as something special or different but, rather, is viewed as being part of a fully integrated picture. In the process, Japanese firms now carefully target how they are going to use information technology and try hard to neither overrate nor underrate its role and importance. A good contrast is provided by Seven-Eleven Japan and NSK, one of the world's leading bearings and auto component manufacturers.

In the case of Seven-Eleven Japan, the company has aggressively invested in IT and used this system to monitor and meet customer needs. For example, Japanese consumers place a high premium on product freshness. Many years ago the company began using its IT system to create a just-in-time arrangement that relied on multiple daily deliveries of products. Today, each store's fresh food changes over entirely three times a day, which allows managers to change their unit's physical layout throughout the day, as the flow of customers shifts from housewives to students to working people. Moreover, the company's just-in-time system allows the stores to be extraordinarily responsive to consumers' shifting tastes. For example, if a particular kind of take-out lunch sells out by noon, extra stock can be in the store within an hour. Conversely, if it is raining, the IT system will remind cash register operators to put umbrellas on sale next to the register. This level of responsiveness is made possible by a sophisticated point-of-sale data-collection system and an electronic ordering system that links individual stores to a central distribution center.

In the case of NSK, the company uses a combination of both highly integrated technology systems and low-tech systems. For example, for simulation and analysis in component design, engineers rely on the firm's flexible-engineering information control system and an array of databases and expert systems. Quality engineers use handheld terminals to monitor quality data, which are automatically recorded from in-line sensors and inspection machines. Salespeople can search sophisticated databases and narrow the range of products that they will suggest to a customer. At the same time, NSK has a number of low technology islands where the personnel use machinery and equipment that is over a decade old and rely on their own judgment in making decisions and processing information. By choosing the best mix of information technology, the company is able to maintain its competitiveness.[31]

Other contrasts between the ways in which IT issues are addressed by Western firms and Japanese companies are provided in Table 11–2. A close analysis of these contrasts shows that the integration of IT into the overall organizing process can have a dramatic effect on the performance of an organization.

■ Use of Subsidiary Boards of Directors

Organizing begins at the top, with boards of directors. These boards are responsible for overseeing the corporation and ensuring that senior managers are operating in accord with the overall policies and objectives established by the board. As firms increase their international focus, many are finding that subsidiary boards of directors are useful in helping to shape and guide the activities of global operations.

A **subsidiary board of directors** oversees and monitors the operations of a foreign subsidiary. In recent years, this organizational arrangement has become increasingly popular. Some of the best-known multinationals use this arrangement, including Dow Chemical; Hewlett-Packard; Pilkington Bros., Ltd.; Honda Motor; and Matsushita Electric.

There are a number of reasons for this trend toward subsidiary boards. The main one is that as the external environment in which MNCs operate becomes extremely complex, rapid decision making gains in importance. To meet this need for immediate response, subsidiaries must be given more authority for local operations. At the same time, however, the corporate board would like to ensure that the subsidiary does not become too autonomous. The solution

Subsidiary board of directors
A board that overseas and monitors the operations of a foreign subsidiary.

Table 11–2
Contrasting Approaches to Using Information Technology: Western and Japanese Views

Key Issue	How Western Firms Address the Matter	How Japanese Firms Address the Matter
How to decide the information systems needed by the business.	Develop an IT strategy that aligns with the company's business strategy.	Determine the basic way the firm competes, driven particularly by its operations goals, and use this to determine the IT investment.
How to determine if the investments in IT are worthwhile.	Adapt the capital budgeting process to manage and evaluate the IT investment.	Judge investments based on operational performance improvements.
When trying to improve a business process, how technology fits into management's thinking.	Assume that technology offers the smartest, cheapest way to improve performance.	Identify a performance goal and then select a technology that will help the firm achieve this goal in a way that supports the people doing the work.
How IT users and IT specialists should connect in the organization.	Teach specialists about business goals and develop technically adept, business-savvy Chief Information Officers.	Encourage integration by rotating managers through the IT function and giving IT oversight to executives who oversee other functions.
How systems to improve organization performance can be designed.	Design the most technically elegant system possible and ask employees to adapt to it.	Design a system that makes use of the tacit and explicit knowledge that employees already possess.

Source: Adapted from M. Bensaou and Michael Earl, "The Right Mind-set for Managing Information Technology," *Harvard Business Review,* September–October 1998, p. 121.

to this dilemma is a local board, which can play an important linking role between the two groups. The subsidiary board also can assist the unit in planning and controlling activities.

Four major areas in which MNCs use subsidiary boards have been identified. One is to advise, approve, and appraise local management. A second is to help the unit respond to local conditions. A third is to assist in strategic planning, and a fourth is to supervise the subsidiary's ethical conduct. These areas are spelled out in greater detail in Table 11–3, where survey responses from U.S., Canadian, Japanese, and European samples are provided. A close look at the table shows that the Japanese and the Swedes tend to place greater importance on these boards than Europeans and Americans, although all countries report important benefits from the use of these boards. Will the future see increasing use of this organizational arrangement? Very likely, the answer is yes.

■ Organizational Characteristics of MNCs

Although MNCs have similar organizational structures, they do not all operate the same way. A variety of factors have been identified that help to explain the differences.[32] These include overall strategy, employee attitudes, and local conditions. Of particular significance to this discussion are the organizational characteristics of formalization, specialization, and centralization.

Formalization

Formalization
The use of defined structures and systems in decision making, communicating, and controlling.

Formalization is the use of defined structures and systems in decision making, communicating, and controlling. Some countries make greater use of formalization than others; in turn, this affects the day-to-day organizational functioning. One large research study of Korean firms found that unlike employees in the United States, Korean workers perceive more positive work environments when expectations for their jobs are set forth more

Table 11–3

Importance of Subsidiary Boards over the Next 5 to 10 Years
Mean Ratings (1 = Low; 5 = High)

	United States (n=31)	Canada (n=9)	Japan (n=14)	Europe, excluding Sweden (n=28)	Sweden (n=8)
Local management					
Advising local management	3.50	3.67	4.15	3.43	4.00
Approving budgets and short-term plans of the subsidiary	2.48	3.00	4.36	2.75	3.13
Monitoring operating performance and corrective measures in the subsidiary	2.81	3.00	4.00	2.71	3.38
Appraising the subsidiary's top management performance and top officers' compensation	2.10	2.33	3.64	2.46	2.63
Deciding the amount to remit as dividends	2.39	2.33	3.57	2.18	2.00
Local country contacts and conditions					
Facilitating the establishment of contacts with local leaders and institutions	2.90	3.56	3.62	3.32	3.88
Identifying and responding to concerned stakeholders (e.g., environmentalists and consumer groups)	2.10	1.44	3.50	1.68	1.00
Ensuring compliance with local legal requirements	3.50	2.67	4.23	3.00	3.75
Providing knowledge of local economic, political, and social conditions	3.48	3.44	4.00	3.39	4.25
Appraising and minimizing the subsidiary's political risk	3.00	2.89	3.79	2.57	2.57
Strategic plan					
Participating in drawing up the subsidiary's strategic plan	2.52	3.00	4.29	2.54	2.88
Ethical issues					
Supervising the subsidiary's ethical conduct	2.94	2.67	3.64	2.82	2.75

Source: Adapted from Mark P. Kriger and Patrick J. J. Rich, "Strategic Governance: Why and How MNCs Are Using Boards of Directors in Foreign Subsidiaries," *Columbia Journal of World Business,* Winter 1987, p. 43. Copyright 1987, reprinted with permission.

strictly and formally. In short, Koreans respond very favorably to formalization.[33] Korean firms tend to be quite formal, but this may not hold throughout Asia. For example, a study that investigated whether Japanese organizations are more formalized than U.S. organizations found that although Japanese firms tend to use more labor-intensive approaches to areas such as bookkeeping and office-related work than their U.S. counterparts, no statistical data support the contention that Japanese firms are more formalized.[34]

Another study of U.S. and Japanese firms in Taiwan divided formalization into two categories: objective and subjective.[35] Objective formalization was measured by things such as the number of different documents given to employees, organizational charts, information booklets, operating instructions, written job descriptions, procedure manuals, written policies, and work-flow schedules and programs. Subjective formalization was measured by the extent to which goals were vague and unspecified, use of informal controls, and use of culturally induced values in getting things done. The findings of this study are reported in Table 11–4.

Commenting on differences in the use of formalization, the researchers concluded that

> American and Japanese firms appear to have almost the same level of written goals or objectives for subordinates, written standards of performance appraisals, written schedules, programs, and

Table 11–4

Organizational Characteristics of U.S. and Japanese Firms in Taiwan

Characteristics	U.S. Firms (n=38)	Japanese Firms (n=85)
Formalization (subjective)	3.54	3.47
Formalization (objective)	11.39	10.91
Horizontal specialization	12.89	10.02
Vertical specialization	7.04	7.75
Job routinization	2.25	2.86
Job autonomy	2.78	2.62
Foreign expatriates per 1,000 employees	4.2	16.6
Ratio of firms using quality circles (in percentages)	24	32

Note: The highest score for the subjective formalization index, job routinization index, and autonomy index is 6; the lowest score is 1. The highest score for the objective formalization index is 19; the lowest score is 0. The highest score for the horizontal specialization index is 16; the lowest score is 0. Ratios of foreign expatriates to total employees are calculated on the basis of firms with 50 or more employees.

Source: Adapted from Rhy-song Yeh and Tagi Sagafi-nejad, "Organizational Characteristics of American and Japanese Firms in Taiwan," *National Academy of Management Proceedings,* 1987, p. 113. Used with permission.

work specifications, written duties, authority and accountability. However, managers in Japanese firms perceive less formalization than do managers in American firms. Less reliance on formal rules and structure in Japanese firms is also revealed by the emphasis on face-to-face or behavioral mode of control indicated by the ratio of foreign expatriates to total employees in subsidiaries.[36]

The study also found that U.S. MNCs tend to rely heavily on budgets, financial data, and other formalized tools in controlling their subsidiary operations. This contrasts with Japanese MNCs, in which wider use is made of face-to-face, informal controls. These findings reveal that although the outward structural design of overseas subsidiaries may appear to be similar, the internal functioning in characteristics such as formalization may be quite different.

In recent years, this formal/informal characteristic of organizations has become the focal point of increased attention.[37] One reason is because MNCs now realize there are two dimensions of formality/informality that must be considered: internal and external. Moreover, to a large degree, these formal/informal relationships require effective networking of a different type. As Yoshino and Rangan noted, there are

> two approaches that firms that must compete globally—and that includes most major firms—employ to achieve the layering of competitive advantages: (1) development of extensive *internal networks* of international subsidiaries in major national or regional markets and (2) forging *external networks* of strategic alliances with firms around the world. These approaches are not mutually exclusive, and increasingly firms are striving to build both types of networks.[38]

What is particularly interesting about these networking relationships is that each places a different set of demands on the MNC. In particular, external networking with joint-venture partners often involves ambiguous organizational mandates, less emphasis on systems and more on people, and ambiguous lines of authority. This is a marked difference from internal networking characteristics, where formality is much stronger than informality and the enterprise can rely on a shared vision, clear organizational mandates, and well-developed systems and lines of authority.[39] Table 11–5 summarizes the characteristics of these internal and external networks.

Table 11–5
Internal vs. External Networks

Managerial Dimensions	Internal Network	External Network
Shared vision	Yes	No
Animating mindset	Cooperation	Cooperation and competition
Organizational mandates	Clear	Ambiguous
Organizational objective	Global optimization	Develop win-win approaches
Emphasis on systems	More	Less
Emphasis on people	Less	More
Lines of authority	Clear	Ambiguous at best

Source: Information drawn from Michael Yoshino and N. S. Rangan, *Strategic Alliances* (Boston: Harvard Business School Press, 1995), p. 203.

Specialization

As an organizational characteristic, **specialization** is the assigning of individuals to specific, well-defined tasks. Specialization in an international context can be classified into horizontal and vertical specialization.

Horizontal specialization assigns jobs so that individuals are given a particular function to perform, and people tend to stay within the confines of this area. Examples include jobs in areas such as customer service, sales, recruiting, training, purchasing, and marketing research. When there is a great deal of horizontal specialization, personnel will develop functional expertise in one particular area.

Vertical specialization assigns work to groups or departments where individuals are collectively responsible for performance. Vertical specialization also is characterized by distinct differences between levels in the hierarchy such that those higher up are accorded much more status than those further down, and the overall structure usually is quite tall.

In the earlier, comparative study of 55 U.S. and 51 Japanese manufacturing plants, Japanese organizations had lower functional specialization of employees. Specifically, three-quarters of the functions listed were assigned to specialists in the U.S. plants, but less than one-third were assigned in the Japanese plants.[40] Later studies with regard to formalization have echoed this finding on specialization. As shown in Table 11–4, U.S. subsidiaries have more specialists than Japanese firms do.

By contrast, studies find that the Japanese rely more heavily on vertical specialization. They have taller organization structures in contrast to the flatter designs of their U.S. counterparts. Japanese departments and units also are more differentiated than those in U.S. organizations. Vertical specialization can be measured by the amount of group activity as well, such as in quality circles. Table 11–4 shows that Japanese firms make much greater use of quality circles than the U.S. firms. Vertical specialization also can result in greater job routinization. Because one is collectively responsible for the work, strong emphasis is placed on everyone's doing the job in a predetermined way, refraining from improvising, and structuring the work so that everyone can do the job after a short training period. Again, Table 11–4 shows that the Japanese organizations make much wider use of job routinization than U.S. organizations.

Centralization

Centralization is a management system in which important decisions are made at the top. In an international context, the value of centralization will vary according to the local environment and the goals of the organization. Many U.S. firms tend toward **decentralization,** pushing decision making down the line and getting the lower-level personnel involved.

Specialization
An organizational characteristic that assigns individuals to specific, well-defined tasks.

Horizontal specialization
The assignment of jobs so that individuals are given a particular function to perform and tend to stay within the confines of this area.

Vertical specialization
The assignment of work to groups or departments where individuals are collectively responsible for performance.

Centralization
A management system under which important decisions are made at the top.

Decentralization
Pushing decision making down the line and getting the lower-level personnel involved.

German MNCs centralize strategic headquarter-specific decisions independent of the host country and decentralize operative decisions in accordance with the local situation in the host country. The accompanying sidebar, "Organizing in Germany," describes how relatively small German MNCs have been very successful with such a decentralization strategy. In some cases large firms have also been very successful using a decentralized approach. Nokia, for example, has been described as "one of the least hierarchical big companies on earth, a place where it is often profoundly unclear who's in charge."[41] This hands-off approach promotes creativity, entrepreneurial effort, and personal responsibility. At the same time, however, in order to prevent operations from spinning out of control, the company exercises very tight financial discipline. In contrast, researchers have found that Japanese organizations delegate less formal authority than their U.S. counterparts, but they permit greater involvement in decisions by employees lower in the hierarchy. At the same time, however, the Japanese manage to maintain strong control over their lower-level personnel by limiting the amount of authority given to the latter and carefully controlling and orchestrating worker involvement and participation in quality circles.[42] Other studies show similar findings.[43]

When evaluating the presence of centralization by examining the amount of autonomy that Japanese give to their subordinates, one study concluded:

> In terms of job autonomy, employees in American firms have greater freedom to make their decisions and their own rules than in Japanese firms. . . . Results show that managers in American firms perceive a higher degree of delegation than do managers in Japanese firms. Also, managers in American firms feel a much higher level of participation in the coordinating with other units, . . . in influencing the company's policy related to their work, and in influencing the company's policy in areas not related to their work.[44]

The finding related to influence is explained in more detail in Table 11–6; U.S. managers in Taiwanese subsidiaries felt that they had greater influence than did their Japanese counterparts. Moreover, when statistically analyzed, these data proved to be significant.

Putting Organizational Characteristics in Perspective

MNCs tend to organize their international operations in a manner similar to that used at home. If the MNC tends to have high formalization, specialization, and centralization at its home-based headquarters, these organizational characteristics probably will occur in the firm's international subsidiaries.[45] Japanese and U.S. firms are good examples. As the researchers of the comparative study in Taiwan concluded: "Almost 80 percent of Japanese firms and more than 80 percent of American firms in the sample have been operating in Taiwan for about ten years, but they maintain the traits of their distinct cultural origins even though they have been operating in the same (Taiwanese) environment for such a long time."[46]

These findings also reveal that many enterprises view their international operations as extensions of their domestic operations, thus disproving the widely held belief that convergence occurs between overseas operations, and local customs. In other words, there is far less of an "international management melting pot" than many people realize. European countries are finding that as they attempt to unify and do business with each other, differing cultures (languages, religions, and values) are very difficult to overcome. A major challenge for the years ahead will be bringing subsidiary organizational characteristics more into line with local customs and cultures.

The World of *Business Week*—Revisited

In this chapter there were a number of different organizational arrangements discussed. Some of these were fairly standard approaches that have been traditionally used by MNCs. Others represent hybrid or flexible arrangements and emerging networks that are geared specifically to utilize advanced information technology and the

International Management in Action

Organizing in Germany

www.stihlusa.com/chainsaws

Similar to the rest of the world, Europe in general and Germany in particular have gone through economic ups and downs and the future is very uncertain. German labor unions, the most powerful in Europe, were having to give ground, and major corporations were scaling back operations and reporting losses. At the same time, a number of medium- and small-sized German companies continued to be some of the most successful in the world. Part of this success resulted from their carefully designed decentralized organization structures, a result of company efforts to remain close to the customer. The goal of these German MNCs is to establish operations in overseas locales, where they can provide on-site assistance to buyers. Moreover, these subsidiaries in most cases are wholly owned by the company and have centralized controls on profits.

A common practice among German MNCs is to overserve the market by providing more than is needed. For example, when the auto firm BMW entered Japan, its initial investment was several times higher than that required to run a small operation; however, its high visibility and commitment to the market helped to create customer awareness and build local prestige.

Another strategy is to leave expatriate managers in their positions for extended periods of time. In this way, they become familiar with the local culture and thus the market, and they are better able to respond to customer needs as well as problems. As a result, customers get to know the firm's personnel and are more willing to do repeat business with them.

Still another strategy the German MNCs use is to closely mesh the talents of the people with the needs of the customers. For example, there is considerable evidence that most customers value product quality, closeness to the customer, service, economy, helpful employees, technologic leadership, and innovativeness. The German firms will overperform in the area that is most important and thus further bond themselves to the customer.

A final strategy is to develop strong self-reliance so that when problems arise, they can be handled with in-house personnel. This practice is a result of German companies' believing strongly in specialization and concentration of effort. They tend to do their own research and to master production and service problems so that if there is a problem, they can resolve it without having to rely on outsiders.

How well do these German organizing efforts pay off? Many of these relatively small companies hold world market shares in the 70 to 90 percent range. These are companies that no one has ever heard about, such as Booder (fish-processing machines), Gehring (honing machines), Korber/Hauni (cigarette machines), Marklin & Cle (model railways), Stihl (chain saws), and Webasto (sunroofs for cars). Even so, every one of these companies is the market leader not only in Europe but also in the world, and in some cases, its relative market strength is up to 10 times greater than that of the nearest competitor.

Table 11–6
Managers' Influence in U.S. and Japanese Firms in Taiwan

Managers' Work-Related Activity	U.S. Firm Average	Japanese Firm Average
Assigning work to subordinates	4.72	3.96
Disciplining subordinates	4.07	3.82
Controlling subordinates' work (quality and pace)	3.99	3.82
Controlling salary and promotion of subordinates	3.81	3.18
Hiring and placing subordinates	3.94	3.24
Setting the budget for own unit	3.45	3.16
Coordinating with other units	3.68	3.52
Influencing policy related to own work	3.22	2.85
Influencing policy not related to own work	2.29	1.94
Influencing superiors	3.02	3.00

Note: The highest score of means is 5 (very great influence); the lowest score is 1 (very little influence). The *T*-value for all scores is significant at the .01 level.

Source: Adapted from Rhy-song Yeh and Tagi Sagafi-nejad, "Organizational Characteristics of American and Japanese Firms in Taiwan," *National Academy of Management Proceedings,* 1987, p. 114. Used with permission.

needs of the new global marketplace. Which one of the organizational approaches that were described in this chapter do you think would be of most value to Kraft as it tries to develop an enterprise that is moving away from a heavily North American dependency and toward a more worldwide focus? How do you think this new arrangement will impact on its organizational characteristics, specifically formalization, specialization, and centralization?

Summary of Key Points

1. A number of different organizational structures are used in international operations. Many MNCs begin by using an export manager or subsidiary to handle overseas business. As the operation grows or the company expands into more markets, the firm often will opt for an international division structure. Further growth may result in adoption of a global structural arrangement, such as a global production division, global area division structure, global functional division, or a mixture of these structures.

2. Although MNCs still use the various structural designs that can be drawn in a hierarchical manner, they recently have begun merging or acquiring other firms or parts of other firms, and the resulting organizational arrangements are quite different from those of the past. The same is true of the many joint ventures now taking place across the world. Perhaps the biggest change, however, stems from the Japanese concept of *keiretsu*, which involves the vertical integration and cooperation of a group of companies. Although the Mitsubishi Group, with its 28 core member firms, is one of the best examples of this organizational arrangement, U.S. MNCs also are moving in this direction. Other examples of new MNC organizational arrangements include the emergence of electronic networks, new roles for organizational synergy, new approaches to organizing for production development, and the more effective use of IT.

3. Some multinationals have subsidiary boards of directors that oversee and monitor the operations of a foreign subsidiary. As MNCs' worldwide operations increase, these boards likely will gain in popularity.

4. A variety of factors help to explain differences in the way that international firms operate. Three organizational characteristics that are of particular importance are formalization, specialization, and centralization. These characteristics often vary from country to country, so that Japanese firms will conduct operations differently from U.S. firms. When MNCs set up international subsidiaries, they often use the same organizational techniques they do at home without necessarily adjusting their approach to better match the local conditions.

Key Terms

centralization, *329*

decentralization, *329*

formalization, *326*

global area division, *314*

global functional division, *315*

global product division, *312*

horizontal specialization, *329*

international division structure, *311*

keiretsu, 320

mixed organization structure, *315*

specialization, *329*

subsidiary board of directors, *325*

transnational network structure, *316*

vertical specialization, *329*

Review and Discussion Questions

1. A small manufacturing firm believes there is a market for handheld tools that are carefully crafted for local markets. After spending 2 months in Europe, the president of this firm believes that his company can create a popular line of these tools. What type of organization structure would be of most value to this firm in its initial efforts to go international?

2. If the company in question 1 finds a major market for its products in Europe and decides to expand into Asia, would you recommend any change in its organization structure? If yes, what would you suggest? If no, why not?

3. If this same company finds after 3 years of international effort it is selling 50 percent of its output

overseas, what type of organizational structure would you suggest for the future?

4. Why are *keiretsus* becoming so popular? What benefits do they offer? How can small international firms profit from this development? Give an example.

5. In what way do formalization, specialization, and centralization have an impact on MNC organization structures? In your answer, use a well-known firm such as IBM or Ford to illustrate the effects of these three characteristics.

Internet Exercise: Organizing for Effectiveness

Every MNC tries to drive down costs by getting its goods and services to the market in the most efficient way. A good example are auto firms such as Ford Motor and Volkswagen which have worldwide operations. In recent years Ford has begun expanding into Europe and VW has begun setting up operations in Latin America. By building cars closer to the market, these companies hope to reduce their costs and be more responsible to local needs. At the same time this strategy requires a great deal of organization and coordination. Visit the web sites for both of these firms and examine the scope of their operations. The address for Ford Motor is **www.ford.com** and for Volkswagen it is **www.vw.com**. Then, based on your findings, answer these questions: What type of organizational arrangement(s) do you see the two firms are using in coordinating their worldwide operations? Which of the two companies has the more modern arrangement? Do you think this increases that firm's efficiency or does it hamper the company's efforts to contain costs and be more competitive? Why?

Australia

Australia is the smallest continent but the sixth-largest country in the world. It lies between the Indian and the Pacific Oceans in the southern hemisphere and has a land mass of almost 3 million square miles (around 85 percent the size of the United States). Referred to as being "down under" because it lies entirely within the southern hemisphere, it is a dry, thinly populated land. The outback is famous for its bright sunshine, enormous numbers of sheep and cattle, and unusual wildlife, such as kangaroos, koalas, platypuses, and wombats. Over 19 million people live in this former British colony, and 20 million are projected by the next couple of years. Although many British customs are retained, Australians have developed their own unique way of life. One of the world's most developed countries, Australia operates under a democratic form of government somewhat similar to that of Great Britain. Gross domestic product is over $400 billion, with the largest economic sectors being services, trade, and manufacturing.

A large financial-services MNC in the United States has been examining the demographic and economic data of Australia. This MNC has concluded that there will be increased demand for financial services in Australia during the next few years. As a result, the company is setting up an operation in the capital, Canberra, which is slightly inland from the two largest cities of Sydney and Melbourne.

This financial-service firm began in Chicago and now has offices in seven countries. Many of these foreign operations are closely controlled by the Chicago office. The overseas personnel are charged with carefully following instructions from headquarters and implementing centralized decisions. However, the Australian operation will be run differently. Because the country is so large and the population spread along the coast and to Perth in the west, and because of the "free spirit" cultural values of the Aussies, the home office feels compelled to give the manager of Australian operations full control over decision

making. This manager will have a small number of senior-level managers brought from the United States, but the rest of the personnel will be hired locally. The office will be given sales and profit goals, but specific implementation of strategy will be left to the manager and his or her key subordinates on site.

The home office believes that in addition to providing direct banking and credit card services, the Australian operation should seek to gain a strong foothold in insurance and investment services. As the country continues to grow economically, this sector of the industry should increase relatively fast. Moreover, few multinational firms are trying to tap this market in Australia, and those that are doing so are from British Commonwealth countries. The CEO believes that the experience of the people being sent to Australia (the U.S. expatriates) will be particularly helpful in developing this market. He recently noted, "We know that the needs of the Australian market are not as sophisticated or complex as those in the United States, but we also know that they are moving in the same direction as we are. So we intend to tap our experience and knowledge and use it to garner a commanding share of this expanding market."
www.csu.edu.au/australia

Questions

1. What are some current issues facing Australia? What is the climate for doing business in Australia today?

2. What type of organizational structure arrangement is the MNC going to use in setting up its Australian operation?

3. Can this MNC benefit from any of the new organizational arrangements, such as a joint venture, the Japanese concept of *keiretsu,* or electronic networks?

4. Will this operation be basically centralized or decentralized?

Getting In on the Ground Floor

The EU currently is developing a strategy that will help member countries beat back the threat of U.S. and Asian competition and develop a strong technological base for new product development. European multinational firms currently are strong in a number of different areas. For example, Germany's Hoechst and BASF and Switzerland's Sandoz and Hoffman-LaRoche are major companies in chemicals and pharmaceutics. Philips of the Netherlands invented compact discs and is dominant in the television market. Many strong European-based MNCs could provide a solid base for the EU to defend itself from outside economic invasion.

Ruehter Laboratories, a high-tech R&D firm located in New Jersey, holds a number of important pharmaceutic patents and would like to expand its operation worldwide. The company is considering buying a small, but highly profitable, Dutch insulin-maker. "This acquisition will help us enter the European market by getting in on the ground floor," noted the president.

Although the Dutch firm is quite small, it has strong R&D prowess and likely will play a major role in biotechnology research during the years ahead. Ruehter has talked to the Dutch firm, and the two have arrived at a mutually acceptable selling price. While waiting for the lawyers to work out the final arrangements, Ruehter intends to reorganize its overall operations so that the home-office management can work more closely with its new Dutch subsidiary. There are three areas that Ruehter intends to address in its reorganization efforts: (1) how the subsidiary will be structurally integrated into the current organization; (2) whether a subsidiary board will be an effective method of overseeing the Dutch operation; and (3) whether there can be any joint R&D efforts between the two groups.

Questions

1. What type of organization design would you recommend that Ruehter use?

2. Would a subsidiary board of directors be of any value in overseeing the Dutch operation?

3. If there were joint R&D efforts, would this be a problem?

Chapter 12

Decision Making and Controlling

Objectives of the Chapter

Although they are not directly related to internationalization, decision making and controlling are two management functions that play critical roles in international operations. In decision making, a manager chooses a course of action among alternatives. In controlling, the manager evaluates results in relation to plans or objectives and decides what action, if any, to take. How these functions are carried out is influenced by the international context. For example, the amount of decision-making authority given to subsidiaries is influenced by a number of international factors, such as the philosophy of the company and the amount of competition in the local environment. These factors may result in one international unit's having much more decision-making authority than another. Similarly, the tools and techniques that are used to control one subsidiary may differ from those used to control another.

This chapter examines the different decision-making and controlling management functions used by MNCs, notes some of the major factors that account for differences between these functions, and identifies the major challenges of the years ahead. The specific objectives of this chapter are:

1. **PROVIDE** comparative examples of decision making in different countries.

2. **PRESENT** some of the major factors affecting the degree of decision-making authority given to overseas units.

3. **COMPARE** and **CONTRAST** direct controls with indirect controls.

4. **DESCRIBE** some of the major differences in the ways that MNCs control operations.

5. **DISCUSS** some of the specific performance measures that are used to control international operations.

BusinessWeek

The World of *Business Week*

Wal-Mart's Not-So-Secret British Weapon

Allan Leighton has just gotten one of the hottest jobs in retailing—president and chief executive of Wal-Mart Europe. His mandate: Turn Wal-Mart's European incursion into an all-out assault. And leading the assault will be Asda, the giant British retailer Wal-Mart bought last July and which Leighton ran until he got his new title.

Asda's own home-grown philosophy of low prices and aggressive expansion fits neatly with Wal-Mart's worldview, so the giant U.S. chain sees it as the perfect cornerstone for its European plans. And Leighton is wasting no time. On Jan. 10, scarcely a month after his promotion, he announced plans to open six new Asda stores, expand six others, build a dozen or so distribution centers for online shopping, and add 27,000 new jobs to the Asda/Wal-Mart payroll in Britain by 2005.

That's the kind of blistering pace Wal-Mart needs to achieve its foreign ambitions. Buying Asda doubled Wal-Mart's international sales to almost $25 billion, overnight. But that's still a fraction of overall sales of $165 billion. Wal-Mart wants international operations to account for a third of sales growth by 2004. Analysts figure that could mean $72 billion in international revenue within four years. Other regions, like Latin America, will contribute. But the big action will be in Europe, where Wal-Mart has 95

stores in Germany under its own name, and 231
Asda outlets in Britain.

Germany is a key market, but Wal-Mart is losing
about $150 million annually there because of reno-
vation costs and the impact of price wars. Asda, in
contrast, is nicely profitable.

Asda's stores were known for good deals on
groceries, apparel, and electronics even before
Wal-Mart bought the chain for $11 billion. But
since Wal-Mart took over, Asda has embarked on
its biggest discount drive ever, pledging to roll back
prices by 5% to 10% on 10,000 items. The price
offensive is putting serious pressure on leading
British rivals Tesco, Safeway, and Sainsbury, whose
publicly traded shares have been battered by the
Wal-Mart invasion. There are even signs that
Wal-Mart-induced price wars are lowering inflation
in food prices. "Anywhere Wal-Mart goes, a disin-
flationary trend follows, because Wal-Mart is seen
as an agent for prices going down," says Credit
Suisse First Boston's director of retail research,
David M. Shriver.

Leighton, who rose through the ranks at Asda, is
turning up the heat further. Asda defied British price
protections on over-the-counter drugs by lowering
the cost of Nicorette gum by 20%, to $7.40 a pack.
"It's not right to sell ordinary health-care items at
rip-off prices," says Leighton. He's bringing the
price wars to the Web, too. Wal-Mart's first European
online venture, Asda@Home, plans free access to
the Internet, low prices on goods, and free delivery
to British consumers. Asda's inexpensive but hip
clothing brand, George, may be rolled out across
the Continent.

Prowling

Good start. Leighton also plans to roll out Wal-Mart's
super-efficient logistics systems from the U.S. to all
European operations. But other European giants are
bulking up to meet the Wal-Mart threat. France's
Carrefour is integrating French rival Promodes
Group, which it bought for $16.5 billion in August.
Other retailers, including Germany's Metro and
Royal Ahold in the Netherlands, are on the prowl.

So to add heft fast, Leighton will have to consider
takeovers. In Germany, "Wal-Mart does not have
enough of a presence yet," says Merrill Lynch
Europe retail analyst Vera Diehl. Possible German
targets for Wal-Mart could include retail co-operative
Ava or Metro's hypermarket business, Real. In
France, discounters Casino and Auchan could make
for interesting acquisitions. The timing is right too to
make shrewd buys: Share prices for European retailers are off about 11% from a year ago.

Meanwhile, Asda is managing to teach Wal-Mart
a few lessons. Burt P. Flickinger III of U.S. retail
consultancy Reach Marketing says Asda is helping
Wal-Mart improve its productivity in selling food and
restocking grocery shelves. Asda may even inspire

Wal-Mart to offer some novel incentives. A current staff incentive program offers the top-performing employee free use of a Jaguar for a week. Trunk's kind of small for groceries, though.

By Kerry Capell and Heidi Dawley in London, with Wendy Zellner in Dallas and Karen Nickel Anhalt in Berlin

---

Source: **Reprinted from January 24, 2000, p. 132 issue of** *Business Week* **by special permission, copyright © 2000 by McGraw-Hill Companies, Inc.**

Decision making
The process of choosing a course of action among alternatives.

Controlling
The process of evaluating results in relation to plans or objectives and deciding what action, if any, to take.

This opening news story explains Wal-Mart's basic strategy for becoming a major competitor in the European retail industry. The company's decisions to buy Asda, in order to get a strong foothold in the United Kingdom, and to open stores in Germany under its own name seem appropriate because they focus operations in two of the largest and strongest EU economies. Wal-Mart's challenge now will be to carefully monitor local operations and to use its time-proven approach of controlling inventory and prices to gain market share. However, the firm will also have to evaluate the benefits of using the approach that has worked so well in the United States with the changes that might be needed in dealing with the challenges it will face in this international marketplace. The news story focuses on Europe, Wal-Mart also has operations in South America (Argentina and Brazil) and Asia (China and South Korea). So the company will need to adapt its decision-making styles and controlling procedures to meet the needs of its worldwide operations. For example, the way in which decision making is carried out in the U.K. is going to be different from the way managers do it in Germany or Brazil or China. Similarly, the way in which operations are controlled in terms of evaluating both store operations and personnel performance will vary from one country to another. If Wal-Mart can adapt its approach and address these differences, its goal of generating one-third of all sales from the international market may become a reality.

■ The Decision-Making and Controlling Linkages

Decision making and controlling are two vital and often interlinked functions of international management. For example, in the mid-1990s Dell Computer's market share in Europe was a scant 2.5 percent and the company troubles on the continent helped produce the firm's first-ever loss. Five years later Dell was one of the fastest-growing PC makers in Western Europe, taking market share from such major rivals as IBM. How did the company accomplish this feat? By fine-tuning its U.S. approach for success and installing new managers to make the right decisions and better control its German and French operations. For example, Dell's managers made the decision to continue focusing on direct selling to European consumers. Many critics claimed the U.S. approach would never work with Europeans. Yet, this decision resulted in sales growth five times faster than that of the market. Now the challenge is to control this growth to maintain quality and profitability.

Another example is provided by Boeing and General Motors, two well-known MNCs that have signed major deals with the Chinese government. Boeing has agreed to sell the Chinese Civil Aviation Administration five 777-200 jetliners for approximately $685 million; and General Motors has finalized a $1.3 billion joint venture with a Shanghai automotive company to build Buick Century and Regal cars in China. The Boeing deal came after the giant aerospace MNC had been shut out of a number of contract bids in China and offers strong promise of even more business from the Chinese government. The GM deal is a 50/50 venture between the automotive MNC and the Shanghai Automotive Industry Corporation, a state-owned company. Both of these developments are viewed by the management decision makers of the respective American-based MNCs as opportunities to further open the China market and with proper controls increase their sales growth and profitability.[1]

Still another example is offered by Universal Studios Japan. In an effort to attract visitors to its Osaka location, this new theme park was specially built based on feedback from Japanese tourists at Universal parks in Orlando and Los Angeles. The company wanted to learn what these visitors liked and disliked and then use this information in its Osaka park. One theme clearly emerged: the Japanese wanted an authentic American experience, while also expecting the park to cater to their own cultural preferences. In the process, thousands of decisions were made regarding what to include and what to leave out. In terms of food, for example, seafood pizza and gumbo-style soup were put on the menu while a fried-shrimp concoction with colored rice crackers was rejected. In a musical number based on the movie *Beetlejuice,* it was decided that the main character should talk in Japanese while his sidekicks would speak and sing in English; but the decision to put in a restaurant called Shakin's, based on the 1906 San Francisco earthquake, was not a good idea because Osaka has had terrible earthquakes that killed thousands of people. Other decisions that were made related to giving the park a uniquely Japanese flavor.

The nation's penchant for buying edible souvenirs inspired a 6,000-square-foot confection shop packed with Japanese sweets like Dinosaur-shaped bean cakes. Restrooms include Japanese-style squat toilets. Even the park layout caters to the tendency of Japanese crowds to flow clockwise in an orderly manner, contrary to more-chaotic U.S. crowds that steer right. And on the Jurassic park water slide, millions of dollars were spent to widen the landing pond, redesign boat hulls, and install underwater wave-damping panels to reduce spray. Why? Many fastidious Japanese don't like to get wet, even on what's billed as one of the world's biggest water slides.[2]

Over the next few years, as the company evaluates the park's revenues and feedback from the visitors, it will be able to judge how well it is doing in giving its customers an American experience in an environment that also addresses cultural considerations.

■ The Decision-Making Process

As shown in the above examples, a number of decision-making areas currently are receiving attention in international management. One of these is the way that decisions are made in terms of centralization and decentralization. If centralized decision making is in place, most important decisions are made at the top; if decentralized decision making is in place, decisions are delegated to operating personnel. Another issue is how decision making is used to help the subsidiary respond to the economic and political demands of the country. Sometimes, these decisions are heavily economic in orientation and may concentrate on things such as return on investment for overseas operations. Other times, decisions are a result of cultural differences. For example, Ford Motor has designed and built an inexpensive vehicle, the Ikon, for the Indian market. In doing so, engineers took apart the Ford Fiesta and totally rebuilt the car to address buyer needs. Some of the changes that were made included raising the amount of rear headroom to accommodate men in turbans, adjusting doors so that they opened wider in order to avoid catching the flowing saris of women, fitting intake valves to avoid auto flooding during the monsoon season, toughening shock absorbers to handle the pock-marked city streets, and adjusting the air-conditioning system to deal with the intense summer heat.[3] As a result of these decisions, the car is selling very well in India.

The way in which decision making is carried out will be influenced by a number of factors. One of the best ways to illustrate some of these differences is with comparative examples.

Comparative Examples of Decision Making

Do decision-making philosophies and practices differ from country to country? Research shows that to some extent they do, although there also is evidence that many international operations, regardless of foreign or domestic ownership, use similar decision-making norms.

Most British organizations are highly decentralized. One major reason is that many upper-level managers do not understand the technical details of the business. Top-level managers depend heavily on middle managers to handle much of the decision making by decentralizing to their level.

Codetermination
A legal system that requires workers and their managers to discuss major decisions.

Ringisei
From Japan, decision making by consensus.

Tatemae
A Japanese term which means "doing the right thing" according to the norm.

Honne
A Japanese term which means "what one really wants to do."

The French use a different approach. One observer has noted that many top French managers graduated from the Grand Écoles, and they often lack confidence in their middle managers.[4] As a result, decision making tends to be centralized.

In Germany, managers place a greater focus on productivity and quality of goods and services than they do on managing subordinates. In addition, management education is highly technical in focus, and a legal system called **codetermination** requires workers and their managers to discuss major decisions. As a result, German MNCs tend to be fairly centralized, autocratic, and hierarchical. Scandinavian countries also have codetermination, but the Swedes focus much more on quality of work life and the importance of the individual in the organization. As a result, decision making is heavily decentralized and participative.

The Japanese are somewhat different from the Europeans. They make heavy use of a decision-making process called **ringisei,** or decision making by consensus.

> Under this system any changes in procedures and routines, tactics, and even strategies of a firm are organized by those directly concerned with those changes. The final decision is made at the top level after an elaborate examination of the proposal through successively higher levels in the management hierarchy, and results in acceptance or rejection of a decision only through consensus at every echelon of the management structure.[5]

Sometimes Japanese consensus decision making can be very time-consuming. However, in practice most Japanese managers know how to respond to "suggestions" from the top and to act accordingly—thus saving a great deal of time, but many outsiders misunderstand how Japanese managers make such decisions. In Japan, what should be done is called **tatemae,** while what one really feels, which may be quite different, is **honne.** Because it is vital to do what others expect in a given context, situations arise that often strike Westerners as the common game known as charades. However, it is very important in Japan to play out the situation according to what each person believes others expect to happen. To clarify this complicated but important Japanese decision-making process, here is a specific example offered by a Japanese scholar of a Mr. Seward, a Western employee of a Japanese firm.

> [Mr. Seward] joined a meeting as one of eight employees tasked with deciding where to go for a company trip. When the result of the vote was taken, it appeared that the group favored going to a place named Izu. At this point, one of the president's secretaries spoke up, saying, "The president wants to visit Suwa." In a tense atmosphere a second vote was taken, considering the president's opinion, and it turned out that the entire group, except Seward, voted for Suwa. Mr. Seward protested the procedure, insisting that, if members were forced to follow the president's opinion, there was no point in meeting and voting, but his objections were overridden and the company trip was set for Suwa.[6]

Many Westerners would ask why the president did not simply send out a memo announcing the destination of the meeting. The answer is that for the president having the meeting and taking a vote was *tatemae*—the right thing to do according to the normal procedure for reaching this kind of decision. At the same time, going to Suwa was *honne*—what the president wanted to do. Similarly, for the Japanese members of the committee, voting for Suwa was *tatemae* once the president's desires were made clear, while going to Izu was *honne,* what the employees really wanted to do. Obviously such culturally based subtleties make understanding whether decision making is centralized or decentralized across cultures becomes very difficult.

MNCs based in the United States tend to use fairly centralized decision making in managing their overseas units. This approach provides the necessary control for developing a worldwide strategy, because it ensures that all units are operating according to the overall strategic plan.

As shown in these examples, a number of decision-making approaches are used around the world. Most evidence, however, indicates that the overall trend currently is toward centralization. For example, in terms of both delegation and decision-making authority of overseas subsidiaries, there is evidence of a fair degree of centralization in areas such as marketing policies, financial matters, use of expatriate personnel, and decisions on production capacity. The results of a comparative study are summarized as follows:

The convergence in organizational practices in general, and decision making in particular, is taking place rapidly. This can be seen from the results of our recent study of United States, German, British, Japanese, and Swedish multinational companies. The results showed the United States management practices concerning decision making are the norms being followed by other nations. Other countries' practices correlated strongly with those of United States practices.[7]

A number of reasons help to account for this trend toward centralized decision making in international management areas. One is an advanced information technology as well as the desire to increase economies of scale and to attain higher operational efficiency. Such centralized decision making, however, can stifle the creativity and flexibility needed by the subsidiary. In resolving this dilemma, effective MNCs try to manage each overseas operation on its own merits.

Factors Affecting Decision-Making Authority

A number of factors will influence international managers' conclusions about retaining or delegating decision making to a subsidiary. Table 12–1 lists some of the most important situational factors, and the following discussion looks at each in detail.

Company size influences decision making in that large organizations have a greater need for coordination and integration of operations. To ensure that all subsidiaries are effectively managed, the MNC will centralize the authority for a number of critical decisions. This centralization is designed to increase the overall efficiency of operations, and to the extent that centralization creates the desired uniformity and coordination, this is precisely what happens.

The greater the MNC's capital investment, the more likely that decision making will be centralized. The home office wants to keep a tight rein on its investment and to ensure that everything is running smoothly. The subsidiary manager will be required to submit periodic reports, and on-site visits from home-office personnel are quite common.

The more important the overseas operation is to the MNC, the closer the MNC will control it. Home-office management will monitor performance carefully, and the subsidiary manager usually will not be allowed to make any major decisions without first clearing them with the MNC senior management. In fact, in managing important overseas operations, the home office typically will appoint someone who they know will respond to their directives and will regard this individual as an extension of the central management staff.

Table 12–1

Factors that Influence Centralization or Decentralization of Decision Making in Subsidiary Operations

Encourage Centralization	Encourage Decentralization
Large size	Small size
Large capital investment	Small capital investment
Relatively high importance to MNC	Relatively low importance to MNC
Highly competitive environment	Stable environment
Strong volume-to-unit-cost relationship	Weak volume-to-unit-cost relationship
High degree of technology	Moderate to low degree of technology
Strong importance attached to brand name, patent rights, etc.	Little importance attached to brand name, patent rights, etc.
Low level of product diversification	High level of product diversification
Homogeneous product lines	Heterogeneous product lines
Small geographic distance between home office and subsidiary	Large geographic distance between home office and subsidiary
High interdependence between the units	Low interdependence between the units
Fewer highly competent managers in host country	More highly competent managers in host country
Much experience in international business	Little experience in international business

In domestic situations, when competition increases, management will decentralize authority and give the local manager greater decision-making authority. This reduces the time that is needed for responding to competitive threats. In the international arena, however, sometimes just the opposite approach is used. As competition increases and profit margins are driven down, home-office management often seeks to standardize product and marketing decisions to reduce cost and maintain profitability. More and more upper-level operating decisions are made by central management and merely implemented by the subsidiary, although in recent years there has been a trend toward decentralizing authority and letting those decisions be made at the local level.

If there is a strong volume-to-unit-cost relationship, firms that are able to produce large quantities will have lower cost per unit than those that produce smaller amounts. Under these conditions, home-office management typically will centralize decision making and assume authority over sourcing and marketing-related matters as well as overall strategy. This helps to ensure that the subsidiary's unit cost remains low.

The more sophisticated the level of technology, the greater the degree of centralized decision making. The MNC will attempt to protect these resources by making technology-related decisions at the home office. This is particularly true for high-tech, research-intensive firms such as computer and pharmaceutic companies, which do not want their technology controlled at the local level.

If strong importance is attached to brand name, patent rights, and so forth, decision making likely will be centralized. The MNC will want to protect its rights by making these types of decisions in the home office.

The greater the amount of product and service diversification, the greater the decentralization of the decision-making process, because the MNC typically will not have the staff or the resources for coordinating these diversified offerings on a worldwide basis. The home-office management will rely on the subsidiary management to handle this task. In addition, as the overseas unit becomes increasingly skilled in manufacturing and marketing products at the local level, the chance of the home management's recentralizing decision making becomes more remote.

If product and service lines are heterogeneous, differences often exist in the socio-economic, political, legal, and cultural environments in the various countries where the firm is operating. These differences typically result in the MNC's turning over operating control to the local subsidiaries. In addition, the greater the differences in the environment between the home country and the subsidiary, the more likely the MNC will decentralize the decision-making process.

If the subsidiary and home office are far apart, decentralization is more likely than if the subsidiary is located near the home office. There is evidence that U.S. subsidiaries in North America are more closely controlled than those in South America and that those in the Far East are least controlled of all. The farther away the subsidiary, the more likely the home office will give it increased autonomy.

The greater the degree of interdependence among the units, typically the greater the centralization of decision making. The home office will want to coordinate and integrate the units into an effective system, usually from headquarters.

If the subsidiary has highly competent local managers, the chances for decentralization are increased, because the home office has more confidence in delegating to the local level and less to gain by making all the important decisions. Conversely, if the local managers are inexperienced or not highly effective, the MNC likely will centralize decision making and make many of the major decisions at headquarters.

If the firm has had a great deal of international experience, its operations likely will be more centralized. This finding is in accord with the research cited earlier, which shows a convergence toward more centralization by multinational firms.

In some areas of operation, MNCs tend to retain decision making at the top (centralization); other areas fall within the domain of subsidiary management (decentralization). It is most common to find finance, research and development, and strategic planning decisions being made at MNC headquarters, and the subsidiaries must work within the parameters established by the home office. In addition, when the subsidiary is selling new products in growing markets, centralized decision making is more likely. As the product line matures and the subsidiary managers gain experience, however, the company will start to rely more on decentralized decision making. These decisions involve planning and budgeting systems, performance evaluations, assignment of managers to the subsidiary, and use of coordinating committees to mesh the operations of the subsidiary with the worldwide operations of the MNC. The right degree of centralized or decentralized decision making can be critical to the success of the MNC.

■ Decision-Making Issues

There are a number of decision-making issues and challenges with which MNCs currently are being confronted. Three of the most prominent include total quality management decisions, use of joint ventures and other forms of cooperative agreements, and strategies for attacking competition in the international marketplace. The following examines some of the latest developments in each area.

Total Quality Management Decisions

To achieve world-class competitiveness as outlined in Chapter 3, MNCs are finding that a commitment to total quality management is critical. **Total quality management (TQM)** is an organizational strategy and accompanying techniques that result in delivery of high-quality products and/or services to customers.[8] The concept and techniques of TQM, which were introduced in Chapter 9 in relation to strategic planning, also are relevant to decision making and controlling.

> **Total quality management (TQM)**
> An organizational strategy and the accompanying techniques that result in the delivery of high-quality products and/or services to customers.

One of the primary areas where TQM is having a big impact is in manufacturing. For example, in recent years, U.S. automakers have greatly improved the quality of their cars, but the Japanese have continuous improvement of quality and thus still have the lead. A number of TQM techniques have been successfully applied to improve the quality of manufactured goods. One is the use of concurrent engineering/interfunctional teams in which designers, engineers, production specialists, and customers work together to develop new products. This approach involves all the necessary parties and overcomes what used to be an all-too-common procedure: The design people would tell the manufacturing group what to produce, and the latter would send the finished product to retail stores for sale to the customer. Today, MNCs taking a TQM approach are customer-driven. They use TQM techniques to tailor their output according to customer needs and they require the same approach from their own suppliers.[9] IBM followed a similar approach in developing its AS/400 computer systems. Customer advisory councils were created to provide input, test the product, and suggest refinements. The result was one of the most successful product launches in the company's history.

A particularly critical issue is how much decision making to delegate to subordinates. TQM uses employee **empowerment.** Individuals and teams are encouraged to generate and implement ideas for improving quality and given the decision-making authority and necessary resources and information to implement them. Many MNCs have had outstanding success with empowerment. For example, General Electric credits employee empowerment for cutting in half the time needed to change product-mix production of its dishwashers in response to market demand, and Kodak used the empowerment of its workers to increase productivity by teaching them how to inspect their own work, keep track of their own performance, and even fix their own machines.

> **Empowerment**
> The process of giving individuals and teams the resources, information, and authority they need to develop ideas and effectively implement them.

Another TQM technique that MNCs are successfully employing to develop and maintain world-class competitiveness is rewards and recognition. These range from increases in pay and benefits to the use of merit pay, discretionary bonuses, pay-for-skills and knowledge plans, plaques, and public recognition. The important thing to realize is that the rewards and recognition approaches that work well in one country may be ineffective in another. For example, individual recognition in the United States may be appropriate and valued by workers, but in Japan, group rewards are more appropriate as Japanese do not like to be singled out for personal praise. Similarly, although putting a picture or plaque on the wall to honor an individual is common practice in the United States, these rewards are frowned on in Finland as they remind the workers of how their neighbor, the Russians, used this system to encourage people to increase output (but not necessarily quality) and now the Russian economy is in shambles.

Kaizen
A Japanese term that means continuous improvement.

Still another technique associated with TQM is the use of ongoing training to achieve continual improvement. This training takes a wide variety of forms, ranging from statistical quality control techniques to team meetings designed to generate ideas for streamlining operations and eliminating waste. In all cases, the objective is to apply what the Japanese call **kaizen,** or continuous improvement. By adopting a TQM perspective and applying the techniques discussed earlier, MNCs find that they can both develop and maintain a worldwide competitive edge. A good example is Zytec, the world-class, Minnesota-based manufacturer of power supplies. The customer base for Zytec ranges from the United States to Japan to Europe. One way in which the firm ensures that it maintains a total quality perspective is to continually identify client demands and then work to exceed these expectations. Another is to totally revise the company's philosophy and beliefs regarding what quality is all about and how it needs to be implemented. Table 12–2 provides some examples of the new thinking that is now emerging regarding quality.

Indirectly related to TQM is ISO 9000. This refers to the International Standards Organization (ISO) certification to ensure quality products and services. Areas that are examined by the ISO certification team include design (product or service specifications), process control (instruction for manufacturing or service functions), purchasing, service

---

Table 12–2
The Emergence of New Beliefs Regarding Quality

Old Myth	New Truth
Quality is the responsibility of the people in the Quality Control Department.	Quality is everyone's job.
Training is costly.	Training does not cost, it saves.
New quality programs have high initial costs.	The best quality programs do not have up-front costs.
Better quality will cost the company a lot of money.	As quality goes up, costs come down.
The measurement of data should be kept to a minimum.	An organization cannot have too much relevant data on hand.
It is human to make mistakes.	Perfection—total customer satisfaction—is a standard that should be vigorously pursued.
Some defects are major and should be addressed, but many are minor and can be ignored.	No defects are acceptable, regardless of whether they are major or minor.
Quality improvements are made in small, continuous steps.	In improving quality, both small and large improvements are necessary.
Quality improvement takes time.	Quality does not take time, it saves time.
Haste makes waste.	Thoughtful speed improves quality.
Quality programs are best oriented toward areas such as products and manufacturing.	Quality is important in all areas including administration and service.
After a number of quality improvements, customers are no longer able to see additional improvements.	Customers are able to see all improvements including those in price, delivery, and performance.
Good ideas can be found throughout the organization.	Good ideas can be found everywhere, including in the operations of competitors and organizations providing similar goods and services.
Suppliers need to be price competitive.	Suppliers need to be quality competitive.

Source: Reported in Richard M. Hodgetts, *Measures of Quality and High Performance* (New York: American Management Association, 1998), p. 14.

(e.g., instructions for conducting after-sales service), inspection and testing, and training. ISO 9000 certification is becoming a necessary prerequisite to doing business in the EU, but it also is increasingly used as a screening criterion for bidding on contracts or getting business in the United States and other parts of the world. For example, after a year of hard work, Foxboro Corporation, based in Massachusetts, obtained certification, and its business greatly increased.

Strategic Alliances

Besides TQM, another area where decision making has a particular impact on MNCs is creating and nurturing strategic alliances.[10] One of the most common is **international joint ventures (IJVs),** which are formal arrangements with foreign partners who typically, although not always, are located in the country where the business will be conducted. A good example is provided by Ford Motor and Mazda. For a number of years now the two have had a strategic alliance. Today, with guidance from its American partner, Mazda is trimming costs and introducing a host of popular new models in Asia. At the same time the company is beginning to gain ground in both North America and Europe. Part of this success is accounted for by Ford executives who better controlled Mazda's freewheeling engineers and forced them to share auto platforms and to source more components overseas. Mazda also began following Ford's advice to use customer clinics, thus helping the company to develop low-priced, compact sport vehicles that are proving very popular in the Japanese market. Over the next few years Mazda intends to continue growing its market shares in North America and Europe. At the same time the two firms are working closely together in Asia.

IJVs and other strategic alliances are also becoming extremely popular because of the benefits they offer to both parties. In particular, they provide large firms with an opportunity to gain a foothold in new markets. Starbuck's Coffee International of Seattle, Washington, is a good example. This very successful MNC recently entered into a joint venture with the Beijing Mei Da Coffee Company to open coffee houses in China. Getting local consumers to switch from tea to coffee is likely to be a major challenge. However, for the moment the joint venture is focusing on the training of local managers who will run the coffee shops. Recruits are sent to Tacoma, Washington, to learn how to make the various types of Starbuck's coffee and to get a first-hand look at the company's culture. As one of the general managers for the Mei Da company put it, "People don't go to Starbucks for the coffee but for the experience. Focusing on the development of employees so that they can deliver that experience is our priority for now."[11] Part of Starbuck's strategy is also to show the new recruits that there are career and personal development opportunities in this new venture. This is an important area of emphasis for the firm because there is a major shortage of management personnel in China. As a result, many companies raid the management ranks of others, offering lucrative financial arrangements to those who are willing to change companies. One way that Starbuck's is trying to deal with this is by encouraging the trainees to take responsibility, question the system, take risks, and make changes that will keep the customers coming back. Many foreign MNCs in China want the employees to do as they are told. Starbuck's believes that its IJV emphasis on developing talent will give it an edge—and discourage people from leaving for higher financially attractive offers.

As shown in these examples, multinationals are and will be making a host of decisions related to IJVs. In Russia, the current trend is to renegotiate many of the old agreements and seek smaller deals that entail less bureaucratic red tape and are easier to bring to fruition. At the same time, the U.S. administration is trying to create a plan for providing assistance to the former Soviet republics, and this likely will generate increased interest in the use of IJVs.

Besides the former Soviet Union, other areas of the world that also were previously closed to foreign investment are beginning to open up. One of these is Vietnam which had a very auspicious beginning in the early 1990s when investors began flocking there. During this time period, for example, Japan's Idemitsu Oil Development Company signed a

International joint ventures (IJVs)

Formal arrangements with foreign partners who typically, although not always, are located in the country where the business will be conducted.

deal with the Vietnamese government that gave the company the right to explore an offshore oil and gas field in the Gulf of Tonkin. A number of U.S. companies also targeted Vietnam for investment and Citibank and Bank of America both were approved for branch status by the government. The bulk of their business was to be in wholesale banking and, in the case of Bank of America, advising the government on financing the rebuilding of the nation's weak power sector. Other firms that began giving serious consideration to Vietnam included AT&T, Coca-Cola, General Electric, Mobil, and Ralston Purina, to name but five. As a result, by 1996 the country was attracting over $8 billion annually in foreign direct investment (FDI). Since then, however, FDI has dropped sharply.

In 2000 the Vietnam General Department of Statistics reported that annual FDI was in the range of a mere $300 million. Despite its promises, the bureaucratic communist government had not created an attractive environment. Ford Motor, for example, had spent over $100 million to build a factory near Hanoi, but because of pressure from its local rival, the Vietnam Motor Corporation, it had taken 16 months for Ford to get approval to sell its Laser sedan. By the end of 2000 the company had sold less than 1,000 vehicles, a far cry from the 14,000 that had been initially projected.[12] Many other firms reported similar experiences. At present the Vietnamese government is trying to turn things around and promote investment and strategic alliances; and the latest trade agreement with the United States requires that the country open up its own markets in return for favorable treatment in the American market.[13] Among other things, the country's coffee production is skyrocketing and Vietnam currently exports over 20 percent of its coffee to the U.S.; so it is in the best interests of the country to open its markets.[14] At the same time, a growing number of multinationals are reexamining Vietnam's potential and looking to create strategic alliances that will help it establish a foothold in one of the more promising emerging economies in Asia.[15]

Decisions for Attacking the Competition

Another series of key decisions relates to MNC actions that are designed to attack the competition and gain a foothold in world markets. The accompanying box, International Management in Action: "Kodak Goes Digital, Making Film Obsolete" gives an example. Another is General Motors' decision to establish production operations on a worldwide basis and to be a major player throughout Asia, Australia, Europe, and South America, as well as select areas of Africa. As a result of this decision, the company is now closing U.S. factories and building new assembly plants abroad. Between 1995–1999 GM opened up a host of new facilities including a plant in Brazil that has an annual capacity of 120,000 units, and factories in Poland, India, Mexico, Thailand, and Shanghai, each of which has annual capacity of 100,000 units. By locating closer to the final customer and offering a well-designed and efficiently built car, the company has been able to increase its worldwide market share, thus more than offsetting the downturn it has encountered in the U.S. market where overall share has dropped below 30 percent.

GM's expansion decisions, in many cases, have been designed to help it capture the lower end of the market with small, inexpensive cars. However, the company is also intent on appealing to the upper-level buyer as well, as seen by its decision to sell Cadillacs in Europe. This market is quite different from that in the United States. European luxury car buyers often settle for far less comfort and far more handling and performance. GM hopes to appeal to these buyers with many of the changes it has introduced into the Cadillac Sevilles that it has now begun selling in Europe. Examples of some of the differences between this car and the one marketed in the United States include: (a) right-hand-drive version for the United Kingdom; (b) less clutter inside the car including unobtrusive cup holders; (c) simpler, more elegant interiors; (d) a shorter auto length; (e) tighter suspension, wider wheel tracks, and better tires for driving at high speeds; and (f) floor-mounted shifts for automatic transmission.[16]

Will this decision result in greater sales for Cadillac in Europe? It is still too early to tell, but the company's decision certainly does not have firms such as BMW or Mercedes

International Management in Action
Kodak Goes Digital, Making Film Obsolete

Kodak has been attacking the competition in a number of ways. One has been to file a complaint with the U.S. government accusing its main competitor, Fuji, of blocking Kodak growth in the Japanese market and asking the administration to take steps to correct this situation. This is only a short-term strategy designed to increase the growth of Kodak film in one country, however. Of far more future importance are technological developments such as the emergence of inexpensive cameras that use digital technology, which will make film obsolete.

Under its current management, Kodak is in the throes of reorganizing and focusing its efforts on new growth areas while continuing to extract as much sales and profit as possible from its current product lines. For example, the firm recently created a digital imaging unit, thus gathering most of the firm's digital talent into one division. Before this, efforts at digital product development were spread through the divisions. At the same time, Kodak is working to reignite overall growth by focusing on the Asian market. The company believes that it can double its growth rate in photography, a tough challenge given that the world market is growing very slowly.

The real focus of Kodak's effort is in digital technology, however, and the company's strategy in this area finally appears to be getting into focus. Still, this digital thrust will not be easy, because of both the difficulty in generating research and development breakthroughs and in marketing the new products. Some of Kodak's earlier efforts were anything but spectacular. For example, the photo-CD, which is a compact disk that Kodak developed to store photographs for viewing on TV screens or PC monitors, flopped as a consumer product. Buyers balked at paying $500 for a player that plugs into a TV plus $20 per disk. Fortunately, the company did find a ready market among small businesses such as desktop publishers and real-estate agents, which used the unit to display their offerings. The lesson is clear: Creating a new technologic product is not enough; it also is important to carefully identify the market where it can be sold successfully.

Kodak knows that the industry is going digital and the film business eventually will die out. Therefore the company must be prepared to meet the future with new products such as the digital camera. In the interim, the firm also must push ahead in the film business and with new camera offerings such as its single-use, throwaway cameras, which really is nothing more than an inexpensive cardboard-and-plastic box with a roll of film inside. Kodak also has extended this line to include telephoto, panoramic, portrait, and underwater versions of the camera. Most recently the company acquired Ofoto Inc., a leading online photography service. This acquisition is designed to facilitate the move into the online photography market and to help stimulate more rapid adoption of digital and online services by providing users with an easy way to store, share, and print pictures online. The firm hopes that all these efforts will help them to attack the competition successfully while continuing to develop and perfect digital products that will appeal to the masses.

---

concerned. The luxury car market in Europe is highly competitive and Europeans take pride in placing performance over comfort. Buyers like tight steering, rear-wheel drive, and smaller cars that provide greater gas mileage. Cadillac is not known for any of these. Nor does the car have a reputation for high-speed performance, something that people on the continent like, given that on European freeways it is common to find the traffic moving at 80–100 miles per hour.

Another example of decision making for attacking the competition is provided by BMW. While GM is trying to tap the upper market, BMW has made the decision to move down the line and gain small-car market share. The company is now in the process of building small cars with a sales price in the range of $20,000. By sharing engines, gearboxes, and electrical systems from its other offerings, the firm intends to reduce its development and production costs and offer a reliable and competitively priced auto.[17] Other firms including Mercedes and Audi have done this and have not been particularly profitable, but BMW believes that it can succeed where they have not.

NEC offers a third example of how decision making is being used for attacking the competition. In 2001 the company held 8 percent of the world market for mobile transmitting infrastructure and was vying with major competitors such as Ericsson, Lucent, Nokia, and Nortel. Most of NEC's revenues come from its contracts with NTT, Japan's phone monopoly. However, now the company is moving aggressively into the worldwide arena. Its prowess in fiber optics has resulted in its winning a big AT&T network installation contract;

and as the demand for fiber optics increases, NEC intends to exploit this strength.[18] The firm recently announced that it had developed a fiber-optic cable that is four times more powerful than that currently on the market. The company is also a world leader in manufacturing mobile handsets and the semiconductors used in mobiles and other devices. Its folding phones, for example, account for 40 percent of the Internet-capable handset market in Japan, and NEC is now looking to expand its international sales of these products.

Intel is another good example. The company has made a number of interesting decisions designed to stymie the competition. One is to bring out a new version of its Pentium chip at a much lower price than expected and cut the prices of its other chips, thus creating a strong demand for its products and forcing the competition to cut their price. In a market where overall demand has been slowing down, this strategy wreaks havoc on the competition. At the same time, however, lower prices mean that Intel must sell more products in order to increase revenues. One of the ways that the firm is trying to do this is with an extension of its Xeon microprocessor family, which is aimed at more powerful desktop workstations and server systems than the firm has targeted in the past. Intel's server offerings had generally been used in relatively lightweight machines such as those that serve up Web pages. However, this new push is designed to provide chips that are used in midsize servers such as those that run databases as well as some larger systems used in mission-critical tasks. These machines typically cost millions of dollars and run on dozens of microprocessors operating in parallel.[19] The company has also teamed up with Hewlett-Packard to develop the Itanium chip that offers greater speed because it can process 64 bits of data at a time rather than 32 bits. Working with HP, Intel is now building servers for telecommunications and making three-in-one chips that have the ability to radically reduce the size of cell phones and hand-held computers.

■ The Controlling Process

As indicated in the introduction to this chapter, controlling involves evaluating results in relation to plans or objectives and deciding what action to take. An excellent illustration is Mitsubishi's purchase of 80 percent of Rockefeller Center in the late 1980s. The Japanese firm paid $1.4 billion for this choice piece of Manhattan real estate, and it looked like a very wise decision. Over the next 6 years, however, depressed rental prices and rising maintenance costs resulted in Mitsubishi sinking an additional $500 million into the project. Finally, in late 1995, the company decided it had had enough and announced that it was walking away from the investment. Mitsubishi passed ownership to Rockefeller Center Properties Inc., the publicly traded, real-estate investment trust that held the mortgage on the Center. The cost of keeping the properties was too great for the Japanese firm, which decided to cut its losses and focus efforts on more lucrative opportunities elsewhere.

Another example is provided by Dana Corporation, the giant auto parts-supply company, which in the last few years has sold off some of its units, bought others, and refocused its business. Some of the units that Dana has sold include its clutch and transmission operation and heavy frame operations. In each case the company's control process concluded that the unit had low return on sales or investment, slow growth, operating losses, and/or eroding market share. At the same time, Dana has purchased a piston rings and cylinder liners unit, a transmission unit, and a couple of axle units. Today this $12 billion company provides complete integrated systems engineering to auto manufacturers worldwide, and is the largest independent supplier of fluid transfer, fluid power, and materials transfer components and systems in the vehicular and industrial markets.[20] The firm is also able to build complete modular chassis assemblies that fit right into trucks and cars.[21] Thanks to its control function and to effective decision making, in a highly competitive industry Dana has been able to succeed.

Another example of how the control process is being used by MNCs is in the personal computer (PC) business. Until about five years ago, PCs were built using the traditional model shown in Figure 12–1. However, today the direct sales model and the hybrid model are the most common. (See Figure 12–1.) PC firms are finding that they must keep

Figure 12–1   **Models of PC Manufacturing**

Traditional Model

Based on sales forecasts, a manufacturer orders parts for the PCs.	The parts are warehoused until they are needed by the manufacturer.	The manufacturer builds the PCs and stores them in the warehouse.	The units are ordered by distributors and shipped to the latter's warehouse.	Orders are then received from retailers and the PCs are shipped to them by the distributors.	Customers buy the PCs from the retailers and receive assistance in setting up the entire system.

Direct-Sales Model

The manufacturer orders a small number of parts from its suppliers.	Business and individual customers place order by phone or over the Internet.	The manufacturer builds computers to customer's exact specifications.	The manufacturer ships the computer directly to the customer.

Hybrid Model

The computer manufacturer builds shells: a case, power supply, floppy disc, basic circuitry.	The shells are shipped to the distributors, and component suppliers establish a parts inventory with, or near, that of the distributor.	The customer orders a computer through a retailer or directly from the manufacturer, and the order is forwarded to the distributor.	The distributor gathers the parts to assemble the computer to the customer's specifications.	On the dealer's behalf, the distributor ships the computer directly to the customer. The dealer then provides set up and additional services for a separate fee.

on the cutting edge more than any other industry because of the relentless pace of technological change. This is where the control function becomes especially critical for success. For example, stringent controls keep the inventory in the system as low as possible. PCs are manufactured using a just-in-time approach (as in the case of a customer who orders the unit and has it made to specifications) or an almost just-in-time approach (as in the case of a retailer who orders 30 units and sells them all within a few weeks). Because technology in the PC industry changes so quickly, any units that are not sold in retail outlets within 60 days may be outdated and must be severely discounted and sold for whatever the market will bear. In turn, these costs are often assumed by the manufacturer. As a result, PC manufacturers are very much inclined to build to order or to ship in quantities that can be sold quickly. In this way the firm's control system helps to ensure that inventory moves through the system and profitability does not suffer.[22]

In many ways, the control function is conceptually and practically similar to decision making. Like decision-making, the approaches used by multinationals in controlling their operations have long been an area of interest. Of particular concern has been how companies attempt to control their overseas operations to become an integrated, coordinated unit. Unfortunately, a number of control problems arise. Examples include: (1) the objectives of the overseas operation and the corporation conflict; (2) the objectives of joint-venture partners and corporate management are not in accord; (3) the amount of experience and competence in planning are widely diverse among managers running the various overseas units; and (4) there are basic philosophic disagreements about the objectives and policies of international operations, largely because of cultural differences between home- and host-country managers. The following discussion examines the various types of control that are used in international operations and the approaches that are often employed in dealing with these types of problems.

Types of Control

There are two common, complementary ways of looking at how MNCs control operations. One way is by determining whether the enterprise chooses to use internal or external control in devising its overall strategy. The other is by looking at the ways in which the organization uses direct and indirect controls.

Internal and External Control

From an internal control standpoint, an MNC will focus on the things that it does best. At the same time, of course, management wants to ensure that there is a market for the goods and services that it is offering. So the company first needs to find out what the customers want and be prepared to respond appropriately. This requires an external control focus. Naturally, every MNC will give consideration to both internal and external perspectives of control. However, one is often given more attention than the other. In explaining this idea, Trompenaars and Hampden-Turner have set forth four management views regarding how a control strategy should be devised and implemented. The four are these:

1. No one dealing with customers is without a strategy of sorts. Our task is to find out which of these strategies work, which don't, and why. Devising our own strategy in the abstract and imposing it downwards only spreads confusion.

2. No one dealing with customers is without a strategy of sorts. Our task is to find out which of these strategies work and then create a master strategy from proven successful initiatives by encouraging and combining the best.

3. To be a leader is to be the chief devisor of strategy. Using all the experience, information and intelligence we can mobilize, we need to devise an innovative strategy and then cascade it down the hierarchy.

4. To be a leader is to be the chief devisor of strategy. Using all the experience, information and intelligence we can mobilize, we must create a broad thrust, while leaving it to subordinates to fit these to customer needs.

Trompenaars and Hampden-Turner ask managers to rank each of these four statements by placing a "1" next to the one they feel would most likely be used in their company, a "2" next to the second most likely, on down to a "4" next to the one that would be the last choice. This ranking helps managers better see whether they use an external or an internal control approach. Answer 1 above focuses most strongly on an external-direct approach and rejects the internal control option. Answer 3 represents just the opposite. Answer 2 affirms a connection between an external-directed strategy and an inner-directed one, whereas answer 4 does just the opposite.[23]

Cultures differ in the control approach they use. For example, among U.S. multinationals it is common to find managers using a more internal control approach. Among Asian firms an external control approach is more typical. Table 12–3 provides some contrasts between the two.

Direct controls
The use of face-to-face or personal meetings for the purpose of monitoring operations.

Direct Controls

Direct controls involve face-to-face or personal meetings to monitor operations. A good example is International Telephone and Telegraph (ITT), which holds monthly management meetings at its New York headquarters. These meetings are run by the CEO of the company, and reports are submitted by each ITT unit manager throughout the world. Problems are discussed, goals set, evaluations made, and actions taken that will help the unit to improve its effectiveness.

Another common form of direct control is visits by top executives to overseas affiliates or subsidiaries. During these visits, top managers, can learn firsthand the problems and challenges facing the unit and offer assistance.

A third form is the staffing practices of MNCs. By determining who to send overseas to run the unit, the corporation can directly control how the operation will be run. The company will want the manager to make operating decisions and handle day-to-day matters, but the individual also will know which decisions should be cleared with the home office. In fact, this approach to direct control sometimes results in a manager who is more responsive to central management than to the needs of the local unit.

Table 12–3
The Impact of Internal and External-Oriented Cultures on the Control Process

Key Differences between	
Internal Control	**External Control**
Often dominating attitude bordering on aggressiveness towards the environment.	Often flexible attitude, willing to compromise and keep the peace.
Conflict and resistance means that a person has convictions.	Harmony, responsiveness, and sensibility are encouraged.
The focus is on self, function, one's own group, and one's own organization.	The focus is on others such as customers, partners, and colleagues.
There is discomfort when the environment seems "out of control" or changeable.	There is comfort with waves, shifts, and cycles, which are regarded as "natural."
Tips for Doing Business with	
Internally Controlled (for externals)	**Externally Controlled (for internals)**
Playing "hard ball" is legitimate to test the resilience of an opponent.	Softness, persistence, politeness, and long, long patience will get rewards.
It is most important to "win your objective."	It is most important to maintain one's relationships with others.
Win some, lose some.	Win together, lose apart.

Source: Adapted from Fons Trompenaars and Charles Hampden-Turner, *Riding the Waves of Culture: Understanding Diversity in Global Business,* 2nd ed. (New York: McGraw-Hill, 1998), pp. 160–161.

A fourth form is the organizational structure itself. By designing a structure that makes the unit highly responsive to home-office requests and communications, the MNC ensures that all overseas operations are run in accord with central management's desires. This structure can be established through formal reporting relationships and chain of command (who reports to whom).

Indirect Controls   **Indirect controls** use reports and other written forms of communication to control operations. One of the most common examples is the use of monthly operating reports that are sent to the home office. Other examples, which typically are used to supplement the operating report, include financial statements, such as balance sheets, income statements, cash budgets, and financial ratios, that provide insights into the unit's financial health. The home office will use these operating and financial data to evaluate how well things are going and make decisions regarding necessary changes. Three sets of financial statements usually are required from subsidiaries: (1) statements prepared to meet the national accounting standards and procedures prescribed by law and other professional organizations in the host country; (2) statements prepared to comply with the accounting principles and standards required by the home country; and (3) statements prepared to meet the financial consolidation requirements of the home country.

Indirect controls are particularly important in international management because of the great expense associated with direct methods. Typically, MNCs will use indirect controls to monitor performance on a monthly basis, whereas direct controls are used semiannually or annually. This dual approach often provides the company with effective control of its operations at a price that also is cost-effective.

Indirect controls
The use of reports and other written forms of communication to control operations.

Approaches to Control

International managers can employ many different approaches to control. These approaches typically are dictated by the MNC's philosophy of control, the economic environment in which the overseas unit is operating, and the needs and desires of the managerial personnel who staff the unit. Working within control parameters, MNCs will structure their processes so that they are as efficient and effective as possible. Typically, the tools that are used will give the unit manager the autonomy needed to adapt to changes in the market as well as to attract competent local personnel. These tools will also provide for coordination of operations with the home office, so that the overseas unit is in harmony with the MNC's strategic plan.

Some control tools are universal. For example, all MNCs use financial tools in monitoring overseas units. This was true as long as three decades ago, when the following was reported:

> The cross-cultural homogeneity in financial control is in marked contrast to the heterogeneity exercised over the areas of international operations. American subsidiaries of Italian and Scandinavian firms are virtually independent operationally from their parents in functions pertaining to marketing, production, and research and development; whereas, the subsidiaries of German and British firms have limited freedom in these areas. Almost no autonomy on financial matters is given by any nationality to the subsidiaries.[24]

Some Major Differences   MNCs control operations in many different ways, and these often vary considerably from country to country. For example, how British firms monitor their overseas operations often is different from how German or French firms do. Similarly, U.S. MNCs tend to have their own approach to controlling and it differs from both European and Japanese approaches. When Horovitz examined the key characteristics of top management control in Great Britain, Germany, and France, he found that British controls had four common characteristics: (1) financial records were sophisticated and heavily emphasized; (2) top management tended to focus its attention on major problem areas and did not get involved in specific, detailed matters of control; (3) control was used more for general guidance than for surveillance; and (4) operating units had a large amount of marketing autonomy.[25]

This model was in marked contrast to that of German managers, who employed very detailed control and focused attention on all variances large and small. These managers also placed heavy control on the production area and stressed operational efficiency. In achieving this centralized control, managers used a large central staff for measuring performance, analyzing variances, and compiling quantitative reports for senior executives. Overall, the control process in the German firms was used as a policing and surveillance instrument. French managers employed a control system that was closer to that of the Germans than to the British, however. Control was used more for surveillance than for guiding operations, and the process was centrally administered. Even so, the French system was less systematic and sophisticated.[26]

How do U.S. MNCs differ from their European counterparts? One comparative study found that a major difference is that U.S. firms tend to rely much more heavily on reports and other performance-related data. Americans make greater use of output control, and Europeans rely more heavily on behavioral control. Commenting on the differences between these two groups, the researcher noted: "This pattern appears to be quite robust and continues to exist even when a number of common factors that seem to influence control are taken into account."[27] Some specific findings from this study include:

1. Control in U.S. MNCs focuses more on the quantifiable, objective aspects of a foreign subsidiary, whereas control in European MNCs tends to be used to measure more qualitative aspects. The U.S. approach allows comparative analyses between other foreign operations as well as domestic units; the European measures are more flexible and allow control to be exercised on a unit-by-unit basis.

2. Control in U.S. MNCs requires more precise plans and budgets in generating suitable standards for comparison. Control in European MNCs requires a high level of companywide understanding and agreement regarding what constitutes appropriate behavior and how such behavior supports the goals of both the subsidiary and the parent firm.

3. Control in U.S. MNCs requires large central staffs and centralized information-processing capability. Control in European MNCs requires a larger cadre of

capable expatriate mangers who are willing to spend long periods of time abroad. This control characteristic is reflected in the career approaches used in the various MNCs. Although U.S. multinationals do not encourage lengthy stays in foreign management positions, European MNCs often regard these positions as stepping stones to higher offices.

4. Control in European MNCs requires more decentralization of operating decision than control in U.S. MNCs.

5. Control in European MNCs favors short vertical spans or reporting channels from the foreign subsidiary to responsible positions in the parent.[28]

As noted earlier in the discussion of decision making, these differences help to explain why many researchers have found European subsidiaries to be more decentralized than U.S. subsidiaries. On the one hand, Europeans rely on the managerial personnel they assign from headquarters to run the unit properly. Americans tend to hire a greater percentage of local management people and control operations through reports and other objective, performance-related data. The difference results in Europeans' relying more on socioemotional control systems and Americans' opting for task-oriented, objective control systems.

Evaluating Approaches to Control   Is one control approach any better than the other? The answer is that each seems to work best for its respective group. Some studies predict that as MNCs increase in size, however, they likely will move toward the objective orientation of the U.S. MNCs. Commenting on the data gathered from large German and U.S. MNCs, the researchers concluded:

> Control mechanisms have to be harmonized with the main characteristics of management corporate structure to become an integrated part of the global organization concept and to meet situational needs. Trying to explain the differences in concepts of control we have to consider that the companies of the U.S. sample were much larger and more diversified. . . . Accordingly, they use different corporate structures, combining operational units into larger units and integrating these through primarily centralized, indirect, and task-oriented control. . . . The German companies have not (yet) reached this size and complexity, so a behavioral model of control seems to be fitting.[29]

Approaches to control also differ between U.S. and Japanese firms. For example, one study surveyed the attitudes of a large sample of Japanese and U.S. controllers and line managers. Respondents were drawn from the 500 largest industrial firms in both countries, and some of the results are presented in Table 12–4.

One overall finding of the research was that Japanese controllers and managers prefer less participation in the control process than their U.S. counterparts do. In addition, the Japanese have longer-term planning horizons, view budgets as more of a communication device than a controlling tool, and prefer more slack in their budgets than the Americans. These results are extremely important in terms of adapting U.S. approaches to Japanese-owned subsidiaries. The study results suggest the following:

> U.S. managers who wish to design control systems for foreign divisions in Japan (or vice-versa) may wish to consider modifications to the typical domestic system, or they should at least be aware of the potential differences in responses to the system in the areas of budget development, evaluation against budgets, long-run/short-run orientation of budgets, the use of budget slack, and the use of analytic tools in developing inputs to the budget process to name a few.[30]

It is also important to understand why Japanese managers act as they do. Yoshimura and Anderson recently conducted a detailed analysis of white-collar middle managers in Japan in order to determine what foreign managers need to know about these "salarymen." One thing that the researchers found was that Japanese managers place human relationships ahead of economic efficiency. As a result, when Western managers try to penetrate Japanese markets by offering superior technology or lower price as their levers, they often find that these strategies do not work. If a Japanese company has had a satisfactory relationship with a supplier, the company may continue doing business with this firm even if it means accepting higher costs. Second, when dealing with a Japanese company, nothing

Table 12–4
Selected Beliefs Related to Planning and Control

| | Statement of Results—Average Responses[a] | | | |
| | Japan | | United States | |
	Managers	Controllers	Managers	Controllers
To be useful in performance evaluation of managers, a budget must be revised continuously throughout the year.	3.07	3.14	2.70	2.48
It is important that budgets be very detailed.	3.38	3.31	2.93	2.97
It is appropriate to charge other activities when budgeted funds are used up.	3.01	2.91	1.96	1.52
Budgets should be developed from the bottom up rather than from the top down.	3.13	3.01	3.68	3.96
Budgets are useful in communicating the goal and planned activities of the company.	4.54	4.68	4.11	4.23
Budgets are useful in coordinating activities of various departments.	4.24	4.46	3.78	4.02
A manager who fails to attain the budgets should be replaced.	2.56	2.67	2.00	1.92
Top management should judge a manager's performance mainly on the basis of attaining budget profit.	3.25	3.38	2.27	2.07
It is important that executive compensation depend on a comparison of actual and budgeted performance.	3.18	3.18	3.55	3.56
It is important that managers who perform exceptionally well receive more money than other managers in similar positions.	3.84	3.92	4.28	4.14
It is important for a manager to have quantitative or analytic skills as opposed to people skills.	3.12	3.15	2.04	1.96
The best way to determine the value of capital projects is through the use of quantitative analysis.	3.61	3.80	3.23	3.37

Note:[a] The response scale was as follows:

strongly disagree	1
disagree	2
neutral	3
agree	4
strongly agree	5

Source: Adapted from Lane Daley, James Jiambalvo, Gary L. Sundem, and Yasumasa Kondo, "Attitudes toward Financial Control Systems in the United States and Japan," *Journal of International Business Studies,* Fall 1985, pp. 100–102. Used with permission.

is more important than a supplier's ability to meet this customer's expectations. When salarymen complain about non-Japanese companies and the products or service they provide, they usually contend that consistency is missing.

They want their suppliers to understand customer expectations without being told explicitly, and they want assurance that even "unreasonable" expectations, such as midnight service, will be met. They don't want their relationship manager changed frequently because of turnover; a new contact may not understand their expectations immediately. Japanese overseas subsidiaries do business with their traditional suppliers because they want to maintain continuity in relationships, even if lower-cost local firms are available. The Japanese believe that, in the long run, if both parties contribute to the relationship in good faith, results will take care of themselves.[31]

Another thing that the researchers discovered is that sometimes performance results are not as high as they could be because of the fear of embarrassing others in the organization. For example, even though some decisions might result in higher returns on investment for the company, if these decisions put others in a bad light, they will not be made. This means that if a bank has two groups that are charged with buying and selling foreign currency and one of the groups concludes that the U.S. dollar is going to decline against the Japanese yen, it would be wise for this group to sell those dollars and buy yen. On the other hand, if there is another group in the bank that has a large position in dollars and will be unable to unload this currency very quickly, the first group might refuse to sell its dollars because this would end up making the group that held dollars look foolish and this is something that Japanese salarymen try very hard to avoid.

In fact, the avoidance of embarrassment or saving "face" is one reason that many Japanese firms focus on long-term objectives rather than short-term ones. While their pronouncements seem to emphasize the long-term orientation of their company, in truth this approach is a way of deflecting embarrassment. After all, no one knows what will happen in the long run, so by pretending to be highly interested in 50-year goals, the management sidesteps any likelihood that its current performance will be criticized. After all, it can always argue that in the long run it will achieve high level performance, despite the fact that it is not doing very well at present. So in deciding which form of control to use, MNCs must determine whether they want a more bureaucratic or a more cultural control approach; and from the cultural perspective, it must be remembered that this control will vary across subsidiaries.

■ Control Techniques

A number of performance measures are used for control purposes. Three of the most common types are those related to financial performance, quality performance, and personnel performance.

Financial Performance

Financial performance evaluation of a foreign subsidiary or affiliate usually is based on profit and return on investment. **Profit** is the amount remaining after all expenses are deducted from total revenues. **Return on investment (ROI)** is measured through dividing profit by assets; some firms use profit divided by owners' equity (returns on owners' investment, or ROOI) in referring to the return-on-investment performance measure. In any case, the most important part of the ROI calculation is profits, which often can be manipulated by management. Thus, the amount of profit directly relates to how well or how poorly a unit is judged to perform. For example, if an MNC has an operation in both country A and country B and taxes are lower in country A, the MNC may be able to benefit if the two units have occasion to do business with each other. This benefit can be accomplished by having the unit in country A charge higher prices than usual to the unit in country B, thus providing greater net profits to the MNC. Simply put, sometimes differences in tax rates can be used to maximize overall MNC profits. This same basic form of manipulation can be used in transferring money from one country to another, which can be explained as follows:

> Transfer prices are manipulated upward or downward depending on whether the parent company wishes to inject or remove cash into or from a subsidiary. Prices on imports by a subsidiary from a related subsidiary are raised if the multinational company wishes to move funds from the receiver to the seller, but they are lowered if the objective is to keep the funds in the importing subsidiary. . . . Multinational companies have been known to use transfer pricing for moving excess cash from subsidiaries located in countries with weak currencies to countries with strong currencies in order to protect the value of their current assets.[32]

The so-called bottom-line (i.e., profit) performance of subsidiaries also can be affected by a devaluation or revaluation of local currency. For example, if a country devalues its currency, then subsidiary export sales will increase, because the price of these goods

Profit
The amount remaining after all expenses are deducted from total revenues.

Return on investment (ROI)
Return measured by dividing profit by assets.

will be lower for foreign buyers, whose currencies now have greater purchasing power. If the country revalues its currency, then export sales will decline because the price of goods for foreign buyers will rise, since their currencies now will have less purchasing power in the subsidiary's country. Likewise, a devaluation of the currency will increase the cost of imported materials and supplies for the subsidiary, and a revaluation will decrease these costs because of the relative changes in the purchasing power of local currency. Because devaluation and revaluation of local currency are outside the control of the overseas unit, bottom-line performance sometimes will be a result of external conditions that do not accurately reflect how well the operation actually is being run.

Of course, not all bottom-line financial performance is a result of manipulation or external economic conditions. Sometimes there are other forces that account for the problem. For example, one of Volkswagen's goals for a recent year was to earn a pretax 6.5 percent on revenues. The firm fell far short of this goal, earning only 3.5 percent before taxes. One reason for this poor performance was that labor costs in Lower Saxony, where approximately half of its workforce is located, are very high. Workers here produce only 40 vehicles per employee annually in contrast to the VW plant in Navarra, Spain, which turns out 79 vehicles per employee per year. Why doesn't VW move work to lower-cost production sites? The major reason is because the state of Lower Saxony owns 19 percent of the company's voting stock and so the workers' jobs are protected.[33] Simply put, relying solely on financial results to evaluate performance can result in misleading conclusions.

Quality Performance

Just as quality has become a major focus in decision making, as discussed earlier under TQM, it also is a major dimension of the modern control process of MNCs. The term "quality control" (QC) has been around for a long time, and it is a major function of production and operations management. Besides the TQM techniques of concurrent engineering/interfunctional teams, employee empowerment, reward/recognition systems, and training, which were discussed under decision making, another technique more directly associated with the control function is the use of quality circles, which have been popularized by the Japanese. A **quality control circle (QCC)** is a group of workers who meet on a regular basis to discuss ways of improving the quality of work. This approach has helped many MNCs to improve the quality of their goods and services dramatically.

Why are Japanese-made goods of higher quality than those of many other countries? The answer cannot rest solely on technology, because many MNCs have the same or superior technology or the financial ability to purchase it. There must be other causal factors. The accompanying sidebar, "How the Japanese Do Things Differently," gives some details on these factors. One study attempted to answer the question by examining the differences between Japanese and U.S. manufacturers of air conditioners.[34] In this analysis, many of the commonly cited reasons for superior Japanese quality were discovered to be inaccurate. One theory was that Japanese focus their production processes on a relatively limited set of tasks and narrow product lines, but this was not so. Nor was support found for the commonly held belief that single sourcing provided Japanese firms with cost advantages over those using multiple sourcing; the firms studied regularly relied on a number of different suppliers. So, what were the reasons for the quality differences?

One reason was the focus on keeping the workplace clean and ensuring that all machinery and equipment was properly maintained. The Japanese firms were more careful in handling incoming parts and materials, work-in-process, and finished products than their U.S. counterparts. Japanese companies also employed equipment fixtures to a greater extent than U.S. manufacturers in ensuring proper alignment of parts during final assembly.

The Japanese minimized worker error by assigning new employees to existing work teams or pairing them with supervisors. In this way, the new workers gained important experience under the watchful eye of someone who could correct their mistakes.

Another interesting finding was that the Japanese made effective use of QCCs. Quality targets were set, and responsibility for their attainment then fell on the circle while management provided support assistance. This was stated by the researcher as follows:

Quality control circle (QCC)
A group of workers who meet on a regular basis to discuss ways of improving the quality of work.

International Management in Action
How the Japanese Do Things Differently

There are a number of things that Japanese firms do extremely well. One is to train their people carefully, a strategy that many successful U.S. firms also employ. Another is to try and remain on the technological cutting edge. A third, and increasingly important because of its uniqueness to the Japanese, is to keep a keen focus on developing and bringing to market goods that are competitively priced.

In contrast to Western firms, many Japanese companies use what is called a "target cost" approach. Like other multinational firms, Japanese companies begin the new product development process by conducting marketing research and examining the characteristics of the product to be produced. At this point, however, the Japanese take a different approach. The traditional approach used by MNCs around the world is next to go into designing, engineering, and supplier pricing, then to determine if the cost is sufficiently competitive to move ahead with manufacturing. Japanese manufacturers, on the other hand, first determine the price that the consumer most likely will accept, and then they work with design, engineering, and supply people to ensure that the product can be produced at this price. The other major difference is that after most firms manufacture a product, they will engage in periodic cost reductions. The Japanese, however, use a kaizen approach, in which there are continuous cost-reduction efforts.

The critical difference between the two systems is that the Japanese get costs out of the product during the planning and design stage. Additionally, they look at profit in terms of product lines rather than just individual goods, so a consumer product that would be rejected for production by a U.S. or European firm because its projected profitability is too low may be accepted by a Japanese firm because the product will attract additional customers to other offerings in the line. A good example is Sony, which decided to build a smaller version of its compact personal stereo system and market it to older consumers. Sony knew that the profitability of the unit would not be as high as usual, but it went ahead because the product would provide another market niche for the firm and strengthen its reputation. Also, a side benefit is that once a product is out there, it may appeal to an unanticipated market. This was the case with Sony's compact personal stereo system. The unit caught on with young people, and Sony's sales were 50 percent greater than anticipated. Had Sony made its manufacturing decision solely on "stand alone" profitability, the unit never would have been produced.

These approaches are not unique to Japanese firms. Foreign companies operating in Japan are catching on and using them as well. A good example is Coca-cola Japan. Coke is the leading company in the Japanese soft drink market, which sees the introduction of more than 1,000 new products each year. Most offerings do not last very long, and a cost accountant might well argue that it is not worth the effort to produce them. However, Coca-Cola introduces one new product a month. Most of these sodas, soft drinks, and cold coffees survive less than 90 days, but Coke does not let the short-term bottom line dictate the decision. The firm goes beyond quick profitability and looks at the overall picture. Result: Coca-Cola continues to be the leading soft drink firm in Japan despite competition that often is more vigorous than that in the United States.

In supporting the activities of their QCC's, the Japanese firms in this industry routinely collected extensive quality data. Information on defects was compiled daily, and analyzed for trends. Perhaps most important, the data were made easily accessible to line workers, often in the form of publicly posted charts. More detailed data were available to QCC's on request.[35]

This finding pointed out an important difference between Americans and Japanese. The Japanese pushed data on quality down to the operating employees in the quality circles, whereas Americans tended to aggregate the quality data into summary reports aimed at middle- and upper-level management.

Another important difference is that the Japanese tend to build in early warning systems so that they know when something is going wrong. A good example is that incoming field data are reviewed immediately by the quality department, and problems are assigned to one of two categories: routine or emergency. Special efforts then are made to resolve the emergency problems as quickly as possible. High failure rates attributable to a single persistent problem are identified and handled much faster than in U.S. firms.

Still another reason is that the Japanese work closely with their suppliers so that the latters' quality increases. In fact, research shows that among suppliers that have contracts with both American and Japanese auto plants in the U.S., the Japanese plants get higher performance from their suppliers than do the Americans.[36] The Japanese are able to accomplish this because they work closely with their suppliers and help them develop lean manufacturing capabilities. Some of the steps that Japanese manufacturers take in doing this include: (1) leveling their own production schedules in order to avoid big spikes in demand, thus allowing their suppliers to hold less inventory; (2) encouraging their suppliers to ship only what is needed by the assembly plant at a particular time, even if this means sending partially filled trucks; and (3) creating a disciplined system of delivery time windows during which all parts have to be received at the delivery plant. A close look at Table 12–5 shows that the 91 suppliers who were working for both Japanese and American auto firms performed more efficiently for their Japanese customers than for their American customers.

Management attitudes toward quality also were quite different. The Japanese operate under the philosophy of "anything worth doing in the area of quality is worth overdoing." Workers are trained for all jobs on the line, even though they eventually are assigned to a single workstation. This method of "training overkill" ensures that everyone can perform every job perfectly and results in two important outcomes: (1) if someone is moved to another job, he or she can handle the work without any additional assistance; and (2) the workers realize that management puts an extremely high value on the need for quality. When questioned regarding whether their approach to quality resulted in spending more money than was necessary, the Japanese managers disagreed. They believed that quality improvement was technically possible and economically feasible. They did not accept the common U.S. strategy of building a product with quality that was "good enough."

These managers were speaking only for their own firms, however. Some evidence shows that at least in the short run, an overfocus on quality may become economically unwise. Even so, firms must remember that in the long run, quality goods and services lead to repeat business, which translates into profits and growth. From a control standpoint, however, the major issue is how to identify quality problems and resolve them as efficiently as possible. One approach that has gained acceptance in the United States is outlined by Genichi Taguchi, one of the world's foremost authorities on quality control. Taguchi's approach is to dispense with highly sophisticated statistical methods unless

Table 12–5
Performance of Suppliers When Serving U.S. and Japanese-owned Auto Plants

Performance Indicators	Chrysler Suppliers (n = 26)	Ford Suppliers (n = 42)	GM Suppliers (n = 23)	Honda Suppliers (n = 22)	Nissan Suppliers (n = 16)	Toyota Suppliers (n = 37)
Inventory turnover	28.3	24.4	25.5	38.4	49.2	52.4
Work in process	3.0	3.9	7.2	4.0	3.8	3.0
Finished goods storage time	4.8	5.4	6.6	5.3	4.9	3.2
Inventory on the truck	2.1	4.5	2.6	2.8	2.08	1.61
Inventory maintained at the customer's site	3.5	4.8	3.1	4.0	2.8	2.3
Percentage change in manufacturing costs compared to the previous year	0.69%	0.58%	0.74%	–0.9%	–0.7%	–1.3%
Percentage of late deliveries	4.4%	7.70%	3.04%	2.11%	1.08%	0.44%
Emergency shipping cost (per million sales dollars) in previous year	$1,235	$446	$616	$423	$379	$204

Source: Adapted from Jeffrey K. Liker and Yen-Chun Wu, "Japanese Automakers, U.S. Suppliers and Supply-Chain Superiority," *Sloan Management Review,* Fall 2000, p. 84.

more fundamental ways do not work. Figure 12–2 provides an example of how his approach was used to identify the cause of defects in the paint on a minivan hood. This approach to solving quality control problems is proving to be so effective that many MNCs are adopting it. They also are realizing that the belief that Japanese firms will correct quality control problems regardless of the cost is not true. As Taguchi puts it, "the more efficient approach is to identify the things that can be controlled at a reasonable cost in an organized manner, and simply ignore those too expensive to control."[37] To the extent that U.S. MNCs can do this, they will be able to compete on the basis of quality.

Personnel Performance

Besides financial techniques and the emphasis on quality, another key area of control is personnel performance evaluation. This type of evaluation can take a number of different forms, although there is a great deal of agreement from firm to firm when looking at the overall criteria that are measured. Table 12–6 provides a list of the 25 most admired global companies. What makes these MNCs so successful? Consultants at the Hay Group made an analysis of the best global firms in a recent year and concluded that there were seven common themes that emerged.

1. Top managers at the most admired companies take their mission statements seriously and expect everyone else to do the same.
2. Success attracts the best people—and the best people sustain success.
3. The top companies know precisely what they are looking for.
4. These firms see career development as an investment, not a chore.
5. Whenever possible, these companies promote from within.
6. Performance is rewarded.
7. The firms are genuinely interested in what their employees think and they measure work satisfaction often and thoroughly.[38]

One of the most common approaches to personnel performance evaluation is the periodic appraisal of work performance. Although the objective is similar from country to

Figure 12–2   Solving a Quality Problem: Taguchi Method vs. Traditional Method

Traditional Method Possible causes are studied one by one while holding the other factors constant.

Taguchi Method Brainstorming and a few bold experiments seek to quickly find the problem.

Source: From information reported in John Holusha, "Improving Quality, the Japanese Way," *New York Times,* July 20, 1988, p. 35.

Table 12–6
The Most Admired Global Companies

Ranking	Company
1	General Electric (electronics, electrical equipment)
2	Cisco Systems (network communications, Internet technology)
3	Microsoft (computer hardware, software)
4	Intel (computer hardware, software)
5	Wal-Mart Stores (retail: general, specialty)
6	Sony (electronics, electrical equipment)
7	Dell Computer (computer hardware, software)
8	Nokia (network communications, Internet technology)
9	Home Depot (retail: general, specialty)
10	Toyota Motor (motor vehicles)
11	Southwest Airlines (airlines)
12	Lucent Technologies (network communications, Internet technology)
13	Goldman Sachs (securities, diversified financials)
14	Berkshire Hathaway (insurance: property, casualty)
15	Coca-Cola (beverages)
16	Charles Schwab (securities, diversified financials)
17	Johnson & Johnson (pharmaceuticals)
18	Citigroup (securities, diversified financials)
19	Ford Motor (motor vehicles)
20	Pfizer (pharmaceuticals)
21	Merck (pharmaceuticals)
22	Walt Disney (entertainment)
23	American Express (securities, diversified financials)
24	United Parcel Service (mail, packaging, freight delivery)
25	Enron (energy transmission providers)

Source: Fortune, October 2, 2000, p. 184.

country, how performance appraisals are done differs. For example, what is effective employee performance in one country is not always judged to be effective in another. This is particularly important when expatriate managers evaluate local managers based on home-country standards. A good example came out of a survey that found Japanese managers in U.S.-based manufacturing firms gave higher evaluations to Japanese personnel than to Americans. The results led the researcher to conclude: "It seems that cultural differences and diversified approaches to management in MNCs of different nationalities will always create a situation where some bias in performance appraisal may exist."[39] Dealing with these biases is a big challenge facing MNCs.

Another important difference is how personnel performance control actually is conducted. A study that compared personnel control approaches used by Japanese managers in Japan with those employed by U.S. managers in the United States found marked differences.[40] For example, when Japanese work groups were successful because of the actions of a particular individual, the Japanese manager tended to give credit to the whole group. When the group was unsuccessful because of the actions of a particular individual, however, the Japanese manager tended to perceive this one employee as responsible. In addition, the more unexpected the poor performance, the greater the likelihood that the individual would be responsible. In contrast, individuals in the United States typically were given both the credit when things went well and the blame when performance was poor.

Other differences relate to how rewards and monitoring of personnel performance are handled. Both U.S. and Japanese managers offered greater rewards and more freedom from close monitoring to individuals when they were associated with successful performance, no matter what the influence of the group on the performance. The Americans carried this tendency further than the Japanese in the case of rewards, however, including giving high rewards to a person who is a "lone wolf."[41]

A comparison of these two approaches to personnel evaluation shows that the Japanese tend to use a more social or group orientation, while the Americans are more individualistic. The researchers found that overall, however, the approaches were quite similar, and that the control of personnel performance by Japanese and U.S. managers is far more similar than different.

Such similarity also can be found in assessment centers used to evaluate employees. An **assessment center** is an evaluation tool that is used to identify individuals with the potential to be selected or promoted to higher-level positions. Used by large U.S. MNCs for many years, these centers also are employed around the world. A typical assessment center would involve simulation exercises such as: (1) in-basket exercises that require managerial attention; (2) a committee exercise in which the candidates must work as a team in making decisions; (3) business decision exercises in which participants compete in the same market; (4) preparation of a business plan; and (5) a letter-writing exercise. These forms of evaluation are beginning to gain support, because they are more comprehensive than simple checklists or the use of a test or an interview and thus better able to identify those managers who are most likely to succeed when hired or promoted.

Assessment center
An evaluation tool used to identify individuals with potential to be selected or promoted to higher-level positions.

The World of *Business Week*—Revisited

This chapter focused very heavily on two areas that are going to be critical to Wal-Mart's international success: decision making and controlling. During this decade Wal-Mart is going to continue its efforts to gain market share in Europe by opening new stores and by acquiring retail operations on the continent. In the process, the company is going to face a number of challenges. One is to determine the amount of decision-making authority that its units will need in order to respond effectively to local customer needs. The firm will have to decentralize decision making but, at the same time, be able to maintain sufficient authority for effectively coordinating worldwide operations. Another challenge will be to create the necessary controls for ensuring that financial, quality, and personnel performance are meeting standards. As Wal-Mart expands its operations into more and more countries, the need for such control will become increasingly more important. Now that you have read the material in this chapter, apply the information to Wal-Mart's international operations by answering these questions. What is one way in which decision making in the company's Asian operations might be different from its EU operations? What kinds of direct control might the company use with all of its international operations? When measuring quality performance, what are two areas that the company will need to examine?

Summary of Key Points

1. Decision making involves choosing from among alternatives. Some countries tend to use more centralized decision making than others, so that more decisions are made at the top of the MNC than are delegated to the subsidiaries and operating levels.

2. A number of factors help to influence whether decision making will be centralized or decentralized, including company size, amount of capital investment, relative importance of the overseas unit to the MNC, volume-to-unit-cost relationship, level of product diversification, distance between the home office and the subsidiary, and the competence of managers in the host country.

3. There are a number of decision-making issues with which MNCs currently are being confronted. Three of the most important include total quality management (TQM) decisions, use of joint ventures and other forms of cooperative agreements, and strategies for attacking the competition.

4. Controlling involves evaluating results in relation to plans or objectives, then taking action to correct deviations. MNCs control their overseas operations in a number of ways. Most combine direct and indirect controls. Some prefer heavily quantifiable methods, and others opt for more qualitative approaches. Some prefer decentralized approaches; others opt for greater centralization.

5. Three of the most common performance measures used to control subsidiaries are in the financial, quality, and personnel areas. Financial performance typically is measured by profit and return on investment. Quality performance often is controlled through quality circles. Personnel performance typically is judged through performance evaluation techniques.

Key Terms

assessment center, *361*

codetermination, *340*

controlling, *338*

decision making, *338*

direct controls, *350*

empowerment, *343*

honne, 340

indirect controls, *351*

international joint ventures (IJVs), *345*

kaizen, 344

profit, *355*

quality control circle (QCC), *356*

return on investment (ROI), *355*

ringisei, 340

tatemae, 340

total quality management (TQM), *343*

Review and Discussion Questions

1. A British computer firm is acquiring a smaller competitor located in Frankfurt. What are two likely differences in the way these two firms carry out the decision-making process? How could these differences create a problem for the acquiring firm? Give an example in each case.

2. Would the British firm in the question above find any differences between the way it typically controls operations and the way that its German acquisition carries out the control process?

3. How do U.S. and Japanese firms differ in the way they go about making decisions and controlling operations? How are the two similar? In each case, provide an example.

4. How are U.S. multinationals trying to introduce total quality management (TQM) into their operations? Give two examples. Would a U.S. MNC doing

business in Germany find it easier to introduce these concepts into German operations, or would there be more receptivity to them back in the United States? Why? What if the U.S. multinational were introducing these ideas into a Japanese subsidiary?

5. What are some common control approaches used by U.S. firms at home that may not work well in Europe? Identify and describe three. In your answer, be sure to explain how U.S. multinationals must change their approach in each of these examples.

6. Why are Japanese firms likely to have trouble using their personnel performance evaluation techniques in the United States? Cite two reasons. What do these firms need to realize to make the necessary adjustments in their approach? Are these changes possible, or will the Japanese firms continue to have trouble?

Internet Exercises: Looking at the Best

In Table 12–6 the most admired 25 global companies were listed. Each of these companies uses decision making and controlling to help ensure its success in the world market. Visit two of these company sites: Sony and Nokia. The addresses are **http://www.sony.com** and **http://www.nokia.com**. Carefully examine what these firms are doing. For example, what markets are they targeting? What products and services are they offering?

What new markets are they entering? Then, after you are as familiar with their operation as possible, answer these two questions: (1) What types of factors may influence future management decision making in these two companies? (2) What types of control criteria would you expect them to use in evaluating their operations and determining how well they are doing?

Spain

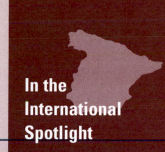

Spain, which covers 195,000 square miles, is located on the Iberian peninsula at the southwest corner of Europe; its southernmost tip is directly across from Morocco. The country has a population of approximately 40 million and a gross domestic product of about $660 billion ($16,500 per capita). Until the mid-1990s, Spain, known for its sunny climate, colorful bullfights, and storybook castles, was one of the most underdeveloped countries in Western Europe. Now, it is an industrialized country whose economy relies heavily on trade, manufacturing, and agriculture. Many of the old Spanish customs, such as taking a siesta (nap or rest) after lunch, are less common. The democratic government uses a constitutional monarchy, which was adopted in 1978, in which the king is head of state and commander-in-chief of the armed forces, but the legislative power rests in a bicameral parliament consisting of a Congress of Deputies and a Senate.

Investors Limited, a partnership based in Hong Kong and headed by Stanley Wong, owns 17 medium and large hotels throughout Asia and a total of 9 others throughout the United Kingdom, France, and Germany. The group now plans on buying a large hotel in Madrid. This hotel was built at the turn of the century but was completely refurbished in 1990 at a cost of $20 million. The current owners have since decided that the return on investment, which has been averaging 5.2 percent annually, is too small to justify continuing the operation. They have offered the hotel to the Wong group for $60 million. One-half is payable immediately, and the rest will be paid in equal annual installments over five years.

Stanley Wong believes that this is a good investment and has suggested to his partners they accept the offer. "Europe is going to boom during the new millennium," he told them, "and Spain is going to be an excellent investment. This hotel is one of the finest in Madrid, and we are going to more than triple our investment by the end of the decade."

In the past, the partnership has handled all hotel investments in the same way. A handful of company-appointed managers are sent in to oversee general operations and monitor financial performance, and all other matters continue to be handled by those personnel who have been with the hotel before acquisition. The investment group intends to handle the Madrid operation in the same way. "The most important thing," Stanley noted recently, "is that we keep control of key areas of performance such as costs and return on investment. If we do that and continue to offer the best possible service, we'll come out just fine."

www.sispain.org
www.red2000.com/spain/index.html

Questions

1. What are some current issues facing Spain? What is the climate for doing business in Spain today?

2. Do you think the Wong group, in running the hotel, should use centralized or decentralized decision making?

3. What types of direct controls might the Wong group use? What types of indirect control might be employed?

4. What are some likely differences between the control measures that the Wong group would use and those that typically are used in countries such as Spain?

Expansion Plans

Kranden & Associates is a very successful porcelain-manufacturing firm based in San Diego. The company has six world-renowned artists who design fine-crafted porcelain statues and plates that are widely regarded as collectibles. Each year, the company offers a limited edition of new statues and plates. Last year, the company made 30 new offerings. On average, 2,500 of each line are produced, and they usually are sold within six months. The company does not produce more than this number to avoid reducing the value of the line to collectors; however, the firm does believe that additional statues and plates could be sold in some areas of the world without affecting the price in North America. In particular, the firm is thinking about setting up production facilities in Rio de Janeiro, Brazil, and Paris, France.

The production process requires skilled personnel, but there are people in both Rio de Janeiro and Paris who can do this work. The basic methods can be taught to these people by trainers from the U.S. plant, because the production process will be identical.

The company intends to send three managers to each of its overseas units to handle setup operation and get the production process off the ground. This should take 12 to 18 months. Once this is done, one person will be left in charge, and the other two will return home.

The company believes that it will be able to sell just as much of the product line in Europe as it does in the United States. The South American market is estimated to be one-half that of the United States. Over the last five years, Kranden has had a return on investment of 55 percent. The company charges premium prices for its porcelain but still has strong demand for its products because of the high regard collectors and investors have for the Kranden line. The quality of its statues and plates is highly regarded, and the firm has won three national and two international awards for creativity and quality in design and production over the past 18 months. Over the last 10 years, the firm has won 17 such awards.

Questions

1. In managing its international operations, should the firm use centralized or decentralized decision making?

2. Would direct or indirect controls be preferable in managing these operations?

3. What kinds of performance measures should the company use in controlling these international operations?

Integrative Case 1

KNP, N.V.

Koninklijke Nederlandse Paperfabrieken, N.V. (KNP), or Royal Dutch Papermills, produces and sells paper and board products to printing and packaging industries throughout the world. The firm originated in 1850 as a small papermill in Maastricht, the Netherlands. One of the firm's three papermaking mills operates in the city today. Another papermill is located across the Maas River in Belgium. The firm also produces packaging materials at various European locations and has investments in paper merchant operations in a number of countries.

The company's headquarters are in a modern office building in a newer section of the ancient and historic city of Maastricht. It is here that Wilmer Zetteler, the commercial director of KNP België, ponders the emerging international business strategy of KNP and the decisions that will be necessary to meet the challenges faced by the firm.

KNP and the World Paper Industry

The evolution of the papermaking industry and the emergence of the modern European economic system have shaped KNP. In the year following World War II, the relatively undamaged but depreciated plant at Maastricht produced only 10,000 tons of paper. By 1950 the firm was pioneering the production of coated paper. KNP was the first European producer of such papers to use technology obtained under a license from the Consolidated Paper Company in the United States. A companion plant that produces top grade coated paper for brochures, art books, and catalogs is located at Nijmegen on the Waal River. Another mill at Meerssen, a town outside Maastricht, produces colored and watermarked paper.

The oil price shock of 1973 led the firm to reconsider its fundamental strategy and further specialize in the production of high-grade coated papers to gain prominence in international markets. The firm was already well known for this specialty, but managed to expand its position. A mill was constructed at Lanaken, across the Maas in Belgium, just north of the Albert Canal, to produce more lightweight coated paper. This paper is used for magazines, brochures, catalogs, and promotional material.

A separate packaging division of KNP has nine plants that produce various forms of carton board for the packaging industry and other industrial applications. These products include solid, folding, corrugated, and other board products for making boxes. In addition, the plants at Oude Pekela and Sappemeer produce a greyboard for jigsaw puzzles, books and various types of deluxe packaging.

The plant at Oude Pekela in the Netherlands also produces solid board that is used in making boxes for shipping flowers, vegetables, fruits and various exports. This board product is manufactured on machines similar to those that make paper, but the board machines at KNP use wastepaper rather than virgin pulp as a raw material in the manufacturing process. The firm owns and operates eight wastepaper collection firms that handle 250,000 tons of raw material a year. Some 30,000 tons of capacity were added in 1986 when two more firms were purchased.

A factory in the Dutch town of Eerbeek produces folding box board. The pharmaceutical and food industries use this product, which also is manufactured from wastepaper. Overall, KNP processes 500,000 tons of wastepaper a year.

KNP acquired in 1986 the German firm of Herzberger Papierfabrik Ludwig Osthushenrich GmbH and Co. KG, which manufactures boxes in four locations in western Germany. The Oberstot plant, gained in the Herzberger acquisition, also produces liner and corrugated board used in boxes and other packaging applications. The Herzberg and Oberau plants that were acquired also produce the corrugated materials used in box converting operations. These acquisitions increased the capacity of the packaging division of KNP by 60 percent.

In addition to the four German packaging plants, KNP owns box-making operations in the Netherlands, Italy, and Spain. Each is supplied with board stock manufactured by other divisions of the firm. KNP also has a joint venture with Buhrman-Tetterode, nv in operating a mill that can produce 350,000 tons of paper for the manufacture of corrugated board. With the addition of a fourth machine at the mill in 1986, this joint venture has become one of the principal suppliers of packaging paper of the European market.

KNP began a series of acquisitions of paper merchants beginning in the late 1970s. Each acquisition was a defensive strategy to prevent competitors from capturing existing channels of distribution of KNP products. KNP has paper merchant operations in Belgium, France, and the United Kingdom. The firm also owns a 35 percent interest in Proost en Brandt, one of the two largest paper merchants in the Netherlands, and a 51 percent share in Scaldia Papier B.V. in Nijmegen.

Exhibit 1 displays the group structure of KNP, while Exhibits 2 and 3 summarize the plant capacity of the principal divisions of the company. Exhibit 4 shows the location of facilities in the Netherlands.

Exhibit 1

KNP, N.V. Group and Divisional Organization

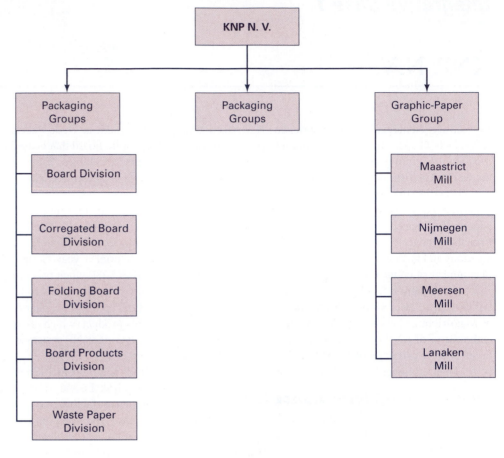

Exhibit 2

KNP, N.V. Plant Capacities of Packaging Group

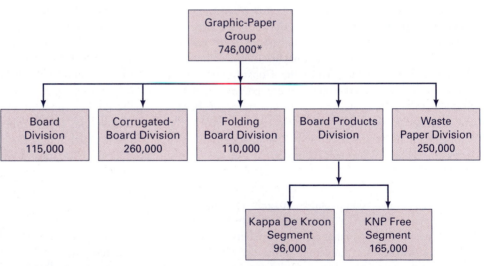

* Tons per annum

Internationalizing of the Firm

KNP's activity outside the Netherlands is not surprising. As with most Dutch manufacturers, the firm has always been an exporter and maintained an international perspective. The market for paper in the Netherlands is insufficient to support a plant. Europe is KNP's principal market. In 1986, 75 percent of its paper and 45 percent of its packaging materials were sold outside the Netherlands.

The modern, manufacture of paper products depends upon machines that produce large volumes. KNP has state-of-the-art technology that can produce such volumes.

The Netherlands has a population of 15 million, not nearly enough people to support a single modern paper manufacturing plant. On the other hand, the European Community has a population of about 275 million and a modern economy that can easily support a number of competing paper firms.

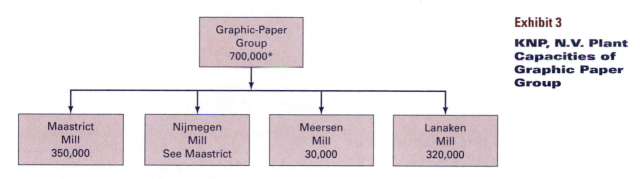

Exhibit 3

KNP, N.V. Plant Capacities of Graphic Paper Group

* Tons per annum

Exhibit 4

KNP Plant Locations

In most European countries, paper is traditionally marketed through paper merchants who distribute products to converters and printers. These merchants serve national or sub-national markets.

Yet sometimes market development is not straightforward. When the demand for lightweight machine-coated paper emerged in the United States, KNP had a paper merchant on each coast for other products of the firm. But the lightweight coated product requires a more direct approach to the printing customer. KNP skirted traditional distributors and developed an exclusive relationship with the Wilcox-Walter-Furlong Paper Company, a paper merchant in Philadelphia that stocked KNP's product in the eastern United States. In the western United States, the firm marketed its product through the offices of MacMillan Bloedel, a firm with a 30 percent stock interest in KNP.

KNP's foreign activities can be divided into two segments and two stages. Part of the first stage has existed since the firm began exporting to adjacent nations in the early 19th century.

The second stage began with the development of the European Community, which was an important factor in the growth of KNP. The development of the company after World War II was typical of other manufacturers in Europe.

Management knowledge and skill was necessary to seize the opportunity provided by the reconstruction of the European economy.

The European Community is designed to break down barriers that prevent economic activity. As the community emerged, paper firms and other businesses use skilled sales agents who were proficient in dealing with the new market. Firms succeeded in extending their markets by meeting the needs of each nation.

Language was not a barrier at KNP, where executives typically speak a number of European languages. Cultural differences also were not a factor.

Outside Europe, KNP initially exported specialized products to Africa and the Middle East. In the early 1980s, the company began exporting to Australia and the Far East and began testing markets in the United States and Canada. No special cultural and language barriers emerged because of the company's previous experience in exporting to European nations.

KNP penetrated the United Kingdom market by working through a sales agent with contacts in the printing trades. Later, the company solidified its position in the United Kingdom by hiring an English paper merchant, Contract Papers Limited, to distribute its products. KNP now owns 45 percent interest in the company.

KNP today is one of Europe's largest exporters of coated paper and a leading producer of board. According to KNP's 1986 annual report, 31 percent of sales were in the Netherlands, 55 percent elsewhere in the European Community, and 14 percent elsewhere in the world.

Globalization of the Firm

KNP cannot be considered a fully globalized company because it does not manufacture products in the markets it serves.

While the specialized paper products of KNP are global products, their manufacture does not fit the global integrated strategy as described by Yves Doz and other theorists of international business. Therefore, KNP would be best described as following a multi-focal international business strategy.

The paper industries of Europe and North America have different configurations. American firms tend to be more fully integrated vertically and horizontally in respect to the full range of forest products. European firms, with the exception of the Scandinavians, have little opportunity to buy extensive woodlands in their home countries. Because North American firms have woodlands and a large domestic market, it is difficult for European firms to become established in the market. The Swedes and Finns, on the other hand, have forest resources, but they are handicapped by poor markets for finished paper in their countries.

KNP has acquired foreign paper merchants with connections in various world markets. KNP owns Papetries Libert S.A. in Paris. The firm has a 51 percent holding in Saldiaa Papier, N.V. in Wilrijk, Belgium, and a 45 percent stake in Contract Papers (Holdings) Ltd. in London. In the Netherlands, KNP has a 35 percent interest in Proost en Brandt, N.V. in Amsterdam, and a 51 percent interest in Scaldia Papier B.V. in Nijmegen.

These acquisition were made in 1978 and 1979 as a defensive move against competitors in the European Community. Competitors had begun acquiring paper merchants that sold KNP products and threatened to use them to promote their own products. Meanwhile, the paper merchants acquired by KNP continue to stock a full range of goods, including those produced by competitors.

No distinct figures are available on KNP's foreign revenues. Overall, distribution provided 2 percent of operating results, while the paper group provided 62.9 percent of operating revenues and 71.7 percent of operating results. The packaging group produced 29.2 percent of operating revenue and 26.3 percent of operating results. These figures ignore the influence of internal transfers, which made up 8.2 percent of the total operating activity of the firm.

Other Aspects of Globalization

In many respects, the creation of KNP België, N.V. in Lanaken is a prime example of the establishment of a greenfield manufacturing operation in a foreign country. The Lanaken paper manufacturing operation was established at the point when the business strategy of the firm shifted toward the production of special grades of coated paper for the printing trades. This decision, just before the energy crisis in the early 1970's, enabled the firm to exploit those grades of specialty paper that had a higher value added in manufacture. The creation of the greenfield operation at Lanaken supported an offensive European niche strategy, while the acquisition of paper merchants in France, Belgium and the United Kingdom was a defensive maneuver to prevent erosion of existing channels of distribution that supported the more extensive range of products produced by KNP.

The plant that was finally constructed at Lanaken had to be located somewhere in the heavy industrial triangle of northwest Europe to minimize transportation costs to key European markets. The Liege-Limburg-Aachen area is close to the heart of this triangle and has the necessary infrastructure for paper production. The nearby Albert Canal provides direct access to the facilities of the port of Antwerp and pulp shipments from worldwide sources.

The situation is somewhat different at the packaging materials operations of KNP in Germany, Italy, and Spain. Raw materials are shipped from KNP operations in the Netherlands and Germany. These location are strategically situated to minimize transportation costs.

Future Globalization

A more important question is whether KNP would ever consider harvesting forest resources, given the limited opportunity to manufacture pulp in the Netherlands. In contrast, some American and Japanese firms have been enticed by less developed nations to develop and harvest forests so that they have sure sources of pulp. This is one example of globalization. Another example is shipping antiquated paper machines or converting equipment to less developed countries where labor and energy costs are lower.

Future Strategic Developments

The top management team at KNP is aware of these developments in the world paper industry. Zetteler will take these features into account as he helps plan KNP's future, as marketing and production strategies in the industry are already showing signs of change. For example, the firm in early 1987 started a 70,000 ton capacity chemi-thermomechanical pulp line in at the Lanaken mill. This is KNP's first integrated production operation that uses softwood drawn from the Ardennes, instead of the chemical pulp purchased in the international commodity markets. The firm is considering doubling this integrated capacity with a second pulp line in the next few years.

The emergence of KNP and other firms of integrated European producers of special papers would enhance competition in various world markets. The U.S. market has already been penetrated because of the declining value of the dollar and the superior quality of certain European paper products. Any firm that entered the U.S. market, however, would have to consider transportation costs and the advantages of U.S. producers that have forest resources.

1. In formulating its strategy for the next decade, what are the first steps that KNP should undertake?

2. What type of organizational arrangement does the firm use currently? If it expanded operations into North America, what type of structure would you recommend it use? What other organizational changes would you recommend?

3. In controlling operations, on what types of performance should KNP be focusing its attention? If the firm were to expand operations into South America and Asia, how would this impact on the way it would need to control operations? Explain.

By Alan Bauerschmidt, Professor of Management, University of South Carolina, and Daniel Sullivan, Professor of Management, Tulane University. Used with permission.

Cultural Differences Doom a Seemingly Perfect Alliance Between Corning and Vitro

Vitro is a Mexican glass manufacturer located in Monterrey, Mexico. Vitro's product line concentrates on drinkware but includes dozens of products, from automobile windshields to washing machines. Vitro has a long history of successful joint ventures and is globally oriented.

Corning, Inc., is most famous for its oven-ready glass wear; however, Corning has diversified into fiberoptics, environmental products, and laboratory services. Like Vitro, Corning has a long history of successful joint ventures and globalization. Vitro and Corning share similar corporate cultures and customer-oriented philosophies.

After realizing such similarities and looking to capitalize on NAFTA by accessing the Mexican market, Corning, Inc., entered into a joint venture with Vitro in the fall of 1992. The similarities in history, philosophy, culture, goals, and objectives of both companies would lead to the logical conclusion that this alliance should be an instant success. However, as Francisco Chevez, an analyst with Smith Barney Shearson in New York, said, "The cultures did not match . . . it was a marriage made in hell." As history reveals, Corning and Vitro dissolved the joint venture 25 months after the agreement. Both companies still have an interest in maintaining the relationship and continue to distribute each other's products.

A further look at the strategic history of Corning and the joint venture between Corning and Vitro will lead to a better understanding of the difficulties that are involved in creating and maintaining foreign alliances. A more in-depth investigation also will reveal the impact of culture on business transactions.

The Strategic History of Corning

Corning, Inc., has been an innovative leader in foreign alliances for over 73 years. One of the company's first successes was an alliance with St. Gobain, a French glass maker, to produce Pyrex cookware in Europe during the 1920s. Corning has formed approximately 50 ventures over the years. Only 9 have failed, which is a phenomenal number considering one recent study found that over one-half of foreign and national alliances do not succeed. Over the last 5 years, Corning's sales from joint ventures were over $3 billion, which contributed more than $500 million to its net income.

Corning enters into joint ventures for two primary reasons, which are best explained through examples of its past ventures. The first is to gain access to markets that it cannot penetrate quickly enough to obtain a competitive advantage. Corning currently has multiple ventures that exemplify market penetration. Samsung–Corning is an alliance in which Corning provided its distinctive competency of television tube production while Samsung provided expansion into the television market. Corning was able to achieve a strong market share in the Asian market, with sales in excess of $500 million.

The second reason is to bring its technology to market. For example, the strategic alliance of Corning with Mitsubishi led to the creation of Cometec, Inc. Corning produces the ceramic substrates in automotive catalytic converters. The venture employs coating technology developed by Mitsubishi that extends Corning's business into stationary pollution control. Corning reports that the venture is quite successful.

Corning's CEO, James R. Houghton, summarizes the major criteria for deciding whether an equity venture is likely to succeed as follows:

1. You need a solid business opportunity.
2. The two partners should make comparable contributions to the new enterprise.
3. The new enterprise should have a well-defined scope and no major conflicts with either parent company.
4. The management of each parent firm should have the vision and confidence to support the venture through its inevitable rough spots.
5. An autonomous operating team should be formed.
6. Responsibility cannot be delegated.

Houghton also emphasizes that the most important dimension of a successful joint venture is trust between the partners.

Corning's track record indicates that it has been able to establish and run a large number of joint ventures successfully. What went wrong with the recent Vitro venture? Vitro and Corning seemed to have similar operating procedures, and Vitro's product line complemented Corning's consumer business. Therefore, how could a seemingly perfect alliance fail so miserably? Probing deeper into the Corning–Vitro joint venture reveals the important role that culture may play in international alliances.

Background on the Corning–Vitro Joint Venture

The Corning–Vitro venture seemed to be ideal. However, a strong Mexican peso, increased overseas competition, and strong cultural differences spelled trouble for the alliance. The economic problems are understandable, but the cultural differences should have been given more attention before the alliance was entered.

Although both companies appeared so similar on the surface, they really were quite different. Cultural clashes erupted from the very beginning of the venture because of differing approaches to work. One example was in the marketing area. Vitro's sales approach was less aggressive than the Americans at Corning thought necessary; the slower, deliberate approach to sales in Mexico was a result of the previously highly controlled economy. Corning's sales approach, on the other hand, was more quick-action oriented and aggressive, which had developed from decades of competition.

Once in the venture, the Mexicans thought the Americans were too forward, and the Americans believed that their Mexican partners wasted time being too polite. The Americans perceived the Mexican characteristics to include an unwillingness to acknowledge problems and faults. With respect to speed, the Mexicans thought Corning moved too quickly, while the Americans thought Vitro moved too slowly.

Another obvious cultural difference was the conflicting styles and time allotment for decision making. Vitro is bureaucratic and hierarchical, and loyalty is to family members and patrons in the ranks of the company. Decisions often are left either to a member of the controlling family or to top executives, while middle-level managers seldom are asked to contribute their opinions, let alone to make important decisions. Mr. Loose (Corning's chief executive of the joint venture) observed, "If we were looking at a distribution decision, or a customer decision, we would have a group of people in a room, they would do an assessment, figure alternatives and make a decision, and I as chief executive would never know about it. My experience on the Mexican side is that someone in the organization would have a solution in mind, but then the decision had to be kicked up a few levels."

These examples indicate that culture was an especially sensitive issue between Corning and Vitro, and the alliance was not able to overcome these problems. Corning felt that the cross-cultural differences were depriving both companies of the flexibility to take the fast management action that is necessary in the dynamic business climate of both countries. Vitro basically agreed. Corning gave Vitro back its $130 million investment, and the joint venture was called off. The companies still recognize the opportunity to continue business with each other, however. They have changed their relationship into a mutual distribution of each other's products.

The Aftermath of the Breakup

Vitro and Corning each responded publicly to the dissolution of their alliance, and each indicated the strong differences in culture. Corning wanted to discuss the problems and learn from them, while Vitro was hesitant to criticize anyone, especially a visible U.S. partner like Corning. The Mexicans preferred to concentrate on continuation of the marketing arrangement between the companies. Houghton, the Corning CEO, openly spoke of the alliance as one that stopped making sense. He stated that cross-cultural differences inhibited the potential of the alliance. Corning's chief executive of the venture, Mr. Loose, openly acknowledged the different decision-making styles between the two cultures. Vitro executives were defensive and disappointed that Mr. Loose had expressed his views so frankly in public. "It is unfortunate that he made those comments," said an anonymous Vitro executive. The president of Vitro, Eduardo Martens, flatly denied that the cultural differences were any greater than in other alliances. In an interview with the Harvard Business Review, however, he admitted, "Business in Mexico is done on a consensus basis, very genteel and sometimes slow by U.S. standards."

Corning feels they learned a lesson in the failed Vitro alliance; both foreign and domestic alliances require additional skills and more management time. CEO Houghton says that alliances carry a lot of risk and misunderstandings, but they can be significantly beneficial to the operations of a company if they are done carefully and selectively. Corning continues to analyze why the cultural differences with Vitro were too strong to overcome.

1. Identify and discuss Corning's strategic predisposition toward a joint venture with Vitro.

2. Cultural clashes among partners in joint ventures are not a new issue. Discuss why an MNC, and specifically Corning, would be interested in fully understanding the culture of a potential partner before deciding on an alliance.

3. If Corning and Vitro had decided to remain in the alliance, how could they have overcome their differences to make the partnership a success?

4. Discuss why both companies would continue to distribute each other's products after the joint venture failed. What impact might the public statements about the failure have on this relationship?

Source: This case was written specially for this book by Professor Cara Okleshen, University of Georgia.

Integrative Case 3

Can Reliance Compete?

Recently, the Indian government did something unusual: It decided to reverse a policy that would have helped one of the nation's most formidable business empires. It's a curious tale. Early in the year, New Delhi had announced that, for a nominal fee, fixed-line phone operators would be allowed to offer limited mobile services without actually having to buy a mobile license. To foreign and local telecom outfits that had spent billions on such licenses, the announcement was a shock.

Industry execs soon figured out the biggest beneficiary of the policy would be Reliance Industries Ltd., a Bombay-based conglomerate with considerable political leverage. Time and again over the years, the government has altered regulations and policies in industries that Reliance has subsequently dominated. If the January telecom rule had prevailed, the group could have undercut its rivals on price, a key advantage in a business in which Reliance is only a peripheral player. The group denies exerting improper pressure on regulators and insists the change was meant to benefit consumers. And it has vowed to forge ahead anyway with its plans to offer cheap mobile service across India.

Still, the government's reversal must have been a wake-up call for a group that has been getting its way since a textile trader named Dhirubhai H. Ambani founded it in 1966. Over the years, Ambani and his sons, Anil, 42, and Mukesh, 44, have sold themselves to sympathetic officials as defenders of the Indian consumer—a gambit that has paid off handsomely. In the early 1990s, Reliance told New Delhi that the group could help reduce what the nation spends each year on refined oil imports if it built its own refinery. The government provided Reliance with incentives to build one in 1993—and India's purchases of refined oil supplies did indeed decline. In its telecom bid, Reliance promised to offer wireless calls for less than a quarter of the going rate.

"In the Past"

The Ambanis have come in for a fair amount of criticism, however. Their close ties with officialdom rankle rivals—though there is a long tradition of such relationships in India. Besides, insists the group's joint managing director, Anil Ambani, Reliance is a model corporate citizen. "Political linkages and controversy," he told *Business Week* in March, "are all in the past. There is no substitute for performance." (Reliance subsequently refused to cooperate for this story.) Still, the Ambanis' putative power to shape

> ### An Indian Giant: Reliance Industries
>
> **The Business**   India's biggest private producer of textiles and refined oil products. Sales almost $13 billion. Stock has returned 27 percent on average over the past five years
>
> **The Family**   Patriarch Dhirubhai Ambani founded the company in 1966. His sons, Anil and Mukesh, now run Reliance day-to-day.
>
> **The Future**   The Ambanis want to dominate India's telecom industry by investing heavily in fiber-optics and offering cheap mobile service.
>
> **The Challenge**   Taking on entrenched foreign telecom giants like AT&T, SingTel, and Hutchison.

a nation's destiny has taken on almost mythic dimensions. When Reliance goes head-to-head with another company, the rival is almost invariably vanquished.

Yet the Ambanis also get high marks for their entrepreneurial grit and savvy use of capital markets. Nobody has built a major company in India as fast as this family. In less than 40 years, Reliance has grown so big that its production of oil products and petrochemicals accounts for 3 percent of India's GDP. The group is consistently profitable; last year, it earned $900 million on revenues of $12.9 billion, up 10 percent over 1999. Reliance is a favorite of Indian and overseas investors, while its creditors applaud its fiscal management.

What's not clear, however, is if Reliance knows how to compete against the world's best companies. It operates in a transitional India, where tariffs as high as 41 percent still protect some of its operations and tax breaks go straight to the bottom line. Many of its rivals are inefficient state companies. And Reliance's main market is its home market. Hence, Reliance faces a major test with its foray into telecom, where the likes of AT&T, Hutchison Whampoa, and Singapore Telecom already are active.

Reliance faces pressure on other fronts. Profit growth in its petrochemical business slowed last quarter amid slackening demand and expectations of a supply glut. In April, Raashid Alvi, a member of parliament, produced a 1,600-page report alleging that in 1993 Reliance diverted at least $230 million from its public oil company into private companies controlled by the Ambanis. They deny it.

In a sign that all may not be well, the group's share price has softened in recent weeks. And in May, Reliance postponed a listing of its subsidiary Reliance Petroleum

Steady Earner

Steady Earner

Reliance Net Profits

Millions of Dollars

Data: Reliance Industries

Ltd. on the *NYSE,* saying it would instead divest 14 percent of its stake in the oil producer, worth $750 million, on the Luxembourg exchange, where listing rules are less stringent. "Reliance has always benchmarked itself globally," says R. Ravimohan, managing director of rating agency Credit Rating Information Services of India, which rates Reliance Industries as AAA. "But the real risk lies going forward—when it comes face-to-face with competition."

A few years ago, Reliance seemed untouchable—thanks mostly to its canny founder. A teacher's son who grew up in western Gujarat state, Dhirubhai Ambani burned to take on India's industrial dynasties, which had carved out monopolies with licenses bestowed on them by the state. In the early days, Ambani lacked the clout to extract the cheap government loans being doled out to better-connected businessmen. So in October, 1977, he issued 2.8 million shares in Reliance Textile Industries, raising $1.8 million—one of the larger public issues in India at the time.

It was a turning point. Realizing that stock placements were the key to expansion, Ambani made sure investors were well-rewarded. And he still does: Over the past five years, Reliance investors have earned an average annual return of 27.5 percent. "At a time when other Indian companies were ripping off shareholders," says Ajay Sondhi, country head for UBS Warburg in Bombay, "Ambani figured out that if he made shareholders happy, they'd give him more money."

Ambani senior, 69, and his sons are today a formidable troika. The father remains the controlling patriarch and resident genius. He focuses on long-term plans, and his sons execute them. Stanford University-educated Mukesh is the quiet, clever strategist; even rivals admit he is a "world-class" businessman. Flamboyant Anil, a Wharton graduate,

is the group's public face. The brothers are often spied after midnight toiling in their office in Nariman Point, Bombay's financial district, not far from their palatial home.

Penny a Call

Much of their time is now taken with telecom. Reliance is spending $5 billion to build a 37,000-mile fiber-optic backbone through India and hopes to dominate domestic and global data and voice traffic. "We want to be a carrier's carrier," Anil says. He dismisses the recent controversy: "How can you contest the idea [that] a phone call will cost 75 percent less for ordinary Indians?"

Analysts say Reliance will find the telecom business hard going. For starters, its budget calling plan won't pay without government subsidies or artificially high long-distance rates. Other telecom players won't agree to that without demanding similar advantages. More important, Indians may not want to pay for such services as broadband and Internet data. And Reliance must do well against foreign rivals with deep pockets and local expertise.

Reliance insists it has done its homework and will pull in some $5 billion a year in revenues by decade's end in the Indian telecom market. Clearly, the company has staying power. It generates $1.4 billion in cash a year, which it's willing to spend to learn the business. "Reliance should be one of the leading players, given its finances and execution ability," says Sanjeev Prasad of Kotak Securities in Bombay.

It's testing time for Reliance. The giant started as the iconoclast of India's socialist economy, an upstart that mastered the system to break the back of India's industrial empires. Now, as India joins the global economy, Reliance wants to be there, too. To succeed, it will have to adopt new strategies. If Reliance pulls it off, the Ambanis may at least reap the one thing that has eluded them: universal respect.

By Manjeet Kripalani in Bombay

1. What strategy has the Reliance owners used to gain favorable treatment from the Indian government? Do you think this is smart? What are the positives and the negatives?

2. Do you think Reliance can compete against outside MNCs who do business in India? Do you agree with analysts who say Reliance will find the telecom business hard going?

Source: Reprinted from June 25, 2001, pp. 50–52 of *Business Week* by special permission, copyright © 2001 by the McGraw-Hill Companies, Inc.

Part Four

Organizational Behavior and Human Resource Management

Chapter 13

Motivation Across Cultures

Objectives of the Chapter

Motivation is closely related to the performance of human resources in modern organizations. When motivation is applied to international management, it must be remembered that although the motivation process may be the same across cultures, the content of what motivates people often is culturally based. What motivates employees in the United States may only be moderately effective in Japan, France, or Nigeria. Therefore, although motivation is the concept of choice for analyzing employee performance, an international context requires country-by-country, or at least regional, examination of differences in motivation.

This chapter examines motivation as a psychological process and how motivation can be used in understanding and improving employee performance. It also identifies and describes internationally researched work motivation theories and discusses their relevance for international human resource management. The specific objectives of this chapter are:

1. **DEFINE** "motivation," and explain it as a psychological process.

2. **EXAMINE** the hierarchy-of-needs, two-factor, and achievement motivation theories, and assess their value to international human resource management.

3. **DISCUSS** how an understanding of employee satisfaction can be useful in human resource management throughout the world.

4. **EXAMINE** the value of process theories in motivating employees worldwide.

5. **RELATE** the importance of job design, work centrality, and rewards in understanding how to motivate employees in an international context.

BusinessWeek

The World of *Business Week*

Executive Pay

Joseph M. Magliochetti watched helplessly as his market crumbled. The CEO of auto-parts maker Dana Corp. saw North American heavy-truck production tumble, the Big Three Detroit auto makers scale back production, and demand for replacement parts weaken. Despite his best efforts, sales at the Toledo company fell 6%, profits plummeted 44%, and Dana's stock lost more than half its value, turning most of Magliochetti's stock options into so much worthless paper.

By almost any measure, Magliochetti was still rewarded handsomely. The Dana board gave him the $850,000 salary it had promised him, based on strong sales and profits, and an option grant to bring him in line with his peers. But it stripped him of his bonus and stock grant. The board cited his failure to beat goals for net income growth and return on invested capital. In all, Magliochetti's pay came to $948,363, down 63% from the previous year, making him one of only a handful of top executives to bring home less than $1 million. That's right: In setting Magliochetti's pay, the board in effect said: "The company failed to prosper, and we're holding you accountable."

Makes sense, right? Not in the world of executive compensation. In fact, Dana's actions are extraordinary compared with the way most corporations respond to sluggish performance. While shareholders got hammered, many compensation committees scrambled to cushion their chief executives from feeling any real pain, granting massive blocks of new stock options in some cases and in others forgiving corporate loans. The average CEO, riding a still-hot market for top management talent, earned a stupendous $13.1 million last year, according to the results of *BusinessWeek*'s 51st annual Executive Pay Scoreboard, compiled with Standard & Poor's Institutional Market Services, a division of The McGraw-Hill Companies. Cash compensation for the CEOs at 365 of the largest U.S. companies increased 18% in 2000, while total pay increased 6.3%. That far exceeds the 4.3% pay hike that salaried workers got last year, and it widens still further the yawning gap between the boss and the rank and file.

As usual, compensation committees handed out perks like candy. Retirees were showered with the standard gifts: lucrative consulting jobs, company cars, and hefty pensions. John F. Welch of General Electric Co. got a pay package valued at $122.6 million in recognition of his "20 years of outstanding service as CEO." And you didn't have to leave to be generously rewarded. Apple Computer Inc.'s Steven P. Jobs landed the mother of all bonuses after three years of working for free: his own $90 million jet, a Gulfstream V.

In Tears

But while the CEO gravy train hasn't run off the rails, it is slowing down. The reason had little to do with

anything decided by boards of directors, though: The same market crash that had investors in tears made many executives' stock options worthless. And with far fewer executives able to cash in, overall CEO pay growth slowed. Still, there was some evidence that more boards, like Dana's, were toying with the notion that CEOs should suffer along with their shareholders.

All of which raises an interesting question: Will compensation committees wield a carrot or a stick as they meet to calculate CEO rewards? Some boards are building tough performance goals into future stock and option awards, raising the possibility that some big-name executives who don't meet the goals could walk home with much less. Says Peter Chingos, head of the executive compensation practice at consultants William M. Mercer Cos.: "We're seeing a more conservative movement in compensation increases, largely because of what happened with stock prices. I don't think this is going to go away overnight."

Incentives

Still, after years of paying lip service to the idea of pay for performance, at least a few companies took extraordinary steps to link the two. At Coca-Cola Co., CEO Douglas N. Daft was granted $87.2 million in restricted shares—but he will get the full amount only if he manages to increase earnings per share by 20% a year for five years, a task analysts say may be difficult, if not impossible. Coke compensation committee Chairman Herbert A. Allen said that management considers the goals "aggressive but realistic," adding, "we'll see in five years." Staples Inc. CEO Thomas G. Stemberg got 100,000 restricted shares, worth $1.4 million, which vest in 2005—or earlier if earnings goals are met. Says Stemberg: "Our philosophy is one of low pay combined with strong equity rewards." Of course, low pay is a relative term: Stemberg also took home nearly $1 million in salary and bonus. His $2.4 million total pay, while down 27%, was hardly a pittance.

Those were the exceptions. Overall, the link between CEO pay and company performance remained fuzzy. The top spot for shareholder return relative to pay went to David M. Rickey of Applied Micro Circuits Corp., who delivered a giant 4,751% for a mere $4.5 million in pay from 1998 through 2000—in marked contrast to last year's winner, David S. Wetherell of CMGI Inc., who was paid $1 million less and delivered returns nearly three times as good. Rickey also sold millions of dollars' worth of stock in December and January, and the stock has since lost 80% of its value. At the bottom of the performance heap, Charles B. Wang of Computer Associates International Inc. (CA) earned $698.2 million from 1998 through 2000 and produced a dismal shareholder return of –63%, making last year's loser, Eisner of Walt Disney, look like a bargain. Eisner was paid $60 million less from 1997 through 1999 and earned 28% for shareholders during the same period. CA says Wang helped increase shareholder value 901% in the 1990s. He also agreed to return more than 20% of his 1998 pay—2.7 million shares, or $150 million, according to the company—to settle shareholder lawsuits over a special grant of stock to Wang and other top company executives.

Compensation consultants say the growing gap between pay and performance is partly the result of companies' using new measures to gauge performance. By using comparisons such as earnings per share and return on equity, a CEO whose stock is going to the dogs can still sometimes come out ahead in pay. Case in point: CMGI. The Internet incubator more than doubled Wetherell's bonus, to $481,400, on the strength of operating income—even though the company ended its 2000 fiscal year in July with a $1.3 billion net loss and with the stock down 18%. CMGI says Wetherell was underpaid compared with his peers and deserved the boost based on the prior year's performance. Says Scott Olsen, leader of the executive compensation practice at consultants Towers Perrin: "If the board likes a CEO, it's likely to do whatever it takes to keep him."

But rewarding a CEO when the stock is plummeting presents its own set of dilemmas. For one thing, option grants have to be bigger: A $10 million grant costs a company only 100,000 shares when the stock is trading at $100, but 5 million shares when it's trading at $2. And few institutional investors are willing to put up with that kind of dilution. A showdown is brewing over the issue. This year, institutional investors have filed more than 50 shareholder proposals targeting executive pay that will be voted on at annual meetings.

At the same time, top executives who have been burned by the market are starting to demand tangible rewards in the here and now: more cash, bigger bonuses, and other perks to offset the risk of options. In a booming economy, options were the incentive of choice because gains could be astronomical, and they belonged to the executive whether he stayed at the company or left. Now there's a new favorite: restricted shares, which typically vest after several years provided the executive remains employed at the company, and are safer than options because they always retain at least some value. A few years ago, says consultant Olsen, executives would hold out for the biggest option grants possible. Cash and bonuses were viewed as positively dowdy. "I don't hear as many people saying that now," Olsen says.

When the economy and stock markets were roaring, CEO pay rocketed along as well. Now that the longest expansion in U.S. history has ground to a halt, though, few companies seem eager to transfer the pain to executive paychecks. If anything, the market for top-flight CEOs is as tight as ever, says Patrick S. Pittard, CEO of executive search firm Heidrick & Struggles International Inc., as troubled companies seek would-be saviors. "It has never been more expensive," he says. Still, if share-holders continue to suffer the kinds of market losses dished out in the first quarter, even the thickest-skinned boards may have a hard time upping the pay for under-performing CEOs in 2001. In that case, look for the gravy train to creak to a halt.

With Frederick F. Jespersen and bureau reports

Source: **Reprinted from April 16, 2001, pp. 76–80 issue of** *Business Week* **by special permission, copyright © 2001 by McGraw-Hill Companies, Inc.**

This opening news story focuses on one of the ways in which multinational enterprises are motivating their chief executive officers: money. The examples are all from U.S. MNCs, they all do business internationally, and their competitors outside the United States have similar compensation for their own executives. In fact, when one considers the perks pro-vided to many international managers, including housing, entertainment allowances, trans-portation, and sundry expenses, it becomes obvious that the salaries and bonuses paid to German and Japanese executives, for example, are often just as high as their U.S. counter-parts. As discussed in the article, the linkage between performance and pay in U.S. MNCs is the goal, but may be breaking down. This chapter is not only concerned with top level compensation, but also the background, research, and implications of motivating interna-tional managers and others across cultures.

■ The Nature of Motivation

Motivation is a psychological process through which unsatisfied wants or needs lead to drives that are aimed at goals or incentives. Figure 13–1 shows this motivation process. The three basic elements in the process are needs, drives, and goal-attainment. A person with an unsatisfied need will undertake goal-directed behavior to satisfy the need. Motiva-tion is an important topic in international human resource management, because many MNC managers assume they can motivate their overseas personnel with the same approaches that are used in the home country. Is this true, or do major differences require tailor-made, country-by-country motivation programs? As described in earlier chapters (especially Chapter 5), there obviously are some motivational differences caused by cul-ture. The major question is: Are these differences highly significant, or can an overall the-ory of work motivation apply throughout the world? Considerable research on motivating human resources has looked at motivation in a large number of countries; however, before reviewing these findings, two generally agreed-on starting assumptions about work moti-vation in the international arena should be made.

Motivation
A psychological process through which unsatisfied wants or needs lead to drives that are aimed at goals or incentives.

The Universalist Assumption

The first assumption is that the motivation process is universal. All people are motivated to pursue goals they value—what the work-motivation theorists call goals with "high valence" or "preference." Although the process is universal, however, the specific content and goals that are pursued will be influenced by culture. For example, one recent analysis suggests that the key incentive for many U.S. workers is money; for Japanese employees, it is respect and power; and for Latin American workers, it is an array of factors, includ-ing family considerations, respect, job status, and a good personal life. Similarly, the pri-mary interest of the U.S. worker is him- or herself; for the Japanese, it is group interest; and for the Latin American employee, it is the interest of the employer.[1] Simply put, moti-vation differs across cultures. Adler sums up the case against universality of motivation as follows:

> Unfortunately, American as well as non-American managers have tended to treat American the-ories as the best or only way to understand motivation. They are neither. American motivation

Figure 13–1

The Basic Motivation Process

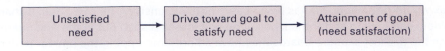

Unsatisfied need → Drive toward goal to satisfy need → Attainment of goal (need satisfaction)

theories, although assumed to be universal, have failed to provide consistently useful explanations outside the United States. Managers must therefore guard against imposing domestic American theories on their multinational business practices.[2]

In the United States, personal achievement is an important need, and individual success through promotions and more money may be an important goal. In China, however, group affiliation is an important need, and harmony is an important goal. Therefore, the ways to motivate U.S. employees are quite different from those used with Chinese workers. The motivational process is the same, but the needs and goals are not because of differences between the two cultures. This conclusion was demonstrated in a study by Welsh, Luthans, and Sommer that examined the value of extrinsic rewards, behavioral management, and participative techniques among Russian factory workers. The first two motivational approaches worked well to increase worker performance, but the third did not. The researchers noted that

> this study provides at least beginning evidence that U.S.-based behavioral theories and techniques may be helpful in meeting the performance challenges facing human resources management in rapidly changing and different cultural environments. We found that two behavioral techniques—administering desirable extrinsic rewards to employees contingent upon improved performance, and providing social reinforcement and feedback for functional behaviors and corrective feedback for dysfunctional behaviors—significantly improved Russian factory workers' performance. By the same token, the study also points out the danger of making universalist assumptions about U.S.-based theories and techniques. In particular, the failure of the participative intervention does not indicate so much that this approach just won't work across cultures, as that historical and cultural values and norms need to be recognized and overcome for such a relatively sophisticated theory and technique to work effectively.[3]

At the same time, however, it is important to remember that as a growing number of countries begin moving toward free market economies and new opportunities for economic rewards emerge, the ways in which individuals in these nations are motivated will change. Commenting on the management of Chinese personnel, for example, Sergeant and Frenkel have pointed out that new labor laws now allow both state enterprises and foreign-invested Chinese enterprises to set their own wage and salary levels. However, the companies have to be careful about believing that they can simply go into the marketplace, pay high wages, and recruit highly motivated personnel. In particular, the researchers note that:

> Devising reward packages for Chinese employees has been difficult because of the range and complexity of nonwage benefits expected by workers as a legacy of the "iron rice bowl" tradition. However, health and accident insurance, pensions, unemployment and other benefits are increasingly being taken over by the state. There are two cultural impediments to introducing greater differentials in pay among workers of similar status: importance accorded to interpersonal harmony which would be disrupted by variations in earnings; and distrust of performance appraisals because in state enterprises evaluations are based on ideological principles and *guanxi* [connections].[4]

So some of what foreign MNCs would suspect about how to motivate Chinese employees is accurate, but not all. The same is true, for example, about Japanese employees. Many people believe that all Japanese firms guarantee lifetime employment and this practice, in turn, is motivational and results in a strong bond between employer and employee. In truth, much of this is a myth. Actually, less than 28 percent (and decreasing) of the workforce has any such guarantee, and in recent years a growing number of Japanese employees have been finding that their firms may do the best they can to ensure jobs for them—but they will not guarantee this if the company begins to face critical times. As in the West, when a Japanese firm has a crisis, people are often let go. This has been clearly seen in recent years as the Japanese economy has remained stalled and the country's joblessness rate has hit new highs.[5]

The Assumption of Content and Process

The second starting assumption is that work-motivation theories can be broken down into two general categories: content, and process. **Content theories** explain work motivation in terms of *what* arouses, energizes, or initiates employee behavior. **Process theories** of worker motivation explain *how* employee behavior is initiated, redirected, and halted.[6] Most research in international human resource management has been content-oriented, because these theories examine motivation in more general terms and are more useful in creating a composite picture of employee motivation in a particular country or region. Process theories are more sophisticated and tend to focus on individual behavior in specific settings. Thus, they have less value to the study of employee motivation in international settings, although there has been some research in this area as well. By far the majority of research in the international arena has been content driven, but this chapter will examine research findings from both the content and process theories.

The following section examines work motivation in an international setting by focusing on three content theories that have received the greatest amount of attention: the hierarchy-of-needs theory, the two-factor motivation theory, and the achievement motivation theory. Then attention is focused on three process theories: equity theory, goal-setting theory, and expectancy theory. Each offers important insights regarding the motivation process of personnel in international settings.

Content theories
Theories that explain work motivation in terms of what arouses, energizes, or initiates employee behavior.

Process theories
Theories that explain work motivation by how employee behavior is initiated, redirected, and halted.

■ The Hierarchy-of-Needs Theory

The hierarchy-of-needs theory is based primarily on work by Abraham Maslow, a well-known humanistic psychologist now deceased.[7] Maslow's hierarchy of needs has received a great deal of attention in the U.S. management and organizational behavior field, but also for the purposes of this text from international management researchers, who have attempted to show its value in understanding employee motivation throughout the world.[8]

The Maslow Theory

Maslow postulated that everyone has five basic needs, which constitute a need hierarchy. In ascending order, beginning with the most basic, they are physiological, safety, social, esteem, and self-actualization needs. Figure 13–2 illustrates this hierarchy.

Physiological needs consist of food, clothing, shelter, and other basic physical needs. Maslow contended that if someone were deprived of all need satisfaction, the individual's drive to satisfy these physiological needs would be greater than the drive to satisfy any other need. Applied to work motivation, these physiological needs often are satisfied through the wages and salaries paid by the organization.

Safety needs include the desire for security, stability, and absence of pain. Organizations typically help personnel to satisfy these needs through safety programs and equipment and by providing security through medical insurance, unemployment and retirement plans, and similar benefits.

Social needs include the need to interact and affiliate with others and the need to feel wanted by others. This desire for "belongingness" often is satisfied on the job through social interaction within the work group, in which people give and receive friendship. Besides the formally assigned work group, the formation of informal groups and acquaintanceships also is typical.

Esteem needs involve the needs for power and status. These result in individuals' needing to feel important and receive recognition from others. Promotions, awards, and feedback from the boss lead to feelings of self-confidence, prestige, and self-importance.

Self-actualization needs are desires to reach one's full potential by becoming everything that one is capable of becoming. Although less is known about this highest-level need, most closely associated would be the ideas concerning human potential. In the organization, this may not be a promotion but instead may involve mastering one's environment as well as setting and achieving attainable goals.[9]

Physiological needs
Food, clothing, shelter, and other basic, physical needs.

Safety needs
The desire for security, stability, and the absence of pain.

Social needs
The need to interact and affiliate with others and the need to feel wanted by others.

Esteem needs
The needs for power and status.

Self-actualization needs
The desire to reach one's full potential by becoming everything one is capable of becoming.

Figure 13–2

Maslow's Need Hierarchy

Maslow's theory, translated over the years, includes a number of basic assumptions. One is that lower-level needs must be satisfied before higher-level needs become motivators. A second is that once a need is satisfied, it no longer serves as a motivator. A third is that there are more ways to satisfy higher-level than lower-level needs. Some of these assumptions came from Maslow's original work, some from others' work, and some have been modified by Maslow. These assumptions have driven much of the international research on the theory.

International Findings on Maslow's Theory

Do people throughout the world have needs that are similar to those described in Maslow's need hierarchy? Research generally shows that they do. For example, in a classic study undertaken by Haire, Ghiselli, and Porter, a sample of 3,641 managers from 14 countries was surveyed. This study is quite dated but still the most comprehensive and relevant one for showing the different cultural impacts on employee motivation. Countries in this survey included the United States, Argentina, Belgium, Chile, Denmark, England, France, Germany, India, Italy, Japan, Norway, Spain, and Sweden.[10] With some minor modification, the researchers examined the need satisfaction and need importance of the four highest-level needs in the Maslow hierarchy. The esteem need was divided into two groups: esteem and autonomy. The first examined the importance of self-esteem and prestige; the second examined the importance of authority and the opportunity for independent thought and action.

The results of this study showed that all these needs were important to the respondents across cultures. It should be remembered, however, that the subjects in this huge international study were managers, not rank-and-file employees. Upper-level needs were of particular importance to these managers. These findings, for select country clusters (Latin Europe, United States/United Kingdom, and Nordic Europe), show that autonomy and self-actualization were the most important needs for the respondents. Interestingly, these same managers also reported that these needs were those with which they were *least* satisfied, which led Haire and his associates to conclude:

> It appears obvious, from an organizational point of view, that business firms, no matter what country, will have to be concerned with the satisfaction of these needs for their managers and executives. Both types of needs were regarded as relatively quite important by managers, but, at the present time at least, the degree to which they were fulfilled did not live up to their expectations.[11]

Since this classic study, a number of others have examined management groups from other countries. One follow-up study surveyed managers in eight East Asian countries and found that autonomy and self-actualization in most cases ranked high; however, the degree of satisfaction/dissatisfaction varied much more widely than that reported by Haire and his associates. Some East Asian managers apparently were quite dissatisfied with their ability to satisfy autonomy and self-actualization needs.

Both research studies indicate the value of examining motivation of human resources (in this case, managers) in terms of country or geographic clusters. Each country or geographic region appears to have its own need-satisfaction profile. In using this information to motivate managers, MNCs would be wise to consider the individual country's or region's profile and adjust their approach accordingly.

Some researchers even have suggested modifying Maslow's hierarchy by reranking the order of needs. Nevis believes that the Maslow hierarchy reflects a culture that is Western-oriented and focused on the inner needs of individuals.[12] Obviously, not all cultures function this way. Asian cultures emphasize the needs of society. As a result, Nevis suggested that the Chinese hierarchy of needs has four levels, which from lowest to highest are: (1) belonging (social); (2) physiological; (3) safety; and (4) self-actualization in the service of society. If this is true, MNCs attempting to do business in China must consider this revised hierarchy and determine how they can modify their compensation and job-design programs to accommodate the requisite motivational needs. In any event, Nevis's idea is worth considering, because it forces the multinational firm to address work motivation based on those cultural factors that are unique to it.

The discussion so far indicates that even though it is culturally specific, the need-hierarchy concept is a useful way to study and apply work motivation internationally. Others such as the well-known Dutch researcher Geert Hofstede, however, have suggested that need-satisfaction profiles are *not* a very useful way of addressing motivation, because there often are so many different subcultures within any given country that it may be difficult or impossible to determine which culture variables are at work in any particular work setting. The Haire and follow-up studies dealt only with managers, but Hofstede has found that job categories are a more effective way of examining motivation. He reported a linkage between job types and levels and the need hierarchy. Based on survey results from over 60,000 people in more than 50 countries who were asked to rank a series of 19 work goals (see Tables 13–1 and 13–2), he found that:

Table 13–1

Top-Ranking Goals for Professional Technical Personnel from a Large Variety of Countries

Rank	Goal	Questionnaire Wording
1	Training	Have training opportunities (to improve your present skills or learn new skills)
2	Challenge	Have challenging work to do—work from which you can get a personal sense of accomplishment
3	Autonomy	Have considerable freedom to adopt your own approach to the job
4	Up-to-dateness	Keep up-to-date with the technical developments relating to your job
5	Use of skills	Fully use your skills and abilities on the job
6	Advancement	Have an opportunity for advancement to higher-level job
7	Recognition	Get the recognition you deserve when you do a good job
8	Earnings	Have an opportunity for high earnings
9	Cooperation	Work with people who cooperate well with one another
10	Manager	Have a good working relationship with your manager
11	Personal time	Have a job which leaves you sufficient time for your personal or family life
12	Friendly department	Work in a congenial and friendly atmosphere
13	Company contribution	Have a job which allows you to make a real contribution to the success of your company
14	Efficient department	Work in a department which is run efficiently
15	Security	Have the security that you will be able to work for your company as long as you want to
16	Desirable area	Live in an area desirable to you and your family
17	Benefits	Have good fringe benefits
18	Physical conditions	Have good physical working conditions (good ventilation and lighting, adequate work space, etc.)
19	Successful company	Work in a company which is regarded in your country as successful

Source: Geert H. Hofstede, "The Colors of Collars," *Columbia Journal of World Business,* September 1972, p. 74. Used with permission.

Table 13–2
The Four Most Important Goals Ranked by Occupational Group and Related to the Need Hierarchy

Goals Ranked in "Need Hierarchy"	Professionals (Research Laboratories)	Professionals (Branch Offices)	Managers	Technicians (Branch Offices)	Technicians (Manufacturing Plants)	Clerical Workers (Branch Offices)	Unskilled Workers (Manufacturing Plants)
High—Self-actualization and esteem needs:							
Challenge	1	2	1	3	3		
Training		1		1			
Autonomy	3	3	2				
Up-to-dateness	2	4		4			
Use of skills	4						
Middle—Social needs:							
Cooperation			3/4			1	
Manager			3/4		4	2	
Friendly department						3	
Efficient department						4	
Low—Security and physiological needs:							
Security				2	1		2
Earnings					2		3
Benefits							4
Physical conditions							1

Source: Geert H. Hofstede, "The Colors of Collars," *Columbia Journal of World Business*, September 1972, p. 78. Used with permission.

- Professionals ranked all four top goals corresponding to "high" Maslow needs.
- Clerks ranked all four top goals corresponding to "middle" Maslow needs.
- Unskilled workers ranked all four top goals corresponding to "low" Maslow needs.
- Managers and technicians showed a mixed picture—with at least one goal in the "high" Maslow category.[13]

The tables from Hofstede's research show that self-actualization and esteem needs rank highest for professionals and managers. Conversely, security, earnings, benefits, and physical working conditions are most important to low-level, unskilled workers. These findings illustrate that job categories and levels may have a dramatic effect on motivation and may well offset cultural considerations. As Hofstede noted, "There are greater differences between job categories than there are between countries when it comes to employee motivation."[14]

In deciding how to motivate human resources in different countries or help them to attain need satisfaction, researchers such as Hofstede recommend that MNCs focus most heavily on giving physical rewards to lower-level personnel and on creating a climate in which there is challenge, autonomy, the ability to use one's skills, and cooperation for the middle- and upper-level personnel. Of course, this does not mean that executives are unmotivated by large compensation packages (as seen in this chapter's opening news story) or that new employees are not looking for flexible compensation. As seen in "International Management in Action: Rethinking the Motivation Equation," compensation packages for the personnel in Japan is beginning to change.

Overall, there seems to be little doubt that need-hierarchy theory is useful in helping to identify motivational factors for international human resource management. This theory alone is not sufficient, however. Other content theories, such as the two-factor theory, add further understanding and effective practical application for motivating personnel.

■ The Two-Factor Theory of Motivation

The two-factor theory was formulated by well-known work-motivation theorist Frederick Herzberg and his colleagues. Similar to Maslow's theory, Herzberg's has been a focus of attention in international human resource management research over the years. This two-factor theory is closely linked to the need hierarchy.

The Herzberg Theory

The **two-factor theory of motivation** holds that two sets of factors influence job satisfaction: hygiene factors and motivators. The data from which the theory was developed were collected through a critical incident methodology that asked the respondents to answer two basic types of questions: (1) When did you feel particularly good about your job? and (2) When did you feel exceptionally bad about your job? Responses to the first question generally related to job content and included factors such as achievement, recognition, responsibility, advancement, and the work itself. Herzberg called these job-content factors **motivators.** Responses to the second question related to job context and included factors such as salary, interpersonal relations, technical supervision, working conditions, and company policies and administration. Herzberg called these job-context variables **hygiene factors.** Table 13–3 lists both groups of factors; a close look at the two lists shows that the motivators are heavily psychological and relate to Maslow's upper-level needs and that the hygiene factors are environmental in nature and relate more to Maslow's lower-level needs. Table 13–4 illustrates this linkage.

The two-factor theory also holds that these two sets of factors relate to employee satisfaction. This relationship is more complex than the traditional view that employees are either satisfied or dissatisfied; according to the two-factor theory, if hygiene factors are not taken care of or are deficient, there will be dissatisfaction (see Figure 13–3). Importantly, however, if hygiene factors are taken care of, there may be no dissatisfaction, but there also may not be satisfaction. Only by providing the motivators will there be satisfaction. In short, hygiene factors help to prevent dissatisfaction (thus the term "hygiene," as it is used

Two-factor theory of motivation
A theory that holds there are two sets of factors that influence job satisfaction: hygiene factors and motivators.

Motivators
In the two-factor motivation theory, the job content factors which include achievement, recognition, responsibility, advancement, and the work itself.

Hygiene factors
In the two-factor motivation theory, job context variables that include salary, interpersonal relations, technical supervision, working conditions, and company policies and administration.

International Management in Action

Rethinking the Motivation Equation

For many years Japanese firms have used a traditional approach to motivating their personnel. Twice a year workers would be paid a bonus, and when they retired they would receive an additional lump sum payment that was tied to their salary and length of time with the company. Additionally, there was a package of perquisites that the company would provide for those who were going to be staying with the firm for their entire career. Today, however, this traditional approach is undergoing radical change. A growing number of companies, Matsushita being a good example, are starting to offer their personnel a more flexible benefits package—and a growing number of employees are beginning to take it.

One reason for the change is that Japanese companies are coming to realize that their standard benefits package is not the best for all of their people. In particular, a growing number of personnel are now changing jobs and moving to other firms. In 1995, for example, approximately 80 percent of all workers in Japan were still with the same company with which they had begun their careers. By 1998 this percentage had dropped to 70 percent and by the year 2010 traditional lifetime employment in many Japanese companies will be a thing of the past.

Since many people will not be staying with their firm in the future, a growing number of companies are now offering more flexible options. For example, in some enterprises an employee who has special skills but does not intend to stay with the firm for a long time can command higher pay and is allowed to take advances on his or her pension. In turn, of course, the individual agrees to give up some benefits. And for those who want even more flexibility, there is the option of putting one's pension payments into savings plans rather than simply having the company provide a lump sum amount upon retirement.

One reason for the change in the traditional approach is that many firms now believe that they must do business a different way. Rather than giving people lifetime employment, they want to be able to hire new recruits who have skills and abilities not possessed by current personnel; and rather than having to keep the older personnel as well, they can move them out. In addition, companies such as Matsushita are now moving from a seniority-based management reward system to a merit-based one.

Will this new approach prove motivational? Many young Japanese believe that it will because it offers them more control over their retirement option and it is based on a pay-for-performance philosophy. Older Japanese workers are not sure. However, one thing is certain: A growing number of major Japanese corporations are rethinking the motivation equation and looking for a different approach to motivating their people and maintaining world-class organizations in the face of growing worldwide hypercompetition. A recent example is Fujitsu, one of the first Japanese corporations to introduce performance-based pay. Now, after eight years of using this system, the company is reviewing it with an eye toward making a host of changes. In particular, Fujitsu feels that its current performance-based system does not fit very well with the Japanese business culture. As a result, while the company does not intend to bring back the old seniority-based approach, it does want to create a motivation system that is both equitable and effective. One of the problems with the current system is that it allows employees to set their own goals. As a result, many have continually chosen targets that are easy to attain, thus ensuring themselves of raises and promotions. Another problem with the current system is that by tying rewards to performance it encourages people to pursue short-term goals and to avoid ambitious projects that might produce hit products but which will take time to accomplish. A third problem is that the system does not reward some types of performance that are important. For example, after-sale customer service is not rewarded; as a result, this end of the business has begun to suffer. Fujitsu plans on revamping its motivation system and addressing these problems. By rethinking the motivation equation, the company believes that it will be able to increase the performance of its workforce.

in the health field), but only motivators lead to satisfaction. Therefore, according to this theory, motivating human resources must include recognition, a chance to achieve and grow, advancement, and interesting work.

Before examining the two-factor theory in the international arena, it is important to note that Herzberg's theory has been criticized by some organizational-behavior academics. One criticism surrounds the classification of money as a hygiene factor and not as a motivator. There is no universal agreement on this point, and some researchers report that salary is a motivator for some groups, such as blue-collar workers, or those for whom money is important for psychological reasons, such as a score-keeping method for their power and achievement needs.

Table 13–3
Herzberg's Two-Factor Theory

Hygiene Factors	Motivators
Salary	Achievement
Technical supervision	Recognition
Company policies and administration	Responsibility
Interpersonal relations	Advancement
Working conditions	The work itself

A second line of criticism is whether Herzberg has developed a total theory of motivation. Some argue that his findings actually support a theory of job satisfaction. In other words, if a company gives its people motivators, they will be satisfied; if it denies them motivators, they will not be satisfied; and if the hygiene factors are deficient, they may well be dissatisfied. Much of the international research on the two-factor theory discussed next is directed toward the satisfaction/dissatisfaction concerns rather than complex motivational needs, drives, and goals.

International Findings on Herzberg's Theory

International findings related to the two-factor theory fall into two categories. One consists of replications of Herzberg's research in a particular country; that is, do managers in country X give answers similar to those in Herzberg's original studies? The other consists of cross-cultural studies that focus on job satisfaction; that is, what factors cause job satisfaction and how do these responses differ from country to country? The latter studies are not a direct extension of the two-factor theory, but they do offer insights regarding the importance of job satisfaction in international human resource management.

Two-Factor Replications   A number of research efforts have been undertaken to replicate the two-factor theory, and in the main, they support Herzberg's findings. George Hines, for example, surveyed 218 middle managers and 196 salaried employees in New Zealand using ratings of 12 job factors and overall job satisfaction. Based on these findings, he concluded that "the Herzberg model appears to have validity across occupational levels."[15]

Table 13–4
The Relationship between Maslow's Need Hierarchy and Herzberg's Two-Factor Theory

Maslow's Need Hierarchy	Herzberg's Two-Factor Theory
Self-actualization	Motivators
	Achievement
	Recognition
	Responsibility
Esteem	Advancement
	The work itself
Social	Hygiene factors
	Salary
	Technical supervision
Safety	Company policies and administration
	Interpersonal relations
Physiological	Working conditions

Figure 13–3

Views of Satisfaction/ Dissatisfaction

Traditional View

Dissatisfaction ——————————————— Satisfaction

Two-Factor View
(hygiene factors)

Absent ——————————————— Present
(dissatisfaction)   (no dissatisfaction)

(motivators)

Absent ——————————————— Present
(no satisfaction)   (Satisfaction)

Another similar study was conducted among 178 managers in Greece who were Greek nationals. Overall, this study found that Herzberg's two-factor theory of job satisfaction generally held true for these managers. The researchers summarized their findings as follows:

> As far as job dissatisfaction was concerned, no motivator was found to be a source of dissatisfaction. Only categories traditionally designated as hygiene factors were reported to be sources of dissatisfaction for participating Greek managers. . . . Moreover . . . motivators . . . were more important contributors to job satisfaction than to dissatisfaction . . . (66.8% of the traditional motivator items . . . were related to satisfaction and 31.1% were related to dissatisfaction). Traditional hygiene factors, as a group, were more important contributors to job dissatisfaction than to job satisfaction (64% of the responses were related to dissatisfaction and 36% were related to satisfaction).[16]

Another study tested the Herzberg theory in an Israeli kibbutz (communal work group). Motivators there tended to be sources of satisfaction and hygiene factors sources of dissatisfaction, although interpersonal relations (a hygiene factor) were regarded more as a source of satisfaction than of dissatisfaction. The researcher was careful to explain this finding as a result of the unique nature of a kibbutz, however, where interpersonal relations of a work and nonwork nature are not clearly defined, thus making difficult the separation of this factor on a motivator/hygiene basis. Commenting on the results, the researcher noted, "the findings of this study support Herzberg's two-factor hypothesis: Satisfactions arise from the nature of the work itself, while dissatisfactions have to do with the conditions surrounding the work."[17]

Similar results on the Herzberg theory have been obtained by research studies in developing countries. For example, one study examined work motivation in Zambia, employing a variety of motivational variables, and work motivation was a result of six factors: work nature, growth and advancement, material and physical provisions, relations with others, fairness/unfairness in organizational practices, and personal problems. These variables are presented in Figure 13–4. They illustrate that, in general, the two-factor theory of motivation was supported in this African country.[18]

Cross-Cultural Job-Satisfaction Studies A number of cross-cultural studies related to job satisfaction also have been conducted in recent years. These comparisons show that Herzberg-type motivators tend to be of more importance to job satisfaction than are hygiene factors. For example, one study administered the Job Orientation Inventory (JOI) to MBA candidates from four countries.[19] As seen in Table 13–5, the relative ranking placed hygiene factors at the bottom of the list and motivators at the top. What also is significant is that although Singapore students do not fit into the same cultural cluster as the other three groups in the study, their responses were similar. These findings provide evidence that job-satisfaction-related factors may not always be culturally bounded.[20]

Another, more comprehensive study of managerial job attitudes investigated the types of job outcomes that are desired by managers in different cultures. Data were gathered from

<---- High dissatisfaction ———— Neutral point ———— High satisfaction ———>

Growth opportunity

Work nature

Material and physical provisions

Relations with others

Fairness in organizational practices

Personal problems

−2.00   −1.00   +1.00   +2.00

Average standard score of frequency of mention of items

Figure 13–4

Motivation Factors in Zambia

Source: Adapted from Peter D. Machungwa and Neal Schmitt, "Work Motivation in a Developing Country," *Journal of Applied Psychology,* February 1983, p. 41. Used with permission.

lower- and middle-management personnel who were attending management development courses in Canada, the United Kingdom, France, and Japan.[21] The researchers sought to identify the importance of 15 job-related outcomes and how satisfied the respondents were with each other.

The results indicated that job content is more important than job context. Organizationally controlled factors (**job context factors,** such as conditions, hours, earnings, security, benefits, and promotions) for the most part did not receive as high a ranking as internally mediated factors (**job content factors,** such as responsibility, achievement, and the work itself). The data also show that managers from the four countries differ significantly regarding both the perceived importance of job outcomes and the level of satisfaction experienced on the job with respect to these outcomes. These differences are useful in shedding light on what motivates managers in these countries and, in the case of MNCs, in developing country-specific human resource management approaches. The most striking contrasts were between the French and the British. Commenting on the applicability of this research to the formulation of motivational strategies for effective human resource management, the researchers noted the following:

> The results suggest . . . that efforts to improve managerial performance in the UK should focus on job content rather than on job context. Changes in the nature of the work itself are likely to be more valued than changes in organizational or interpersonal factors. Job enrichment programs which help individuals design their own goals and tasks, and which downplay formal rules and structure, are more likely to improve performance in an intrinsically oriented society such as Britain, where satisfaction tends to be derived from the job itself, than in France, where job context factors such as security and fringe benefits are more highly valued. The results suggest that French managers may be more effectively motivated by changing job situation factors, as long as such changes are explicitly linked to performance.[22]

In summary, Herzberg's two-factor theory appears to reinforce Maslow's need hierarchy through its research support in the international arena. As with the application of Maslow's theory, however, MNCs would be wise to apply motivation–hygiene theory on a country-by-country or a regional basis. Although there are exceptions, such as France, there seems to be little doubt that job content factors are more important than job context factors in motivating not only managers but also lower-level employees around the world, as Hofstede pointed out.

Job context factors
In work motivation, those factors controlled by the organization, such as conditions, hours, earnings, security, benefits, and promotions.

Job content factors
In work motivation, those factors internally controlled, such as responsibility, achievement, and the work itself.

Table 13–5
The Results of Administering the JOI to Four Cross-Cultural Groups

	Relative Rankings			
	United States (*n*=49)	Australia (*n*=58)	Canada (*n*=25)	Singapore (*n*=33)
Achievement	2	2	2	2
Responsibility	3	3	3	3
Growth	1	1	1	1
Recognition	10	10	8	9
Job status	7	7	7	7
Relationships	5	5	10	6
Pay	8	8	6	8
Security	9	9	9	10
Family	6	6	7	5
Hobby	4	4	4	4

Source: G. E. Popp, H. J. Davis, and T. T. Herbert, "An International Study of Intrinsic Motivation Composition," *Management International Review,* vol. 26, no. 3, 1986, p. 31. Used with permission.

■ Achievement Motivation Theory

In addition to the need-hierarchy and two-factor theories of work motivation, achievement motivation theory has been given a relatively great amount of attention in the international arena. Achievement motivation theory has been more applied to the actual practice of management than the others, and it has been the focus of some interesting international research.

The Background of Achievement Motivation Theory

Achievement motivation theory
A theory which holds that individuals can have a need to get ahead, to attain success and to reach objectives.

Achievement motivation theory holds that individuals can have a need to get ahead, to attain success, and to reach objectives. Note that like the upper-level needs in Maslow's hierarchy or like Herzberg's motivators, the need for achievement is learned. Therefore, applied to the international scene, in the United States, where entrepreneurial effort is encouraged and individual success promoted, the probability is higher that there would be a greater percentage of people with high needs for achievement than, for example, in China, Russia, or other Eastern European countries,[23] where cultural values have not traditionally supported individual, entrepreneurial efforts.

Researchers such as the late Harvard psychologist David McClelland have identified a characteristic profile of high achievers.[24] First, these people like situations in which they take personal responsibility for finding solutions to problems. They want to win based on their own efforts and not on luck or chance. Second, they tend to be moderate risk-takers rather than high or low risk-takers. If a decision-making situation appears to be too risky, they will learn as much as they can about the environment and try to reduce the probability of failure. In this way, they turn a high-risk situation into a moderate-risk situation. If the situation is too low-risk, however, there usually is an accompanying low reward, and they tend to avoid situations with insufficient incentive.

Third, high achievers want concrete feedback on their performance. They like to know how well they are doing, and they use this information to modify their actions. High achievers tend to gravitate into vocations such as sales, which provide them with immediate, objective feedback of how they are doing. Finally, and this has considerable implications for human resource management, high achievers often tend to be loners. They typically do not like or get along well with other people. They do not form warm, close relationships, and they have little empathy for others' problems. This last characteristic may distract from their effectiveness as managers of people.

Researchers have discovered a number of ways to develop high achievement needs in people. These involve teaching the individual to do the following: (1) obtain feedback on performance, and use this information to channel one's efforts in areas where success likely will be attained; (2) emulate people who have been successful achievers; (3) develop an internal desire for success and challenge; and (4) daydream in positive terms by picturing oneself as successful in the pursuit of important objectives.[25] Simply put, the need for achievement can be taught and learned.

Before examining international research on achievement motivation theory, it is important to realize that the theory has been cited as having a number of shortcomings. One is that it relies almost solely on the projective personality Thematic Apperception Test (TAT) to measure individual achievement and a number of recent studies have questioned the validity and reliability of this approach.[26] Another concern is that achievement motivation is grounded in individual effort, but in many countries group harmony and cooperation are critically important to success. Simply put, the original theory does not satisfactorily explain the need for achievement in cultures where individual accomplishment is neither valued nor rewarded.[27]

International Findings on Achievement Motivation Theory

A number of international researchers have investigated the role and importance of high achievement needs in human resource management.[28] One study, discussed under the two-factor theory, used the JOI scale and found that achievement or a sense of accomplishment ranked as the second most important work-reward factor.[29] Remember, however, that these results were obtained with MBA students from various countries who were studying in the United States. It should not be surprising that these respondents who came to the United States for advanced study of business, regardless of their home country, would have a high need for achievement. The question remains as to what degree people throughout the world have this need.

Early research among Polish industrialists found that many of them were high achievers.[30] The average high-achievement score was 6.58, which was quite close to that of the U.S. managers' score of 6.74. This led some to conclude there is evidence that managers in countries as diverse as the United States and those of former Soviet-bloc Central Europe have high needs for achievement.[31] In later studies, however, researchers did *not* find a high need for achievement in Central European countries. One study, for example, surveyed Czech industrial managers and found that the average high-achievement score was 3.32, considerably lower than that of U.S. managers.[32] Because the need for achievement is learned, differences in these samples can be attributed to cultural differences. By the same token, given the dramatic, revolutionary changes that occurred in Central and Eastern Europe with the end of communism and centrally planned economies, one could argue that the achievement needs of post-communist Europeans, once they are allowed to be freely expressed, may well be high today. The important point, however, is that because achievement is a learned need and thus largely determined by the prevailing culture, it is not universal and may change over time.

China is a good example of a country where a high need for achievement has traditionally been absent. In recent years, however, a growing segment of the population, especially the younger well-educated Chinese, seem to have this need. In high-achieving societies, work goals such as autonomy, challenge, promotions, and earnings are valued. The need for affiliation and safety rank far down the list; the high achiever is not very interested in these. In China, achievement-oriented goals traditionally have not ranked very high, although government-sponsored economic programs and free enterprise may be changing this.[33] Table 13–6 reports standardized scores on work goals for four East Asian countries. Note that there are five variables to which high achievers would tend to give high scores: autonomy, challenge, earnings, recognition, and promotion. The managers from the People's Republic of China gave high scores to only one of these: autonomy. On the other four high-achievement responses, two were the lowest and the other two second lowest among the four countries. Conversely, high achievers would not give

Table 13–6
Standardized Scores on Work Goals for Managers from Four Countries

Variables	People's Republic of China	Hong Kong	Taiwan	Singapore
Making a contribution	671	—	—	—
Coworkers who cooperate	635	579	571	624
Autonomy	603	512	480	532
Training	583	596	657	611
Efficiency	578	—	—	—
Skills	—	555	577	536
Challenge	515	548	548	571
Working relationship with manager	483	522	524	551
Earnings	454	567	442	552
Security	450	452	506	437
Recognition	446	487	487	442
Benefits	439	323	363	439
Area	—	477	438	362
Favorable physical conditions	433	436	407	432
Promotion	364	640	630	593
Time for nonwork activities	345	307	372	348

Note: Data, except those for the People's Republic, are from Geert Hofstede's book *Culture's Consequences: International Differences in Work-Related Values* (Beverly Hills: Sage, 1980). For the variables of the People's Republic, the skills goals are included in the training goal and the area goal is irrelevant.

Source: Oded Shenkar and Simcha Ronen, "Structure and Importance of Work Goals among Managers in the People's Republic of China," *Academy of Management Journal,* September 1987, p. 571. Used with permission.

high scores to affiliation-related variables or security-related goals such as cooperation with coworkers, security, benefits, physical conditions, and time for nonwork activities. Yet some of these rated relatively high in the Chinese sample.

On the other hand, as China's economy continues to grow and the government allows more market-based efforts, the achievement motivation drive likely will increase among the general population. This finding has been reinforced by a recent study of Chinese and U.S. businesses that found Chinese employees were economically oriented and favored reward systems giving more to some individuals than to others. Among other things, the study concluded that, "The Chinese differential preferences . . . are consistent with efforts to encourage individual responsibility and to link reward to performance . . ."[34] So, the seeds of the achievement motivation drive now appear to be taking root in China.

One of the other countries in Table 13–6, Singapore, had fairly high achievement scores and more recent research reports that indeed this is one of the reasons why the country has done so well. Lee and Chan, for example, recently examined high achievement drive among second-generation Singaporean Chinese businesspeople and found that many of them had the same characteristics that were described by McClelland: a desire for autonomy, individualism, a willingness to take risks, and a willingness to actively search the environment for opportunities, initiative, and ambition. This led the researchers to conclude that "second-generation Chinese entrepreneurs in Singapore possess numerous characteristics which are highly consistent with . . . major related research studies on entrepreneurial characteristics."[35] This may well be one of the reasons why, despite a downturn in the Southeast Asian economy, Singapore has continued to be relatively economically successful.[36]

These results show there is considerable cultural impact on achievement motivation theory. The ideal profile for high-achieving societies can be described in terms of the cultural dimensions examined in Chapter 5. In particular, two cultural dimensions identified

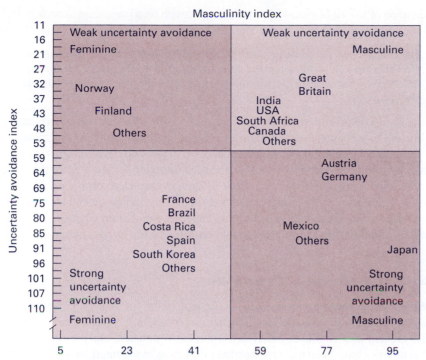

Figure 13–5

Selected Countries on the Uncertainty Avoidance and Masculinity Scales

Source: Adapted from Geert Hofstede, "The Cultural Relativity of Organizational Practices and Theories," *Journal of International Business Studies,* Fall 1983, p. 86. Used with permission.

by Hofstede in Chapter 5 best describe high-achieving societies. First, these societies tend to have low uncertainty avoidance. Those in high-achieving societies are not afraid to take at least moderate risks or to live with ambiguity. Second, these societies tend to have moderate to high masculinity (Hofstede's term), as measured by the high importance assigned to the acquisition of money and other physical assets and the low value given to caring for others and for the quality of work life. This combination is found almost exclusively in Anglo countries or in nations that have been closely associated with them through early colonization or treaty, such as India, Singapore, and Hong Kong (countries in their history that have been associated with Great Britain) and the Philippines (which has been associated with the United States). This is seen in Figure 13–5.

Countries that fall into one of the other three quadrants in Figure 13-5 will not be very supportive of the high need for achievement. MNCs in these geographic regions, therefore, would be wise to formulate a human resource management strategy for either changing the situation or adjusting to it. If they decide to change the situation, they must design jobs to fit the needs of their people or put people through an achievement motivation training program to create high-achieving managers and entrepreneurs.

A number of years ago, McClelland was able to demonstrate the success of such achievement motivation training programs with underdeveloped countries. For example, in India, he conducted such a program with considerable success. In following up these Indian trainees over the subsequent 6 to 10 months, he found that two-thirds were unusually active in achievement-oriented activities. They had started new businesses, investigated new product lines, increased profits, or expanded their present organizations. For example, the owner of a small radio store opened a paint and varnish factory after completing the program. McClelland concluded that this training appeared to have doubled the natural rate of unusual achievement-oriented activity in the group studied.[37]

If international human resource managers cannot change the situation or train the participants, then they must adjust to the specific conditions of the country and formulate a motivation strategy that is based on those conditions. In many cases, this requires consideration of a need-hierarchy approach blended with an achievement approach. Hofstede offers such advice in dealing with the countries in the various quadrants of Figure 13–5.

> The countries on the feminine side . . . distinguish themselves by focusing on quality of life rather than on performance and on relationships between people rather than on money and things. This means *social motivation:* quality of life plus security and quality of life plus risk.[38]

In the case of countries that are attempting to introduce changes that incorporate values from one of the other quadrants in Figure 13–5, the challenge can be even greater.

In summary, achievement motivation theory provides additional insights into the motivation of personnel around the world. Like the need-hierarchy and two-factor theories, however, achievement motivation theory must be modified to meet the specific needs of the local culture. The culture of many countries does not support high achievement. However, the cultures of Anglo countries and those that reward entrepreneurial effort do support achievement motivation, and their human resources should probably be managed accordingly.

■ Select Process Theories

While content theories are useful in explaining motivation for managing international personnel, process theories can also lead to better understanding. As noted earlier, the process theories explain how employee behavior is initiated, redirected, and halted; and a number of these theories have been used to examine motivation in the international arena. Among the most widely recognized are equity theory, goal-setting theory, and expectancy theory. The following briefly examines each of these three and their relevance to international human resource management.

Equity Theory

Equity theory

Equity theory focuses on how motivation is affected by people's perception of how fairly they are being treated.

Equity theory focuses on how motivation is affected by people's perception of how fairly they are being treated. The theory holds that if people perceive that they are being treated equitably, this will have a positive effect on their job performance and satisfaction and there is no need to strive for equity. Conversely, if they believe they are not being treated fairly, especially in relation to relevant others, they will be dissatisfied and this will have a negative effect on their job performance and they will strive to restore equity.

There is considerable research to support the fundamental equity principle in western work groups.[39] However, when the theory is examined on an international basis the results are mixed. Yuchtman, for example, studied equity perceptions among managers and nonmanagers in an Israeli kibbutz production unit.[40] In this setting everyone was treated the same and the managers reported lower satisfaction levels than the workers. This was because the managers perceived their contributions to be greater than those of any other group in the kibbutz. As a result, they felt that they were undercompensated for their value and effort. These findings support the basic concepts in equity theory.

On the other hand, there are a number of studies that cast doubt on the relevance of equity theory in explaining motivation in an international setting. Perhaps the biggest shortcoming is that the theory appears to be culture bound. For example, equity theory postulates that when people are not treated fairly, they will take steps to reduce the inequity. Typical ways include doing less work, filing a grievance, or getting a transfer to another department. In Asia and the Middle East, however, employees often readily accept inequitable treatment in order to preserve group harmony. Additionally, in countries like Japan and Korea, men and women typically receive different pay for doing the same work, yet because of years of cultural conditioning these women may not feel they are being treated inequitably.[41] Some researchers have explained this finding by suggesting that these women compare themselves only to other women, and in this regard they feel they are being treated equitably. While this may be true, the results still point to the fact that equity theory is not universally applicable in explaining motivation and job satisfaction. In short, while the theory may help explain why "equal pay for equal work" is a guiding motivation principle in countries like the U.S. and Canada, it may have limited value in other areas of the world including Asia and Latin America, where compensation differences based on gender, at least traditionally, have been culturally acceptable.

Goal-Setting Theory

Goal-setting theory focuses on how individuals go about setting goals and responding to them and the overall impact of this process on motivation. Some of the specific areas that are given attention in goal-setting theory include the level of participation in setting goals, goal difficulty, goal specificity, and the importance of objective, timely feedback related to progress toward goals. Unlike many theories of motivation, goal-setting has been continually refined and developed.[42] There is considerable research evidence showing that employees perform extremely well when they are assigned specific and challenging goals that they have had a hand in setting.[43] On the other hand, most of these studies have been conducted in the U.S., while few of them have been carried out in other cultures.[44] One study that did examine goal-setting in an international setting looked at Norwegian employee participation in goal-setting.[45] They found that the Norwegian employees shunned participation and preferred to have their union representatives work with management in determining work goals. This led the researchers to conclude that individual participation in goal-setting was seen as inconsistent with the prevailing philosophy of participation through union representatives. Unlike the U.S. where employee participation in setting goals is motivational, it had no value for the Norwegian employees in this study.

Similar results to the Norwegian study have been reported by Earley, who found that workers in the U.K. responded more favorably to a goal-setting program sponsored by the union stewards than by management. This led Earley to conclude that the transferability across cultural settings of management concepts such as participation in goal-setting may well be affected by the prevailing work norms.[46] In order to further test this proposition, Erez and Earley studied American and Israeli subjects and found that participative strategies led to higher levels of goal acceptance and performance in both cultures than did strategies in which objectives were assigned by higher-level management.[47] In other words, the value of goal-setting theory may well be determined by culture and in the case, for example, of Asian and Latin work groups where collectivism is very high, the theory may have limited value for MNC managers in selected countries.

Expectancy Theory

Expectancy theory postulates that motivation is largely influenced by a multiplicative combination of a person's belief that effort will lead to performance, that performance will lead to specific outcomes, and that these outcomes are valued by the individual.[48] In addition, the theory predicts that high performance followed by high rewards will lead to high satisfaction.[49] Does this theory have universal application? Eden used it in studying workers in an Israeli kibbutz and found some support;[50] and Matsui and Terai reported that the theory could be applied successfully in Japan.[51] On the other hand, it is important to remember that expectancy theory is based on employees having considerable control over their environment, a condition that does not exist in many cultures around the world (e.g., Asia). In particular, in societies where people believe that much of what happens is beyond their control, this theory may have less value. It would seem that expectancy theory is best able to explain worker motivation in those cultures where there is a strong internal locus of control (e.g., in the U.S.). In short, the theory seems culture bound and international managers must be aware of this in their efforts to apply this theory to motivate human resources.

■ Motivation Applied: Job Design, Work Centrality, and Rewards

Content and process theories provide important insights and understanding into how to motivate human resources in international management. So, too, do applied concepts such as job design, work centrality, and rewards.

Goal-setting theory
Goal-setting theory focuses on how individuals go about setting goals and responding to them and the overall impact of this process on motivation.

Expectancy theory
Expectancy theory postulates that motivation is influenced by a person's belief that effort will lead to performance, performance will lead to specific outcomes, and that these outcomes are valued by the individual.

Job Design

Job design
A job's content, the methods that are used on the job, and the way the job relates to others in the organization.

Job design consists of a job's content, the methods that are used on the job, and the way in which the job relates to others in the organization. The job design typically is a function of the work to be done and the way in which management wants the job to be carried out. These factors help to explain why the same type of work may have a different impact on the motivation of human resources in various parts of the world and result in different quality of work life.

Quality of Work Life: The Impact of Culture
Quality of work life (QWL) is not the same throughout the world. For example, assembly line employees in Japan will work at a rapid pace for hours and have very little control over their work activities. In Sweden, assembly line employees work at a more relaxed pace and have a great deal of control over their work activities. U.S. assembly line employees are somewhere in between; they typically work at a pace that is less demanding than that in Japan but more structured than that in Sweden.

What accounts for these differences? One answer is found in the culture of the country. QWL is directly related to culture. Table 13–7 compares the three industrialized nations mentioned earlier using the four cultural dimensions described in Chapter 5. A brief look shows that each country has a different cultural profile, helping to explain why similar jobs may be designed quite differently from country to country. Assembly line work is a good comparative example.

In Japan, there is strong uncertainty avoidance. The Japanese like to structure tasks so there is no doubt regarding what is to be done and how it is to be done. Individualism is low, so there is strong emphasis on security and individual risk-taking is discouraged. The power distance index is high, so Japanese workers are accustomed to taking orders from those above them. The masculinity index for the Japanese is high, which shows that they put a great deal of importance on money and other material symbols of success. In designing jobs, the Japanese structure tasks so that the work is performed within these cultural confines. Japanese managers work their employees extremely hard. Although Japanese workers contribute many ideas through the extensive use of quality circles, Japanese managers give them very little say in what actually goes on in the organization (in contrast to the erroneous picture often portrayed by the media, which presents Japanese firms as highly democratic and managed from the bottom up[52]) and depend heavily on monetary rewards, as reflected by the fact that the Japanese rate money as an important motivator more than the workers in any other industrialized country do.

In Sweden, however, uncertainty avoidance is low, so job descriptions, policy manuals, and similar work-related materials are more open-ended or general as opposed to the detailed procedural materials developed by the Japanese. In addition, Swedish workers are encouraged to make decisions and take risks. Swedes exhibit a moderate to high degree of individualism, which is reflected in their emphasis on individual decision making (in

Table 13–7 **Cultural Dimensions in Japan, Sweden, and the United States**					
	Degree of Dimension				
Cultural Dimension	**High/Strong** X ←		**Moderate** — X —		**Low/Weak** → X
Uncertainty avoidance	J			USA	S
Individualism	USA	S		J	
Power distance		J	USA	S	
Masculinity	J		USA		S

Source: Adapted from Geert Hofstede, "The Cultural Relativity of the Quality of Life Concept," *Academy of Management Review,* July 1984, pp. 391, 393. Used with permission.

contrast to the collective or group decision making of the Japanese). They have a weak power distance index, which means that Swedish managers use participative approaches in leading their people. Swedes score low on masculinity, which means that interpersonal relations and the ability to interact with other workers and discuss job-related matters are important. These cultural dimensions result in job designs that are markedly different from those in Japan.

Cultural dimensions in the United States are closer to those of Sweden than to those of Japan. In addition, except for individualism, the U.S. profile is between that of Sweden and Japan (again see Table 13–7). This means that job design in U.S. assembly plants tend to be more flexible or unstructured than that of the Japanese but more rigid than that of the Swedes.

This same pattern holds for many other jobs in these countries. All job designs tend to reflect the cultural values of the country. The challenge for MNCs is to adjust job design to meet the needs of the host country's culture. For example, when Japanese firms enter the United States, they often are surprised to learn that people resent close control. In fact, there is evidence that the most profitable Japanese-owned companies in the United States are those that delegate a high degree of authority to their U.S. managers.[53] Similarly, Japanese firms operating in Sweden find that quality of work life is a central concern for the personnel and that a less structured, highly participative management style is needed for success. Some of the best examples are provided by sociotechnical job designs.

Sociotechnical Job Designs

Sociotechnical designs are job designs that blend personnel and technology. The objective of these designs is to integrate new technology into the workplace so that workers accept and use these developments to increase overall productivity. Because technology often requires people to learn new methods and, in some cases, work faster, employee resistance is typical. Effective sociotechnical design can overcome these problems. There are a number of good examples, and perhaps the most famous is that of Volvo, the Swedish automaker. Sociotechnologic changes that were reflective of the cultural values of the workers were introduced at the firm's Kalmar plant. Autonomous work groups were formed and given the authority to elect their own supervisors as well as to schedule, assign, and inspect their own work. Each group was allowed to work at its own pace, although there was an overall output objective for the week and each group was expected to attain this goal.[54] The outcome was very positive and resulted in Volvo's building another plant that employed even more sophisticated sociotechnical job design concepts. More recently, however, Volvo's plant layout has not prevented the firm from having some problems. Both Japanese and North American automakers have been able to produce cars in far less time, putting Volvo at a cost disadvantage. As a result, the economic downturn in Asia, coupled with weakening demand for its product lines in both Europe and the United States, has resulted in the firm beginning to lay off workers and take steps to increase its efficiency.[55]

Without sacrificing efficiency, a number of other firms have introduced sociotechnical designs for better blending of their personnel and technology. A well-known U.S. example is General Foods, which set up autonomous groups at its Topeka, Kansas plant to produce Gaines pet food. Patterned after the Volvo example, the General Foods project allowed workers to share responsibility and work in a highly democratic environment. Other U.S. firms also have opted for a self-managed team approach. In fact, research reports that the concept of multifunctional teams with autonomy for generating successful product innovation is more widely used by successful U.S., Japanese, and European firms than any other form of teamwork concept.[56] Its use must be tempered by the cultural situation, however. And even the widely publicized General Foods project at Topeka in the United States had some problems. Some former employees there indicate that the approach has steadily eroded and that some managers were openly hostile because it undermined their power, authority, and decision-making flexibility. The most effective job design will be a result of both the job to be done and the cultural values that support a particular approach.[57] For MNCs, the challenge will be to make the fit between the design and the culture.

Sociotechnical designs
Job designs that blend the personnel and the technology.

At the same time, it is important to realize that functional job descriptions now are being phased out in many MNCs and replaced by more of a process approach. This new approach is explained as follows:

> Process management differs from managing a function in three ways. First, it uses external objectives. Old-line manufacturing departments, for example, tend to be measured on unit costs, an intradepartmental number that can lead to overlong production runs and stacks of unsold goods. By contrast, an integrated manufacturing and shipping process might be rated by how often it turns over its inventory—a process-wide measurement that reveals how all are working together to keep costs down. Second, in process management, employees with different skills are grouped to accomplish a complete piece of work. . . . Third, information moves straight to where it's needed, unfiltered by a hierarchy. If you have a problem with people upstream from you, you deal with them directly, rather than asking your boss to talk to theirs.[58]

The result is a more horizontal network that relies on communication and teamwork. This approach also is useful in helping to create and sustain partnerships with other firms.

Work Centrality

Work centrality
The importance of work in an individual's life relative to other areas of interest.

Work centrality, which can be defined as the importance of work in an individual's life relative to his or her other areas of interest (family, church, leisure), provides important insights into how to motivate human resources in different cultures.[59] After conducting a review of the literature, Bhagat and associates found that Japan has the highest level of work centrality, followed by moderately high levels for Israel, average levels for the United States and Belgium, moderately low levels for the Netherlands and Germany, and low levels for Britain.[60] These findings indicate that successful multinationals in Japan must realize that although work is an integral part of the Japanese lifestyle, work in the United States must be more balanced with a concern for other interests. Unfortunately, this is likely to become increasingly more difficult for Japanese firms in Japan because the stagnant population growth is creating a shortage of personnel. As a result, a growing number of Japanese firms are now trying to push the mandatory retirement age to 65 from 60 and, except for the U.S., the Japanese workers put in the most hours.[61]

Value of Work   Although work is an important part of the lifestyles of most people, there still are a large number of misconceptions. For example, one reason that Americans and Japanese work such long hours is that the cost of living is high and hourly employees cannot afford to pass up the opportunity for extra money. Among salaried employees who are not paid extra, most Japanese managers expect their subordinates to stay late at work, and this has become a requirement of the job. Moreover, there is recent evidence that Japanese workers may do far less work in a business day than outsiders would suspect.

Many people are unaware of these facts and have misperceptions regarding both why the Japanese work so hard and the importance of work to these employees. The same is true for Germans and Americans. In recent years, the number of hours worked annually by German workers has been declining, while the number for Americans has been on the rise. What accounts for this trend? Some observers have explained it in cultural terms, noting that Germans place high value on lifestyle and often prefer leisure to work, while their American counterparts are just the opposite. In fact, research reveals that culture may have little to do with it. A recent study by the National Bureau of Economic Research (NBER) has found that there is a far wider range of wages within American companies than there is in German firms, and this large pay disparity has created incentives for American employees to work harder. In particular, many U.S. workers believe that if they work harder their chances of getting pay hikes and promotions will increase, and there is historical data to support this belief. An analysis of worker histories in the U.S. and Germany has led NBER researchers to estimate that American workers who increase their working time by 10 percent, for example from 2,000 to 2,200 hours annually, will raise their future earnings by about 1 percent for each year that they put in extra hours. Pulling together all of their data, the NBER researchers conclude:

In sum, workers in both nations appear to log more time on the job when pay scales are unequal, but the impact is much weaker in Germany, where wages are far less variable and where greater job security, high jobless benefits, and a national health system cushion the adverse effects of layoff. Americans work longer hours mainly because of the lure of big wage gains . . . they're also responding to the higher risk of losing income and health coverage if the boss lets them go.[62]

Another important area of consideration is the importance of work as a part of overall lifestyle. In the case of Japanese workers, in particular, there has been a growing interest in the impact of overwork on the physical condition of employees. A report by the Japanese government has noted that one-third of the working age population suffers from chronic fatigue, and a recent survey by the Japanese prime minister's office has found that a majority of those who were surveyed complained of being chronically tired and feeling emotionally stressed.[63] Fortunately, as seen in the accompanying sidebar, "*Karoshi, or Stressed Out in Japan*," the effects of overwork or job burnout are beginning to be recognized as a real social problem.

Karoshi
Overwork or job burnout, in Japanese.

Job Satisfaction In addition to the implications that value of work has for motivating human resources across cultures, another interesting contrast is job satisfaction. For example, one study has found that Japanese office workers may be much less satisfied with their jobs than their U.S., Canadian, and EU counterparts are. The Americans, who reported the highest level of satisfaction in this study, were pleased with job challenges, opportunities for teamwork, and ability to make a significant contribution at work. Japanese workers, however, were least pleased with these three factors.[64] Similar findings were uncovered by Luthans and his associates, who reported that U.S. employees had higher organizational commitment than Japanese or Korean workers in their cross-cultural study. What makes these findings particularly interesting is that a large percentage of the Japanese and Korean workers were supervisory employees, who could be expected to be more committed to their organization than nonsupervisory employees, and a significant percentage of these employees also had lifetime guarantees.[65] This study also showed that findings related to job satisfaction in the international arena often are different than expected.[66]

Conventional wisdom not always being substantiated has been reinforced by cross-cultural studies that found Japanese workers who already were highly paid, and who then received even higher wages, experienced decreased job satisfaction, morale, commitment, and intention to remain with the firm. This contrasts sharply with U.S. workers, who did not experience these negative feelings.[67] These findings show that the motivation approaches used in one culture may have limited value in another.[68]

Research by Kakabadse and Myers also has brought to light findings that are contradictory to commonly accepted beliefs. These researchers examined job satisfaction among managers from the United Kingdom, France, Belgium, Sweden, and Finland. It has long been assumed that satisfaction is highest at the upper levels of organizations; however, this study found varying degrees of satisfaction among managers, depending on the country. The researchers reported that

> senior managers from France and Finland display greater job dissatisfaction than the managers from the remaining countries. In terms of satisfaction with and commitment to the organization, British, German and Swedish managers display highest levels of commitment. Equally, British and German managers highlight that they feel stretched in their job, but senior managers from French organizations suggest that their jobs lack sufficient challenge and stimulus. In keeping with the job related views displayed by French managers, they equally indicate their desire to leave their job because of their unsatisfactory work-related circumstances.[69]

On the other hand, research also reveals that some of the conditions that help to create organizational commitment among U.S. workers also have value in other cultures. For example, a large study of Korean employees ($n = 1192$ in 27 companies in eight major industries) found that consistent with U.S. studies, Korean employees' position in the hierarchy, tenure in their current position, and age all related significantly to organizational commitment. Also, like previous studies in the United States, as the size of the Korean

International Management in Action

Karoshi, or Stressed Out in Japan

Doing business in Japan can be a real killer. Overwork, or **karoshi,** as it is called in Japan, claims 10,000 lives annually in this hard-driving, competitive economic society according to Hiroshi Kawahito, a lawyer who has founded the National Defense Council for Victims of Karoshi.

One of the cases is Jun Ishii of Mitsui & Company. Ishii was one of the firm's only speakers of Russian. In the year before his death, Ishii made 10 trips to Russia, totaling 115 days. No sooner would he arrive home from one trip than the company would send him out again. The grueling pace took its toll. While on a trip, Ishii collapsed and died of a heart attack. His widow filed a lawsuit against Mitsui & Company, charging that her husband had been worked to death. Tokyo labor regulators ruled that Ishii had indeed died of *karoshi,* and the government now is paying annual worker's compensation to the widow. The company also cooperated and agreed to make a one-time payment of $240,000.

The reason that the case received so much publicity is that this is one of the few instances in which the government has ruled that a person died from overwork. Now regulators are expanding *karoshi* compensation to salaried as well as hourly workers. This development is receiving the attention of the top management of many Japanese multinationals, and some Japanese MNCs are beginning to take steps to prevent the likelihood of overwork. For example, Mitsui & Company now assesses its managers based on how well they set overtime hours, keep subordinates healthy, and encourage workers to take vacations. Matsushita Electric has extended vacations from 16 days annually to 23 days and now requires all workers to take this time off. One branch of Nippon Telegraph & Telephone found that stress made some workers irritable and ill, so the company initiated periods of silent meditation. Other companies are following suit, although there still are many Japanese who work well over 2,500 hours a year and feel both frustrated and burned out by job demands.

On the positive side, the Ishii case likely will bring about some improvements in working conditions for many Japanese employees. Experts admit, however, that it is difficult to determine if *karoshi* is caused by work demands or by private, late-night socializing that may be work-related. Other possible causes include high stress, lack of exercise, and fatty diets, but whatever the cause, one thing is clear: More and more Japanese families no longer are willing to accept the belief that *karoshi* is a risk that all employees must accept. Work may be a killer, but this outcome can be prevented through more carefully implemented job designs and work processes.

At the same time, recent reports show that there is still a long way to go. In Saku, Japan, for example, the city's main hospital has found that 32 percent of the patients hospitalized in the internal medicine and psychiatric ward are being treated for chronic fatigue syndrome, a diagnosis that is made only after six months of severe, continuous fatigue in the absence of any organic illness. Japanese doctors attribute this explosion of chronic fatigue syndrome to stress. Moreover, during the prolonged economic downturn a growing number of business people have found themselves suffering from these symptoms. And to make matters worse, there is a growing concern with alcoholism among workers. Over the past four decades, the per capita alcohol consumption in most countries has declined but in Japan it has risen fourfold. The per capita consumption of alcohol in Japan is equal to that in the U.S. Even this comparison is misleading because researchers have found that most Japanese women do not drink at all, but Japanese men in their 50s drink more than twice that of their American counterparts. Additionally, young Japanese employees find that drinking is considered necessary and some of them have raised complaints about *alru-hara* or alcohol harassment (forced/pressured alcohol consumption).

Dealing with overwork will continue to be a challenge for both Japanese firms and the government. The same is true for the growing problems associated with alcohol that is being brought on by stress and business cultures that have long supported alcohol consumption as a way of doing business and fitting into the social structure.

organizations increased, commitment decreased, and the more positive the climate perceptions, the greater the commitment.[70] In other words, there is at least beginning evidence that the theoretic constructs predicting organizational commitment may hold across cultures.

Also related to motivation are job attitudes toward quality of work life. Recent research reports that EU workers see a strong relationship between how well they do their jobs and the ability to get what they want out of life. U.S. workers were not as supportive of this relationship, and Japanese workers were least likely to see any connection.

This finding raises an interesting motivation-related issue regarding how well, for example, American, European, and Japanese employees can work together effectively. Some researchers have recently raised the question of how Japanese firms will be able to have effective strategic alliances with American and European companies, if the work values of the partners are so different. Tornvall, after conducting a detailed examination of the work practices of five companies—Fuji-Kiku, a spare parts firm in Japan, Toyota Motor Ltd. of Japan, Volvo Automobile AB of Sweden, SAAB Automobile AB, Sweden, and the General Motors plant in Saginaw, Michigan—concluded that there were benefits from the approaches used by each. This led him to recommend what he calls a "balance in the synergy" between the partners.[71] Some of his suggestions included the following:

Moving away from	Moving toward
Logical and reason-centered, individualistic thinking.	A more holistic, idealistic, and group thinking approach to problem solving.
Viewing work as a necessary burden.	Viewing work as a challenging and development activity.
The avoidance of risk-taking and the feeling of distrust of others.	An emphasis on cooperation, trust, and personal concern for others.
The habit of analyzing things in such great depth that it results in "paralysis through analysis."	Cooperation built on intuition and pragmatism.
An emphasis on control.	An emphasis on flexibility.

In large degree, this balance will require all three groups—American, Europeans, and Asians—to make changes in the way they approach work.

In conclusion, it should be remembered that work is important in every society. The extent of importance will vary, however, and much of what is "known" about work as a motivator often is culture-specific. The lesson to be learned for international management is that although the process of motivation may be the same, the content may change from one culture to another.

Reward Systems

Besides the content and process theories, another important area of motivation is that of rewards. Managers everywhere use rewards to motivate their personnel. Sometimes these are financial in nature such as salary raises, bonuses, and stock options. Other times they are nonfinancial such as feedback and recognition.[72] The major challenge for international managers is that there are often significant differences between the reward systems that work best in one country and those that are most effective in another. Some of these differences are a result of the competitive environment[73] or of government legislation which dictates such things as minimum wages, pensions, and perquisites.[74] In other cases, however, the differences are accounted for very heavily by culture.[75] For example, while many American companies like to use merit-based reward systems, firms in Japan, Korea, and Taiwan, where individualism is not very high, often feel that this form of reward system is too disruptive of the corporate culture and traditional values.[76]

Incentives and Culture

Use of financial incentives to motivate employees are very common, especially in countries with high individualism. In the United States, as seen in the opening news story, a number of chief executive officers have earned over $100 million a year thanks to bonuses, stock options, and long-term incentive payments.[77] These pay systems are common where companies attempt to link compensation to performance. Typically, these systems range from individual incentive-based pay in which workers are paid directly for their output to systems in which employees earn individual bonuses based on how well the organization at large achieves certain goals such as sales growth, total revenue, or total profit. These reward systems are designed to stress *equity*. However, they are not universally accepted. In many cultures compensation is based on group membership or group effort. In these cases the systems are designed to stress *equality* and employees will oppose the use of individual incentive plans. One example of this is the American multinational corporation that decided to institute an individually based bonus system for the sales representatives in its Danish subsidiary. However, the sales force rejected the proposal because it favored one group over another and the employees felt that everyone should receive the same size bonus.[78] Another example, reported by Vance and associates, was Indonesian oil workers who rejected a pay-for-performance system that would result in some work teams making more money than the others.[79]

While financial rewards such as pay, bonuses, and stock options are important motivators, in many countries workers are highly motivated by other things as well. For example, Sirota and Greenwood studied employees of a large multinational electrical equipment manufacturer with operations in 40 countries. They found that in all of these locales the most important rewards involved recognition and achievement. Second in importance were improvements in the work environment and employment conditions including pay and work hours.[80] Beyond this, a number of differences emerged in terms of preferred types of rewards. For example, employees in France and Italy highly valued job security while for American and British workers it held little importance. Scandinavian workers placed high value on concern for others on the job and for personal freedom and autonomy, but they did not rate "getting ahead" as very important. German workers ranked security, fringe benefits, and "getting ahead" as very important, while Japanese employees put good working conditions and a congenial work environment high on their list but ranked personal advancement quite low.

Very simply, the types of incentives that are deemed important appear to be culturally influenced. Moreover, culture can even affect the overall cost of an incentive system. For example, in Japan efforts to introduce western-style merit pay systems typically leads to an increase in the overall labor costs because the companies find that they cannot reduce the pay of less productive workers for fear of causing them to lose face and thus disturb group harmony.[81] As a result, everyone's salary increases. Culture also impacts on profit in that people tend to perform better under management systems that are supportive of their own values. Nam, for example, studied two Korean banks that operated under different management systems.[82] One was owned and operated as a joint venture with an American bank and the other was owned and operated as a joint venture with a Japanese bank. The American bank put into place management practices and personnel policies that were common in its own organization. The Japanese bank put together a blend of Japanese and Korean human resource management policies. Nam found that employees in the joint venture with the Japanese bank were significantly more committed to the organization than their counterparts in the American joint venture and the Japanese-affiliated bank had significantly higher financial performance.

At the same time, however, reward systems can sometimes be transferred and used successfully. For example, Welsh, Luthans, and Sommer examined the effectiveness of common western incentive systems in a Russian textile factory.[83] They found that both contingently administered extrinsic rewards and positive recognition and attention from the supervisor led to significantly enhanced job performance, while participative techniques had little impact on job behavior and performance. Similarly, while many people believe that large annual financial packages and lucrative golden parachutes are used only in American firms, this is untrue. Senior-level managers in many MNCs now earn large salaries and the use of large financial packages for executives who are terminated or have their company acquired by another firm are gaining in popularity, especially in Europe.[84] In other words, the type of rewards that are used are not culture-bound.

Overall, however, cultures do greatly influence the effectiveness of various rewards. What works in one country may not work in another. For example, research shows that Swedish workers with superior performance often prefer a reward of time off rather than additional money, while high-performing Japanese workers tend to opt for financial incentives—as long as they are group-based and not given on an individual basis.[85] It is also important to realize that the reasons why workers choose one form of motivation over another, for example days off rather than more money, may not be immediately obvious or intuitively discernible. For example, research has found that Japanese workers tend to take only about half of their annual holiday entitlements, while French and German workers take all of the days to which they are entitled. Many people believe it is because the Japanese want to earn more money, but the primary reason is that they believe taking all of these days shows a lack of commitment to their work group. The same is true for overtime; those individuals who refuse to work overtime are viewed as selfish. One of the results of these cultural values is *karoshi,* which was discussed earlier in the chapter.

The World of *Business Week*—Revisited

The opening news story examined the pay of chief executives of some major U.S. multinationals. These executives are earning huge compensation packages because their firms have performed well. This "pay for performance" approach, as explained in the chapter, is more common in the U.S. and other countries with high individualism than it is in more collectivist cultures such as in Asia. In fact, for many employees around the globe money is not the most important motivator. Many workers worldwide tend to be motivated by a host of nonmonetary factors including interesting work, challenge, a friendly environment, feedback, and recognition. So the challenge for international managers is to put together a motivational package that addresses the specific needs of the employee and/or group. In applying this idea, answer these questions: (1) What are some of the things that successful MNCs do to effectively motivate their Japanese employees? (2) What are some of the things that they do in effectively motivating their European employees, specifically German workers? (3) How important is culture as a factor in the motivation equation?

Summary of Key Points

1. Two basic types of theories explain motivation: content and process. Content motivation theories have been given much more attention in international management research, because they provide the opportunity to create a composite picture for motivation of human resources in a particular country or region of the world. In addition, content theories apply more directly to providing ways for managers to improve the performance of their human resources.

2. Maslow's hierarchy-of-needs theory has been studied in a number of different countries. Researchers have found that regardless of country, managers have to be concerned with the satisfaction of these needs for their human resources.

3. Some researchers have suggested that satisfaction profiles are not very useful for studying motivation in an international setting, because there are so many different subcultures within any country or even at different levels of a given organization. These researchers have suggested that job categories are more effective for examining motivation, because job level (managers versus operating employees) and the need hierarchy have an established relationship.

4. Like Maslow's theory, Herzberg's two-factor theory has received considerable attention in the international arena, and his original findings from the United States have been replicated in other countries. Cross-cultural studies related to job satisfaction also have been conducted. The data show that job content is more important than job context to job satisfaction.

5. The third content motivation theory that has received a great amount of attention in the international arena is the need for achievement. Some current findings show that this need is not as widely held across cultures as was previously believed. In some parts of the world, however, such as Anglo countries, cultural values support people to be high achievers. In particular, Dutch researcher Geert Hofstede has suggested that an analysis of two cultural dimensions, uncertainty avoidance and masculinity, helps to identify high-achieving societies. Once again, it can be concluded that different cultures will support different motivational needs, and that international managers developing strategies to motivate their human resources for improved performance must recognize cultural differences.

6. Process theories have also contributed to the understanding of motivation in the international arena. Equity theory focuses on how motivation is affected by people's perception of how fairly they are being treated and there is considerable research to support

the fundamental equity principle in western work groups. However, when the theory is examined on an international basis the results are mixed. Perhaps the biggest shortcoming of the theory is that it appears to be culture bound. For example, in countries like Japan and Korea, men and women typically receive different pay for doing precisely the same work and this is at least traditionally not perceived as inequitable to women.

7. Goal-setting theory focuses on how individuals go about setting goals and responding to them and the overall impact of this process on motivation. There is evidence showing that employees perform extremely well when they are assigned specific and challenging goals that they made a contribution in setting. On the other hand, most of these goal-setting studies have been conducted in the U.S.; few of them have been carried out in other cultures. Additionally, research results on the effects of goal-setting at the individual level are very limited and culture may well account for these outcomes.

8. Expectancy theory postulates that motivation is largely influenced by a multiplicative combination of a person's belief that effort will lead to performance, that performance will lead to specific outcomes, and that these outcomes are valued by the individual. There is mixed support for this theory's value. Many researchers believe that the theory best explains motivation in those countries that emphasize an internal locus of control.

9. Although content and process theories provide important insights into the motivation of human resources, three additional areas that have received a great deal of recent attention in the application of motivation are job design, work centrality, and reward systems. Job design is influenced by culture as well as the specific methods that are used to bring together the people and the work. Work centrality helps to explain the importance of work in an individual's life relative to other areas of interest. In recent years work has become a relatively greater part of the average U.S. employee's life and perhaps less a part of the average Japanese worker's life. Research also indicates that Japanese office workers are less satisfied with their jobs than are U.S., Canadian, and EU workers, suggesting that MNCs need to design motivation packages that address the specific needs of different cultures. This idea is also true in the case of rewards. Research shows that the motivational value of monetary and nonmonetary rewards is influenced by culture. Countries with high individualism such as the U.S. and the U.K. tend to make wide use of individual incentives, while collectivistic countries such as in Asia tend to prefer group-oriented incentives. At the same time, research shows that some motivational approaches in the U.S. have been successfully used in Russia. So while the importance of focusing on the importance of motivation in the international arena is unquestioned, the use of specific applications continues to be challenging for MNC managers.

Key Terms

achievement motivation theory, *390*	job content factors, *389*	process theories, *381*
content theories, *381*	job context factors, *389*	safety needs, *381*
equity theory, *394*	job design, *396*	self-actualization needs, *381*
esteem needs, *381*	*karoshi, 399*	social needs, *381*
expectancy theory, *395*	motivation, *379*	sociotechnical designs, *397*
goal-setting theory, *395*	motivators, *385*	two-factor theory of motivation, *385*
hygiene factors, *385*	physiological needs, *381*	work centrality, *398*

Review and Discussion Questions

1. Do people throughout the world have needs similar to those described in Maslow's need hierarchy? What does your answer reveal about using universal assumptions regarding motivation?

2. Is Herzberg's two-factor theory universally applicable to human resource management, or is its value limited to Anglo countries?

3. What are the dominant characteristics of high achievers? Using Figure 13–5 as your point of reference, determine which countries likely will have the great-

est percentage of high achievers. Why is this so? Of what value is your answer to the study of international management?

4. A U.S. manufacturer is planning to open a plant in Sweden. What should this firm know about the quality of work life in Sweden that would have a direct effect on job design in the plant? Give an example.

5. What does a U.S. firm setting up operations in Japan need to know about work centrality in that country? How would this information be of value to the multi-

national? Conversely, what would a Japanese firm need to know about work centrality in the United States? Explain.

6. In managing operations in Europe, which process theory—equity theory, goal-setting theory, or expectancy theory—would be of most value to an American manager? Why?

7. What do international managers need to know about the use of reward incentives to motivate personnel? What role does culture play in this process?

Internet Exercise: Motivating Potential Employees

In order for multinationals to continue expanding their operations, they must be able to attract and retain highly qualified personnel in many countries. Much of their success in doing this will be tied to the motivational package that they offer including financial opportunities, benefits and perquisites, meaningful work, and an environment that promotes productivity and worker creativity. Automotive firms, in particular, are a good example of MNCs that are trying very hard to increase their worldwide market share. So for them, employee motivation is an area that is getting a lot of attention. Go to the Web and look at the career opportunities that are currently being offered by Ford Motor (**www.ford.com**), Volvo (**www.volvo.com**), and Volkswagen (**www.vw.com**). Each of these companies provides information about career opportunities in their firm. Based on this information, answer these three questions: (1) What are some of the things that all three firms offer in terms of motivating new employees? (2) Which of the three had the best motivational package? Why? (3) Were there any major differences between Ford and its European rivals? What conclusion can you draw from this?

Singapore

Singapore is an island city-state that is located at the southern tip of the Malay Peninsula. The small country covers 239 square miles and is connected by train across the Johore Strait to West Malaysia in the north. The Straight of Malacca to the south separates Singapore from the Indonesian island of Sumatra. There are approximately 4 million people in Singapore, resulting in a population density per square mile of almost 18,000 people. About three-fourths of Singaporeans are of Chinese descent, 15 percent are Malays, and the remainder are Indian and European. The gross domestic product of this thriving country is over $95 billion, and per-capita GDP is around $24,000. One of the so-called newly industrialized countries or Four Tigers (along with Korea, Taiwan, and Hong Kong), Singapore in recent years has been affected by the economic uncertainty around the world, but the currency and prices have remained relatively stable. The very clean and modern city remains as the major commercial and shipping center of Southeast Asia. The government of this former British colony consists of a cabinet headed by Prime Minister Goh Chok Tong and a parliament of 81 members, who are elected by universal suffrage.

For the last 6 months, the Madruga Corporation of Cleveland has been producing small electronic toys in Singapore. The small factory has been operated by local managers, but Madruga now wants to expand the Singapore facilities as well as integrate more expatriate managers into the operation. The CEO explained: "We do not want to run this plant as if it were a foreign subsidiary under the direct control of local managers. It is our plant and we want an on-site presence. Over the last year we have been staffing our Canadian and European operations with headquarters personnel, and we are now ready to turn attention to our Singapore operation." Before doing so, however, the company intends to conduct some on-site research to learn the most effective way of managing the Singapore personnel. In particular, the Madruga management team is concerned with how to motivate the Singaporeans and make them more productive. One survey has already been conducted among the Singapore personnel; this study found a great deal of similarity with the workers at the U.S. facilities. Both the Singapore and U.S. employees expressed a preference for job content factors such as the chance for growth, achievement, and increased responsibility, and they listed money and job security toward the bottom of the list of things they looked for in a job.

Madruga management is intrigued by these findings and believes that it might be possible to use some of the same motivation approaches in Singapore as it does in the United States. Moreover, one of the researchers sent the CEO a copy of an article showing that people in Singapore have weak uncertainty avoidance and a general cultural profile that is fairly similar to that of the United States. The CEO is not sure what all this means, but she does know that motivating workers in Singapore apparently is not as "foreign" a process as she thought it would be.

www.sg

Questions

1. What are some current issues facing Singapore? What is the climate for doing business in Singapore today?

2. Based on the information in this case, determine the specific things that seem to motivate human resources in Singapore.

3. Would a knowledge of the achievement motive be of any value to the expatriate managers who are assigned to the Singapore operation?

4. If you were using Figure 13–5 to help explain how to motivate Singapore human resources effectively, what conclusions could you draw that would help provide guidelines for the Madruga management team?

Motivation Is the Key

Over the last 5 years, Corkley & Finn, a regional investment brokerage house, has been extremely profitable. Some of its largest deals have involved cooperation with investment brokers in other countries. Realizing that the world economy is likely to grow vigorously over the next 25 years, the company has decided to expand its operations and open overseas branches. In the beginning, the company intends to work in cooperation with other local brokerages; however, the company believes that within 5 years, it will have garnered enough business to break away and operate independently. For the time being, the firm intends to set up a small office in London and another in Tokyo.

The firm plans on sending four people to each of these offices and recruiting the remainder of the personnel from the local market. These new branch employees will have to spend time meeting potential clients and building trust. This will be followed by the opportunity to put together small financial deals and, it is hoped, much larger ones over time.

The company is prepared to invest whatever time or money is needed to make these two branches successful. "What we have to do," the president noted, "is establish an international presence and then build from there. We will need to hire people who are intensely loyal to us and use them as a cadre for expanding operations and becoming a major player in the international financial arena. One of our most important challenges will be to hire the right people and motivate them to do the type of job we want and stay with us. After all, if we bring in people and train them how to do their jobs well and then they don't perform or they leave, all we've done is spend a lot of money for nothing and provide on-the-job training for our competitors. In this business, our people are the most important asset, and clients most often are swayed toward doing business with an investment broker with whom they think they can have a positive working relationship. The reputation of the firm is important, but it is always a function of the people who work there. Effective motivation of our people is the key to our ultimate success in these new branches."

Questions

1. In motivating the personnel in London and Tokyo, would the company find that the basic hierarchical needs of the workers were the same? Why or why not?

2. How could an understanding of the two-factor theory of motivation be of value in motivating the personnel at both of these locations? Would hygiene factors be more important to one of these groups than to the other? Would there be any difference in terms of the importance of motivators?

3. Using Figure 13-5 as a point of reference, what recommendation would you make regarding how to motivate the personnel in London? In Tokyo? Are there any significant differences between the two? If so, what are they? If not, why not?

Chapter 14

Leadership Across Cultures

Objectives of the Chapter

Leadership often is credited for the success or failure of international operations. Note that like the other topics discussed so far, effective leadership styles and practices in one culture are not necessarily effective in others. For example, the leadership approach used by effective U.S. managers would not necessarily be the same as that employed in other parts of the world. Even within the same country, effective leadership tends to be very situation-specific; however, also like the other areas studied in international management, certain leadership styles and practices transcend international boundaries. This chapter examines these leadership differences and similarities.

First the basic foundation for the study of leadership is reviewed. Next, leadership in various parts of the world, including Europe, East Asia, the Middle East, and developing countries, is examined. The specific objectives of this chapter are:

1. **DESCRIBE** the basic philosophic foundation and styles of managerial leadership.

2. **EXAMINE** the attitudes of European managers toward leadership practices.

3. **COMPARE** and **CONTRAST** leadership styles in Japan with those in the United States.

4. **REVIEW** leadership approaches in China, the Middle East, and developing countries.

5. **EXAMINE** recent findings regarding universalism in leadership.

6. **DISCUSS** the relationship of culture clusters and leader behavior on effective leadership practices.

BusinessWeek

The World of *Business Week*

Defiant Daimler

Jürgen E. Schrempp is exasperated. The athletic ceo of DaimlerChrysler is a risk-taker who always trusts his instincts—in the African bush or in the boardroom. To him, the need for bold moves is so evident that it's annoying when investors question his strategy. So when asked by reporters why he didn't stick to the high-margin luxury segment Daimler knows best—powerful Mercedes-Benz cars—he springs out of his chair to explain. On a blackboard, he draws a big rectangle that represents the luxury-car market and then begins: "Let's say you only made Mercedes S- or E-Class cars with very high margins. And there you would live peacefully forever because no one would attack you? What nonsense! Everyone's moving into that segment. Everyone." That, he explains, is why he bought Chrysler: to outflank his rivals before they outflanked him.

These days, however, Schrempp must spend much of his time defending himself and his aggressive expansion strategy. Since Daimler-Benz merged with Chrysler in November, 1998, the stock has plunged. While the luxury Mercedes-Benz Div. is humming along, Chrysler is experiencing one setback after another.

Crazy Discounts

That's not what investors had in mind when they endorsed the merger. They wanted to see payoffs from synergy, runaway hit models, and a supremely capable management from the German-American fusion. Instead, they've got a Chrysler that's discounting like crazy just to move the metal. Meanwhile, Schrempp's new Japanese partner, Mitsubishi Motors Corp., is losing money hand over fist, while Hyundai Motor in South Korea, Schrempp's newest auto alliance, is wracked by family feuds.

Yet just two years ago, Schrempp was flying high. Almost single-handedly, he engineered the biggest industrial merger ever when his Daimler-Benz swallowed No. 3 U.S. auto maker Chrysler Corp. The watershed deal set off a wave of consolidation in the automotive industry and signaled that German companies were prepared to play aggressively on the world stage. Inside Germany, it marked the beginnings of a shift from traditional bureaucratic capitalism to market-based competition.

Schrempp epitomized the changes. He had transformed Daimler-Benz from a money-losing mess when he took the top job in 1995 to a company with $5.7 billion in profits in 1998. He liked to test his top deputies' allegiance to shareholder value by quizzing them without warning on the company's share price. In an early spot check, eight of the managers he phoned couldn't even offer an answer, and two got it wrong.

Today, the same guys would get it right. But nobody—not Schrempp, his managers, or his shareholders—is happy with the answer. Schrempp complains that investors just don't get it: "The merger is judged on the basis of the stock price, which I appreciate is not where it should be. But that's not the point. The point is, we are a solid company."

It's a message that's not getting through. Since the $36 billion Chrysler merger, Schrempp has articulated a grand vision for the group to compete in every segment of every major market. And he's well on his way to putting the pieces in place.

Moving downmarket into small and midsize cars is at the heart of Schrempp's strategy. He is committed to the tiny Smart car. He established a foothold in Asia by acquiring stakes in Japan's Mitsubishi Motors and Korea's Hyundai Motor for $2.4 billion. Next he wants to expand into auto insurance and other services. "We have the whole spectrum of products, and we're the most technologically intensive car company in the world," Schrempp says.

Schrempp flogs this vision to investors tirelessly. One former insider recounts how Schrempp rehearsed for two days for the first DaimlerChrysler annual meeting. "Nothing he does is by accident," says this former executive.

The big question: Can Schrempp the dealmaker earn his stripes as Schrempp the manager? The 55-year-old native of Freiburg rose through the Daimler ranks buying, closing, or selling businesses based on his gut instincts. But it's one thing to put four carmakers together, and another to run them. BMW gave up this year on its six-year-old British acquisition, Rover, and dumped it. It took Ford Motor Co. a decade to get Jaguar in shape.

Schrempp's idea is to win by leveraging Daimler-Chrysler's excellent but costly technology across a much larger range of products. "Everything that you see in technology in cars has been invented here—everything," he says. Daimler-Benz' recent innovations

409

include night-vision and anticollision radar systems but it's fuel-cell engines that Schrempp sees as the next big thing. Fuel-cell cars are powered by electric engines that can run on clean fuels such as hydrogen. The shift to hydrogen will take decades, but Schrempp and his team figure the mammoth costs involved will completely vindicate the logic of the DaimlerChrysler merger.

Rocky

But has it really been a merger in the full sense? The promise of the deal was to save nearly $3 billion a year from achieving huge efficiencies in purchasing and technology sharing—everything a global company can do. But right now, a real, synergy-producing merger between the two giant companies seems to have stalled.

The Daimler-Chrysler marriage has been rocky from the start. Cultural differences between the Germans and Americans proved difficult to overcome. Little wonder, then, that in September, 1999, Schrempp decided it was best to let Chrysler and Mercedes operate as separate business units. That may have smoothed ruffled feathers, but it suddenly diluted the benefits of the merger. Says the ex-president of the U.S. operation, Thomas T. Stallkamp, himself a casualty of the culture wars: "Obviously, when you run a company as [separate] business units, you do redundant things, and you can't run as efficiently as when you put things together."

Insiders say big synergies will come with time. "You don't just instantly have everything combined," says Holden. "There's a lot going on behind the scenes." Through a joint Automotive Council, engineers are already collaborating. They meet quarterly to compare product designs and look for components that could be shared. "That is where the money lies, and [it's] how you should run a company," says Schrempp.

Schrempp also already has a model for global integration: the Mercedes truck division, which has increased its margins despite harsh market conditions. Mercedes' Freightliner unit has skillfully absorbed Ford's heavy-truck business, with Stuttgart coordinating the sharing of engines, transmissions, and axles. "The important thing is to integrate activities around the world," says truck boss Dieter Zetsche.

Schrempp's executives have made a start at duplicating Zetsche's efforts. Chrysler and Mercedes have started combining their research and development operations for key technologies such as fuel cells. Last year, Mercedes began building its M-Class sport-utility vehicle in Chrysler's plant in Graz, Austria. Still, achieving synergies will take time. "Many things you can only implement in one generation of products, which takes four to five years," says Schrempp.

Too Pricey?

Yet investors gripe that Schrempp is not forthcoming enough about the merger's synergies. After announcing that DaimlerChrysler had saved $1.4 billion in 1999, the first full year of the merger, through joint purchasing of steel and other commodities, Schrempp says he will no longer disclose any information on synergies because it is now one company. "DaimlerChrysler's unwillingness to break out synergies creates the impression that they're not coming through at the anticipated rate," says Christian Breitsprecher, an auto analyst at Deutsche Bank.

The friction of the merger has certainly sent many Chrysler middle managers fleeing. Most senior executives retired shortly after the merger anyway, but what really hurt was the defection of several highly regarded engineers and manufacturing executives. The latest executive preparing to leave: Treasurer Thomas Capo. Yet Holden says the atmosphere has improved lately. "The fear of the Germans is gone." Schrempp himself, at Holden's request, is regularly holding "town hall" meetings with Chrysler employees.

A series of hits would do plenty to wipe away the anxiety about the merger. The red-hot PT Cruiser is a good start. And this fall, Chrysler will release a stream of new cars and trucks, including a new generation of minivans and a new family of midsize sedans and coupes. "The pipeline is still so full that their lineup will remain one of the freshest on the market," says John Casesa, an analyst at Merrill Lynch & Co.

DaimlerChrysler has little flags in all the right places—the U.S., Europe, and Asia. But managing its Asian partnerships will be tricky. Mitsubishi President Katsuhiko Kawasoe insists on running his operations independently, while DaimlerChrysler has three board members and only two senior management posts. Schrempp does not, he says, want to trigger the same "fears and anxieties" at Mitsubishi that were aroused at Chrysler.

Handling Chrysler, cajoling Asian partners, developing a new engine technology, building a world-beating small car: These tasks would tax the best manager in the world. Schrempp manages this raft of tasks in this way: communication, confrontation, and competition. He values personal contact with senior managers, logging 600 hours of flight time last year. A former Daimler executive says Schrempp likes to play people off each other: "For almost everything, there's a red team and a green team—with the guys competing against each other. That can drive you crazy."

To date, no one has used the stock's tumble and Chrysler's woes to challenge Schrempp. He still seems to have the support of the supervisory board. "There's probably no other company in the car industry that performs as well and is rated so badly in the stock market as DaimlerChrysler," says one supervisory board member. The question persists, though: How many operations can he actually merge?

For his part, though, Schrempp has no doubts: "Our message will change the market's perception into the right one . . . DaimlerChrysler is a unique company, uniquely positioned." Supremely confident, as always. But if Jürgen Schrempp fails, he will be remembered as the man who mangled the world's most prestigious carmaker and a cherished American brand.

By Christine Tierney, Matt Karnitschnig, and Joann Muller,
with Rafael Mrowczynski in Stuttgart, Ken Belson in
Tokyo, Moon Ihlwan in Seoul, and bureau reports

Source: Reprinted from August 7, 2000, pp. 90–94 of *Business Week* by special permission, copyright © 2000 by the McGraw-Hill Companies, Inc.

This opening news story provides an excellent example of the challenges of global leadership. In the auto industry, over the last decade, there have been a number of mergers and acquisitions by Ford, General Motors, and Volkswagen, to name but three. Daimler did not want these competitors to gain an important step on it by picking up auto firms that could round out their line and/or give them entrée to new markets. So Daimler's acquisition of Chrysler was important, as was taking an equity position in Mitsubishi. While this strategy can be very useful in ensuring Daimler's future competitiveness, however, it has also created problems. Chrysler's operations are in the red and Schrempp is having trouble straightening things out. As the story noted, Daimler may have bought in just as Chrysler was about to have major problems. So much of what has been going wrong may have nothing to do with Schrempp's leadership. On the other hand, it is his job to correct the situation and get both major auto units of DaimlerChrysler into the profit column. In doing this, a great deal of attention has been focused on Schrempp's style of leadership. Is he too authoritarian? Does he know how to deal effectively with American managers and workers? Is the style that has worked well for him in Europe going to be as useful in the U.S.? Additionally, what about Mitsubishi? With such a large equity position, DaimlerChrysler will have a lot to say about what happens at Mitsubishi Motors. Will Schrempp be able to integrate this Japanese company into his MNC's worldwide strategy? These questions all raise issues that will be addressed in this chapter from the types of leadership styles that work best in different cultures to the possibility of using one style worldwide. We begin our investigation of leadership by looking at its basic foundations.

■ Foundation for Leadership

Leadership
The process of influencing people to direct their efforts toward the achievement of some particular goal or goals.

When one realizes that much of history, political science, and the behavioral sciences is either directly or indirectly concerned with leadership, the statement that more concern and research has focused on leadership than on any other topic becomes believable. With all this attention over the years, however, there still is no generally agreed-on definition, let alone sound answers to which approach is more effective than others in the international arena. For present purposes, however, **leadership** can be defined as the process of influencing people to direct their efforts toward achievement of some particular goal or goals.[1] Leadership is widely recognized as being very important in the study of international management, but relatively little effort has gone to systematically studying and comparing leadership approaches throughout the world. Most international research efforts on leadership have been directed toward a specific country or geographic area.

The following two comparative areas provide a foundation for understanding leadership in the international arena: (1) the philosophic grounding of how leaders view their subordinates; and (2) leadership approaches as reflected through use of autocratic-participative characteristics and behaviors of leaders. The philosophies and approaches used in the United States often are quite different from those employed by leaders in overseas organizations, although these differences often are not as pronounced as is commonly believed.

Philosophic Background: Theories X and Y

One primary reason that leaders behave as they do is their philosophy or beliefs regarding how to direct their subordinates most effectively. Managers who believe their people are naturally lazy and work only for money will use a leadership style that is different from those who believe their people are self-starters and enjoy challenge and increased responsibility. Douglas McGregor, the pioneering leadership theorist, labeled these two sets of philosophic assumptions with the terms "Theory X" and "Theory Y."

Theory X manager
A manager who believes that people are basically lazy and that coercion and threats of punishment often are necessary to get them to work.

A **Theory X manager** believes that people are basically lazy and that coercion and threats of punishment must be used to get them to work. The specific philosophic assumptions of Theory X leaders are:

1. By their very nature, people do not like to work and will avoid it whenever possible.
2. Workers have little ambition, try to avoid responsibility, and like to be directed.
3. The primary need of employees is job security.
4. To get people to attain organizational objectives, it is necessary to use coercion, control, and threats of punishment.[2]

Theory Y manager
A manager who believes that under the right conditions people not only will work hard but will seek increased responsibility and challenge.

A **Theory Y manager** believes that under the right conditions, people not only will work hard but seek increased responsibility and challenge. In addition, a great deal of creative potential basically goes untapped, and if these abilities can be tapped, workers will provide much higher quantity and quality of output. The specific philosophic assumptions of Theory Y leaders are:

1. The expenditure of physical and mental effort at work is as natural to people as resting or playing.
2. External control and threats of punishment are not the only ways of getting people to work toward organizational objectives. If people are committed to the goals, they will exercise self-direction and self-control.
3. Commitment to objectives is determined by the rewards that are associated with their achievement.
4. Under proper conditions, the average human being learns not only to accept but to seek responsibility.

5. The capacity to exercise a relatively high degree of imagination, ingenuity, and creativity in the solution of organizational problems is widely distributed throughout the population.

6. Under conditions of modern industrial life, the intellectual potential of the average human being is only partially tapped.[3]

The reasoning behind these beliefs, however, will vary by culture. U.S. managers believe that to motivate workers, it is necessary to satisfy their higher-order needs. This is done best through a Theory Y leadership approach. In China, Theory Y managers act similarly—but for different reasons. After the 1949 revolution, two types of managers emerged: Experts and Reds. The Experts focused on technical skills and primarily were Theory X advocates. The Reds, skilled in the management of people and possessing political and ideologic expertise, were Theory Y advocates. The Reds also believed that the philosophy of Chairman Mao supported their thinking (i.e., all employees had to rise together both economically and culturally). Therefore, both U.S. and Chinese managers support Theory Y, but for very different reasons.[4]

The same is true in the case of Russian managers. In a survey conducted by Puffer, McCarthy, and Naumov, 292 Russian managers were asked about their beliefs regarding work.[5] Table 14–1 shows the six different groupings of the responses. The results, reported in Table 14–2, clearly indicates that some Russian managers endorsed certain beliefs about work more than others. In particular, top-level executives scored higher on organizational beliefs and lower on both participation and Marxist-related beliefs than did other managers. Additionally, managers 40 years of age or older had stronger agreement than those in their twenties and thirties regarding work ethic beliefs and the importance of leisure. Also, as shown in Table 14–2, women more strongly endorsed humanistic, participative, leisure, and Marxist-related beliefs than did men.

Drawing together the findings of the study, the researchers pointed out the importance of Westerners going beyond the stereotypes of Russian managers and learning more about the latters' beliefs, so that it is possible to be more effective in working with them as both employees as well as joint venture partners. Quite obviously, assuming that Russian managers are strict adherents of Theory X may be a common assumption, but it may also be an erroneous one.[6]

These philosophic assumptions of both the Chinese and Russian managers help to dictate the leadership approach that is used. They most easily are seen in behaviors used by managers, such as giving orders, getting and giving feedback, and creating an overall climate within which the work will be done.

Leadership Behaviors and Styles

Leader behaviors can be translated into three commonly recognized styles: (1) authoritarian; (2) paternalistic; and (3) participative. **Authoritarian leadership** is the use of work-centered behavior that is designed to ensure task accomplishment. As shown in Figure 14–1, this leader behavior typically involves the use of one-way communication from manager to subordinate. The focus of attention usually is on work progress, work procedures, and roadblocks that are preventing goal attainment. Although this leadership style often is effective in handling crises, some leaders employ it as their primary style regardless of the situation. It also is widely used by Theory X managers, who believe that a continued focus on the task is compatible with the kind of people they are dealing with. Many people believe this is Jurgen Schrempp's style in leading DaimlerChrysler (see the opening *Business Week* article). Given the situation he has been facing with Chrysler reporting massive annual losses and Mitsubishi Motors deeply in debt, it may well be the most effective style for dealing with this difficult situation.[7]

Paternalistic leadership uses work-centered behavior coupled with a protective employee-centered concern. This leadership style can be best summarized by the statement, "work hard and the company will take care of you." This approach was described in Figure

Authoritarian leadership
The use of work-centered behavior designed to ensure task accomplishment.

Paternalistic leadership
The use of work-centered behavior coupled with a protective employee-centered concern.

Table 14–1
Russian Managerial Beliefs about Work

A. **Humanistic Beliefs**
Work can be made meaningful.
One's job should give one a chance to try out new ideas.
The workplace can be humanized.
Work can be made satisfying.
Work should allow for the use of human capabilities.
Work can be a means of self-expression.
Work should enable one to learn new things.
Work can be organized to allow for human fulfillment.
Work can be made interesting rather than boring.
The job should be a source of new experiences.

B. **Organizational Beliefs**
Survival of the group is very important in an organization.
Working with a group is better than working alone.
It is best to have a job as part of an organization where all work together even if
    you don't get individual credit.
One should take an active part in all group affairs.
The group is the most important entity in any organization.
One's contribution to the group is the most important thing about one's work.
Work is a means to foster group interests.

C. **Work Ethic**
Only those who depend on themselves get ahead in life.
To be superior a person must stand alone.
A person can learn better on the job by striking out boldly on his own than by
    following the advice of others.
One must avoid dependence on other persons whenever possible.
One should live one's life independent of others as much as possible.

D. **Beliefs about Participation in Managerial Decisions**
The working classes should have more say in running society.
Factories would be better run if workers had more of a say in management.
Workers should be more active in making decisions about products, financing,
    and capital investment.
Workers should be represented on the board of directors of companies.

E. **Leisure Ethic**
The trend towards more leisure is not a good thing. (R)
More leisure time is good for people.
Increased leisure time is bad for society. (R)
Leisure time activities are more interesting than work.
The present trend towards a shorter workweek is to be encouraged.

F. **Marxist-Related Beliefs**
The free enterprise system mainly benefits the rich and powerful.
The rich do not make much of a contribution to society.
Workers get their fair share of the economic rewards of society. (R)
The work of the laboring classes is exploited by the rich for their own benefit.
Wealthy people carry their fair share of the burdens of life in this country. (R)
The most important work is done by the laboring classes.

Notes: 1. The survey is from Buchholz (1977).
2. Response scales ranged from 1 (strongly disagree) to 5 (strongly agree).
3. (R) denotes reverse-scoring items.
4. The 45-individual items contained in the 6 belief clusters were presented to respondents in a mixed fashion, rather than categorized by cluster as shown above.
5. Participation was a subset of Marxist-related values in Buchholz's original study, but was made a separate cluster in his later work.

Source: Adapted from Sheila M. Putter, Daniel J. McCarthy, and Alexander I. Naumov, "Russian Managers' Beliefs about Work: Beyond the Stereotypes," *Journal of World Business,* vol. 32, no. 3, 1997, p. 262.

> **Table 14–2**
> **Russian Beliefs about Work by Managerial Level, Age, and Gender**

Managerial Groups	Humanistic	Organi-zational	Work Ethic	Participation	Leisure	Marxist-Related
Total sample (n=292)	4.71	3.81	3.70	3.20	3.18	2.99
Managerial Levels						
Executives (n=110)	4.71	**3.95**	3.70	**3.03**	3.16	**2.91**
Other managers (n=177)	4.72	3.73	3.71	**3.26**	3.18	3.05
Age groups						
20–29 (n=106)	4.71	3.67	**3.68**	3.18	**3.04**	2.92
30–39 (n=87)	4.69	**3.73**	**3.61**	3.05	**3.18**	3.00
40+ (n=92)	4.75	**4.05**	**3.83**	3.33	**3.35**	3.09
Gender						
Men (n=171)	**4.67**	3.82	3.71	**3.08**	3.12	**2.90**
Women (n=116)	**4.77**	3.79	3.71	**3.34**	3.26	**3.12**

Notes: 1. Numbers in bold denote statistically significant differences within subgroups for a specific work value, as found in t-tests and analyses of variance. For example, executives rated organizational beliefs higher than did lower-level managers, while the latter group rated participation and Marxist-related beliefs higher. Significant differences were at the .05 level. Exceptions were Marxist-related beliefs for managerial level, and leisure ethic for gender, which were significant at the .10 level.
2. Standard deviations and alpha reliability coefficients for the total sample are: humanistic (.34 SD, .64 alpha), organizational (.66, .72), work ethic (.58, .43), participation (.90, .58), leisure ethic (.70, .66), and Marxist (.61, .45).
3. In addition to the above findings, analyses of variance found a significant 3-way interaction for participation, such that women over age 40 in nonexecutive managerial positions were the strongest reporters of worker participation in decision making.
Source: Adapted from Sheila M. Puffer, Daniel J. McCarthy, and Alexander I. Naumov, "Russian Managers' Beliefs about Work: Beyond the Stereotypes," *Journal of World Business,* vol. 32, no. 3, 1997, p. 263.

13–5 and perhaps is best supported by cultures such as those found in Japan. Paternalistic leaders expect everyone to work hard; in turn, the employees will be guaranteed employment and given security benefits such as medical and retirement programs. Paternalistic leaders often are referred to as "soft" Theory X leaders because of their strong emphasis on strictly controlling their employees coupled with concern for their welfare. They often treat their employees as strict but caring parents would their children. A good example was provided by the chairman of the Daewoo Motor Company of Korea, who recently laid off thousands of employees. Having made this decision, the chairman then went throughout the company apologizing for having to take such drastic action and telling each person that he was determined to help them find another job. When asked about his approach, he said, "I'm the father of my employees. I need to bring back hope to everyone."[8]

One way of contrasting authoritative and paternalistic leaders is in terms of Likert's management systems or leadership styles, as presented in Table 14–3. As shown, an authoritarian leader is characterized by Likert's system 1, and a paternalistic leader is characterized by system 2.

Participative leadership is the use of both a work-centered and people-centered approach. Participative leaders typically encourage their people to play an active role in assuming control of their work, and authority commonly is highly decentralized. In terms of Likert's four systems shown in Table 14–3, participative leaders are characterized by system 3. (Likert's system 4 leaders are fully democratic and go beyond the participative style.) Another way of characterizing participative leaders is in terms of the managerial grid, which

Participative leadership
The use of both a work- or task-centered and people-centered approach to leading subordinates.

Figure 14–1

Leader-Subordinate Interactions

One-way downward flow of information and influence from authoritarian leader to subordinates.

Continual interaction and exchange of information and influence between leader and subordinates.

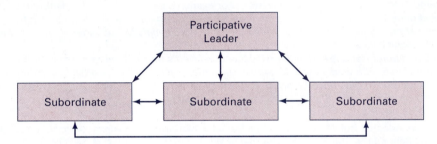

Continual interaction and exchange of information and influence between leader and subordinates.

Source: Adapted from Richard M. Hodgetts, *Modern Human Relations at Work,* 8th ed. (Fort Worth: Houghton, 2002), p. 264.

is a traditional, well-known method of identifying leadership style. As shown in Figure 14–2, participative leaders are on the 9,9 position of the grid. This is in contrast to paternalistic leaders, who tend to be about 9,5 and autocratic leaders, who are more of a 9,1 position on the grid. Participative leadership is very popular in many technologically advanced countries. Such leadership has been widely espoused in the United States, England, and other Anglo countries, and it currently is very popular in Scandinavian countries as well. For example, at General Electric, managers are encouraged to use a participative style that delivers on commitment and shares the values of the firm, which is an approach that also is common in these other nations. The accompanying box, "International Management in Action: Welch Led the Way," provides some additional insights regarding how former CEO Jack Welch put his own brand of leadership on General Electric. The remainder of the chapter gives more details and research results relating leadership styles by country and area of the world.

■ Leadership in the International Context

How do leaders in other countries attempt to direct or influence their subordinates? Are their approaches similar to those used in the United States? Research shows that there are both similarities and differences. Most international research on leadership has focused on Europe, East Asia, the Middle East, and on developing countries such as India, Peru, Chile, and Argentina.

Table 14–3
Likert's Systems or Styles of Leadership

Leadership Characteristic	System 1 (Exploitive Autocratic)	System 2 (Benevolent Autocratic)	System 3 (Participative)	System 4 (Democratic)
Leadership processes used (extent to which superiors have confidence and trust in subordinates)	Have no confidence and trust in subordinates	Have condescending confidence and trust, such as master has in servant	Substantial but not complete confidence and trust, still wish to keep control of decisions	Complete confidence and trust in all matters
Character of motivational forces (underlying motives tapped)	Physical security, economic needs, and some use of the desire for status	Economic needs and moderate use of ego motives (e.g., desire for status, affiliation, and achievement)	Economic needs and considerable use of ego and other major motives (e.g., desire for new experiences)	Full use of economic, ego, and other major motives such as motivational forces arising from group goals
Character of communication process (amount of interaction and communication aimed at achieving organization's objectives)	Very little	Little	Quite a bit	Much, with both individuals and groups
Character of interaction influence process (amount and character of interaction)	Little interaction and always with fear and distrust	Little interaction and usually with some condescension by superiors; fear and caution by subordinates	Moderate interaction, often with fair amount of confidence and trust	Extensive friendly interaction with high degree of confidence and trust
Character of decision-making process (at what level in organization are decisions formally made)	Bulk of decisions at top of organization	Policy at top; many decisions with prescribed framework made at lower levels but usually checked with top before action is taken	Broad policy decision at top; more specific decisions of lower levels	Decision making widely done throughout organization, although well integrated through linking process provided by overlapping groups
Character of goal setting or ordering (manner in which usually done)	Orders issued	Orders issued, opportunity to comment may exist	Goals are set or orders issued after discussion with subordinates of problems and planned action	Except in emergencies, goals are usually established by group participation

Source: Adapted from Rensis Likert, *The Human Organization* (New York: McGraw-Hill, 1967). Used with permission.

Figure 14–2

The Managerial Grid

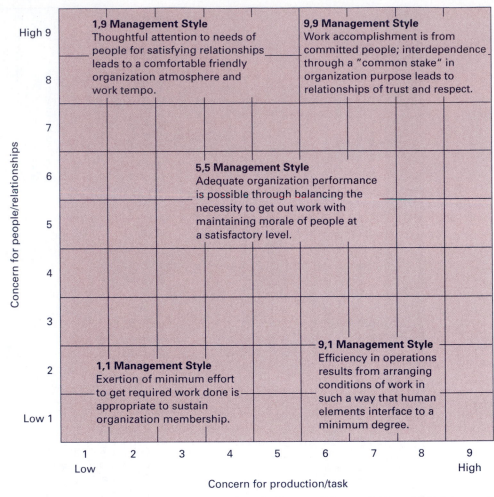

Source: Adapted from Robert S. Blake and Jane S. Mouton, "Managerial Facades," *Advanced Management Journal,* July 1966, p. 31.

Attitudes of European Managers Toward Leadership Practices

In recent years, much research has been directed at leadership approaches in Europe. Most effort has concentrated on related areas, such as decision making, risk-taking, strategic planning, and organization design, that have been covered in previous chapters. Some of this previous discussion is relevant to an understanding of leadership practices in Europe. For example, British managers tend to use a highly participative leadership approach. This is true for two reasons: (1) the political background of the country favors such an approach; and (2) because most top British managers are not highly involved in the day-to-day affairs of the business, they prefer to delegate authority and let much of the decision making be handled by middle- and lower-level managers. This preference contrasts sharply with that of the French and the Germans,[9] who prefer a more work-centered, authoritarian approach. In fact, if labor unions did not have legally mandated seats on the boards of directors, participative management in Germany likely would be even less pervasive than it is, a problem that currently confronts firms like Volkswagen that are trying to reduce sharply their overhead to meet increasing competition in Europe.[10] Scandinavian countries, however, make wide use of participative leadership approaches, with worker representation on the boards of directors and high management–worker interaction regarding workplace design and changes.

As a general statement, most evidence indicates that European managers tend to use a participative approach. They do not entirely subscribe to Theory Y philosophical assumptions, however, because an element of Theory X thinking continues. This was made clear by the now-classic Haire, Ghiselli, and Porter study of 3641 managers from 14 countries.[11]

International Management in Action

Welch Led the Way

When Jack Welch became chief executive officer of General Electric in 1981, the company had a market value of $12 billion. When he retired 20 years later, the firm's market value was in excess of $300 billion. His leadership and effectiveness in running the firm resulted in a host of accolades. One leading management writer called him "the greatest corporate leader of the 20th century," and in Japan, for example, his leadership concepts are still used as examples to be followed. In the latter case, what is particularly interesting is that many Japanese firms do not subscribe to all of his ideas. For example, most are very reluctant to cut their workforces or sell losing businesses, something that Welch espoused and did not hesitate to do regardless of the fact that some people might be hurt in the process. In fact, when he was once asked by a Japanese interviewer if getting rid of losing businesses was not the cruelest form of management, he replied, "God almighty, do you want to go in and watch people with their heads down, no smiling, working in hopeless situations. That is crazy! That's not culture, that's not kindness; that's cruelty." Few people who have studied Welch's leadership style believe he was cruel. In fact, his approach resulted in outstanding success for GE year after year. Why? Because he did a series of critical things very well.

First, he believed that effective leaders kept their customers happy. For him this meant doing whatever was necessary to meet client needs. As a result of this emphasis, GE significantly reduced its bureaucracy and streamlined operations. In the process, the company created an "informal" enterprise in which communications now flow in an unfettered manner and departments and units cooperate in an almost "boundaryless" enterprise. Result: worldwide teamwork.

Second, closely coupled with this emphasis on customers was consideration of employee satisfaction and cash flow. Welch continually contended that a leader needs to focus on just three areas of information: customer feedback, employee feedback, and cash flow. If the customers like the goods and services they are receiving, the employees are pleased with their work environment, and there is enough money to keep the doors open—the leaders are doing a good job.

Another of Welch's leadership beliefs was that managers have to focus on developing three things in their followers: speed, simplicity, and self-confidence. People have to work faster because speed is critical to worldwide success. Employees also have to learn how to do their job simply and correctly, so that greater speed is possible. Finally, employees have to be confident of their own abilities because this is the ultimate key to success.

In getting his managers to do these things, Welch set out a vision and used himself as the model for achieving it. Those who worked for him emulated his style and approach and, in turn, so did their subordinates. So there was consistency of leadership throughout the organization. This also included the way managers rewarded their personnel. Welch believed strongly in differentiated pay. People who do the best job should get the biggest rewards. Under his leadership, gone were the days when everyone who did well would get a 5 percent raise. Noted one observer:

> Although GE set an overall 4% salary increase as a target last year, base salaries can rise by as much as 25% in a year without a promotion. Cash bonuses can increase as much as 150% in a year, to between 20% and 70% of base pay. Stock options, once reserved for the most senior officers at GE, have been broadly expanded under Welch. Now, some 27,000 employees get them, nearly a third of GE's professional employees. More than 1,200 employees, including over 800 below the level of senior management, have received options that are now worth over $1 million.

Many observers believe that what made Welch most successful was that his ideas transcended national boundaries. Bureaucracy-bashing is as useful to operations in Toledo, Ohio as they are in Toledo, Spain. Leaders who are successful in achieving high customer and employee satisfaction ratings in Paris, France are as effective as those who do this in Paris, Texas. The criteria by which effective leaders must be measured remains the same and, as a result, Welch's ideas work just as well in Athens, Georgia as they do in Athens, Greece.

(The motivation-related findings of this study were reported in the previous chapter.) The leadership-related portion of this study sought to determine whether these managers were basically traditional (Theory X, or system 1/2) or democratic-participative (Theory Y, or system 3/4) in their approach. Specifically, the researchers investigated four areas relevant to leadership:

1. *Capacity for leadership and initiative.* Does the leader believe that employees prefer to be directed and have little ambition (Theory X), or that characteristics such as initiative can be acquired by most people regardless of their inborn traits and abilities (Theory Y)?

2. *Sharing information and objectives.* Does the leader believe that detailed, complete instructions should be given to subordinates and that subordinates need only this information to do their jobs, or does the leader believe that general directions are sufficient and that subordinates can use their initiative in working out the details?

3. *Participation.* Does the leader support participative leadership practices?

4. *Internal control.* Does the leader believe that the most effective way to control employees is through rewards and punishment or that employees respond best to internally generated control?

Overall Results of Research on Attitudes of European Managers   Responses by managers to the four areas covered in the Haire, Ghiselli, and Porter study, as noted in the last chapter, are quite dated, but these responses still are the most comprehensive available and are relevant to the current discussion of leadership similarities and differences. The specifics by country may have changed somewhat over the years, but the leadership processes revealed should not be out of date. The clusters of countries studied by these researchers are shown in Table 14–4. Results indicate that none of the leaders from various parts of the world, on average, were very supportive of the belief that individuals have a capacity for leadership and initiative. The researchers put it this way: "In each country, in each group of countries, in all of the countries taken together, there is a relatively low opinion of the capabilities of the average person, coupled with a relatively positive belief in the necessity for democratic-type supervisory practices."[12]

An analysis of standard scores compared each cluster of countries against the others, and it revealed that Anglo leaders tend to have more faith in the capacity of their people for leadership and initiative than do the other clusters. They also believe that sharing information and objectives is important; however, when it comes to participation and internal control, the Anglo group tends to give relatively more autocratic responses than all the other clusters except developing countries. Interestingly, Anglo leaders reported a much stronger belief in the value of external rewards (pay, promotion, etc.) than did any of the clusters except that of the developing countries. These findings clearly illustrate that attitudes toward leadership practices tend to be quite different in various parts of the world.

The Role of Level, Size, and Age on European Managers' Attitudes toward Leadership   The research of Haire and associates provided important additional details within each cluster of European countries. These findings indicated that in some countries, higher-level managers tended to express more democratic values than lower-level managers; however, in other countries, the opposite was true. For example, in England, higher-level managers responded with more democratic attitudes on all four leadership dimensions, whereas in the United States, lower-level managers gave more democratically oriented

Table 14–4
Clusters of Countries in the Haire, Ghiselli, and Porter Study

NORDIC-EUROPEAN COUNTRIES	ANGLO-AMERICAN COUNTRIES
Denmark	England
Germany	United States
Norway	
Sweden	
	DEVELOPING COUNTRIES
LATIN-EUROPEAN COUNTRIES	Argentina
	Chile
Belgium	India
France	
Italy	JAPAN
Spain	

responses on all four. In the Scandinavian countries, higher-level managers tended to respond more democratically; in Germany, lower-level managers tended to have more democratic attitudes.

Company size also tended to influence the degree of participative-autocratic attitudes. There was more support among managers in small firms than in large ones regarding the belief that individuals have a capacity for leadership and initiative; however, respondents from large firms were more supportive of sharing information and objectives, participation, and use of internal control.

There were findings that age also had some influence on participative attitudes. Younger managers were more likely to have democratic values when it came to capacity for leadership and initiative and to sharing information and objectives, although on the other two areas of leadership practices older and younger managers differed little. In terms of specific countries, however, some important differences were found. For example, younger managers in both the United States and Sweden espoused more democratic values than their older counterparts; in Belgium, just the opposite was true.

Conclusion about European Leadership Practices   Data from the classic Haire and associates study show differences in the attitudes toward leadership practices between European managers. In most cases, these leaders tend to reflect more participative and democratic attitudes, but not in every country. In addition, organizational level, company size, and age seem to greatly influence attitudes toward leadership. Because many of the young people in this study now are middle-aged, European managers in general are highly likely to be more participative than their older counterparts of the 1960s and 1970s; however, no empirical evidence proves that each generation of European managers is becoming more participative than the previous one. Also, just because they express favorable attitudes toward participative leadership does not mean that they actually practice this approach, although it is certainly true that boards of directors of U.S. multinationals operating in Europe are becoming more international and that this multicultural mix may indeed promote participative management. More research that actually observes today's European managers' style in their day-to-day jobs is needed before any definitive conclusions can be drawn.

Japanese Leadership Approaches

Japan is well known for its paternalistic approach to leadership. As noted in the previous chapter's Figure 13–5, Japanese culture promotes a high safety or security need, which is present among home country-based employees as well as MNC expatriates. For example, one study examined the cultural orientations of 522 employees of 28 Japanese-owned firms in the United States and found that the native Japanese employees were more likely to value paternalistic company behavior than their U.S. counterparts.[13] Another study found that Koreans also value such paternalism.[14] However, major differences appear in leadership approaches used by the Japanese and those in other locales.

For example, the comprehensive Haire, Ghiselli, and Porter study found that Japanese managers have much greater belief in the capacity of subordinates for leadership and initiative than do managers in most other countries.[15] In fact, in the study, only managers in Anglo-American countries had stronger feelings in this area. The Japanese also expressed attitudes toward the use of participation to a greater degree than others. In the other two leadership areas, sharing information and objectives and using internal control, the Japanese respondents were above average but not distinctive. Overall, however, this classic study found that the Japanese respondents scored highest on the four areas of leadership combined. In other words, these findings provide evidence that Japanese leaders have considerable confidence in the overall ability of their subordinates and use a style that allows their people to actively participate in decisions.

In addition, the leadership process used by Japanese managers places a strong emphasis on ambiguous goals. Subordinates are typically unsure of what their manager wants them to do. As a result, they spend a great deal of time overpreparing their assignments. Some observers believe that this leadership approach is time-consuming and wasteful. However, it has a number of important benefits. One is that the leader is able to maintain stronger control of the followers because the latter do not know with certainty what is expected of them. So they prepare themselves for every eventuality. Second, by placing the subordinates in a position where they must examine a great deal of information, the manager ensures that the personnel are well prepared to deal with the situation and all of its ramifications. Third, the approach helps the leader maintain order and provide guidance, even when the leader is not as knowledgeable as the followers.

Two experts on the behavior of Japanese management have noted that salarymen (middle managers) survive in the organization by anticipating contingencies and being prepared to deal with them. So when the manager asks a question and the salaryman shows that he has done the research needed to answer the question, the middle manager also shows himself to be a reliable person. The leader does not have to tell the salaryman to be prepared; the individual knows what is expected of him.

> Japanese managers operate this way because they usually have less expertise in a division's day-to-day business than their subordinates do. It is the manager's job to maintain harmony, not to be a technical expert. Consequently, a senior manager doesn't necessarily realize that E, F, G, and H are important to know. He gives ambiguous directions to his subordinates so they can use their superior expertise to go beyond A, B, C, and D. One salaryman explained it this way: "When my boss asks me to write a report, I infer what he wants to know and what he needs to know without being told what he wants." Another interviewee added that subordinates who receive high performance evaluations are those who know what the boss wants without needing to be told. What frustrates Japanese managers about non-Japanese employees is the feeling that, if they tell such a person they want A through D, they will never extract E through H; instead, they'll get exactly what they asked for. Inferring what the boss would have wanted had he only known to ask is a tough game, but it is the one salarymen must play.[16]

Differences Between Japanese and U.S. Leadership Styles

In a number of ways, Japanese leadership styles differ from those in the United States. For example, the Haire and associates study found that except for internal control, large U.S. firms tend to be more democratic than small ones, whereas in Japan, the profile is quite different.[17] A second difference is that younger U.S. managers appear to express more democratic attitudes than their older counterparts on all four leadership dimensions, but younger Japanese fall into this category only for sharing information and objectives and in the use of internal control.[18] Simply put, evidence points to some similarities between U.S. and Japanese leadership styles, but major differences also exist.

A number of reasons have been cited for these differences. One of the most common is that Japanese and U.S. managers have a basically different philosophy of managing people. Table 14–5 provides a comparison of seven key characteristics that come from the work of William Ouchi, author of the widely recognized *Theory Z,* which combines Japanese and U.S. assumptions and approaches. Note in the table that the Japanese leadership approach is heavily group-oriented, paternalistic, and concerned with the employee's work and personal life. The U.S. leadership approach is almost the opposite.[19]

Another difference between Japanese and U.S. leadership styles is how senior-level managers process information and learn. Japanese executives are taught and tend to use **variety amplification,** which is the creation of uncertainty and the analysis of many alternatives regarding future action. By contrast, U.S. executives are taught and tend to use **variety reduction,** which is the limiting of uncertainty and the focusing of action on a limited number of alternatives.[20] Some specific characteristics of these two approaches, based on research by Sullivan and Nonaka, are shown in Table 14–6.

When this study of processing information and learning examined the leadership styles used by Japanese and U.S. senior managers, it found that the Japanese focused

Variety amplification
The creation of uncertainty and the analysis of many alternatives regarding future action.

Variety reduction
The limiting of uncertainty and the focusing of action on a limited number of alternatives.

Table 14–5
Japanese vs. U.S. Leadership Styles

Philosophical Dimension	Japanese Approach	U.S. Approach
Employment	Often for life; layoffs are rare	Usually short-term; layoffs are common
Evaluation and promotion	Very slow; big promotions may not come for the first 10 years	Very fast: those not quickly promoted often seek employment elsewhere
Career paths	Very general; people rotate from one area to another and become familiar with all areas of operations	Very specialized; people tend to stay in one area (accounting, sales, etc.) for their entire careers
Decision making	Carried out via group decision making	Carried out by the individual manager
Control mechanism	Very implicit and informal; people rely heavily on trust and goodwill	Very explicit; people know exactly what to control and how to do it
Responsibility	Shared collectively	Assigned to individuals
Concern for employees	Management's concern extends to the whole life, business and social, of the worker	Management concerned basically with the individual's work life only

Source: Adapted from William Ouchi, *Theory Z: How American Business Can Meet the Japanese Challenge* (Reading, MA: Addison-Wesley, 1981).

Table 14–6
Japanese and U.S. Senior Management Approaches to Processing Information

Japanese Senior Management Approach (Variety Amplification)	U.S. Senior Management Approach (Variety Reduction)
State a policy that all phenomena are relevant	State a policy that focuses only on relevant issues and sources of information
Require all employees to be identifiers of corporate problems and opportunities	Identify specific employees who will identify problems and opportunities
Seek a large quantity of information from the environment	Seek only high-quality information from the environment
State a desire for the firm to attain an idea—a dream	State a desire for the firm to attain a realistic level—a goal
Focus on creating challenges—barriers to hurdle and problems to solve	Focus on taking advantage of opportunities—holes in the barrier to crawl through
Vitalize people	Direct people

Source: Adapted from Jeremiah J. Sullivan and Ikujiro Nonaka, "The Application of Organizational Learning Theory to Japanese and American Management," *Journal of International Business Studies,* Fall 1986, pp. 130–131. Used with permission.

very heavily on problems while the U.S. managers focused on opportunities.[21] The Japanese were more willing to allow poor performance to continue for a time so that those who were involved would learn from their mistakes, but the Americans worked to stop poor performance as quickly as possible. Finally, the Japanese sought creative approaches to managing projects and tried to avoid relying on experience, but the Americans sought to build on their experiences.

Still another major reason accounting for differences in leadership styles is that the Japanese tend to be more ethnocentric than their U.S. counterparts. The Japanese think of themselves as Japanese managers who are operating overseas; most do not view themselves as international managers. As a result, even if they do adapt their leadership approach on the surface to that of the country in which they are operating, they still believe in the Japanese way of doing things and are reluctant to abandon it.

Similarities Between Japanese and U.S. Leadership Styles

Although differences exist and get considerable attention in both research and the popular media, important similarities in leadership approaches also exist between the Japanese and the Americans. For example, a somewhat dated, but still relevant, study examined the ways in which leadership style could be used to influence the achievement motivation of Japanese subjects.[22] Achievement motivation was measured among a series of participants, and two major groups were created: one consisted of Japanese high achievers, the other of Japanese low achievers. Four smaller groups of high-achieving participants and four more of low-achieving participants then were created. Each high-achieving group was assigned a supervisor who used a different leadership style. The same pattern was used with the low-achieving groups.

In each of the two major clusters (high achievers and low achievers), one group was assigned a leader who focused on performance (called "P supervision" in the study). The supervisor used a 9,1 (high on task, low on people) type of style on the managerial grid (see Figure 14–2, which identifies all the styles on the grid). This supervisor was work-centered, took the initiative in solving problems that impeded performance, and ensured that all rules were followed, exhorting the workers to "hurry up," "work more quickly," and "don't fool around; get to work." The supervisor also compared this group with the others, related how far behind they were, and pressed them to catch up.

In a second group within each major cluster, the supervisor's leadership style focused on maintaining and strengthening the group (called "M supervision" in the study). The individual used a 1,9 (low on task, high on people) leadership style on the managerial grid. The supervisor was open to suggestions, never pushed personal opinions on the workers, and encouraged a warm, friendly environment. This supervisor often said, "Let's be pleasant and cheerful," and "Let's be more friendly." The supervisor also was sympathetic when things did not go well and worked to improve interpersonal relations by reducing tensions and increasing the sociability of the environment.

In a third group within each major cluster, the supervisor focused on both performance and maintenance (called "PM supervision" in the study). This supervisor put pressure on the workers to do their work but, at the same time, offered encouragement and support to the workers. In other words, this supervisor used a 9,9 leadership style from the managerial grid.

In the fourth group within each major cluster, the supervisor focused on neither performance nor maintenance (called "pm supervision" in the study). This supervisor simply did not get very involved in either the task or the people side of the group being led. In other words, the supervisor used a 1,1 leadership style on the grid.

The results of these four leadership styles among the high-achieving and low-achieving groups are reported in Figures 14–3 and 14–4. In the high-achieving groups, the PM (or 9,9) leadership style that emphasized both the task and human dimension was the most effective throughout the entire experiment, and the pm (or 1,1) leadership style was consistently ineffective. The P (or 9,1 [high on task, low on people]) leadership style was the second most effective during the early and middle phases of the study, but it was supplanted by the M (or 1,9 [low on task, high on people]) leadership style in the later phases. Among the low-achieving groups, the P (or 9,1) supervision was most effective. The M (or 1,9) leadership style was the second most effective during the early sessions, but it soon tapered off and produced negative results in later sessions. The PM (or 9,9) style was moderately ineffective during the first three sessions but improved rapidly and was the second most effective by the end of the seventh session. The pm (or 1,1) leadership style was consistently effective until the fifth session, then productivity began to level off.

The results of this study are similar to those that would be expected among high- and low-achieving groups of U.S. managers. In addition, the study showed that high-achieving groups of Japanese tend to be more productive than low-achieving groups. Thus, this study shows some degree of convergence or similarity between Japanese and U.S. managers regarding the most effective types of leadership styles given the achievement motivation of the group members.

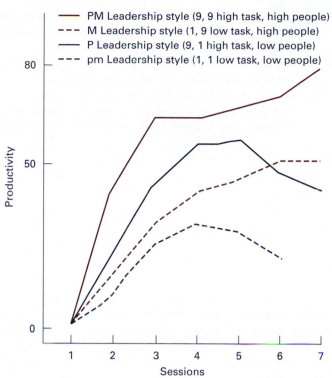

Figure 14–3

Productivity of Japanese Groups with High-Achievement Motivation under Different Leadership Styles

Source: Adapted from Jyuji Misumi and Fumiyasu Seki, "Effects of Achievement Motivation on the Effectiveness of Leadership Patterns," *Administrative Science Quarterly,* March 1971, p. 57. Used with permission.

Figure 14–4

Productivity of Japanese Groups with Low-Achievement Motivation under Different Leadership Styles

Source: Adapted from Jyuji Misumi and Fumiyasu Seki, "Effects of Achievement Motivation on the Effectiveness of Leadership Patterns, *Administrative Science Quarterly,* March 1971, p. 57. Used with permission.

Recent findings support these conclusions and suggest they can be extended to other countries as well. For example, in the United States the Saturn has proved to be one of General Motors' most successful new auto offerings. The approach used in managing workers in the Saturn plant is quite different from that employed in other GM plants. Strong attention is given to allowing workers a voice in all management decisions, and pay is linked to quality, productivity, and profitability. Japanese firms such as Sony use a similar approach, encouraging personnel to assume authority, use initiative, and work as a team. Major emphasis also is given to developing communication links between management and the employees and to encouraging people to do their best. Korean firms also are relying more heavily on a 9,9 leadership style. Sang Lee and associates have reported that among Korea's largest firms, a series of personality criteria are used in screening employees, and many of these directly relate to 9,9 leadership: harmonious relationships with others, creativeness, motivation to achieve, future orientation, and a sense of duty.[23]

Another common trend is the movement toward team orientation and away from individualism. The accompanying sidebar, "Global Teams," illustrates this point.

Leadership in China

In the past few years a growing amount of attention has been focused on leadership in China. In particular, international researchers are interested in learning if the country's economic progress is creating a new cadre of leaders whose styles are different from those of the past. In one of the most comprehensive studies to date, Ralston and his colleagues found that, indeed, a new generation of Chinese leaders are emerging and that they are somewhat different from those of the past in terms of work values.[24]

The researchers gathered data from a large number of managers and professionals ($n=869$) who were about to take part in management development programs. These individuals were part of what the researchers called the "New Generation" of Chinese organizational leaders. The researchers wanted to determine if this new generation of managers had the same work values as those of the "Current Generation" and "Older Generation" groups. In their investigation, the researchers focused their attention on the importance that the respondents assigned to three areas: individualism, collectivism, and Confucianism. Individualism was measured by the importance assigned to self-sufficiency and personal accomplishments. Collectivism was measured by the person's willingness to subordinate personal goals to those of the work group with an emphasis on sharing and group harmony. Confucianism was measured by the importance the respondent assigned to societal harmony, virtuous interpersonal behavior, and personal and interpersonal harmony.

The researchers found that the new generation group scored significantly higher on individualism than did the current and older generation groups. In addition, the new generation leaders scored significantly lower than the other two groups on collectivism and Confucianism. These values appear to reflect the period of relative openness and freedom, often called the "Social Reform Era," during which these new managers grew up. They have had greater exposure to western societal influences and this may well be resulting in leadership styles similar to those of western managers.

These research findings show that leadership is culturally influenced, but as the economy of China continues to change and the country moves more and more toward capitalism, the work values of managers may also change. As a result, the new generation of leaders may well use leadership styles similar to those in the West, something that has also occurred in Japan as seen by Figures 14–3 and 14–4.

Leadership in the Middle East

Research also has been conducted on Middle East countries to determine the similarities and differences in managerial attitudes toward leadership practices. For example, in a follow-up study to that of Haire and associates, mid-level managers from Arab countries were surveyed and found to have higher attitude scores for capacity for leadership and initiative than those from any of the other countries or clusters reported in Table 14–4.[25] The

---

International Management in Action

Global Teams

International leaders now put increasing focus on developing global teams that are capable of overcoming cultural barriers and working together in an efficient, harmonious manner. At Dallas-based Maxus Energy (a wholly owned subsidiary of YPF, the largest Argentinean corporation in the world), teams consist of Americans, Dutch, British, and Indonesians who have been brought together to pursue a common goal: maximize oil and gas production. Capitalizing on the technical expertise of the members and their willingness to work together, the team helped the company to achieve its objective and add oil reserves to its stockpiles—an almost unprecedented achievement. This story is only one of many that help to illustrate the way in which global teams are being created and used to achieve difficult international objectives.

In developing effective global teams, companies are finding there are four phases in the process. In phase one, the team members come together with their own expectations, culture, and values. In phase two, members go through a self-awareness period, during which they learn to respect the cultures of the other team members. Phase three is characterized by a developing trust among members, and in phase four, the team begins working in a collaborative way. How are MNCs able to create the environment that is needed for this metamorphosis? Several specific steps are implemented by management, including:

1. The objectives of the group are carefully identified and communicated to the members.

2. Team members are carefully chosen so that the group has the necessary skills and personnel to reinforce and complement each other.

3. Each person learns what he or she is to contribute to the group, thus promoting a feeling of self-importance and interdependency.

4. Cultural differences between the members are discussed so that members can achieve a better understanding of how they may work together effectively.

5. Measurable outcomes are identified so that the team can chart its progress and determine how well it is doing. Management also continually stresses the team's purpose and its measurable outcomes so that the group does not lose sight of its goals.

6. Specially designed training programs are used to help the team members develop interpersonal, intercultural skills.

7. Lines of communication are spelled out so that everyone understands how they can communicate with the other members of the group.

8. Members are continually praised and rewarded for innovative ideas and actions.

MNCs now find that global teams are critical to their ability to compete successfully in the world market. As a result, leaders who are able to create and lead these interdisciplinary, culturally diverse groups are finding themselves in increasing demand by MNCs.

Arab managers' scores for sharing information and objectives, participation, and internal control, however, all were significantly lower than those of managers in the other countries and clusters reported in Table 14–4. The researcher concluded that the results were accounted for by the culture of the Middle East region. Table 14–7 summarizes not only the leadership differences between Middle Eastern and Western managers but also other areas of organization and management. The researcher noted that

> management should recognize the Middle Eastern executive's desire to have the opportunity to become more of an integral part of the management team. His democratic attitude towards individual's capacity for leadership and, yet, classical attitude towards other management practices (participation, sharing information and internal control) are largely a function of his cultural values, and to a much lesser degree, of western influence in education and work setting and their countries' stage of economic development.[26]

More recent research provides some evidence that there may be much greater similarity between Middle Eastern leadership styles and those of Western countries.[27] In particular, the observation was made that Western management practices are very evident in the Arabian Gulf region because of the close business ties between the West and this oil-rich geographic area.

Table 14–7
Differences in Middle Eastern and Western Management

Management Dimensions	Middle Eastern Management	Western Management
Leadership	Highly authoritarian tone, rigid instructions. Too many management directives.	Less emphasis on leader's personality, considerable weight on leader's style and performance.
Organizational structures	Highly bureaucratic, over centralized, with power and authority at the top. Vague relationships. Ambiguous and unpredictable organization environments.	Less bureaucratic, more delegation of authority. Relatively decentralized structure.
Decision making	Ad hoc planning, decisions made at the highest level of management. Unwillingness to take high risk inherent in decision making.	Sophisticated planning techniques, modern tools of decision making, elaborate management information systems.
Performance evaluation and control	Informal control mechanisms, routine checks on performance. Lack of vigorous performance evaluation systems.	Fairly advanced control systems focusing on cost reduction and organizational effectiveness.
Personnel policies	Heavy reliance on personal contacts and getting individuals from the "right social origin" to fill major positions.	Sound personnel management policies. Candidates' qualification are usually the basis for selection decisions.
Communication	The tone depends on the communicants. Social position, power, and family influence are ever-present factors. Chain of command must be followed rigidly. People relate to each other tightly and specifically. Friendships are intense and binding.	Stress usually on equality and a minimization of difference. People relate to each other loosely and generally. Friendships not intense and binding.

Source: Adapted from M. K. Badawy, "Styles of Mid-Eastern Managers," *California Management Review,* Spring 1980, p. 57. Copyright 1980 by the Regents of the University of California. Reprinted by permission of the Regents.

This study used a questionnaire survey among 381 managers in the two top levels of 10 multinational organizations that were engaged in either production or marketing in the Persian Gulf region.[28] The questionnaire was designed to determine which of Likert's leadership styles or systems these Middle Eastern managers were using. (See Table 14–3 for Likert's systems or styles.) Organization climate characteristics that were measured included communication flows, decision-making practices, concern for employees, influence on departments, and motivation of employees. The findings showed that almost all managers were operating in a system 3 (participative) style, the same approach that was used by their U.S. counterparts.[29] These findings indicate more similarity between leadership styles of Middle Eastern and Western managers than previously thought. Once again, we see the danger of generalizations and stereotypes in international management.

Leadership Approaches in Developing Countries

Some research has focused on leadership styles in developing countries such as India, Peru, Chile, and Argentina. These studies have examined leadership in terms of Likert's systems or styles (see Table 14-3) and the managerial attitudes toward the four dimensions of leadership practice from the Haire, Ghiselli, and Porter study.

Because of India's long affiliation with Great Britain, leadership styles in India would seem more likely to be participative than those in the Middle East or other developing countries. Haire and associates found some degree of similarity between leadership styles in India and Anglo-American countries, but it was not significant. The study found Indians to be similar to the Anglo-Americans in terms of managerial attitudes toward capacity for leadership and initiative, participation, and internal control. The difference is in sharing information and objectives. The Indian managers' responses tend to be quite similar to those of managers in other developing countries.[30]

Other early research on leadership styles in India found that a highly controlling superior had a positive effect on subordinates' job satisfaction.[31] Other research that focused more on Indian industrial firms, however, indicates that the most effective leadership style used by Indian managers often is a more participative one. One study, for example, found that the job satisfaction of Indian employees increases as leadership style becomes more participative.[32] Still another study reached similar conclusions based on interviews and surveys conducted with managers in a cross-section of industries in northern and western India using a questionnaire that identified Likert systems or styles of leadership.[33] Of the 120 respondents, 14 percent classified their organization as operating under exploitive autocratic leadership (system 1), 63 percent as benevolent autocratic (system 2), and 23 percent as consultative participative (system 3). None viewed their firm as operating under fully democratic leadership (system 4). In addition, this study found that the more autocratic the leadership style (systems 1 and 2), the lower the level of job satisfaction.[34]

These findings from India show that participative leadership style may be more common and more effective in developing countries than has been reported previously. Over time, developing countries (as also shown in the case of the Persian Gulf nations) may be moving toward a more participative leadership style.

A similar situation exists in Peru. There is little reason to believe that managerial attitudes toward leadership practices would have been any different from those reported by Haire and associates for other South American countries, such as Argentina or Chile. The results from the Haire and associates study for those two developing countries were similar to those for India.[35] More recent research, however, has found that leadership styles in Peru may be much closer to those in the United States than was previously assumed.

Stephens conducted research among three large textile plants in an urban area in Peru.[36] These three Peruvian plants were matched with three U.S. plants of similar size in urban settings in the southwest United States. Because these Peruvian and U.S. firms all were in the same industry and faced similar competitive pressures, this study was an excellent opportunity to compare intercultural leadership profiles and identify any significant differences. Using the same four dimensions of leadership practice that were used in the Haire and associates study, Stephens found that the leadership profiles of the Peruvian and U.S. managers were similar. Commenting on the results, he noted that

> there is little reason to conclude that leader styles are much different in Peru than in the U.S. Absolutely, U.S. leaders appear to perceive workers as having more initiative, being more internally motivated, and therefore more capable of meaningful participation. However, the differences for initiative and locus of control were not statistically significant and differences for sharing of information and objectives showed Peruvians to be statistically more inclined to share than U.S. managers. Taken in total, this does not suggest a more participative, democratic leader style in the U.S. and an authoritarian, external control oriented style in Peru.[37]

As in the case of Middle Eastern managers, these findings in South America indicate there indeed may be more similarities in international leadership styles than previously assumed. As countries become more economically advanced, participative styles may well gain in importance. Of course, this does not mean that MNCs can use the same leadership styles in their various locations around the world. There still must be careful contingency application of leadership styles (different styles for different situations); however, many of the more enlightened participative leadership styles used in the United States and other economically advanced countries, such as Japan, also may have value in managing international operations even in developing countries as well as the emerging Eastern European countries.

Recent Findings Regarding Universalism in Leadership

In recent years researchers have begun raising the question of universality of leadership behavior. Do effective leaders, regardless of their country culture or job, act similarly? A second, and somewhat linked, research inquiry has focused on the question: Are there a host of specific behaviors, attitudes, and values that leaders in the twenty-first century will need in order to be successful? Thus far the findings have been mixed. Some investigators have found that there is a trend toward universalism for leadership; others have concluded that culture continues to be a determining factor and an effective leader, for example, in Sweden will not be as effective in Italy if he or she employs the same approach. One of the most interesting recent efforts has been conducted by Bass and his associates and has focused on the universality and effectiveness of both transformation and transactional leadership.

Transformational leaders
Leaders who are visionary agents with a sense of mission and who are capable of motivating their followers to accept new goals and new ways of doing things.

Transactional leaders
Individuals who exchange rewards for effort and performance and work on a "something for something" basis.

Transformational and Transactional Leadership **Transformational leaders** are visionary agents with a sense of mission who are capable of motivating their followers to accept new goals and new ways of doing things. **Transactional leaders** are individuals who exchange rewards for effort and performance and work on a "something for something" basis.[38] Do these types of leaders exist worldwide and is their effectiveness consistent in terms of performance? Bass, drawing on an analysis of studies conducted in Canada, India, Italy, Japan, New Zealand, Singapore, and Sweden, as well as the United States, discovered that very little of the variance in leadership behavior could be attributed to culture. In fact, in many cases he found that national differences accounted for less than 10 percent of the results. This led him to create a model of leadership and conclude that "although this model . . . may require adjustments and fine-tuning as we move across cultures, particularly into non-Western cultures, overall, it holds up as having considerable universal potential."[39]

Simply stated, Bass discovered that there was far more universalism in leadership than had been believed previously. Additionally, after studying thousands of international cases, he found that the most effective managers were transformational leaders and they were characterized by four interrelated factors. For convenience, the factors are referred to as the "4 I's" and they can be described this way:

1. *Idealized influence.* Transformational leaders are a source of charisma and enjoy the admiration of their followers. They enhance pride, loyalty, and confidence in their people and they align these followers by providing a common purpose or vision which the latter willingly accept.

2. *Inspirational motivation.* These leaders are extremely effective in articulating their vision, mission, and beliefs in clear-cut ways, thus providing an easy-to-understand sense of purpose regarding what needs to be done.

3. *Intellectual stimulation.* Transformational leaders are able to get their followers to question old paradigms and to accept new views of the world regarding how things now need to be done.

4. *Individualized consideration.* These leaders are able to diagnose and elevate the needs of each of their followers through individualized consideration, thus furthering the development of these people.[40]

Bass also discovered that there were four other types of leaders. All of these are less effective than the transformational leader, although the degree of their effectiveness (or ineffectiveness) will vary. The most effective of the remaining four types was labeled the contingent reward (CR) leader by Bass. This leader clarifies what needs to be done and provides both psychic and material rewards to those who comply with his or her directives. The next most effective manager is the active management-by-exception (MBE-A) leader. This individual monitors follower performance and takes corrective action when deviations from standards occurs. The next manager in terms of effectiveness is the passive management-by-exception (MBE-P) leader. This leader takes action or intervenes in situations only when standards are not met. Finally, there is the laissez-faire (LF) leader. This person avoids intervening or accepting responsibility for follower actions.

Bass has found that through the use of higher-order factor analysis it is possible to develop a leadership model that illustrates the effectiveness of all five types of leaders: I's (transformational), CR, MBE-A, MBE-P, and LF. Figure 14–5 presents this model. The higher the box in the figure and the farther to right on the shaded base area, the more effective and active the leader. Notice that the 4 I's box is taller than any of the others in the figure and it is located more to the right than any of the others. The CR box is second tallest and second closest to the right, on down to the LF box which is the shortest and farthest from the right margin.

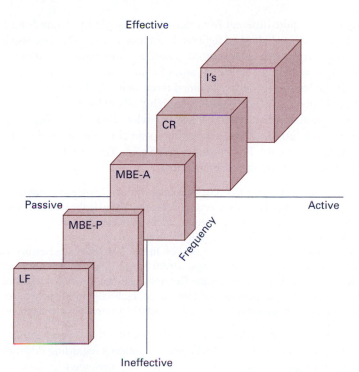

Figure 14–5

An Optimal Profile of Universal Leadership Behaviors

Source: Adapted from Bernard M. Bass, "Is There Universality in the Full Range Model of Leadership?" *International Journal of Public Administration,* 1996, vol. 16, no. 6, p. 738.

Bass also found that the 4 I's were positively correlated with each other, but less so with contingent reward. Moreover, there was a near zero correlation between the 4 I's and management-by-exception styles, and there was an inverse correlation between these four factors and the laissez-faire leadership style.

Does this mean that effective leader behaviors are the same regardless of country? Bass has concluded that this statement is not quite true—but there is far more universalism than people have believed previously. In putting his findings in perspective, he has concluded that there certainly would be differences in leadership behavior from country to country.[41] For example, he has noted that transformational leaders in Honduras would have to be more directive than their counterparts in Norway. Moreover, culture can create some problems in using universal leadership concepts in countries such as Japan, where the use of contingent reward systems is not as widely used as in the west. These reward systems can also become meaningless in Arab and Turkish cultures where there is a great belief that things will happen "if God wills" and not because a leader has decided to carry them out. Yet, even after taking these differences into consideration, Bass contends that universal leadership behavior is far more common than many people realize.[42]

> I cannot and do not want to dismiss the evidence of systematic differences in beliefs, values, implicit theories, traits associated with leadership, decision styles, paternalism, trait and institutional historical and legal differences that shape leader-subordinate relations. Nevertheless, although the model of transformational or transactional leadership may have needs for adjustments and fine-tuning as we move across cultures, particularly into non-Western, overall, it holds up as having a lot of universal potential. Generally speaking, transformation leadership is more effective than managing-by-exception and managing-by-exception is more effective than laissez-faire leadership. Secondly, transformation leadership augments transactional leadership, it does not replace it. Thirdly, the ideals and implicit leadership theories of leadership people carry around in their heads are more transformational than transactional.[43]

Qualities for Successful Leaders Another recent research approach that has been used to address the issue of international leadership is that of examining the characteristics that companies are looking for in their new executive hires. Are all firms seeking the same types of behaviors or qualities or, for example, are companies in Sweden looking for executives with qualities that are quite different from those being sought by Italian firms? The answer to this type of question can help shed light on international leadership because it helps focus attention on the behaviors that organizations believe are important in their managerial workforce. It also helps examine the impact, if any, of culture on leadership style.

Tollgerdt-Andersson recently examined thousands of advertisements for executives in the European Union (EU). She began by studying ads in Swedish newspapers and journals, noting the qualities, characteristics, and behaviors that were being sought. She then expanded her focus to publications in other European countries including Denmark, Norway, Germany, Great Britain, France, Italy, and Spain. The results are reported in Table 14–8. Based on this analysis, she concluded that:

> Generally, there seem to be great differences between the European countries regarding their leadership requirements. Different characteristics are stressed in the various countries. There are also differences concerning how frequently various characteristics are demanded in each country. Some kind of personal or social quality is mentioned much more often in the Scandinavian countries than in the other European countries. In the Scandinavian advertisements, you often see many qualities mentioned in a single advertisement. This can be seen in other European countries too, but it is much more rare. Generally, the characteristics mentioned in a single advertisement do not exceed three and fairly often, especially in Mediterranean countries (in 46–48% of the advertisements) no personal or social characteristics are mentioned at all.[44]

At the same time, Tollgerdt-Andersson did find that there were similarities between nations. For example, Italy and Spain had common patterns regarding desirable leadership characteristics. Between 52–54 percent of the ads she reviewed in these two countries stated specific personal and social abilities that were needed by the job applicant. The same pattern was true for Germany and Great Britain where 64–68 percent of the advertisements set forth the personal and social abilities required for the job. In the Scandinavian countries these percentages ranged between 80–85.

Admittedly, it may be difficult to determine the degree of similarity between ads in different countries (or cultural clusters) because there may be implied meanings in the messages or it may be the custom in that country not to mention certain abilities but simply to assume that applicants know that these will be assessed in making the final hiring decision. Additionally, Tollgerdt-Andersson did find that all countries expected executive applicants to have good social and personal qualities. So there was some degree of universalism uncovered in terms of leadership behaviors. On the other hand, the requirements differed from country to country, showing that effective leaders in northern Europe may not be able to transfer their skills to the southern part of the continent with equal results. This led Tollgerdt-Andersson to conclude that multicultural understanding will continue to be a requirement for effective leadership in the twenty-first century. She put it this way: "If tomorrow's leaders possess international competence and understanding of other cultures it will, hopefully, result in the increased competitive cooperation which is essential if European commerce and industry is to compete with, for example, the USA and Asia."[45]

Culture Clusters and Leader Effectiveness

While the above discussion indicates there is research to support universalism in leadership behavior, recent findings also show that effective leader behaviors tend to vary by cultural cluster. Brodbeck and his associates conducted a large survey of middle-level managers ($n = 6052$) from 22 European countries.[46] The respondents were given 112 questionnaire items containing descriptions of leadership traits and behaviors. For each attribute the respondents were asked to rate how well it fit their concept of an outstanding business leader. Some of the results, grouped by cluster, are presented in Table 14–9. A close look at the data shows that while there are similarities between some of the cultures, none of the lists of leadership attributes is identical. For example, managers in the Anglo cluster reported that the five most important attributes of an effective manager were a performance-orientation, an inspirational style, having a vision, being a team integrator, and being decisive. Managers in the Nordic culture ranked these same five attributes as the

Table 14–8
Qualities Most Demanded in Advertisements for European Executives

Quality	Sweden (N=225)	Denmark (N=175)	Norway (N=173)	Germany (N=190)
Ability to cooperate (interpersonal ability)	25	42	32	16
Independence	22	22	25	9
Leadership ability	22		16	17
Ability to take initiatives	22	12	16	
Aim and result orientation	19	10	42	
Ability to motivate and inspire others	16	11		
Business orientation	12			
Age	10	25		13
Extrovert personality/contact ability	10	8	12	11
Creativity	9	10	9	9
Customer ability	9			
Analytic ability		10		
Ability to communicate		12	15	
High level of energy/drive			12	
Enthusiasm and involvement			14	14
Organization skills				7
Team builder				
Self-motivated				
Flexibility				
Precision				
Dynamic personality				
Responsibility				

Quality	Great Britain (N=163)	France (N=164)	Italy (N=132)	Spain (N=182)
Ability to cooperate (interpersonal ability)	7	9	32	18
Independence			16	4
Leadership ability	10		22	16
Ability to take initiatives			10	8
Aim and result orientation	5			2
Ability to motivate and inspire others		9	26	20
Business orientation				8
Age		12	46	34
Extrovert personality/contact ability				
Creativity	5			4
Customer ability				2
Analytic ability			10	
Ability to communicate	23			8
High level of energy/drive	8			20
Enthusiasm and involvement				
Organization skills		6	12	12
Team builder	10	5		
Self-motivated	10			
Flexibility				2
Precision		7		
Dynamic personality		6		6
Responsibility				10

Note: The qualities most demanded in Swedish, Danish, Norwegian, German, British, French, Italian, and Spanish advertisements for executives are expressed in percentage terms. N = total number of advertisements analyzed in each country. Each entry represents the percentage of the total advertisements requesting by each quality.

Source: Adapted from Ingrid Tollgerdt-Andersson, "Attitudes, Values and Demands on Leadership—A Cultural Comparison among Some European Countries," in Pat Joynt and Malcolm Warner (eds.), *Managing across Cultures* (London: International Thomson Business Press, 1996), p. 173.

Table 14–9

Rankings of the Most Important Leadership Attributes by Region and Country Cluster

North/West European Region

Anglo Culture (Great Britain, Ireland)	Nordic Culture (Sweden, Netherlands, Finland, Denmark)	Germanic Culture (Switzerland, Germany, Austria)	Czech Republic	France
Performance-oriented	Integrity	Integrity	Integrity	Participative
Inspirational	Inspirational	Inspirational	Performance-oriented	Non-autocratic
Visionary	Visionary	Performance-oriented	Administratively-skilled	
Team integrator	Team integrator	Non-autocratic	Inspirational	
Decisive	Performance-oriented	Visionary	Non-autocratic	

South/East European Region

Latin Culture (Italy, Spain, Portugal, Hungary)	Central Culture (Poland, Slovenia)	Near East Culture (Turkey, Greece)	Russia	Georgia
Team integrator	Team integrator	Team integrator	Visionary	Administratively-skilled
Performance-oriented	Visionary	Decisive	Administratively-skilled	Decisive
Inspirational	Administratively-skilled	Visionary	Inspirational	Performance-oriented
Integrity	Diplomatic	Integrity	Decisive	Visionary
Visionary	Decisive	Inspirational	Integrity	Integrity

Source: Adapted from: Felix C. Brodbeck, *et al.,* "Cultural Variation of Leadership Prototypes across 22 European Countries," *Journal of Occupational and Organizational Psychology,* vol. 73, 2000, p. 15.

most important but not in this order. Moreover, while the rankings of clusters in the North/West European region were fairly similar, they were quite different from those in the South/East European regions which included the Latin cluster, countries from Eastern Europe that were grouped by the researchers into a Central cluster and a Near East cluster, and Russia and Georgia that were listed separately.

The data in Table 14–9 seems to indicate that culture influences effective leadership behavior. Moreover, the importance of these behaviors varies by cluster, although those that are geographically close to each other, such as the Anglo and Nordic clusters, tend to report similar leadership prototypes which are different from those located farther away, such as the Central and Near East clusters. This research also shows that there is some degree of universalism in leadership behavior when examined on an intra-cluster level, but when examined across clusters the impact of culture can be significant.[47]

Leader Behavior and Leader Effectiveness

Culture is also important in helping explain how leaders *ought* to act in order to be effective. A good example is provided by the difference in effective behaviors in Trompenaars's categories (covered in Chapter 5) of affective (or emotional) cultures and neutral cultures. In affective cultures, such as the United States, leaders tend to exhibit their emotions. In neutral cultures, such as Japan and China, leaders do not tend to show their emotions. Moreover, in some cultures people are taught to exhibit their emotions but not let it affect their making rational decisions, while in other cultures the two are intertwined. Trompenaars explains it this way:

Table 14–10	
Leadership Tips for Doing Business in Affective and Neutral Cultures	
When Managing or Being Managed in	
Affective Cultures	**Neutral Cultures**
Avoid a detached, ambiguous, and cool demeanor because this will be interpreted as negative behavior.	Avoid warm, excessive, or enthusiastic behaviors because these will be interpreted as a lack of personal control over one's feelings and be viewed as inconsistent with one's high status.
Find out whose work and enthusiasm is being directed into which projects, so you are able to appreciate the vigor and commitment they have for these efforts.	Extensively prepare the things you have to do and then stick tenaciously to the issues.
Let people be emotional without personally becoming intimidated or coerced by their behavior	Look for cues regarding whether people are pleased or angry and then amplify their importance
When Doing Business with Individuals in	
Affective Cultures (for Those from Neutral Cultures)	**Neutral Cultures (for Those from Affective Cultures)**
Do not be put off stride when others create scenes and get histrionic; take time-outs for sober reflection and hard assessments.	Ask for time-outs from meetings and negotiations where you can patch each other up and rest between games of poker with the "impassive ones."
When others are expressing goodwill, respond warmly.	Put down as much as you can on paper before beginning the negotiation.
Remember that the other person's enthusiasm and readiness to agree or disagree does not mean that the individual has made up his or her mind.	Remember that the other person's lack of emotional tone does not mean that the individual is disinterested or bored, only that the person does not like to show his or her hand.
Keep in mind that the entire negotiation is typically focused on you as a person and not so much on the object or proposition that is being discussed	Keep in mind that the entire negotiation is typically focused on the object or proposition that is being discussed and not on you as a person.
Recognize the Way in Which People Behave in	
Affective Cultures	**Neutral Cultures**
They reveal their thoughts and feelings both verbally and nonverbally.	They often do not reveal what they are thinking or feeling.
Emotions flow easily, vehemently, and without inhibition.	Emotions are often dammed up, although they may occasionally explode.
Heated, vital, and animated expressions are admired.	Cool and self-possessed conduct is admired.
Touching, gesturing, and strong facial expressions are common.	Physical contact, gesturing, or strong facial expressions are not used.
Statements are made fluently and dramatically.	Statements are often read out in a monotone voice.

Source: Adapted from Fons Trompenaars and Charles Hampden-Turner, *Riding the waves of Culture: Understanding Diversity in Global Business.* 2nd ed. (New York: McGraw Hill, 1998), pp. 80–82.

Americans tend to exhibit emotion, yet separate it from "objective" and "rational" decisions. Italians and south European nations in general tend to exhibit and not separate. Dutch and Swedes tend not to exhibit and to separate . . . there is nothing "good" or "bad" about these differences. You can argue that emotions held in check will twist your judgments despite all efforts to be "rational." Or you can argue that pouring forth emotions makes it harder for anyone present to think straight. Similarly, you can scoff at the "walls" separating reasons from emotions, or argue that because of the leakage that so often occurs, these should be thicker and stronger.[48]

Researchers have also found that the way in which managers speak to their people can influence the outcome. For example, in Anglo Saxon cultures it is common for managers to raise their voice in order to emphasize a point. In Asian cultures managers generally speak at the same level throughout their communication, using a form of self-control that shows respect for the other person. Latin managers, meanwhile, vary their tone of voice continually, and this form of exaggeration is viewed by them as showing that they are very interested in what they are saying and committed to their point of view. Knowing how to communicate can greatly influence leadership across cultures. Here is an example:

> A British manager posted to Nigeria found that it was very effective to raise his voice for important issues. His Nigerian subordinates viewed that unexpected explosion by a normally self-controlled manager as a sign of extra concern. After success in Nigeria he was posted to Malaysia. Shouting there was a sign of loss of face; his colleagues did not take him seriously and he was transferred.[49]

One of the keys to successful global leadership is that of knowing what style and behavior works best in a given culture and adapting appropriately. In the case of affective and neutral cultures, for example, Trompenaars and Hampden-Turner have offered the specific tips provided in Table 14–10.

The World of *Business Week*—Revisited

As seen in the opening news story, the leadership challenges facing Jurgen Schrempp are many and diverse. DaimlerChrysler has major operations worldwide and through its acquisitions owns Chrysler and holds a controlling interest in Mitsubishi Motors. Effective global leadership is going to be crucial in getting all of these operations to work synergistically. In this chapter, it was noted that effective leadership is often heavily influenced by culture. The approach that is effective in the U.S. is different from that employed in Germany, and in Japan effective managers often use a still different approach. At the same time, there are threads of universalism. This was seen, for example, in the case of Japanese and U.S. leadership styles in managing both high- and low-achievement workers. The approach used with both groups was similar. The research by Bass, depicted in Figure 14–5 also lends support to universalism. On the other hand, in applying the chapter information to Daimler-Chrysler, can Schrempp rely on the leadership style that has served him well in Germany to oversee operations in the U.S. and Japan? Given the condition of both Chrysler and Mitsubishi Motors, he is going to have to work hard to turn things around. In linking this chapter material to the news story, answer these questions: In managing Chrysler's operations in North America, what do Schrempp and the other senior-level managers in Germany need to know about effective leadership practices in the U.S.? When working with managers at Mitsubishi Motors, what do they need to know about effective leadership practices in Japan? If the company decides to move into Eastern Europe and build plants there, how will effective leadership practices be different from those in Germany?

Summary of Key Points

1. Leadership is a complex and controversial process that can be defined as influencing people to direct their efforts toward the achievement of some particular goal or goals. Two areas warrant attention as a foundation for the study of leadership in an international setting; philosophical assumptions about people in general, and leadership styles. The philosophical foundation is heavily grounded in Douglas McGregor's Theories X and Y. Leadership styles relate to how managers treat their subordinates and incorporate authoritarian, paternalistic, and participative approaches. These styles can

be summarized in terms of Likert's management systems or styles (systems 1 through 4) and the managerial grid (1,1 through 9,9).

2. The attitudes of European managers toward dimensions of leadership practice, such as the capacity for leadership and initiative, sharing information and objectives, participation, and internal control, were examined in a classic study by Haire, Ghiselli, and Porter. They found that Europeans, as a composite, had a relatively low opinion of the capabilities of the average person coupled with a relatively positive

belief in the necessity for participative leadership styles. The study also found that these European managers' attitudes were affected by hierarchical level, company size, and age. Overall, however, European managers espouse a participative leadership style.

3. The Japanese managers in the Haire and associates study had a much greater belief in the capacity of subordinates for leadership and initiative than managers in most other countries. The Japanese managers also expressed a more favorable attitude toward a participative leadership style. In terms of sharing information and objectives and using internal control, the Japanese responded above average but were not distinctive. In a number of ways, Japanese leadership styles differed from those of U.S. managers. Company size and age of the managers are two factors that seem to affect these differences. Other reasons include the basic philosophy of managing people, how information is processed, and the high degree of ethnocentrism by the Japanese. However, some often overlooked similarities are important, such as how effective Japanese leaders manage high-achieving and low-achieving subordinates.

4. Leadership research in China shows that the new generation of managers tends to have a leadership style that is different from both the current generation and the older generation. In particular, new generation managers assign greater importance to individualism as measured by such things as self-sufficiency and personal accomplishments. They also assign less importance to collectivism as measured by subordination of personal goals to those of the group and to Confucianism as measured by such things as societal harmony and virtuous interpersonal behavior.

5. Leadership research in the Middle East traditionally has stressed the basic differences between Middle Eastern and Western management styles. More recent research, however, shows that many managers in multinational organizations in the Persian Gulf region operate in a Western-oriented Likert system 3 (participative) style. Such findings indicate that there may be more similarities of leadership styles between Western and Middle Eastern parts of the world than has previously been assumed.

6. Leadership research also has been conducted among managers in developing countries, such as India, Peru, Chile, and Argentina. These studies show that Likert's system 3 (participative) leadership styles are more in evidence than traditionally has been assumed. Although there always will be important differences in styles of leadership between various parts of the world, participative leadership styles may become more prevalent as countries develop and become more economically advanced.

7. In recent years there have been research efforts that focused on the topic of universalism in the leadership process. Bass has found that there is a great deal of similarity from culture to culture and transformational leaders, regardless of culture, tend to be the most effective. At the same time, however, he has found that culture continues to be a mitigating factor. This same conclusion has been reached by research focused on the qualities needed in new managers. The qualities that are demanded by companies in Scandinavia, for example, are not the same as those required by firms in Italy. Similar findings have been offered by Brodbeck and his associates who have found that the leadership attributes that managers feel are important for effectiveness are culturally driven. This study found that the responses from managers in the Anglo culture, for example, were quite different from those in the Germanic culture, and these differed from the responses from other cultures including Nordic, Latin, and Near East, to name but three. Trompenaars echoes these sentiments, noting that leader behavior needs to be adapted to the culture. In summary, current research reveals that effective leadership styles and behaviors are at least partly culture-driven.

Key Terms

authoritarian leadership, *413*

leadership, *412*

participative leadership, *415*

paternalistic leadership, *413*

Theory X manager, *412*

Theory Y manager, *412*

transactional leaders, *430*

transformational leaders, *430*

variety amplification, *422*

variety reduction, *422*

Review and Discussion Questions

1. Using the results of the classic Haire and associates study as a basis for your answer, compare and contrast managers' attitudes toward leadership practices in Nordic-European and Latin-European countries. (The countries in these clusters are identified in Table 14–4.)

2. Is there any relationship between company size and the attitude toward participative leadership styles by European managers?

3. Using the Haire and associates study results and other supporting data, determine what Japanese managers believe about their subordinates. How are these beliefs similar to those of U.S. and European managers? How are these beliefs different?

4. A U.S. firm is going to be opening a subsidiary in Japan within the next 6 months. What type of leadership style does research show to be most effective when leading high-achieving Japanese? Low-achieving

Japanese? How are these results likely to affect the way that U.S. expatriates should lead their Japanese employees?

5. A British firm is in the process of setting up operations in the Middle East Gulf States. What Likert system or style of leadership do managers in this region seem to use? Is this similar to that used by Western managers?

6. What do U.S. managers need to know about leading in the international arena? Identify and describe three important guidelines that can be of practical value.

7. Is effective leadership behavior universal or does it vary from culture to culture? Explain.

Internet Exercise: Taking a Closer Look

Over the last decade, one of the most successful global firms has been General Electric. In the International Management in Action box in this chapter, some of the basic leadership ideas of the company's recent CEO, Jack Welch, were described. Now we are going to take a closer look at the firm and the role of leadership in its success. Go to the company's web site at **www.ge.com** and review its latest annual report. Pay close attention to the MNC's international operations and to its product lines. Also read about the new members on the board of directors and look through the information on the company's six sigma program. Then, aware of what GE is doing worldwide as well as in regard to its quality efforts, answer these questions:

On how many continents does the company currently do business? Based on this answer, is there one leadership style that will work best for the company or is it going to have to choose managers on a country-by-country basis? Additionally, if there is no one universal style that is best, how can current CEO Jeffrey Immelt effectively lead so diverse a group of worldwide managers? In what way would an understanding of the managerial grid be useful in explaining leadership behaviors at GE? Finally, if GE were advertising for new managers in England, Italy, and Japan, what qualities would you expect them to be seeking in these managers? Would there be a universal list or would it be different on a country-by-country basis?

Germany

A unified Germany has become a major event of modern times. Although problems remain, Germany remains a major economic power in the world. The single Germany is big but still only about the size of the state of Nevada in the United States, and with a population of about 84 million, Germany has about three times the population of California. In addition, the one Germany still is way behind the economic size of Japan and 20 percent that of the United States. Because Germany has rebuilt almost from the ground up since World War II, however, many feel that Germany, along with Japan, is an economic miracle of modern times. Unified Germany's GDP of $1.8 trillion is behind that of both the United States and Japan, but Germany exports more than Japan, its gross investment as a percent of GDP is higher than that of the United States, and its average compensation with benefits to workers is higher than that of the United States or Japan. It is estimated that Germany has direct control of about one-fourth of Western Europe's economy, which gives it considerable power in Europe. The German people are known for being thrifty, hardworking, and obedient to authority. They love music, dancing, good food and beer, and fellowship. The government is a parliamentary democracy headed by a chancellor.

For the last 13 years the Wiscomb Company has held a majority interest in a large retail store in Bonn. The store has been very successful and also has proved to be an excellent training ground for managers whom the company wanted to prepare for other overseas assignments. First, the managers would be posted to the Bonn store and, then, after 3 or 4 months of international seasoning, they would be sent on to other stores in Europe. Wiscomb has holdings in the Netherlands, Luxembourg, and Austria. The Bonn store has been the primary training ground because it was the first one the company had in Europe, and the training program was created with this store in mind.

A few months ago, the Wiscomb management and its German partners decided to try a new approach to selling. The plan called for some young U.S. managers to be posted to the Bonn store for a 3-year tour while some young German managers were sent stateside. Both companies hoped that this program would provide important training and experience for their people; however, things have not worked out as hoped. The U.S. managers have reported great difficult in supervising their German subordinates. Three of their main concerns are: (1) their subordinates do not seem to like to participate in decision making, preferring to be told what to do; (2) the German nationals in the store rely much more heavily on a Theory X approach to supervising than the Americans are accustomed to using, and they are encouraging their U.S. counterparts to follow their example; and (3) some of the German managers have suggested to the young Americans that they not share as much information with their own subordinates. Overall, the Americans believe that the German style of management is not as effective as their own, but they feel equally ill at ease raising this issue with their hosts. They have asked if someone from headquarters could come over from the United States and help to resolve their problem. A human resources executive is scheduled to arrive next week and meet with the U.S. contingent.

Questions

1. What are some current issues facing Germany? What is the climate for doing business in Germany today?

2. Are the leadership styles used by the German managers really much different from those used by the Americans?

3. Do you think the German managers are really more Theory X-oriented than their U.S. counterparts? Why, or why not?

4. Are the German managers who have come to the United States likely to be having the same types of problems?

An Offer from Down Under

The Gandriff Corporation is a successful retail chain in the U.S. Midwest. The St. Louis-based company has had average annual growth of 17 percent over the last 10 years and would like to expand to other sections of the country. Last month, however, it was made a very interesting offer by a group of investors from Australia. The group is willing to put up $100 million to help Gandriff set up operations Down Under. The Australian investors believe that Gandriff's management and retailing expertise could provide it with a turnkey operation. The stores would be built to Gandriff's specifications, and the entire operation would be run by Gandriff. The investors would receive 75 percent of all profits until they recovered their $100 million plus an annual return of 10 percent. At this point the division of profits will then become 50-50.

Gandriff management likes the idea but feels there is a better chance for higher profit if they were to set up operations in Europe. The growth rate in European countries, it is felt, will be much better than that in Australia. The investors, all of whom are Australian, are sympathetic and have promised Gandriff that they will invest another $100 million in Europe, specifically England, France, and Germany, within 3 years if Gandriff agrees to first set up and get an Australian operation running. The U.S. firm believes this would be a wise move but is delaying a final decision, because it still is concerned about the ease with which it can implement its current approach in foreign markets. In particular, the management is concerned as to whether the leadership style used in the United States will be successful in Australia and in European countries. Before making a final decision, management has decided to hire a consultant specializing in leadership to look into the matter.

Questions

1. Will the leadership style used in the United States be successful in Australia, or will the Australians respond better to another?

2. If the retailer goes into Europe, in which country will it have the least problem using its U.S.-based leadership style? Why?

3. If the company goes into Europe, what changes might it have to make in accommodating its leadership approach to the local environment? Use Germany as an example.

Chapter 15

Human Resource Selection and Repatriation

Objectives of the Chapter

MNCs annually select thousands of people to staff not only their home-country facilities but also their subsidiaries around the world. Who should be selected for a foreign assignment, and how are they handled when they get back? Chapter 15 focuses on potential human resources that can be used for overseas assignments, criteria that are used in the selection process, and how MNCs handle repatriation of the managers back to their country of origin (in most cases, home-country managers are returning to headquarters or to local operations). The specific objectives of this chapter are:

1. **IDENTIFY** the three basic sources that MNCs can tap in filling management vacancies in overseas operations.

2. **SET FORTH** some of the most common selection criteria used in identifying the best people for overseas assignments.

3. **DESCRIBE** the selection procedures used in making the final decisions on the part of both the organization and the individual manager.

4. **DISCUSS** the reasons for people's returning from overseas assignments and present some of the strategies used in ensuring a smooth transition back into the local operation.

BusinessWeek

The World of *Business Week*

Repairing the Coke Machine

First, the good news for Douglas N. Daft: After one year as chief executive of Coca-Cola Co., there's no doubt that he's vanquished the old regime at his Atlanta headquarters. Daft announced his boldest management shakeup, including the departure of his second-in-command, President and Chief Operating Officer Jack L. Stahl and the hiring of a highly regarded senior executive from the media industry. A 20-year veteran, Stahl apparently couldn't get with Daft's new program. "Daft had been waiting for Jack to seize responsibility, and he didn't do it," says one Coke insider. (Stahl was not available for comment.) Around the same time, Coke's board offered Daft a generous incentive package that could be worth as much as $87.2 million over five years.

Now the bad news. In order to earn that pay, he'll have to hit aggressive performance targets. And the cleanup job that Daft signed up for has turned out to be much messier than anyone anticipated—including him. Even though he has laid out a bold plan to move Coke beyond soda and into the faster-growing markets for bottled water, juices, and other noncarbonated drinks, Daft has not convinced Wall Street that he can reignite Coke's brands anytime soon.

Cautionary Tale

How long will investors—or Coke's board—be willing to wait? Wall Street investment banker and board member Herbert A. Allen says the Coke directors back Daft. Whereas M. Douglas Ivester, his predecessor, paid little heed to the board—resisting their entreaties to name a president or cut Coke's bloated bureaucracy—Daft has been more willing to delegate, tackle dirty tasks like the restructuring, and consult regularly with directors such as Allen and investor Warren Buffett. "He has made very significant achievements in a fairly short period of time," Allen says.

Coke may be the world's most powerful brand, but for years the company has been unable to capitalize on that. Soda sales have been flat in the all-important U.S. market—and a reinvigorated Pepsi has moved aggressively into the nonsoda business. Still, under Ivester, there was no sense of danger at the Coke headquarters, no real focus on new products. That's changed. Last year, to make the company more nimble, Daft canned one-fifth of Coke's 29,000 workers and eased out or reassigned 30 of Coke's top 32 managers. The moves were intended to smash what Daft viewed as a stifling bureaucracy and give more decision-making to his field managers.

Unlike Ivester, a low-key accountant who made decisions by the numbers, Daft is a passionate, idea-a-minute manager who acts off the intuitions developed during his 24 years climbing up the ranks of Coke's Asia-Pacific operations. "Doug Daft likes to make decisions. The problem is, he likes to make them every five minutes," jokes one Coke vice-president.

So far, however, few of those ideas have trickled through to the bottom line. That's partly because Daft spent much of the past year putting out fires. He had to contend with a high-profile racial discrimination suit, the political fallout in Europe from a soda-contamination scare, and a backlash by financially strapped bottlers who felt that Coke was profiting largely at their expense. "Nobody realizes the garbage that was on his table," says retired Coke President Donald R. Keough, whom Daft retained as an adviser last year. For his part, the 57-year-old Australian allows that the past year was a difficult one. Says Daft: "There was certainly a lot more to do than I envisioned. Every time you squeeze one side, something else popped up."

Daft's management reshuffling should make Coke more responsive. He created four new division presidents reporting directly to him. Daft has just hired Steven Heyer from AOL Time Warner's Turner Broadcasting to head what will be known as the New Business Ventures unit. Jeffrey T. Dunn, who runs the North American business, will head the Americas; Charles S. Frenette will continue to oversee Europe and Africa; and Alexander "Sandy" Allan remains in charge of Asia. While Stahl was once viewed as the perfect backup to Daft—providing knowledge of Wall Street and the U.S. market that he lacked—sources say Daft had become increasingly frustrated by Stahl's reluctance to break from Coke's old ways. However, the price to be paid for the shuffle is that after a series of high-level departures, Daft now has a talented but largely untested executive team. Meanwhile, the board is still likely to press Daft to eventually elevate one of his four division chiefs to second-in-command.

Daft is pushing managers to think outside of the box, generating everything from new products to different ways of gathering consumer research. At a recent retreat in San Francisco with two dozen Coke executives from around the world, Daft prodded his staff for smart ideas—and then funded four of them, with $250,000 each, right on the spot. "He said: 'Consider it done,'" recalls Vinita Bali, whom Daft appointed in December to create an internal think tank in New York. "And he told everyone: 'If you're being stalled, you get back to me.'" Similarly, company sources say Daft will shortly announce an "incubator" project in which Coke will provide office space—and seed money—to startups with innovative ideas that could benefit Coke.

Much of that energy will go into building up Coke's noncarbonated business. During the global boom of the 1980s, Coke enjoyed explosive growth with a simple business model: building out an expansive bottling network around the world, and then pushing its four core brands—Coke, Diet Coke, Sprite, and Fanta—through this network. But when the global boom went bust in the late '90s, sales slumped and haven't revived. Coke realized there may be a limit to the world's appetite for carbonated sodas, particularly in maturing markets such as the U.S.

Historically, Coca-Cola has struggled to parlay its killer distribution and hefty marketing resources into a meaningful presence in the high-margin "premium" beverage market dominated by the likes of Snapple, AriZona, SoBe, and Gatorade. Consider the company's first direct attempt to challenge Snapple, with Fruitopia. After years of trying to mimic Snapple's wide-mouth bottles and all-natural ingredients, sales were tepid, and Coke retrenched with a product that's more like a soft drink and easier to produce—but doesn't command premium prices.

Just Crumbs?

That's why analysts question whether Daft can build the same kind of economies from his noncarbonated business as from soda, which generates gross margins of 80% and the high volume runs that Coke's bottlers love. Right now noncarbonated drinks account for only 10% of sales. And they fear that in his haste to push further into juice and chips, Daft let P&G get the better end of its deal. "Coke gave up half the profits from Minute Maid, which still has good growth potential, in exchange for two declining brands in Pringle's and Sunny Delight," says Sanford C. Bernstein & Co. analyst William Pecoriello, who lowered Coke to "market perform" after the P&G announcement.

Coke boasts that putting Pringle's onto its army of delivery trucks will get the brand into as many as 16 million stores worldwide, vs. the 1.6 million that Pringle's reaches now. But industry analysts doubt the wisdom of taking on PepsiCo in the chip business where its entrenched Frito-Lay brand boasts a 60% market share, vs. 6% for Pringle's.

Fitting these myriad ventures together into a new Coke machine is a daunting task that could take years. But for Daft, as for Coke, there's no turning back.

By Dean Foust in Atlanta, with Gerry Khermouch
in New York and bureau reports

Source: **Reprinted from March 19, 2001, pp. 86–88 issue of** *Business Week* **by special permission, copyright © 2001 by McGraw-Hill Companies, Inc.**

This opening news story points out some of the steps that Coca-Cola is taking to try and bolster performance. Marketing and innovation are going to be critical in this effort. At the same time, the company is cutting staff and shifting jobs from Atlanta to the regional offices. All this restructuring is going to prove useful only if the field personnel can perform profitably and this is where the firm's human resource challenge comes into the picture. In particular, Coke needs to grow its worldwide market share by developing products that appeal to the varied tastes of people from Europe to Asia. Local managers are going to have to step up and make the right product decisions. If it can do these things, the firm's stock price will start back up and the board and the stockholders will be pleased. If not, the company is likely to again restructure and seek new managers, both in Atlanta and world-wide, who can create the changes needed to increase revenues and profits. In the final analysis, the firm's human resource selection and repatriation process is going to play a key role in this effort.

■ Sources of Human Resources

There are four basic sources that MNCs can tap for positions: (1) home-country nationals; (2) host-country nationals; (3) third-country nationals; and (4) inpatriates. The following sections analyze each of these major sources.

Home-Country Nationals

Home-country nationals are managers who are citizens of the country where the MNC is headquartered. In fact, sometimes the term "headquarters nationals" is used. These managers commonly are called **expatriates,** or simply "expats," which refers to those who live and work away from their home country. Historically, MNCs have staffed key positions in their foreign affiliates with home-country nationals or expatriates.[1] Based on research in U.S., European, and Japanese firms, Rosalie Tung found that U.S. and European firms used home-country nationals in less-developed regions but preferred host-country nationals in developed nations. The Japanese, however, made considerably more use of home-country personnel in all geographic areas, especially at the middle- and upper-level ranks.[2]

More recent research, however, reveals that the pattern reported by Tung may be undergoing change. Richards, for example, investigated staffing practices for the purpose of determining when companies are more likely to use an expatriate rather than a local manager. He conducted interviews with senior-level headquarters managers at 24 U.S. multinational manufacturing firms and with managers at their U.K. and Thai subsidiaries. This study found that local managers were most effective in subsidiaries located in developing countries or those that relied on a local customer base. In contrast, expatriates were most effective when they were in charge of larger subsidiaries or those with a marketing theme similar to that at headquarters.[3]

There are a variety of reasons for using home-country nationals. One of the most common is to start up operations. Another is to provide technical expertise. A third is to help the MNC maintain financial control over the operation.[4] Other commonly cited reasons include

> the desire to provide the company's more promising managers with international experience to equip them better for more responsible positions; the need to maintain and facilitate organizational coordination and control; the unavailability of managerial talent in the host country; the company's view of the foreign operation as short lived; the host country's multiracial population, which might mean that selecting a manager of either race would result in political or social problems; the company's conviction that it must maintain a foreign image in the host country; and the belief of some companies that a home country manager is the best person for the job.[5]

In the past, expatriates were almost always men, but over the last decade there has been a growing number of female expatriates as companies have come to realize that women do want international assignments and are prepared to assume the challenges that accompany these jobs. Stroh, Arma, and Valy-Durbin, for example, recently surveyed 261 female expatriates and 78 of their supervisors and, among other things, found that these women felt that their gender did not stand in the way of their doing their jobs and, in fact, was sometimes an advantage because it gave them greater visibility, enabled them to build stronger interpersonal relationships with clients, and helped them to adapt better to life as an outsider.[6]

In recent years, there definitely has been a trend away from using home-country nationals. This is true even among Japanese firms, which long preferred to employ expats

Home-country nationals
Expatriate managers who are citizens of the country where the multinational corporation is headquartered.

Expatriates
Those who live and work away from their home country. They are citizens of the country where the multinational corporation is headquartered.

and were reluctant to allow local nationals a significant role in subsidiary management. Beamish and Inkpen recently conducted an analysis of over 3,200 Japanese subsidiaries and found that the percentage of expats in larger units has been declining steadily over the last four decades.[7] Table 15–1 shows the precise breakdown. What has caused this? Four reasons for the declining use of Japanese expats have been cited. First, as the number of Japanese subsidiaries worldwide have increased, it has become more difficult to find the requisite number of qualified expats to handle these assignments. Second, there are a growing number of effective local managers that make it no longer necessary to rely as heavily on expats. Third, the high cost of keeping expats overseas is having a strong negative effect on company profits. Fourth, Japanese human resource management policies are changing and the old "rice paper ceiling" which prevented non-Japanese from being promoted into the upper management ranks of subsidiaries is now beginning to disappear. This latter development, in the United States in particular, is a result of Japanese firms realizing that their American subsidiaries have not been able to compete effectively. Japanese expat managers have been outflanked by their American counterparts. In particular, Japanese managers have not known how to fine-tune products for the U.S. market; did not understand how to tailor market approaches to different customer segments; and were unable to develop the speed, flexibility, and responsiveness needed to compete with the Americans.[8] It is highly likely that MNCs from other countries besides Japan are also following this trend of using local managers in lieu of expats.

Host-Country Nationals

Host-country nationals
Local managers who are hired by the MNC.

Host-country nationals are local managers who are hired by the MNC. For a number of reasons, many multinationals use host-country managers at the middle- and lower-level ranks: Many countries expect the MNC to hire local talent, and this is a good way to meet this

---

Table 15–1
Number of Japanese Expatriates per Subsidiary by Subsidiary Entry Date

When Subsidiary Was Started	Number of Japanese Expatriate Managers					Number of Subsidiaries
	0	**1–2**	**3–5**	**6–10**	**over 10**	
pre-1960	5 10.6%	9 19.1%	8 17.0%	8 17.0%	17 36.2%	47
1961–1965	11 13.4%	18 22.0%	18 22.0%	19 23.2%	16 19.5%	82
1966–1970	42 19.1%	59 26.8%	49 22.3%	39 17.7%	31 14.1%	220
1971–1975	83 14.1%	164 28.3%	142 24.5%	111 19.1%	80 13.8%	580
1976–1980	53 12.6%	143 34.1%	122 29.1%	60 14.3%	41 9.8%	419
1981–1985	87 17.6%	156 31.6%	109 22.1%	90 18.2%	52 10.5%	494
1986–1990	148 12.4%	406 33.9%	346 28.9%	184 15.4%	113 9.4%	1,197
1991–1993	35 15.6%	85 37.9%	66 29.5%	25 11.2%	13 5.8%	224
All Subsidiaries	**464** **14.2%**	**1,040** **31.9%**	**860** **26.4%**	**536** **16.4%**	**363** **11.1%**	**3,263**

Note: The first number in each cell is the number of subsidiaries; the second number is the row percentage.

Source: Adapted from Paul W. Beamish and Andrew C. Inkpen, "Japanese Firms and the Decline of the Japanese Expatriate," *Journal of World Business*, vol. 33, no. 1, 1998, p. 40.

expectation. Also, even if it wanted to staff all management positions with home-country personnel, the MNC is unlikely to have this many available managers, and the cost of transferring and maintaining them in the host country would be prohibitive.

Although top management positions typically are filled by home-country personnel, this is not always the case. For example, many U.S. MNCs use home-country managers to get the operation started; then they turn things over to host-country managers. However, there are exceptions even to this pattern. An early study found that U.S. managers often were put in charge of subsidiaries in MNCs that were in the process of marketing a product worldwide.[9] As the product was introduced into each new country, however, the local manager was replaced by a home-country manager. Then, when the international effort was completed, host-country managers were again put in charge.

This traditional pattern of managerial positions filled by home- and host-country personnel illustrates why it is so difficult to generalize about staffing patterns in an international setting. An exception would be in those cases where government regulations dictate selection practices and mandate at least some degree of "nativization." In Brazil, for example, two-thirds of the employees in any foreign subsidiary traditionally had to be Brazilian nationals. In addition, many countries exert real and subtle pressures to staff the upper-management ranks with nationals. In the past, these pressures by host countries have led companies such as Standard Oil to change their approach to selecting managers.

In European countries, home-country managers who are assigned to a foreign subsidiary or affiliate often stay in this position for the remainder of their career. Europeans are not transferred back to headquarters or to some other subsidiary, as is traditionally done by U.S. firms. Another approach, although least common, is always to use a home-country manager to run the operation.

U.S. firms tend to rely fairly heavily on host-country managers. Tung has identified four reasons that U.S. firms tend to use host-country managers: (1) these individuals are familiar with the culture; (2) they know the language; (3) they are less expensive than home-country personnel; and (4) hiring them is good public relations. European firms who use host-country managers gave the two major reasons of familiarization with the culture and knowledge of the language, whereas Japanese firms gave the reason that the host-country national was the best-qualified individual for the job.[10] The accompanying box, "International Management in Action: Important Tips on Working for Foreigners," gives examples of how Americans can better adapt to foreign bosses.

Third-Country Nationals

Third-country nationals are managers who are citizens of countries other than the one in which the MNC is headquartered or the one in which they are assigned to work by the MNC. Available data on third-country nationals are not as extensive as those on home- or host-country nationals. Tung found that the two most important reasons that U.S. MNCs use third-country nationals were that these people had the necessary expertise or were judged to be the best ones for the job. European firms gave only one answer: The individuals were the best ones for the job.[11]

Third-country nationals
Managers who are citizens of countries other than the one in which the MNC is headquartered or the one in which the managers are assigned to work by the MNC.

Phatak reports that U.S. MNCs use third-country nationals only from highly developed countries, and this is the ultimate promotion for this person.[12] Unlike U.S. managers, who commonly are put in a foreign position to gain experience before being routed back to headquarters, the third-country national assigned to head a foreign subsidiary or affiliate will tend to remain there indefinitely.

Third-country nationals (TCNs) more typically are found in MNCs that have progressed through the initial and middle stages of internationalization and now are in the more advanced stages.[13] Figure 15–1 shows that the number of third-country subsidiary managers in the U.S. companies studied was greatest during the stable growth period and into the stage characterized by political and competitive threat. Among European firms, a somewhat different pattern was found. Beginning with the initial manufacturing stage, these European MNCs began using third-country managers and continued to do so until political and

---

As the Japanese, South Koreans, and Europeans continue to expand their economic horizons, increased employment opportunities will be available worldwide. Is it a good idea to work for foreigners? Those who have done so have learned that there are both rewards and penalties associated with this career choice. Here are some useful tips that have been drawn from the experiences of those who have worked for foreign MNCs.

First, although most U.S. managers are taught to make fast decisions, most foreign managers take more time and view rapid decision making as unnecessary and sometimes bad. In the United States, we hear the cliché that "the effective manager is right 51 percent of the time." In Europe, this percentage is perceived as much too low, which helps to explain why European managers analyze situations in much more depth than most U.S. managers do. Americans working for foreign-owned firms have to focus on making slower and more accurate decisions.

Second, most Americans are taught to operate without much direction. In Latin countries, managers are accustomed to giving a great deal of direction, and in East Asian firms, there is little structure and direction. Americans have to learn to adjust to the decision-making process of the particular company.

Third, most Americans go home around 5 p.m. If there is more paperwork to do, they take it with them. Japanese managers, on the other hand, stay late at the office and often view those who leave early as being lazy. Americans have to either adapt or convince the manager that they are working as hard as their peers but in a different physical location.

Fourth, many international firms say that their official language is English. However, important conversations always are carried out in the home-country's language, so it is important to learn that language.

Fifth, many foreign MNCs make use of fear to motivate their people. This is particularly true in manufacturing work, where personnel are under continuous pressure to maintain high output and quality. For instance, those who do not like to work under intense conditions would have a very difficult time succeeding in Japanese auto assembly plants. Americans have to understand that humanistic climates of work may be the exception rather than the rule.

Finally, despite the fact that discrimination in employment is outlawed in the United States, it is practiced by many MNCs, including those operating in the United States. Women seldom are given the same opportunities as men, and top-level jobs almost always are reserved for home-office personnel. In many cases, Americans have accepted this ethnocentric (nationalistic) approach, but as Chapter 4 discussed, ethics and social responsibilities are a major issue in the international arena and these challenges must be met now and in the future.

---

competitive threats were faced (stage 6). At this point, as for the U.S. firms, use of third-country managers began to decline; they were replaced by host-country nationals.

A number of advantages have been cited for using TCNs. One is that the salary and benefit package usually is less than that of a home-country national, although in recent years, the salary gap between the two has begun to diminish. A second reason is that the TCN may have a very good working knowledge of the region and/or speak the same language as the local people. This helps to explain why many U.S. MNCs have hired English or Scottish managers for the top positions at subsidiaries in former British colonies such as Jamaica, India, the West Indies, and Kenya. It also explains why successful multinationals such as Gillette, Coca-Cola, and IBM recruit local managers and train them to run overseas subsidiaries. Other cited benefits of using TCNs include:

1. In terms of control, these TCN managers, particularly those who have had assignments in the headquarters country, can often achieve corporate objectives more effectively than expatriates or local nationals. In particular, they frequently have a deep understanding of the corporation's policies from the perspective of a foreigner and can communicate and implement those policies more effectively to others than can expats.

2. During periods of rapid expansion, TCNs cannot only substitute for expatriates in new and growing operations, but they offer different perspectives that can complement and expand on the sometimes narrowly focused viewpoints of both local nationals and headquarters personnel.

Figure 15–1   **MNC Internationalization**

Source: Lawrence G. Franco, "Who Manages Multinational Enterprises?" *California Management Review,* Summer 1973, p. 33. Copyright © 1973 by the Regents of the University of California. Reprinted by permission of the Regents.

3. In joint ventures, TCNs can demonstrate a global or transnational image and bring unique cross-cultural skills to the relationship.[14]

Inpatriates

In recent years a new term has emerged in international management—inpatriates. An **inpatriate** is an individual from a host country or a third-country national who is assigned to work in the home country. Even Japanese MNCs are now beginning to rely on inpatriates to help them meet their international challenges. Harvey and Buckley have reported that:

> The Japanese are reducing their unicultural orientation in their global businesses. Yoichi Morishita, president of Matsushita, has ordered that top management must reflect the cultural diversity of the countries where Matsushita does business. Sony sells 80 percent of its products overseas and recently recognized the need to become multicultural. It has appointed two foreigners to its board of directors and has plans to hire host-country nationals who are to be integrated into the top management of the parent organization. At the same time, the Chairman of Sony has stated that in five years the board-of-directors of Sony will reflect the diversity of countries that are important to the future of the company. Similarly, Toshiba plans to have a more representative top management and board of directors to facilitate long-run global strategies.[15]

This growing use of inpats is helping MNCs better develop their global core competencies. As a result, today a new breed of multilingual, multiexperienced, so called global managers or transnational managers is truly emerging.[16]

These new managers are part of a growing group of international executives who can manage across borders and do not fit the traditional third-country nationals mold. With a unified Europe and other such developments in North America and Asia, these global managers are in great demand. Additionally, with labor shortages developing in certain regions of the world, there is a wave of migration from regions with an abundance of personnel to those where the demand is strongest.[17]

Inpatriate

An individual from a host country or a third-country national who is assigned to work in the home country.

■ Selection Criteria for International Assignments

International selection criteria
Factors used to choose personnel for international assignments.

Making an effective selection decision for an overseas assignment can prove to be a major problem. Typically, this decision is based on **international selection criteria,** which are factors used to choose international managers. These selections are influenced by the MNC's experience and often are culturally based. For example, Hoecklin has noted that in

> Anglo-Saxon cultures, what is generally tested is how much the individual can contribute to the tasks of the organization. In these cultures, assessment centers, intelligence tests and measurements of competencies are the norm. In Germanic cultures, the emphasis is more on the quality of education in a particular function. The recruitment process in Latin and Far Eastern cultures is very often characterized by ascertaining how well the person "fits in" with the larger group. This is determined in part by the elitism of higher educational institutions, such as the *grandes ecoles* in France or the University of Tokyo in Japan, and in part by their interpersonal style and ability to network internally. If there are tests in Latin cultures, they will tend to be more about personality, communication and social skills than about the Anglo-Saxon notion of "intelligence."[18]

Sometimes as many as a dozen criteria are used, although most MNCs give serious consideration to only five or six.[19] Table 15–2 reports the importance of some of these criteria as ranked by Australian, expatriate, and Asian managers from 60 leading Australian, New Zealand, British, and U.S. MNCs with operations in South Asia.[20]

General Criteria

Some selection criteria are given a great deal of weight; others receive, at best, only lip service. A company sending people overseas for the first time often will have a much longer list of criteria than will an experienced MNC that has developed a "short list." For example, in one study, Tung found that personnel sent overseas by MNCs could be grouped into four categories—chief executive officer, functional head, troubleshooter, and operative—and each category had its own criteria for selection.[21] Chief executive officers had to be good communicators, and they had to have management talent, maturity, emotional stability, and the ability to adapt to new environmental settings. Functional heads had to be mature and have emotional stability and technical knowledge about their job.

Table 15–2
Rank of Criteria in Expatriate Selection

	Australian Managers n=47	Expatriate Managers[a] n=52	Asian Managers n=15
1. Ability to adapt	1	1	2
2. Technical competence	2	3	1
3. Spouse and family adaptability	3	2	4
4. Human relations skill	4	4	3
5. Desire to serve overseas	5	5	5
6. Previous overseas experience	6	7	7
7. Understanding of host country culture	7	6	6
8. Academic qualifications	8	8	8
9. Knowledge of language of country	9	9	9
10. Understanding of home country culture	10	10	10

Note: [a]U.S., British, Canadian, French, New Zealand, or Australian managers working for an MNC outside their home countries.

Source: Raymond J. Stone, "Expatriate Selection and Failure," *Human Resource Planning,* vol. 14, no. 1, 1991, p. 10. Used with permission.

Troubleshooters had to have technical knowledge of their business and be able to exercise initiative and creativity. Operatives had to be mature, emotionally stable, and respectful of the laws and people in the host country. In short, the nature of the job determined the selection factors.

Typically, both technical and human criteria are considered. Firms that fail to consider both often find that their rate of failure is quite high. For example, Tung investigated both U.S. and Japanese companies and found that many U.S. firms had poor success in choosing people for overseas assignments; meanwhile, the Japanese firms were quite successful. The primary difference between the two was that the Americans tended to focus most heavily on technical considerations, whereas the Japanese also considered behavioral or relational skills, such as the ability of the managers to deal with clients, customers, superiors, peers, and subordinates.[22] More recently Peterson, Napier, and Shul-Shim investigated the primary criteria that MNCs use when choosing personnel for overseas assignments and found that the Japanese and American MNCs in their survey ranked both technical expertise and interpersonal skills as very important.[23] The following sections examine some of the most commonly used selection criteria for overseas assignments in more depth.

Adaptability to Cultural Change

Overseas managers must be able to adapt to change. They also need a degree of cultural toughness. Research shows that many managers are exhilarated at the beginning of their overseas assignment. After a few months, however, a form of culture shock creeps in, and they begin to encounter frustration and feel confused in their new environment. One analysis noted that many of the most effective international managers suffer this cultural shock.[24] This may be a good sign, because it shows that the expatriate manager is becoming involved in the new culture and not just isolating himself or herself from the environment. Here is an example provided by a North American who was assigned to the Middle East:

> My third day in Israel, accompanied by a queasy stomach, I ventured forth into the corner market to buy something light and easy to digest. As yet unable to read Hebrew, I decided to pick up what looked like a small yogurt container that was sitting near the cheese. Not being one hundred percent sure it contained yogurt, I peered inside; to my delight, it held a thick white yogurt-looking substance. I purchased my "yogurt" and went home to eat—soap, liquid soap. How was I to know that soap came in packages resembling yogurt containers, or that market items in Israel were not neatly divided into edible and inedible sections, as I remembered them in the United States. My now "clean" stomach became a bit more fragile and my confidence waned.[25]

As this initial and trying period comes to an end, an expatriate's satisfaction with conditions tends to increase. In fact, as seen in Figure 15–2, after the first 2 years, most people become more satisfied with their overseas assignment than when they first arrived. Research also shows that men tend to adjust a little faster than women, although both sexes exhibit a great deal of similarity in terms of their degree of satisfaction with overseas assignments. In addition, people over 35 years of age tend to have slightly higher levels of satisfaction after the first year, but managers under 35 have higher satisfaction during the next 3 to 4 years. In all cases, however, these differences are not statistically significant.[26]

Organizations examine a number of characteristics in determining whether an individual is sufficiently adaptable. Examples include work experiences with cultures other than one's own, previous overseas travel, a knowledge of foreign languages (fluency generally is not necessary), and recent immigration background or heritage. Others include: (1) the ability to integrate with different people, cultures, and types of business organizations; (2) the ability to sense developments in the host country and accurately evaluate them; (3) the ability to solve problems within different frameworks and from different perspectives; (4) sensitivity to the fine print of differences of culture, politics, religion, and ethics, in addition to individual differences; and (5) flexibility in managing operations on a continuous basis despite lack of assistance and gaps in information.

Figure 15–2

Development of Satisfaction in Host Country Over Time

Note: Satisfaction scale: 1 = extremely low; 7 = extremely high.
Source: Ingemar Torbiorn, *Living Abroad* (New York: John Wiley & Sons, 1982), p. 98. Copyright 1982 by John Wiley & Sons. Used with permission.

In research recently conducted among expatriates in China, Selmar found that those who were best able to deal with their new situation had developed coping strategies characterized by sociocultural and psychological adjustments including: (1) feeling comfortable that their work challenges can be met; (2) being able to adjust to their new living conditions; (3) learning how to interact well with host-country nationals outside of work; and (4) feeling reasonably happy and being able to enjoy one's day-to-day activities.[27] And Caligiuri, after examining how host nationals help expatriates adjust, has reported that certain types of personality characteristics are important in this process. In particular, her findings suggest that greater contact with host nationals helps with cross-cultural adjustment when the person also possesses the personality trait of openness. She also found that sociability was directly related to effective adjustment.[28]

Independence and Self-Reliance

In many overseas assignments, managers must carry out responsibilities and functions at levels higher than those to which they are accustomed. At the same time, managers have fewer people to call on for assistance and guidance. At company headquarters, a large staff of technical advisors may be available to provide assistance and guidance. In foreign assignments, managers often must be more self-reliant. One analysis reported that some of the determinants of independence and self-reliance include prior field experience (domestic or foreign), special project or task force experience, a hobby or avocation that requires a high degree of self-reliance, and a record of extracurricular college activities or community service activities.[29]

Physical and Emotional Health

Most organizations require that their overseas managers have good physical and emotional health. Some examples are fairly obvious. An employee with a heart condition would be rejected for overseas assignment; likewise, an individual with a nervous disorder would not be considered.

The psychological ability of individuals to withstand culture shock also would be considered, as would the current marital status as it affects the individual's ability to cope in a foreign environment. For example, one U.S. oil company operating in the Middle East considers middle-aged men with grown children to be the best able to cope with cultural shock, and for some locations in the desert, people from Texas or southern California make better risks than those from New England.

Age, Experience, and Education

Most MNCs strive for a balance between age and experience. There is evidence that younger managers are more eager for international assignments. These managers tend to be more "worldly" and have a greater appreciation of other cultures than older managers do. By the same token, young people often are the least developed in terms of management experience and technical skills; they lack real-world experience. To gain the desired balance, many firms send both young and seasoned personnel to the same overseas post. As Blue and Haynes put it, "Ideally, that team should be selected for both its youth and its experience, taking into consideration reporting relationships, specific responsibilities, authority and professional judgment as the determinants of whether youth or experience is best suited to a specific job."[30]

Many companies consider an academic degree, preferably a graduate degree, to be of critical importance to an international executive; however, universal agreement regarding the ideal type of degree is nonexistent. As one expert observed:

> Companies with highly technical products tend to prefer science degrees. Other firms feel that successful management requires depth, drive, imagination, creativity, and character-and that the type of person exemplified by these traits is more likely to be produced by a liberal arts education. But the overall prize-winning combination seems to be an undergraduate degree combined with a graduate business degree from a recognized business school.[31]

MNCs, of course, use formal education only as a point of departure for their own training and development efforts. For example, Siemens of Germany gives its international management team specific training designed to help them deal more effectively with the types of problems they will face on the job.

Language Training

One recognized weakness of many MNCs is that they do not give sufficient attention to the importance of language training. English is the primary language of international business, and most expatriates from all countries can converse in English. Those who can speak only English are at a distinct disadvantage when doing business in non-English-speaking countries, however. One study asked 1,100 Swedish expatriates how satisfied they were with knowledge of the local language. These Swedish managers expressed particular dissatisfaction with their understanding of Japanese and Middle Eastern languages.[32] In other words, language can be a very critical factor, and international experts have referred to it as "a most effective indirect method of learning about a country . . . as well as the value systems and customs of its people."[33]

Traditionally, U.S. managers have done very poorly in the language area. For example, a survey of 1,500 top managers worldwide faulted U.S. expatriates for minimizing the value of learning foreign languages. Executives in Japan, Western Europe, and South America, however, placed a high priority on speaking more than one language. The report concludes that "these results provide a poignant indication of national differences that promise to influence profoundly the success of American corporations."[34]

Motivation for a Foreign Assignment

Although individuals being sent overseas should have a desire to work abroad, this usually is not sufficient motivation. International management experts contend that the candidate also must believe in the importance of the job and even have something of an element of idealism or a sense of mission. Applicants who are unhappy with their current situation at home and are looking to get away seldom make effective overseas managers.

Some experts believe that a desire for adventure or a pioneering spirit is an acceptable reason for wanting to go overseas. Other motivators that often are cited include the desire to increase one's chances for promotion and the opportunity to improve one's economic status. For example, many U.S. MNCs regard international experience as being critical for promotion to the upper ranks. In addition, thanks to the supplemental wage and benefit package, U.S. managers sometimes find that they can make, and especially save, more money than if they remained stateside.

Spouses and Dependents or Work-Family Issues

Spouses and dependents are another important consideration when a person is to be chosen for an overseas assignment. If the family is not happy, the manager often performs poorly and may either be terminated or simply decide to leave the organization. Shaffer and her associates recently collected multisource data from 324 expatriates in 46 countries and found that the amount of organizational support that an expatriate feels he or she is receiving and the interplay between this person's work and family domains have a direct and unique influence on the individual's intentions regarding staying with or leaving the enterprise.[35] For this reason, some firms interview both the spouse and the manager before deciding whether to approve the assignment. This can be a very important decision on the part of the firm because it focuses on the importance of family as an issue. In fact, in a survey that she conducted of over 400 expats, Tung found that people had very firm views in this area regarding what they would and would not do. Here is how expats responded to select work-family issues on a scale that ranged from 1 (strongly disagree) to 5 (strongly agree).[36]

I am willing to forgo an important function at home if it conflicts with an important job-related function.	3.37
I would accept an international assignment even if it means that my spouse/partner has to make career sacrifices.	3.07
I place my career above my family.	2.21
I would accept an international assignment even if my family objected to the assignment.	1.83
I would accept an international assignment even if my family will not be able to relocate with me.	1.69

Adaptability screening
The process of evaluating how well a family is likely to stand up to the stress of overseas life.

One popular approach in appraising the family's suitability for an overseas assignment is called **adaptability screening.** This process evaluates how well the family is likely to stand up to the rigors and stress of overseas life. The company will look for a number of things in this screening, including how closely knit the family is, how well it can withstand stress, and how well it can adjust to a new culture and climate. The reason this family criterion receives so much attention is that MNCs have learned that an unhappy executive will be unproductive on the job and the individual will want to transfer home long before the tour of duty is complete. These findings have been affirmed and extended by Borstorff and her associates, who examined the factors associated with employee willingness to work overseas and concluded that:

1. Unmarried employees are more willing than any other group to accept expat assignments.
2. Married couples without children at home or those with non-teenage children are probably the most willing to move.
3. Prior international experience appears associated with willingness to work as an expatriate.
4. Individuals most committed to their professional careers and to their employing organizations are prone to be more willing to work as expatriates.
5. Careers and attitudes of spouses will likely have a significant impact on employee willingness to move overseas.
6. Employee and spouse perceptions of organizational support for expatriates are critical to employee willingness to work overseas.[37]

These findings indicate that organizations cannot afford to overlook the role of the spouse in the expat selection decision process. What, in particular, can be done to address their concerns?[38] Table 15–3 provides some insights regarding this answer. Additionally, the table adds a factor that is often overlooked in this process—situations in which the wife is being assigned overseas and the husband is the "other" spouse. While many of the concerns of the male spouse are similar to those of spouses in general, a close look at Table 15–3 shows that some of the concerns of the males are different in terms of their rank ordering.

Leadership Ability

The ability to influence people to act in a particular way, commonly called "leadership," is another important criterion in selecting managers for an international assignment. Determining whether a person who is an effective leader in the home country will be equally effective in an overseas environment can be difficult, however. In determining whether an applicant has the desired leadership ability, many firms look for specific characteristics, such as maturity, emotional stability, the ability to communicate well, independence, initiative, creativity, and good health. If these characteristics are present and the person has been an effective leader in the home country, MNCs assume that the individual also will do well overseas.

Table 15–3
Activities that Are Important for Expatriate Spouses (scale: 1-5, 5 = very important)

Mean Score	Activity
Average	From all respondents:
4.33	Company help in obtaining necessary paperwork (permits, etc.) for spouse
4.28	Adequate notice of relocation
4.24	Predeparture training for spouse and children
4.23	Counseling for spouse regarding work/activity opportunities in foreign location
4.05	Employment networks coordinated with other international networks
3.97	Help with spouse's reentry into home country
3.93	Financial support for education
3.76	Compensation for spouse's lost wages and/or benefits
3.71	Creation of a job for spouse
3.58	Development of support groups for spouses
3.24	Administrative support (office space, secretarial services, etc.) for spouse
3.11	Financial support for research
3.01	Financial support for volunteer activities
2.90	Financial support for creative activities
Average	From male spouses:
4.86	Employment networks coordinated with other international organizations
4.71	Help with spouse's reentry into home country
4.71	Administrative support (office space, secretarial services, etc.) for spouse
4.57	Compensation for spouse's lost wages and/or benefits
4.29	Adequate notice of relocation
4.29	Counseling for spouse regarding work/activity opportunities in foreign location
3.86	Predeparture training for spouse and children
3.71	Creation of a job for spouse
3.71	Financial support for volunteer activities
3.43	Financial support for education
3.14	Financial support for research
3.14	Financial support for creative activities
3.00	Development of support groups for spouses

Source: Adapted from Betty Jane Punnett, "Towards Effective Management of Expatriate Spouses," *Journal of World Business,* vol. 33, no. 3, 1997, p. 249.

Other Considerations

Applicants also can take certain steps to prepare themselves better for international assignments. Tu and Sullivan have suggested the applicant can carry out a number of different phases.[39] In phase one, they suggest focusing on self-evaluation and general awareness. This includes answering the question: Is an international assignment really for me? Other questions in the first phase include finding out if one's spouse and family support the decision to go international and collecting general information on the available job opportunities.

Phase two is characterized by a concentration on activities that should be completed before being selected. Some of these include: (1) conducting a technical skills match to ensure that one's skills are in line with those that are required for the job; (2) starting to learn the language, customs, and etiquette of the region where one will be posted; (3) developing an awareness of the culture and value systems of this geographic area; and (4) making one's superior aware of this interest in an international assignment.

The third phase consists of activities to be completed after being selected for an overseas assignment. Some of these include: (1) attending training sessions provided by the company; (2) conferring with colleagues who have had experience in the assigned region; (3) speaking with expatriates and foreign nationals about the assigned country; and (4) if possible, visiting the host country with one's spouse before the formally scheduled departure.

■ International Human Resource Selection Procedures

Besides considering the selection criteria discussed so far, MNCs use a number of selection procedures. The two most common are tests and interviews. Some international firms use one; a smaller percentage employ both. Recently, theoretical models containing the variables that are important for adjusting to an overseas assignment have been developed. These adjustment models can help contribute to more effective selection of expatriates. The following sections examine traditional testing and interviewing procedures, then present an adjustment model.

Testing Procedures

Some evidence suggests that although testing is used by some firms, it is not extremely popular. For example, an early study found that almost 80 percent of the 127 foreign operations managers who were surveyed reported that their companies used no tests in the selection process.[40] This contrasts with the more widespread testing these firms use when selecting domestic managers. A number of comments were offered regarding why testing was not used. Here is a sampling of the reasons:

> Tests are too expensive and you have to be a mathematical and psychological wizard to construct and interpret them. What you get for your money and effort is not worth it.

> Testing and predicting success are inseparable partners. We know this and selectors in other firms know this. However, measuring managerial performance in overseas operations is something that is taking time to pinpoint. Thus, until we make progress in measuring success it is our belief that there is no reason why we should become involved in constructing tests for overseas managerial candidates.

> We have used tests in the past and found that they did not improve the selection process. If something does not pay its own way we discard it. Testing did not pay and had to be eliminated as a screening device. We now use the candidate's domestic record and our personal opinions about his adaptability potential. We think that our overseas experience enables us to be excellent judges about a candidate's probability of succeeding abroad.[41]

These reasons are still valid today. For example, MNCs doing business in China are finding that selection tests have limited value. For example, one large U.S. consumer goods firm has reported that the analytical problem-solving tests that it uses in screening applicants in North America and Europe will eliminate half of these individuals, but only 12 percent of Chinese applicants are screened out with these tests.[42] This is a result of the outstanding analytical training that these individuals receive at prestigious Chinese universities. So the company needed to find other tests for identifying the very best applicants. Similarly, the use of psychological testing or western-style assessment center exercises have not proven very effective. For one thing, the Chinese education system does not train students to analyze open-ended hypothetical situations. As a result, expatriate evaluators find it hard to draw conclusions about the suitability of the Chinese candidates based on their performance in problem-solving exercises.

Interviewing Procedures

Many firms use interviews to screen people for overseas assignments. One expert notes: "It is generally agreed that extensive interviews of candidates (and their spouses) by senior executives still ultimately provide the best method of selection."[43] Tung's research supports these comments. For example, 52 percent of the U.S. MNCs she surveyed reported that in the case of managerial candidates, MNCs conducted interviews with both the manager and his or her spouse, and 47 percent conducted interviews with the candidate alone. For technically oriented positions, 40 percent of the firms interviewed both the candidate and the spouse, and 59 percent conducted interviews with the candidate alone. German MNCs follow a pattern similar to that of U.S. companies. In the case of management positions, 41 percent interviewed both the candidate and the spouse, and 59 percent interviewed the candidate only. For technically oriented positions, these percentages were 62 and 39, respectively. Concerning these findings, Tung concluded:

> These figures suggest that in management-type positions which involve more extensive contact with the local community, as compared to technically oriented positions, the adaptability of the spouse to living in a foreign environment was perceived as important for successful performance abroad. However, even for technically oriented positions, a sizable proportion of the firms did conduct interviews with both candidate and spouse. This lends support to the contention of other researchers that MNCs are becoming increasingly cognizant of the importance of this factor to effective performance abroad.[44]

In addition, a growing number of MNCs are modifying the approaches they use in conducting their interviews. For example, many multinationals have found that in interviewing Chinese job applicants in the PRC it is useful to employ both expatriate and local interviewers. The expatriate is there to ensure that attention is focused on the key selection criteria so that those who are offered jobs will indeed have the abilities, skills, and training to do the work. The local person is there because this individual knows the local culture and customs and can provide insights regarding the applicant's responses and other behaviors that might go unnoticed by the expatriate. So together the two are able to help identify those candidates most likely to do the best job.[45]

An Adjustment Model

In recent years, international human resource management scholars have developed theoretical models that help to explain the factors involved in effectively adjusting to overseas assignments.[46] These adjustment models help to identify the theoretical underpinnings of effective selection of expatriates. Figure 15–3 provides an example of one such adjustment model.[47]

As shown, there are two major types of adjustments that an expatriate must make when going on an overseas assignment. One is the anticipatory adjustment. This is carried out before the expat leaves for the assignment. The other is the in-country adjustment, which takes place on-site.

The anticipatory adjustment is influenced by a number of important factors. One individual factor is the predeparture training that is provided. This often takes the form of cross-cultural seminars or workshops, and it is designed to acquaint expats with the culture

Figure 15–3   **A Theoretic Model for Explaining International**
Adjustment of Expatriates

Source: J. Stewart Black, Mark Mendenhall, and Gary Oddou, "Toward a Comprehensive Model of International Adjustment: An Integration of Multiple Theoretical Perspectives," *Academy of Management Review,* April 1991, p. 303. Used with permission.

and work life of the country to which they will be posted. Another individual factor affecting anticipatory adjustment is the previous experience the expat may have had with the assigned country or those with similar cultures. These two individual factors, training and previous experience, help to determine the accuracy of the expat's expectations.

The organizational input into anticipatory adjustment is most directly related and concerned with the selection process. Traditionally, MNCs relied on only one important selection criteria for overseas assignments: technical competence. Obviously, technical competence is important, but it is only one of a number of skills that will be needed. If the MNC concentrates only on technical competence as a selection criterion, then it is not properly preparing the expatriate managers for successful adjustment in overseas assignments. Expats are going to go abroad believing that they are prepared to deal with the challenges awaiting them, and they will be wrong.

Once the expatriate is on-site, a number of factors will influence his or her ability to adjust effectively. One factor includes the expat's ability to maintain a positive outlook in the face of a high-pressure situation, to interact well with host nationals, and to perceive and evaluate the host country's cultural values and norms correctly. A second factor is the job itself, as reflected by the clarity of the role the expat plays in the host management team, the authority the expat has to make decisions, the newness of the work-related challenges, and the amount of role conflict that exists. A third factor is the organizational culture and how easily the expat can adjust to it. A fourth input is nonwork factors, such as the toughness with which the expatriate faces a whole new cultural experience and how well his or her family can adjust to the rigors of the new assignment. A fifth and final factor identified in the adjustment model is the expat's ability to develop effective socialization tactics and to understand "what's what" and "who's who" in the host organization.

These anticipatory and in-country factors will influence the expatriate's mode and degree of adjustment to an overseas assignment. As identified in Figure 15–3, these factors cover a wide continuum of considerations. They can help to explain why effective selection

Figure 15–4

The Relocation Transition Curve

Perceived Competence

7. **Integration** of new skills and behavior. Acceptance of the new environment

2. **Fantasia** The feeling of enchantment and excitement in the new environment

3. **Interest** A deeper exploration of the environment and a realization that it is fundamentally different from home

6. **Search** for meaning. Understanding reasons for success and failure. New models/personal theories created

5. **Experimentation** and testing of new approaches. Practice phase, trying to do things differently. Feedback of results, success and failure

1. **Unreality** The feeling that the relocation is a dream

4. **Acceptance of reality** "Letting go" of past comfortable attitudes. The realization that you are a stranger in a strange land

Beginning of transition

Time

Source: Adapted from Iain McCormick and Tony Chapman, "Executive Relocation: Personal and Organizational Tactics," in Pat Joynt and Malcolm Warner (eds.), *Managing across Cultures: Issues and Perspectives* (London: International Thomson Business Press, 1996), p. 368.

of expatriates is multifaceted and can be very difficult and challenging. On the other hand, if all works out well the individual can become a very important part of the organization's overseas operations. McCormick and Chapman have illustrated this by showing the changes that an expat goes through as he or she seeks to adjust to the new assignment.[48] As seen in Figure 15–4 early enthusiasm often gives way to cold reality and the expat typically ends up in a search to balance personal and work demands with the new environment. In many cases, fortunately, everything works out well. Additionally, one of the ways that MNCs often try to put potential expats at ease about their new assignment is by presenting an attractive compensation package.

■ The Compensation Issue

One of the reasons why there has been a decline in the number of expats in recent years is that MNCs have found that the expense can be prohibitive. Reynolds has estimated that, on average, "expats cost employers two to five times as much as home-country counterparts and frequently ten or more times as much as local nationals in the country to which they are assigned."[49] As seen in Figure 15–5, the cost of living in some of the major cities is extremely high and these expenses must be included somewhere in the compensation package.

Common Elements of Compensation Packages

The overall compensation package often will vary from country to country. As Bailey has noted:

> Compensation programs implemented in global organization will not mirror an organization's domestic plan because of differences in legally mandated benefits, tax laws, cultures, and employee expectation based on local practices. The additional challenge in compensation design is the requirement that excessive costs be avoided and at the same time employee morale be maintained at high levels.[50]

Figure 15–5   **Relative Cost of Living in Selected Cities**
New York = 100

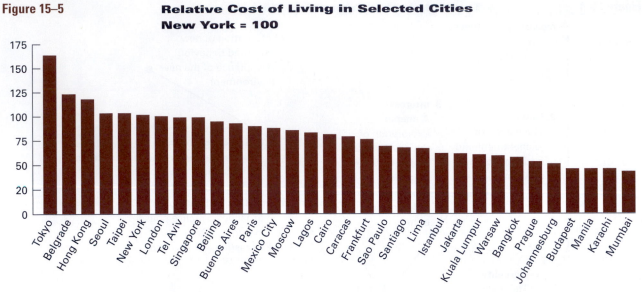

Source: Economist Intelligence Unit, 2000.

There are, however, five common elements in the typical expatriate compensation package. These include base salary, benefits, allowances, incentives, and taxes.

Base Salary   Base salary is the amount of money that an expatriate normally receives in the home country. In the United States this has been around $175,000 for upper-middle managers in recent years, and this rate is similar to that paid to managers in both Japan and Germany. The exchange rates, of course, also affect the real wages.

Expatriate salaries typically are set according to the base pay of the home countries. Therefore, a German manager working for a U.S. MNC and assigned to Spain would have a base salary that reflects the salary structure in Germany. U.S. expatriates have salaries tied to U.S. levels. The salaries usually are paid in home currency, local currency, or a combination of the two. The base pay also serves as the benchmark against which bonuses and benefits are calculated.

Benefits   Approximately one-third of compensation for regular employees is benefits. These benefits compose a similar, or even larger, portion of expat compensation. A number of thorny issues surround compensation for expatriates, however. These include:

1. whether MNCs should maintain expatriates in home-country benefit programs, particularly if these programs are not tax-deductible;
2. whether MNCs have the option of enrolling expatriates in host-country benefit programs and/or making up any difference in coverage;
3. whether host-country legislation regarding termination of employment affects employee benefits entitlements;
4. whether the home or host country is responsible for the expatriates' social security benefits;
5. whether benefits should be subject to the requirements of the home or host country;
6. which country should pay for the benefits;
7. whether other benefits should be used to offset any shortfall in coverage; and
8. whether home-country benefits programs should be available to local nationals.[51]

Most U.S.-based MNCs include expatriate managers in their home-office benefits program at no additional cost to the expats. If the host country requires expats to contribute to their social security program, the MNC typically picks up the tab. Fortunately, several international agreements between countries recently have eliminated such dual coverage and expenses.

Additionally, MNCs often provide expatriates with extra vacation and with special leaves. The MNC typically will pay the airfare for expats and their families to make an annual visit home, for emergency leave, and for expenses when a relative in the home country is ill or dies.[52]

Allowances   Allowances are an expensive feature of expatriate compensation packages. One of the most common parts is a cost-of-living allowance—a payment for differences between the home country and the overseas assignment. This allowance is designed to provide the expat with the same standard of living that he or she enjoyed in the home country, and it may cover a variety of expenses, including relocation, housing, education, and hardship.

Relocation expenses typically involve moving, shipping, and storage charges that are associated with personal furniture, clothing, and other items that the expatriate and his or her family are (or are not) taking to the new assignment. Related expenses also may include cars and club memberships in the host country, although these perks commonly are provided only to senior-level expats.

Housing allowances cover a wide range. Some firms provide the expat with a residence during the assignment and pay all associated expenses. Others give a predetermined housing allotment each month and let expats choose their own residence. Additionally, some MNCs help those going on assignment with the sale or lease of the house they are leaving behind; if the house is sold, the company usually pays closing costs and other associated expenses.

Education allowances for the expat's children are another integral part of the compensation package. These expenses cover costs such as tuition, enrollment fees, books, supplies, transportation, room, board, and school uniforms. In some cases, expenses to attend postsecondary schools also are provided.

Hardship allowances are designed to induce expats to work in hazardous areas or an area with a poor quality of life. Those who are assigned to Eastern Europe, China, and some Middle Eastern countries sometimes are granted a hardship premium. These payments may be in the form of a lump sum ($10,000 to $50,000) or a percentage (15% to 50%) of the expat's base compensation.

Incentives   In recent years some MNCs have also been designing special incentive programs for keeping expats motivated. In the process a growing number of firms have dropped the ongoing premium for overseas assignments and replaced it with a one-time, lump-sum premium. For example, in the early 1990s over 60 percent of MNCs gave ongoing premiums to their expats. Today that percentage is under 50 percent and continuing to decline. Peterson and his colleagues, for example, recently examined the human resource policies of 24 U.S., British, German, and Japanese subsidiaries and found that in only 10 cases did the multinational have a policy of paying expatriates higher compensation than they would have received if they had stayed in their home country.[53]

The lump sum payment has a number of benefits. One is that expats realize that they will be given this payment just once—when they move to the international locale. So the payment tends to retain its value as an incentive. A second is that the costs to the company are less because there is only one payment and no future financial commitment. A third is that because it is a separate payment, distinguishable from regular pay, it is more readily available for saving or spending.

The specific incentive program that is used will vary, and expats like this. Researchers, for example, have found that some of the factors that influence the type and amount of incentive include whether the person is moving within or between continents and where the person is being stationed. Table 15–4 provides some of the latest survey information related to worldwide employer incentive practices.

Table 15–4
Employer Incentive Practices around the World

MNCs Paying for Moves within Continents				
	Asia	Europe	North America	Total
Type of premium				
Ongoing	62%	46%	29%	42%
Lump sum	21	20	25	23
None	16	27	42	32
MNCs Paying for Moves between Continents				
	Asia	Europe	North America	Total
Type of premium				
Ongoing	63%	54%	39%	49%
Lump sum	24	18	30	26
None	13	21	27	22

Source: Derived from Geofferey W. Latta, "Expatriate Incentives: Beyond Tradition," *HR Focus,* March 1998, p. S4.

Finally, it is important to recognize that a growing number of MNCs are beginning to phase out incentive premiums. Instead, they are focusing on creating a cadre of expats who are motivated by nonfinancial incentives.

> More companies are starting to take an entirely different approach, paying no premiums to expatriates regardless of where they send them. According to this philosophy, an assignment itself is its own reward. It's an opportunity for an employee to achieve personal and career growth. In some organizations, succession planning for senior-level positions requires international experience. Others view expatriate assignments as a step toward achieving globalization. Companies that subscribe to the philosophy of paying no premiums only consider cost-of-living issues, not motivational rewards, when designing pay packages.[54]

Taxes   The other major component of expatriate compensation is tax equalization. For example, an expat may have two tax bills, one from the host country and one from the U.S. Internal Revenue Service, for the same pay. IRS Code Section 911 permits a deduction of up to $70,000 on foreign-earned income. Top-level expats often earn far more than this, however; thus, they may pay two tax bills for the amount by which their pay exceeds $70,000.

Usually, MNCs pay the extra tax burden. The most common way is by determining the base salary and other extras (e.g., bonuses) that the expat would make if based in the home country. Taxes on this income then are computed and compared with the taxes due on the expat's income. Any taxes that exceed what would have been imposed in the home country are paid by the MNC, and any windfall is kept by the expat as a reward for taking the assignment.[55]

Tailoring the Package

Working within the five common elements just described, MNCs will tailor-make compensation packages to fit the specific situation. For example, senior-level managers in Japan are paid only around four times as much as junior staff members. This is in sharp contrast to the United States, where the multiple is much higher. A similar situation exists in Europe, where many senior-level managers make far less than their U.S. counterparts and stockholders, politicians, and the general public oppose U.S.-style affluence. For example, when Daimler-Benz bought Chrysler there was controversy regarding the differences in the executive pay packages. German companies believe that executive pay should be closer to that of the average employee. American companies, on the other hand, reward executives with bonuses and stock options. Here is a contrast between the compensation packages of the chairman and chief executive at both companies at the time of the merger.[56]

	Chrysler Chairman and CEO	Daimler-Benz Chairman and CEO
Salary	$1,612,500	$1,137,300
Bonus	3,000,000	—
Other annual payments (dividends, tax reimbursement)	218,903	—
Other programs (matching payment to savings plan)	77,400	—
Performance shares	1,209,701	—
Options granted (estimate of value)	4,753,000	796,100
Options exercised (granted in previous years)	5,259,600	—
Total	$16,131,104	$1,933,400

These data help pinpoint a thorny problem: Can a senior-level U.S. expat be paid a salary that is significantly higher than local senior-level managers in the overseas subsidiary, or will this create morale problems? This is a difficult question to answer and must be given careful consideration. One solution is to link pay and performance to attract and retain outstanding personnel. For example, at Salomon Brothers, the U.S. investment bank, employees are well paid if they do well and penalized if they do poorly—and this system is acceptable to all concerned. One report noted:

> The result is that in exceptionally good years Salomon's new system appears to offer its employees exceptional returns, but it will be less generous than at present when times are hard. The firm's aim is to make staff behave as if they own the business, rather than merely work for it. It is a big gamble. Some of the firm's most profitable traders may be tempted away by fatter bonuses elsewhere. Alan Howard, one of its top traders in London, left Salomon after the pay deal was confirmed, moving to Japan's Tokai Bank for a two-year package reputedly worth a guaranteed [$7.5 million].[57]

In formulating the compensation package, a number of approaches can be used. The most common is the **balance sheet approach,** which involves ensuring that the expat is "made whole" and does not lose money by taking the assignment. A second, and often complementary approach, is negotiation, which involves working out a special, ad hoc arrangement that is acceptable to both the company and the expat. A third approach is called **localization** and involves paying the expat a salary that is comparable to those of local nationals. This approach most commonly is used with individuals early in their careers and who are being given a long-term overseas assignment. A fourth approach is the **lump sum method,** which involves giving the expat a predetermined amount of money and letting the individual make his or her own decisions regarding how to spend it. A fifth is the **cafeteria approach,** which entails giving expats a series of options and then letting them decide how to spend the available funds. For example, if expats have children, they may opt for private schooling; if expats have no children, they may choose a chauffeur-driven car or an upscale apartment. A sixth method is the **regional system,** under which the MNC sets a compensation system for all expats who are assigned to a particular region. Therefore, everyone going to Europe falls under one particular system, and everyone being assigned to South America is covered by a different system.[58]

The most important thing to remember about global compensation is that the package must be cost effective and fair. If it meets these two characteristics, it likely will be acceptable to all parties.

Balance sheet approach
An approach to developing an expatriate compensation package that is based on ensuring the expat is "made whole" and does not lose money by taking the assignment.

Localization
An approach to developing an expatriate compensation package that involves paying the expat a salary comparable to that of local nationals.

Lump sum method
An approach to developing an expatriate compensation package that involves giving the expat a predetermined amount of money and letting the individual make his or her own decisions regarding how to spend it.

Cafeteria approach
An approach to developing an expatriate compensation package that entails giving the individual a series of options and letting the person decide how to spend the available funds.

Regional system
An approach to developing an expatriate compensation package that involves setting a compensation system for all expats who are assigned to a particular region and paying everyone in accord with that system.

■ Individual and Host-Country Viewpoints

Until now, we have examined the selection process mostly from the standpoint of the MNC: What will be best for the company? However, two additional perspectives for selection warrant consideration: (1) that of the individual who is being selected; and (2) that of the country to which the candidate will be sent. Research shows that each has specific desires and motivations regarding the expatriate selection process.

Candidate Motivations

Why do individuals accept foreign assignments? One answer is a greater demand for their talents abroad than at home. For example, a growing number of senior U.S. managers have moved to Mexico because of Mexico's growing need for experienced executives.

A number of researchers have investigated overall candidate motivations. One early study administered an opinion questionnaire to 13,000 employees of a large electrical equipment manufacturing firm with operations in 46 countries. There were 200 multiple-choice items in the questionnaire, and the instrument was translated into 12 foreign languages to accommodate all groups of people.[59] Fourteen goals were found to have varying degrees of importance. These extended from a desire for training to the need to work for a successful company. Table 15–5 presents a brief description of the 10 most important goals.

This study found that the importance of each goal was somewhat influenced by the individual's occupation. Table 15–6 shows this breakdown. The most important objectives related to achievement; the least important related to what the organization gives to its employees.

In drawing together their findings, these researchers grouped the participating countries into clusters: Anglo (Australia, Austria, Canada, India, New Zealand, South Africa, Switzerland, United Kingdom, and United States); Northern European (Denmark, Finland, Norway); French (Belgium and France); northern South American (Colombia, Mexico, and Peru); southern South American (Argentina and Chile); and Independent (Brazil, Germany, Israel, Japan, Sweden, and Venezuela). Based on these groupings, they were able to identify major motivational differences. Some of their findings included:

1. The Anglo cluster was more interested in individual achievement and less interested in the desire for security than any other cluster.

2. The French cluster was similar to the Anglo cluster, except that less importance was given to individual achievement and more to security.

3. Countries in the Northern European cluster were more oriented to job accomplishment and less to getting ahead; considerable importance was assigned to jobs not interfering with personal lives.

4. In South American clusters, individual achievement goals were less important than in most other clusters. Fringe benefits were particularly important to South American groups.

5. Germans were similar to those in the South American clusters, except that they placed a great emphasis on advancement and earnings.

6. The Japanese were unique in their mix of desires. They placed high value on earnings opportunities but low value on advancement. They were high on challenge but low on autonomy. At the same time, they placed strong emphasis on working in a friendly, efficient department and having good physical working conditions.[60]

Another study investigated the reasons why personnel accept overseas positions.[61] The study sampled 135 U.S. expatriate managers at the upper-middle ranks of three foreign subsidiaries of three major U.S. MNCs. Four major sets of variables explained why people go overseas. The most important reason was the enhancement of one's international business career. This included things such as increased promotion potential, the opportunity to improve career mobility, and the opportunity for greater responsibility. The second

Table 15–5
Goal Ranking among Overseas Personnel

Rank	Goal	Questionnaire Wording
1	Training	Have training opportunities (to improve your present skills or learn new skills)
2	Challenge	Have challenging work to do—work that gives you a personal sense of accomplishment
3	Autonomy	Have considerable freedom to adopt your own approach to the job
4	Earnings	Have opportunity for high earnings
5	Advancement	Have an opportunity for advancement to higher-level jobs
6	Recognition	Get the recognition you deserve for doing a good job
7	Security	Have job security (steady work)
8	Friendly department	Work in a department where the people are congenial and friendly to one another
9	Personal time	Have a job which leaves you sufficient time for your personal and/or family life
10	Company contribution	Have a job which allows you to make a real contribution to your company's success

Source: Adapted from David Sirota and J. Michael Greenwood, "Understand Your Overseas Workforce," *Harvard Business Review,* January–February 1971, p. 55.

Table 15–6
Goal Ranking by Occupation

Goal	Average Rank		
	Salespeople	Technical Personnel	Service Personnel
Training	2	1	1
Challenge	1	2	2.5
Autonomy	3	3	7
Earnings	4	4.5	4
Advancement	5	6	5
Recognition	6	4.5	9
Security	10	11	2.5
Friendly department	9	8	8
Personal time	11	7	6
Company contribution	7.5	9.5	10

Source: Adapted from David Sirota and J. Michael Greenwood, "Understand Your Overseas Workforce," *Harvard Business Review,* January–February 1971, p. 56.

most important reason was the attraction to overseas assignments. This included the opportunity to go overseas, the desire to live in a particular locale, and encouragement from one's family to take the assignment. The third most important reason was technical competence. The individual had knowledge of the particular job to be done and/or had proven performance or capability in this area of work. The fourth was that the assignment was viewed as necessary for one's career. For example, some candidates felt that all managers who wanted to reach the upper ranks had to have international experience and/or these jobs were necessary in gathering knowledge and experience for future assignments.

Another interesting focus of attention has been on those countries that expatriates like best. The Torbiorn study cited earlier found that the 1,100 Swedish expatriates surveyed were at least fairly well satisfied with their host country, and in some cases were very satisfied. Five of the countries that they liked very much included Switzerland, Belgium,

Figure 15–6

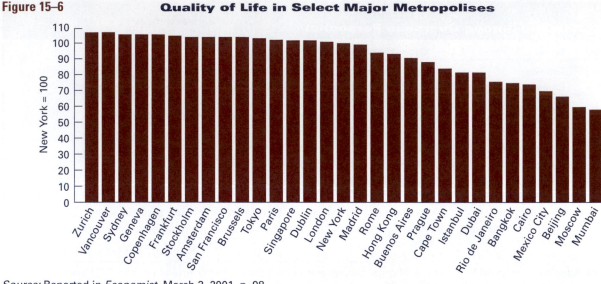

Quality of Life in Select Major Metropolises

Source: Reported in *Economist,* March 3, 2001, p. 98.

England, the U.S., and Portugal.[62] Today these countries are still quite popular, although the specific city is typically of even greater importance. What are the best cities? One way of answering this question is by determining the quality of life in the metropolis. This is usually done by measuring a host of criteria including the city's educational system, recreational facilities, communication system, transportation system, cost of living, and the degree of personal safety one can expect to find there. Figure 15–6 reports the recent quality of life in 31 major cities worldwide.

Host-Country Desires

Although many MNCs try to choose people who fit in well, little attention has been paid to the host country's point of view. Whom would it like to see put in managerial positions? One study surveyed over 100 host-country organizations (HCOs) in five countries: Germany (*n*=38), England (*n*=33), France (*n*=16), Holland (*n*=16), and Belgium (*n*=8). The respondents were either chief executive officers of the HCO or heads of departments that interacted extensively with expatriate managers heading the subsidiary. Data were collected via a questionnaire survey and a comprehensive interview. The 200-item questionnaire was designed to determine both present and desired personnel policies and patterns of managerial behavior.[63] The findings are presented in Table 15–7.

The results showed that in the main, accommodating the wishes of HCOs can be very difficult. They are highly ethnocentric in orientation. They want local managers to head the subsidiaries; and they set such high levels of expectation regarding the desired characteristics of expatriates that anyone sent by the MNC is unlikely to measure up. These findings help to explain why many MNCs welcome input from their host-country nations regarding staffing decisions but do not let themselves be totally swayed by these opinions. Quite obviously, many MNCs are as guilty of ethnocentric behavior as their host-country counterparts. The accompanying sidebar, "Recruiting Managers in Japan," provides a detailed example of Japanese ethnocentricity.

■ **Repatriation of Expatriates**

Repatriation
The return to one's home country from an overseas management assignment.

For most overseas managers, **repatriation,** or the return to one's home country, occurs within 5 years of the time they leave. Few expatriates remain overseas for the duration of their stay with the firm.[64] When they return, these expatriates often find themselves facing readjustment problems, and some MNCs now are trying to deal with these problems through use of transition strategies.

Table 15–7
Beliefs of Home-Country Organization Expats

Beliefs	Percentage of Respondents Who Agree				
	Holland	England	Germany	Belgium	France
All top managers of foreign subsidiaries should be host-country nationals.	87.5	78.0	35.1	42.9	81.3
Expatriate managers should be of West European ethnic origin.	90.0	95.0	96.3	100.0	58.3
Expatriate managers should be thoroughly familiar with the culture of the host country.	93.8	90.3	78.9	100.0	81.3
Expatriate managers should adhere to local managerial patterns of behavior.	87.5	96.9	73.7	100.0	93.3
Expatriate managers should be proficient in the host-country language.	100.0	100.0	100.0	100.0	100.0
Expatriate managers should have a working knowledge of the host country's social characteristics.	93.3	96.9	84.2	100.0	100.0
Expatriate managers should be thoroughly familiar with the history of the host country.	93.3	83.9	81.6	100.0	100.0

Source: Adapted from Y. Zeira and M. Banai, "Attitudes of Host-Country Organizations toward MNCs' Staffing Policies: A Cross-Country and Cross-Industry Analysis," *Management International Review,* vol. 21, no. 2, 1981, p. 42. Used with permission.

Reasons for Returning

The most common reason that expatriates return home from overseas assignments is that their formally agreed-on tour of duty is over. Before they left, they were told that they would be posted overseas for a predetermined period, often 2 to 3 years, and now are returning as planned. A second common reason is that expatriates want their children educated in a home-country school, and the longer they are away, the less likely this will happen.[65]

A third reason that expatriates return is because they are not happy in their overseas assignment. Sometimes this is a result of poor organizational support by the home office which results in the manager feeling that the assignment is not a good one and it is best to return as soon as possible. Kraimer, Wayne, and Jaworski have found that lack of this kind of support has a negative effect on the expat's ability to adjust to the assignment.[66] Other times an expat will want to return home early because the spouse or children do not want to stay, and the company feels that the loss in managerial productivity is too great to be off-set by short term personal unhappiness. Therefore, the individual is allowed to come back even though typically the cost is quite high.[67]

A fourth reason that people return is failure to do a good job. Such failure often spells trouble for the manager. As a director of employee relations of a large U.S. MNC put it: "If a person flunks out overseas . . . we bring him home. . . . He's penalized indirectly because the odds are that if he flunked out over there, he's in trouble over here. But we bring him back and, generally, he has a tough row to hoe."[68]

Readjustment Problems

While many companies say that they want their people to have international experience, they often seem unsure of what to do with these managers when they return. One recent survey of midsize and large firms found that 80 percent of these companies send people abroad and more than half of them intend to increase the number they have on assignment overseas. However, the responses from the returning expats point to problems. Three-quarters of the respondents said that they felt their permanent position upon returning home was a demotion. Over 60 percent said that they lacked the opportunities to put their foreign experience

International Management in Action

Recruiting Managers in Japan

Recruiting managers in host countries can be a very difficult chore. For example, small U.S. firms in Japan report that local managers often do not want to work for them because they are unfamiliar with the company and do not want to run the risk of joining a business that may be around for only a short time. Larger, highly visible MNCs, such as IBM, Coca-Cola, and Ford Motor, do not have this problem, but there are other recruiting challenges for human resource management in Japan that are just as formidable.

One of these challenges facing an MNC in Japan is the significant amount of time it takes to recruit a Japanese manager. In the United States, when an MNC wants to hire an identified manager from another company, it will either have a headhunter contact the individual or have someone from the MNC do it. In either case, the MNC doing recruiting in the United States will quickly find out if the person is interested in changing jobs. If the answer is yes, a tentative offer will be made, and negotiations will begin. Quite often, the entire process will take only two or three meetings spread over a few weeks. Managers are recruited quite differently in Japan. There, the recruitment process is very slow and very deliberate, often taking 6 months to a year. The extended time is necessary, because there are a number of rules of business etiquette that must be followed.

A multinational doing recruiting in Japan typically goes through the following steps. A top manager from the multinational that is seeking to hire a manager away from a Japanese firm will first meet with that person's manager, and perhaps even the person's family, and request permission to negotiate with the individual. The MNC will have to provide assurances regarding this person's future position, security, and opportunities. Only then will meetings and negotiations with the manager begin. Moreover, the higher up the organization the recruited manager is located, the more delicate and slow-moving the process tends to be. There is little that the multinational can do, however, because it needs to recruit the top local talent.

The primary reason why it is so important for MNCs doing business in Japan to have local managers is because the Japanese are extremely ethnocentric. Japanese consumers and firms prefer to buy from Japanese businesses. They prefer local products to imports. In selecting people, MNCs in Japan typically put a Japanese national in charge of the subsidiary or make the individual the number-two person. They also recruit a large percentage of the managerial work force from the local market and do everything they can to give their subsidiary a "local look." In fact, in many Japanese subsidiaries of MNCs, there are no visible foreign managers.

One of the most important things that MNCs have learned about doing business in Japan is that they must be regarded as a local firm if they hope to succeed. MNCs such as IBM have done this so well that they are regarded as "Japanese" by the locals. As a result, many of the barriers that prevent other multinationals from doing business in Japan do not exist for companies such as IBM, which clearly understands the value of recruiting managers in Japan.

---

to work, while 60 percent said that their company had not communicated clearly about what would happen to them when they returned. Perhaps worst of all, within a year of returning, 25 percent of the managers had left the company.[69] These statistics are not surprising to those who have been studying repatriation problems. In fact, one researcher reported the following expatriate comments about their experiences:

> My colleagues react indifferently to my international assignment. . . . They view me as doing a job I did in the past; they don't see me as having gained anything while overseas.

> I had no specific reentry job to return to. I wanted to leave international and return to domestic. Working abroad magnifies problems while isolating effects. You deal with more problems, but the home office doesn't know the details of the good or bad effects. Managerially, I'm out of touch.

> I'm bored at work. . . . I run upstairs to see what [another returning colleague] is doing. He says, "Nothing." Me, too.[70]

A study by Tung found that in general, the longer the duration of an off-shore assignment, the more problem the expatriate has being reabsorbed into the home office. Here are the major reasons:

1. The "out of sight, out of mind" syndrome is common.

2. Organizational changes made during the time the individual was abroad may make his or her position in the parent headquarters redundant or peripheral.

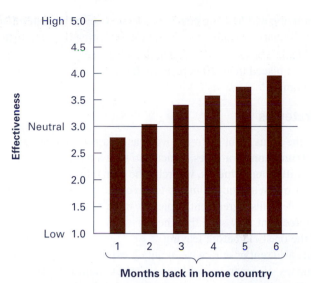

Figure 15–7

**Effectiveness
of Returning
Expatriates**

Months back in home country

Source: Nancy J. Adler, *International Dimensions of Organizational Behavior,* 2nd ed. (Boston: PWS-Kent, 1991), p. 238. Copyright © 1991 by Wadsworth, Inc. Reprinted by permission of PWS-Kent Publishing Company, a division of Wadsworth, Inc.

3. Technological advances in the parent headquarters may render the individual's existing skills and knowledge obsolete.[71]

Still another problem is adjusting to the new job back home. It sometimes takes from 6 months to 1 year before managers are operating at full effectiveness. Figure 15–7 provides an illustration.

Other readjustment problems are more personal in nature. Many expatriates find that the salary and fringe benefits to which they have become accustomed in the foreign assignment now are lost, and adjusting to this lower standard of living is difficult. In addition, those who sold their houses and now must buy new ones find that the monthly cost often is much higher than when they left. The children often are placed in public schools, where classes are much larger than in the overseas private schools. Many also miss the cultural lifestyles, as in the case of an executive who is transferred from Paris, France, to a medium-sized city in the United States, or from any developed country to an underdeveloped country. Additionally, many returning expatriates have learned that their international experiences are not viewed as important. Many Japanese expatriates, for example, report that when they return, their experiences should be downplayed if they want to "fit in" with the organization. In fact, reports one recent *New York Times* article, a substantial number of Japanese expatriates "are happier overseas than they are back home."[72]

Other research supports the findings noted here and offers operative recommendations for action. Based on questionnaires completed by 174 respondents who had been repatriated from four large U.S. MNCs, Black found the following:

1. With few exceptions, individuals whose expectations were met had the most positive levels of repatriation adjustment and job performance.

2. In the case of high-level managers in particular, expatriates whose job demands were greater, rather than less, than expected reported high levels of repatriation adjustment and job performance. Those having greater job demands may have put in more effort and had better adjustment and performance.

3. Job performance and repatriation adjustment were greater for individuals whose job constraint expectations were undermet than for those individuals whose expectations were overmet. In other words, job constraints were viewed as an undesirable aspect of the job and having them turn out to be less than expected was a pleasant surprise that helped adjustment and performance.

4. When living and housing conditions turned out to be better than expected, general repatriation adjustment and job performance were better.

5. Individuals whose general expectations were met or overmet had job evaluations that placed them 10 percent higher than those whose general expectations were unmet.[73]

Transition Strategies

Transition strategies
Strategies used to help smooth the adjustment from an overseas to a stateside assignment.

Repatriation agreements
Agreements whereby the firm tells the individuals how long she or he will be posted overseas and promises to give the individual, on return, a job that is mutually acceptable.

To help smooth the adjustment from an overseas to a stateside assignment, some MNCs have developed **transition strategies,** which can take a number of different forms. One is the use of **repatriation agreements,** whereby the firm tells the individual how long she or he will be posted overseas and promises to give the individual, on return, a job that is mutually acceptable. This agreement typically does not promise a specific position or salary, but the agreement may state that the person will be given a job that is equal to, if not better than, the one held before leaving.[74]

Some firms also rent or otherwise maintain expatriates' homes until they return. The Aluminum Company of America and Union Carbide both have such plans for managers going overseas. This plan helps to reduce the financial shock that often accompanies home shopping by returning expatriates.

A third strategy is to use senior executives as sponsors of managers abroad, as described here:

It is the responsibility of a sponsor to monitor the performance, compensation, and career paths of expatriate managers who are under their wings, and to plan for their return. Sponsors begin scouting anywhere from six months to a year prior to an expatriate's return for a suitable position that he or she can come back to. Union Carbide and IBM are two companies who make use of such sponsors, but there are others as well.[75]

Still another approach is to keep expatriate managers apprised of what is going on at corporate headquarters and to plug these managers into projects at the home office whenever they are on leave in the home country. This helps maintain the person's visibility and ensures the individual is looked on as a regular member of the management staff.

In the final analysis, a proactive strategy that provides an effective support system to allay expatriate concerns about career issues while serving abroad may work best. Tung found that the successful U.S., European, Japanese, and Australian MNCs that she studied had: (1) mentor programs (one-on-one pairing of an expatriate with a member of home-office senior management); (2) a separate organization unit with primary responsibility for the specific needs of expatriates; and/or (3) maintenance of constant contacts between the home office and the expatriate.[76]

Recent research supports and expands these findings. One study surveyed 99 employees and managers with international experience in 21 corporations.[77] The reactions of the respondents to statements regarding the repatriation experience are provided in Table 15–8. The findings reveal that cultural re-entry, financial implications, and the nature of job assignments are three major areas of expatriate concern. In particular, some of the main problems of repatriation identified in this study include: (1) adjusting to life back home; (2) facing a financial package that is not as good as that overseas; (3) having less autonomy in the stateside job than in the overseas position; and (4) not receiving any career counseling from the company. To the extent that the MNC can address these types of problems and others presented in Table 15–8, the transition will be smooth, and the expatriate's performance effectiveness once home will increase quickly. Some additional steps suggested by experts in this area include:

1. Arrange an event to welcome and recognize the employee and family, either formally or informally.

2. Establish support to facilitate family reintegration.

3. Offer repatriation counseling or workshops to ease the adjustment.

4. Assist the spouse with job counseling, resume writing, and interviewing techniques.

5. Provide educational counseling for the children.

Table 15–8
Assessment of Repatriate Experience

Survey Categories	Mean Score[a]
Cultural Reentry	
1. The transition back to the American lifestyle was very easy.	3.71
2. I do not miss the people I worked with in the overseas assignment.	5.27
3. I felt comfortable giving up the friendships that I had developed overseas.	4.69
4. *If my spouse and/or children joined me overseas,* their transition back to the American lifestyle was very easy.	4.10
5. My family and friends back in the U.S. were interested in hearing about my experiences living overseas.	3.93
6. *If my spouse and/or children joined me overseas,* their friends in the U.S. were interested in hearing about the overseas experience.	4.23
7. Life back in the States seems exciting in comparison with the cultural experience I had during my overseas assignment.	4.95
8. My company provided me with help regarding relocation problems like housing and transportation.	3.44
Financial Implications	
1. The total financial package that I received in my new U.S. job assignment was better than my total financial package overseas.	5.42
2. The salary offer in the U.S. job assignment was better than my salary overseas.	4.20
3. The fringe benefits in the new U.S. job assignment were better than when I was working overseas.	5.65
4. *If you did not own your house or apartment in the U.S. while working overseas,* the cost of buying one upon returning from overseas was very reasonable.	5.87
5. My personal finances since returning from overseas are in better shape than was true before I left for the overseas assignment.	3.23
6. My company provided me bridge loans or other interim financial assistance when I returned from overseas.	5.31
7. My company provided me with considerable accounting advice/financial planning upon my return from overseas.	5.40
Nature of Job Assignment	
1. It was clear to me what permanent job I would have when I first returned from overseas.	3.42
2. I experienced more autonomy in my new job than had been the case in my overseas assignment.	5.37
3. My job status is less in my new job than had been the case in my overseas assignment.	4.54
4. I have less political influence in the company in my new job than had been the case in my overseas assignment.	4.69
5. *If it applies,* my mentor was helpful in apprising me of company developments when I first returned from overseas.	4.92
6. *If it applies,* my mentor helped in finding a good job assignment for me when I returned from overseas.	4.50
7. The present job is less challenging than the one I held overseas.	4.38
8. I consider that the company was fair with me in terms of identifying a suitable job assignment for me when I returned from overseas.	3.68
9. I view my present job assignment as very permanent.	3.96
10. I feel a high sense of job (employment) security with my present company.	3.02
11. Looking back at it, I consider that the overseas assignment benefitted me in terms of career opportunities in the company.	3.41
12. Overall, the managerial skills I gained overseas are being utilized by my employer now that I am working back in the U.S.	4.20
13. I was placed in a "holding pattern" when I first returned from the overseas assignment.	2.76
14. My company was helpful in providing me with career counseling when I returned from overseas.	5.88
15. My company provided my spouse with considerable help with career counseling when I returned from overseas.	6.51

[a]1 = strongly agree; 7 = strongly disagree.

Source: Nancy K. Napier and Richard B. Peterson, "Expatriate Re-entry: What Do Expatriates Have to Say?" *Human Resource Planning,* vol. 14, no. 1, 1991, pp. 26–27. Used with permission.

6. Provide the employee with a thorough debriefing by a facilitator to identify new knowledge, insights, and skills and to provide a forum to showcase new competencies.

7. Offer international outplacement to the employee and reentry counseling to the entire family if no positions are possible.

8. Arrange a postassigned interview with the expatriate and spouse to review their view of the assignment and address any repatriation issues.[78]

Hammer and his associates echo these types of recommendations. Based on recent research they conducted in two multinational corporations among expats and their spouses, they concluded that:

> The findings from the present study suggest that one of the key transitional activities for returning expatriates and their spouses from a corporate context should involve targeted communication from the home environment concerning the expectations of the home office toward the return of the repatriate executive and his/her family (role relationships). Further, reentry training should focus primarily on helping the repatriate manager and spouse align their expectations with the actual situation that will be encountered upon arrival in the home culture both within the organizational context as well as more broadly within the social milieu. To the degree that corporate communication and reentry training activities help the returning executive and spouse in expectation alignment, the executive's level of reentry satisfaction should be higher and the degree of reentry difficulties less.[79]

Additionally, in recent years many MNCs have begun using inpatriates to supplement their home-office staff and some of the same issues discussed here with repatriation come into play.

The World of *Business Week*—Revisited

The *Business Week* story that opened this chapter explained some of the things that Coca-Cola is doing to increase its worldwide revenue and profits. Now that you have read the material in this chapter, you are aware of the importance of selecting the best people for international assignments and why this is so important for a big internationally dispersed MNC like Coke. In particular, the firm has operations in almost every country of the world and a large percentage of the international staff are managers. So Coke not only has to carefully select expatriates for overseas assignments, but it also has to be able to choose the right host-country and home-country nationals to manage local operations and inpats for home country operations. In drawing together this chapter information and applying it to multinational firms, answer these questions: (1) In choosing people for overseas assignments in locales where the economies remain weak, how much reliance should MNCs be putting on expats? Host-country nationals? Third-country nationals? Inpats? (2) What criteria do you think would be important to MNCs in screening people for jobs in Asia? What is the reasoning behind your choices? (3) What type of compensation program do you think MNCs should be looking at in order to motivate managers to take jobs in their Asian operation? Will this program be different from the one you would offer to managers in their European operations? (4) Will the repatriation strategy that is used for American managers returning to the States from overseas assignments be the same as the one that should be used with inpats who are leaving the States and returning to their home country?

Summary of Key Points

1. MNCs can use four basic sources for filling overseas positions: home-country nationals (expatriates), host-country nationals, third-country nationals, and inpatriates. The most common reason for using home-country nationals, or expatriates, is to get the overseas operation under way. Once this is done,

many MNCs turn the top management job over to a host-country national who is familiar with the culture and language and who often commands a lower salary than the home-country national. The primary reason for using third-country nationals is that these people have the necessary expertise for the job. The use of inpatriates (a host-country or third-country national assigned to the home office) recognizes the need for diversity at the home office. This movement builds a transnational core competency for MNCs.

2. Many criteria are used in selecting managers for overseas assignments. Some of these include adaptability, independence, self-reliance, physical and emotional health, age, experience, education, knowledge of the local language, motivation, the support of spouse and children, and leadership.

3. Those who meet selection criteria then are given some form of screening. Some firms use psychological testing, but this approach has lost popularity in recent years. More commonly, candidates are given interviews. A recent development, theoretic models that identify important anticipatory and in-country dimensions of adjustment, offers help in effective selection.

4. Compensating expatriates can be a difficult problem, because there are many variables to consider. However, most compensation packages are designed around four common elements: base salary, benefits, allowances, and taxes. Working within these elements, the MNC will tailor-make the package to fit the specific situation. In doing so, there are six different approaches that can be used, including the balance sheet approach, the complementary approach, localization, lump sum method, the cafeteria approach, and the regional method. Whichever one (or combination) is used, the package must be both cost-effective and fair.

5. A manager might be willing to take an international assignment for a number of reasons, including: increased pay, promotion potential, the opportunity for greater responsibility, the chance to travel, and the ability to use his or her talents and skills. Research shows that most home countries prefer that the individual who is selected to head the affiliate or subsidiary be a local manager, even though this often does not occur.

6. At some time, most expatriates return home, usually when the predetermined tour is over. Sometimes, managers return because they want to leave early; other times, they return because of poor performance on their part. In any event, readjustment problems can happen back home, and the longer the managers have been gone, the bigger the problems usually are. Some firms now are developing transition strategies to help expatriates adjust to their new environments.

Key Terms

adaptability screening, *454*

balance sheet approach, *463*

cafeteria approach, *463*

expatriates, *445*

home-country nationals, *445*

host-country nationals, *446*

inpatriate, *449*

international selection criteria, *450*

localization, *463*

lump sum method, *463*

regional system, *463*

repatriation, *466*

repatriation agreements, *470*

third-country nationals, *447*

transition strategies, *470*

Review and Discussion Questions

1. A New York-based MNC is in the process of staffing a subsidiary in New Delhi, India. Why would it consider using expatriate managers in the unit? Local managers? Third-country managers?

2. What selection criteria are most important in choosing people for an overseas assignment? Identify and describe the four that you judge to be of most universal importance, and defend your choice.

3. Building on your answer to the question above, discuss some theoretical dimensions that may affect anticipatory and in-country adjustment of expats. How can these be turned into selection criteria?

4. What are the major common elements in an expat's compensation package? Besides base pay, which would be most important to you? Why?

5. Why are individuals motivated to accept international assignments? Which of these motivations would you rank as positive reasons? Which would you regard as negative reasons?

6. Why do expatriates return early? What can MNCs do to prevent this from happening? Identify and discuss three steps they can take.

7. What kinds of problems do expatriates face when returning home? Identify and describe four of the most important. What can MNCs do to deal with these repatriation problems effectively?

Internet Exercise: Going International with Coke

As seen in this chapter, the recruiting and selecting of managers is critical to effective international management. This is particularly true in the case of firms that are expanding their international operations or who currently do business in a large number of countries. These MNCs are continually having to replace managers who are retiring or moving to other companies. Coca-Cola in the opening *Business Week* story is an excellent example. Go to the company's website at **www.coke.com** and look at the career opportunities that it offers overseas. In particular, pay close attention to current opportunities in Europe, Africa, and Asia. Read what the company has to say and then contact one of the individuals whose e-mail address is provided. Ask this company representative about the opportunities and challenges of working in that country or geographic area. Then, using this information, coupled with the chapter material, answer these questions: (1) From what you have learned from the Coca-Cola inquiry, what types of education or experience would you need to be hired by the company? (2) What kinds of international career opportunities does Coke offer? (3) If you were hired by Coke, what type of financial package could you expect?

Russia

Russia is by far the largest republic in the former Soviet Union. Russia stretches from Eastern Europe across northern Asia and to the Pacific Ocean. The 150 million people consist of 83 percent Russians, 4 percent Tartars, and a scattering of others. The largest city and capital is Moscow, with about 9 million people. At present, there is continuing social and economic turmoil in Russia. Although prices are no longer controlled and privatization is well under way, the value of the ruble continues to deteriorate. At the same time, however, there are many pockets of prosperity in the country and under President Vladimir Putin positive efforts are under way to bolster the economy.

By the beginning of the millennium, the country's GDP was over $600 billion and Russia is still considered to be a potentially good place to do business by some MNCs. One that has been extremely interested in the country is Earth, Inc. (EI), a farm-implement company that is headquartered in Birmingham, Alabama. EI recently entered into an agreement with the government of Russia to set up operations near Moscow in a factory that was operating at about one-half of capacity. The factory will produce farm implements for the newly emerging Eastern European market. EI will supply the technical know-how and product design as well as assume responsibility for marketing the products. The Russian plant will build the equipment and package it for shipping.

The management of the plant operation will be handled on a joint basis. EI will send a team of five management and technical personnel from the United States to the Russian factory site for a period of 12 to 18 months. After this time, EI hopes to send three of them home, and the two who remain would continue to provide ongoing assistance. At the same time, EI intends to hire four middle-level managers and eight first-level supervisors from Italy and Germany, because the operation will need Europeans who are more familiar with doing manufacturing in this part of the world. Very few locals have inspired EI with confidence that they can get the job done. However, over a 2-year period, EI intends to replace the third-country nationals with trained local managers. "We need to staff the management ranks with knowledgeable, experienced people," the CEO explained, "at least until we get the operation up and running successfully with our own people. Then we can turn more and more of the operation over to local management, and run the plant with just a handful of headquarters people on-site."

This arrangement has been agreed to by the Russian government, and EI currently is identifying and recruiting managers both in the United States and Europe. Initially, the firm thought that this would be a fairly simple process, but screening and selecting are taking much longer than anticipated. Nevertheless, EI hopes to have the plant operating within 12 months.

Questions

1. What are some current issues facing Russia? What is the climate for doing business in Russia today?

2. What are some of the benefits of using home-country nationals in overseas operations? What are some of the benefits of using host-country nationals?

3. Why would a multinational such as EI be interested in bringing in third-country nationals?

4. What criteria should EI use in selecting personnel for the overseas assignment in Russia?

A Selection Decision

The Star Corporation is a California-based manufacturing firm that is going to do business in mainland China. The company's contract with the Chinese government calls for it to supply technical know-how and machinery for producing consumer electronics. These products are not state-of-the-art, but they will be more than adequate for the needs of the Chinese consumers. Star has agreed to sell the Chinese its plant, which was being closed because it no longer was competitive.

The Chinese will pay to move all the machinery and equipment to the mainland and install it in a factory that currently is being modified for this purpose. The two then will become partners in the venture. Star will provide the management and technical expertise to run the plant, and the Chinese government will provide the workers and be responsible for paying for all output. Star will receive an annual fee of $1 million and 5 percent of all sales.

The Star management is very pleased with the arrangement. Although they are of Chinese descent, they have lived in the U.S. all their lives and know relatively little about doing business either with or in mainland China. To provide Star with the necessary information and assistance, a native of Beijing, educated there but living in California for the past 5 years, was brought in. The individual told the company the following facts about mainland China:

- Chinese managers do not plan. They usually are told what to do and they do it. Planning is handled by others and simply passed on to them.

- Chinese managers are not concerned with profit or loss. They simply do their jobs and let the government worry about whether the operation is making money.

- No rewards are given to workers who perform well; everyone is treated the same. If there is no work, the workers are still paid, although they may not be required to come to the factory.

- There is a basic aversion to individual decision making; most decisions are collective efforts.

- The current government of China would like its managers to learn how to run a profit-oriented operation and eventually eliminate the need for forcing managerial assistance.

- When outsiders tell the Chinese how to do things, they have to be careful not to insult or offend the Chinese, who often are sensitive about the way they are treated.

Questions

1. What selection criteria would you recommend to Star when deciding whom to send to mainland China?

2. What procedures should the company use in making the final selection?

3. What type of repatriation agreement would you recommend the firm use? Be specific regarding some things you would suggest be contained in the agreement.

Chapter 16

Human Resource Development Across Cultures

Objectives of the Chapter

Firms conducting international business need to be particularly concerned with training and organization development to better prepare their personnel for overseas assignments.[1] This chapter examines how successful multinational organizations prepare personnel to go overseas. A specific focus is the reasons for training and development and the various types of training that commonly are offered. Training by use of cultural assimilators is discussed, and their value in providing effective acculturation is analyzed. Broader-based organization development also is considered—how it works as well as its value in helping to resolve human problems in an international setting. The specific objectives of this chapter are:

1. **IDENTIFY** the training process as used in international management, and note that people from different cultures often have different learning styles.

2. **DISCUSS** the most common reasons for training and the types of training that often are provided.

3. **EXPLAIN** how cultural assimilators work and why they are so highly regarded.

4. **IDENTIFY** the term "organization development," and discuss its use in international management.

BusinessWeek

The World of *Business Week*

John Malone's European Tour

Europe has no equivalent to the U.S. media wheeler-dealer John C. Malone. He rose to dominate the distribution of cable television in the U.S. through his company Telecommunications Inc., then sold out to AT&T in 1998 for $52 billion. Of course, a tycoon like this can never leave the game. Sure enough, Malone has quickly accumulated a portfolio of investments through a new vehicle, Liberty Media Corp. There were fears, however, that the master had lost his touch. He put $500 million, for example, into ICG Communications Inc. seven months before the telecom company declared bankruptcy last November.

Now, the king of cable is back—but on a different continent. Malone cut a deal with Deutsche Telekom to pay an estimated $4 billion for the German phone giant's stakes in six regional cable-TV companies that serve 10 million households, nearly half the cable-connected homes in Germany. Malone will be the biggest cable operator not only in Germany but in Europe. He already indirectly owns a substantial stake in UPC, the Dutch cable company that has the biggest subscriber base of any European cable company. "It's a very exciting move," says Adam Bird, leader of the European media and entertainment practice for Booz, Allen & Hamilton Inc. in Munich. "The European cable industry has been very fragmented."

That's not all. Once you tack on the new German customers to Malone's other cable holdings in Japan, Argentina, Chile, and Puerto Rico, he will have controlling interests in companies with wires into 25 million homes worldwide. That's double the 12.5 million households TCI had served when Malone sold it to AT&T. Throw in the number of homes located close enough to Malone's wires to hook up in the future for high-speed data, digital video, and telephony, and the number of actual and potential hookups is 50 million. "What he has done is create a giant footprint again," says Larry Petrella.

Slimmed-Down Field

Malone is once again living up to his reputation as a consummate dealmaker. Cash-rich Liberty, with just 40 employees operating from a suburban Denver office and assets valued at $50 billion, has seized an opportunity in Europe by making an offer at a time when tough capital markets have slimmed the field of potential buyers. Deutsche Telekom, Germany's former phone monopoly and biggest Internet service provider, is being pushed by regulators to sell its cable business for conflict-of-interest reasons. Industry sources say Liberty will cover a substantial part of the purchase price with its own shares.

It's easy to see why Malone is ready to jump into Germany. Cable is an undervalued and underdeveloped asset in Europe. Malone will have lots of room to upgrade Germany's outmoded cable infrastructure, which Deutsche Telekom neglected, and introduce

broadband as well as compelling programming packages. "If there's anybody that knows how to do this, it's John Malone and his team," says Bird. Malone's holdings in programmers such as Discovery Channel and Rupert Murdoch's News Corp., is a big advantage, particularly in Germany where original cable programming has been scant.

The most important member of Malone's team is A. Gary Klesch, a London-based investor who helped broker the Liberty deal. Klesch has an option to buy up to 24.9% of this newly created German cable company and will operate it for Malone.

As impressive as the move is, Malone is taking a huge risk. The fragmented German cable market is full of hazards, ranging from wary regulators to stingy viewers unwilling to pay for premium services. German viewers pay as little as $4 a month for basic cable service. In the U.S., cable operators have used premium services to persuade viewers to shell out an average of $40 a month. Thousands of local cable operators offer rudimentary service across Germany. Because of local laws, private operators ranging from corner electronics shops to building associations control the last few meters of cable that connect the Deutsche Telekom network with some 6.6 million homes. In other words, Liberty will control the pipes, but not always the spigot.

"Malone will suffer his first defeat here," warns Heinz-Peter Labonte, founder of PEPCOM, a company based in Bingen, near Frankfurt, that is buying up smaller cable operators in Germany. That prediction may be too dire. But Malone's move is already stirring opposition from established interests. The Association of Private Broadcasting & Telecommunications, which represents established German players such as Kirch Group, the film distributor and pay-TV operator, has called for regulators to keep a close eye on Liberty Media. One of its demands is that viewers on Malone's cable network be allowed to choose from competing set-top decoders. "Nobody should be shut out," says Thorsten Grothe, deputy director of the broadcasters' group. Regulators are already making sympathetic noises.

Tough Fight

The broadcasters also worry that they are trading one obnoxious monopoly for another. Malone is known for driving a hard bargain, and they wonder what kind of tolls he may demand once he owns the infrastructure. Moreover, they fear he'll give favorable treatment to his own media holdings, which include a 21% stake in USA Networks.

Malone is doing little to assuage the broadcasters' fears. Sources close to the deal say Malone's primary aim is to secure distribution for his company's content. But he's a shrewd political player and likely to make sure there is a fair amount of local content.

Assuming Malone can battle his way through all these obstacles, he'll then face the toughest challenge of all: German couch potatoes. With access to more than 30 free channels on basic cable, including two all-sports channels and movie channels such as ProSieben, German viewers are notoriously reluctant to pay for extra services. Just ask Leo Kirch, who has been struggling for five years to make money with digital pay TV and is still years from breaking even.

No one should underestimate Malone's drive or business savvy. And he seems to recognize the hazards. He initially plans a relatively modest investment of about $400 million a year to upgrade the existing system so it can handle more channels and interactive services. But that's still big money. And Malone will need all his smarts if he wants to see it again.

By Jack Ewing in Frankfurt, with Tom Lowry in New York,
Ronald Grover in Los Angeles, and Carol Matlack in Paris

This opening news story presents a very good example of why human resource development (HRD) across cultures is so important to multinational firms. Malone's Liberty Media Corporation has holdings worldwide in an industry that has tremendous potential. At the same time, however, there are a great deal of challenges that have to be met. In Germany, for example, not only are there regulatory restrictions in this industry, but buyers are unaccustomed to paying for extra TV services. So Malone will need a well-trained and developed staff in order to offer the best services and to ensure that he can achieve a satisfactory return on the $3 billion he is investing in this German venture. He will also need to have highly competent, well-trained people managing his other holdings that extend from the Netherlands to Puerto Rico and from Argentina and Chile to Japan. Malone has an opportunity to sell services to 25 million homes worldwide, but a good portion of his success will be dictated by how well Liberty Media can meet the HRD challenge. Many of the concepts and techniques discussed in this chapter can be of value to this and all MNCs and may well determine their overall success in the highly competitive international arena.

Training
The process of altering employee behavior and attitudes in a way that increases the probability of goal attainment.

■ Training in International Management

Training is the process of altering employee behavior and attitudes in a way that increases the probability of goal attainment. This training process is particularly important in preparing employees for overseas assignments[2] because it helps ensure that their full potential will be tapped.[3] One of the things that training can do is to help expat managers better understand the customs, cultures, and work habits of the local people and thus avoid blunders such as the following:

> An American company eager to do business in Saudi Arabia sent over a sales manager to "get something going." The salesman began calling contacts soon after his arrival on Monday. . . . After many disappointing appointments, the salesman ran into an old buddy who gave him an introduction to some basic rules of Saudi etiquette and how to do business with the Arabs. The salesman learned that he had repeatedly insulted his contacts by his impatience, refusal of coffee, the "all business talk" attitude and aggressive selling. Even incidental acts such as handing people papers with his left hand and exposing the sole of his shoe while sitting on the floor were improper Saudi customs.[4]

The simplest training, in terms of preparation time, is to place a cultural integrator in each foreign operation. This individual is responsible for ensuring that the operation's business systems are in accord with those of the local culture. The integrator advises, guides, and recommends actions needed to ensure this synchronization.[5] The "International Management in Action: The Cultural Integrator," accompanying box, describes in detail the use of such a person.

Unfortunately, although using an integrator can help, it is seldom sufficient. Recent experience clearly reveals that in creating an effective global team, the MNC must assemble individuals who collectively understand the local language, have grown up in diverse cultures or neighborhoods, have open, flexible minds, and who will be able to deal with high degrees of stress.[6] In those cases where potential candidates do not yet possess all of these requisite skills or abilities, MNCs need a well-designed training program that is administered before the individuals leave for their overseas assignment (and, in some cases, also on-site) and then evaluated later to determine its overall effectiveness. One review of 228 MNCs found that cross-cultural training, which can take many forms, is becoming increasingly popular. Some of these findings included the following:

1. Of organizations with cultural programs, 58 percent offer training only to some expatriates, while 42 percent offer it to all of them.

2. Ninety-one percent offer cultural orientation programs to spouses, and 75 percent offer them to dependent children.

3. The average duration of the cultural training programs is 3 days.

4. Cultural training is continued after arrival in the assignment location 32 percent of the time.

5. Thirty percent offer formal cultural training programs.

6. Of those without formal cultural programs, 37 percent plan to add such training.[7]

The most common topics covered in cultural training include social etiquette, customs, economics, history, politics, and business etiquette. However, the MNC's overall philosophy of international management and the demands of the specific cultural situation are the starting point. This is because countries tend to have distinctive human resource management (HRM) practices that differentiate them from other countries. For example, the HRM practices that are prevalent in the United States are quite different from those in France and Argentina. This has been clearly illustrated by Sparrow and Budhwar, who compared data from 13 different countries on the basis of HRM factors. Five of these factors included the following:

1. Structural empowerment that is characterized by flat organization designs, wide spans of control, the use of flexible cross-functional teams, and the rewarding of individuals for productivity gains.

2. Accelerated resource development that is characterized by the early identification of high potential employees, the establishment of both multiple and parallel career paths, the rewarding of personnel for enhancing their skills and knowledge, and the offering of continuous training and development education.

International Management in Action

The Cultural Integrator

In recent years, some international management experts have suggested that firms use a cultural integrator to deal with the cultural differences they face overseas. The basic concept of integration is not new; MNCs long have tested their products in foreign markets to ensure that any necessary modifications are made before full-scale selling begins. Similarly, many of these firms have trained and developed their people before sending them to foreign assignments. In most cases, however, the personnel are not totally prepared to deal with the day-to-day cultural challenges, because they lack field experience. This is where the cultural integrator enters the picture.

The integrator is responsible for helping handle problems between the subsidiary and host cultures. Among other things, the person advises management about the consequences of those actions that can negatively affect its position in the host country and market, and he or she works with management in developing an appropriate response.

Some companies send the cultural integrator from the home office. Many choose a host-country national who has intimate knowledge of the multinational's culture and can view operations from both sides. Quite often, the individual holds a staff position and can only advise and recommend courses of action; the person has no authority to demand implementation of such actions. For this reason, the integrator needs proficiency in both conceptual and human relations skills. He or she must be able to envision the relationships between the MNC and host country that will result in the best "fit" for both. At the same time, the individual must be able to persuade the managers to accept her or his point of view.

Will the coming years see greater use of cultural integrators? This trend appears to be very likely.

As more corporations expand internationally, there is a greater need to integrate their operations into foreign societies. It cannot be expected that an international manager can function effectively in all host societies. Nor can it be expected that a manager will remain in a society long enough to gain the cultural familiarity necessary to function effectively there, since one of the competitive advantages of an international firm is its managerial mobility. The cultural integrator offers a clear resolution to this dilemma, allowing international organizations to achieve their full potential.

---

3. Employee welfare emphasis that is characterized by firms offering personal family assistance, encouraging and rewarding external volunteer activities, and promoting cultures that emphasize equality in the workplace.

4. An efficiency emphasis in which employees are encouraged to monitor their own work and to continually improve their performance.

5. Long termism that stresses long-term results such as innovation and creativity rather than just weekly and monthly short-term productivity.[8]

When Sparrow and Budhwar used these HRM approaches on a comparative country-by-country basis, they found that there were worldwide differences in human resource management practices. Table 16–1 shows the comparative results, after each of the 13 countries was categorized as being either high or low on the respective factors.

These findings reveal that countries are unique in their approach to human resource management. What works well in the United States may have limited value in France. In fact, a close analysis of Table 16–1 shows that none of the 13 countries had the same profile; each was different. This was even true in the case of Anglo nations such as the United States, Canada, Australia, and the United Kingdom where differences in employee welfare emphasis, accelerated resource development, long efficiency orientation, and long termism resulted in unique HRM profiles for each. Similarly, Japan and Korea differed on two of the factors, as did Germany and France; and India, which many people might feel would be more similar to an Anglo culture, because of the British influence, than to an Asian one, differed on two of factors with Canada, on three of the factors with both the United States and the United Kingdom, and on four factors with Australia.[9]

These findings point to the fact that MNCs in the new millennium will have to focus increasingly on HRM programs designed to meet the needs of local personnel. A good example is provided in the former communist countries of Europe where international

Table 16–1
Human Resource Management Practices in Select Countries

	Structural Empowerment		Accelerated Resource Development		Employee Welfare Emphasis		Efficiency Emphasis		Long-Termism	
	High	Low	High	Low	High	Low	High	Low	High	Low
United States	X		X		X		X			X
Canada	X		X		X			X		X
United Kingdom	X		X			X		X		X
Italy		X	X			X		X		X
Japan		X	X		X		X		X	
India		X	X		X			X	X	
Australia	X			X		X	X		X	
Brazil	X			X	X			X	X	
Mexico	X			X	X			X		X
Argentina		X		X	X			X		X
Germany		X		X		X		X	X	
Korea		X		X		X	X		X	
France		X		X		X	X			X

Source: Adapted from Paul R. Sparrow and Pawan S. Budhwar, "Competition and Change: Mapping the Indian HRM Recipe Against Worldwide Patterns," *Journal of World Business,* vol. 32, no. 3, 1997, p. 233.

managers are discovering that in order to effectively recruit college graduates their firms must provide training programs that give these new employees opportunities to work with a variety of tasks and to help them specialize in their particular fields of interest. At the same time the MNCs are discovering that these recruits are looking for companies that offer a good social working environment. A recent survey of over 1,000 business and engineering students from Poland, the Czech Republic, and Hungary found that almost two-thirds of the respondents said that they wanted their boss to be receptive to their ideas; 37 percent wanted to work for managers who had strong industry experience; and 34 percent wanted a boss who was a good rational decision maker. These findings indicate that multinational human resource management is now becoming much more of a two-way street: both employees and managers need to continually adjust to emerging demands.[10]

The Impact of Overall Management Philosophy on Training

The type of training that is required of expatriates is influenced by the firm's overall philosophy of international management. For example, some companies prefer to send their own people to staff an overseas operation; others prefer to use locals whenever possible.[11] Briefly, four basic philosophic positions of multinational corporations (MNCs) can influence the training program:

1. An **ethnocentric MNC** puts home-office people in charge of key international management positions. The MNC headquarters group and the affiliated world company managers all have the same basic experiences, attitudes, and beliefs about how to manage operations. Many Japanese firms follow this practice.

2. A **polycentric MNC** places local nationals in key positions and allows these managers to appoint and develop their own people. MNC headquarters gives the subsidiary managers authority to manage their operations just as long as these operations are sufficiently profitable. Some MNCs use this approach in East Asia, Australia, and other markets that are deemed too expensive to staff with expatriates.

Ethnocentric MNC
An MNC that stresses nationalism and often puts home-office people in charge of key international management positions.

Polycentric MNC
An MNC that places local nationals in key positions and allows these managers to appoint and develop their own people.

Regiocentric MNC
An MNC that relies on local managers from a particular geographic region to handle operations in and around that area.

Geocentric MNC
An MNC that seeks to integrate diverse regions of the world through a global approach to decision making.

3. A **regiocentric MNC** relies on local managers from a particular geographic region to handle operations in and around that area. For example, production facilities in France would be used to produce goods for all EU countries. Similarly, advertising managers from subsidiaries in Italy, Germany, France, and Spain would come together and formulate a "European" advertising campaign for the company's products. A regiocentric approach often relies on regional group cooperation of local managers. The Gillette MNC uses a regiocentric approach.

4. A **geocentric MNC** seeks to integrate diverse regions of the world through a global approach to decision making. Assignments are made based on qualifications, and all subsidiary managers throughout the structure are regarded as equal to those at headquarters. IBM is an excellent example of an MNC that attempts to use a geocentric approach.

All four of these philosophical positions can be found in the multinational arena, and each puts a different type of training demand on the MNC.[12] For example, ethnocentric MNCs will do all training at headquarters, but polycentric MNCs will rely on local managers to assume responsibility for seeing that the training function is carried out.

The Impact of Different Learning Styles on Training and Development

Learning
The acquisition of skills, knowledge, and abilities that results in a relatively permanent change in behavior.

Another important area of consideration for development is learning styles. **Learning** is the acquisition of skills, knowledge, and abilities that results in a relatively permanent change in behavior.[13] Over the last decade a growing number of multinationals have tried to become a "learning organization" (discussed in Chapter 3), which is typified by a continual focus on activities such as training and development. In the new millennium this learning focus applied to human resource development may go beyond learning organizations to "teaching organizations." For example, Tichy and Cohen, after conducting an analysis of world-class companies such as General Electric, PepsiCo, AlliedSignal, and Coca-Cola, found that teaching organizations are even more relevant than learning organizations because they go beyond the belief that everyone must continually acquire new knowledge and skills and focus on ensuring that everyone in the organization, especially the top management personnel, pass their learning on to others. Here are their conclusions:

> In teaching organizations, leaders see it as their responsibility to teach. They do that because they understand that it's the best, if not only, way to develop throughout a company people who can come up with and carry out smart ideas about the business. Because people in teaching organizations see teaching as critical to the success of their business, they find ways to do it every day. Teaching every day about critical business issues avoids the fuzzy focus that has plagued some learning organization efforts, which have sometimes become a throwback to the 1960s- and 1970s-style self-exportation and human relations training.[14]

There are many examples of how successful leaders are doing this teaching. One of the best is Jack Welch of General Electric, who spent close to 30 percent of his own time teaching and developing. Moreover, Welch insisted that all other GE leaders also teach. Larry Bossidy, former CEO of AlliedSignal, followed a similar approach. When he began transforming the company, he started by teaching his senior-level people about strategy and spent hundreds of days each year with other managers throughout the company. In his first year on the job, he personally met and worked with over 15,000 employees. As a result, Bossidy began to show his people how to create a mindset for growing a business that was operating in a mature market. This learning helped the firm become the best performing company on the Dow Jones Industrial Average within five years.[15]

Of course, the way in which training takes place can be extremely important. A great deal of research has been conducted on the various types and theories of learning.[16] However, the application of these ideas in an international context often can be quite challenging because cultural differences can affect the learning and teaching. Prud'homme van Reine and Trompenaars, commenting on the development of expats, have noted that national cultural differences typically affect the way MNCs train and develop their people. For example, Americans like an experiential learning style while Germans prefer a theoretical-analytical learning approach.[17] Moreover, there can be sharp learning preferences between groups that are quite similar in terms of culture. Hayes and Allinson, after studying cultural differences in the learning styles of managers, have reported that, "Two groups can be very similar in ecology and climate and, for example, through a common legacy of colonialism, have a similar language and legal, educational and governmental infrastructure, but may be markedly different in terms of beliefs, attitudes, and values."[18] Moreover, research shows that people with different learning styles prefer different learning environments, and if there is a mismatch between the preferred learning style and the work environment, dissatisfaction and poor performance can result.[19]

One study investigated learning styles by giving a learning style questionnaire to British middle managers, Indian midcareer managers, and East African midcareer managers. Two dimensions of learning style were measured: analysis and action. The analysis dimension measures the extent to which the learner adopts a theory-building and test approach as opposed to using an intuitive approach. The action dimension measures the extent to which the learner uses a trial-and-error approach as opposed to employing a contemplative or reflective approach.[20] The researchers found important differences in learning style between the three cultures. Indian managers were much higher on analysis than the other two groups. British managers were much higher on action. East African managers were the lowest on both analysis and action scores. The results were summarized as follows:

> The results of this study advance the argument . . . and raise questions about not only the aims and content of management development activities in different cultures but also about the nature of the learning process and the design of learning environments employed. . . . It may well be that the kind of learning environments and activities which promote effective learning in some cultures may not promote the same outcomes in other cultures where different learning styles predominate. This could have important implications for the design of learning environments, the composition of training groups and the location of training (in host country, regional center or home country) undertaken by transnational organizations.[21]

In addition to these conclusions, those responsible for training programs must remember that even if learning does occur, the new behaviors will not be used if they are not reinforced. For example, if the head of a foreign subsidiary is highly ethnocentric and believes that things should be done the way they are in the home country, new managers with intercultural training likely will find little reward or reinforcement for using their ideas. This cultural complexity also extends to the way in which the training is conducted. A corporate trainer and specialist for Esso Production Malaysia recently offered the following advice for training in cross-cultural settings:

> Start with a problem-oriented approach—avoid using complicated theories and definitions. Focus on here and now and "how to's." For teaching in cross-cultural settings, start with affirming the values of the participants, especially those which are part of their cultural heritage and are the basis of their shared practices. Once these values are identified, begin to look for gaps in performance and create an awareness of what is needed. The trainer will then focus on the steps to be taken to develop the new skills repertoire. A word of caution—if the skills have to do with interpersonal skills, it is better to have some contribution from the local participants. In this instance the trainer's task is to inform not to instruct.[22]

Reasons for Training

Training programs are useful in preparing people for overseas assignments for many reasons. These reasons can be put into two general categories: organizational and personal.

Organizational Reasons Organizational reasons for training relate to the enterprise at large and its efforts to manage overseas operations more effectively.[23] One primary reason is to help overcome **ethnocentrism,** the belief that one's way of doing things is superior to that of others. Ethnocentrism is common in many large MNCs where managers believe

Ethnocentrism
The belief that one's own way of doing things is superior to that of others.

that the home office's approach to doing business can be exported intact to all other countries, because this approach is superior to anything at the local level. Training can help home-office managers to understand the values and customs of other countries so that when they are transferred overseas, they have a better understanding of how to interact with local personnel. This training also can help managers to overcome the common belief among many personnel that expatriates are not as effective as host-country managers. This is particularly important given that an increasing number of managerial positions now are held by foreign managers in U.S. MNCs.[24]

Another organizational reason for training is to improve the flow of communication between the home office and the international subsidiaries and branches. Quite often, overseas managers find that they are not adequately informed regarding what is expected of them while the home office places close controls on their operating authority. This is particularly true when the overseas manager is from the host country. Effective communication can help to minimize these problems.

Finally, another organizational reason for training is to increase overall efficiency and profitability. Research shows organizations that closely tie their training and human resource management strategy to their business strategy tend to outperform those that do not.[25] Stroh and Caligiuri recently conducted research on 60 of the world's major multinationals and found that effective HRM programs pay dividends in the form of higher profits. Additionally, their data showed that the most successful MNCs recognized the importance of having top managers with a global orientation. One of the ways in which almost all of these organizations did this was by giving their managers global assignments that not only filled technical and managerial needs but also provided developmental experiences for the personnel—and this assignment strategy included managers from every geographic region where the firms were doing business. Drawing together the lessons to be learned from this approach, Stroh and Caligiuri noted that:

> The development of global leadership skills should not stop with home country nationals. Global HR should also be involved in developing a global orientation among host country nationals as well. This means, for example, sending not only home-country managers on global assignments but host national talent to the corporate office and to other divisions around the world. Many of the managers at the successful MNCs talked about how their companies develop talent in this way. In addition, they described a "desired state" for human resources, including the ability to source talent within the company from around the world. Victor Guerra, an executive at Prudential, commented: *We need to continually recognize that there are bright, articulate people who do not live in the home country. U.S. multinationals are especially guilty of this shortsightedness.* Acknowledging that talent exists and using the talent appropriately are two different issues—one idealist, the other strategic.[26]

Personal Reasons   Although there is overall organizational justification, the primary reason for training overseas managers is to improve their ability to interact effectively with local people in general and their personnel in particular. One early study that surveyed 75 countries in England, Holland, Belgium, and Germany found that some of the biggest complaints about managers by their personnel revolved around personal shortcomings in areas such as politeness, punctuality, tactfulness, orderliness, sensitivity, reliability, tolerance, and empathy.[27] As a result, an increasing number of training programs now address social topics such as how to take a client to dinner, effectively apologize to a customer, appropriately address one's overseas colleagues, communicate formally and politely with others, and learn how to help others "save face."[28] These programs also focus on dispelling myths and stereotypes by replacing them with facts about the culture. For example, in helping expatriates better understand Arab executives, the following guidelines are offered:

1. There is a close relationship between the Arab executive and his environment. The Arab executive is looked on as a community and family leader, and there are numerous social pressures on him because of this role. He is consulted on all types of problems, even those far removed from his position.

2. With regard to decision making, the Arab executive likely will consult with his subordinates, but he will take responsibility for his decision himself rather than arriving at it through consensus.

3. The Arab executive likely will try to avoid conflict. If there is an issue that he favors but is opposed by his subordinates, he tends to impose his authority. If it is an issue favored by the subordinates but opposed by the executive, he will likely let the matter drop without taking action.

4. The Arab executive's style is very personal. He values loyalty over efficiency. Although some executives find that the open-door tradition consumes a great deal of time, they do not feel that the situation can be changed. Many executives tend to look on their employees as family and will allow them to bypass the hierarchy to meet them.

5. The Arab executive, contrary to popular beliefs, puts considerable value on the use of time. One thing he admires most about Western or expatriate executives is the use of their time, and he would like to encourage his own employees to make more productive use of time.[29]

Another growing problem is the belief that foreign language skills are not really essential to doing business overseas. Effective training programs can help to minimize these personal problems.

A particularly big personal problem that managers have in an overseas assignment is arrogance. This is the so-called Ugly American problem that U.S. expatriates have been known to have. Many expatriate managers find that their power and prestige are much greater than they were in their job in the home country. This often results in improper behavior, especially among managers at the upper and lower positions of overseas subsidiaries. This arrogance takes a number of different forms, including rudeness to personnel and inaccessibility to clients. Zeira and Harari made the following observations:

> Another manifestation of expatriate managers' arrogance is their widespread tendency to ignore invitations to become participant observers in HCOs [host-country organizations]. The underlying idea behind these invitations involves rotating expatriate managers in various HCO departments to enable them to observe patterns of organizational behavior at various hierarchical levels. The purpose of this observation is to familiarize expatriate managers, especially those new in their jobs or about to begin to assume them, with the goals, policies, procedures, formal and informal norms, and expectations of HCOs regarding expatriate managers and their respective subsidiaries.[30]

Another common problem is expatriate managers' overruling of decisions, often seen at lower levels of the hierarchy. When a decision is made by a superior who is from the host country and the expatriate does not agree with it, the expatriate may appeal to higher authority in the subsidiary. Host-country managers obviously resent this behavior, because it implies that they are incompetent and can be second-guessed by expatriate subordinates.

Still another common problem is the open criticizing by expatriate managers of their own country or the host country. Many expatriates believe that this form of criticism is regarded as constructive and shows them to have an open mind. Experience has found, however, that most host-country personnel view such behavior negatively and feel that the manager should refrain from such unconstructive criticism. It just creates bad feelings and lack of loyalty.

In addition to helping deal with these types of personal problems, training can be useful in improving overall management style. Research shows that many host-country nationals would like to see changes in some of the styles of expatriate managers, including their leadership, decision making, communication, and group work. In terms of leadership, the locals would like to see their expatriate managers be more friendly, accessible, receptive to subordinate suggestions, and encouraging to subordinates to make their best efforts. In decision making, they would like to see clearer definition of goals, more involvement in the process by those employees who will be affected by the decision, and greater use of group meetings to help make decisions. In communication, they would like to see more exchange of opinions and ideas between subordinates and managers. In group work, they would like to see more group problem solving and teamwork. When Harari and Zeira researched the attitudes in six subsidiaries of non-Japanese MNCs, three in Japan and three from outside (United States, France, and Israel), they found that all host-country nationals wanted to see the use of more behavioral management techniques.[31]

The specific training approach used must reflect both the industrial and the cultural environment. For example, there is some evidence that Japanese students who come to the United States to earn an MBA degree often find this education of no real value back home. One graduate noted that when he tactfully suggested putting to use a skill he had learned during his U.S. MBA program, he got nowhere. An analysis of Japanese getting an outside education concluded:

> Part of the problem is the reason that most Japanese workers are sent to business schools. Whatever ticket the MBA degree promises—or appears to promise—Americans, the diploma has little meaning within most Japanese companies. Rather, companies send students abroad under the life-time employment system to ensure that there will be more English speakers who are familiar with Western business practices. Some managers regard business schools as a kind of high-level English language school, returning students say, or consider the two years as more or less a paid vacation.[32]

However, as the Japanese economy continues to have problems, American-style business education is beginning to receive attention and respect. In the 1980s American managers went to Japan to learn; now Japanese managers are coming to the United States in increasing numbers to see what they can pick up to help them better compete.

■ Types of Training Programs

There are many different types of multinational management training programs.[33] Some last only a few hours; others last for months. Some are fairly superficial; others are extensive in coverage. Figure 16–1 shows some of the key considerations that influence development of these programs. As shown, there are nine phases. In the first phase the overall objective of the program to increase the effectiveness of expats and/or repatriated executives is emphasized. The second phase focuses on recognition of the problems that must be dealt with in order to reach the overall objective. The third phase is the identification of the developmental objectives. The fourth phase consists of determining the amount of development that will be needed regarding each of these objectives. The fifth phase entails choosing the specific methods to be used in the development process from types or predeparture training to language instruction to reentry training. The sixth phase is an intermediate evaluation of how well things are going and the institution of any needed midstream corrections. The seventh phase is an evaluation of how well the expat managers are doing, thus providing evaluation feedback of the developmental process. The eighth phase is devoted to reentry training for returning expats. The ninth, and final, phase is an evaluation of the effectiveness of the executives after they have returned. By carefully laying out this type of planning model, MNCs ensure that their development training programs are both realistic and productive. In this process they often rely on both standardized and tailor-made training and development approaches.

Standardized vs. Tailor-Made

Some management training is standard, or generic. For example, participants often are taught how to use specific decision-making tools, such as quantitative analysis, and regardless of where the managers are sent in the world, the application is the same. These tools do not have to be culturally specific. For example, Osman-Gani recently surveyed managers from a host of countries regarding the content that was important in their expatriate training programs. The results are reported in Table 16–2. It shows that there is a fair

Figure 16–1   **A Model for the Development of Multinational Managers**

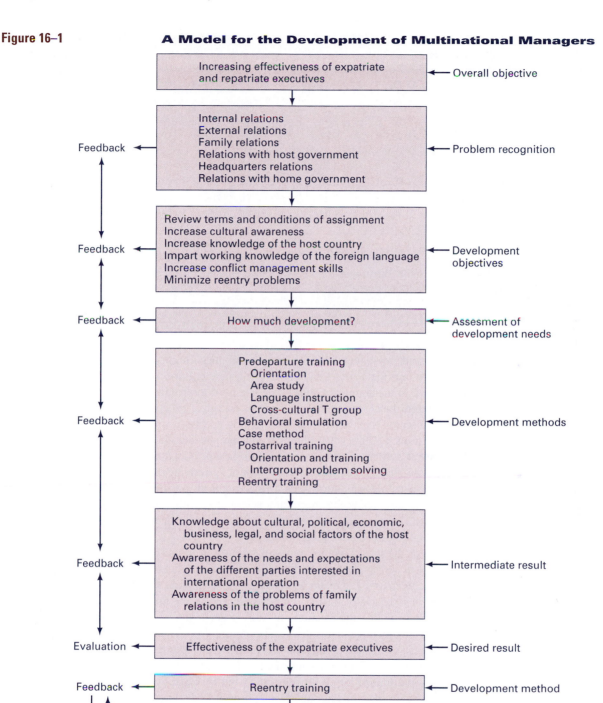

amount of agreement among countries regarding training content.[34] Research also shows that small firms usually rely on standard training programs. Larger MNCs, on the other hand, tend to design their own. Some of the larger MNCs are increasingly turning to specially designed video and power-point programs for their training and development needs.

Tailor-made training programs are created for the specific needs of the participants. Input for these offerings usually is obtained from managers who currently are working (or have worked) in the country to which the participants will be sent as well as from local

Table 16–2
Content Deemed Important in Expatriate Training Programs

Content	U.S.	Germany	Japan	South Korea	Singapore
General management factors	3.57	3.58	3.61	3.43	3.40
Human resource and labor factors	3.68	3.46	3.56	3.13	3.60
Sociocultural factors	3.58	3.51	3.27	2.86	3.53
Accounting, financial, and taxation factors	3.35	3.26	3.29	3.60	3.27
Legal and environmental factors	3.40	3.36	3.36	3.24	3.49
Production and technology factors	3.25	3.25	3.20	2.90	3.23
Marketing factors	3.40	3.46	3.23	3.30	3.43

Note: 1 = least important
5 = most important

Source: Aahad M. Osman-Gani, "Developing Expatriates for the Asia-Pacific Region: A Comparative Analysis of Multinational Enterprise Managers from Five Countries Across Three Continents," *Human Resource Development Quarterly,* vol. 11, no. 3, Fall 2000, p. 226.

managers and personnel who are citizens of that country. These programs often are designed to provide a new set of skills for a new culture. For example, MNCs are now learning that in managing in China, there is a need to provide directive leadership training because many local managers rely heavily on rules, procedures, and orders from their superiors to guide their behaviors.[35] So training programs must explain how to effectively use this approach. Quite often, the offerings are provided before the individuals leave for their overseas assignment; however, there also are postdeparture training programs that are conducted on-site. These often take the form of systematically familiarizing the individual with the country through steps such as meeting with government officials and other key personnel in the community; becoming acquainted with managers and employees in the organization; learning the host-country nationals' work methods, problems, and expectations; and taking on-site language training.

One of the most common types of training in both standard and tailor-made packages is that of self-evaluation. Participants in such training are provided personal insights about their behaviors. For example, managers will be given tests to determine if their managerial style is basically factual, intuitive, analytical, or normative. A **factual manager** looks at the available information and makes decisions based on the data. An **intuitive manager** is imaginative, innovative, and can jump from one idea to another. An **analytical manager** is systematic, logical, and carefully weighs alternatives to problems. A **normative manager** is idealistic and concerned with how things should be done. Every manager will be some combination of all four types, but by learning their individual preferences, participants gain insights into their own approach to dealing with people.

Table 16–3 shows how these managerial styles will influence the way that an individual plans, appraises performance, makes decisions, and coaches. For example, a factual manager will focus on how things are done here-and-now, while an intuitive manager will focus more on the future. Similarly, an analytical manager will integrate consideration of the past, present, and future into his or her planning activities, while a normative manager will focus heavily on reviewing what has happened in the past and use this to determine new directions. Simply put, different managers use different styles in doing their jobs. This is an important finding because it shows that when these managers are being trained, the trainer must keep in mind the trainees' personal orientations. Some people learn best with factual styles, others do better with intuitive, analytical, or normative styles.

Table 16–4 illustrates this in more depth by showing how each of the management styles will differ based on the cultural background of the trainees. A close look at the table, for example, shows that a factual management style applied in European cultures would need to emphasize theoretical as opposed to factual information, while in North America a

Factual manager
A manager who looks at the available information and makes decisions based on that data.

Intuitive manager
A manager who is imaginative, innovative, and able to jump from one idea to another.

Analytical manager
A manager who is systematic and logical and carefully weighs alternatives to problems.

Normative manager
A manager who is idealistic and concerned with how things should be done.

Table 16–3
Cultural Characteristics of Managerial Styles and Activities

Activity	Factual Style	Intuitive Style	Analytical Style	Normative Style
Planning	Focus on the present, on the here-and-now. The manager clarifies the existing situation, what is.	Focus on the future. The manager sets up objectives.	Relate past, present, and future. The manager works on strategies and tactics.	Focus on the past. The manager reviews and assesses what has been done to direct new action.
Performance appraisal	Deal with skills. (Register the facts.)	Concentrate on potential. (Look for possibilities.)	Assess performance according to several factors. (The individual, the situation, the manager, the environment.)	Insist on the perform-ance appraisal process, the relationship, the sharing of perceptions. (To understand each other is the aim.)
Decision making	Decision are based on facts and on thorough investigations; they are always well documented.	Decision are related to hunches, imagination, guesses, trial and error, risk-taking.	Decisions are the result of a systematic way to iden-tify options, alternatives and weigh them according to a set of well-analyzed pros and cons.	Decisions are closely linked to the value systems which exist in the team, organization, or culture concerned.
Coaching	Each individual has to find his or her own way. The manager can only facilitate the process by clarifying the facts.	The manager moti-vates the employee in describing a "could be" situation appealing to him or her.	Coaching is systematically organized, in a kind of step-by-step approach: "This is what has to be done to change what is into what should be."	The basic assumption that underlines the evaluative approach toward coaching is that weaknesses and strengths should be fairly evaluated and taken care of.

Source: This information is found in Pierre Casse, *Training for the Multicultural Manager* (Washington, DC: Society for Intercultural Education, Training and Research, 1982), p. 41.

much more pragmatic approach would be required if the training were to be effective. Similarly, when using an intuitive management style, North American trainees tend to look for ideas which can be applied, while in African cultures perceptions are often given much greater importance than basic facts, and in South American cultures the intuitive style often results in a great deal of excitement and emotion regarding how the information can be used—in sharp contrast to the more subdued approach used by North Americans. Additionally, when an analytical style is used in European cultures, the focus is often on getting things done through a hierarchical, bureaucratic design, while North Americans tend to process analytical information in terms of how it can be used in a decentralized, empow-ered structure. Both of these approaches are quite different, for example, from those of African cultures where the analytical style would focus on the process used to get things done, and from Asian cultures where ambiguity is widely accepted and the training partic-ipants would not feel that there was only one right way to do things. In South American cultures, meanwhile, the analytical approach is more problematic because of the belief that many times things should just be allowed to take their own course and not be overly con-trolled through analysis. Finally, a normative approach will also have to be modified to meet the needs of the participant's culture. Europeans place a great deal of attention on quality of work life and are often overly critical of how things are done. North Americans are far less critical and put their focus on getting things done and achieving self-esteem for their professional accomplishments. In contrast, African cultures value interpersonal rela-tions and the training must reflect these needs. Meanwhile, Asians like to avoid conflict and prize simplicity and humility, so many of the ideas that might get active discussion in European and North American training sessions receive very little, if any, attention. Finally, in South American cultures dignity and personal relations are important and nor-mative ideas are dealt with accordingly.

Table 16–4
Management Styles Applied to Five Cultures

Management Style	European Cultures	North American Cultures	African Cultures	Asian Cultures	South American Cultures
Factual	• Meanings are in individuals • Theoretic as opposed to practical • Inconsistent	• Individuals rely on the spoken words • Professional experiences are perceived as important • Pragmatic	• Meanings come from the environment • Time is viewed as flexible; it is not rigid • "Things" are alive	• Meanings are everywhere; in people, things • No clear-cut separation between the internal and external worlds • Sensing is an illusion	• Touching is an important part of the communication process • Sensual • Attracted to poetry, art, literature
Intuitive	• Like to play with ideas • Creative and imaginative • Enjoy exploring new avenues	• Look for ideas which can be used • Enjoy learning • Can be perceived as "naive" at times (simplistic ideas)	• Superstitious • Ideas come from group interactions • What is perceived is at least as important as what is	• Highly "spiritual" • A great sense of unity is shared by many people • Metaphysical	• Enjoy disagreements on principles, ideas; the stimulation of an exchange of opinions • Jump from one idea to another • Emotional when talking about possibilities and opportunities
Analytical	• Deductive • Rigid organizational structures • Centralized decision-making process	• Inductive • Flexible organization cultures • Decentralized decision-making process	• Are process oriented • Thinking is highly internalized (visual thinking) • Thinking is assimilated to "feeling"	• Accept ambiguity • Open to many options (there is not just "one way") • Integrate polarities and contradictions	• A certain fatalism (faith is valued) • *Mañana* concept • Disorganized and highly centralized
Normative	• Overcritical • Quality of life is highly valued • Conflicts are enjoyable	• Getting the job done is the priority • People like to be liked at the same time that they "push" people around • Self-esteem is based largely on professional accomplishments	• The concept of kinship is highly valued • Friendship comes before business and is lasting • Interpersonal relationships are based on sincerity	• Simplicity and humility are highly valued • Peacefulness is what counts above all • Enjoy flowing with situational forces	• *Machismo* (conservative) • *Dignita* • *Personalismo*

Source: This information is found in Pierre Casse, *Training for the Multicultural Manager* (Washington, DC: Society for Intercultural Education, Training and Research, 1982), p. 43.

A close evaluation of the material in Table 16–4 shows that the training approaches that are successful in one geographic region of the world may need to be heavily modified if they are to be as effective elsewhere. This finding has been echoed by Sergeant and Frenkel who recently conducted interviews with expatriate managers with extensive experience in China.[36] Their objective was to identify HRM issues and the ways in which they need to be addressed

Table 16–5
Human Resources Management Challenges Facing MNCs in China

Human Resource Management Function	Comments/Recommendations
Employee recruitment	The market for skilled manual and white-collar employees is very tight and characterized by rapidly rising wages and high turnover rates. Nepotism and overhiring remain a major problem where Chinese partners strongly influence HR policies; and transferring employees from state enterprises to joint ventures can be difficult because it requires approval from the employee's old work unit.
Reward system	New labor laws allow most companies to set their own wage and salary levels. As a result, there is a wide wage disparity between semiskilled and skilled workers. However, these disparities must be balanced with the negative effect they can have on workers' interpersonal relations.
Employee retention	It can be difficult to retain good employees because of poaching by competitive organizations. In response, many American joint-venture managers are learning to take greater control of compensation programs in order to retain high-performing Chinese managers and skilled workers.
Work performance and employee management	Local managers are not used to taking the initiative and are rarely provided with performance feedback in their Chinese enterprises. As a result, they tend to be risk-averse and are often unwilling to innovate. In turn, the workers are not driven to get things done quickly and they often give little emphasis to the quality of output. At the same time, it is difficult to dismiss people.
Labor relations	Joint-venture regulations give workers the right to establish a trade union to protect employee rights and to organize. These unions are less adversarial than in the West and tend to facilitate operational efficiency. However, there is concern that with the changes taking place in labor laws and the possibility of collective bargaining, unions may become more adversarial in the future.
Expatriate relations	Many firms have provided little cross-training to their people and family, education, and health issues limit the attractiveness of a China assignment. Some of the major repatriation problems include limited continuity in international assignments and difficulties of adjusting to more specialized and less autonomous positions at home, lack of career prospects, and undervaluation of international experience. Management succession and the balancing of local and international staff at Chinese firms are also problematic.

Source: Adapted from Andrew Sergeant and Stephen Frenkel, "Managing People in China: Perceptions of Expatriate Managers," *Journal of World Business,* vol. 33, no. 1, 1998, p. 21.

by MNCs going into China. As seen in Table 16–5, many of the human resource management approaches that are employed are different from those used in the United States or other developed countries because of the nature of both the Chinese culture and its economy.

In the final analysis, the specific training program to be used will depend on the needs of the individual. Tung, after surveying managers in Europe, Japan, and the United States, has found that there are six major types of cross-cultural training programs:

1. Environmental briefings used to provide information about things such as geography, climate, housing, and schools
2. Cultural orientation designed to familiarize the individual with cultural institutions and value systems of the host country
3. Cultural assimilators using programmed learning approaches designed to provide the participants with intercultural encounters
4. Language training
5. Sensitivity training designed to develop attitudinal flexibility
6. Field experience, which sends the participant to the country of assignment to undergo some of the emotional stress of living and working with people from a different culture[37]

Surprisingly, Tung found that only 32 percent of the U.S. firms she surveyed had formal training programs to prepare individuals for foreign assignments. This contrasted sharply with the 57 percent of Japanese firms and 69 percent of European companies that had formal programs. Table 16–6 reports the findings based on type of program and functional task. She concludes the following:

> Results indicate that for both the U.S. and West European samples, most of the firms that had training programs recognized the need for more rigorous training for the CEOs and functional heads than for trouble-shooters and operatives. In contrast, the Japanese firms that sponsored training programs appear to provide slightly more rigorous training for operatives. This could arise from the fact that since CEOs have more extensive records of overseas work experience, the need to subject them to the more rigorous programs was perceived as less important.[38]

Some organization now have extended this idea to include cross-cultural training of family members, especially children who will be accompanying the parents. The accompanying sidebar, "U.S.-Style Training for Expats and Their Teenagers," explains how this approach to cultural assimilation is carried out.

In addition to training expats and their families, effective MNCs also are developing carefully crafted programs for training personnel from other cultures who are coming into their culture. These programs, among other things, have materials that are specially designed for the target audience. Some of the specific steps that well-designed cultural training programs follow include:

1. Local instructors and a translator, typically someone who is bicultural, observe the pilot training program and/or examine written training materials.

2. The educational designer then debriefs the observation with the translator, curriculum writer, and local instructors.

3. Together, the group examines the structure and sequence, ice breaker, and other materials that will be used in the training.

4. The group then collectively identifies stories, metaphors, experiences, and examples in the culture that will fit into the new training program.

Table 16–6
Frequency of Training Programs in U.S., European, and Japanese Samples (percent)

Training Programs	Job Category											
	CEO			Functional Head			Troubleshooter			Operating Personnel		
	U.S.	Eur.	Japan.	U.S.	Eur.	Japan.	U.S.	Eur.	Japan.	U.S.	Eur.	Japan.
Environmental briefing	52	57	67	54	52	57	44	38	52	31	38	67
Cultural orientation	42	55	14	41	52	14	31	31	19	24	28	24
Culture assimilator	10	21	14	10	17	14	7	10	14	9	14	19
Language training	60	76	52	59	72	57	36	41	52	24	48	76
Sensitivity training	3	3	0	1	3	0	1	3	5	0	3	5
Field experience	6	28	14	6	24	10	4	3	10	1	7	24

Source: Rosalie L. Tung, "Selection and Training Procedures of U.S., European, and Japanese Multinationals," *California Management Review,* Fall 1982, p. 66. © 1982 by the Regents of the University of California. Reprinted from the *California Management Review,* vol. 25, no. 1. By permission of the Regents.

International Management in Action

U.S.-Style Training for Expats and Their Teenagers

One of the major reasons why expatriates have trouble with overseas assignments is that their teenage children are unable to adapt to the new culture, and this has an impact on the expat's performance. To deal with this acculturation problem, many U.S. MNCs now are developing special programs for helping teenagers assimilate into new cultures and adjust to new school environments. A good example is provided by General Electric Medical Systems Group (GEMS), a Milwaukee-based firm that has expatriates in France, Japan, and Singapore. As soon as GEMS designates an individual for an overseas assignment, this expat and his or her family are matched up with those who have recently returned from this country. If the family going overseas has teenage children, the company will team them up with a family that had teenagers during its stay abroad. Both groups then discuss the challenges and problems that must be faced. In the case of teenagers, they are able to talk about their concerns with others who already have encountered these issues, and the latter can provide important information regarding how to make friends, learn the language, get around town, and turn the time abroad into a pleasant experience. Coca-Cola uses a similar approach. As soon as someone is designated for an overseas assignment, the company helps initiate cross-cultural discussions with experienced personnel. Coke also provides formal training through use of external cross-cultural consulting firms who are experienced in working with all family members.

A typical concern of teenagers going abroad is that they will have to go away to boarding school. In Saudi Arabia, for example, national law forbids expatriate children's attending school past the ninth grade, so most expatriate families will look for European institutions for these children. GEMS addresses these types of problems with a specially developed education program. Tutors, schools, curricula, home-country requirements, and host-country requirements are examined, and a plan and specific program of study are developed for each school-age child before he or she leaves.

Before the departure of the family, some MNCs will subscribe to local magazines about teen fashions, music, and other sports or social activities in the host country, so that the children know what to expect when they get there. Before the return of the family to the United States, these MNCs provide similar information about what is going on in the United States, so that when the children return for a visit or come back to stay, they are able to quickly fit into their home-country environment once again.

An increasing number of MNCs now give teenagers much of the same cultural training they give their own managers; however, there is one area in which formal assistance often is not as critical for teens as for adults: language training. While most expatriates find it difficult and spend a good deal of time trying to master the local language, many teens find that they can pick it up quite easily. They speak it at school, in their social groups, and out on the street. As a result, they learn not only the formal language but also clichés and slang that help them communicate more easily. In fact, sometimes their accent is so good that they are mistaken for local kids. Simply put: The facility of teens to learn a language often is greatly underrated. A Coca-Cola manager recently drove home this point when he declared: "One girl we sent insisted that, although she would move, she wasn't going to learn the language. Within two months she was practically fluent."

A major educational benefit of this emphasis on teenagers is that it leads to an experienced, bicultural person. So when the young person completes college and begins looking for work, the parent's MNC often is interested in this young adult as a future manager. The person has a working knowledge of the MNC, speaks a second language, and has had overseas experience in a country where the multinational does business. This type of logic is leading some U.S. MNCs to realize that effective cross-cultural training can be of benefit for their workforces of tomorrow as well as today.

5. The educational designer and curriculum writer make the necessary changes in the training materials.

6. The local instructors are trained to use the newly developed materials.

7. After the designer, translator, and native-language trainers are satisfied, the materials are printed.

8. The language and content of the training materials are tested with a pilot group.[39]

In developing the instructional materials, culturally specific guidelines are carefully followed so that the training does not lose any of its effectiveness.[40] For example, inappropriate pictures or scenarios that might prove to be offensive to the audience must be screened out. Handouts and other instructional materials that are designed to enhance the learning process are provided for all participants. If the trainees are learning a second language, generous use of visuals and live demonstrations will be employed. Despite all of these efforts, however, errors sometimes occur. One consultant, whose team was working with Japanese trainers and managers, reported the following story:

> We assumed that the Japanese trainers would be extemporaneous. But we found that they expected to "blend" into a rigorous manual and follow it to the letter. They also expected to follow an exact time schedule and work through all of the material without veering too far from the lesson plan, even to respond to trainees' questions. What's more, we American trainers were criticized for our behavior in the training sessions. We thought we were being professional. But, to the Japanese trainers, anything that wasn't in the manual was considered "out of form." From the Japanese perspective, harmony in training comes from conforming. But our trainers from the United States felt as if the Japanese expected them to be robots. In the Japanese culture, if a trainer's behavior and activities lack form, trainees may view the trainer as irresponsible.[41]

Cultural Assimilators

Cultural assimilator
A programmed learning technique designed to expose members of one culture to some of the basic concepts, attitudes, role perceptions, customs, and values of another culture.

The cultural assimilator has become one of the most effective approaches to cross-cultural training. A **cultural assimilator** is a programmed learning technique that is designed to expose members of one culture to some of the basic concepts, attitudes, role perceptions, customs, and values of another. These assimilators are developed for each pair of cultures. For example, if an MNC is going to send three U.S. managers from Chicago to Caracas, a cultural assimilator would be developed to familiarize the three Americans with Venezuelan customs and cultures. If three Venezuelan managers from Caracas were to be transferred to Singapore, another assimilator would be developed to familiarize the managers with Singapore customs and cultures.

In most cases, these assimilators require the trainee to read a short episode of a cultural encounter and choose an interpretation of what has happened and why. If the trainee's choice is correct, he or she goes on to the next episode. If the response is incorrect, the trainee is asked to reread the episode and choose another response. Table 16–7 provides an example.

Choice of Content of the Assimilators   One of the major problems in constructing an effective cultural assimilator is deciding what is important enough to include. Some assimilators use critical incidents that are identified as being important. To be classified as a critical incident, a situation must meet at least one of the following conditions:

1. An expatriate and a host national interact in the situation.
2. The situation is puzzling or likely to be misinterpreted by the expatriate.
3. The situation can be interpreted accurately if sufficient knowledge about the culture is available.
4. The situation is relevant to the expatriate's task or mission requirements.[42]

These incidents typically are obtained by asking expatriates and host nationals with whom they come in contact to describe specific intercultural occurrences or events that made a major difference in their attitudes or behavior toward members of the other culture. These incidents can be pleasant, unpleasant, or simply nonunderstandable occurrences.

Validity
The quality of being effective, of producing the desired results. A valid test or selection technique measures what it is intended to measure.

Validation of the Assimilator   The term **validity** refers to the quality of being effective, of producing the desired results. It means that an instrument—in this case, the cultural assimilator—measures what it is intended to measure. After the cultural assimilator's critical incidents are constructed and the alternative responses are written, the process is validated. Making sure that the assimilator is valid is the crux of its effectiveness. One way to test an assimilator is to draw a sample from the target culture and ask these people to read the scenarios that have been written and choose the alternative they feel is most appropriate. If a large percentage of the group agrees that one of the alternatives is preferable, this scenario is used in the assimilator. If more than one of the four alternatives receives strong support, however, either the scenario and/or the alternatives are revised until there is general agreement or the scenario is dropped.

Table 16–7
A Cultural Assimilator Situation

Sharon Hatfield, a school teacher in Athens, was amazed at the questions that were asked of her by Greeks whom she considered to be only casual acquaintances. When she entered or left her apartment, people would ask her where she was going or where she had been. If she stopped to talk, she was asked questions like, 'How much do you make a month?" or "Where did you get that dress you are wearing?" She thought the Greeks were very rude.

Page X-2

Why did the Greeks ask Sharon such "personal" questions?

1. The casual acquaintances were acting like friends do in Greece, although Sharon did not realize it.

Go to page X-3

2. The Greeks asked Sharon the questions in order to determine whether she belonged to the Greek Orthodox Church.

Go to page X-4

3. The Greeks were unhappy about the way in which she lived and they were trying to get Sharon to change her habits.

Go to page X-5

4. In Greece such questions are perfectly proper when asked of women, but improper when asked of men.

Go to page X-6

Page X-3

You selected 1: The casual acquaintances were acting like friends do in Greece, although Sharon did not realize it.

Correct. It is not improper for in-group members to ask these questions of one another. Furthermore, these questions reflect the fact that friendships (even "casual" ones) tend to be more intimate in Greece than in America. As a result, friends are generally free to ask questions which would seem too personal in America.

Go to page X-1

Page X-4

You selected 2: The Greeks asked Sharon the questions in order to determine whether she belonged to the Greek Orthodox Church.

No. This is not why the Greeks asked Sharon such questions. Remember, whether or not some information is "personal" depends upon the culture. In this case, the Greeks did not consider these questions too "personal." Why? Try again.

Go to page X-1

Page X-5

You selected 3: The Greeks were unhappy about the way in which she lived and they were trying to get Sharon to change her habits.

No. There was no information given to lead you to believe that the Greeks were unhappy with Sharon's way of living. The episode states that the Greeks were acquaintances of Sharon.

Go to page X-1

Page X-6

You selected 4: In Greece such questions are perfectly proper when asked of women, but improper when asked of men.

No. Such questions are indeed proper under certain situations. However, sex has nothing to do with it. When are these questions proper? Try to apply what you have learned about proper behavior between friends in Greece. Was Sharon regarded as a friend by these Greeks?

Go to page X-1

Source: Adapted from Fred E. Fiedler, Terence Mitchell, and Harry C. Triandis, "The Culture Assimilator: An Approach to Cross-Cultural Training," *Journal of Applied Psychology,* April 1971, pp. 97–98.

A second validation step is to ask the sample group to rate how important each episode is. This helps to identify those incidents that should be included and those that are of only marginal value and can be omitted.

After the final incidents are chosen, they are sequenced in the assimilator booklet and today can be put on-line to be taken electronically. Similar cultural concepts are placed together and presented, beginning with simple situations and progressing to more complex ones. Most cultural assimilator programs start out with 150 to 200 incidents, of which 75 to 100 eventually are included in the final product.

The Cost-Benefit Analysis of Assimilators   The assimilar approach to training can be quite expensive. A typical 75- to 100-incident program often requires approximately 800 hours to develop. Assuming that a training specialist is costing the company $50 an hour including benefits, the cost is around $40,000 per assimilator. This cost can be spread over many trainees, however, and the program may not need to be changed every year. An MNC that sends 40 people a year to a foreign country for which an assimilator has been constructed is paying only $200 per person for this programmed training. In the long run, the costs often are more than justified. In addition, the concept can be applied to virtually all cultures. Many different assimilators have been constructed, including Arab, Thai, Honduran, and Greek, to name but four. Most importantly, research shows that these assimilators improve the effectiveness and satisfaction of those being trained as compared with other training methods.

Other Approaches

In addition to assimilators, a variety of other approaches are used in preparing managers for international assignments. These include visits to the host country, briefings by host-country managers, in-house management programs, training in local negotiation techniques, and an analysis of behavioral practices that have proven most effective.[43]

The best "mix" of training often is determined by the individual's length of stay. The longer that a person will be assigned to an international locale, the greater the depth and intensity of the training should be. Figure 16–2 illustrates this idea. Using the model in this figure, if the expected level of interaction is low and the degree of similarity between the individual's culture and the host culture is high, the length of the training should be less than a week, and methods such as area and cultural briefings should be used. Conversely, if the level of interaction is going to be high and the individual will be gone for 1 to 3 years, use of assessment centers, field experiences, and simulations should be considered. The degree, type, and length of training is a result of expected integration and length of stay. Simply put, today's MNCs use a contingency approach in developing their training strategy.

■ Organization Development

Organization development (OD) has been broadly defined as the deliberate and reasoned introduction, establishment, reinforcement, and spread of change for the purpose of improving an organization's effectiveness and health. The OD process has been widely used in the United States and Western Europe to help organizations identify problems that are associated with change and to formulate effective solutions.

Nature of OD

A basic purpose of OD is to reconcile individual-group-organization differences. Two of the most common reasons for this reconciliation are: (1) individual or group conflicts in the organization are resulting in a loss of overall effectiveness; and (2) the organization is introducing changes, such as new technology, and efforts must be made to gain acceptance by the personnel.

Most OD efforts are led by an individual who is skilled in the behavioral sciences and knows how to guide and facilitate the introduction and implementation of change effectively. This OD change agent typically will use one or more OD interventions. **OD intervention** is a catchall term used to describe the structured activity in which targeted individuals, groups, or units engage in accomplishing task goals that relate to organization development. There are many examples of OD interventions. Some are fairly simple and designed to improve individual or interpersonal behavioral skills. Others are more

Organization development (OD)
The deliberate and reasoned introduction, establishment, reinforcement, and spread of change for the purpose of improving an organization's effectiveness.

OD intervention
The structured activity in which targeted individuals, groups, or units engage in accomplishing task goals that are related to organization development.

Figure 16–2   **A Contingency Approach to Cross-Cultural Training**

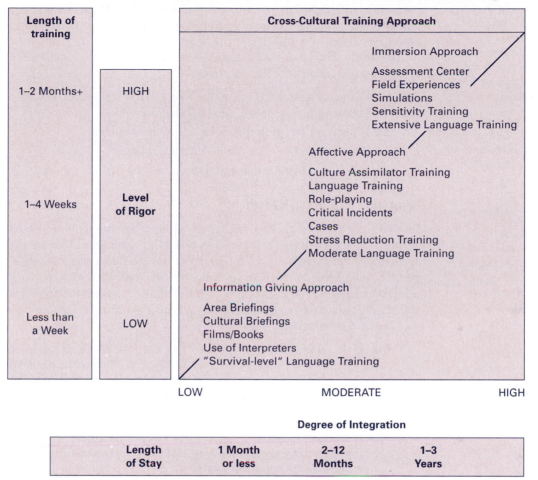

Source: M. E. Mendenhall, E. Dunbar, and G. R. Oddou, "Expatriate Selection, Training and Career-Pathing: A Review and Critique," *Human Resource Management,* Fall 1987, p. 338. Used with permission. © 1987. Reprinted by permission of John Wiley & Sons, Inc.

sophisticated and involve large groups or even the entire organization. Some of the most common OD interventions include the following:

- **Team building.** An extension of classic T-groups (training groups) and sensitivity training, which were designed to help the participants better understand themselves and each other, team building is geared more to improving organizational effectiveness through cooperation and a "team" effort by key personnel.

- **Management by objectives (MBO).** A management system for the joint setting of subordinate goals, coaching and counseling the personnel, and providing feedback on their performance.

- **Confrontation meetings.** The gathering and analysis of information related to intra- or intergroup conflict, followed by formulation of a plan of action by the participants to resolve these problems.

- **Third-party peacemaking.** The diagnosis of group conflict followed by use of an outside party (usually the OD change agent) to facilitate a constructive resolution of the situation.

- **Survey feedback.** Often more detailed and long-range than the confrontation meeting, this intervention involves the gathering and analysis of information related to group behavior and problems and the feeding back of this information to develop effective action plans.

Team building
An extension of classic T-groups (training groups) and sensitivity training that is geared to enhancing organizational effectiveness through cooperation and a "team" effort of key personnel.

Management by objectives (MBO)
A management system for the joint setting of subordinate goals, coaching and counseling personnel, and providing feedback on their performance.

Confrontation meetings
The gathering and analysis of information related to intra- and intergroup conflict followed by the formulation of a plan of action by the participants for the purpose of resolving these problems.

Third-party peacemaking
The diagnosis of group conflict followed by the use of an outside party (usually the OD change agent) to facilitate a constructive resolution of a problem.

Survey feedback
An OD intervention that involves the gathering and analysis of information related to group behavior and problems and the feeding back of this information to develop effective action plans.

These interventions can focus on the individual, groups of two or three people, large groups, intergroup relations, or the total organization. The OD intervention that is used will be determined by the particular problems that are uncovered after an OD change agent analyzes the situation.

Research shows that in most cases, success of an OD intervention depends on a number of important conditions. These include:

1. Use of an outside OD consultant who will collect the data, determine how best to deal with the problem, and lead the intervention.

2. Support for the effort from all levels of management.

3. Proper implementation of the OD intervention.

4. Follow-up to ensure that once things are improved, they do not slip back.

OD in International Settings

Can OD techniques be applied successfully in international settings? Researchers have found that although OD interventions can be useful, some limitations are caused by cultural barriers. For example, Lau and Ngo report that individual interventions which require openness and candor are ineffective with Chinese employees, who are skeptical toward such OD techniques.[44] Also, Bourgeois and Boltvinik have noted that the way managers in the U.S. communicate and use participative decision making in getting things does not work well in South America. They observe:

> Authoritarian management styles are not only accepted, but practically demanded by both Latin American workers and subordinate managers. Recent research has confirmed that, at least among Mexican managers, the perceived need to share information and objectives with subordinates is less than it typically is among American managers; there is also less belief in participative management styles. Any offer made to a Latin American subordinate to participate in decision making would not only be met with bewilderment but would result in a lowering of respect for the superior. With the acceptance of autocratic style comes complete faith in the superior's competence and wisdom. Any request for subordinate input would erode this faith and be perceived as a sign of weakness.[45]

Another major problem is language. Some of the words and concepts that are used in OD do not translate into Spanish. For example, although there in concept, the actual word *compromise* does not exist in Spanish. As a result, there may be confusion and many of the conditions critical to the success of OD change efforts are missing. Thus, many OD techniques will not work well in South American cultures.

There also are problems in applying OD in regions such as Europe, Asia, and Australia. As noted in Chapter 5, four cultural dimensions are given major attention. Two of these are power distance and uncertainty avoidance. In a typical OD intervention, participants are asked to share information, be open and honest in their communications, listen to what is being said by others, and work as a team to identify and resolve problems. This process requires the individuals to let down their guard and take the chance that they will be embarrassed or have their egos bruised. Participants who do these things must have low power distance. They must be willing to treat everyone else as an equal and not allow hierarchical rank or status to affect their interaction with the other individuals.

At the same time, participants must have low uncertainty avoidance. They must be able to live with ambiguity. Hofstede's research shows that few countries have these two dimensions of low power distance and low uncertainty avoidance. He found the four countries that best fit this cultural pattern are Denmark, Sweden, Ireland, and Great Britain. Jamaica also is a good candidate because of its low uncertainty avoidance, although it does have moderately high power distance. The United States, Canada, Australia, and others in that cluster also are good candidates for OD, although not as good as the Denmark cluster.[46] The overall conclusion is fairly obvious: OD interventions in many cases do not work well overseas, because the culture does not lend itself to these techniques. This is particularly true of unstructured interventions such as team building.[47]

Even management by objectives, which is so popular in the United States, has not been widely accepted. Comparing its success in the United States with that in Germany and France, Jaeger has noted that

> in Germany, which scores quite a bit higher on uncertainty avoidance, MBO has become management by joint goal setting, mitigating some of the risk and emphasizing the team approach, which is in line also with the lower individualism present in the German culture.
>
> In France, MBO has generally run into problems. . . . The original DPO (Director par Objectifs) became DPPO (Direction Participative par Objectifs) after the 1968 student revolts: "anything that fostered participation and decentralization was welcomed." Nevertheless, the high power distance to which the French are accustomed from childhood ultimately has thwarted the successful utilization of MBO as a truly participative process. Trepo notes that the problem is not necessarily with MBO per se but its implementation by French managers. He describes examples of managers who are unaware that they are trying to exert control through the implementation of the objectives of MBO almost by fiat.[48]

Similarly, the confrontation meeting, with its strong emphasis on low uncertainty avoidance and power distance, is particularly inappropriate in areas such as South America, the Mediterranean, Japan, Pakistan, Iran, Thailand, and Taiwan. However, some OD interventions do seem to have value. Third-party peacemaking is particularly compatible in many cultures, and if handled correctly, survey feedback could be used in countries with high uncertainty avoidance and power distance. Jaeger comments:

> Survey feedback generates data that at first may be looked at in a dispassionate way, without generating uncertainty or raising questions that would overstep the boundaries of hierarchy. Thus, an evaluation of the data can proceed slowly and not reach sensitive issues very quickly, if at all. With survey feedback one also has some control over the type of data generated, as the consultant can decide which questions are asked. A culturally sensitive consultant can therefore put together a questionnaire that generates data in such a way that a problem can be defined and discussed without upsetting the power relationships present. Hence, survey feedback could be an appropriate intervention even in those countries . . . that have high uncertainty avoidance and high power distance.[49]

In addition, OD practitioners can improve the chances of effectively using these techniques by accepting that cross-cultural OD interventions must be adapted to local conditions. Joint efforts with local practitioners can be of particular value. OD practitioners also need to learn the language of the country where the intervention is used to facilitate the exchange of information between participants and the OD change agent. The change agent can gain participant assistance in modifying the intervention for local use. As Bourgeois and Boltvinik have noted: "The straightforward transfer of American organizational development technologies to an alien cultural setting could have deleterious consequences for both the focal organization and the individuals in it if a concerted effort is not made to recognize and compensate for the potential conflicts inherent in applying its value-laden techniques in foreign organizations."[50]

Organizational Behavior Modification

Attention was briefly given to organizational behavior modifications or O.B. Mod. research in Chapters 6 and 13, where it was noted that in motivating and leading international personnel, U.S.-based theories and techniques often need to be modified. At the same time, however, recent research reveals that a behavioral management approach, if applied properly, can prove to be very valuable in improving performance across cultures. The basic O.B. Mod. application model is presented in Figure 16–3. As shown, the five major steps include:

1. *Identification of performance behaviors.* The first step of the O.B. Mod. application model is to identify the critical, observable, performance-related behaviors. In this way high-impact behaviors that may account for most of the performance outcomes are targeted for primary consideration.

Figure 16–3 **The Organizational Behavior Modification Model**

Source: Fred Luthans, Alex Stajkovic, Brett C. Luthans, and Kyle W. Luthans, "Applying Behavioral Management in Eastern Europe," *European Management Journal,* vol. 16, no. 4, 1998, p. 469. This model was originally formulated in Fred Luthans and Robert Kreitner, *Organizational Behavior Modification* (Glenview, IL: Scott, Foresman, 1975) and refined by Alex Stajkovic and Fred Luthans, "A Meta-Analysis of the Effects of Organizational Behavior Modification, 1975–1995," *Academy of Management Journal,* vol. 40, 1997, pp. 1122–1141.

2. *Measurement of the behavior.* The next step is to measure the baseline frequencies of the behaviors that were identified in Step 1. This is typically done through approaches such as direct observation, time sampling, and the gathering and analysis of existing records.

3. *Functional analysis of the behavior.* The next step consists of a functional analysis of the antecedents—behavior—contingent consequences of the behavior. Antecedents are identified in order to determine those factors that cue or set the occasion for the behavior to be carried out. Behaviors are the actions that follow from the antecedents. Contingent consequences are what determine the subsequent behavior and give power to the antecedent cues; these are reinforcers and punishers.

4. *Develop and implement an intervention strategy.* This action step accelerates and strengthens the identified functional behaviors that are increasing performance, while weakening the dysfunctional ones. The main intervention strategy is to use positive reinforcement to increase desirable, functional behaviors. Corrective feedback is used to decrease undesirable, dysfunctional behaviors, followed by positive reinforcement of the desired alternative behaviors. While positive reinforcers can be anything that increases performance behavior, they typically take forms such as monetary rewards, performance feedback, and social attention and recognition. Moreover, the performance feedback uses the guideline of being positive, immediate, graphic, and specific.

5. *Evaluate to ensure performance improvement.* The last step in the O.B. Mod. behavioral management approach is to systematically evaluate the effectiveness in improving performance. During this phase four levels of evaluation are encouraged: reaction, learning, behavioral change, and performance improvement. Reaction is measured to assess whether the process was well-liked and well-received by those involved in the program because the better the reaction the better the chance of the process being used effectively. Learning is measured to assess how well O.B. Mod. is understood by the participants. Behavioral change is assessed in order to see if there has been any change from the baseline measures obtained in Step 2. Performance improvement is measured to assess outcomes such as the quantity and quality of goods and services that are being produced.

Research by Stajkovic and Luthans found that O.B. Mod. had a very positive impact on employee performance in both manufacturing and service settings primarily in the United States.[51] A meta-analysis of 19 studies that employed the O.B. Mod. approach found that it resulted in a 17 percent average improvement in performance. This was higher than results from meta-analysis on such widely recognized approaches as goal setting. Yet, can O.B. Mod. be of value in the international arena?

As briefly noted in Chapter 13, research on O.B. Mod. by Welsh, Luthans, and Sommer was conducted in the largest textile mill in Russia. The purpose of this investigation was to examine the value of transferring U.S.-based organizational behavior/HRM techniques in a Russian factory. Using a field experimental design, the researchers tested whether both a participative and an O.B. Mod. approach (independent variables) would have a positive impact on Russian workers' productivity (dependent variable). It was found that the participative technique did not work, but the O.B. Mod. approach, using both extrinsic and social reward interventions, did lead to highly significant increases in the performance of the Russian workers.

> Both administration of desired extrinsic rewards and the trained supervisors deliberately providing attention, recognition and feedback contingent upon the workers exhibiting the impact behaviors identified in step one of the O.B. Mod. led to highly significant increases in performance. Importantly, since this was a field experimental research design, we can confidently conclude that the O.B. Mod. was indeed the cause for the performance to significantly improve.[52]

These findings for Russia were recently broadened by Fey and Bjorkman, who investigated the relationship between human resource management and the performance of 101 foreign-owned subsidiaries in Russia and found strong support for a positive relationship between

HRM practices and subsidiary performance.[53] There is also evidence to generalize that O.B. Mod. and other HRM techniques such as multisource feedback and self-managed teams are needed to develop the human resource core competency across cultures.[54]

Global Leadership Development

Another current trend of human resource development is to focus on leadership. Tichy has noted that a number of leadership training approaches can be used.[55] As shown in Figure 16–4, these range from awareness to cognitive and conceptual understanding to the development of skills and then on to new problem-solving approaches and, ultimately, fundamental change. In this process, management development becomes deeper, involves greater risk, incorporates a longer-term time horizon, and focuses on organization (rather than just individual) change.

At the same time, effective MNCs now encourage strong leadership in the areas of both hard and soft organizational issues. Examples of hard issues include the budget, manufacturing, marketing, distribution, and finance; soft issues address values, culture, vision, leadership style, and innovative behavior. In exercising strong leadership on hard organizational issues, attention is focused on becoming a low-cost provider of goods and services. In exercising strong leadership on soft organizational issues, the emphasis is on developing and maintaining innovativeness.

GLP Program   One of the best examples of the emerging leadership development programs used by MNCs is the Global Leadership Program (GLP), which is a consortium of leading U.S., European, and Japanese firms, global faculty, and participating host countries. Here is how the GLP has been described:

> The companies are part of an ongoing partnership started in 1988 jointly committed to research and development on issues of globalization. The program design, facilities, and support staff are directed by core faculty from universities in the United States, Europe, and Japan. The members of the consortium participate in a research partnership and in an intensive 5-week Global Leadership Program designed for senior executives with CEO potential.[56]

Figure 16–4

The Tichy Development Matrix

Source: Reported in Noel M. Tichy, "Global Development," in Vladimir Pucik, Noel M. Tichy, and Carole K. Barnett (eds.), *Globalizing Management* (New York: John Wiley, 1993), pp. 206–224.

The GLP is designed to provide participants with an intensive international experience to develop a global mindset, instill cross-cultural competency, and provide the opportunity for global networking. The program is 5 weeks in duration, but before attending, each person is given specially prepared briefing materials about the country that he or she will visit. At the beginning, participants are asked to complete the survey instruments that are designed to assess the individual's perceptions regarding the characteristics of a global organization, dimensions of global leadership, and the way that managers carry out their global responsibilities.

The core of the program is a 2-week, on-site, country assessment carried out by cross-cultural teams. Each group of trainees is required to use information from the assessment to produce investment opportunities and entry strategy recommendations as well as video documentaries as part of their country assessment. Among other things, each team of trainees spends 2 weeks preparing for the country assessment by working on its personal global leadership capabilities and its global mindset and team skills. Preparation also includes a weekend at an Outward Bound school and a 2-day assessment in Washington, DC.

The GLP is designed to blend rigorous intellectual development of global leaders, beginning with each individual's map of his or her own personal global mindset. Then, these are shared with the members of each team, who then are responsible for creating an analytical framework to guide its assessment of a major geopolitical region of the world. By the second week of the program, the teams have started on their country assessment. During the third and fourth weeks, the participants split up and travel to their respective countries. During the fifth and last week of the program, the individuals write their reports and make their video documentaries and presentations. Because of its strong emphasis on involvement and action learning, the GLP has become one of the best recognized development programs for training global leaders for MNCs.

The World of *Business Week*—Revisited

As seen in the *Business Week* article that opened this chapter, Liberty Media faces a host of challenges in the German market, among others. Some of these can be addressed through the careful application of human resource development strategies. Of course, the fact that the MNC has operations on three continents means that some of the HRM approaches that work well in Europe, for example, will have limited, if any, value in developing company resources in South America or Asia. So a great deal of attention has to be given to fashioning specific programs for each culture. Moreover, if the company does well in Germany, it is likely that it will try to expand into other EU countries and this, again, will require careful tailoring of human resource development efforts.

In linking this chapter to the opening article, briefly review the story and the major concepts that were presented. Then answer the following three questions: (1) Using Table 16–1 as your guide, how would the training and development programs that Liberty Media uses in Germany be different from those that it uses in Argentina? (2) Again using Table 16–1, how would the programs that it uses in Puerto Rico be different from those employed in Japan? (3) How could the company profit from the creation of a global leadership development program? If it chose to do this, what would you expect to be included in the program?

Summary of Key Points

1. Training is the process of altering employee behavior and attitudes to increase the probability of goal attainment. Many expatriates need training before (as well as during) their overseas stay. A number of factors will influence a company's approach to training. One is the basic type of MNC: ethnocentric, polycentric, regiocentric, or geocentric. Another factor is the learning style of the trainees.

2. There are two primary reasons for training: organizational and personal. Organizational reasons include overcoming ethnocentrism, improving communication, and validating the effectiveness of training programs. Personal reasons include improving the ability of expatriates to interact locally and increasing the effectiveness of leadership styles. There are two types of training programs: standard and tailor-made. Research shows that small firms usually rely on standard programs and larger MNCs tailor their training. The six major types of training include environmental briefings, cultural orientation, cultural assimilators, language training, sensitivity training, and field experience.

3. A cultural assimilator is a programmed learning approach that is designed to expose members of one culture to some of the basic concepts, attitudes, role perceptions, customs, and values of another. Assimilators have been developed for many different cultures. Their validity has resulted in the improved effectiveness and satisfaction of those being trained as compared with other training methods.

4. Organization development (OD) is the deliberate and reasoned introduction, establishment, reinforcement, and spread of change for the purpose of improving an organization's effectiveness. The basic purpose of OD is to reconcile individual-group-organization differences, often accomplished through the use of OD interventions such as team building, MBO, confrontation meetings, third-party peacemaking, and survey feedback.

5. Research shows that OD interventions often are less effective in international settings. One primary reason is that many cultures do not have low power distance or low uncertainty avoidance, which are two key dimensions for successful OD efforts. This is why team building has not worked well and MBO has been greatly modified. On the other hand, third-party peacemaking and survey feedback have been successful, because they can be adapted to the two cultural dimensions of power distance and uncertainty avoidance. Also, proven techniques such as O.B. Mod. have been shown to hold considerable potential for improving employee performance across cultures.

Key Terms

analytical manager, *490*

confrontation meetings, *500*

cultural assimilator, *496*

ethnocentric MNC, *483*

ethnocentrism, *485*

factual manager, *490*

geocentric MNC, *484*

intuitive manager, *490*

learning, *484*

management by objectives (MBO), *499*

normative manager, *490*

OD intervention, *498*

organization development (OD), *498*

polycentric MNC, *483*

regiocentric MNC, *484*

survey feedback, *500*

team building, *499*

third-party peacemaking, *500*

training, *480*

validity, *496*

Review and Discussion Questions

1. How do the following types of MNCs differ: ethnocentric, polycentric, regiocentric, and geocentric? Which most likely would provide international management training to its people? Which would least likely provide international management training to its people?

2. IBM is planning on sending three managers to its Zurich office, two to Madrid, and two to Tokyo. None of these individuals has any international experience. Would you expect the company to use a standard training program or a tailor-made program for each group?

3. Ford Motor now is in the process of training managers for overseas assignments. Why might this MNC want to learn the managerial styles (factual, intuitive, analytical, and normative) of each person? Of what

value would this be in the training process? Give two examples.

4. Zygen, Inc., a medium-sized manufacturing firm, is planning to enter into a joint venture in China. Would training be of any value to those managers who will be part of this venture? If so, what types of training would you recommend?

5. Hofstadt & Hoerr, a German-based insurance firm, is planning on expanding out of the EU and opening offices in Chicago and Buenos Aires. How would a cultural assimilator be of value in training the MNC's expatriates? Is the assimilator a valid training tool?

6. Why would an MNC be interested in using OD techniques? What are their benefits? What are their limitations? On balance, how useful are they?

Internet Exercise: Searching On-Line for Excellence

This chapter focused on human resource management approaches that are used by MNCs to develop their international workforce as well as to better prepare their home-office personnel to meet the international challenge. Two of the firms that are particularly interested in developing effective HRM programs and practices are PepsiCo and Honeywell. Visit the web sites of these companies at **www.pepsico.com** and **www.honeywell.com**. In each case, look carefully at the firm's current operations and international expansion activities. In most cases the organization's current annual report will provide you with much of this information, but also look at special product lines and new developments that are taking place. Then tie your findings to the chapter material by answering these four questions: (1) In what areas of the world is each firm beginning to focus more of its attention? (2) What types of training and development programs do you believe will be of value to each company in these efforts? Be specific and describe the tools and techniques that you would expect the firms to use. (3) What challenges do you think each will face in creating these programs and what are some steps that will be of value in minimizing these challenges? (4) Do you think a global leadership program such as the one discussed at the end of this chapter and used by General Electric would have value to any of these three firms in developing their leadership programs? Why or why not?

Argentina

Argentina occupies most of the southern part of South America. The country covers a triangular area of approximately 1.1 million square miles. It is bordered on the west by Chile, on the north by Bolivia and Paraguay, and on the east by Uruguay and the Atlantic Ocean. There are approximately 38 million people in the country (in South America, only Brazil is larger and has more people). People from many European countries settled in Argentina, but most came from Spain and Italy. The urban Argentines thus have many European customs and continue to draw from them in terms of fashion, art, literature, and architecture. Much of the country's wealth comes from the land (Argentina exports more beef than any other country). The economy has had continuing economic problems. However, by 2002 the country reached the depths with riots, many changeovers in the government, and the devaluation of the peso. The economic outlook for the future remains risky, and very uncertain.

For the last 2 years Warren Worthy's U.S.-based company has been operating two shopping malls in Buenos Aires and one in Cordoba. The operations have not been profitable, but they are making more money than the rest of the retail industry in the country.

Earlier this year, Warren sent one of his senior-level management people, Paul Flexner, to look over the mall operations and see if there were any changes that might be made or whether they should cut their losses and get out of these investments altogether. Paul was met at the airport by one of the eight U.S. managers who held the top jobs in the Buenos Aires and Cordoba operations. Paul was accompanied by an interpreter. During his stay, Paul had an opportunity to look over the operations of the shopping malls and talk to many relevant parties. Paul is convinced the economy will be okay in the long run and was able to put together a number of recommendations that he was convinced could be useful. Overall, the major operational problem he felt was that the Americans being sent down from the United States did not have enough training or orientation to Argentinean culture and language. When Paul asked one of the expatriate managers about this, he was tersely told, "Oh, we pick up things as we go along. If there's something I don't understand, I ask my interpreter. These guys are worth their weight in gold down here."

Paul also noticed that the U.S. managers remained aloof in terms of involvement. Their style was to give orders and then depend on the Argentineans who worked for them to implement the decisions. Paul believes that the reason for this approach is that the Americans are not really sure of how to do things, so they prefer not to get too involved. On his return to the United States, Paul is going to recommend that a detailed training program be put together and that no one be sent to Argentina until he or she has successfully completed this course. In particular, Paul wants to see major emphasis given to culture and language training. Before leaving, he mentioned some of his ideas to one of the U.S. managers, but the expatriate did not seem very receptive. "Oh, it's not necessary to go through all of that trouble," he told Paul. "We're doing just fine by relying on interpreters."

www.invertir.com

Questions

1. What are some current issues facing Argentina? What is the climate for doing business in Argentina today?

2. Do you agree with Paul that language training is needed?

3. Should the firm develop a standardized or a tailor-made training program?

4. What are some things that Americans need to know about management styles in South America? In your answer, incorporate data from Table 16–4.

A Southern Expansion

A small but rapidly growing U.S. irrigation equipment company is thinking about expanding its operation into the South American market. Founded 8 years ago, the firm has annual sales of $25 million and is growing at a 25 percent annually compounded rate. Most of these sales are in the United States, although the company has been trying to penetrate the Indian market and had sales of $1 million there last year.

The company sells a patented piece of irrigation equipment that has proven performance capabilities. The biggest problem for the firm is that many buyers prefer better-known companies' products, so it has to compete vigorously based on price. Thus, the board of directors is considering entering markets that are not as competitive. "There is very little irrigation equipment selling in South America," the chair of the board recently told top management. "Why don't we look into this market and see if we can develop a foothold. Admittedly, the agricultural community down there won't be as knowledgeable as they are in the states, but we could end up getting in on the ground floor."

Following up this suggestion, the company sent three representatives to South America to investigate the market. These individuals all agreed that there is a large, untapped potential in the region that could be the base for a very profitable foreign venture. As a result, the company has drafted a preliminary plan of action for doing business in Venezuela, Brazil, Chile, and Peru. If sales are sufficient in these four countries, the firm will then expand to other South American locations. The company wants to enter into a business arrangement with foreign partners whereby the firm provides the equipment and the partners handle the selling activities. Each country would have a central sales office that would serve as the link between the firm and its local foreign-run outlets. The head of this sales office would be a U.S. American appointed by company headquarters' senior management. This individual would be responsible for providing assistance to the local outlets and keeping headquarters' senior management informed about developments in the region. The sales office head would have a small staff consisting of two expatriates and three locals.

Initial plans call for setting up the first unit in each country within the next 18 months and, if things go according to plan, expanding coverage to an average of three outlets per country within the first 3 years. In each case, the company will set up the initial units in the country's agricultural centers and then slowly expand into other areas.

Questions

1. What type of training would you recommend for the expatriate managers?

2. Would you recommend the use of cultural assimilators? If no, why not? If yes, for whom?

3. If there are operating problems, would it be possible to use OD techniques to resolve them?

Chapter 17

Labor Relations
and Industrial Democracy

Objectives of the Chapter

Besides personnel selection and repatriation (Chapter 15) as well as training and organization development (Chapter 16), another critical part of managing human resources in the international arena is how the MNC handles its labor relations. How domestic firms deal with their labor relations and determine union contracts can differ significantly from country to country. A second challenge, especially for those MNCs operating in Europe and Asia, is industrial democracy, which is much more prevalent there than in other parts of the world. A third challenge is the need to coordinate worldwide efforts through formulation of an effective labor relations strategy.

This chapter addresses these challenges. Initially, it examines labor relations in the international arena using the United States as the point of comparison. Next, the internationalism of labor unions is explored. The chapter then looks at the various approaches to industrial democracy that are employed in Europe and Asia. Finally, how MNCs attempt to integrate industrial relations into their overall strategy is reviewed. The specific objectives of this chapter are:

1. **DEFINE** "labor relations," and examine the approaches used in the United States and other countries.

2. **REVIEW** the international structure of labor unions.

3. **EXAMINE** the nature of industrial democracy, and note some of the major differences that exist throughout the world.

4. **DESCRIBE** the philosophical views and strategic approaches that are used by MNCs in managing international industrial relations and future strategies.

BusinessWeek

The World of *Business Week*

Car Power

Karla Fabiola Valdez' eyes sparkle as she talks about her new job. The 30-year-old mother of three became one of the first women to join the assembly line at Ford Motor Co.'s car plant in Hermosillo in northern Mexico. After two months of intense training, Valdez now takes home around $437 a month, a princely sum for this Mexican family, which had been living off the meager wages that Valdez' husband, Gabriel, earned as a restaurant worker. "We'll be solid middle class," she says. "We're going to fix up our house, and [we] are dreaming of buying a car."

Some 5,600 miles away in Betim, in Brazil's southeast, Paulo Durães also thinks he has found his dream job. The 33-year-old is one of a team of 160 Brazilian mechanical engineers who collaborated with colleagues in Italy on development of Fiat's Palio subcompact. Durães and his compatriots put their knowledge of Brazil's tropical climate and rough road conditions to work on the project. Their contributions—from special shock absorbers to custom-designed dust filters—are now features in Palios worldwide. "Ever since I was a boy I wanted to be an auto engineer. But I thought I would have to move to Detroit," says Durães, who began working for Fiat in Brazil at the age of 18. "Thank heavens, I've been able to do everything an engineer could want without leaving home."

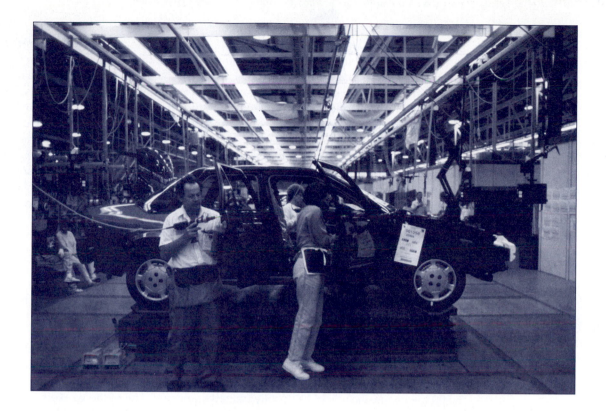

Valdez and Durães are part of the cast of thousands that is staging a manufacturing revolution in Latin America. Spurred on by a decade of market reforms and an ever-expanding web of free-trade agreements, foreign auto makers have embarked on an unprecedented spending spree. In the past five years, companies have plowed almost $40 billion into car-assembly and auto-parts plants in Latin America.

Car manufacturing has a long history in the region, of course. But until recently, high tariff walls forced companies to maintain operations in each country, where they were confined to selling locally. Now, the Latin American auto industry is entering a new era. With barriers to imports falling, manufacturers can now supply several countries from a single plant, realizing the economies of scale that had long eluded them.

So carmakers have been centralizing production in the biggest markets—Mexico, Brazil, and, to a lesser extent, Argentina. In their eternal quest for greater efficiency, auto manufacturers have transformed their freshly minted factories in Latin America into laboratories of sorts. And workers have become active participants in these experiments.

Export Platform

Employees are more than willing to undergo months of intensive training, in the hopes that their new skills will catapult them into the region's small but growing middle-class. And their bosses know that the money they lay out for education will be repaid in the form of higher-quality vehicles. That has allowed U.S., Japanese, and European car companies to turn Mexico into an export platform for some of the world's hottest new cars. DaimlerChrysler's new PT Cruiser is made only in Toluca, outside Mexico City. General Motors is assembling the Aztek sport-utility vehicle exclusively in Ramos Arizpe, near Monterrey. Production of Nissan's New Sentra is centralized in Aguascalientes. And VW manufactures its popular New Beetle in just one location on the whole planet: Puebla.

One of the most interesting trends is the level of experimentation taking place, particularly in Brazil and Mexico. These countries have become convenient testing grounds for innovative production processes, such as modular assembly and lean manufacturing, which shave hours off the time it takes to build a new vehicle. At Volkswagen's truck plant in Resende in Brazil's Rio de Janeiro state, most of the assembly work is performed by parts suppliers—not VW's workers. Militant auto unions in Europe and the U.S. would not stand for that. "It's much easier to do these things here than in the Old World, with its more rigid [labor] practices," says Herbert Demel, president of VW South America.

Mexico, for its part, has become one of the world's most dynamic car exporters. The country has signed free-trade agreements with 23 nations over the past decade, making it an ideal location for auto manufacturers. Ford led the way, back in 1986, when it became the first major auto maker to produce cars in Mexico primarily for export to the U.S. Fifteen years later, Ford's Hermosillo factory is still considered one of its most efficient in the world. Other standouts are GM's plant in Silao, Guanajuato state, where it produces the Suburban and Yukon Excel, and Chrysler's facility in Saltillo, Coahuila state, where Ram trucks are built. "These plants are doing tremendous things, often implementing lean manufacturing better than they do in the U.S. and Canada," says Laurie Felax, vice-president at Harbour & Associates Inc., a Troy (Mich.) consulting firm. Proof that Mexican plants can turn out a world-class product is in the trade numbers. Mexico exported $29 billion worth of autos and auto parts last year. "Fifteen years ago, it would have been unthinkable for auto makers to have so much confidence in Mexico that they could make it the pioneer launching facility for a new product," says Scott Martin, a professor at Sarah Lawrence College who tracks the auto industry in Latin America.

Little wonder that Mexico and Brazil are now key stepping stones to top executive positions in Detroit's Big Three and European auto companies. "When I was down there, Mexico was a $6 billion business and I ran it all," recalls Theodor R. Cunningham, who served as president of Chrysler de México between 1996 and 1998. "You get to run every entity of the business and learn what they do." Cunningham is now executive vice-president for global sales and marketing, responsible for the Chrysler, Plymouth, Jeep, and Dodge brands at DaimlerChrysler.

Companies are also grooming local talent, actively promoting Mexican and Brazilian engineers to replace expatriates once plants have been set up. At Nissan's huge factory in Aguascalientes, there are just 45 Japanese employees, compared with 5,000 Mexicans, including 400 locally trained engineers. "All of the workers, if given an opportunity, are eager to learn," says Nissan Mexicana chief Hiroshi Yoshioka.

And auto makers are investing in developing the rank and file on the assembly line. In Mexico, an assembly line worker earns $2.10 to $2.60 an hour, compared with $21 an hour in the U.S. and $19 in Germany. Because wages are low, companies can afford to lay on an unusual amount of training. VW trains new employees for three years, taking in students as young as 15. And each year, it sends 100 of its Brazilian engineers to Germany to observe production processes there. Such cross-continental pollination helps build a loyal and able workforce that can churn out world-quality cars—even though production costs run $300 to $1,500 lower per car than in the U.S.

At the same time, auto makers have begun exporting some of the cutting-edge manufacturing methods pioneered at their Mexican and Brazilian plants to other countries. The modular assembly schemes that have been perfected in Brazil, for instance, will be introduced in the U.S. and Germany as new plants are built or old ones are revamped. "We're building a book of knowledge about production systems, policies, and best practices from our experiences in plants around the world," says Frederick "Fritz" Henderson, president of the Latin America, Africa, and Mideast regional operations at GM.

Latin American nations, meanwhile, are benefiting from the boost in employment and incomes that the foreign-owned car factories provide. In Mexico, auto jobs are multiplying. The industry as a whole employs more than 611,000, up 50% in the past five years. Brazil presents a slightly different picture. Although the country has received the lion's share of auto investment over the past five years, employment in the industry has actually shrunk by nearly 20%, to 261,500, mostly owing to consolidation and streamlining, particularly in the labor-intensive parts sector. But new investments since 1996 have created more than 25,000 fresh jobs, many at factories yet to come on line. And in Brazil, as in Mexico, the new auto jobs tend to be toward the high end of the pay scale for manufacturing employment.

Thanks to NAFTA, Mexico's automotive industry is now virtually an extension of that of North America. Since the accord entered into force in 1994, Mexico has logged in $13.6 billion in auto investments. Meanwhile, U.S.-Mexico trade in vehicles and parts has skyrocketed from $14.6 billion in 1994, to $37.6 billion last year. And that commerce will increase when NAFTA tariffs on autos finally reach zero in 2003.

Ramping Up

Mexico is now anticipating a new wave of transatlantic investment. A free-trade agreement with the European Union that slashes tariffs on autos and auto parts moving in either direction took effect in July. European carmakers and their suppliers are expected to take advantage of the accord to ramp up operations in Mexico. Renault, which pulled out of the country in 1986, has begun manufacturing the Scénic, a compact SUV, at Nissan's assembly plant in Cuernavaca. This will be the companies' first joint experience in manufacturing since Renault acquired operating control of the Japanese carmaker. Patrice Ratti, general director of Renault de México, says the accord helps: "If we want to, we can import motors from France at zero tariff [in 2003]."

Brazil is fast developing into an auto center that can match Mexico. Lured by a market of 160 million consumers, GM, Ford, VW, and Fiat have been in Brazil for decades. But others piled in after the country conquered hyperinflation in the mid-1990s. Since 1995, auto makers have committed some $21 billion for new plants and upgrades of existing ones. Brazil's installed production capacity will soon reach 3 million vehicles a year.

Until now, Mexico's and Brazil's auto industries have remained worlds apart. But that situation may be about to change: Earlier this year, the two countries signed a ground-breaking one-year agreement allowing 40,000 vehicles to be shipped back and forth with a tariff of just 8%. This is well below the 35% tariff Brazil levies on imports of finished cars and the 20% duty that Mexico applies to imports from countries with which it doesn't have free-trade agreements. Major auto companies are already lobbying to make the temporary Brazil-Mexico accord permanent, and they want to include auto parts in the deal. "We're pushing very hard to sign a long-term, comprehensive auto agreement quickly," says César Flores, president of Mexico's Automobile Industry Assn.

In the meantime, foreign auto makers will continue pouring money into Brazil and Mexico. Fifteen years ago, Hermosillo was a sleepy farming and cattle ranching outpost in the middle of the desert. Today, it is home to Ford's manufacturing facility and dozens of auto-parts suppliers. To cement worker loyalty and reduce turnover, Ford built 500 modest, two-bedroom homes near its assembly plant back in 1990. Many of the homes have since been enlarged and painted bright hues of orange, blue, pink, and green. The neighborhood is called Renacimiento, which means "Rebirth." It's an appropriate name for a place that might never have existed without the Ford plant.

By Geri Smith in Mexico City and Jonathan Wheatley
in São Paulo, with Jeff Green in Detroit

The 21st century is ushering in a host of opportunities and challenges for international management. As seen in this opening news story, trade barriers in Latin America are falling and automakers are targeting the region for investment and expansion. A thriving auto industry throughout this region has emerged, and, if things go according to plan, auto MNCs there will achieve strong growth and profit. At the same time, however, these MNCs are going to face a number of labor relations challenges. One reason is because both the labor relations environment and the approaches that are used by automakers in dealing with unions tend to be different from one region to another. The way in which unions and management interact and negotiate in the United States is different from the way they do in other parts of the world. When the labor relations situation tends to be tough, then American unions can be quite confrontational. However, labor relations in Japan are quite the opposite. A more docile and accommodating approach is used. In the EU, compared to the U.S., unions have a great deal of power that is given to them by law including, in some cases, seats on the board of directors of companies. In Latin America the approaches to dealing with unions are different yet. In short, each region of the world has its own distinctive approach that is influenced by the local culture and the national economy. So the approach that works well for Ford Motor in the U.S. is not the same one that is used in the EU or Japan, and it will be modified again in managing its Brazilian operations. The same is true for all of the other automotive MNCs from Volkswagen of Germany to Honda of Japan. In this chapter, we will be studying the ways in which multinationals deal with labor relations and industrial democracy. We will also address the issue of how companies try to integrate their overall operations by using concepts such as strategic fit and strategic stretch.

■ Labor Relations in the International Arena

Labor relations

The process through which management and workers identify and determine the job relationships that will be in effect at the workplace.

The term **labor relations** can be defined as the process through which management and workers identify and determine the job relationships that will be in effect at the workplace. These relationships often are communicated verbally, but in some cases, they also are written in the form of a contract, particularly when workers are represented by a union and a management-labor contract is negotiated and agreed to by both parties. The percentage of workers who are union members varies widely by country. In Sweden, in recent years over 85 percent of employees have been unionized, while in France and the United States, only 12 percent are unionized. Therefore, depending on the countries where it does business, an MNC will face varying degrees of organized labor challenges.

As in other areas of international human resource management, the specific approaches to labor relations will vary from country to country. Some nations employ a labor negotiation process similar to that in the United States, in which both sides have power; others are characterized by either a strong management group or a highly powerful union. This is true in terms of the way that labor agreements are negotiated and enforced as well as the way industrial conflicts are resolved. Using the U.S. approach to labor relations as a benchmark, the following sections discuss how the labor relations process is carried out in selected countries around the globe.

The U.S. Approach to Labor Relations

Collective bargaining

The process whereby formal labor agreements are reached by union and management representatives; it involves the negotiation of wages, hours, and conditions of employment and the administration of the labor contract.

Union

An organization that represents the workers and in collective bargaining has the legal authority to negotiate with the employer and administrator the labor contract.

In the United States, formal labor agreements result from **collective bargaining,** in which union and management representatives negotiate wages, hours, and conditions of employment and administer the labor contract. A **union** is an organization that represents the workers and, in collective bargaining, has the legal authority to negotiate with the employer and to administer the labor contract. How collective bargaining is carried out in the United States often differs from how it is done in other countries because of the nature of U.S. labor laws.

For a work group to unionize in the United States, 30 percent of the workers must first sign authorization cards requesting that a specific union represent them in bargaining with the employer. If this percentage is met, the union can petition the National Labor Relations Board (NLRB) to hold an election. When this is done, it will be certified as the bargaining agent if the union receives more than 50 percent of the workers' votes. The two sides then will meet and hammer out a labor contract. This agreement typically remains in effect for 2 to 3 years. When it expires, a new agreement is negotiated, and assuming that the union continues to represent the workers, the cycle continues anew. If the workers are dissatisfied with their representation, they can vote out the union and go back to things the way they were before.

Note that if the workers support the union but that union is unable to negotiate a labor agreement that is acceptable to them, the workers may go on strike to pressure management to agree to their terms. Management, however, can bring sanctions of its own, including locking out employees or hiring strike breakers (called "scabs" by union members) to fill the positions of those who refuse to work. Such a lockout occurred by the owners in the

National Basketball Association strike in the 1998–1999 season. Unlike those in most other countries, however, labor strikes in the United States, such as the NBA, almost always are confined to periods when the contract is being renegotiated. Strikes seldom are used in the middle of the labor contract agreement, because mechanisms such as a grievance procedure can be employed.

Steps of a Grievance Procedure   A **grievance** is a complaint brought by an employee who feels that he or she has been treated improperly under the terms of the labor agreement. In the United States, efforts are made to solve these problems at the lowest level of the hierarchy and as quickly as possible. The contract will spell out the specific steps in the grievance procedure. The first step usually involves a meeting of the union representative at the operating level (commonly called the "shop steward") and the supervisor, who attempt to agree on how to solve the grievance. If it is not solved at this level, the grievance may go to the next steps, involving union officials and higher-level management representatives. These conciliatory approaches usually solve the grievance to the satisfaction of both parties. Sometimes, however, the matter ends up in the hands of a mediator or an arbitrator.

Mediation and Arbitration   A **mediator** brings both sides together and helps them to reach a settlement that is mutually acceptable. An **arbitrator** provides a solution to a grievance that both sides have been unable to resolve themselves and that both sides agree to accept. A number of arbitration approaches typically are used. In resolving wage-related issues, for example, three of the most common include: (1) splitting the difference between the demands of the two parties; (2) using an either-or approach, in which one side's position is fully supported and the other side's rejected; and (3) determining a fair wage based on market conditions.

Importance of Positive Labor Relations   Labor relations are important, because they directly determine labor costs, productivity, and eventually, even profits. The accompanying box, "International Management in Action: They're Leading the Pack," gives details on some of the benefits from healthy labor relations. If the union and management do not have good relations, the organization's cost of doing business likely will be higher than it otherwise would be. In fact, in recent years, many MNCs entering the United States have been looking for sites where they can set up nonunion plants. They are convinced that unions make them less competitive. This conviction certainly is debatable (e.g., highly successful Southwest Airlines is highly unionized), although some MNCs have been effective by keeping out unions. One example is the productive Japanese Nissan plant in Smyrna, Tennessee, which continually defeats union efforts.

Labor Relations in Other Countries

Because labor relations strategies vary greatly from country to country, MNCs find that the strategy used in one country sometimes is irrelevant or of limited value in another. A number of factors can account for this. One is the economic development of the country, given that general labor relations strategies often change as a country's economic situation changes. In addition, entry strategies often must be modified as the firm begins to settle in. Changes in the political environment also must be taken into consideration. For example, under the Thatcher government, British labor unions had a difficult time; in fact, prounion recognition provisions that were legislated in the mid-1970s were repealed in the 1980s. With the reelection of Tony Blair in the UK, the Labor Party now dominates, although its policies are decidedly more middle-of-the-road than that of previous labor governments.

Still another factor is strike activity. Unions in many countries often call strikes in the middle of a contract period. These strike decisions often catch the company unprepared and result in lost productivity and profit as the firm tries to negotiate with the union and/or transfer work to other geographic locales and minimize the economic effect.

Other differences are more regional in nature. For example, labor relations throughout Europe are somewhat similar, but they differ sharply from those in the United States. Some of these differences in European labor relations include:

Grievance
A complaint brought by an employee who feels that he or she has been treated improperly under the terms of the labor agreement.

Mediator
A person who brings both sides (union and management representatives) together and helps them to reach a settlement that is mutually acceptable.

Arbitrator
An individual who provides a solution to a grievance that both sides (union and management representatives) have been unable to resolve themselves and that both sides agree to accept.

International Management in Action

They're Leading the Pack   www2.ford.com

Many believe that MNCs are attracted to lesser developed countries because of labor relations policies that are conducive to cooperation, low wages, and productivity. In truth, the United States is still proving to be one of the most attractive locations for international firms. Although the power of U.S. labor unions is declining, the labor relations climate is conducive to rising productivity. Today, the United States is not only the most productive nation in the world, its overall productivity is increasing faster than that of the other major industrial powers, such as Japan, Germany, and France. The Japanese economy has been having trouble since the early 1990s, and the surging value of the yen has reduced its international competitiveness. Despite having some of the most successful MNCs in the world (e.g., Hitachi, Mitsubishi, Sony, and Toyota), Japan is experiencing some difficulties. The same is true in Europe. Many MNCs on the continent now are engaged in painful restructuring that is designed to make them more efficient and competitive in world markets. Their governments fight such downsizing, however, because of the negative impact on employment. As a result, firms such as Volkswagen in Germany and Alcatel Alsthom in France continue to face the challenge of becoming more efficient on the one hand and accommodating government directives to hire more people on the other. These are problems that U.S. MNCs do not yet face, and it helps them to maintain high productivity. There also are other reasons why U.S. productivity is doing so well relative to the rest of the world.

One is that the U.S. work ethic seems to be stronger than ever. For example, U.S. workers now are working more hours per week than they did 20 years ago. Other major economic powers such as Germany and Japan are finding just the opposite; their people are working shorter workweeks than at any time in the past. In Japan, for example, the average manufacturing worker today puts in approximately 20 percent fewer hours than in 1960, and this downward trend likely will continue. A couple of reasons are that many Japanese feel they already make enough money to take care of their needs, and many claim that they are fed up with hard work. Even Japanese union members oppose lengthening the workweek, despite efforts from their leadership to cooperate with the companies and put in more hours. Part of this opposition is a belief among the rank-and-file Japanese workers that the union represents the company's interests rather than their interests.

A second factor is that labor costs in the United States actually are lower in recent years than in most other major industrial countries. Thanks to union-management cooperation, U.S. companies have been able to introduce high-tech, efficient machinery. As a result, firms such as Ford now can manufacture cars at lower prices than foreign competitors can. Moreover, as Ford continues closing outmoded plants and running others at close to capacity, costs per car should decline even further. Much of this outcome is a result of effective labor relations strategies and shows that U.S. manufacturers not only are back in the ballgame but, in many cases, may be leading the pack.

1. In Europe, firms typically negotiate their agreements with unions at the national level, through employer associations representing their particular industries, even when there also is local, within-company negotiations. This national agreement establishes certain minimum conditions of employment that frequently are augmented through bargaining with the union at the firm or the local level.

2. Unions in many European countries have more political power than those in the United States, so when employers deal with their union(s), they in effect often are dealing directly or indirectly with the government. Unions often are allied with a particular political party—generally referred to as the labor party, although in some countries these alliances are more complex, such as a number of different political parties, each supported and primarily identified with a particular union or set of unions.

3. There is a greater tendency in Europe for salaried employees, including those at managerial levels, to be unionized, often in a union of their own.

4. Unions in most European countries have existed longer than those in the United States. Consequently, they occupy a more accepted position in society and are less concerned about gaining approval.[1]

The following sections examine industrial relations approaches in a number of selected countries.

Great Britain   In contrast to the situation in the United States, the labor agreement in Great Britain is not a legally binding contract. It is merely an "understanding" among the parties that sets forth the terms and conditions of employment that are acceptable at present. Violations of the agreement by the union or management carry no legal penalties, because the contract cannot be enforced in court. Additionally, while unions are relatively powerful and strikes are more prevalent than in the United States, British union membership has declined in recent years.[2]

Labor agreements in Great Britain typically are less extensive than those in the United States. These understandings usually contain provisions that define the structure of the relationships among the parties and set forth procedures for handling complaints. Typically, however, there is no provision for arbitration of disagreements or grievances, although both mediation and arbitration on occasion are used.

Germany   Traditionally, unions and management in Germany have had a more cooperative relationship than those in the United States, where an adversarial relationship often has existed. While some observers believed that the unification of West and East Germany would increase labor conflict, this has not happened. In fact, as integration continues, labor harmony seems to be improving. Certainly, on an overall basis, there is a spirit of cooperation between German management and labor brought about by, among other things, the use of industrial democracy, in which workers serve on the board of directors and ensure that the rank and file are treated fairly. A detailed discussion of industrial democracy is given toward the end of this chapter.

Union power in Germany is still quite strong. Although union membership is voluntary, there generally is one union in each major industry. This powerful industry union will negotiate a contract with the employers' federation for the industry, and the contract will cover all major issues, including wages and terms of employment. All firms that are members of the employers' federation then will pay the agreed-on wages. Firms that are not members of the federation typically will use the contract as a guide to what they should pay their people. Although a minority of the labor force is organized, unions set the pay scale for about 90 percent of the country's workers, with wages determined by job classifications. If an individual is replaced because of automation or laid off because of declining business, the workers' wage settlement also is handled according to the previously determined agreement. Still other agreements are hammered out to cover general working conditions, work hours, overtime pay, personal leave, and vacations.

If there is a conflict over interpretation or enforcement of the agreement, the situation typically is negotiated between the company and the worker with participation of a union representative and/or work council. If an impasse is reached, the situation can be referred to a German labor court for final settlement.

By the mid-1990s, some German unions became more adversarial. For example, IG Metall union began adopting an approach in dealing with employers that was more like that used in the United States. However, more recent economic developments have resulted in a softening of this union position. In fact, the labor relations climate in Germany traditionally is much more serene than in the United States, and most unions lack the firepower to engage in prolonged strikes. One reason is that the rights of workers are addressed more carefully by management. A second is that even though they are covered by a labor contract, individual workers are free to negotiate either individually or collectively with management to secure wages and benefits that are superior to those in the agreement. In recent years some unions have been merging in order to create what are called "super unions" and, in the process, increase their political clout and bargaining power.[3]

Japan   Unions and management have a cooperative relationship in Japan. One reason is social custom, which dictates nonconfrontational union-management behavior. The provisions in Japanese labor agreements usually are general and vague, although they are legally enforceable. Disputes regarding the agreement often are settled in an amicable manner. Sometimes, they are resolved by third-party mediators or arbitrators. Labor commissions have been established by law, and these groups, as well as the courts, can help to resolve negotiations impasses.

Japanese unions are most active during the spring and again at the end of the year, because these are the two periods during which bonuses are negotiated. Recently, Japanese unions, like the German unions, have been trying to extend wage bargaining to cover all firms in a particular industry. This would provide the union with greater negotiating power over the individual firms within the industry. Their success in this industrywide bargaining strategy would have particular impact on MNCs operating in Japan. Compared with those of most other industrialized countries, however, Japanese unions remain relatively weak.

How Industrial Conflict Is Handled Around the World

When the union and management reach an impasse in contract negotiations or over some issue, conflict results. The union may call for a strike, or management may have a lockout. A **strike** is a collective refusal to work to pressure management to grant union demands. In recent years, strikes have been less common in most countries; however, when measured in terms of working days lost per 1,000 employees, strikes are still a powerful weapon in dealing with industrial conflict. For example, between 1990 and 1999 economically advanced countries lost an average of 59 working days per 1,000 employees because of labor disputes. In the last half of this decade, the average strike rate fell by nearly 50 percent in the EU. Figure 17–1 shows the annual average of days lost during this ten-year period. A **lockout** is the company's refusal to allow workers to enter the facility. Other typical union strategies resulting from conflict include slowdowns, sabotage, sit-ins, and boycotts. The following sections show how these approaches are handled around the world.

United States   Most U.S. labor contracts have a specific provision that outlaws strikes; thus, sudden or unauthorized strikes (commonly called "wildcat strikes") are uncommon. If either party to the contract feels that the other is not acting in good faith or living up to the terms, the grievance procedure is used to resolve the matter peacefully. However, once the contract period is over and if a new one is not successfully negotiated, the workers may strike or continue to work without a contract while threatening to walk out. On the other side, management also may lock out the workers, although this is much more rare. The modern position of more and more U.S. unions is that a philosophy of "us against them" is not as conducive to the long-range welfare of the union as is a strategy of working together to find common ground. In this regard, U.S. unions are moving closer to the approach that is used by many unions in other countries.

Great Britain   In Great Britain, labor unions are relatively powerful (although this power has been eroded in recent years), and strikes are more prevalent than in the United States. Labor agreements typically do not prohibit strikes, and the general public is more used to and tolerant of them. Strikes in Britain often are brief, however, and do not involve a large number of people, although British miners have had prolonged strikes.

Some labor experts believe that industrial conflict in Britain results in more problems than in the United States, because the system is not geared toward the efficient resolution of problems. For example, many in the British general public as well as the workers believe that it is management's job to look after workers, and failure to do so is a breach of management's social responsibility. This climate often results in hard feelings and impedes rapid solutions. In addition, the procedure for handling grievances, in contrast to that used in the United States, often is informal, cumbersome, and sometimes results in fragmented efforts with the outcome costly in terms of both time and money. Sometimes, management uses the lockout to vent its frustration over the bureaucratic delays in resolving labor-related problems. Although things have been changing for the better in recent years, the British in general still appear willing to accept conflict with resulting strikes and lockouts as the price of protecting the rights of the workers.

Strike
A collective refusal to work to pressure management to grant union demands.

Lockout
A company's refusal to allow workers to enter the facility during a labor dispute.

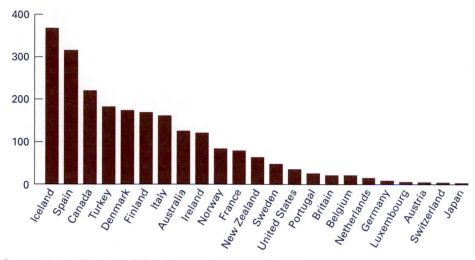

Figure 17–1

Annual Average Days Lost Due to Labor Disputes in Economically-Advanced Nations: 1990–1999

Source: United Kingdom, Office for National Statistics, 2001.

Germany A number of similarities exist between the United States and Germany in terms of managing labor conflicts. As in the United States, strikes and lockouts are prohibited in Germany during the period when a labor agreement is in effect. A strike is legal, however, when the contract has run out and a new one has not yet been ratified by the workers. Although German unions tend to be industrywide, quite often several agreements are in force in a particular company, and these agreements do not have the same termination dates. Therefore, one group of workers may be striking or working out a contract while another is working under contract. In addition, different terms and conditions of employment exist for different groups of workers, just as in the United States. Similarly, there sometimes are strikes in the middle of a contract period in clear violation of the labor agreement, indicating that the German preference for orderly and well-defined work relationships is not always present. Overall, however, there tends to be a fair amount of cooperation between management and labor because of the way labor relations are legally structured.

Japan Strikes and lockouts in Japan are very rare. Following World War II, there was a period of severe labor unrest coupled with massive, and sometimes crippling, labor strikes. Today, however, strikes are of short duration and used only to drive home a particular, minor point, not to cripple an industry or inconvenience the public. One knowledgeable observer has explained it this way:

> Since threats are generally unnecessary, a strike in Japan is merely a way to embarrass management, and thus may last from a couple of hours to a couple of days, with those of a week or more considered very long. But an equally important reason for strikes' being so short is the strong social pressure to keep the conflict quiet and resolve it quickly and quietly without having to resort to the law. In Japan the law is regarded as the instrument with which the state imposes its will. Hence, the Japanese do not like the law and will try to stay as far away from it as possible.[4]

Sometimes, strikes occur when a Japanese union is negotiating with management during industrywide negotiations. These strikes are aimed at showing that the workers support their union and are not designed to indicate any particular grievance or complaint with management. This is understood by both sides. The issues over which both sides might disagree are fairly limited. This is true for two reasons: (1) An individual's term of employment never exceeds those provided for in the labor contract, because this would indicate that this worker was more important than the other members of the work group; and (2) the law establishes standards for minimum wages, hours, overtime, rest periods, vacations, sick leaves, sanitary conditions, and discharge. Therefore, individual needs or desires are not given a great deal of attention by the union; however, Japanese unions still try to gain benefits for their people, as seen in recent efforts to win wage increases and cuts in working hours.

An insight into Japanese labor relations is provided by the cultural value of *Wa,* which implies that individuals should subordinate their interests and identities to those of the group. This cultural value helps to account for a great deal of the harmony that exists between management and labor in Japan.

■ International Structure of Unions

So far, this discussion has centered on the international implications of labor relations, but the structure of unions themselves also has important implications. Most labor unions are locally or nationally based, but some are internationally active. Union internationalization has been achieved in three basic ways: (1) through use of intergovernmental organizations; (2) through use of transnational union affiliations; and (3) through extension of domestic contracts.

Intergovernmental Organizations

There are two important intergovernmental organizations. The **International Labour Office (ILO)** is a United Nations affiliate that consists of government, industry, and union representations. The ILO has worked to define and promote fair labor standards regarding health and safety, working conditions, and freedom of association for workers throughout the world. A number of years ago, the ILO published a study of social policy implications of MNCs. Some topics in that study included investment concentration by area and industry, capital and technology transfers, international trade, workforce efforts, working conditions, and industrial relations effects. The study concluded by noting the different views and concerns of employers and workers, and it recommended that the social problems and benefits specific to MNCs be identified and studied further.

The ILO has also conducted a series of industry-specific studies on MNCs in Western Europe, and country studies on the employment effects of MNCs, including jobs lost and gained as a result of MNCs as well as the quality of jobs within MNCs. Some of its important conclusions were: (1) jobs were growing faster in MNCs than in non-MNCs; (2) white-collar positions were increasing at the expense of blue-collar jobs; and (3) one key reason for this employment growth was the R&D intensity of MNCs.

The **Organization for Economic Cooperation and Development (OECD)** is a government, industry, and union group that was founded in 1976 and that has established a voluntary set of guidelines for MNCs. These guidelines include MNCs' obligation to respect the laws and regulations of foreign countries, and in turn, these foreign countries are obliged to provide national treatments to MNCs within their borders. In recent years, these guidelines have been used to help countries regulate the operations of MNCs within their national boundaries.

Transnational Union Affiliations

There are four basic types of international trade affiliations: global, regional, specialized, and industrial operations. **Global international trade union affiliations** cut across regional and industrial groups and are heavily concerned with political activities. The **International Confederation of Free Trade Unions (ICFTU)** is the most important global international union confederation. Most of the **regional internationals** are subdivisions of the globals, and the regionals' activities are application of the globals' activities. **Specialized internationals,** such as the ILO, the Trade Union Advisory Committee in the OECD, and the European Trade Union Congress, which represents workers' interests at the European Union level, function as components of intergovernment agencies and lobby within these agencies. The **industrial internationals** also are affiliates of the global internationals. In the ICFTU, they are called International Trade Secretaries (ITS), and there is an individual ITS for each major industry group.

Also of transnational interest are worldwide company councils that have been formed under the auspices of the International Trade Secretaries (ITS). For example, there is a General Motors Council, which consists of union representatives from GM plants

Margin glossary

International Labour Office (ILO)
A United Nations affiliate, consisting of government, industry, and union representatives, that works to promote fair labor standards regarding health and safety, working conditions, and freedom of association for workers.

Organization for Economic Cooperation and Development (OECD)
A government, industry, and union group founded in 1976 that has established a voluntary set of guidelines for MNCs.

Global international trade union affiliations
Trade union relationships that cut across regional and industrial groups and are heavily concerned with political activities.

International Confederation of Free Trade Unions (ICFTU)
The most important global international union confederation.

Regional internationals
Subdivisions of the global affiliation; regional applications of the global's activities.

Specialized internationals
Trade union associations that function as components of intergovernmental agencies and lobby within these agencies.

Industrial internationals
Affiliates of the global international union groups that focus on a particular industry.

throughout the world. This council meets periodically to share information about collective bargaining, working conditions, and other developments that can be valuable to unions in gaining comparable treatment for their people in country-level bargaining.

The international structure of the ITS provides a union vehicle that is parallel to the international structure of an MNC. On occasion, an ITS representative has sought to intervene at the global headquarters of an MNC on behalf of a member union having difficulty in its dealings with a subsidiary of the MNC at the national level. Some labor relations experts believed that when worldwide company councils were developing during the 1970s, they would become vehicles for transnational collective bargaining with MNCs; however, the diverse legal and cultural environments of the various countries have been a major barrier to this development.

Extensions of Domestic Contracts

Some U.S. unions have sought to deal with MNCs by bargaining with them on a global basis. The International Union of Electrical (IUE) workers, for example, invited union representatives from General Electric's overseas plants to participate in its collective bargaining. These foreign representatives were only observers, however, because U.S. labor law limits collective bargaining to matters that relate to the U.S. labor unit. In another action, the IUE contended that GE was transferring work overseas and charged that this was an unfair labor practice under the provisions of the collective bargaining agreements; however, the general counsel for the National Labor Relations Board rejected the charge and held that the union had not substantiated its claim. Overall, unions have been unsuccessful in attempting to prevent companies from transferring work overseas, although this certainly will continue to be a major focal point in the years ahead.

■ Industrial Democracy

Industrial democracy involves the rights of employees to participate in significant management decisions. This participation by labor includes areas such as wage rates, bonuses, profit sharing, vacations and holiday leaves, work rules, dismissals, and plant expansions and closings. Industrial democracy is not widely used in the United States, where management typically refuses to relinquish or share its authority (commonly called "managerial prerogatives") to make major decisions. In many other countries, however, and especially in Europe, the right of industrial democracy is guaranteed by national law. This right can take a number of different forms.

Industrial democracy
The rights that employees have to participate in significant management decisions.

Common Forms of Industrial Democracy

As the EU consolidates its goal of unification, the head of the European Commission has stated that a primary objective is to obtain a minimum threshold of social rights for workers, to be negotiated between a "European union" and employers. At present, several forms of industrial democracy exist in European countries and elsewhere. In some countries, one form may be more prevalent than others, but it is common to find a number of these forms existing simultaneously.

Codetermination Codetermination, which was discussed briefly in Chapter 12, involves the participation of workers on boards of directors. The idea began right after World War II in Germany to prevent the re-emergence of Nazism in the coal and steel industries. By the mid-1970s, European countries besides Germany, such as Austria, Denmark, the Netherlands and Sweden, all had legally mandated codetermination. In most cases, boards of directors had to consist of one-third worker representatives. In the late 1970s, Germany increased this to 50 percent for private companies with 2,000 or more employees. Most recently the EU Council of Ministers issued a directive that now requires all companies with 50 or more employees by 2008 to "inform and consult" workers' representatives about company strategy.[5] Despite such efforts, some researchers report that the workers are not greatly impressed with codetermination; many regard such participation on boards as merely a cosmetic attempt to address the substantive issue of true industrial democracy.

Work Councils   To varying degrees, work councils exist in all European countries. These councils are a result of either national legislation or collective bargaining at the company–union level. Their basic function is to improve company performance, working conditions, and job security. In some firms, these councils are worker- or union-run, whereas in others, members of management chair the group. Workers typically are elected to serve on the council, and management representatives are appointed by the company. The amount of council power will vary. In England, France, and Scandinavia, the groups tend not to be as powerful as in Germany, the Netherlands, and Italy. Moreover, in small firms many managers feel that these councils reduce the company's flexibility and make it less competitive. As observed in Germany:

> Under current law, a workers council can block decisions on hiring and firing workers. It must approve employee transfers from one job to another, as well as management requests for workers to put in extra hours. Workers councils also have the right to propose changes on many policies and the right to be informed in advance if a company plans to reduce its workforce. If a company does not intend to eliminate jobs, the workers council has the right to approve the plan for compensating dismissed employees.[6]

On the other hand, both unions and management acknowledge that companies have found a variety of ways to reduce codetermination by hiring temporary workers and outsourcing work to other firms. So the negative impact of work councils is often minimized in practice.

Shop Floor Participation   A wide number of approaches are used to achieve shop floor participation. Some of the most common include worker involvement programs, quality circles, and other forms of participative management discussed in earlier chapters. QWL (quality of work life) programs such as those used in the Scandinavian countries and currently very popular in manufacturing and assembly plants throughout Europe and the United States are excellent examples.

Financial Participation   Financial participation takes a number of forms. One of the most common is profit sharing between management and workers. In some cases, productivity or gain sharing plans are used, whereby management shares productivity gains in a predetermined ratio, such as 50-50, with the workers. This motivates workers to recommend efficiency measures and develop shortcuts to doing their jobs in return for a share of the increased profits. Overall, financial participation has not been widely adopted overseas, although it has gained a foothold in a number of U.S. firms, especially those using gain sharing as a team incentive for performance improvement.

Collective Bargaining   If no specific forms of industrial democracy are in effect, collective bargaining itself can become the mechanism to obtain industrial democracy for workers. As noted previously, the ability of unions to bargain collectively is legally restricted in some countries (e.g., a majority vote of the bargaining unit is required in the United States) and is not widely used in others. However, some nations, such as Sweden, require collective bargaining and allow many matters that in the United States are considered to be managerial prerogatives and not applicable to bargaining, such as work rules and production standards, to be open for negotiation with the workers.

Industrial Democracy in Selected Countries

Industrial democracy takes a number of different forms depending on the country. For example, the approach used in the United States differs from those used in Europe and Asia. The following discussion briefly highlights some of these differences.

United States   In the United States, the most common form of industrial democracy is collective bargaining, whose guidelines are spelled out by law. A union that is certified by the NLRB becomes the exclusive bargaining agent for employees in the unit and is authorized to represent workers in the negotiation and administration of a labor–management contract. During the last decade, other forms of industrial democracy have gained ground, most notably employee participation in the form of problem-solving teams, special purpose teams, and self-managing teams.

Problem-solving teams meet weekly to discuss ways of improving quality, efficiency, and the overall work environment. While they generally are not empowered to implement their ideas, their suggestions often result in more efficient operations. These teams have begun to gain widespread support as managers turn to employees for help in improving performance.

Special purpose teams design and introduce work reforms and new technology. In unionized firms, both management and labor will collaborate on operational decisions at all levels. This involvement often creates the necessary environment for both quality and productivity improvements. These teams are continuing to gain popularity, especially in unionized operations.

Self-managing teams consist of individuals who learn all the tasks of all group members, which allows them to rotate from job to job. These teams also take over supervisory duties such as scheduling work, ordering materials, and determining vacation times. These teams have been so effective that in some cases, productivity has increased and quality has risen dramatically. In recent years, these teams have become increasingly popular, and the future will probably see even greater use of them.

The three types of industrial democracy described here represent a radical departure from the way that U.S. firms traditionally have been managed. The old approach of a top-down management holding on to all the authority now is being replaced with an industrial democracy philosophy of sharing power with the workers. Spurred on more by creative human resource management and the total quality movement, the currently popular empowerment of employees, defined in Chapter 3 as the process of giving employees the resources, information, and authority needed to carry out their jobs effectively, is bringing U.S. firms more into step with the industrial democracy approach taken by firms in other countries over the years.

Great Britain   Industrial democracy is not new to England. Self-governing workshops (worker cooperatives) existed as early as the 1820s; however, Great Britain has not become the hub of industrial democracy in the twentieth century. For example, unlike many workers in Germany and Scandinavia, British workers are not legally mandated to have seats on the board of directors. During the mid-1970s, it appeared that this would happen, but by the early 1990s, indications were that it would not occur in the near future, if at all. As in the United States, however, there is industrial democracy in Great Britain in the form of collective bargaining and worker representation through the use of teams.

Work groups within a British company or plant will elect a chief spokesperson or steward from their ranks to act as their interface with management. If the employees are unionized, a union council will represent them. These councils help to ensure that workers are treated fairly by management. Unfortunately, this sometimes creates a problem, because spokespersons or stewards in the firm may not agree with the union councils.

During the coming years, British firms likely will begin relying more heavily on participative approaches such as those used in the empowerment process in the United States and Northern Europe. The primary reason is that competitive nations have been able to show that shop floor democracy is a key element in reducing production costs and increasing product quality. However, even with the Labor government now in power, legally mandated industrial democracy measures are unlikely in Great Britain any time in the near future.

Germany   Industrial democracy and codetermination are very strong in Germany, especially in the steel and auto industries. Although the union is charged with handling the collective bargaining, internal boards have been established by law for ensuring codeterminism in the workplace. As noted earlier, the full impact of unifying with East Germany is yet to be determined, but all firms with 2,000 or more employees (1,000 or more in the steel industry) presently must have boards composed of workers. One supervisory board is

Problem-solving teams
Employee groups that discuss ways of improving quality, efficiency, and the overall work environment.

Special purpose teams
Employee groups that design and introduce work reforms and new technology.

Self-managing teams
Employee groups that take over supervisory duties and manage themselves; teams consist of individuals who learn all the tasks of all the group members, allowing team members to rotate jobs.

made up of an equal number of representatives who are elected by both the shareholders and the employees, and of one additional, neutral person. This supervisory board in German companies is similar to the board of directors in U.S. firms. The other type of board in German firms is the management board, which is responsible for daily operation. Employees in each plant also elect a plant work council; if it is a multiplant company, members of the plant work council serve on a company work council as well.

Work councils perform a number of important functions, including negotiating wage rates above the contractually established minimums, negotiating benefits, setting wage rates for new jobs, and re-evaluating pay when workers are transferred between jobs. In multiplant operations, these councils sometimes have difficulty finding out what is happening at the shop floor, so they rely heavily on meetings with employees and communication with shop stewards. As a result, German workers have two groups working for them: the union, which is bargaining collectively with management; and the work council, which is negotiating employment issues relating to that particular plant.

Because of the strong degree of codeterminism, some German managers have argued that the process undermines their ability to operate efficiently. They contend that the legally established industrial democracy hampers their efforts; however, research does not support such a position. For example, Scholl conducted a study of both managers and work councils to determine whether codetermination results in more complex, and thus slower, decision making.[7] He focused on decisions that related to both investment and personnel matters. In general, the study found that the ability of German firms to make decisions is not hampered by codeterminism. However, German businesses must continue to push for changes that make them more competitive worldwide.

Denmark Industrial democracy ensures that Danish workers participate in the management of their firms both directly and indirectly. The direct form includes use of semiautonomous work groups that provide ideas on enhancing productivity and quality and on scheduling the work. The indirect form includes use of shop stewards on the work floor, representation on boards of directors, cooperation committees consisting of worker and manager representatives, safety groups made up of a supervisor and an elected employee representative, and participation on safety committees that are headed by a manger. Figure 17–2 provides an organizational illustration of these employee participation and industrial democracy arrangements.

Unlike the situation in Germany, where the participation of workers on boards of directors is perceived as cosmetic, cooperation committees of firms in Denmark seem particularly important in ensuring a true feeling of industrial democracy on the part of Danish workers. For example, one study found that most Danish workers felt the cooperation committees contributed heavily to openness, coordination of effort, and a feeling of importance.

Sweden Industrial democracy in Sweden is directed very heavily toward ensuring quality of work life (QWL) and worker participation in the operation of the enterprise. QWL efforts are closely associated with Sweden's Volvo approach. The creation of semiautonomous work teams and development of a cooperative spirit between management and workers are key elements in Volvo and the Swedish approach to industrial democracy. In addition, councils and committees encourage employee involvement in identifying and implementing changes, which lead to improved QWL, which helps to sustain high morale and positive attitudes of workers and to improve productivity and quality of products and services. There is some evidence, however, that the early, glowing reports from Volvo may have been overstated, and that instead of returning dignity to the workers, the assembly lines are just more efficient but not really reaching the standards that are required for world-class competition.

Swedish firms also have workers who are members of the board of directors. To ensure that these worker board participants are competent in handling their tasks, they typically are given formal training and spend time with other workers on the board in learning how to do things such as analyze and evaluate financial statements, read reports, and focus on both long-range and short-range issues.

Figure 17–2

**Employee
Participation in
All Levels of
Danish Firms**

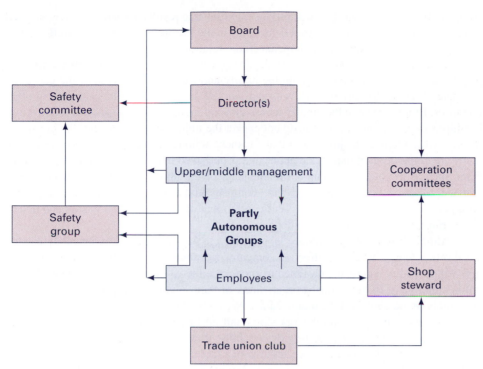

Source: Adapted from Reinhard Lund, "Industrial Democracy in Denmark," *International Studies of Management & Organization,* Summer 1987, p. 18. Used with permission.

China   China has the largest workforce in the world, but even now, little is known to outsiders about how industrial democracy really works there. Similar to the situation in Eastern Europe, many changes have occurred in China. Unlike what has happened in Eastern Europe, many of the reforms and Westernized policies and practices in China, including the nature of industrial democracy, are closely related to the current political climate.

Chinese enterprises traditionally had two policy-making committees; one contained Communist party leaders and members, and the other included managers and worker representatives. Which committee had more power depended on the political climate, but after reforms in the 1980s, the workers (not the party members) represented industrial democracy in communist countries; however, worker participation in management decision making is less open than Westerners may expect. One study of a variety of enterprises in Beijing found that the number of employees who participate in management decisions is not very high but that the scope was quite broad and important (sales and business plans, production operations decisions, wages and bonuses, employee benefits, housing allocations, transfer of funds, and termination of problem employees).[8] Only time will tell what course industrial democracy will take in China. However, the government did recently agree to an ambitious program of cooperation with the ILO. According to the agreement, the ILO will provide advice on such things as job creation, workplace safety, collective bargaining, and the settlement of labor disputes.[9] Given that illegal strikes and worker protests have become common as China continues to move toward a market-driven system that has left millions of people out of work, and left others toiling in arduous or unsafe conditions, this ILO agreement may well prove to be helpful to the government, the workers, and the MNCs doing business there.

Japan   Unlike the situation in Europe and China, industrial democracy in Japan is not closely tied to political philosophy. Like in the United States, Japan is oriented more to the operating philosophy of enhancing worker performance. The best example is quality circles, in which Japanese workers are encouraged to identify and help solve job-related problems that are associated with quality and flow of work. Management is particularly

Enterprise unions
Unions that represent both the hourly and salaried employees of a particular company.

receptive to workers' ideas that will produce bottom-line results. Except for a few unusual cases, Japan has very little industrial democracy in the European sense. This is reflected by the basic nature of Japanese union–management relations.

There are over 70,000 unions in Japan, and most of them are **enterprise unions,** which means that they represent both the hourly and salaried employees of the particular company. Including salaried employees is a marked departure from labor unions in other countries. Employees join the union because they are members of the firm and union membership is expected; however, they do not expect the union to negotiate and win big salary increases for them. A major reason that Japanese unions are relatively weak is because many are company-dominated, a practice that is outlawed in the United States. In the large firms such as Toyota, for example, the president of the union typically is a middle-level manager who has been nominated by the company and elected by the membership. This arrangement ensures that the unions act in harmony with the company's wishes and undermines European-style industrial democracy.

Although there sometimes are labor strikes in Japan, as noted earlier, they usually are short-lived and have little effect on company operations. In fact, these strikes often are just ceremonial in nature and designed to encourage the workers to think of themselves as union employees. In truth, most workers think of themselves as company employees who are simply associated with the union. Moreover, it is not uncommon to find a union strike in a company with two or three work shifts and no loss of work output. This is because when the strikers are done picketing or marching, they go to work and the group coming out of the factory takes up the strike activity. In a factory with three shifts, a line employee will work a full shift, picket for a while, go home to eat and sleep, and then return to the factory for her or his shift.

Of all the industrialized nations, Japan faces the greatest challenge from industrial democracy during the years ahead. Japanese MNCs in Europe, and to a growing degree in the United States, will find that they must relinquish more control over operations to the workers if they hope to achieve the same productivity results they have at home. Conversely, MNCs in Japan report that Japanese white-collar workers are too used to working in a disciplined, corporate environment and fail to make decisions and take initiative. Therefore, changes are needed at home as well.

■ Strategic Management of International Labor Relations

The strategic management of international labor relations will be a major challenge facing MNCs in the years ahead, because so many different approaches can be taken. The approach used in U.S. firms may not be the same as that employed in other countries, including Anglo nations. In Great Britain, as noted earlier, unions do not have the power they once had. In many other European countries, such as Germany, however, unions continue to be quite strong, and especially as the Eastern European traditions of industrial democracy become infused in the EU, the workers will continue to have a great deal of authority in determining what the firm will do. It also is important to realize that those strategies benefitting unions in one country may have no value in others. This sometimes can be a conflict between international unions. For example, when Ford Motor felt that the labor climate in Britain was unfavorable to further investing, the company was approached by a group of Dutch businesspeople and urged to consider the Netherlands for future investment. Despite the strong criticism of British unions, the leadership of the Dutch trade unions did not object to these suggestions that investment funds be transferred to their country.[10]

The Philosophical Backdrop

As noted in earlier chapters, MNCs can use a number of philosophies as a starting point for their approach to management functions, including labor relations. For instance, under an ethnocentric philosophy, the MNC will take an approach to labor relations in other countries that is identical to its approach at home. Cultural, legal, and economic factors of the host country will not be considered in industrial relations efforts. This approach, quite obviously, generally is not effective and can even have disastrous results; as companies begin going international, they soon abandon such an approach.

A second approach is to use a polycentric philosophy in managing international industrial relations. Under this philosophy, the MNC will evaluate each country or geographic region as a separate entity. The MNC's international industrial relations strategy will be a series of different approaches depending on the country.

A third approach is a geocentric philosophy that is characterized by an effort to understand the interrelationships between the various geographic locations and a strategy to link them with a unifying thread and a composite industrial relations approach. The primary difference between a polycentric and a geocentric philosophy is that the latter considers the interrelationships between the various groups. Here are some examples of how industrial relations in one country can affect those in others:

1. Opel (General Motors' German subsidiary) negotiates an *increase* in the basic workweek hours with Belgian unions as it adds a second shift at its Belgian assembly plant. The intent of management is to keep the costs of production there competitive with those at a similar Opel plant in Germany. The intent of the Belgian workers is to expand employment and enhance job security.

2. A U.S. electronics firm cuts back its U.S. manufacturing output by 10 percent through laying off a like percentage of its U.S. workers. Its French subsidiary picks up the resulting product market slack. By cutting back employment in the United States, the firm avoids the large payments to workers that French law would have required if the cutback had been made by the French subsidiary.

3. Workers at a German company's British subsidiary go out on strike to support their demand for improved wages. Operations at the company's German plants continue, providing substantial cash inflows (revenues) to the entire system. The British workers completely forgo their cash inflows—their wages—during the strike. The company is less severely pressed financially than these workers are and can sustain a long strike if need be.

4. Ford of Europe integrates production among several European subsidiaries. For certain models of cars, the engines are British-made, the power train and some stampings are German-made, the wheels and other stampings are Belgian-made, and so on. A strike by workers in Belgium could shut down plants in Britain, Germany, and elsewhere. This gives the Belgian workers operational leverage vis-à-vis management and enhances their power in collective bargaining.[11]

The Japanese also make an interesting case study of the need for a geocentric philosophy toward industrial relations. Japanese auto firms long have realized that auto capacity is outstripping demand both in North America and Europe. As Japan continues to increase its foothold in North America, it will have to pay greater attention to its industrial relations approaches and modify them to meet the local labor market. Japan also will need to coordinate its worldwide holdings with a carefully formulated geocentric strategy toward labor relations.

Labor Costs

Another major area of consideration in formulating an international labor relations strategy is labor costs. Wages that are paid in one country often differ considerably from those in other countries for the same job. In some countries, workers are grossly exploited. From China to Bangladesh[12] to El Salvador,[13] employee sweatshops produce clothing for the world market and workers toil for long hours, in unsafe conditions, for minimum pay. At the same time, however, a growing number of MNCs are refusing to do business with these firms and are beginning to closely monitor their suppliers to ensure that workers are treated well. These developments, of course, will lead to an increase in labor costs, but this is certainly the socially responsible thing to do. On the other hand, in some countries labor costs are extremely high. In manufacturing, for example, hourly rates in Germany have been substantially greater than those paid elsewhere. Some of the latest data,[14] complemented by the average weekly hours worked in manufacturing, reveal the following:

Country	Average Total Hourly Compensation in U.S. Dollars for Production Workers	Average Weekly Hours Worked
Germany	$31.87	29.0
France	19.34	31.7
Italy	18.08	35.0
United States	17.74	37.9
Great Britain	14.19	35.6

A close analysis of this information shows, in the main, that there is an inverse relationship between hourly compensation and hours worked. By holding down weekly hours, unions have been able to increase the hourly pay of their members. At the same time, however, while real wages have increased, research shows that a growing number of high paid workers have found themselves priced out of the market. Businesses are finding it easier to transfer work to other geographic locales than to pay these high prices. Also, companies are now trying to develop innovative plans in order to increase the number of workers while simultaneously controlling labor costs. A recent example was provided by Volkswagen's proposal to hire 5,000 unemployed and unqualified workers at a flat salary of DM 5,000 (approximately $2,200) per month. Depending on auto demand, seasonal fluctuations, and their speed in fulfilling daily production targets, these employees would have worked an average of 28.8 to 42.5 hours per week, including Saturdays. The unions rejected the plan, however, because they felt it undermined the basic pay contracts that set an upper limit of 35 hours a week and called for extra pay for Saturday work.[15] Given the rising cost of labor in Germany, these types of innovative pay schemes are becoming more common and unions are having to face the likelihood that if companies cannot produce output at competitive prices, they will outsource the work to those who can. In addition, a growing number of German employees now have "flexible" working hours typified by night work and weekend or holiday shifts. The number of jobless Germans has increased over the last decade and today almost 50 percent of the workforce has had to accept these flexible hours,[16] although average hourly wages in many industries still remain relatively high by international standards.

Figure 17-3 shows some of the most current data related to the real wages of low-paid employees in North America, Australia, and Europe. The average annual percentage change in the United States, Canada, and Australia during this time period was negative compared, for example, to Norway, Italy, Sweden, and Germany, where it was over 1.5 percent. Clearly, something had to be done to make the labor rates in the European countries more reasonable, to make them more competitive. The Dutch provide a good example of some of the latest changes that are being implemented. These changes combine the flexibility found in America with the security that is so common in Germany. In particular, the Dutch:

> have made part-time work easier by permitting part-timers to be paid less than full-timers for the same job. This has helped Dutch companies to adjust their workforce to the demand for labour and has helped unemployed people get back into work. At the same time, centralised wage bargaining has helped build a consensus in favour of wage restraint. Dutch wages in manufacturing have been moderate, compared with Germany and France, where bargaining occurs sector by sector. Finally, the Dutch have tried to provide incentives to work, because sickness benefits were busting the social security-budget. As long ago as 1985 the value of both unemployment insurance and disability insurance was cut to 70% of final pay from 80%. In 1991 and 1995 the government made it harder to qualify for unemployment; in 1995 it removed the coverage for those who chose to become unemployed. The system has also gradually shifted the burden of supporting the sick on to companies. In 1996, for example, firms became responsible for the benefits paid during the first year of illness.[17]

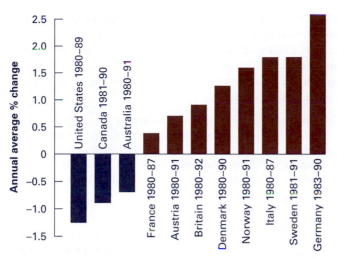

Figure 17–3

**Real Wages
of Low-Paid
Workers***

Note: *Tenth percentile of earnings for men (both sexes for Norway and Denmark) deflated by consumer-price inflation.
Source: Organization for Economic Cooperation and Development, 1997.

New Labor Force Trends

In recent years there have been pronounced new labor force trends in the international arena. As discussed above, this is particularly true in Europe, and to a lesser degree in Asia, where companies are trying to regain some of the competitiveness they lost through high labor costs. In the process, many of these firms are going through the same approach that their counterparts did in the United States a decade ago: The workforce is being downsized, and a strong focus is being placed on providing higher quality output at lower costs.[18]

Some of these recent changes are being fought by the unions, but a growing number of informed observers seem to agree that during the first decade of the new millennium workers are going to have to realize that when national values collide with the realities of global competition, the latter is likely to win. Renault offers a good example. In the 1990s the French auto firm tried to strike a deal with Volvo to build trucks. However, the agreement collapsed when it became clear that Renault would have to cut its own workforce and close some inefficient production operations. This was not something the firm was prepared to do. Since then, however, faced with competitive reality, Renault has cut 25 percent of its workforce and is continuing to make cost-related changes—and the unions are finding that they must accommodate these new decisions or face the fact that work will be moved elsewhere and members will lose their jobs. This is a strategy that has been employed by other European automakers such as Volkswagen and Fiat, which have set up new factories in Latin America, Asia, and Europe in recent years. Additionally, companies that fail to proactively revise their labor agreements and become more competitive are going to find competition seeking them out.

Another trend that is affecting labor forces is that of immigration. A number of major industrial countries need to sharply increase immigration in order to have the necessary workforce to maintain their economic momentum. The United States, for example, has long encouraged immigration and has been able to attract many talented people. Canada has done the same and is currently taking steps to further bolster its pool of skilled immigrant workers.[19] In contrast, Japan, for example, has long opposed bringing in foreign labor, although a growing number of Japanese business leaders have been urging the government to open the country wider to foreign workers. Demographic data show that this is good advice. A recently released United Nations report has presented a dire projection for Japan. In particular, the report notes that Japan will need to bring 609,000 immigrants a year for a half century in order to sustain its working age population of 87.2 million through 2050.[20]

Germany faces a similar situation and the fact that its labor market is closely regulated by the government only adds to the problem.[21] As a result, many firms have difficulty hiring all of the people they need. Siemens, for example, recruits extensively at German universities and hires hundreds of graduates each year. However, the big German MNC needs still more engineers and typically finds it hard to get government approval to bring them in from other countries. Siemens is not alone.

> Some German companies, frustrated by how hard it is to import talent, have opened shop abroad. Take Conceptware AG, an Internet-software company based in Eschborn. Half of its 40 programmers here are non-Germans, but despite its relative success in obtaining work permits, the company late last year opened an office in Canada. There, it is now hiring some of the very programmers from India for whom it couldn't get approval from Germany.[22]

In response to this challenge, the German government has been opening wider the door for immigrants.[23] Today, there are over 7 million foreigners in Germany. This constitutes 9 percent of the population, the highest proportion of immigrants of any of the major European economies.[24] In addition, the German government has recently endorsed proposals from a high-level independent commission whose recommendations would dramatically reshape the nation's current approach to immigration. Among other things, the commission has recommended that each year 20,000 skilled workers be given permanent residency. In addition, 20,000 more would be given five-year permits to work in sectors experiencing labor shortages, and an additional 10,000 trainees would be given temporary permits.[25] Even with these changes, however, Germany will still face critical labor shortages if it does not further increase immigration; and there are strong political factions in the country that are opposed to even these latest changes.[26] As a result, Germany will undoubtedly continue to face labor shortages in critical areas for the foreseeable future.

European firms are beginning to respond to global competition in a number of ways. One is with flexible working arrangements that help contain costs and better link work demands with the employees. Four of the most prominent of these flexible arrangements include the use of part-time workers, greater reliance on shift work, the introduction of temporary contracts, and increased reliance on subcontracting.

Part-Time Work   Part-time work is the most widely used form of flexibility in Europe. Today one in seven people in the EU is a part-time worker; and during the last few years this form of employment accounted for more new jobs than did any other. The OECD has estimated that during the years 1983–1996 the percentage of part-time workers in the labor force increased substantially in many European countries. In Ireland, for example, it rose from 6.7 percent of the workforce up to 11.6 percent; in France it increased from 9.6 percent up to 16 percent; in Germany it went from approximately 12 percent of the labor force up to 16 percent; and in the Netherlands it zoomed from 21 percent of the labor force up to 36.5 percent.[27] Moreover, far more employers are now increasing their use of part-time workers than reducing them with the greatest increase occurring in northern Europe.[28]

In the United States there are also a large number of part-time workers. Wal-Mart, for example, employs thousands of them. So, too, does Microsoft, which recently settled an 8-year class action lawsuit in which temp workers claimed they were actually permanent employees and were entitled to the same benefits as regular workers.[29] Simply put, a growing number of MNCs are using part-time and temporary contract workers.

Shiftwork   Shiftwork has become very popular in Europe. In particular, it is widely used in newspaper production, public transportation, utilities, food production, delivery services, hospitals, emergency services, telephone sales, and banking. Additionally, it is very popular with employers in Italy, Sweden, Belgium, England, France, and Germany.

Nonpermanent Employment   Nonpermanent employment refers to any form of employment other than permanent open-ended contracts. Typical examples include temporary and fixed-term contractual agreements. In recent years nonpermanent employment has been popular in southern European countries such as Greece, Portugal, and Spain, where it accounts for over 15 percent of the workforce. It is far less popular in countries such as Luxembourg, Belgium, and Italy, where only 5 percent of the employees have nonpermanent employment contracts. As would be expected, all of these workers would like to see the arrangements changed and permanent jobs assigned to them. However, many managers feel there are too many benefits to be derived from the use of nonpermanent employment. These benefits include:

1. Many managers know that work needs to be done, but they do not know how long the demand will last or whether further work will accrue. Nonpermanent employment allows them to hedge on the conservative side. A good example is provided by Rank Xerox, which transformed its United Kingdom copier and printer business in the face of Asian competition. Because Rank Xerox did not know whether it could sustain the growth, the firm chose to use only temporary employees until things became clearer.

2. Employers know that some jobs will require only a limited period of time. A typical example is seasonal work As a result, they opt for nonpermanent employment arrangements as in the case of American Express which relies heavily on temporary workers.

3. Organizations believe that short-term recruitment is a cost-effective human resources approach because very little money needs to be spent on the selection of these individuals. The process can be simple and inexpensive. Additionally, these temporary employees do not get benefits, one of the largest factors in labor costs. These are some of the reasons that British Telecom has chosen to use temporary workers.

4. Enterprises are convinced that short-term recruiting is an excellent way to deal with situations where special skills are needed and the firm does not have the time, nor want to invest the money, to develop these skills internally. Additionally, when these workers are no longer needed, it is easy to terminate them.

5. Managers feel that short-term employment is a good way to determine if someone will "fit in" on a permanent basis. British Air and Lufthansa, for example, hire new employees as temporary workers and then, after evaluating their performance, decide those who will be offered full-time jobs.[30]

Subcontracting Subcontracting involves replacing employment contracts with commercial contracts. This approach is widely used in construction where workers simply move from one contract to another or are laid off until the contractor lands a new client. Subcontracting in Europe is also very popular in public sector organizations, as well as in private organizations that prefer to focus on their core business and to subcontract the other activities. Research shows that in recent years there has been an increase in subcontracting in all major western European countries. Based on their international survey research, Brewster, Mayne, and Tregaskis have found that in recent years subcontracting has increased among half of the organizations in Germany and the Netherlands and among one-third or more in enterprises in Finland, France, Ireland, Spain, Switzerland, and the United Kingdom.[31]

Many of the subcontracting approaches that are being used are quite creative. For example, a Swedish businessman who used to run Saab's human resources department realized that sometimes the company would need to quickly hire more employees to meet increasing work demands and at other times it would have more people than it needed. He then formulated a plan of action.

> If area manufacturers got together and formed a labor pool, they could pluck workers out of it whenever they needed them and give them back when they didn't. [He] took his plan to 10 big companies, including Saab, ABB and Ericsson. Within a few months, he left Saab to start Industrie Competens, a sort of temp agency for engineers, skilled technicians and assembly-line workers. One of the agency's temps is Niclas Arkstal . . . a technician who has assembled air conditioners for NAF AB and telephones for Ericsson. At both, he says, he became bored after a while. Joining Industrie Kompetens was the perfect tonic. "It's so flexible," he says, "I don't worry about boredom anymore."[32]

The discussion in this section shows that flexible work arrangements are now becoming much more common in Europe, a situation that has existed in the United States for quite some time. However, the specific approach that is used tends to vary based on country. Here is a summary observation of the current situation:

> The evidence shows a clear and widespread trend to increase flexibility across Europe. However, the trend is starting from markedly different bases. The form, extent and nature of flexible working that employers are most likely to use is different in the different countries. . . . Interestingly, despite this national variability, flexibility is not determined by employment legislation per se. The North/South divide on the use of part-time and nonpermanent work, which emerges from much of the data, indicates that there is a complex set of factors involved in the use of particular forms of flexibility. Both high-regulated and low-regulated countries use considerable amounts of flexibility and in many cases show very similar levels of increase . . . employers are facing the same pressures to use their human resources in the most cost-effective manner. The national context is a more powerful predictor of the use of flexibility by employers than size of organization or sector, although within the national boundaries these variables may also be important.[33]

When analyzed in terms of total labor costs, recent statistics show that during most of the past decade countries have faced rising costs for two major reasons: higher local wages (rates expressed in local currency) and higher costs in terms of U.S. dollars (when local currencies are converted to reflect prices in dollars). Figure 17–4 shows these changes from 1990–1997. The data reveal that unit labor costs among Japanese manufacturing firms were almost unchanged when measured in yen (the local currency). The 0.1 percent annual increase only marginally outpaced productivity gains. However, when measured in dollar terms, the yen had strengthened considerably against the dollar during these years. As a result, the total cost of labor required to produce a unit of output in Japanese manufacturing rose in dollar terms by 2.8 percent annually during these years. This is in marked contrast, for example, to the United States where unit labor costs fell by 0.1 percent a year in dollar terms, thus making the U.S. manufacturing more competitive in labor costs than that of Japan's. The accompanying sidebar "German Unions Become More Flexible—and Do Better" shows some of the ways in which unions are now beginning to address this problem.

Figure 17–4

Manufacturing Labor Costs (per unit of output, annual average percentage change: 1990–1997)

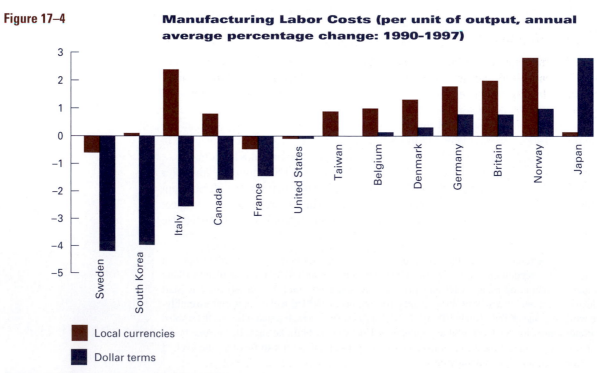

■ Local currencies

■ Dollar terms

Source: U.S. Bureau of Labor Statistics, 1998.

International Management in Action

German Unions Become More Flexible-and Do Better

In recent years, unions in countries such as Germany have become less confrontational with management and, as a result, are becoming more successful in persuading companies not to send work elsewhere. This is a turnaround from just a few years ago when German wage levels were not just the highest, but were increasing more quickly than those of other nations. What has led to this new flexibility? One answer is that German unions are finding that with high unemployment throughout the country, especially in the East, there is less room for negotiating. They have to accommodate the needs of German firms or risk losing membership through layoffs and plant closings. Moreover, many union workers now seem more willing to adjust their job schedules and accept lower wages in return for continued employment. As a result, in the eastern part of Germany union employees now earn much less than their counterparts in the western part of the country (approximately $32 hourly including benefits). In fact, recent statistics show that hourly rates in the east are very competitive vis-à-vis other parts of the continent including the Netherlands ($22 hourly) and Italy ($18 hourly).

There are a growing number of German companies that are winning concessions from their unions. One is CED Informationstechnik GmbH, a small firm that assembles personal computers. The company's union contract allows it to cut back the workforce when orders are weak. And since CED focuses on delivery of computers within 24 hours of receiving an order, it has no need to build inventory. So the workforce size is tied directly to the amount of orders on hand, thus allowing CED to operate with a basic crew of only 200 people. In turn, another group of approximately 40 workers has contracts guaranteeing them at least 1,000 hours of work annually, so these people can count on approximately 20 hours a week on average—although this is all tied to work orders. The remaining 300 employees at CED work as needed and can find after a month or two of large orders that things dry up and they have no work for the next couple of months. It is a chance they have to take.

While all of this is a big change from the days when the unions used to dictate terms, it is one that is accepted by both the workers and the CED's worker council. The head of the council explained it this way, "You can only keep your job when the company does well. These agreements have to be adopted everywhere if we're going to protect jobs." This attitude is reflective of a growing number of German unions. For example, the IG Chemie chemical workers union signed a milestone agreement that conditionally allows troubled employers to cut wages in return for job security. The contract, which covers approximately 1,700 companies, is designed to trade wages and other financial benefits for job security. In turn, the newfound flexibility offers the promise of making German industry more competitive than it has been in a long time.

Organizing International Industrial Relations

In organizing international industrial relations, a number of factors help to explain the relative degree of centralized and decentralized control and employment flexibility that is exercised. The following compares the organizational dimensions of U.S. and European MNCs that are critical to labor relations:

1. A number of studies have shown that compared with European MNCs, U.S. firms tend to concentrate authority at corporate headquarters, with greater emphasis on formal management controls and a close reporting system (particularly within the area of financial control) to ensure that planning targets are met.

2. European MNCs tend to deal with labor unions at the industry level (frequently via employer associations) rather than the company level. The opposite is more typical for U.S. firms. In the United States, employer associations have not played a key role in the industrial relations system, and company-based labor relations policies are the norm.

3. A final factor is the extent of the home product market. If domestic sales are large relative to overseas operations (as in the case with many U.S. companies), it is more likely that overseas operations will be regarded by the parent company as an extension of domestic operations. This is not the case for many European MNCs, whose international operations represent the major part of their business.[34]

In addition, when compared with British firms, U.S. MNCs are much more likely to be involved in collective bargaining and strike settlement issues of their overseas subsidiaries. British firms tend to adopt a more "hands off" approach and confine themselves to giving advice and guidance to their subsidiaries, allowing local management to deal with day-to-day industrial relations matters. These examples point out that industrial relations practices differ from country to country, and MNCs need to be concerned with coordinating these activities.

A number of alternative approaches can be used in managing labor relations in different cultures. For example, one study found that labor relations often is delegated to the local management, except in the case of pension issues, which are handled by the MNC headquarters.[35] The foreign subsidiary is not totally on its own when it comes to labor relations, however. A great deal of guidance and advice still comes from the home office, and hiring and staffing policies also ensure that headquarters plays a role in industrial relations. In addition, many expatriate subsidiary managers use the same industrial relations approach, or a modified version of the approach, that they used back home.

The linkage between the subsidiary and headquarters often is handled by a home-based industrial relations staff, which provides advice and assistance. This industrial relations staff typically gathers information related to wages, benefits, and working conditions around the world as well as at the location of the particular subsidiary. This helps local managers to determine the labor contract that should be negotiated or, in the case of nonunionized operations, the level of wages and benefits that should be paid.

The MNC industrial relations staff also provides assistance in dealing with labor disputes and grievances. The staff can provide information as to how similar problems have been handled in other locales and can be of particular importance to the subsidiary. Many local managers may be unaware of the variety of approaches that can be used in negotiating labor agreements and resolving related problems.

Information provided by the MNC headquarters industrial relations staff can be used by upper-level management in determining when and where to make changes in production work worldwide as well. For example, if wage rates in France go up 10 percent next year, will this reduce the MNC's competitiveness in that market? If it will, what costs are associated with moving some of this work to the MNC's plant in Barcelona? The industrial relations staff at headquarters can help to answer this question in terms of wages, salaries, and benefits. When this information is coupled with that provided by the staffs in manufacturing, marketing, and legal, the MNC then is in a position to make a final decision regarding the wisdom of transferring the work to another locale.

■ A Final Word

In this book, a great deal has been said about how to effectively manage international operations. In closing, two points merit consideration: the inevitability of joint partnering, and the need for ongoing research and learning.

Joint Partnering

Virtual corporation
A network of companies that come together to exploit fast-changing opportunities and share costs, skills, and access to global markets.

Current trends leave no doubt that the world of international management will be one of joint partnerships and agreements. Transnationals will be boundaryless companies in the twenty-first century, because this is the only way that they will be able to survive. Sometimes called a **virtual corporation,** defined as a network of companies that come together to exploit fast-changing opportunities and share costs, skills, and access to global markets,[36] good examples would be IBM, Toshiba, and Siemens. These MNCs created a joint venture to develop state-of-the-art, "benchmark" (best in the world) memory chips. These chips will be able to store 256 million bits of data each, which is equivalent to 10,000 pages of typed text. Large-capacity chips will make it much easier for businesses in the twenty-first century to store information as well as open the door for computer scientists to achieve breakthroughs in areas such as computer speech recognition, machine vision, and computer reasoning.

One main reason for this joint venture is to help control the expenses of research and production. In the early 1990s, it cost approximately $500 million to build a manufacturing plant capable of producing the most advanced chips, which at one time could store 16 million bits of information. By the end of the decade, the cost of these high-tech plants had risen sharply and was now in the neighborhood of $1 billion. No computer firm could afford to take such a large risk, hence the need for a joint venture. These types of arrangements will become increasingly prevalent in the next century. Here is what Rosabeth Kantor, a widely recognized management of change expert, has to say about such partnering and collaborating:

> To gain strength to compete in more demanding global markets, companies collaborate—e.g., to achieve speed and quality through closer integration with suppliers and customers, to attain scale through alliances, or to redefine an industry. Yellow Springs Instruments lists its strategic partners next to the balance sheet in its annual report. Software companies, for whom ties with independent developers, venture partners, and customers are a critical asset, dedicate senior executives and large departments solely to the management of alliances and partnerships. Companies like Disney that once licensed rights to others and stepped away now want to get more value from those arrangements, using them to gain ideas for innovation or intelligence about new country markets—or to push more Disney-branded product through those channels, with more influence over partners' businesses.[37]

She also notes that this collaboration in a way follows the well-established Japanese *keiretsus,* Korean *chaebols,* or the interlocking companies in Southeast Asian conglomerates. However, the emerging arrangement of MNC collaboration tend to be looser, with a wider range of partners and fewer permanent, contractual commitments.

Another reason for partnering is that the success of MNCs depends heavily on a strong worldwide economy, a genuine commitment to helping nations improve the well-being of their citizens, and a willingness to share success with other businesses, MNCs and local firms alike. Akio Morita, the late chairman of Sony and a leading proponent of worldwide partnering, suggested that Japanese MNCs take the following steps:

- Manufacture more products locally in the United States—reducing exports from Japan and creating high-quality jobs for U.S. workers.
- Discover and develop more parts and components suppliers among U.S. firms in the United States.
- Augment U.S. "human capital" by training workers in the most advanced aspects of Japanese production processes, and do advanced R&D locally.
- Build business partnerships, including technology exchanges and transfers, with like-minded U.S. corporations.
- Practice "borderless" policies within Japanese corporations—internationalizing management as much as possible and offering equal training and promotional opportunities to all employees.
- Participate fully as "corporate citizens" in community activities and philanthropic endeavors in the United States, with special attention to supporting education, skills training, and scientific research.
- Work to reduce trade-related imbalances by identifying high-quality companies and products in the United States that can be introduced to the Japanese market.[38]

Such suggestions clearly reinforce the need for cooperation and joint partnering as well as key mergers and acquisitions.[39] They also illustrate that the international environment now is, and in the century ahead will be, markedly different from that of the past.

Continued Research and Learning

A great many theories have relevance to the study of international management. Many have been discussed in this book, but all must be continually subjected to review, analysis, and reformulation. A good example is the theory of lifetime employment in Japan. For many years, international management experts have argued that lifetime employment creates a highly motivated workforce and that Western organizations should emulate this approach. More recent research, however, reveals that lifetime employment is less useful as a motivator than as a control tool for ensuring worker loyalty and performance. In return for guaranteed employment, the personnel stay with the firm for their entire career, work hard, and are compliant to management's wishes. Based on an analysis of empirical data collected on this topic, two researchers concluded: "Lifetime employment is offered within a . . . context of loyalty and benevolence based on cultural values. Its impact, however, is to increase the control of Japanese employees by managers."[40] Moreover, these researchers found that lifetime employment was not widely used by firms in tight labor markets, because it was not possible to control the workers, who could easily find jobs with other companies and derived little motivation from such guarantees.

International management research also is important because it generates new hypotheses for testing. For example, as workers in large companies with guaranteed lifetime employment near retirement (55 to 65 years of age), will management replace them with younger people who are not given such guarantees? As the competitive environment increases, will MNCs stop offering these guarantees because they reduce the firms' flexibility in responding to changing conditions? Will young workers entering the Japanese workforce during this decade be motivated by such guarantees, or will they turn them down because they are unwilling to commit their career to one firm in return for job security? These types of questions must be focal points for international management research and learning, because changing economic, cultural, and social environments are creating new conditions in which MNCs must compete. Research can help to shed light on the effect of these changes. A comprehensive summary of research on Japanese management practices concluded the following:

1. The cultural underpinnings of Japanese society are shifting toward Western values, although this shift is not uniform across culture and is not rapid in all sectors.

2. Industrial organization in Japan, especially the *keiretsu,* will continue to provide competitive advantages and is being extended internationally.

3. Long-range planning is becoming more formal and moving toward a Western style, although it will retain a more visionary perspective.

4. Manufacturing productivity per employee in the United States is rapidly approaching or exceeding parity with Japan. Advantages for Japanese companies appear in certain areas such as R&D and product design, but these appear to be heavily supported by governmental and vertical alliances.

5. The Japanese possess some advantages in the management of quality processes; however, the gap between Japanese and U.S. quality management is closing, though perhaps more slowly than the productivity gap.

6. In neutral countries, the quality image of Japanese products continues to slightly exceed those of the United States, largely because of distribution, promotion, and service advantages.

7. The Japanese will continue to invest more heavily in R&D than U.S. firms and to introduce new products both faster and more economically than the United States by using superior organizational, communicative, and integrative arrangements, discriminatory patent protection, superior governmental funding, and exceptional support by *keiretsus.* These advantages will be aggressively protected and enhanced in the future.

8. Traditional Japanese human resource management practices, including lifetime employment, seniority-based systems, and company unions, are rapidly disappearing and cannot be relied on to produce future competitive advantage. Transplanted Japanese organizations have had limited success in implementing these practices and will make fewer attempts to do so in the future.

9. Because of the rapidly converging parity of U.S. and Japanese productivity and quality, as well as diminishing human resource management advantages, future competitive advantages of the Japanese, if they persist, will derive largely from managerial and organization learning excellence, strengthened by structural systems that promote information amplification, and bolstered by even greater reliance on the *keiretsu* and the Ministry of International Trade and Industry.[41]

Only time will tell how accurate these predictions prove to be, but such information is valuable to the field of international management.

Research also will play an increasing role in helping to uncover how and why multinationals succeed. In particular, greater attention must be given to research designed to explain why some MNCs do better than others and how the strategies are changing. For example, traditional international business strategy gave strong support to the concept of **strategic fit,** in which an organization must align its resources in such a way as to mesh with the environment. Auto firms had to design and build cars that were in demand, and this might mean a variety of models and accessories depending on the number of markets being served. Analogously, electronics firms had to maintain state-of-the-art technology to meet consumer demands for new, high-quality, high-performance products. Today, successful multinationals do much more than attempt to attain a strategic fit. The rapid pace of competitive change requires linkages between all segments of the business, from manufacturing on down to point-of-purchase selling, in the supply chain and in every phase of operation, there must be attention to value-added concepts.[42]

Recently, the concept of strategic fit is being supplemented by the concept of **strategic stretch,** which is the creative use of resources to achieve ever more challenging goals.[43] It is important for MNCs to employ strategic stretch, because without it, they find that what is immediately feasible drives out what is ultimately desirable. Without strategic stretch, Percy Barnevik never would have been able to build ABB into a global giant, and Ted Turner never would have dared to dream of creating CNN. Those multinationals with the greatest amount of resources today will not be the leaders in tomorrow's international arena if they fail to use the creative judgement that is fundamental to strategic stretch. Scarcity of resources can be offset by creativity and risk-taking, and this can make all the difference in besting competitors whose primary strength is an abundance of resources. Commenting on this, Hamel and Prahalad have noted:

> We believe that companies like NEC, Charles Schwab, CNN, Sony, Glaxo, Canon, and Honda were united more by the unreasonableness of their ambition and the creativity exhibited in getting the most from the least than they were by a common cultural or institutional heritage. If further evidence is needed, consider the less-than-sterling performance of Japan's largest banks and brokerages in world markets. Almost unique among Japan's multinationals, these firms possessed immense resource advantages where they entered world markets. Yet material advantages have proved to be a poor substitute for the strategic creativity engendered by resource scarcity.[44]

Of course, it is unlikely there will ever be agreement on all aspects of international management strategy, if only because the specific environmental demands made on one company or industry will require a response different from that needed in another. However, there will continue to be efforts to find overriding strategic principles that have broad value and can be used by most transnationals. A good example was provided by Sullivan and Bauerschmidt, who surveyed managers of large multinationals in an effort to discover those international management strategy principles that were of most value. They found that three were of critical importance to large MNCs: (1) the ability to optimize efficiency; (2) rapid response to environmental changes; and (3) the ability to develop distinct, proprietary advantages.[45] In the case of small firms, major emphasis was needed on innovation, because this helps to make up for the companies' lack of expertise in international manufacturing and marketing.[46]

Another good example is provided by Kanter, whose research shows that the successful MNC of the twenty-first century will empower its people and leverage relationships,

Strategic fit
An approach to strategically managing an organization that involves aligning resources in such a way as to mesh with the environment.

Strategic stretch
The creative use of resources to achieve ever more challenging goals.

both inside and outside its boundaries. As a result, successful MNCs will be able to reach further and faster to both gain and spread knowledge. In this process, it will:

1. Connect its people and partners globally, using horizontal networks to take advantage of all of the resources in the entire extended enterprise of business units, suppliers, customers, and alliances to create value for end users;

2. Craft global strategies and standards but encourage and learn from local customization and innovation, neither commanding everything from the center nor letting each unit or territory act on its own;

3. Use collaborative methods—networks, cross-boundary teams, supply chain partnerships, strategic alliances—to support innovation and then spread knowledge from local innovations everywhere quickly; and

4. Shape a shared culture of unity that appreciates and derives strength from diversity, and develop common tools and measurements to put everyone "on the same page," while also encouraging everyone to "break the mold."[47]

In other words, successful twenty-first century MNCs will be connected, innovative, and build strength and competitive advantage from their diversity.[48]

The World of *Business Week*—Revisited

As seen in the opening *Business Week* article, automotive MNCs are greatly expanding their operations into Latin America. In applying the information in this chapter to these developments, it is clear that industrial relations are going to be a key area of consideration for these firms as they begin producing more and more cars for both local sale and regional distribution. One of the keys to their success will be how well they can develop and maintain effective relations with the unions both at home and in their international locations. Although much of the information in this chapter focused on the major economies such as the United States, the EU, and Japan, these patterns will provide important input and experience for effective labor relations in Latin America. Review the material in this chapter and then use it to revisit the news story and answer these questions: (1) What are two major issues that unions in Latin America are most likely to negotiate with the automakers? (2) Would you expect the industrial relations approaches that are used in Latin America to be more similar to those employed in the United States, Asia, or EU countries, and if the latter, which ones in particular? (3) In what way are the auto firms in Latin America using strategic stretch in their operations?

Summary of Key Points

1. Labor relations is the process through which management and workers identify and determine the job relationships that will be in effect at the workplace. In the United States, these agreements result from negotiation at the union–management bargaining table. In other countries, the approach is different. For example, the labor agreement in Great Britain is not a binding contract. In Germany, however, it is binding, and the unions are particularly influential in determining wages, salaries, and working conditions. In Japan, labor agreements usually are general and vague, although they are legally enforceable.

2. From time to time, industrial conflicts result from disagreements between management and the union.

In the United States, these often are solved through use of a grievance procedure, the steps of which are spelled out in the union contract. In Great Britain, the conflict resolution process often is fragmented and costly, because the system is not designed to deal with such problems. The approach in Germany is similar to that in the United States. In Japan, industrial conflict is minimal because of the way that unions are formed and led.

3. Unions have attempted to become internationally active in three basic ways. One is through use of intergovernmental organizations such as the ILO (International Labour Office) and the OECD (Organization for Economic Cooperation and Development).

Another is through transnational union affiliations. A third is by extending domestic contracts into the international arena.

4. Industrial democracy is the rights that employees have to participate in significant management decisions. Such decisions include wage rates, bonuses, profit sharing, vacations and holiday leaves, work rules, dismissals, and plant expansions and closings. Except for the recent emphasis given to empowerment in total quality and human resource management, traditionally defined industrial democracy is not as widespread in the United States as it is in other countries, especially in Germany and the Scandinavian countries. Some of the most common forms of industrial democracy include codetermination, work councils, shop floor participation, financial participation, and collective bargaining.

5. In formulating a strategy and managing international industrial relations, MNCs can draw on a number of philosophies. The most effective tends to be a geocentric philosophy that is characterized by an effort to understand the interrelationships between the various

geographic locations and a strategy to link them with a composite unifying theme. This approach to labor relations can be helpful in dealing with compensation policy issues as well as in providing assistance to the worldwide subsidiaries on labor issues or challenges that they face.

6. In recent years a growing number of unions, especially in Europe, have been adopting flexible work contracts. These contracts allow companies to adjust their staffing levels to meet work demands by using non-full-time workers. Four of the most prominent of these flexible work arrangements include use of part-time workers, greater reliance on shift work, the introduction of temporary contracts, and increased reliance on subcontracting.

7. Trends for the future point to the inevitability of joint partnering and the need for ongoing research and learning. Collaboration will become a way for MNCs to compete effectively in the global economy, and continued international research is needed to learn and to innovate for future success.

Key Terms

arbitrator, *515*

collective bargaining, *514*

enterprise unions, *526*

global international trade union affiliations, *520*

grievance, *515*

industrial democracy, *521*

industrial internationals, *520*

International Confederation of Free Trade Unions (ICFTU), *520*

International Labour Office (ILO), *520*

labor relations, *514*

lockout, *518*

mediator, *515*

Organization for Economic Cooperation and Development (OECD), *520*

problem-solving teams, *523*

regional internationals, *520*

self-managing teams, *523*

specialized internationals, *520*

special purpose teams, *523*

strategic fit, *537*

strategic stretch, *537*

strike, *518*

union, *514*

virtual corporation, *534*

Review and Discussion Questions

1. What are three major differences between the way that labor–management agreements are reached in the United States and in Great Britain? Germany? Japan? Compare and contrast the process in all four countries.

2. How are industrial conflicts handled in the United States? Great Britain? Germany? Japan? Compare and contrast the process in all four countries.

3. A U.S. MNC is considering opening a plant in Germany. What are three labor relations and industrial democracy developments that this firm needs to know about? Identify and describe each.

4. A French firm is talking to state officials in Indiana about setting up a new plant in Terre Haute. What

types of labor relations issues should the company be investigating so that it can have the most efficient and effective operation?

5. How would each of the following philosophical views affect the formulation of strategy and the management of international industrial relations: ethnocentric, polycentric, and geocentric?

6. A Japanese MNC is considering setting up a manufacturing plant east of Los Angeles. How is the firm likely to organize and control the industrial relations strategies and practices of this overseas subsidiary? Are there any particular problems the home office is likely to confront? Be complete in your answer.

Internet Exercise: Challenges of a New World Auto Industry

Labor relations is a critical area for multinationals, especially among those firms that are expanding their worldwide operations. A good example is provided by the major auto firms headquartered in North America, Europe, and Asia, which are now pushing into emerging markets as well as setting up factories in current market locales. Visit four of these firms—General Motors, Volvo, Toyota, and Honda—and find out what they have been up to in the last year. Their web site addresses are the following: **www.gm.com**, **www.volvo.com**, **www.toyota.com**, and **www.honda.com**. At the General Motors site, look closely at some of the new developments that are occurring in the company, review its annual reports, and examine some of its new innovations. In the case of Volvo, look at new developments in the company. In the case of Toyota, focus on both its manufacturing efforts and its community service. At the Honda site, concentrate your attention on recent community press releases and what the company is doing in the area of research and development. When you have finished this assignment, answer these three questions: (1) What recent changes have been taking place in these major auto firms in the manufacturing area? (2) How do you think these changes will impact the firms' labor relations policies and practices? (3) What changes would you expect to take place in the way these companies manage their labor forces in the years ahead?

Denmark

Denmark is a small country in Northern Europe that is surrounded by water except for a 42-mile border shared with Germany to the south. The country is approximately 17,000 square miles of small green farms, blue lakes, and white coastal beaches. The population is 5.2 million, one-fourth of whom live in Copenhagen. Although poor in natural resources, the Danes are famous for their dairy products, processed foods, and beautifully designed manufactured goods, including furniture and silverware. Since the time of the Vikings, the Danes have been a seafaring people. Denmark maintains large shipping and fishing industries. The prosperous Danes have a high standard of living, and the economy is fairly stable and relatively strong. A fairly rich country, per capita GDP is around $24,000. Denmark has been a constitutional monarchy for over 130 years. Legislative power is in the hands of a parliament whose members are elected for 4-year terms, and a prime minister heads the government.

Two months ago, a medium-sized, high-tech firm based in Seattle, called Seattle Tech, Inc. (STI), entered into a joint venture with a Danish electronics manufacturing firm. STI is going to invest $1.4 million and give its Danish partner the right to use its patents to manufacture a portable facsimile machine. The Danish company is going to renovate one wing of its factory and devote this area to the production of these machines.

There are two reasons that STI wanted to enter into this agreement: One is that the arrangement provides it entry into the EU. A second is an analysis that indicated overall costs for producing the fax machines in Denmark would be about 25 percent less than if they were made in the United States and shipped over. Cost is a very important factor in STI's decision. Control also is important. STI insists that the units be produced according to the master blueprint that is being provided. "Quality is a key factor in the success of these machines," the vice president of production noted, "and this means that we must produce them to a strict manufacturing tolerance. We can't have anyone making arbitrary changes in the process."

Everything appeared to be going well until earlier this week, when the CEO of STI was talking to the top management of the Danish company in Copenhagen. There, for the first time, he learned that the board of directors consists of seven members of management and six members of the union. Moreover, to his surprise, he learned that Danish workers often get involved in shop floor decision making and make recommendations regarding how to change production flows and techniques to increase productivity and quality. The president is happy to learn that the workers are so interested in trying to improve output and quality, but he is concerned that any tinkering with the production process for the facsimile machines could result in major quality problems. He explained these concerns to his counterpart in the Danish firm, but he feels that his points were not well received. "We may have made a major mistake," the CEO of STI told his assistant when they returned from their meeting in Copenhagen. "It may be necessary for us to back out of this venture and look for a different partner." **www.geocities.com/thetropics/4597**

Questions

1. What are some current issues facing Denmark? What is the climate for doing business in Denmark today?

2. Do the workers have to be included on the board of directors? Can the company force them off?

3. How important is worker participation in decision making in Denmark?

4. What would you recommend that STI do at this point?

They're Back

During the 1970s, Volkswagen was the leading U.S. foreign car importer. By 1979 the German firm was selling 300,000 cars and had 2.8 percent of the total U.S. market. The next year saw sales slip to 275,000 units, but because of the general decline of industry sales as a whole, Volkswagen's share of the U.S. market rose to 3 percent, and the next year it did slightly better. However, this was the company's zenith. By 1982 sales had fallen to 160,000, and market share was down to 1.8 percent. The firm was being overrun by Japanese imports and revitalized German lines such as Mercedes and BMW. In an effort to cut costs, the company closed its U.S. manufacturing plant in Pennsylvania in 1988, eventually moving production to Mexico.

In recent years, Volkswagen has made a stunning comeback in the U.S. market. Its biggest initial success was the New Beetle that it introduced in March 1998. By the end of that year, the company had sold almost 56,000 of these cars. In addition, its Jetta, Passat, and Cabrio lines all did exceptionally well, resulting in total sales of just under 220,000 units. This was an increase of 59.3 percent over the previous year and the company's best showing in almost two decades. By the end of 1998, Volkswagen held 3.4 percent of the American car market—its highest share ever and the New Beetle was chosen as the 1999 North American Car of the Year by an independent jury. The award is based on consumer appeal, quality, and driving characteristics. The New Beetle garnered more than double the number of votes of the second place finisher. Since then, the New Beetle's sales have floundered but the company's overall sales have risen. In 1999 Volkswagen sold over 315,000 cars in the American market and over 355,000 in 2000. As a result, today VW is the number-one European brand in the U.S. auto market. Quite clearly, Volkswagen is back!

Questions

1. What was the logic behind Volkswagen's decision to close its U.S. plant?

2. How critical will labor relations be in helping Volkswagen further increase its market share in the United States? Defend your answer.

3. What would you recommend that Volkswagen do in coordinating its worldwide labor operations so as to produce the lowest-price car and thus further increase its competitiveness?

Can This Man Save Chrysler?

The midsummer sun was setting over Upper Long Lake in Bloomfield Hills, Mich., as Chrysler Group's new CEO, Dieter Zetsche, sipped wine and chatted with Detroit's elite at a fund-raiser for the United Way. Now that the German executive is a captain of U.S. industry, he receives invitations to all kinds of charity events. What made Zetsche's presence at this party so remarkable, however, was that the host was James P. Holden, the American he had replaced.

At the end of the evening, Holden cornered Zetsche on the terrace to ask some pointed questions about Chrysler's troubles. It was the first time they had spoken since November, when DaimlerChrysler CEO Jürgen E. Schrempp fired Holden after less than a year on the job and dispatched Zetsche to take over the struggling U.S. unit. As a member of DaimlerChrysler's management board, Zetsche had frequently second-guessed Holden when Chrysler's business began to sour in the summer of 2000. Now, in the most professional way possible, of course, Holden in effect said: "I told you so. Fixing Chrysler is a little more complicated than it looked, isn't it?" Zetsche didn't argue.

What could he say? Not so long ago—in 1998, say, when Daimler-Benz and Chrysler linked up—Chrysler earned more on each vehicle than any other major carmaker and it had a well-deserved reputation for eye-catching design. Today, it is bleeding money: It will lose at least $2 billion this year, and by its own calculations probably won't make a dollar of profit until 2003. Although it offers huge discounts, Chrysler's market share is shrinking. Since the merger, it has fallen from 16.2 percent to just 13.5 percent. And after bringing out the new, $17,000 Jeep Liberty sport-utility and an updated, $18,000 Dodge Ram pickup this year, Chrysler won't launch another major vehicle until early 2004. Even then, there's no telling if what's in development will be enough to revive Chrysler.

Cash Hoard

The merger didn't lead to this sorry state, but the turmoil that followed didn't help either. For the first two years, Chrysler's executives floundered as they tried to work with their German colleagues, and almost two-thirds of the senior management was fired or resigned. At the same time, Chrysler's fortunes were shifting rapidly. The company owed much of its success to its ability to avoid competition by creating such innovative, high-margin vehicles as the minivan. But as more efficient rivals such as Honda Motor Co. and Toyota Motor Corp. moved swiftly into the U.S. with similar vehicles and prices began to fall, Chrysler continued to add more expensive features. Before too long, the U.S. auto maker started to suffer. Now, Zetsche, 48, has to turn Chrysler into something it hasn't been for a while: a low-cost producer. "I'm pretty confident we'll get our act together," says Zetsche. "But it's taking longer than I thought when I first came in."

For Daimler, the acquisition has proved costly indeed. In 2000, Chrysler's operating profit tumbled 90 percent, to just $500 million, on $64.2 billion in sales. As a result, Stuttgart itself reported only $4.9 billion in profits, a 49 percent drop, on sales of $152 billion. It will probably take two more years before DaimlerChrysler even comes close to the profit level it enjoyed during the first full year of the merger. Investors have seen their shares lose more than half their value since peaking in January, 1999, at $108. The stock now trades at about $43. Still, DaimlerChrysler has plenty of cash on hand, some $11.5 billion. And Schrempp has often dismissed the possibility that he might walk away from Chrysler. The company is integral to his global strategy, he says, and he's not about to abandon that simply because of Chrysler's current problems. "In the financial markets, there is great support for our strategy— and still a question mark about whether we are able to implement it, which I think is a fair assessment," he says.

It is Zetsche who has to prove that Schrempp is right about Chrysler. In February, he started a three-year, $3.9 billion restructuring. He has announced 26,000 layoffs and has wrested big concessions from dealers and suppliers. Zetsche is also driving out inefficiencies in Chrysler's vehicle-development process to reduce costs and boost quality: DaimlerChrysler ranks only fifth among the seven largest auto makers, according to J. D. Power & Associates Inc. Certainly sharing some Mercedes components should help down the road. In all, he hopes to save $8.1 billion by 2003. "We're feeling more positive," says Klaus Martini, chief investment officer at Frankfurt's DWS Investment, which owns 1 percent of DaimlerChrysler's stock.

Along the way, the German engineer has confounded his critics in Detroit, who included almost everybody he works with, by turning out to be a decent, even likable fellow. He has spread a lot of misery, but he has done it with such sensitivity—and often in person—that potential antagonists usually decide to cooperate instead. After so many layoffs, no one expected Zetsche to address a United Auto Workers convention in Las Vegas in March. Indeed, few CEOs have ever ventured to speak at the union's gatherings. Zetsche not only gave a speech but also mingled with the delegates for five hours. "The union and the company are working very well together," says UAW Vice-President Nate Gooden, who handles relations with Chrysler.

While trying to blend in at Chrysler, Zetsche is slowly insinuating himself into Detroit's clubby community. He joined Detroit Renaissance, a nonprofit group of CEOs dedicated to revitalizing the city's economy and has jumped right into the discussions, especially those on school reform. "He's intellectually curious," says the group's president, Paul Hillegonds. These days, Zetsche speaks well of the state he now calls home: His family passed up their usual European summer vacation to explore the wilds of northern Michigan. And they recently bought a new, lakefront house. Zetsche is no golfer, so he wasn't interested in joining the Bloomfield Hills Country Club, where the auto set gathers. Instead, he can be found at the Bloomfield Hills Hunt Club coaching his 13-year-old daughter in show jumping, or more likely, he laughs, "cleaning up [manure]." Zetsche himself used to be a competitive stunt rider.

Grim Facts

But even Zetsche admits his new posting would have been a lot rougher if the auto market hadn't been as strong as it was last year. And "was" is the operative word. Chrysler's sales fell 24 percent in August from a year earlier, and the grim reality that it won't introduce any new mass-market vehicles until 2004 poses a real danger. "The company's not prepared to deal with the competitive onslaught," says John Casesa, an auto analyst at Merrill, Lynch & Co. For now, Zetsche has to resort to such risky tactics as lowering prices in hopes of moving away from incentives for good.

Of course, Zetsche is also trying to restart development of higher-margin, must-have vehicles, in the vein of the retro PT Cruiser. "We can do it," says Zetsche. "It's in our genes." An even more macho and smooth-riding Dodge Ram pickup that will sell for almost $1,000 less than current models should help Chrysler compete against the offerings from Ford Motor Co. and General Motors Corp. Zetsche is also keen on expanding the Jeep lineup: He'll probably start with an entry-level vehicle priced below the $15,000 Wrangler. And by working with Mitsubishi Motors Corp., the struggling Japanese auto maker in which DaimlerChrysler holds a controlling stake, Zetsche hopes to reinvigorate Chrysler's car business. They will develop small and midsize cars to sell in North America and Asia.

Making Chrysler more efficient is a manageable, if time-consuming, problem for Zetsche. Making Daimler-Chrysler the carmaker that Schrempp had in mind, however, is another sort of challenge altogether. The $36 billion deal was the biggest ever among carmakers, and it pushed rivals around the globe to seek out partners of their own. Schrempp's idea was to create a company that would

...Chrysler has offered steeper discounts

Dollar Incentive Per Vehicle

*Through July

...but customers aren't biting...

Percent Share of U.S. Light-Vehicle Sales

...profits have hit the skids...

Operating Profits

Data: UBS Warburg, Ward's AutoInfo Bank, DaimlerChrysler, Bloomberg Financial Markets, Deutsche Bank

couple Mercedes' engineering with Chrysler's marketing and design savvy to develop a vehicle for every kind of driver, a colossus that would sell cars everywhere from Buenos Aires to Beijing. It would be extremely competitive: Chrysler and Mercedes could share parts and the cost of developing expensive new technologies. It would be an unprecedented combination of prestige and market power. It would be the global standard.

But so far, the merger has fallen disastrously short of that goal. Distrust between Auburn Hills and Stuttgart has made cooperation on even the simplest of matters difficult. Coming to terms with such prickly issues as deciding which parts image-conscious Mercedes-Benz would share with scrappy, mass-market Chrysler was all but impossible. Meanwhile, the U.S. company was deteriorating quickly. By the time Schrempp sent Zetsche over, Chrysler had become Daimler's biggest problem.

Dire Straits

Predictably enough, that's what seems to have finally forced the two to attempt to make their union work. Of course, for the Germans it helps that one of their own is now in charge in Detroit. The first Chrysler vehicle to use Mercedes parts extensively will be the Crossfire, a sensuous two-seat roadster that will be available in 2003. Insiders say it will include a Mercedes transmission, engine, and axles. And starting in 2004, Zetsche plans to install Mercedes parts in a widening array of mainstream Chrysler cars, from the next-generation Grand Cherokee SUV to the Dodge Intrepid sedan. But even so, it will be years before DaimlerChrysler can live up to its promise. In the meantime, it may well be that the greatest benefit for the two companies will be that they share technology. It will be a success, but a smaller one.

If Zetsche manages to rebuild Chrysler and integrate it into Daimler, he will vindicate his boss, the 56-year-old Schrempp. And Zetsche will no doubt greatly improve his chances of one day running the auto giant. But if Zetsche fails, the deal will be condemned as one of the biggest flops in corporate history—and both men could find themselves on the wrong side of the DaimlerChrysler supervisory board. "This is a test of a young executive with a lot of brains and charisma," says Ronald Harbour, president of automotive research firm Harbour & Associates. "It really

doesn't matter how good he is. He couldn't have a tougher time to try to make this transformation."

Chrysler has been in dire straits before. It took a federal bailout to save the company in 1979 and a complete product overhaul to recover from near-bankruptcy a decade later. Today, however, globalization has transformed the industry. Japanese and European auto makers have edged out the Big Three in the car market and are pushing into trucks and SUVs as well. That's a particular threat to Chrysler, which last year looked to its minivans, Jeeps, and pickups for 80 percent of sales. While Zetsche is careful not to criticize Holden or any other former executives, he's certain that the strategy Chrysler used to great advantage in the 1990s wouldn't work in today's more brutal environment. "Competition is everywhere," he says.

That's why Daimler Benz and Chrysler began their grand experiment in globalization. But the Germans and the Americans have been out of sync from the start: The two proud management teams resisted working together, were wary of change, and weren't willing to compromise. Daimler and Chrysler have combined nothing beyond some administrative departments, such as finance and public relations. Talk of synergy might as well have been *verboten*. Mercedes executives worried their buyers might feel cheated if they shared parts with the American auto maker; Chrysler resented the implication that its technology was inferior.

The strange truth today is that only a German can save the American icon. Even Holden admits Zetsche has a better chance of succeeding at Chrysler than any U.S. executive would. Zetsche wants to be called a "Chrysler guy," but the fact that he worked at Daimler for 25 years makes all the difference. First, he has Schrempp's confidence:

Dieter Zetsche

"It's all about credibility and confidence. If you don't disappoint people, they won't disappoint you"

Born   May 5, 1953, in Istanbul to German parents working abroad. Two years later, the family returned to Germany.

Education   Master's degree in electrical engineering, University of Karlsruhe, 1976; PhD in mechanical engineering, Paderborn Technical University, 1982.

Current   Position President and CEO of Chrysler Group; member of the management board at DaimlerChrysler.

First Job   Driving a beverage truck in Frankfurt.

First Car   1971 Volkswagen Beetle.

Teenage Passion   Competed in the sport of equestrian vaulting, which involves performing acrobatic stunts on a galloping horse.

Career Breaks   Impressed his bosses at Daimler Benz a decade ago by rescuing Mercedes in Argentina and Freightliner in the U.S. He returned to Germany to help overhaul the Mercedes brand.

Getting Acclimated   Instead of their usual European vacation this summer, Zetsche and his family rented a cottage in northern Michigan. And he joined the Bloomfield Hills Hunt Club, where his daughter stables her horse.

Family   Married for 18 years, to Gisela. Three teenage children—and one cocker spaniel, Carlito.

Holden was fired after predicting that Chrysler wouldn't turn a profit until 2003. When Zetsche made the same forecast, Schrempp accepted it. And Zetsche's relationships with managers in Stuttgart—especially Mercedes boss Jürgen Hubbert—have made it easier for him to pry loose technologies and components that no American could get his hands on. Of course, the crisis helped. For example, DaimlerChrysler may save $100 million in engineering costs by cloning a Mercedes transmission for Chrysler sedans coming out in 2004. "Being in trouble makes it easier to understand that you have to change," says Zetsche. "In Germany, they understand we are in one boat." But it took a German to make them understand.

Few were surprised that Schrempp chose Zetsche to take on DaimlerChrysler's greatest challenge. He's fast, decisive, and an experienced troubleshooter. Zetsche revived Daimler's Freightliner truck business, in Portland, Ore., by cutting a quarter of the workforce and reducing capacity. (The company and the U.S. industry, however, are now in a slump.) As chief engineer at Mercedes in the early 1990s, he fought off Japanese rivals by expanding his lineup and making development more efficient. At 38, he was the youngest member ever of Daimler's management board. Later, he took over Mercedes' sales and marketing and came away with a keen understanding of the consumer side of the business.

Decisive

As it turned out, Zetsche had just the combination of humility and warmth to ease tensions among Chrysler's demoralized staff. He eats in the cafeteria, interrupts plant tours to talk with workers, and even promised to shave his head (he's already half-bald) if the new Dodge Ram again topped the J.D. Power & Associates quality survey. His town hall meetings are so popular that plant officials resort to a lottery to choose participants.

Zetsche's decisive leadership is welcome relief for an outfit that drifted aimlessly after the merger. "There's not an employee around here who didn't know this company was in trouble," says James D. Donlon III, senior vice-president and controller. "They just needed somebody to get up and tell it like it is." That's true for those outside Chrysler as well. Three weeks into the job, Zetsche demanded that suppliers swallow an immediate 5 percent price cut. That alone should save Chrysler $2 billion this year. And to keep Chrysler's business, suppliers must wring out a further 10 percent by 2003, which should cut Chrysler's costs by an additional $4 billion. Zetsche has explained to many suppliers just how dire things are. While about one-tenth of them walked away, among those remaining "the violent anger is gone," says Neil DeKoker, managing director of the Original Equipment Suppliers, which represents auto-parts makers. "It has been replaced with sincere frustration. You wish you could help."

So far, Zetsche is ahead of schedule in his cost-cutting, partly because more people than expected retired early and plant managers found unexpected ways to save. Shutting down the escalators at one factory, for instance, saved $80,000 a year. Manufacturing boss Gary L. Henson says he can probably cut $1 billion annually, three times his target. A second-quarter operating loss of just $125 million was a better result than Wall Street had predicted.

But as sales continue to slow, Zetsche needs to keep buyers coming in the door without offering big incentives. "We need to find the sweet spot between volume and profits," he says. To get away from the rebate game, he is lowering base prices: The 2002 Jeep Grand Cherokee will now start at $25,400—$2,000 less than the sticker price of the 2001 model—and the 300M sedan will sell for $28,300—$1,200 less than last year's model. It's a potentially dangerous move, however, since other auto makers could respond with their own aggressive cuts.

In terms of product development, Zetsche wants Chrysler to balance style with thrift—an approach he calls "disciplined pizzazz." He is overhauling the vehicle-development process to put more focus on the earliest stages. By pulling

---

All In the Family

Chrysler shares almost no components with its sister companies, Mercedes and Mitsubishi. But Zetsche's plan hinges on changing that in four crucial segments:

Small and Specialty Cars	Midsize Cars	Big Cars	SUVs, Trucks, Other
Dodge Neon Crossfire	Chrysler Sebring Dodge Stratus	Dodge Intrepid Chrysler Concorde	Jeep Grand Cherokee PT Cruiser
The 2003 Crossfire gets several Mercedes parts. Mitsubishi will engineer the 2005 Neon's underpinnings; Chrysler will design the interior and body.	Chrysler will handle most of the engineering for 2006 models and share the platform with Mitsubishi. Chrysler expects each joint project to save $100 million.	Chrysler will design 2004 replacements for these cars using Mercedes E-Class rear-wheel drive transmission, electronics, and steering column.	This year, Chrysler will offer Mercedes diesel engines in Europe, and its 2005 Grand Cherokee will share components with the Mercedes M-Class SUV.

together teams from all areas of the company—design, engineering, marketing, manufacturing, and purchasing—Zetsche hopes to reduce waste and resolve nagging quality problems without diminishing Chrysler's creative instincts. It's an approach that Chrysler itself pioneered in 1989 but couldn't stick with. Zetsche is also borrowing Mercedes' system of "quality gates." This allows Zetsche and his team to review a vehicle at each of 11 checkpoints throughout the three-year development cycle. If they don't think the vehicle is ready to pass through, they send it back for work. "If he can combine Chrysler's passion for design with German engineering and drivability, he may pull it off," says Christopher W. Cedergren, an analyst at Nextrend, Inc., a Thousand Oaks (Calif.) research firm.

Still, skeptics contend that selling $50,000 sedans has not prepared Zetsche to deal with the cutthroat business of moving Dodges. "He's got experience in America, but it's with Mercedes. It's not trying to put Neons over the curb," says Steve Rossi, who was a public relations executive for both Chrysler and Mercedes in the U.S. and is now CEO of McLaren Performance Technologies.

Certainly nobody rolled out the welcome wagon when Zetsche arrived in Detroit in November. For resentful company veterans, Zetsche's appointment confirmed their worst fear: that Chrysler had lost what remained of its independence. Naturally, tensions were high at an early press conference when a reporter asked the question on nearly everyone's mind: "How many more Germans are you going to bring over?" Zetsche leaned into the microphone and answered: "Four." A wry smile appeared through his enormous moustache. "My wife and three kids."

Diplomacy

That disarming response, brilliantly timed, helps explain why the workout guy from Germany is one of the most popular executives in Detroit these days. He's diplomatic in an industry more used to hostile encounters. In January, he told Chrysler dealers the company planned to take away subsidies worth $300 to $500 per vehicle. This could save Chrysler as much as $1 billion. When dealers balked, Zetsche agreed to consider alternatives that would deliver the same result. In the end, he accepted a proposal that would allow dealers to make up the lost money with bonuses for beating new sales targets.

In putting together the cost-cutting initiatives, Zetsche has counted on Wolfgang Bernhard, 40, his bright, German chief operating officer. (O.K., so he brought five Germans over.) Bold and at times brash, the high-energy Bernhard is a sharp contrast to the thoughtful, analytical Zetsche. But the two have a close working relationship, partly because they're outsiders. "When we came over, it was just the two of us," explains Bernhard. "You feel like you're in a life raft in the ocean. You can only work together if you have complete confidence in each other."

Zetsche is also devoting a good deal of time to making sense of the merger. DaimlerChrysler is expected to announce soon that by yearend Chrysler will offer Mercedes diesel engines in the Grand Cherokees and the PT Cruisers it sells in Europe. The Crossfire will be only a niche model, but it wowed enthusiasts at this year's auto shows, and Chrysler hopes it will generate excitement about the company's full-size sedan and its next-generation Jeep Grand Cherokee, which will borrow parts from the updated Mercedes M-Class SUV.

Zetsche admits that a "not-invented-here" syndrome kept Chrysler and Mercedes from sharing much in the beginning. It took a group of senior executives several months to put together what Schrempp calls the company's brand bible, which decrees what is sacred about both Mercedes and Chrysler. In fact, it was Zetsche and Holden who led the effort; Zetsche jokingly called himself the brand pope. And while each request is still carefully debated in Stuttgart by a newly established executive automotive committee, "certainly the momentum is stronger now," he says. Schrempp agrees: "It's as if somebody took their foot off the brake."

Potholes Up Ahead

Zetsche wants to rev up Chrysler by cutting costs and boosting revenues, but he faces plenty of obstacles

Supplier Revolt	Dealer Unrest	Productivity Limits	Rebate Treadmill	Dry Pipeline
Zetsche demanded that parts suppliers reduced prices by 5% immediately—and by a further 10 percent over the next two years. But these outfits are already struggling, and they say Chrysler is squeezing too hard.	Chrysler angered dealers when it cut financing and marketing support by $300 to $500 per vehicle. The two sides negotiated a more acceptable solution.	A lack of factory flexibility, along with labor pacts that ban plant closings, are hampering efficiency efforts.	Kicking the incentive habit is proving harder than expected in the hypercompetitive U.S. market.	Chrysler rolled out the Jeep Liberty and new Dodge Ram this year. It won't launch other major products until early 2004.

No Rancor

Zetsche is paying close attention to vehicles already in the works when he arrived, especially a sport wagon due in 2003 (it will look like an SUV but drive like a car). Chrysler had planned to sell the vehicle as a luxury car, in the range of $35,000 to $38,000. But Zetsche persuaded the planners to make it more affordable by stripping out a few features: Now, it will start around $28,000. "He has a great way of removing some of the emotion," says Richard O. Schaum, executive vice-president for product development and quality. Zetsche also felt "there wasn't enough tension" in the design of the sport wagon's grille. And he told the engineers to reinforce the car's structure to ensure it would earn a five-star crash rating from the government, even though it meant a six-month delay at a crucial time.

But executives have to know when to trust their managers, too. Consider the case of Aerosmith—that's right, the heavy-metal rock band. A few months ago, James C. Schroer, the Ford executive Zetsche recruited to head Chrysler's sales and marketing, presented him with the idea of using Aerosmith to promote the new Ram. Zetsche asked a few sharp questions and then agreed, although he was only vaguely familiar with the band. He made a point to find out, though. Two weeks later, he, Schroer, and other Chrysler executives attended the Aerosmith concert kicking off the campaign. Zetsche liked the match of the band's in-your-face music and the brawny Ram, but there was nothing on stage that said Dodge. Zetsche leaned over to Schroer, smiled, and shouted: "I see more Dodge Ram or I cancel the program." It was the kind of brush-back Zetsche is known for: humorous, not rancorous.

Still, it must be galling to Zetsche that he's in such a precarious position. But no one has ever become a Chrysler guy without going through a near-death experience. And if he can actually help turn DaimlerChrysler into a successful global auto company, then Zetsche can pretty much call himself whatever he wants. Otherwise, his name will likely join the list of other casualties of a $36 billion mistake.

By Joann Muller in Auburn Hills, Mich., with Christine Tierney in Frankfurt

1. Explain the statement that the DaimlerChrysler merger didn't lead to the sorry state Chrysler now finds itself, but the turmoil that followed didn't help either.

2. Can the change of leadership help Chrysler get back on track? Why or why not?

3. What are the steps the new leader of Chrysler is taking? Do you agree with these? What organizational behavior and human resource management initiatives would you recommend he should implement?

4. Evaluate the statement: "The strange truth today is that only a German can save the American icon (Chrysler)."

Source: Reprinted from September 17, 2001, pp. 88–94 of *Business Week* by special permission, copyright © 2001 by the McGraw-Hill Companies, Inc.

Integrative Case 2

Chiba International, Inc.

Ken Morikawa, the general manager for administration of a Japanese manufacturing plant under construction in rural Georgia, was troubled. Earlier that morning, his American personnel manager, John Sinclair, had walked eagerly across the temporary, open-plan office and announced, "I've found a professor of Japanese at Georgia State University who is willing to help translate our corporate philosophy. I'd like to hire him for the job." He felt pressured. In his mind, Sinclair, like many Americans, was expecting too much of Japanese companies. The company philosophy that he, Ken, had learned to live by in Tokyo would continue to guide him, but he did not feel that Americans would welcome or even understand a Japanese company philosophy.

Ken had a very large task in supervising the building of a plant that might one day provide jobs for up to 2,000 employees, in a region where very few workers had any industrial experience. He wanted to show them that his company cared about the welfare of its workers and their job security and could be trusted to treat them fairly and not to lay them off. He believed that such a philosophy, if it could be properly explained to workers and carefully implemented, would help build a high morale among the employees. And that would improve productivity.

Ken also wanted to ensure that high morale be maintained while the workforce expanded to full capacity. Aside from issues of ease of transportation and distribution, the characteristics of the local workforce—mainly their "Japanese" work ethic—had been one of the primary reasons for establishing the plant here. He believed that the training costs involved in transforming very "green" workers were well worth it. With training, you could avoid people who had picked up "bad habits" or had had their morale lowered in prior industrial jobs. In Japan, Ken knew, teaching company philosophy was an important part of the company's introductory training program. But would it work in rural Georgia?

Ken wondered if his new administrative duties were lowering his concern for personnel matters. Ever since he'd read Alfred Sloan's *My Years with General Motors* during the company training program and had written a review that focused on human resource issues, he had held positions in HR. Even though he had majored in mathematical economics in college, his first assignment had been in the personnel "design center," which controlled training and salary administration for white-collar employees. After two years, he was sent to a district office as a salesman. He returned after 13 months to the employee welfare section of the personnel department at the head office, administering such programs as house loans and recreational activities. Eight years with the company had passed by the time he was sent to an American college to study personnel related subjects and improve his English.

After receiving his MBA, he returned to the head office. His most recent assignment before coming to Georgia was in personnel development research, planning new wages systems. In this new job in Georgia, it was expected that he would eventually hand the reins over to an American general manager and remain only in an advisory capacity. However, at this vital stage he felt that the corporation depended on his human relations expertise to set the scene for future success. Was he neglecting an area in which he had been trained to be sensitive?

He brought the subject up at lunch with John Sinclair. "Let me tell you something, John. I have a hunch why the Japanese are more successful in achieving high quality and productivity than Americans have been recently. It has to do with application, rather than ideas. Many great ideas have come from the United States, but the Japanese concentrate on applying them very carefully. Americans emphasize creating something new and then moving on. The Japanese meticulously analyze a problem from all angles and see how a solution might be implemented. However, John, as they say, Rome wasn't built in a day. I'm not sure our American workers will understand what it really means to have a company philosophy. Let's take it slowly and see what kind of people we hire and then see what best meets their needs."

John, who had worked at a rather traditional U.S. company for 11 years and had become increasingly interested in how Japanese companies managed their U.S. employees, had been eager to join a Japanese company. He wanted to see in action such "Japanese" strategies as long-term employment, the expression of a company philosophy, and careful attention to integrating the employees into the company. He answered comfortingly, "Ken, I know you hate conflict. But you also think it's important to gather information. One of our purchasing agents, Billy, told me about a Japanese company he recently visited, Chiba International. Apparently, they have already fully implemented their company philosophy, and I understand that they're doing very well with it. Why don't we go out to California and talk with their management and try and understand how and why they concentrated on communicating their philosophy to their American workforce."

"And soak up some sun, too," beamed Ken. "You're on!"

The Company

Chiba International, Inc. in San Jose, California, makes high-precision, sophisticated electronics parts used in the final assembly of customized and semicustomized integrated circuits, particularly the expensive memory chips used in computers and military hardware. In such products, reliability is everything (price is a lesser consideration). The similar, but cheaper, parts that manufacturers use once a product reaches high volume are left for others to make.

Chiba International is a subsidiary of Chiba Electronics Company. *Nihon Keizai Shimbun,* Japan's preeminent business paper, recently ranked Chiba Electronics as one of the foremost companies in Japan on the basis of its management earnings stability and performance, ahead of such better-known giants as Sony, Matsushita Electric, and Toyota Motor. Chiba Electronics has 70 percent of the $350 million-a-year world market for its products. Chiba International likewise has a 70 percent share of the $250 million-a-year U.S. market.

Chiba International started with a small sales office in the United States 12 years ago. A manufacturing plant that had been losing $100,000 to $200,000 a month was acquired from an American competitor. The American management was replaced by a team of Japanese headed by a Canadian-born Japan-reared executive. They succeeded in turning it around in two years.

Today, 14 out of the 24 top executives and 65 out of 70 salesmen at Chiba are Americans. All the employees in other categories are also American.

Chiba's Philosophy

> As the sun rises brilliantly in the sky,
> Revealing the size of the mountain, the market,
> Oh this is our goal.
> With the highest decree of mission in our heart we serve our industry
> Meeting the strictest decree of customer requirement.
> We are the leader in this industry and our future path
> Is ever so bright and satisfying.

"That's a translation of our company song," said a high-ranking Japanese executive, one of the group of Japanese and American managers who had agreed to meet with Ken and John. "But we haven't introduced it to our employees yet. That's typical of the way we brought the company philosophy to our employees—slowly and carefully. Every line worker gets a leaflet explaining our company philosophy when he or she starts work. We don't have a specific training session on it and we don't force them to swallow it. It's up to them to digest and understand it."

"What about when you acquire a company, as you have done over the past few years?" asked John.

"The same thing: It's very gradual. If we force it, it causes nothing but indigestion. Here it has been easy: The work is very labor intensive, repetitive, tedious assembly.

In other places, the soil is different. At one, for example, almost all the employees are salaried. They understand the philosophy, but won't necessarily go by it. Engineers and technical people also seem to be less receptive than people in sales, personnel and administration. In other sites, though, where the technology is more similar to this one, we have had no problems at all."

One of the other managers present in the group, an American, interrupted to show Ken and John a copy of the leaflet. It was quite rhetorical in tone and a few paragraphs struck them as particularly interesting.

The Leaflet

Management philosophy: Our goal is to strive toward both the material and spiritual fulfillment of all employees in the Company, and through this successful fulfillment, serve mankind in its progress and prosperity.

Management policy: Our purpose is to fully satisfy the needs of our customers and in return gain a just profit for ourselves. We are a family united in common bonds and singular goals. One of these bonds is the respect and support we feel for our fellow family coworkers.

Other exhortations: When there is a need, we all rally to meet it and consider no task too menial or demeaning; all that matters is that it should be done! We are all ready to sweep floors, sort parts, take inventory, clean machines, inspect parts, load trucks, carry boxes, wash windows, file papers, run furnaces, and do just about anything that has to be done.

Meetings

"Daily meetings at the beginning of each shift are held in the courtyard," explained a manager. "All the workers stand in lines (indicated by metal dots in the asphalt). Each day, a different member of management speaks for about five minutes. On Mondays, executives speak; on Tuesdays, personnel and administration are represented. Wednesdays are about safety concerns and on Thursdays and Fridays, members of production and sales speak. They are all free to say whatever they like. The shift workers tend to develop favorites, especially among the more extroverted sales managers.

"Then a personnel coordinator delivers news about sports events and so on, and perhaps a motivational message, and goes on to lead the group in exercises for one minute. These calisthenics are voluntary, but most of the employees join in. After that, the large group breaks up for brief departmental meetings.

"Again, in the departmental meetings, a speaker is chosen for the day and speaks for about five minutes. Even people at the lowest exempt ('salaried') level speak. Then the department manager discusses yesterday's performance, today's schedule and any other messages such as that housekeeping is inadequate or that certain raw materials are in short supply.

"Once a month, there is an announcement of total company performance versus plans. This is important, as all company employees share at the same rate in the annual company bonus, which is based on profitability and usually equals about one month's salary or wages."

Another Japanese manager continued: "Years ago, there were complaints about having so many meetings, but I haven't heard any for a long time now. The employees like to hear important announcements and even less important ones, such as who is selling theater tickets, bowling league reports, and tennis match dates."

The American personnel manager chimed in. "I was the one who came up with the idea of exercises. I saw it on my visit to Japan. They are just a part of the rituals and symbols that you need in order to get better mutual understanding. The atmosphere was right and the timing was good. Even so, because they weren't mandatory, it took about one-and-a-half years until everyone joined in. Now most people understand the meaning behind it. If we were to stop it now, we'd get complaints.

"Besides the morning meeting, we have served other meetings. On Mondays, we have a very large liaison meeting for information sharing. All the executives attend: sales managers and staff managers, the plant manager and the assistant plant manager. On Tuesdays, we have a production meeting attended by the production managers and any staff involved with their problems. On Monday at four o'clock every second week we have a supervisors' meeting, mainly for one-way communication to them. On the alternating weeks, we have a training meeting. The whole personnel department also meets every week.

"Less formally, we have many sales meetings about, for example, new products. We have combination sales and production meetings, which are called on as an as-needed basis. Team meetings on the production lines are also called whenever needed.

"All these formal meetings are supplemented by many company-sponsored activities. We have a company bowling league, tennis matches, softball, fishing, and skiing. We often organize discount tickets. We're planning the Christmas party. Each employee can bring a guest, so it costs us about $40,000. Our company picnic costs $29,000."

"It sounds very well-worked out for the non-exempts," said John. "What about for the exempts?"

Sales Force

The company started with the largely American sales force. "They're a very different species. They have tremendous professional pride. Most of the American sales engineers have a very arrogant take-it-or-leave-it attitude. Our attitude is almost the complete opposite. We try to serve our customer's needs. Almost like a geisha girl, who makes her customer feel that he is the only one served by her," explained one of the Chiba managers.

"We try to communicate the following motto to them:

S	incerity
A	bility
L	ove
E	nergy
S	ervice

"Sincerity is the basic attitude you have to have as well as the ability to convince the customer. You must love the products that you sell, or you can't convince the customer. You must have energy because, at the end of the day, it's always the case that you could have done one more thing or made one more sales call. Finally, the mentality of serving the customer is the most important.

"We communicate that to our sales force and they like it, especially when they don't have to tell white lies to customers or put up with harassment from customers. We also want them to be honest with us, even about their mistakes. Quite often, we depend on input from the salespeople for our understanding of customers, so an objective daily report by telex or phone is very important to us.

"No one in our company works on a commission basis, not even salesmen. We would lose market share for products that are difficult to promote. Also, the nature of different sales territories would make commissions unfair.

"Although we pay on straight salary only, we don't just have a unilateral sales quota. The salespeople discuss targets with their boss. They are purposely set high, so good performance against goals is grounds for a merit increase the next year.

"We don't really have a marketing department. We feel that it is an expensive luxury. We have a vice president in charge of marketing, but this is almost a corporate sales staff function."

U.S. Management

John was curious about how American line managers reacted to working in a Japanese company. A Japanese manager explained. "When Americans join us, they expect the usual great deal of internal politicking. They scan people in meetings, looking for those with real power; looking, to use our expression, for whose apple they should polish. It takes time for them to realize that it's unnecessary.

"When we interview American executives for a job, we do it collectively, so five to ten interviews are present. That usually puzzles the interviewees. They wonder whom they will report to. We reply that they will be hired by the *company,* although they may report to one individual. As in Japan, the company will take care of them, so it does not depend on their loyalty to one individual."

"What about your company criteria for hiring managers?" asked John.

"We focus on a manager's way of thinking, not necessarily on ability. Although a Harvard MBA is welcomed, it is not essential. In fact no one here has one. We don't provide an elegant fit to his or her social elite. There are no private offices. Salary and benefits are up to par for the location (and industry), but not especially high. We work long hours.

"We're looking for devotion and dedication as well as an aggressive attitude. We conduct two or three long interviews for an important position. We ask questions like 'what is your main shortcoming?' We're interested not in the answer itself but in the kind of thinking behind it. We do make mistakes sometimes, but our batting average is good.

"Sometimes there's a very deep communication gap between Japanese management and U.S. management because we believe in dedication and devotion to the company. They do too, but only up to a certain point. We often tell them that the joy of working for the company can be identical to personal happiness with the family. I ask my wife for her understanding of that, and I work six days a week from seven o'clock to ten o'clock. Their wives place demands on them to come home at six o'clock. U.S. executives put personal and family happiness first. I'm not telling you which is right. But it is second nature for me to think about the future of the company. So long as I have challenging assignments and job opportunities, I will put the company before my personal happiness."

"What do American interviewees feel about all this?" inquired John.

"One problem is that they ask, 'What's my real future? Can I be considered for president?' There's no real answer because it probably will be a Japanese. However, we don't like to close those doors to a really capable American.

"The issue of communication between Japanese and Americans is still a problem. After the Americans go home, the Japanese get together at seven or eight o'clock and talk in Japanese about problems and make decisions without the Americans present. Naturally, this makes the Americans feel very apprehensive. We're trying to rectify it by asking the Japanese managers not to make decisions alone and by asking the Americans to stay as late as possible.

"More important, if we could really have our philosophy permeate the American managers, we Japanese could all go back to Japan and not worry about it. Our mission is to expedite that day by education and training.

"So far, however, there is a gap. Americans are more interested in individual accomplishment, remuneration, and power. When they are given more responsibility, they don't feel its heavy weight, rather they feel that it extends their sovereign area so that they have more of a whip. That creates power conflicts among U.S. managers."

"Let me tell you, though," summarized the American personnel manager. "I like it. I was recruited by a headhunter.

Now, I've been with the company five years and the difference from my former employer is astounding. I don't have to get out there and be two-faced, fudging to keep the union out, hedging for the buck. In general, it's hard to find an American employer that really, sincerely cares for the welfare of the low-level employee. This company went almost too far in the opposite direction at first. They wanted to do too much for the employees too quickly, without their earning it. That way, you don't get their respect."

Financial Principles

"Our financial people throughout the company are proud because of our impressive company performance," said one of the Chiba team. "Only 20 percent of our financing is through debt, in contrast to many Japanese companies. We also have a rather unique way of treating some of our raw materials internally. We try to expense everything out. It's derived from our founder's very conservative management. We ask the question: 'If we closed down tomorrow, what would our liquid assets be?' In line with that, for example, internally we put our inventory at zero.

"We follow the 'noodle peddler theory.' The noodle peddler is an entrepreneur. He has to borrow his cart, his serving dishes and his pan to make ramen. He has to be a good marketer to know where to sell. He has to be a good purchasing director and not overbuy noodles, in case it rains. He could buy a fridge, but he would need a lot of capital, the taste of the noodles would deteriorate, and he would need additional manpower to keep an inventory of the contents of the fridge. The successful noodle peddler puts dollars aside at the end of the day for depreciation and raw materials for tomorrow. Only then does he count profits. That's also why we don't have a marketing department. The successful peddler doesn't have time to examine opportunities in the next town.

"This is the way a division manager has to operate. In order to maximize output with minimum expenditure, every effort is made to keep track on a daily basis of sales, returns, net shipment costs, and expenses."

Open Communication

"I understand all that you've said so far," mused John, "but how exactly do you take all these abstract philosophical ideas and make them real?"

"Oh, open communications is the key. We have a fairly homogeneous workforce. Most are intelligent, some are even college graduates. Most are also very stable types with dependents or elderly parents they send money to.

"We're lucky, but of course, it's not as homogeneous as in Japan, where everyone has experienced one culture. So here, the philosophy has to be backed up by a great deal of communication.

"We mentioned the meetings. We also have a suggestion box, and we answer all the suggestions in print in the company newspaper. Also, one person from personnel tours the plant all day, for all three shifts, once a week, just chatting and getting in touch with any potential problems as they arise. It's kind of a secondary grievance systems. We're not unionized and I guess we'd rather stay that way as it helps us so much with flexibility and job changes among our workforce.

"In the fall, when work is slow, we have many *kompas*. You may not know about this, John. A *kompa* is a small gathering off-premises after work. Eight to eighteen people participate, and the company pays for their time and for refreshments. They're rarely social: They have an objective. For example, if two departments don't get along and yet they need to work together, they might hold a *kompa*. A *kompa* can take place at all levels of the company. Those groups that do it more frequently tend to move on from talking about production problems to more philosophical issues."

Appraisal and Reward Systems

"It all sounds great," sighed Ken, "just as good as Japan. But tell me, how does it tie with wages and salaries, because people here are used to such different systems?"

"Well, we don't have lifetime employment, but we do have an explicit no-layoff commitment. We are responsible for our employees. This means that employees also have to take responsibility and have broad job categories, so we don't have to redo paperwork all the time. We have tried to reduce the number of job classifications to the raw minimum, so we have two pay grades covering 700 workers. At the higher levels, we have three pay grades for craftsmen and two for technicians."

John ventured: "I guess an example of your job flexibility in action is the mechanic you mentioned when we toured the plant."

"Yes, the person you spoke with was a dry press mechanic. He's doing menial labor this week, but his pay hasn't been cut and he knows he wouldn't be taken off his job if it weren't important."

"We don't hire outside, if we can avoid it," added the personnel manager, "only if the skill is not available in-house. The bulk of our training is on the job. We don't utilize job postings. We promote when a person's skills are ripe or when there is a need.

"The job of a 'lead' or team leader is the stepping-stone to supervisor. It's not a separate job status within our system, but the lead is given a few cents an hour extra and wears a pink, not a yellow, smock. Leads are carefully groomed for their position, and although a lead might be demoted because a specific need for them no longer existed, a lead would rarely be demoted for lack of skills or leadership ability.

"Rewards are for service and performance. Plant workers, unskilled and semiskilled, are reviewed every six months. The lead completes the evaluation form [see Exhibit 1]. This is checked or confirmed by the supervisor, and the overall point score translates into cents per hour. There are two copies, one for the supervisor and one for the employee. Depending on the supervisor, some employees get a copy, some don't.

"The office clerical staff are all reviewed on April 1st and October 1st. The review form for managers [see Exhibit 2] is used to determine overall letter scores. All the scores are posted on a spread sheet and compared across departments, through numerous meetings of managers and personnel people, until the scores are consistent with one another. Then the scores are tied to dollars. Some managers provide feedback, some don't.

"Salaried staff are reviewed on April 1st and, as a separate process, the spread procedure just outlined is carried out. At least two managers review any exempt employee, but feedback is usually minimal. The reason is that we encourage feedback all year. If there are no surprises for your subordinate at review time, then you've managed well.

"Agreements on reviews for exempt personnel take place in many meetings at various levels. The process is very thorough and exceptionally fair, and contributes to the levels of performance we get."

Quality and Service

A question from John as to how Chiba International was doing as a result of all this elicited much pride.

"Turnover is 2-1/2 percent a month, which is very satisfactory for our kind of labor, given a transient society. We rarely have to advertise for new employees now. The community knows about it. But we do select carefully. The personnel department does the initial screening and then the production managers and supervisors get together and interview people.

"The lack of available, technically trained people used to be a big problem, but over the years, we've developed the expertise internally. Our productivity is now almost as high as in Japan."

Ken and John asked what other aspects of the company they had not yet discussed. They were told that quality, and hence customer service, was another central part of the philosophy. "Our founder, Mr. Amano, firmly believes in zero defect theory. Doctor Deming taught us the concept of quality control. Unfortunately, many American companies did not emphasize this. During World War II, the concept of acceptable quality level was developed in the United States. The idea was that, with mass production, there will be some defects. Rather than paying for more inspectors on the production line, real problems, for example, with cars, could be identified by the consumer in the field and repaired in the field.

"We don't allow that. We have 100 percent visual inspection of all our tiny parts, which only cost $50 per 1,000 units. We inspect every finished package under a

Exhibit 1 **Semiannual Performance Review**

Employee's name	Clock no.	Dept.	Shift	Over last six-month period			
				Days absences	Number tardies	Number early exits	Work days leave of absence
Employee's job title	Anniversary						

Rate on factors below		Numerical score			
		L	S	M	F
1. Loyalty/Dedication:	Faithful to the company cause, ideals, philosophy, and customers; devoting or setting aside time for company purposes.				
2. Spirit/Zeal:	Amount of interest and enthusiasm shown in work; full of energy, animation, and courage; eagerness and ardent interest in the pursuit of company goals.				
3. Cooperation:	A willingness and ability to work with leaders and fellow employees toward company goals.				
4. Quantity of work:	Volume of work regularly produced; speed and consistency of output.				
5. Quality of work:	Extent to which work produced meets quality requirements of accuracy, thoroughness, and effectiveness.				
6. Job knowledge:	The fact or condition of knowing the job with familiarity gained through experience, association and training.				
7. Safety attitude:	The willingness and ability to perform work safely.				
8. Creativeness:	The ability to produce through imaginative skill.				
9. Attendance:	Includes all types of absence (excused or unexcused), tardies, early exits, LOAs from scheduled work.				
10. Leadership:	The ability to provide direction, guidance, and training to others.				
Overall evaluation of employee performance:					

Supervisor's approval	Manager's approval	Personnel dept. approval

Do not write below this line – for human resource department use only

microscope, so we have 130 inspectors, which is about one sixth of our production staff.

"Mr. Amano, has said to us, 'We try to develop every item our customers want. Being latecomers, we never say no, we never say we can't.' Older manufacturers would evaluate a proposal on a cost basis and say no. Yet we have been profitable from the start."

As the interview drew to a close, one Japanese manager reflected, "Mr. Amano has a saying:

Ability $\times$ philosophy $\times$ zeal = performance.

"If the philosophy is negative, performance is negative because it's a multiplicative relationship.

"But in our company, which now numbers 2,000, we must also start to have different kinds of thinking. The Japanese sword is strong because it is made of all different kinds of steel wrapped around one another. The Chinese sword is also very strong, but because it's all one material, it's vulnerable

to a certain kind of shock. We must bear that in mind so that we have differences within a shared philosophy.

"We're thinking of writing a book on our philosophy, addressing such issues as what loyalty is, by piecing together events and stories from our company history. This would be a book that would assist us in training."

Ken and John walked out into the parking lot. "Whew!" sighed John. "It's more complicated than I thought."

"Oh yes! You need a great deal of patience," responded Ken paternally.

"So we'd better get started quickly," said John, enthusiastic. "Where shall we begin? Perhaps I should call the translator."

Ken wasn't sure what his answer should be.

1. Of all the information that Ken and John have learned at Chiba International, what human resources ideas do you think were the most important? Why?

Exhibit 2   **Example of Completed Performance Review**

Values

Below average						Average	Above average						DOE, John
Unsatisfactory	Fair				Good			Very good			Excellent		
E−	E	D−	D−	D+	C−	C	C+	B−	B	B+	A−	A	
1	2	3	4	5	6	7	8	9	10	11	12	13	

Factors

Factor	Description	Grade	Score
1. Loyalty/Dedication:	Faithful to the company cause, ideals, philosophy, and customers; devoting or setting aside, time for company purposes.	B+	11
2. Spirit/Zeal:	Amount of interest and enthusiasm shown in work; full of energy, animation, and ardent interest in the pursuit of company goals.	C	7
3. Consultation:	The ability to consult and listen to subordinates, fellow employees, superiors in an effort to arrive at the best possible direction.	C−	6
4. Communications:	The ability to communicate effectively with subordinates, fellow employees, superiors and business associates.	C+	8
5. Philosophy:	The willingness to learn and practice company philosophy; the ability to train others regarding company philosophy.	B−	9
6. Method of thinking:	The ability, good sense and judgment to discern inner qualities and relationships to determine the best course of action.	D	4
7. Cooperation:	A willingness and ability to work with leaders and fellow employees toward company goals.	A	13
8. Job knowledge:	The fact or condition of knowing the job with familiarity gained through experience, association and training.	B−	9
9. Attendance:	This factor includes reliability, dependability and punctuality; one's ability to be "on-the-job."	A−	12
10. Results:	The efforts which have brought about a beneficial effect in line with company goals.	E	2

Overall comment | C+ |

$\dfrac{81}{10} = 8.1$

2. What will be the greatest challenges in implementing what they have learned at Chiba back at their manufacturing plant?

3. If you were in charge of operations at the manufacturing plan, which of the ideas from Chiba would you implement first? Choose three and give your reasoning.

Source: This case was written by Professors Vladimir Pucik (IMD) and Nina Hatvany (formerly of Columbia University) as a basis for class discussion rather than to illustrate either effective or ineffective handling of a business situation. Copyright © 1998 by IMD—International Institute for Management Development, Lausanne, Switzerland. Not to be used or reproduced without written permission directly from IMD. Reprinted with permission.

Integrative Case 3

The Road to Hell

John Baker, chief engineer of the Caribbean Bauxite Company of Barracania in the West Indies, was making his final preparations to leave the island. His promotion to production manager of Keso Mining Corporation near Winnipeg—one of Continental Ore's fast-expanding Canadian enterprises—had been announced a month before, and now everything had been tidied up except the last vital interview with his successor, the able young Barracanian, Matthew Rennalls. It was crucial that this interview be successful and that Rennalls leave his office uplifted and encouraged to face the challenge of a new job. A touch on the bell would have brought Rennalls walking into the room, but Baker delayed the moment and gazed thoughtfully through the window, considering just exactly what he was going to say and, more particularly, how he was going to say it.

John Baker, an English expatriate, was 45 years old and had served 23 years with Continental Ore in East Asia, several African countries, Europe, and for the last 2 years, the West Indies. He hadn't cared much for his previous assignment in Hamburg and was delighted when the West Indian appointment came through. Climate was not the only attraction. Baker had always preferred working overseas (in what were termed "the developing countries"), because he felt he had an innate knack—better than most other expatriates working for Continental Ore—of knowing just how to get along with the regional staff. After 24 hours in Barracania, however, he realized that he would need all this "innate knack" to deal effectively with the problems that awaited him in this field.

At his first interview with Hutchins, the production manager, the problem of Rennalls and his future was discussed. There and then it was made quite clear to Baker that one of his most important tasks would be "grooming" Rennalls as his successor. Hutchins had pointed out that not only was Rennalls one of the brightest Barracanian prospects on the staff of Caribbean Bauxite—at London University he had taken first-class honors in the BSc engineering degree—but being the son of the minister of finance and economic planning, he also had no small political pull.

The company had been particularly pleased when Rennalls decided to work for it rather than the government in which his father had such a prominent post. The company ascribed his action to the effect of its vigorous and liberal regionalization program, which since World War II had produced 18 Barracanians at mid-management level and given Caribbean Bauxite a good lead in this respect over all other international concerns operating in Barracania.

The success of this timely regionalization policy led to excellent relations with the government.

This relationship was given an added importance when Barracania, 3 years later, became independent—an occasion that encouraged a critical and challenging attitude toward the role that foreign interests would play in the new Barracania. Therefore, Hutchins had little difficulty in convincing Baker that the successful career development of Rennalls was of primary importance.

The interview with Hutchins was now 2 years old, and Baker, leaning back in his office chair, reviewed his success in grooming Rennalls. What aspects of the latter's character had helped and what had hindered? What about his own personality? How had that helped or hindered? The first item to go on the credit side would, without question, be the ability of Rennalls to master the technical aspects of the job. From the start, he had shown keenness and enthusiasm and often impressed Baker with his ability in tackling new assignments as well as the constructive comments he invariably made in departmental discussions. He was popular with all ranks of Barracanian staff and had an ease of manner that placed him in good stead when dealing with his expatriate seniors. These were all assets, but what about the debit side?

First and foremost, there was his racial consciousness. His 4 years at London University had accentuated this feeling and made him sensitive to any sign of condescension on the part of expatriates. It may have been to give expression to this sentiment that as soon as he returned from London, he threw himself into politics on behalf of the United Action Party, which later won the preindependence elections and provided the country with its first prime minister.

The ambitions of Rennalls—and he certainly was ambitious—did not lie in politics, because staunch nationalist that he was, he saw that he could serve himself and his country best—for bauxite was responsible for nearly half the value of Barracania's export trade—by putting his engineering talent to the best use possible. On this account, Hutchins found that he had an unexpectedly easy task in persuading Rennalls to give up his political work before entering the production department as an assistant engineer.

Baker knew that it was Rennalls' well-repressed sense of race consciousness that had prevented their relationship from being as close as it should have been. On the surface, nothing could have seemed more agreeable. Formality between the two men was at a minimum. Baker was delighted to find that his assistant shared his own peculiar "shaggy dog" sense of humor so that jokes were continually being exchanged; they entertained each other at their houses and often played tennis together—and yet the barrier remained invisible, indefinable, but ever present. The existence of this "screen" between them was a constant source of frustration to Baker, because it indicated a weakness that he was loath to accept. If he was successful with all other nationalities, why not with Rennalls?

At least he had managed to "break through" to Rennalls more successfully than any other expatriate. In fact, it was the young Barracanian's attitude—sometimes overbearing, sometimes cynical—toward other company expatriates that had been one of the subjects Baker had raised last year when he discussed Rennalls' staff report with him. He knew, too, that he would have to raise the same subject again in the forthcoming interview, because Jackson, the senior draftsperson, had complained only yesterday about the rudeness of Rennalls. With this thought in mind, Baker leaned forward and spoke into the intercom, "Would you come in, Matt, please? I'd like a word with you." As Rennalls entered the room, Baker said, "Do sit down," and offered a cigarette. He paused while he held out his lighter, then went on.

"As you know, Matt, I'll be off to Canada in a few days' time, and before I go, I thought it would be useful if we could have a final chat together. It is indeed with some deference that I suggest I can be of help. You will shortly be sitting in this chair doing the job I am now doing, but I, on the other hand, am 10 years older, so perhaps you can accept the idea that I may be able to give you the benefit of my longer experience."

Baker saw Rennalls stiffen slightly in his chair as he made this point. Consequently, he added in explanation, "You and I have attended enough company courses to remember those repeated requests by the personnel manager to tell people how they are getting on as often as the convenient moment arises and not just the automatic 'once a year' when, by regulation, staff reports have to be discussed."

Rennalls nodded his agreement, and Baker went on. "I shall always remember the last job performance discussion I had with my previous boss back in Germany. He used what he called the 'plus and minus' technique. His firm belief was that when a senior, by discussion, seeks to improve the work performance of his staff, his prime objective should be to make sure that the latter leaves the interview encouraged and inspired to improve. Any criticism must, therefore, be constructive and helpful. He said that one very good way to encourage a person—and I fully agree with him—is to tell him about his good points-the plus factors—as well as his weak ones—the minus factors. I thought, Matt, it would be a good idea to run our discussion along these lines."

Rennalls offered no comment, so Baker continued. "Let me say, therefore, right away, that, as far as your own work performance is concerned, the plus far outweighs the minus. I have been most impressed, for instance, with the way you have adapted your considerable theoretic knowledge to master the practical techniques of your job—that ingenious method you used to get air down to the fifth-shaft level is a sufficient case in point—and at departmental meetings I have invariably found your comments well-taken and helpful. In fact, you will be interested to know that only last week I reported to Mr. Hutchins that, from the technical point of view, he could not wish for a more able man to succeed to the position of chief engineer."

"That's very good indeed of you, John," cut in Rennalls with a smile of thanks. "My only worry now is how to live up to such a high recommendation."

"Of that I am quite sure," returned Baker, "especially if you can overcome the minus factor which I would like now to discuss with you. It is one that I have talked about before, so I'll come straight to the point. I have noticed that you are more friendly and get on better with your fellow Barracanians than you do with Europeans. In point of fact, I had a complaint only yesterday from Mr. Jackson, who said you had been rude to him—and not for the first time either.

"There is, Matt, I am sure, no need for me to tell you how necessary it will be for you to get on well with expatriates, because until the company has trained sufficient people of your calibre, Europeans are bound to occupy senior positions here in Barracania. All this is vital to your future interests, so can I help you in any way?"

While Baker was speaking on this theme, Rennalls sat tensed in his chair, and it was some seconds before he replied. "It is quite extraordinary, isn't it, how one can convey an impression to others so at variance with what one intends? I can only assure you once again that my disputes with Jackson—and you may remember also, Godson—have had nothing at all to do with the color of their skins. I promise you that if a Barracanian had behaved in an equally peremptory manner I would have reacted in precisely the same way. And again, if I may say it within these four walls, I am sure I am not the only one who has found Jackson and Godson difficult. I could mention the names of several expatriates who have felt the same. However, I am really sorry to have created this impression of not being able to get along with Europeans—it is an entirely false one—and I quite realize that I must do all I can to correct it as quickly as possible. On your last point, regarding Europeans holding senior positions in the company for some time to come, I quite accept the situation. I know that Caribbean Bauxite—as it has been doing for many years now—will promote Barracanians as soon as their experience warrants it. And, finally, I would like to assure you, John—and my father thinks the same too—that I am very happy in my work here and hope to stay with the company for many years to come."

Rennalls had spoken earnestly. Although not convinced by what he heard, Baker did not think he could pursue the matter further except to say, "All right, Matt, my impression *may* be wrong, but I would like to remind you about the truth of that old saying, 'What is important is not what is true but what is believed.' Let it rest at that."

But suddenly Baker knew he didn't want to "let it rest at that." He was disappointed once again at not being able to break through to Rennalls and having yet again to listen to his bland denial that there was any racial prejudice in his makeup. Baker, who had intended to end the interview at this point, decided to try another tactic.

"To return for a moment to the 'plus and minus technique' I was telling you about just now, there is another plus factor I forgot to mention. I would like to congratulate you not only on the calibre of your work but also on the ability you have shown in overcoming a challenge which I, as a European, have never had to meet. Continental Ore is, as you know, a typical commercial enterprise—admittedly a big one—which is a product of the economic and social environment of the United States and Western Europe. My ancestors have all been brought up in this environment for the past 200 or 300 years, and I have, therefore, been able to live in a world in which commerce (as we know it today) has been part and parcel of my being. It has not been something revolutionary and new that has suddenly entered my life." Baker went on, "In your case, the situation is different, because you and your forebears have had only some 50 or 60 years in this commercial environment. You have had to face the challenge of bridging the gap between 50 and 200 or 300 years. Again, Matt, let me congratulate you—and people like you—once again on having so successfully overcome this particular hurdle. It is for this very reason that I think the outlook for Barracania—and particularly Caribbean Bauxite—is so bright."

There was a pause, and for a moment, Baker thought hopefully that he was about to achieve his long-awaited breakthrough, but Rennalls merely smiled back. The barrier remained unbreached. There remained some 5 minutes of cheerful conversation about the contrast between the Caribbean and Canadian climate and whether the West Indies had any hope of beating England in the Fifth Test before Baker drew the interview to a close. Although he was as far as ever from knowing the real Rennalls, he nevertheless was glad that the interview had run along in this friendly manner and, particularly, that it had ended on such a cheerful note.

This feeling, however, lasted only until the following morning. Baker had some farewells to make, so he arrived at the office considerably later than usual. He had no sooner sat down at his desk than his secretary walked into the room with a worried frown on her face. Her words came fast, "When I arrived this morning, I found Mr. Rennalls already waiting at my door. He seemed very angry and told me in quite a peremptory manner that he had a vital letter to dictate that must be sent off without any delay. He was so worked up that he couldn't keep still and kept pacing about the room, which is most unlike him. He wouldn't even wait to read what he had dictated. Just signed the page where he thought the letter would end. It has been distributed, and your copy is in your tray."

Puzzled and feeling vaguely uneasy, Baker opened the confidential envelope and read the following letter:

From: Assistant Engineer

To: Chief Engineer,
         Caribbean Bauxite Limited

                                        14 August

*Assessment of Interview between Baker
and Rennalls*

It has always been my practice to respect the advice given me by seniors, so after our interview, I decided to give careful thought once again to its main points and so make sure that I had understood all that had been said. As I promised you at the time, I had every intention of putting your advice to the best effect.

It was not, therefore, until I had sat down quietly in my home yesterday evening to consider the interview objectively that its main purport became clear. Only then did the full enormity of what you said dawn on me. The more I thought about it, the more convinced I was that I had hit upon the real truth—and the more furious I became. With a facility in the English language which I, a poor Barracanian, cannot hope to match, you had the audacity to insult me (and through me every Barracanian worth his salt) by claiming that our knowledge of modern living is only a paltry 50 years old whereas yours goes back 200 or 300 years. As if your materialistic commercial environment could possibly be compared with the spiritual values of our culture. I'll have you know that if much of what I saw in London is representative of your most boasted culture, I hope fervently that it will never come to Barracania. By what right do you have the effrontery to condescend to us? At heart, all you Europeans think us barbarians; as you say amongst yourselves, we are "just down from the trees."

Far into the night I discussed this matter with my father, and he is as disgusted as I. He agrees with me that any company whose senior staff think as you do is no place for any Barracanian proud of his culture and race—so much for all the company "clap-trap" and specious propaganda about regionalization and Barracania for the Barracanians.

I feel ashamed and betrayed. Please accept this letter as my resignation, which I wish to become effective immediately.

cc: Production Manager
       Managing Director

1. What mistake did John Baker make? Why did he not realize this mistake when it occurred?

2. What would you recommend that Baker do now? Explain.

3. What does this case illustrate about human resource management in the international environment? Be complete in your answer.

Source: This case was prepared by Gareth Evans and is used with permission.

Experiential Exercises for International Management

1. The Culture Quiz

Objectives

- To stimulate awareness of cultural differences
- To promote consideration of the impact of cultural differences in a global economy
- To stimulate dialogue between domestic and international students
- To explore issues raised by culturally diverse workforces

Background

Few, if any, traditions and values are universally held. Many business dealings have succeeded or failed because of a manager's awareness or lack of understanding of the traditions and values of his/her foreign counterparts. With the world business community so closely intertwined and interdependent, it is critical that managers today become increasingly aware of the differences that exist.

How culturally aware are you? Try the questions below.

Instructions

Working alone or with a small group, answer the questions (without peeking at the answers). When you do look at the answers, be sure to read the explanations. If you are taking the quiz with students from other countries than your own, explore what the answer might be in your country and theirs.

1. In Japan, loudly slurping your soup is considered to be
   a. rude and obnoxious.
   b. a sign that you like the soup.
   c. okay at home but not in public.
   d. something only foreigners do.

2. In Korea, business leaders tend to
   a. encourage strong commitment to teamwork and cooperation.
   b. encourage competition among subordinates.
   c. discourage subordinates from reporting directly, preferring information to come through well-defined channels.
   d. encourage close relationships with their subordinates.

3. In Japan, virtually every kind of drink is sold in public vending machines except for
   a. beer
   b. diet drinks with saccharin.
   c. already sweetened coffee.
   d. soft drinks from U.S. companies.

4. In Latin America, managers
   a. are most likely to hire members of their own families.
   b. consider hiring members of their own families to be inappropriate.
   c. stress the importance of hiring members of minority groups.
   d. usually hire more people than are actually needed to do a job.

5. In Ethiopia, when a woman opens the front door of her home, it means
   a. she is ready to receive guests for a meal.
   b. only family members may enter.
   c. religious spirits may move freely in and out of the home.
   d. she has agreed to have sex with any man who enters.

6. In Latin America, businesspeople
   a. consider it impolite to make eye contact while talking to one another.
   b. always wait until the other person is finished speaking before starting to speak.
   c. touch each other more than North Americans do under similar circumstances.
   d. avoid touching one another as it is considered an invasion of privacy.

7. The principal religion in Malaysia is
   a. Buddhism.
   b. Judaism.
   c. Christianity.
   d. Islam.

8. In Thailand
   a. it is common to see men walking along holding hands.
   b. it is common to see a man and a woman holding hands in public.

c.   it is rude for men and women to walk together.

d.   men and women traditionally kiss each other on meeting in the street.

9.   When eating in India, it is appropriate to

a.   take food with your right hand and eat with your left.

b.   take food with your left hand and eat with your right.

c.   take food and eat it with your left hand.

d.   take food and eat it with your right hand.

10. Pointing your toes at someone in Thailand is

a.   a symbol of respect, much like the Japanese bow.

b.   considered rude even if it is done by accident.

c.   an invitation to dance.

d.   the standard public greeting.

11. American managers tend to base the performance appraisals of their subordinates on performance, while in Iran, managers are more likely to base their performance appraisals on

a.   religion.

b.   seniority.

c.   friendship.

d.   ability.

12. In China, the status of every business negotiation is

a.   reported daily in the press.

b.   private, and details are not discussed publicly.

c.   subjected to scrutiny by a public tribunal on a regular basis.

d.   directed by the elders of every commune.

13. When rewarding a Hispanic worker for a job well done, it is best not to

a.   praise him or her publicly.

b.   say "thank you."

c.   offer a raise.

d.   offer a promotion.

14. In some South American countries, it is considered normal and acceptable to show up for a social appointment

a.   ten to fifteen minutes early.

b.   ten to fifteen minutes late.

c.   fifteen minutes to an hour late.

d.   one to two hours late.

15. In France, when friends talk to one another

a.   they generally stand about three feet apart.

b.   it is typical to shout.

c.   they stand closer to one another than Americans do.

d.   it is always with a third party present.

16. When giving flowers as gifts in Western Europe, be careful not to give

a.   tulips and jonquils.

b.   daisies and lilacs.

c.   chrysanthemums and calla lilies.

d.   lilacs and apple blossoms.

17. The appropriate gift-giving protocol for a male executive doing business in Saudi Arabia is to

a.   give a man a gift from you to his wife.

b.   present gifts to the wife or wives in person.

c.   give gifts only to the eldest wife.

d.   not give a gift to the wife at all.

18. If you want to give a necktie or a scarf to a Latin American, it is best to avoid the color

a.   red.

b.   purple.

c.   green.

d.   black.

19. The doors in German offices and homes are generally kept

a.   wide open to symbolize an acceptance and welcome of friends and strangers.

b.   slightly ajar to suggest that people should knock before entering.

c.   half-opened suggesting that some people are welcome and others are not.

d.   tightly shut to preserve privacy and personal space.

20. In the area that was formerly West Germany, leaders who display charisma are

a.   not among the most desired.

b.   the ones most respected and sought after.

c.   invited frequently to serve on boards of cultural organizations.

d.   pushed to get involved in political activities.

21. American managers running business in Mexico have found that by increasing the salaries of Mexican workers, they

a.   increased the numbers of hours the workers were willing to work.

b.   enticed more workers to work night shifts.

c.   decreased the number of hours workers would agree to work.

d.   decreased production rates.

22. Chinese culture teaches people

a.   to seek psychiatric help for personal problems.

b.   to avoid conflict and internalize personal problems.

c.   to deal with conflict with immediate confrontation.

d.   to seek help from authorities whenever conflict arises.

23. One wedding gift that should not be given to a Chinese couple would be

    a. a jade bowl.

    b. a clock.

    c. a basket of oranges.

    d. shifts embroidered with dragon patterns.

24. In Venezuela, New Year's Eve is generally spent

    a. in quiet family gatherings.

    b. at wild neighborhood street parties.

    c. in restaurants with horns, hats, and live music and dancing.

    d. at pig roasts on the beach.

25. If you order "bubble and squeak" in a London pub, you will get

    a. two goldfish fried in olive oil.

    b. a very cold beer in a chilled glass, rather than the usual warm beer.

    c. Alka Seltzer and a glass of water.

    d. chopped cabbage and mashed potatoes fried together.

26. When a stranger in India wants to know what you do for a living and how much you earn, he will

    a. ask your guide.

    b. invite you to his home and, after getting to know you, will ask.

    c. come over and ask you directly, without introduction.

    d. respect your privacy above all.

27. When you feel you are being taken advantage of in a business exchange in Vietnam, it is important to

    a. let the anger show in your face but not in your words.

    b. say that you are angry, but keep your facial expression neutral.

    c. not show any anger in any way.

    d. end the business dealings immediately, and walk away.

28. When a taxi driver in India shakes his head from side to side, it probably means

    a. he thinks your price is too high.

    b. he isn't going in your direction.

    c. he will take you where you want to go.

    d. he doesn't understand what you're asking.

29. In England, holding your index and middle fingers up in a vee with the back of your hand facing another person is seen as

    a. a gesture of peace.

    b. a gesture of victory.

    c. a signal that you want two of something.

    d. a vulgar gesture.

Answers to the Culture Quiz

1. *b.* Slurping your soup or noodles in Japan is good manners in both public and private. It indicates enjoyment and appreciation of the quality. (Source: Eiji Kanno and Constance O'Keefe, *New Japan Solo.* Japan National Tourist Organization: Tokyo, 1990, p. 20.)

2. *b.* Korean managers use a "divide-and-rule" method of leadership that encourages competition among subordinates. They do this to ensure that they can exercise maximum control. In addition, they stay informed by having individuals report directly to them. This way, they can know more than anyone else. (Source: Richard M. Castaldi and Tjipyanto Soerjanto, "Contrasts in East Asian Management Practices." *The Journal of Management in Practice,* 2:1, 1990, pp. 25–27.)

3. *b.* Saccharine-sweetened drinks may not be sold in Japan by law. On the other hand, beer, a wide variety of Japanese and international soft drinks, and so forth, are widely available from vending machines along the streets and in buildings. You're supposed to be at least 18 to buy the alcoholic ones, however. (Source: Eiji Kanno and Constance O'Keefe, *New Japan Solo.* Japan National Tourist Organization: Tokyo, 1990, p. 20.)

4. *a.* Family is considered to be very important in Latin America, so managers are likely to hire their relatives more quickly than hiring strangers. (Source: Nancy J. Adler, *International Dimensions of Organizational Behavior,* 2nd ed., PWS-Kent: Boston, 1991.)

5. *d.* The act, by a woman, of opening the front door, signifies that she has agreed to have sex with any man who enters. (Source: Adam Pertman, "Wandering No More," *Boston Globe Magazine,* June 30, 1991, p. 10 ff.)

6. *c.* Touching one another during business negotiations is common practice. (Source: Nancy J. Adler, *International Dimensions of Organizational Behavior,* 2nd ed., PWS-Kent: Boston, 1991.)

7. *d.* Approximately 45 percent of the people in Malaysia follow Islam, the country's "official" religion. (Source: Hans Johannes Hoefer, ed., *Malaysia.* Prentice-Hall: Englewood Cliffs, NJ, 1984.)

8. *a.* Men holding hands is considered a sign of friendship. Public displays of affection between men and women, however, are unacceptable. (Source: William Warren, Star Black, and M.R. Priya Rangsit, eds., *Thailand.* Prentice-Hall: Englewood Cliffs, NJ, 1985.)

9. *d.* In India, as in many Asian countries, toilet paper is not used. Instead, water and the left hand are used, after which the left hand is thoroughly cleaned. Still, the left hand is considered to be polluted and therefore inappropriate for use during eating or touching another person. (Source: Gitanjali Kolanad, *Culture Shock! India*. Graphic Arts Center Publishing Company: Portland, Oregon, 1996, p. 117.)

10. *b.* This is especially an insult if it is done deliberately, since the feet are the lowest part of the body. (Source: William Warren, Star Black, and M.R. Priya Rangsit, eds., *Thailand*. Prentice-Hall: Englewood Cliffs, NJ, 1985.)

11. *c.* Adler suggests that friendship is valued over task competence in Iran. (Source: Nancy J. Adler, *International Dimensions of Organizational Behavior*. 2nd ed., PWS-Kent: Boston, 1991.)

12. *b.* Public discussion of business dealings is considered inappropriate. Kaplan, et al. report that, "the Chinese may even have used a premature announcement to extract better terms from executives," who were too embarrassed to admit that there was never really a contract. (Source: Frederic Kaplan, Julian Sobin, Arne de Keijzer, *The China Guidebook*. Houghton Mifflin: Boston, 1987.)

13. *a.* Public praise for Hispanics and Asians is generally embarrassing because modesty is an important cultural value. (Source: Jim Braham, "No, You Don't Manage Everyone the Same," *Industry Week*, February 6, 1989.) In Japan, being singled out for praise is also an embarrassment. A common saying in that country is, "The nail that sticks up gets hammered down."

14. *d.* Though being late is frowned upon in the United States, being late is not only accepted but expected in some South American countries. (Source: Lloyd S. Baird, James E. Post, and John F. Mahon, *Management: Functions and Responsibilities*. Harper & Row: New York, 1990.)

15. *c.* Personal space in most European countries is much smaller than in the United States. Americans generally like at least two feet of space around themselves, while it is not unusual for Europeans to be virtually touching. (Source: Lloyd S. Baird, James E. Post, and John F. Mahon, *Management: Functions and Responsibilities*. Harper & Row: New York, 1990.)

16. *c.* Chrysanthemums and calla lilies are both associated with funerals. (Source: Theodore Fischer, *Pinnacle: International Issue*. March–April 1991, p. 4.)

17. *d.* In Arab cultures, it is considered inappropriate for wives to accept gifts or even attention from other men. (Source: Theodore Fischer, *Pinnacle: International Issue*. March–April 1991, p. 4.)

18. *b.* In Argentina and other Latin American countries, purple is associated with the serious fasting period of Lent. (Source: Theodore Fischer, *Pinnacle: International Issue*. March–April 1991, p. 4.)

19. *d.* Private space is considered so important in Germany that partitions are erected to separate people from one another. Privacy screens and walled gardens are the norm. (Source: Julius Fast, *Subtext: Making Body Language Work*. Viking Penguin Books: New York, 1991, p. 207.)

20. *a.* Though political leaders in the United States are increasingly selected on their ability to inspire, charisma is a suspect trait in what was West Germany, where Hitler's charisma is still associated with evil intent and harmful outcomes. (Source: Nancy J. Adler, *International Dimensions of Organizational Behavior*. 2nd ed., PWS-Kent: Boston, 1991, p. 149.)

21. *c.* Paying Mexican workers more means, in the eyes of the workers, that they can make the same amount of money in fewer hours and thus have more time for enjoying life. (Source: Nancy J. Adler, *International Dimensions of Organizational Behavior*. 2nd ed., PWS-Kent: Boston, 1991, pp. 30 and 159.)

22. *b.* Psychological therapy is not an accepted concept in China. In addition, communism has kept most Chinese from expressing opinions openly. (Source: James McGregor, "Burma Road Heroin Breeds Addicts, AIDS Along China's Border." *Wall Street Journal*, September 29, 1992, p. 1.)

23. *b.* The Chinese regard a clock as a bad omen because the word for clock, pronounced *zhong*, is phonetically similar to another Chinese word that means the end. Jade is highly valued as symbolizing superior virtues, and oranges and dragon patterns are also auspicious symbols. (Source: Dr. Evelyn Lip, "Culture and Customs." *Silver Kris*, February 1994, p. 84.)

24. *a.* Venezuelans do the reverse of what most people in other countries do on Christmas and New Years. On Christmas, they socialize. While fireworks are shot off on both nights, most restaurants are closed, and the streets are quiet. (Source: Tony Perrottet, ed., *Venezuela*. Houghton Mifflin: Boston, 1994, p. 97.)

25. *d.* Other popular pub food includes Bangers and Mash (sausages and mashed potatoes), Ploughman's lunch (bread, cheese, and pickled onions), and Cottage pie (baked minced meat with onions and topped with mashed potatoes). (Source: Ravi Desai, ed., *Let's Go: The Budget Guide to Britain and Ireland*. Pan Books: London, 1990, p. 83.)

26. *c.* Indians are generally uninhibited about staring at strangers and asking them about personal details in their lives. Social distance and personal privacy are not common social conventions in India. (Source:

Frank Kusy, *India.* The Globe Pequo Press: Chester, Conn., 1989, p. 27.)

27. *c.* Vernon Weitzel of the Australian National University advises never to show anger when dealing with Vietnamese officials or businesspeople. Showing anger causes you to lose face and is considered rude. Weitzel also recommends always smiling, not complaining or criticizing anyone, and not being inquisitive about personal matters. (Source: Daniel Robinson and Joe Cummings, *Vietnam, Laos & Cambodia.* Lonely Planet Publications: Australia, 1991, p. 96.)

28. *c.* What looks to Westerners like a refusal is really an Indian way of saying "yes." It can also express general agreement with what you're saying or suggest that an individual is interested in what you have to say. (Source: Gitanjali Kolanad, *Culture Shock! India.* Graphic Arts Center Publishing Company: Portland, Oregon, 1996, p. 114.)

29. *d.* In England, this simple hand gesture is considered vulgar and obscene. In a report to *The Boston Globe,* an American who had been working in London wrote, "I wish someone had told me before I emphatically explained to one of the draftsmen at work why I needed two complete sets of drawings." (Source: "Finger Gestures Can Spell Trouble," *The Berkshire Eagle:* January 26, 1997, p. E5.)

2. Using Gung Ho to Understand Cultural Differences

Background

There is no avoiding the increasing globalization of management. Few, if any, current students of business can expect to pursue a successful career without some encounter of an international nature. Gaining early and realistic exposure to the challenges of cross-cultural dynamics will greatly aid any student of business.

The Pacific Rim will continue to play a dominant role in North American transnational organization and global markets. The opening doors to China offer an unprecedented market opportunity. Korea, Singapore, and Taiwan continue to be unsung partners in mutually beneficial trading relationships. And, of course, Japan will always be a dominant player in the international arena.

An important aspect of cross-cultural awareness is understanding actual differences in interpersonal style and cultural expectations, and separating this from incorrect assumptions. Many embellished stereotypes have flourished as we extend our focus and attention abroad. Unfortunately, many of these myths have become quite pervasive, in spite of their lack of foundation. Thus, North American managers frequently and confidently err in their cross-cultural interactions. This may be particularly common in our interactions with the Japanese. For example, lifetime employment has long been touted as exemplifying the superior practices of Japanese management. In reality, only one-third of Japanese *male* employees enjoy this benefit, and in 1993, many Japanese firms actually laid off workers for the first time. Also, Japan is promoted as a collectivist culture founded on consensus, teamwork, and employee involvement. Yet Japan is at the same time one of the most competitive societies, especially when reviewing how students are selected for educational and occupational placement.

Films can provide an entertaining yet potent medium for studying such complex issues. Such experiential learning is most effective when realistic and identifiable with one's own likely experiences. Case studies can be too sterile. Role plays tend to be contrived and void of depth. Both lack a sense of background to help one "buy into" the situation. Films on the other hand can promote a rich and familiar presentation that promotes personal involvement. This exercise seeks to capitalize on this phenomenon to explore cross-cultural demands.

Procedure

Step I. (110 minutes). Watch the film *Gung Ho.* (This film can be obtained at any video store.)

Step II. (30 minutes). Use one of the following four formats to address the discussion topics.

Option A Address each issue in an open class forum. This option is particularly appropriate for moderate class sizes (40 students) or for sections that do not normally engage in group work.

Option B Divide the class into groups of four to seven to discuss the assigned topics. This is a better approach for larger classes (60 or more students). This approach might also be used to assign the exercise as an extracurricular activity if scheduled class time is too brief.

Option C Assign one group to adopt the American perspective and another group to take the Japanese perspective. Using a confrontation meeting approach (Walton, 1987), have each side describe its perception and expected difficulties in collaborating with each other. Then, have the two sides break into small mixed groups to discuss methods to bridge the gap (or avoid its extreme escalation as portrayed in the film). Ideas should extend beyond those cited in the movie. Present these separate discussions to the class as a whole.

Option D Assign students to groups of four to seven to watch the film and write a six-page analysis addressing one or more of the discussion topics.

Discussion Topics

1. In the opening Scenes, Hunt observes Kaz being berated in a Japanese "management development center." According to at least one expert, this is a close representation of Japanese disciplinary practices. Would such an approach be possible in an American firm? How does this scene illustrate the different perspectives and approaches to motivation? To reinforcement? To feedback?

Source: Steven M. Sommer, University of Nebraska, Lincoln. Used with permission.

2. The concepts of multiculturalism and diversity are emerging issues in modern management environments. The importance of recognizing and responding to racial, ethnic, and other demographic factors has been widely debated in the popular press. What does *Gung Ho* offer to the discussion (both within and across the two groups)? How does each culture respond to different races, genders, cultures?

3. Individualism and collectivism represent two endpoints on a continuum used to analyze different cultural orientations. Individualism refers to a sense of personal focus, autonomy, and compensation. Collectivism describes a group focus, self-subjugation, obligation, and sharing of rewards. How do you see American and Japanese workers differing on this dimension? You might compare the reactions of the Japanese manager whose wife was about to give birth with those of the American worker who had planned to take his child to a doctor's appointment.

4. How does the softball game illuminate cultural differences (and even similarities)? You might consider this question in reference to topic 3; to approaches to work habits; to have "fun"; to behavioral norms of pride, honor, sportsmanship.

5. On several occasion we see George Wendt's openly antagonistic responses to the exercise of authority by Japanese managers. Discuss the concept of authority as seen in both cultures. Discuss expectations of compliance. How might George's actions be interpreted differently by each culture? Indeed, would they be seen as different by an American manager as compared with a Japanese manager?

6. Throughout the film, one gains an impression of how Americans and the Japanese might differ in their approach to resolving conflict. Separately describe how each culture tends to approach conflict, and how the cultures might be different from each other.

7. Experienced conflict between work and family demands has also gained attention as an important managerial issue. How do both cultures approach the role of work in one's life? The role of family? How does each approach balance competing demands between the two? Have these expectations changed over time (from twenty years ago, forty years ago, sixty years ago)? How might they change now in the twenty-first century?

8. In reality, Japanese managers would be "shamed" if one of their subordinates was seriously injured on the job (the scene where the American worker's hand is caught in the assembly line belt). Taking this into account, what other issues in the film might be used to illustrate differences or similarities between American and Japanese management and work practices?

3. "When in Bogotá . . ."*

As Jim Reynolds looked out the small window of the Boeing 757, he saw the glimmer of lights in the distance. After a five-hour flight, he arrived in Bogotá, Colombia at 9:35 P.M. on a clear Friday evening. It had been nearly five years since Jim had seen his best friend, Rodrigo Cardozo. The two had met in college and kept in touch over the years. During their school years, Rodrigo would often accompany Jim when he went home to Chicago for the holidays.

Entering the main terminal, Jim found himself in what looked like a recently bombed building. Piles of debris were everywhere. Lights hung from the ceiling by exposed electrical wires, and the walls and floors were rough, unfinished concrete. "Certainly, aesthetics are not a major concern at the Bogotá International Airport," Jim thought.

As he came to the end of the long, dimly lit corridor, an expressionless customs official reached out his hand and gestured for Jim's travel documents.

"Passaporte, por favor. Bienvenidos a Bogotá, Señor Reynolds. Estás en vacacciones?"

"Sí," Jim replied.

After a few routine questions, Jim was allowed to pass through customs feeling relatively unscathed.

"Loquillo! Loquillo! Estamos quií! Jim, Jim," a voice shouted.

Trying to find the origin of the voice among the dense crowd, Jim finally spotted Rodrigo. "Hey, man. How've you been? You look great!"

"Jim, it's so good to see you. How've you been? I would like you to meet my wife, Eva. Eva, this is my best friend, Jim. He's the one in all those pictures I've shown you."

Late Night Begins the Day

Close to an hour later, Jim, Rodrigo, and Eva arrived at Rodrigo's parents' house on the other side of Bogotá from the airport. As Jim was aware, it is customary for couples to live with their parents for a number of years after their marriage, and Rodrigo and Eva were part of that custom.

Darío, Rodrigo's father, owned an import/export business in Bogotá. He was a knowledgeable and educated man and, from what Jim knew, a master of business negotiations. Over the years, Darío had conducted business with people in nearly every country in Central and South America, the United States, Europe, Hong Kong, and some parts of Africa. Jim had first met Darío with Rodrigo in Boston in 1989.

"Jim, welcome to my house," Darío boomed effusively as the group walked in. "I am so pleased that you're finally in Bogotá. Would you like something to drink—whiskey, bourbon, Aguardiente?"

"Aguardiente!" Rodrigo urged.

"Yes, Jim would like some Aguardiente. I understand you're going to Bahía tonight," Darío added.

"Where?" Jim asked, looking around. "I didn't know we were going anywhere tonight."

"Don't worry, Jim, todo bien, todo bien," Rodrigo assured him. "We're going dancing, so get dressed. Let's go."

The reality of being in Colombia hit Jim at about 11:15 that night when he and his friends entered Bahía, a Bogotá nightclub. The rhythms of salsa and merangue filled the club. Jim's mind flashed back to the Latin dance parties he and Rodrigo had had in Boston with their friends from Central and South America.

"Jim, this is my cousin, Diana. She'll be your partner tonight," Rodrigo said. "You'll get to practice your Spanish too; she doesn't speak a word of English. Have fun."

For the next six hours, they danced and drank. This is the Colombian way. At 5:30 the next morning, Rodrigo decided it was time to leave to get something to eat. On the drive home, they stopped at an outdoor grill in the mountains where many people had congregated for the same reason. Everyone was eating arepas con queso and mazorca, and drinking Aguardiente.

Next, they continued to an outdoor party just down the street. Here, they danced and drank until the sun crested over the mountains of Bogotá. It was about 7:00 A.M. when they decided to conclude the celebration—for now.

Saturday was spent recovering from the previous evening and also touring some local spots in the country. However, Saturday night was a repeat of Friday. After being in Colombia for three days, Jim had slept a total of about four hours. Fortunately, Monday was a national holiday.

Business Before Pleasure Before Business?

Although Jim was having a great time, he had also scheduled a series of business meetings with directors of business schools at various Bogotá universities for the week to come. Jim worked as an acquisitions editor for Academia Press, a major publisher of college-level business textbooks. The purpose of the meetings was to establish business contacts in the Colombian market. It was hoped that these initial contacts would lead to others in Latin America.

*Copyright 1994 by Matthew B. Shull. Used with permission.

567

At Academia Press headquarters in New York, Jim and Caroline Evans, his boss, had discussed the opportunities in Latin America. Although Academia Press routinely published international editions of its texts, total international sales never represented more than 15 percent of their gross. Consequently, international markets had never been pursued aggressively. Caroline, however, saw the Latin American markets as having a lot of potential within the next three to five years. She envisioned this market alone could, in time, represent 15 to 20 percent of gross sales. Moreover, she felt that within the next ten years, international sales could reach 40 percent if developed properly. With numbers like that, it was evident to Jim that this deal was important, not only to the company but to his career as well. If Jim was able to open these markets, he might receive a promotion and be able to continue to work in Central and South America.

Jim's first meeting was scheduled for 11:00 A.M. on Tuesday, the second on Wednesday at 11:00 A.M., and the third on Friday at 3:00 P.M. At precisely 11:00 A.M. on Tuesday, Jim arrived at Javeriana University where he was to meet with Professors Emilio Muñoz, Diana Espitia, and Enrique Ronderos. When he arrived, Professor Muñoz was waiting for him in the conference room.

"Señor Reynolds, I am delighted to meet you. How was your flight?"

"Wonderful," Jim replied.

"And how do you like Bogotá so far? Have you been able to sightsee?"

"No, I haven't had the chance to get around the city yet. I hope to see some things later in the week."

"Well, before you leave, you must visit *El Museo de Oro*. It is the finest collection of gold artifacts from the various indigenous Indian tribes in Colombia. Although much of the gold was stolen by the Spanish, many pieces have survived." For the next thirty minutes, Professor Muñoz spoke of everything from the upcoming presidential elections to world cup soccer.

Jim looked at his watch, concerned about the other professors who had not yet arrived and about the meeting for which he had prepared.

"Is there something wrong, Señor Reynolds?"

"No, no, I was just wondering about the others; it's 11:30."

"Don't worry. They'll be here shortly. Traffic in Bogotá at this hour is terrible. They're probably caught in a traffic jam."

Just then, Professors Espitia and Ronderos walked in.

"Muy buenas, Señor Reynolds," Professor Espitia said warmly. "Please forgive us for the delay. Traffic is simply awful at this time of day."

"Oh, that's not necessary. I understand. Traffic in New York can be absolutely horrendous as well," Jim replied. "Sometimes it takes two hours to get from one end of the city to the other."

"Have you had lunch yet, Señor Reynolds?" asked Professor Ronderos.

Jim shook his head.

"Why don't we go to lunch, and we can talk there?" Professor Ronderos suggested.

After discussing the restaurants in the area, the professors decided on El Club Ejecutivo. It was nearly 12:30 P.M. when they arrived.

"It's been an hour and a half, and we haven't discussed anything," Jim thought. He was concerned that the Colombians were not very interested in what he had to offer. Throughout lunch, Jim grew increasingly concerned that the professors were more interested in his trying typical Colombian dishes and visiting the sights in Bogotá than in Academia's textbooks. They were fascinated that Jim knew how to dance salsa and merangue and impressed that he spoke Spanish with a slight Colombian accent; Señorita Espitia said she found it amusing. That seemed much more important than his knowledge of business textbooks and publishing in general.

By the end of lunch, Jim was nearly beside himself. It was now after 2:30 P.M. and nothing had been accomplished.

"Why don't we all go to Monserate tomorrow? It's absolutely beautiful up there, Señor Reynolds," Professor Ronderos suggested, going on to describe the mountain that overlooks Bogotá and the myths and traditions that surround it.

"That's a wonderful idea," Professor Espitia added.

"Monserate it is then. Jim, it has been a pleasure. I look forward to our meeting tomorrow," Professor Ronderos said with a slight bow.

"Señor Reynolds, would you like a ride home?" Professor Muñoz asked.

"Yes, if it's not too much trouble."

On the way home, Jim was relatively quiet.

"Do you feel okay?"

"It must be jet lag catching up to me. I'm sure it's nothing," Jim responded. Concerned about the way the meeting had gone, Jim realized that he had never even had a chance to mention Academia Press's various titles and how these texts could be used to create a new curriculum or supplement an existing curriculum at the professors' business school.

When in Bogotá

On arriving at the house, Jim went upstairs and sat in the living room glumly sipping a cup of aguapanela. "I just don't get it," he thought. "The Colombians couldn't have been happier with the way the meeting turned out, but we didn't do anything. We didn't even talk about one book. I just don't understand what went wrong."

In a short time, Darío arrived. "Muy buenas, Jim. How did your meetings go today with the directors?" he asked.

"I don't know. I don't know what to think. We didn't do anything. We didn't talk about business at all. We talked more about the sights I should see and the places I should visit before I leave Colombia. I'm supposed to call my boss this afternoon and tell her how the initial meeting went. What am I going to tell her. 'Sorry, we just decided to plan my vacation in Colombia instead of discussing business.' I can't afford to have this deal fall through."

Darío laughed.

"Señor, I'm serious."

"Jim, I understand. Believe me. Tell me about your meeting today."

Jim recounted every detail of the meeting to Darío, who smiled and nodded his head as he listened.

"Jim, you have to understand one thing before you continue negotiating with the directors."

"What's that?"

"You're in Colombia now," Darío said simply.

Jim stared at him with a puzzled look. "And?"

"And what, Jim?"

"Is there something else I should know?"

"That's where you need to start. You let the directors set the tone of the meeting. It's obvious they felt very comfortable with you, or they wouldn't have invited you to Monserate. Here in Colombia, Jim, we do business differently. Right now, you're building friendship. You're building their trust in you. This is very important in doing business in all of Latin America."

"Jim," Darío continued, "would you rather do business with a friend or someone you hardly know?"

As Darío went on to analyze the meeting, Jim realized that his perception of the situation had been formed by his experiences in the United States. "When in Bogotá," he thought, "I guess I had better think like the Colombians."

"Jim, you've gained the respect and the trust of the directors. In my opinion, your first meeting was a complete success."

"What should I expect in the meetings to come?" Jim asked.

"Don't worry," he responded. "Just let the directors worry about that. You'll come to an agreement before the end of the week. I guarantee it."

Questions for Discussion

1. What differences does Jim notice between life in the United States and life in Colombia?

2. What differences does Jim notice between doing business in the United States and doing business in Colombia? How might these same factors differ in other countries?

3. What advice would you give Jim for closing his deals? Why?

4. The International Cola Alliances

Objectives

- To introduce some of the complexities involved in doing business across international borders
- To examine what happens when countries seek to do business with one another without the benefit of a common language and customs

Background

Even with a common language, communication can break down, and interpretations of words and actions often can confound understanding and incur negative attributions of purpose. Add to this the differences of personal needs that exist from individual to individual, as well as national and cultural needs that exist from country to country. These limitless variables make cooperation across borders even that much more complex.

The Story

You are a delegation from a country that would like to enter into a large cooperative effort with a number of other countries for the production and distribution of a popular soft drink produced by the American company International Cola. In the past, countries in your region of the world have been resistant to allowing foreign soft drinks into their markets, despite consumer demands. However, recent thinking is that the advantages of allowing this competition outweigh the disadvantages.

International Cola has expressed an interest in setting up a bottling plant, a regional corporate headquarters, and four distribution depots. Their goal, of course, is to do this in the most economically efficient way possible to maximize profits. However, because the executives at International Cola believe this area to be a rich new market with outstanding potential and are therefore eager to get in, they have ceded to the demands of the various governments in the proposed alliance. These require International Cola to allow for local control of the facilities; to maintain only 49 percent interest in the facilities with local partners holding 51 percent ownership; and to allow the participating governments to work out among themselves the details of where the facilities will be located.

For the countries involved, having one or more of these facilities located within their borders will bring jobs, revenue, and a certain amount of prestige. (It is possible for a single country to have all six of the facilities: regional headquarters, bottling plant, distribution depots.)

Each of the countries involved shares at least two borders with the other countries. This has not always been the most peaceful area. Border skirmishes are frequent, most stemming from minor misunderstandings that became inflated by vast cultural and religious differences.

These distinct cultural differences between your country and your neighbors will likely become even more evident as you pursue the negotiation. It will be up to you to decide how to respond to them. While it is important for you to retain your own cultural integrity—for example, when you first meet a delegate from another country you will likely greet him or her in the cultural style of your country—you understand the importance of being sensitive to one another. If you understand, for example, that the cultural style of another country is to bow on meeting, whereas you shake hands, you may wish to bow instead.

Since you are negotiating the venture across borders, and each country has a different primary language, you have agreed to negotiate in English, but none of you is entirely fluent. Therefore, a few phrases will creep in from your own languages.

Wear your country's flag in a visible place at all times.

Instructions

Step 1 (*30–40 minutes—may be done before class*)
Working in small groups (5–7), develop a profile of your country and its people based on profile sheets 1 and 2.

You will also be given a third profile sheet that details cultural norms within your country. Information given will include the ways in which people in your country deal with areas such as time, personal physical space, gender, social mores, and oral communication.

After you have completed profile sheets 1 and 2 and everyone in your group has read profile sheet 3, briefly discuss them to be sure there is mutual understanding of what the group's behavior and negotiating stance are to be during the negotiation.

Step 2 (*20 minutes—may be done before class*)
Based on the profile sheets, decide which International Cola facilities you believe you should have in your country and why you believe they should be in your country rather than one of the others that will be represented. For example,

if you have a highly educated population, you may argue that you should be the home of the regional corporate headquarters; be aware, however, that another country might argue that you should not have bottling and distribution facilities because these do not require a highly educated or skilled labor force.

On the negotiation sheet, make a list of the facilities you believe your country should have and some notes as to what your arguments will be for having them. Also, make some notes on what you believe the other countries' counterarguments will be and how you expect to respond to them.

Step 3 (30–45 minutes—in class)

Everyone in your group should pin a copy of your country's flag and motto on himself or herself in a visible place. One to three representatives from your group (delegation) should negotiate the arrangements for International Cola's facilities with the representatives from the other delegations. Be sure to use the cultural norms of your country during the negotiation, but *do not tell* the others what your social norms are.

Representatives should introduce themselves to one another on an individual basis. After personal introductions, representatives should form a circle in the center of the room with their delegations behind them, briefly describe their countries, state their positions, and begin negotiations. During negotiations, representatives should make an effort to use their new language at least three times. They should not use English for any of the six phrases listed.

Delegation representatives and the other members of their groups may communicate with one another at any point during the negotiation, but only in writing. Group members may also communicate among themselves, but only in writing during the negotiation.

Any group or representative may ask for a side meeting with one or more of the other groups during the negotiation. Side meetings may not last more than five minutes.

At any time in the negotiation, the delegation may change its representative. When such a change is made, the new representative and the other delegates must reintroduce themselves and greet one another.

Those members of each delegation who are not directly negotiating should be active observers. Use the observer sheet to record situations in which other groups insulted them, shamed them, or were otherwise offensive.

At the end of 45 minutes, the negotiation should be concluded whether or not an agreement has been reached.

Step 4 (open-ended)

Class discussion. Each group should begin by reading their profile sheet 3 aloud. A reporter should note some of the events in which members of other delegations caused them shame, embarrassment, and so forth. Open discussion of the meaning of what took place should follow.

Questions for Discussion

1. What role did cultural differences play in the various phases of the negotiation process? Be careful not to overlook the introductory phase. Was the negotiation frustrating? Satisfying? Other? Why?

2. At any time, did delegations recognize the cultural differences between themselves and the others? If so, was any attempt made to try to adapt to another country's norms? Why? Why not? Would there have been a benefit in doing so? Why?

3. What role did language differences play during the negotiation? What was the effect of lack of understanding or miscommunication on the process?

4. Did the delegations from various countries attempt to find mutual goals and interests despite their differences? In what ways were the best interests of the overall plan subjugated to the individual interests of each country? What rhetoric was used to justify the personal interests?

5. To what degree did groups construct their countries to best justify their position? In situation where this happened, did it work? Why? Why not?

Profile Sheet 1

1. Select a name for your country:

   _____

Be sure that the name of your country appears on or around the flag (see below).

2. In the space below, design your country's flag or emblem. Make enough copies so that each member of your group has one to wear.

3. Write a slogan for your country that best embodies your country's ideals and goals. Include the slogan on or around the flag.

   _____

   _____

   _____

4. Make up a partial language with a vocabulary of up to twenty-five (25) words into which you should translate the following phrases for use during negotiations:

Phrase	*Translation*
I agree.	_____
I disagree.	_____
This is unacceptable.	_____
I don't understand your point.	_____
	_____
You have insulted me.	_____
Please repeat that.	_____

5. Briefly describe how people in your country react when they have been insulted.

_____

_____

_____

_____

_____

_____

Profile Sheet 2

Describe your country by selecting one element from each of the following lists. After you have made your selections, list the elements that make up your country's description on a separate piece of paper and add any additional elements you wish.

Population Density

_____ high density with overpopulation a problem

_____ moderate density-high end

_____ moderate density-average

_____ moderate density-low end

_____ low density

Average Educational Level

_____ less than 3 years—large percent totally illiterate

_____ 3–6 years—widespread functional illiteracy

_____ 6–9 years—functional illiteracy a problem in scattered areas

_____ 9–12 years—most read and write at functional levels

_____ 12+ years—a highly educated and functioning population

Per Capita Income

_____ under $1,000 per year

_____ $1,000–5,000 per year

_____ $5,000–10,000 per year

_____ $10,000–20,000 per year

_____ $20,000–30,000 per year

_____ $30,000–40,000 per year

_____ $40,000+ per year

Climate

_____ tropical

_____ arctic

_____ mixed in different areas

_____ runs range from season to season

Form of Government

_____ socialist

_____ democratic

_____ communist

_____ monarchy

_____ dictatorship

_____ other (specify)

Dominant Racial-Ethnic Group

_____ Asian

_____ black

_____ white

_____ other (specify)

Dominant Religion

_____ animist

_____ atheist/agnostic

_____ Buddhist

_____ Catholic

_____ Hindu

_____ Jewish

_____ Mormon

_____ Protestant (specify)

_____ other (specify)

Negotiation Sheet

1. What facilities do you believe your country should have?

_____

_____

_____

_____

2. What facilities of those listed above are you willing to relinquish to reach agreement?

_____

_____

_____

3. On what bases will you justify your need or desire for having the facilities you have listed?

_____

_____

_____

_____

_____

_____

_____

_____

_____

Observer Sheet

1. List actions taken by members of other delegations that were insulting, created shame for you and your delegation, or were otherwise offensive based on your country's norms. Include notes on the context in which the actions were taken.

    _____

    _____

    _____

    _____

    _____

    _____

    _____

    _____

2. Based on the above list, what happened to your interest in forming an alliance and your belief that a mutual agreement could be reached?

    _____

    _____

    _____

    _____

    _____

    _____

    _____

    _____

    _____

    _____

5. Who to Hire?

Objectives

- To explore participants' cultural biases and expectations
- To examine cultural differences
- To consider the impact culture has on hiring decisions

Instructions

Step 1 (10–15 minutes)

Read the background information and descriptions of each of the applicants. Consider the job and the cultures within which the individual to be hired will be operating. Rank the candidates from 1 to 5, with 1 being your first choice, and enter your rankings on the ranking sheet in the column marked "My Ranking." Briefly, list the reasons for each of your rankings.

Do not discuss your rankings with your classmates until told to do so.

Step 2 (30–40 minutes)

Working with three to four of your classmates, discuss the applicants, and rank them in the order of group preference. Do not vote.

Rank the candidates from 1 to 5, with 1 being the group's first choice, and enter your group rankings on the ranking sheet in the column marked "Group Ranking." Briefly list the reasons for each of the group's rankings.

If your group represents more than one culture, explore the ways in which each person's cultural background may have influenced his or her individual decisions.

Step 3 (open-ended)

Report your rankings to the class, and discuss the areas of difference that emerged within your group while you were trying to reach consensus.

Questions for Discussion

1. Was your group able to explore openly any culturally based biases that came up-for example, feelings about homosexuality, religion, personality traits, politics?
2. Did you make any comments or observations that you feel would have been fully acceptable in your own culture but were not accepted by the group? Explain.
3. If the answer to number 2 was yes, how did the reaction of the group make you feel about your membership in it? How did you handle the situation?
4. What implications do you believe these cultural differences would have in business dealings?

Background

You are a member of the management committee of a multinational company that does business in 23 countries. While your company's headquarters are in Holland, your offices are scattered fairly evenly throughout the four hemispheres. Primary markets have been in Europe and North America; the strongest emerging market is the Pacific Rim. Company executives would like to develop what they see as a powerful potential market in the Middle East. Sales in all areas except the Pacific Rim have shown slow growth over the past two years.

At present, your company is seeking to restructure and revitalize its worldwide marketing efforts. To accomplish this, you have determined that you need to hire a key marketing person to introduce fresh ideas and a new perspective. There is no one currently in your company who is qualified to do this, and so you have decided to look outside. The job title is "vice-president for international marketing"; it carries with it a salary well into six figures (US$), plus elaborate benefits, an unlimited expense account, a car, and the use of the corporate jet. The person you hire will be based at the company's headquarters and will travel frequently.

A lengthy search has turned up five people with good potential. It is now up to you to decide whom to hire. Although all the applicants have expressed a sincere interest in the position, it is possible that they may change their minds once the job is offered. Therefore, you must rank them in order of preference so that if your first choice declines the position, you can go on to the second, and so on.

Applicants
Park L, age 41, Married with Three Children

Park L. is currently senior vice president for marketing at a major Korean high technology firm. You have been told by the head of your Seoul office that his reputation as an expert in international marketing is outstanding. The market share of his company's products has consistently increased since he joined the company just over fifteen years ago. His company's market share is now well ahead of that of competing producers in the Pacific Rim.

Mr. Park started with his present company immediately after his graduation from the University of Seoul and has worked his way up through the ranks. He does not have a graduate degree. You sense that Mr. Park has a keen understanding of organizational politics and knows how to play them. He recognizes that because the company he works for now is family controlled, it is unlikely that he will ever move much higher than his present situation. Mr. Park has told you that he is interested in the growth potential offered at your company.

In addition to his native tongue, Mr. Park is able to carry on a reasonably fluent conversation in English and has a minimal working knowledge of German and French. His wife, who appears quiet and quite traditional, and his children speak only Korean.

Kiran K., age 50, Widow with One Adult Child

Kiran K. is a Sikh woman living in Malaysia. She began her teaching career while finishing her DBA (doctorate in business administration) at the Harvard Business School and published her first book on international marketing 10 months after graduation. Her doctoral dissertation was based on the international marketing of pharmaceuticals, but she has also done research and published on other areas of international marketing.

Two months after the publication of her book, Kiran went to work in the international marketing department of a Fortune 500 company, where she stayed for the next 10 years. She returned to teaching when Maura University offered her a full professorship with tenure, and she has been there since that time. her academic position has allowed her to pursue a number of research interests and to write authoritative books and papers in her field. At present, she is well published and internationally recognized as an expert on international marketing. In addition, she has an active consulting practice throughout Southeast Asia.

You have learned through your office in Kuala Lumpur that Kiran's only child, a 23-year-old son, is severely mentally and physically disabled. You sense that part of her interest in the job with your company is to have the income to guarantee his care should anything happen to her. Her son would go with her to Holland, should she be given the job, where he will need to be enrolled in special support programs.

In addition to fluency in Malay, English, and Hindi, Kiran speaks and writes German and Spanish and is able to converse in Japanese and Mandarin.

Peter V., age 44, Single

Peter is a white South African. He had worked in a key position in the international marketing division of an American Fortune 100 company until the company pulled out of his country eight months ago. While the company wanted to keep him on, offering to move him from Johannesburg to its New York headquarters, Peter decided that it was time to look elsewhere. He had begun to feel somewhat dead-ended in his position and apparently sees the position at your company as an opportunity to try out new

territory. Like your other candidates for the position, Peter has a long list of accomplishments and is widely recognized as outstanding in his field. People in your company who have had contacts with him say that Peter is creative, hard working, and loyal. In addition, you have been told that Peter is a top-flight manager of people who is able to push his employees to the highest levels of performance. And, you are told, he is very organized.

Peter has a PhD in computer science from a leading South African university and an MBA from Purdue's Krannert School of Business.

Peter had been a vehement opponent of apartheid and is still very much a social activist. His high political visibility within South Africa had made his life there difficult, and even now, with the end of apartheid, he would like to get out. His constant male companion, P. K. Kahn, would be coming with him to Holland, and Peter would like your personnel office to help P. K. find an appropriate position.

Peter speaks and reads English, Dutch, Afrikaans, and Swahili and can converse in German.

Tex P., age 36, Divorced with One Child

Tex is currently job hunting. His former job as head of marketing for a single-product high-technology firm—highly specialized work stations for sophisticated artificial intelligence applications—ended when the company was bought out by Texas Instruments. Tex had been with his previous company virtually from the time the company was started six years earlier. Having to leave his job was an irony to Tex as it was largely due to the success of his efforts that the company was bought out. You sense that he is a little bitter, and he tells you that jobs offered to him by TI were beneath him and not worthy of consideration.

Tex has both his undergraduate and MBA degrees from Stanford University. In addition, he was a Rhodes Scholar and won a Fulbright scholarship, which he used to support himself while he undertook a two-year research project on the marketing of high-technology equipment to Third World countries.

You have learned through your New York office that Tex has a reputation for being aggressive and hard driving. Apparently he is a workaholic who has been known to work eighteen to twenty hours a day, seven days a week. He seems to have little time for his personal life.

In addition to his native English, Tex has a minimal command of French—which he admits he hasn't used since his college days.

Zvi C., age 40, Married with Five Children

Zvi began his career after receiving his MBA from the Sloan School of Management at the Massachusetts Institute of Technology (MIT). His first job was as marketing manager for a German company doing business in Israel.

Zvi's phenomenal success with this company led to his being hired away by an international office equipment company in England. Again, he proved to be outstanding, boosting the company's market share beyond all expectations within two years. After five years, Zvi was offered a chance to go back to Israel, this time to oversee and coordinate all the international marketing programs for an industrial park of fourteen companies run as an adjunct to Israel's leading scientific research institution. It has been his responsibility to interface the research component with product development and sales as well as to manage the vast marketing department. Again, he has shown himself to be a master.

You have learned through your Haifa office that Zvi is highly respected and has extensive contacts in the scientific and high-tech worlds. He is exceptionally creative in his approach to marketing, often trying bold strategies that most of his peers would dismiss as too risky. Zvi, however, has made them work and work well.

Zvi is a religious man who must leave work by noon on Friday. He will not work Saturdays nor any of his religion's major and minor holidays—about eighteen a year. He will, however, work on Sundays.

In addition to his native language, Dutch (Zvi and his family moved to Israel form Holland when Zvi was six), he speaks and writes fluent Hebrew, English, German, and Arabic.

Ranking Sheet

Rank candidates from one to five with one as your first choice.

Applicant	Rank	Group Reasons	Ranking	Reasons
Park L.				
Kiran K.				
Peter V.				
Tex P.				
Zvi C.				

References

CHAPTER 1

Privatization in Great Britain   John Moore, "British Privatization—Taking Capitalism to the People," *Harvard Business Review,* January–February 1992, pp. 115–124; Paula Dwyer and Wendy Zellner, "This Splice Could be Golden," *Business Week,* February 8, 1993, pp. 36–37; Robert Neff, "Japan Airlines Cinches Its Seat Belt," *Business Week,* February 1, 1993, p. 42; "A Great Train Crash," *Economist,* January 5, 1995, p. 20; and Nicholas Bray, "Britain's Labor, Miming Tories, Unveils 3-Year Privatizing Plan," *Wall Street Journal,* June 12, 1998, p. A9.

International Management in Action: Separating Myths from Reality   Stanley J. Modic, "Myths about Japanese Management," *Industry Week,* October 5, 1987, pp. 49–53; Richard M. Hodgetts and Fred Luthans, "Japanese HR Management Practices: Separating Fact From Fiction," *Personnel,* April 1989, pp. 42–45; Jon Wonoroff, *The Japanese Management Mystique* (Chicago: Probus Publishing, 1992); and Howard W. French, "A Postmodern Plague Ravages Japan's Workers," *New York Times,* February 21, 2000, p. A4.

In the International Spotlight: India   John F. Burns, "India Now Winning U.S. Investment," *New York Times,* February 6, 1995, pp. C-1, C-5; "The Trouble With Democracy, Part 2," *Economist,* December 17, 1994, pp. 17–18; Rahual Jacob, "India Gets Moving," *Fortune,* September 5, 1994, pp. 101–102; Saritha Rai, "Enron Unit Moves to End India Contract for Power," *New York Times,* May 22, 2001, p. W 1; 67; and Jon E. Hilsenrath, "Honda Venture Takes the Bumps in India," *Wall Street Journal,* August 2, 2000, p. A18.

CHAPTER 2

The U.S. Goes to the Mat   Robert Neff, Brian Bremner, and Edith Updike, "The Japanese Have a New Thirst for Imports," *Business Week,* June 5, 1995, pp. 52, 54; Gabriella Stern and Nichole M. Christian, "GM Plans to Sell Saturn Line in Japan in Network of Stand-Alone Dealerships," *Wall Street Journal,* June 2, 1995, p. A4; Keith Bradsher, "U.S. Called Ready to Compromise on Date for Japan Trade Talks," *New York Times,* June 1, 1995, pp. C1, C15; and Bhushan Bahree, "Auto Talks by U.S., Japan Seem Set for Geneva in June," *Wall Street Journal,* June 1, 1995, p. A11.

In the International Spotlight: Vietnam   Frederik Balfour, "Back on the Radar Screen," *Business Week,* November 20, 2000, pp. 56–57; Jon E. Hilsenrath, "U.S. Investors See Hope in Vietnam Trip," *Wall Street Journal,* November 17, 2000, p. A17; Benjamin Fulford, "Capitalism Creeps into Vietnam," *Forbes,* May 17, 1999, pp. 174, 176; and Roy Rowan, "25 Years After the Fall," *Fortune,* May 1, 2000, pp. 208–222.

CHAPTER 3

International Management in Action: Quality Wins Out   Larry Armstrong, "And the Checkered Flag Goes to—Korea," *Business Week,* May 29, 2000, pp. 216, 218; Robyn Meredith and Matthew Swibel, "Class Meets Mass," *Forbes,* May 14, 2001, pp. 205–206; Jennifer Ordonez, "Starbucks Satisfies Investors' Craving for Robust Results," *Wall Street Journal,* February 2, 2001, p. B4; Benjamin Fulford, "Smell the Beans," *Forbes,* September 4, 2000, p. 56; and David A. Kaplan and Katrina Woznicki, "Trouble Brewing," *Newsweek,* July 19, 1999, pp. 40–41.

International Management in Action: Bit Players Bite the Dust   Amy Borrus, Edith Hill, and Keith Naughton, "This Trade Gap Ain't What It Used to Be," *Business Week,* March 18, 1996, p. 50; Brian Bemner and

Steven Brull, "At Last—Sayonara to the Blahs," *Business Week,* January 22, 1996; and Andrew Pollack, "Japan Inc.'s Dying Bit Players," *New York Times,* May 27, 1995, pp. 17–18.

In the International Spotlight: France   Stewart Toy, Linda Bernier, and Bill Javetski, "Now, the Whirlwind," *Business Week,* May 22, 1995, p. 59; Stewart Toy et al., "Can Anyone Fix This Country?" *Business Week,* May 8, 1995, pp. 56–58; Philip R. Harris and Robert T. Moran, *Managing Cultural Differences,* 3rd ed. (Houston: Gulf Publishing, 1991), pp. 464–471; *The World Almanac and Book of Facts: 2001* (Mahwah, NJ: World Almanac Book, 2001), pp. 788–789; and www.france.com.

CHAPTER 4

Getting Tough . . . Or Else   Amy Borrus, Dexter Roberts, and Joyce Barnathan, "Counterfeit Disks, Suspect Enforcement," *Business Week,* September 18, 1995, p. 68; Pete Engardio and Joyce Barnathan, "China: Strife at the Top May Spark a War on Corruption," *Business Week,* March 6, 1995, p. 53; Seth Faison, "Razors, Soap, Cornflakes: Pirating in China Balloons," *New York Times,* February 17, 1995, pp. A1, C2; "Copy to Come," *Economist,* January 7, 1995, pp. 51–52; and Richard Behar, "Beijing's Phony War on Fakes," *Fortune,* October 30, 2000, pp. 189–208; and Robin Stanley Snell and Choo-sin Tseng, "Ethical Dilemmas of Relationship Building in China," *Thunderbird International Business Review,* March–April 2001, pp. 171–200.

CHAPTER 5

Business Customs in Japan   William Morrow, "Speaking the Japanese Business Language," *European Business,* Winter 1974, pp. 45–46; Ted Holden and Suzanne Wolley, "The Delicate Art of Doing Business in Japan," *Business Week,* October 2, 1989, p. 120; Roger E. Axtell, *Dos and Taboos around the World,* 2nd ed. (New York: Wiley, 1990), pp. 33, 90; and Richard D. Lewis, *When Cultures Collide* (London: Nicholas Brealey Publishing, 1999), pp. 400–415.

International Management in Action: Common Personal Values   George W. England, "Managers and Their Value Systems: A Five-Country Comparative Study," *Columbia Journal of World Business,* Summer 1978, pp. 35–44; Geert Hofstede, *Culture's Consequences: International Differences in Work-Related Values* (Beverly Hills, CA: Sage Publishing, 1980); Geert Hofstede, *Cultures and Organizations: Software of the Mind* (London: McGraw-Hill U.K., Ltd., 1991); and Martin J. Gannon, *Understanding Global Cultures,* 2nd edition (Thousand Oaks, CA: Sage, 2001), pp. 35–56.

In the International Spotlight: Taiwan   Michael J. Marquardt and Dean W. Engel, *Global Human Resource Development* (Englewood Cliffs, NJ: Prentice-Hall, 1993), pp. 183–186; "China (Taiwan)," *Europa World Year Book 1995,* vol. 1 (London: Europa Publications, 1995), pp. 833–842; Brian Bremner et al., "Asia: The Big Chill," *Business Week,* April 2, 2001, pp. 48–49; Andy Reinhardt, "A Silicon Chameleon Challenges Intel," *Business Week,* May 29, 2000, pp. 102–106; and Raj Aggarwal, "Assessing the Recent Asian Economic Crises: The Role of Virtuous and Vicious Cycles," *Journal of World Business,* vol. 34, no. 4, 1999, pp, 392–408.

CHAPTER 6

International Management in Action: Ten Key Factors for MNC Success   James F. Bolt, "Global Competitors: Some Criteria for Success,"

Business Horizons, January–February 1988, pp. 34–41; Alan S. Rugman and Richard M. Hodgetts, *International Business,* 2nd edition (London: Pearson, 2000), Chapter 1; and Sheida Hodge, *Global Smarts: The Art of Communicating and Deal Making Anywhere in the World* (New York: Wiley, 2000).

Managing in Hong Kong   J. Stewart Black and Lyman W. Porter, "Managerial Behaviors and Job Performance: A Successful Manager in Los Angeles May Not Succeed in Hong Kong," *Journal of International Business Studies,* First Quarter 1991, pp. 99–112; Geert Hofstede, *Cultures and Organizations: Software of the Mind* (London: McGraw-Hill U.K., Ltd., 1991), Chapters 4–6; and Alan S. Rugman and Richard M. Hodgetts, *International Business,* 2nd edition (London: Pearson, 2000), Chapter 20; and Benjamin Fulford, "Microwave Missionaries," *Forbes,* November 13, 2000, pp. 136–146.

In the International Spotlight: Mexico   David Wessel, Paul B. Carroll, and Thomas T. Vogel, Jr., "How Mexico's Crisis Ambushed Top Minds in Officialdom, Finance," *Wall Street Journal,* July 6, 1995, pp. A1, A4; Craig Torres and Paul B. Carroll, "Mexico's Mantra for Salvation: Export, Export, Export," *Wall Street Journal,* March 17, 1995, p. A6; "Mexico," *Europa* (London: Europa Publications, 1995), pp. 429-444; Carlta Vitzthum and Nicole Harris, "Telefonica Makes Its Move into Mexico," *Wall Street Journal,* October 5, 2000, p. A19; and Joel Millman, "Mexico Factories See Growth Unchecked," *Wall Street Journal,* November 6, 2000, p. A29.

CHAPTER 7

International Management in Action: Matsushita Goes Global
P. Christopher Earley and Harbir Singh, "International and Intercultural Management Research: What's Next," *Academy of Management Journal,* June 1995, pp. 327–340; Karen Lowry Miller, "Siemens Shapes Up," *Business Week* May 1, 1995, pp. 52–53; Christine M. Riordan and Robert J. Vandenberg, "A Central Question in Cross-Cultural Research: Do Employees of Different Cultures Interpret Work-Related Measures in an Equivalent Manner?" *Journal of Management,* vol. 20, no. 3., 1994, pp. 643–671; and Brenton R. Schlender, "Matsushita Shows How To Go Global," *Fortune,* July 11, 1994, pp. 159–166.

CHAPTER 8

International Management in Action: Doing It Right the First Time
www.jetro.gp.ip/JETROINFO/DOING/4.html; Alan Rugman and Richard M. Hodgetts, *International Business,* 2nd edition (London: Pearson, 2000), Chapter 17; Philip R. Harris and Robert T. Moran, *Managing Cultural Differences,* 3rd ed. (Houston: Gulf Publishing, 1991), pp. 393–406; Sheila Hodge, *Global Smarts* (New York: John Wiley, 2000), p. 76; and Richard D. Lewis, *When Cultures Collide* (London: Nicholas Brealey, 1999), pp. 414–415.

Communicating in Europe   Karen Matthes, "Mind Your Manners When Doing Business in Europe," *Personnel,* January 1992, p. 19; Philip R. Harris and Robert T. Moran, *Managing Cultural Differences: High-Performance Strategies for a New World of Business,* 4th ed. (Houston: Gulf Publishing, 1994), Chapter 13; Alan Rugman and Richard M. Hodgetts, *International Business,* 2nd edition (London: Pearson, 2000), Chapter 16; and Richard Lewis, *When Cultures Collide* (London: Nicholas Brealey, 1999).

CHAPTER 9

International Management in Action: Point/Counterpoint   Wendy Bonds, "Fuji, Accused by Kodak of Hogging Markets, Spits Back: 'You Too,'" *Wall Street Journal,* July 31, 1995, pp. A1, A5; "Photo Wars: Shuttered," *Economist,* August 5, 1995, pp. 59–60; Mark Maremont, "Next a Flap Over Film," *Business Week,* July 10, 1995, p. 34; "Japan's Fuji Photo Film's Group Operating Profit Rose in FY 2000," *Asia Pulse,* May 8, 2001; and "Kodak Says Profit Outlook Unchanged," *Reuters,* May 23, 2001.

Joint Venturing in Russia   Keith A. Rosten, "Soviet-U.S. Joint Ventures: Pioneers on a New Frontier," *California Management Review,* Winter 1991, pp. 88–108; Steven Greenhouse, "Chevron to Spend $10 Billion to Seek Oil in Kazakhstan," *New York Times,* May 19, 1992, pp. A1, C9; Louis Uchitelle, "Givebacks by Chevron in Oil Deal," *New York Times,* May 23, 1992, pp. 17, 29; Craig Mellow, "Russia: Making Cash from Chaos," *Fortune,* April 17, 1995, pp. 145–151; Daniel J. McCarthy and Sheila M. Puffer, "Strategic Investment Flexibility for MNE Success in Russia," *Journal of World Business,* vol. 32, no. 4, 1997, pp. 293–318; and R. Bruce Money and Debra Colton, "The Response of the 'New Consumer' to Promotion in the Transition Economies of the Former Soviet Bloc," *Journal of World Business,* vol. 35, no. 2, 2000, pp. 189–206.

You Be the International Consultant: Go East, Young People, Go East   Amy Borrus et al., "The Asians Are Bracing for a Trade Shoot-Out," *Business Week,* May 1, 1989, pp. 40–41; John W. Verity, "If It Looks Like a Slump and Crawls Like a Slump . . . ," *Business Week,* May 1, 1989, p. 27; and Geoff Lewis, "Is the Computer Business Maturing?" *Business Week,* March 6, 1989, pp. 68–78.

CHAPTER 10

International Management in Action: Sometimes It's All Politics
John Stackhouse, "India Sours on Foreign Investment," *Globe and Mail,* August 10, 1995, Sec. 2, pp. 1–2; Peter Galuszka and Susan Chandler, "A Plague of Disjointed Ventures," *Business Week,* May 1, 1995, p. 55; Marcus W. Brauchli, "Politics Threaten Power Project in India," *Wall Street Journal,* July 3, 1995, p. A14; "Enron, and On and On," *Economist,* April 21, 2001, pp. 56–57; and Saritha Rai, "Enron Unit Moves to End India Contract for Power," *New York Times,* May 22, 2001, pp. W1, W7.

Negotiating with the Japanese   Rosalie J. Tung, "How to Negotiate with the Japanese," *California Management Review,* Summer 1984, pp. 62–77; Carla Rapoport, "You Can Make Money in Japan," *Fortune,* February 12, 1990, pp. 85–92; Margaret A. Neale and Max. H. Bazerman, "Negotiating Rationally," *Academy of Management Executive,* August 1992, pp. 42–51; Martin J. Gannon, *Understanding Global Cultures,* 2nd ed. (Thousand Oaks, CA: Sage, 2001), pp. 35–56; Sheila Hodge, *Global Smarts* (New York: Wiley, 2000), Chapter 14; and Richard D. Lewis, *When Cultures Collide* (London: Nicholas Brealey Publishing, 1999), pp. 400–415.

CHAPTER 11

Organizing in Germany   Hermann Simon, "Lessons from Germany's Midsize Giants," *Harvard Business Review,* March–April 1992, pp. 115–123; Carla Rapoport, "Europe's Slump Won't End Soon," *Fortune,* May 3, 1993, pp. 82–87; and Robert Neff and Douglas Harbrecht, "Germany's Mighty Unions Are Being Forced to Bend," *Business Week,* March 1, 1993, pp. 52–56.

CHAPTER 12

International Management in Action: Kodak Goes Digital   Wendy Bonds, "Fuji, Accused by Kodak of Hogging Markets, Spits Back: 'You Too,'" *Wall Street Journal,* July 31, 1995, pp. A1, A5; Kodak Completes Acquisition of Leading Online Photo Service," June 4, 2001, Kodak Company news release.

How the Japanese Do Things Differently   Ford S. Worthy, "Japan's Smart Secret Weapon," *Fortune,* August 12, 1991, pp. 72–75; Brenton R. Schlender, "Hard Times for High Tech," *Fortune,* March 22, 1993, p. 98; Ronald Henkoff, "Companies that Train Best," *Fortune,* March 22, 1993; Jim Carlton, "Sega Leaps Ahead by Shipping New Player Early," *Wall Street Journal,* May 11, 1995, pp. B1, B3; and Jeffrey K. Liker and Yen-Chun Wu, "Japanese Automakers, U.S. Suppliers and Supply-Chain Superiority," *Sloan Management Review,* Fall 2000, pp. 81–93.

CHAPTER 13

International Management in Action: Rethinking the Motivation Equation Bayan Rahman and Ken Hijino, "Japan Moves Towards US-Style Pensions," *Financial Times,* June 23/24, 2001, p. 4; Miki Tanikawa, "Fujitsu Decides to Backtrack on Performance-Based Pay," *New York Times,* March 22, 2001, p. W1; and Stephanie Strom, "Japan's New 'Temp' Workers," *New York Times,* June 17, 1998, pp. 1–4.

***Karoshi,* or Stressed Out in Japan** Michael Zielenziger, "Alcohol Consumption a Rising Problem in Japan," *Miami Herald,* December 28, 2000, p. 10A; Howard K. French, "A Postmodern Plague Ravages Japan's Workers," *New York Times,* February 21, 2000, p. A 4; William S. Brown, Rebecca E. Lubove, and James Kwalwasser, "*Karoshi:* Alternative Perspectives of Japanese Management Styles," *Business Horizons,* March–April 1994, pp. 58–60; and Karen Lowry Miller, "Now, Japan Is Admitting It: Work Kills Executives," *Business Week,* August 3, 1992, p. 35.

CHAPTER 14

International Management in Action: Welch Led the Way Peter Landers, "In Japan, the Words of Chairman Jack Are Revolutionary," *Wall Street Journal,* February 9, 2000, pp. A1, A12; and John A. Byrne, "Jack: A Close-up Look at How America's #1 Manager Runs GE," *Business Week,* June 8, 1998, pp. 91–111.

International Management in Action: Global Teams Jitao Li, Katherine R. Xin, Anne Tsui, and Donald C. Hambrick, "Building Effective International Joint Venture Leadership Teams in China," *Journal of World Business,* vol. 34, no. 1, 1999, pp. 52–68; Charlene Marmer Solomon, "Global Teams: The Ultimate Collaboration," *Personnel Journal,* September 1995, pp. 49–58; Andrew Kakabdse and Andrew Myers, "Qualities of Top Management: Comparison of European Manufacturers," *Journal of Management Development,* vol. 14, no. 1, 1995, pp. 5–15; and Noel M. Tichy, Michael I. Brimm, Ram Chran, and Hiroraka Takeuchi, "Leadership Development as a Lever for Global Transformation," in Vladimir Pucik, Noel M. Tichy, and Carole K. Barnett, (eds.), *Globalizing Management: Creating and Leading the Competitive Organization* (New York: John Wiley & Sons, 1993), pp. 47–60.

CHAPTER 15

International Management in Action: Important Tips on Working for Foreigners Martin J. Gannon, *Understanding Global Cultures,* 2nd edition (Thousand Oaks, CA: Sage Publishing, 2001); Richard D. Lewis, *When Cultures Collide* (London: Nicholas Brealey, 1999); Roger E. Axtell (ed.), *Do's and Taboos Around the World* (New York: Wiley, 1990); John Holusha, "No Utopia but to Workers It's a Job," *New York Times,* January 29, 1989, Section 3, pp. 1, 10; and Faye Rice, "Should You Work for a Foreigner?" *Fortune,* August 1, 1988, pp. 123–124.

Recruiting Managers in Japan James C. Morgan and J. Jeffrey Morgan, *Cracking the Japanese Market* (New York: Free Press, 1991); Richard M. Hodgetts and Fred Luthans, "U.S. Multinationals'

Expatriate Compensation Strategies," *Compensation & Benefits Review,* January–February 1993, p. 61; Philip R. Harris and Robert T. Moran, *Managing and Cultural Differences: High-Performance Strategies for a New World of Business,* 3rd ed. (Houston: Gulf Publishing, 1991), p. 393; and Alan M. Rugman and Richard M. Hodgetts, *International Business,* 2nd ed. (London: Pearson, 2000), pp. 495–499.

You Be the International Consultant: A Selection Decision William H. Davidson, "Creating and Managing Joint Ventures in China," *California Management Review,* Summer 1987, pp. 77–94; Denis Fred Simon, "After Tiananmen: What Is the Future for Foreign Business in China?" *California Management Review,* Winter 1990, p. 106; and S. Gordon Redding, *The Spirit of Chinese Capitalism* (New York: Walter de Gruyter, 1990).

CHAPTER 16

International Management in Action: The Cultural Integrator Robert C. Maddox and Douglas Short, "The Cultural Integrator," *Business Horizons,* November–December 1988, pp. 57–59; Peter J. Dowling and Randall S. Schuler, *International Dimensions of Human Resource Management* (Boston: PWS-Kent, 1990); and Michael J. Marquardt and Dean W. Engel, *Global Human Resource Development* (Englewood Cliffs, NJ: Prentice-Hall, 1993).

U.S. Style Training for Expats and Their Teenagers Dawn Anfuso, "HR Unites the World of Coca-Cola," *Personnel Journal,* November 1994, pp. 112–121; Karen Dawn Stuart, "Teens Play a Role in Moves Overseas," *Personnel Journal,* March 1992, pp. 72–78; Richard M. Hodgetts and Fred Luthans, "U.S. Multinationals' Expatriate Compensation Strategies," *Compensation & Benefits Review,* January–February 1993, p. 61; and Philip R. Harris and Robert T. Moran, *Managing Cultural Differences: High-Performance Strategies for a New World of Business,* 3rd ed. (Houston: Gulf Publishing, 1991), Chapter 9.

CHAPTER 17

International Management in Action: They're Leading the Pack Steven R. Weisman, "More Japanese Workers Demanding Shorter Hours and Less Hectic Work," *New York Times,* March 3, 1992, p. A6; Germany's Mighty Unions Are Being Forced to Bend," *Business Week,* March 1, 1993, p. 52; Christopher Farrell and Michael J. Mandel, "Riding High," *Business Week,* October 9, 1995, pp. 134–146; and Tony Czuczka, " 'Lazy' Germany Showing Signs of Declining Work Ethic," *Miami Herald,* April 22, 2001, p. 7A.

Unions Become More Flexible—and Do Better Edmund L. Andrews, "German Union Gives Opening for Wage Cuts," *New York Times,* June 5, 1997, pp. A1, C5; Greg Steinmetz, "One Union Accepts Reality, Breaking with Inflexible Past," *Wall Street Journal,* June 12, 1997, p. A14; Greg Steinmetz, "Under Pressure, Germany's Unions Bend," *Wall Street Journal,* July 29, 1997, p. A10; and Edmund L. Andrews, "Germans Cut Labor Costs with a Harsh Export: Jobs," *New York Times,* March 21, 1998, pp. A1, 3.

Endnotes

Chapter 1 Endnotes

1. Bhushan Bahree, "BP Amoco Commits Up to $2 Billion in China," *Wall Street Journal,* March 24, 2000, p. A15.

2. "New Dell Plant in Ireland," *New York Times,* February 5, 2000, p. B2.

3. Peter Landers, "For American Firms, Rare Japanese Finds," *Wall Street Journal,* October 19, 2000, p. A22.

4. David Rocks, "IBM's Hottest Product Isn't a Product," *Business Week,* October 2, 2000, p. 118.

5. Jim Rohwer, "GE Digs Into Asia," *Fortune,* October 2, 2000, pp. 165–178.

6. Geri Smith, Jonathan Wheatley, and Jeff Green, "Car Power," *Business Week,* October 23, 2000, pp. 72–82.

7. David Welch, "GM Tries to Show Who's Boss," *Business Week,* March 12, 2001, pp. 54–55.

8. Christopher Marquis, "Bush Says He'll Press Effort for Hemisphere Trade Pact," *New York Times,* April 18, 2001, p. A4.

9. Thomas Kamm, Brian Coleman, and Cacilie Rohwedder, "EU Takes First Steps Toward Single Currency," *Wall Street Journal,* May 4, 1998, p. A17; Nicholas Bray, "Euro Is Expected to Level Exchange-Rate Playing Field," *Wall Street Journal,* May 8, 1998, p. A13; and Craig R. Whitney, "Europeans Accept a Single Currency Despite Late Snag," *New York Times,* May 3, 1998, pp. A1, A10.

10. Alan M. Rugman and Richard M. Hodgetts, *International Business,* 2nd edition (London: Pearson, 2000), p. 111.

11. Matt Murray, "GE Capital Goes Bargain Hunting in Troubled Asia," *Wall Street Journal,* March 12, 1998, p. B4.

12. Rebecca Buckman, "Microsoft Buys 60% of Japan's No. 2 Cable Firm," *Wall Street Journal,* April 12, 2000, p. B5.

13. Emily Thornton, "Carload of Trouble?" *Business Week,* March 27, 2000, p. 56.

14. Alan M. Rugman and Richard M. Hodgetts, "The End of Global Strategy," *European Management Journal,* September 2001, in press.

15. Johnnie L. Roberts, "He Owns the Songs," *Newsweek,* June 1, 1998, pp. 52–53.

16. David Luhnow, "Mexico Lowers Expectations for 2001 Economic Growth," *Wall Street Journal,* April 21, 2001, p. A19.

17. Leigh Gallagher, "Half Right, Senor Ross," *Forbes,* May 15, 2000, p. 62.

18. Joel Millman, "Mexico Weaves More Ties with the U.S.," *Wall Street Journal,* August 21, 2000, pp. A12, A13.

19. Elizabeth Malkin, "Holding Off Asia's Assault," *Business Week,* April 13, 1998, pp. 44–45.

20. Joel Millman, "Mexico Is Becoming Auto-Making Hot Spot," *Wall Street Journal,* June 23, 1998, p. A17.

21. Julia Preston, "Mexican Retail Conglomerate Buying Rest of CompUSA," *New York Times,* January 25, 2000, p. C3.

22. Joel Millman, "The World's New Tiger on the Export Scene Isn't Asian; It's Mexico," *Wall Street Journal,* May 9, 2000, pp. A1, A10.

23. Geri Smith, Elisabeth Malkin, and William Echikson, "Mexico Pulls Off Another Trade Coup," *Business Week,* February 7, 2000, p. 56.

24. Millman, *op. cit.,* p. A1.

25. For some of the country's current problems see Toby Muse, "Fly the Beloved Country," *Business Week,* September 11, 2000, p. 62 E8.

26. Also see Jennifer L. Rich, "A Startling Bank Privatization in Brazil," *New York Times,* November 21, 2000, p. W1.

27. "Emerging Market Indicators," *Economist,* March 7, 1998, p. 114.

28. Pamela Druckerman, "Latin Web Firms Venture out to Markets in Spain, U.S.," *Wall Street Journal,* April 12, 2000, p. A23.

29. Henri Thompson and Hugo Toledo, "Bolivia and South American Free Trade," *International Trade Journal,* Spring 2001, pp. 113–126.

30. Paul Starobin and Catherine Belton, "The Crumbling of Russia," *Business Week,* September 11, 2000, p. 60.

31. Jonathan Sapsford, Norihiko Shirouzu, and David P. Hamilton, "IMF Sets $22.6 Billion Loan Accord with Russia," *Wall Street Journal,* July 14, 1998, pp. A12, A14.

32. Jeanne Whalen and Bhushan Bahree, "How Siberian Oil Field Turned into Minefield," *Wall Street Journal,* February 9, 2000, p. A21.

33. See for example Hugh Pope, "Corruption Stunts Growth in Ex-Soviet States," *Wall Street Journal,* July 5, 2000, pp. A17–18.

34. Fred Luthans and Laura T. Riolli, "Albania and the Bora Company: Lessons Learned Before the Recent Chaos," *Academy of Management Executive,* August 1997, pp. 61–72.

35. See Jim Rohwer, "Asia's Economy: A Precarious Balancing Act," *Fortune,* June 26, 2000, pp. 211–218; and Raj Aggarwal, "Assessing the Recent Asian Economic Crises: The Role of Virtuous and Vicious Cycles," *Journal of World Business,* Vol. 34, No. 4, pp. 392–408.

36. Stephanie Strom, "Japanese Majority Owner Forces Bankruptcy of Rockefeller Center," *New York Times,* May 12, 1995, pp. A1, C4; and Mitchell Pacelle and Steven Lipin, "Japanese Firm Turns to Laws on Bankruptcy," *Wall Street Journal,* May 15, 1995, p. A4.

37. Stephanie Strom, "Deflation Shackles Japan, Blocking Hope of Recovery," *New York Times,* March 12, 2001, pp. A1, A5.

38. "Will Tokyo Finally Clean House?" *Economist,* June 27, 1998, p. 71.

39. For more on this see Andrew Pollack, "Japanese Banks Cutting Back on U.S. Presence," *New York Times,* July 10, 1998, pp. C1–2; and Mortimer B. Zuckerman, "Land of the Sinking Sun?" *U.S. News & World Report,* July 13, 1998, p. 64.

40. Phred Dvorak, "Corporate Bankruptcies in Japan Hit Record High," *Wall Street Journal,* April 16, 2001, p. A12.

41. Karby Leggett, "China's Economy Expanded by 8% Over Past Year," *Wall Street Journal,* January 2, 2001, p. A6.

42. Karby Leggett and Jason Dean, "China's Growth Surges—but Qualms Persist," *Wall Street Journal,* July 19, 2000, pp. A16, A18; Ian Johnson, "China's Economic Health Raises Doubts," Wall Street Journal, May 31, 2000, p. A22; and Karby Leggett, "China's Economy Rallies, but the Outlook Is Fragile," *Wall Street Journal,* April 19, 2000, p. A25.

43. "Mixed reviews for East Asian Economies," *Wall Street Journal,* September 19, 2000, p. A23.

44. Karby Leggett, "Foreign Investment in China Rebounds," *Wall Street Journal,* April 12, 2000, p. A21.

45. See "Slackening Seen in Export Growth," *New York Times,* December 18, 2000, p. C22.

46. Elizabeth Weldon and Wilfried Vanhonacker, "Operating in a Foreign-Invested Enterprise in China: Challenges for Managers and Management Researchers," *Journal of World Business,* Vol. 34, No. 1, 1999, pp. 94–107; and John Child and David K. Tse, "China's Transition and Its Implications for International Business," *Journal of International Business* Studies, First Quarter 2001, pp. 5–21.

47. Also see Dexter Roberts et al., "Will China Follow WTO Rules?" *Business Week,* June 5, 2000, pp. 42–48.

48. Jim Rohwer, "Asia's Meltdown," *Fortune,* February 16, 1998, p. 88.

49. "South Korea Announces Plans for Privatizing Its Industries," *New York Times,* July 4, 1998, p. B5.

50. Brian Bremner and Moon Ihlwan, "Korea's Digital Quest," *Business Week,* September 25, 2000, pp. 68–76.

51. Larry Armstrong, "And the Checkered Flag Goes To—Korea," *Business Week,* May 29, 2000, pp. 216, 218.

52. Jesse Wong and Peter Wonacott, "In Hong Kong: Persuasion or Pressure?" *Wall Street Journal,* July 21, 2000, pp. A8–9.

53. Frederik Balfour, "Back on the Radar Screen," *Business Week,* November 20, 2000, pp. 56–57; Benjamin Fulford, "Capitalism Creeps into Vietnam," *Forbes,* May 17, 1999, pp. 174, 176; and Roy Rowan, "25 Years After the Fall," *Fortune,* May 1, 2000, pp. 208–222.

54. Ann Marsh, "Mapping a Pan-African Market," *Red Herring,* March 6, 2001, pp. 54–60.

Chapter 2 Endnotes

1. See Karby Leggett, "China's Economy Rallies, but the Outlook Is Fragile," *Wall Street Journal,* April 19, 2000, p. A25.

2. Ian Johnson, "China's Jiang Outlines Privatization Steps," *Wall Street Journal,* July 31, 1997, p. A14.

3. "Can China Reform Its Economy?" *Business Week,* September 29, 1997, p. 120.

4. Ian Johnson, "China to Lift Restrictions on Foreign Business," *Wall Street Journal,* January 10, 2000, p. A17.

5. Elizabeth Weldon and Wilfried Vanhonacker, "Operating a Foreign-Invested Enterprise in China: Challenges for Managers and Management Researchers," *Journal of World Business,* Vol. 34, No. 1, 1999, pp. 97–98.

6. John Child and David K. Tse, "China's Transition and Its Implications for International Business," *Journal of International Business Studies,* First Quarter 2001, pp. 5–21.

7. Matt Forney and Pui-Wing Tam, "Qualcomm Learns from Its Mistakes in China," *Wall Street Journal,* June 7, 2000, pp. A21–22.

8. Robyn Meredith, "So You Really Want to Do Business in China?" *Forbes,* July 24, 2000, p. 93.

9. Helene Cooper, "All of Europe Watches as Britain's Tony Blair Hacks Away at Welfare," *Wall Street Journal,* June 25, 1998, p. A18.

10. "Economic Health," *Economist,* March 17, 2001, p. 78.

11. Also see David Fairlamb, *et al.,* "The Euro Mess," *Business Week,* October 2, 2000, pp. 140–146.

12. Daniel J. McCarthy, Sheila M. Puffer, and Alexander I. Naumov, "Russia's Retreat to Statization and the Implications for Business," *Journal of World Business,* Vol. 35, No. 3, 2000, p. 258.

13. Paul Starobin and Catherine Belton, "The Crumbling of Russia," *Business Week,* September 11, 2000, p. 60.

14. Paul Starobin and Olga Kravchenko, "Russia's Middle Class," *Business Week,* October 16, 2000, p. 80.

15. *Ibid.,* p. 79.

16. Hugh Pope, "Corruption Stunts Growth in Ex-Soviet States," *Wall Street Journal,* July 5, 2000, p. A17, A18.

17. Guy Chazan, "Russia Business Practices Face Scrutiny," *Wall Street Journal,* July 5, 2000, p. A18.

18. Sabrina Tavernise, "G.M. in Partnership to Make Cars in Russia," *New York Times,* February 28, 2001, p. W1.

19. For more on this see Trevor Buck, Igor Filatotchev, Peter Nolan, and Mike Wright, "Different Paths to Economic Reform in Russia and China: Causes and Consequences," *Journal of World Business,* Vol. 35, No. 4, 2000, pp. 379–400.

20. "Is Central Europe, Along with Hungary, Turning Right?" *Economist,* May 30, 1998, pp. 49–50.

21. "Czech Finance Ministry Raises 2001 Growth Outlook to 3.5 Percent," *Central Europe on Line,* April 28, 2001.

22. John Graham, "Foreign Corruption Practices Act: A Manager's Guide," *California Management Review,* Summer 1987, p. 9.

23. For more on this see Tipton F. McCubbins, "Somebody Kicked the Sleeping Dog—New Bite in the Foreign Corrupt Practices Act," *Business Horizons,* January–February 2001, pp. 27–32.

24. Howard R. French, "Japan Prime Minister Avoids Factions in Forming Cabinet," *Miami Herald,* April 27, 2001, p. 9A.

25. Brian Bremner and Ken Belson, "Dark Before Dawn?" *Business Week,* March 19, 2001, pp. 54–55.

26. Bay Fing, "Will China's Army Get Out of Business?" *U.S. News & World Report,* August 3, 1998, p. 43.

27. Russell Flannery, "Big Chip Makers Join to Develop New DRAM Technology," *Wall Street Journal,* January 18, 2000, p. A21.

28. Niall McKay, "Hidden Agendas," *Red Herring,* March 6, 2001, p. 98.

29. "Small Screens, Big Market," *Red Herring,* April 2000, p. 176.

30. "Stat Box," *Newsweek,* June 12, 2000, p. 76J.

31. "How the U.S. Rates in the Wired World," *Business Week,* March 19, 2001, p. 10.

32. For additional insights see Anoop Madhok and Thomas Osegowitsch, "The International Biotechnology Industry: A Dynamic Capabilities Perspective," *Journal of International Business Studies,* Second Quarter 2000, pp. 325–335.

33. William Echikson, Carol Matlack, and David Vannier, "American E-Tailers Take Europe by Storm," *Business Week,* August 7, 2000, pp. 54–55.

34. Robert L. Simison, "GM Retooling to Sell Custom Cars Online," *Wall Street Journal,* February 22, 2000, p. B23.

35. Marcus Walker, "Deutsche Bank Overhauls Retail Network," *Wall Street Journal,* August 4, 2000, p. A9.

36. Tanluja Singh, Jay V. Jayashankar, and Jasvinder Singh, "E-Commerce in the U.S. and Europe—Is Europe Ready to Compete?" *Business Horizons,* March–April 2001, p. 7.

37. See Kelley Holland and Amy Cortese, "The Future of Money," *Business Week,* June 12, 1995, pp. 66–78.

38. Also see Timothy A. Lavery, "Cross-Border Payments Hold Promise for Expediting International Payroll," *HRM Magazine,* March 1998, pp. 39–39.

39. See "In Peru, a Cellular Revolution," *Miami Herald,* May 22, 1995, p. 6A.

40. "Reality Bytes," *Wall Street Journal,* April 9, 2001, p. B6.

41. William Echikson, "Wiring Europe the American Way," *Business Week,* July 31, 2000, pp. 77–78.

42. Jan Syfert, "Up There with the Best," *Productivity SA,* November/December 1998, p. 49.

43. Chen May Yee, "High-Tech Lift for India's Women," *Wall Street Journal,* November 1, 2000, pp. B1, B4.

Chapter 3 Endnotes

1. Chris Gaither, "Intel Product Could Set Off a Price War," *New York Times,* April 23, 2001, Section C, pp. 1, 9.

2. Cliff Edwards and Andy Reinhardt, "Intel Inside the War Room," *Business Week,* April 30, 2001, p. 40.

3. Gautam Naik, "Motorola Still Is Struggling in Europe," *Wall Street Journal,* February 11, 2000, p. A12.

4. Gary McWilliams, "Motorola Joins Technology-Outsourcing Wave," *Wall Street Journal,* June 1, 2000, p. B6.

5. Also see Joseph B. White, "Nissan Can Cut Supplier Costs, President Says," *Wall Street Journal,* April 18, 2000, p. A4.

6. Suzanne Kapner, "Ericsson to Farm Out Production," *New York Times,* January 27, 2001, p. B1.

7. Stephanie Strom, "In Japan: Outsourcing Without a Capital 'O,'" *New York Times,* July 16, 2000, Section 4, p. 4.

8. Pete Engardio, "The Barons of Outsourcing," *Business Week,* August 28, 2000, p. 178.

9. *Ibid.*

10. Michael E. Porter, *Competitive Advantages of Nations* (New York: Free Press, 1990).

11. Julian Birkinshaw and Neil Hood, "Unleash Innovation in Foreign Subsidiaries," *Harvard Business Review,* March 2001, pp. 132–133.

12. 3M Company website.

13. Joe Hutsko, "88 Million and Counting," *New York Times,* March 25, 2000, p. B1.

14. Daniel Michaels, "No-Frills Irish Airline Flies High," *Wall Street Journal,* September 6, 2000, pp. B1, B4.

15. See for example David Welch, "Say Good-bye to the Shake, Rattle, and Roll," *Business Week,* November 27, 2000, pp. 212–213.

16. Joseph B. White, "Japanese, European Auto Makers Top Survey," *Wall Street Journal,* May 5, 2000, p. A4.

17. Scott Miller, "Ford Must Rebuild Europe Market Share," *Wall Street Journal,* January 26, 2000, p. A19.

18. Edmund L. Andrews, "G.M. and Ford Losing Out in the European Market," *New York Times,* March 3, 2001, p. B2.

19. See Todd Zaun, "Honda's Profit Fell 12% Last Year, Pressured by Its Losses in Europe," *Wall Street Journal,* April 30, 2001, p. A15.

20. Also see Frederic M. Biddle, "Boeing Is Placing Its Bets on Smaller, Cheaper Airlines," *Wall Street Journal,* July 6, 1998, p. A22.

21. "Boeing and Airbus: A Phoney War," *Economist,* May 5, 2001, pp. 56–57.

22. "Silicon Valley, PRC," *Economist,* June 27, 1998, pp. 64–65.

23. Also see Mark L. Clifford *et al.,* "Asia's Future," *Business Week,* November 27, 2000, pp. 132–136.

24. Michael E. McGill, John W. Slocum, Jr., and David Lei, "Management Practices in Learning Organizations," *Organizational Dynamics,* Summer 1992, pp. 10–16. For additional insights to learning organizations, see J. Bernard Keys, Robert A. Wells, and L. Trey Denton, "Japanese Managerial and Organizational Learning," *Thunderbird International Business Review,* May/April 1998, pp. 119–139.

25. Also see Fred Luthans, Michael Rubach, and Paul Marsnik, "Going Beyond Total Quality: The Characteristics, Techniques and

Measures of Learning Organizations," *International Journal of Organizational Analysis,* January 1995, pp. 24–44.

26. John A. Mathews and Dong-Sung Cho, "Combinative Capabilities and Organizational Learning in Latecomer Firms: The Case of the Korean Semiconductor Industry," *Journal of World Business,* Vol. 34, No. 2, 1999, pp. 139–156.

27. See Luthans, Rubach, and Marsnik, p. 11.

28. Albert Bandura, *Social Foundations of Thought and Action* (Englewood Cliffs, NJ: Prentice-Hall, 1986); and Albert Bandura, *Self-Efficacy: The Exercise of Control* (New York: W. H. Freeman and Company, 1997).

29. Alexander D. Stajkovic and Fred Luthans, "Social Cognitive Theory and Self-Efficacy: Going Beyond Traditional Motivational and Behavioral Approaches," *Organizational Dynamics,* Spring 1998, p. 66.

30. Alexander D. Stajkovic and Fred Luthans, "Self-Efficacy and Work-Related Performance: A Meta-Analysis," *Psychological Bulletin,* vol. 124, 1998, pp. 240–261.

31. See Richard M. Hodgetts, *Measures of Quality and High Performance* (New York: American Management Association, 1998), pp. 146–149; and Stephane Brutus, John W. Fleenor, and Manuel London, "Does 360-Degree Feedback Work in Different Industries," *Journal of Management Development,* vol. 17, no. 3, 1998, pp. 177–190.

32. John J. Keller, "AT&T Bypasses Normal Suppliers in Local-Phone Race," *Wall Street Journal,* March 30, 1997, p. B4.

33. Michael E. Porter, *Competitive Advantage of Nations,* p. 103.

34. Jonathan Friedland, "VW Puts Suppliers on Production Line," *Wall Street Journal,* February 15, 1996, p. A11.

35. Jeffrey Pfeffer, *The Human Equation* (Boston: Harvard Business School Press, 1998), pp. xv–xvi.

36. *Ibid.,* p. xvi.

37. Richard M. Hodgetts, *Implementing TQM in Small- and Medium-Sized Organizations* (New York: American Management Association, 1996), Chapter 7.

38. Edmund L. Andrews, "Wal-Mart Lowers Its Prices at Stores Across Germany," *New York Times,* January 4, 2000, p. C4.

Chapter 4 Endnotes

1. *Source:* Courtesy of Johnson & Johnson.

2. Georges Enderle, "A Worldwide Survey of Business Ethics in the 1990s," *Journal of Business Ethics,* December 1997, pp. 1475–1483.

3. Stephanie Strom, "Donation Scandal Growing in Japan," *Miami Herald,* August 3, 2000, p. 8A.

4. Stephanie Strom, "Top Advisor to Japan's Premier at Center of Political Scandal," *New York Times,* August 3, 2000, p. A11.

5. Greg Wiegand, "Arrests Put Focus on Ethics in Japan," *USA Today,* January 20, 1998, p. 2B.

6. Sheryl WuDunn, "Japan's Corruption Fighter Is Shunted Aside," *New York Times,* August 14, 1998, p. C4.

7. See also "Never Mind the Quality," *Economist,* June 28, 1997, p. 15.

8. Benjamin Fulford, "Japan's Dirty Secrets," *Forbes,* October 30, 2000, p. 69.

9. *Ibid.,* pp. 67–68.

10. Todd Zuan, "Mitsubishi Covered Up Complaints," *Wall Street Journal,* August 23, 2000, pp. A14, A18.

11. Miki Tanikawa, "Mitsubishi Shares Tumble After Police Raid on Headquarters," *New York Times,* August 29, 2000, p. C4.

12. Irene M. Kunii, "Was There a Cover-Up at Mitsubishi?" *Business Week,* October 9, 2000, p. 68.

13. Miki Tanikawa, "Manual For Fooling Inspectors," *New York Times,* November 7, 2000, p. W1.

14. Andrew Pollack, "In Japan, It's See No Evil; Have No Harassment," *New York Times,* May 7, 1996, p. C5.

15. Howard W. French, "Diploma at Hand, Japanese Women Find Glass Ceiling Reinforced with Iron," *New York Times,* January 1, 2001, p. A4.

16. Peter Elstrom and Steven V. Brull, "Mitsubishi's Morass," *Business Week,* June 3, 1996, p. 35.

17. Pat Choate, *Agents of Influence* (New York: Knopf, 1991).

18. Helmut Becker and David J. Fritzsche, "A Comparison of the Ethical Behavior of American, French, and German Managers," *Columbia Journal of World Business,* Winter 1987, pp. 87–95.

19. *Ibid.,* p. 92.

20. *Ibid.,* p. 94.

21. Evelyne Serdjenian, "Women Managers in France," in Nancy J. Adler and Dafna N. Izraeli (eds.), *Competitive Frontiers: Women Managers in a Global Economy* (Cambridge, MA: Blackwell Publishing, 1994), pp. 199–200.

22. *Ibid.,* p. 204.

23. Adriane Berthoin Antal and Camilla Krebsbach-Gnath, "Women in Management in Germany: East, West, and Reunited," in Nancy J. Adler and Dafna N. Izraeli (eds.), *Competitive Frontiers: Women Managers in a Global Economy* (Cambridge, MA: Blackwell Publishing, 1994), pp. 210–211.

24. Suzanne Kapner, "Britain's Legal Barriers Start to Fall," *New York Times,* October 4, 2000, p. W1.

25. Cara Buckley, "Worldwide Music Piracy Costs Industry $5 Billion," *Miami Herald,* October 3, 2000, pp. C1, C10.

26. Richard Behar, "Beijing's Phony War on Fakes," *Fortune,* October 30, 2000, p. 193.

27. Craig S. Smith, "A Tale of Piracy: How the Chinese Stole the Grinch," *New York Times,* December 12, 2000, p. A3.

28. Craig S. Smith, "Piracy a Concern as the China Trade Opens Up," *New York Times,* October 5, 2000, p. W1. Also see Dexter Roberts et al., "China's Piracy Plague," *Business Week,* June 5, 2000, pp. 44–48.

29. Seth Faison, "China Appears to Crack Down on CD Pirating," *New York Times,* April 7, 1997, pp. A1, A6; and Seth Faison, "U.S. and China Agree on Pact to Fight Piracy," *New York Times,* June 18, 1996, pp. A1, A8.

30. "Better Than the Real Thing," *Economist,* January 24, 1998, pp. 65–66.

31. Behar, *op. cit.,* pp. 198–199. Also see Dexter Roberts *et al.,* "Will China Follow WTO Rules?" *Business Week,* June 5, 2000, pp. 42–48.

32. Edward A. Robinson, "China's Spies Target Corporate America," *Fortune,* March 30, 1998, p. 119.

33. Dexter Roberts, Christopher Power, and Stephanie Anderson Forest, "Cheated in China?" *Business Week,* October 6, 1997, p. 142.

34. Also see Lu Xiaohe, "Business Ethics in China," *Journal of Business Ethics,* October 1997, pp. 1509–1518.

35. Karen Korabik, "Managerial Women in the People's Republic of China: The Long March Continues," in Nancy J. Adler and Dafna N. Izraeli (eds.), *Competitive Frontiers: Women Managers in a Global Economy* (Cambridge, MA: Blackwell Publishers, 1994), p. 124.

36. Alan M. Rugman and Richard M. Hodgetts, *International Business,* 2nd edition (London: Pearson, 2000), pp. 9–10.

37. For example, see Matt Moffett, "U.S. Child-Labor Law Sparks a Trade Debate over Brazilian Oranges," *Wall Street Journal,* September 9, 1998, pp. A1, A9.

38. Robert S. Greenberger, "Foreigners Use Bribes to Beat U.S. Rivals in Many Deals, New Report Concludes," *Wall Street Journal,* October 12, 1995, pp. A3, A17.

39. Tipton F. McCubbins, "Somebody Kicked the Sleeping Dog—New Bite in the Foreign Corrupt Practices Act," *Business Horizons,* January–February 2001, p. 27.

40. Greg Steinmetz, "U.S. Firms Are Among Least Likely to Pay Bribes Abroad, Survey Finds," *Wall Street Journal,* August 25, 1997, p. 5.

41. Edmund L. Andrews, "29 Nations Agree to Outlaw Bribing Foreign Officials," *New York Times,* November 21, 1997, p. C2.

Chapter 5 Endnotes

1. Pat Joynt and Malcolm Warner, "Introduction: Cross-Cultural Perspectives," in Pat Joynt and Malcolm Warner (eds.), *Managing across Cultures: Issues and Perspectives* (London: International Thomson Business Press, 1996), p. 3.

2. For additional insights see Gerry Darlington, "Culture—A Theoretical Review," *Managing across Cultures: Issues and Perspectives,* pp. 33–55.

3. Fred Luthans, *Organizational Behavior,* 7th ed. (New York: McGraw-Hill, 1995), pp. 534–535.

4. Gary Bonvillian and William A. Nowlin, "Cultural Awareness: An Essential Element of Doing Business Abroad," *Business Horizons,* November–December 1994, pp. 44–54.

5. Roger E. Axtell (ed.), *Dos and Taboos around the World,* 2nd ed. (New York: Wiley, 1990), p. 3.

6. Lillian H. Chaney and Jeanette S. Martin, *Intercultural Business Communication* (Englewood Cliffs, NJ: Prentice-Hall, 1995), p. 115.

7. Fons Trompenaars and Charles Hampden-Turner, *Riding the Waves of Culture: Understanding Diversity in Global Business,* 2nd ed. (New York: McGraw-Hill, 1998), p. 23.

8. Christopher Orpen, "The Work Values of Western and Tribal Black Employees," *Journal of Cross-Cultural Psychology,* March 1978, pp. 99–111.

9. William Whitely and George W. England, "Variability in Common Dimensions of Managerial Values due to Value Orientation and Country Differences," *Personnel Psychology,* Spring 1980, pp. 77–89.

10. *Ibid.,* p. 87.

11. George W. England and Raymond Lee, "The Relationship between Managerial Values and Managerial Success in the United States, Japan, India, and Australia," *Journal of Applied Psychology,* August 1974, pp. 418–419.

12. George W. England, "Managers and Their Value Systems: A Five-Country Comparative Study," *Columbia Journal of World Business,* Summer 1978, p. 39.

13. A. Reichel and D. M. Flynn, "Values in Transition: An Empirical Study of Japanese Managers in the U.S.," *Management International Review,* vol. 23, no. 4, 1984, pp. 69–70.

14. Hermann F. Schwind and Richard B. Peterson, "Shifting Personal Values in the Japanese Management System," *International Studies of Management & Organization,* Summer 1985, pp. 60–74.

15. *Ibid.,* p. 72.

16. Yumiko Ono and Bill Spindle, "Japan's Long Decline Makes One Thing Rise: Individualism," *Wall Street Journal,* December 29, 2000, pp. A1, A4.

17. Sang M. Lee and Suzanne J. Peterson, "Culture, Entrepreneurial Orientation, and Global Competitiveness," *Journal of World Business,* vol. 35, no. 4, 2000, pp. 411–412.

18. Geert Hofstede, *Culture's Consequences: International Differences in Work-Related Values* (Beverly Hills: Sage Publications, 1980).

19. Geert Hofstede, *Cultures and Organizations: Software of the Mind* (London: McGraw-Hill U.K., Ltd., 1991), pp. 251–252.

20. Geert Hofstede and Michael Bond, "The Need for Synergy among Cross-Cultural Studies," *Journal of Cross-Cultural Psychology,* December 1984, p. 419.

21. A. R. Negandhi and S. B. Prasad, *Comparative Management* (New York: Appleton-Century-Crofts, 1971), p. 128.

22. For additional insights, see Mark F. Peterson et al., "Role Conflict, Ambiguity, and Overload: A 21-Nation Study," *Academy of Management Journal,* June 1995, pp. 429–452.

23. Hofstede, *Culture's Consequences.*

24. *Ibid.*

25. *Ibid.*

26. Also see Chao C. Chen, Xiao-Ping Chen, and James R. Meindl, "How Can Cooperation Be Fostered? The Cultural Effects of Individualism–Collectivism," *Academy of Management Review,* vol. 23, no. 2, 1998, pp. 285–304.

27. Hofstede, *Culture's Consequences,* pp. 419–420.

28. *Ibid.,* p. 420.

29. Simcha Ronen and Allen I. Kraut, "Similarities among Countries Based on Employee Work Values and Attitudes," *Columbia Journal of World Business,* Summer 1977, p. 90.

30. *Ibid.,* p. 95.

31. See for example, David A. Ralston, Carolyn P. Egri, Sally Stewart, Robert H. Terpstra, and Yu Kaicheng, "Doing Business in the 21st Century with the New Generation of Chinese Managers: A Study of Generational Shifts in Work Values in China," *Journal of International Business Studies,* Second Quarter 1999, pp. 415–428.

32. Simcha Ronen and Oded Shenkar, "Clustering Countries on Attitudinal Dimensions: A Review and Synthesis," *Academy of Management Journal,* September 1985, pp. 435-454.

33. *Ibid.,* p. 452.

34. Fons Trompenaars, *Riding the Waves of Culture* (New York: Irwin, 1994), p. 10.

35. Talcott Parsons, *The Social System* (New York: Free Press, 1951).

36. Also see Lisa Hoecklin, *Managing Cultural Differences* (Workingham, England: Addison-Wesley Publishing, 1995).

37. Charles M. Hampden-Turner and Fons Trompenaars, "A World Turned Upside Down: Doing Business in Asia," in Pat Joynt and Malcolm Warner (eds.), *Managing across Cultures: Issues and Perspectives* (London: International Thomson Business Press, 1996), p. 279.

38. *Ibid.,* p. 288.

39. Trompenaars, *Riding the Waves of Culture,* p. 131.

40. *Ibid.,* p. 140.

Chapter 6 Endnotes

1. Nancy J. Adler, *International Dimensions of Organizational Behavior,* 3rd ed. (Cincinnati, OH: Southwestern, 1997).

2. See Clifford C. Clarke and Douglas Lipp, "Contrasting Cultures," *Training & Development Journal,* February 1998, pp. 21–31.

3. For more insights into what Nissan is doing see Victoria Emerson, "An Interview with Carlos Ghosn, President of Nissan Motors, Ltd. and Industry Leader of the Year," *Journal of World Business,* vol. 36, no. 1, 2001, pp. 3–10.

4. A detailed discussion of the company's recent history and strategy can be found in John Tagliabue, "Renault Pins Its Survival on a Global Gamble," *New York Times,* July 2, 2000, Section 3, pp. 1, 6.

5. For more examples of what car companies are doing in the North American market, see Norihiko Shirouzu, "Tailoring World's Cars to U.S. Tastes," *Wall Street Journal,* January 15, 2001, pp. B1, B6.

6. Fons Trompenaars and Charles Hampden-Turner, *Riding the Waves of Culture: Understanding Diversity in Global Business,* 2nd ed. (New York: McGraw-Hill, 1998), p. 188.

7. For a more detailed analysis, see Allen J. Morrison, David A. Ricks, and Kendall Roth, "Globalization versus Regionalization: Which Way for the Multinational?" *Organizational Dynamics,* Winter 1991, pp. 17–28.

8. Lisa Hoecklin, *Managing Cultural Differences* (Workingham, England: Addison-Wesley, 1995), pp. 98–99.

9. "The Personal Touch: Making McDonald's and Coca-Cola Less American," *Economist,* May 15, 1998, p. 5.

10. Bill Spindle, "Cowboys and Samurai: The Japanizing of Universal," *Wall Street Journal,* March 22, 2001, pp. B1, B6.

11. Bruce Orwall and Evan Ramstad, "Web's Reach Forces Hollywood to Rethink America-First Policy," *Wall Street Journal,* June 12, 2000, pp. A1, A8.

12. Linda M. Randall and Lori A. Coakley, "Building a Successful Partnership in Russia and Belarus: The Impact of Culture on Strategy," *Business Horizons,* March–April 1998, pp. 15–22.

13. *Ibid.,* p. 21.

14. Trompenaars and Hampden-Turner, p. 202.

15. See for example Anisya S. Thomas and Stephen L. Mueller, "A Case for Comparative Entrepreneurship: Assessing the Relevance of Culture," *Journal of International Business Studies,* Second Quarter 2000, pp. 287–301.

16. Adapted from Richard Mead, *International Management* (Cambridge, MA: Blackwell, 1994), pp. 57–59.

17. Yumiko Ono, "U.S. Superstores Find Japanese Are a Hard Sell," *Wall Street Journal,* February 14, 2000, pp. B1, B4.

18. Fred Luthans, Richard M. Hodgetts, and Stuart A. Rosenkrantz, *Real Managers* (Cambridge, MA: Ballinger Publishing, 1988).

19. Fred Luthans, Dianne H. B. Welsh, and Stuart A. Rosenkrantz, "What Do Russian Managers Really Do? An Observational Study with Comparisons to U.S. Managers," *Journal of International Business Studies,* Fourth Quarter 1993, pp. 741–761.

20. Diane H. B. Welsh, Fred Luthans, and Steven M. Sommer, "Organizational Behavior Modification Goes to Russia: Replicating an Experimental Analysis across Cultures and Tasks," *Journal of Organizational Behavior Management,* vol. 13, no. 2, 1993, pp. 15–35; Diane H. B. Welsh, Fred Luthans, and Steven M. Sommer, "Managing Russian Factory Workers: The Impact of U.S.-Based Behavioral and Participative Techniques," *Academy of Management Journal,* February 1993, pp. 58–79.

21. Welsh, Luthans, and Sommer, "Organizational Behavior Modification," p. 31. The summary of positive (17 percent average) performance from O. B. Mod. for U.S. samples can be found in Fred Luthans and Alexander Stajkovic, "Reinforce for Performance," *Academy of Management Executive,* vol. 13, no. 2, 1999, pp. 49–57.

22. Steven M. Sommer, Seung-Hyun Bae, and Fred Luthans, "The Structure-Climate Relationship in Korean Organizations," *Asia Pacific Journal of Management,* vol. 12, no. 2, 1995, pp. 23–36. Also see: Steven Sommer, Seung-Hyun Bae, and Fred Luthans, "Organizational Commitment across Cultures," *Human Relations,* vol. 49, no. 7, pp. 977–993.

23. Sommer, Bae, and Luthans, "The Structure-Climate Relationship."

24. Trompenaars and Hampden-Turner, p. 196.

25. Shari Caudron, "Lessons for HR Overseas," *Personnel Journal,* February 1995, p. 92.

26. Richard M. Hodgetts and Fred Luthans, "U.S. Multinationals' Compensation Strategies for Local Management: Cross-Cultural Implications," *Compensation & Benefits Review,* March–April 1993, pp. 42–48.

27. Also see Randall S. Schuler and Nikolai Rogovsky, "Understanding Compensation Practice Variations across Firms: The Impact of National Culture," *Journal of International Business Studies,* First Quarter 1998, pp. 159–177.

28. Tara Parker-Pope, "Culture Clash," *Wall Street Journal,* April 12, 1995, p. R7.

29. Rochelle Kopp, "International Human Resource Policies and Practices in Japanese, European, and United States Multinationals," *Human Resource Management,* Winter 1994, p. 590.

30. Philip M. Rosenzweig and Nitin Nohria, "Influences on Human Resource Management Practices in Multinational Corporations," *Journal of International Business Studies,* Second Quarter 1994, pp. 229–251.

31. Miki Tanikawa, "In Japan, Some Shun Lifetime Jobs to Chase Dreams," *New York Times,* June 25, 1995, p. F11.

32. Also see Richard W. Wright, "Trends in International Business Research: Twenty-Five Years Later," *Journal of International Business Studies,* Fourth Quarter 1994, pp. 687–701; Schon Beechler and John Zhuang Yang, "The Transfer of Japanese-Style Management to American Subsidiaries: Contingencies, Constraints, and Competencies," *Journal of International Business Studies,* Third Quarter 1994, pp. 467–491.

33. See for example Leslie Chang, "China Lists New Rules in Telecoms," *Wall Street Journal,* October 11, 2000, p. A21.

34. Eric W. K. Tsang, "Can Guanxi Be a Source of Sustained Competitive Advantage for Doing Business in China?" *Academy of Management Executive,* vol. 12, no. 2, 1998, p. 64.

35. Stephen S. Standifird and R. Scott Marshall, "The Transaction Cost Advantage of Guanxi-Based Business Practices," *Journal of World Business,* Vol. 35, No. 1, 2000, pp. 21–42.

36. Lee Mei Yi and Paul Ellis, "Insider-Outsider Perspective of *Guanxi,*" *Business Horizons,* January–February 2000, p. 28.

37. Rosalie L. Tung, "Managing in Asia: Cross-Cultural Dimensions," in Pat Joynt and Malcolm Warner (eds.), *Managing Across Cultures: Issues and Perspectives* (London: International Thomson Business Press, 1996), p. 239.

38. Richard D. Lewis, *When Cultures Collide* (London: Nicholas Brealey Publishing, 1999), p. 390.

39. For more on this topic, see Philip R. Harris and Robert T. Moran, *Managing Cultural Differences,* 3rd ed. (Houston: Gulf Publishing, 1991), pp. 410–411.

40. Ming-Jer Chen, *Inside Chinese Business* (Boston: Harvard Business School Press, 2001), p. 153.

41. William B. Snavely, Serguel Miassaoedov, and Kevin McNeilly, "Cross-Cultural Peculiarities of the Russian Entrepreneur: Adapting to the New Russians," *Business Horizons,* March–April 1998, pp. 10–13.

42. Jeanne Whalen and Bhushan Bahree, "How Siberian Oil Field Turned into a Minefield," *Wall Street Journal,* February 9, 2000, p. A21.

43. Snavely, pp. 10–13.

44. For additional insights into how to interact and negotiate effectively with the Russians see Lewis, *When Cultures Collide,* pp. 314–318.

45. Snavely, p. 13.

46. Jonathan Karp, "India Again Is Alluring to Foreign Telecoms," *Wall Street Journal,* February 10, 2000, pp. A13, A15.

47. See "Enron, and on, and on," *Economist,* April 21, 2001, pp. 56–57; and "Indian State to Pay Enron in Power Spat," *Wall Street Journal,* April 26, 2001, p. A17.

48. Jess Pesta, "Investing in India Becomes Easier, but Foreigners May Not Care," *Wall Street Journal,* May 11, 2001, pp. A11, A12.

49. Adapted from Harris and Moran, *Managing Cultural Differences,* p. 447.

50. Also see Lewis, *When Cultures Collide,* pp. 341–346.

51. Jean-Louis Barsoux and Peter Lawrence, "The Making of a French Manager," *Harvard Business Review,* July–August 1991, pp. 58–67.

52. Adapted from Harris and Moran, *Managing Cultural Differences,* p. 471.

53. Lewis, *When Cultures Collide,* pp. 231–232.

54. Changiz Pezeshkpur, "Challenges to Management in the Arab World," *Business Horizons,* August 1978, p. 50.

55. Adapted from Harris and Moran, *Managing Cultural Differences,* p. 503.

Chapter 7 Endnotes

1. Lisa Hoecklin, *Managing Cultural Differences* (Workingham, England: Addison-Wesley, 1995), p. 146.

2. Edgar H. Schein, *Organizational Culture and Leadership,* 2nd edition (San Francisco: Jossey Bass, 1997), p. 12.

3. Fred Luthans, *Organizational Behavior,* 9th ed. (New York: McGraw-Hill/Irwin, 2002), p. 123.

4. In addition see W. Mathew Jeuchter, Caroline Fisher, and Randall J. Alford, "Five Conditions for High-Performance Cultures," *Training & Development Journal,* May 1998, pp. 63–67.

5. Greg Steinmetz and Matt Marshall, "How a Chemical Giant Goes about Becoming a Lot Less German," *Wall Street Journal,* February 18, 1997, p. A18.

6. Miriam Jordan, "Penney Blends Two Business Cultures," *Wall Street Journal,* April 5, 2001, pp. A15, A17.

7. Hoecklin, *Managing Cultural Differences,* p. 145.

8. Andre Laurent, "The Cultural Diversity of Western Conceptions of Management," *International Studies of Management and Organization,* Spring–Summer 1983, pp. 75–96.

9. Nancy J. Adler, *International Dimensions of Organizational Behavior,* 2nd ed. (Boston: PWS-Kent Publishing, 1991), pp. 58–59.

10. Robert Frank and Thomas M. Burton, "Cross-Border Merger Results in Headaches for a Drug Company," *Wall Street Journal,* February 4, 1997, p. A1.

11. Hoecklin, *Managing Cultural Differences,* p. 151.

12. Carla Rapoport and Justin Martin, "Retailers Go Global," *Fortune,* February 20, 1995, pp. 102–108.

13. Rita A. Numeroff and Michael N. Abrams, "Integrating Corporate Culture from International M&As," *HR Focus,* June 1998, p. 12.

14. See Maddy Janssens, Jeanne M. Brett, and Frank J. Smith, "Confirmatory Cross-Cultural Research: Testing the Viability of a Corporation-Wide Safety Policy," *Academy of Management Journal,* June 1995, pp. 364–382.

15. Richard Gibson and Matt Moffett, "Why You Won't Find any Egg McMuffins for Breakfast in Brazil," *Wall Street Journal,* October 23, 1997, pp. A1, 8.

16. *Ibid.*

17. Fons Trompenaars, *Riding the Waves of Culture: Understanding Diversity in Global Business* (Burr Ridge, IL: Irwin, 1994), p. 156.

18. *Ibid.,* p. 164.

19. *Ibid.,* p. 167.

20. *Ibid.,* p. 172.

21. Fons Trompenaars and Charles Hampden-Turner, *Riding the Waves of Culture: Understanding Diversity in Global Business,* 2nd ed. (New York: McGraw-Hill, 1998), p. 182.

22. For more see Rose Mary Wentling and Nilda Palma-Rivas, "Current Status of Diversity Initiatives in Selected Multinational Corporations," *Human Resource Development Quarterly,* Spring 2000, pp. 35–60.

23. Adler, *International Dimensions of Organizational Behavior,* p. 121.

24. Noboru Yoshimura and Philip Anderson, *Inside the* Kaisha (Boston: Harvard Business School Press, 1997).

25. Edmund L. Andrews, "Meet the Maverick of Japan, Inc." *New York Times,* October 12, 1995, pp. C1, 4.

26. Sheryl WuDunn, "Incubators of Creativity," *New York Times,* October 9, 1997, pp. C1, 21.

27. Adler, *International Dimensions of Organizational Behavior,* p. 132.

28. Adele Thomas and Mike Bendixen, "The Management Implications of Ethnicity in South Africa," *Journal of International Business Studies,* Third Quarter 2000, pp. 507–519.

29. John M. Ivencevich and Jacqueline A. Gilbert, "Diversity Management: Time for a New Approach," *Public Personnel Management,* Spring 2000, pp. 75–92.

30. Joseph J. Distefano and Martha L. Maznevski, "Creating Value with Diverse Teams in Global Management," *Organizational Dynamics,* Summer 2000, pp. 45–63.

31. See for example Betty Jane Punnett and Jason Clemens, "Cross-National Diversity: Implications for International Expansion Decisions," *Journal of World Business,* vol. 34, no. 2, 1999, pp. 128–138.

32. Adler, *International Dimensions of Organizational Behavior,* p. 137.

33. Wellford W. Wilms, Alan J. Hardcastle, and Deone M. Zell, "Cultural Transformation at NUMMI," *Sloan Management Review,* Fall 1994, p. 103.

34. *Ibid.,* p. 111.

Chapter 8 Endnotes

1. See Lillian H. Chaney and Jeanette S. Martin, *Intercultural Business Communication* (Englewood Cliffs, NJ: Prentice-Hall, 1995), p. 102.

2. Paul R. Lawrence and Charalambos A. Vlachoutsicos, *Behind the Factory Walls: Decision Making in Soviet and U.S. Enterprises* (Cambridge, MA: Harvard University Press, 1990), p. 282. Also see James E. McLauchlin, "Communicating to a Diverse Europe," *Business Horizons,* January–February 1993, pp. 54–56.

3. See Fred Luthans, Dianne H. B. Welsh, and Stuart A. Rosenkrantz, "What Do Russian Managers Really Do? An Observational Study with Comparisons to U.S. Managers," *Journal of International Business Studies,* 4th Quarter, 1993, pp. 741–761; Fred Luthans, Richard Hodgetts, and Stuart A. Rosenkrantz, *Real Managers* (Cambridge, MA: Ballinger, 1988).

4. Richard Tanner Pascale, "Communication and Decision Making across Cultures: Japanese and American Comparisons," *Administrative Science Quarterly,* March 1978, pp. 91–110.

5. *Ibid.,* p. 103.

6. E. T. Hall and E. Hall, "How Cultures Collide," in G. R. Weaver (ed.), *Culture, Communication, and Conflict: Readings in Intercultural Relations* (Needham Heights, MA: Ginn Press, 1994).

7. Noboru Yoshimura and Philip Anderson, *Inside the* Kaisha: *Demystifying Japanese Business Behavior* (Boston: Harvard Business School Press, 1997), p. 59.

8. William C. Byham and George Dixon, "Through Japanese Eyes," *Training and Development Journal,* March 1993, pp. 33–36; Linda S. Dillon, "West Meets East," *Training and Development Journal,* March 1993, pp. 39–43.

9. Fons Trompenaars and Charles Hampden-Turner, *Riding the Waves of Culture: Understanding Diversity in Global Business,* 2nd ed. (New York: McGraw-Hill, 1998), p. 204.

10. Nancy J. Adler, *International Dimensions of Organizational Behavior,* 2nd ed. (Boston: PWS-Kent Publishing, 1991), pp. 75–76.

11. Giorgio Inzerilli, "The Legitimacy of Managerial Authority—A Comparative Study," *National Academy of Management Proceedings,* Detroit, 1980, pp. 58–62.

12. *Ibid.,* p. 62.

13. Philip R. Harris and Robert T. Moran, *Managing Cultural Differences,* 3rd ed. (Houston: Gulf Publishing, 1996), pp. 36–37.

14. Richard Tanner Pascale and Anthony G. Athos, *The Art of Japanese Management* (New York: Warner Books, 1981), pp. 82–83.

15. Justin Fox, "The Triumph of English," *Fortune,* September 18, 2000, pp. 209–212.

16. See "Double or Quits," *Economist,* February 25, 1995, pp. 84–85.

17. Brock Stout, "Interviewing in Japan," *HR Magazine,* June 1998, p. 73.

18. *Ibid.,* p. 75.

19. H. W. Hildebrandt, "Communication Barriers between German Subsidiaries and Parent American Companies," *Michigan Business Review,* July 1973, p. 9.

20. John R. Schermerhorn, Jr., "Language Effects in Cross-Cultural Management Research: An Empirical Study and a Word of Caution," *National Academy of Management Proceedings,* 1987, p. 103.

21. Brenda R. Sims and Stephen Guice, "Differences between Business Letters from Native and Non-Native Speakers of English," *Journal of Business Communication,* Winter 1991, p. 37.

22. James Calvert Scott and Diana J. Green, "British Perspectives on Organizing Bad-News Letters: Organizational Patterns Used by Major U.K. Companies," *The Bulletin,* March 1992, p. 17.

23. *Ibid.,* pp. 18–19.

24. Mi Young Park, W. Tracy Dillon, and Kenneth L. Mitchell, "Korean Business Letters: Strategies for Effective Complaints in Cross-Cultural Communication," *Journal of Business Communication,* July 1998, pp. 328–345.

25. As an example see Jeremiah Sullivan, "What Are the Functions of Corporate Home Pages?" *Journal of World Business,* Vol. 34, No. 2, 1999, pp. 193–211.

26. Joseph Kahn, "Fraying U.S.-Sino Ties Threaten Business," *Wall Street Journal,* July 7, 1995, p. A6; Nathaniel C. Nash, "China Gives Big Van Deal to Mercedes," *New York Times,* July 13, 1995, pp. C1, C5; and Seth Faison, "China Times a Business Deal to Make a Point to America," *New York Times,* July 16, 1995, pp. 1, 6.

27. David A. Ricks, *Big Business Blunders: Mistakes in Multinational Marketing* (Homewood, IL: Dow Jones-Irwin, 1983), p. 39.

28. *Ibid.,* p. 55.

29. Edwin Miller, Bhal Bhatt, Raymond Hill, and Julian Cattaneo, "Leadership Attitudes of American and German Expatriate Managers in Europe and Latin America," *National Academy of Management Proceedings,* Detroit, 1980, pp. 53–57.

30. Abdul Rahim A. Al-Meer, "Attitudes Towards Women as Managers: A Comparison of Asians, Saudis and Westerners," *Arab Journal of the Social Sciences,* April 1988, pp. 139–149.

31. Sheryl WuDunn, "In Japan, Still Getting Tea and No Sympathy," *New York Times,* August 27, 1995, Section E, p. 3.

32. Fathi S. Yousef, "Cross-Cultural Communication: Aspects of the Contrastive Social Values between North Americans and Middle Easterners," *Human Organization,* Winter 1974, p. 385.

33. Robert A. Guth, "Knowing Art of Deal Makes Japanese Banker a Commodity," *Wall Street Journal,* September 29, 2000, pp. C1, C16.

34. R. Bruce Money, "Word-of-Mouth Referral Sources for Buyers of International Corporate Financial Services," *Journal of World Business,* Vol. 35, No. 3, 2000, pp. 314–329.

35. Yousef, *"Cross-Cultural Communication,"* p. 383.

36. See Roger E. Axtell (ed.), *Dos and Taboos around the World* (New York: Wiley, 1990), Chapter 2.

37. Jane Whitney Gibson, Richard M. Hodgetts, and Charles W. Blackwell, "Cultural Variations in Nonverbal Communication," *55th Annual Business Communication Proceedings,* San Antonio, November 8–10, 1990, pp. 211–229.

38. William K. Brandt and James M. Hulbert, "Patterns of Communications in the Multinational Corporation: An Empirical Study," *Journal of International Business Studies,* Spring 1976, pp. 57–64.

39. Hildebrandt, "Communication Barriers," p. 9.

40. See for example George Ming-Hong Lai, "Knowing Who You Are Doing Business with in Japan: A Managerial View of Keiretsu and Keiretsu Business Groups," *Journal of World Business,* Vol. 34, No. 4, 1999, pp. 423–449.

41. Nicholas Athanassiou and Douglas Nigh, "Internationalization, Tacit Knowledge and the Top Management Teams of MNCs," *Journal of International Business Studies,* Third Quarter 2000, pp. 471–487.

42. Also see Linda Beamer, "Bridging Business Cultures," *China Business Review,* May/June 1998, pp. 54-58.

43. Michael D. Lord and Annette L. Ranft, "Organizational Learning about New International Markets: Exploring the Internal Transfer of Local Market Knowledge," *Journal of International Business Studies,* Fourth Quarter 2000, pp. 573–589.

44. Jennifer W. Spencer, "Knowledge Flows in the Global Innovation System: Do U.S. Firms Share More Scientific Knowledge than Their Japanese Rivals?" *Journal of International Business Studies,* Third Quarter 2000, pp. 521–530.

45. Kenichi Ohmae, "The Global Logic of Strategic Alliances," *Harvard Business Review,* March–April 1989, p. 154.

Chapter 9 Endnotes

1. Neel Chowdhury, "Can Citibank Crack the China Market?" *Fortune,* September 18, 2000, pp. 222–228.

2. Trevor Merriden, "U.S. Investments in Europe," *Management Review,* July/August 1998, p. 26.

3. Fara Warner, "Ford Uses Aggressive Marketing Approach in Thailand," *Wall Street Journal,* June 3, 1998, p. B4.

4. G. Bruce Knecht, "Bertelsmann Breaks through a Great Wall with Its Book Clubs," *Wall Street Journal,* September 18, 1998, pp. A1, 6.

5. For more on this company see Jack Ewing, "Can Bertelsmann Take Wing?" *Business Week,* February 7, 2000, pp. 54–55.

6. Jack Ewing, "Siemens Climbs Back," *Business Week,* June 5, 2000, p. 79.

7. Christopher Rhoades, "Low-Key GE Capital Expands in Europe," *Wall Street Journal,* September 17, 1998, p. A18.

8. www.gecapital.com.

9. Anant R. Negandhi, *International Management* (Boston: Allyn & Bacon, 1987), p. 230.

10. James M. Hulbert and William K. Brandt, *Managing the Multinational Subsidiary* (New York: Holt, Rinehart and Winston, 1980), pp. 35–64.

11. Noel Capon, Chris Christodoulou, John U. Farley, and James Hulbert, "A Comparison of Corporate Planning Practice in American and Australian Manufacturing Companies," *Journal of International Business Studies,* Fall 1984, pp. 41–45.

12. Martin K. Welge, "Planning in German Multinational Corporations," *International Studies of Management and Organization,* Spring 1982, pp. 6–37.

13. Martin K. Welge and Michael E. Kenter, "Impact of Planning on Control Effectiveness and Company Performance," *Management International Review,* vol. 20, no. 2, 1988, pp. 4–15.

14. See for example Masaaki Kotabe, "Global Sourcing Strategy in the Pacific: American and Japanese Multinational Companies," in Michael R. Czinkota and Masaaki Kotabe (eds.), *Trends in International Business: Critical Perspectives* (Malden, MA: Blackwell Publishing, 1998), pp. 237–256.

15. Joan Magretta, "Fast, Global, and Entrepreneurial: Supply Chain Management, Hong Kong Style," *Harvard Business Review,* September–October 1998, p. 108.

16. Nikhil Deogun, "For Coke in India, Thums Up Is the Real Thing," *Wall Street Journal,* April 29, 1998, pp. B1, 6.

17. Richard M. Hodgetts, *Measures of Quality and High Performance* (New York: American Management Association, 1998).

18. Sang M. Lee, Fred Luthans, and Richard M. Hodgetts, "Total Quality Management: Implications for Central and Eastern Europe," *Organizational Dynamics,* Spring 1992, pp. 44–45.

19. Miki Tanikawa, "Nissan's Head Says Revival Is a Success," *New York Times,* May 18, 2001, p. W1.

20. Christine Y. Chen, "How Nortel Stole Optical," *Fortune,* October 2, 2000, p. 144.

21. Thomas Carlgren, "How Swede It Is," *Forbes,* July 24, 2000, p. 56.

22. Quentin Hardy, "Motorola, Broadsided by the Digital Era, Struggles for a Footing," *Wall Street Journal,* April 22, 1998, p. A1, 14.

23. Mark Tatge, "Major Hang Up," *Forbes,* March 5, 2001, pp. 70–72.

24. Jonathan Friedland and Louise Lee, "The Wal-Mart Way Sometimes Gets Lost in Translation Overseas," *Wall Street Journal,* October 8, 1997, p. A12.

25. Michael Flagg, "U.S. Firm to Pioneer China's Interactive TV," *Wall Street Journal,* May 15, 2001, p. A21.

26. Rebecca Buckman, "Microsoft Buys 60% of Japan's No. 2 Cable Firm," *Wall Street Journal,* April 12, 2000, p. B5.

27. Scott Miller, "Ford Trims Its Capacity in Europe," *Wall Street Journal,* May 15, 2000, pp. A25, A28.

28. Scott Miller, "Enough Already: Ford of Europe Means to Find Its Footing," *Wall Street Journal,* August 11, 2000, p. A12.

29. Sea Jin Chang, "International Expansion Strategy of Japanese Firms: Capacity Building Through Sequential Entry," *Academy of Management Journal,* April 1995, p. 402.

30. David A. Andelman, "Merging across Borders," *Management Review,* June 1998, p. 45.

31. Jathon Sapsford, "Real-Estate Buyers Circle Japan," *Wall Street Journal,* March 11, 1998, p. B10.

32. Graham Gori, "Investors Are Rushing to Mexico, Despite Slowing Growth," *New York Times,* May 25, 2001, p. W1.

33. Craig Torres, "Foreigners Snap Up Mexican Companies: Impact Is Enormous," *Wall Street Journal,* September 30, 1997, p. A1.

34. John Garland and Richard N. Farmer, *International Dimensions of Business Policy and Strategy* (Boston: Kent Publishing, 1986), pp. 62–63.

35. Harry I. Chernotsky, "Selecting U.S. Sites: A Case Study of German and Japanese Firms," *Management International Review,* vol. 23, no. 2, 1983, pp. 45–55.

36. Also see Roland Calori, Leif Melin, Tugrul Atamer, and Peter Gustavsson, "Innovative International Strategies," *Journal of World Business,* vol. 35, no. 4, 2000, pp. 333–354.

37. Christos Pantzalis, "Does Location Matter? An Empirical Analysis of Geographic Scope and MNC Market Valuation," *Journal of International Business Studies,* First Quarter 2001, pp. 133–155.

38. Ian Johnson, "China's Venture Ban Could Cost Foreign Firms," *Wall Street Journal,* September 23, 1998, p. A14; and Elisabeth Rosenthal, "U.S. Trade Official Says China Market Is Closed Tighter," *New York Times,* September 23, 1998, p. C2.

39. Youssef M. Ibrahim, "British Petroleum Is Buying Amoco in $48.2 Billion Deal," *New York Times,* August 12, 1998, pp. A1, C5; and Charles Goldsmith and Steven Lipin, "BP to Acquire Amoco in a Huge Deal Spurred by Falling Oil Prices," *Wall Street Journal,* August 12, 1998, pp. A1, 8.

40. Keith Bradsher, "Industry's Giants Are Carving Up the World's Market," *New York Times,* May 8, 1998, pp. C1, 4; and Robyn Meredith, "A Joining of Opposites Could Help Customers," *New York Times,* May 8, 1998, p. C4.

41. Bill Vlasic and Bradley A. Stertz, "Taken for a Ride," *Business Week,* June 5, 2000, pp. 84–92.

42. Harry G. Barkema and Freek Vermeulen, "International Expansion through Start-up or Acquisition: A Learning Perspective," *Academy of Management Journal,* February 1998, pp. 7–26.

43. For additional insights to joint ventures see William Newbury and Yoram Zeira, "General Differences between Equity International Joint Ventures (EIJVs), International Acquisitions (IAs) and International Greenfield Investments (IGIs): Implications for Parent Companies," *Journal of World Business,* vol. 32, no. 2, 1997, pp. 87–102.

44. Also see David Lei, Robert A. Pitts, and John W. Slocum, Jr., "Building Cooperative Advantage: Managing Strategic Alliances to Promote Organizational Learning," *Journal of World Business,* vol. 32, no. 3, 1997, pp. 203–222.

45. For more on this see Ana Valdes Llaneza and Esteban Garcia-Canal, "Distinctive Features of Domestic and International Joint Ventures," *Management International Review,* vol. 38, no. 1, 1998, pp. 49–66.

46. Kevin J. Delaney, "Alcatel and Fujitsu Plan to Create a Joint Venture," *Wall Street Journal,* May 3, 2000, p. A23.

47. John B. Cullen, Jean L. Johnson, and Tomoaki Sakano, "Success Through Commitment and Trust: The Soft Side of Strategic Alliance Management," *Journal of World Business,* vol. 35, no. 3, 2000, pp. 223–240.

48. Khanh T. L. Tran and Julia Angwin, "Sony, AOL Join Up to Link PlayStation 2 to Internet in Move to Outflank Microsoft," *Wall Street Journal,* May 15, 2000, p. A3.

49. M. Tina Dacin, Edward Levitas, and Michael A. Hitt, "Selecting Partners for Successful International Alliances: Examination of U.S. and Korean Firms," *Journal of World Business,* vol. 32, no. 1, 1997, pp. 14–15.

50. For more on this see Donald F. Kuratko and Richard M. Hodgetts, *Entrepreneurship: A Contemporary Approach,* 5th edition (Ft. Worth, TX: Harcourt, 2001), pp. 529–535.

51. Das Narayandas, John Quelch, and Gordon Swartz, "Prepare Your Company for Global Pricing," *Sloan Management Review,* Fall 2000, pp. 61–70.

Chapter 10 Endnotes

1. Douglas Frantz, "Turkey Tries to Step Up Sell-Off of State Companies," *New York Times,* January 19, 2001, p. W1.

2. Seth Faison, "China Applies Brakes on Move toward Market Economy," *New York Times,* September 30, 1998, p. C3.

3. Dexter Roberts, Frederik Balfour, Paul Magnusson, Peer Engardio, and Jennifer Lee, "China's Piracy Plague," *Business Week,* June 5, 2000, pp. 44–48.

4. Benjamin Fulford, "Microwave Missionaries," *Forbes,* November 13, 2000, p. 146.

5. Jennifer Lee, "China's Censor Is Customer No. 1," *New York Times,* August 17, 2000, pp. C1, C8.

6. Jesse Wong and Peter Wonacott, "In Hong Kong: Persuasion or Pressure?" *Wall Street Journal,* July 21, 2000, pp. A8, A9.

7. Elisabeth Rosenthal, "U.S. Trade Official Says China Market Is Closed Tighter," *New York Times,* September 23, 1998, p. C2.

8. Jonathan Karp, "Indian's Legal System Bedevils Foreigners," *Wall Street Journal,* July 11, 1997, p. A10.

9. Mark Landler, "Back to Vietnam, This Time to Build," *New York Times,* September 13, 1998, section 3, pp. 1, 11.

10. Seth Mydans, "Bump in Hanoi's Capitalist Road: Jockeying in U.S. Congress," *New York Times,* May 8, 2001, p. A6.

11. Chris Adams, "Ailing Steel Industry Launches a Battle Against Imports," *Wall Street Journal,* October 1, 1998, p. B4; and Chris Adams, "U.S. Steelmakers to File Trade Complaint," *Wall Street Journal,* September 29, 1998, p. A2.

12. David Stout, "Agency Rejects High Duties on Imported Steel," *New York Times,* March 4, 2000, pp. B1, B2.

13. Michael M. Phillips, "WTO Rules Against U.S. Dumping Law," *Wall Street Journal,* June 7, 2000, p. A2.

14. Betsy McKay and Brandon Mitchener, "EC Raids Coke Bottlers in Antitrust Investigation," *Wall Street Journal,* May 19, 2000, p. A3.

15. Edmund L. Andrews, "Why U.S. Giants Are Crying Uncle," *New York Times,* October 11, 2000, p. W1.

16. David A. Schmidt, "Analyzing Political Risk," *Business Horizons,* July–August 1986, pp. 43–50.

17. Matthew Brzezinski, "Russia Kills Huge Oil Deal with Exxon," *Wall Street Journal,* August 28, 1997, p. A2.

18. For more, see Thomas A. Pointer, "Political Risk: Managing Government Intervention," in Paul W. Beamish, J. Peter Killing, Donald J. LeCraw, and Harold Crookell (eds.), *International Management: Text and Cases* (Homewood, IL: Irwin, 1991), pp. 119–133.

19. Elise Campbell and Jeffrey J. Reuer, "International Alliance Negotiations: Legal Issues for General Managers," *Business Horizons,* January–February 2001, pp. 19–26.

20. David K. Tse, June Francis, and Ian Walls, "Cultural Differences in Conducting Intra- and Inter-Cultural Negotiations: A Sino-Canadian Comparison," *Journal of International Business Studies,* Third Quarter 1994, pp. 537–555.

21. Nancy J. Adler, *International Dimensions of Organizational Behavior,* 2nd ed. (Boston: PWS-Kent Publishing, 1991), p. 197.

22. Jeanne M. Brett, Debra L. Shapiro, and Anne L. Lytle, "Breaking the Bonds of Reciprocity in Negotiations," *Academy of Management Journal,* August 1998, pp. 410–424.

23. Stephen E. Weiss, "Negotiating with 'Romans'—Part 2," *Sloan Management Review,* Spring 1994, p. 89.

24. Fons Trompenaars and Charles Hampden-Turner, *Riding the Waves of Culture: Understanding Diversity in Global Business,* 2nd ed. (New York: McGraw-Hill, 1998), p. 112.

25. John L. Graham, "Brazilian, Japanese, and American Business Negotiations," *Journal of International Business Studies,* Spring/Summer 1983, pp. 47–61; John L. Graham, "The Influence of Culture on the Process of Business Negotiations in an Exploratory Study," *Journal of International Business Studies,* Spring 1983, pp. 81–96.

26. *Ibid.,* pp. 84, 88.

Chapter 11 Endnotes

1. Roger O. Crockett, "Chris Galvin Shakes Things Up—Again," *Business Week,* May 28, 2001, pp. 38–39.

2. Christopher Rhoads, "A Contrarian Motorola Picks Germany," *Wall Street Journal,* October 10, 1997, p. A18.

3. Craig S. Smith, "Motorola Expands Operations in China," *Wall Street Journal,* June 12, 1998, p. A9.

4. William Echikson and Dean Foust, "For Coke, Local Is It," *Business Week,* July 3, 2000, p. 122.

5. Norihiko Shirouzu, "Driven By Necessity—And by Ford—Mazda Downsizes, U.S. Style," *Wall Street Journal,* January 5, 2000, pp. A1, A8.

6. Joan Magretta, "Fast, Global, and Entrepreneurial: Supply Chain Management, Hong Kong Style," *Harvard Business Review,* September–October 1998, p. 106.

7. See George S. Yip, *Total Global Strategy* (Englewood Cliffs, NJ: Prentice-Hall, 1995), Chapter 8.

8. A. V. Phatak, *International Dimensions of Management,* 2nd ed. (Boston: PWS-Kent, 1989), pp. 92–93.

9. Karby Leggett, "France's Alcatel Plans to Set Up Asian Headquarters in Shanghai," *Wall Street Journal,* January 18, 2000, p. A23.

10. Robert A. Guth, "Sony of Japan Announces Yet Another Restructuring," *Wall Street Journal,* March 30, 2001, p. A13.

11. Reported in Peter J. Dowling, Randall S. Schuler, and Denice E. Welch, *International Dimensions of Human Resource Management,* 2nd ed. (Belmont, CA: Wadsworth Publishing, 1994), p. 33.

12. John Tagliabue, "Renault Agrees to Buy Troubled Samsung Motors of Korea," *New York Times,* April 22, 2000, pp. B1, B3.

13. Stephanie Strom, "DaimlerChrysler Buying a Third of Mitsubishi for $2.1 Billion," *New York Times,* March 28, 2000, p. C4.

14. Also see Andrew C. Inkpen and Adva Dinur, "Knowledge Management Processes and International Joint Ventures," *Organization Science,* July–August 1998, pp. 454–468.

15. See for example Hemant Merchant, "Configurations of International Joint Ventures," *Management International Review,* vol. 40, no. 2, 2000, pp. 107–140.

16. Pien Wang, Chow Hou Wee, and Peck Hiong Koh, "Establishing A Successful Sino-Foreign Equity Joint Venture: The Singapore Experience," *Journal of World Business,* vol. 34, no. 3, 1999, pp. 287–306.

17. Gus Gordon and Thurmon Williams, "How Do You Spell Success in Mexico? CALICA," *Business Horizons,* January–February 2001, pp. 11–18.

18. Matthew Schifrin, "Partner or Perish," *Forbes,* May 21, 2001, p. 27.

19. Seth Faison, "Morgan Stanley Establishes a Joint Venture in China," *New York Times,* August 12, 1995, p. 18.

20. For some insights regarding the importance of networking, see "The Battle for Ukraine," *Economist,* February 11, 1995, p. 56.

21. Miki Tanikawa, "Electronics Giants Join Forces in Japan," *New York Times,* May 24, 2001, p. W1.

22. Also see Eric W. K. Tsang, "A Preliminary Typology of Learning in International Strategic Alliances," *Journal of World Business,* vol. 34, no. 3, 1999, pp. 211–229.

23. Kevin J. Delaney, "IBM Signs Outsourcing Contracts in Europe with Value in Billions," *Wall Street Journal,* May 24, 2001, p. B12.

24. Kerry A. Dolan, "The Irish Way," *Forbes,* May 21, 2001, p. 46.

25. Schifrin, "Partner or Perish," p. 27.

26. Thomas W. Malone and Robert J. Laubacher, "The Dawn of the E-Lance Economy," *Harvard Business Review,* September–October 1998, p. 148.

27. Julian Birkinshaw and Neil Hood, "Unleash Innovation in Foreign Subsidiaries," *Harvard Business Review,* March 2001, pp. 131–137.

28. For more on this see Michael Goold and Andrew Campbell, "Desperately Seeking Synergy," *Harvard Business Review,* September–October 1998, p. 133.

29. *Ibid.,* p. 134.

30. Durward K. Sobek, II, Jeffrey K. Liker, and Allen C. Ward, "Another Look at How Toyota Integrates Product Development," *Harvard Business Review,* July–August 1998, p. 49.

31. For more on this see M. Bensaou and Michael Earl, "The Right Mind-set for Managing Information Technology," *Harvard Business Review,* September–October 1998, pp. 119–128.

32. Anne-Wil Harzing, "An Empirical Analysis and Extension of the Bartlett and Ghoshal Typology of Multinational Companies," *Journal of International Business Studies,* First Quarter 2000, pp. 101–120.

33. Steven M. Sommers, Seung-Hyun Bae, and Fred Luthans, "The Structure-Climate Relationship in Korean Organizations," *Asia Pacific Journal of Management,* vol. 12, no. 2, 1995, pp. 23–36.

34. James R. Lincoln, Mitsuyo Hanada, and Kerry McBride, "Organizational Structures in Japanese and U.S. Manufacturing," *Administrative Science Quarterly,* September 1986, p. 356.

35. Rhy-song Yeh and Tagi Sagafi-nejad, "Organizational Characteristics of American and Japanese Firms in Taiwan," *National Academy of Management Proceedings,* 1987, pp. 111–115.

36. *Ibid.,* p. 113.

37. Abbass F. Alkhafaji, *Competitive Global Management: Principles and Strategies* (Delray Beach, FL: St. Lucie Press, 1995), pp. 390–391.

38. Michael Yoshino and N. S. Rangan, *Strategic Alliances* (Boston: Harvard Business School Press, 1995), p. 195.

39. For additional insights, see Anant K. Sundaram and J. Stewart Black, *The International Business Environment: Text and Cases* (Englewood Cliffs, NJ: Prentice-Hall, 1995), pp. 314–315.

40. Lincoln, Hanada, and McBride, "Organizational Structures," p. 349.

41. Justin Fox, "Nokia's Secret Code," *Fortune,* May 1, 2000, p. 170.

42. Mark Lehrer and Kazuhiro Asakawa, "Unbundling European Operations: Regional Management and Corporate Flexibility in American and Japanese MNCs," *Journal of World Business,* vol. 34, no. 3, 1999, pp. 267–286.

43. Masumi Tsuda, "The Future of the Organization and the Individual to Japanese Management," *International Studies of Management & Organization,* Fall–Winter 1985, pp. 89–125.

44. Yeh and Sagafi-nejad, "Organizational Characteristics," p. 113.

45. Also see Valerie Reitman, "Toyota Names a New Chief Likely to Shake Up Global Auto Business," *Wall Street Journal,* August 11, 1995, pp. A1, A4.

46. Tsuda, "The Future of the Organization," p. 114.

Chapter 12 Endnotes

1. Kathy Chen and Hilary Stout, "Boeing, GM Obtain China Agreements," *Wall Street Journal,* March 25, 1997, p. A3.

2. Bill Spindle, "Cowboys and Samurai: The Japanizing of Universal," *Wall Street Journal,* March 22, 2001, p. B6.

3. Jon E. Hilsenrath, "Ford Designs Ikon to Suit Indian Tastes," *The Globe and Mail,* August 8, 2000, p. B10.

4. Raghu Nath, *Comparative Management: A Regional View* (Cambridge, MA: Ballinger Publishing, 1988), p. 126.

5. *Ibid.,* pp. 74–75.

6. Noboru Yoshimura and Philip Anderson, *Inside the* Kaisha (Boston: Harvard Business School Press, 1997), p. 44.

7. Anant R. Negandhi, *International Management* (Boston: Allyn & Bacon, 1987), p. 193.

8. Sang M. Lee, Fred Luthans, and Richard M. Hodgetts, "Total Quality Management: Implications for Central and Eastern Europe," *Organizational Dynamics,* Spring 1992, p. 45.

9. Daewoo Park and Herna A. Krishnan, "Understanding Supplier Selection Practices: Differences Between U.S. and Korean Executives," *Thunderbird International Business Review,* March–April 2001, pp. 243–255.

10. For example, see Robert L. Simison and Michael Schuman, "Hyundai Gears Up for a Grueling Global Race," *Wall Street Journal,* March 13, 2000, A 23; and Robyn Meredith, "In Policy Shift, G.M. Will Rely On Alliances," *New York Times,* January 18, 2000, pp. C1, C14.

11. Joanne Lee-Young, "Starbucks' Expansion in China Is Slated," *Wall Street Journal,* October 5, 1998, p. A27C.

12. Frederick Balfour, "Back on the Radar Screen," *Business Week,* November 2000, p. 27.

13. Jon E. Hilsenrath, "U.S. Investors See Hope in Vietnam Trip," *Wall Street Journal,* November 17, 2000, p. A 17.

14. Benjamin Fulford, "Capitalism Creeps into Vietnam," *Forbes,* May 17, 1999, p. 176.

15. See Roy Rowan, "25 Years After the Fall," *Fortune,* May 1, 2000, pp. 208–222.

16. Rebecca Blumstein, "Cadillac Has Designs on Europe's Luxury Car Buyers," *Wall Street Journal,* September 9, 1997, p. B1.

17. Scott Miller, "BMW to Try Again in Small-Car Market," *Wall Street Journal,* November 24, 2000, p. A10.

18. Benjamin Fulford, "NEC Talks Invasion," *Forbes,* February 5, 2001, pp. 86–88.

19. Dan Goodin, "Intel Aims New Chips at High-End Market," *Wall Street Journal,* May 21, 2001, p. B9.

20. Dana Corporation, Annual Report 2000.

21. Robert L. Simison, "New Dana Illustrates Reshaping of Auto Parts Business," *Wall Street Journal,* September 2, 1997, p. B4.

22. For more on this system see Saul Hansell, "Is This the Factory of the Future?" *New York Times,* July 26, 1998, Section 3, pp. 1, 12–13.

23. Fons Trompenaars and Charles Hampden-Turner, Riding the Waves of Culture: *Understanding Diversity in Global Business,* 2nd ed. (New York: McGraw-Hill, 1998), pp. 157–159.

24. John D. Daniels and Jeffrey Arpan, "Comparative Home Country Influences on Management Practices Abroad," *Academy of Management Journal,* September 1972, p. 310.

25. Jacques H. Horovitz, "Management Control in France, Great Britain and Germany," *Columbia Journal of World Business,* Summer 1978, pp. 17–18.

26. *Ibid.,* p. 18.

27. William G. Egelhoff, "Patterns of Control in U.S., U.K., and European Multinational Corporations," *Journal of International Business Studies,* Fall 1984, p. 81.

28. *Ibid.,* pp. 81–82.

29. M. Kreder and M. Zeller, "Control in German and U.S. Companies," *Management International Review,* vol. 28, no. 3, 1988, pp. 64–65.

30. Lane Daley, James Jiambalvo, Gary L. Sundem, and Yasumasa Kondo, "Attitudes toward Financial Control Systems in the United States and Japan," *Journal of International Business Studies,* Fall 1985, pp. 91–110.

31. Yoshimura and Anderson, *Inside the* Kaisha, p. 55.

32. A. V. Phatak, *International Dimensions of Management,* 2nd ed. (Boston: PWS-Kent, 1989), p. 154.

33. Christopher Watts, "VW Misses Its Mark," *Forbes,* February 19, 2001, pp. 78, 80.

34. David A. Garvin, "Japanese Quality Management," *Columbia Journal of World Business,* Fall 1984, pp. 3–12.

35. *Ibid.,* p. 6.

36. Jeffrey K. Liker and Yen-Chun Wu, "Japanese Automakers, U.S. Suppliers and Supply-Chain Superiority," *Sloan Management Review,* Fall 2000, pp. 81–93.

37. Cited in John Holusha, "Improving Quality, the Japanese Way," *New York Times,* July 20, 1988, p. 25.

38. "Key To Success: People, People, People," *Fortune,* October 27, 1997, p. 232.

39. Golpira Eshgi, "Nationality Bias and Performance Evaluations in Multinational Corporations," *National Academy of Management Proceedings,* 1985, p. 95.

40. Jeremiah Sullivan, Terukiho Suzuki, and Yasumasa Kondo, "Managerial Theories and the Performance Control Process in Japanese and American Work Groups," *National Academy of Management Proceedings,* 1985, pp. 98–102.

41. *Ibid.*

Chapter 13 Endnotes

1. Abbass F. Alkhafaji, *Competitive Global Management* (Delray Beach, FL: St. Lucie Press, 1995), p. 118.

2. Nancy L. Adler, *International Dimensions of Organizational Behavior,* 2nd ed. (Boston: PWS-Kent, 1991), p. 160.

3. Dianne H. B. Welsh, Fred Luthans, and Steven Sommer, "Managing Russian Factory Workers: The Impact of U.S.-Based Behavioral and Participative Techniques," *Academy of Management Journal,* February 1993, p. 75.

4. Andrew Sergeant and Stephen Frenkel, "Managing People in China: Perceptions of Expatriate Managers," *Journal of World Business,* vol. 33, no. 1, 1998, p. 21.

5. Stephanie Strom, "A Surprising Jump in Japanese Joblessness," *New York Times,* April 29, 1998, p. C3.

6. For a more detailed discussion, see Fred Luthans, *Organizational Behavior,* 9th ed. (New York: Irwin/McGraw-Hill, 2002), Chapter 8.

7. A. H. Maslow, "A Theory of Human Motivation," *Psychological Review,* July 1943, pp. 390–396.

8. For more information on this topic, see Richard Mead, *International Management Cross-Cultural Dimensions* (Cambridge, MA: Blackwell Publishers, 1994), pp. 209–212.

9. See Richard M. Hodgetts, *Modern Human Relations at Work,* 8th ed. (Hinsdale, IL: Dryden press, 2002), Chapter 2.

10. Mason Haire, Edwin E. Ghiselli, and Lyman W. Porter, *Managerial Thinking: An International Study* (New York: John Wiley & Sons, 1966).

11. *Ibid.,* p. 75.

12. Edwin C. Nevis, "Cultural Assumption and Productivity: The United States and China," *Sloan Management Review,* Spring 1983, pp. 17–29.

13. Geert H. Hofstede, "The Colors of Collars," *Columbia Journal of World Business,* September 1972, pp. 72–78.

14. *Ibid.,* p. 72.

15. George H. Hines, "Cross-Cultural Differences in Two-Factor Motivation Theory," *Journal of Applied Psychology,* December 1973, p. 376.

16. Donald D. White and Julio Leon, "The Two-Factor Theory: New Questions, New Answers," *National Academy of Management Proceedings,* 1976, p. 358.

17. D. Macarov, "Work Patterns and Satisfactions in an Israeli Kibbutz: A Test of the Herzberg Hypothesis," *Personnel Psychology,* Autumn 1972, p. 492.

18. Peter D. Machungwa and Neal Schmitt, "Work Motivation in a Developing Country," *Journal of Applied Psychology,* February 1983, pp. 31–42.

19. G. E. Popp, H. J. Davis, and T. T. Herbert, "An International Study of Intrinsic Motivation Composition," *Management International Review,* vol. 26, no. 3, 1986, pp. 28–35.

20. Also see Rabi S. Bhagat et al., "Cross-Cultural Issues in Organizational Psychology: Emergent Trends and Directions for Research in the 1990s," in C. L. Cooper and I. Robertson (eds.), *International Review of Industrial and Organizational Psychology* (New York: John Wiley & Sons, 1990), p. 76.

21. Rabindra N. Kanungo and Richard W. Wright, "A Cross-Cultural Comparative Study of Managerial Job Attitudes," *Journal of International Business Studies,* Fall 1983, pp. 115–129.

22. *Ibid.,* pp. 127–128.

23. Fred Luthans, "A Paradigm Shift in Eastern Europe: Some Helpful Management Development Techniques," *Journal of Management Development,* vol. 12, no. 8, 1993, pp. 53–60.

24. For more information on the characteristics of high achievers, see David C. McClelland, "Business Drive and National Achievement," *Harvard Business Review,* July–August 1962, pp. 99–112.

25. For more detail on the achievement motive, see Luthans, *Organizational Behavior,* pp. 253–256.

26. S. Iwawaki and R. Lynn, "Measuring Achievement Motivation in Japan and Great Britain," *Journal of Cross-Cultural Psychology,* vol. 3, 1999, pp. 219–220.

27. For more on this see J. C. Abegglen and G. Stalk, *Kaisha: The Japanese Corporation* (New York: Basic Books, 1985); and R. M. Steers, Y. K. Shin, and G. R. Ungson, *The Chaebol: Korea's New Industrial Might* (New York: McGraw-Hill, 1989).

28. Fred Luthans, Brooke R. Envick, and Mary F. Sully, "Characteristics of Successful Entrepreneurs: Do They Fit the Cultures of Developing Countries?" *Proceedings of the Pan Pacific Conference,* 1995, pp. 25–27.

29. For an earlier example of similar findings using sample groups of male Australian MBA candidates and University of California-Berkeley MBA candidates, see Theodore T. Herbert, Gary E. Popp, and Herbert J. Davis, "Australian Work-Reward Preferences," *National Academy of Management Proceedings,* 1979, pp. 289–292.

30. These data were reported in David C. McClelland, *The Achieving Society* (Princeton, NJ: Van Nostrand, 1961), p. 294.

31. E. J. Murray, *Motivation and Emotion* (Englewood Cliffs, NJ: Prentice-Hall, 1964), p. 101.

32. David J. Krus and Jane A. Rysberg, "Industrial Managers and N ach: Comparable and Compatible?" *Journal of Cross-Cultural Psychology,* December 1976, pp. 491–496.

33. Oded Shenkar and Simcha Ronen, "Structure and Importance of Work Goals among Managers in the People's Republic of China," *Academy of Management Journal,* September 1987, pp. 564–576.

34. Chao C. Chen, "New Trends in Rewards Allocation Preferences: A Sino-U.S. Comparison," *Academy of Management Journal,* April 1995, p. 425.

35. Jean Lee and Havihn Chan, "Chinese Entrepreneurship: A Study in Singapore," *Journal of Management Development,* vol. 17, no. 2, 1998, p. 139.

36. Erik Guyot, Christina Mungan, and Richard Borsuk, "Streamlined Singapore Gives Hong Kong a Run for the Big Money," *Wall Street Journal,* November 19, 1998, p. A19.

37. David C. McClelland, "Achievement Motivation Can Be Developed," *Harvard Business Review,* November–December 1965, p. 20.

38. Geert Hofstede, "Motivation, Leadership, and Organization: Do American Theories Apply Abroad?" *Organizational Dynamics,* Summer 1980, pp. 55–56.

39. For more on this see Richard M. Steers and Carlos J. Sanchez-Runde, "Culture, Motivation, and Work Behavior" in Martin J. Gannon and Karen L. Newman (eds.), *Handbook of Cross-Cultural Management* (London: Basil Blackwell, 2002).

40. E. Yuchtman, "Reward Distribution and Work-Role Attractiveness in the Kubbutz: Reflections on Equity Theory," *American Sociological Review,* vol. 37, 1972, pp. 581–595.

41. R. M. Steers, S. J. Bischoff, and L. H. Higgins, "Cross-Cultural Management Research: The Fish and the Fisherman," *Journal of Management Inquiry,* vol. 1, 1992, pp. 321–330; and Ken I. Kim, Hun-Joon Park, and Nori Suzuki, "Reward Allocations in the U.S., Japan, and Korea: A Comparison of Individualistic and Collectivistic Cultures," *Academy of Management Journal,* March 1990, pp. 188–198.

42. Fred Luthans, *Organizational Behavior,* 9th edition (Burr Ridge, IL: Irwin/McGraw, 2002), p. 520.

43. Edwin A. Locke and Gary P. Latham, *A Theory of Goal-Setting and Task Performance* (Englewood Cliffs, NJ: Prentice-Hall, 1990).

44. M. Erez, "The Congruence of Goal-Setting Strategies with Socio-Cultural Values and Its Effect on Performance," *Journal of Management,* vol. 12, 1986, pp. 585–592.

45. J. P. French, J. Israel, and D. As, "An Experiment in a Norwegian Factory: Interpersonal Dimension in Decision-Making," *Human Relations,* vol. 13, 1960, pp. 3–19.

46. P. C. Earley, "Supervisors and Shop Stewards as Sources of Contextual Information in Goal-Setting," *Journal of Applied Psychology,* vol. 71, 1986, pp. 111–118.

47. M. Erez and P. C. Earley, "Comparative Analysis of Goal-Setting Strategies Across Cultures," *Journal of Applied Psychology,* vol. 72, no. 4, 1987, pp. 658–665.

48. Victor Vroom, *Work and Motivation* (New York: Wiley, 1964).

49. Lyman W. Porter and Edward E. Lawler, III, *Managerial Attitudes and Performance* (Homewood, IL: Irwin, 1968).

50. Dov Eden, "Intrinsic and Extrinsic Rewards and Motives: Replication and Extension with Kibbutz Workers," *Journal of Applied Social Psychology,* vol. 5, 1975, pp. 348–361.

51. T. Matsui, T. Kakuyama, and M. L. Onglatco, "Effects of Goals and Feedback on Performance in Groups," *Journal of Applied Psychology,* vol. 72, 1987, pp. 407–415.

52. For a systematic analysis of this and other myths of Japanese management, see Richard M. Hodgetts and Fred Luthans, "Japanese HR Management Practices," *Personnel,* April 1989, pp. 42–45.

53. "Japanese Employers Are 'Locking Out' Their U.S. Managers," *Business Week,* May 7, 1990, p. 24.

54. For more on this topic, see Noel M. Tichy and Thore Sandstrom, "Organizational Innovations in Sweden," *Columbia Journal of World Business,* Summer 1974, pp. 18–28.

55. Almar Latour, "Volvo Plans to Lay Off Workers," *Wall Street Journal,* November 18, 1998, p. A17.

56. "Product Innovation Gains Worldwide Importance," *HR Focus,* March 1992, p. 12.

57. Eric Sundstrom, Kenneth P. DeMeuse, and David Futrell, "Work Teams: Application and Effectiveness," *American Psychologist,* February 1990, pp. 120–133.

58. Thomas A. Stewart, "The Search for the Organization of Tomorrow," *Fortune,* May 18, 1992, p. 95.

59. See Lillian H. Chaney and Jeanette S. Martin, *Intercultural Business Communication* (Englewood Cliffs, NJ: Prentice-Hall, 1995), pp. 46–47.

60. Bhagat et al., "Cross-Cultural Issues," p. 72.

61. Stephanie Strom, "Japan's New 'Temp' Workers," *New York Times,* June 17, 1998, p. 4; and Steven Greenhouse, "Report Shows Americans Have More Labor Days," *New York Times,* September 1, 2001, p. A6.

62. Gene Koretz, "Why Americans Work So Hard," *Business Week,* June 11, 2001, p. 34.

63. Howard W. French, "A Postmodern Plague Ravages Japan's Workers," *New York Times,* February 21, 2000, p. A4.

64. "Satisfaction in the USA, Unhappiness in Japanese Offices," *Personnel,* January 1992, p. 8.

65. Fred Luthans, Harriette S. McCaul, and Nancy G. Dodd, "Organizational Commitment: A Comparison of American, Japanese, and Korean Employees," *Academy of Management Journal,* March 1985, pp. 213–219.

66. For other research on this topic see Shahid N. Bhuian, Eid S. Al-Shammari, and Omar A. Jefri, "Work-Related Attitudes and Job Characteristics of Expatriates in Saudi Arabia," *Thunderbird International Business Review,* January–February 2001, pp. 21–31.

67. David I. Levine, "What Do Wages Buy?" *Administrative Science Quarterly,* September 1993, pp. 462–483.

68. David Heming, "What Wages Buy in the U.S. and Japan," *Academy of Management Executive,* November 1994, pp. 88–89.

69. Andrew Kakabadse and Andrew Myers, "Qualities of Top Management: Comparisons of European Manufacturers," *Journal of Management Development,* vol. 14, no. 1, 1995, p. 6.

70. Steven M. Sommer, Seung-Hyun Bae, and Fred Luthans, "Organizational Commitment across Cultures: The Impact of Antecedents on Korean Employees," *Human Relations,* 1996, vol. 49, no. 7, pp. 977–993.

71. Anders Tornvall, "Work-Values in Japan: Work and Work Motivation in a Comparative Setting," in Pat Joynt and Malcolm Warner, (eds.), *Managing across Cultures: Issues and Perspectives* (London: International Thomson Business Press, 1996), p. 256.

72. Stephen Kerr, "Practical, Cost-Neutral Alternatives That You May Know, but Don't Practice," *Organizational Dynamics,* Summer 1999, pp. 61–70.

73. Joel Millman, "Mexico Is Perk Paradise for U.S. Middle Managers," *Wall Street Journal,* May 23, 2000, pp. B1, B18.

74. See for example Geoff Winestock, "Social Security Reform Rocks the World," *Wall Street Journal,* October 30, 2000, p. A21.

75. In the case of money, for example, see Swee Hoon Ang, "The Power of Money: A Cross-Cultural Analysis of Business-Related Beliefs," *Journal of World Business,* vol. 35, no. 1, 2000, pp. 43–60.

76. J. Milliman, S. Nason, M. A. von Glinow, P. Hou, K. B. Lowe, and N. Kim, "In Search of 'Best' Strategies Pay Practices: An Exploratory Study of Japan, Korea, Taiwan, and the United States," in S. B. Prasad (ed.), *Advances in International Comparative Management* (Greenwich, CT: JAI Press, 1995), pp. 227–252.

77. Louis Lavelle, "Executive Pay," *Business Week,* April 16, 2001, pp. 76–80.

78. S. C. Schneider, S. A. Wittenberg-Cox, and L. Hansen, *Honeywell Europe* (Insead, 1991).

79. C. M. Vance, S. R. McClaine, D. M. Boje, and H. D. Stage, "An Examination of the Transferability of Traditional Performance Appraisal Principles Across Cultural Boundaries," *Management International Review,* vol. 32, no. 4, 1992, pp. 313–326.

80. David Sirota and J. Michael Greenwood, "Understand Your Overseas Workforce," *Harvard Business Review,* January–February 1971, pp. 53–60.

81. D. E. Sanger, "Performance Related Pay in Japan," *International Herald Tribune,* October 5, 1993, p. 20.

82. S. H. Nam, "Culture, Control, and Commitment in International Joint Ventures," *International Journal of Human Resource Management,* vol. 6, 1995, pp. 553–567.

83. Dianne H. B. Welsh, Fred Luthans, and Steven Sommer, "Managing Russian Factory Workers: The Impact of U.S.-Based Behavioral and Participative Techniques," *Academy of Management Journal,* February 1993, pp. 58–79.

84. Anita Raghavan and G. Thomas Sims, "'Golden Parachutes' Emerge in European Deals," *Wall Street Journal,* February 14, 2000, pp. A17, 18.

85. Susan C. Schneider and Jean-Louis Barsoux, *Managing across Cultures* (London: Prentice-Hall, 1997).

Chapter 14 Endnotes

1. Richard M. Hodgetts, *Modern Human Relations at Work,* 8th ed. (Ft. Worth: Harcourt, 2002), p. 255. Also see Daniel Goleman, "What Makes a Leader?" *Harvard Business Review,* November–December 1998, pp. 93–102.

2. Douglas McGregor, *The Human Side of Enterprise* (New York: McGraw-Hill, 1960), pp. 33–34.

3. Ibid., pp. 47–48.

4. See Nancy J. Adler, *International Dimensions of Organizational Behavior,* 2nd ed. (Boston: PWS-Kent, 1991), p. 150.

5. Sheila M. Puffer, Daniel J. McCarthy, and Alexander I. Naumov, "Russian Managers' Beliefs about Work: Beyond the Stereotypes," *Journal of World Business,* vol. 32, no. 3, 1997, pp. 258–276.

6. For other insights into this area see Manfred F. R. Kets de Vries, "A Journey into the 'Wild West': Leadership Style and Organizational Practices in Russia," *Organizational Dynamics,* Spring 2000, pp. 67–80.

7. See Alex Taylor III, "Can the Germans Rescue Chrysler?" *Fortune,* April 30, 2001, pp. 106–112; Holmman W. Jenkins, Jr., "The Limits of Schremppism," *Wall Street Journal,* December 6, 2000, p. A23; and Edmund L. Andrews, "No Apologies from Stuttgart," *New York Times,* December 2, 2000, pp. B1, B2.

8. Hae Won Choi, "Daewoo's CEO Is Sad He Had to Lay Off Members of the Family," *Wall Street Journal,* June 26, 2001, pp. A1, A14.

9. Karen Lowry Miller, "The Toughest Job in Europe," *Business Week,* October 9, 1995, pp. 52–53.

10. See for example Uta Harnischfeger, "Unions Reject Innovative Pay Scheme at VW," *Financial Times,* June 27, 2001, p. 3.

11. Mason Haire, Edwin E. Ghiselli, and Lyman W. Porter, *Managerial Thinking: An International Study* (New York: John Wiley & Sons, 1966).

12. Ibid., p. 21.

13. James R. Lincoln, Mitsuyo Hanada, and Jon Olson, "Cultural Orientation and Individual Reactions to Organizations: A Study of Employees of Japanese-Owned Firms," *Administrative Science Quarterly,* March 1981, pp. 93–115; also see Karen Lowry Miller, "Land of the Rising Jobless," *Business Week,* January 11, 1993, p. 47.

14. Sangjin Yoo and Sang M. Lee, "Management Style and Practice of Korean Chaebols," *California Management Review,* Summer 1987, pp. 95–110.

15. Haire, Ghiselli, and Porter, *Managerial Thinking,* p. 29.

16. Noboru Yoshimura and Philip Anderson, *Inside the* Kaisha (Boston: Harvard University Press, 1997), p. 167.

17. Haire Ghiselli, and Porter, *Managerial Thinking*, p. 140.

18. *Ibid.*, p. 157.

19. For more on this topic, see Edgar H. Schein, "SMR Forum: Does Japanese Management Style Have a Message for American Managers?" *Sloan Management Review*, Fall 1981, p. 55–68.

20. Jeremiah J. Sullivan and Ikujiro Nonaka, "The Application of Organizational Learning Theory to Japanese and American Management," *Journal of International Business Studies*, Fall 1986, pp. 127–147.

21. *Ibid.*, pp. 130–131.

22. Iyuji Misumi and Fumiyasu Seki, "Effects of Achievement Motivation on the Effectiveness of Leadership Patterns," *Administrative Science Quarterly*, March 1971, pp. 51–59.

23. Sang M. Lee, Sangjin Yoo, and Tosca M. Lee, "Korean Chaebols: Corporate Values and Strategies," *Organizational Dynamics*, Spring 1991, p. 41.

24. David A. Ralston, Carolyn P. Egri, Sally Stewart, Robert H. Terpstra, and Yu Kaicheng, "Doing Business in the 21st Century with the New Generation of Chinese Managers: A Study of Generational Shifts in Work Values in China," *Journal of International Business Studies*, Second Quarter 1999, pp. 415–428.

25. M. K. Badawy, "Managerial Attitudes and Need Orientations of Mid-Eastern Executives: An Empirical Cross-Cultural Analysis," *National Academy of Management Proceedings*, 1979, pp. 293–297.

26. *Ibid.*, p. 297.

27. Abdulrahman, Al-Jafary and A. T. Hollingsworth, "An Exploratory Study of Management Practices in the Arabian Gulf Region," *Journal of International Business Studies*, Fall 1983, pp. 143–152.

28. *Ibid.*

29. *Ibid.*, p. 146.

30. Haire, Ghiselli, and Porter, *Managerial Thinking*, p. 22.

31. Robert D. Meade, "An Experimental Study of Leadership in India," *Journal of Social Psychology*, June 1967, pp. 35–43.

32. Sudhir Kakar, "Authority Patterns and Subordinate Behavior in Indian Organizations," *Administrative Science Quarterly*, September 1971, pp. 298–307.

33. Bikki Jaggi, "Job Satisfaction and Leadership Style in Developing Countries: The Case of India," *International Journal of Contemporary Sociology*, October 1977, pp. 230–236.

34. *Ibid.*, p. 233.

35. Haire, Ghiselli, and Porter, *Managerial Thinking*, p. 22.

36. D. B. Stephens, "Cultural Variations in Leadership Style: A Methodological Experiment in Comparing Managers in the U.S. and Peruvian Textile Industries," *Management International Review*, vol. 21, no. 3, 1981, pp. 47–55.

37. *Ibid.*, p. 54.

38. Hodgetts, *Modern Human Relations at Work*, pp. 275–276.

39. Bernard M. Bass, "Is There Universality in the Full Range Model of Leadership?" *International Journal of Public Administration*, vol. 16, no. 6, 1996, p. 731.

40. *Ibid.*, pp. 741–742.

41. *Ibid.*, p. 731.

42. For additional insights to recent research by Bass and his associates, see Bruce J. Avolio and Bernard M. Bass, "You Can Drag a Horse to Water but You Can't Make It Drink Unless It Is Thirsty," *Journal of Leadership Studies*, Winter 1998, pp. 4–17.

43. Bass, "Is There Universality in the Full Range Model of Leadership?" pp. 754–755.

44. Ingrid Tollgertd-Andersson, "Attitudes, Values and Demands on Leadership—A Cultural Comparison Among Some European Countries," in Pat Joynt and Malcolm Warner (eds.), *Managing across Cultures* (London: International Thomson Business Press, 1996), p. 172.

45. *Ibid.*, p. 176.

46. Felix C. Brodbeck, *et al.*, "Cultural Variation of Leadership Prototypes Across 22 European Countries," *Journal of Occupational and Organizational Psychology*, vol. 73, 2000, pp. 1–29.

47. For more on culture and leadership see Jangho Lee, Thomas W. Roehl, and Soonkyoo Choe, "What Makes Management Style Similar and Distinct Across Borders? Growth, Experience and Culture in Korean and Japanese Firms," *Journal of International Business Studies*, Fourth Quarter, 2000, pp. 631–652; Uzoamaka P. Anakwe, Magid Igbaria, and Murugan Anandarajan, "Management Practices across Cultures: Role of Support in Technology Usage," *Journal of International Business Studies*, Fourth Quarter, 2000, pp. 653–666; and Graeme L. Harrison, Jill L. McKinnon, Anne Wu, and Chee W. Chow, "Cultural Influences on Adaptation to Fluid Workgroups and Teams," *Journal of International Business Studies*, Third Quarter, 2000, pp. 489–505.

48. Fons Trompenaars and Charles Hampden-Turner, *Riding the Waves of Culture: Understanding Diversity in Global Business*, 2nd ed. (New York: McGraw-Hill, 1998), p. 74.

49. *Ibid.*, p. 77.

Chapter 15 Endnotes

1. Also see Kenneth Groh and Mark Allen, "Global Staffing: Are Expatriates the Only Answer?" *HR Focus*, March 1998, pp. S1–2.

2. Rosalie L. Tung, "Selection and Training Procedures of U.S., European and Japanese Multinationals," *California Management Review*, Fall 1982, p. 59.

3. Malika Richards, "U.S. Multinational Staffing Practices and Implications for Subsidiary Performance in the U.K. and Thailand," *Thunderbird International Business Review*, March–April 2001, pp. 225–242.

4. Richard B. Peterson, Nancy K. Napier, and Won Shul-Shim, "Expatriate Management: A Comparison of MNCs across Four Parent Countries," *Thunderbird International Business Review*, March–April 2000, p. 150.

5. Arvind V. Phatak, *International Dimensions of Management*, 2nd ed. (Boston: PWS-Kent Publishing, 1989), p. 106.

6. Linda K. Stroh, Arup Varma, and Stacey J. Valy-Durbin, "Why Are Women Left at Home: Are They Unwilling To Go on International Assignments?" *Journal of World Business*, vol. 35, no. 3, 2000, pp. 241–256.

7. Paul W. Beamish and Andrew C. Inkpen, "Japanese Firms and the Decline of the Japanese Expatriate," *Journal of World Business*, vol. 33, no. 1, 1998, pp. 35–50.

8. *Ibid.*, pp. 44–45.

9. Lawrence G. Franco, "Who Manages Multinational Enterprises?" *Columbia Journal of World Business*, Summer 1973, pp. 30–42.

10. Tung, "Selection and Training Procedures," pp. 61–62.

11. *Ibid.*

12. Phatak, *International Dimension of Management*, p. 107.

13. Franco, "Who Manages Multinational Enterprises?" p. 33.

14. Calvin Reynolds, "Strategic Employment of Third Country Nationals," *HR Planning*, vol. 20, no. 1, 1997, p. 38.

15. Michael G. Harvey and M. Ronald Buckley, "Managing Inpatriates: Building a Global Core Competency," *Journal of World Business*, vol. 32, no. 1, 1997, p. 36.

16. For some additional insights regarding inpatriates and worldwide staffing see Michael Harvey and Milorad M. Novicevic, "Staffing Global Marketing Positions: What We Don't Know Can Make a Difference," *Journal of World Business*, vol. 35, no. 1, 2000, pp. 80–94.

17. Jennifer Smith, "Southeast Asia's Search for Managers," *Management Review*, March 1998, p. 9.

18. Lisa Hoecklin, *Managing Cultural Differences* (Workingham, England: Addison-Wesley, 1994), p. 124.

19. Winfred Arthur, Jr. and Winston Bennett, Jr., "The International Assignee: The Relative Importance of Factors Perceived to Contribute to Success," *Personnel Psychology,* Spring 1995, pp. 99–114.

20. Also see Michael G. Harvey, Milorad M. Novicevic, and Cheri Speier, "An Innovative Global Management Staffing System: A Competency-Based Perspective," *Human Resource Management,* Winter 2000, pp. 381–394.

21. Rosalie L. Tung, "U.S. Multinationals: A Study of Their Selection and Training Procedures for Overseas Assignments," *National Academy of Management Proceedings,* Atlanta, 1979, pp. 298–299.

22. Rosalie L. Tung, "Human Resource Planning in Japanese Multinationals: A Model for U.S. Firms?" *Journal of International Business Studies,* Fall 1984, p. 141.

23. Peterson *et al.,* "Expatriate Management," p. 151.

24. Indrei Ratiu, "Thinking Internationally: A Comparison of How International Executives Learn," *International Studies of Management & Organization,* Spring–Summer 1983, pp. 139–150.

25. Nancy J. Adler, *International Dimensions of Organizational Behavior,* 2nd ed. (Boston: PWS-Kent Publishing, 1991), pp. 228–229.

26. Ingemar Torbiorn, *Living Abroad* (New York: John Wiley, 1982), pp. 100–101.

27. Jan Selmer, "Effects of Coping Strategies on Sociocultural and Psychological Adjustment of Western Expatriate Managers in the PRC," *Journal of World Business,* vol. 34, no. 1, 1999, pp. 41–51.

28. Paula M. Caligiuri, "Selecting Expatriates for Personality Characteristics: A Moderating Effect of Personality on the Relationship Between Host National Contact and Cross-cultural Adjustment," *Management International Review,* vol. 40, no. 1, 2000, pp. 61–80.

29. Jeffrey L. Blue and Ulric Haynes, Jr., "Preparation for the Overseas Assignment," *Business Horizons,* June 1977, p. 63.

30. *Ibid.,* p. 65.

31. Jean E. Heller, "Criteria for Selecting an International Manager," *Personnel,* May–June 1980, p. 50.

32. Torbiorn, *Living Abroad,* p. 128.

33. Blue and Haynes, "Preparation for the Overseas Assignment," p. 64.

34. The survey was conducted by executive recruiters for Korn-Ferry International and the Columbia Business School. Excerpts were reported in "Report: Shortage of Executives Will Hurt U.S.," *Omaha World Herald,* June 25, 1989, p. 1G.

35. Margaret A. Shaffer, David A. Harrison, K. Matthew Gilley, and Dora M. Luk, "Struggling for Balance Amid Turbulence on International Assignments: Work-Family Conflict, Support, and Commitment," *Journal of Management,* vol. 27, 2001, pp. 99–121.

36. Rosalie Tung, "A Study of the Expatriation/Repatriation Process," A report prepared under the auspices of Arthur Andersen, 1997, p. 6.

37. Patricia C. Borstorff, Stanley G. Harris, Hubert S. Field, and William F. Giles, "Who'll Go? A Review of Factors Associated with Employee Willingness to Work Overseas," *Human Resource Planning,* vol. 20, no. 3, 1997, p. 38.

38. See Betty Jane Punnett, "Towards Effective Management of Expatriate Spouses," *Journal of World Business,* vol. 33, no. 3, 1997, pp. 243–256.

39. Howard Tu and Sherry E. Sullivan, "Preparing Yourself for an International Assignment," *Business Horizons,* January–February 1994, p. 68.

40. James C. Baker and John M. Ivancevich, "The Assignment of American Executives Abroad: Systematic, Haphazard or Chaotic?" *California Management Review,* Spring 1971, p. 41.

41. *Ibid.*

42. Ingmar Bjorkman and Yuan Lu, "A Corporate Perspective on the Management of Human Resources in China," *Journal of World Business,* vol. 34, no. 1, 1999, p. 19.

43. Heller, "Criteria for Selecting an International Manager," p. 53.

44. Tung, "Selection and Training Procedures," p. 65.

45. Bjorkman and Lu, "A Corporate Perspective," p. 20.

46. This section is based on J. Stewart Black, Mark Mendenhall, and Gary Oddou, "Toward a Comprehensive Model of International Adjustment: An Integration of Multiple Theoretical Perspectives," *Academy of Management Review,* April 1991, pp. 291–317.

47. For more on this area see Jaime Bonache, Chris Brewster, and Vesa Suutari, "Expatriation: A Developing Research Agenda," *Thunderbird International Business Review,* January–February 2001, pp. 3–20.

48. Iain McCormick and Tony Chapman, "Executive Relocation: Personal and Organizational Tactics," in Pat Joynt and Malcolm Warner (eds.), *Managing across Cultures: Issues and Perspectives* (London: International Thomson Business Press, 1996), pp. 326–337.

49. Calvin Reynolds, "Expatriate Compensation in Historical Perspective," *Journal of World Business,* vol. 32, no. 2, 1997, p. 127.

50. Elaine K. Bailey, "International Compensation," in Oded Shenkar (ed.), *Global Perspectives of Human Resource Management* (Englewood Cliffs, NJ: Prentice-Hall, 1995), p. 148.

51. See Hodgetts and Luthans, *Compensation & Benefits Review,* pp. 58–59.

52. For additional insights see Joel Millman, "Mexico Is Perk Paradise for U.S. Middle Managers," *Wall Street Journal,* May 23, 2000, pp. B1, B18.

53. Peterson, Napier, and Shul-Shin, "Expatriate Management," p. 155.

54. Geoffrey W. Latta, "Expatriate Incentives: Beyond Tradition," *HR Focus,* March 1998, p. S4.

55. Also see "Income Tax, 1998," *Economist,* April 4, 1998, p. 113.

56. Greg Steinmetz and Gregory L. White, "Chrysler Pay Draws Fire Overseas," *Wall Street Journal,* May 26, 1998, p. B1.

57. "Bonus Points," *Economist,* April 15, 1995, pp. 71–72.

58. See Dennis R. Briscoe, *International Human Resource Management* (Englewood Cliffs, NJ: Prentice-Hall, 1995), pp. 111–120.

59. David Sirota and J. Michael Greenwood, "Understand Your Overseas Workforce," *Harvard Business Review,* January–February 1971, pp. 53–60.

60. *Ibid.,* pp. 59–60.

61. Edwin L. Miller and Joseph L. C. Cheng, "Circumstances That Influenced the Decision to Accept an Overseas Assignment," *National Academy of Management Proceedings,* Kansas City, 1976, pp. 336–429; Edwin L. Miller and Joseph L. C. Cheng, "A Closer Look at the Decision to Accept an Overseas Position," *Management International Review,* vol. 18, no. 3, 1978, pp. 25–33.

62. Torbiorn, *Living Abroad,* p. 127.

63. Y. Zeira and M. Banai, "Attitudes of Host-Country Organization toward MNCs' Staffing Policies: A Cross-Country and Cross-Industry Analysis," *Management International Review,* vol. 21, no. 2, 1981, pp. 38–47.

64. Chi-Sum Wong and Kenneth S. Law, "Managing Localization of Human Resources in the PRC: A Practical Model," *Journal of World Business,* vol. 34, no. 1, 1999, pp. 28–29.

65. Torbiorn, *Living Abroad,* p. 41.

66. Maria L. Kraimer, Sandy J. Wayne, and Renata A. Jaworski, "Sources of Support and Expatriate Performance: The Mediating Role of Expatriate Adjustment," *Personnel Psychology,* vol. 54, 2001, pp. 71–99.

67. Zeira and Banai, "Selection of Expatriate Managers," p. 34.

68. John S. McClenahan, "The Overseas Manager: Not Actually a World Away," *Industry Week,* November 1, 1976, p. 53.

69. Jobert E. Abueva, "Return of the Native Executive," *New York Times,* May 17, 2000, p. C1.

70. Adler, *International Dimensions of Organizational Behavior,* p. 236.

71. Rosalie L. Tung, "Career Issues in International Assignments," *The Academy of Management Executive,* August 1988, p. 242.

72. Howard W. French, "Japan Unsettles Returnees, Who Yearn to Leave Again," *New York Times,* May 2, 2000, p. A12.

73. J. Stewart Black, "Coming Home: The Relationship of Expatriate Expectations with Repatriate Adjustment and Job Performance," *Human Relations,* vol. 45, no. 2, 1992, p. 188.

74. Wong and Law, "Managing Localization of Human Resources," p. 36.

75. Phatak, *International Dimensions of Management,* p. 126.

76. Tung, "Career Issues in International Assignments," p. 243.

77. Nancy K. Napier and Richard B. Peterson, "Expatriate Reentry: What Do Expatriates Have to Say?" *Human Resource Planning,* vol. 14, no. 1, 1991, pp. 19–28.

78. Charlene Marmer Solomon, "Repatriation: Up, Down or Out?" *Personnel Journal,* January 1995, p. 32.

79. Mitchell R. Hammer, William Hart, and Randall Rogan, "Can You Go Home Again? An Analysis of the Repatriation of Corporate Managers and Spouses," *Management International Review,* vol. 38, no. 1, 1998, p. 81.

Chapter 16 Endnotes

1. Karen Roberts, Ellen Ernst Kossek, and Cynthia Ozeki, "Managing the Global Workforce: Challenges and Strategies," *Academy of Management Executive,* November 1998, pp. 93–106.

2. See Barbara Kres Beach, "The Canadians Are Training, The Canadians Are Training," *Training and Development Journal,* February 1998, pp. 38–39.

3. See for example, Mark C. Blino and Daniel C. Feldman, "Increasing the Skill Utilization of Expatriates," *Human Resource Management,* Winter 2000, vol. 39, no. 4, pp. 367–379; and Ben L. Kedia and Ananda Mukherji, "Global Managers: Developing a Mindset for Global Competitiveness," *Journal of World Business,* vol. 34, no. 3, 1999, pp. 230–251.

4. Lennie Copeland, "Making Costs Count in International Travel," *Personnel Administrator,* July 1984, p. 47.

5. Robert C. Maddox and Douglas Short, "The Cultural Integrator," *Business Horizons,* November–December 1988, pp. 57–59.

6. Michael Hickins, "Creating a Global Team," *Management Review,* September 1998, p. 6.

7. Charlene Marmer Solomon, "Global Operations Demand that HR Rethink Diversity," *Personnel Journal,* July 1994, p. 50.

8. Paul R. Sparrow and Pawan S. Budhwar, "Competition and Change: Mapping the Indian HRM Recipe Against Worldwide Patterns," *Journal of World Business,* vol. 32, no. 3, 1997, p. 231.

9. In addition see Chi-Sum Wong and Kenneth S. Law, "Managing Localization of Human Resources in the PRC: A Practical Model," *Journal of World Business,* vol. 34, no. 1, 1999, pp. 32–33.

10. Bodil Jones, "What Future European Recruits Want," *Management Review,* January 1998, p. 6.

11. Filiz Tabak, Janet Stern Solomon, and Christine Nielsen, "Managerial Success: A Profile of Future Managers in China," *SAM Advanced Management Journal,* Autumn 1998, pp. 18–26.

12. Also see Allan Bird, Sully Taylor, and Schon Beechler, "A Typology of International Human Resource Management in Japanese Multinational Corporations: Organizational Implications," *Human Resource Management,* Summer 1998, pp. 159–176.

13. Fred Luthans, *Organizational Behavior,* 9th ed. (New York: Irwin/McGraw-Hill, 2002), Chapter 16.

14. Noel M. Tichy and Eli Cohen, "The Teaching Organization," *Training and Development Journal,* July 1998, p. 27.

15. *Ibid.,* p. 28.

16. Fred Luthans, Alex Stajkovic, Brett C. Luthans, and Kyle W. Luthans, "Applying Behavior Management in Eastern Europe," *European Management Journal,* vol. 16, no. 4, 1998, pp. 466–475.

17. Peter Prud'homme van Reine and Fons Trompenaars, "Invited Reaction: Developing Expatriates for the Asia-Pacific Region," *Human Resource Development Quarterly,* vol. 11, no. 3, Fall 2000, p. 238.

18. J. Hayes and C. W. Allinson, "Cultural Differences in the Learning Styles of Managers," *Management International Review,* vol. 28, no. 3, 1988, p. 76.

19. *Ibid.,* p. 79.

20. *Ibid.,* pp. 75–80.

21. *Ibid.,* p. 79.

22. John R. Schermerhorn, "Intercultural Management Training: An Interview with Asma Abdullah," *Journal of Management Development,* vol. 13, no. 3, 1994, pp. 60–61.

23. See for example, Jennifer Smith, "Southeast Asia's Search for Managers," *Management Review,* June 1998, p. 9.

24. Also see Schon Beechler and John Zhuang Yang, "The Transfer of Japanese-Style Management to American Subsidiaries: Contingencies, Constraints, and Competencies," *Journal of International Business Studies,* Third Quarter 1994, pp. 467–491.

25. Allan Bird and Schon Beechler, "Links Between Business Strategy and Human Resource Management Strategy in U.S.-Based Japanese Subsidiaries: An Empirical Investigation," *Journal of International Business Studies,* First Quarter 1995, p. 40.

26. Linda K. Stroh and Paula M. Caligiuri, "Increasing Global Competitiveness through Effective People Management," *Journal of World Business,* vol. 33, no. 1, 1998, p. 10.

27. Yoram Zeira and Ehud Harari, "Host-Country Organizations and Expatriate Managers in Europe," *California Management Review,* Spring 1979, p. 42.

28. For more on this, see Tomoko Yoshida and Richard W. Breslin, "Intercultural Skills and Recommended Behaviors," in Oded Shenkar (ed.), *Global Perspectives of Human Resource Management* (Englewood Cliffs, NJ: Prentice-Hall, 1995), pp. 112–131.

29. Alan M. Barrett, "Training and Development of Expatriates and Home Country Nationals," in Oded Shenkar, *Global Perspectives of Human Resource Management* (Englewood Cliffs, NJ: Prentice-Hall, 1995), p. 135.

30. Zeira and Harari, "Host-Country Organizations," p. 43.

31. For more on this topic, see Ehud Harari and Yoram Zeira, "Training Expatriates for Managerial Assignments in Japan," *California Management Review,* Summer 1978, pp. 56–62.

32. Yukimo Ono, "Japanese Firms Don't Let Masters Rule," *Wall Street Journal,* May 4, 1992, p. B1.

33. See also Stalislav Shekshnia, "Western Multinationals' Human Resource Practices in Russia," *European Management Journal,* August 1998, pp. 460–465.

34. AAhad M. Osman-Gani, "Developing Expatriates for the Asia-Pacific Region: A Comparative Analysis of Multinational Enterprise Managers from Five Countries Across Three Continents," *Human Resource Development Quarterly,* vol. 11, no. 3, Fall 2000, pp. 213–235.

35. In addition see Chi-Sum Wong and Kenneth S. Law, "Managing Localization of Human Resources in the PRC: A Practical Model," *Journal of World Business,* vol. 34, no. 1, 1999, pp. 32–33.

36. See Andrew Sergeant and Stephen Frenkel, "Managing People in China: Perceptions of Expatriate Managers," *Journal of World Business,* vol. 33, no. 1, 1998, pp. 17–34.

37. Rosalie L. Tung, "Selection and Training Procedures of U.S., European, and Japanese Multinationals," *California Management Review,* Fall 1982, p. 65.

38. *Ibid.,* pp. 66–67.

39. Michael J. Marquardt and Dean W. Engel, *Global Human Resource Management* (Englewood Cliffs, NJ: Prentice-Hall, 1995), p. 44.

40. Ingmar Bjorkman and Yuan Lu, "A Corporate Perspective on the Management of Human Resources in China," *Journal of World Business,* vol. 34, no. 1, 1999, pp. 20–21.

41. Cynthia L. Kemper, "Global Training's Critical Success Factors," *Training and Development Journal,* February 1998, p. 37.

42. Fred E. Fiedler, Terence Mitchell, and Harry C. Triandis, "The Culture Assimilator: An Approach to Cross-Cultural Training," *Journal of Applied Psychology,* April 1971, p. 97.

43. See for example Frits K. Pil and John Paul MacDuffie, "What Makes Transplants Thrive: Managing the Transfer of 'Best Practice' at Japanese Auto Plants in North America," *Journal of World Business,* vol. 34, no. 4, 1999, pp. 372–391.

44. Chung-Ming Lau and Hang-Yue Ngo, "Organization Development and Firm Performance: A Comparison of Multinational and Local Firms," *Journal of International Business Studies,* First Quarter 2001, pp. 95–114.

45. L. J. Bourgeois III and Manuel Boltvinik, "OD in Cross-Cultural Settings: Latin America," *California Management Review,* Spring 1981, p. 77.

46. Geert Hofstede, "The Cultural Relativity of Organizational Practices and Theories," *Journal of International Business* Studies, Fall 1983, p. 84.

47. Alfred M. Jaeger, "The Applicability of Organization Development Overseas: Reality or Myth?" *National Academy of Management Proceedings,* Boston, August 12–15, 1984, pp. 95–104.

48. Alfred M. Jaeger, "Organization Development and National Culture: Where's the Fit?" *Academy of Management Review,* January 1986, p. 185.

49. Alfred M. Jaeger, "The Appropriateness of Organization Development Outside North America," *International Studies of Management & Organization,* Spring 1984, p. 32.

50. Bourgeois and Boltvinik, "OD in Cross-Cultural Settings," p. 80.

51. A. D. Stajkovic and F. Luthans, "A Meta-Analysis of the Effects of Organizational Behavior Modification on Task Performance, 1975–1995," *Academy of Management Journal,* vol. 40, 1997, pp. 1122–1141.

52. Dianne H. B. Welsh, Fred Luthans, and Steven Sommer, "Managing Russian Factory Workers: The Impact of U.S.-Based Behavioral and Participative Techniques," *Academy of Management Journal,* February 1993, p. 74.

53. Carl F. Fey and Ingmar Bjorkman, "The Effect of Human Resource Management Practices on MNC Subsidiary Performance in Russia," *Journal of International Business Studies,* First Quarter 2001, pp. 59–75.

54. Fred Luthans, Richard M. Hodgetts, and Brett C. Luthans, "The Role of HRM in Sustaining Competitive Advantage into the 21st Century," *National Productivity Review,* Winter 1997, pp. 73–81.

55. Noel M. Tichy, "Global Development," in Vladimir Pucik, Noel M. Tichy, and Carole K. Barnett (eds.), *Globalizing Management* (New York: John Wiley, 1993), pp. 206–224.

56. *Ibid.,* p. 219.

Chapter 17 Endnotes

1. Dennis R. Briscoe, *International Human Resource Management* (Englewood Cliffs, NJ: Prentice-Hall, 1995), p. 159.

2. Jeffrey P. Kotz and Stanley W. Elsea, "A Framework for Assessing International Labor Relations: What Every Human Resource Manager Needs to Know," *Human Resource Planning,* 1997, vol. 20, no. 4, p. 22.

3. Konstantin Richter, "European Super-Unions Face Challenges," *Wall Street Journal,* January 11, 2000, p. A23.

4. Keith Atkinson, "State of the Unions," *Personnel Administrator,* September 1986, p. 58.

5. "Inform, Consult, Impose," *Economist,* June 16, 2001, p. 63.

6. Edmund L. Andrews, "Germany Weighs Overhaul of 'Consensus' Capitalism," *New York Times,* February 14, 2001, p. W1.

7. Wolfgang Scholl, "Codetermination and the Ability of Firms to Act in the Federal Republic of Germany," *International Studies of Management & Organization,* Summer 1987, pp. 27–37.

8. See Irene Hall-Siu Chow and Oded Shenkar, "HR Practices in the People's Republic of China," *Personnel,* December 1989, pp. 41–47.

9. Erik Eckholm, "China Accepts U.N. Advice to Help Ease Labor Strife," *New York Times,* May 20, 2001, p. 15.

10. Peter J. Dowling, Randall S. Schuler, and Denise E. Welch, *International Dimensions of Human Resource Management,* 2nd ed. (Belmont, CA: Wadsworth, 1994), pp. 198.

11. Robert Grosse and Duane Kujawa, *International Business: Theory and Managerial Applications* (Homewood, IL: Irwin, 1988), p. 447.

12. Barry, Bearak, "Lives Held Cheap in Bangladesh Sweatshops," *New York Times,* April 15, 2001, pp. 1, 12.

13. Leslie Kaufman and David Gonzalez, "Labor Progress Clashes with Global Reality," *New York Times,* April 24, 2001, pp. A1, A10.

14. Also see "3% Raise for German Union," *New York Times,* March 29, 2000, p. D4.

15. Uta Harnischfeger, "Unions Reject Innovative Pay Scheme at VW," *Financial Times,* June 27, 2001, p. 3.

16. Tony Czuczka, "'Lazy' Germany Showing Signs of Declining Work Ethic," *Miami Herald,* April 22, 2001, p. 7A.

17. "Europe Hits a Brick Wall," *Economist,* April 5, 1997, p. 22.

18. See for example Richard Waters, "Alcatel Planning to Slash Another 2,500 Jobs in US," *Financial Times,* July 10, 2001, p. 17.

19. Julian Beltrame, "Canada Is Taking Steps to Boost Immigration," *Wall Street Journal,* July 10, 2000, p. A24.

20. Masayoshi Kanabayashi, "Calls Grow for Foreign Workers in Japan," *Wall Street Journal,* May 26, 2000, p. A20.

21. Cecilie Rohwedder, "Germany Tackles Joblessness, but Misses," *Wall Street Journal,* May 8, 2001, p. B11A.

22. C. Pascal Zachary, "As High-Tech Jobs Go Begging, Germany Is Loath to Import Talent," *Wall Street Journal,* January 17, 2000, p. A10.

23. G. Pascal Zachary and Cecilie Rohwedder, "Germany Widens Door for Immigrants," *Wall Street Journal,* July 2, 2001, pp. A8, A10.

24. Roger Cohen, "How Open to Immigrants Should Germany Be? An Uneasy Country's Debate Deepens," *New York Times,* May 13, 2001, p. 9.

25. Hugh Williamson, "Immigration Plan Hailed by Schroder," *Financial Times,* July 5, 2001, p. 2.

26. David Wessel and Cecilie Rohwedder, "Immigration Issue Flares Up in Germany," *Wall Street Journal,* April 4, 2000, p. A21.

27. Edmund L. Andrews, "Only Employment for Many in Europe Is Part-Time Work," *New York Times,* September 1, 1997, pp. A1, B7.

28. Chris Brewster, Lesley Mayne, and Olga Tregaskis, "Flexible Working in Europe," *Journal of World Business,* vol. 32, no. 2, 1997, p. 138.

29. Steven Greenhouse, "Temp Workers at Microsoft Win Lawsuit," *New York Times,* December 13, 2000, pp. C1, C7.

30. Brewster, Mayne, and Tregaskis, pp. 141–142.

31. *Ibid.,* pp. 133–151.

32. Helene Cooper and Thomas Kamm, "Much of Europe Eases Its Rigid Labor Laws, and Temps Proliferate," *Wall Street Journal,* June 4, 1998, p. A6.

33. Brewster, Mayne, and Tregaskis, pp. 143–144.

34. Reported in Dowling, Schuler, and Welch, *International Dimensions,* p. 188.

35. Grosse and Kujawa, *International Business,* pp. 463–464.

36. Also see "Global Risk," *Business Week,* October 12, 1998, pp. 113–125.

37. Rosabeth Moss Kanter, "Change Is Everyone's Job: Managing the Extended Enterprise in a Globally Connected World," *Organizational Dynamics,* Summer 1999, p. 12.

38. Akio Morita, "Partnering for Competitiveness: The Role of Japanese Business," *Harvard Business Review,* May–June 1992, p. 78.

39. See "The Auto Baron," *Business Week,* November 16, 1998, pp. 82–90.

40. See for example, "America vs. The New Europe," *Fortune,* December 21, 1998, pp. 149–156.

41. J. Bernard Keys, Luther Trey Denton, and Thomas R. Miller, "The Japanese Management Theory Jungle—Revisited," *Journal of Management,* vol. 20, no. 2, 1994, pp. 373–402.

42. See Thomson A. Stewart, "Toward the Century of Quality: A Conversation with Joseph Juran," *Fortune,* January 11, 1999, pp. 168, 170.

43. Gary Hamel and C. K. Prahalad, *Competing for the Future* (Boston: Harvard Business School Press, 1994), p. 23.

44. *Ibid.,* p. 156.

45. Daniel Sullivan and Alan Bauerschmidt, "The 'Basic Concepts' of International Business Strategy: A Review and Reconsideration," *Management International Review,* Special Issue 1991, pp. 111–124.

46. Also see B. Joseph Pine II and James H. Gilmore, "Welcome to the Experience Economy," *Harvard Business Review,* July–August 1998, pp. 97–105.

47. Kanter, "Change Is Everyone's Business," p. 17.

48. Gary Hamel, *Leading the Revolution* (Boston: Harvard Business School Press, 2000).

Glossary

Achievement culture   A culture in which people are accorded status based on how well they perform their functions.

Achievement motivation theory   A theory which holds that individuals can have a need to get ahead to attain success and to reach objectives.

Act of state doctrine   A jurisdictional principle of international law which holds that all acts of other governments are considered to be valid by U.S. courts, even if such acts are illegal or inappropriate under U.S. law.

Adaptability screening   The process of evaluating how well a family is likely to stand up to the stress of overseas life.

Adaptive organizations   Organizations that are characterized by reaction to required changes but failure to anticipate them and stay on or ahead of the cutting edge.

Administrative coordination   Strategic formulation and implementation in which the MNC makes strategic decisions based on the merits of the individual situation rather than using a predetermined economically or politically driven strategy.

Analytical manager   A manager who is systematic and logical and carefully weighs alternatives to problems.

Arbitrator   An individual who provides a solution to a grievance that both sides (union and management representatives) have been unable to resolve themselves and that both sides agree to accept.

Ascription culture   A culture in which status is attributed based on who or what a person is.

Assessment center   An evaluation tool used to identify individuals with potential to be selected or promoted to higher-level positions.

Authoritarian leadership   The use of work-centered behavior designed to ensure task accomplishment.

Balance sheet approach   An approach to developing an expatriate compensation package that is based on ensuring the expat is "made whole" and does not lose money by taking the assignment.

Benchmarking   The process of identifying what leading-edge competitors are doing and then using this information to produce improved products or services.

Bicultural group   A group in which two or more members represent each of two distinct cultures, such as four Mexicans and four Taiwanese who have formed a team to investigate the possibility of investing in a venture.

Cafeteria approach   An approach to developing an expatriate compensation package that entails giving the individual a series of options and letting the person decide how to spend the available funds.

Centralization   A management system under which important decision are made at the top.

Chaebols   In South Korea, very large, family-held conglomerates, including internationally known firms, in which many key managers have attended school in the West and use this education to help formulate successful international strategies for their firms. *Chaebols* have considerable political and economic power in Korea.

Chromatics   The use of color to communicate messages.

Chronemics   The way in which time is used in a culture.

Civil or code law   Law that is derived from Roman law and is found in the non-Islamic and nonsocialist countries.

Codetermination   A legal system that requires workers and their managers to discuss major decisions.

Collective bargaining   The process whereby formal labor agreements are reached by union and management representatives; it involves the negotiation of wages, hours, and conditions of employment and the administration of the labor contract.

Collectivism   A culture in which people tend to belong to groups or collectives and to look after each other in exchange for loyalty.

Common law   Law that derives from English law and is the foundation of legislation in the United States, Canada, and England, among other nations.

Communication   The process of transferring meanings from sender to receiver.

Communitarianism   Refers to people regarding themselves as part of a group.

Confrontation meetings   The gathering and analysis of information related to intra- and intergroup conflict followed by the formulation of a plan of action by the participants for the purpose of resolving these problems.

Conglomerate investment   A type of high-risk investment in which goods or services produced are not similar to those produced at home.

Content theories   Theories that explain work motivation in terms of what arouses, energizes, or initiates employee behavior.

Context   Information that surrounds a communication and helps to convey the message.

Controlling   The process of evaluating results in relation to plans or objectives and deciding what action, if any, to take.

Cross-cultural school of management thought   An approach to international management holding that effective managerial behavior is a function of the specific culture: A successful manager in one location may not be effective in another location around the world.

Cultural assimilator   A programmed learning technique designed to expose members of one culture to some of the basic concepts, attitudes, role perceptions, customs, and values of another culture.

Culture   The acquired knowledge that people use to interpret experience and to generate social behavior. This knowledge forms values, creates attitudes, and influences behavior.

Decentralization   Pushing decision making down the line and getting the lower-level personnel involved.

Decision making   The process of choosing a course of action among alternatives.

Delayed differentiation   A manufacturing strategy in which all products are manufactured in the same way for all countries or regions until as late in the assembly process as possible, with differentiation of features or components introduced in the final stages of production.

Diffuse culture   A culture in which both public and private space are similar in size and individuals guard their public space carefully, because entry into public space also affords entry into private space as well.

Direct controls   The use of face-to-face or personal meetings for the purpose of monitoring operations.

Doctrine of comity   A jurisdictional principle of international law which holds that there must be mutual respect for the laws, institutions, and government of other countries in the matter of jurisdiction over their own citizens.

Downward communication   The transmission of information from superior to subordinate.

Economic imperative   A worldwide strategy based on cost leadership, differentiation, and segmentation.

Eiffel Tower culture   A culture that is characterized by a strong emphasis on hierarchy and orientation to the task.

Emotional culture   A culture in which emotions are expressed openly and naturally.

Empowerment   The process of giving individuals and teams the resources, information, and authority they need to develop ideas and effectively implement them.

Enterprise unions   Unions that represent both the hourly and salaried employees of a particular company.

Environmental scanning   The process of providing management with accurate forecasts of trends related to external changes in geographic areas where the firm currently is doing business and/or is considering setting up operations.

Equity theory   A theory which holds that people's motivation is determined by how fairly they feel they are being treated.

Esteem needs   The needs for power and status.

Ethics   The study of morality and standards of conduct.

Ethnocentric MNC   An MNC that stresses nationalism and often puts home office people in charge of key international management positions.

Ethnocentric predisposition   A nationalistic philosophy of management whereby the values and interests of the parent company guide the strategic decisions.

Ethnocentrism   The belief that one's own way of doing things is superior to that of others.

European Research Cooperation Agency (Eureka)   An agency that funds projects in the fields of energy, medical technology, biotechnology, communications, and the like, with the objective of making Europe more productive and competitive in the world market.

Expatriates   Those who live and work away from their home country. They are citizens of the country where the multinational corporation is headquartered.

Expectancy/valence theory   A theory which postulates that motivation is influenced by a person's belief that effort will lead to performance, that performance will lead to specific outcomes, and that these outcomes are valued by the individual.

Expropriation   The seizure of businesses by a host country with little, if any, compensation to the owners.

Factual manager   A manager who looks at the available information and makes decisions based on that data.

Family culture   A culture that is characterized by a strong emphasis on hierarchy and orientation to the person.

Femininity   A situation in which the dominant values in society are caring for others and quality of life.

Foreign Corrupt Practices Act (FCPA)   Made into U.S. law in 1977 because of concerns over bribes in the international business arena, this act makes it illegal to influence foreign officials through personal payment or political contributions.

Formalization   The use of defined structures and systems in decision making, communicating, and controlling.

Franchise   A business arrangement under which one party (the franchisor) allows another (the franchisee) to operate an enterprise using its trademark, logo, product line, and methods of operation in return for a fee.

Geocentric MNC   An MNC that seeks to integrate diverse regions of the world through a global approach to decision making.

Geocentric predisposition   A philosophy of management whereby the company tries to integrate a global systems approach to decision making.

Global area division   A structure under which global operations are organized on a geographic rather than a product basis.

Global functional division   A structure which organizes worldwide operations primarily based on function and secondarily on product.

Global international trade union affiliations   Trade union relationships that cut across regional and industrial groups and are heavily concerned with political activities.

Globalization   The production and distribution of products and services of a homogeneous type and quality on a worldwide basis.

Globalization imperative   A belief that one worldwide approach to doing business is the key to both efficiency and effectiveness.

Global product division   A structural arrangement in which domestic divisions are given worldwide responsibility for product groups.

Global sourcing   The use of worldwide suppliers, regardless of where they are located geographically, who are best able to provide the needed output.

Goal-setting theory   A theory that focuses on how individuals set goals and the impact of this process on their motivation.

Grievance   A complaint brought by an employee who feels that he or she has been treated improperly under the terms of the labor agreement.

Groupthink   Social conformity and pressures on individual members of a group to conform and reach consensus.

Guanxi   In China means good connections.

Guided missile culture   A culture that is characterized by a strong emphasis on equality in the workplace and orientation to the task.

Haptics   Communicating through the use of bodily contact.

Home-country nationals   Expatriate managers who are citizens of the country where the multinational corporation is headquartered.

Homogeneous group   A group that is characterized by members who share similar backgrounds and generally perceive, interpret, and evaluate events in similar ways.

Honne   A Japanese term which means "what one really wants to do."

Horizontal investment   An MNC investment in foreign operations to produce the same goods or services as those produced at home.

Horizontal specialization   The assignment of jobs so that individuals are given a particular function to perform and tend to stay within the confines of this area.

Host-country nationals   Local managers who are hired by the MNC.

Hygiene factors   In the two-factor motivation theory, job context variables that include salary, interpersonal relations, technical supervision, working conditions, and company policies and administration.

Incubator culture   A culture that is characterized by a strong emphasis on equality and orientation to the person.

Indigenization laws   Laws that require that nationals hold a majority interest in the operation.

Indirect controls   The use of reports and other written forms of communication to control operations.

Individualism   A culture in which people tend to look after themselves and their immediate family only.

Industrial democracy   The rights that employees have to participate in significant management decisions.

Industrial internationals   Affiliates of the global international union groups that focus on a particular industry.

Inpatriate   An individual from a host country or a third-country national who is assigned to work in the home country.

Integrative techniques   Techniques that help the overseas operation become a part of the host country's infrastructure.

International Confederation of Free Trade Unions (ICFTU)   The most important global international union confederation.

International division structure   A structural arrangement that handles all international operations out of a division created for this purpose.

International joint ventures (IJVs)   Formal arrangements with foreign partners who typically, although not always, are located in the country where the business will be conducted.

International Labour Office (ILO)   A United Nations affiliate, consisting of government, industry, and union representatives, that works to promote fair labor standards regarding health and safety, working conditions, and freedom of association for workers.

International management   The process of applying management concepts and techniques in a multinational, multicultural environment.

International selection criteria   Factors used to choose personnel for international assignments.

Intimate distance   Distance between people that is used for very confidential communications.

Intuitive manager   A manager who is imaginative, innovative, and able to jump from one idea to another.

Islamic law   Law that is derived from interpretation of the Qur'an and the teachings of the Prophet Mohammed and is found in most Islamic countries.

Job content factors   In work motivation, those factors internally controlled, such as responsibility, achievement, and the work itself.

Job context factors   In work motivation, those factors controlled by the organization, such as conditions, hours, earnings, security, benefits, and promotions.

Job design   A job's content, the methods that are used on the job, and the way the job relates to others in the organization.

Joint venture   An agreement in which two or more partners own and control an overseas business.

Kaizen   A Japanese term that means continuous improvement.

Karoshi   Overwork or job burnout, in Japanese.

Keiretsu   In Japan, a newly emerging organizational arrangement in which a large, often vertically integrated group of companies cooperate and work closely with each other to provide goods and services to end users; core members may be bound together by cross-ownership, long-term business dealings, interlocking directorates, and social ties.

Key factor for success (KFS)   A factor necessary for a firm to effectively compete in a market niche.

Kinesics   The study of communication through body movement and facial expressions.

Labor relations   The process through which management and workers identify and determine the job relations that will be in effect at the workplace.

Leadership   The process of influencing people to direct their efforts toward the achievement of some particular goal or goals.

Learning   The acquisition of skills, knowledge, and abilities that results in a relatively permanent change in behavior.

Learning organizations   Organization that are able to transform themselves by anticipating change and discovering new ways of creating products and services; they have learned how to learn.

License   An agreement that allows one party to use an industrial property right in exchange for payment to the other party.

Localization   An approach to developing an expatriate compensation package that involves paying the expat a salary comparable to that of local nationals.

Lockout   A company's refusal to allow workers to enter the facility during a labor dispute.

Lump sum method   An approach to developing an expatriate compensation package that involves giving the expat a predetermined amount of money and letting the individual make his or her own decisions regarding how to spend it.

Macro political risk analysis   Analysis that reviews major political decisions likely to affect all enterprises in the country.

Management by objectives (MBO)   A management system for the joint setting of subordinate goals, coaching and counseling personnel, and providing feedback on their performance.

Maquiladora industry   An arrangement created by the Mexican government that permits foreign manufacturers to send materials to their Mexican-based plants, process or assemble products, and ship them back out of Mexico with only the value added being taxed.

Masculinity   A culture in which the dominant values are success, money, and things.

Mass customization   Tailor-making mass-production products to meet the expectations of the customers.

Mediator   A person who brings both sides (union and management representatives) together and helps them to reach a settlement that is mutually acceptable.

Micro political risk analysis   Analysis directed toward government policies and actions that influence selected sectors of the economy or specific foreign businesses in the country.

Ministry of International Trade and Industry (MITI)   A governmental agency in Japan that identifies and ranks national commercial pursuits and guides the distribution of national resources to meet these goals.

Mixed organization structure   A structure that is a combination of a global product, area, or functional arrangement.

Monochronic time schedule   A time schedule in which things are done in a linear fashion.

Motivation   A psychologic process through which unsatisfied wants or needs lead to drives that are aimed at goals or incentives.

Motivators   In the two-factor motivation theory, the job content factors which include achievement, recognition, responsibility, advancement, and the work itself.

Multicultural group   A group in which there are individuals from three or more different ethnic backgrounds, such as three U.S., three German, three Uruguayan, and three Chinese managers who are looking into mining operations in South Africa.

Multidomestic   A firm that operates production plants in different countries but makes no attempt to integrate overall operations.

National responsiveness   The need to understand the different consumer tastes in segmented regional markets and respond to different national standards and regulations imposed by autonomous governments and agencies.

Nationality principle   A jurisdictional principle of international law which holds that every country has jurisdiction over its citizens no matter where they are located.

Negotiation   The process of bargaining with one or more parties for the purpose of arriving at a solution that is acceptable to all.

Neutral culture   A culture in which emotions are held in check.

Nonreciprocal trade partners   Nations that sell (export) goods to other countries but do not buy (import) from them.

Nonverbal communication   The transfer of meaning through means such as body language and the use of physical space.

Normative manager   A manager who is idealistic and concerned with how things should be done.

North American Free Trade Agreement (NAFTA)   A free trade agreement, including the United States, Canada, and Mexico, that will effectively eliminate trade barriers between the three countries.

Oculesics   The areas of communication that deal with conveying messages through the use of eye contact and gaze.

OD intervention   The structured activity in which targeted individuals, groups, or units engage in accomplishing task goals that are related to organization development.

Operational risks   Government policies and procedures that directly constrain management and performance of local operations.

Organization development (OD)   The deliberate and reasoned introduction, establishment, reinforcement, and spread of change for the purpose of improving an organization's effectiveness.

Organization for Economic Cooperation and Development (OECD)   A government, industry, and union group founded in 1976 that has established a voluntary set of guidelines for MNCs.

Organizational culture   A pattern of basic assumptions that are developed by a group as it learns to cope with problems of external adaptation and internal integration and that are taught to new members as the correct way to perceive, think, and feel in relation to these problems.

Ownership-control risks   Government policies or actions that inhibit ownership or control of local operations.

Paradox   A statement that appears to be contradictory but is not, such as "increases in product quality often result in a decline of the cost of producing the goods."

Parochialism   The tendency to view the world through one's own eyes and perspectives.

Participative leadership   The use of both a work- or task-centered and people-centered approach to leading subordinates.

Particularism   The belief that circumstances dictate how ideas and practices should be applied and something cannot be done the same everywhere.

Paternalistic leadership   The use of work-centered behavior coupled with a protective employee-centered concern.

Perception   A person's view of reality.

Personal distance   In communicating, the physical distance used for talking with family and close friends.

Physiologic needs   Food, clothing, shelter, and other basic, physical needs.

Political imperative   Strategic formulation and implementation utilizing strategies that are country responsive and designed to protect local market niches.

Political risk   The likelihood that a business's foreign investment will be constrained by a host government's policies.

Polycentric MNC   An MNC that places local nationals in key positions and allows these managers to appoint and develop their own people.

Polycentric predisposition   A philosophy of management whereby strategic decisions are tailored to suit the cultures of the countries where the MNC operations.

Polychronic time schedule   A time schedule in which people tend to do several things at the same time and place higher value on personal involvement than on getting things done on time.

Power distance   The extent to which less powerful members of institutions and organizations accept that power is distributed unequally.

Practical school of management thought   A traditional approach to international management, which holds that effective managerial behavior is universal: a successful manager in one location will be effective in any other location around the world.

Principle of sovereignty   An international principle of law which holds that governments have the right to rule themselves as they see fit.

Problem-solving teams   Employee groups that discuss ways of improving quality, efficiency, and the overall work environment.

Process theories   Theories that explain work motivation by how employee behavior is initiated, redirected, and halted.

Product proliferation   The creation of a wide array of products that the competition cannot copy quickly enough.

Profit   The amount remaining after all expenses are deducted from total revenues.

Protective and defensive techniques   Techniques that discourage the host government from interfering in operations.

Protective principle   A jurisdictional principle of international law which holds that every country has jurisdiction over behavior that adversely affects its national security, even if the conduct occurred outside that country.

Proxemics   The study of the way people use physical space to convey messages.

Public distance   In communicating, the distance used when calling across the room or giving a talk to a group.

Quality control circle (QCC)   A group of workers who meet on a regular basis to discuss ways of improving the quality of work.

Quality imperative   Strategic formulation and implementation utilizing strategies of total quality management to meet or exceed customers' expectations and continuously improve products and/or services.

Regiocentric MNC   An MNC that relies on local managers from a particular geographic region to handle operations in and around that area.

Regiocentric predisposition   A philosophy of management whereby the firm tries to blend its own interests with those of its subsidiaries on a regional basis.

Regional internationals   Subdivisions of the global affiliation; regional applications of the global's activities.

Regional system   An approach to developing an expatriate compensation package that involves setting a compensation system for all expats who are assigned to a particular region and paying everyone in accord with that system.

Repatriation   The return to one's home country from an overseas management assignment.

Repatriation agreements   Agreements whereby the firm tells the individual how long she or he will be posted overseas and promises to give the individual, on return, a job that is mutually acceptable.

Return on investment   Return measured by dividing profit by assets.

Ringisei   From Japan, decision making by consensus.

Safety needs   In Maslow's hierarchy of needs, the desire for security, stability, and the absence of pain.

Self-actualization needs   In Maslow's hierarchy of needs, the desire to reach one's full potential by becoming everything one is capable of becoming.

Self-efficacy   A person's belief or confidence in his or her abilities to marshal the motivation, resources, and courses of action needed to successfully accomplish a specific task.

Self-management teams   Employee groups that take over supervisory duties and manage themselves; teams consist of individuals who learn all the tasks of all the group members, allowing team members to rotate jobs.

Simplification   The process of exhibiting the same orientation toward different culture groups.

Smallest space analysis (SSA)   A nonparametric multivariate analysis. This mathematic tool maps the relationship among the countries by showing the distance between each. By looking at this two-dimensional map, it is possible to see those countries that are similar to each other and those that are not.

Social distance   In communicating, the distance used to handle most business transactions.

Social needs   The need to interact and affiliate with others and the need to feel wanted by others.

Socialist law   Law that comes from the Marxist socialist system and continues to influence regulations in countries formerly associated with the Soviet Union as well as China.

Sociotechnical designs   Job designs that blend the personnel and the technology.

Special purpose teams   Employee groups that design and introduce work reforms and new technology.

Specialization   An organizational characteristic that assigns individuals to specific, well-defined tasks.

Specialized internationals   Trade union associations that function as components of intergovernmental agencies and lobby within these agencies.

Specific culture   A culture in which individuals have a large public space they readily share with others and a small private space they guard and share only with close friends and associates.

Strategic fit   An approach to strategically managing an organization that involves aligning resources in such a way as to mesh with the environment.

Strategic planning   The process of determining an organization's basic mission and long-term objectives, then implementing a plan of action for attaining these goals.

Strategic stretch   The creative use of resources to achieve ever more challenging goals.

Strategy implementation   The process of providing goods and services in accord with a plan of action.

Strike   A collective refusal to work to pressure management to grant union demands.

Subsidiary board of directors   A board that oversees and monitors the operations of a foreign subsidiary.

Survey feedback   An OD intervention that involves the gathering and analysis of information related to group behavior and problems and the feeding back of this information to develop effective action plans.

Tatemae   A Japanese term which means "doing the right thing" according to normal models of decision making.

Team building   An extension of classic T-groups (training groups) and sensitivity training that is geared to enhancing organizational effectiveness through cooperation and a "team" effort of key personnel.

Technology paradox   (Also see **Paradox**) That high-tech businesses can thrive at the very moment that their prices are falling the fastest.

Territoriality principle   A jurisdictional principle of international law which holds that every nation has the right of jurisdiction within its legal territory.

Theory X manager   A manager who believes that people are basically lazy and that coercion and threats of punishment often are necessary to get them to work.

Theory Y manager   A manager who believes that under the right conditions people not only will work hard but will seek increased responsibility and challenge.

Third-country nationals   Managers who are citizens of countries other than the one in which the MNC is headquartered or the one in which the managers are assigned to work by the MNC.

Third-party peacemaking   The diagnosis of group conflict followed by the use of an outside party (usually the OD change agent) to facilitate a constructive resolution of a problem.

Token group   A group in which all members but one have the same background, such as a group of Japanese retailers and a British attorney.

Total quality management (TQM)   An organizational strategy and the accompanying techniques that result in the delivery of high-quality products and/or services to customers.

Training   The process of altering employee behavior and attitudes in a way that increases the probability of goal attainment.

Transactional leaders   Individuals who exchange rewards for effort and performance and work on a "something for something" basis.

Transfer risks   Government policies that limit the transfer of capital, payments, production, people, and technology in and out of the country.

Transformational leaders   Leaders who are visionary agents with a sense of mission and who are capable of motivating their followers to accept new goals and new ways of doing things.

Transition strategies   Strategies used to help smooth the adjustment from an overseas to a stateside assignment.

Transnational corporations (TNCs)   Multinational corporations that view the world as one giant market.

Transnational network structure   A multinational structural arrangement that combines elements of function, product, and geographic designs, while relying on a network arrangement to link worldwide subsidiaries.

Two-factor theory of motivation   A theory that holds there are two sets of factors that influence job satisfaction: hygiene factors and motivators.

Uncertainty avoidance   The extent to which people feel threatened by ambiguous situations and have created beliefs and institutions that try to avoid these.

Union   An organization that represents the workers and in collective bargaining has the legal authority to negotiate with the employer and administer the labor contract.

Universalism   The belief that ideas and practices can be applied everywhere in the world without modification.

Upward communication   The transfer of meaning from subordinate to superior.

Validity   The quality of being effective, of producing the desired results. A valid test or selection technique measures what it is intended to measure.

Values   Basic convictions that people have regarding what is right and wrong, good and bad, and important or unimportant.

Variety amplification   The creation of uncertainty and the analysis of many alternatives regarding future action.

Variety reduction   The limiting of uncertainty and the focusing of action on a limited number of alternatives.

Vertical investment   The production of raw materials or intermediate goods that are to be processed into final products.

Vertical specialization   The assignment of work to groups or departments where individuals are collectively responsible for performance.

Virtual corporation   A network of companies that come together to exploit fast-changing opportunities and share costs, skills, and access to global markets.

Virtual organization   An organization that is able to conduct business as if it were a very large enterprise when, in fact, it is much smaller, made up of core business competencies and the rest outsourced.

Wholly owned subsidiary   An overseas operation that is totally owned and controlled by an MNC.

Work centrality   The importance of work in an individual's life relative to other areas of interest.

World-class organization (WCOs)   Enterprises that are able to compete with anybody, anywhere, anytime.

World Trade Organization (WTO)   Started in 1995 to replace GATT, the WTO has power to enforce rulings in trade disputes and monitor trade policies.

Photo Credits

Name and Organization Index

Aaron, Marcia, 107

ABB, 63, 65, 537

Abrahams, Michael N., 175

Accenture, 138, 139, 162

Adler, Nancy J., 172, 182, 183, 188, 204, 212, 294, 301, 379–380, 469

Advanced Micro Devices, 54

Airbus Industrie, 58

Air Europa, 58

Akiba, Toshiharu, 238

Alcan Aluminum, 286

Alcatel, 18, 267, 314

Alcatel Alsthom, 260, 516

Alexiadus, Peter, 74

Allan, Alexander "Sandy," 443

Allen, Herbert A., 442–443

AlliedSignal, 484

Allinson, C. W., 485

All Nippon Airways, 58

Alonso Risteos, Pilar, 106

Alsusuisse Lonza Group, 286

Aluminum Company of America, 470

Alvi, Raashid, 372

Amazon.com, 42

Ambani, Anil, 372, 373

Ambani, Dhirubhai H., 372, 373

Ambani, Mukesh, 373

American Airlines, 12, 13

American Business Centers, 289

American Cyanamid, 10

American Express, 44–45, 360

America Online, 267

Ameritech, 44

Amersham International, 263

Amgen, 83

Amoco, 48, 266, 318

Andersen Consulting, 139

Anderson, Philip, 202, 353–354

Anderson, R. G. S., 101

Anheuser-Busch Cos., 14, 168, 169, 170

Antal, Adriane Berthoin, 79

AOL Time Warner, 443

Appeal Corp., 279

Apple Computer Inc., 254, 377

Applied Micro Circuits Corp., 378

Arasawa, Koichi, 198

Arby's, 14

ARCO, 10, 48

Armstrong, Larry, 248–251

Asda, 336–338

ASEAN (Association of Southeast Asian Nations), 7, 96

Asian Development Bank, 21

Asia-Pacific Economic Cooperation group, 15, 93

Associated British Ports, 16

Association of Private Broadcasting & Telecommunications, 480

Aston Martin Lagonda, 318

AT&T, 10, 12, 23, 48, 346, 347–348, 372, 478, 479

AT&T Wireless Group, 307

Auchan, 337

Auger, Robert, 91

Autokonzern, 18

Autolatina, 318

Automotive Council, 410

Ava, 337

Avtovaz, 5–6, 37, 196

Awata, Fusahao, 238

Badawy, M. K., 428

Bailey, Elaine K., 459

Baillot, Jean Louis, 230

Baker, John, 556–558

Baker, Stephen, 98

Balfour, Frederick, 103–104

Bali, Vinita, 444

Banai, M., 467

Bandura, Albert, 61

Bankers Trust, 263

Bank for International Settlements, 13

Bank of America, 346

Bank of Japan, 76

Barnard, Kurt, 108

Barnett, Carole K., 504

Barnevik, Percy, 537

Bartlett, Christopher A., 143, 317

BASF, 10, 263

Subject Index

Russia
  communication in, 200
  economic status and issues of, 16–18
  joint ventures in, 268
  leadership in, 413, 414, 415, 434
  managing across cultures, 157–158
  organizational behavior modification in, 503–504
  political environment of, 36–37
  political risk and, 283, 289
  spotlight on, 475
  transition to market economy, 7

Safety needs, 381
Saudi Arabia
  communication in, 203
  spotlight on, 91
Scandal, in Japan, 76–77
Self-actualization needs, 381
Self-awareness, 62
Self-efficacy, 61–63
Self-managing teams, 523
Self-reliance, in employee selection, 452
Sexual harassment, in Japan, 77–78
Shiftwork, 530
Shop floor participation, 522
Simplification, 147–149
Singapore
  cultural values in, 132, 151
  economic status and issues of, 22
  motivation in, 392, 393
  organizational culture in, 185
  spotlight on, 406
Slovenia, leadership in, 434
Smallest space analysis (SSA), 123
Smart cards, 43
Social distance, 214
Socialist law, 38
Social needs, 381
Social responsibility, 86–88. *See also* Ethics
Sociotechnical designs, 397–398
South America, 14–15, 492. *See also names of specific countries*
Southeast Asia, 23
Sovereignty, 38
Spain
  communication in, 218
  cultural values in, 132, 151
  leadership in, 433, 434
  organizational culture in, 174
  retailing in, 106–108, 131–133
  spotlight on, 363

Specialization, 329
Specialized internationals, 520
Special purpose teams, 523
Specific culture, 129, 146
Spouses, in employee selection, 454–455
Standardized training programs, 488–496
Strategic alliances
  decision-making in, 345–346
  organizational arrangements for, 319–320
Strategic fit, 537
Strategic planning, 248–274
  approaches to, 254–258
  basic steps in formulation, 259–262
  benefits of, 254
  defined, 252
  need for, 252–253
  strategic dispositions in, 258–259
  strategy implementation, 262–272
Strategic stretch, 537
Strategy implementation, 262–272
  defined, 262
  entry considerations in, 265–270
  functional areas in, 271–272
  location considerations in, 263–265
  ownership considerations in, 265–270
Strikes, defined, 518
Subcontracting, 531–532
Subsidiary boards of directors, 325–326
Succinct communication, 201, 202
Survey feedback, 499, 500, 501
Sweden
  communication in, 203
  industrial democracy in, 524
  job design in, 396–397
  leadership in, 433, 434
  organizational characteristics of firms in, 327
Switzerland
  cultural values in, 133
  leadership in, 434
  political environment of, 36
Synergy, 322–323

Tailor-made training programs, 488–496
Taiwan
  cultural values in, 151
  economic status and issues of, 22–23
  motivation in, 392
  organizational characteristics of firms in, 328, 331
  spotlight on, 135
Tatemae, 340
Taxes, in employee compensation, 462